THE RISE AND DEVELOPMENT OF

WESTERN CIVILIZATION

THE RISE
AND DEVELOPMENT OF
WESTERN CIVILIZATION

The Emergence of Man to The Present

ONE VOLUME EDITION

JOHN L. STIPP
Knox College

ALLEN W. DIRRIM
Ohio University

With the Assistance of

C. WARREN HOLLISTER
University of California, Santa Barbara

HAROLD L. BAUMAN
University of Utah

JOHN WILEY & SONS, INC.,   New York · London · Sydney · Toronto

To our parents

Preface

This edition of the *Rise and Development of Western Civilization* presents the sweep of Western man's past in shortened form. Its purpose is shaped to meet the needs of the growing number of courses which concentrate, within a limited period, on an encompassing overview of the Western experience. To say that the whole flavor of that experience is offered in but half the space used in the two-volume edition is patently foolish; it is not. On the other hand, no part of the basic presentation has been omitted in this volume. And, where time permits, even the fuller flavor may be tasted by judicious use of the many and easily available paperback books dealing with particular periods and events.

Several assumptions underlie this account of the rise and development of Western civilization. One is that the modern college student possesses a quickened intellectual curiosity. Given a reasonably comprehensive body of data, he may be trusted to reach responsible judgments on his own. Another—only seemingly contradictory to the first—is that he needs some guidelines to keep him on the main paths; otherwise he may easily get lost in a forest of facts. The present work deliberately focuses attention on pivotal decisions and developments. Where they are encountered, the tempo slows to allow such treatment in depth as a one-volume narrative allows. Where they are not present, the narrative passes over details mainly of interest only to the specialist. For the most part, the

problems which invite this kind of study are problems whose nature or "solution" bears upon our own times.

A third premise, closely related to the second, rests in the belief that historical trends or movements deserve emphasis over separate, particular events. Of course this does not mean neglect of the latter; the pages of this volume actually contain almost a distressing amplitude of them. The point is that a sustained effort is made to present them so that they reveal the larger concerns of man and the spirit of the times that envelops them.

A fourth assumption is that no meaningful understanding of the various facets of human experience—religion, politics, literature, economics, art, philosophy—can come from studying them in isolation. Repeatedly the literature or art of a particular "period" is considered in intimate connection with political and economic activity.

Finally, encompassing these beliefs is a fundamental faith that the collective memory of man which we call history is not, in essence, an academic—and sometimes dispensable—discipline, but a requisite for the enlargement of man. The eminent historian, Carl Becker, phrased this faith in compelling words:

"The value of history is, indeed, not scientific but moral: by liberalizing the mind, by deepening the sympathies, by fortifying the will, it enables us to control, not society, but ourselves—a much more important thing; it prepares us to live more humanely in the present and to meet rather than to foretell the future."

The results of recent research, published in articles and monographic and general works, have been used throughout. Naturally they have modified a number of opinions and conclusions once firmly held. But a critical, and at times stubborn, insistence that new findings prove to be more than merely *new* has saved, it is hoped, both writers and readers from misunderstanding in the name of new understanding. At all times we have stood ready, where it seemed necessary, to report that from the available evidence no conclusions could be reached, however important the event or object under study. On a few occasions we have had to confess that from the evidence it seemed that no conclusions were ever likely to be reached. On the whole, however, we are left with the feeling that the material in the pages that follow offers opportunities enough, for those who want to know, to learn where Western man has been and how he got where he now is. Any lesser purpose seems hardly worthwhile.

John L. Stipp
C. Warren Hollister
Allen W. Dirrim

Acknowledgments

In the production of a work of such large proportions as this, we are naturally indebted to many persons. We express appreciation to a number of our colleagues who have carefully read portions of the manuscript and have made many helpful suggestions. They are not, of course, to be held accountable for any errors of fact or interpretation, for which we must bear sole responsibility.

Klaus Baer, University of California (Berkeley)
Loren Baritz, University of Rochester
R. Davis Bitton, University of California (Santa Barbara)
William J. Bouwsma, University of California (Berkeley)
Gene A. Brucker, University of California (Berkeley)
Sidney A. Burrell, Boston University
Mortimer Chambers, University of California (Los Angeles)
Gerald D. Feldman, University of California (Berkeley)
John G. Gagliardo, University of Illinois (Chicago)
Boyd H. Hill, University of California (Los Angeles)
Jeffry Kaplow, Columbia University
Ann D. Kilmer, University of California (Berkeley)
Walter LeFeber, Cornell University
Gordon Leff, University of Manchester
Orest Ranum, Columbia University
Carl E. Schorske, University of California (Berkeley)

William G. Sinnigen, Hunter College
William B. Slottman, University of California (Berkeley)
George H. Stein, State University of New York (Binghamton)
Edward R. Tannenbaum, New York University
George V. Taylor, University of North Carolina
Richard S. Westfall, Indiana University

We also express our collective debt to Jere Donovan of *Time* magazine for maps that have made portions of this history instructively graphic beyond the power of words. We are under especial obligation to Nancy Lipscomb, Associate Editor of John Wiley and Sons, who bore the heavy editorial responsibilities for seeing this edition through the press. And, as always and above all, we owe grateful thanks to our chief editor, William L. Gum, for his steady encouragement and his thorough, sensitively informed general supervision of a very long and very complicated task. Each of us is under special obligation to particular individuals. We should like to express this obligation in separate statements.

Although this volume represents a joint effort, particular responsibilities are involved: John L. Stipp for Chapters 1 to 7, and 24 to 32; C. Warren Hollister for the chapters on the medieval world and for general editorial advice and concern; and Allen W. Dirrim for his work in the earlier editions. Since Allen W. Dirrim, one of the three original authors, was unable, because of earlier commitments, to devote full time to this abridged version, we were unusually fortunate to have the immeasurable help of Harold L. Bauman for the period 1300 to about 1850.

Grateful acknowledgments are made to: my wife Cleo, not only for patient understanding throughout, but for careful reading of galley proof of many sections of my portions; Mrs. Elizabeth B. Wilson for critically reading most of the chapters on the ancient world and for making countless helpful suggestions; Mrs. Jo Ann Robinson, for typing early versions of various chapters, for perceptive criticism, and for sustained interest in the whole work; Mr. Mark Lawrence and other members of the Seymour Library Staff for their inestimable help; and Miss Mary Mangieri, who bore prime responsibility for transmuting many corrected and condensed chapters into new, clean copy.

J. L. S.

For her patience and the assumption of additional family responsibilities over the several years of preparing my portions of this work, no word of thanks can repay my wife, Loretta. I also wish to express my appreciation to colleagues, notably Professor Darrell Morse, for testing ideas and providing suggestions; to Mrs. Virginia (Gay) Hayden, for her efficient typing and editorial assistance during the early stages of this work; to Mrs. Earle Field, for assistance on some of the illustrations; and to Barbara Delman, for her editorial work on Chapter 15. Especial acknowledgment is due Perry Viles, University of Pennsylvania, who provided most of Chapter 19.

A. W. D.

Contents

Part   *A*

Beginnings

Chapter	1. Emergent Man and Egyptian Society	1
Chapter	2. Mesopotamia and Crete	29
Chapter	3. Small States, Empires, and the Hebrews	45

Part   *B*

The Greco-Roman World

Chapter	4. The Greek Way: Phoenix	67
Chapter	5. The Greek Way: Prometheus — and Epimetheus	91
Chapter	6. The Roman World: The Republic	115
Chapter	7. The Roman World: Empire and the Christian Community	143

Part   *C*

Medieval Life

Chapter	8. Rome's Three Heirs: Byzantium, Western Europe, Islam	183
Chapter	9. Carolingian Europe and the New Invasions	219
Chapter	10. The High Middle Ages: Economic, Territorial, and Religious Frontiers	257
Chapter	11. Church and State in the High Middle Ages	291
Chapter	12. Literature, Art, and Thought in the High Middle Ages	335

Part   D

Centuries of Crises

Chapter 13. The Renaissance 1300–c. 1520   369
Chapter 14. The Confessional Age: The Reformations of the
             Sixteenth Century   405
Chapter 15. The Century of Crises – 1560–1660   431

Part   E

The Shaping of the Modern World

Chapter 16. Governments and Societies in the Age of
             Absolutism   465
Chapter 17. The Secularization of Thought – The Seventeenth
             and Eighteenth Centuries   491
Chapter 18. The Decline of Absolutism, 1720 to 1787   515

Part   F

Nationalism, Industrialism, Scientism

Chapter 19. A Generation of Revolution, 1787 to 1815   541
Chapter 20. Reaction and Revolution, 1815 to 1850   567
Chapter 21. The Industrialization of Society   593
Chapter 22. Intellectual and Ideological Ferment in the Age
             of Realism and Science   619

Part   G

Politics of the New Industrialism

Chapter 23. The Politics of Emergent Industrial Society –
             About 1850 to 1914   643
Chapter 24. The New Imperialism and the Posture of
             Aggression   675
Chapter 25. Power Politics, 1875 to 1914 – The Entangling
             Web   699

Part **H**

From War to War

Chapter 26. World War I and Its Settlement   723
Chapter 27. In the Wake of War: 1919 to 1930s   747
Chapter 28. The Collectivist Trend between the Wars:
       Russia; Italy   773
Chapter 29. The Collectivist Trend between the Wars:
       Germany; the United States   799
Chapter 30. The World at War Again, 1939 to 1945   823

Part **I**

The World in Flux

Chapter 31. The World in Flux, 1940s to 1960s   865
Chapter 32. The Travail of Contemporary Man   909

Illustration Credits   925

Index   929

List of Color Inserts

Period I. Man in the Ancient World   *follows page*   158

II. Man in the Medieval World   270

III. Man in the World of the Renaissance
and Reformation   414

IV. Man in the Baroque and Classical World   526

V. Man in the Nineteenth Century   622

VI. Man in the Twentieth Century   814

The colored illustrations in this book attempt a survey of how man has viewed his world throughout recorded time. With history divided into six principal periods, each illustration has been carefully selected to portray an important aspect of man's life during a particular era. The four strata of society—the nobility and the upper, middle, and lower or peasant classes—from the countries most prominent in that period are represented in each group. Because, as the authors contend in their preface, no meaningful understanding of human experience is possible without reference to literature and art, most of the illustrations are from the fine and decorative arts. Through his work the artist often records a true and telling account of his times.

List of Maps

Maps by J. Donovan

Ancient Egypt	8
Mesopotamia	31
The Aramean "Trade Empire"	48
Assyrian Empire, *c.* 650 B.C.	50
Chaldean Empire, *c.* 550 B.C.	51
Persian Empire, *c.* 500 B.C.	52
Palestine, 1200 B.C.	57
Early Greek Settlements	71
Greek and Phoenician Colonization	82
Hellenistic Kingdoms in the Third Century B.C.	104
Early Migrations into Italian Peninsula, Sicily and Carthage	116
Some Roads of Ancient Rome	124
Roman Provinces during the Reign of Augustus	146
Movement of Germanic Tribes to *c.* A.D. 450	166
Early Christian Settlements, *c.* A.D. 65	172
The Germanic Invasions	191
Europe at Clovis's Death, A.D. 511	192
Conquests of Justinian	200
Europe around 600	205
The Islamic Empire	213
The Carolingian Empire	227
Partition of the Empire, 843	236
Invasions: Vikings, Moslems, Hungarians	240
England about 885	242
The Holy Roman Empire in 962	249
Reconquest of Spain	264
The Crusader States	270
German Settlements to the East, 800–1400	274
The Holy Roman Empire in 1190	301
Angevin Empire in 1154	315
Growth of the French Royal Domain	328
Italy, *c.* 1490	387
Spain at the time of Ferdinand and Isabella	390
France after the Hundred Years' War	392
The Empire and Central Europe, *c.* 1490	395
Expansion of Muscovy to 1533	396
The Holy Roman Empire about 1520	407
Europe in 1526	413
Religions, 1560	420
Explorations and Colonial Empires	434–435
Division of the Netherlands, 1579–1609	442
Religious and Political Divisions of France, 1585–1598	447
Central Europe after 1648	450
Sweden's Baltic Empire	453
English Civil Wars	454
France of Louis XIV	474
Western Europe after Utrecht, 1721	477
Expansion of the Danubian Monarchy	478
Rise of Brandenburg-Prussia	479
Expansion of Petrine Russia	482
The West Indies at the Time of Walpole	519
Europe, about 1763	521
Partitions of Poland	525
Napoleonic Empire at Its Height	560
Europe, 1815, after the Congress of Vienna	562
Major Languages of Europe	576
Uprisings of the 1820s	578

Latin American Independence, about
  1824   580
Major Revolutions and Reforms,
  1848 and 1849   585
Europe's Expanding Railway Net   602
Unification of Italy   657
Unification of Germany   661
Africa, about 1875   682
The Imperial Thrust into Southeast
  Asia, about 1890   689
The "Middle Kingdom" in the Age of
  Imperialism   690
Africa, about 1900   708
Europe, 1914   725
The Western Front, 1914 to 1918   728
Russian Losses, 1918   734

Europe, 1929   750
Expansion of Hitler's Reich, 1938 to
  1939   830
World War II, Germany Dominated
  Europe, 1942   838
World War II, Mediterranean Area,
  1940 to 1943   841
World War II, Far East   844
World War II, Russian Counter-
  thrust, 1943 to 1945   849
The German Invasion, 1940 to 1941   852
The Allied Victory, D-Day, June 6,
  1944 — V-E Day, May 8, 1945   853
Asia, 1967   887
The New Africa, 1967   892
Europe, 1967   896

A

BEGINNINGS

Emergent Man and Egyptian Society

EMERGENT MAN

The Genesis of Man

Man stands small amid the immensities and mysteries of the universe. Above him stretch measureless space and countless heavenly bodies. Among these bodies our solar system is part of a galaxy so vast that 200,000,000 years or so are required for it to revolve about its axis. And there are millions of galaxies, some of them larger than our "Milky Way." Underfoot, the Earth abounds in complexities. Its crust, a mere thirty or forty miles thick, has been barely scratched; its four thousand miles of mantle and core are more subjects of conjecture than of verifiable description.

The mere mention of these immensities and complexities is enough to suggest how wrong man once was to view everything in anthropomorphic terms. But they may also serve to place man in a perspective that reveals power and promise. If we confess that astronomically man is an infinitesimally small speck, we ought not overlook the corollary—that man is the astronomer. Likewise, if we are tempted to think of the works of man as puny and passing, we should make sure we are weighing them in a realistic time-scale. One earth scientist, for example, has pointed out that if "the 4.5 billion year age of the earth is thought of as one year, the 500 million years of fossil record is equivalent to about forty days. The time of humans, assuming that it is about one million years, would amount to less than two hours, and that of modern man, giving him fifty thousand years [perhaps a generous estimate], is a little more than five minutes."[1] Another account carries the comparison further: ". . . the Pyr-

1. Ruth Moore, *The Earth We Live On*, Knopf, New York, 1956, p. 406 fn.

1

amids of Egypt were built two minutes ago; Caesar was murdered fifty seconds ago! By this same schedule, the American republic has existed for less than five seconds." Viewed in this light the human condition, so often in our times the object of gloomy prophecies, takes on a new aspect. If in "two hours" man can develop from a slouching hominid to an Einstein and a Gandhi, the hours and days ahead may seem not too foreboding.

The Emergence of Homo Sapiens

There is disagreement among anthropologists over the age of man either as hominid (subman) or as *Homo sapiens* (thinking man). The former appeared perhaps as early as 2,000,000 years ago; *Homo sapiens* may have appeared about 50,000 years ago. The difficulties and harassing uncertainties that continually beset anthropological probing are illustrated by a controversy of the mid-1960s. In 1959, the noted African anthropologist L. S. B. Leakey reported a find which seemed to revolutionize the chronology of pre-historic man. Leakey discovered certain skeletal remains which indicated the existence, some 1,700,000 years ago, of a hominid which he called *Zinjanthropus boisie*. His study of the bone fragments caused him to conclude that *Zinjanthropus* was in the direct evolutionary line which eventually led to modern man. The evidence, and his reasoning from it, persuaded many of his colleagues—though by no means all—to rebranch the hominid tree. With this discovery the life of genus Homo was extended back more than a million years. Shortly thereafter Leakey unearthed another find in Africa even more sensational than his first. Skull fragments and parts of an upper and lower jaw permitted him to reconstruct a creature he believed to be older than *Zinjanthropus*. The new find—dubbed *Homo habilis*, "resourceful man"—stood about four feet tall and, unlike the vegetarian *Zinjanthropus,* was an omnivore, as is modern man. In fact, the new discovery forced Leakey and many of his followers to conclude that *habilis* not only preceded *Zinjanthropus* but definitely relegated him to a deadend evolutionary line. Other anthropologists currently question both the meaning of *Homo habilis* and the downgrading of *Zinjanthropus*. In the meantime, most authorities have come to believe that a much earlier find—*Australopithecus africanus*—should now be backdated about 1,000,000 years; that is, to about 1,700,000 years ago. Thus *africanus,* once regarded as the first true hominid, lost his place of distinction to a supposedly much more ancient rival only to have a million years more recently added to his age and be thrust again close to the rank of senior hominid.

Such scholarly buffetings and about-faces warn us of the futility of either demanding or accepting "definitive" answers to our very natural questions about the evolution of man. Given this caution we may briefly note some tentative judgments that seem fairly sound at the present writing.

The cranial capacities of *Zinjanthropus boisie* and *Australopithecus africanus* hardly exceeded that of present-day chimpanzees. On the other hand, their spines were sufficiently erect to allow them to walk in a manner suggesting human locomotion. But for reasons presently unknown they seemed unable to make further progress toward "Homo-hood." Some 500,000 years ago they gave way to two more advanced species, commonly called Java Man and Peking Man. Both walked fairly upright and both possessed cranial cavities larger than their predecessors. Peking Man lived in caves, learned to make fire, and used crude, stone tools. He was followed, some 50,000 years later, by Heidelberg Man, the first hominid to possess definitely human teeth. Perhaps 300,000 years later, Swanscombe Man evolved. His fossil remains suggest a type well advanced along the road to modern man. Indeed, a few authorities, for example Herbert Wendt, believe him to be the first *Homo sapiens.*

TABLE I

Geologic Ages	Cultural Stages	Glacial Record	Evolution of Man
present Holocene	Civilization Food-Producing	Post Fourth Glacial Age	
25,000			
50,000		Fourth Ice Age (75,000 years' duration)	Cro-Magnon and Grimaldi Man
100,000			Neanderthal Man
		Third Interglacial Age (40,000 years)	Swanscombe Man
150,000		Third Ice Age (50,000 years)	
200,000			
250,000			
300,000		Second Interglacial Age (200,000 years)	
350,000			
400,000		Second Ice Age (40,000 years)	Heidelberg Man
450,000			
500,000		First Interglacial Age (75,000 years)	*Pithecanthropus pekinensis* (Peking Man)
550,000			*Pithecanthropus erectus* (Java Man)
600,000– 1,500,000		First Ice Age (75,000 years)	*Zinjanthropus boisie* *Australopithecus africanus* *Homo habilis*

Left-hand vertical labels (spanning the table):
AGE / PLEISTOCENE
FOOD-GATHERING AND COLLECTING STAGE (Paleolithic Age)

(Some authorities substantially update certain periods)

Neanderthal Man appeared at the beginning of the last ice age, about 100,000 years ago. Some authorities consider him a regressive development, or perhaps an anthropological blind alley because, despite his late appearance, he still possessed a very thick skull and a somewhat bent spine. He apparently yielded to modern man in two ways: by extermination, and by absorption. Some evidence seems to indicate that our direct ancestor, Cro-Magnon Man (for Africans, Grimaldi Man) whose spine was wholly erect and whose brain was actually larger than ours, intermarried with female Neanderthalers. In any event, about 50,000 to 25,000 years ago modern man, as we know him today, came to dominate all *homo* forms, and finally to eliminate them.

As other Primates, he had an opposable thumb; that is, he could manipulate his thumb in conjunction with his fingers in such a way that his hand became a tool user. But no other Primate had the two features that made modern *Sapiens* the "sharer of creativity" that he became—an erect spine and, especially, a reflective thinking apparatus. The erect spine enabled him to go about "on two" instead of four, thus freeing his hands for toolmaking and tool using. But it was man's reflective thinking apparatus that gave substantial meaning to his existence. Other animals think, but not reflectively. No cow, for instance, reflects as she chews her cud on the particular joy that will be hers when the spring rains come and the grass grows greener and thicker (or if she does, our total human experience becomes fantastically unreliable). The cow, of course, is aware; but she is not aware that she is aware. Of all living creatures only man possesses this attribute.

As we conclude our rapid survey of the birth of *Homo sapiens* we may be tempted to fret over his lowly beginnings and to feel that his evolution by "natural selection" reduces human life to a thing of chance and purposelessness. The famous anthropolo-

gist, Ernest Hooton, pertinently answers this dolorous query: "We need not," he says, "give man and his ancestors the credit of developing their own intelligence, but if a human being is not a manifestation of an intelligent design, there is no such thing as intelligence." [2]

Preliterate Culture

Food-Gatherers

As paleontologists and anthropologists study the fossil remains of man in an effort to reconstruct his primitive physical history, so archeologists and social anthropologists try to reconstruct his preliterate cultural history by examining the artifacts (buildings, utensils, tools, weapons, etc.) and nonartifactual materials (bones, grains, shells, etc.) he left behind. Although they have been at it scarcely more than a century, their work has already sketched the fundamental aspects of earliest human existence.

From his emergence as a hominid, man was fundamentally a gatherer or collector of food. This is not to imply that his whole time and energy were spent in food-gathering or that the basic significance of his experiences lay in his economic activity. Still, the evidence is clear that this parasitic existence molded a substantial portion of the pattern of early man's motivational life.

He lived in groups, but the groups were quite small (for that matter, it must be understood, hominids *in toto* were few). Sometime after Java Man our early ancestors learned the miracle of firemaking, one of the greatest discoveries in human history. Plentiful archeological evidence shows that these forebears of ours—scattered across parts of Europe, Africa, and Asia—used various crude tools of stone, bone, and antler. During the long period of the last European glacier, homes were built

2. Quoted in Gustav H. R. von Koenigswald, *Meeting Prehistoric Man*, translator M. Bullock, Harpers, New York, 1956, pp. 52–53.

in caves (where they existed; otherwise in the vast open spaces) from which forays went forth for the purpose of slaying the bison and other large game which roamed the tundras that bordered the European ice-sheet.

It is certain that very early man formulated and consistently practiced burial rites. The significance of these rites is a matter of dispute among prehistory specialists — some infer religious meaning, others deny this, holding rather that a fear of "bad luck" probably gave rise to these customs.

Already, during the very late years of the food-gathering stage, the trend toward racial differentiation had probably set in, although the various cultures identified by archeologists do not necessarily bear a race-culture relationship; in other words, the same basic complex of customs might be created and experienced by differing races, such as the sub-Sahara Negroes and the Eastern European Caucasians. Both clothes and homes were probably made of animal skin. The atl-atl — a bone or wood device with thongs attached to its ends, designed to accelerate the speed and force of a stone or spear projected from it — was conceived and effectively used. At this time, too, "hunting drives" were organized. Men of a settlement or "station" would form themselves into two bands of hunters. One band would seek out the game, the other would lie in ambush to fall upon whatever prey was chased into the trap. With greater food supplies available, the human population increased and societal life became correspondingly complex.

Probably as a magical means of insuring good hunting, Cro-Magnon man developed art forms which present-day artists frankly call beautiful by their own standards. Bison, deer, and other animal forms were represented on the ceilings and walls of caves, usually in such a way as to suggest the mastery of man over beasts.

By this time the last great ocean of ice that (about 75,000 years earlier) had spread over great areas of Eurasia, affecting not

Cro-Magnon art about 20,000 B.C.: wall painting of a bison from the Altamira caves.

only its own climates and conditions of living but those of Africa and the Americas as well, had shrunk almost to the vanishing point. As the cold weather retreated, a much changed flora and fauna developed. For example, in northern Africa a "drying out" took place which turned the grasslands into desert while it made more inhabitable the valley of the Nile.

In Europe forests sprang up and man was confronted with a series of new and bewildering environments. In response to these challenges he relied heavily upon the newly developed bow and arrow. Along with the ice, mammoths, bison, and oxen vanished; thus man was forced to concentrate on the smaller, swifter animals which took the place of the retreating or vanishing big game. "Another 'invention' for hunting was the dog, whose parentage is not exactly known. . . . Dogs are affable beings, and the chances are good that they took to hanging around the human camps hoping for scraps and were tolerated in this way and later allowed to come along and make themselves useful in the hunt, long before they were actually 'domesticated' and bred."[3] The domestication of other animals, particularly sheep, goats, and oxen, occurred soon after the domestication of dogs.

3. William W. Howells, *Back of History . . .*, Doubleday, New York, 1954, p. 115.

Food-Producers

In Europe the food-gathering stage lasted until 4000 B.C. and later. But as early as *c.* 9000 B.C., an agricultural revolution took place in Asia (and Africa?) which swiftly led men into ways we call civilized. The central feature of this cataclysmic event was the discovery, possibly by woman, that wild grain—barley and wheat especially—which was used to supplement early man's meat diet, contained seeds which, when deposited in the earth, produced more grain. Thereafter man gradually replaced his chasing and *collecting* habits (although not altogether, of course) with *food-producing* practices. It is this that Gordon Childe refers to when he speaks of "that revolution whereby man ceased to be merely parasitic and, with the adoption of agriculture and stock raising, became a creator emancipated from the whim of his environment." [4] Indeed it is not an exaggeration to say that this revolution was as destiny-laden as the industrial revolution which occurred some ten thousand years later.

Thus man left savagery and entered barbarism. It is not known whether this triumph over environment stimulated man—or, again, more probably woman—to still another epochal discovery, but in any case it was during this period that pottery was invented, in which food and drink were stored for later use. Moreover, not only were more efficient tools produced—the polished stone ax-head, for example—but

a new thrust of creative designing was applied to the concept of *tools to make tools.*

With the agricultural revolution came the settlement of sizable villages and, later, towns. In short, man's wandering days were over (but of course not for all men; nomads still roam certain regions of the earth); now he could settle down and produce food and the materials for clothing instead of chasing around after them. Soon improved grains, possibly the use of manure for fertilizer, plows, hoes, sickles, and techniques for breadmaking (and, it may be added, the brewing of beer) were developed by the farmer-villager. The towns were still small—although Jericho (modern Tell es-Sultan), founded about 9000 years ago and now believed by some experts to be the first "city" in human history, probably had considerably more than the ten to twenty households of the usual precivilization settlement. Since the revolution resulted in a distinct increase in population, clearly urbanism was not far off—no further, actually, than man's solution of two problems that kept primitive society primitive: unceasing war and the lack of adequate food reserves. The time required to establish a food-producing ("Neolithic") culture—in portions of Asia and, somewhat later, in northeast Africa—was brief compared to the long millennia of the food-gathering age; but its accomplishments were tremendous. In the Nile and Euphrates valleys man was ready to effect the "urban revolution," and to establish what we proudly call civilization.

EGYPT — SPHINX AND FALCON

Predynastic History

Settlement of the Valley

About six or seven thousand years ago, late Neolithic peoples began to move into the Nile region. The Valley itself was still

too swampy to permit immediate settlement. On the other hand, beyond the lush strip on either side of the Valley stretched forbidding deserts. Nature and the venture-

4. *New Light on the Most Ancient Near East,* Grove Press, New York, 1957 (?), 4th ed., pp. 1–2.

TABLE II

From Caves to Cities

All dates B.C.

3000	Formal political state, writing, monumentality in art — "civilization"	Mesopotamia
3500	Incipient urbanization; "political" organization of communities	Mesopotamia
4500	Systematized farming; appearance of market towns; migration into valley areas	Mesopotamia
7500	Permanent villages appear	Hilly flanks north and east of Mesopotamia ("Neolithic times")
9000	Incipient agriculture developed; intensification of planned food-collection	Hilly flanks north and east of Mesopotamia ("Neolithic times")
12,000	Food-gathering yielding to "planned collection" of food	Hilly flanks north and east of Mesopotamia ("Neolithic times")
1,500,000–1,000,000	Cave-dwelling hunters, fishers; random food-gathering	Food-gathering (Paleolithic) Near East

Adapted from a chart originally constructed by Professor Robert J. Braidwood who, however, has asked that responsibility for this redraft rest altogether upon the author (J. L. S.).

some human spirit, however, combined to produce a compromise. Flanking spurs, neither swamp nor desert, fringed the life-bearing river, and here the Badarians and the later Nagadians (as archeologists have designated them) settled. The encounter with the Nile had begun.

Artifacts found in graves and settlement sites prove that the Nile dwellers were advanced in the manufacture of flint tools, the materials for which they quarried systematically. Houses or huts of the scattered villages were round, with mud foundations. The Asiatic origin of the settlers' grains and animals suggest migration from the east; almost certainly they were not descendants of the early food-gathering peoples who roamed over North Africa before the last glaciation.

Their religion was characterized by worship of a host of human and animal gods and goddesses. A female figurine of the earliest period shows a fertility goddess cupping her breasts in her hands. Other figures combined human and animal features. Probably the worship of Horus, the falcon god who later came to play a central role in the religio-political life of Egypt, was introduced by invading conquerors (from the Arabian peninsula?) who suddenly debouched into the valley of the upper Nile about 500 years after the Badarians and Nagdians had settled on the river's spurs.

The invaders gradually spread north and south from Nagade (see map), absorbing or displacing the earlier inhabitants; in the north (that is, lower Egypt) the old cultures maintained themselves. Thus there de-

ANCIENT EGYPT

Mediterranean Sea

Nile Delta

Sea of Galilee
•Megiddo
Jerusalem•
Dead Sea

•Tanis

•Heliopolis
Memphis• *Sinai*
LOWER EGYPT *Peninsula*

Mt. Sinai

Fayum Depression

Akheton
(Tell-el-Amarna)

UPPER *Nile River* EGYPT
Abydos• •Nagade
•Thebes
(Karnak; Luxor)

Red Sea

0   50   100   150 mi.
Map by J. Donovan

veloped a Lower Egypt and an Upper Egypt, giving rise to the appellation "Land of Two Lands."

Local communities (nomes, in later terminology), formed about their clan leaders and animal-god totems, slowly evolved group practices and social sanctions. In ways yet impossible from lack of evidence to trace, each of the "Lands" gravitated toward the establishment of a central authority. Thus in the several centuries before 3000 B.C. there came into being the twin kingdoms of the Nile, equipped with bureaucratic systems, owing allegiance to central authority and poised, quite unconsciously, on the brink of history.

Probably the decisive thrust into literate life came from Sumer. There the creation of writing as well as other marks of

civilization had already been achieved. Presumably the invention of writing was marked by two stages. In the first, pictures of objects were drawn—man, tree, boat. In the second, the rebus-principle * was used to convey notions not easily communicable by picture drawing. Since the very earliest Egyptian writing of which we have any record already included the second stage, it is not easy to avoid the assumption that the Egyptians took over both the idea and principles of written expression from Sumerian originals. Among the borrowings were the cylinder seal and the monumental style of architecture, a style which, as we shall see, was so perfected by the Egyptians as to constitute a lasting mark of their genius.

Founding of the First Dynasty

The founding of the First Dynasty involved a physical phenomenon resting on a metaphysical assumption. Both archeological and historical evidence clearly point to a conquest of Lower Egypt by a king from Upper Egypt around 3100 B.C. Although the unity thus created suffered later disruptions, they were temporary. For approximately two thousand years Egypt towered in the Ancient East, truly a colossus.

The Physical Conquest

The physical conquest was effected by "Menes." † From his native town of Thinis, near Abydos, he moved his forces some three hundred miles down the Nile, subjugating the Lower Kingdom's nomes as he went. To serve as a permanent base of operations and administration, a new city which we know as Memphis was built. In Egyptian accounts it was referred to merely as the White Walls. Here the boundaries of the two kingdoms met so that the choice of the site was probably symbolic as well as strategic. Evidence indicates that the struggle for unification was long-lasting, continu-

---

* Symbols with phonetic value of the objects depicted. For instance, the mouth (*ro* in Egyptian) for the consonant *r*.

† According to Egyptian tradition. We do not know the name of the actual conqueror.

CHRONOLOGICAL TABLE (all dates B.C.)

c. 5000 to 3100

Badarians and Nagadians move into Valley (from Asia?)
   established food-producing economy
   worship of most of the traditional Egyptian gods introduced
"New Egyptians" invade and settle Valley
   borrowings from Sumeria:
      writing
      monumental architecture
   population clusters in North and South
   steady urbanization of Egyptian culture
   formation of central authority in Upper (and Lower?) Egypt

c. 3100 to 2700

Founding of First Dynasty
   the "Two Lands" united by "Menes"
   copper mines in Sinai and Nubia worked
Development of administration
General consolidation and organization of cultural gains

c. 2700 to c. 2200

Old Kingdom
   artistic surgence
   isolationist self-consciousness
   highly centralized political theocracy
   rise of nomarchies in the provinces
   wisdom literature first appears

c. 2200 to c. 2050

First Intermediate Period
   collapse of centralized authority
   nomarchical chaos
   literary flowering
   "democratization of the hereafter"

c. 2050 to c. 1800

Middle Kingdom
   redevelopment of political cohesion
   refinement of arts
   economic prosperity
   first really large-scale irrigation project (the Fayum, see map, p. 8)

c. 1800 to c. 1570

Hyksos Invasion—Second Intermediate Period
   foreign rule

c. 1570 to c. 1100

Empire (New Kingdom)
   independence and unity reestablished
   conquest of other lands; period when "Egypt ruled the East"
   foreign influence in religion, culture
   "Amarna" period
   at end: decline of economy, power, political and private morality
      settlement of foreigners (especially Libyans) in Egypt who gradually
         came to dominate the army

King Narmer's palette (c. 3000 B.C.) *shows this Upper Egyptian pharaoh bringing the northern "Land" under his subjection. Narmer is one of several southern pharaohs whose combined efforts unified Egypt.*

ing throughout most of the First Dynasty. The period of cultural consolidation was equally protracted, extending over three or four centuries. But by about 2700 B.C. national dynastic control was a physical reality.

The Metaphysical Assumption

By this time, too, the metaphysical assumption had become firmly fixed. Its essence is simplicity itself; the king (or pharaoh, a word originally designating the royal residence) was a god — not, it must be noted, a delegate or regent of the gods but a god himself. By about 2500 B.C. the notion had become so accepted that pharaohs called themselves sons of the chief god, Re. In our scientific and democratic times such an idea is so patently unthinkable that a school child would reject it, probably along with the notion that human beings seriously could ever have believed it. Yet the Egyp-

tians did. The pharaoh was god; even more, "he, as god, *was* the state." Geographic conditions and the particular Egyptian state of mind may have led to the formulation and acceptance of this belief. Egypt was, indeed, the gift of the Nile, that magic ribbon of water that made the land a livable one; yet Egyptians knew their land was *two.* Here was a mystery of the gods, paramount in their national life but permanently beyond their comprehension. Only a god could reconcile the conflicting forces of the universe, including the contrasts of the Two Lands.

Moreover, the Egyptians were given neither to ventures in mysticism nor to what we would call scientific inquiry. As patient pragmatists, they were willing to try different means to gain their ends. To them, all matter and motion were of the divine substance. They sensed no essential difference in the multiple components of the universe. They ranged easily from the world of men to the realm of gods, and thus readily accepted the idea of the pharaoh as actually a god living on earth in order to rule Egypt.

The Old Kingdom

Government and Economic Life

In the five centuries of the Old Kingdom, elaborate institutions were created many of which, for better or worse, were to endure across the next 2000 years. Theoretically, the pharaoh owned the whole land and all its produce. In practice, this meant that the state, then as now, had the right to tax, draft, and confiscate. Naturally he needed subordinates to help him administer the manifold duties of government. Originally the chief of these came from his family and circle of noble friends. Later a kind of civil service system was worked out which recruited talent wherever it could be found (though usually from the children of officials); in this very limited sense an element of democracy was introduced.

Taxes were levied by the pharaoh and his

advisors and brought into the exchequer by his staff of tax collectors. Each of the "two lands" was divided into approximately twenty nomes, or provinces, ruled by lieutenants selected by the pharaoh. The provincial governors in turn appointed hosts of lesser officials such as treasury and military officers and scribes, who periodically submitted reports on affairs in their nomes. By Dynasty V (see chart, p. 23) these nomarchs were successful in persuading the pharaoh to make their offices hereditary. Thereafter their influence steadily increased, especially in the south. Eventually they sought, sometimes successfully, to usurp royal power when times of trouble beset the king-gods.

A lively foreign trade flourished throughout the whole period of the Old Kingdom. Numerous accounts tell us of the importations of cedar, ivory, ebony, gums, resins, and myrrh. Sometimes these accounts were written to make it seem that the importations were tributes from conquered peoples. But this is hardly likely, for other records speak of Egyptian products, especially manufactured goods, going in the other direction. But agriculture, then and for the long centuries to follow, constituted the basic strength of the nation's economy. Emmer, barley, and cattle formed the bulk of the produce. From the peasants' toil, about one-third to one-half went to the state and to the landlord. In times of famine, large-scale starvation and death were suffered. The ordinary peasant was conscious of his status—superior to animals, far inferior to landowners and even craftsmen. Generally, he seems to have accepted his lot ungrudgingly. Unable to escape burdensome tasks, he sang through his chores when his spirits needed lifting. Where simple guile would serve, he used it; he could also bend under his burdens and bear them.

Women and Marriage

Although Old Kingdom society was essentially man-centered and man-dominated, women were not regarded as chattels. Like men they could own and control property; occasionally they might become officials. But perhaps the best notion of their status, at least during the Old Kingdom period, can be obtained from this excerpt from the writing of an Egyptian in that period:

If thou art a man of standing, thou shouldst found thy household and love thy wife as is fitting. Fill her belly, clothe her back. Ointment is the prescription for her body. Make her heart glad as long as thou livest. She is a profitable field for her lord. Thou shouldst not contend with her at law, and keep her far from gaining control. . . .[5]

The pharaoh possessed a number of concubines; among those who could afford it, polygamy was commonly practiced. Since succession to the throne was provided in large part through matriarchal channels, the habit of brother-sister marriage early developed as a kind of accession insurance, a custom continued down to Roman times. But, contrary to popular belief, no one but royalty practiced it. On the other hand, first-cousin marriages were not only permitted but were favored.

Science and Writing

Science, as we know it today, did not exist. Nowhere does the record indicate an interest in knowing in order to know, or an interest in living what the later Greeks called the "examined life." Egyptian thought was utilitarian. But when he found it useful, the Egyptian pursued knowledge assiduously, and his achievements were remarkable. Early in the Third Dynasty a solar calendar was devised. This had been preceded by two other calendars. The first was constructed to mark the rhythmic flow of the Nile—inundation, seed time, harvest. The second was based on the waxing and waning of the moon, to regulate social, religious, and civil celebrations. But neither satisfied the long-run administrative needs

5. James B. Pritchard, ed., *Ancient Near Eastern Texts* . . . , Princeton University Press, 1955, p. 413.

This basalt slab, inscribed by Egyptian priests in the Hellenistic period, was found by troops of Napoleon in 1799. It contains an inscription written in hieroglyphs, demotic script, and Greek. With this key, scholars were able to decipher hieroglyphic writing and to bring much of Egypt's life into history.

of the complex government apparatus. By patient, tedious observation and calculation, Egyptian officials discovered the 365-day average lapse between the commencement of inundation activities. This average, set up as a standard of time, could then be geared into the wheeling movement of a fixed star, thus giving them a dependable frame of reference.

A numbering system was early devised. With it, Egyptians were able to reckon complicated sums and deal with quantitative differentials. They also worked out some of the fundamental propositions of geometric progression, which gave them a working knowledge of the simpler properties of such figures as they needed to plan the construction of houses, temples, and pyramids.

Medicine was a mixture of knowledge gained by shrewd observation and plain unadulterated magic. The centrality of the function of the heart in the complex of bodily processes was well known. The kind, position, and functions of the bones were early learned. In a surviving papyrus, extensive passages deal with the "scientific" treatment of fractures. But much medical lore included fantastic incantations designed to propitiate or exorcise evil spirits.

Although the idea and basic principles of written language were borrowed from Mesopotamia, both were creatively reworked. Egyptian scribes soon discovered the principle of writing, for example, " ⬜⬜⬜ , the picture of a house, received the value $p + r$ because the Egyptian word for house was *por*, whence—the vowels being felt of as little account—the hieroglyph ⬜⬜⬜ was adopted for writing of a number of words, for example *pire* 'to go forth' which possessed the sounds $p + r$ in that order." [6] It is evident that when such a sound stood for a word of one consonant only (Gardiner gives as an example ⬭ , *ro*—mouth) the Egyptian stood on the verge of alphabet making. That he did not take this imaginative leap—as Phoenician scribes, profiting from this development, later did—hardly detracts from this solid achievement.

Moreover, Egyptian copyists, busy with the expanding affairs of the growing nation, soon found any kind of pictographic writing too cumbersome for rapid, easy use. So they adopted the practice of indicating only the barest outline of each picture or phonetic symbol, thus inventing a cursive that we call hieratic. As writing became a more widespread practice, especially in the Empire period (though it remained throughout the whole of Egyptian history the property of the minority), it tended to become more cursive. Out of this cursive eventually developed the so-called Demotic script (in the seventh century B.C.) which, from about 700 B.C. on, became the writing of those engaged in business.

6. Stephen R. K. Glanville, *Legacy of Egypt*, Oxford University Press, Oxford, 1942, p. 64.

Architecture and Sculpture

It is commonly acknowledged that Egyptian architects employed mass as no people had done before or since. The tombs and temples of the Old Kingdom are enduring wonders. The largest of the pyramid tombs, built by Khufu (Cheops), is properly known simply as the Great Pyramid. About 2 million blocks of stone, some weighing 15 tons, were required to give it the form and substance its creators desired. More than a third the height of the Empire State building, the tomb covered an area of more than 13 acres. Elaborate corridors and chambers were an integral part of the structural design. The King's Chamber, for example, made of granite, had a ceiling constructed of 9 slabs, each weighing over 4 tons.

Beyond superb handling of mass, Egyptian designers solved the architectural problem of space by inventing the column, the arch, and the dome, although the latter two were not used much. Later, Greek architects were to follow Egyptian models in fashioning their own chaste Doric columns.

Sculptors worked both in the round and in relief. Again, in neither was their aim to evoke an aesthetic or intellectual response. Their purpose, instead, was to facilitate the subject's transition from this world to the next and, at the same time, to eternalize his earthly life. So it was customary to set the carefully wrought statues — many of which (like the sitting figure of Khafre) rightfully belong in the category of masterpieces — in the tomb chapels and mortuary temples of the pharaohs or nobles. To depict the form and features of royalty and nobility, a style was early set and faithfully maintained, except for the brief Amarna period. It was characterized by impassive calm and enduring nobility, calculated to suggest and perhaps even in part to effect the eternal existence of the subject. On the other hand, when the models came from the nonruling classes or from the animal world, these stylistic conventions were often abandoned in favor of vivacious realism.

Religion

For the most part the arts flourished in the service of religion. We need now to note some aspects of that religion with its catholic touch, its demanding and ultimately smothering embrace.

Because of the central position of the tomb in Egyptian life, we are naturally inclined to regard the Egyptians as a people morbidly preoccupied with death. Precisely the opposite was true. Egyptians found life zestful and unendingly rewarding. The security they enjoyed, once the goal of political and cultural consolidation was achieved by the leaders of the early dynasties, contributed in large measure to this attitude. Also, a benign climate warmed and brightened the land, while the unfailing rhythm of the mysterious Nile heightened the sense of security and anticipation. From the vantage point of their valley it seemed to the Egyptians that the whole universe conspired for good — their good. This thesis is not meant, of course, to deny or to play down the vicissitudes of life that beset this (as every other) people — sickness and suffering, extended periods of want, famine, class cruelties, and oppressions large and small. It argues merely against the common notion that Egypt was a land of the dead where the goal was the grave.

In short, the Egyptian paid much attention to death because he so much loved life. The pious European ascetic of medieval times might seek death as a prelude to eternal spiritual bliss. But the Egyptian wooed this life; he was anything but spiritual. It was almost impossible for him to think in metaphysical terms. True, he spoke of his *ba*, the soul, and of a *ka*, a kind of generalized and superior personality. But both were thought of as ongoing, glorified magnifications of his earthly being. Very definitely, Egyptian religion was a religion of life.

Originally, only the pharaoh enjoyed immortality by intrinsic right. But this doctrine was soon modified to include his family and his noble retainers. Since the daily life of the masses was dependent upon the eternal existence of the ruler, everything was done to give assurance that this immortality was not endangered. Very likely the pyramid assumed its form and glorified spaciousness for this reason. In Memphite theology, Ptah, the creator, raised an island from chaos—the watery depths—from which he could operate to bring phenomena into existence. This Primeval Hill, as it was called, may have been the original model of the pyramid. One scholar believes that the idea was introduced by Zoser (Djoser), a pharoah of the Third Dynasty. Other authorities suppose that the pyramidal form symbolized the god-king's intermediate position between eternal and temporal existence. In any case, the pyramid-tombs epitomized the link between gods and man, between the now and the hereafter, serving as the specific instrument by which the pharaoh-god Horus became the god Osiris.

Like modern Christianity, Egyptian religion had many forms and often conflicting aspects. In one system, Ptah created all gods and lesser creatures. "And so Ptah was satisfied (or, so Ptah rested), after he had made everything, as well as all the divine order. He . . . had made the cities, he had founded nomes, he had put the gods in their shrines . . . he had made their bodies like that (with which) their hearts were satisfied. . . . So all the gods, as well as their *ka's,* gathered themselves to him, content and associated with the Lord of the Two Lands." [7]

Geography and climate conspired to emphasize the primacy of three gods—Re, Osiris, and Horus. The blazing Egyptian sun dominated cloudless skies and, in a sense, the whole realm; it was natural that the sun god should take a commanding position in the first community of the gods.

7. From the Shabaka Stone, James B. Pritchard, ed., *Ancient Near Eastern Texts . . . ,* Princeton University Press, Princeton, New Jersey, 1955, p. 5.

---

* The emphasis here is upon grain, not the river itself which was associated with its own god, Ha'py.

Similarly the vital, rhythmic flow of the grain-producing Nile occasioned perennial appeals to Osiris.* Although present evidence does not establish it as a fact, it reasonably may be conjectured that Egyptians thought of the eternal winds of the desert, ridden by the high flying falcon, as enveloping the whole life of the "now," epitomized in Horus, the pharaoh-god whose emblem was the falcon. Re was thought of as making his daily journey across the sky from east to west in a boat, a vehicle naturally suggesting itself to a river people. Each night he was rowed back through the Underworld, to reappear triumphantly the next morning. Thus a cycle of birth, death, and rebirth daily impressed itself upon the land, symbolizing and reenforcing belief in the eternality of life. In the same way, the legend of Osiris' death and resurrection gave assurance that endless todays linked forever with endless tomorrows, especially as this same god was the pharaoh who "lived in death," as well as the god of endlessly recurring harvests.

The theology constructed and elaborated in the Old Kingdom made a place for moral and ethical conduct, but it did not give it primacy. The individual was urged to be honest, just, dutiful, and considerate; but chiefly for narrowly selfish ends. That is, moral behavior was sanctioned for the sake of practical expediency—a kind of honesty-is-the-best-policy approach—and to propitiate the gods, themselves almost invariably practical-minded.

Time of Troubles—The First Intermediate Period

By the end of the Sixth Dynasty (around 2200 B.C.), a gradually deepening crisis reached climax. Although the Valley was rich in resources it could not supply the needs of its inhabitants under a "pyramid economy." As this economy declined, its principal units—estates of the nobles—became more restrictively self-contained.

Moreover, as the affairs of the Old Kingdom became more complex and large-proportioned, the authority of the local governor, the nome leader, increased. It is natural to assume that with the increase in power came an increase in the appetite for power. In any case, the evidence is clear that by around 2200 B.C. central authority had become seriously weakened and the powers of the nome leaders had become correspondingly greater.

The interlude between the fading of the Old Kingdom and the flourishing of the Middle Kingdom is called the First Intermediate Period. It lasted about two hundred years.

During this period the land of the Two Kingdoms, now split into a hodgepodge of contending nomarchies, was characterized by a kind of feudal anarchy. Although records show the existence of what were called the Seventh and Eighth Dynasties, their pharaohs were shadowy figures. Individual nome leaders exercised what control they could over their local areas. During the Ninth Dynasty of Herakleopolis, nomarchs fought each other in Middle and Upper Egypt for control of the Valley. In the meantime, numerous Asians from the Fertile Crescent had filtered into the defenseless delta. Eventually a new dynasty (the Eleventh) arose in Thebes and consolidated its position in the southern part of Upper Egypt. For about three generations, the Theban kings of the Eleventh Dynasty fought the Herakleopolitan Tenth and its vassal nomarchs in middle Egypt and succeeded once more in bringing unity and order to Egypt. The invaders were either expelled from the land or were absorbed into the population.

A scribe of these troubled times has left an account of the bewildering and anarchic conditions which is worth quoting in part:

Why really the Nile is in flood, (but) no one plows for himself, (because) every man says: "We do not know what may happen to the land!"

Why, really, women are dried up, and none can conceive. Khnum ["the potter god (who)

shaped infants on his wheel"] cannot fashion (mortals) because of the state of the land. . . .

Why really, the land spins as a potter's wheel does. The robber is (now) the possessor of riches. . . .

[Why] really, the desert is (spread) throughout the land. The homes are destroyed. Barbarians from outside have come to Egypt. . . . There are really no people anywhere. . . .

Why really, all maid-servants make free with their tongues. When the mistresses speak, it is burdensome to the servants. . . .

So Lower Egypt weeps. The storehouse of the king is a (mere) come-and-get-it for everybody, and the entire palace is without its taxes. . . .[8]

Thus there appeared in the land a spirit of doubt and dismay, of disbelief in gods and men, and a corresponding tendency to live a life of abandon and sensationalism, reminding us of our own century's Jazz Age, with its theme of "Running Wild."

But Egypt's confidence and optimism were clouded, not killed; eventually the dynast of a Theban house successfully brought an end to the chaos and restored unity to the land.

The Middle Kingdom

The new nation that slowly formed is called by modern historians the Middle Kingdom to distinguish it from the Old Kingdom and the Empire (or New Kingdom) which followed it after another interlude of darkness. But the aptness of the term goes somewhat beyond chronological classification. For in politics, art, morals, and religion a new note was struck, characterized by a groping for sophisticated moderation and a refined concern for a more humane way of life.

The new pharaohs (almost all of the Twelfth Dynasty), although continuing to give lip service to the concept of their divine nature, infallible and omnipotent, did not wholly act the part. Nome leaders, for example, were granted a degree of decision-making unheard of in the grand days of the

8. Pritchard, *op. cit.,* pp. 441–443, *passim.*

Old Kingdom. Occasionally a pharaoh frankly confessed that he had made mistakes, an admission unthinkable in the Old Kingdom rulers. Throne names reflected the new attitude. That of Amenemhet II, for example, was "He Who Takes Pleasure in Ma'at"; that of Senusert II, "He Who Makes Ma'at Appear." In Egyptian thought, *ma'at* meant concern for the good way of life, for "right justice," and at least a measure of tolerant understanding.

In this period the copper mines of Mount Sinai were systematically worked and tin was added to the refined ore, so that the Bronze Age began. Trading was carried on with peoples of the eastern Mediterranean shore as well as with sea peoples to the north and Nubians to the south. One of the most ambitious projects carried out by the kings of Dynasty XII was the conversion of portions of the Fayum depression (see map, p. 8) into a large flood-control area designed to serve the needs of Lower Egypt. In addition, certain areas adjacent to the Fayum were brought under cultivation for the first time. Although economic affluence was still restricted to official classes, some amelioration of the lot of workers seems to have occurred; and some laborers became artisans or independent farmers. Political as well as economic changes were effected; for the dual program was of a nature so ramifying and complex that large-scale cooperation of many settlements was required, thus knitting together many hitherto semi-isolated communities.

Religion and the Arts

In religious thought the Egyptian of this time was in a transitional state between dynamism, animism, pantheism, and monotheism. By 2000 B.C. the Nile dweller, though cautiously, had come to probe the meaning of his traditional belief in God as force and God as many. It is possible that some Egyptian intellectuals were beginning to suspect that one pulsing power made up the universe. If so, they were in-

deed close to pantheism. And an indication of how close the times came to investing religion with ethical concern appears in an excerpt from the "king's instruction," noted above, an excerpt that easily could pass for a line from the writings of one of the later Hebrew prophets: "More acceptable is the character of one upright of heart than the ox of the evil doer." * Here the inner moral worth of the individual is weighted more heavily than oblations, incantations, and sacrifices. But, in actual fact, neither the road to pantheism nor to ethical (or any other kind of) monotheism was taken by the Middle Kingdom Egyptian.

Preeminently the arts flourished, and even the crafts achieved a distinction of rare quality. The exquisite jewelry that belonged to the royal princesses reveals the dexterity and subtle craftsmanship of Egyptian workmen. Fortunately for us, many treasures of the Dahshur necropolis escaped the attention of tomb robbers; otherwise we might never have known of the artistic capabilities of the Middle Kingdom craftsmen.

Writers of the period excelled in their creations, ranging feelingly and subtly over many subjects. Some of the tales were of such heroic proportions and continuing worth that they have influenced modern literature (for example, "The Story of Sinuhe"; see readings list at end of this chapter). In architecture, pyramids became less mountainous; some sculptured works were cast in less massive molds. Altogether, the artistic sensibilities of the Valley people were given ample scope for creative expression.

Thus for over 200 years the reunited Two Lands gave promise of a new freedom. Although periodic raids reached into the outside world, in the main the nation pursued the arts of peace. For a while it

---

* Compare, for example, with Micah's sentiments, where he denounces ritualistic sacrifice and asks, "What doth the Lord require of thee but to love mercy, do justly, and walk humbly with thy God?"

seemed that the collective genius of the human spirit might flower into the chaste grandeur of true sophistication. But the challenge proved too great. The Middle Kingdom began to show signs of inability to "survive national prosperity and the renewal of materialism." Provincial privileges, fed by parochial pride, weakened the fabric of national life. Sesostris III arrested the development by eliminating the powerful nomarchs of Middle Egypt, who suddenly disappeared in his time. But the drift toward political particularism was resumed at his death. Soon the second act of the Egyptian drama was over; the Middle Kingdom had had its opportunity—and its day.

The Second Intermediate Period, and Imperial Egypt— The Hyksos Interlude

Evidence indicates that the Hyksos—a term signifying "rulers of foreign lands"—swept into Egypt from the Palestine area about 1670 B.C. They brought with them advanced fighting equipment (the composite bow, for example) with which they were able to subdue most of Egypt.

The capital was moved to Tanis in the delta region, into which flowed booty and tribute from all parts of the kingdom. Since Egyptian culture was superior to that

brought in by the "barbarians," the newcomers took over what they could understand and use. This, it developed, was not a little; indeed before they were expelled they had become almost completely Egyptianized. If the arts did not flourish under the new rulers they at least did not markedly decline. A number of scientific observations recorded by Egyptian scribes were recopied and presumably studied. And a reasonable order and justice seemed to prevail throughout a large part of the nation. Still, in the main, civilization marked time in the Valley.

Sometime around 1600 signs of serious restiveness appeared. As in the First, so in the Second Intermediate Period Thebes served as the nucleus of opposition and of unifying activity. Though most of the high officials seemed satisfied with the status quo, royalty was not. The struggle to oust the invaders was begun by Sekeneure Ta'o II, continued by Kamos whose premature death gave the movement's leadership to his brother Ahmose who, in his eleventh reigning year, finally succeeded in capturing Tanis. Even this triumph was not enough. For over a hundred years the sacred land had suffered foreign rule. If left at the delta's edge, might not the foreign hosts return? So they were pursued to Sharuhen, near the first Palestinian settlements, which the Egyptians took after a three years' siege. Once again the Two

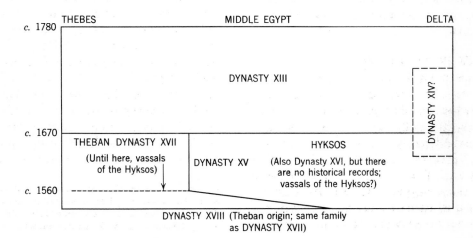

Kingdoms were one; once again Egypt was the Valley of the Gods. Still, haunting questions remained: Might not history repeat itself? Might not the sacred Valley again suffer profane violation at the hands of new barbarians?

Imperial Egypt

The Resort to Conquest

The Amenhoteps and Thutmoses (four of each) of the Eighteenth Dynasty thought they knew the answer: the conquest and occupation of other lands. In the beginning the reasoning was deceptively simple. Foreign invaders had come from the north. If a buffer state was created there, Egypt would be secure. So the region immediately adjacent to the delta was brought under control. But then—what of *its* future security? As added insurance, Egyptian legions conquered areas farther north. Before Ahmose (the first of the Eighteenth Dynasty rulers) had died, Egypt's new borders had been extended to about 70 miles from Jerusalem. As we shall presently note, a long pause then followed while the Land of the Two Lands was reknit internally. Thereafter the imperialist impulse drove all before it until checked by Mitanian troops along the great bend of the Euphrates—all, that is, in Palestine, Phoenicia, and practically the whole of Syria.

Centuries before, pharaohs had probed the northland. But those thrusts were sporadic and more in the nature of raids than attempts to build an empire. Why the great drive now? Documentary evidence does not spell out the answer. But the inference seems clear. The shock of foreign invasion, the build-up of vengeful patriotism, the victorious sweep of "foreign devils" from the land had worked a change in Egypt's image of itself and of the world about. One may perhaps liken the psychological shift somewhat to that experienced by Japan in the latter half of the nineteenth century. For ages Japan had been an island kingdom, turned within herself, unaware or but con-temptuously aware of the world around her. "Opened" by Americans in the 1850s she suddenly sensed the power and potential hostility of the outer world, and "awakened" to her own latent powers and demanding needs; within a century's span she was in control of a large portion of Southeast Asia.

Ahmose's two successors drove south to conquer Nubia (to Egyptians, the land of "Kush") and checked Libyan raids in the west. But the long century of Hyksos rule had wrought too many disruptive changes to give the Valley people's kings time or energy for external adventures. The land of the gods had been scarred and profaned; a time of healing and reconstruction was required. Under Hatshepsut (1486–1468 B.C.), thorough national renovation was effected. New buildings and temples were constructed, cults were reestablished, and the offended gods were propitiated. Within a generation, Egypt seemed herself again.

The Spread of Empire

Her successor, Thutmose III, spent the next three decades creating an empire such as the ancient world had never seen. In Egyptian nomenclature the region of present-day Palestine and the coastland of Phoenicia was called Djahi; that lying between Beirut and Damascus, Coelesyria; * the lands to the north, so far as the Euphrates, Retenu. In none of these areas was there a strongly consolidated state; rather, each was made up of many small communities endlessly quarreling among themselves. The retreating Hyksos, it is true, had formed a loosely organized confederation in parts of Palestine which, led by the king of Kadesh, tried to stand against the advancing Egyptians. They took their stand at Megiddo (see map, p. 8) east of the Sea of Galilee. To get at them the legions of pharaoh had to file through a narrow pass and at great risk debouch into

---

* Greek equivalent of the Egyptian word denoting "hollow Syria."

the valley of Esdraelon. Why the Kadesh chieftain allowed them to negotiate this route without harassment is unknown. The two armies fell upon each other in the open plain, where in a one-day battle the northern forces were completely routed. If the booty they left behind had not been so tempting they might have been destroyed before escaping behind the protective walls of Megiddo. Even so, complete capitulation was only postponed, for after a seven-months' siege by the Egyptians they were starved into surrender. According to a contemporary Egyptian account:

Then that fallen one [the chief of Kadesh], together with the chiefs who were with him, caused all their children to come forth to my majesty with many products of gold and silver, all their horses with their trappings, their great chariots of gold and silver with their painted equipment, all their implements of war—those things, indeed, with which they had come to fight against my majesty. And now they brought them as tribute to my majesty while they stood on their walls giving praise to my majesty in order that the breath of life might be given to them.

Then my majesty caused them to swear an oath, saying: "Never again will we do evil against Menkheperre [praenomen of Thutmose III]—may he live forever—our lord, in our lifetime, for we have witnessed his power. Let him only give breath to us according to his desire. . . ."

Then my majesty allowed to them the road to their cities, and they went, all of them, on donkeys. For I had taken their horses, and I carried off their citizens to Egypt and their property likewise.[9]

Thereafter, Thutmose III undertook the subjugation of all the peoples of Coelesyria and Retenu. In two campaigns the conquering Pharaoh burned and battled his way to the Euphrates. Although rebellions broke out from time to time, necessitating reconquest, the near East, from Sharuhen to Naharin, and from the Mediterranean coast

to the Euphrates River, ultimately acknowledged the overlordship of the living Horus. So fearfully renowned had he and his rampaging forces become that the conquest of Nubia, to the south, was accomplished with hardly a struggle.

The "New" Egypt

A steady stream of wealth flowed into Egypt from the conquered lands—cattle and slaves, gold and silver, coniferous woods (particularly the "cedars of Lebanon"), and vases of alabaster, wines and oils, grains and furniture—the list is endless. A great amount of this "tribute" went to the god Amon and his priests. Temples were erected and priests were supplied to attend them. The new wealth was also used to pay and provision mercenary troops. Much, too, was spent on the rapidly multiplying personnel recruited to staff the ever-growing civil bureaucracy. On the other hand, little trickled down to the masses. Actually, in one sense their lot became worse: for whereas formerly a degree of social mobility marked Egyptian life, in most of the Empire period a sharp class cleavage existed. Indeed, a general change, reaching far beyond class cleavage, came over Egyptian life. Although at no time in its history, including the Empire Period, did urbanization as we know it today develop, a cosmopolitan air settled over the land. On the surface, the hold of tradition seemed strong; but change and a desire for the new infiltrated the multiple interstices of the whole society. Changes ranged from such simple innovations as random tree planting in landscape gardening (in place of "orderly rows of trees planted in careful balance") to a reformulation of the spirit of the people. The old, secure "folk society" was gone. And with its going, alarms and fears beset ordinary citizens and officials alike. None knew when new invaders might threaten again. The bureaucratic apparatus was expanded and military preparations were increased. But such security measures apparently made the people feel only more inse-

9. George Steindorff and Keith C. Seele, *When Egypt Ruled the East,* University of Chicago Press, Chicago, 1942, p. 55.

cure. On the other hand, imperial power and wealth encouraged a restless search for new experiences, giving to the land something of the atmosphere of our "Gilded Age."

During the latter part of the Eighteenth and a substantial portion of the Nineteenth Dynasties (roughly the three hundred years from 1550 to 1250 B.C.), artists of the Empire Period responded to the quickened pulse of the new life. At Thebes (Karnak) and Luxor, its suburb, colossal colonnaded halls, courts, temples, obelisks, and statuary "produced an impression both of gorgeous detail and overwhelming grandeur of which the sombre ruins . . . impressive as they are, offer little hint at the present day." In literature new genres appeared. Especially noteworthy was the evolution of a delicate love poetry. The following is a fair sample of the new form:

> Seven days from yesterday I have not
>   seen my beloved
> And sickness hath crept over me,
> And I am become heavy in my limbs
> And am unmindful of mine own body.
> If the master-physicians come to me,
> My heart hath no comfort of their remedies,
> And the magicians, no resource is in them,
> My malady is not diagnosed.
> · · · · · · · · · · · · · ·
> Better for me is my beloved than any
>   remedies, . . .
> My salvation is when she enteres from
>   without,
> When I see her, then am I well;
> Opens she her eye, my limbs are young
>   again, . . .
> And when I embrace her, she banishes evil,
> And it passes from me for seven days.[10]

The Religious Revolution

In religion a curious paradox developed. Outwardly the forms and symbols were the same as they always had been. A citizen of the Old Kingdom, returning to the expansive Empire, would have found himself at home in almost any temple of the land. But

the "true believer" of Old Kingdom days, to say nothing of the probing seeker of the Middle Kingdom period, was gone. True, temples and priests multiplied as never before. But the rites were practiced mechanically, without conviction; and dependence upon sheer magic and the power of incantations deepened. Two thousand years of civilized life had failed to produce an enriched and enlightened metaphysic.

After two centuries of imperial grandeur, military conquest, territorial expansion, and moral and religious deterioration, a religiously grounded reaction set in. The revolution, aesthetically seeded in the reign of Amenhotep III (1413–1377 B.C.), erupted suddenly following the accession to the throne of Amenhotep IV (Akhenaton, 1377 B.C.). He and his sister-wife— the beautiful Nefertiti—were profoundly dissatisfied with the spiritual foundations of the Empire. The close association of Amon-Re with the imperial banners, the rituals of that god's growing army of priests (who were, moreover, part of the control group which today we call the power elite), the hypocritical abuse of Ma'at—these and other developments caused the king and his consort to throw off the yoke of tradition and to attempt to create a new cult concentrated on a single god, an exceedingly un-Egyptian enterprise.

Repudiating Amon-Re and his ubiquitous priests the young pharaoh, whom Breasted has called the first *individual* in history, dropped his original throne name (Ahmenhotep—"Amon is satisfied") in favor of Akhenaton ("Beneficial to the Aton"). From Thebes the machinery of government was moved to a new site, about midway between Thebes and Memphis, especially chosen as ground for the new capital (the modern Tel el Amarna).

Central in Akhenaton's system was his worship—and through him that of all Egyptians—of the Aton whose representative he was. He stressed natural living. For example, the Pharaoh directed royal artists and sculptors to give up the stylized pat-

10. Alan H. Gardiner, "Writing and Literature," in Glanville, *op. cit.*, p. 77.

terns of the past and to portray him as he was—and everyone else as they were. Since the king's own physique was rather unusual—sloping shoulders, heavy hips, a distinct pot belly—the direction was at least courageous. In an attempt to erase the memory of Amon and the other gods, Akhenaton ordered references to them chiseled out of all the monuments in the land.

The new religion emphasized the central sway of one god who ruled not only Egypt but the whole world. Every land, according to the famous "Hymn to the Aton," was filled with the god's beauty which extended "to the outermost limits of all that thou hast made." Every man was put in his own place; every people was provided with its own language; they were distinguished from one another by the color of their skin, as well as by their speech. For Egypt there was the life-giving Nile; but the Aton had caused "Niles in the heaven" to water the soils of other peoples, and thus give them opportunity to sow and to reap and to live. To administer the practices of the new religion, Akhenaton created his own hierarchy of priests. They saw to it that Aton was never represented in human or animal form but always as the life-giving sun. Magical incantations disappeared. They were replaced by prayers to the Aton. No longer were tomb walls decorated with representations of various life-time activities of the one entombed. Instead, all paintings and relief works centered in worship scenes glorifying Aton and his pharaoh-son. Whether these drastic changes tokened a developing monotheism is debatable. Some specialists, such as Breasted and Frankfort, have argued that they do; others, particularly Wilson, believe they point not to monotheism but to syncretism or monolatry. In any case, the changes were basic.

Amon-Re's priests, to say nothing of the bewildered average Egyptian whose whole way of life was outraged by such large-scale innovations, resented the loss of position, security, and in general the familiar con-

Akhenaton and his family worshipping the Aton.

ditions of the old life. Within a few years a strong reaction had set in. There is reason to believe that the Pharaoh himself was toying with some kind of a compromise solution when after a decade of strenuous effort to convert his people, he died, leaving his young son-in-law, Tutankhamon, to deal with the growing unrest. Still a boy, Tutankhamon and his regents quickly yielded to public and government pressure. Within a short time the governmental apparatus was returned to Thebes and Memphis, and the revolution was over. (Our stress has been on the religious motivation of Akhenaton's innovations. Some scholars believe Akhenaton was less concerned with religious reform than with breaking the power of Amon's priests.)

The few years remaining to the Eighteenth Dynasty (1360–1320 B.C.) were spent reestablishing the old regime and consolidating the remaining empire in Asia. On the surface at least, Egypt had returned to her ancient ways.

Imperial Ventures Renewed

To the early pharaohs of the succeeding Nineteenth Dynasty it seemed that the Empire of Thutmose III could and should be reconquered. Consequently Egyptian legions marched again. Under Seti I (c. 1300 B.C.), a large part of Palestine was brought under subjugation and the frontier was extended into Syria. Here, however, a new threat loomed. For some time a new people, the Hittites, had been consolidating their strength in southeastern Anatolia (see Chapter 3). Egypt's new push for power and imperial glory coincided with similar Hittite ambitions. In the first skirmishes that followed, the Egyptians came off victors. Thereafter, however, a long drawn-out tug developed that seriously sapped the strength of both contestants. In an effort to deal a decisive blow to the northern "barbarians," Ramses II led a large army against them (c. 1285 B.C.). Things did not turn out well. For one thing, Hittite strength had grown disproportionate to Egypt's strength. For another, the new expedition was none too wisely led. Hoping to drive the increasingly aggressive Hittites from their stronghold of Kadesh (in Syria), Ramses blunderingly led his armies into a trap. Although he personally escaped death or capture—indeed, he returned home to boast of a great victory—the Hittites were not driven back, and the Egyptians, for all their Pharaoh's boasting, had to abandon plans of conquering all of Syria.

Eventually both states recognized the need to come to some kind of terms. The Hittites might have beat down the one-time masters of the East if they had had only Egypt to contend with. But by the thirteenth century, as we shall see later, various "Sea Peoples" were forcing their way into the narrow corridor and areas adjacent to it. These continuing attacks drained off a substantial portion of Hatti's war potential. About 1280 B.C. an alliance was concluded that called for each to recognize a vaguely defined neutralized zone in Syria, to help the other if attacked by a third major power, and to exchange what today we would call "displaced persons." The lengthy document was written in the international language of the day (Akkadian cuneiform) and appropriately was attested to by a host of divine witnesses. All the evidence—and there is considerable—points to the treaty's lasting effects. Neither side ever again sent its forces against the other; reciprocal aid was extended; and a highly publicized state marriage set a special seal on the arrangements (when a young Hittite princess was made wife of the not-so-young Ramses II). But it could not save Hatti from the steadily stepped-up assaults of the Sea Peoples and the Assyrians. By the end of the thirteenth century she was overrun and occupied, leaving Egypt alone before the gathering hosts.

"The Empty Years"

About 1200 B.C. a prince of one of the "northern barbarian" states battered his way into Egypt. According to the plaintive terms of an Egyptian document, the Syrian conqueror "set the entire land as tributary before him. One joined his companion so that their property might not be plundered. They treated the gods like the people, and no offerings were presented in the temples." [11] Under Ramses III the foreigners were driven out, and imperial glory faintly beckoned again. The Sea Peoples were repulsed, and Palestine was retaken.

11. John A. Wilson, *The Burden of Egypt,* University of Chicago Press, 1951, p. 257 (later published under the title *The Culture of Ancient Egypt* as a Phoenix paperback).

CHRONOLOGICAL TABLE OF PERIODS, DYNASTIES, AND PHARAOHS

With certain exceptions, dates are given in rounded figures. Before 2000 B.C. a margin of 100 years or so should be allowed; after 2000 B.C. the margin may be reduced within a range of 50 to 5 years. Since all dates are B.C., these initials are not repeated in the table. It should be noted that not all of the pharaohs are included.

Predynastic Period	about 5000 to 3100
Dynasties I and II	3100 to 2700
Old Kingdom	2700 to 2200
Dynasty III	2700 to 2650
Zoser	2700
Dynasty IV	2650 to 2500
Seneferu	2650
Khufu (Cheops) "Pyramid Age"	2630
Khafre	2600
....	......
Dynasty V	2550 to 2400
Dynasty VI	2400 to 2250
First Intermediate Period	2250 to 2050
Dynasties VII and VIII	2225 to 2155
Dynasties IX, X and XI (period of confused claims to throne)	2115 to 2000
Middle Kingdom	2050 to 1780
Dynasty XII	1991 to 1780
Amenemhet I	1991 to 1961
Senusert I	1971 to 1926
Amenemhet II	1929 to 1894
Senusert II	1897 to 1878
Amenemhet III	1840 to 1792
Second Intermediate Period	1780 to 1550
(see chart, p. 17)	
Kamose	1585
Empire	1570 to 1090
Dynasty XVIII	1570 to 1320
Ahmose I	1570 to 1545
Amenhotep I	1545 to 1525
Thutmose I	1525 to 1495
....	......
Hatshepsut	1486 to 1468
Thutmosis III (conqueror of Palestine and Syria)	1490 to 1436
Amenhotep II	1436 to 1413
....	....
Amenhotep III	1403 to 1366
Amenhotep IV – Akhenaton (Ikhnaton)	1377 to 1360
Tutankhamon	1360 to 1351
....	......
Haremhab	1347 to 1319
Dynasty XIX	1319 to 1205
Ramses I	1319 to 1318
Seti I	1318 to 1304
Ramses II (period of Exodus of Jews?)	1304 to 1238
....	......
Dynasty XX	1200 to 1090
Post-Empire Period	1090 to 664
Dynasties XXI to XXV	1090 to 664
Saite Period	664 to 525
Persian Conquest	525
Conquest by Alexander the Great	332

The above is a somewhat modified version of Wilson's "Chronology" from his *Burden of Egypt*, pp. vii–viii.

But the elan of Egypt was weak, and her people were tired. Under Ramses IV all foreign territories were lost forever. With the flow of tribute stopped, economic hard times beset the land. Goods became scarce, prices rose, and inflation spread throughout the Valley. To make things worse, iron had by now become the dominant metal; Egypt had no iron mines, no means to purchase iron products. Thus stricken, the nation degenerated into a jungle of warring nomes hacking away at each other, and at ever-bolder invaders. Libyan chieftains carved out provinces in the west. Ethiopian princes drove down from the south and, for a while, set up a ruling dynasty (XXV, 712–664 B.C.). In the later years of their ascendancy, Assyrian conquerors overran Lower Egypt and dictated internal and external affairs under puppet pharaohs. The wings of Horus, the falcon god who once had ridden triumphantly the high winds of imperial conquest, drooped in defeat. Now could the mournful dirge of an earlier time of troubles speak again to the stricken people: "Why really, laughter has disappeared, and is [no longer] made. It is wailing that pervades the land, mixed with lamentation."

Even so, the end was not yet. In the seventh century Assyria was forced by threats from the north to withdraw from her garrison sites. A prince from Sais, in Lower Egypt, founded a new dynasty (XXVI, 664–525). Once again the land was united; once again the future seemed bright. Trade flourished, especially with the Greek city-states, and with communities along the Phoenician coast. Foreign powers, busy holding each other in check, left the Land of Two Lands alone and in peace. But it was a peace of cultural stasis, of spiritual retrogression. Apprehensive of the new and seemingly cowed by its challenges, Saite Egypt reached back into the past for security and serenity. Old and Middle Kingdom customs, literary genres, and art forms became sacrosanct models.

Such posturing before the mirror of history could not hope to develop meaningful growth or even to maintain itself. Any storm, from within or without, would destroy it. For modern readers Cleopatra's Egypt evokes a certain sense of excitement and curiosity. In reality the scenes of her day were sterile and empty — and had been for a half millennium before her. The storm came in 525 B.C. when the Persians swept down into the Valley and exploited the land. In 332 B.C. Alexander the Great repeated the process as, with melancholy monotony, did the Romans, the Moslems and, in the century before ours, the British. The Hebrew prophet, Isaiah, concerned over his own people turning from the Lord to seek refuge in military alliances, looked to Egypt as a lesson and warned in the voice of Jehovah: "And I will set the Egyptians against the Egyptains: and they shall fight everyone against his brother, and everyone against his neighbor. . . . And the spirit of Egypt shall fail in the midst thereof."

The long drama of the Sphinx and the Falcon was over.

SELECTED READINGS

Emergent Man

Braidwood, Robert J., *Prehistoric Men,* University of Chicago Press, 1963 (6th ed.).
> Probably the best introductory work on the subject. Professor Braidwood has made a special effort to present the material in a style inviting to the lay reader. Some prehistorians will not agree with certain of his conclusions, but the reader is given fair warning of their controversial nature.

Ceram, C. W. (Kurt W. Marek), *The March of Archeology,* Alfred A. Knopf, New York, 1958.
> The author's frank statement that his book "is not basically a scientific but a literary work" should not deter the serious student from its careful study. There is no more interesting and useful introduction to archeology than this work. Almost every page is illustrated by either a halftone or color plate, an illuminating chart, or a helpful chronological table.

*Childe, Gordon, *New Light on the Most Ancient Near East,* Grove Press, New York, 1952.

A standard work which any serious student of the genesis of civilization should read. The author's argument for the "urban revolution" has been challenged in recent years, as have his diffusionist views.

*Childe, Gordon, *What Happened in History,* Pelican, New York, 1957.

A general and highly readable account of human development from earliest times through the "decline and fall of the ancient world."

Clark, Grahame, *World Prehistory: An Outline,* Cambridge University Press, Cambridge, 1961.

A general survey of prehistoric human life ranging in subjects from man's place in nature to recent aboriginal culture; and ranging in time from the glacial periods to present nonliterate cultures.

Clark, Grahame, and Stuart Piggott, *Prehistoric Societies,* Alfred A. Knopf, New York, 1965.

An attempt by two trained scholars to present the data of the specialists to lay readers. Its theme leaves the current of pessimistic evaluations of human development. It frankly aims at restoring "a little confidence not only in man's capacity to endure the frequent catastrophes of human existence but also in his intellectual abilities."

Coon, Carlton S., *The Story of Man . . . ,* Alfred A. Knopf, New York, 1962.

This book presents a reliable account of what anthropologists have discovered about the development of man from his hominid origins through his emergence as a reflectively thinking creature. Except for the author's use of contemporary primitive societies as guides for interpreting some anthropological data, this work is probably more generally accepted by scholars in the field than any other.

Engle, Shirley H., *New Perspectives in World History,* National Council for Social Studies, New York, 1964.

A collection of essays by various specialists. For a good brief account of how man evolved from lower animal life, and for details of new hominid findings, see Chapter 6.

* Asterisk (*) denotes paperback.

Hawkes, Jacquetta, and Sir Leonard Wooley, *Prehistory and the Beginnings of Civilization,* George Allen and Unwin, London, 1963.

This is the first volume of Unesco's grand design to bring out a multivolumed history of the cultural and scientific development of mankind. The date of publication is somewhat misleading. Because of its unusually long period of preparation, some of the volume's conclusions became outdated before it went to press.

The extensive notes placed at the end of each chapter are a mixed blessing for the non-specialist. Some are more useful than the textual comment to which they refer; others are simply uncalled for or, at worst, an encumbrance. The reader has to fend for himself as best he can.

Leakey, L. S. B., *The Progress and Evolution of Man in Africa,* Oxford University Press, London, 1961.

This small book can be read in one sitting. It seeks in one chapter to trace and place the evolution of Africa's earliest "near men." The other chapter (actually the first; both were originally lectures delivered to English university audiences) presents a lively argument for the upgrading of our understanding of African culture.

Moore, Ruth, *The Earth We Live On,* Alfred A. Knopf, New York, 1956.

An attempt, in the main successful, to explain in lay terms the views and findings of earth scientists from about 1700 to mid-twentieth century. For a general understanding of the basic structure, changing forms, and fundamental forces that constitute and characterize our planet it is worth reading. But it should be kept in mind that the author is not a scientist, and that some of the data she deals with are not in the current stream of scholarly study.

Parks, Henry B., *Gods and Men: The Origin of Western Culture,* Alfred A. Knopf, New York, 1959.

Special emphasis is given to Hellenic concepts and Judeo-Christian beliefs. The author disdains the "objective" approach in his study of our cultural heritage. In a very real sense he is an advocate of a way of life.

Egyptian Society

Baumgartel, Elsie J., *The Cultures of Prehistoric Egypt,* Oxford University Press, London, 1955.

This is the most satisfactory, indeed almost the only, study of Egyptian society before the rule of the dynasts. Miss Baumgartel considers these questions: who were the earliest post-Paleolithic inhabitants; what parts of Egypt were settled; what environmental conditions favored and hindered settlement; what were the religious and economic habits of the settlers; what were the relations between the peoples of Upper and Lower Egypt?

Breasted, James A., *A History of Egypt,* Charles Scribner's Sons, New York, 1912.

This pioneering, comprehensive work on the civilization of Egypt is still very useful. Probably no other historian of this civilization offers to the student such penetrating insights and profound understanding; but it should be used with the works of Wilson, and Steindorff and Seele, cited below.

*Edwards, I. E. S., *The Pyramids of Egypt,* Pelican, New York, 1961.

This is a revised edition of the original 1947 publication and not a reprint. It is sound, interestingly written, and comprehensive.

Frankfort, Henri, *Kingship and the Gods,* University of Chicago Press, Chicago, 1948.

Easily the best work on this subject. The duties of the king are described in detail, as are the devices and ceremonies of royal succession and the relationship of kingship and divine powers. Egyptian views and practices are described in the first half of the book, Mesopotamian in the second.

Glanville, R. K., *The Legacy of Egypt,* Oxford University Press, London, 1942.

A series of articles by specialists. The essays consider such items as mechanical and technical processes in ancient Egypt, science and medicine, and calendars and chronology. They are dated but still worth using.

Janson, H. W., *History of Art,* Prentice-Hall, Englewood Cliffs, New Jersey, 1962.

This lavish and enlightening display of Egyptian art (pp. 35–49) should be used with Pritchard's texts.

Kees, Hermann, *Ancient Egypt,* University of Chicago Press, Chicago, 1961.

Given access to and use of Wilson and Breasted, students may pass over parts one and two of this book. Part three describes in detail particular cities and areas such as Memphis, Abydos, Amarna, the Delta region, and the Fayum.

Montet, Pierre, *Eternal Egypt,* Doreen Weightman, translator, Weidenfeld and Nicholson, London, 1964.

An internationally known Egyptologist here presents in 300 pages a lucid, readable account of Egyptian life. Its topical arrangement makes it especially attractive when used with Breasted's work which, of course, it updates.

Moscati, Sabatino, *The Face of the Ancient Orient,* University of Chicago Press, Chicago, 1960.

An interpretive study of the fundamental characteristics of the civilizations of the ancient Near East. The author presents the main features of the "components": Sumerians, Babylonians, Assyrians, Egyptians; describes the catalytic effect upon these features of various small states; and the grand synthesis effected by Persia. Generous and pertinent selections from original source materials give flavor and weight to this valuable study.

Pritchard, James B., ed., *Ancient Near Eastern Texts . . . ,* Princeton University Press, Princeton, New Jersey, 1955.

A collection of myths, epics, legal and historical texts, descriptions of festivals, hymns, prayers, wisdom literature, songs, poems, and letters. Some of the manuscripts are difficult to make sense of because of their fragmentary nature. But in general the collection gives a sense of identification no historical narrative could possibly impart. The organization is faulty; but the Contents is so detailed that it somewhat compensates for the misarrangement of the items, many of which are of great interest and significance.

Steindorff, G., and Kenneth Seele, *When Egypt Ruled the East,* University of Chicago Press, Chicago, 1956 (2nd ed.).

After very brief introductory material on

the early periods, the authors present a detailed account of Egypt under Thutmose III and his successors. For this portion of Egyptian history the book is really an updating of Breasted's work.

*Wilson, John A., *The Culture of Ancient Egypt,* University of Chicago Press, Chicago, 1956.

This is a reprinting of his *The Burden of Egypt.* In this work the author is interested primarily in interpreting data rather than recording it. As an evaluative study of the Egyptian mentality and pattern of values it has no serious competitor.

For a good fictional account of Egypt in the days of the Empire see M. T. Waltari, *The Egyptian.* The novel is based on an Egyptian source, "The Story of Sinuhe."

2

Mesopotamia and Crete

MESOPOTAMIA

Soil, Cities, and Strife

The valley cradled by the Tigris and Euphrates rivers was originally settled by Sumerians, a "Mediterraneanoid" people who probably entered the valley from the East sometime during the fifth millennium B.C. Somewhat later, a Semitic people settled farther up the valley around Akkad, south of present-day Baghdad. Sumer contained about 25,000 square miles of territory; Akkad even less. Yet these tiny portions of land, together hardly larger than our state of Ohio, offered economic allurements that vaster surrounding stretches could not match. Annual flooding of the rivers left heavy silt deposits that made portions of the land richly fertile. When compared to the hilly and desert regions around it, it was virtually a paradise (indeed, the Garden of Eden, conceived in the folk memory of the ancients, was located here).

For over a thousand years Sumerian and Akkadian cities multiplied in number and advanced in cultural development. But at no time during this long period was a genuine nation or even a confederacy established. Instead, the opposite was true. Jealous guardianship of water rights and agrocommercial advantages led each community to be wary of its neighbors, so that a mosaic of warring units rather than an enduring nation resulted.

Occasionally, serious overflooding of the rivers brought catastrophic loss of life and property. Around 2900 B.C. the valley was deluged by raging waters about 16 feet in depth. Not only whole cities but clusters of them were destroyed. Subsequently, Mesopotamians came to believe that the gods, disgusted with the faults and frailties of mankind, had sent the flood to destroy their recalcitrant children (undoubtedly the source of the Biblical account of Noah and the flood).

MESOPOTAMIAN CHRONOLOGY, 4500–1100

Approximate dates

4500–3500 [1]	UBADIANS ("Proto-Euphrateans") origins unknown; conjecture: infiltration of Semites from west and north, non-Semites from east; fusion
3500–3000	SUMERIANS – Protoliterate Period origins uncertain; from Caspian Sea area? entered valley from Elam? mixed with "native" peoples
3000–2350	SUMERIANS – Early Dynastic Period first Dynasty of Kish, about 3000 first Dynasty of Ur, about 2700 King Lugal-Zuggesi of Lagash, about 2400
2350–2150	AKKADIANS – Sargonid Period Sargon the Great, about 2350 Akkadian ascendance, 2350–2150
2150–1900	SUMERIANS Resurgence under Gudea of Lagash, about 2100
1900–1500	BABYLONIANS (Amorites) Hammurabi
1500–1100	KASSITES Invaded from east; no development of inherited culture

1. Some authorities believe first settlements were made about one thousand years earlier. Compare Samuel Kramer, *The Sumerians,* University of Chicago Press, Chicago, 1963, p. 40.

Not long after this catastrophe, Sumerian city-states succeeded in establishing control over the northern Akkadian communities. This hegemony lasted about four hundred years, surely enough time and more to fashion a state. But instead of unity, greater disunity resulted. Soon, too, original primitive democracy gave way to royal despotism and pitiless exploitation of the peasants. Seemingly this left the people with neither the heart nor the vision to embark on the challenging task of state-making. Equally important, neither the city-states nor their royal masters could leave off indulging particularistic ambitions. Exaggerating for emphasis, one may say that everybody fought everybody most of the time. True, one king, Lugal-Zaggesi of Lagash (*c.* 2400 B.C.), succeeded for a time in bringing the greater part of Sumer-Akkad under his rule. But before lasting consolida-

tion could be effected, the Akkadians found a leader to shake off "alien" domination.

Under this extraordinarily energetic king – the fabled Sargon the Great – the Akkadians moved against Sumer which now paid for its prolonged political follies by being brought under complete Semitic domination. Once again unification opportunities were offered. Although differing in ethnic backgrounds, Sumer and Akkad had much in common. For two millennia, Akkad had absorbed Sumerian culture so completely that the two peoples had become virtually one in language, arts, religion, and general social habits.

Despite these affinities, Sumerian communities chafed under "foreign" control and finally succeeded (*c.* 2150 B.C.) in destroying the power of the ranging empire. Thereafter, for nearly two centuries (except for one passing interlude), the old pattern of intercity strife was monotonously and fatally repeated. When a new, vigorous people, the Amorites (Babylonians), struck eastward from their Syrian base (*c.* 1900 B.C.), they found a tired and divided land unable to stand against them. "Having wasted its youth in fratricidal wars, Sumer in its old age died for lack of blood." Politically, it never experienced a resurrection.

But culturally no rebirth was needed, for in patterns of civilized living the Mesopotamians pioneered for the ages, in religion, language and literature, and architecture and sculpture.

Religious Concepts

For their city god and the higher gods of the pantheon, the Valley people felt close and abiding concern. Man-made troubles were always threatening; but the unpredictable habits of the natural elements gave rise to even profounder feelings of insecurity and tension. As earlier noted, raging waters and overflowing river and canal banks could and did work indescribable havoc. On the other hand, devastating droughts occurred from time to time. Often in some and occasionally in all areas the intense summer heat prostrated multitudes. Thus beset by human and natural violence, Mesopotamia wrought her achievements in a deeply disturbed atmosphere.

Hence religious concern was characterized by elaborate efforts to propitiate the gods, to beguile them with offerings and ceremonial practices in the hope that a modicum of good fortune and tranquility might be experienced. Subsuming such efforts were certain commonly accepted metaphysical postulates. One of these postulates was the belief that human life was eternally shaped by an overarching Fate which was basically indifferent to the needs of mankind, and, indeed, of the gods and their occasionally rewarding response. But one could never be sure. A second assumption, seemingly in contradiction to the first, held that the lowly human being was given a divine word now

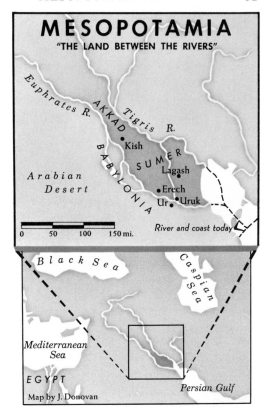

MESOPOTAMIA
"THE LAND BETWEEN THE RIVERS"

Euphrates R. *Tigris R.* *AKKAD* *BABYLONIA* Kish *SUMER* Lagash *Arabian Desert* Erech Ur Uruk

0   50   100   150 mi.

River and coast today

Black Sea *Caspian Sea*

Mediterranean Sea

EGYPT

Persian Gulf

Map by J. Donovan

and then which might enable him to pattern his life in a purposeful, satisfying manner. It is probably going too far to closely associate the "word" with the later Platonic or Christian doctrine of the *Logos.* Still, there is some relation. To the Mesopotamians, thunder from the heavens signified the intention of the gods to communicate—for good or for ill—with man. If, by liturgical or other appropriate ceremonies, man prepared himself to receive the word, he might have some share, however humble, in the shaping of events.

Besides such metaphysical venturing, Sumerians and others of the region established a definite hierarchy of gods, thus creating mankind's first systematic polytheistic religion. In this system, cosmogony —description of the creation of the universe—played an important part. In the beginning, according to the most ancient Sumerian writings (for the most part, coming down to us through Semitic sources), there were Apsu, primeval god of fresh water, and Tiamat, primeval goddess of salt water. Their coming together (at the delta of the Tigris-Euphrates?) produced An, who, overthrowing his father, became sky god and brought order out of chaos; En-lil, god of the wind, or storm god; Tammuz, god of vegetation; Ea, god of water; Inanna, queen of heaven, goddess of love and fertility; Ningirau, god of the spring rains; and many others. Later peoples, through a kind of creative borrowing, modeled their own gods after these. The Egyptian Osiris, for example, bears a marked resemblance to Tammuz. The Semitic Ishtar is Inanna under another name. En-lil is clearly similar to the later Roman Jupiter. And the Great Mother, of the classical world, may be likened to Tiamat and Inanna.

Language and Literature

There is little doubt that the Sumerians invented written language. From the beginning, they used both pictograms and arbitrary (syllabic) phonetic symbols.* It is important for us to keep in mind this concurrent usage. Otherwise we may easily, and erroneously, conclude that Sumerian script evolved simply by gradual adaptation from pictures or images. Originally

Blackstone tablet showing early Sumerian pictograms.

(when a straight stick was used to scratch or draw the signs) the sign for sun or day was ⊃⊂ ; later, when all the writing was turned 90 degrees, it became 〇 ; still later, in early Babylonian (when the triangular stylus producing wedge shapes was developed), ; and finally, in Assyrian (when all signs became simplified),

Thus it is true that in some instances images served as the starting point. But in many they did not. Completely arbitrary symbols were often employed as, for example, ⊗ , which signified sheep. Moreover, very soon phonetic values were substituted for some notion-signs. At first the drawing of an arrow simply meant that weapon. Originally the vocal sound for arrow approximated "ti," which happened also to be the sound for "life." It thus became relatively easy to transmute the image-sign into a phonetic symbol, and to let the drawing for arrow represent either. In order to keep the two meanings apart, another sign was placed before it—a determinative, meaning "wood-object"—when it meant "arrow"; when "life," the sign stood by itself.[1] In this way the reproduction of phonetic symbols began.

Naturally religious and cosmogonic speculations played a large part in Mesopotamian literary creations. In the myth *Innana's Descent to the Netherworld,* vague reassurances were given to Sumerian mortals that Heaven might prevail over Hell. In the *Creation Epic,* composed about 2000 B.C., unknown Babylonian authors drew upon Sumerian legends to explain how the world was brought into being. Among other things, the epic relates the creation of the gods, and their parents' sub-

---

* Unlike the Egyptians, Mesopotamians did not have papyrus resources available. Clay tablets were easy to make, however, and on them they inscribed their signs using a wedge-shaped stylus. From the impression thus made, we call their writing cuneiform, after the Latin word *cuneus,* wedge.

---

1. Henri Frankfort, *The Birth of Civilization in the Near East,* Indiana University Press, 1954, p. 56 fn.

sequent dissatisfaction with them; certainly not the Judeo-Christian "expulsion from Eden" story, but thematically suggestive of it.

Secular as well as religious interests were made the subjects of creative literary activity. The justly famous *Epic of Gilgamesh*, originally sketched by the Sumerians and finally shaped in the form we know it by the Babylonians, sensitively deals with a theme that has haunted humanity across the ages—what is man's ultimate destiny. Of course, not all Mesopotamian literature was of epic proportions. Here, for example, is part of a delicate lyrical verse, thought by one Sumerologist to be the first love song ever written:

> Bridegroom, dear to my heart,
> Goodly is your beauty, honeysweet,
> Lion, dear to my heart,
> Goodly is your beauty, honeysweet.
>
> You have captivated me, let me stand
>   tremblingly before you,
> Bridegroom, I would be taken by you to
>   the bedchamber,
> You have captivated me, let me stand
>   tremblingly before you,
> Lion, I would be taken by you to thy
>   bedchamber.[2]

Besides epic tales and lyrical verses, Sumero-Akkadian writings took many other forms—historical texts, hymns and prayers, incantations, legal texts, letters, "lamentations," scholarly disputations, scientific compendia, economic texts and, the largest body of all, the "omen" texts (a Semitic contribution).

Architecture and Sculpture

For the most part, Mesopotamian monumental architecture consisted of palaces and temple towers. Temple towers, called ziggurats, were almost invariably of a conventional shape and construction. Generally they rested upon carefully chosen elevated sites. Superimposed on the base was

2. Samuel Kramer, *History Begins at Sumer*, Anchor Books, New York, 1959, pp. 213–214.

Sumerian cylinder seal, c. *1900* B.C.

a series of terraces, culminating in the sanctuary, the whole resembling (as, indeed, it was) a stepped tower. In the sanctuary were a niche for statuary and an altar. The altar was attended by priests whose quarters were often provided on one of the lower terraces. To break the drab expanse of brick wall, varied patterns of recesses and buttresses were commonly employed. The arch and vault were used sparingly. Because the walls were necessarily very thick, supporting columns were unnecessary. Most of these temple towers have long since crumbled. Among those surviving, as ruins, are the fabled ziggurats of Ur and Babylon, the latter celebrated in Biblical literature as the tower of Babel.

Sculpture in the round was faltering in conception and awkward in workmanship. But Mesopotamian relief, especially in the later Akkadian and Babylonian periods, was boldly and skillfully executed. Martial and hunting scenes were favorite subjects. Often the sculptor portrayed a mighty warrior-king leading his hosts into the thick of battle. The dead enemy, arrow-pierced, lay under the heels or chariot wheels of the conquering legions. Other favored carved reliefs featured the winged bull and a lion with a human head. Especially finely wrought were cylinder seals, used chiefly as signatures or official stamps.

Science

In the arts, Mesopotamians were both imaginative creators and talented craftsmen. Does the record show comparable achievements in science? Much depends upon how we define the term. If we mean a body of verifiable data collected and assessed in an objective, orderly manner (that is, by means of what today we call "the scientific method"), then we may say flatly that science was unknown to these early people. However, if we define its essence as measurement, the answer is quite different, for the Mesopotamians invented its basic concepts and techniques. As we have seen, the Egyptians came close to determining the true span of the solar year. But this was merely a refinement of earlier pioneering by Sumerians who long before had calculated a 360-day year. Since Mesopotamian cosmology postulated a direct relationship between human affairs and divine activities, movements of the heavenly body were closely observed. If men could gain some understanding of the ways of the gods they might be able to predict and shape events to come, at least in a vague and general way. The gods themselves, of course, could never actually be seen. But the intimate association of some of them with certain celestial bodies permitted an indirect observation of their habits and, hopefully, purposes. In this way, astrology was born. Across many centuries this pseudoscience built up a corpus of data which ultimately served as the foundation for the true science of astronomy.

Five of the planets were identified, joining with the sun and moon to give further substance to Mesopotamian belief in the sacred properties of the number seven. From this may have come the division of the week into seven days. And because they found 12's more easy to work with than 10's—though they also used the decimal system—they fixed upon 12 double hours as the day's span.

This table is intended to help in the computation of the area of square fields. The first column (left) gives the length of the side (s a g) measured in g a r - d u (1 g a r - d u = 6 yards approx.). The second column (middle) gives the length of the other side, stating that it is equal (s á) to the first side. The third column (right) gives the area measured in iku (1 i k u = 100 g a r - d u^2). Thus to obtain the area in g a r - d u^2, multiply the results given in the third column by 100.

Note that a special set of number signs is used in surface measurements:

$\bigcirc$ = 1080 iku $\diamondsuit$ = 180 iku $\circ$ = 18 iku

etc.

$$
\begin{aligned}
600 \text{ sag gar-du} \times 600 \text{ sá} &= 1080 \times 3 + 180 \times 2 &&= 3600 \text{ iku} \\
(60 \times 9)(60 \times 9) &= 1080 \times 2 + 180 \times 4 + 18 \times 2 &&= 2916 \text{ iku} \\
(60 \times 8)(60 \times 8) &= 1080 \times 2 + 180 \times 8 &&= 2304 \text{ iku} \\
(60 \times 7)(60 \times 7) &= 1080 + 180 \times 3 + 18 \times 8 &&= 1764 \text{ iku} \\
(60 \times 6)(60 \times 6) &= 1080 + 180 + 18 \times 2 &&= 1269 \text{ iku} \\
(60 \times 5)(60 \times 5) &= 180 \times 5 &&= 900 \text{ iku} \\
(60 \times 4)(60 \times 4) &= 180 \times 3 + 18 \times 2 &&= 576 \text{ iku} \\
(60 \times 3)(60 \times 3) &= 180 + 18 \times 8 &&= 324 \text{ iku} \\
(60 \times 2)(60 \times 2) &= 18 \times 8 &&= 144 \text{ iku}
\end{aligned}
$$

etc.

From Kramer, *The Sumerians*, pp. 93–94.

Mesopotamian medicine was mostly magic, as early as about 2200 B.C. Sumerian physicians had identified a number of chemical properties and processes. In medical texts of this period we note, for example, that potassium nitrate was included in certain prescriptions. And some recovered tablets classify diseases, symptoms, and treatments with an orderliness, though often not with factual accuracy, that compares favorably with modern texts.

Economic Conditions

Under a system that has been called theocratic socialism, collective labor was used on all temple lands; but for the rest, private enterprise prevailed. Most of the population were peasants, and most peasants were tenants who, in return for their toil, received subsistence portions of the land's produce. Artisans were but little better off; the metal they worked, the cloth they wove, and the pottery they shaped were bought up by traders at low prices often fixed by royal decree. Merchants, on the other hand, fared well. As the Near East's first civilized society, Mesopotamia early developed elaborate commercial connections with its less advanced neighbors; and then, as now, the middleman garnered greater profits than either producer or wage-earning consumer. Thousands of clay tablets uncovered by archeologists, such as bills of sale, letters of credit, and promissory notes, attest to both the range and volume of trade and the profits made by traders. Even so, however, the greatest wealth was owned by royalty, nobility, and the priests.

Pax Babylonica

In the early years of the second millennium B.C., political dominance passed to conquering Semitic tribes pressing in from the west (see p. 31). Originally called Amorites by the Valley people (after Amurru, land to the west; roughly, modern Syria), the conquerors made Babylon their

This shell plaque from Ur reveals the artist's acute sense of animal forms. It appears to illustrate a myth: the hero is in the top panel, the other panels show animals performing human tasks.

By the beginning of the second millennium, Mesopotamians had become so adept in the theory and practice of numeration that they were as proficient as modern man in problems of multiplication. They constructed tables with multipliers for integers up to 20 and by decades above 20. Fractions and large numbers were handled with ease. Problems of various kinds—for instance, the areas of circles and squares, and calculations needed to excavate artificial waterways—were solved by application of intricate geometric formulations. Although

Upper part of the stele inscribed with Hammurabi's Code; Hammurabi is confronting the sun-god.

capital. Eventually, under Hammurabi and his successors, they ruled an empire embracing Sumer, Akkad, and a number of surrounding countries. For about three centuries the newcomers brought stability, peace, and unity to the land. Under this *Pax Babylonica* both consolidation and spatial expansion of Sumero-Akkadian culture were effected. Especially significant was Babylonia's nurturing of the Valley's achievements in literature and law.

For example, the Sumerian forerunners of the Gilgamesh saga were reworked so masterfully in the *Epic of Gilgamesh* that in some respects a new creation was produced. Certain episodes and motifs, of course, were retained, but Babylonian writers refashioned the central theme so thoroughly that we are justified in comparing the borrowing to the kind later employed by Virgil, Molière, and Shakespeare. The new rulers were equally gifted in refining and codifying statutory enactments. The famous code of Hammurabi, for example, mirrors in detail the social milieu of his time. About 300 laws set forth behavioral "do's" and "don'ts." Sample provisions follow.

On marriage, divorce, and sexual practices:

> If a man has taken a wife and has not executed a marriage contract, that woman is not a wife.

> If a man's wife be caught lying with another, they shall be strangled and cast into the water. If the wife's husband would save his wife, the king can save his servant.

> If her husband has said, I will not divorce her [a wayward wife] he may take another woman to wife; the wife shall live as a slave in her husband's house.

On good workmanship:

> If a builder constructs a house for a man, and has not made his work sound, and the house falls, causing the death of the owner, that builder shall be put to death.

Note the Code's recognition of class discrimination:

> If a man has knocked out the eye of a patrician, his eye shall be knocked out. If a man has knocked out the eye of a plebeian, he shall pay one mina of silver.

On debtor-relief:

> If a man has incurred a debt and a storm has flooded his field or carried away the crop, or the corn had not grown because of drought, in that year he shall not pay his creditor. Further, he shall post-date his bond and shall not pay interest on that debt.[3]

Blanketed by the Code's many provi-

3. C. H. W. Johns, *Babylonian and Assyrian Laws, Contracts, and Letters,* Charles Scribner's Sons, New York, 1904, pp. 44–47, *passim.*

sions and ruled by a succession of gifted dynasts, Babylonian society enjoyed a period of unity, peace, and prosperity. In the meantime, however, Kassite hordes from the east had established themselves in areas flanking the Valley which soon became for them a tempting prize. Under their ceaseless pressure the Empire gradually gave way until, about 1500 B.C., it crumbled completely.

CRETE

Cretan Civilization

Pivotally located vis-à-vis three continents, blessed with a mild, salubrious climate, and large enough to hold a sizable population, Crete was ideally endowed to cradle one of the early civilizations of the Ancient Near East. But it was not until our own century that archeologists uncovered evidences of its extraordinary achievements. Even now, after the diligent labor of two generations of scholars, our understanding of its nature and significance is provokingly fragmentary.

From the absence of paleolithic artifacts we must conclude that the first migrants came to the island only some six or seven thousand years ago; we cannot be sure from where, nor what routes were used. For about two thousand years the settlers enjoyed and suffered experiences common to other food-gathering societies. From caves they graduated to round adobe huts and then, for some, to squarish houses of unworked stone. Like other peoples of this period they used tools of stone or bone. In later centuries they imported obsidian from neighboring islands from which they shaped hard cutting instruments and arrowheads. Throughout this early period they practiced little agriculture, relying upon hunting, fishing, and stock-raising for their livelihood. Their pottery, though polished, was crudely formed as were the many statuettes they modelled to represent fertility goddesses and other divine beings.

Cultural Achievements

After 3000 B.C. a series of migrations, the causes of which are little understood, reshuffled populations in many parts of the Near East. Various tribes from the Balkans, it seems, moved south into the Greek mainland. Farther south and east other groups, of Mediterranean stock, migrated to Crete, the peninsula, and its islands to the east (the Cyclades). The first settlements at Hissarlik (later Troy) were founded, Cyprus inhabited, and various Syrian cities formed trade connections with Egypt. Moreover copper was discovered, an achievement which soon marked, for this region, the end of "neolithic" culture. For Crete the overall consequence of the impact of these developments was an upward civilizing thrust which eventually set it off as one of the most advanced regions of the ancient world. Pottery decorations reflected a refined and subtle sense of line and color. Stone and ivory carvings showed an acutely sensitive taste. Many tombs, yielding their secrets in recent years, contained precious objects of art, and other items denoting an advanced standard of living. Pictographic writing, herald of a later linear script, was introduced, inspired perhaps by Egyptian hieroglyphics. Other evidence indicates clearly that Anatolian influences bore heavily upon receptive Cretan culture.

In the following millennium, which, as we have seen, witnessed the flowering and fading of the Old Kingdom in Egypt and the rise and decline of Sumer and Akkad in Mesopotamia, Crete sustained a steady advance in the arts that civilize. Further "immigration explosions" pushed new groups from Asia and Europe into northern and central Greece and the off-shore islands to the southeast. Other groups made new settlements along the western fringe of Asia Minor. The resulting increase in volume and tempo of trade naturally benefited Crete where, because of its location, many lanes of commerce tended to converge. Moreover the introduction of bronze further improved its position. Tin, the alloy which when combined with copper produces bronze, was chiefly obtainable from the farther north and west—from the Cornish tip of England, from Gaul and Spain, and from western Italy (though some was got from peoples in the Caucasus regions). Lying between the sources of supply on the one hand and markets on the other, Crete became both an exchange center and a producing workshop. Thus nurtured by commerce and the cultural forces that flow with it the Cretans became, by 2000 B.C., the dominant sea people of the Mediterranean world.

For centuries thereafter the nature and achievements of their civilization were rivalled only by the Hittites and Old Babylonians and surpassed, if at all, by the resurgent Egyptians (during the Middle Kingdom and Empire periods). Whether or not Crete's capital city, Knossos, is "the parent city of Western civilization" is doubtful. But the claim suggests something of the enduring significance of this civilization. The apex of its development was reached about 1700 B.C. and was sustained for nearly three hundred years. Then, about 1450 B.C., Mainland Mycenaeans, as these early Greeks are called, conquered the island

and brought to an end the independent, autonomous Cretan society that had flourished for well over a thousand years.

Palace Political System

In their own right and because collectively they constituted an important link between the old world of the Near East and the new Western world to be patterned by the Greeks, the chief features of this society are worth examining.

Of the governmental apparatus of earliest Cretan society not much is known. For the first thousand years, it is supposed, the population was grouped into clans, each dominated by its elders. Among the clans there seems to have been no close association. Later two cities, Knossos on the northern rim of the island and Phaistos on the southern, seem to have vied for cultural (and political?) predominance. Eventually Knossos triumphed. For a while (shortly before 1700 B.C.) it appeared that the triumph might be short-lived, for archeological finds clearly show the almost complete destruction of the city's palace buildings. About a generation later, however, a new and grander palace complex (the legendary Labyrinth?) was constructed under the supervision of a new dynasty established, perhaps, by Minos.* Within a remarkably short time a ramifying bureaucratic system emerged which provided centralized controls hitherto lacking. Doubtless many cities retained a modicum of self-government; but there can be little doubt that local chieftains were subservient to the central government when, indeed, the latter did not appoint royal governors in their places.

The king gradually gathered into his hands not only political power but also dominant religious authority. To these power-categories still a third was added, for available evidence makes plain that the rulers soon became the country's foremost entrepreneurs. They owned the large workshops that produced such articles as porcelain ware, beautiful—and expensive—pot-

---

* We do not know whether Minos was the personal name for the first king of this dynasty or his title. In any case this word and its variant forms are commonly used by archeologists to designate Cretan society generally.

tery, and various commodities wrought from precious metals, often embellished by exquisite jewel inlays. Thus by the seventeenth century an effective political system, at once close-knit and wide-ranging, dominated by the palace and centered in Knossos, undergirded a substantial portion, if not all, of Cretan society.

Economic and Religious Life

Economic support for this system—as well as for the general societal fabric—came from agriculture and trade in agricultural products. The wooden plow, the bronze sickle, and the extensively found *pithoi* (grain receptacles) amply testify to common and continuing cultivation of the soil. But great wealth, such as was needed to support the kingdom's advanced urban culture, was channeled through the ports and landing quays which circled the island. Important exports were oil (from the ubiquitous olive), wine, luxury items from the workshops of metal-smiths and ceramic factories, finely wrought tools, and weapons produced by armorers unexcelled throughout the Near East. In exchange the Cretans imported foodstuffs, ivory, and heavy stone from Egypt; porphyry, amber, and obsidian from nearby islands and the mainland; tin from the farther west; and various luxury items from Asia Minor and Mesopotamia.

Because of agriculture's dominant role in the economy, it generated both the basic force and the dominant forms of this society's religious life. The central figure in Cretan religion was the Mother Goddess, creator and sustainer of all life. Extant figurines emphasize her lifegiving breasts, either cupped in the goddess's hands, resting on her folded arms, or bare and thrust forward. One signet relief shows her seated under a sacred tree, breasts supported with one hand, while with the other hand she holds aloft a floral symbol, receiving offerings from two women and a young girl. In other scenes she is shown holding coiled snakes; between rampant lions as "Our Lady of the Sea"; or in the form of a bird.

Cretan Snake Goddess.

Though supreme, she was not the only divinity. Lesser male gods were worshiped, especially one whom, according to the conjecture of some authorities, the later Greeks called Zeus. Whether the later Zeus or not, he was given noble anthropomorphic features. Sometimes he was represented as an animal, particularly the bull; at other times as a man, when he was invariably and quite naturally Minos. Occasionally he assumed the features of both and hence became the Minotaur who, according to later Greek legend, demanded from time to time the sacrifice, in his elaborate labyrinth, of specially chosen Greek men and maidens. In Greek mythology the Mother Goddess tended to merge into Hera or Demeter; sometimes with the Eileithyiae, goddesses of childbirth. Other Greek amalgams of earlier Cretan folk-faith included Ariadne, who successfully supervised Theseus' journey through the labyrinth, and Dionysos, son of Zeus.

39

For many centuries ritualistic worship of the goddesses and gods took place in natural settings—on hilltops, or on "slopes from which fruitful waters splashed," or in caves. Sacrifice of animals, especially bulls and boars, constituted the central rite. Others included the parade of acolytes and worshipers before priestesses who received offerings and bestowed benedictions on behalf of the goddesses whose surrogates they were. Later men took part in the cult rites, but never on a par with women. Holy festivals, some of which were later taken over by the Greeks, celebrated special occasions such as the vernal equinox and the harvesting of the olive crop. On such occasions religious dances and long processionals marked the Cretan effort to propitiate divine powers and to invoke their aid. As with the festive days, some of these liturgical exercises were later incorporated into Greek religious practices.

Humane Character of Cretan Society

Cretan society, then, conformed to the general pattern of all ancient societies: religion subsumed and supported it (without possessing, again quite normally, any real ethical content). In certain other respects, however, it differed from the common pattern. In contrast to Asian and African societies, for example, it did not fortify its cities or maintain large armies. It is true that its efficient and well-equipped navy controlled the sea. But even here commerce and self-defense were prime considerations rather than imperial aggrandizement, though by 1770 B.C. Crete probably possessed an empire of sorts. The place of women also set it apart. We have already noted their prominence in religious affairs. In other activities they played an active part, quite in contrast to the habits of the average home-hidden female of ancient times. Of course women did the work of the home. But they felt—and were—free to leave it for other pursuits as their interests and means might prompt. They partici-

pated, for example, in the hunt, in chariot races, and in acrobatic exhibitions, particularly as bull-leapers and occasionally as pugilists.* Though the archeological evidence is slight, from what there is we may suppose that woman's legal position was strong. Her position in the home certainly was.

Moreover, Cretan life in general seemed to be relatively free from constraint and class-stratification. Certainly we cannot claim that Cretan civilization was characterized by substantial economic and political equality. There were the very rich and the very poor; but it seems that the contrasts were less sharp than in other Near Eastern societies. And one may speculate that they enjoyed a sense of "release of energy" to a degree unmatched by any people before the Greeks.

Art

Conditions of openness and creative energy are reflected in their art which, though derivative, excelled that of any of their contemporaries. In Egypt and Mesopotamia the artistic genius of man abundantly showed itself, but it was devoted almost exclusively to the glorification of rulers and gods. For the Cretans "art extends to everything and to all men. . . . At table they want jugs and cups of graceful form adorned with brilliant painting or fine engraving. They like to see about them the play of oblique light in their rooms, and, on the walls, the lively images of all that pleases them in nature and increases their joy of life." [4]

Diggings reveal, particularly at Hagia Triada, the refined sensitivity and master craftsmanship which enabled them to paint large mural scenes which capture the elan of life. Multihued flowers and plants frame

---

* For a fuller description of feminine life in Cretan society see Gustave Glotz, *The Aegean Civilization*, Alfred A. Knopf, 1925, pp. 142–145, from which the above statements are drawn.

4. Glotz, *op. cit.*, pp. 303–304.

the movements of animal and human figures caught in arresting postures—bounding rabbit, crouching wildcat, treading bull; dancing women and kneeling priestess. Other compositions, especially in the palace at Knossos, vividly portray the activities and attitudes of court life, or grandly reproduce the majestic Minos. Perspective was never really mastered, and almost to the end the island artists retained certain Egyptian stylistic conventions (for example, frontal shoulders atop a body in profile). But overall Cretan art was adaptable and aesthetically satisfying.

In contrast to the masters of fresco painting, with their grand designs, Cretan sculptors almost invariably produced creations of diminutive dimensions. Whether working with relief or in the round the typical artist turned out objects which for delicacy, imaginative treatment, and technical craftsmanship were hardly equalled in the ancient world. A good example in relief is the Chieftain Vase. Here a king is represented receiving homage from a vassal accompanied by troops. Circumscribed by the severe space limitations of an object just over 3 inches high with a circumference diminishing from top to bottom, the artist managed to portray the full significance of the ceremony. At the same time, he could work in such intricate detail as the kings' "triple necklace reaching from shoulder to shoulder." A civilization must necessarily have long since passed its adolescence before such a masterpiece of artistic conception and execution could be produced. Other sculptures depict animal scenes such as the wild goat with its young and representations of men and beasts. But it was in the ceramic arts that Cretan genius found its fullest expression. By 1800 B.C. potter-painters were turning out ware exquisite in symmetry, line, and color. Rich contrasting colors were combined with sinuous spirals to decorate vases whose swelling curves were at once voluptuously bold and demurely alluring. One could almost say the Cretan vase, in its disciplined exuberance

Octopus Vase.

and refined elan, symbolized the essence of Cretan civilization.

Language and Literature

So much can be said of Cretan art because many examples of it have been unearthed in the island and throughout the Aegean world. Unfortunately the same cannot be said of this people's language and literature. Indeed, to date no remains of its literature and little of its language have been found. It is true that many seals, stones, and jars show inscribed characters, hieroglyphs or ideograms suggesting Egyptian (or Anatolian?) influence. But so far no one has been able to read them. In addition excavations have brought to light two scripts, labelled by Evans simply as Linear A and Linear B. The latter, discussed when we take up Mycenaean civilization, has been deciphered and found to be archaic Greek. Linear A is certainly Cretan but no cryptographer has yet succeeded in forcing it to yield its secrets. We know that it was used at least as early as 1700 B.C. (and the hieroglyphs, of course, still earlier); and that Linear B was adapted from it for use by Mycenaeans when those early Greeks invaded and for a while ruled the island kingdom (c. 1400–?–1200 B.C.). But we cannot safely go beyond these few and relatively barren facts. The next chapter in Cretan history must await another triumph by the linguist.

SELECTED READINGS

Mesopotamia

Braidwood, Robert J., *The Near East and the Foundations for Civilization,* Oregon State System of Higher Education, Eugene, Oregon, 1952.

> A series of lectures which challenge Childe's theory of the urban revolution as the catalyst of civilization, as well as the traditional chronological and terminological frame of reference for prehistoric times. A highly stimulating work. Some of it is now outdated by the author's own study, but it remains a valuable source of information and interpretation.

*Childe, Gordon, *New Light on the Most Ancient Near East,* Grove Press, New York, 1952 (see notation in Chapter I). See Chapters VI, VII, VIII, and X. See also Childe's *What Happened in History* (cited in Chapter I), Chapter V.

*Kramer, Samuel, *History Begins at Sumer,* Anchor Books, New York, 1959.

> Twenty-seven "firsts" in history, among them the first schools, legal precedent, "farmer's almanac," animal fables, tale of resurrection, literary borrowing, and love song.

Kramer, Samuel, *The Sumerians,* University of Chicago Press, Chicago, 1963.

> Dean of Sumerologists, Professor Kramer has packed in these 350 pages an abundance of findings of and opinions about ancient Sumerians. The first 300 pages cover archeology, kings, the Sumerian city, religion, literature and education, and the Sumerian "character." The last 50 pages (of appendices) deal with Sumerian writing and language, votive inscriptions, date-formulas, letters, and a "farmer's almanac."

Moscati, Sabatino, *The Face of the Ancient Orient* (see notation in Chapter I). See Chapters I–III.

Oppenheim, A. Leo, *Ancient Mesopotamia,* University of Chicago Press, Chicago, 1964.

> Two caveats: despite the title, Sumeria is omitted; despite the author's aim to write for the general reader, the book is not at all easy to read, chiefly because of his conceptual and organizational preferences. Still the general reader, with sufficient effort and patience, will find in this book a complex of facts and an overall view of the "Mesopotamian" past seldom encountered in other texts.

Pritchard, James, ed., *Ancient Near Eastern Texts* (see notation in Chapter I). See pp. 37–120; 217–219; 265–269; 331–346; 382–393; 425–427; 434–441; 455–467.

Pritchard, James, ed., *The Ancient Near East in Pictures,* Princeton University Press, Princeton, New Jersey, 1954.

> A selection of halftones presenting "people and their dress," "daily life," writing, and religious scenes and figures. The second half of the book is made up of detailed notes describing the pictures.

Crete

Bury, J. B., *A History of Greece,* Macmillan and Co., London, 1959 (revised by Russell Meiggs). Chapter 2 views Cretan life more or less in the manner of Hammond, cited below.

Clark, Grahame, *World Prehistory* (see notation in Chapter I), Ch. 6.

Evans, Arthur, *The Palace of Minos . . . ,* Macmillan and Co., London, 1921–1936, 6 vols.

> This elaborate work, by the "discoverer" of Minoan civilization, is exhaustive in factual material and now highly controversial in his interpretation of it. For years his thesis that Crete was the "cradle of western civilization" was accepted by many scholars. Since 1960 this view has been seriously challenged by Leonard Palmer and others (for Palmer see below).

Hammond, N. G. L., *A History of Greece to 322* B.C., Clarendon Press, Oxford, 1959.

> In Book I, pp. 19–35, Professor Hammond cites the sources of knowledge for this civilization, deals generally with the origins of Minoan culture, and refers briefly to Mycenaean Linear Script tablets found at Knossos. His views are disputed by a number of other scholars, notably C. G. Starr, cited below.

Palmer, Leonard R., *Mycenaeans and Minoans,* Alfred A. Knopf, New York, 1962.

In this book Professor Palmer presents evidence to refute the Evans contention that Crete fundamentally influenced its northern neighbors in the Peloponnese. See especially Chapters VI and VII. Palmer's chief argument concerns the stratigraphy of the Linear B findings at Pylos.

Starr, C. G., "The Myth of the Cretan Thalassocracy," *Historia III,* 1955, pp. 283–291.

See also Starr, *A History of the Ancient World,* Oxford University Press, New York, 1965, pp. 104–108; *The Origins of Greek Civilization,* Alfred A. Knopf, New York, 1961, pp. 36–39.

A good fictional account of ancient Cretan life is found in Mary Renault, *The King Must Die,* Pantheon, New York, 1958.

Asterisk (*) denotes paperback.

3

Small States, Empires, and the Hebrews

HITTITES, PHOENICIANS, ARAMEANS, AND LYDIANS

The partial disintegration of the fabric of Mesopotamian civilization which occurred, as we have seen, sometime after 1500 B.C. invited "outsiders" to raid and infiltrate into the region. Some of them, such as the Indo-European Hittites and the Hurrians, came from the highlands of the northwest or northeast. Others, particularly the Semitic Hebrews, Phoenicians, and Arameans, trekked north from the desert stretches of Arabia. Later, still others (such as Lydians, Phrygians, and Philistines) drove down from the Balkan Peninsula or across the Aegean Sea.

Thus genesis and exodus combined to close one era and to open another as the original civilizations entered into decline and migrant streams, pressing into the favored lands, absorbed their advanced ways of living. Out of these lands the components of civilization flowed into all of Western Asia, touching finally the coastal region where they formed a base for the birth of western culture.

Although we cannot, in a brief, introductory history, take account of all of these peoples, we should realize that each absorbed Mesopotamian culture and fused it with their own customs, religions, and traditions. The spread and quickening of such cultural developments, while naturally bringing benefits enjoyed by these "small peoples," also acted as catalytic agents destined to serve the needs of the great synthesizers to come, especially the Assyrians and the Persians. Here we can note the catalytic effect of only four nations — Hatti, Phoenicia, Aramea, and Lydia.

45

The Hittite Empire

The Old Empire

Long before their conquest of neighboring peoples, the Hittites had firmly established themselves in northern Anatolia in the great bend of the Halys River. We do not know their point of origin nor the exact time of their migrations. The evidence suggests what one authority has called "a repeated and prolonged penetration" from the Black Sea area, at about the same time that the Amorites moved into Sumer and Akkad (*c.* 2000 B.C.?). Almost certainly these invading Indo-European speaking tribes intermarried with indigenous peoples and, after a century or so, succeeded in setting up a cluster of city-states.

In this early period the government was made up of a council of nobles and an elective king. One of the kings, Labarnas (*c.* 1680–*c.* 1650 B.C.), sent out military forces from his capital city, Hattusas (modern Boghazkoy), and eventually created what we have come to call the Old Empire, comprising a large part of the Anatolian Peninsula.

Outstanding among the features of this Empire was its "federalist" character. Conquest was not followed by ruthless subjugation, wholesale killings, or dispersion. Instead, the records show that a surprisingly advanced concept of international law was applied to the conquered lands. The latter were encouraged to sign treaties with the victor in which mutual rights and obligations were set forth, though naturally the conquerors' advantages outran those of the conquered. Following its consolidation of Anatolian dominance, Hatti turned south, to Amurru (Syria) and adjacent lands. For a time its fortunes fluctuated, due principally to rising ambitions among the nobles to usurp royal power. In the 1500s a strong king forced through constitutional reforms which gave the monarch the right to name his successor. Thereafter the southward push was resumed, finally culminating in the extension of Hittite hegemony to the Syrian border. There Egyptian legions stood against the challenging power.

The New Empire

It is probably at this juncture that the New Empire emerged. It was characterized by the complete destruction of remaining noble prerogatives, and by extensive plans to deal with the Egyptian threat. Under Suppilulimas I (1375–1335 B.C.), the Hammurabi of the Hittites, the Hittite Empire absorbed the Hurrians and took over a number of Amurru's border towns. Egyptians and Hittites had clashed before, but now they engaged in a long series of encounters which ultimately sapped the strength of both. In 1296 B.C. at Kadesh on the Orontes, armies of the two empires met in an extended battle which proved that neither could conquer the other. Even worse, it became clear that each state, by its endless fighting, had bled itself weak beyond recovery. Less than a half century later the marauding Sea Peoples poured into Anatolia and the Palestinian region, scattering the imperial forces of both powers. By 1200 B.C. the Hittite Empire, as a Near Eastern power-state, had disappeared from history.

Despite their control of a substantial portion of Asia Minor for nearly a millennium the Hittites never succeeded in creating a civilization after the manner of the Egyptians and Mesopotamians. That is, they failed to make of the cultural elements which they absorbed an organic whole, a meaningful ethos. But if their history lacked a central theme, their institutions clearly reflected what has been called the principle of federalism. In religion, for example, all their neighbors' gods were honored. Thus we find Anu and Ea worshipped along with Ishtar and their own Telipinus, the latter (the incarnation of a one-time king) behaving remarkably like Osiris. Whereas other mountain peoples had one storm god, the Hittites tolerantly included in their pantheon a number of gods, "varying from place to place . . . and . . . sometimes imported from abroad like the Hurrian weather-god Teshu. . . ." Somehow all were loosely linked together under the sun goddess of Arinna and her consort, the Weather-god of Heaven. In further conformity to the principle of tolerant eclecticism, the ceremonies and liturgies of various peoples were brought together into a loose commingling.

In short, most of the salient features of Hittite civilization were derivative in origin and were generally inferior to the cultures of those from whom they freely borrowed. But a degree of genius was clearly reflected in their skillful juxtaposing of many seemingly disparate elements. Superior sensitivity and talent, too, were shown in their construction of legal texts. Here they brought a humane touch unmatched by any earlier society (and many later ones). For in Hittite justice the "principle of an eye for an eye had no place. . . . We may say that the guiding principle throughout was reparation rather than the prevailing *lex talionis* or law of retaliation." But if other advances were made, knowledge of them must await new archeological finds.

Phoenicians, Arameans, Lydians

As a branch of the Canaanites, the Phoenicians had early settled along the fringes of the eastern Mediterranean coast. Originally the rich soil of the Lebanon coastal plains encouraged an agrarian culture. But steady growth of population stimulated the communities to turn to the sea. Harbors (many now silted up) were numerous. Moreover, extensive cedar forests covering the Lebanon spurs provided an abundance of shipbuilding materials (resin as well as timber).

Under these influences the Phoenicians ventured into the Mediterranean and eventually became the greatest sea merchants of ancient times. Their own waters yielded a shellfish whose secretion provided a dye which made Tyrian purple a universal trade

name. From eastern nomadic tribes they obtained wool which they wove into garments and carpets. From Africa came ebony and ivory. Metal ware was manufactured from Cyprus's copper and Cornwall's tin. Spices and perfumes were imported from Arabia. And always and from everywhere Phoenicians purchased or stole slaves to supply a market that finally ringed the whole Mediterranean basin.

Although trade rather than colonization was their chief interest they planted a number of settlements ranging from Cyprus to Spain. Of these states Carthage, settled in the northern tip of what is now Tunisia (*c.* 725 B.C.), became the most prominent. Ultimately it became the chief commercial power of the western Mediterranean world.

As the Near East's middleman, the Phoenician merchant naturally tended to develop efficient systems of contract-making and accounting. From this economic prod —as well as from the long centuries of language-making dating from earliest Egypto-Sumerian times—he fashioned a series of symbols which came to be adopted by those with whom he traded. These symbols, representing neither pictures, ideas, nor phonetic syllables, were arbitrary signs denoting consonantal sounds, twenty-two in all. In this way was born (*c.* 1400 B.C.) the alphabet that we use today (except for vowel signs later added by the Greeks).

In the meantime another "small people," the Arameans, had taken advantage of the decline of the river powers to develop a culture and pattern of life of their own. Although archeologists have yet to do much more digging before we can speak authoritatively of their culture, we know that the Arameans, like the Phoenicians, were a Semitic people who migrated early from the desert regions of Arabia into the middle land.

Their chief state was Aram. Its capital, Damascus, was strategically located, as were virtually all Aramean cities, along the main caravan routes running from Mesopotamia to Egypt (see map). As a conse-

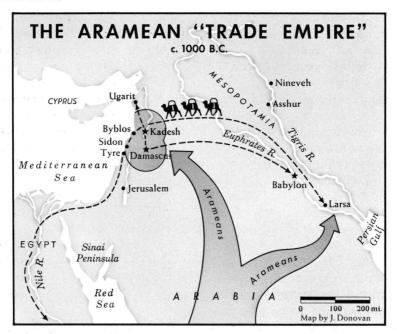

THE ARAMEAN "TRADE EMPIRE"
c. 1000 B.C.

Map by J. Donovan

quence, this people became (by *c.* 1000 B.C.) the foremost inland traders of the ancient Orient. From the Phoenicians they borrowed alphabetic writing and spread it wherever their trade carried them. Sometime after the beginning of the first millennium B.C. the Aramean language had become so popular that it dominated all other systems of speech and writing in the Near East. By Jesus' day it had supplanted them so thoroughly that the son of Joseph, "of the seed of David," Hebrew born and raised, spoke Aramaic, not Hebrew.* A portion of this far-ranging people migrated to southern Mesopotamia, around Babylon, where they took the name "Chaldeans."

Equally spotty is the record of another people of this era, the Lydians. Since, to date, none of their literature has been recovered, we must go to the accounts of others, chiefly the Greeks. Probably the original Lydians migrated around 1200 B.C. from the Balkan area into west central Asia Minor where they intermarried with native peoples. By about 700 B.C. they had formed a kingdom whose boundaries had gradually expanded westward until they reached the sea, and eastward as far as the Halys River. Within a century or so Lydia was recognized as the strongest power in Asia Minor.

Although precious metals had long been used as a medium of exchange, no earlier people had thought of minting coins which bore the official stamp of its government. Appearing in the eighth or seventh century B.C., this Lydian innovation naturally stimulated international trade. By the reign of the famous King Croesus (569–546 B.C.), Lydia had become renowned for its wealth. Even more significant was its role as cultural mediator between East and West. For example, the philosophic and cosmological speculations of certain Ionians such as Thales, Anaximenes, and Anaximander (speculations which initiated the Greek venture in rational thought) rested partially upon Lydian absorption and transmission of Eastern lore.

At the height of its power (*c.* 550 B.C.), the Lydian empire controlled most of the western half of the plateau, including the

---

* But it should be noted that for official documents Akkadian continued to be used in neo-Assyrian and neo-Babylonian times.

Greek settlements along the coast. Under the tolerant Croesus the Greeks were allowed to retain their local traditions and governmental forms; were recognized, even, as already possessing a superior culture. So a beneficent reciprocal relationship was established. The Greeks had much to learn from the ancient East; their clearly superior talents could serve a wider world. Lydia thus served as both bridge and buffer between the old and the new.

Assyrian Empire

The Assyrians

Viewed from the perspective of our own times the history of the Ancient Near East may be divided into three major epochs: the genesis and growth of the Valley civilizations; their decline and the rise of numerous small states which fed upon, developed, and spread their achievements; and the effecting of a climactic cultural synthesis wrought by the newly formed empires of Assyria, Chaldea, and Persia.*

Actually the Assyrians, a Semitic people originating in the desert lands, entered Mesopotamia long before the rise of the small states. For nearly two millennia they lived in a restricted area of the highland country, fighting to wrest subsistence from the sullen soil and rugged terrain and, periodically, against neighboring tribes competing for choicer lands and booty. From the Akkadians and Babylonians they borrowed writing and other cultural tools and techniques. For example, the Assyrian legal code was but a modification of Hammurabi's Code. The Gilgamesh epic was taken over and made their own, with certain names and episodes changed to suit

* Sabotino Moscati, in his *Face of the Ancient Orient,* Quadrangle Books, Chicago, 1960, popularized the concepts of "components" (the Valley civilizations), "catalysts," and "synthesis." While acknowledging our debt to him we should point out that unlike his treatment, here the synthesis includes Assyria and Chaldea.

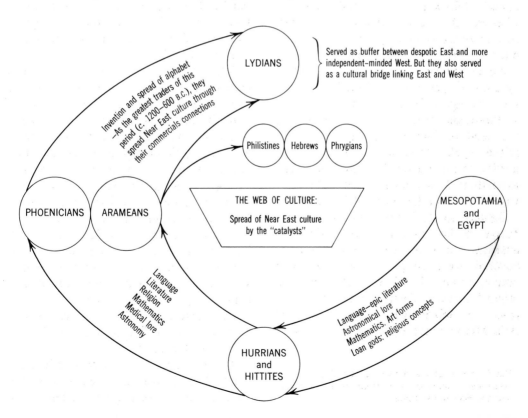

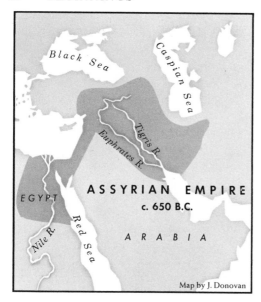

ASSYRIAN EMPIRE
c. 650 B.C.

Map by J. Donovan

instrument of imperial policy has its limits, and by the seventh century B.C. the burden of mass misery had passed beyond the bearable. When, therefore, the Chaldeans and Medes to the south dared to raise the banner of revolt, nation after nation joined in the attack. Within a dozen years the Empire had collapsed. Some notion of the fury of the oppressed peoples can be gauged by the treatment meted out to Nineveh, capital and symbol of Assyrian might. Capture and sacking did not suffice. Building by building, stone by stone, the city was dismantled so that not even a charred skeleton remained. The ground itself was slashed and churned by shards. In the end, Assyria died as it had lived, by the sword.

The Assyrian Synthesis

For all their raw savagery the Assyrians were not so stupid as to seek the complete destruction of all the lands and peoples they conquered. Numerically an insignificant

their own ethos and local conditions. With the collapse of the Valley empires, visions of booty and living space had come to their warrior kings. For several centuries the small states were able to maintain their independence. But in the ninth century B.C. Assyrian might swept forward in a relentless push until most of the Near Orient, from the Persian Gulf to the Lake Van region, then westward to Phoenicia and southward into Egypt, was dominated by the surrogates of the great god Assur.

In 722 B.C., under Sargon II (722–705 B.C.), Israel's ten tribes were conquered and dispersed (the "ten lost tribes"). Shortly before, Damascus had been captured and its people deported. In 689 B.C., Senhacharib sacked and burned Babylon. Egypt's turn was next, succumbing under the hammer blows of Esarhaddon and Ashur-bani-pal (626 B.C.).

But Ashur-bani-pal's successors were unable to hold the Empire together. For nearly two centuries much of the Near East lay under the heavy hand of the cruelest conqueror of ancient times. By terror the Assyrians had subdued scores of people and by terror they had sought to keep them from thoughts of rebellion. But terror as an

This colossal winged bull with human head, a favorite subject of Assyrian sculptors, is from one of the gates of the Citadel of Sargon II (c. 725 B.C.). Altogether, the gate was made up of four of these giant guardian demons.

nation, they realized that their imperial dreams depended upon the exploitation of the lands and products, the muscles and minds, of many peoples. So with the same efficiency that marked their destructive ways they set about putting together the greatest empire the world had yet seen—indeed, the first true empire.*

The basic imperial pattern was simple. Peoples which had for one reason or other escaped the full fury of Assyrian conquest (for example, the Hebrews of Judah) were made tributary states and required to make annual payments in goods or coin or both. Others were allowed to keep their princes whose rule, however, was placed under the supervision of governors sent out from Nineveh. The remaining states were annexed outright. As the needs of Empire multiplied, naturally the bureaucratic apparatus expanded. By *c.* 700 B.C., most of the Ancient Near East thus found itself bound together under the sway of an iron-willed dominant minority.

The Assyrian policy of ruthlessly deporting and resettling foreign populations of course inflicted traumatic experiences upon the conquered. But it also exploited to the fullest the earlier catalytic functions of the smaller states. In this sense it tremendously stimulated the diffusion of culture, helped to break down narrow, provincial views and, though in embryonic form, introduced the concept of one world. No matter how mean and inhumane his motivation, man ventured here, at this time and in this place, his first attempt to create the ecumenical state.

The Chaldeans

Less than a century later a greater and even more significant consolidation of lands and states was effected by the Persians, but before considering this new synthesis we must briefly note the precipitous rise and fall of the Chaldean Empire. We have already seen that the Chaldeans and Medes spearheaded spreading revolts

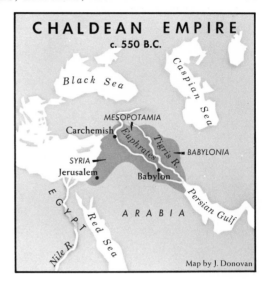

which brought down Assyria. Sometime around 600 B.C. its sprawling empire was divided up, Media taking the eastern portion, Chaldea the western.

The remote origins of the Chaldeans are not known. A Semitic people of the desert (late Aramean tribes?), they settled in and around Babylon which, long before the fall of Assyria, they had rebuilt on a grand scale. Allied with Cyaxares of Media, their king, Nabopolassar, led them in the attack on Nineveh and, after its fall, garrisoned the lands from the Valley to the sea. At his death his son Nebuchadnezzar inherited a fair-sized empire and a taste for further conquest. During the next half century (from 605–561 B.C.) he extended Chaldean rule, defeating the Egyptians at Carchemish, and captured Jerusalem from which he sent thousands of Jews in captivity to Babylon. But not all of Nebuchadnezzar's energies were spent in battle. Interested in beautifying Babylon, he erected magnificent temples and palaces and even,

* Egypt had never been able to extend its dominion into the lands of the Tigris-Euphrates Valley; except for very limited periods, Babylonia restricted its expansion to this Valley. In short, they were empires dominating particular regions of the Near East. Assyria linked valley to valley and both to southern Anatolia.

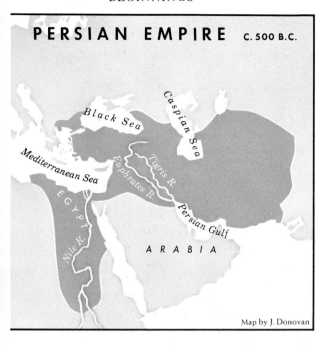

PERSIAN EMPIRE C. 500 B.C.

Black Sea

Caspian Sea

Mediterranean Sea

Euphrates R.

Tigris R.

Persian Gulf

EGYPT

Nile R.

ARABIA

Map by J. Donovan

The Persians

Beginnings

The Persians were an Indo-European people whose roots go back to the third millennium B.C. and to regions east of the Caspian Sea. They were of the same stock as those who, around 2000 B.C., migrated westward, finally sifting down into the Aegean and Italian peninsulas, and of those who trekked in the opposite direction, settling eventually in India. By the time of the Kassite invasion (*c.* 1600 B.C.) several tribes, probably fleeing from the domination of their cousins, the Medes, had set up a loose confederacy at the head of the Persian Gulf. For the next thousand years they increased in population, absorbed Mesopotamian culture, and welded it to their own complex of customs, ideologies, and expansionist dreams.

Imperial Achievements

Around the middle of the sixth century B.C., as we have noted, these dreams began to take on reality as Cyrus led his forces to victory over Medes, Lydians, and Chaldeans. In scarcely more than a decade he had subjugated the whole of Anatolia (including the Greeks on the coastal fringe), the Syro-Palestinian corridor, and then turning east, established Persian hegemony as far as the Indus River. Before his death in 529 B.C. he had created the greatest empire the world had yet known, and had laid plans for its further expansion.

For unknown reasons the reign of his successor, Cambyses (529–521 B.C.), was cut short, but not before he had conquered Egypt and joined it to the sprawling state. In 521 B.C. Cyrus's son-in-law, the great Darius (521–485 B.C.), became king and continued his predecessor's conquering ways. Aryan states in northwest India were added to the empire. Turning west, the Great King invaded Europe where he subjugated Thrace and established overlord-

to please his Median queen who missed the mountains of her homeland, constructed for her a many-tiered ziggurat.

His death in 561 B.C. brought on a bout of royal infighting for the throne and marked the beginning of the Empire's disintegration. In 538 B.C. Persian legions were sent against Babylon. Internal strife and royal degeneracy had developed to such an extent that the city surrendered without a struggle, and the Chaldean empire whimpered out.

But the brief half century of Chaldean rule was marked by two significant cultural developments. One was the further conjoining and deeper rooting of elements of the grand cultural synthesis begun by the Assyrians. The other was a remarkable resurgence of interest in astrology and the mathematical calculations required to probe the movement and patterns of celestial bodies. Out of this renewed interest came almost all of the findings used by the Persians in their great scientific breakthrough several centuries later.

ship of Macedonia. But military venturesomeness and vigor were not the sole or major determinants of the cultural synthesis which was effected. What marked and made Persian hegemony so outstanding were enlightened policies and refined administrative procedures. Among the policies was the principle that non-Iranian peoples should not merely be allowed but encouraged to retain and develop their own pattern of culture. Yahwehism, for example, was recognized as the official religion of the Hebrews, and the Jews in Babylon were permitted to return to Palestine. Other peoples were similarly treated. This substitution of tolerance for monolithic structuring, of catholic sympathy for vindictive parochialism, laid strong foundations for the construction of a universal state.

To administer the new ecumenical community, Cyrus and his successors divided it into twenty satrapies (provinces) ruled over by a governor whose official title was "protector of the Kingdom." Basic laws, applicable throughout the Empire, were determined by the King. Within the framework of these laws, provincial codes were drawn up by the local governors and their advisors, many of whom were natives of the region. To make sure that the governor neither abused the royal system of justice nor conspired to set himself up as an autonomous ruler, the King created a corps of "king's messengers" whose business it was to make annual inspection of provincial affairs. Since distances within the Empire were so great, an elaborate system of roads was laid out to facilitate rapid exchange of news and reports and, of course, the efficient dispatch of military units to trouble spots.

The Persian Amalgam

For nearly two centuries, under the aegis of the "King of Kings" and his bureaucratic apparatus, a multitude of Near Eastern institutions, tongues, habits, and outlooks was diffused and, to a degree, blended into a cosmopolitan civilization. To a reflective citizen of the times it might have appeared that the river of life, across the millennia, had drawn from the streams of every age to issue into one channeled current. Or, to change the figure of speech, that the Crescent had acted as a magnet, drawing into itself and refining the energies, visions, and talents of the surrounding desert and mountain peoples.

In art this synthesis was particularly marked. Old Babylonian forms merged with those of Assyria and Chaldea to reflect the universality of the empire of empires. Colored bricks, for example, were used in the time of Hammurabi and before. On the Persian palace at Susa, well over a thousand years later, we find a frieze made up of colored bricks, depicting scenes that clearly suggest the later art forms of Assyria, in particular the typical winged animal with human head. Darius himself, as we find in a royal inscription, called attention to the many sources drawn upon to construct one of his palaces—Lebanon for cedars, Carmania for *yaka* wood, Bactria for gold, Egypt for silver and ebony, and Assyria, Ionia, Media, and Chaldea for laborers and artisans.

In the same way language served at once as a kind of cultural sponge and spray. To issue royal orders, transact business, commemorate inscriptions, and like pronouncements a cuneiform (Old Persian?) script was used, its syllabary probably invented by the Medes. To give direction to complicated administrative affairs, imperial officials wrote on a different material and used a language without a syllabary. Hieroglyphics were used by those engaged in the conduct of Egyptian affairs.

Zoroastrianism

Paradoxically, one of the most significant and lasting influences of Persian culture—its religion—had in its original form little of the imitative or eclectic. Its founder, Zoroaster (Zarathustra), probably lived in the seventh or sixth century B.C. For reasons and under conditions unknown to us, this prophet took it upon himself to re-create the ancient religious lore of his people. Early Aryan (that is, Iranian) faiths held that the world was ruled by many spirits, some good, some evil. Of the good the greatest were Ahura, the divine creator, and Mazda, the spirit of wisdom. Lesser deities were called *devas* if kindly, *daevas* if evil. From the lore of this religion, Zoroaster created a monotheistic faith in which Ahura and Mazda were merged into the Creating Word. Existing before the world was formed, the Word brought all forms of life into being. Over all brooded the Holy Spirit of Ahura-Mazda, boding good for species of every kind, particularly for Man. That man might, through struggle, appreciate more meaningfully and win the intended goodness, a twin of the Holy Spirit, Ahriman, the Evil One, was created by Ahura. Thenceforth all life became a contest between truth and error, light and dark, good and evil.

Zoroaster dismissed the various *devas* and *daevas* as chimeras, conjured out of human fears and insecurity. Nor did he allow a place for statuary, elaborate rituals, or a priestly caste. Any person seeking the good and the true could find them. Similarly anyone, if he wished, could reject them or pervert them into evil. At death the virtuous passed on into the eternal bliss of heaven. Practitioners of evil, on the other hand, descended into the everlasting torment of hell. Later this doctrine was modified to hold that a great climacteric final day of judgment would come when the creator's Holy Spirit would weigh all souls in the balance and grant everlasting life to those who had followed the Righteous Way, and visit destruction upon those who had turned aside from it.

The *Gathas,* Zoroaster's collected work, contain certain key words and phrases which are repeated over and over: "the Holy One," "Good Thought," "Righteousness," "Piety," and "Salvation." The ethical content of its teachings combined with its monotheistic character to place Zoroastrianism far in advance of the religious concepts and practices of any other peoples of his time (except, as we shall see, the Hebrews). In fact, the new faith was so far beyond its milieu that, like Akhenatonism, it failed to receive ready acceptance by the masses. It is not surprising, therefore, that at Zoroaster's death his teachings underwent changes destined to minimize its abstractions and to emphasize symbols, sacrifice, liturgy, and priestly mediation. Before long the ancient Aryan Mother Goddess, Anahita, was returned to the pantheon as was Mithra, god of light. Thus in time Zoroastriansim, originally a reforming protest against polytheism and empty formalism, took on characteristics of the paganism it had sought to supplant. Even so, then and thereafter many disciplined and devout minds "found in [Zoroaster's] doctrines something so new, so fresh, so bracing that his influence may be detected in the majority of the later religious movements. It is no accident that the *Gathas* of Zoroaster sound so much like the first New Testament."[1]

Astronomy

With the later corrupted form of Zoroastrianism was linked, as was true of all early religions, an intensive study of heavenly phenomena. But now astrology showed unmistakable signs of yielding to disciplined reason. Before the Persians, the Chaldeans had divided the heavens into the twelve signs of the zodiac. Even earlier, as we have seen, the solar year, the lunar month, and the division of the day into twenty-four hours had been worked out by priests and astrologers. Now Persian savants, collecting, collating, and refining previous studies, produced a corpus of data not significantly added to until the

1. A. T. Olmstead, *History of the Persian Empire,* University of Chicago Press, Chicago, 1948, p. 106.

Copernican revolution. In the fifth and fourth centuries B.C. astronomical observations were combined with mathematical calculations to ascertain and systematically formulate the cycles of the planets, major movements of the stars, eclipses of the sun and moon, and the length of the seasons. Although much of this learning was still yoked with religio-astrological lore and used to predict events in the lives of individuals and nations, this could not fundamentally detract from the soaring achievements of ancient astronomy, "the one science the Orient gave the West full grown."

The Amalgam Dissolved

Added, then, to this synthesis of ancient eastern culture were Persia's own contributions to religion and science. By *c.* 500 B.C., three thousand years of civilized refinements to the art of living had been brought by this Empire to a grand flowering. Judged by this performance the Iranian promise was bright. But both performance and promise failed. The facts themselves are simple. In the early fifth century B.C.

the Empire challenged the Greeks and was defeated. About 150 years later it lay in ruins, bestrode by a Macedonian conqueror. In this brace of centuries an amazing breakthrough in politics, philosophy, art, and science had occurred; but these achievements were the Greeks'. The old world had lost its vision and lay moribund. But it is unlikely that the facts, so simply stated, will soon or ever yield the secret of their causative impulses. Why did the Persian amalgam dissolve? Why did not the Iranians, instead of their Greek cousins, achieve the breakthrough to a new vision of life? One can conjecture that the material power and glory of imperial dominion sapped their spiritual elan. Or one can suppose that the weight of three thousand years' of tradition smothered their spirit. Or that both of these influences, combined perhaps with unknown others, robbed the Persians at the moment of their victory of their most meaningful achievement—the development of the beautiful and the good. Whatever the hypothesis, the fact remained: the East had spent its genius. Henceforth the West would mold and fashion afresh the creative forces of life.

THE HEBREWS—CHOSEN OF YAHWEH

Early History

Chronologically the Hebrews should have been considered in our earlier study of the so-called smaller states. They are taken up here because their history is intricately and fundamentally connected with the development of Western man which we will examine next.

Originally the term *Hebrew* (from *Habiru; Ibri*) meant transient, nomad, wanderer. As such it was applied to many groups of peoples who roamed throughout the Near East during the millennium 2000–

1000 B.C., non-Semitic as well as Semitic. In the earlier centuries the word was invariably used to denote drifters, alien nobodies. The origins and migrations of the Hebrews are difficult to pin down. Abraham was probably their first patriarchal leader. Conjecture places his birth in the region of Ur during the reign of Hammurabi. From Ur, Abraham migrated to Harran, along the upper reaches of the Euphrates where dwelt the Hurrians. When a number of the Hurrians migrated to Palestine, Abraham and a portion of his tribe accompanied them. In this peaceful, non-dramatic manner the first Hebrews entered the Promised Land. Since the more productive regions of Palestine were already settled—the littoral of the eastern Mediterranean and the valley of the Jordan—the wanderers had to be content with the hilly central portion. And in the main, they were content. Settled here and there in small units, with grazing their chief occupation, the Hebrews established a pattern of life that, although primitive, was satisfying. Heads of families, patriarchs such as Isaac, Jacob, and Joseph, ruled over their tribes with paternalistic devotion. Pastoral life constituted their common economic bond.

But far outweighing this material condition as a unifying element was the covenant concept originally shaped, according to Biblical tradition, by Abraham. In essence the covenant was a reciprocal promise. On the one hand, Abraham undertook to commit himself and his people to one god, Yahweh (*El* or *Elohim*), beside whom there should be no other. In return, Yahweh promised to protect and develop one people, the Hebrews of the house of Abraham.

This commitment, however, should not be understood to imply a monotheistic faith. Yahweh was "God of Abraham," not of the universe. Canaanite tribes had their Baals; Egyptians their Re, Osiris, Amun; Aegeans still other gods; and so on. These early Hebrews are rightly called monolatrists—believers in one *tribal* god. But even so, the Hebrew advance is significant. Except for the reformers of the Akhenaton period in Egypt, no people before the Biblical Hebrews had either sufficiently refined insights or sufficient faith and daring to accept the dictum that "there must not be to you other gods against my face." *

Eisodus and Exodus

The searching quest for God and his truth was accompanied by an equally restless probing for more mundane satisfactions, chief of which was economic well-being. The region of central Palestine afforded subsistence and even a modest measure of abundance. But occasional poor seasons and the natural tendency of man to better his lot impelled some Hebrews to trek farther south, particularly into the fabled land of Egypt.

Typical of this sporadic migrant movement was Abraham's visit to, and his son Isaac's sojourn in, what the Bible calls the land of Goshen, the delta area of the Nile. When their ethnic cousins, the Hyksos, conquered Egypt (see Chapter 1, p 17), other Jewish groups poured in. Some individuals among them, such as Joseph, actually achieved positions of considerable power. Others became minor officials, and all enjoyed advantages that went with their close association with the conquerors. For several generations this Eisodus—"going into"—continued, quite naturally influencing Jewish habits and thoughts as the superior culture of Egypt made itself felt. But when, as we have seen, the Egyptians finally ousted the Hyksos, the lot of the remaining Hebrews became oppressive. As the Old Testament has it:

> Now there arose a new king over Egypt, who did not know Joseph. . . . [The Egyptians] therefore . . . set taskmasters over them to afflict them with heavy burdens . . . and made their living bitter with hard service, in mortar and brick, and of [sic] all kinds of work in the field. . . .

Intermittently Egyptian legions raided Hebrew communities in Palestine and sent many prisoners back as slaves. As oppression increased these captives and their descendants naturally yearned for a deliverer who would lead them out of the land of bondage and, hopefully, into a land they could call their own. Such a leader did

---

* A number of scholars have claimed otherwise. An example of this position is found in W. F. Albright's article in *The American Scholar,* VII (1938), p. 138 and in his *Archeology of Palestine and the Bible,* New York, 1932, p. 163 (cited in *Hebrew Origins,* T. H. Meek, Harper and Row, Torchbook edition, New York, 1960, p. 205).

appear about 1200 B.C. But before we consider the dramatic Exodus led by Moses, brief attention must be given to Hebrew life in the half-millennium after Abraham.

During this long period three clusters of Jewish settlements were established in Palestine (or Canaan). One was in the north where a number of Abraham's people lingered when their leader pushed farther south. Shechem and Dothan subsequently became centers of this cluster (see map, p. 57, for these and other locations referred to). Another was in central Palestine, around Bethel and Jericho. A third was formed to the south, in the Negeb, particularly around Beersheba.

It appears that after the conquest of Jericho (probably long before the Exodus, contrary to traditional belief), Joshua turned north to Shechem. There he organized the Hebrews into an amphectony (confederacy with strong religious bonds). As we learn in the book of Joshua (24:20 ff.) he exhorted his people to "put away foreign gods which are among you, and incline your heart under the Lord God of Israel."

In a similar way Hebrews who had settled in the central and southern portions of Palestine were urged by their "judges" (leaders) to resist the temptation to bow down to local gods, forsaking Yahweh. In the main, the response was similar to that of their kinsmen in the north. From many references in the Old Testament, however, we know that periods of backsliding were not uncommon. After all, wherever the Jews settled in Palestine neighboring tribes greatly outnumbered them. Moreover, because the migrations and conquests occurred at different times and in rather widely separated areas, no secure feeling of unity had developed. It is not altogether strange, therefore, that for most of this early period the concept "God of the Hebrews" was slow to form. Even then, it only imperfectly influenced the daily life of the Jews.

Much of this, however, was soon to change. For one thing, the long years of grinding servitude in Egypt had made many Hebrews willing to risk almost anything to escape the pharaoh's rule. For another, Egypt, by the end of the thirteenth century, had become so weakened from her wars with the Sea Peoples and so torn with internal dissension that the risk seemed not too great. Finally, there was at hand an inspired man of vision who was determined

PALESTINE 1200 B.C.

Map by J. Donovan

to lead his people out of bondage. In short, the Eisodus of Abraham, of Jacob, and of Joseph was now to issue into an Exodus under Moses.

The great venture was set in motion around 1200 B.C. Along some routes (which authorities are unable to agree upon), Moses led his people across the Red Sea (or "Reed Sea" – Bitter Lakes?) into the Sinai Peninsula. For a generation or longer – the Biblical account reckons it as 40 years – a number of Hebrew tribes, Levites, Reubenites, and others sought both to unify themselves and to push their way northward where they hoped to found a permanent homeland.

The task was not easy. Hard desert experiences led many to question their decision to leave Egypt where, though unfree, they at least had plenty to eat.

Over seemingly endless dissensions and doubts, however, Moses' faith and vision prevailed. With patient understanding, with clear and sometimes sharp exhortation, and by personal example he led his people not into a promised land – others were to do that – but into a new covenant.* It was this experience which was to make the Jews a unique people, and ultimately to shape some of the most basic features of Western life. Under the triple impact of the Exodus, long wanderings, and the genius of Moses' leadership, these southern Hebrews formed themselves into a nation. More important, they dedicated themselves to one God – Yahweh. Thus out of historic conditions and inner resources there came for the Jews a revelation; out of this revelation, an abiding faith.

To symbolize the new nation's common devotion to one god, a Tabernacle – "Tent of Meeting" – was constructed (portable, as required by a people on the march). In return for his continuing guidance and protection, Yahweh demanded of his chosen people a pattern of behavior compatible

with his nature. Research has made it abundantly clear that the details of this pattern were not at the time spelled out as clearly as they appear in the two decalogues of Exodus (20: 2–17; 34: 17–26, commonly called the Ten Commandments). But it is equally clear that the main features of the code were shaped by Moses and accepted by his people: "Thou shalt not take the name of the Lord thy God in vain . . . ; honor thy father and mother . . . ; thou shalt not kill; thou shalt not commit adultery . . . ; thou shalt not bear false witness"; etc. Quite probably, too a wooden chest (the Ark) was built to enshrine the sacred commands. In this way, then, Hebrew *ethical* monolatry was born and a hinge of Western civilization forged.

The New Nation

But the newly formed, God-centered people were as yet without a homeland. True, the land of Canaan (or, more correctly, a part of it) had been infiltrated by their ancestors. Against this fact, however, was actual and longstanding control of the land by the Egyptians and the Canaanites, the latter a complex of peoples (including the Phoenicians) of Semitic origins. It was into this area – "Canaan Land" – that the successors of Moses led the Israelites in the belief that Yahweh had singled it out for their possession.

The conquest was neither quick nor complete. From *c.* 1165 to *c.* 1050 B.C., Israelite judges – religious and military leaders – pitted their armies against Canaanite garrisons, now winning battles, now losing them. Probably they would have had fewer successes if the land had not been under invasion at the same time by one of the Sea Peoples, the Philistines. Under this double thrust, Canaanite control collapsed. By *c.* 1050 B.C., the two conquerors stood poised against each other.

Two circumstances favored the Israelites. For several centuries their tribal groups, as we have seen, had settled in the

---

* Destined slowly to replace the earlier tribal covenants of Abraham, Isaac, and Jacob.

region. Many of them now joined their kinsmen against the Sea People. Also, to gain the strength which combined efforts bring, they agreed to unite under a single king, Saul (c. 1020 B.C.). Under these conditions the Philistines were routed and confined to a small area along the Mediterranean coast. God's Chosen had found their home.

Saul's reign, however, was a troubled one, ending in his suicide. Shortly thereafter David, his young rival, assumed the throne. Under David, Israelite gains were consolidated and extended until the new nation became something of a power. Upon his death (c. 960 B.C.), his son Solomon was acclaimed king. His forty-year reign raised Israel's prestige to the greatest temporal heights it was ever to achieve. From Dan to Beersheba and from the coast to the Jordan River, Palestine blazed in martial and material splendor. Trade and mining brought extraordinary prosperity. To symbolize the permanence and majesty of Israel's position, Solomon built a great Temple, in the Holy of Holies of which the Ark was enshrined.

But outward splendor belied Israel's inner life. In the nearly three hundred year span from the Exodus to the death of Solomon, the one-time flaming fire of devotion to Yahweh faded into a flicker of formal incense burning. Delivered from Egyptian bondage, successfully led out of the wilderness, victoriously established in the land of Canaan, many of the Jewish people became indifferent to the strict demands of the New Covenant. In short, apostasy fed on material success. Others— descendants of those who had not made the trek to Egypt—had always been sympathetic to the Canaanite worship of Baal. By Solomon's time the religious prod, to change the figure of speech, source of this people's genius, had been blunted and converted into a perfunctory, even soothing, pat.

Political Collapse

Another influence fostering decline was the complex of differences separating northern Jews and their southern kinsmen. Long settled in Palestine, the former had quite naturally absorbed many Canaanite social and religious habits. In addition they were superior to the Jews of the Exodus in both numbers and affluence. The death of Solomon (a southerner whose reign, moreover, was marked by excessive taxation borne especially by the people of the north) proved a good excuse for a separation long brewing. In c. 925 B.C. the ten northern tribes seceded and set themselves up as an independent nation, which they called Israel. The remaining southern tribes constituted what came to be called the kingdom of Judah.*

Corrupted spiritually, sundered politically, and lying athwart one of the main trade and military routes connecting three continents, the two little states could hardly survive for long. In c. 722 B.C., Assyria conquered and destroyed Israel, so completely dispersing its people that thereafter they were known as the "ten lost tribes." Something over a century later the Chaldeans, under their conquering King Nebuchadnezzar, overran Judah, sacked Jerusalem, destroyed the Temple, and took many citizens captive to Babylon. Jewish life seemed ended. Politically it was. But spiritually the issue was quite different. In the realm of religious experience, where its genius lay, this harassed people made a most remarkable advance, destined both to remake their own life, and to keep shape the rise of Western civilization.

---

* From which "Jew" is derived. The terminology applicable to the Jews is somewhat complicated. Originally Jewish as well as a number of other tribes were called Hebrews. From about 1000 B.C. the northern kingdom was called Israel, and the southern Judah. Later the northern group, or what was left of it, took the name Samaria, after its chief city. By Jesus' day, Judeans considered themselves exclusively the Jewish people; references to their northern kinsmen—Samaritans—were consistently of a derogatory nature (hence the power of the parable of the Good Samaritan).

Religious Developments

The foundations for it were laid before the Jews suffered their humiliations of defeat and dispersal. Such prophets as Elijah and Elisha, for example, clearly sensed the catastrophic drift affairs were taking. They boldly confronted even kings, pointing out the backsliding of the times and declaring in the name of Yahweh, "Behold, I will bring evil upon you, and will take away your prosperity."

A century later (in the 700's B.C.) the equally forthright Amos surveyed conditions and felt overwhelming disgust at the growing tendency to substitute empty ceremony for moral behavior. In the fifth chapter of the book that bears his name the prophet has the Lord declare: "I hate, I despise your feast days, and I will not smell of the sacrifices of your solemn assemblies. Though you offer me burnt offerings, I will not accept them, neither will I pay any attention to your peace offerings of fatted beasts. Take away from me the noise of your songs; I will not listen to the melody of your viols. Rather let judgment run down as waters, and righteousness as a mighty stream."

Another prophet of this period, Hosea, used the vivid imagery of sexual infidelity to warn Israelites of the sin of idolatry which they were committing, and the price they would pay for it. Likening Yahweh to a husband and Israel to a faithless wife, Hosea (in II: 2 ff.) has the Lord admonishing his children thus:

Plead with your mother, plead; for she is not my wife, neither am I her husband [since Israel, by worshiping Baal and other gods, had broken the tie with Yahweh]. Let her therefore put away her whoredoms out of my sight, and her adulteries from between her breasts. Otherwise I shall strip her naked, and set her as in the day she was born, and make her a wilderness. . . .[2]

At the time, the adjurations of the prophets went unheeded. The northern kingdom fell under the fury of the Assyrian legions; later Chaldea conquered the southern kingdom. Nonetheless the words burned deeply in the Jewish conscience. Later they served to create an attitude of God-centeredness that made the Hebrews not only a unique people, but a light for many nations in the ages that followed. For if the ninth- and eighth-century prophets did not construct ethical monotheism, they substantially prepared the way for it; and in the sixth century their southern colleagues perfected it.

Preeminent in this creative achievement were the labors of Jeremiah and the second Isaiah. For example, in Jeremiah:

And it shall come to pass . . . in those days that people will not ask after the ark of the covenant [merely a thing of wood]. They shall call Jerusalem the throne of the Lord, and all the nations shall be gathered unto it, in the name of the Lord. . . .

And in Isaiah, as he speaks in the Lord's name:

Let all the end of the earth look to one to be saved, for I am God and there is none else. I have sworn in righteousness that unto me every knee shall bend; every tongue shall swear. People shall say, surely in the Lord have we righteousness and strength. To him all men shall come.

This triumphant call may seem inconsonant with the actual conditions of the times. Jerusalem had been sacked, the Temple destroyed, the people themselves (though not all of them) taken captive into a strange land. Earlier their nation had suffered disruption, and their northern kinsmen had been dispersed. How, then, could a triumphant note be struck?

Changing Concepts of the Universe and History

In the exilic period, despair was rejected out of the Jew's response to a new prophetic and priestly vision. Fundamentally, it de-

---

2. This and the following quoted excerpts are from F. C. Cook, ed., *The Holy Bible. . . .*, Charles Scribner and Co., New York, 1871.

veloped from a fresh assaying of the nature of the world and the meaning of history. For centuries the Hebrews had been content to think of Yahweh as their God who had led them to the promised land of peace and plenty. Other regions, other peoples, other gods, to say nothing of the cosmos in its entirety, interested them very little. Yahweh had covenanted with them; that was enough. Now, captives in a foreign land, surrounded by strange institutions and practices (*after,* it must be kept in mind, the experiences and implications of the Exodus), the Jews were forced to rethink their previous cosmology, if it could be called such, and the meaning of historic existence.

From this reevaluation, the world took on for them greater and more varied dimensions. Jerusalem did not disappear from or cease to be important in their hopes. But it no longer constituted the only meaningful part of the universe. In the same way their understanding of the significance of historic existence changed. In scarcely more than a century Israel and Judah had been conquered and dispersed. How, then, were they a chosen people? What was the meaning of the Covenant—or of life itself?

Out of the torment of such frank probing came new appreciations and a larger faith. One of the results of this probing, as we have seen, was the fashioning of pure ethical monotheism. Yahweh was not just their God, but the merciful Father of all peoples. Beyond this concept, grand as it was, other understandings developed. Since their peoplehood had been destroyed, the idea of collective moral responsibility was untenable. In its place arose the idea of individual responsibility. One of the greatest of the exilic prophets, Ezekiel, boldly declared in Yahweh's name:

What do you mean by using this proverb of the land of Israel: "The fathers have eaten sour grapes and set their children's teeth on edge"? As I live, . . . you shall never again have occasion to use this proverb . . . Behold, all souls are mine; as the soul of a father, so also the soul of the son is mine; and the soul that sinneth

shall die. But if a man be just and right . . . he shall surely live.

Quite understandably, this shift to individual responsibility resulted in lessening emphasis upon political nationalism and its religious significance. It would be going too far to say that the Jews forgot their homeland or their mystical faith in the high places of Palestine. Nonetheless, salvation no longer rested merely in God-given national sovereignty. Instead, it was founded in the Law now made more rigid and elaborate. In short, a spiritual rather than a purely geographical homeland was envisioned. A new order of religious officials, the Scribes, marked out in legalistic detail the features of the new Promised Land.

New Concepts of God and Man: *Job*

Equally important was a new insight gained concerning man's understanding of the ways of God. As the Jews reflected upon the miseries that had befallen them, they naturally came to ask, "How can a just god so treat his chosen people?" True, more than once they had fallen into backsliding. But always they had returned and repented, seeking forgiveness. Was Yahweh really a god of mercy and compassion? Or had their faith from the time of Abraham been one long elaboration of delusion? Were the good rewarded and the evil punished; or was life shaped by blind chance, by forces indifferent to human welfare?

The vivid drama we call the Book of Job came out of this doleful pondering. It provided believing Jews (and, later, Christians) with an answer which seemed, however grim, to be consonant with divine nature and human misery. Briefly the answer was this: such questions are not true questions. Finite man has not the right so to interrogate his infinite creator. God, though present in every living second of every life, is also far removed from man, transcendent, perfect, altogether holy. "My thoughts are not your thoughts, saith the Lord." Man may indeed propose, but God disposes. It is not for us to demand explanations. What seems to be fortuitous, unjust, or even malicious must be accepted in a faith larger than our reasoning can ever make sense of. And with this man must be content. If one objects, "how can human beings live sensibly and rationally without eternally putting questions?" Job implicitly replies, certainly man must question, but the questions and hoped for answers must lie within the scope of human understanding. Man has not formed his faith out of nothing, but rather out of actual, meaningful experience. It is unreasonable to frame questions which deny the reality of this experience. So long as you are man, do not play God.

Zoroastrian Influences

It is difficult to believe that such profound and extensive changes in religious thought came from Jewish experience and introspection alone. Earlier we noted the development of Zoroastrianism in Babylon. Certain influences from this religion, with which the Jews rubbed elbows for so long, almost surely made themselves felt. The doctrine of death and judgment—eschatology—for example, figures little if at all in the religious thought of the Jews before the captivity. During and after this period it came to play if not a prominent certainly a substantial part in their thought. Since Zoroastrianism emphasized this doctrine, one must believe that the Hebrews borrowed from their captors. Thus we find second Isaiah speaking of the Last Day, when "the glory of the Lord shall be revealed, and all flesh shall see it together." When we come to study the rise and development of Christianity, this and other loan ideas will be considered more fully.

Climaxing the eschatological content of the Hebrew's exilic faith (though not itself deriving altogether from Babylonian influences) is the idea of the suffering servant who finally reconciles sinful man to his

sinless creator. Pre-exilic and exilic experiences not only had taught the Jews that Yahweh was not just theirs but the world's God; it confirmed their conviction that they were a chosen people. But "chosen" took on added significance. Now it meant that by virtue of both their special insights and their sufferings, the Jews were to serve as the vehicle of universal redemption. Singled out by Yahweh as his special servants, the Hebrews were privileged to apprehend before all other peoples the Lord's majesty and love. But by the same token they were destined to experience hardships and sufferings by which they—and vicariously through them, all mankind—ultimately would be saved.

The Messianic Promise

Finally, some of the prophets came to believe that one person rather than the whole nation would mediate salvation for mankind. One suffering servant, "of the seed of David," would take unto himself all the sins of mankind and atone for them. In other words he would be a Messiah:

[once] despised and rejected of men, a man of sorrows and acquainted with grief. And we hid, as it were, our faces from him; and he was despised, and we esteemed him not. Surely he has borne our griefs and carried our sorrows . . . he was wounded for our transgressions and bruised for our iniquities. The whole of our chastisement is upon him, and by his stripes we are healed.[3]

Released from captivity when the Persians conquered Chaldea, most of the Jews in exile returned to Palestine. With them they took their reformed religion and entrusted its administration to the Pharisees, their priestly caste. Under a new government they lived against the day when the Redeemer would come and usher in the new, universal, eternal Kingdom of God. A few centuries after their return one group of this chosen people believed that in Jesus

3. Adapted from Cook, *op. cit.,* Vol. V, pp. 267–268.

their deliverer had appeared, and Christianity was born. Most, however, rejected this savior as the truly anointed. For them and their coreligionists today the Redeemer is still the Promised One.

SELECTED READINGS

Frye, Richard N., *The Heritage of Persia,* Weidenfeld and Nicholson, London, 1962.

The first three chapters constitute one of the most useful summaries in English of the origin, political development, and economic and religious life of the greatest empire of pre-Alexandrian ancient times. The author frankly states his unconcern with "recent clever or brilliant surmises" which, in his opinion, have "no concrete evidence behind them."

*Gaster, Theodor H., *The Dead Sea Scrolls,* Anchor, New York, 1956.

Though now somewhat outdated by more recent studies this book is, in our opinion, the best single source for undergraduate study of the famous scrolls. Nine-tenths of it is devoted to the scrolls themselves and notes explaining and interpreting particular passages. The 30-page introduction is marked by scholarly insights, bold interpretation, and good humor.

Harden, Donald, *The Phoenicians,* Frederick A. Praeger, New York, 1962.

One of the multivolumed series *Ancient Peoples and Places* under the general editorship of Glyn Daniel. Its topical treatment of Phoenician history includes consideration of the homeland of the Phoenicians, their colonies, religion, towns, industry, and art.

The Interpreter's Bible, Vol. I, Abingdon-Cokesbury Press, New York, 1952.

The section entitled "The Old Testament World," by William F. Albright, contains a summary account of the ancient Near East from prehistoric man to Alexander's conquest of the Persian empire. Much of it is now outdated, but the work is still valuable, for it is studded with excerpts from ancient

sources as they bear upon historical interpretation. The following section, "The History of Israel," by Theodore H. Robinson, is both simply and soundly written.

*Meek, Theophile James, *Hebrew Origins,* Harper Torchbooks, New York, 1960.

A scholarly account, though in places somewhat controversial, of the beginnings of the Hebrew people, law, conception of God, priesthood, prophecy, and monotheism.

Moscati, Sabatino, *The Face of the Ancient Orient* (see notation in previous chapters).

Chapters 5 and 6 give concise, informative, and well-written accounts of the Hittites, Hurrians, Canaanites, and Arameans. Generous excerpts from ancient sources clearly outline the values and habits of these peoples.

Olmstead, A. T., *History of the Persian Empire,* University of Chicago Press, Chicago, 1948.

The standard English work on the ancient Persians. Although somewhat out of date, its full treatment of almost every element of this civilization makes it required reading for anyone who would become closely informed on affairs of the Achaemenid world.

Oppenheim, A. Leo, *Mesopotamia* (see notation in previous chapters).

Chapter III contains essays on Babylonian and Assyrian history.

*Orlinsky, Harry M., *Ancient Israel,* Cornell University Press, Ithaca, New York, c. 1954.

A summary history of the Israelites from their origins to the post-exilic period. Especially interesting when used in conjunction with Meek's book.

Parkes, Henry B., *Gods and Men* (see notation in previous chapters).

Chapter 4 is good for an overall view of Near Eastern imperialism.

Pritchard, James, *Ancient Near Eastern Texts* . . . . (see notation in previous chapters).

See especially pp. 120–159 (Hittite and Ugaritic myths, epics, and legends), 199–207 (Hittite treaties), 274–301 (assorted Assyrian documents), 499–506 (Canaanite and Aramaic inscriptions).

Asterisk (*) denotes paperback.

THE GRECO-ROMAN WORLD

4

The Greek Way: Phoenix

Preclassical Greeks—
The Mycenaeans

As we have seen, Cretan civilization shaped and sustained its greatest glories in the period *c*. 1750 to *c*. 1450. Not long before, an Indo-European speaking people had pushed probing settlements into the northern portion of the Peloponnese, had mixed with the native population, and had given increasing indications of making their presence felt in the wider Aegean world. The Greeks had arrived.

Because our civilization traces many of its roots to the Greeks we have given long and close study to this people (who eventually came to call their land Hellas and themselves Hellenes). We are tempted to think of them as a special breed. Certainly to some they appear as a race of giants whose magical genius sparked into exist-

ence, out of practically nothing, a brave new world compounded of political democracy, profound philosophic constructs, the scientific attitude, and a unique and unsurpassed art and literature. The actual historic record does, indeed, confirm brilliant achievements in all of these fields. But the further grand and sweeping generalizations it must leave to the panegyrist. As accepted by most historians, the record is silent, for instance, on the question of a "special breed." Nor can we say with confidence who the "original" Greeks were, or from where they came. As for creating out of the void, they did nothing of the kind. We know, for example, that the Mycenaeans borrowed generously from the whole Aegean world including the Syro-Palestinian coastal civilizations, and particularly from the Cretans. The classical Greeks did, indeed, as this statement implies, work great changes in their Mycenaean heritage; but it is important to keep in mind the distinction between cultivating a heritage and creating a way of life *de novo*.

Thus we need, at the outset, to place the creative genius of the classical Greeks in historical perspective, lest their later glory blind us to the way of truth they themselves so stubbornly cherished.

Ionian Greek culture of the seventh and sixth centuries B.C. reflects the interaction between East and West. Epic poetry arose among the Greeks of Asia at a time when European Greece was narrowly provincial and relatively inarticulate. We must overcome our long habit of attributing systematic classification of observed data and formulation of theories to the Greeks, and reconsider our notion that the achievements of the Egyptians and Babylonians had been stumbled upon by some rule of thumb. These generalizations imply that somehow the Greeks were a unique people. They were not. They were different, they were gifted; they were not superhuman. What may make them seem so is essentially a matter of their appearance in time; they

came into history when conditions were ripe for their talents.

"The glory that was Greece" is solid in its own right; it does not need the fancy ideas and the fancier phrases of the rabid Hellenophile.

Whoever they were and from wherever they came, the original Mycenaeans — sometimes called Achaeans, the first of a series of "waves" to be followed by Dorian tribes — were a primitive people (see map, p. 71). When they came down into the peninsula they were illiterate, unsophisticated in their religious concepts, crude in artistic skills, uninformed in the arts of husbandry, and suspicious of the sea that lapped around them. But they were bold and energetic, eager to learn. From the indigenous population with whom they mingled they learned the peasant's craft. Climate, soil, and terrain did not encourage grain cultivation, so they became, as those before them, cultivators of the vine and the olive tree. From Cretan seamen and settlers they learned of the sea routes and ports of the Aegean world and how to construct and

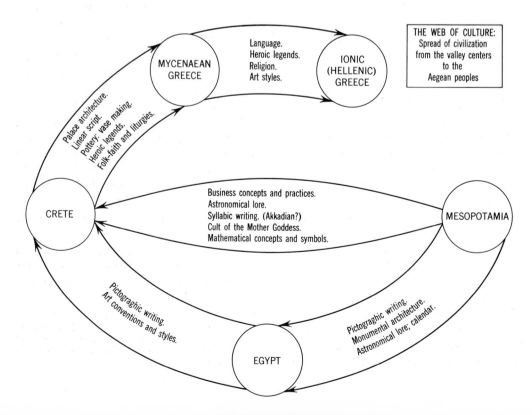

maneuver ships. By 1600 B.C. they had made the Peloponnese their own, fashioned a viable economy, and formed numerous politically well-organized urban centers (for example, Mycenae, Tiryns, and Pylos). Around 1450 B.C. they felt strong enough to challenge Cretan dominance, and soon occupied Knossos and other portions of the island.

There can be little doubt that Cretan scribes taught the Greeks how to write. But the newcomers preferred, naturally, to write in their own language. For many years archeologists believed certain tablets found at Knossos by Sir Arthur Evans (1900) to be inscribed with Minoan signs. They called the writing "Linear B." Nearly four decades later many similar tablets were found on the mainland, first at Pylos and later at a number of other sites of ancient Mycenaean cities. Scholars' suspicions that the writing was not Minoan were confirmed when Michael Ventris, an amateur cryptographer, successfully deciphered the script in 1952 and found it to be an early form of Greek writing. Evidence indicates that the new written language was constructed around 1400 B.C.

Meanwhile Mycenaean seamen and merchants had learned the craft of maritime commerce so well that, by the fifteenth century, they had usurped the position held by their teachers. Henceforth, until the 1100s, Greek ships and Greek traders were predominant in the Mediterranean. In short, their energetic, steady advance in material power and cultural refinement apparently led them to challenge (c. 1450 B.C.) the whole structure of the Cretan thalassocracy. Archeological and philological evidence may point to Mycenaean control of Knossos itself around this time, in which case the challenge was successful.

Mycenaean Culture

The next two centuries (from c. 1400 to c. 1200 B.C.) marked the full flowering of Mycenaean culture. Magnificent many-roomed palaces were built and richly fur-nished. Walls of the more important rooms as well as of the traditional great hall (megaron) were often covered with frescoed murals. Some basic structural forms were borrowed from Crete, as was the plain round column with its base slightly smaller than its top where a large circular capital rested. Elaborate beehive tombs (designated tholos tombs) housed royal remains. ". . . so excellent was the construction of one of the latest (built around 1330 B.C.), the corbel dome of the so-called 'Tomb of Agamemnon' . . . that this chamber has survived intact to the present day. To stand within this chamber and peer into the dim heights of its vaults . . . is an impressive experience. The technical skill and excellence of workmanship . . . make it one of the outstanding architectural achievements of antiquity." [1]

Reference has already been made to the Mycenaean use of loan-gods. But it should not be supposed that the Greek religious fabric was of a piece with the Cretan. It is true that in both the Mother Goddess was supreme. But already male divinities (Zeus and Poseidon, for example) were showing challenging strength. Dionysos (and perhaps Apollo) appeared early. Increasingly, too, Mycenaean religious thought tended to move the gods closer to man — or man closer to the gods (a tendency which, in classical Greece, became a fixed pattern).

The Hellenic practice of establishing colonies along the rim of the Mediterranean derived from Mycenaean precedent. The Ahhijava people, for example (in the Levant?), were settlers from the Mycenaean mainland, so large and powerful that they have been called "a power second only to Egypt and the Hittites."

Probably the political and cultural center of this early Greek civilization was the city of Mycenae itself. Evidence suggests that

1. J. Walter Graham, "Mycenaean Architecture," *Archeology*, Vol. 13, No. 1 (Spring, 1960), pp. 48–49. The date of the construction of this tomb lies more probably in the thirteenth than the fourteenth century.

its king exercised a kind of control—how loose or strong we cannot say—over other princes such as those ruling in Pylos, Knossos, Athens, and Argolis. Under his leadership various military campaigns were conducted including, quite probably, the attack on Troy around 1220 B.C. Probably the main objective of the attack was control over trade routes along the western coast of Asia Minor. In the war that followed, Troy was destroyed and with it, presumably, the restrictions to commerce. But the Greek victory was an empty one, for within a generation or so Mycenaean civilization underwent rapid deterioration.

What caused the flourishing Mycenaean culture to fade so quickly and so completely? Four events seem to bear the main responsibility. One was a series of devastating intercity wars, for which scholars as yet can find no satisfactory explanation. Another was widespread raids throughout the Aegean world, carried on during the 1200s B.C. by certain "Sea Peoples," whose original homes were probably in the Balkan area. Some hired out as mercenaries for various states then involved in sundry disastrous wars, particularly the Hittites, Egyptians, and Phoenicians. Their sea raids and later land migrations throughout this area, especially in Asia Minor and Palestine, created pressures that caused other groups in turn to move about and themselves to become "sea peoples." The resulting vacuum brought anarchy into the region, inviting the Sea Peoples to step up the tempo and scope of their marauding activities.

As a consequence of such activities, orderly commercial relations, upon which the prosperity of the Aegean world by now depended, were destroyed. Quite naturally the web of Mycenaean civilization was torn and weakened. Shortly thereafter (in the late 1100s and throughout the 1000s) a fourth disruptive force thrust its way into the sundering Aegean world. For reasons again unknown, a crude but vigorous tribe of Greeks from the northwest, the Dorians,

spilled into the Mycenaean and Cretan lands, conquering and destroying as they came. Caught between destructive pressures from both the East and the West, and visited by economic stagnation and international chaos, Mycenaean civilization collapsed. To escape from poverty and invaders alike, many mainland Greeks migrated eastward: to Attica (where, according to probably reliable tradition, Athens was spared invasion); to the south-central fringe of Asia Minor; and to the islands lying off it. Eventually these mass migrations to and resettlements in what came to be called Ionia contributed to the shaping of classic Hellenic civilization. In the meantime, however, many generations of Aegean peoples retrogressed into a shadowy world of subsistence living, little literary activity, and dimming memories. Thus, by 1000–900 B.C., a new Dark Age, not unlike that out of which it had emerged 1000 years before, blacked out Mycenaean civilization.

The Ionian Renaissance

People and Places

But this so-called darkness was compounded of dawn as well as of dusk. For the new settlements based their transplanted, cruder life upon past, though currently diminished, achievements and upon dim but persistent memories of earlier glories. Moreover, the disintegration of the Hittite state gave almost unlimited opportunities for creative reconstruction to the bewildered refugees who streamed into the political vacuum. The burden of ancient, binding customs was shed. Although admittedly far-fetched, the analogy of Puritan America is worth considering: migrating Englishmen in the seventeenth century of our era left their homes and settled in a land so institutionally unencumbered that they could rear, almost as they pleased, their City of God. In much the same way, refugee Greeks settled in an area so far from the centers of oriental

Achaeans and Aeolians

onians

Dorians

MACEDONIA

THRACE

Black Sea

Aegean Sea

ASIA MINOR

CYCLADES

RLY GREEK SETTLEMENTS

CRETE

Mediterranean Sea

80   160 mi.

y J. Donovan

not in Hellas but in Asia Minor. (Athens, which for unknown reasons seems not to have been overrun by invaders, is an important exception to this generalization.)

Almost certainly these displaced Greeks, and for that matter the mainlanders from whom they parted, had no notion of the glories to come. Although the art of writing may not have been forgotten, it was so little used that, until Homer, we have virtually no literate records. For several generations at least, pottery decorations also reflected cultural retrogression; the intricate and skillful designs in Cretan and Mycenaean times from plant and animal life were but crudely imitated. The record is too scanty to give more than a general picture. But, as such, it tends to show scattered and insecure migrant groups feeling out new lands and neighbors. From these they sought social and psychic satisfactions toward which their traditions and genius pointed.

Conditions prevailing for the next several centuries invited a cultural renaissance. After the decline of the Hittites and Egyptians there existed no great power capable of impressing its domination over the newcomers. Moreover, their nearest neighbor of substantial size, Lydia (from *c.* 800 on), stood as a buffer between them and potential aggressors. In addition to serving as a shield, this state made significant cultural contributions to the coastal colonies: coinage, art motifs, and astronomical data. Other peoples, especially the Phoenicians, siphoned off the lore of older Mesopotamian cultures and, through trade and travel, fed it into Greek life. They also taught the fringe communities new secrets of the sea as an exploitable avenue of commerce and colonization. Most importantly, they developed alphabetic writing which the Greeks eventually adapted to their own language (chiefly by adding vowels).

For nearly a half millennium (*c.* 1050–*c.* 550 B.C.)—until an aggressive Persian empire emerged—the Greeks thus enjoyed advantages which allowed them to fashion

despotism—though not so far that the fingers of culture could not reach them—that they were free to construct, eventually, their own City of Man.

Each dialect-tribe selected that portion of the coastal fringe which the logic of geography dictated. Many Mycenaeans (Achaeans) crossed into Attica where some joined pioneering Ionians in treks either to the Cyclades or to the coast directly to the east. Aeolians, from Thessaly and Boeotia, settled along the northern strip from Troy to Smyrna; while those Dorians who did not choose to remain in their newly won Laconian base occupied areas along the southern coast (see map). Hellenic history * thus began "in the night of the eleventh, tenth, and ninth centuries,"

* As distinguished from the earlier Mycenaean phase of Greek history. The Greeks, it may be added, did not call themselves by this name (which comes from a later Roman designation). Sometime around 1000–900 B.C. they began referring to themselves as Hellenes, and their collective lands as Hellas. Before this, they probably called themselves Achaeans.

the fabric of a revitalized civilization. Nor were mainland Greeks unaffected by these developments. For throughout most of this period Athens, as well as other cities in western Greece, especially Ionian and Aeolean cities, maintained close and continuing relations with their Asian brothers.

The spade of the archeologist will one day undoubtedly turn up sufficient evidence to fill in the details of the Ionian renaissance. Until then, however, we must rely mainly on Homer's two epic masterpieces, the *Iliad* and the *Odyssey*. We know that the material of both poems had a long oral tradition before being given literate, artistic expression (probably around 750 B.C.) * Mycenaean minstrels sang of man-like gods and godlike men, weaving historic fact into heroic legend. Athena's winning ways with Odysseus, the ambitions, conflicts, and conquests of mighty lords, and, later, the story of Achaean (Mycenaean) destruction of haughty Troy—these and other themes, sifted and refined by generations of critical acclaim, were organized and given unity by the genius of Homer. There can be no doubt that much of the eighth-century Homeric epics quite faithfully described late Mycenaean society. For example, we read in the *Odyssey:*

> And Meriones gave Odysseus bow and quiver and a sword, and on his head set a helmet made of leather, and with many a thong was it stiffly wrought within, while without the white teeth of a boar of flashing tusks were arranged thick set on either side, well and cunningly, and in the midst was fixed a cap of felt.

No such headgear as Homer thus describes was used in his own times. But . . . "just such a helmet was discovered in a tholos tomb of Dendra in the Argolid." [2] Homer also describes bronze weapons, war chariots, and gold cups of a certain style which were not common in his own day when iron had come into use. Moreover, the poet refers to flourishing cities which, by the eighth century B.C., were but dust and ashes.

Political Organization; Religion

From the *Iliad* and the *Odyssey* we can discern the outlines of early political developments which eventually led, in the Periclean age, to the patterns perfected by Athens and Sparta. We learn that the citizen-body—the Assembly (originally a military institution)—periodically met to indicate by its acclaim or silence its attitude toward propositions affecting the general populace, propositions presented to it by the king. It is true that the ruler was not bound by this expression of citizen opinion. But then, as now, a lack of community morale could render nugatory arbitrary dictation. To advise him on policy the king relied upon a council of elders made up of prominent members of the most powerful clans. These favored aristocrats were the real political power in the budding city-state; from *c.* 850 B.C. on (to *c.* 600 B.C.), they gradually edged out the king completely. (In Sparta and a number of other Dorian cities this pattern was not followed; the contrasting systems, as they finally developed, are discussed on pp. 74–81.)

Into the socioeconomic warp of Greek life the weft of religion was closely threaded. Much has been made, and should be, of the man-centered nature of Greek society. But it is a careless assessment of that society which leads to the conclusion that the Greeks were godless humanists. By the mid-sixth century and increasingly in the fifth century B.C. inspired poets (who, contrary to Hebrew and Roman experience, shaped the national religion) pictured human life as bounded by divine justice.

Probably in the beginning their religion was based on the simple, human recognition

---

* The Homeric questions—Was there really such a poet, and if so did he write the Greek epics?—are too confused and too irrelevant to be considered here. Scholarly consensus tends to confirm Homer's historicity and his authorship of the *Iliad*. Most scholars believe that another poet, or other poets, wrote the *Odyssey*. Here the phrase "Homeric poems" is used as convenient rhetoric.

2. J. B. Bury, *A History of Greece,* Macmillan, London, England, 1959, p. 51.

of "Otherness" in life. As did other peoples, the Greeks encountered frustration or hurt or emptiness. And when they did they sought surcease or help from the elemental force or forces which had brought forth creation. Gradually they constructed a complex of religious concepts designed to allow them to live in happiness and in harmony with the necessities of existence, means which would benevolently link them with the "Other."

In this effort they borrowed symbols and ideas from various peoples, particularly the Cretans. But to borrowing they added insights and inspirations of their own. By the time of the period we are now considering (500s B.C.), the fundamental features of their religion had developed somewhat as follows. In the beginning there was chaos out of which *Moira* (Destiny or Fate) brought order. Although they were, across the centuries, to modify many other features and articles of their religious faith, this concept remained basic and inviolate. It clearly indicates the rationalistic bent of Greek religious thought. The gods may act by whim; mortal men may be foolish or wise. But neither gods nor mortals could alter the basic structure and slant of the Cosmos (the Greek word for order). This, of course, did not mean that men could not probe the secrets of the universe. Indeed, an abiding cosmic imperative ordained this very probing, the aim of which was always to bring man and order into alignment and a harmonious relationship. Such an attitude and such probing, as one scholar has pointed out, necessarily invited man "to contend with the Angel." The call of the heroic haunted the Greek and prompted him toward self-realization and self-enlargement. From this nagging prod came his greatest achievements.

But from it, too, came brokenness and tragedy, for the line between enlargement and aggrandizement is hard to draw and still harder to honor in the actual give-and-take of life. Part of the price of the achievement of power is resistance to the tempta-

Attic amphora showing Athena, dressed for battle, springing from the head of Zeus.

tion to abuse it, to confuse the created with the creator and hence to arrogate to the human self superhuman attributes. From wisdom, later acquired, such great Greek tragedians as Aeschylus, Sophocles, and Euripides spent their genius in laboring this theme—the delusions of *Hubris* (pride) and the sufferings endured from the inevitable visitation of *Nemesis* (retributive justice).

In the centuries that cradle the Ionian renaissance, however, this subtle refinement of religious thought had not yet developed. The *Iliad* hymns the praises of the aristocratic warrior-hero; the *Odyssey* of a hero's conquest of the sea and its perils and the obstacles separating man from country and home. Zeus, son of Cronos, whom he deposed as "sky-god"; Poseidon, god of the sea; Athena, goddess of wisdom; Apollo, patron of poetry and music—these and a host of other gods made up the pantheon of divinities which ruled over the Homeric Greeks. Recognized by all Hellenes everywhere, they served to impart a feeling of unity, of national identity. But each *polis* had its own local god who often played a more prominent part in the villager's life than the major figures named above. The community or clan chief acted also as chief priest, so that no strict hierarchy of religious officers ever evolved. Nor did dogma or official creed develop. Thus in religious as well as secular affairs the Greek propensity for independent inquiry was encouraged.

Political Particularism

Out of the darkness of their times of troubles there emerged then (by the 800s and 700s) the pattern of a resurgent Greek society. By this time Greeks of the Asian coastal fringe islands and mainland, fed by the experiences, observations, and inventions of the old societies of the East, had knit together the basic elements of a new civilization. Undergirding this emerging society was a growing realization that they were a "peculiar people."

They might and did admire other peoples, especially the Egyptians, Lydians, and Phoenicians. Or they might look down upon ethnic groups (such as the Cimmerians from the Caucasus region who had not developed the advanced tastes and insights that they themselves enjoyed). But whether others were admired or scorned, all were called "barbarians," that is, peoples whose speech was cacophonic noises—bar-bar-bar—to their ears; or, more simply, as the outer world of non-Greeks.

But, if new glories beckoned, new ills beset them too, interlaced with the ancient and abiding evil of political particularism. For in spite of the dawning consciousness of ethnic and linguistic bonds and of a common core of traditions, the Greek city-states found then, as later, the obstacle of disunity too great to overcome. Athens,

Sparta, Corinth, Thebes, to name but four of the hundreds of city-communities, could indeed arrange joint projects such as the Olympic games (instituted in 776 B.C.) or the religious festivals at Delphi. In the face of great danger from abroad they could merge military units in common defense, as in the Persian Wars; but even then, only with the greatest reluctance, and only temporarily. To examine in detail the great divergence among the Greek states, as well as to consider their intrinsic significance, we now turn to the development of two states which stood out above all others—Athens and Sparta.

Athenian Society

Long before the Persian Wars the Athenian community had revealed the promise of coming greatness. It will be remembered that it had been spared the fierce thrusts of the Dorian invasion (in the eleventh century B.C.). By that time, too, it had probably spread beyond its original site, nestling in the valley of three mountains and protected westward by the sea, to include a fair part of the Attic subpeninsula.

Social Factors: Economic and Political

Even so, for a very long time the lot of the average Athenian was a hard one. The thin Attic soil had long since wasted away; in some areas it was tillable only at the barest subsistence level. Moreover the better soil had long since been preempted by leaders of the stronger clans—by the Eupatridae, the aristocratic "beautiful and good." With good bottom land—the Plain—thus out of reach, the commoners retreated to the hill country to scratch for themselves what living they could. Some, commanding more energy and talent than others, abandoned agriculture altogether and took to the sea as sailors or traders; others, in time, turned to artisan crafts. Ultimately there developed, in this way, three social classes: the aristocrats of the Plain, the peasants and laborers of the Hills, and the commercialists and artisans of the Coast.

Like many another *polis,* Athens by the seventh century B.C. had substituted the rule of the landed few for monarchy. Theoretically, all citizens, as members of the Assembly, or *Ecclesia,* could help shape national policy. Actually, the Council of Areopagus, with its members selected from the lords, made all law and policy (see chart, p. 77).

About 630 B.C. an abortive attempt by one Cylon to set up a tyranny * favorable to the commoners failed. The "little people," in truth, were still too ignorant, too gullible, and too insecure to form an effective followership. To forestall the evolution of such a movement the aristocrats in 621 B.C. appointed one of their own class, Draco, to set down the law in writing, an obvious move of appeasement. The Draconian codification may appear to modern eyes as a sorry sop indeed to the grievance of the little man. One item, for example, provided the death penalty for cabbage stealing; others were of such severity that the word "Draconian" was used later to describe all harsh, retributive legislation. Nonetheless an advance had been made. Although severe, the law at least was known and beyond capricious whim. The state had become the guardian of justice.

Solonian Reforms

But since little had been done to alleviate the hardships of the yeoman and commercial classes, troubled and troubling restiveness continued. Once more Athenian aristocrats saved some of their power by agreeing to share it. In 594 B.C. Solon, aristocrat by birth, wealthy merchant by profession, and poet by avocation, was asked to revise the city's constitution.

His archonship proved a turning point in Athenian history. The rule of the masses,

he believed, would invite anarchy; the continued exploitive rule of the landed few, bloody chaos. He therefore chose a middle course. Tempering rather than destroying class distinctions, he decreed the abolition of debt for slavery, made more land available to the commoners, reformed the coinage system, and offered membership in the *Ecclesia* to the *Thetes,* the lowest citizen class. Perhaps most significantly, he created the *Heliaea,* popular courts whose members were chosen by lot. With this innovation the commonest of the commoners could participate in the actual administration of justice. In addition a new body—the Council of Four Hundred—was created to prepare legislation for approval by the *Ecclesia.* All citizens except *Thetes* were eligible for membership. In short, timocracy was substituted for the aristocratic rule of the "well born." To Athenians it invited a substantial enlargement of life. A man can make money; he cannot make ancestors.

Not suprisingly, the Plain faction sabotaged the new regime whenever it could. And those of the Hill also felt aggrieved, insisting that reform had not gone far enough. Nor was the Coast altogether satisfied, feeling that the nobles had been let off too lightly while the commoners had been granted undue advantages. So the new constitution, although undoubtedly preparing the way for later democratic institutions, left so many groups dissatisfied that a season of turmoil blighted the nation. In short, the day of the "tyrant" had come.

Pisistratus and Cleisthenes

In 546 B.C. a new leader, Pisistratus, though himself an aristocrat, came to power as "the people's champion." Highly gifted in the art of persuasion, well endowed with leadership qualities and supported enthusiastically by the commoners, Pisistratus wrought important changes in the Athenian way of life. Loans to newly settled commoners were made easy, recalcitrant nobles were sent packing and their land confis-

* For an explanation of this much misunderstood title and office, turn to page 83.

cated. Interest rates were lowered. The *Demos* — the people — were increasingly reminded that they were the real power of the state. This steady emphasis, fructifying the principle that when an image is strongly presented over a long period of time the odds are great that semblance becomes substance, helped eventually to produce a real democratic life.

Unsatisfied with mere politico-economic reforms, far reaching though they were, Pisistratus labored to increase Athenian appreciation of the city's spiritual genius and the growing esteem many Hellenes held for it. To this end he fostered the Panathenaea, an elaborate festival designed to glorify the *polis'* protective goddess Athena. Music, athletic contests, and competitive recitations featured this celebration to which contestants from all over Hellas were invited. Pisistratus himself established rules for the declaiming of poetry. He also brought to Athens, from a nearby village, the Festival of Dionysos. Dramatic works were exhibited at this festival with emphasis given to the performances of tragedies. (It was from the latter, indeed, that the forms and themes of classic Greek Tragedy later developed.)

Unfortunately, Pisistratus' successors were more interested in self-aggrandizement than in political and cultural progress,* and another time of troubles plagued his people. When the aristocrats attempted to reinstate oligarchic rule, the *polis* became wracked again by violence and demoralizing intrigue. Out of the confusion and spreading chaos, a new tyrant emerged.

Emergent Democracy

In 507 B.C. Cleisthenes, by birth an aristocrat, by late — and reluctant — persuasion a democrat, inaugurated a program of far-reaching reforms. In place of the four tribes he substituted ten purely geographic divisions, thus rooting out the clan system

---

* But compare Thucydides, *The Peloponnesian War,* 6.54, pp. 5–6.

inherent in the long prevailing tribal pattern.

The *Areopagus* or Council of Elders, ancient citadel of aristocratic power, was not abolished. But its remaining prerogatives were transferred to a new Council of Five Hundred, formed of 50 democratically selected representatives from each of the ten divisions. Among its duties was the preparation of legislation for the *Ecclesia,* now a power in fact as well as in theory. The members of the latter became truly sovereign since they no longer felt the threat of aristocratic discipline if they disapproved a suggested law.

The archons — judicial, religious, political, and military administrators — continued to be elected by and held responsible to the *Ecclesia.* But within a generation the military archon (the Polemarch) and many of his administrators had yielded most of their power to new officers, the *Strategoi.* This metamorphosis arose out of two developments. Eventually the archons came to be chosen by lot from a panel selected by the *Ecclesia.* This practice quite naturally led to a watering down of the quality of such officers. Moreover they were limited to but a year's tenure without eligibility of reelection. Under Cleisthenes each tribe elected its own general, the *Strategos* noted above. Time and experience proved the latter, more carefully selected and eligible for reelection, to be of distinctly greater competence. Hence the ten generals came to be entrusted with affairs quite beyond their military commands and soon became the state's chief administrators. Logically enough the president of the *Strategoi* eventually functioned, although without specific legal sanction, as a kind of prime minister. It was in this capacity that Pericles, elected *Strategos* some thirty times, shaped policies during the great age that bears his name (see chart, p. 77).

Also, whether introduced by Cleisthenes or by some later statesman, there came into use (*c.* 485 B.C.) the institution called *Ostrakismos* (ostracism). Periodically the *Eccle-*

OUTLINE OF ATHENIAN POLITICAL STRUCTURE

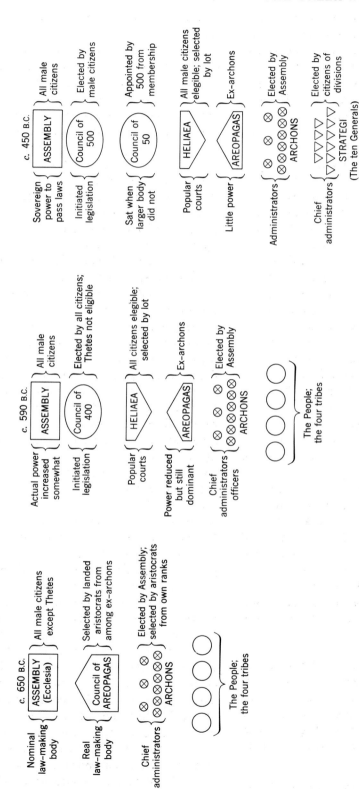

sia gave the citizenry an opportunity to decide whether any, and if so who, among its politicians ought for the state's safety to be sent into exile. Although *Ostrakismos* did not at all take the place of party responsibility—which really never existed in all Athenian history—it did serve somewhat to keep ambitious statesmen from overreaching themselves.

By the early 400s B.C., then, Athens had achieved a substantial degree of democracy. Its laws were sanctioned by the whole (male, free) citizenry and administered and interpreted by democratically selected representatives. Under such leaders as Themistocles, Cimon, Ephialtes, and Pericles, the Attic city-state emerged in the period *c.* 480 to 430 B.C. as a kind of wonder society. In the south and west, Sparta tried several times in the early part of this period to stay Athenian advance, but each time she and her allies were given serious setbacks. The art, philosophy, and literature of the age—the Periclean age—we shall presently consider. Altogether, her glory shone round about her so luminously that her citizens themselves were sometimes hard put to take it in.

Despite her power and her glory she was and remained but a part of Greece. Many another city-state, it is true, came willingly or through coercion under her control. But many did not; paramount among those who stood apart from and often against the Attic commonwealth was Sparta.

Spartan Society

Settlement and Conquest

Not much of this community's early history is known. The original Spartans were Dorians who, in the eleventh century, flooded down into the Peloponnese and settled in a region they came to call Laconia (or Lacedamonia). Unlike Athens, they did not develop an abiding interest in the sea. Rather they soon established themselves in the rich Eurotas Valley, took over the choice lands, and imposed upon conquered peoples a distinct and distressing serfdom. In time a number of the valley villages grouped themselves together into a sprawling city-state which, as Sparta, ultimately brought the whole Laconian plain into one or another form of subservience.

By the eighth century B.C. their numbers had increased beyond the land's productivity, fertile as it was. Other city-states met a similar challenge by turning to trade or to colonization or to both. Sparta's response was annexation of more alien territory—with fateful results. To the west lay Messenia, broad in expanse and rich of soil; and to this inviting region she turned for living space. The conquest proved far more difficult than the invaders had anticipated. Indeed, if the scanty records are to be relied upon a full score of years (*c.* 737–*c.* 715 B.C.) was needed before the conquerors finally were able to divide the land among their own nobility and force the sullen Messenians into serfdom. Even then their hold was anything but strong. For many years the conquered chafed under the yoke and plotted for freedom. Around the middle of the seventh century B.C. they rose in a fierce and long continued revolt (*c.* 640–*c.* 620 B.C.) which taxed the Spartans to the limit of their resources.

In the end they were able to reimpose control, but the bloody interlude fundamentally changed their way of life. Down to about 650 B.C. the Spartan community had been touched by and had responded to the same aesthetic impulses that had marked Greek genius elsewhere. Their work in ivories, for example, so early perhaps as the ninth century, clearly showed a delicate and refined artistic talent and taste. Poetry and drama, dancing and festivals, had gladdened their days and lifted their spirits. But Sparta, unlike much of Greece as it evolved toward modern manners and outlooks, stubbornly perpetuated traditional habits and attitudes. The long, drawn-out Messenian rebellion led Spartans to believe that perpetual readiness for war was imperative if they were to keep their dominant position in the subpeninsula. There was neither leisure nor incentive for cultivating the arts and refinements which distinguished other Greeks.

Government

So to keep the Messenian serf forever in his place — and for that matter their own — and to prevent another uprising which might the next time overwhelm the small body of elite nobility, the Spartan aristocrats now turned their community into a garrison state. Every Greek community, then and later, relied upon military force to serve its interests when they seemed threatened, as states still do. But under the constitutional "reforms" of Lycurgus the whole of Sparta was turned into a permanent armed camp.

Dating from the village mergers which had made Sparta a city-state, two kings — probably representing the two strongest tribes — had shared royal power. But except during times of war the real power lay in the *Gerousia*, or Council of Elders, made up of representatives of the leading clans. Ostensibly the *Apella* — or Assembly, composed of all citizens — could disapprove laws framed by the Council. But the Elder elite exercised virtually sovereign powers. The Lycurgan constitution recognized all three of these institutions. In addition it raised from obscurity the Ephorate, made up of five nobles who presided over the *Apella* and exercised judicial functions. It also created the *Crypteia*, or Secret Police, with functions soon to be described. In effect, the Lycurgan "reforms" froze the class structure and provided instruments to guarantee its perpetuity.

Class Structure and Economic Life

With the final conquest of Messenia, Sparta's serf population (*helots*) came to outnumber the citizen population about fifteen to one. The mere arithmetic of the situation was frightening. A fair American analogue may be found in the antebellum

Spartan soldier draped in a cloak; his helmet, of the Corinthian type, protects both his face and head.

South where, in some states, Negro slaves so outnumbered their masters that the latter lived in real and unending fear of servile insurrection. To insure the military strength necessary to cope with such an uprising, all Spartan children were subjected at birth to physical examination. Babies showing deformities or structural

79

weaknesses were dispatched at once (as often were female infants regardless of their physical condition). Those who later developed deficiencies rendering them unfit for military service were segregated into a kind of second-class citizenship.

To keep the *Helot* population permanently cowed, the *Ephors* annually declared war on them and sent out the *Crypteia* to do its work. This consisted of routine—and wanton—slaying of such numbers of serfs as would serve to keep the masses in proper subjection. On the other hand, to keep Spartan war youth in prime condition a fantastic regimen was developed. At the age of seven each young Spartan was taken from his home and directed to join a Youth Pack. There he was subjected to rigorous discipline; for example, going "barefoot in winter . . . clad in a single cloak." In order to develop cunning and daring he was encouraged to forage about the countryside stealing produce from farms to supplement his Pack fare which, for this purpose, was deliberately kept to a bare subsistence level. Successful foraging earned merits which might point to Pack leadership. Detection of his crimes, on the other hand, brought condemnation and demerits. Annually the Packs convened at the Artemis shrine to undergo the ordeal of whipping when the bravest proved themselves by standing up under the lash after others had fallen or fled. After twelve years of Pack life the Spartan youth was assigned to a barracks where he underwent ten years of drill and general military training. During this period marriage was permitted, even encouraged; but the regimen called for the warrior husband to steal away from barracks for only brief liaisons with his wife.* From the ages of 30 to 60 the Spartiate male was enrolled in the regular armed forces where he participated in endless maneuvers interspersed with campaigns against recalcitrant allies or foreign foes.

Although Spartan nobles were allowed to own private property, much of the land was worked under supervision of the state.

Helots, of course, worked the fields, giving to designated nobles a stated portion of each year's yield, illogically demanded in good times or bad. Thus members of the warrior caste were assured of economic security, although they were prohibited from exploiting the land for personal profit. Under the Lycurgan constitution male citizens were denied the opportunity to engage in commerce, even when they had reached retirement age. Furthermore, to discourage trade, gold and silver were prohibited (until the 300s B.C.) as media of exchange; in their place cumbersome iron pieces were used.

However, such restrictions did not hold for citizens of those city-states that ringed Sparta and had been brought under her hegemony. These "people round about," the *Perioikoi,* were free to engage in any activity they chose; it was therefore among this group that traders and artisans were found. Noninterference even extended to their social and political institutions. Three things only were demanded of them—annual tribute, armed contingents, and acquiescence in Spartan direction of their foreign affairs. On the negative side they were denied Spartan citizenship or even the right to marry Spartan women.

Spartan Hegemony

In this way Sparta, by the fifth century B.C., came to dominate the whole of the Peloponnese. At the core of her state was the warrior caste. Tilling the soil—and also

---

* Upon occasion the state sanctioned "breeding leaves" when the soldiers, single or married, were given permission to mate with watever women were handy, providing only that the latter were Spartan citizens. The marital status of either partner was regarded as immaterial. Compare Bury, *op. cit.,* p. 133, who says of Spartan women, "They were, proverbially, ready to sacrifice their maternal instincts to the welfare of their country. Such was the spirit of the place." Such was the spirit of Nazi Germany, too. Himmler, for example, specifically directed his SS elite to breed with whatever good Aryan women they could find; for this purpose, leaves were granted even when *Festung Europa* was being encircled by Allied troops.

conscripted for battle when exigencies de-manded it—were the toiling *Helots*. Round about, the *Perioikoi* supplied tools and weapons. States too large or too far away for *Perioikoi* status were grouped, under Sparta's firm leadership, in the Pelopon-nesian League. This League, which rivaled the Athenian-led Delian League, included almost all of the flourishing city-states of the Peloponnese—Corinth, Sicyon, Megara, Tegea, and others. With the in-ternal affairs of these League members Sparta interfered not at all. Indeed, several came to consider themselves rivals of the leader (Corinth, for example). But until the 300s B.C., when the whole Hellenic world crumbled in the violence and after-math of the Peloponnesian War, none cared to push its claims too far.

For this position of power, of course, Sparta paid a heavy price. A single war, or even a series of wars, conceivably may stimulate the aesthetic talents and impulses of a people. But when war becomes a total and permanent way of life, cultural horizons close down. So it was with Sparta. In all of Greece its warriors were regarded with fear and respect. Its monolithic structure was even admired, eventually, by such philosophers as Plato and Aristotle. But out of such a community come no poets or dramatists, no sculptors or gifted architects, no political theorists or creative thinkers. The garrison state may produce a cultural iron age; it can never give birth to a golden age. And, in the end, even its warriors may fail as, indeed, did Sparta's.

Colonization and Class Struggle

Power of the Aristocracy

In considering the disparate societies of Athens and Sparta we have bypassed cer-tain developments of Greek society gen-erally. Throughout most of the mainland and Asian coastal regions the "beautiful and the good," as the aristocrats called themselves, had established control by the late 700s. The qualities that they prized above all others were blood and land. Pos-sessing these, they believed that they had both the right and the duty to oversee the affairs of society.

But under this aristocratic rule the lot of the little man steadily and grievously worsened. Such conditions, of course, were common enough in the ancient cultures of the Fertile Crescent where binding custom and political despotism had crusted over free play of the human spirit. There the commoner and the slave, the "unbeautiful," had long since accepted their status as ordained by fate. The Asian coastal fringe and Greece, however, were far enough re-moved from these lands to constitute a pioneer region. And pioneers are noto-riously sensitive to humiliations fostered by static, class-stratified societies. So the little man fought back, occasionally enlist-ing the aid of the wealthier, but also the underprivileged, merchants and artisans, with results which we shall presently ex-amine.

Some notion of the spirit of the times may be obtained from the *Works and Days* of Hesiod (*c.* 725 B.C.). The poet's father, it seems, had left his home in Asia Minor to settle in Boeotia (an example of reversal of the migration trend of several hundred years before?) where he hoped to find a way out of his poverty. The piece of land he was able to acquire was diligently worked and, with his death, duly passed on to his sons Perses and Hesiod. Perses received the fairer portion of the estate, a circumstance that undoubtedly contributed to the bitter-ness that shows through much of the poet's work. In his *Works and Days* he describes five ages of mankind. The first was a golden age, free of evil. The following silver age was "less noble by far." Men of the third period were even more degenerate—"They ate no bread, but were hard of heart like adamant, fearful men who were finally destroyed by their own hands and passed to the dark house of chill Hades, and left no name." Grown temporarily more merci-

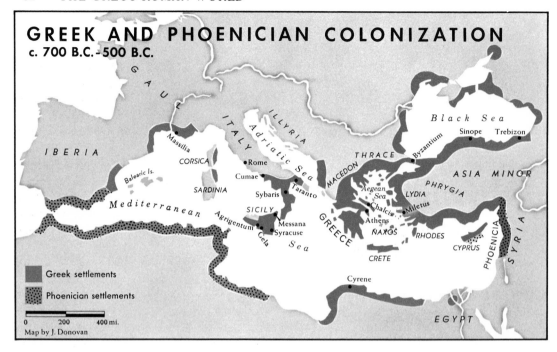

GREEK AND PHOENICIAN COLONIZATION
c. 700 B.C. - 500 B.C.

Greek settlements

Phoenician settlements

0   200   400 mi.

Map by J. Donovan

ful, Zeus created a fourth race, some of whom fought and destroyed the Trojans and thereafter lived "untouched by sorrow in the islands along the shore of deep swirling ocean." But the fifth generation was so steeped in misery that the poet lamented that he had not "died before or been born afterwards. For now truly is a race of iron, and men who never rest from labour and sorrow by day and from perishing by night; and the gods shall lay sore trouble upon them." [3]

Colonization

In a sense, these sufferings constituted the pangs of a new Hellenic birth of freedom, part of the glory to come. But many commoners — led by lesser nobles edged out of positions of power by their own elite — preferred the risks of a new land to what seemed the permanent insecurities of their homeland. Thus there developed (c. 750–c. 550 B.C.) what is called the Greek age of colonization (see map). Originally the

pioneers sought expansion in the Anatolian hinterland, but Phrygia and Lydia stopped such attempts before they were well started. Colonization efforts in Cyprus and Syria were precluded by a stubborn Phoenician veto. Perforce, therefore, other areas were settled. Miletus, for example (probably the strongest Greek community in Asia Minor), sent colonists to Trebizon and other Black Sea areas; Megarans founded Byzantium; the Euboean cities of Chalcis and Eretria colonized Thrace (until halted by the Persians in the 500s B.C.). Chalcis was especially active, turning west as well as to the north and east, establishing Cumae (c. 750 B.C.) about one hundred miles south of Rome, from which restless pioneers moved on to found Naples. Other Chalcidians settled colonies in Sicily, as Naxos and Messana. Greeks from the island of Rhodes colonized Gela in Sicily, which sent an offshoot to Agrigentum (c. 580 B.C.). On the southern tip of the Italian peninsula, Achaeans located at Sybaris, Spartans at Taras (Taranto). Other Greeks ventured farther west, colonizing Massilia (Marseilles) on the present French Riviera.

3. Hugh G. Evelyn-White, *Hesiod . . .*, G. P. Putnam and Sons, New York, 1920, pp. 11 ff.

In northern Africa Dorians established a flourishing settlement at Cyrene. Thus by the early sixth century B.C. migrant Greeks had ringed the Mediterranean with carbon copies of their home *poleis*.

Unlike the Phoenicians, the Greeks were interested not only in commercial ventures but in establishing communities. They took with them, of course, their language, habits, and customs (much as pioneering Puritans and Cavaliers were to do when they settled the Atlantic seaboard of the New World over two thousand years later). Far from discouraging emigration, most of the home communities facilitated such efforts in every way they could; for the freer they became of potential malcontents the more they could rest secure—or hoped they could—in their own privileged positions. Once established, the Greek colonists made their way not only as enterprising merchants and independent yeomen but also as cultural links which hooked the barbarian hinterland to the developing genius of the Ionian way of life. So effective were they as diffusionists that by Roman times Sicily and much of southern Italy was called, simply and quite appropriately, Magna Graecia.

Commercial Class

But if the stay-at-home aristocrats hoped, with commoners moving out, to avoid a democratic day of reckoning they were soon disillusioned. For one thing, and paradoxically, by breaking old family ties and thereby enhancing the position and place of the individual, the migrations actually gave impetus to the democratic impulse in the home communities. For another, increasing commercial relations led to a relatively rapid acceptance of coined money as a medium of exchange. Until about 640 B.C. when the officially stamped coin was invented (by the Lydians), commerce had been forced to employ such media of exchange as goods themselves, that is, barter, or pieces of gold and silver validated by weight rather than by the offi-

cial seal of a government. During the seventh century B.C. the new invention steadily advanced in general acceptance, making possible a systematic accumulation of capital. "Henceforth value was placed not on blue blood, but on what a man was and what he had." In short, a commercial class grew in numbers and affluence; and would soon, in its efforts to wrest control from the landed gentry, make plain its willingness to join hands with other commoners.

These economic developments led to a third influence weakening aristocratic control. The new quasi-business class could now afford the military equipment formerly the distinguishing mark of the landed elite. It must be understood that there was no such class consciousness as developed later in Western history. The new factor in seventh-century Greece was the presence of money in new hands. Thus the defense of the city-state became as much the responsibility of nonaristocrats as of the nobility. Sensitive to the political implications of the new situation the trading class now began to challenge tradition—and to back up their challenge with the power of the purse and threats of a military strike. Well might the highly conservative poet Alcaeus (a contemporary of the gifted Sappho) complain that the aristocratically piloted ship of state was in grave danger of foundering:

> I cannot understand how the winds are set against each other. Now from this side and now from that the waves roll. We between them run with the wind in our black ship driven hard pressed and laboring under the giant storms. All around the mast-step washes the sea we shipped. You can see through the sails already while there are opening rents within it. . . .[4]

Emergence of Tyrants

Perhaps one aspect of the "giant storms" Alcaeus, as a conservative aristocrat, found hard to understand was the develop-

4. From Moses Hadas, ed., *The Greek Poets*, The Modern Library, Random House, New York, 1953, p. 186.

ment of the institution of "tyranny." For modern students the term is an unfortunate one. It easily brings to mind a Mussolini, a Hitler, a Stalin. In ancient times "tyrannis" designated a leader who had seized power from a legitimate ruler. The overthrown ruler was as likely—indeed, far more likely—to have played what we today think of as the tyrant's role than the usurper. Originally the tyrant was essentially a reliever of oppression. Alcaeus was himself (as a type) an excellent example of a prime mover of the "giant storms" he so deplored. For he and his aristocratic colleagues had badly bungled affairs of state by stubbornly refusing to recognize the deserved rights of those not in their charmed circle. As one authority has put it, the poet was "obsessed by his own troubles, but his troubles and so his poems were mainly political; an embittered aristocrat, his attitude goes far to explain why his world was breaking up around him." By the sixth century B.C., not only the newly rich merchant—who, in any case, was not then a numerous breed—but the inquiring commoner had learned what not to endure. Often, as we saw in the section on Athens, the succoring tyrant was a renegade aristocrat (as in our own times was Franklin D. Roosevelt). But the phenomenon was not peculiar to Athens. It could occur in any part of the Greek world; before formal constitutional government was introduced, it often did.

Finally, the adaptation of the Phoenician alphabet to the Greek language (sometime after 800 B.C.) gave winged power to ideas hitherto crippled and cramped by awkward and inadequate syllabaries. The creative talents of the Greek, freedom biased, could now sing eloquently of woes not to be borne, of dimly remembered glories of the past, and of a way of life—the "examined life"—that would surpass them all. Thus by the eighth century B.C. a new Greek world, Hellas, emerged from the long night of the "second dark age," probing the promise of man and eventually laying, in large part,

the foundations upon which our own Western society was built. Before turning to a detailed study of the Golden Age which flowered and faded in the fifth and fourth centuries, we need to take an overall view of the general state of society as it existed in the late 600s and 500s, and to consider briefly the Persian Wars which helped to bring the Great Age into being.

Prelude to Glory: Greek Society, 600–500 B.C.

Religion and Philosophy

Some changes took place in Greek religion that are worth noting. Stesichorus, a lyric poet living in Sicily (*c.* 600 B.C.), is credited with modifying the ancient Atrean legend which told of Clytemnestra's murder of her husband, Agamemnon, and of her own death at the hands of her son. Stesichorus made of this a moral tale, a version that Aeschylus and other later tragedians used as a model. In addition to this new emphasis upon morality the Greeks began to show a curiosity about the afterlife and a "desire for personal contact with the supernatural."

Out of these concerns were born several important religious movements. One was the Orphic cult, named after the poet-priest Orpheus. Into the popular religion its leaders wove a metaphysic which sought to relate man to the powers of the underworld. It also initiated a complex system of rites and practices designed not only to give man a place in the next life but to regulate his behavior in this one.

Another was the Eleusinian cult—so called after Eleusis, a city near Athens—where certain ceremonies came annually to be held. These derived from the legend of Hades' abduction of Persephone, "The Maiden of Grain." Ordered by Zeus to return the maiden to earth, Hades proved stubborn, and a bargain was finally struck: Persephone would remain with Hades four months of the year, returning to the world of life for the remaining eight months. According to one interpretation of the legend, the latter period coincided with the first fall plantings and ran through the harvesting and threshing of the grain in June. Across the centuries, however, this folk-myth of the year's seasons and man's dependence upon them took on metaphysical overtones. In this new elaboration man has his season of life and growth, nurtured by Mother Earth. Upon his death he is buried and in his turn "nourishes the plants of the earth." After a season the renourished earth brings forth another harvest of grain to sustain the living who, in due time, return to the earth which is thus again enabled to produce another harvest—and so on endlessly.

Much more direct and profound was the Greek venture into philosophy, begun as early as *c.* 600 B.C. Interested originally in astronomy, Thales of Miletus, called "the father of Greek, and thereby of European, philosophy and science," came to probe the question of the origin of the world of materiality. His deliberations led him to conclude that in spite of the various shapes and seemingly diverse natures of the phenomena about him, all partook of and evolved from a single substance. Anaximander (flourished *c.* 575 B.C.), Thales' student, agreed with his master on the abstract principle of causation but argued that a "boundless mass," not water, was the primordial force out of which all things came and into which all things returned. Associated with him another Ionian, Anaximenes, held that although a basic force did indeed give form and life to all things this form was neither water nor "the Unlimited," but air. Its expansion and contraction, he supposed, created phenomenal differences which separated each being from another and gave each its identity.

In a subtly conceived synthesis the mystical elements of the Orphic cult were combined with the new trend toward rationalism by Pythagoras (*c.* 530 B.C.), a Greek migrant to southern Italy. Pythagoras taught that numbers were the stuff of creation.

From his study of what might be called the physics of music he concluded that tonal pitch was strictly and absolutely related to measurable physical properties. The length of the lyrestring, for example, determined the tone which its plucking would bring forth. He thus postulated the thesis that all phenomena are reducible to number combinations.

Particularly important was the seminal thought of Parmenides and Heraclitus. Parmenides (*b.* 514? B.C.) followed Xenophanes in holding that total existence is one basic being, without beginning or end, unchanging forever. The changes that men think they experience are illusions created by the false promptings of our senses. The way to truth is found by logic and reason alone. Properly used, they reveal the encompassing unity of all phenomena and, contrariwise, the sham of seeming pluralism. Heraclitus (flourished 500 B.C.), on the other hand, denied the reality of permanence. All things, according to him, are in a state of flux. Nothing *is,* everything is *becoming*—"you cannot step into the same stream twice."

Literature, Art, and Everyday Life

Until the 600s B.C. Greek poetry was almost exclusively devoted to the recounting of grand, heroic deeds. But at that time a break was made from the Homeric school of thought and expression with the invention of a new genre, the lyric poem. The following excerpt is a good illustration of the new emphasis upon the "inner" community:

> Tossed on a sea of troubles, Soul, my soul
> Thyself do thou control; . . .
> Rejoice in joyous thing—nor overmuch
> Let grief thy bosom touch
> Midst evil, and still bear in mind
> How changeful are the ways of human kind.[5]

5. From Moses Hadas, ed., *The Greek Poets,* The Modern Library, Random House, New York, 1953, pp. 183–184.

Simonides of Amorgos used the new meter to give vent to his rather sour views on the worth of women. On the other hand, Sappho (*c.* 600 B.C.), acknowledged as "the greatest woman poet of antiquity," employed it to frame such passionate lines as these:

> . . . should I but see thee a moment,
>   Straight is my voice hushed;
> Yea, my tongue is broken, and through
>   and through me
> Neath the flesh impalpable fire runs ting-
>   ling;
> Nothing see my eyes, and a noise of
>   roaring
>   Waves in my ear sounds;
> Sweat runs down in rivers, a tremor seizes
> All of my limbs, and paler than grass in
>   autumn,
> Caught by pains of menacing death,
>   I falter,
>   Lost in the love-trance.[6]

Traditionally, many Greek city-states, to celebrate their godgiven well-being, or to plead for it, had set aside certain days for public performances. Commonly a chorus, dancing in stately steps to flute music, would chant praises or imprecations to one of the greater gods, such as Dionysos. In the mid-sixth century B.C. Thespis of Athens introduced a dramatic element destined to flower into that wondrous creation we call Greek Tragedy. Into the metrical sweep of the strophic-antistrophic choric odes he introduced the independent reciter of lines. This actor, almost always impersonating a god, would sound a warning or a note of prophecy, setting off a choral response of lamentation or jubilation.

The imaginative leaps in literature were marked by similar advances in art, especially pottery-making and sculpture. The fetching prearchaic geometric designs yielded to a new style. Geometric patterns were still used, but now they were juxtaposed with graceful animals and live human

6. Moses Hadas, *loc. cit.*

A typical example of "black figure" painting. On the reddish clay, black figures were painted in silhouette. As on this vase, the lace-like details were scratched in with a fine-pointed instrument.

forms to make the vase's beauty outreach its utilitarian function. This "orientalizing ware" (so called from obvious borrowing of naturalistic styles from the Near East) exhibited an exuberant spirit which gave full play to emotional expression.

It should not, of course, be supposed that these seventh and sixth century developments in religion, philosophy, literature, and art consumed all the waking hours of the average Greek. Then, as now, the bread and butter aspects of life occupied most of man's attention and energy. For the average Greek a new day meant but return to the field where olives were beaten from the trees; or where ploughing was resumed; or to the threshing floor where chaff was winnowed from the grain; or to the grape pit where his bare feet trod out the juice of wine-to-be. Boys attended grammar school where music and rhetoric were taught. Girls stayed at home with their mothers where they learned the arts of homecraft — and their position as a woman, which was distinctly and frankly inferior to man's.

Athletic activities played a large part in the life of the Greek male. Games and contests were featured at various seasons in almost every *polis,* culminating in elaborate annual tournaments in some cities. Moreover, every four years a week was set aside for a great socioreligious festival — the Olympic Games. Work and fighting ceased while contestants from all over the Greek world gathered at Olympus to display their prowess in foot and chariot races, in the javelin throw, in boxing bouts, and in jousting. From time to time the literati gathered at Delphi to compete in dramatic and musical contests. These great gatherings, held in the third and fourth years of each Olympiad, gave the Greeks unexampled opportunities to practice the educational trinity they preached: the disciplined synchronization of body, mind, and soul; and, incidentally, the only meaningful national unity they were ever to know.

Nature and Significance of the Persian Wars

By the middle of the sixth century B.C. there had emerged, we will recall, the challenging Persian empire. As it spread into western Asia Minor and the Greek world on its fringe, "East-West" friction developed. Succeeding monarchs, Cyrus, Cambyses, and Darius (*c.* 545–*c.* 485 B.C.), grew increasingly impatient with Greek "recalcitrance"; and Darius eventually established satraps instructed to brook no nonsense.

Naturally the mainland Greeks, led by Athens, looked askance at the rolling Persian tide and asked themselves where it would end and whether Greece itself would not one day be washed under. Coupled with this fear was fraternal sympathy for their Asian kin, to whom they gave support when the latter sporadically rose in revolt. As Greeks and Persians girded themselves for a showdown, Athens sounded a general alarm, warning other *poleis* that its doom would spell doom for all. But when the first blow fell Athens was almost alone in standing up to it.

In 490 B.C. a large contingent of Persian troops sailed into the Bay of Marathon, about 20 miles northeast of Athens. The Persian plan was to meet and crush Greek infantrymen between the marshy stretches below Marathon while other Persian forces sailed southward around the bay to march directly against Athens. The scheme was plausible, but certain circumstances combined to render it impracticable. For one thing, it seems the cavalry units were included in the second group. This resulted in Persian inability to envelop swiftly the flanks of the Greek army (itself without cavalry) when the latter advanced onto the plains of Marathon. For another, defense of the homeland often engenders a spirit and tenacity hard to equal by an invader. In the ensuing battle Athenian infantrymen succeeded in driving the Persians into the sea. At this point a third development served to wreck Persian strategy completely. Sensing the destination and mission of the enemy convoy Miltiades, the Athenian commander, called upon his victorious but weary troops to march, at once and without rest, to the defense of their supposedly beleaguered city. Actually their forced march brought them into position before the Persian ships could disembark their troops. Seeing the futility of an attempted landing, Datis, the Persian commander, called off the attack and returned home.

The effect of this double victory over the vaunted Persian hordes was tremendous. All Hellas rejoiced in the .miracle of Marathon. To the Greek world Athens appeared as a city apart, a *polis* of heroic stature. To Athens the victories gave a sharp impetus to the Hellenic leadership she was then shaping.

But the Persians were not discouraged. Darius laid new plans to conquer these western upstarts; when he died in 485 B.C. Xerxes, his son, pushed these plans with all the vigor of his aggressive sire.

Well understanding the ordeal ahead, Athens on the advice of her gifted leader, Themistocles, concentrated on the construction of a large navy. For her part, Sparta rallied the support of about 30 city-states and formed a defensive Panhellenic League. When Xerxes began his march in 480 B.C.—this time across the Hellespont and down through Thessaly—the Greeks were probably as ready as ever they had been or were to be for action in a common enterprise. At Thermopylae valiant Spartan forces met the Persians and stood them off until, through treachery, the latter learned of a route which enabled them to skirt the pass and attack the defenders in the rear. The Persian flood then poured into Attica. City after city capitulated. Athens itself was captured and burned; the way seemed opened for conquest of the whole peninsula. But at this point the foresight and wisdom of Themistocles decided the issue. The Greek navy, well equipped and daringly led, maneuvered the Persian armada into a fight in the Bay of Salamis, just off the Athenian coast. There the Persians suffered a decisive defeat. With half his fleet wiped out and bereft of supplies and logistical requisites, Xerxes was placed in a serious dilemma. To stay with his stranded army would not only invite disaster but encourage fresh revolts among restive Ionians along the Asian coast. To withdraw his forces northward and back across the pontoon bridge would save his army but lose the war. The Persian king's decision was both reasonable and fatal. Leaving the army under the command of an able general, Mardonius, to try a stand at Plataea (the port of Athens), Xerxes hastened back

to Asia Minor to superintend the containment of Ionian rebellion and to assemble, so far as he could, a relieving navy.

Enspirited by success the Greeks, in the spring of 479 B.C., inflicted a crushing defeat upon Mardonius' army. Similarly inspired Ionian Greeks joined their mainland brothers in a battle off Miletus—at Cape Mycale—where Persian forces were again routed. Thereafter the coastal cities vied with one another in ridding themselves of their Persian overlords. For the second time in hardly more than a decade the mighty Persian empire had been humbled.

It is customary to argue that Greek victories at Marathon, Salamis, and Plataea held back the Persian flood and saved Europe from drowning in the murky sea of Oriental despotism. The European way of life, it is claimed, was thus given a chance to root itself in the Greek ethos and eventually to flower in disciplined thought, democracy and vaulting aesthetic expression. Although it is hard to accept the argument that Europe would have died aborning had the hosts of Xerxes won the day, it is nevertheless true that these events were of high significance. Two great Hellenic communities were, at a crucial juncture of their development, spared Eastern domination; were allowed, rather, to create their own image—or, in the case of Sparta, to maintain the institutions it had already developed—as their native talents dictated. If it be objected that the Spartan image turned out a rather sorry thing, it must also be conceded that the Athenian way of life came to shape some of the basic features of later European society (and ultimately our own). We need not go the whole way with those historians who link the birth of freedom with this Greek victory. But we may reasonably hold that without that victory the creative development of Western man's mind and Western institutions would have been seriously retarded. If the Persian Wars did not create Western man, they unquestionably permitted an early flowering of Hellenic society.

SELECTED READINGS

*Andrews, A., *Greek Tyrants,* Harper Torchbook, New York, 1963.

A competent, thorough analysis of these much misunderstood statesmen.

Bonnard, André, *Greek Civilization,* George Allen and Unwin, London, 1957–1961, 3 vols.

It is not uncommon for translators to disclaim acceptance of some of the views of the works they translate. Both translators do so in these volumes. They are joined by a number of other scholars in disassociating themselves from Bonnard's controversial approach and interpretations. Nevertheless, in my opinion these volumes make up one of the most meaningful studies of Greek culture to be published in our times when used with such standard works as those of Bury, Hammond, and Starr cited below. (J. L. S.)

Bowra, C. M., *The Greek Experience,* Weidenfeld and Nicholson, London, 1957.

Topical treatment of Greek religion, the *polis,* philosophy, art, literature, and, in Chapter 5, the "good life."

Bury, J. B., *A History of Greece to the Death of Alexander the Great,* Macmillan and Co. Ltd., London, 1959.

Professor Meigg's updating of this classic study assures its continuing reputation as one of the most significant works on Greek history. If only one work were to be read this should be it.

Dodds, E. R., *The Greeks and the Irrational,* University of California Press, Berkeley and Los Angeles, 1951.

This should be required reading for those who still hold that Hellenic civilization and rational living are synonymous.

Ehrenberg, Victor, *The Greek State,* Barnes and Noble, New York, 1960.

A sociopolitical analysis of the *polis.* One of the most authoritative brief accounts available of the life and problems of the Greek citizen.

Ehrenberg, Victor, *Society and Civilization in Greece and Rome,* Harvard University Press, Cambridge, Massachusetts, 1964.

Asterisk (*) denotes paperback.

The first three essays are interpretive lectures on Homeric Greece, the Archaic age, and "the Athenian century." They deal, in part, with the impact of things upon thought, the significance of social customs and habits, and the relationship between poetry and "education."

Finley, M. I., *The Ancient Greeks,* Viking Press, New York, 1963.

A delightful and informative essay—a "personal analysis"—of certain cultural aspects of Greek civilization. Especially useful when read with Bury, Hammond, or Starr.

Hale, William Harlan, *The Horizon Book of Ancient Greece,* American Heritage Publishing Co., New York, 1965.

A fascinating account written for popular reading. The illustrations are superb; the maps are strikingly graphic; the text, though not always consistent with the findings of scholarly research, is imaginatively organized and highly readable.

Hammond, N. G. L., *A History of Greece to 322 B.C.,* Clarendon Press, Oxford, 1959.

A close second to Bury's work. Professor Hammond takes some positions sharply challenged by some other (mostly American) scholars, especially in the first 100 or so pages. Here it is useful to compare Starr's *Origins* (noted below).

*Homer, *The Iliad,* and *The Odyssey,* E. V. Rieu, translator, Penguin, New York, 1950.

No reading, however extensive, about the heroic age can substitute for "Homer's" own accounts of it. These translations are perhaps the best.

*Kitto, H. D. F., *The Greeks,* Pelican, Baltimore, 1951.

Many of Kitto's interpretations are as subjectively arrived at as are Bonnard's. The book is not a narrative history of the Greek people so much as an evaluative essay of certain aspects of their culture, for example the Greeks as warriors and thinkers.

Muller, Herbert J., *Freedom in the Ancient World,* Harper and Brothers, New York, 1961.

Chapters 6–8 should be read with Toynbee's work cited below. Both works have the same basic approach; the comparable and contrasting emphases should stimulate the reader's own imaginative reconstruction of the Hellenic genius.

Palmer, Leonard R., *Mycenaeans and Minoans,* Alfred A. Knopf, New York, 1962.
   Professor Palmer seeks in this book to interpret the script deciphered by Ventris; in doing so he challenges the basic thesis of Evans' *Palace of Minos* (see notation in Chapter II). Can be profitably read with Miss Vermeule's work cited below.

Parkes, Henry Bamford, *Gods and Men* (see notation in Chapter III).
   Pages 147–304 treat of Hellenic and Hellenistic culture from the standpoint of one mainly interested in examining "social myths" and the "spiritual" core of civilized mores.

Robinson, Cyril E., *Hellas: A Short History of Ancient Greece,* Beacon Press, Boston, 1955.
   If Bury, Hammond, or Starr is not read, this work should be. It is sound in scholarship, balanced in interpretations, and readable.

Starr, Chester G., *The Origins of Greek Civilization,* Alfred A. Knopf, New York, 1961.
   This book contains an abundance of facts describing early Greek culture, down to the period of colonization. In one sense it presents too many facts—thematic treatment suffers from an urge to include data that cloud rather than clarify some concepts.

Toynbee, Arnold J., *Hellenism,* Oxford University Press, New York, 1959.
   A philosophic approach to the problem of Greek humanism and its bearing on the rise and decline of Greek culture.

Ventris, Michael, and John Chadwick, *Documents in Mycenaean Greek,* Cambridge University Press, Cambridge, 1956.
   Much of the language is technical. But despite this the lay reader can feel some excitement as he is led stage by stage through the maze of cryptography and philological venturing which resulted in cracking the once (and still somewhat) baffling Linear B script.

Vermeule, Emily, *Greece in the Bronze Age,* University of Chicago Press, Chicago, 1964.
   An up-to-date, highly readable, and controversial account of Mycenaean history. Miss Vermeule has ideas of her own, but a scholarly conscience as well. All aspects of Mycenaean culture are included in her survey: politics, economics, art, religion, palace life, language, shaft graves. Especially worthwhile when read with Palmer and Webster.

Webster, T. B. L., *From Mycenae to Homer,* Methuen and Co. Ltd., London, 1958.
   A detailed and scholarly study of Mycenaean art and poetry. The last chapter connects the Mycenaean heritage to Greek culture in Homeric times.

5

The Greek Way: Prometheus—
and Epimetheus

The School of Hellas:
Mind

Pre-Socratic Philosophy

We have already seen how, in Ionia, the Milesian school of philosophers prefigured the inquiring mind. In the fifth and fourth centuries B.C. that mind was brought to a maturity hardly, if at all, surpassed today. Democritus (flourished 425 B.C.), for example, propounded a seminal notion which was destined to languish two and a half millennia before bearing fruitful development—the atomic theory. According to this Thracian philosopher, all matter was reducible to minute solid corpuscles moving about in infinite void, "the first really atheistic doctrine in the ancient Greek world." All flora and fauna were, in his view, explicable by investigation and understanding of the laws of attraction and combination. Essentially—that is, literally in the essence of each—man and mud were identical; only by the manner in which

atoms combined were they different. Not only was the individual atom identical with every other, it was also indestructible. Its appearance (in combinations perceived by man) could change, but its basic being existed in eternity. Thus Democritus anticipated, besides the atomic theory, the first law of thermodynamics which holds that the fundamental stuff of life can never be destroyed.

Democritus' distinguished older contemporary (though possibly his pupil) was Protagoras (c. 481–411 B.C.), architect of the Sophist school of thought, Pericles' tutor, and friend to two of Athens' most gifted dramatists, Sophocles and Euripides. Protagoras, though not unmindful of the importance of cosmological probing, was primarily interested in the human response to man's phenomenal environment. Bypassing arguments over the nature of ultimate reality, he sought to place men meaningfully in actual existence. This first of the philosophical humanists thus argued that "man is the measure of all things." Outer phenomena exist. But only man can *reflect* upon these phenomena; only man is aware that he is aware. Man is more significant than other beings because he can and does manipulate his environment to enhance the superior quality of his being. Hence the "meanings" of all other things are (for man) what he judges them to be.

Sophism and Socrates

Of Protagoras' many pupils (of whom Socrates was one) a number developed ramifying lines of thought which collectively came to be known as Sophism—the thought of the "wise ones." For several reasons this variegated philosophy attained, for a short time, a wide popularity. One reason was Protagoras' own ambiguity which invited a multitude of reactions. Also, by about 460 B.C. the demands of pure democracy clearly called for rhetorical and dialectical skills which only professional logicians could teach. Finally, Athens' increasing wealth accentuated natural tendencies to find solutions in compromise and expediency. Almost certainly a number of the practitioners were sincere seekers after truth. Gorgias, for example, was no fee-splitting logician casing the market for what today might be called culture vultures. His view that man can never really *know* anything and that virtue is dependent upon milieu and moment may seem defeatist and dour but there can be little doubt that it came from sincere and prolonged inquiry. But other sophists sold their dialectical wares in a robust seller's market, holding one day this position, another day the opposite, and sometimes the propriety of both—or neither. Soon Athens became dotted with what one scholar calls thinkshops which gladly sold what the buyer demanded. Thus in the world of ideas and

attitudes everything became relative, amorphous, chameleonlike.

Out of this morass of intellectual stock-jobbery came Socrates (469–399 B.C.), preaching the validity of definable verities. Unlike his fee-conscious and prose-conscious contemporaries, he wrote nothing and taught without charge. To Socrates the Sophists had become "intoxicated with the exuberance of their own verbosity." For him, truth existed, eternal and absolute. But it could not be found by fancy speech or clever formulas. The path to truth was rather by honest and disciplined examination of the incongruous and seemingly contradictory. An example might run like this: A holds that democracy produces the good society, B that it results in evil. Which is true, if either; or to what extent may both be right? A may ask B what evil democracy produces; B responds with two statements. A is forced to grant the validity of the first proposition, but points out a fallacy in the second. B replies that for reasons *a, b,* and *c* the remaining proposition seems true. A then shows how *a* cannot be true if the first proposition, agreed to by both, is sound; and that *b* and *c* depend upon *a.* Upon reflection, B concedes that the second proposition cannot, after all, stand. And so the dialectic goes on until the husks of error, half-truth, and prejudice are peeled away revealing the kernel of absolute truth. Neither A nor B may particularly like the truth that is thus uncovered. But granting honesty and intelligence—prerequisites of the Socratic method—both accept the result. Its evaluation and application, however, invite varying and again contradictory views, when once more the dialectic is set to work.

Curiously, the man who held that the virtues existed and were knowable, for himself claimed no knowledge except knowing that he did not know. But only his method of inquiry, he insisted, could produce knowledge. He made his dialectic thoroughly familiar to other Athenian philosophers and, through them, their students, and ultimately to all the great thinkers of the Western world. With it, he questioned everything, even the most sacred and seemingly secure institutions. In the end the State, finding his ceaseless proding unbearable, put him to death; but not before some of the most gifted minds of his age—preeminently, of course, Plato—had become converted to their master's way.

Plato

Of fundamental importance in Plato's political thought is the concept of the tripartite nature of Man. Some human beings are given the gift of profound, intuitive insight; these are the men of *reason*. Others possess a *power of will* which enables them to execute the plans of the men of reason. The masses are devoid of both high reason and powerful will. Motivated mainly by the *impulse to acquire material gain,* they are designed by nature to produce and distribute the material goods of life.

Accordingly, the ideal society is a graded, hierarchical structure where the ruler is the wise man (or men) whose policies, executed by the men of will, confer unending blessings upon the whole realm. A Platonic fable, seeking to emphasize this threefold structure of society, depicts the philosopher as the Man who compacts with the soldier-administrator Lion to discipline and keep in check the Many-Headed Beast, the masses. In this regimen, the last learn to know the value of obedience, the men of will develop the courage and initiative which maintain and protect the State, while the creative ruler ceaselessly probes the secrets of universal justice.

Necessarily, then, the ruler is the only possessor of knowledge which Plato, like Socrates, equates with virtue. The soldier-administrator, under the tutelage of the leader, may probe past and present conditions and form *opinions*. When based upon serious and disciplined study, such opinions are not merely useful in the life of the re-public but actually indispensable. They do not, however, touch eternal truth. Rather they result from keen perception of the changing shadow world. The acquiring masses, busy with the bread-and-butter business of life, do not even form clear perceptions of the shadows. For the most part they live in a state of the Great Unknowing, recognizing meaning only in superficial phenomena or through directives given to them by their superiors.

Subserving this premised political structure was an elaborate metaphysic dealing with the nature of reality of which only the barest outline may be given here. According to this metaphysic reality resides and subsists wholly in Ideas (in Plato's thought, *idea* meant what we today would more likely call essence). In the beginning God, out of a desire to share his goodness and being, created many ethereal forms of truth: humankind, vegetation, the animal kingdom, inanimate objects, fire, and water, for example. But to invest these forms with a species of sovereignty—not to do so would be but to play with sharing—God, out of void and time, created a corporeal world of concrete objects or instances. Thus there were two worlds, spiritual forms where actual and whole truth existed, and the world of "parallel shadows" out of which might come, man willing, the journey to the world of reality. This is man's destiny, to travel, if he will, from the seeming to the real. Or if he will not, to pass from shadows to hell, that is, from convertible to incovertible and eternal error.

To be specific, Plato argued that in this corporeal world it is impossible for any human being to know, let us say, a real river. Man's perceptual sense, it is true, may discern the banked water and its flowing course. But such constitute only an imperfect instance of the Idea (or essence) of *riverness*. Similarly, it is impossible for perfect justice to manifest itself or exist in the world in which we live. A specific act may partake of the essence of justice, for example, the appreciative returning of a borrowed object. But this act or instance can in no way embrace the totality of the essence of justice.

Aristotle

Born about two hundred miles to the north and east of Athens (in Stagira, hence his cognomen "the Stagirite"), Aristotle found in that city the atmosphere of learning he yearned for and in Plato the master he was seeking. But his own genius was too vaulting to be confined by another's. After Plato's death he founded a school of

Aristotle.

his own in Athens—the Lyceum—and there spent the rest of his life remodeling the mansion of philosophy.

But if he altered the Platonic structure he did not destroy it. Like Plato he believed that the essence of reality is found in ideas, which he called "forms" (we would think of them as universals). Unlike his master, however, he did not believe reality resided exclusively in ideas. On the contrary he held that it was also found in the substance of matter which the forms prefigured. Thus, for example, a particular tree, although modeled by the universal of "treeness," partook of reality as truly as the idea which shaped it.

For Aristotle, then, the individual man was real. Man's purpose—true of all forms of life—was to realize his potentials which, since man's genius lay in his unique reflective thinking apparatus, meant to think; ultimately, indeed, to experience a life of pure thought.

But if man is to know himself he must necessarily know the nature and relationship of all other phenomena which are also real—for instance, rain, trees, and bees. Such understanding, Aristotle believed, could result only and exclusively from the use of a particular mode of inquiry. He called it *logic;* our phrase today would be the scientific method. A basic element of this mode of inquiry was what he called the syllogism, a species of deductive reasoning in which there are set up major and minor premises which lead by necessity to an inescapable conclusion. A simple example would be: all human beings breathe; John is a human being; therefore John breathes.

With this intellectual tool and its refinement, Aristotle set for himself the chore of learning all the secrets of nature and of life. That he naturally failed to achieve this fantastic goal is less significant than the pioneering paths he blazed for others to follow. For he not only gathered and collated an enormous mass of data in a number of disciplines but created the disciplines themselves. His *Politics* exemplifies this.

Before his time, from "Menes" through Solon and Plato, many minds had grappled with the nature and function of political organization. But none had identified and explicated the scientific principles which subsume civic life. To accomplish this, Aristotle collected over 150 Greek constitutions, subjecting their aims and provisions to scientific scrutiny. From this labor he adduced fundamental political propositions that have continued to serve state-makers and politicians to our own day.

In the same way he created disciplines in the life sciences. His *History of Animals* sets up classifications, never before attempted, of various species. To effect this categorization he resorted again to long continued observation and critical analysis. Similarly, he grouped and classified the plant world, probably being aided in this task by receiving an almost endless stream of specimens from scholars who accompanied the far-ranging armies of his former pupil, Alexander.

Almost no field of study escaped his patient exploration. In his *Poetics* he examined the nature and purpose of literary creation. No art is valid, according to Aristotle, unless it evokes pleasure which comes from the harmonious union of the true (or the probable) and the good. There is thus nothing of "art for art's sake" in the Aristotelian doctrine.

By his death in 323 B.C. he had brought into being the sciences of logic, physics, biology, psychology (in its incipient form), and ethics. Moreover, he had refashioned Platonic metaphysics and had created the canons of artistic expression. Critics who labor his many errors and false judgments — and there are very many of both — quite miss the point. We know now that Darwin erred and, on more than one occasion, formulated serious misjudgments; yet no informed person would care to denigrate the Darwinian contribution. It is in this perspective that Aristotle's achievements should be judged. Indeed his place, secure in the human record, looms larger today than when he strode the walk of the Lyceum.

The School of Hellas: Word

Literature

Greek tragedy encompassed virtually all of the basic purposes that were the concern of Greek philosophy. It is a mistake, therefore, to assume that the great Greek tragedians, Aeschylus, Sophocles, and Euripides, used their creative gifts to embroider heroic legends with existentialist fantasies. No more sound, either, is the commonly held view that their works proclaim the inexorable doom of man. As a matter of fact, it is to hope, not despair, that they point. All were didactically motivated — interested not in the notion that "the play's the thing" but in conveying a message.

We have already seen how, in earlier days, the Eupatridae mercilessly exploited the underprivileged and made their life a kind of hell. Here were the historic conditions which first impelled the Greek dramatist to tragic response, as they impelled the masses and their tyrant leaders to political struggle. Not long after came a new threat, from the East, when again the Greeks stood to the test and, at Marathon and Salamis, threw back the aggressor. From both, extended trials, suffering, degradation, and violent death came as intimate and abiding companions. Although from each period the Greek world emerged victorious, the demanding experience prompted grave questioning. Whence came the evils they suffered? Were there such things as cosmic justice and harmony? Were the gods indifferent to human fate or, even worse, was Fate itself fashioned to preclude the human achievement of permanent goodness and happiness? These questions and their logical implications lie at the root of the dramatic confrontations Greek writers made to their times of troubles.

Aeschylus

Of about seventy plays written by Aeschylus (525–456 B.C.), more than sixty are lost. The extant few, however, are masterpieces which have shaped and inspired the works of most subsequent tragedians. Of these perhaps the *Oresteia*, a trilogy made up of *Agamemnon,* the *Choephori*, and the *Eumenides*, best serves the purposes of our study. In all three the dramatist's basic theme is the relation of human endeavor to destiny. In each his aim is to align earthly struggle and suffering with divine harmony and justice. *Agamemnon* deals with murder, injustice, and impiety. To rescue Helen from the Trojans the Mycenaean king storms and sacks the city of Troy. Becoming enamored of Cassandra, daughter of the Trojan king, he brings her with him on his return home. Long since, his own wife, Clytemnestra, has taken a paramour of her own. In her fury compounded of guilt, desire for her lover, and indignation at *Agamemnon's* infidelity, she hacks him to pieces within an hour of his return. In justification she reminds the people of Agamemnon's wanton slaying of their daughter, Iphigenia, in propitiation of the supposed wrath of the gods, and points to her husband's flaunting a mistress in her face. The drama ends in this melange of murder and mean intrigue.

In *Choephori*, the main theme is vengeance, or "the failure of man's efforts to struggle against Destiny." Orestes and his sister Electra, offspring of the doomed Agamemnon and his murderous spouse, cannot suffer the spectacle of their faithless mother openly cavorting with her caddish lover. At this point the god Apollo intervenes, laying upon Orestes the command to destroy his mother. Although he recoils against such a mandate, Orestes realizes that man cannot stand against the gods, and in the end he murders both Clytemnestra and her lover. "Thus the chain of crime and vengeance seems as though it may be endless."

But in *The Eumenides* a reconciliation among the gods and between them and humankind is effected. In this third portion of the trilogy the Furies haunt and harass Orestes ceaselessly. Before they destroy him, however, the goddess Athena intervenes and proposes a solution. Let the citizens of the city make up a jury. Let the evidence on both sides be presented; and let the verdict decide Orestes' fate. So a panel of his countrymen sit in judgment and hear the arguments for and against him (with, appropriately, the god Apollo as counsel for the defendant). With the evidence in and the jury polled, Orestes is declared guilty by exactly one half the panel and innocent by the other half. At this juncture Athena appears and casts the deciding vote for acquittal. The vicious chain was broken. Moreover the goddess worked a divine miracle by transforming the vengeance-hungry Furies into benign spirits—the *Eumenides*. In this fashion both divine and human justice and harmony were established.

Sophocles, Euripides, and Aristophanes

Thus Aeschylus, responding to the challenge of his times, sought to probe the larger meanings and purposes of life, the nature of justice and destiny, and the relationship between the human and the divine. A generation later Sophocles (495–406 B.C.) took up the same theme and produced works that some critics hold in even higher esteem than those of his predecessor. *Oedipus Rex, Oedipus at Colonus, Antigone*, and *Electra* are four of the many tragedies he wrote. His contemporary, Euripides (480–406 B.C.), concentrated on the secular and interpersonal conflicts of mundane existence (as in his *Medea, Hippolytus* and *Iphigenia at Aulis*). These works moved Sophocles to remark that "he painted them as they are," a remark that pointed to "the most important change wrought by the last of the great tragedians in the Greek drama." [1]

Somewhat ironically the dramatist whose

characters most vividly bring alive the spirit of this period was Aristophanes, no tragedian, but a writer of comedies. Within his life span (*c.* 450–389 B.C.) Athens both achieved its peak and began its downward plunge. In the new milieu of violence and spreading chaos, Aristophanes sought with the scorn of his biting satire to expose the fatal drift that affairs had taken. In *The Acharnians* and *Lysistrata* he caricatured both the person of the warrior and the spirit of war.

Other targets of his lampooning wit were democratic demagogues (*The Knights*), those of his own craft whom he considered bowed down with their own weightiness (*The Frogs,* aimed at Euripides, no less!), and the sophists, of whom Aristophanes considered Socrates the pompous master wordmonger (*The Clouds*). With his death a century of classic drama closed.

Of lyric and epic poetry of this period there is not much to examine, since tragic drama seemed to absorb the Greek genius. But at least one lyricist, Pindar (*c.* 515–*c.* 435 B.C.), wrote verse graced by an enduring nobility. To Pindar the gods' greatest gift to man was heroic action, particularly as it exhibited itself in athletic contests and war.

Herodotus and Thucydides

In the fifth century B.C. the Greek mind, following in the tradition of knowledge-seeking established a century earlier, turned to the question, "What are the past events that have given rise to certain current events?" Here the discipline of history was born; here was the question *before* the answer; indeed, *for* the answer.

Acclaimed by later generations as the Father of History, Herodotus (*c.* 484–*c.* 428 B.C.) spent the early years of his life traveling over a large portion of the civilized world known to him—the Greek mainland and islands, Asia Minor and Mesopotamia, Crete and Egypt. Everywhere he went he probed with a prodigious energy and curiosity, collecting data of all kinds: on geography, genealogy, political and social institutions, historic annals, and folklore.

Sometime in the 450s B.C. he began to compose his account of the Persian Wars. To Herodotus these wars constituted an epochal turning point in human affairs. They demonstrated the superiority of the Greek way over that of all other peoples, although Persian virtues and values as well as those of other nations were liberally included in his story.

It may be argued that if Herodotus had been Persian rather than Greek, his history would have shown the superiority of the Persian way. Or that he may have had an inkling of his conclusion before he had finished his probing, or had even begun it. The merit or lack of merit in either argument makes really little difference. For Herodotus *did* have genuine curiosity and genuine questions; he *did* labor long and hard for answers; he *did* confine his work to human affairs. With whatever faith he followed his own concept and method of inquiry (and most modern historians would grade him well on both counts), the more important fact is his creation of them.

His successor, Thucydides, was less catholic in his interests but more precise in his method. He sought to discover the course and significance of the Peloponnesian War in which for a while he himself participated. He tried to divest himself of bias the better to learn stark truth. He disciplined himself to put aside impinging interests that might cloud his understanding of what answers he might find to his main question. The most famous portions of his history may seem to the modern student examples of how history should not be written. They are speeches, long speeches, which by Thucydides' own admission were put together by himself. But the substance of the speeches was not invented. This historian spent many years in close study

1. George Howe and G. S. Harrer, eds., *Greek Literature in Translation,* Harper and Brothers, New York, 1924, p. 284.

The School of Hellas: Form

Sculpture and Architecture

Before its decline into grandiose sophistry the afflatus of the Hellenic world worked its wonders in other artistic disciplines, particularly sculpture and architecture. Already by the early fifth century Greek talent had achieved a monumental breakthrough in the plastic arts. By this time it had effected a marriage of imagination and technique which produced works characterized by exquisite tension between the real and the ideal.

Dramatically heralding the new art are the works of Myron (480–445 B.C.), es-

Delphic Charioteer, *an early fifth-century work already showing the trend toward realism.*

Cleobis *and* Biton, *early sixth-century figures, clearly indicate the Greek sculptor's debt to his Cretan and Egyptian mentors.*

of sources, both written and oral. He subjected these data to checking and rechecking. And at all times, it should be said again, he sought to stay outside of the material. He began with no thesis; he shrank from no information that was personally offensive. From such study he learned an amplitude of facts about both events and the men who were involved in them. Only then, according to his own assertion, did he "put into the mouth of the speaker the sentiments proper to the occasion, expressed as I thought he would be likely to express them." If modern historians dare not use this particular part of the Thucydidean method they do not unduly berate him for using it. Indeed, it is because he was so insistent upon maintaining an impartial spirit and upon examining critically accounts which might and often did contain error and deception that he is called the creator of "scientific" history.

pecially his famous *Discobulus* and the *Marsyas with Athena.* In the *Discobulus,* Myron portrays a discus thrower at the climax of his windup, at the moment when disciplined energy and muscles tauten the whole body for release.

Myron's contemporary, Phidias (490–417 B.C.), approached perfection in the explication of the ultimate relationship between the human and the divine. Called by a Greek traveler and geographer of Roman times the "maker of gods," Phidias portrayed the divine in human form, suggesting simultaneously the closeness of the gods to men, and human potentials for making "what is" into "what ought to be." In the famous *Lemnian Athena,* Phidias humanized divinity while inviting man to let his reach exceed his grasp. The later years of his life were spent supervising the decoration of the Parthenon; he designed and executed an undetermined number of its

Discobulus. *This work of Myron* (c. 455) *is a measure of the growth of Greek genius in the century since* Cleobis *and* Biton.

Hermes, *by Praxiteles. The hand of the missing right arm held a bunch of grapes for which the infant Dionysos is reaching.*

reliefs as well as the huge *Athena* that was its aesthetic center.

The culmination of this classical religio-humanistic impulse, this supremely creative effort to build the world of man according to the model of the world of the gods, is found in the statues of Polyclitus (flourished 452–415 B.C.). In his *Doryphorous* (lance-bearer) and *Diadumenus* (victorious athlete) we move beyond masterly expression of the moment of action to equally masterly representation of *man becoming* or, more broadly, "the conception of a society that is becoming more than itself." Here, viewers

99

Panathenaic Procession. Part of a frieze showing the celebration of a festival held every five years in honor of Athena.

may well have felt, is what we are and what we may become, conscious of the reality around us and sensitive to the spirit that beckons us god-ward.

The heights reached by Greek sculpture in the fifth century B.C. were matched by those achieved in architecture. Indeed, these were usually united in the same artistic effort. The most conspicuous example of this union of aesthetic disciplines is the Parthenon, temple of the virgin goddess Athena.

In its basic design the Parthenon is simplicity itself: a double-columned rectangular building with a colonnaded portico on each end—"a marble poem." The columns are of the chaste Doric design. To give the effect of symmetrical solidity the four treadways are of unequal dimensions. Indeed, the whole embodies a number of deliberate and subtly calculated dis-

Parthenon from the west. Even the ruins of today suggest the chaste grandeur of this once "marble poem."

proportions and imbalances. The step sur-faces, for example, are given a slight swel-ling toward the center in order to offset the otherwise optical illusion of concavity. The same is true of the floor.

Before the century ended three other buildings adorned the Acropolis. Designed by Mnesicles, the Propylaea, occupying the westernmost portion of the Acropolis and serving as its gateway, combined the more slender Ionic column with the Doric. Its five entrances invited assorted throngs, religious processionals, individual wor-shippers, and ordinary sightseers. To the southwest, Callicrates erected a miniature shrine to the city's great protectress, the *Athena Nike,* containing his delightfully informal representation of the goddess tying her sandal. Several hundred feet be-yond it rose the two-levelled Erechtheum, an elegant Ionic structure.

Hellas' Great Age was relatively short-lived, encompassing scarcely two genera-tions. But for posterity perhaps a portion of the famous remark made in another context by former Prime Minister Churchill aptly applies—never was so much owed by so many to so few.

Power Politics, Social Lag, and the Peloponnesian War

Politics: Rivalries and Alliances

The battle of Plataea had freed Greece from the Persian threat. But how long would security last? Would not the great Eastern horde mount a third attack? And if it did, could the miracle of 479 be re-peated?

In spite of the ambiguity of the situation, almost immediately after Plataea the Greek weakness for particularism again showed it-self. Each city-state returned, or tried to return, to the world of its own *polis*. Except for the period of the Persian Wars, Sparta had long looked upon Athens as an evil second only to the Persian "barbarians," a feeling fully reciprocated by the Athenians. Argos, Corinth, and Thebes, among others, feared both city-states and sought ways to counter their power.

Nonetheless, Athens was able to per-suade a number of other communities to join in a league (478 B.C.) to guard the peninsula and to free the Ionians still under Persian rule. This Delian Confederacy—so-called from locating the common treas-ury and council on the island of Delos—did succeed in keeping the Persians Asia-bound. But for the allies the price was high. From the beginning, Athens made it clear that she intended to call the tune, demand-ing ships or their money equivalent as she saw fit. Two states which declined to join (Scyros and Carystus) were promptly con-quered and made subject to Athenian rule. Naxos, wishing to withdraw, was occupied. When Xerxes showed signs of regathering his forces for another offensive he was attacked and decisively beaten before he could leave Asian waters. Following this victory (Eurymedon, 468 B.C.), Athenian ambitions knew no limits. Thasos, off the Thracian coast, was overrun in 465 B.C. A few years later both the League council and treasury were moved from Delos to Athens. By then the defensive alliance, which eventually came to number some 470 cities, had been turned into an Athenian Empire.

By this time the democrats under the leadership of Pericles had taken most of their power from the conservative Areo-pagites. They had also begun the rebuilding of the Acropolis which, they hoped, would serve not only as the "school of Hellas" but as the symbol of Athenian supremacy. From the steadily increased levies, abun-dant wealth was at hand together with, as we have seen, almost a plethora of intellec-tual and artistic talents. And unification of the *poleis* into a Greek confederacy was long overdue.

With what can only be called tribute money the great Attic city did indeed adorn the Acropolis. But creation of a confederated Hellas was quite another matter. For one thing certain decisions of the government, dominated now for a generation by Pericles and his subordinates, made the city suspect. In the period 454 to 451 B.C., pay for public service, especially court service (in the *Heliaea*), was instituted. Also a new law was passed restricting citizenship to those who could claim both parents as citizens of Athens. On the surface, neither law seemed reprehensible. If the poorer commoner was to exercise his office-holding privileges he must be compensated. And since *metics* * and other foreigners increasingly made up a substantial portion of the population, the Athenian genius seemed threatened. But, in the long run, state pay tended to make many an Athenian a kind of idle, professional citizen. And citizenship restrictions kept much fresh political talent from participating in the democratic development of Athenian life.

Moreover two wars, in the 450s and 440s B.C., found Athens again at grips with Persia in the east and with Sparta in the west. The treaties which concluded them were fair enough. But the martial appetite, it seems, grew with feeding; in any case, the peace treaties marked only a lull. At the same time, the war experiences coarsened the spirit of the people. For example, in 440 B.C. Miletus was attacked without any legal sanction, its walls torn down, its warships seized, and an indemnity of over one million dollars imposed.†

The Peloponnesian War

Thus constituted, with imperial designs motivated by *hubris,* in proud ignorance of the *nemesis* to come, Athens cast about for more worlds to conquer. To the east Persia temporarily lay powerless. But to the west

Sparta and her allies seemed an intolerable challenge. It is true that during the period 445 to 431 B.C. a treaty of peace kept the rivals on nominally good terms. But, according to Thucydides, each side during that period was actually readying itself for a showdown. In 431 B.C. it came, desired by both but precipitated by Athens.

In a survey such as this, it is not possible to consider the details of wars, temporary truces, individual battles, and factional strife. To the student who has a special interest in the bitter and prolonged military struggle between Athens and Sparta, Thucydides is available. In his classic work may be found an extended analysis of the motivations and aspirations of each side, the war's tortuously complex course, and its conclusion and significance. Here we may only note that it lasted, with interruptions, nearly thirty years; that it nurtured rapacity and violence in the Greek soul; accentuated the drift from religious faith to sophist philosophy; mutilated what many had prized as the democratic way of life; and increased the natural and fatal Greek tendency to exalt *polis* over people.

In a loose sense the long struggle may be called a kind of world war. Not only were almost all of the major Greek cities involved at one time or another, but Athens and Sparta alternately courted and received Persian aid and thus invited the ancient enemy of both to fish anew in their troubled waters. To the north, rising Macedonia, neither Greek nor barbarian, lent diplomatic support now to this side, now to that. Westward, colonies of the mother cities felt the lapping waves of fury and became embroiled in the martial tempest, particularly Corinthian Syracuse. And Carthage, poised on the tip of modern Tunisia, did what she could to weaken the efforts of any and all who might threaten her command of the Great Sea's (Mediterranean) western lanes of commerce. In a much closer sense the 30-year conflict was also a class war. Oligarchs fought democrats for control of particular city-states, "the Athenians being

---

* Residents of foreign birth.

† Another example is Athens' ruthless destruction of Melos in 416 B.C. when, bluntly asserting the "law of nature," Athenians murdered all men of military age and enslaved the others.

called in everywhere by the democratic leaders and the Spartans by the oligarchs."

In 404 B.C. the once invincible Athens capitulated to the Peloponnesian power she had goaded into war. But Sparta no more than Athens could create a lasting empire. Most of the next 100 years were taken up with assorted civil and foreign wars. Thebes, Corinth, and Argos periodically enjoyed passing dominance. Occasionally Sparta and Athens would again show signs of establishing hegemony, as Persia threw her purchased weight to one side or the other. Internally, as during the original struggle, oligarchies and democracies were torn down and propped up with startling speed and impermanence. Wealth, strength, hope, and vision, all were battered in the seemingly endless melee of intraparty and international strife.

Arms and the Man: The Alexandrian Empire

Rise of Macedonia

In the early years of the fourth century Macedonia, growing in strength and ambition as the once proud *poleis* of the south killed off one another, looked to the spreading chaos with mounting interest. By 350 B.C. she considered the time ripe for some adventuring of her own. Sensing this new danger a Greek orator and statesman, Demosthenes, delivered in the Athenian assembly a series of prophetic warnings (the famous Philippics). But sustained vigor and purpose had been drained from Greece. At Chaeronea, in 338 B.C., rough and rude warriors of the northern kingdom rode down the forces of the stricken cities. The peninsula lay prostrate before a new conqueror. Later the fabric of Greek civilization, threaded with various patterns from the East, would clothe a new Western society; but for the present it was a garment rent. The glory of classical Greece had departed.*

Shortly after the battle of Chaeronea its victor, Philip, died (336 B.C.). To the Greeks, anxious to throw off the new Macedonian yoke and anxious also to resume their own intercity fighting, the death of this fearsome war lord from the north seemed a gift from Apollo. But they were soon disillusioned. For Philip's successor, Alexander III (356–323 B.C.), had plans of his own and, though but a stripling of twenty years, ample ability to realize them.

Alexander the Great

In 335 B.C. Alexander turned to the north where strong Balkan tribes had shown signs of breaching the frontier of civilization. Within the year he had defeated both the Getae and Triballi, brought the Celts of the region into alliance, cowed the Scyths, and reestablished Macedonian hegemony in Thrace. Soon a wish-fathered rumor that Alexander had been slain in the campaign reached the Greeks. Thebes at once rose in revolt. To make clear once and for all who was master Alexander, by forced marches, descended upon the rebel city and overwhelmed its defenders. Acting as "agent" for a terrified Greek league, he leveled it to the ground, sparing only the temples and Pindar's house. All of its inhabitants, young and old, were sold into slavery and its outlying lands distributed to nearby cities. The lesson was not wasted on the rest of Greece.

The remainder of his brief life—barely a dozen years—was spent in the subjugation of Egypt and Western Asia. This fantastic saga has been retold many times and cannot be detailed here. It must suffice to note that in the battles of Granicus River, 334 B.C., and Issus, 333 B.C. (see map, p. 104), Persian forces under Darius III were defeated, permitting Alexander to move south and wrest Egypt from Persian control. From

---

* In our study of the Roman world in the following chapter we shall see that in 338 B.C. Rome dissolved the Latin League and soon thereafter consolidated its control of the Italian peninsula. Never before or since in human history have signs clearly heralding the death of one great civilization and the birth of another been so dramatically juxtaposed within the space of a single year.

here the conqueror turned east where at Guagamela in 331 B.C. he routed the hosts of Darius for the third time. Thereafter he conquered with monotonous regularity whatever kingdoms and armies stood between him and India. Even India was invaded, but his troops had had enough and Alexander was forced to turn back. Before he could ready new plans for the conquest of Arabia, bypassed in his rush to the east, he fell ill in Babylon and died in the summer of 323 B.C. At his death he left an empire that sprawled from the Adriatic Sea to the Indus River.

It is difficult to conjecture what impact East and West might have had upon each other as a result of this forced and artificial union had Alexander been conqueror only. But he was much more than this. Added to his vaulting martial ambitions was a seemingly genuine desire to merge Greeks and Persians into one people, one vast community. To effect it he encouraged mass intermarriage (himself setting the example). To this end, too, he founded about twenty cities scattered from the Nile to the Indus, settled by Macedonians and Greeks. Liberally equipped with libraries and other cultural paraphernalia, and administered by commissions made up of both Asians and

Europeans, these population centers invited a blending of eastern and western ways. The grand community, of course, never materialized. But important changes were wrought, nevertheless. Language and law moved east. By the time of the birth of Christ, *koine,* a common version of classic Greek, was used by Asians and Europeans alike. On the other hand, the Macedonian type of government, monarchy, was so strongly supported by Oriental custom that Greek democracy and oligarchy both gradually yielded to it. It can be argued, of course, that both East and West (especially the West), wearied by burdens of wars, would have changed, Alexandrian thrust or not. But the thrust is history and must be duly recorded.

Division of Alexander's Empire

With Alexander's death in 323 B.C. a long struggle for imperial control began among his leading generals. In the end the Empire was partitioned. Macedonia, with its hegemony over a number of Greek cities, was taken over by Antigonus (and his successors, the Philips and others). Much of Asia Minor and most of Syria and Mesopotamia fell to Seleucus (some of whose successors were the several Antiochuses).

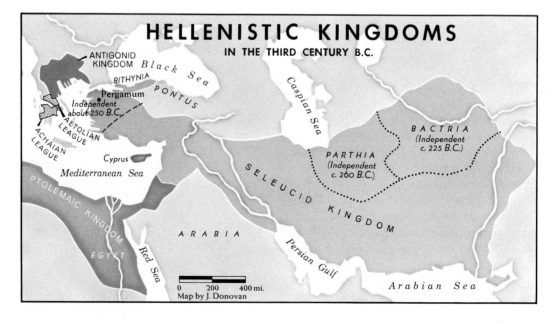

Ptolemy, another Macedonian war lord, carved out an empire made up of Egypt, Palestine, and part of Syria. Most of India, never conquered by Alexander, continued to maintain its independent existence. In northwestern Asia Minor along the littoral of the Black Sea, Pontus, ruled by a local dynasty, resisted Seleucid attacks. Later, Attalus Philadelphus freed Pergamum from Seleucid rule, as did various local leaders in other sections of the empire. In Greece proper two new leagues, the Aetolian and Achaean, preserved in their respective spheres a kind of home rule. (For delineation of these areas, see map.)

Although the faint promise of peace initially held out by the partition never materialized, it should not be concluded that unending violence disrupted life in the cities. As a matter of fact, most post-Alexandrian communities enjoyed an orderly existence either under royal bureaucratic officials or, more commonly, their own semiautonomous (or, at least, locally based and controlled) municipal officers. Still, if intercity life was relatively stable and peaceful, interdynastic relations were not. But wars and violence, endemic as they were, were not all that marked the Hellenistic period. Gradually there came into being a new spirit, changed economic and social conditions, new philosophies and literature, different approaches to science and art, and new religions.

The Departure from the Golden Mean: Hellenistic Society

From Polis to Cosmopolis

From 430 until about 145 B.C., by which time a large part of the Hellenistic world had come under Roman rule, internecine wars drained the *poleis* of their energy and wealth. Most of them were eventually absorbed into one or another of the larger empires. In the process much of the *elan* and *virtus* that had given the Greek his

genius was lost. Where there had been *polis*-man there was now *personal*-man, uprooted, disoriented, insecure. Essentially this is what the vaunted individualism of Hellenistic times came to mean. Concurrently, with the disappearance of the city-state and the creeping merger of East and West, *ecumene*-consciousness evolved, for with the city no longer the Greek's world, the world became his city. *Polis* became *cosmopolis*. To the modern student individualism and cosmopolitanism connote progress in human sophistication. To some extent this reasoning holds for Hellenistic man, but to a greater degree it does not. True, the world was wider. But the old order and the old sign posts were gone. And if the meeting of East and West, the merging of city with city, made the Greek less provincial, it also made him less Greek. The old ideal of the golden mean faded before the frameless discontents of the people and the scrambling of the *nouveaux riches* for materialistic power and glory. Even criticism of the new spirit was given a kind of amused tolerance: "When Apemantus the Cynic invaded the feast of Timon of Athens to denounce waste and worldliness, he was welcomed by the *bons vivants* as a kind of sauce to the fatted calf."

Social Conditions

Perhaps in an effort to create a cultural microcosm that would substitute for the city, many Greeks, both in the homeland and those abroad, established clubs whose officers bore titles resembling those of *polis* officials. Neither political nor professional in nature, they were designed to afford an outlet for the Greek spirit which had flowered in the city-state. Basically they functioned as recreational and social associations whose members—typically of the times, often a mixture of Greek and "barbarian"—found in the brotherhoods a sense of community which was lacking in the macrocosm of the new *ecumene*. In a sense the associations were a kind of graduate school for gentlemen, with membership open to those who had gone through the grammar, poetry, rhetoric, and physical education courses offered in the numerous private schools.

There is even some evidence that here and there women joined in such associations. If they did—and there is positive evidence of one in Alexandria—this would seem to argue an advance in the status of women. Strengthening this thesis is the prominent role which at least a few women played in political affairs. In both Macedonia and Egypt royal control was shared occasionally by such outstanding individuals as Olympias and the famous line of Cleopatras. But, on the other hand, evidence is strong that most women of the time—the wife of the typical burgher, artisan, or peasant—remained as underprivileged as her Hellenic sisters. Girl babies, for example, continued to be abandoned. Those who were allowed to survive lived, as Tarn has phrased it, on a different and lower level from that of men even though informal "relations between the sexes became less cramped and more rational." And the record clearly shows that female slaves outnumbered bondsmen, especially among the "house-born."

Economic Conditions

Economic conditions underwent a marked change. To be sure, mainland Greeks continued to experience grinding poverty, save for speculators and favored tradesmen. But in Asia Minor, Mesopotamia, and Egypt boom times were nurtured by the Alexandrian amalgam. For one thing Alexander's plans to explore little known lands were carried out, at least in part, by the dynasts who succeeded him. The first Seleucus, for example, probed areas of the Persian Gulf and settled colonies in the region. Later the coasts of Arabia and Upper Egypt were explored and trading opportunities exploited. To the north the hinterland of the Caspian Sea attracted both settlers and merchants. And though India remained strong enough to repel invaders, envoys and traders were allowed beyond the Indus River who eventually gave the Hellenistic world a vastly expanded understanding of this mysterious land.

Quite naturally, the creation of large empires and continued exploration stimulated trade. Throughout most of this period two great routes served to expedite both the exchange of goods and the diffusion of culture. The most important route was the sea lane that ran from the delta of the Indus across the Indian Ocean, up the Persian Gulf, overland to Antioch and thence to all parts of the Western world. The second, or southern, route connected India with southern Arabia. Through these great arteries flowed goods of all kinds: gold and silver, quicksilver (important in the manufacture of vermilion), grains, wines, oil, fruits and nuts, sugar, linen and other textiles, papyrus, glassware, marble, ebony and other rare woods, ivory, diamonds and other precious stones, spices, frankincense, and an unending stream of slaves.

To serve this trade many cities were founded or enlarged; for example, Antioch, Seleucia, Ephesus, and the many Alexandrias. In other words the old producing centers turned into transit-trade centers. This, of course, meant the aggrandizement of the merchant bourgeois class. But not this class alone. In Egypt especially, but also in Asia, monarchs were not only rulers but often the chief entrepreneurs. The huge fortunes amassed by merchants and kings gave the general impression of great prosperity (save for mainland Greece). But it is important to note that this affluence did not seep down to the commoners; so that in contrast to, say, fifth century Athenians the masses of Greece, Egypt, and Asia were separated from the wealthy few by an ominous and ever-widening gulf.

Hellenistic Philosophy

In response to these changed socioeconomic conditions and the development of a different spirit and outlook, Hellenistic philosophers labored to provide a rationale that would give sense and purpose to their new world. Their way had already been prepared by the Cynics.* The welter of wars and the courting of *hubris* made a mockery of the doctrine of the "middle way" once so persuasively preached by Greek philosophers, dramatists, and artists. So in the early post-Periclean age there arose a school of thought, or better, a way of life, dedicated to renunciation of the false values and perverted practices that had dissolved the way of the golden mean. Led by Antisthenes (*c.* 450–366 B.C.) and his disciples, Cynicism peeled away the pretensions of conventional life and called for a return to primitive virtue. Especially attacked were the prerogatives of wealth, race, and caste which, in the eyes of the Cynics, made life a jungle of jealousies, a desolate wasteland where "ignorant armies clash by night." Everything invited their bitter denunciation: the foolish and fatal pride of the *polis;* the demeaning distinction between Greek and barbarian, master and slave, man and woman; the madness that status seekers confused with glory; the continued erection of elaborate temples while the shrine in the soul was prostituted; the catering to the appetite for things rather than thought; and the fondness for finely spun theoretical speculation as the ancient world slowly crumbled into chaos.

Related to Cynicism but differing from it in at least one important respect were the teachings of the Skeptics. Introduced by Timon, an associate of Alexander the Great, the doctrine of the unknowability of anything and all things came into a brief flowering in the third century B.C. The Skeptics argued that the consistency with which the greatest thinkers—as, for example, Heraclitus and Parmenides—eternally contradicted one another proved the impossibility of attainment of true knowledge. The search for the true and the good should frankly yield to cultivated indifference to the ineffable mystery of life and death.

Of incomparably greater influence, then and thereafter, were the teachings of Zeno (late fourth and early third century B.C.). A Phoenician who had come to Athens, which was still regarded as the school of Hellas, Zeno gathered about him on the Painted Porch (the Stoa, hence the name Stoics for his followers) a group of students disillusioned of the worth of Platonism and Aristotelianism, and especially unsatisfied with the offerings of Cynicism and Skepticism. Zeno was fundamentally interested in what today we would call the human situation. But since man is a creature he cannot be understood apart from his creator. So Zeno began with a theological postulate: God was the fiery ether out of which all things came, in which all things rest, and to which all things return. By necessity there is therefore a spark of the divine in man; all are God's children and brothers one to another. Thus the Stoics taught, in the words of Plutarch, that "there should not be different City-States, each distinguished from the rest by its own peculiar system of justice: *all* men should be fellow citizens; and there should be one life and one order, as a flock pasturing together, which feeds together by a common law."

According to this philosophy man's basic response to the conditions of life is to seek the true and the good, as prompted by the divine impulse within him. So motivated he will come, through reason, to an understanding of the nature of his Creator, of himself, and of his relationship to all things, giving him power to achieve the good and endure the evil. Although such understanding comes only through individual effort Stoicism, in contrast to Cynicism and Epicureanism, by no means preached the

---

* The word suggests to the modern student something rather different from the original connotation, which was derived from the Greek word for dog. In their contempt for current customs and behavior these practical philosophers cast off the garment of convention and revelled in primitivism. Many adopted the very simplest kind of garb, some even disdaining physical cleanliness—hence their designation as "dog people."

doctrine of the essential solitude of man or of man's need to retire to the cultivation of his own garden; instead, quite the opposite. Since all are brothers, all are involved in a common life. Hence each is bound by duty and conscience to probe life unceasingly for that which is worthy and purposed by God for all. Being sons of God, men will seek to build the heavenly kingdom. Being finite, they will err and sin. For the Stoic, the good was to be sought and lived in humble appreciation of the Creator's grace. By this same grace man must learn to tolerate the results of human error and sin.

Throughout most of Hellenistic times Epicureanism had a greater following than Stoicism. In Zeno's own time and that of his disciples Epicureanism also had a more immediate influence. Like Zeno, Epicurus (341–270 B.C.) subordinated all interests to ethical considerations. Unlike him he repudiated pantheism and elaborated a system of mechanistic materialism. With Democritus, Epicurus argued that the essence of all things is atoms which combine by chance to produce objects, "dissolving if unfit, persisting as individuals and species if fit. . . ." There is no God, or if there is, he is wholly unrelated, by reason of his necessary perfection, to imperfect objects including, of course, man. All religions, therefore, are superstitions which stand between man and the goal of human life, which is the achievement of inner tranquillity. To the extent that man places his trust in religious myth he neglects reason and reason's method of comprehending the universe. All about man is discord and discord's products — endless possibilities of harassment and disturbances. Only the disciplined mind can bring order to the world of sensation in which we live. Necessarily this order is inner and personal.

By insisting upon the need for the individual to create his own spiritual world, tolerant and tranquil, Epicureanism came by some to be considered as a kind of salvation through disciplined selfishness. Actually, however, Epicurus based his teach-

ings upon the doctrine of sacrificial altruism. If he will, man may through reason transmute selfish drives into compassion; indeed he must, since reason links all men to one another. And no man, conscious of this and faithful in the use of his talents, can fail to understand that personal serenity is incompatible with indifference to the inner well being of others. On the other hand Epicureanism, in its concentration upon the creation of the inner citadel of security, disavowed all interest in public affairs. As the conditions of Hellenistic life became more hectic and man more concerned with material things, this way of life became, in the hands of dilettante philosophers, almost diametrically opposite that of its original nature and form. It became, in short, the refuge of debauchees who used it to justify their own escapist attitude of "eat, drink and be merry, for tomorrow we die."

Science

More compelling for the Hellenistic world than the pull of philosophy was the attraction of science. The *ecumene* created by Alexander, the continuing explorations after his death, and the materialistic approach prompted by, among other motivations, commerce and industry tended to incline the Greek mind toward observation, measurement, and analysis of natural phenomena (although interest in the occult and in religion did not die out).

The tendency of the Hellenistic Greek toward scientific inquiry was given focus, especially in astronomy, by the lore of Babylonia where the disciplined use of recorded astronomical observations had its origin. Kidinnu and his predecessor, Aristarchus of Samos (c. 310–230 B.C.) postulated the startling thesis that the earth orbits the sun and not vice versa. This suggestion, as Tarn points out, "should have been epoch-making." But the theory died at birth, for Aristarchus made the orbits of the planets circular rather than elliptical and geometricians of the day had no difficulty in conclusively proving that the sun could not rest in the center of a circle.

Similarly leaning upon Babylonian lore, Hipparchus (flourished 161–126 B.C.) charted the heavens, positioning no less than 805 fixed stars. It is thought that he may also have discovered the regular movement of the sun across the equator, thus establishing the pattern of the progression of the seasons. The moon's distance from the earth and its diameter were calculated with approximate accuracy. Because of the close relationship of the methods and processes of mathematics to philosophy, Hellenistic intellectuals were particularly attracted to it. Since the system of notation was as yet unformed, the Greeks developed geometry rather than algebra. Compiling and systematizing the advances made in this field, Euclid (c. 300 B.C.) produced a textbook that served students down to our own century. Archimedes of Syracuse (c. 287–212), though professing to believe that knowledge was gained only for knowledge's sake, was as much at home with applied mathematics and its derivatives as with theory. For example, when his friend Hiero, king of Syracuse, asked him to determine whether a certain royal crown was pure gold or contained some silver, as he suspected, Archimedes mulled over the problem for days. The key to the solution came to him in his bath. The displacement of water by his body suggested to him the idea of measuring the displacement of water by both gold and silver objects. In this way he hit upon the law of specific gravity.

Similarly motivated was his discovery of the laws of leverage. When Rome was planning an attack against Syracuse, Hiero again applied to the mathematician for help. In this case the problem was how to launch the *Syracusia,* a war vessel of far greater than normal tonnage. Working out the laws governing the mechanics of the pulley, Archimedes devised an instrument that permitted the king himself, unaided by any force beyond his own muscular

strength, to launch the outsized ship. He also invented the endless screw, subsequently much used in the irrigation of fields. His *On Plane Equilibria or Center of Gravity of Planes* laid the foundation of theoretical mechanics, as his *On Floating Bodies* created the study of hydrostatics, a branch of physics dealing with the pressure and equilibrium of liquids. He also "calculated the limits for the value of π . . . [and] laid the foundations of the calculus of the infinite."

In geography Eratosthenes (c. 275–195 B.C.) not only extended the use of the parallels of latitude and the meridians of longitude but succeeded in measuring within a remarkably small margin of error (less than 200 miles) the circumference of the earth. Anticipating Vasco da Gama by about 1700 years he argued that one could sail from Spain to India by rounding Africa. He correctly guessed that all the oceans lap into one another, and constructed the best maps that the ancient world produced.

Hippocrates (flourished 400 B.C.), father of the science of medicine, developed the canon and basic practices of the healing arts. He believed that symptoms could be effectively treated only if case histories were kept and consulted. So he introduced the practice of keeping a detailed account of a particular illness, its response to treatment, and the seeming permanence of the cure, or seeming causes of the disease's resistance to treatment.* But he was not satisfied with mere technical competence. Just as important, he believed, was the social and moral standard of values held by the physician. Out of this concern he drew up an oath which has lasted to our day. In it the promise is made that the practitioner will be governed solely by the needs of the patient, not by fees; that (implicitly) he will

---

* He also introduced, most unhappily, a theory of disease the influence of which bedeviled patient and practitioner alike for centuries. In essence the theory held that all bodily disorders originate in a malfunctioning of one or more of the four "humors"—yellow bile, black bile, blood, and phlegm.

not practice mercy killing; and that all statements made by patient to doctor will be kept in strict confidence.

Literature

The steady advance in science was not matched by similar achievements in literature. Not that writers were scarce or their production limited; actually the age was drenched with a flood of literary works. New and efficient means of processing the papyrus reed supported the steadily rising rate of literacy. Also, public libraries sprang up in many cities, for example in Rhodes, Pergamum, Antioch, and Alexandria. At one time the library at Alexandria could boast of a collection of nearly a million rolls. Here, too, the Ptolemys set up and maintained a museum—a first in man's history—where devotees of the muses spent their lives in genteel practice of the arts. But little of this tremendous output of creative energy has survived the test of the ages.

Aratus of Soli wrote, among dozens of other works, a long poem detailing the positions and clusters of the stars. Of itself it is scarcely worth mentioning. But somehow its hexameters intrigued, some two centuries later, the great Virgil who used it as a kind of model for his *Georgics*. Even more influential was the epigram invented by Antimachus and developed, among others, by Callimachus (*c.* 310–245 B.C.).

Besides the epigram, other poetic forms were devised by Hellenistic writers, particularly the idyll and the pastoral. But their virtues ran to perfection of structure and pretty turns of speech rather than to probing insights expressed in disciplined, unpretentious form. Equally mediocre, or worse, were the tragedies produced by dramatists who sought the profound and found, at best, only the precious. Of all their works—and Tarn points out that they were "manufactured in quantities"—not one of worth remains. In comedy the record is better, especially in the works of Menander, upon whom many later Roman

writers leaned heavily. But the "new comedy" bore little resemblance, either in structure or content, to the Aristophanean model. For one thing the chorus disappeared. For another, the content tended to deal almost exclusively with manners. The plot, moreover, was usually a melange of impossible coincidences, mistaken identities, and contrived endings.

History

Our chief authority for the development of events during the half century after Alexander's death is Hieronymus (*c.* 250 B.C.), who was both politician and historian. Besides serving as a source for Plutarch in the writing of his *Lives,* the works of Hieronymus helped later historians to put flesh on the skeletal outline of this period. Following him, Polybius (*c.* 198–117 B.C.) produced a narrative of events from about 230 to about 145 B.C. A Greek captured by the Romans, he became virtually a Roman himself, much admired by his contemporaries and much used by subsequent historians. We depend upon him for a great deal of what we know of the second and third Punic Wars, and of the story of Rome's conquest of the Mediterranean world. Although strongly biased in favor of the Romans, he nonetheless dealt justly with Hannibal and generally tried to find and present the truth as his abilities and sources allowed. By modern historians he is often ranked second only to Thucydides.

The Plastic Arts

In whatever medium of expression, style always reflects the spirit of a people. So the new spirit of Hellenistic man evoked a new style in the plastic arts, as in all others. It would be folly to hold that Hellas, even in her golden period, perfectly practiced the *sophrosyne* she preached. Still she conceptualized, idealized, and seriously tried to live by it. In Hellenistic times this was not true. With the Peloponnesian War and the Alexandrian conquests came a new world, larger in dimensions, smaller in hopes, psychically restless, impatient of all faiths. It was eager to probe and to find, if it could, the *real* for what increasingly it came to regard as the grand illusions of the golden days. With such feelings and outlook it was inevitable that art styles of the Hellenistic world would be different from those of the Hellenic world. For modern man it is easy, if he is an ardent admirer of the Greek genius of the fifth century B.C., to look upon its successor as degenerate or prettily precious or both. But it is also easy to overlook the terms of existence of an age, and therefore to do injustice to their artistic expression. Judged by those terms the Hellenistic practitioner of the plastic arts possessed his own genius.

Sculpture and architecture—we cannot speak of painting and music since almost no remains are extant—clearly reflected the new mood, the new spirit. The trend toward realism, the *what is* in contrast to *what ought to be,* perhaps is best exemplified in the famous head of Euthydemus, a

Bactrian king (*c.* 200 B.C.). He is of the earth, earthy; "in his sunhelmet, his eyes squinting against the desert sun, his nose beaked like an eagle, his mouth hard and cynical . . . the type of empire builder of

Euthydemus, a Bactrian king (c. *200* B.C.).

Capuan Venus, c. *300* B.C.

Old Market Woman, *a striking example of the raw realism of Hellenistic art.*

Sleeping Hermaphrodite.

all ages." Other subjects were often equally mundane—Negroes of the Sudan, fishermen, naked beggars, old women. Another genre included the crippled, dwarfs, and gnomes. The passion for naturalism reached its apogee (or nadir) in the great altar frieze at Pergamum. Commissioned by King Eumenes II to celebrate a great Pergamenian victory over northern barbarians, the frieze is a kind of carnival of raw naturalism. Covering 450 feet, it is alive with action and passion, civilizations pitted against each other, giants battling gods to the death, all executed with such finesse in the portrayal of ferocity and violence that later the Christian writer of the book of Revelation referred to the whole as "Satan's Throne." Famous, too, is the *Laocoon,* depicting father and sons caught in the coils of entwining serpents. The expressions of horror and pain in this work are detailed with almost unbearable realism.

Other works of the period, executed by artists whose technical skills equalled and eventually surpassed those of their Hellenic masters, were of quite another appeal. The *Capuan Venus,* dating from around 300 B.C., is a Hellenistic artist's effort to bring to life the compelling force of victorious Aphrodite. That the artist succeeded is further proved by the many copies that were turned out (including the famous *Venus de Milo?*) in the Roman period and later. The *Nike of Samothrace* (*c.* 250 B.C.?) shows Victory alighting from a flight. Housed in the Louvre it evokes, even in its present mutilated form, an emotional response that testifies to the sculptor's

genius. Equally arresting is the *Sleeping Hermaphrodite* in which the artist combined to a remarkable degree romantic sensualism with austere classicism.

For the most part architects were content to use models of the Hellenic and Eastern past. Although faith in Olympian gods had faded, numerous temples in their honor continued to be erected. For example, at Didyma, off the coast of Asia Minor, an imposing temple was dedicated to Apollo, even larger and more elaborate than that god's shrine on the Acropolis. As in the other arts, Hellenistic departure from the golden mean is plainly evident, the Didyma temple's frontal columns typically forsaking the chaste Doric model, and the whole showing a strong Egyptian influence. In time the ornate and eventually gingerbreaded Corinthian column replaced both the Doric and Ionian styles. Secular basilicas—the form of which was copied by builders of the first Christian churches—gained popularity in the second and first centuries B.C. being used mostly for marketing purposes or to house bureaus and offices of city officials.

Religion

As philosophy, literature, and the arts underwent change in the post-Alexandrian world, so too did religion. We have already noted that with the decline of the city-state the gods of Greece faded into fuzzy myth. Alexander indeed conquered the East, but the conquest "was by the sword alone, not the spirit." The essential weakness of the Greek was his sense of being cut adrift. Protecting Athena was gone; gone, too, as sources of spiritual renewal, were the powers of Zeus and Apollo. As for the philosophic systems of Zeno and Epicurus, the average person could not master their intricacies and did not try. A new religion was needed. The East offered not one but many including magic, Babylonian astrology, and the various mystery cults. In the following chapter brief reference will be made to the cult of the Phrygian Great

Mother, a cult which flourished in the centuries preceding the advent of Christ. Here particular attention must be given to a mystery religion which attracted an even greater number of votaries, the cult of the goddess Isis.

To the lost little man—and woman—of Hellenistic times, Isis appeared as the supreme savior. Through the loss of her husband-son Osiris (see Chapter I, p. 14) she knew the sorrows of humankind. Through her boundless will and infinite mercy she had conquered death in the restoration of Osiris, and thus promised everlasting life to all believers. Here was a message the Hellenistic mortal was waiting for. The old familiar world had dissolved; the new was frameless and chaotic. To the rootless masses Isis offered salvation for eternity, and they turned to her in ever increasing numbers.

In 430 B.C., as the Peloponnesian War opened, Pericles had lauded Athens as the School of Hellas. Three centuries later both the School and Hellas lay prostrate. Peace and order were to come, but Hellenes were not to make the one or construct the other. For by this time the Roman world had absorbed the Greek Way. Another chapter in the development of Western civilization had opened.

SELECTED READINGS

Many of the books cited in Chapter 4 may be consulted for various topics of this chapter. Particularly pertinent are: Bury, *A History of Greece;* Hammond, *A History of Greece to 332* B.C.; Finley, *The Ancient Greeks;* Kitto, *The Greeks;* Robinson, *Hellas;* Parkes, *Gods and Men;* Toynbee, *Hellenism;* Muller, *Freedom in the Ancient World;* Bowra, *The Greek Experience;* and Dodds, *The Greeks and the Irrational.* In addition, the following works are recommended.

Bonnard, André, *Greek Civilization* (see notation in Chapter 4).

Asterisk (*) denotes paperback.

Provocative—and often controversial—views and evaluations of all of the chief figures discussed in this chapter.

Bowra, C. M., *Sophoclean Tragedy,* Oxford University Press, Oxford, 1944.
Compare with Bonnard, II (see notation in Chapter 4), Chapter IV.

Cary, Max, *History of the Greek World from 323 to 146* B.C., Methuen, London, 1951 (2nd ed.)
A scholarly standard work, well conceived and well written.

*Cornford, F. M., *Before and After Socrates,* Cambridge Paperbacks, Cambridge, 1960.
One of the most stimulating and enlightening discussions of the development of human inquiry.

*Cornford, F. M., *The Origin of Attic Comedy,* Anchor, New York, 1961.
Like Dodds, Cornford stresses the deep, and to him decisive, strain of irrationality which he believes is found under the deceptive layer of rational thought and behavior so often mistaken for the true Greek "way." In the final chapter he discusses Greek Comedy as a derivative of Greek Tragedy.

Ehrenberg, Victor, *The People of Aristophanes,* Basil Blackwell, London, 1951.
A fascinating account of Greek social life in the Comedies. Farmers, traders, slaves, neighbors, citizens—these and others are given flesh and character.

*Jaeger, Werner, *Aristotle,* Oxford Paperback, New York, 1962.
This is probably the most reliable account of the views of and the method of inquiry used by Aristotle.

Martin, Seymour G., et al., *A History of Philosophic Thought,* R. S. Crofts, New York, 1947.
A useful survey of the main-traveled roads of seekers of the why and what of human existence.

Rostovtzeff, M. I., *Social and Economic History of the Hellenistic World,* Oxford University Press, Oxford, 1941, 3 vols.
This detailed study is comprehensive in coverage and cogent in argument. In spite of being outdated it is still worth careful reading.

Tarn, W. W., and G. T. Griffith, *Hellenistic Civilizations,* St. Martins Press, New York, 1952 (3rd ed.).

> Probably the best general account. Tarn died before certain important researches were completed, but Professor Griffith has competently woven them into the earlier text.

Winspear, A. D., *The Genesis of Plato's Thought,* S. A. Russell, New York, 1956 (2nd ed.).

> A plainly written exposition of the ideas and values that still form much of the content of philosophic thought.

For good translations of all the major works of Greek philosophers, poets, and historians consult appropriate titles in the *Loeb Classical Library.*

6

The Roman World: The Republic

Early Settlements and Culture

The founding of the city of Rome about 650 B.C.* had been preceded by many millennia of human movement and endeavor in the narrow bootlike Italian peninsula. Cave paintings and stone tools point to the flourishing of paleolithic pre-*Homo Sapiens* culture well over 100,000 years ago. Some time after *c.* 2300 B.C. a number of migrant groups poured into the peninsula and mixed with the native population. Some came over the Alpine passes from Switzerland, some came down into the peninsula from southern Germany.

A third wave, the *Terramaricoli* (so designated from the black, bitter earth on which they later built their pile-raised huts) settled in the Po Valley around 1700 B.C.

* Here "founding" denotes the consolidation of several village-towns settled much earlier.

Archeological evidence suggests that they came from the Danube basin, probably from the vicinity of present-day Hungary. Their farming techniques were advanced as were, indeed, their culture patterns generally. If they did not introduce the use of bronze they certainly made it a common feature of Italian culture.

About 900 B.C. another band of invaders settled in Latium and Etruria. Later a number of them migrated to the north, around Bologna (whence they are called Villanovans after a village near Bologna where their remains were first found). Authorities dispute their place of origin. Recent evidence indicates that they were a Balkan people who crossed the Adriatic, lived for a while on lands east of the Apennines, then crossed the mountains to settle, eventually, in Latium and Etruria. To Italy's by now burgeoning culture they contributed the use of iron. Through intermarriage with

115

EARLY MIGRATIONS
INTO ITALIAN PENINSULA, SICILY AND CARTHAGE

Map by J. Donovan

the *Terramaricoli* and other early groups they helped to provide the main ethnic base for the general complex of Italic peoples (of which the most important were the Umbrians, the Samnites, and the Latins).

Thus by around the beginning of the first millennium B.C. the peninsula had been settled from end to end by either indigenous tribes or migrants or by the descendants of the fusion of these two groups. The economy was of course agrarian, though loose commercial relations were maintained among tribal communities and, in Umbria at least, an iron-mongering industry had developed. Linguistically, a complex of tongues prevailed in spite of the common, fundamentally Indo-European pattern. None had a written language; none had developed political organizations beyond primitive village-states.

The religions of the Italic peoples were as different from one another as their various dialects and modes of cantonal life. Local earth and river gods were placated by farmers anxious for good harvests and good fortune generally. In art their talents were undeveloped except for the Villanovans, whose efforts were modest enough.

Human ingenuity and industry had shaped a culture in the Italian Peninsula but it was clearly inferior to the ancient societies to the east. Adventuring bands from the Aegean world had settled in Sicily a thousand years before. But continuing relations had failed to develop, and the western frontier lagged far behind the East.

Greeks and Etruscans

Sometime after 800 B.C., however, enduring contact was established as a result of two population movements. Eruptive political and military events sent a new wave of migrants (whom the Romans came to call Etruscans) to the "new west." And population pressures, combined with commercial expansion, produced a Greek exodus to southern Italy and to Sicily.

On the eve of these fateful invasions an equally significant development occurred in Latium without which their impact would certainly have had quite different consequences. The plains of Latium lie in a pocket about 25 miles wide and about 60 miles long, south and east of the angle formed by the Tyrrhenian Sea and the Tiber River. So active were the many volcanoes in this region and so swampy and malaria-infested was the land that natives and migrants alike shunned it. Not until about the ninth century B.C. when volcanic activity had largely ceased and the soil had become fertile and tillable did this neglected pocket draw settlers. Then migrant groups began to test its subsistence possibilities, merging finally into a melange of about 40 tribe-complexes, of which one took the name Romans.

Hardly had the Latins emerged from their period of ethnic incubation when the Eastern invaders settled along the Italian coast, flanking them north and south. From about 800 to about 700 B.C. the Etruscans spread out in Latium and Campania (later in the Po Valley), conquering as they went. The Greeks were, in the main, content to trade with other peoples though among themselves they practiced the same intramural fighting which, as we have seen, prevented their political consolidation in the East. It was probably this fatal fascination for self-destruction that prevented them from coming into eventual control of the peninsula, for their cultural achievements were unquestionably superior to those of either the *Italici* or the Etruscans. Even so, they probably gave the Etruscans their alphabet, which the latter subsequently passed on to the Romans. Moreover the Greeks "introduced into Italy the cultivation of the vine and the olive . . . and so took the first steps by which the country was converted into the 'garden of Europe.' " And, of course, their widespread commercial contacts effectively served as agents of cultural diffusion.

Far more immediately important than Greek influence, however, was that of the Etruscans who stimulated the prepared potentials of the Latins in a variety of ways. They established regular trade routes with the Gauls and other Indo-Europeans to the north; excelled in the production of realistic statuary in terra-cotta; set the style in house construction; introduced expert workmanship in metals, especially gold, and popularized Greek design and decoration in pottery. Although the phrase "scientific farming" cannot be used to describe Etruscan development of the economy, their elaborate and effective drainage systems augmented agricultural output. Of yet greater significance was their influence on urbanization. It is probably not an exaggeration to say that the Etruscans found the Romans semitribal villagers and left them fairly sophisticated city-dwellers.

By the seventh century, population pressure and economic opportunities prompted Etruscan merchants (and later craftsmen) to settle in the Roman villages. Eventually they brought into these backward settlements most of their own arts and industries. Possibly the very name of the city was given to it by the Rumulo, thought to be the first Etruscan family to settle in Rome. There is no doubt that subsequent Etruscan leaders, especially the Tarquins, ruled Rome as elective kings. But their dominion, of whatever kind, was short-lived. Their city-states could no more form a permanent union than could those of the Greeks. Around the end of the sixth century they were battered so badly by Latin tribes and Syracusan Greeks that their dominance was broken. Roman leaders, naturally welcoming the event, set up political housekeeping for themselves in what is commonly called the Revolution of 509.

The Vital Center of Latium: Emergent Rome

Why Rome?

The desire to understand why it was the Romans rather than the Samnites or Umbrians or another Italic people who accomplished the unification of Italy is reasonable enough, but difficult to satisfy. Rome's location in the center of western Italy is surely part of the answer. For being so situated Rome could build and control roads running north and south, thus gaining both economic and military advantages. The seven hills which as a cluster constituted the locale of what eventually became the city of Rome afforded further military advantages. Another advantage was Rome's location near the Tiber. Salt beds near the mouth of the Tiber attracted many miners and merchants. But since the most convenient trails leading to them were eventually dominated by the Etruscans, the miners and merchants took to using Rome as a bridge to get to and from the salt beds.

Proximity to aggressive foreign peoples undoubtedly constituted another prod. By the sixth century Rome and her neighboring towns were flanked by ambitious Etruscans, Greeks, and raiding hill tribes. To fully gain and preserve their own autonomy, particularly against the warlike proclivities of the Etruscans, the natives were forced into extreme military measures. As occupants of the area closest to the Etruscan threat the Romans must have felt this military imperative more keenly than the other Latin tribes. It is reasonable to suppose that with the failure of the Etruscans to effect consolidated rule the primary responsibility for ejecting them devolved upon Rome. This, of course, is quite another matter from the unification of Italy. To say that Roman character accounts for it is to say very little. Whence came Roman character? It is true that age-long tradition had hallowed certain basic virtues — family solidarity, sober industry, respect for authority, and devotion to the idea of order. However, the Romans were not alone in these virtues.

In any case, by what the Romans came to think of as a great revolutionary thrust —which many modern historians consider rather a prolonged evolutionary development—they assumed the posture of leadership. But the following of other peoples did not develop automatically. For one thing, no one knew when resubjugation of Latium might be attempted, for the Etruscans were only defeated, not destroyed; for many years they continued to keep nostalgic account of doings in the rich Latin plains. For another, most of the other neighboring towns did not relish the prospect of Roman rule. Moreover other Italic tribes, notably the Sabines, Aequi, and Volsci, had territorial ambitions of their own. Even so, the emergence of Italy as a people and as a power is essentially the story of the rise of Rome.

Politics and Culture of the Early Republic

Territorial Expansion

Because the evidence is meager, the Republic's early history must be sketched in general and tentative terms.

Four broad themes predominate: territorial expansion; the development of political institutions; class struggle between the patricians and plebeians; and the unplanned, fatal drift into imperial conquest.* After driving out her foreign rulers Rome faced the problem of dealing with raiding marauders from the east and south. Rome's solution of the problem was to set a pattern for most of her later conquests, a pattern marked by winning an ally to defeat a common foe followed by subjugation of the ally. At various times in the early fifth century B.C. the Sabines, Aequi, and Volsci harassed Latium by their fierce excursions into the plains. In order to stay these "thieving, covetous hillsmen," Rome and her Latin allies banded together as closely as their own conflicting interests allowed. For years they won and lost battles in the seesaw contest. Finally, in the latter half of the fifth century B.C. Roman leaders reorganized their armed forces, mounted new attacks against the raiders, and drove them back to the hills. But the peace was soon broken when the citizens of Veii, close by Rome, simply by being rich, powerful, and Etruscan, acted as a magnet upon the metal of Roman ambition. For several years Roman troops, supported by levies from the cities of the Latin league, relentlessly pressed against the river stronghold. So vigorous was the resistance that for a time it appeared that Rome would suffer defeat and Etruscan dominance would reemerge. Eventually the stubborn Roman assaults proved more than the Veitians could stand and they were forced to capitulate. As was now their practice, the Romans settled their own colonists in choice portions of the land. Some colonists, thus rewarded, were newly recruited plebeians.

Within a decade, however, catastrophe befell the rising power. Restless Gauls, raiding far beyond their borders to the north, drove into central Italy and surprised the Romans who, in the battle of Allia (*c.* 390 B.C.) suffered complete rout.

---

* By "imperial conquest" is meant extension of control over non-Italian peoples and places beyond the peninsula. The phrase should *not* be understood to mean conquest and consolidation of the peninsula.

For a while the Celtic hordes occupied Rome, leaving only when a sizable indemnity was paid. This humiliating experience taught the Romans a lesson they long remembered. Now more than ever patricians found it necessary to yield to demands put forward by the plebeians as the latter became an increasingly indispensable reservoir of military strength. Encouraged by the apparent vulnerability of their erstwhile conquerors, the Aequi and Volscians resumed their attacks upon Rome which (with the grudging help of the other Latin cities who feared the hill people above all others) rallied and inflicted upon them lasting defeat. Once again Roman colonists were settled in conquered territory; and for added protection permanent garrisons were set up among the defeated tribes.

As a result of these conquests Roman territory now spread out over about three hundred square miles. Clearly, so far as peninsular affairs were concerned, the city-state was beginning to feel the tug of manifest destiny. The significance of this development was not, of course, lost upon the members of the Latin League who, though willing enough to join with others against aggression from Gauls and Volscians, wanted to preserve intact their own independence and tribal customs. To Rome, such desires seemed unreasonable and dangerous. Anticipating a conflict, she besought an alliance with the Samnites to the east and south who, respectful of Roman power and ever fearful of their own neighbors, accepted the offer. Thus strengthened, Rome maneuvered her one-time allies into declaring war and proceeded, by 338 B.C., to reduce them to a politically subordinate position. In the settlement that followed, the genius of the rising new state showed itself at its best. Instead of humiliating terms, citizens of the Latin towns were offered privileges of an economic and social nature that were substantially the same as those enjoyed by the Romans. Indeed, citizenship rights were granted to those migrants who chose to move into Roman territory and establish residence. Of course, in return, Rome required certain concessions, particularly the right to raise Latin levies when needed.

It would be tedious to recount the remaining and repetitious details of Roman conquest and consolidation. By 275 B.C. nearly the whole of the peninsula was confederated under one rule, and the Republic extended from the Po Valley to the Mediterranean Sea. From Rome, its vital center where an intricate system of government had developed, came a general overall policy for the entire land.

Political Institutions

In the beginning this system of government had been, in concept and practice, quite simple. The citizen body originally was made up of three tribes whose main business was to contribute needed revenues and military levies. Each tribe was divided into ten *curiae,* artificial units created to determine local policy and admission into the citizen body. When these units met together they were known as the *Comitia Curiata* or Assembly. In their turn the *curiae* were made up of groups of families, called *gentes.* Quite naturally the citizen-body was divided into the few high-born landed aristocrats (*patricians,* after *patres,* fathers) and the many poor plebeians (or commoners).

After the Revolution of 509 the Assembly, dominated by the patricians, abandoned monarchy as a form of government. Two leaders—called consuls—were selected from among the most outstanding nobles to administer the affairs of state. Their power was complete except that persons suffering sentences of death or exile might appeal to the Assembly. Advising the consuls was the Senate, originally made up of patricians nominated by the consuls. In theory the Senate could neither initiate nor pass laws. Suggested legislation was brought by the consuls (or dictator, referred to presently) to the Assembly which, without debate, either confirmed or rejected it. But, in practice, Senators had much to do with law making. Commonly the consuls sought the Senate's advice before introducing legislation; indeed it was only in the Senate that full and free debate on policy occurred. Since both Senators and consuls were patricians (until about 400 B.C.) and since the Senate was a continuing body, mainly made up of experienced ex-magistrates, its advice more often than not was accepted. Furthermore, it is likely that considerable legislation was actually, though informally, initiated by Senators who always had easy access to the consuls. Naturally, as the Republic grew in size, population, and complexity, the two consuls were unable personally to attend to all necessary duties. Hence, in the century following the Revolution of 509, additional magistracies were added.

Chief among these magistracies were the *Pontifex Maximus,* who supervised the celebration of major religious ceremonies; *aediles,* entrusted with the administration of the city's water supply, common markets, and the like; *censors,* whose functions will be described shortly; and *quaestors* and *praetors,* the former charged with regulating financial affairs, the latter selected mainly to assist the consuls.

Normally the consuls performed their functions harmoniously enough (often dividing the year into six months work for each, the better to avoid serious conflict). But when, as happened upon occasion, they canceled out each other and chaos threatened or when the state was gravely menaced by foreign foes and the consuls seemed unequal to the emergency, a dictator was appointed. His tenure, however, was strictly limited to six months and, until the latter days of the Republic, was unrenewable, an arrangement obviously calculated to ensure the permanent hegemony of the senatorial order which did not want a dictator to become king.

From military necessity the Assembly lost most of its power around the middle of the fifth century, when foreign foes were pressing hard upon the state. Feeling the need for army reorganization so as to make her legions tactically more maneuverable, Rome divided her adult population (according to wealth) into five groups; each group, in turn, was subdivided into companies of 100 men, or *centuriae.* The necessary enumeration of the population was entrusted to two new officials — census-takers, or censors — who drew up the official list of male citizens and decided to which group each citizen belonged. The new Assembly, now called the *Comitia Centuriata,* held regular meetings which soon took on a political cast. By about 425 B.C. the new *Centuriate Assembly* came to supersede the *Comitia Curiata,* though technically the latter continued in existence functioning for the most part as a religious body.

Class Struggle: Patricians Versus Plebeians

In spite of the disproportionate weight given the vote of the wealthy in the "centuries," the plebes gained advantages vis-à-vis their former condition by reason of their use of the military strike, soon to be considered. Their appetite grown with this feeding, they increasingly resented patrician conservatism. This period marks, then, the beginning of the long struggle of the commoners for first-class citizenship. Going on concurrently with the fight for consolidation, this "conflict of the orders" potentially held even greater good than unification if a liberal, republican society be reckoned a supreme good. That she prized and lost this goal is at once Rome's glory and her shame.

The glory began in 494 B.C. when, heavily in debt and threatened with wholesale slavery (which normally followed failure to maintain solvency), the commoners were called upon by their patrician rulers to rally for another struggle against another foe. This time the plebes rebelled. But not by a violent show of force. They simply made a mass pilgrimage to their sacred mount, the Aventine, and after deliberation formed a state (extralegally, of course) of their own. Paralleling the Curiate Assembly dominated by the patricians they set up their own *Concilium Plebis* (hereafter referred to as the Tribal Assembly or *Comitia Tributa*),* a popular body which elected two, later ten, *Tribunes* whose duty it was to intervene for them when patrician rule became harsh or extreme. Naturally the patricians resented this recalcitrance; but in the face of endless pressures from foes and the very real need for plebeian help they yielded.

In essence, a veto power was exercised by the Tribunes. They listened to appeals by commoners convicted of crimes carrying the penalty of exile or death, and if in their joint or individual opinion justice had miscarried they forbade execution of the sentence. Two circumstances lent power and permanence to their vetoes: the sacred vow of the whole plebeian order to take vengeance if any of their Tribunes should suffer violence; and the Tribunes' judicious and temperate use of their power. Another demand proved so reasonable that the patricians found themselves unable to oppose it, imbued as they were from long habit with devotion to duty and to responsibility. This demand called for a written expression of the "sense of the community," the unwritten laws of custom. In 451 B.C., specially elected *Decemvirs* set themselves to this task, completing it the next year. The result was the famous Law of Twelve Tables which codified all existing laws and spelled out the political, social, and economic rights and duties of all Roman citizens. Henceforth the plebes knew where they stood (though they often complained,

* Authorities disagree over the date of the first secession. Cary, for example, believes that the annalists and later historians (such as Livy) err in setting the date at 494 B.C.; instead, he believes, the first withdrawal occurred in 449 B.C. It is difficult to decide, and the above account should be taken with an open mind and tentatively.

with increasing success, of particularly harsh provisions of the Tables).

Emergent Plebeian Power

Not infrequently modifications of the code were effected by another plebeian innovation, the *Plebiscita*. In addition to electing Tribunes, the *Comitia Tributa,* from time to time, expressed the legislative wishes of the commoners. Although these plebiscites did not have the binding effect of law they served as prods inducing the Centuriate Assembly to take cognizance of plebeian needs. The middle of the fifth century was a busy period for the plebeians. In 449 B.C. the Horatian Laws widened the scope of their powers still further. These laws filled a lacuna in the Tables which had failed to include the plebeian right of appeal.

Before long the two orders clashed over yet another issue: eligibility to the consulship. Although the contest went on for about eighty years its outcome was never really in doubt. For by then Rome had come to depend heavily upon plebeian arms. In 367 B.C. the Licinian-Sextian Laws granted the plebeian demand. Henceforth "middle-class" commoners—called *novi homines,* new men—could and did become consuls and other magistrates. This betokened a still more significant development. Since by now the magistrates almost automatically became, at the end of their year's term, members of the Senate, that august body came to be made up of citizens of both orders. It would be wrong to conclude, however, that this constituted a decisive democratic advance. In actual fact the plebeian leaven oftener than not was more affected than the patrician lump it was intended to change, especially since, by another law of 445 B.C., plebeians were granted the privilege of marrying into patrician families, whose outlooks and habits they soon took over.

Nevertheless the commoners' surge which continued throughout the fourth century was real and of substantial pro-

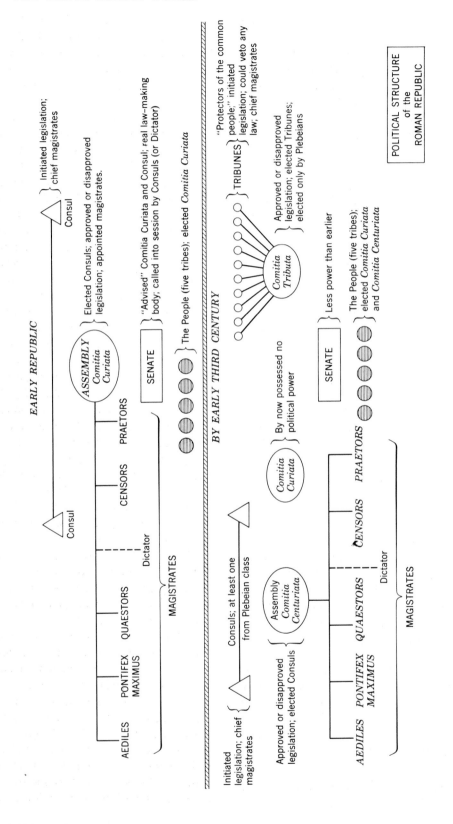

POLITICAL STRUCTURE
of the
ROMAN REPUBLIC

portions. Shortly after the gains effected by the Licinian-Sextian legislation the plebes won the mandate to fill at least one of the consulships.* Further, the Tribal Assembly was granted the right to legislate for all citizens, not just plebeians. At first this right was qualified by a provision requiring Senate approval. But in 287 B.C. the Hortensian Law was passed making this approval automatic. Rome had become, in form, a democracy. Commoners and patricians alike voted laws into existence; members from either order were eligible for all magistracies; and the Senatorial veto, invariably conservative, was legally eliminated. Two hundred and twenty-two years after the Revolution, Italy had become confederated; and a substantial portion of its people lived under a nonautocratic form of government. No other people of ancient times could claim such an achievement.

Early Republican Culture

From meager sources scholars can thus piece together the broad political developments of the early Republic. But these sources hardly avail for a satisfactory account of Rome's nonpolitical life—social, religious, and literary experiences and patterns. As we have seen, written language came late to the *Italici.* Its early forms, quite understandably, were employed for more pedestrian uses than grand epics and stirring prose creations. Still, in "banquet" ballads, epitaphs, and *annales,* the beginnings of a literature appear. Undoubtedly the ballads embodied many early folk myths so intricately embroidered by later writers.

From the beginning Roman religious life was marked by a sense of awe and sober effort to learn and live the will of the spirits—*numina*—which figured existence and gave animation, for good or ill, to all things. Twin foci, the field and the home,

were central in the spatial and functional framework of the spiritual life developed by the Romans. As farmers they had a deep and abiding reverence for nature and her vital, mysterious ways and for nature's greatest gift, the family and home. The will of the *numina* worked in all things: soil, river, wind, rain; threshold, hearth, storeroom. The earliest religious festivities celebrated features of rural life such as the seasons of sowing and harvesting.

In the home the chief religious functionary was the *paterfamilias,* and the chief object of worship was his Genius, or protecting spirit. If the Genius of the head of the family was ill disposed toward that head the whole family suffered; if well disposed, all members of the family were favored. In the early days of the Republic, before a degree of urbanization was effected and before an intricate state cult had developed, the *paterfamilias,* standing in awe of his Genius and soberly performing the rites necessary for health and good fortune, was the vital center of all family life. In public affairs special officers, the *Pontifex Maximus* and his priests, propitiated the gods and ascertained, by such practices as interpretation of the formation of flights of birds and examination of the entrails of animals, whether the time was right (or the auspices good) for an official state action or ceremony.

Meetings of the Assemblies, for example, invariably were preceded by such searching for signs; if the priests' findings were negative, the assemblies postponed or cancelled their deliberations.

Although there was no true hierarchy, some gods were recognized as having significance beyond a particular place and specific function. Especially was this true of Jupiter (or Jove) who, while thought of as the skygod, was understood to symbolize the highest powers of all the gods. Under his vaulting domain all creatures lived and in his name men made their most solemn pledges. "Mars . . . another god to develop early . . . started as an agricultural numen,

---

* From now on, that is, at least one of the consuls *must* be a plebeian.

perhaps the averter of disease and bad weather, but soon became also the averter of violence. . . ." Through the head of the family or the priest, prayers to these and other gods were addressed together, often, with sacrificial offerings. Early Roman religion thus permeated every facet of life — social, economic, and political. It is true that ethical content was lacking. Romans reverently understood that powers greater than themselves existed but this understanding expressed itself in propitiatory prayers and sacrifices rather than ethical behavior.

Except for fresco painting and some temple building, early Roman art and architecture remained undeveloped. In certain practical arts, however, Roman genius early showed itself. From the fifth century through the years of the Empire such a great system of roads was constructed as the world had never seen before nor, in some respects, since. Across the mountainous terrain of the peninsula the Romans flung out roads in all directions. The famed Appian Way, begun by Appius Claudius in the late fourth century, stretched ultimately from Rome to Brun-

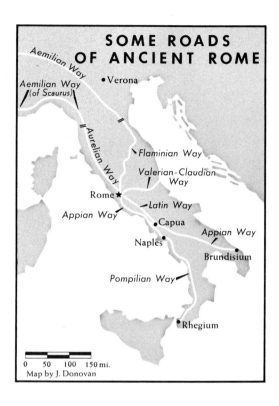

This modern photograph testifies to the enduring qualities of Roman roads. This is the Appian Way, constructed over 2000 years ago.

disium, some 300 miles to the south and east. The Flaminian Way, running another 300 miles northward, connected Rome with the eastern coast of present-day Venezia. These and all the other important throughways were constructed in such a manner that they bore, with little repair, the tramp of legions, the grinding wear of commercial and military wagons, and the pounding of cavalry for periods not of years but of centuries; parts of some, indeed, are still in existence. With the same skill they constructed gigantic aqueducts which provided Rome and other cities with clear mountain water. Some of these, too, are still intact. Much of her culture was derivative (though more so in the Empire than in the Republic). But in the practical arts Rome had no equal in ancient, and few in modern, times.

Economically Rome was the same agrarian society in, say, 250 B.C., that she had been 500 years before. After the Punic Wars, it is true, the capital of the Republic became to a very limited extent a sort of middleman receiving goods it did not produce and distributing them at a profit. But this was the business of the economic elite only. The masses, from early Etruscan times, were obliged to give unremitting toil to the land. Much of the produce went to their masters who were either Etruscan or Roman large landowners. This is not to say that commoners were not themselves landowners; actually more often than not they were. Always, however, the economic tune was called by the landed nobles.

The Imperial Impulse

The First Punic War

Unlike Rome, Carthage—founded in the eighth century B.C. by venturing Phoenicians—had early concentrated on trading activities. By 275 B.C. this state had become the master merchant of the western Mediterranean, controlling almost all the important ports of call except a few held by such Greek centers as Messina (Messana) and Syracuse, in Sicily.

Some time in the early part of the third century a ruffian band of Greek mercenaries, demobilized by Rome after the Pyrrhic wars, migrated to Messina, a trading city in Sicily just off the toe of the Italian boot. Within a short time they had taken over the town and used it thereafter as a base for various piratical and marauding raids. Both to eliminate this disturbance and to extend their territory, Greeks of the nearby city-state of Syracuse sent off an expeditionary force. The Messina pirates, now divided into factional groups, sought help, some appealing to Carthage, some to Rome. Thus Roman legions for the first time since the founding of the city set foot on soil beyond the peninsula and, in 264 B.C., casually challenged the greatest Empire in the western Mediterranean. They could not know the hinge of history they had forged.

Accepting the challenge, Carthage readied a large force at Agrigentum, on the southern coast of Sicily. In reply, Roman commanders swiftly drove their columns southward, laid the Carthaginian base under siege and, in 262 B.C., captured and sacked the city. But one defeat did not bring Carthage to Roman terms. Instead, the Punic power readied new and larger forces. At this point Rome realized the scope of the encounter. If Messina was to be preserved from Carthaginian control the whole island must be swept clear of Carthaginian troops. More than this, the surrounding sea lanes must be dominated by the Roman navy, which was then practically nonexistent. So a large commitment of land troops and the creation of a strong navy were requisites for Roman victory. Within two years a fleet of over 150 ships had been constructed and equipped, a remarkable achievement which later historians were to make into a much embellished legend.

Thereafter followed a prolonged and bloody duel which our brief account cannot follow. In 241 B.C. the weary Carthaginians at last sued for peace, taking what terms they could get. These were short and harsh—the surrender to Rome of all Sicily (save for a few scattered Greek cities which had been Roman allies) and the payment of a huge indemnity. Thus, in 241 B.C., the first Punic War ended and a new imperial power was established in the West. Contrary to her usual practice, Rome extended neither citizenship nor partnership to the people of the conquered island. Instead the Senate, now risen to dominance over the popular assemblies by reason both of its continuing tenure and the extended period of emergency, sent out a governor to rule as Rome decreed. Similar rule was instituted in Corsica and Sardinia which Carthage was forced to yield to the new Empire in 238 B.C.

Although the victor, Rome was almost as exhausted by the long and terrible ordeal as her defeated foe. Gaulish hordes, encouraged by Roman exhaustion, again swept down from the Po Valley. Initial successes encouraged them to attempt permanent conquest, and for the next 10 years Roman resources were strained to the limit.

Probably the deciding factor was the loyalty of her Italian allies who, even if they had not long since become convinced of the beneficence of Roman order, feared above all things the yoke of the Celtic barbarian. By 222 B.C. the invaders were finally conquered and all of north Italy from the Apennines to the Alps was annexed by Rome.

The Second Punic War

But the severest test was still to come. In the 20 years following her defeat Carthage made an amazing comeback under the aggressive leadership of Hamilcar, a gifted general and statesman, and under his even more talented son, Hannibal. Stripped of her island possessions in the war with Rome, Carthage turned to Spain for imperial recovery. By 220 B.C. she was master of most of the Iberian peninsula. Rome's concern over the resurgence of Punic power led her to fear for her own new power status. Carthage, for her part, was determined to brook no Roman veto in the peninsula. When that veto seemed to materialize, as Rome interfered with Punic expansion in 218 B.C., Carthage badgered Rome into declaring war.

In the Second Punic War the initiative was taken by Hannibal. He performed a kind of military miracle when he led his forces, which included elephant trains, across southern France and down through the Alpine passes in the snows of late autumn. In northwest Italy Publius Scipio, consular commander of the Roman army (and father of the later famous Scipio Africanus) was the first to taste of the many bitter defeats Hannibal was to inflict. Stinging under their own recent rout and heartened by new hope of reversing fortune, the Gauls jubilantly joined the fray. By the next year the invaders were in Etruria where, at Lake Trasimene, they smashed another Roman army under Flaminius. The road to Rome now seemed open. But the city's strong defenses and Hannibal's lack of an adequate supply base to support a long siege led the aggressive general to bypass it and head south. Under a dictator, Q. Fabius Maximus,* a new policy of delaying actions was adopted which gave little opportunity for Hannibal to display his genius. But the *Comitia Tributa,* growing impatient with indecisive guerilla warfare, overruled the Senate and appointed two new commanders, eager for battle. On the open plains of Apulia, near Cannae, the two armies met head on. The result was the greatest catastrophe the Republic had yet suffered. With the loss of but 6000 men, Hannibal cut the Roman legions to pieces. When Capua, in Campania, went over to the invader, King Philip of Macedonia, who had been carefully watching events, indicated he was ready to take up where Pyrrhus had left off.

But Roman doggedness again showed itself. Young boys and even bondsmen were pressed into service; Fabian tactics were again resorted to. Its judgment vindicated, the Senate thereafter made decisions without further challenge. By clever diplomatic maneuvering it stirred up Philip's enemies in Greece to keep that monarch fully occupied at home. In 207 B.C. Roman forces met and defeated a large Carthaginian contingent under Hasdrubal (the battle of the Metaurus River); and Hannibal was forced to begin a series of retreats. The Senate had earlier sent new legions to Spain; under the Scipios they eventually won complete control of the peninsula. The Senate also maintained a large navy which served both to supply Roman troops in Spain and to break up enemy communications.

In Italy some of the newly raised forces reconquered Capua, while others continued to harass the weary Hannibal. When Philip once again showed signs of changing his mind, Roman troops were landed in Greece. Although they did not bring him to heel, they found allies (especially Pergamum, in Asia Minor) who once more kept the am-

---

* From this general and his policy of harassment rather than frontal assault has come the phrase "Fabian tactics."

bitious monarch too busy to venture abroad. In the meantime, from newly won Spain the younger Scipio mounted a massive assault against Carthage itself. To meet this attack Hannibal was now forced to return home. In 202 B.C., at Zama, about 50 miles south of Carthage, the two armies met in the final battle of the war. There the forces of the once invincible Punic commander suffered a defeat greater than they had inflicted upon the Romans at Cannae. The next year, Carthage gave up the struggle and accepted a Roman peace much harsher than the first—payment of an enormous indemnity and cession of the whole of her European empire.*

The Decline of the Republic

Political and Economic Changes

But if the victor gained imperial grandeur it lost republican glory. For the Rome which emerged from the Punic Wars was quite different from the Rome which had so casually entered into them. The old Rome was basically an ethnic unit; although all were not citizens, few were subjects and still fewer slaves. Though its political structure had been shaped perhaps as much by improvisation as by deliberate plan it was, nevertheless, well suited in the main to the developing needs of the Italian people. On the other hand, the imperial necessities of the new Rome were glaringly inconsonant with the services offered by a republican constitution.

Equally significant was the change that occurred in class structure. Two generations of yeoman farmers had been taken from the fields and, under terms of service sometimes running to twenty years, fed into the armed forces. In many instances the unhusbanded farms were sold to the ever-growing army of speculators. In this

way the new rich developed large estates— *latifundia*—worked by slaves provided by the seemingly endless wars. The returning landless yeomen increasingly drifted to the cities, particularly Rome. There they constituted an unemployed mob eager to exchange their votes for promises of governmental largess. To curry favor with this uprooted, restless multitude, candidates for office promised greater and greater benefits which usually took the form of doles and contrived amusement—the famous bread and circuses.

In these circumstances a permanent proletariat formed. Its endless demands further debased political officialdom which, across the war years, already had grown alarmingly corrupt. Rome's more extensive involvement in commerce (which naturally followed the ebbing of Punic hegemony), her increased profits from conquest, and financial and land speculation combined to give rise to a new class, the *Equites*. The main interest of this middle-class order was, very simply, to make money. Its members cared nothing for democratic development, nor for republican order, nor for any order at all save as it prevented turmoil that interfered with business. Although they did not enjoy the social prestige and perquisites of the old landed aristocracy, they ranked substantially above the yeomen and artisans. They were, in short, an evolving middle class.

The Militarization of Roman Life

Quite naturally, modifications of the old Roman way went beyond political and economic changes. It is hardly reasonable to suppose that the long years of fighting, which subordinated normal civic privileges and responsibilities to wartime exigencies, could fail to affect the spirit and habits of the Roman people. Though always ready to fight when they believed their interests were threatened they had never practiced violence as a way of life. But the Punic Wars were "marked by many brutalities, the Romans in particular being guilty of

---

* About fifty years later, the remaining stub of the great Carthaginian state was rooted out in the third brief, vicious Punic War (149 to 146 B.C.).

indiscriminate plundering and massacre in the towns recovered by them." It is difficult to believe that a coarsening of the spirit did not result. A related sign of the deterioration of the republican way of life was manifest in the tendency of field commanders to flout senatorial directives, flattered as they were by the subservience of the conquered and emboldened as they were by the power of their own fiat. With growing frequency these leaders ventured on forays not only without but sometimes contrary to the Senate's dictum, hinting of an eventual practice that would turn the later Empire into an outright military autocracy.

Thus the great Roman victory at Zama in 202 B.C. marked more than the end of a war. It signified the end of an age. Gifted Republican leaders, as we shall see, would try to save the Republic; but they would fail. Empire and world rule beckoned.

The Conquest of the East

Within two generations after Zama, Rome controlled directly or indirectly the greater part of the old Alexandrian Empire—all of Greece, most of the present-day Balkans, a substantial portion of Asia Minor, and Egypt (as "protector"). This *what* of history can be validly documented, as can most of its *how*. But when we come to the important *why* our sources are incomplete and confusing. Perhaps we must be satisfied with these bare clues: Rome had learned to distrust the word of Philip V of Macedonia and to fear somewhat his aggressive policy of expansion to the south and particularly to the west (especially as such designs might touch Ilyria). Her new position of power attracted the attention of small states in the East, the more so as they feared the increasingly expansive designs of the great empire builders. By this time, too, Rome (consciously or unconsciously) had begun to think of herself in relation to "lesser" powers and peoples

in vague but developing terms of patron and clients. The half century from 200 to 150 B.C. was marked by constant strife in the East as the kings of Macedonia tried to refashion the old expansive Alexandrian Empire. In 200 B.C. a new Macedonian war opened and Roman legions marched again in the name of freedom and order.

If there were eager Roman leaders who thought in terms of a glorious summer campaign they were soon disillusioned. For the next half century Rome learned hard lessons in the "school of Athens." Not that Roman legions had lost their winning ways. Without exception all of the major military engagements fought throughout this long period resulted in smashing Italian victories. In 197 B.C. at Cynoscephalae, for example, Flaminius easily conquered the oversanguine Philip and ended the war in one season of fighting. In 171 B.C. Perseus, son of Philip, renewed his father's fight, and received from Aemilius Paulus the same kind of trouncing his sire had received from Flaminius.

The Roman problem seemed to be not how to win wars but how to secure peace. After Cynoscephalae, Roman legions had returned home after their leader had proudly announced to the hysterically grateful Greeks that they were now free to live their own lives. No sooner had the liberator gone, however, than the liberated fell upon each other, ending up not only castigating Rome for allowing such discord to develop but inviting the Syrian leader Antiochus to move in. With the return of the legions and the defeat of the Syrian monarch, the same tableau was reenacted—again Roman troops withdrew, and again another aggressor (rejuvenated Macedonia) took to the field. The process seemed both pointless and unending.

By the middle of the second century, then, Rome had indeed "gone East." By that time she had become so deeply and inextricably involved in the turbulence of that part of the Mediterranean world that unless she resigned herself to living with turmoil it seemed imperative to impose outright domination. She would hardly choose turmoil. So domination it was. Ironically, at the very time she succeeded in imposing order abroad she lost it at home. To this highly un-Roman phase of Roman history we must now turn.

A Century of Struggle, 145–31 B.C.

"The Degradation of the Democratic Dogma"

The century following the last Macedonian War—this is, about 145 to 30 B.C.—was throughout a time of troubles. Economic conditions were especially confused. If an economic census could have been taken it probably would have shown a tremendous leap over previous years in what today would be called gross national income. We have already noted the development of large estates, the growing influx of slaves and tribute, the emergence of Rome as the exchange center of the Mediterranean world, and the rise of a moneyed class. All this economic bustle and stir, however, only meant that the rich were getting richer. The masses, whether they remained on the farm or went to the cities for nonexistent jobs, lived on the near side of starvation. As the *latifundia* waxed, yeoman holdings correspondingly waned, so that increasingly the little farmer was forced either to try to compete on unequal terms—an obvious impossibility—or to give up rural life altogether. To use a borrowed phrase, a Grand Barbecue was being held to which the proletariat were not invited. Naturally the plebes' misery and resentment sought political channels for expression and redress. Just as naturally the beneficiaries under the status quo opposed any suggestion of change. So the makings of a new class struggle were at hand.

If these conditions had existed before the Punic Wars (a none too realistic reference since the wars produced the conditions), popular remedial resources would have been available, particularly the Tribunes and the Tribal Assembly. Technically they still were. But the long, terrible years of fighting had changed the substance if not the form of Roman politics. For one thing, the Senate had again become supreme. Also, under the relentless pressures of the Hannibalic war the safeguard of annual consular elections could no longer be relied upon.

Moreover, even before the wars, a significant change had taken place in the *Tribunate,* a change that definitely pointed to "the degradation of the democratic dogma." Originally the voice of the sacrosanct Tribune was literally the voice of the people. But with intermarriage occurring between the classes, the Tribunes tended to become "integrated into the new patricio-plebeian senatorial oligarchy" (and with the establishment of policy by assassination, soon to develop, certainly not sacrosanct). Thus by 200 B.C. the supreme representatives of the plebeians had themselves joined the elite. There seemed no one and no place for the commoner to turn to. Nevertheless, many came to believe that conditions were so bad that little could be lost by a fight to improve them. By the middle of the second century B.C. they were ready for the effort. The attempted revolution—for it amounted to that—was fathered, paradoxically, by a representative of an old noble plebeian family. Believing that the crux of Rome's troubles lay in the gentry's monopoly of land—particularly as it compounded the problem of what to do with the proletarian mobs in the capital city—Tiberius Sempronius Gracchus stood for election as tribune (133 B.C.) on a platform calling for a rather radical redistribution of the public land. Naturally the Senate vigorously objected.

The Gracchan Revolution and Its Aftermath

In circumstances that the wars had made normal, the political machine of the nobility should have had little difficulty in insuring Gracchus' defeat. For over a century the Senate had made war and peace, directed military campaigns, manipulated the magistrates, usurped almost complete judicial powers; in short, had acted as the oligarchic dictatorship that it was. True, commoners could vote, but only in Rome, which long since had become a kept city. One important feature was new. By the last quarter of the second century the equestrian order, the *Equites,* had created a machine of their own. It is true that both the "knights" and the nobles were capitalists with interests that usually drew them together when the masses became restive. But as entrepreneurs, the *Equites* had grievances of their own, and occasionally landed and entrepreneurial interests clashed. Then the *Equites* found it convenient to draw a little closer to the "forgotten men." This situation existed in 133 B.C. when the great challenge was made. Combined with the appeal of Gracchus' platform and oratory and the desperate temper of the masses, it accounted for an overwhelming popular victory.

At his first opportunity Tiberius introduced a bill authorizing the redistribution of public lands. The Assembly, for once disregarding the Senate's advice, prepared to pass it. Before a vote could be taken, however, the Senate induced (bribed is the more accurate word) another tribune to veto the bill's formal presentation. At this point the Gracchan movement clearly showed its revolutionary nature. Arguing that the people's will had been thwarted by an unworthy political maneuver, Tiberius asked the Assembly to unseat his colleague. The Assembly promptly did and, as promptly, enacted the land bill into law. At once the Senate charged Tiberius with violating the constitution—as he had—and made preparation to assert its will. When his one-year term as a tribune expired Tiberius, contrary to custom which forbade tribunes to succeed themselves, announced his candidacy for reelection. By this time the city was seething with plots and coun-

terplots. During the campaign, gangs fought gangs as the proletariat, aided by the *Equites,* sought to keep its champion in power. In the rioting, Tiberius was killed. "This was practically the first bloodshed in Rome's long record of political struggles. The peaceful record of the past was almost matchless in political history. But this day established a precedent which was to be followed more than once, and for which the Senators of a later day were to pay a heavy price."[1]

The Senate immediately appointed a judicial commission which ruthlessly purged the Gracchan followers of their more prominent spokesmen, and set about to restore the former order. Once again a cry went up from the commoners and once again a Gracchus—Gaius, the former tribune's brother—offered himself as the people's leader. Although twice elected to the Tribunate, Gaius made scarcely more headway than his brother. And he met the same fate in 121 B.C. when a consular bodyguard, acting on the Senate's order, charged a meeting he was haranguing and demanded his surrender and appearance before a judicial commission. Rather than accept purging at the hands of the Senate he took his own life. The triumphant nobles proceeded to round up as many of the fallen leader's lieutenants as they could for the peremptory treatment that was now becoming a part of the normal political pattern.

To cope as it had with the second Gracchus the Senate devised a practice which set a dangerous precedent commonly followed thereafter. To justify sending troops to apprehend the popular leader the Senate passed what came to be called the *senatus consultum ultimum,* the "last decree." This decree declared martial law and gave the consul absolute power to do what he thought was necessary to preserve the state.

Probably few Romans in, say, 120 B.C.,

---

1. Tenney Frank, *History of Rome,* Jonathan Cape, London, p. 198.

took occasion quietly to sit down and assess the fundamental troubles which were steadily drawing them into chaos, chaos which ultimately seemed to sanction autocracy as the only way out. If they had assessed their troubles, the appraisal might have looked like this:

Extreme maldistribution of wealth had given luxury to the few and bare subsistence to the masses.

The steady, century-old crumbling of constitutional guarantees had added large political grievances to economic distress.

Refusal to extend citizenship to ethnic kin while managing their political lives inexorably was leading to a violent reckoning—the "social war."

The incessant and constantly growing need to protect far-flung frontiers had perforce created permanent large-standing armies and given militarists increasingly greater powers.

In short, the Roman "republic" was in the throes of class struggle, enduring depression (for the many), bitter sectional rivalry, and large-scale imperio-militarist ventures which added up behind the grand imperial facade to mounting distress, disorder, and despair.

"Years of the Sword"

West of Carthage, in Africa, lay Numidia, a Roman protectorate. In 118 B.C. its ruler died and rival princes claimed the throne. One, Jugurtha, soon gained supremacy. His cousin Adherbal at once appealed to Rome. Busy with domestic business the Senate bungled the affair so badly that Roman prestige was seriously compromised. To end the embarrassing impasse—complicated by adroit maneuvering by the *Populares,* as the anti-aristocratic party was coming to be called—the Senate dispatched an army to Africa. In the war that followed, Jugurtha—helped by insurgents in Spain—put up a struggle that seemed beyond the power of the legions to handle.

In these circumstances the *Populares*

took heart and endorsed the consular candidacy of Gaius Marius, a republican general who had made a name for himself in Africa. Backed by the equestrian order and strongly supported by the Tribunes, Marius was overwhelmingly elected. One of his first acts was the establishment of a volunteer, client army to supplement the draft militia system. Thus equipped, Marius quickly brought Jugurtha to surrender. The country now possessed another province and a new hero. From Africa the victor set out at once to deal with the threatening Cimbri and Teutons. There, in three years of hard fighting, he completely annihilated the barbarian armies. Clearly the *Populares* had found a redoubtable champion. They made the most of their discovery.

Exploiting the military glory of the popular chieftain, various other leaders worked diligently to further discredit and weaken the Senate. They pushed through a new grain law which provided for the sale of grain at submarket prices to needy citizens. Another law gave Marius' veterans generous land settlements in Africa. Still another proposed further grants in southern Gaul and the founding of various new colonies. But the last proposal, though it finally carried, displeased many Romans who objected to a provision which gave Marius the right to grant citizenship to colonial settlers. Marius deemed it prudent to disassociate himself from two newly elected Tribunes who showed an alarming taste for violence. One, for example, when running for reelection in 99 B.C., coldly arranged the murder of his conservative opponent.

With popular favor veering away from the extremists the Senate passed its formidable "last decree" and ordered Marius, consul again (now for the sixth time), to execute it. In his bungling attempt to avoid the Senate's directive, Marius failed to afford proper protective custody to his prisoners, who suffered lynching at the hands of an excited Roman mob. The aftermath

Marius, champion of the Populares.

of this shabby series of events returned the aristocratic party to power.

But the Senate, regrettably consistent, continued to ignore fundamental problems in favor of partisan gain. Particularly urgent were the demands of non-Roman Italians for full citizenship. When one of their champions was assassinated they decided to answer violence with violence. In 90 B.C. the long dreaded "social war" became a frightful reality. Picentes, Samnites, Umbrians, Etrurians, and citizens of other second-class states sent their combined armies against Rome. At the head of its legions Rome placed its old warrior Marius (who was glad to get back into action again) and his one-time quaestor, Sulla. But the Italians had fought too long under Roman generals not to have mastered the military tactics that had won Rome her victories. When Marius' troops in the north and Sulla's in the south ran into serious trouble, the Senate saw its hope for any early victory fading. Moreover, a new threat had developed in the East. Mithridates, king of Pontus, had begun to manifest Alexandrian ambitions. In these circumstances

Rome finally offered citizenship to all Italians who would lay down their arms within 60 days; so the social war ended in an Italian victory.

Bloody Civil Strife

The Senate now gave full attention to Mithridates and readied its legions for another pacification of the East. Sulla, now turned conservative, was chosen to head them. Embittered at what they considered a gratuitous insult to the savior of Rome, Marius and his followers sought to reverse the decision. In the violent struggle which followed, Sulla, backed by a professional — and personal — army, ruthlessly crushed the opposition. With Mithridates already consolidating his gains in Asia Minor he had no time to set the Roman house in sound, conservative order. Under the banner of his legions he did succeed in forcing the popular assembly to commit suicide. At his dictation it passed a law making senatorial consent a prerequisite for the enactment of all legislation, thus abrogating the democratic gains of the ancient Hortensian Law.

Upon his departure the "democratic" party, led by L. Cornelius Cinna and at once joined by Marius with his still loyal army, overthrew the conservative government and established a nightmare regime. Systematically the ranks of the nobility were decimated. Marius died within a year (86 B.C.), perhaps worn out by his orgy of hate, but his lieutenants carried on.

Meanwhile, in Asia, Sulla slowly but convincingly settled accounts with Mithridates. Sending ahead blunt warnings that he would spare no one who stood in his way Sulla returned to the hectic city and once more stormed and captured it. Some of the generals sent out to intercept him joined him. Among these were Cn. Pompeius, soon to be styled Pompey the Great, and Marcus Crassus who later, with Pompey and Julius Caesar, formed the First Triumvirate.

Under a new constitution, written by

himself, Sulla held factional disputes and imperial disturbances in check. But shortly after his death (78 B.C.), his elaborate edifice of order collapsed, and once more the way was open for ambitious generals to fight their way to wealth and fame.

The last act of the long drama of the Roman Republic opened with a strange and sanguine struggle between Pompey and his erstwhile collaborator Julius Caesar; and ended, when they had passed from the scene, with a stranger and sharper struggle between Caesar's chief protagonists, Mark Antony and the younger Octavian (soon to be called Augustus).

After Sulla's death the most conspicuous figure in Roman life was Pompey whose fame rested upon a series of impressive military victories. In 70 B.C. he and M. Licinius Crassus, an *Equite* more interested in accumulating wealth than political power, were elected consuls. Although neither trusted the other both saw advantages in working together.

Under their consulship three important laws were passed. The tribunician power, destroyed by Sulla, was restored. This naturally gratified the plebeians (though they had long since lost the disciplined will to make use of it). Jury lists were again drawn from the ranks of the *Equites* (though not from their ranks alone), mollifying this bourgeois order. And to expedite the purging from the Senate of many Sulla-appointed members the office of Censor was reintroduced. Naturally the Senate fought all three measures. But Pompey's legions and Crassus's money prevailed, helped by the oratory of Cicero and the subtle machinations of Julius Caesar, then thirty years old and already impatient with destiny.

When his year's term expired Pompey led new legions against a revived Mithridatic threat. It took him four years to effect it, but by 62 B.C. Asia Minor once more enjoyed a Roman peace. In the same year he re-entered Rome, trailing glory and countless trophies behind him.

Political Intrigues

In the meantime Pompey's colleagues back home were busy with schemes of their own. In 68 B.C. Julius Caesar, with the help of Crassus, was elected quaestor and attached to the *praetorian* office in Spain. There he carefully observed the management of provincial affairs. Elected upon his return to the office of *aedile,* he borrowed further sums from Crassus to stage extravaganzas for the Roman populace. The name of Caesar was beginning to take on a magic glow.

Others were busy with plans and projects of their own, particularly one Sergius Catiline. A man of inordinate ambition unchecked by scruples, Catiline had twice run for the consulship without success, being once beaten by Cicero who regarded him as a dangerous man on horseback. In 62 B.C. he recklessly plotted to overthrow the government and make himself dictator. Once again Cicero thwarted him, exposing the conspiracy before the Senate in orations that have become famous.

Pompey the Great.

At this juncture the vaulting ambitions of Caesar, Crassus, and Pompey brought them into a strange partnership. Long since Crassus had marked Pompey as his chief enemy. Nor could Caesar see himself as master until the great general was somehow eliminated. For his part, Pompey despised Crassus and considered Caesar an annoying upstart. But all professed to be the people's champion; and all were opposed by the stubborn Senate which now seemed to have found in Cicero a new if somewhat strange (to it) leader. In these circumstances, and at the initiative of Caesar, the three pooled their resources and formed what is known as the First Triumvirate.

In 58 B.C. Caesar departed for Gaul, where he hoped to build up an army strong enough to support him in whatever opportunities future circumstances might suggest. The years of the proconsulship won fame for Caesar and the whole of Gaul for Rome. On the other hand, neither Crassus nor Pompey was able to manage so well. Pompey had revived Caesar's old scheme—now strenuously opposed by Caesar—to invade and annex Egypt; but both aristocratic and popular enthusiasm was lacking. With equal lack of success Crassus had schemed to win for himself a provincial governorship.

Caesar Over All

With the death of Crassus in 43 B.C. and the election of Pompey as sole consul the following year, the triumvirate came to an end; and now Pompey and Caesar openly faced each other in the battle for Rome. Yet it is doubtful that Pompey's heart was really in the struggle. Probably what he desired above all else was not mastery over the Republic but recognition as its "first citizen." But for Caesar, prestige, though precious, was not enough. He yearned for power and grand achievement. The years in Gaul had schooled him in both the techniques of battle and the arts of statecraft. They had touched his genius and given him a vision of a remade society. He saw in the shambles of Rome the inevitable product of imperial power and grandeur cracking the ancient mold of republican life. A new structure was required, and he firmly believed fate had singled him out as its architect.

In 49 B.C., therefore, with Gaul finally pacified and his second term as proconsul drawing to a close, he announced his intention of returning to Rome to seek election as consul. Both Pompey and the *Optimates,* having more than an inkling of Caesar's ambition, feared above all just this. To thwart him the Senate, asserting that the proconsul was planning a *coup d'etat,* passed the fateful *senatus consultum ultimum* and authorized Pompey to take whatever action was needed.

In the civil war that followed Caesar's troops, taught and toughened by 10 years of almost continuous combat by the barbarian hordes of Gaul, swept from victory to victory. His army utterly routed, Pompey fled to Egypt to enlist that country's help. But Ptolemy was himself engaged in a civil war with Cleopatra, his half-sister. In the intrigues that followed Pompey was assassinated.

To prevent Egypt from later serving as a base of operations against him, Caesar essayed the task of not only healing the breach between the royal contestants but of winning them as allies. With Ptolemy he was unsuccessful, eventually becoming involved with him in a brief war in which the ruler lost his life. Cleopatra proved more amenable to his approach, and was soon set up as Egypt's sole sovereign under Rome's protection. (Not all of the affairs between the two, it might be added, were confined to the business of statecraft.) For several years, mopping-up operations were required elsewhere—in Asia Minor, Numidia, Spain. With these last remnants of opposition crushed (45 B.C.), Caesar indeed "bestrode the world like a colossus."

Caesar: "Work and Days"

His political accounting was large in scope and was left unfinished by his assassination. The calendar, which because of its anachronistic condition prevented effective execution of public and private business, was given early attention. Under Caesar's supervision a committee of experts, advised by a prominent astronomer brought in from Alexandria, added (46 B.C.) 67 days between the last day of November and the first of December. It also distributed 10 additional days over the other months, and provided for the permanent intercalation of one day every four years to allow for the hiatus of the remaining one quarter of a day. Save for a slight correction authorized by Pope Gregory in the sixteenth century, this calendar has served to our own times.

To rid Rome of the rabble which for years had offered itself to the highest bidder and had made a mockery of stable government, Caesar decreed several wisely conceived laws. One, fostering a back-to-the-land movement, required all large landholders to reduce the number of their slaves in favor of a like number of freemen. Another forced capitalists to invest at least one half of their wealth in land.

To take up the slack of urban unemployment until his laws could be given effect, Caesar set in motion an extensive program of public works (a kind of Roman PWA). He ordered road and canal building, harbor improvement, rechanneling of the Tiber, drainage of the Pontine marshes (completed by Mussolini in our own century), and the construction of temples and other public edifices. Strict laws against crime were passed, backed by energetic enforcement.

All of this, Caesar well knew, required the creation of an autocracy. Not wanting "to lend dignity to old republican offices" he refused the Senate's offer of a 10-year consulship. But when the Senate then voted him the dictatorship for life, he promptly accepted it. Subsequently he combined in his person the functions, indeed the titles as well, of consul, tribune, "prefect of morals," and Pontifex Maximus. Before his planned departure for Parthia, where he hoped to win new imperial victories, he was given the added power of naming the two consuls and one half of the magistracies.

In the main these revolutionary changes met with popular acclaim. The depth and sweep of his program and the magic of his touch promised an end at last to the long years of anarchy and turbulence. To many Romans he seemed a kind of divine savior.

But if subservient Senate and enthusiastic crowds acclaimed Caesar as lord and savior, a stubborn minority of old line republicans fumed in bitter and impotent rage. Brutus and Cassius tried to rally their countrymen against the looming autocracy. When Caesar's laws and agents made their campaign too dangerous they turned to the one remaining weapon, assassination. To Brutus and other representatives of the old order, tyrannicide, far from being a crime, was considered the highest form that patriotism could take. Thus as Caesar swept from power to power, and especially as he came to show signs of restoring the hated monarchy and of becoming a new Alexander, the conspirators made ready for their own "last decree."

Caesar planned to leave for the East immediately after the Ides of March. The conspirators feared he would there proclaim himself god-emperor. So the Republic, if it was to be saved, must be saved at once. Thus it was that on March 15, 44 B.C., avenging daggers struck down the conqueror.

The assassination of Caesar plunged the Roman world again into factional strife and confusion. Antony, strangely spared by the assassins, originally assumed a moderate position in order to see which group would prove stronger. He did not have long to wait. The mobs in Rome cried out against the murder of their idol; and Caesar's troops showed no inclination to yield their power to a bickering Senate. In these circumstances Antony moved easily into the posture of Caesar's avenger.

By his will Caesar had designated his grand-nephew, Octavian, as his heir and adopted son. At the time of Caesar's death, the young man (then eighteen years old) was in Athens under a tutor.* Within the month he appeared in Rome to claim his inheritance. Antony, hardly in a position to repudiate a Caesar while himself fighting under that name, grudgingly made room for him. For the next two years, hectic jockeying for position continued.

In 42 B.C. Antony and Octavian defeated republican forces at Philippi. Perhaps each suspected that the next and final contest must be between themselves. Established in the East, Antony soon came to play the part of an oriental monarch under the heady tutelage of Cleopatra, who found Caesar's lieutenant as attractive and useful as his captain. While Octavian was busy at home establishing order and encouraging the return of prosperity, Antony made Cleopatra "Queen of Kings," and finally designated his two sons, born of Cleopatra, as future rulers of certain eastern provinces. When this became known (32 B.C.), Octavian had little trouble persuading the Senate to declare war (nominally against Egypt), and the issue was joined. The next year, at Actium, the two armies met in what turned out to be an easy victory for Octavian; soon thereafter Antony took his own life. With favorable precedent to guide her Cleopatra coyly invited the victor to a conference. But this time her charms were of no avail; and preferring death to a Roman prison, she followed Antony in suicide. Once more the Roman world had a master; but this time the old pattern was not to be repeated. With Octavian, Rome had come of imperial age.

---

* Some scholars place Octavian in Dalmatia at this time, rather than in Athens.

Roman Culture in the Century of Struggle

Military and political decisions and events constituted the chief forces that worked the pivotal change marking Roman history from *c.* 150 B.C. to the demise of the Republic. But of course literary, philosophical, religious, and economic developments inevitably were part of that history, too. In literature the works of five writers are especially worthy of notice.

Literature: Lucretius and Catullus

T. Lucretius Carus' *De Rerum Natura* was written in the years of agony that characterized the onset of the civil wars. The age, as we have seen, was unsettled by a haunting fear of tomorrow's senseless violence. It suffered from the agony of the dissolution of old frames of reference, from blind groping in a widening void, and from the desperately eager conversion of many to the inviting hopes of alien and esoteric faiths. These and other wracking features of his period stirred Lucretius and set him on his quest for the balm of abiding truth. His search led him to the philosophy of Epicurus where, he came to believe, the final answers lay. Thereafter he became a man with a message. *De Rerum Natura—On the Nature of Things—*is, therefore, actually a homiletical exercise designed to save man from his wretched superstitions and harassments.

Undergirding and feeding this wretchedness, Lucretius believed, were twin evils— religion and man's fear of death. Let man rid himself not only of false gods but of all gods; then let him explore the natural world and learn its secrets. From this bold venture in reason two rewards would be his: serenity that allows acceptance of blind, purposeless life; and welcome rapport with death.

If Lucretius, as a few critics have insisted, had something to do with shaping the work of Catullus (*c.* 84–54 B.C.), the evidence for it is none too plain. Whereas Lucretius sorrowed over the ignorant state of human-kind and laboriously worked out a plan of salvation, Catullus sang of himself, es-pecially of the waxing and waning of his love life. Where Lucretius wrote in the measured, solemn manner of the old Romans, Catullus, affected by the new fashions of the Alexandrine school, scorned archaic syntax, vocabulary, and often meter in favor of the sweetly passionate dicta of the Eastern literary cult. Even their interpretations of the essence of Epicurean philosophy differed. Lucretius found in it solace of mind; Catullus, satiation of the senses. Although Catullus wrote a few longer works, his genius lay in exploiting a Latinized elegiac form, the brief lines of which seared the reader's emotions as a hot brand. His chief subject was his love for "Lesbia," who in real life was Clodia Pulchra, one of Rome's famous courtesans.

Caesar and Cicero

Catullus' contemporary, Julius Caesar (100–44 B.C.), was, as we have seen, more the maker of history than its mirror, though he wrote far more and better than one would suppose a busy warrior could. His literary efforts were broad in scope: ora-tions, essays (on astronomy and grammar, for example), epigrams, drama (still an-other *Oedipus*), love poems, as well as his ten books of commentaries. Save for a few of the orations and, of course, the com-mentaries, all have been lost. His orations were marked by directness and studied simplicity. Although the Alexandrine school was too precious for him, he did not, on the other hand, care to use the polished, rolling periods of Cicero. His severe approach is even more marked in his seven books of commentaries *On the Gallic Wars,* and in his three books *On the Civil War.* It has been said that "his memoirs have no supe-rior as military narratives." In his *Gallic Wars* he went out of his way to eliminate the first person singular; by deliberate cal-culation, it has been charged, he sought in

this way to throw himself into even greater relief. The work is a marvel of compact austere prose.

Far surpassing Caesar in literary talent (though except in his own eyes, in few other ways) was M. Tullius Cicero (106–43 B.C.), after Caesar the most renowned of ancient Romans. There is hardly a form of literary expression that he left untried— poetry, philosophic essays, letters, works on grammar and rhetoric, theological treatises and, preeminently, orations. Of the orations, 57 survive, the most famous being the two Philippics, his passionate indictments of the character and design of Caesar's colleague, Mark Antony. On these especially, and to a lesser extent on his similar diatribes against Cataline, rest his fame as the ancient world's greatest orator after Demosthenes. From the latter ora-tions came his title "savior of his country." From the former came not only lasting acclaim but, tragically for him, his own death warrant; for, as we have seen, Antony had found it impossible to forgive the powerful and damning strictures of his eloquent adversary. Surpassing all, es-pecially in their power to evoke both the spirit and features of his age, are his letters, some eight hundred of which have survived. To our own day they remain the most im-portant single source of historical data dealing with the last days of the Republic.

Sallust

The foremost historian of the period, in-deed saluted by Martial as Rome's first real historian, was Sallust (C. Sallustius Crispus, 86–35 B.C.). A partisan of Caesar's and a one-time Tribune, Sallust retired to private life after Caesar's death and de-voted the remaining nine years of his life to writing. His two major works were *Bellum Catilinarium,* in which he described the political maze of that politician's con-spiracy, and Bellum *Jugurthinum,* a narra-tion and interpretation of Rome's war with Jugurtha. In the first work his aim, ap-parently, was to contrast the worth of

Caesar's rule with that which succeeded it. His second work was based, in broad aim, on Thucydides' history of the Peloponnesian War. In this volume he set the pattern that Roman historians would use as a model. Hitherto, annalists with their bare, dry laying of facts on end had served exclusively as Clio's servants; nor did Caesar's fetching prose attempt more than an unadorned recital of fact. Sallust endeavored to read the meaning of the facts, to discover motives, to discern trends and movements.

Philosophy and Religion

Our study of the literature of this period suggests the trends taken by philosophic and religious thought which were likewise derived from the Greeks. By the time of Augustus, Epicureanism and Stoicism were competing on equal terms. The great systems of the Academies, on the other hand, had gone into eclipse. They had opened brilliantly with the promise that the play of man's mind would lead to the discovery of all truth. But by Augustan times Neoplatonists and Neoaristotelians had despaired of such a grand achievement. Reacting against this failure, most philosophic speculation was inclined to subsume its activity with implicit acknowledgment that first causes were beyond the human ken. For the Epicurean this did not mean averting attention from nature and her ways; as we have seen, for Lucretius it meant precisely the opposite. But the underlying assumption was that while man's mind could and should seek causal connection of events—should forever peck away at the *how*—the basic *why*, or even *what*, was unanswerable. The philosophers' task, therefore, was to seek the partial truth that could be discovered and to fit man's life into it. With this Stoicism agreed, adding the argument of duty. For the Stoic, contemplation for the sake of contemplation was useless, even foolish. He therefore criticized the Epicurean not only for allowing his thought to run to hedonistic seed but, as much, for neglecting the "disciplined doing" which naturally followed a true understanding of the laws of nature.

The Mystery Religions

But to the average person neither Epicureanism nor Stoicism afforded satisfaction. Most persons, then as now, could not grasp philosophy's abstractions or follow its cogently reasoned arguments. Moreover, their lot was often so miserable and destitute of promise that they were hardly likely to subscribe to any system which predicated the acceptance of "things as they were." In addition, masses and intellectuals alike found it impossible, in the actual conditions of life, to hold in eternal abeyance the *why* of existence and the related question of man's destiny after death. Long since, faith in the ancient religion had dimmed. To the state cult, especially as it was nurtured by Augustus and his successors, citizens gave lip service, but more as a political symbol than as a way of life. Out of these promptings the average Roman displayed an increasing willingness to explore the new religions that filtered in from the East. These religions often spoke to the individual and his demanding needs, promising spiritual satisfactions both in this and in the next world.

During the trying days of the Hannibalic War the old Roman gods had seemingly proved unworthy of continued supplication and worship. It was at this time that the cult of Cybele (the Great Mother) made its appearance. The Great Mother was a nature goddess whose benevolent spirit inclined her to listen and attend to the wants of man, to the wants of every man. These she could readily understand because, as the legend proclaimed, her son was human, not divine. Accompanying these articles of faith, mystical rituals and liturgical devices invited emotional responses which served as an effective release from the tensions and fears of life.

Another mystery religion, Isis worship, flourished in the late years of the Republic.

We are familiar with its chief features from our study of Egyptian civilization. Brought to Rome, it underwent some modifications. Serapis became the remote supreme god, "while Isis herself became a gentle queen of the living and the dead." As they were of the cult of the Great Mother, songs, liturgies, and an elaborate priesthood were important features of this religion.

During the war between Pompey and Caesar, Mithraism attracted many followers in Rome. Its influence, especially as it bore on the rise and development of Christianity,* will be considered later. Much of the impetus given to this and other mystery religions came originally from the hordes of migrants pouring in from regions of the ancient Near East where "religion of the spirit" had its birth. By the second century A.D. these faiths had become, together with Christianity, an integral part of the religious life of the West.

Economic Conditions

Thus profound changes marked Roman life during the two hundred years from Hannibal to Octavian. But not every aspect of life. The economic system and its practices remained essentially unaltered. For most Italians, agriculture continued to serve as the main source of livelihood. It is true that under the prodding of the elder Cato new techniques and practices had developed. But the husbandman of Rome at the dawn of the Empire period planted, cultivated, and harvested much as had his forefathers.

The exigencies and opportunities of imperial dominion brought into prominence the equestrian order and created an influential bourgeois class. But much of the trading was still carried on by Greeks whether they lived in Italy, Africa, or in the East. Consequently Italians remained indifferent to tariff policies and regulatory measures, giving them almost no official or sustained attention until the time of Diocletian. This tends to puzzle the modern

* A relationship reversed by some modern historians.

student who is used to thinking of national development in terms of class struggle, duty schedules, money and banking policies, governmental regulation of business, and the like. But we need to keep in mind that for the period we are considering a huge slave supply made genuine class struggle impossible, save for an occasional servile revolt. It even ruled out such common proletarian protests as strikes. For the most part factories were small and locally owned. There were great centers of industry, to be sure, but not in Italy. In the main the equestrian order controlled banking, and hence dominated what we would call the real estate business.

But if the basic structure of the economic system remained unaltered the overall effects produced by it remarkably changed the society it sustained. Particularly significant was the mushrooming of cities, both in size and number. Wealth, though inequitably distributed, increased at such a rate that the age may be called one of luxury. Roman political control made the whole Mediterranean world one great free-trade area. Commerce accordingly flourished, further encouraged by the Roman-built network of roads. The two centuries of the *Pax Romana* that followed witnessed a still greater augmentation of the "gross national product," so that the advent of Octavian heralded an era not only of peace but also of unprecedented prosperity. And the nature of the new state which Octavian set up, the salient features of which we may now examine, guaranteed that these gains would outlive the generation that so rapturously hailed them.

SELECTED READINGS

Boak, A. E. R., and William G. Sinnigen, *A History of Rome to A.D. 565*, Macmillan Co., New York, 1965 (5th ed.).

Any text which survives nearly a half century of reading is worthy of attention. This one is up-to-date, well-balanced in scope (about one-half of it is devoted to preempire periods), and, within the limits imposed by a narrative of some 500 pages, comprehensive. If the works of Cary, Geer, or Heichelheim, cited below, are not used, this one should be.

*Carcapino, Jerome, *Daily Life in Ancient Rome,* Yale University Press, New Haven, Connecticut, 1940.

A highly readable account of the routine activities and common attitudes of Roman citizens.

Cary, Max, *A History of Rome Down to the Age of Constantine,* Methuen and Company, London, 1954 (2nd rev.).

Another standard text, more readable than Boak and Sinnigen's; somewhat out of date, though certainly not so much as to cause it to be passed over lightly.

*Crowell, F. R., *Cicero and the Roman Republic,* Pelican, Harmondsworth, London, 1956.

In our opinion the best book by far on the last hundred years of the Republic. It is exceptionally well organized and exceptionally well written. Unique "Isotype" charts are used to clarify and vivify sequential developments.

Geer, Russell M., *Classical Civilization— Rome.* Prentice-Hall, New York, 1941.

Though even more back-dated than Cary's, this work is still worth reading. Textbooks rarely achieve a "classic" status; this one is an exception. The author has an extraordinary feel for what should be stressed, as well as an unusual talent for clear expression. It treats "cultural" interests more fully and meaningfully than any of the other three texts cited.

Heichelheim, Fritz M., and Cedric A. Yeo, *A History of the Roman People,* Prentice-Hall, Englewood Cliffs, New Jersey, 1962.

Incorporates the findings of recent research. The chapters on Italian prehistory and the Etruscans are particularly worthwhile. Some interpretations are controversial and somewhat faulted by a species of pedantry.

Homo, Léon, *Roman Political Institutions from City to State,* Barnes and Noble, New York, 1962.

Asterisk (*) denotes paperback.

A socio-historical study of the "necessities" of Roman life which shaped Rome's political structure from pre-Etruscan times to the late Empire.

Marsh, Frank B., *A History of the Roman World from 146 to 30* B.C., Methuen and Co., London, 1953 (2nd ed.).

For those who like an amplitude of detail this work on Rome's tumultuous century of change from republic to empire is good solid reading. The notes by Professor Scullard, who readied the second edition for the press, are especially valuable.

Mommsen, Theodore, *The History of Rome.* W. P. Dickinson, translator, J. M. Dent and Sons, London, 1911.

This multivolumed classic will probably continue to be read long after many of the other works cited, valuable as they are, have had their day. For those with sufficient leisure and learning, and who like to lose themselves in the full sweep of the Republic's 500 year history, this great work will continue to offer impelling charm despite its early date and its sometimes tendentious character.

But even Mommsen's work does not allow the savoring of the life of Republican Rome as does a first-hand reading of the works of Caesar, Cicero, and Catullus, available in many modern translations and a variety of paperbacks.

Pareti, Luigi, et al., *The Ancient World,* Vol. II, George Allen and Unwin, London, 1965.

This elaborate work (underwritten by Unesco) is made up of three parts (each a separate volume). The first describes the ancient world from 1200 B.C. to 500 B.C.; the second to the advent of Christ; the third to A.D. 500. In the main it incorporates the latest findings of historical research; but in dealing with some topics (such as the Etruscans) it is stubbornly out of date.

Its organization, like that of its companion volume, is seriously flawed. Events are treated topically at the expense of clear sequential development. Also, as in the first volume, some of the footnotes are unusually enlightening and important while others are quite out of place, often unnecessary.

Pulgram, Ernst, *The Tongues of Italy,* Harvard

University Press, Cambridge, Massachusetts, 1958.

A unique attempt to correlate linguistic and nonlinguistic facets of Italian history. For our purposes the sections entitled "Prehistoric Background," "The Indo-Europeanization of Italy," and "The Latinization of Italy" are particularly worthwhile.

Richardson, Emeline, *The Etruscans,* University of Chicago Press, Chicago, 1964.

Probably the best work on Etruscan origins, art, language, and religion. If the reader's interest is whetted, an extensive topical bibliography may be consulted.

Rostovtzeff, M. J., *History of the Ancient World,* Oxford University Press, Oxford, 1927.

Rather out of date and opinionated, but still worth consulting if used in conjunction with one or more of the other works cited.

Scullard, Howard H., *A History of the Roman World . . . ,* Methuen and Co., London, 1963 (4th ed.).

In our opinion the best single general account of Roman history down to the "century of troubles." Professor Scullard lets the reader know what other scholars think about an event or development at the same time he expresses his own judgment (somewhat oversubtlely at times, it must be admitted). He presents evidence the reader needs without losing either himself or the reader in the mass of details.

Starr, Chester G., *A History of the Ancient World* (see notation in Chapter II).

Mainly concerned with political and economic developments, Chapters 21 to 32 give the reader a generally sound understanding of Rome's emergence, expansion, republican institutions, imperial sway, and eventual decline. Especially recommended for its utilization of recent research. Its style makes for easy reading.

*Syme, Ronald, *Roman Revolution,* Oxford Paperback, New York, 1960.

A scholarly, often controversial, and sometimes puckish account of the forces at work in the remaking of Roman political life and outlook after the Punic Wars. See especially for an interesting view of Pompey.

7

The Roman World: Empire and the Christian Community

THE EMPIRE

The Establishment of the Principate

From Chaos to Order

For 200 years the Romans had lived in a hectic world of change. What started out as a brush with the Carthaginians had turned into a struggle for empire from which the Romans had emerged both triumphant and bewildered. The brave new world into which they had stumbled excited and flattered them. From an undistinguished tribe nestling in the hills along the Tiber they had somehow become masters of the Mediterranean world. But in the process old prizes were lost. In a sense they had become alienated from themselves. The republican surge had faltered and failed. The yeoman farmer still existed but, precariously, his old central position in the state swept away before the servile flood. Old religions, old family customs, the old spirit—all were profoundly changed. For over 100 years civil violence had wracked and torn the corpus of Roman society until it was scarcely recognizable as a society with a future.

These things the Romans experienced rather than understood. They yearned for a way out of disorder, a way that somehow would save the Republic, keep the Empire, and end the chaos. But if the Romans failed to understand their times and themselves, Octavian understood both very well. If he lacked, as he did, a ready-made solution, he had what perhaps was better. His was the genius to sense the spirit of the times, to take a step and test its worth, then another and another until gradually a program evolved which seemed best to fit the Roman facts of life. These things he knew: that there must be peace; that Empire existed; that it was incompatible with the Republic it had succeeded; that his tradition-bound people wanted to eat their republican cake

143

and to keep their Empire; and that his job was to produce a policy which would weld reality with memory and illusion. It is difficult to believe, of course, that the more perceptive Romans did not understand what was going on. History is not innocent of periods in which man deliberately deceives himself in order to do something which one part of him clearly condemns. It may be that the new "Golden Age" was such a period.

Augustus

We do not know whether Octavian (soon to be styled Augustus) himself knew how well he worked. Probably he did not, for there is nothing in his record that suggests the brilliant flashes of insight and introspective analysis of his famous great-uncle. In many ways he resembled America's founding father. Like Washington he possessed an almost unerring judgment of the fit and the proper, of the unglamorous achievable, of the workable compromise and the techniques needed to effect it, and of when to show courage and when to prefer caution. But if he did not have at his command the resources of a superman's *mystique* he knew how to learn from Caesar's malpractice of such magic. As clearly as his predecessor he understood that the Republic was finished. But unlike Caesar he knew this was the last thing his countrymen would admit. The "Revolution of 509" hallowed it; the long "struggle of the orders" had revealed its rich potentials. Now it was gone. But to say so was a kind of suicide. A formula was needed that somehow kept illusion and yet coped with reality. Octavian devoted the next fifteen years to working out precisely such a formula.

Part of his success lay in the almost instantaneous recognition by the public of his basic motivation. Although ambitious, he was driven by a tenacious desire to serve the public weal. He could scheme, but unlike Crassus he was not interested in politics as a game; nor was he touched with Caesar's megalomania. Although he received more than his share of material goods (reserving the whole wealth of Egypt as his private income), he was not out for booty. Although he deliberately and successfully set out to make himself an absolute ruler he was not basically interested in power *per se*. And although he accepted and used an awesome array of titles, he was not glory-mad. Fundamentally he was interested in saving the Roman world from destruction, and the Roman world well understood this. They sensed further that great glories lay ahead; perhaps even the restoration of the Golden Age of the early Republic. And as the repose of peace and the glory of Empire continued and developed decade after decade the sense grew into a conviction: the miracle of restoration had indeed come to pass.

Princeps

Returning in triumph from Egypt, Augustus found the people ready to give him permanent dictatorial powers. But remembering the fate that befell his great-uncle, he let it appear that he asked for nothing. He knew, of course, that the Empire called for some form of absolutism. But he understood also that ancient aspirations and Republican memories were not dead. Somehow he had to foster a faith that was at once unrealizable but necessary if the active cooperation of the orders, without which he could do nothing, was to be gained. In short, a redefinition of the state was called for which sanctioned absolutism without seeming to sanction it.

To achieve this definition Augustus resorted to a bold and dramatic (almost melodramatic) *coup*. On January 13, 27 B.C. he appeared before the Senate and humbly asked to be relieved of all the powers, legal and extralegal, that had been granted him across the previous decade. Peace was won; order had been achieved. It was time, he said, for the Republic to be restored to its rightful rulers, the Senate and the Assemblies. For himself he asked only that he be given surcease from responsibilities and a chance to enjoy life as a private citizen, if the conscript Fathers in their wisdom would allow this.

At once a tumult of protests broke out. So promptly and overwhelmingly did the demonstration occur that it is naive to suppose it was spontaneous. Obviously his followers had been given their cues. But, equally obviously, real concern lay behind the demonstration. Clearly, without Augustus violence would break out afresh. Rome had had its fill of factionalism and anarchy. His task, Romans insisted, was far from complete. Peace and order had been achieved. Now let their champion remain to nurture them. Bowing to this popular demand Augustus humbly agreed to stay at his post, accepting as legal powers all those and more which he had surrendered.

Throughout the drama the Emperor was careful to see that all the forms and practices of the old Roman constitution were faithfully observed. Nonetheless he found himself again elected to the consulship and in a position to effect whatever legislative changes he felt necessary. Even more important, he "consented" to assume responsibility for a number of provinces. As it turned out, these were the provinces in which the most powerful armies were quartered. The fact that his offices were limited in tenure mattered little, since his prestige and wise rule made his reelection automatic. The time soon came, indeed, when his prestige allowed him to give up the consulship altogether, though of course those who thereafter held the offices were his nominees. Soon the tribunician sacrosanctity which had been granted him in 30 B.C. was widened in scope. Ultimately he achieved complete legislative power, quite apart from his control of the consuls. Thus he was in essence supreme commander of the armies, chief lawmaker,* and, as personal "owner" as well as ruler of Egypt, independently wealthy.

But it must be repeated, on the surface this was not at all plain. Nothing belonged to Augustus that the Senate and People had not voted him. To the rule of the Senate, moreover, certain (pacified) provinces were given. Senate meetings were regularly held; and Augustus sat with the rest, though as *princeps senatus*. All of his legislation was submitted for approval to the conscript Fathers (whose ranks had been purged of the "new family" members and reduced in number to 600). Whatever the reality behind it, the facade of Roman life was again republican.

Peace and Prosperity

To signify the coming of a reign of peace Augustus, in 28 (?) B.C., closed the temple of Janus. Moreover he reduced by half the size of the armed forces, settling his discharged veterans upon land in Italy or in the provinces (land paid for out of his own exchequer, not confiscated as had so often been the practice in the past). As a stopgap until his plans could become effective, he spent lavish sums in Rome to entertain the unemployed. He also inaugurated a gigantic building program which gave the economy a much needed stimulus. Construction of various kinds of public edifices was begun, new roads were planned and laid, and about 80 new temples were erected. Drawing upon the riches of his Egyptian "bank," he embarked on an extensive program of what today might be called lend-lease, designed to succor the hard-pressed senatorial class. As business revived the *Equites* rejoiced to find their profits growing ever larger. A decline in the interest rate reflected the stabilization of the economy and helped the peasant, eternally in debt, to share in the overall prosperity. Thus all classes, although unevenly, made material gains in the new period of peace and plenty.

---

* Technically the assemblies were, and long remained, the supreme lawmakers; but only technically. Often Augustus yielded a point to them. But when legislation, believed by Augustus to be of real importance, was under discussion, both the *princeps* and the assemblies knew who would make the decision.

ROMAN PROVINCES
DURING THE REIGN OF AUGUSTUS

Atlantic Ocean

Rhine R.

GERMANIA

SARMATIA

LOWER RHINE

BELGICA

LUGUDUNENSIS

UPPER RHINE

Danube R.

RAETIA

NORICUM

AQUITANIA

ALPINE TER.

PANNONIA

DACIA

NARBONENSIS

TARRACONENSIS

ITALY

DALMATIA

UPPER MOESIA

LOWER MOESIA

Black Sea

LUSITANIA

CORSICA

Rome

MACEDONIA

BITHYNIA

GALATIA

BAETICA

SARDINIA

EPIRUS

ASIA

LYCAONIA

Euphrates R.

NUMIDIA

SICILY

ACHAEA

PAMPHYLIA

CILICIA

SYRIA

CYPRUS

Mediterranean Sea

AFRICA

CYRENAICA

MARMARICA

EGYPT

Nile R.

Imperial Provinces

Senatorial Provinces

0   200   400 mi.

Map by J. Donovan

Nor were the provinces (which, of course, formed the predominant bulk of the Empire) neglected. Indeed, in some respects they benefited the most. During the preceding century and a half they had become dependents of Rome. Many of them had been exploited and despoiled by rapacious governors who had come for their year of misrule and had left with private fortunes. To them the Republic meant not so much glory and order as corruption and legal pillage. So when Augustus instituted a new system characterized by career officials supervised by the Emperor himself, the provinces hailed the new ruler as a veritable god. Indeed, in the East his image was worshiped and shrines were dedicated to his genius.*

The *princeps,* as he preferred to be called, made a strenuous effort to revive ancient religious habits and to resurrect the old concept of the family and of family morality. New temples were heavily subsidized. Sumptuary laws (which proved none too effective) were passed to regulate conduct. To dramatize the coming of the new Golden Age, Augustus arranged a grand celebration, in 17 B.C., of the seventh centenary (rather arbitrarily calculated) of the founding of Rome. For three days the capital was given over to festivities, crowned by a solemn and impressive march through the city of a chorus of young boys

* For a geographical survey of the provinces at the time of Augustus, see map above.

and girls chanting a triumphal ode composed by Horace.

Thus Rome finally seemed to have found herself. After her violent time of troubles she was at peace. A measure of prosperity was enjoyed. An order that gave signs of enduring had been established. The future seemed bright, prefigured by the hope and vision, albeit dim, of the progressive enlargement of man. During the thirty years that still remained of Augustus' rule, golden hopes seemed to take on flesh, to form and to shape themselves into reality.

The Price of Paternalism

But the illusion of the glorious Republic regained was, after all, an illusion. The Republic, in actual fact, had not been restored but had been interred. Behind the show of partnership lay one-man rule—autocracy. Augustus had jerked the state back from the abyss of chaos and corruption. And the state was grateful. As a benevolent autocrat he had imposed order and a kind of well-being. What, though, would happen under another absolutist ruler who happened not to be benevolent? And even assuming, which one certainly could not, that all of Rome's future autocrats would be benevolent—what then? Could the vision of the progressive enlargement of the individual abide permanent paternalism of any sort?

Moreover, social mobility was seriously restricted by finely calculated legislation. Manumission of slaves was made difficult. The freedman was encouraged to be satisfied with his lot by the creation for him of an honorary society (the *Augustales*), an organization of priestly officers dedicated to service in the cult of the Genius of Augustus. Intermarriage between yeomen and equestrian orders was discouraged. Both *Equites* and Senators were given distinct symbols to wear, setting them off from the other orders.

Beyond this, the morale of the senatorial class steadily deteriorated. Increasingly, younger members of this order, knowing they were never to exercise real responsibility and power in governing the state, tended to drift into bored acquiescence. The equestrians, the upper bourgeoisie, became, as their wealth increased under preferred treatment, more and more the victims and exemplars of that crass culture which extravagant riches so often promote. In short, as the state grew in grandeur, the dignity and inner worth of man seemed to shrink in significance, although the full impact of these developments was long in making itself felt.

If history were merely past politics, we should next move on to the succession of emperors and political events that followed the establishment of the Principate. From our habit of thinking so largely in these terms, such a progression seems reasonable enough. But to do so would be to confuse structure for substance. The stuff of human vision, of dream and desire, is expressed in literature and art, in philosophy and religion rather than in politics. Especially was this true of the Augustan Age, the so-called new Golden Age of Rome. Indeed, except as we turn to these developments we can only superficially understand either the Augustan program or the cultural forces which simultaneously shaped and were shaped by it.

Literature and Culture of the Golden Age

Of all the achievements of the Golden Age—although paradoxically not only rooted in the preceding years of struggle but culminating before the imperial period was well begun—one of the greatest was its literary production. Many of the creations of its literary titans—Virgil, Horace, Ovid, Livy—were masterworks that have lived. Save for that of the Greeks and certain portions of the Old Testament, no literature in ancient times matched it in stylistic grace and brilliance, in profundity and subtlety of thought. It therefore deserves more than cursory attention.

Virgil

Sallust's death in 35 B.C. marked the end of what some have called the Ciceronian prelude to the Golden Age. By this time a new and greater constellation of literati had appeared. The greatest of these was Publius Vergilius Maro (70–19 B.C.). Virgil's * life spanned the interval of transition from chaos to order. He has rightly been called both priest and prophet of the new day. Indeed, in a measure he was its creator, sharing the honors with Augustus, his friend and patron. Although it is especially true of his greatest poem, the *Aeneid,* his aim in all his works was to glorify the Italian land and its people, Empire and Emperor, and to herald the coming age.

His earliest work—ten poems (*Eclogues* or *Bucolics*)—is much his slightest. In some of these verses he tested his developing talents on the often-told stories of classical Greece. But, even here, we find his main theme given expression (although the verses were mainly meant to evoke the charms of pastoral life). At the time Virgil wrote the poem of which a brief extract is quoted below Augustus was showing every sign of grooming his young son-in-law, Marcellus, as his successor, a choice much applauded by the Romans. The poet used this projected purpose (which never materialized) as a point from which to take off in celebration of Rome's present glory and the greater glory to come.

> The cycle of great epochs starts anew
> And Virgin Astraea evokes Saturnian
>   sway.
> From heaven now new progeny is sent.
> O chaste Lucina, to this infant boy
> Whose reign shall see the age of iron yield
> And all over the world a golden age begin,
> Be thou propitious—now Apollo reigns.[1]

The *Georgics,* a long poem of four books,

* Technically, the correct spelling is Vergil. Here traditional usage is followed.

1. Adapted from a prose translation, T. A. Buckley, ed., *The Works of Vergil,* Harper and Brothers, 1855, pp. 11–13.

was suggested by Maecenas, the Emperor's gifted political adviser and Virgil's personal friend and benefactor. Like the *Eclogues,* the verses deal with the calm grandeur of Italy's pastoral life (in addition to suggestions on practical farming).

But Virgil's fame rests on the *Aeneid,* a long epic poem justly counted one of the world's greatest masterpieces. The poet's aim in this work, to which he devoted the last ten years of his life, was to provide his countrymen with a kind of spiritual foundation of the new age which he envisioned. He conceived his task as this: to reveal the Roman genius, to evoke the first Golden Age (destroyed sometime after the Punic Wars), to liken it to the Augustan Age, and to silhouette the outlines of the Empire's coming grandeur. His method was partly historical. Using Homer as a model and borrowing freely from him, Virgil chose Aeneas, a warrior from the heroic age of Troy, as the central figure of his poem. As the poet has it, Aeneas—sired by a Trojan prince out of Venus—and a band of his followers fled from the doomed city to embark upon a long series of adventures before settling in Latium. There the hero wooed Lavinia, daughter of the king, and from this union came Rome's founders. According to Virgil, therefore, his countrymen were the product of this merger of Trojan and Latin blood.

Blessing this project was Venus; opposing it, Juno. Most of the mighty adventures recounted in the poem occur as consequences of this divine contest. The *Aeneid* opens with a simple statement of the poet's theme:

> Of arms I sing and the man, that hero who
> Exiled by fate from Troy besought
> The darkling shores of far off Italy.[2]

The denouement is foretold in an early book when Jupiter, in answer to a protest from Venus that his stubborn spouse is playing havoc with fated events, assures her that

2. Buckley, *op. cit.,* p. 103.

> . . . frantic Juno now
> Afret with sullen fear, disturbing seas
> And earth and skies, will one day change
>   her ways
> And join with me to favor over all
> One people, Romans, lords of all the
>   world,
> A nation of the gown. Such is my will.[3]

After recounting the adventures and vicissitudes that befall Aeneas and his band after they had fled from Rome, Virgil brings them to Italy where Aeneas is transported to the world of shades. He is shown the ghosts of those who had lived in the first Golden Age and is told which are destined for a second life on earth. Among others is pointed out to him one who is to be Aeneas' own son, by Lavinia. Other ghosts identified are Julius Caesar, Pompey, Cato, the Gracchi, and the Scipios.

Much of the remainder of the poem centers in the long struggle between Aeneas' Trojans and the Latin armies led by Turnus. In the end Aeneas slays Turnus, and victors merge with vanquished to form a new imperial people.

Horace

Where Virgil's genius lay in the grand epic, that of his contemporary and friend, Quintus Horatius Flaccus (65 to 8 B.C.), is found in the national lyric. Born of lowly parentage (his father was a freedman), Horace nonetheless was given a sound education. After his early years of schooling at Rome he went to Athens for "graduate" study in the liberal arts. While there he learned of the assassination of Julius Caesar. Shortly thereafter, when Brutus fled to Greece to raise an army against Caesar's defenders, the future poet laureate of the Augustan Empire allowed himself to be enrolled in the ranks of the republicans. He fought—and fled—at Philippi, losing, as a consequence, not only status at home but also what little property his father had left him. Returning under the general amnesty he worked quietly for

a time at clerical chores. His early verse attracted Virgil's attention and they soon became close friends. Through Virgil the one-time republican was introduced to Maecenas, Augustus' chief adviser. Subsequently Horace met and became intimate with the Emperor himself. By this time he had come to see the promise of the Augustan age. Although he turned down an offer to become the Emperor's private secretary, he thereafter proved a strong supporter of the regime.

His great period of productivity (c. 35–13 B.C.) saw the publication of two books of *Satires,* a number of *Epodes* ("refrains"), four books of *Odes,* and two of *Epistles.* The *Satires* might be called conversation pieces in verse. Their content included jibes at contemporary figures and comments on current social issues and political problems. They are by no means his best work. The *Epodes* "resemble the *Satires* in their frequent polemical character, the *Odes* in the lyric form in which they were cast." The latter two works marked Horace as a poet of the first rank. His *Epistles,* informal verse essays on matters of day-to-day concern, were similar to the *Satires.*

If Virgil was the prophet of the new age Horace was its moralist, if the term may be used without its sometimes prudish and narrow connotation. This is clearly evident in the concern over the state of society found in his verses, especially those written immediately after his return to Italy from Greece. It is clear, too, in his dawning realization of the significance of the Augustan effort, and in his subsequent calm and mellow meditations on the good life. Rejecting alike Lucretian and Catullan Epicureanism, Horace finally came to infuse his work with a humane Stoicism, lightly overlaid with perfunctory obeisance to traditional and state religion.

The poetic genius of Horace thus served, as did Virgil's, not only to signal the dawn of a new age but in part to create it. Hope was high, the ship of state steady under the firm (if heavy) hand of Augustus, and the

3. Buckley, *op. cit.,* p. 113.

imperial realms encompassed nearly all of the Mediterranean world. The Golden Age, it seemed, had indeed returned.

Ovid

The third great poet of this age, P. Ovidius Naso (43 B.C.–A.D. 18), unlike his two colleagues, was remarkably indifferent to the national renaissance and imperial glory of which his times gave promise. Ovid's genius, indeed, rested upon him but lightly. That genius he had, his contemporaries recognized and history has confirmed. His mastery of the elegiac form, his delicate phrasings, his incisive handling of antithetical themes, and the natural grace of his most casual verse amply demonstrate his native talents. But, for whatever reason, he did not choose to exploit them. He neither plumbed the depths of the individual psyche nor reached for the grand epic theme. The potential profundity of his genius shunned microcosm and macrocosm alike. He preferred, as another has expressed it, to be the sophisticated voice of the smart set of Rome. Almost invariably his treatment, of whatever subject matter, was marked by the urbane touch, the casual approach. He spoke as Rome's great literary *bon vivant.*

Livy

In prose one great name stands out, Titus Livius (*c.* 59 B.C.–A.D. 17). For forty years he labored on a project hardly less stupendous in scope than that of Virgil— nothing less than the history of Rome from its founding to his own times. The accomplishment of this huge task itself made history. Through it Livy promoted, as did Virgil in the *Aeneid,* a developing sense of nationalism. Much as did Horace in his *Odes,* he made his countrymen conscious of the moral virtues which reputedly gave Rome its early strength. In this sense he too was both harbinger and creator of the new Golden Age.

But this is not to suggest that his history is not subject to serious criticism. For one

thing he was not a researcher as modern historians use the term. He leaned heavily upon secondary sources even when, as on a number of occasions, he had access to the primary materials from which others had drawn. When he did use documents he frequently failed to give samples of their exact wording which would have imparted to the reader a livelier sense of the times. In his early books (the whole work ran to 142 books of which, unfortunately, only 35 are extant) he relied too much upon legend. His judgment, when the evidence was more complete and complex, was not always as discriminating as it should have been. Throughout, his chauvinism is clearly apparent. He was as much interested in history as literary art as in history as "objective" inquiry—in itself a good thing except where, as was often the case with him, such interest carries one away. Finally, his understanding of the intricate complexity of his subject left much to be desired. In these and other ways his history was faulty and must be read with guard up.

But, on the other hand, it is not altogether fair to judge an ancient historian by modern standards. And it must be added that he did not deliberately twist evidence to make it fit his story, though he certainly embellished it. Furthermore, literary art of itself deserves a place, and a rather high place, in all worthy historical writing. Finally, it must be admitted that without Livy most later historical works on Republican Rome would dwindle to a shadowy sketch. Indeed, a contemporary authority has argued that if the 107 lost books were found hardly a page of Roman history, as written by modern historians, would escape revision.

Literary Decline

We have noted enough about the literature of the Golden Age to sense that the grand phrase was not a misnomer. Two further observations remain. It is easy to equate chronologically the Golden Age of Roman literature with the famous *Pax*

Romana. This, however, is a mistake. If, not too arbitrarily, we date the latter period from 30 B.C. to the end of the reign of Marcus Aurelius in A.D. 180 we see that though the great literature falls within this epoch, it does so but barely. Lucretius, Catullus, Caesar, Cicero, Sallust—all lived and died before that period. Even Virgil, Horace, Ovid, and Livy had produced their major works before the Age of Peace was well begun. The Golden Age of literature, therefore, does not coincide with the Imperial Age. Indeed, the years of the latter witnessed a distinct falling away from the established standards. It was, we should note, the Silver Age that belonged to the Empire; and even it, as we shall see, failed to sustain itself for more than half that period.

This decline suggests a second observation. The *promise* of the Augustan reforms undoubtedly stirred the creators of the literature we have surveyed. But actual *practice*, belied the glorious auspices. There is, for example, no Cicero in the Augustan and succeeding ages. This is hardly an accident. Authoritarian regimes do not encourage genuine oratory, for this comes only from unfettered thought freely expressed. Artificially bedecked declarations, pretty and precious, there were; but no stirring works of challenge. When, in one instance, an orator did dare to say what he thought about Augustus and his new regime his books and speeches were publicly banned and the offending protestor was sent into exile. When, too, a few recalcitrant judges gave decisions adverse to Augustus' decrees, the *princeps* promptly stipulated that thereafter no acceptable legal advice or opinion could be given except under terms laid down by Augustus himself. Thus under the New Order, which did indeed bring peace and the rule of law, creative imagination (that is, freedom) was stifled and ultimately sacrificed. Under such conditions one does not expect "golden literature" to flourish, nor did it.

Pax Romana— Imperial Rome

Tiberius

A pressing problem for Augustus in his later years was the question of his successor. For one thing, how was he to be chosen? To leave the choice to the Senate would only invite a return of factionalism and violence. Even less eligible to make such a decision was the popular Assembly, for the people had long since drifted away from a sense of participation and responsibility in matters of high statecraft. Besides, by this time it had become in the main merely a nominal power. For Augustus to nominate his own successor would be tantamount to proclaiming the dictatorship he had been at such pains to conceal. Still, in the end, this is what he did. Rather reluctantly (earlier designees having died) he selected his stepson Tiberius, eldest child of his third wife. By way of preparation for the succession Augustus, in his declining years, gave over power to Tiberius until the latter came to share full authority. Accordingly, when the Emperor died in A.D. 14, the Senate lost no time in proclaiming the new *princeps,* and called upon army and people to swear personal allegiance to him. Thus a pattern of succession was set which served for the next half-century, the period of the so-called Julio-Claudian line (A.D. 14–68).

The apprehensions Augustus had begun to feel in his later years proved to be only too well grounded. Tiberius, who ruled from A.D. 14 until his death in A.D. 37, was an able administrator but haughty and tactless, lacking almost completely the knack Augustus had of getting on with people. Well trained and determined in purpose, he faithfully followed Augustan policies, winning the enthusiastic support of the people in the provinces. At home he fared less well. The Senate chafed under a system that increasingly made clear its own subservient position. The Roman masses objected to Tiberius' program of economy which, for them, meant fewer circuses and smaller doles. Plebeians generally resented an imperial edict which frankly recognized that the people no longer elected the magistrates. Even the army, long his supporter, turned sour when he pared down the budget for military expenditures. Friction developed between Drusus, the Emperor's son, and Germanicus, a nephew whom Augustus had forced Tiberius to designate as his successor. When Germanicus suddenly died, the Emperor was suspected of murdering him, although the available evidence does not support this suspicion. A few years later Drusus was poisoned. When Tiberius learned that one of his once most trusted lieutenants had ordered the murder (motivated by imperial ambitions of his own), he gave himself over to vicious temper tantrums. The last years of his reign were marked by absolute tyranny. When he died in 37 he was cordially hated by everyone.

Violence Revisited

For some years following Tiberius' death the morale so carefully fostered by Augustus was badly shaken. Of the six emperors of this period all died by murder or suicide. Tiberius' great-nephew Gaius (better known by his nickname Caligula—"Little Boots") occupied himself during his three-year reign with incest, assassinations, and assorted cruelties. Officers of his own Praetorian Guard finally slew him and forced the Senate, which briefly toyed with the possibility of restoring the old Republic, to proclaim his uncle, Claudius, as the new *princeps*. In 54 Claudius was assassinated at his wife's orders so that Nero, her son by an earlier marriage, might become ruler. One of Nero's early decisions—though delayed in execution—was to get rid of his mother whom he rightly suspected of having ambitions to be the power behind the throne. Fourteen years later Nero fell victim to the violence he spent his tenure cultivating. Within one year (68–69)—the "Year of the Four Emperors"—Galba, Otho, and Vitellius likewise met violent deaths.

Imperial Order

In spite of this outburst of imperial gangsterism the Empire held together, indeed flourished. Troops posted along its borders kept the "barbarians" from attempting more than occasional raids. With the soldiers came Roman culture which the conquered lands gradually absorbed. From time to time the scholar and his paraphernalia accompanied the soldier, so that books and learning edged their way northward with conquest. Soon, amid the general peace and prosperity, cities came to vie with one another for regional honors and glory. Public buildings of all kinds were erected: government offices, public baths, and temples. Private dwellings of the rich were constructed on a grand scale and were handsomely furnished and decorated. Hellenistic culture, siphoned off and modified by Roman colonists, took root and laid the foundation for the later medieval civilization from which our own has developed.

Throughout this period, too, signs appeared of the spread of new faiths, doubtless developing from the westward flow of religious ideas carried by devotees of the mystery cults and by neo-Pythagoreans; and of ethical monotheism, carried by refugee Hebrews, and by those who had come into contact with the earliest Christian missionaries. Although numerically the most insignificant, the last were especially zealous. The crucifixion of Jesus had occurred in Tiberius' reign. Scarcely twenty years later Peter and Paul were effectively spreading the new gospel in lands along the northern rim of the Mediterranean basin. Three of the Christian gospels were composed during this period and, presumably, soon came to be read in the newly formed congregations whose members were eager to carry the "good news" to the whole world.

In the provinces a new breed of citizen

Cubiculum (bedroom) from the villa near Boscoreale.

was emerging. Many of the discharged legionaries stayed on in the regions they had guarded, often as husbands of native women. Since they were Roman citizens their settlement in the provinces meant that Roman law and Roman civic sense came to merge with foreign habits and folkways. Members of auxiliary units, upon their discharge, were often granted citizenship rights. To be a Roman thus came to mean something quite different from what it had meant in the days of the old Republic.

Vespasian

The situation in Rome itself, however, was far too serious to continue without placing in jeopardy the whole realm. In the capital the important question was, would the new emperor preserve the Principate, or would he openly acknowledge the "secret" of the army's power and frankly set up a military autocracy. He chose to follow the Augustan pattern, a decision which, coupled with his very real abilities,

saved the *Pax Romana* from untimely collapse.

Vespasian (69–79; his full name was Titus Flavius Vespasianus, from which he and his successors are called Flavians) was in no way related to the Julio-Claudians. Strictly speaking he was not even a Roman, but a native of the Sabine country. "Coming to the throne in 69 at the age of 60, bald, wrinkled, and tough, he had behind him much administrative and military experience." Within a half dozen years he had reestablished order in the capital, reorganized the Empire's finances, reconstituted the personnel of the Senate, and made provision for his son, Titus, to succeed him. During his regime he founded new colonies and gave "Latin rights" to all freemen in Spain. Vacant civil service posts were filled by competent administrators. Professional informers—the hated *Delatores*—were sent packing. Accordingly, morale among both public officials and private citizens markedly improved. To placate the eternal Roman mob and to win favor in the city generally, Vespasian ordered the construction of a super-amphitheater (the famed Colosseum) where games and exhibitions were staged on a scale never before attempted.

ROMAN RULERS, 27 B.C.–A.D. 180
Julio-Claudian Line

Augustus	27 B.C.–A.D. 14
Tiberius	14–37
Caligula	37–41
Claudius	41–54
Nero	54–68

"The Year of the Four Emperors"

Galba; Otho; Vitellius; Vespasian	68–69

Flavian Line

Vespasian	69–79
Titus	79–81
Domitian	81–96

"The Five Good Emperors"

Nerva	96–98
Trajan	98–117
Hadrian	117–138
Antoninus Pius	138–161
Marcus Aurelius	161 (147)–180

The "Five Good Emperors": Trajan

For a quarter of a century the Flavian restoration healed the wounds of the Caligula-Nero epoch, yielding in 96 to Nerva, the first of the "five good emperors." * Thus from the death of Vitellius in 69 to the end of the *Pax Romana* in 180, citizens of the Empire enjoyed all the benefits that benevolent paternalism could bestow. "The five"—Nerva (96–98); Trajan (98–117); Hadrian (117–138); Antoninus Pius (138–161); Marcus Aurelius (161–180)—were humane and gifted statesmen who brought close to perfect execution the system worked out by Augustus. If in the end they failed, that failure came from the nature of autocracy which the so-called principate masked but could

not essentially alter; that is, from the Augustan attempt to "will the impossible, making inevitable the impracticable."

The advent of Trajan (98) signaled the trend toward cosmopolitanism which came to characterize life in the later Empire. The Julio-Claudians were Romans, members of two of the city's oldest and most honored families. Vespasian, although not Roman, was at least Italian. But Trajan was neither, having been born in Spain of stock which had separated from its Italian roots 300 years before. To him, Aeneas and the Roman gods were merely interesting legends, of little consequence as part of a political rationale designed to meet problems of statecraft. During his reign the commonwealth's most distant boundaries were reached. Dacia—modern Rumania—was added, and generous (overgenerous, for they had soon to be relinquished) portions of the ancient Near East—Armenia and Mesopotamian Parthia. In both old and new provinces new roads were built on a grand scale. Naturally, many were constructed primarily to serve military needs, but many were built to expedite travel and commerce.

With Roman peace, Roman law, and Roman roads serving it, commerce naturally continued its prosperous ways. And as the sprawling Empire thus became an everexpanding free-trade area, correspondingly and causally it served as a cultural magnetic field. As such, it attracted and fused Eastern and Western religions, philosophies, laws, and the forms and substance of literature and art. Steady development of this cosmopolitan trend depended upon the Empire's remaining a manageable unit. Trajan's successors diligently worked to effect this. Hadrian went so far as to construct permanent limits along the Danube and in England (Hadrian's Wall)—a clear indication that imperial boundaries had been set.

* The last Flavian, Domitian, instituted a reign of terror in the last years of his rule; but this was an exception and, fortunately, a brief interlude.

Hadrian

Under Hadrian, Trajan's successor, the cosmopolitan trend was consciously and actively encouraged. Particularly significant was the continuing development of law and jurisprudence. Here the Roman was at home; here, for once, he was creator. We have seen how in the early days the Romans codified law in the Twelve Tables. Subsequently new statutory enactments were added. But the genius of Roman law lay more in interpretation and the place given to precedent than in static legislation. Legislation, the letter of the law as it applied to Roman citizens (the *ius civile*), existed and was sufficiently detailed. But the interpreters of this law, the *praetors* and the *juris prudentes*,* often modified it as they applied it to various kinds of concrete cases.

Moreover, the web of commercial life bound Roman and non-Roman in an intimate association which law and equity served to regulate. The Roman solution was to set up a general imperial system of contractual relationships. These were based upon provisions of the *ius civile* which either were or could be made applicable by imperial edict or judicial interpretation. This wider body of law, progressive in principle and embracing the whole state and not just the Roman part of it, was called the *ius gentium*.

Gradual denationalization was, of course, implicit in this process. Consequently Roman law had become, by the end of the fourth century, universal law. Of still wider scope, though more amorphous and only indirectly applied, was that body of general principles dealing with fundamental human rights—the *ius naturale*. Long since, philosophers and moralists had set forth certain ideas regarding the good life. Imperial jurisprudence came to recognize these as worthy maxims, even if

they were not always practicable. In effect, then, this natural law served as the ideal toward which positive law pointed.

Hadrian's contributions were real and substantial. A number of his judgments came to be embodied in the corpus of Roman law. He collected and collated previous imperial pronouncements which bore upon his own decisions; under him the appointment of Praetorian Prefects was made with due regard for legal talent. "Often enough in Hadrian's decisions are seen the motives which determined him. Humanity, natural equity and a justice that proceeds from deep ethical sources must be the judge's support. . . . In difficult cases philosophers or doctors are referred to as authorities. . . . The final redaction and codification of the Praetorian Edict by the jurist Salvius Julianus, which he made the Senate raise to be a norm, also shows that he desired, in legal matters as in organization of the state, to make the creative will of the ruler prevail." [4]

Antoninus

This progress of developing law, of general peace and prosperity, and of the cosmopolitanization of the imperial state continued in the twenty-three year reign of Antoninus Pius, Hadrian's successor. Indeed, this period marked the apogee of the *Pax Romana*. Antoninus well deserved the title "pius" bestowed upon him by Senate and people. Save for Marcus Aurelius he was the most sensitive, gentle, humane ruler in the whole of Roman history. Accordingly his subjects could not praise him enough. Many had been the exaggerated praises composed by skillful rhetoricians showered upon emperors in the past, even upon such debased rulers as Caligula and Nero. But they had been calculated panegyrics motivated by favor-seeking and greed. The laudations of Antoninus were sincere. Aristides the Sophist, for example, "describes the state of the Roman Empire in terms of glowing

---

* Unofficial jurists whose training and native abilities gave their opinions something of the authority attaching today to the decisions of official members of our higher courts.

4. *Cambridge Ancient History*, Vol. II, p. 314.

admiration. The richness and happiness of the countries of the Empire testify to the excellence of Roman government. Everywhere towns have been founded or restored and a place of honor has been reserved for Hellenic culture. The Roman World is administered as a single household which enjoys a perpetual holiday, and is safeguarded from external aggression by the discipline of the Roman army." [5] Even the Senate, long the ark of anti-imperial sentiment, found in rule and ruler only praiseworthy features. The Mediterranean civilization seemed at last to have achieved permanent political stability. One ruler, one state, and one law combined to produce and sustain an age of peace and plenty.

Marcus Aurelius

Associated with Antoninus during the last fourteen years of his reign was his adopted son, Marcus Aurelius. During these years the younger man's nobility of character had clearly shown itself, and the Empire's peoples confidently looked forward to a continuation of good times. If Plato had been alive at Marcus's accession he might well have believed that in the new ruler his ideal of philosopher-king had been realized. In a sense he would have been right. The new ruler personified to a remarkable degree "the virtues that had been Rome's glory." Preeminently he embodied the essence of *Pietas*. By nature and training a philosopher, he ruled not for glory but rather reluctantly from a sense of duty. His gentle and compassionate stoicism is reflected in his book of devotions which we know as the *Meditations*. In them we sense a quality akin to that which motivated the founders of the world's great religions. He admonished man to "see that the godhead within thee have the guardianship of . . . one who has taken his post like a soldier, who awaits the bugle that shall

sound his recall in all readiness to obey." Like Christ he taught that:

It is peculiar to man to love even those who do wrong. And this happens, if when they do wrong, it occurs to thee that they are kinsmen, and that they do wrong through ignorance and unintentionally, and that soon both of you will die; and above all, that the wrong-doer has done thee no harm, for he has not made thy ruling faculty worse than it was before. [6]

The End of Pax Romana

But in spite of Marcus' genuine talent for statecraft, his devotion to duty, and his noble character, his reign marked the end of the great Roman peace. Virtually the whole period of his rule (161–180) was spent conducting military campaigns. Various portions of the provinces of Germany and Raetia were invaded by tribes from the north. Rebellion broke out in Britain; in the East a whole spate of wars developed. At the same time Rome suffered from one of the most disastrous plagues of her history. And to these troubles were added the harassments of famine. For nearly a score of years Marcus jumped from one trouble spot to another. Not infrequently he was forced to return to the same area when it was discovered that pacification had not been complete. It is true that at his death the frontiers still held; but the signs were ominous. Teutonic tribes to the north had been repulsed; but they were still there, still active, and were to grow bolder. Financial strains were so severe that in one period the Emperor had been forced to auction off family jewels and other valuables to meet military expenses. The felicities of the age had somehow and quite suddenly vanished. "It was as though a mysterious night descended on the bright day."

If, as one authority has warned, "to

---

5. Paraphrased by H. M. D. Parker, *The History of Rome*, Barnes and Noble, New York, 1958 (2nd ed.), p. 38.

6. *The Thoughts of the Emperor M. Aurelius Antoninus*, translated by George Long, G. P. Putnam's Sons, New York and London [n.d.], pp. 194–195 (VII, 22).

speak of a 'decay' of the Roman empire at this period would be premature," it is nonetheless necessary to note the static spirit of the times which blanketed the whole period of the "good emperors" and which passed for contentment. Actually the glossy, brilliant external features of the age masked an inner decay, an imperceptive willingness to expend the cultural capital that the Augustan solution and its hopeful reception had built up. No matter how well-intentioned the rulers were, they made no move to introduce or to allow others to introduce political innovations pointing toward a more independent citizenship, or even decentralized control. No program was devised to reduce the gap between the wealthy few and the impoverished many. No thought was given to the great despoiling of the human soul that the institution of slavery necessarily effected. If the Empire was surrounded by *limites* that retarded invasions, it was also encompassed by psychic *limites* that held back the free play of man's creative powers and needs.

At Marcus' death in 180 the succession passed to his son Commodus who was almost the complete antithesis of his father. The Empire, in fact, witnessed a reenactment of the scenes of Nero's reign. Court favorites were given the highest civil and military positions. Thus released from responsibilities the new emperor gave himself over to the grossest debaucheries. Many of his palace days and nights were spent in open carousing with mistresses and "pretty boys." The demure mask of the Principate that most of his predecessors had been careful to keep in place slipped in his careless hands. All who cared to look could see the imperial power in its raw state. The Praetorian Prefect became a kind of Oriental vizier. Alien Eastern gods were lavishly worshiped in court circles. Just before his death the young Emperor proclaimed a new trinity— Isis, Serapis, and himself. The Senate, alternatively cowed and bribed, offered no opposition. As for the Roman mob, it wildly hailed an emperor who dramatically entered the arena to slay bears and panthers before the thrill-hungry crowds that packed the amphitheater. Either this tragicomedy or the machinery of imperial government had to give way. In 192 desperate conspirators arranged for his athletic trainer to strangle the mad ruler in his bath. Thus ingloriously the Antoinine line petered out.

The year 192, like the year 69, was one of four emperors. For eighty-seven days Pertinax, who had been Commodus' City Prefect, wore the purple. But when he disciplined the Guards who had elevated him to the throne, they cut off his head and paraded it through the city, meanwhile offering his place to the highest bidder. A wealthy senator, M. Didius Julianus, purchased the crown and wore it uneasily for a few weeks. But restive troops along the Danube had other plans. Their favorite was Septimius Severus who, after a citizen-soldier had obligingly assassinated Julianus, rode into the city to be proclaimed by legionaries and Senate alike.*

Under Septimius (Punic born and reared) and his immediate successors, order was restored and the Empire entered its third century intact. But it was a very different empire from the Augustan dream. Living frankly now on the sufferance of the soldiers, it would last only so long as military strength lasted. The Golden Age, heralded by Virgil, planned by Augustus, and winsomely developed by the Antonines, was over. It is true that the Empire was to survive for many years; but not in faith and hope. The vision was gone. If the Virgilian vision is thought of as pointing to a release of purposeful energy it had, in fact, long since faded—possibly as early as the Neronian period. For at no time thereafter did Roman civilization show those

---

* Actually, three other claimants were put forward by different sets of troops; Septimius had to spend several years putting down his rivals.

creative scars which mark the struggle of a dynamic society.

The Culture
of the Silver Age

This reduction of the heroic tension is clearly reflected in the literature of the period, significantly called the Silver Age. Contrary to the less peaceful regimes preceding it the Principate had severely curtailed liberty of expression. The growing material comforts of the times had created a superficial contentment which tended to drug any Ciceronian impulse that might have challenged the imperial censorship. This combination of coercion and self-induced atrophy of the will resulted in a literature that, while often elegant, was rarely inspired or inspiring. When not precious or pedantic it was often bitterly captious. And almost always, whether bourgeois or bitter, it feared its tomorrows. The foibles of the present or the glories of the past were safer.

Literature: Seneca and Pliny

Seneca (3 B.C.–A.D. 65), for a while Nero's adviser, produced nine tragedies and numerous prose essays. The tragedies were brilliantly written but smacked of the contrived display so characteristic of Silver Age literature. Drenched in blood and violence, they caught passing attention; but they are regarded today only as interesting museum pieces. His philosophical essays have fared better. In them he preached benevolent stoicism as a cure for the psychic *malaise* of his society. If he was suspected of not practicing what he preached, still the rhetorical force which marked his presentation of stoic benignity has made his dialogues live.

No less polished and as suavely constructed are the letters of Pliny the Younger (62–113). Most of them were written with an eye to publication and hence lack the spontaneity and unconscious self-revelation of Cicero's correspondence. But

Pliny's touch is so urbane and his ability to turn the winsome phrase so masterly that his letters attract in spite of their artificial flavor. Of special importance for us is the wealth of historical data found in much of his correspondence. As governor of Bithynia during Trajan's reign, Pliny wrote endless inquiries to his master concerning the administrative and social problems that demanded his attention. Through these letters we get a close and detailed picture of one segment of provincial life, and of imperial administration in action. The following excerpt reveals Pliny's puzzlement over the correct treatment to be accorded to a new religious sect.

It is my invariable rule, Sir, to refer to you in all matters where I feel doubtful. . . . Having never been present at any trials concerning those who profess Christianity, I am unacquainted not only of the nature of the crimes, or the measure of their punishment, but how far it is proper to enter into an examination concerning them . . . whether repentance entitles them to a pardon; or if a man has been once a Christian, it avails nothing to desist from his error; whether the very profession of Christianity, unattended by any criminal act, or only the crimes themselves inherent in the profession are punishable; on all these points I am in great doubt. In the meantime the method I have observed towards those who have been brought before me as Christians is this: I asked them whether they were Christians; if they admitted it, I repeated the question twice, and threatened them with punishment; if they persisted, I ordered them to be punished; for I was persuaded, whatever the nature of their opinions might be, a contumacious and inflexible obstinacy certainly deserved correction. . . . it appears to be a matter highly deserving your consideration, more especially as great numbers must be involved in the danger of these prosecutions, which have already extended, and are still likely to extend, to persons of all ranks and ages, and even of both sexes. In fact this contagious superstition is not confined to the cities only, but has spread its infection among the neighboring villages and country. Nevertheless, it still seems possible to restrain its progress . . . it is easy to conjecture what numbers might be reclaimed if a

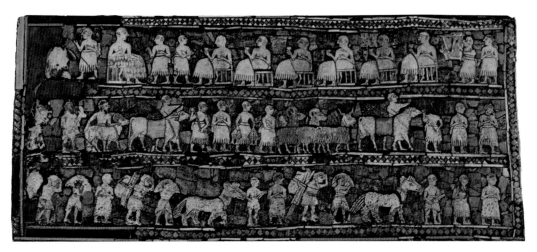

"Royal Standard" of Ur, ca. 3500–3000 B.C. *Early settlers in the valley of the Tigris and Euphrates, the ancient Sumerians developed a high level of craftsmanship, exemplified in this inlaid panel. Believed to be part of a standard carried in ceremonial functions, the panel represents a victory feast at which the spoils of battle, including teams of asses, are being exhibited before the king (seated at the left in the top register) and other celebrants. (Courtesy of the British Museum, London)*

Harvest Scene, *Tomb of Menna, Thebes, ca. 1415 B.C. The high development of Egyptian civilization owed much to the fertility of the land, for the success of this agrarian economy gave people the physical security needed to pursue the arts. Here Menna, the Pharaoh's field scribe, stands in a shelter recording the wheat harvest going on around him. To his right an official surveys the land to determine how much grain per acre is owed in taxes. At Menna's left delinquent taxpayers are being punished. (Scala)*

Duris, School Scenes, Red-figured Kylix, ca. 480 B.C. *To the humanistic Greeks, the goal of education was a man developed to his highest potential, physically perfect and culturally accomplished. Specialization was not encouraged. Boys of the privileged classes were expected to attain proficiency in both* gymnastic, *the cultivation of the body, and* music, *which to the Greeks meant not only singing, composing, and playing instruments, but also the sciences, literature, and the general cultivation of the mind. The outside of this* kylix, *or drinking cup, shows a young boy receiving instruction from schoolmasters trained to set and recite poetry to music, one of the few specialized professions. In the side shown above, the instructor is demonstrating how to play the* aulos, *or double flute, and how to write with a stylus on a wax tablet. In the side shown below, the student is learning to play the lyre and is reciting poetry to his master, who follows along with his scroll. Both sides of the* kylix *picture the boy's slave sitting at the right. (Staatliche Museen, Berlin)*

François Vase, ca. 550 B.C. *Greek religion centered around both mortal heroes and gods endowed with human form and behavior. This famous* krater, *used for mixing wine and water, depicts events in the history of the house of Peleus, whose most famous member was Achilles. The hero himself is shown on the handle. The horizontal bands illustrate the procession of the gods to the wedding of his parents, the funeral games for Achilles' friend Patroclus, and the Caledonian hunt. (Scala, Courtesy of Museo Archeologico, Florence)*

Battle of the Romans and Barbarians, *Ludovisi Sarchophagus,* ca. A.D. 250. *This relief, which shows the Roman cavalry victoriously trampling the barbarian invaders, celebrates the familiar institution through which the vast territories of the Roman Empire had been annexed and defended, the Roman Army. But by the time the relief was carved, the walls of the Empire had already begun to weaken under the barbarian onslaught, and within a century the decline and fall of the Empire was well underway. (Scala)*

View of a Harbor, ca. A.D. 50. *Expert engineers and city planners, the Romans constructed an elaborate system of roads and harbors to accommodate the flourishing trade of the Empire. Harbors such as the one pictured here, on the Bay of Naples, were fully equipped with wharves and warehouses for the unloading and storage of cargo. The goods were then transferred to wagons which carried them along the vast network of Roman roads to their destination. (Scala)*

general pardon were granted to those who shall repent their error.[7]

Juvenal and Martial

The mood of the post-Augustan Age found satire its most acceptable mode of expression. Among the many practitioners of this pungent if oft-times oblique form of critical assessment Juvenal was preeminent (c. 50–130). His themes were the decadent state of society, the exploitive idiosyncracies of man, the dry-crust literature of his day, the almost complete depravity of women (he was a bachelor), the defense mechanisms that shield human conduct, and the like. Very much like him in style although less appealing as a human being was Martial (40–104), whose epigrams have made him as quotable as Pope. Beyond the virtuosity of his rhetorical genius there is almost nothing lovely about the man. Because Domitian found his flattery pleasant Martial paid the dictator the most ridiculous public attention. But when the tyrant was assassinated and Rome made it clear how despised he was, Martial quickly faced about and heaped calumny upon his one-time benefactor. Everything and everybody became grist for his mill. At times he was the indignant champion of virtue, as when he wrote:

Till nightfall you lunch, till nightfall, Turgidius, you dine, and with all sorts of wine day and night you reek. And although you are careful of your person, you are unwilling to take a wife; your unwillingness says: 'A chaste life pleases me.' Turgidius, you lie; this is not a chaste life. Would you have me tell you what is a chaste life? Moderation.

But (more in character) he also wrote, "Aper is abstemious, sober; so what is that to me? A slave I praise so, not a friend." And, "Do you wonder, Aulus, that our good friend Pabullius is so often taken in? A good man is always a greenhorn." [8]

Suetonius and Tacitus

Among the biographers of the period none achieved the eminence of Suetonius whose *Lives of the Caesars* has furnished many historians with delectable anecdotes. Scorning the flourish of so many of his contemporaries Suetonius set down in factual, unadorned fashion the findings of his tireless research. Unfortunately he seemed unable to discriminate between the significant and the trivial, so that we find him accepting court gossip as enthusiastically as the data of the archival material with which he worked. As a matter of fact, his impish habit of retailing scandal of all sorts cost him his job as court scribe. But since he was so close to court circles his works, in spite of the dross which encumbers them, remain of value.

Far surpassing him, and indeed all others of the Silver Age, is Tacitus (c. 55–c. 120), whose fame rests on a much broader base than as the depicter of German tribal habits and folkways. Little is known of his personal life. Active in political affairs (he served one term as consul), Tacitus wrote from the perspective of the "old Roman." His diligent research and his supreme gifts of expression combined to make his histories worthy of the most careful study. It is true they do not suggest some of the advantages that the Empire undoubtedly brought to the Mediterranean world. But his republican bias is so open and obvious that the reader has little difficulty in keeping it in calculation. His most important works are the *Annales*, which detail the events of Roman history during the period of the Julio-Claudian emperors; *Histories*, which carry the story down through Domitian; the *Germania*, our most important single source on primitive Teutonic culture; and *Agricola*, a biography of his father-in-law, who was governor of the province of Britain.

7. F. C. T. Bosouquet, ed., *The Letters of Caius Plinius Caecilius Secundus. . . .* George Bell and Sons, London, 1878, pp. 393–395.

8. Martial, *Epigrams,* Vol. II, tr., W. C. A. Kerr, in *The Loeb Classical Library,* William Heinemann, London 1920, pp. 531, 355, 341. "Aper" is a pun on the word for pig.

Plutarch and Aristides

A contemporary of Tacitus, and a native of Greece, Plutarch (46?–120) has put a host of later historians in his debt. His first work was a series of lives of outstanding Greek political figures. Finding these sketches so well received he paralleled them with their Roman counterparts. These *Lives* have long played a disproportionately large role in shaping the schoolboy's notions of Roman political character.

A fellow Greek, but of a later generation, Aelius Aristides (115–185) produced a number of grave and graceful essays on the general state of society of the Roman world of his time. They are both literature and sociological documents.

Medicine and Astronomy

Although not as literature, the works of two Hellenized provincials may be noted. Galen of Pergamum (131–201) devoted most of his life (apart from his duties as personal physician to three of Rome's emperors) to compiling the "scientific" medical lore of his day. The monumental treatise that he published remained the standard textbook for the next thousand years. Ptolemy (*c.* 150), an Alexandrian scholar, did similar services for astronomy and geography. The Ptolemaic theory of the constitution of the heavens was accepted as late as the seventeenth century, when Galileo was brought to his knees for challenging it.

Architecture

If the trend in literature during the post-Augustan years was downward, developments in architecture moved in the opposite direction. Authorities still argue whether the architectural triumph of the Flavian and Antonine periods reflected native Roman genius or skillful discipleship. Certainly the three Greek orders of the column were directly taken over by the Romans. And the pediment of the Pantheon would have looked quite at home in Periclean Athens. But the Romans were not mere copyists. After a period of tutelage they adapted Hellenistic form to Roman spirit so masterfully that the argument about creativity loses much of its point.

The architectural efforts of the Greeks — and particularly the Athenians — were directed toward the construction of buildings designed to glorify the *polis* and to provide settings for meaningful living. In one degree or another probably these aims also characterized Roman efforts. But glorification of the imperial impulse was certainly the predominant theme. From Augustus on, Rome was deliberately made into a showpiece; and provincial "Romes" tried hard to keep pace with the mother city. It is not without significance that the most outstanding examples of Roman originality in this discipline were the triumphal arch and the commemorative column.

A good example of the former is the Arch of Titus, begun by Vespasian to memorialize Titus's triumph over the Jews. In this massive monument the imperial mood is dramatically expressed. Masterly reliefs on both outer and inner walls of the arch tell the story of this victory. There is the long procession of booty-bearing figures, booty which included the sacred trumpets and the seven-branched candelabrum. Titus looms large as the invincible conqueror, a kind of god, crowned by Victory. The whole work, in short, stirs in the spectator the restless urge to share in the celebration. The even more elaborate Arch of Constantine bespeaks the same exultant pride (although the craftsmanship is second rate). Impressive columns served a like purpose. The Column of Trajan, made of costly marble, reaches a height of 100 feet, topped by a statue of the conqueror; spiraling scenes of his victories over the Dacians make up the intricate sculptured relief.

Since Roman taste ran less to theater than to grand exhibitions, Greek models again were modified. To cater to the Roman yen for spectacles, huge "bowls" were con-

Arch of Constantine.

The Colosseum.

structed; notably the Amphitheatrum Flavianum, truly deserving of the name given it in medieval days—the Colosseum.* Its facade, the features of which are well known to every schoolboy, was probably modeled on that of the Theater of Pompey. But behind the facade are examples of bold, original, skillfully executed structural design. To sustain the burden of a capacity crowd (perhaps 75,000), the barrel vault was abandoned in favor of a new technique —cross or groined vaulting. Another innovation was the triple-entrance hall, dominated by nave and aisles that lost width as they fed their way into the yawning depths. Intricate underground stalls and passageways honeycombed the substructures. From these areas issued the wild beasts and gladiators that brought the cheering multitudes to their feet. To give the Romans a holiday they would not soon forget, Vespasian decreed 100 days of games to celebrate its opening. Much of this glorified stadium still stands, its ruins attracting modern tourists as its bloody spectacles drew Roman crowds 2000 years ago.

The same bold use of cross-vaulting permitted architects to construct magnificent *thermae* or baths. Dozens of them were built in Rome. Hardly an Italian or provincial community dared call itself a city without at least one public bath. Those built by Caracalla and Diocletian were the most famous. One of them could accommodate 3000 bathers; the other was so sumptuously constructed and appointed that Caracalla is scarcely remembered for anything else. The soaring magnificence of its main hall was framed and supported by a series of groined vaults, affording vast space unbroken by supporting columns.† Some rooms were provided with steam baths; others allowed bathers the titilation of hot, warm, and cold sprays. Recreation and games rooms, as well as gossip corners, were elegantly furnished.

In spite of the Augustan impetus given to religion, temples in the Empire period received less attention than in Republican days. Sometimes, almost as an afterthought, they were adjoined to the baths. The most famous example of temple architecture is the Pantheon, rebuilt by Hadrian on the site of the Pantheon of Agrippa erected by Augustus. Its Grecian facade is composed of rearing columns supporting a typical pediment. The central chamber is an enormous room which "has a perfection of form and a restful sense of space that is without equal in the whole world." The dome is of concrete, without vaulted support. At the top is a 20-foot opening through which sunlight could filter to light up the whole. Many official palaces, governmental offices, and palatial private homes were constructed in the Flavian-Antonine period. By the end of the second century, Rome could justly claim that it yielded in splendor to no city of the fabled East.

Sculpture

Reference has already been made to the relief work which profusely adorned arches, columns, and public buildings. Sculptors worked in the round as well. Some of the statuary of this period, particularly of the emperors, rivaled the best efforts of the Greeks. It is true that the Roman penchant for both realistic detail and sumptuous ornamentation ruled out true expression of classic idealism. But any other kind of art would have been un-Roman; what was lost in classic artistry was made up in historical documentation. "The grim smile on Vespasian's dour but not uncongenial countenance, the boyish openness of Titus's face, the hard intellectual cast of Domitian's eyes and forehead, the searching glance of Hadrian and the almost mask-like passivity of M. Aurelius—all these distinguishing features are reproduced to the life." [9] The spiraling

---

* Actually derived from its proximity to a huge statue.
† Copied by the architects of the one-time Pennsylvania Station in New York City.

relief recited history no less than did the pen of Livy and Tacitus (the campaigns of the Dacian and Danubian wars, for example), often filling gaps left by written accounts long since lost. In all, of course, the theme of Empire was dominant.

Economic Conditions

Imperial stirrings which gave rise to the construction of arches, columns, amphitheaters and other edifices stimulated economic development as well as aesthetic impulses. Aping though not matching the grand public projects, private buildings such as villas and baths, constructed by wealthy families, reached unprecedented sumptuousness. Military roads, fanning out in all directions, served commerce no less than military security as they linked up widespread trading centers. By the time of the Antonines the volume of goods produced and distributed throughout Western Europe reached a level as high as any reached across the next 1000 years. Limited commerce was even carried on with portions of the Far East.

The working classes, however, did not partake proportionately in the Empire's affluence. It can be argued that so much prosperity must have offered some material comforts to the servile order, and no doubt it did. But existing evidence suggests that although the mass of slaves received adequate nourishment they lived in the meanest circumstances. And since their numbers were so great, they naturally kept down the wage level of the free worker so that he too lived at a bare subsistence level. Under Nerva and his successors the *alimenta* provided easy loans to free farmers, the interest from which was used as grants to needy families. This program bettered the lot of thousands of citizens; but the very need for such a system makes obvious the serious maldistribution of wealth.

9. Max Cary, *A History of Rome Down to the Age of Constantine,* Methuen and Company, London, 1954 (2nd rev.), pp. 686–687.

In the early part of the third century general economic conditions suffered a serious decline. This was mainly due to three causes. As wealth accumulated in the hands of the new nobility and the equestrian order, extensive investment in real estate (an old Roman habit) was given free play. A large portion of working capital was thus drained from other enterprises. Also, with the end of Roman conquest the Empire, having no new provinces to exploit, was thrown back on its own resources. Potentially such resources were ample enough, but the habit of exploiting new territories rather than applying intensive efforts to opportunities in the old rendered them less remunerative. Finally, from the reign of Marcus Aurelius on, border raids increased in number and scope until there existed what can only be called a permanent state of invasion. Thus, from the end of the second century on, more and more of the Roman world's wealth was diverted into the imperial exchequer to meet the constantly mounting costs of war. In the end, taxes for military purposes soared to such figures that both confidence in the regime and business incentive were killed. In short, as the third century opened, *civilization* slowly yielded to *militarization.*

The Disintegration of the Roman World

"Pamper the Army and Despise the Rest"

Technically the Principate continued in existence throughout most of the third century. But actually the accession of Septimius Severus (193–211) marked its end. For the new ruler frankly acknowledged the army as the force that held the Empire together. His reported advice to his sons epitomizes the change: "Pamper the army and despise the rest." Among the precautions taken by the new ruler was the disbanding of the Praetorian Guard, hitherto made up almost exclusively of

Italians, and the creation of a new one open to soldiers from the provinces. This went far to break the power of the political generals in Rome who so often had made and unmade emperors.

Under Septimius both size and pay of the army were substantially increased, aggravating the already heavy tax burden. Because the Emperor showed promise of preventing a recurrence of the terrible events of 69, probably most citizens were willing enough to pay the stiff price that stability seemed to demand. But had they wanted to protest no effective means were at hand. The assemblies had long since fallen into disuse. For 200 years the Senate had been a kept body. Now under Septimius it was all but abolished. Twenty-nine of its recalcitrant members were executed; the right of Senators to be tried in their own assembly was taken from them; many administrative posts, hitherto held by Senators, were now assigned to equestrians.

The death of Septimius in 211 made way for Caracalla (211–217), who carried on the policies of his father, though without his intelligence and discipline. During his brief reign he decreed citizenship for all free persons in the Empire (212). And he constructed elaborate baths which became forever associated with his name. For the rest, he took up where Nero had left off; and he met the same fate. Several others of the Severi tried to recapture the firm grip of Septimius but without success. From 235 to 285 the Empire can only be described as a shambles. In this period 23 emperors were put up and pulled down by plundering armies. Warfare along the borders became endemic. Everywhere barbarian forces stabbed at the imperial frontiers and infiltrated the regions of their breakthroughs in Italy, Spain, and Gaul. In the East, Mesopotamia and Syria suffered incursions by Persian invaders. Serious plagues broke out, devastating whole regions. To appease the bewildered and panic-stricken populace emperors occasionally ordered a round of Christian persecutions. Municipal administration sank to a fantastic state wherein citizens were drafted to fill offices and forced to remain at their thankless tasks upon pain of death. A further significant symptom of the decay of Roman power was the decision of Aurelianus, Emperor from 270 to 275, to build a protecting wall around Rome. Once world conqueror, the mighty city had itself become an object of foreign aggression.

Temporary Recovery under Diocletian and Constantine

As the third century drew to a close a temporary recovery was effected by Diocletian (284–305) and Constantine (306–337). Diocletian created what has been described as the Dominate. All pretence that the ruler was merely *princeps* was abandoned. To make his point clear Diocletian set up an elaborate court modeled after the absolute despotism of the East. He frankly called himself Lord and added the royal diadem to the ancient republican purple. Citizens were turned into subjects. Officials approached the throne in the posture of abject obeisance, kneeling before the Lord and kissing the hem of his robe. Law was made, interpreted, and administered at the will of the sole ruler. Rome ceased to be the working capital of the state for, with the northern and eastern regions demanding constant attention, it was found advisable to transfer the seat of government to Milan. In the East a sub-capital was set up where an auxiliary Augustus was established, together with a successor-designate who was given the title of Caesar.

Division and Infiltration

Under Constantine the division into western and eastern "empires" was further developed (though not consummated) when the Emperor moved his court to the ancient Greek city of Byzantium, renamed Constantinople (330). For by this time the spilling of the German hordes into the western provinces was marked with such frequency and force that imperial attention in that area was constantly required. The continuing thrusts and eventual conquest of the western Empire by the Germans make it easy to misjudge their actual strength and numbers, to conclude that these northerners swamped the Empire by sheer mass. But in actual fact it is but "picturesque nonsense to speak of the Roman Empire as being overwhelmed by German's 'teeming millions.'" It is true that for several hundred years population pressures had been building up along the Rhine-Danube frontiers. By mid-third century large numbers of Goths, Alamanni, Franks, Saxons, Vandals, Burgundians, and Lombards were on the move as Eurasian peoples relentlessly pushed in from the east (for the groupings and movements of the Germanic tribes see map, p. 166). But at no time did they constitute more than a small minority of the western Empire's population. Moreover, many had peacefully infiltrated the provinces to become Roman subjects. Nor were they at any time a match for the Romans in military organization, tactics, and equipment. The potency of their threat and part of their eventual success lay in the Roman practice of withdrawing legions from border posts to fight each other in the endless game of emperor-making. This game Diocletian and Constantine, by establishing absolutism, halted for a time. But Constantine understood that even under absolute rule the imperial machinery was safer in the East.

Acceptance of Christianity

Even more significant than Constantine's abandonment of Rome was his acceptance of Christianity. For 250 years Christians had suffered intermittent persecution, sometimes mild, sometimes severe. Under a recent Augustus, Galerius (305–311), alternate policies had been tried. From extremely savage repression he swung, just before his death, to granting qualified freedom of worship. After the battle of Milvian Bridge (312) in which Constantine won a great victory over his rival, Maxentius (a victory to which he ascribed the intervention of the Christians' God), Constantine decreed complete religious toleration and restoration of all Church property. Thereafter State and Church worked in close union until, in 392, Christianity was made the sole, official religion.

Barbarian Invasions

With Constantine's death in 337 internal dissension broke out afresh amid, of course, raids and invasions of the ubiquitous Germans. From here on the Empire went into steady and sharp decline. In 378 the Goths defeated imperial troops in the battle of Adrianople. The next year a new emperor, Theodosius (379–395), pacified the invaders by allowing them to settle within the Empire. Upon his death the Empire was divided into its western and eastern sections; Arcadius (395–408) succeeded to power in Constantinople, and Honorius (393–424) in Rome. The latter's long term was a troubled one. The usual plots and factional struggles, while bad enough, were not the chief worry, for by this time the pressure of the German tribes was irresistible. In 410 the Visigoths, under their able chieftain Alaric, attacked Rome and looted the city for three days. Buildings and temples suffered relatively little damage, but Roman morale was crushed. In 452 a marauding army of Huns and their allies, led by Attila, again threatened Rome which somehow was reprieved by the daring intervention of Pope Leo I. In the next century, Justinian (527–565) reunited the two portions of the empire in what, presumably, he thought was a permanent settlement. It was not. Even if the reunion had endured the empire would have been Byzantine, not Roman. The strength and grandeur of Rome had long since faded. Whatever the beliefs and nostalgic yearnings of Westerners of the fifth century, the Roman World had passed into history. (A more detailed account of the Germanic

MOVEMENT OF
GERMANIC TRIBES
to c. A.D. 450

GERMANIC
PEOPLES

SAXONS

FRANKS ALAMANNI

BURGUNDIANS

Empire
boundary

LOMBARDS

OSTROGOTHS

VISIGOTHS   R O M A N   E M P I R E

VANDALS

invasions and their influence in shaping a new society in the West is reserved for the opening section of the following chapter.)

The Fall of Rome

A summary view of Roman history such as ours usually ends with a consideration of the question of why Rome "fell." Scholars agree that there is no single answer; some insist that there are no satisfying multiple answers. But the question has a haunting insistence that cannot be denied. In the present study attention, from time to time, has been deliberately focused on particular decisions and developments that suggest the outlines of a judgment. Hence if the facts presented have been of sufficient scope and pertinence, if their organization has lent itself to reasonably clear understanding, and if the occasional interpretive comment has been rooted in the logic of fact, then there is no need for detailed consideration of the question.

It is only fair, however, to list representative samples of the more commonly argued theses. The first answer was framed by the ancients themselves. Contemporary pagans insisted that Rome fell because Romans deserted their ancient deities for the Chris-

tian God. In their view the Empire had only received the divine wrath it had invited. Against this, St. Augustine (in *The City of God*), held that anarchy, violence, and chaos had often been visited upon ancient empires; and that, anyway, man's true home was heaven, not Rome. In medieval times emphasis was laid upon moral decay. Still later the old pagan argument was given a new turn: the triumph of Christianity had both watered down the Roman will to conquer and rule, and had turned Roman purposes and hopes from this world to the next. At all times many have seen the collapse as merely the result of inexorable barbarian pressures. The twentieth century has added economic arguments, particularly those stressing loss of fertility of the soil, and the debasement of monies by emperors from the third century on. Another case has been made on biological grounds. From the second century B.C., this argument runs, slaves and other migrants flooded into the peninsula from all parts of the Mediterranean world, particularly from the East. Across the centuries the incidence of intermarriage rose until the native vigor of the original Roman stock had been crossbred out of existence. (The latter argument, it might be added, has little support among historians.) If Everyman, as Professor Carl Becker has affirmed, is indeed his own historian, the implicit arguments of this chapter as well as those just listed may or may not find their way into the individual reader's own assessment. But judgment of some kind is inescapable.

The Roman Legacy

In similar case is the question, what is the Roman legacy? Again, if the narrative text has served intended purposes an extensive enumeration of Rome's contributions is supererogatory. But here too a summary review is in order. In language the debt is obvious. Virtually all tongues of Western Europe and the Western Hemisphere either derived from Latin or were substantially shaped by it. Roman law is still the basis of Western jurisprudence. No less important is the idea of the world state. For hundreds of years a large portion of the human race lived under one government and one law. The memory and meaning of that experience lives in and influences our own day—else we are hard put to explain such a contemporary experiment as the United Nations and its forerunner the League of Nations. A final contribution is of still greater import. The *Pax Romana* failed to achieve the Augustan dream. But it gave Rome time and opportunity to form itself into a cultural sponge which could and did absorb the endowments and treasures of Hellenistic civilization, treasures which in turn were passed on to the medieval world and thence to our own. No matter how dubious one may be of the phrase "the grandeur that was Rome," these achievements stand.

THE CHRISTIAN COMMUNITY

Origins of the Christian Faith

Roots of Christianity

As the Augustan dream of world empire faded with passing centuries the Christian vision of another kingdom took on form and features. Rome, the city of man, ruled for a time; but the City of God would endure forever. In this faith Western civilization made a new turning.

The vital center of the new religion is Jesus Christ. But its setting and formative elements reach far back into pre-Christian times. A thousand years before Jesus a God-centered Jewish nation was founded. Yet earlier, Hebrew leaders and judges had implanted in their countrymen the conviction that Yahweh had chosen them as his people. The covenant was clear and binding: in return for abiding faithfulness, God would richly bless them and, in the fullness of time, give them custodianship of his eternal kingdom.

But the straight way of the Lord was hard to keep, and more than once his Chosen had turned from it. Invariably catastrophe had followed—dispersion of the Ten Tribes, Babylonian Captivity, Macedonian conquest and, in the last years of the pre-Christian era, seemingly endless harassment as Alexander's successors used the Holy Land as a pivotal area for imperial conquest. A climax was reached in 168 B.C. when a Seleucid emperor, Antiochus IV, outlawed Judaism. To dramatize his decree he profaned the Temple by ordering the erection within its holy precincts of an altar to Zeus. The Jewish reaction is clearly described by the wirter of one of the apocryphal books of Hebrew scriptures:

In those days, arose Mattathias . . . a priest . . . [who] spoke with a loud voice [saying], Though all the nations that are under [Antiochus'] dominion obey him, and fall away every one from the religion of their fathers, and give consent to his commandments, yet will I and my sons and my brethren walk in the covenant of our fathers. God forbid that we should forsake the law and the ordinances. . . . Then many sought after justice and judgment, went down into the wilderness to dwell there: both they and their children, and their wives, and their cattle; because afflictions increased sore upon them. . . . Then came there unto [Mattathias] a company of Assideans, who were mighty men of Israel, even all such as were voluntarily devoted unto the law. Also all they that fled from persecution joined themselves unto them, and were a stay unto them. So they joined their forces, and smote sinful men in their anger and wicked men in their wrath.[10]

10. Maccabees, 2:1–44, *passim.*

This Maccabean revolt, as it came to be called, was successful, regaining for the Jews not only their right to worship Yahweh but political independence as well. Unfortunately their new kings turned out to be as rapacious and godless as their foreign oppressors. In disgust and desperation a segment of the more pious Hebrews, the Assideans (or Hassidim), withdrew to the desert stretches east of Jerusalem. There, about 135 B.C., they established a number of religious communities under the rule of their own priests. Of the hopes and habits of these puritan Hebrews the newly discovered Dead Sea Scrolls have revealed much. Exilic Hebrews had been extraordinarily influenced by Persian religious ideas. So it was only natural that the Assideans came to combine strict orthodox observance of the Law with certain Zoroastrian beliefs. Among these were the struggle between the sons of light and the sons of darkness, the coming of a Right Teacher who would prepare the way for an anointed one, and a final day of judgment when the Messiah would usher in the eternal Kingdom of God.

Apocalyptic Hopes

As a matter of fact, a number of Gentiles throughout the Mediterranean world held similar apocalyptic beliefs. The times too long had been out of joint. There had been too many wars and too much wickedness. Surely the end of history was at hand when the forces of creation would rescue the elect, destroy the world, and inaugurate a reign of heavenly peace. Such hopes, however, were hard to hold to within the framework of current patterns of religious thought. For the educated, Greek philosophy had undercut these patterns; for the masses, they seemed barren and unprofitable.

Now and then from the prevailing wilderness of discontent and disillusion a voice would cry out in both warning and hope. One such was the strident call of John the Baptist (flourished c. A.D. 25) who urgently preached the need for men to repent against the day of the coming Kingdom. Intended for the whole world, John's Assidean-tinged message actually reached only into scattered Jewish communities. But where it was heard its impact was strong. The Lord, he declared, was interested not in elaborate liturgy but righteous living. Let those whose hearts were dark with sin repent and prepare for the coming of the Eternal Day. The substance of regeneration—inner purification—should be outwardly symbolized by the rite of baptism. But let men not wait, lest the day of the Lord overtake them before they had loosed the bonds of the Evil One. Soon bands of disciples formed to preach the word of the Baptist, spreading it west to the sea and north into Galilee. Among those quickened by the message was Jesus of Nazareth.

Life and Teachings of Jesus

Contemporary references to the life and import of Jesus and to the formation of primitive Christian societies are almost wholly restricted to those found in Christian scriptures. In Mark, probably the first Gospel to be written, we learn that after John the Baptist was imprisoned by Herod, Jesus went forth proclaiming, "The time has come; the Kingdom of God is upon you; repent and believe the Gospel." [11]

For however long his ministry lasted, (one, two, or three years), this was its burden. Although Jesus rarely made specific reference to Satan, the Evil One, he constantly emphasized the conflict between the true and the false, and its imminent resolution. Perhaps his many miracles of healing and of controlling the forces of nature are best understood in this light: the force of evil was great, indeed, but the power of God was greater; and in the end God would prevail. This is not, of course, to imply Jesus' indifference to human want

11. From *The New English Bible,* New Testament, Oxford and Cambridge University Presses, 1961, p. 58.

and suffering. On the contrary his whole mission was motivated by compassion. Explicitly and implicitly he affirmed that God is love, ineffably merciful and total. Whether the Sermon on the Mount as we find it in Matthew is a summary of his teachings or a literal recording of a specific event matters little. It epitomizes Jesus' concept of the meaning of existence:

> How blest are those who hunger and thirst
> to see right prevail;
> they shall be satisfied.
> How blest are those who show mercy;
> mercy shall be shown to them.
> How blest are those whose hearts are pure;
> they shall see God.
> How blest are the peacemakers;
> God shall call them his sons.

And again:

> You have learned that our forefathers were told, "Love your neighbor, hate your enemy." But what I tell you is this: Love your enemies and pray for your persecutors; only so can you be the children of your heavenly Father. . . . You must therefore be all goodness, just as your heavenly Father is all good.

The Lord's prayer reflects this same tension. The Father's name is to be hallowed, not Satan's. His kingdom will come, not the Evil One's. We are to seek God's help in resisting the Devil's lures: "And do not bring us to the test, But save us from the evil one." [12]

There can be little doubt that Jesus believed the end of the world at hand; that his divine mission was to proclaim the good news (that is, "Gospel") of the coming Kingdom; and that his purpose was to prepare for its advent. Theologians differ on the question whether Jesus, during his life on earth, understood that his suffering and death constituted vicarious atonement for man's sins, the reconciliation of God and man (though, of course, this soon came to be and remains still the cardinal truth of orthodox Christianity).

Early in his ministry he chose 12 men, the Apostles, to help him spread the good news. With them he went about the countryside preaching and performing miracles. Most of his time was spent with the common people; as the friend, as Luke has it, "of tax gatherers and sinners." More than once he was chided for living too much with the wayward and lowly. Often he seemed to go out of his way to reprove men of wealth and position. Such men, we must suppose he believed, had succumbed to worldly temptations. To the rich young man who earnestly sought of him how he was to be saved, Jesus finally advised the giving away of all his wealth. On another occasion he plainly said, "how difficult it is for a rich man to enter the kingdom of heaven."

But his sharpest strictures were directed against his own religious leaders. They had become, he felt, corrupted by privilege and power, more interested in forms and legalisms than true spiritual guidance. "Ye tithe mint and cummin, and neglect the weightier matters." He likened them to gleaming coffins of death, "whited sepulchers." Naturally these leaders, drawn mostly from the Sadducees and Pharisees, viewed unfavorably such a man and such a message.

Jewish Reactions

For years the Sadducees had held high priestly offices. From them were recruited the majority of the Sanhedrin, Judah's supreme legislative and judicial body (functioning, of course, under Roman supervision). Conservative in all things, they rejected whatever was not rooted in the ages, such as the doctrine of resurrection and the existence of angels. Both concepts were late in becoming a part of Jewish thought; hence both were, to them, unorthodox additions to the ancient Law. They differed from other sects, also, in holding that man possessed absolute free will. To this elite group Jesus and his teachings seemed heterodox and dangerous.

The Pharisees (and the most learned

12. *The New English Bible*, pp. 8, 10–11, *passim*.

among them, called the Scribes) were the chief spiritual leaders of the Jews. To the written Law they added tradition; and conceived themselves to be the most reliable interpreters of both. Filling the chief offices of the synagogues they came into direct and intimate contact with the people. Modern readers of the New Testament often derive from it a somewhat distorted picture of these leaders. It is true that they often were officious and hypocritical. But unlike the Sadducees they made genuine efforts to keep the ancient Law alive and meaningful by incorporating into it or adding to it concepts and practices consonant with changing times. That they sometimes overreached themselves is undeniable. But their basic intention and function should not be overlooked, nor their courageous work in saving for their people the corpus of the Jewish faith after the destruction of Jerusalem in A.D. 70. In an effort to balance our usually one-sided view it has been argued that

The Pharisees were the only guides and teachers who had a word for the people; and they, and none other, saved from the ruin of the Jewish nation all that could be saved, and spoke to the stricken hearts of their countrymen the words of comfort and hope. The Judaism which has come down through the centuries is essentially Pharisaism.[13]

Nonetheless, the charges leveled against them by Jesus and the Gospel writers were not without substance. Often they *were* interested more in the letter of the Law than in the spirit. At the dawn of the Christian era they often *did* lack vision and nerve; and they could be unbearably stuffy.

In contrast to them was another, smaller sect called the Essenes. No mention is made of them by New Testament writers (because they were so close to the way of life preached by Jesus and his followers?). But secular sources yield some information

about their beliefs and practices. For them the true faith was that proclaimed by the prophets. Long since, they believed, these had become corrupted by the doctors of the Law. Wealth and worldly power were bad, *per se,* and should be renounced in favor of the ascetic life. Prayer, work, and worship, in preparation for the Day of the Lord, almost exclusively occupied their time and directed their energies.

Except for the emphasis upon asceticism, these were essentially the ideas stressed by Jesus. Within a short time his message and his miracles had attracted a large following; too large, as it turned out, for the Sadducees and the Pharisees. To them John the Baptist and Jesus were only two of a lengthening series of prophets who excited and agitated the Jewish people. They stirred up unrest, subverted priestly authority, and made the great Roman rulers uneasy. Especially serious was the latter concern. Many of the multitudes acclaiming Jesus clearly understood him to be the herald of the New Jerusalem. Unchecked, this subversive movement could only result in harsh Roman countermeasures.

To prevent this the Sanhedrin finally acted. Using one of the new prophet's own disciples, the betrayer Judas, the high court arrested Jesus and brought him to trial, charging blasphemy. Witnesses were brought to testify that the prisoner had made claims for himself that only God could make. As Mark relates it,

Then the High Priest stood up in his place and questioned Jesus: "Have you no answer to the charges that these witnesses bring against you?" But he kept silence; he made no reply. Again the High Priest questioned him: "Are you the Messiah, the Son of the Blessed One?" Jesus said, "I am; and you will see the Son of Man seated on the right hand of God and coming with the clouds of heaven." Then the High Priest tore his robes and said, "Need we call further witnesses? You have heard the blasphemy. What is your opinion?" Their judgement was unanimous: that he was guilty and should be put to death.[14]

13. R. T. Herford, *The Pharisees,* p. 52, quoted by M. J. Enslin, *Christian Beginnings,* Harper and Brothers, New York, 1938, p. 113.

Under Roman law the Sanhedrin could not execute a sentence of death. But it could make a petition to the local Roman governor, Pontius Pilate. At first Pilate, satisfied that the accused was not guilty of serious subversion, was inclined to let Jesus off with mild punishment. But the priests and officials were insistent. To pacify them Pilate acquiesced, and thus Jesus' life and ministry were brought to an end.

Collapse and Revival of the Faith

At once the movement seemed to collapse. Many of Jesus' followers had already left him after he made it clear, just before his death, that he was not interested in re-establishing the old Jewish kingdom. Others took his death as proof that the Sanhedrin had been right; another false Messiah had fooled them for a while. Even the eleven remaining Apostles were cast down — one of them, Peter, going so far as to deny he had ever known Jesus. Seemingly another subversive minor movement had had its brief hour and was no more.

But soon the Apostles and others of the disciples regained their courage and faith. For them Jesus had brought a new vision not to be dimmed. That this vision shone brightly is historically demonstrable. Without it the great risks and sufferings gladly accepted by those who, then and long after, lived by the sign of the cross cannot be explained. But what exactly this vision was, what its features and form were, no historian can say. A conjecture may run thus: Jewish understanding of the nature of Yahweh had developed, it is true, far beyond the concept of dread Sovereign; to, indeed, that of kindly Father. But never before had Jews seen Godliness walking the earth, incarnate in man. They had long known what it meant to be God's Chosen People; but to be direct sharers of the Holy Spirit was as ecstatically new as it was past understanding.

Moreover, the gentle love-force emanating from their teacher still moved and enthralled his followers; life could never again be the same. Finally, the crucified one was reported to have risen from his tomb and to have appeared to some of his disciples before his ascension into heaven. Like a fanned flame their spirit flared again. Exaltation replaced despair. Many of his words, ambiguous at the time he spoke them, took on startling significance.

The Son of Man is now to be given up into the power of men, and they will kill him; and three days after being killed he will rise again. . . . Heaven and earth will pass away; my words will never pass away. But about that day or that hour no one knows, not even the angels in heaven, not even the Son; only the Father. . . . Keep awake, then, for you do not know when the master of the house is coming.[15]

So the little band of believers, led by the shamed and chastened Peter, rallied their forces and their hopes. In the synagogue of Jerusalem they naturally formed a group apart. For most Jews the Messiah was still the promised one. For the disciples the Messiah had come, conquered death, ascended to heaven, and would return to establish the eternal Kingdom of God. Their task was to continue to purify themselves, call others to repentance, and generally to prepare for the Day of the Lord. Some Jews, partly persuaded by the Apostles' teachings, asked what they should do. As recorded in Acts (2:38–39) Peter was prompt and incisive in response: "repent . . . and be baptized, every one of you, in the name of Jesus the Messiah for the forgiveness of your sins; and you will receive the gift of the Holy Spirit. For the promise is to you, and to your children, and to all who are far away, every one whom the Lord our God may call." [16]

The Apostle could hardly have realized how very far that call would be carried in the long centuries that lay ahead.

14. *New English Bible*, p. 87.

15. *New English Bible*, pp. 74; 83–84.
16. *New English Bible*, p. 200.

The Spread of the Faith

The Work of Peter and Paul

Peter's reference to the Holy Spirit was probably prompted by the Pentecostal "miracle of tongues." On that day, as reported in Acts, there came to the believers "tongues like the flames of fire which caused a great commotion among the population." Suddenly Jesus' followers seemed able, according to the writer of the book of Acts, to praise God and to prophesy in the language of the foreign residents of Jerusalem—Romans, Parthians, Medians, Egyptians, Arabians. In explanation of the phenomenon Peter pointed out that God had promised that a portion of his spirit would be given to man in the last days. Jesus, past herald and present savior, had brought about the fulfillment of that promise. All who wanted to be saved could be saved. Thereupon, according to Acts (2:41), "those who accepted his word were baptized, and some three thousand were added to their number that day."

Meantime communities of believers beyond Jerusalem had been established. To care for families of Christian hellenized Jews, seven deacons had been appointed in the home church. After one of their number, Stephen, had been stoned to death by some fanatical Pharisees, the rest fled the city. Following this scattering, numerous congregations were formed throughout the land: in Samaria, Caesarea, Joppa, certain Galillean towns, and as far north as as Damascus and Antioch (see map, opposite).

In Damascus there shortly occurred an event of especial significance. One of the most vigorous of the new sect's opponents —by his own words "a Pharisee of Pharisees"—was Saul of Tarsus. He had witnessed the lynching of Stephen at Jerusalem and had busied himself harassing Christians in various cities. The congregation at Damascus attracting his attention, he set out for that city. But his plans strangely miscarried. En route to the city he was struck by a blinding vision of the risen Messiah. As later recorded, Paul (as he soon came to be called) "heard a voice speaking to him, 'Saul, Saul, why are you persecuting me?' 'Who are you, Lord?' he asked. 'I am Jesus whom you are persecuting,' was the reply. 'But stand up now and go into the city and you will there be told what you must do.' " In Damascus Paul met with Christians who baptized him, whereupon "without delay he proclaimed Jesus in the synagogue, declaring that he is the Son of God." [17]

The conversion of Paul marked a turning

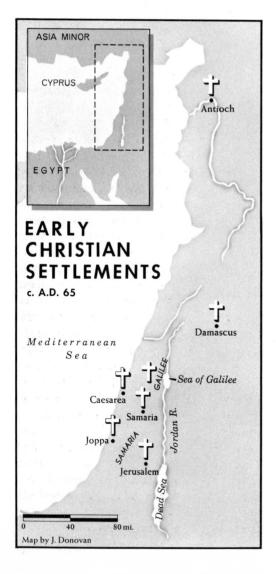

EARLY CHRISTIAN SETTLEMENTS

c. A.D. 65

ASIA MINOR

CYPRUS

Antioch

EGYPT

Mediterranean Sea

Damascus

Sea of Galilee

GALILEE

Caesarea

Samaria

SAMARIA

Joppa

Jordan R.

Jerusalem

Dead Sea

0   40   80 mi.

Map by J. Donovan

point in Christian history. Hitherto Gentiles had, for the most part, been excluded from the disciples' teachings. Believing that his special task was to evangelize the Roman empire Paul set out on a number of missionary journeys which eventually encompassed most of the Mediterranean world. Galatia, Phrygia, "Asia," * Macedonia, Greece, Italy, and possibly Spain heard his preaching and felt the effects of his organizing genius. By the time of his death (c. 65) the Christian Church had become established in communities ranging from one end of the Great Sea to the other; and where it had originally been Jewish it was now almost wholly Gentile. Others such as Peter and Philip were partly responsible for this metamorphosis but Paul was its chief agent.

Nor was this, great as it was, his only influence. For the religion that took root in the Empire was markedly different from that preached along the byways of Galilee. By his own avowal Jesus had come not to destroy the Law but to fulfill it. But for Paul the Law was of little consequence. Jesus had said, repent and be saved. To Paul repentance of sins was no longer enough. One must experience and acknowledge an abiding faith in Christ Jesus as both Messiah and Redeemer. Again, Jesus gave not the slightest hint that he intended to found a church. Paul on the other hand not only spoke of a new church but was its principal creator. Furthermore, though Jesus several times referred to his coming death and resurrection, neither formed the crux of his message. With Paul, Christ crucified and risen became the central article of faith.

17. *The New Testament in Modern English,* tr. by J. B. Philips, The Macmillian Co., New York, 1958, pp. 262–263.

* The reference here is to a Roman province in western Anatolia.

"World" Evangelism: Development and Difficulties

By the end of the first century of our era nearly 50 churches bore witness to the newer, Pauline Christianity. In most of them exhorters, elders, and deacons preached the word and cared for the witnesses. In some, bishops presided over affairs of the congregation. By then, too, it had become apparent that the second coming of Christ was not to be expected on the morrow. Hence a closer concern came to be felt for the establishment of enduring institutions and for increased efforts to evangelize the world.

For the latter the times were ripe. Throughout the Mediterranean world, as we have seen, faith in the ancient religions had waned. Moreover, the democratic hopes of ancient Greece and the yearnings of the commoners of republican Rome lay buried under the brutalizing effects of centuries of imperialist wars and growing authoritarian Roman rule. The world thus held few allurements for the common man; his dissolving faith offered little hope for another chance beyond the grave. He was, in short, materially and spiritually prepared for the "good news" of Christianity. Since the new religion recognized the spiritual equality of the sexes, women especially were drawn to it. In addition, the willing martyrdom of many believers proved an impelling force. Few devotees of the official cults or mystery religions were ready to lay down their lives for their convictions. Many Christians, beginning with St. Stephen, gladly did, causing one early Church Father to declare that "the blood of the martyrs is the seed of the church." Finally, the readiness of Christian leaders to incorporate into their creed and worship ideas from other religions where these appeared compatible with the central message of Christianity added an appeal for those seeking salvation yet loath to part from familiar religious habits.

The multiplication of congregations,

scattered over wide areas, naturally created doctrinal and organizational problems. All Christians, it is true, believed in Jesus as Lord and Savior. But interpretations and practices were far from uniform. In Jerusalem, for example, leaders of the Church emphasized Jewish law and tradition, insisting in particular upon circumcision. On the other hand, many converts in Antioch were so thoroughly hellenized that the mother church felt called upon to send Paul to them lest Jewish roots be lost (though, as we know, quite the opposite result occurred). Farther west, Christians, accustomed to Roman law and procedure, invested their beliefs and practices with a legalism and organizational structure quite at variance with patterns developing in Asia Minor and Palestine.

Formulation of Christian Doctrine

Even more important was growing divergence of doctrinal beliefs. This was almost inevitable. The New Testament was not yet in existence; the only Bible these early Christians knew was the body of canonical Jewish scriptures. Necessarily the experiences of the members of the new congregations had to serve as guides to right interpretation and understanding. But since the particulars of these experiences differed from congregation to congregation, doctrinal beliefs—expressions of such experiences—naturally lacked uniformity.

One example of such variation of beliefs concerned the nature of the Savior. Certain churches in Asia Minor came to hold that Jesus was, to use theological terminology, Very God, but not Very Man. To them the Savior, that is, God, took on the appearance of earthly reality, but not its substance. This concept doubtless grew out of Gnostic doctrine. Gnosticism had developed, probably out of Zoroastrianism, some time before the advent of Jesus. Devotees of this religion believed in the existence of two worlds, the good and the evil. In their view God was, in the be-

ginning, pure spirit and pure goodness. Desiring to share his nature, he permitted another world (or, in Gnostic phraseology, an emanation) to develop out of himself. From this second creation another evolved and then still others until our own world came into existence. But by this time God's nature, his pure spirit and goodness, had become so corrupted that the latest emanation constituted a world far apart from its original essence. In this way, according to Gnosticism, evil was born.

Accordingly, all "earth children," physical creatures worlds removed from God, were born in sin. If they would, however, they could return to primeval goodness. The road back to God was long and difficult but possible by reasons of the existence of "the Primal Man . . . , the man who existed [by God's grace] before the world, the prophet who goes through the world in various forms and finally [according to later Gnostic Christians] reveals himself in Christ." To many early Christians seeking redemption from sin by a good God, such divine knowledge (which is what "gnosticism" means) was welcome. It explained how evil could exist in the world coevally with a good God. It threw light on the Evangelist's affirmation that, "In the beginning was the Word, and the Word was with God, and the Word was God." * And it clarified, for them, the redemptive role of the Savior.

Most Christians, however, found such teachings utterly unacceptable. If Christ only *seemed* to be real, that is, true man, his human suffering necessarily was unreal. It followed that atonement was likewise unreal and hence man was left in sin, unsaved. They also vigorously protested the Gnostic Christians' disregard for the Old Testament. To Gnostic Christians the latter was patently valueless since "it portrayed Yahweh as immoral, or at least amoral; for them one could choose either

---

* An affirmation that identifies Jesus with God and that holds, therefore, to the preexistence of Jesus.

morality or the Jewish scriptures but not both." They chose morality, and in the place of the Old Testament, they increasingly tended to substitute Paul's letters to the churches, Luke's Gospel and its supplement, the book of Acts. To non-Gnostic Christians this was cutting the vine from the roots, and they called for a cleansing in the church to prevent "deceitful schemers" from killing the Word.

So disputes multiplied. Left unchecked, these doctrinal differences could have resulted in the complete fragmentation of the Church. On the other hand, reconciliation of contrary interpretations was quite impossible in the absence of an agreed upon body of writings which set forth the true scheme of salvation. (Even with such, of course, varying interpretations were possible; but this is another question.) Therefore Church authorities set themselves to the task of determining what was revealed truth and what was not.

It was a difficult chore. Paul and his colleagues, it was true, had written many epistles to the early churches. But they certainly did not intend their letters to be taken as inspired scripture. Rather, they sought to admonish erring communities, point out pitfalls, sustain flagging spirits, or counteract the effects of what they considered false teachings or immoral behavior. For their part, the Gospel writers were mainly interested in committing oral Christian history and teachings to permanent written form. But churches found both letters and Gospels so useful and enlightening that they adopted the habit of reading from them at divine services. By the end of the second century this habit, combining with the necessity to combat centrifugal doctrinal tendencies, led the Church Fathers to determine which were truly inspired writings and which were not. The selection came to include thirteen Pauline letters, seven "catholic" or general epistles, the tract called the Hebrews, the book of Revelation, the Acts of the Apostles, and accounts of the Gospel according to Matthew, Mark, Luke, and John. Confirmed by Church councils across the next two hundred years, they came to be considered and called the New Testament, as divinely inspired as the Old.*

Persecution of the New Faith

Meantime a new difficulty beset the spreading faith. So long as Christian communities were small and scattered Roman authorities paid them little heed. But already within a generation after Christ's death they had established themselves in Rome and in other metropolitan areas where they quickly attracted unfavorable attention. Almost invariably they tended to denounce this world as transitory, unreal, and evil. Naturally such a negative attitude was resented by the general populace. In the eyes of the latter, the Christians themselves were most unrealistic. They denied concrete facts which both experience and reason supported. They refused to cooperate in the joint enterprise of day-to-day living. And they were forever decrying enjoyment of physical satisfactions that all normal, sensible human beings sought. Moreover, they met in secret, practicing allegedly unholy and sacrilegious ceremonies. Before long the charge of cannibalism came to be leveled against them; for what was their "holy meal" but the eating of human flesh and the drinking of human blood? Finally, they categorically refused to acknowledge any lord but their own, even when officials made it plain that rejection of required "loyalty ceremonies" clearly proved dissentients to be subversive enemies of the state.

It is hardly surprising, therefore, that they soon became objects of persecution.

* Again, it is hard to avoid oversimplification. Actually, some early Christian communities preferred one or more other letters or gospels to those named above. It was not until around 700 that complete agreement was reached among the main body of Christians. Even as late as the sixteenth century a Council of Church Fathers deemed it necessary to reaffirm the canonicity of several New Testament writings.

As early as the writing of the book of Hebrews (*c.* A.D. 100) we find Christians commiserating with one another and adjuring all to keep the faith. "Remember the days gone by, when, newly enlightened, you met the challenge of great sufferings and stood firm. Some of you were abused and tormented to make a public show, while others stood loyally by those who were so treated."[18] The "public show" may refer to the first great persecution in A.D. 64 under Nero when the Emperor, to quiet Roman mobs distraught over a great fire which destroyed much of their capital city, blamed Christians for the deed and had hundreds of them arrested. According to Tacitus they were, after their conviction,

covered with wild beasts' skins and torn to death by dogs; or they were fastened on crosses, and when the daylight failed, were burned to serve as lamps by night. Nero had offered his Gardens for the spectacle, and gave an exhibition in his Circus, mixing with the crowd in the habit of a charioteer. . . .[19]

Under Domitian (d. 96) persecution seemed to center in the ranks of the so-called upper classes, some (admittedly doubtful) evidence pointing, for example, to the execution of two relatives of the Emperor himself. The book of Revelation, probably written at this time, is almost entirely concerned with the struggle going on between Rome — "the mother of whores" — and the Church. In the second century three prominent Christian leaders, among many nameless fellow-sufferers, were martyred: Ignatius, bishop of Antioch; Polycarp, bishop of Smyrna; and Justin Martyr, one of early Christendom's profoundest philosophers. Not all Roman Emperors, it is true, were active persecutors of the new faith; many were indifferent, some were back-handedly sympathetic.

18. *The New English Bible*, p. 384 (Hebrews 10:32–34).
19. Tacitus, *The Annals*, Harvard University Press, Cambridge, 1937, Vol. IV, p. 285 (the Loeb Classical Library).

But the steadily growing power of the Church, the desperation of city mobs as the Empire slowly declined, and the fierce resolve of the later emperors to stamp out seditious heresy brought to Christians continuing and heightened tribulations.

Christian Apologetics

To answer mounting criticism and to blunt the thrust of growing persecution a number of Christian intellectuals began to publish explanations ("apologies") of their faith and practice. An early and typical example is Justin Martyr (*c.* 100–165) who, about 150, wrote his first *Apology*. In it he explained that Christian congregations met the first day of the week to offer thanks to God for his merciful bounties, to express love for each other (symbolized in the "Kiss of Love"), and to confirm and enlarge their common faith. He took care to make clear that the holy meal was made up of prepared bread and water "mingled with wine." What he called the memoirs of the apostles were read from, together with portions of the writings of the prophets. After the offering of prayers, members were asked to consider the material needs of fellow Christians. "The rich among us come to the aid of the poor, and we always stand together." The collection of offerings concluded the service after which the communicants dispersed to their homes.

Following Justin, other apologists published works designed to prove their faith, combat heresies, and regularize church ceremonies. Irenaeus (125–202), Bishop of Lyons, composed a comprehensive work — *Against Heresies* — which served for centuries as a model of its kind. In it he not only pointed out which beliefs and practices were false but systematized the presentation of orthodox teachings. He made it clear that God's special grace was given to the Apostles through the laying on of hands and, through the Apostles, to the ever-renewed body of clergymen. He listed the canonical books of the New Testament and, at the same time, insisted that the Old

Testament was divinely inspired and hence a basic part of Christian Scriptures. Certain fundamental practices, such as baptism, were categorized and explained.

Church Organization; Petrine Doctrine

In a further effort to guard against ouside attack as well as to guarantee internal harmony, the early Fathers set about effecting a general order and system of Church government. Even during apostolic times, as we have seen, a nuclear organization had evolved. To instruct the faithful and to administer approved rites, presbyters (that is, priests), were needed. To carry out necessary charitable functions others, called deacons, were called upon to serve. Over all activities some administrative agent was needed; hence arose the office of *episcopos* — "overseer" or bishop. By the middle of the second century most churches were organized in this fashion. Since bishops exercised general supervision of all church affairs they soon came to a predominant position of authority. When questions arose over correct doctrine or behavior or when united action was needed to stand against a hostile pagan group most Christians looked to the bishop for leadership; and most bishops readily accepted this responsibility. Later, as congregations multiplied and clustered in given areas, one particular "overseer" within each area came to exercise authority over the others. For the most part, these areas were closely modeled after the Roman province or diocese. Of all the provinces of the Empire, that which had Rome as its capital was regarded as the seat of ultimate authority. Quite naturally, many Christians turned to the Roman diocese — or "see," as the religious province was called — for guidance. In addition, tradition and a particular scriptural passage combined to help fix authority there. In the Gospel according to Matthew (16:18–20) Jesus said to Peter "You are Peter, the Rock; and on this rock I will build my church, and the forces of death will never overpower it. I will give you the keys of the kingdom of Heaven; and what you forbid on earth shall be forbidden in heaven, and what you allow on earth shall be allowed in heaven." Asserting that Peter had founded the Church at Rome, tradition thus held that this Apostle and his successors constituted authority to which all important religious questions must be referred for final settlement. It is true that in the early centuries other diocesan leaders disputed this dictum. And most of the Eastern churches (making up the Greek Orthodox Church) came finally to repudiate it. But in the West this view prevailed and the bishop of Rome, from about the fourth century on, became the Holy Father (*papa,* that is, pope) and head of the visible Church.

Rise of Christian Monasticism

Not all Christians, however, were satisfied with this institutionalization of their faith. To them the world and its ways were pure evil. The Church, in allowing itself to become a part of the world, partook of its evil even when clearly stressing its own redemptive role. Rather what was needed, they felt, was a complete renunciation of the way of the flesh, including marriage and the gratification of sensual appetites. Christians, they argued, could not have it both ways. If earthly existence is basically a struggle between Satan and God, the true believer, by tolerating, or worse, adjusting to the material world, in reality succumbs to Satan and forfeits his place in the Body of Christ. Only complete renunciation could bring salvation.

Very early in Christian history, therefore, some members of the faith, acting singly, practiced the ascetic life. In 285, St. Anthony collected a number of them and founded a monastery in Egypt. In the next century St. Basil, of Caesarea, established another order. In 529 St. Benedict introduced monasticism₁ in the West. At Monte Cassino, near Naples, he set up a community dedicated to celibacy, poverty, and obedience to its leader (abbot). Thereafter the movement spread until monasteries dotted every area of Western Europe.

At first the Church regarded this development with apprehension. How could the Christian flock be shepherded and enlarged if its leaders withdrew from it? Moreover, most communicants were clearly unable to hold to the ideals of celibacy and poverty. On the other hand, could priests and bishops denounce a way of life practiced by Jesus and Paul? Eventually a workable compromise was reached. Monastic ideals admittedly represented the highest demands of the faith. For the few men who could so live, the Church would officially recognize their commitments and exercise general supervision over their communities. For the rest—the vast majority—it would continue to offer a ministry that, though looking to their ultimate salvation, demanded less of weak mortals.

Trials and Triumph

Continuing Threats to Christian Unity

By the fourth century Christianity had spread its faith and its institutions over most of the ancient world, steadily growing stronger as the Roman Empire declined. As we have seen, under Constantine it was given official status and support. Several generations later Theodosius made it the sole, legal religion (392). From a feeble esoteric sect it had become an ecumenical faith. Pagan victory altars had yielded to the cross. Soon its leaders would wield more power than claimants to the imperial throne. Even so, dangers from within and without made its future not altogether certain. For many years theologians had been unable to agree, for example, on the nature of the God they worshiped. The Apostles had spoken of Father, Son, and Holy Spirit. Was God one or three? Many (es-

pecially Eastern) ecclesiastics were inclined to hold the second and third persons of the Trinity as unequal in nature and power to God the Father. On the other hand, some insisted upon the unhumanness of Jesus; or, in creedal language, that the Christ was Very God but not Very Man. In 325 at Nicea (near Constantinople) a great gathering of churchmen met to deal with this question. Leading the forces arguing that the second and third persons were inferior to the creator was Arius, a presbyter of North Africa. Against him were arrayed Athanasius, bishop of Alexandria, and his followers who insisted all were of one substance—that One was Three and Three were One. Eventually the Trinitarians won the council to its position and the mystery of the Trinity became both the foundation of the orthodox creed and an important force in unifying Christian believers. But for a time the question threatened to split the Church asunder.*

Even more menacing than Arianism and other heretical doctrines were rival religions, especially Mithraism and Manichaeism. The former, older than Christianity, was an offshoot of Zoroastrianism. Its central figure, Mithras, was worshipped as the god whose principal mission was to overcome the leader of the sons of darkness and to bring man to a perfect understanding of the power and majesty of Ahura Mazda. By the first century B.C. a number of mystery cults, centering their worship in Mithras as the divine mediator between God and Man, flourished in the East. Several of them reached Rome about the same time as Christianity. For well over two centuries they vied with it for popular acceptance. Like Christianity, Mithraism laid emphasis upon strict moral behavior, preached a day of judgment when the good would win heaven and the evil suffer the

---

* But not all Christians then or now could accept the doctrine. Modern dissenters are called Unitarians.

fires of hell, and looked to a divine savior for atonement of human sins. Authorities still cannot agree on the question of who borrowed from whom. But it is certain that both religions shared common observances and practices—Sunday as the holy day of the week; December 25th as the date of their savior's birth (here evidence seems clear that Christianity borrowed from Mithraism); the use of holy water; and participation in a common sacred meal which offered sustaining grace to believers. It was probably the conversion of Constantine to Christianity which assured the latter its seal of victory over the Mithraic faith, at least at so early a date.

But while one rival was entering decline, another, Manichaeism, was posing a new, even greater challenge. Like Mithraism it was rooted in Zoroastrian sources. Born in the third century, Mani, its founder, combined certain Mesopotamian religious beliefs with those of eastern Christianity to produce a faith which, for a while, seemed destined to conquer not only the Near Orient but the West as well. Even such a Christian stalwart as St. Augustine had been a staunch Manichaean before his conversion. Indeed for a while, particularly in the fifth century, it appeared likely that intellectuals, and the philosophically minded generally, would carry the new religion to a dominant position in the Empire. In essence Manichaeism postulated the existence of two kingdoms—the world of Light and the world of Darkness. For a time God ruled the world of Light in pure love and justice. But Satan, born of Darkness, came to envy God's world and to desire it for his evil rule. To counter Satan, God created Primal Man. But the Evil One overcame the appointed savior so that God was forced to set himself directly in combat with the spirit of darkness. The god of evil was defeated, but not before the world of light had become streaked with satanic shadows. Thus mortal man is a compound of both good and evil with his ultimate salvation depending upon the thorough cleansing of himself of Satan's spirit. To help him achieve this purity God has sent inspired prophets into the world to sustain and counsel all those who would discipline themselves for such mentorship. Included among these prophets were Abraham, Noah, and Jesus. But the last and greatest was Mani who revealed to man the full measure of salvation.

Similar to Christianity in its ethical content, and like it promising eternal life for the saved, Manichaeism attracted to itself thousands of the declining Empire's weary and distraught subjects. Outlawed by emperors, made anathema by popes, for a time it spread in spite of (and like Christianity, probably in part because of) persecution. But though it lingered on, in one form or another, into the Middle Ages—Albigensianism for example, was largely shaped by it—by the eighth or ninth century Manichaeism had lost most of its followers to Christianity. The latter's especial concern for the unlearned masses and the steady support given it by imperial officials probably combined with the Christian faith's intrinsic strengths to effect its victory over this and other competitors.

Final Triumph of Christianity

In spite, then, of persecution, serious internal differences, and rival faiths, Christianity emerged as the dominant religion of the Mediterranean world. And since it had so intimately woven itself into the religiosocial life of this world it became, when Rome fell,* the one universal institution around which the Empire's disoriented subjects could rally in their desperate struggle to survive the collapse of Western civilization. The further account of how society created and stabilized a new order under the aegis of the Church will be taken up in the next chapter.

---

* The reference, of course, is to the Western Empire not the Eastern which survived for another thousand years.

SELECTED READINGS

The Empire

A number of titles suggested in the bibliography for Chapter 6 are useful for this chapter also, especially part 3 of Pareti, *The Ancient World;* Boak and Sinnigan, *A History of Rome to* A.D. *565;* Heichelheim and Yeo, *A History of the Roman People.*

Charlesworth, M. P., *The Roman Empire,* Oxford University Press, London, 1958.
> One of the Home University Library titles. In its 200 pages are packed a surprising abundance of facts touching on, among other subjects, work and taxes, the army and navy, the person and position of the emperor, education, art, and "relaxation."

Gibbon, Edward, *The Decline and Fall of the Roman Empire,* Washington Square Press, New York, *c.* 1936 (edited and abridged).
> Despite new evidence and several generations of attack this work remains a classic exposition of the history of this fateful period.

Larsen, J. A. O., *Representative Government in Greek and Roman History,* University of California Press, Berkeley and Los Angeles, 1955.
> Although a little given to the use of technical language, the author presents a readable account of provincial assemblies and how they were transformed during the late Empire period from their original modes of functioning.

Rowell, Henry Thompson, *Rome in the Augustan Age,* University of Oklahoma Press, Norman, Oklahoma, 1962.
> In this small book of some 200 pages there are good sections on religion, morals, ideas, city life, and Augustus's rise to power. Especially valuable for undergraduate reading is the chapter on the New Order. We know of no other book which so succinctly and satisfactorily explains the Augustan blueprint for the new "golden age."

Waddy, Lawrence, *Pax Romana and the World Peace,* Chapman and Hall, London, 1950.
> An interpretive study of why Rome became a great ruling state, and why she faltered and finally failed. The author often suggests, both implicitly and explicitly, parallels with our own times.
>
> Use should be made of appropriate titles in the Loeb Classical Library, especially for the works of Virgil, Horace, Livy, and Ovid.

The Christian Community

Gough, Michael, *The Early Christians,* Thames and Hudson, London, 1961.
> A brief work based in the main upon archeological evidence. After a short historical sketch of the first three centuries of Christianity, it is concerned with a consideration of the first six centuries of Christian art and architecture.

Guignebert, Charles, *Ancient, Medieval and Modern Christianity,* University Books, New Hyde Park, New York, 1961.
> Originally published in 1921 and 1927, this work is written from the standpoint of a non-Churchman. Orthodox Christians will find it offensive; most readers, whether Christian or not, will find it fascinating as a polemical *tour de force.*

Hutchinson, Paul, and Winfred E. Garrison, *20 Centuries of Christianity,* Harcourt, Brace and Company, New York, 1959.
> Most of this book was written by Garrison, whose basic outlook is that of a liberal Christian. It is sound in scholarship and readable in style.

Kershner, Frederick, *Pioneers of Christian Thought,* The Bobbs-Merrill Co., Indianapolis, Indiana, 1930.
> One of the most useful guides through the labyrinth of early Christian theology. The author's style is lucid, his organization simple and effective, his general outlook liberal. The reader will be surprised to discover how much "heresy" has found its way into both dogma and creed of orthodox Christianity.

Loisy, Alfred, *The Birth of the Christian Religion,* L. P. Jacks, translator, George Allen and Unwin, Ltd., London, 1948.
> An interesting attempt by a noted scholar to set forth the genesis and early development of Christianity *sans* miracles and the often special pleading of the theologian-historian.

Asterisk (*) denotes paperback.

MEDIEVAL LIFE

8

Rome's Three Heirs: Byzantium, Western Europe, Islam

BACKGROUND: THE CHRISTIAN EMPIRE

The Mood of the Late Empire

During the three centuries following the end of the Roman imperial line in the West in A.D. 476, the Mediterranean world underwent a profound transformation. Where once a single state had encompassed the far-flung lands of the Mediterranean basin, now three distinct civilizations were established on the ruins of the old Empire. These three—Byzantium, Western Europe, and Islam—differed sharply from one another in style and outlook; all had broken appreciably from the traditions of Old Rome. Yet each, though to a different degree, was a product of the Greco-Roman past. No longer Roman, all were deeply indebted to the legacy of classical antiquity. The rise of these three great cultures

out of the seedbed of the late-Roman state is the subject of this chapter.

Intensification of Otherworldly Outlooks

Each of Rome's three heirs was animated by a powerful transcendental faith. Each, in its own way, was shaped by the intense religious experience of the late Empire itself. Accordingly, our examination of these three successor civilizations must begin with a fuller study than has been possible thus far of the Roman Empire's Christian phase, that is, of the crucial decades between Constantine's conversion and the fall of the Western Empire, when Church and Caesar worked in tandem toward the Christianization of the ancient world.

As Rome grew old, the allegiance of her people gradually shifted from the traditional

183

gods of hearth, field, and city, to potent transcendental deities of the Orient such as Isis, Mithras, and the Great Mother, who promised the priceless gifts of personal redemption and eternal life. Even in the buoyant years of the "five good emperors," imperial culture and prosperity had failed to affect a vast, wretched substratum of the population. And as the peace of the second century gave way to the turbulence and disintegration of the third, an ever-increasing portion of the Empire's inhabitants were reduced to a state of grinding poverty and futility. To men such as these, the shining dreams of classical humanism — an ordered universe, an ideal republic, a good life — were cruel illusions. For them, the world was not enough, and the salvation cults became their one hope.

The older pagan cults of Jupiter, Minerva, and the other deities of the classical pantheon survived the turmoil of the third century but only in profoundly altered form. They, too, were transformed by the great transcendental upsurge of the age. For during the third century all that was vital in the traditional pagan cults was incorporated into a vast philosophical scheme known as Neoplatonism. One of the most influential philosophers of the Roman era, Plotinus, taught this doctrine of one god, infinite, unknowable, and unapproachable except through a mystical experience. Plotinus' god was the ultimate source of all things, physical and spiritual. All existence was conceived as a vast hierarchy radiating outward from God, like concentric ripples in a pond, diminishing in excellence and significance in proportion to its distance from the divine source. Human reason, which the Greeks had earlier exalted, was now reduced to impotence, for the nexus of reality was an unknowable god that lay beyond reason's scope.

Despite their mystical doctrine of monotheism, the Neoplatonists allowed a place in their system for the manifold deities of paganism. The pagan gods were interpreted as symbols of the Neoplatonic god — crude symbols, but useful nevertheless. The pagan pantheon, so radically unsuited to the deepening mood of otherworldliness, was now galvanized and given new relevance by the overarching structure of Neoplatonic philosophy. So it was that the deities of Old Rome came to participate increasingly in the new trend toward mysticism and monotheism. The distinction between Jupiter and Mithras was steadily fading.

Christianity and the Empire

It was in this atmosphere of mysticism and the supernatural that Christianity won its final victories. By Constantine's time the age of questing rationalism and fallible, anthropomorphic deities had long passed, and with the Emperor's conversion and his subsequent victory at Milvian Bridge the triumph of Christianity over its mystical rivals was all but assured.

The Christians were deeply grateful to Constantine, their first imperial convert. But had they possessed the broad, retrospective view available to the modern historian they might have expressed a kind of gratitude also toward Diocletian, their last imperial persecutor. For the ruthless, authoritarian measures by which Diocletian and Constantine revived the faltering Empire had the effect of postponing imperial collapse in the West for nearly two centuries, and the Christians put this borrowed time to good use. Indeed, Constantine's founding of Constantinople provided the foundation for the Christian Byzantine Empire which endured for a millennium. Had Rome collapsed at the end of the third century — had there been no experience of a Christian Roman Empire — the subsequent history of Europe, North Africa, and Western Asia would surely have been substantially altered.

The fourth-century Empire witnessed mass conversions to Christianity under the benevolent support of Christian emperors. From a vigorous, dedicated minority sect, Christianity expanded during the fourth century to become the dominant religion of the Mediterranean world. No longer persecuted and disreputable, Christianity became official, conventional, respectable. And of course it lost much of its former spiritual élan in the process. Moreover, total victory was accompanied by a new surge of internal dissension. The fourth century was an age of bitter doctrinal struggle, and here, too, the Christian emperors played a commanding role. It was only after strong imperial action that Arianism, the most powerful of the fourth-century heresies, lost its hold on the inhabitants of the Empire. Theodosius I (378–395) condemned the Arians and broke their power, making orthodox Christianity the official religion of the Roman state. Indeed, Theodosius proscribed paganism itself and, deprived of imperial sanction, the old gods of Rome gradually passed into memory.

Orthodox Christianity now dominated the Empire; yet old heresies lingered on and vigorous new ones arose.* And although Arianism was dying in the Empire by the late fourth century, it survived among the Germanic peoples along the frontiers. These barbarians had been converted by Arian missionaries during the course of the century, at a time when Arianism was still strong in the Empire, and the persecutions of the orthodox Emperor Theodosius had no effect on the faith of the Germanic tribes. Consequently, when in time the barbarians built their successor states on the debris of the Western Empire, they were divided from their Roman subjects not only by culture but also by the bitter antagonisms that have traditionally separated rival faiths.

Christianity gained much from Constantine's conversion but it also lost much. The post-Constantine Church was less fervent, less dedicated than before; it was also less independent. For the gratitude of Christians toward Constantine almost reached the point of adulation. He was regarded as

a thirteenth Apostle, as the master of all churches, as a monarch whose office was commissioned by God. His regal presence dominated the great Ecumenical Council of Nicaea in 325, and it was at his bidding that the Council denounced Arianism. In the decades that followed, the Arian-orthodox struggle swayed back and forth according to the inclinations of the emperors. First the Arian leaders were condemned to exile, then the orthodox, until at length, late in the fourth century, Arianism subsided under the pressure of the sternly orthodox Emperor Theodosius I. Good Catholics rejoiced when Theodosius banned Arianism, but they might well have been apprehensive of a situation in which such crucial matters of faith depended upon imperial fiat.

A situation of this sort is traditionally called "caesaropapism." It arises from a political structure in which Church and state are both controlled by a single individual — a "caesar-pope." Caesaropapism was a significant characteristic of the Christian Empire, and in the East it became a fundamental ingredient in the organization of the Byzantine state throughout its age-long history. For a thousand years Church and state tended to merge under the encompassing authority of the emperor at Constantinople. His subjects regarded him not merely as a Caesar but as the supreme ruler of a Christian state (or rather, in the eyes of the East Romans, *the* Christian state). As such, he was usually able to depend on the fervent support of his Christian subjects, and their support gave the Eastern Empire the strength to endure. On the other hand, the Eastern emperor's orthodoxy evoked a spirit of uncompromising hostility in districts where heterodox views held sway. The religious disaffection of these districts — most notably Egypt and Syria — resulted in their eventual loss during the opening stages of the seventh-century Islamic conquests.

Dominant in the East, caesaropapism failed in the West. For the fifth century

* See pp. 178–179.

The fusion of Christian and classical traditions is illustrated in the New Testament themes cast on the bronze doors of this fifth-century church.

brought renewed turbulence and, ultimately, political catastrophe to the Western Empire; Western Christians began to doubt the wisdom of placing all their hope in the imperium. Gradually they came to realize that the disintegration of the Empire did not mean the end of the world or the collapse of the Church. Eastern Christians might indeed regard their Empire as the Ark of Christ, but those in the West wisely refused to bind themselves to a sinking ship. Accordingly, the Western Church slowly began to assert its independence of imperial authority, thereby laying the foundation for the Church-state tension that became such a dominant theme in the evolution of European civilization.

The Latin Doctors

The conversion of Constantine was merely one event in the long and significant process of fusion between Christianity and Greco-Roman civilization. We have already seen this process at work among the early Christian apologists who sought to present their faith in the intellectually respectable context of Greek philosophy. The classical-Christian synthesis was carried still further by great third-century theologians such as Origen of Alexandria who produced a masterful fusion of Christian doctrine and Platonic philosophy. The process reached its climax in the Western Empire during the later fourth and early fifth centuries with the work of three Christian intellectuals, St. Ambrose, St. Jerome, and St. Augustine, who wrote with such erudition and insight that they have come to be regarded as "Doctors of the Latin Church." Working at a time when the Christianization of the Empire was proceeding apace, yet before the intellectual vigor of classical antiquity had faded, these three scholar-saints applied all the sophisticated wisdom of their fine classical educations to the elucidation of the Christian faith. Nearly seven centuries were to pass before Western Europe regained the intellectual level of late Antiquity, and the writings of these three Latin Doctors therefore exerted a powerful influence on the thought of the succeeding ages.

St. Ambrose and St. Jerome

Although Ambrose, Jerome, and Augustine made their chief impact in the realm of intellectual history, all three were deeply involved in the political and ecclesiastical affairs of their day. Saint Ambrose (*c.* 340–397) was bishop of Milan, a great city of northern Italy which in the later fourth century replaced Rome as the imperial capital in the West. Ambrose was a superb administrator, a powerful orator, and a vigorous opponent of Arianism. Thoroughly grounded in the literary and philosophical traditions of Greco-Roman civilization, he enriched his Christian writings by drawing heavily from Plato, Cicero, Virgil, and other great figures of the pagan past. And as one of the first champions of ecclesiastical independence from the authority of the Christian Empire, he stood at the fountainhead of the Church-state controversy that was to affect Western Europe for more than a millennium. For when the powerful orthodox emperor, Theodosius I, massacred the rebellious inhabitants of Thessalonica, St. Ambrose excommunicated him from the Church of Milan, forcing Theodosius to humble himself and beg forgiveness. The Emperor's public repentance set a momentous precedent for the principle of ecclesiastical supremacy in matters of faith and morals—a precedent that would not be forgotten by churchmen of later centuries.

Saint Jerome (*c.* 340–420) was the most scholarly of the three Latin Doctors. A restless, troubled man, he roamed widely through the Empire, living at Rome for a time, then fleeing the worldly city to found a monastery in Bethlehem. Jerome's monks in Bethlehem devoted themselves to the copying of manuscripts, a task that was to be taken up by countless monks in centuries to come and which, in the long run, resulted in the preservation of countless works of Greco-Roman antiquity which would otherwise have vanished. The modern world owes a great debt to St. Jerome and his successors for performing this humble but essential labor.

St. Jerome himself was torn by doubts as to the propriety of a Christian immersing himself in pagan literature. On one occasion Jesus appeared to him in a dream and banished him from paradise with the words, "Thou art a Ciceronian, not a Christian." For a time thereafter Jerome renounced all pagan learning, but he was much too devoted to the charms of classical literature to persevere in this harsh resolve. In the end he seems to have concluded that Greco-Roman letters might properly be used in the service of the Christian faith.

Jerome's supreme achievement lay in the field of scriptural commentary and translation. It was he who produced the definitive Latin translation of the Bible from its original Hebrew and Greek—the so-called Latin Vulgate Bible, which Catholics have used ever since. By preparing a trustworthy Latin text of the fundamental Christian book, he made a notable contribution to the civilization of Western Europe.

St. Augustine

St. Augustine of Hippo (354–430) was the towering intellect of his age. His achievements exceeded those of St. Ambrose, the ecclesiastical statesman, and St. Jerome, the scholar. For St. Augustine too was a statesman and a scholar, and he was a great philosopher as well. As bishop in the important North African city of Hippo he was deeply immersed in the affairs of his day, and his writings were produced in response to vital contemporary issues. Augustine's thought combines profundity and immediacy—the abstract and the human. In his *Confessions* he describes his own intellectual and moral odyssey through paganism and Manichaeism into the orthodox Christian fold. He writes with the hope that others, lost as he once was, might be led by God to the spiritual haven of the Church.

Augustine wrote voluminously against the various pagan and heretical doctrines that threatened Christian orthodoxy in his age. Out of these diverse writings there emerged a lofty system of speculative thought that served as the intellectual foundation for medieval philosophy and theology. Like so many of his predecessors and contemporaries he worked toward the synthesis of classical and Christian thought, but more than any before him he succeeded in welding the two cultures into one. He was disturbed, as Jerome was, by the danger of pagan thought to the Christian soul. But, like Jerome, he concluded that although a good Christian ought not to *enjoy* pagan culture he might properly *use* it for Christian ends. Accordingly, Augustine used the philosophy of Plato and the Neoplatonists as a basis for a new and thoroughly Christian philosophical scheme. As the thirteenth-century philosopher St. Thomas Aquinas said, "Whenever Augustine, who was imbued with the philosophy of the Platonists, found in their teaching anything consistent with faith, he adopted it; those things which he found contrary to faith, he amended."

Thus, Augustine stressed the Platonic notion of ideas and archetypes as the models of tangible things, but instead of placing his archetypes in some abstract "heaven," as Plato did, he placed them in the mind of God. For Augustine, the Platonic archetypes were "divine ideas." These ideas constituted the highest form of reality—the only true knowledge—and the human mind had access to the archetypes through a form of God's grace which Augustine called "divine illumination." Augustine was much too good a Christian to fall into the Zoroastrian notion that matter was worthless or that the human body was evil. But by emphasizing the superiority of ideas over particulars he was led to the conclusion that the material world was less important—less real—than the spiritual world. He concluded that man's body was a prison for his soul, and that the soul's escape from its material body was the chief goal of the Christian life. And he insisted that man, corrupted by the original sin of Adam's fall, was incapable of escaping the prison of his body except through God's grace. Hence, man could not earn his own way into heaven; he was predestined to salvation or damnation by the will of God.

These and other doctrines were developed in the process of St. Augustine's long struggle against the various heretical sects that flourished in his age. In the course of his arguments he examined many of the central problems that have occupied theologians ever since—the nature of the Trinity, the existence of evil in a world created and governed by an omnipotent God, the special power and authority of the priesthood, the compatibility of free will and predestination.

When pagan critics ascribed the Visigothic sack of Rome in 410 to Rome's de-

sertion of her former gods, Augustine met the challenge by writing his profoundly influential *City of God** which set forth a complete Christian philosophy of history. Human development was interpreted not in economic or political terms but in moral terms. Kingdoms and empires rise, prosper, and decline according to a divine plan, ordained from the beginning, yet forever beyond human comprehension. But even though the pattern of history must always elude us, we do know this: that God is not interested in the fate of tribes and empires except insofar as they affect the destiny of individual men—that the chief business of history is the salvation of human souls. And the salvation of souls depends not on the victories of Caesar but on the grace of God. Accordingly, true history has less to do with the struggles of states than with the struggle between good and evil which rages within each state and within each soul. The human race is divided into two distinct classes: not Romans and barbarians as the pagan writers would have it, but those who live in God's grace and those who do not. The former are members of the "City of God," the latter belong to the "City of Evil." The two cities are hopelessly intertwined in this life, but their members will be separated at death by eternal salvation or damnation. The divine plan for human history therefore has one fundamental purpose: the growth and welfare of the City of God. As for the city of Rome, perhaps, in the long run, its decline will be beneficial—perhaps even irrelevant!

The Romans had never excelled in the realm of speculative thought, but with the Christian Augustine, Roman philosophy came into its own at last. He was the Empire's greatest philosopher and, indeed, one of the two or three foremost minds in the history of Christianity. His theory of the two cities, although often simplified and misunderstood in later generations, influ-

* See p. 166.

enced Western thought and politics for a thousand years. His Christian Platonism dominated medieval philosophy until the mid-twelfth century and remains a significant theme in religious thought of this day. His distinction between the ordained priesthood and the laity has always been basic to Catholic theology. And his emphasis on divine grace and predestination was to be a crucial source of inspiration to the Protestant leaders of the sixteenth century.

As a consequence of Augustine's work, together with that of his great contemporaries, Ambrose and Jerome, Christian culture was firmly established on classical foundations. At Augustine's death in 430 the classical-Christian fusion was essentially complete. The strength of the Greco-Roman tradition that underlies medieval Christianity and Western civilization owes much to the fact that these three Latin Doctors and others like them, found it possible to be both Christians and Ciceronians.

The Germanic Barbarians

Fusion of Classical, Christian, and Germanic Cultures

The civilization of medieval Europe built creatively upon a synthesis of three cultures: classical, Christian, and Germanic. The age of Ambrose, Jerome, and Augustine witnessed the virtual completion of the classical-Christian synthesis, but the impact of Germanic culture had only begun to be felt. It was not until the eighth century or thereabouts that a fusion of classical-Christian and Germanic cultures was achieved, and only then can it be said that Western civilization was born. The intervening centuries, which are often called "The Dark Ages," provide a fascinating view of a new civilization in the process of formation. Throughout these turbulent years the classical-Christian tradition was preserved and fostered by the Church while the Germanic tradition governed the political and social organization of the barbarian successor states that rose on the ruins of the Western Empire. To be sure, the barbarians quickly accepted Christianity. Yet for centuries a cultural chasm separated the Church, with its classical-Christian heritage, and the Germanic kingdoms with their primitive, warlike culture. It is true, of course, that churchmen and aristocratic laymen tended, as time went on, to be drawn from the same social milieu. The Church of the Early Middle Ages was therefore able to preserve classical culture only in a simplified and corrupted form. But nevertheless it remained that the great mission of the early medieval Church was to civilize and Christianize the Germanic peoples.

One should be wary of generalizing too broadly on the subject of Germanic culture, for customs and institutions varied considerably from tribe to tribe. Agrarian peoples such as the Angles, Saxons, and Franks migrated slowly, but, once settled, they were exceedingly difficult to drive away. These three tribes were little influenced by Roman civilization and quite untouched by Christianity when they moved into the Empire. Tribes such as the Visigoths, Ostrogoths, and Vandals, on the other hand, were far more mobile and more rootless. All three had been converted to Arianism and had long been in touch with Roman culture. Still, all the tribes shared a common culture, and their political and social structures disclose significant similarities and parallels.

The *Germania,* written by the Roman historian Tacitus in A.D. 98, provides a sympathetic account of early Germanic institutions that is interesting and illuminating but not altogether trustworthy. It is not a dispassionate report, but rather a work of moral indignation written for the purpose of creating an edifying contrast between the "degenerate" Romans and the simple, unspoiled barbarians. Tacitus' descriptions of Germanic political and military institutions and social customs are invaluable, but his eulogy of Germanic virtue and chastity is overdrawn. In reality, the barbarians were at least as prone to dishonesty, lechery, and drunkenness as their Roman contemporaries—perhaps more so.

The barbarians devoted themselves chiefly to tending herds, raising crops, and fighting wars. Each tribe was divided into numerous kindred groups or clans which protected the welfare of their members by means of blood feuds. When a man was killed his clan would avenge him by declaring a feud against the killer and his clan. Since killings were common among the hot-tempered barbarians, the blood feuds constituted a dangerous threat to tribal cohesion. In order to reduce feuds the tribes developed a system of payments known as *wergelds* which might be rendered by the killer to the relatives of his victim to compensate for the killing and to appease their vengeance. The size of the wergeld depended on the social status of the victim. Smaller wergelds were established for lesser injuries such as cutting off a person's arm, leg, or finger, until in time the wergeld schedules came to cover every imaginable injury. Unfortunately, the offender could not always be persuaded to pay a wergeld, nor would the victim or his clan always agree to accept it. Hence, even though the laws of the later Germanic kingdoms abounded in wergeld schedules, the blood feud was never entirely eliminated.

Tacitus describes another important unit within the tribe, entirely distinct from the kindred group, which was known as the *comitatus*. It was a war band in which the warriors and their chief were bound together in an honorable brotherhood by ties of fidelity and mutual respect. The chief of the *comitatus* was expected to set an example for his men in courage and military prowess. The followers were expected to fight bravely at their chief's side and, if the chief should be killed in battle, to avenge him by fighting to the death if need be. The heroic martial virtues of the *comitatus,* so characteristic of the Germanic outlook,

persisted for centuries as the ideology of the medieval warrior nobility.

The members of a Germanic tribe, although subdivided into kindred groups and war bands, were bound together into a larger, tribal unit by their allegiance to a chieftain or king and by their recognition of a common body of customary law. The laws of the barbarian tribes were childish and irrational compared with those of the Roman Empire. Legal decisions often depended on whether the parties were able to adhere precisely to complex procedural formalities. An accused man was presumed guilty unless he could prove his innocence, and in many cases innocence could be established only by the accused submitting to an "ordeal." He might, for example, be required to grasp a bar of red-hot iron and carry it some specified distance. If, after several days, his hand was healing properly, he was adjudged innocent. If his hand was infected, he was guilty. Similarly, he might be required to take a stone from the bottom of a boiling cauldron, or to leap into a lake or pond. If he sank he was innocent; if he floated he was guilty; the pure waters would not "accept" a guilty man. Throughout the Early Middle Ages it was these Germanic customs rather than the majestic and sophisticated concepts of Roman law that governed jurisprudence in Western Europe. Not until the twelfth century did Roman law return to the West. And only gradually did it come to supersede the arbitrary practices of the Germanic legal tradition.

Yet Germanic law, crude though it was, made one crucial contribution to Western thought: implicit in the Germanic system was the concept that law arose from the immemorial customs of the people rather than from the will of the ruler. Since law transcended the royal authority, no king could be absolute. Many kings of the Early Middle Ages put the customs of their people into writing, but few claimed the power to change old laws or create new ones. The constitutional principle of government under the law did not emerge clearly for

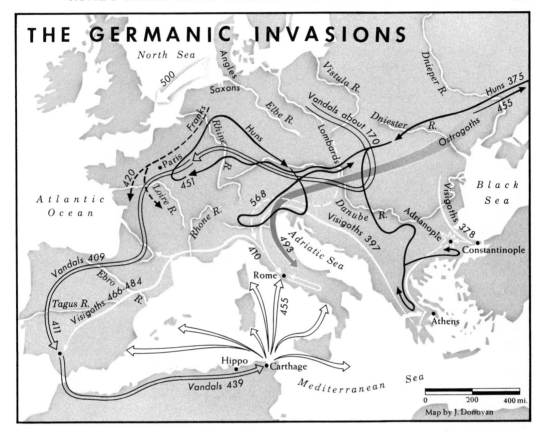

THE GERMANIC INVASIONS

North Sea

Angles

500

Saxons

Vistula R.

Dnieper R.

Huns 375

455

Vandals about 170

Dniester

Ostrogoths

Elbe R.

Huns

Lombards

R.

Franks

Rhine

Paris

420

451

Loire R.

Rhone R.

568

Atlantic Ocean

Danube R.

Visigoths 397

Adrianople

Visigoths 378

Black Sea

Constantinople

Adriatic Sea

410

493

Rome

Vandals 409

Ebro

R.

Tagus R.

Visigoths 466-484

411

455

Athens

Hippo

Carthage

Vandals 439

Mediterranean Sea

0   200   400 mi.

Map by J. Donovan

centuries to come, but when it did appear at last, in the High Middle Ages, it was rooted in the traditions of Europe's Germanic past.

Scholars of the nineteenth century tended to dwell excessively on the seeds of constitutionalism and popular sovereignty which they thought they detected in the customs of the primitive Germanic peoples. Democracy, they suggested, originated in the German forests. Modern historians, on the other hand, have rightly stressed the obvious gulf that separated German tribalism from Victorian constitutionalism. It should be evident that the veneration of customary "folk law" is not uniquely Germanic but is common to many primitive peoples. The significant fact is not that early Germanic kings were limited by customary law, but that the institution of limited monarchy endured and

developed over the centuries of the Middle Ages.

By the time of the major fourth- and fifth-century barbarian invasions, relatively stable royal dynasties had emerged in most of the Germanic tribes. Often a dynasty must have begun with a particularly talented warrior supported by a large *comitatus*. But after a few generations his royal successors were claiming descent from a god. At the death of a king the assembly of a tribe normally chose as his successor the ablest member of his family. The custom of election persisted in most Germanic kingdoms well into the Middle Ages. During the fifth-century invasions it had the effect of preserving the dynasty while at the same time insuring that the tribe was led by an able warrior-king in an age when the western Roman Empire was ruled by weaklings and nincompoops.

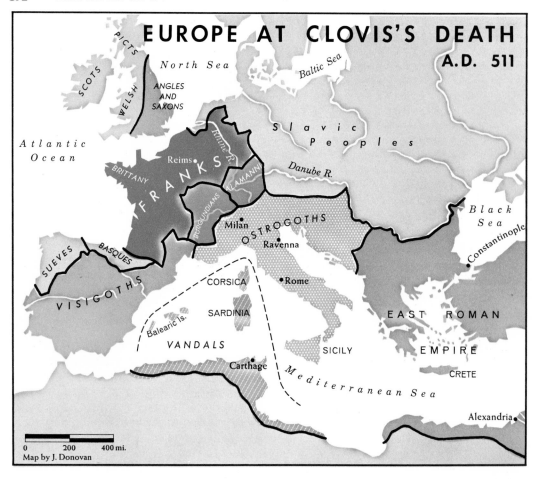

Germanic Successor States

With the fifth-century invasions the Christian Empire came to an end in Western Europe. In its place, by the century's close, a group of barbarian successor states was established. By the early years of the sixth century some of these states were beginning to achieve a degree of cohesion. Britain was then in the process of being conquered by groups of heathen Germanic peoples, known traditionally as the Angles, Saxons, and Jutes, who divided their territories into several small kingdoms. Most of Spain was in the hands of the Arian Visigoths whose kings found their power progressively eroded by a powerful, particularistic Visigothic nobility. A Vandal kingdom was established in North Africa whose Arian king and nobles made themselves hated by persecuting the indigenous orthodox Christians.

The two most powerful states in Western Europe around A.D. 500 were Ostrogothic Italy and Frankish Gaul. By 493 Italy had fallen under the control of the Ostrogoths, led by an able and far-sighted king named Theodoric. The reign of Theodoric in Italy (493–526) brought peace and a degree of prosperity to the long-tormented peninsula. For although Theodoric and his people were Arians, he pursued a policy of toleration toward his indigenous orthodox subjects. Under Theodoric the Italian people began to build once again, erecting new public buildings and repairing roads and aqueducts. Indeed, the improvement in political and economic conditions gave rise to a minor intellectual revival in early sixth-century Italy that contributed significantly to the transmission of classical culture into the Middle Ages. Boethius, a competent philosopher and a high official in Theodoric's regime, produced thoughtful, original essays and Latin translations of important Greek philosophical works. These translations served as basic texts in western European schools for the next 500 years. Boethius' supreme work, *The Consolation of Philosophy*, is an illuminating synthesis of Platonism and Stoicism which proved to be one of the most widely read books in medieval Europe. Another important scholar of Ostrogothic Italy was Theodoric's secretary, Cassiodorus, whose voluminous and flowery writings disclose a broad familiarity with classical culture. Cassiodorus spent the later years of his long life as abbot of a monastery named Vivarium whose monks, following St. Jerome's example, devoted themselves to copying and preserving the great literary works of antiquity, both Christian and pagan.

Frankish Gaul stands in sharp contrast to Ostrogothic Italy. Like the Ostrogoths, the Franks had a great leader, a contemporary of Theodoric named Clovis (481–511), but whereas Theodoric was tolerant and civilized, Clovis was cruel, ruthless, and barbaric. Yet the Frankish kingdom of Gaul, conquered for the most part by Clovis, proved to be far more enduring than Ostrogothic Italy. For the Franks were good farmers as well as fierce warriors, and they established firm roots in the soil of Gaul. Clovis began his career not as an Arian but as a heathen, and in the course of his conquests he became a convert to orthodox Christianity, believing that the Christian God would aid him in his battles. The conversion of Clovis was doubtless a superficial one, yet it was enormously significant to the history of Europe. For when Clovis became a Christian his Frankish people followed him, thereby becoming the first major barbarian tribe to adopt the faith in its orthodox form. In a sense, the conversion of Clovis marks the genesis of Catholic France. Clovis himself remained a savage to the end of his days, but the Church came to regard him as a new Constantine and a stalwart champion of orthodoxy. With the passing of the centuries, the friendship between the Church and the Frankish crown became a fundamental element in the political structure of medieval Europe.

BYZANTIUM

Byzantine State and Culture

The Survival of the Eastern Empire

At the death of Clovis in 511 the old Western Empire had been transformed into a group of political fragments dominated by Germanic tribes—the Anglo-Saxon and Jutish states of Britain, Visigothic Spain, Vandal North Africa, Ostrogothic Italy, Frankish Gaul, and several smaller barbarian kingdoms. But the Eastern emperors, with their capital at Constantinople, retained control of an immense, crescent-shaped empire which girdled the eastern Mediterranean from the Balkans through Asia Minor, Syria, and Palestine, to Egypt. Why was it that the Eastern Empire was able to survive the destructive forces that shattered the West?

To begin with, the Eastern Empire had always been more populous than the West. It had led the Roman Empire from the beginning in industry and commerce, and its civilization was far older and more durable than that of the western provinces. Accordingly, the economic blight that slowly paralyzed the Western Empire was considerably less devastating in the East.

Moreover, the Eastern Empire enjoyed important strategic and geopolitical advantages. Its province of Asia Minor, protected from the barbarian incursions by invulnerable Constantinople, was a crucial reservoir of manpower for the East Roman army and was also a dependable source of imperial taxes. With the rich material and human resources of Asia Minor behind it, the Eastern capital at Constantinople held fast against the barbarian onslaught. This great city, dominating the passage between the Black Sea and the Mediterranean, secure behind its massive landward and seaward walls, was the economic and political heart of the Eastern Empire. So long as the heart continued to beat, the Empire endured. And over the centuries Constantinople's walls remained inviolate against the attacks of barbarians, Persians, and Moslems. Under the circumstances, it is quite understandable that the Germanic tribes should have preferred to carve out their states in the feebler and more vulnerable West.

It would be misleading, however, to assume that the prolonged survival of the Eastern Empire was accompanied by a parallel survival of Roman civilization. The culture of classical antiquity was gradually transformed in the East, just as in the West, even though the line of Eastern emperors proceeded without significant interruption until 1453. Historians recognize this cultural transformation by giving a new name to the East Roman Empire of the Middle Ages. It is called the *Byzantine* Empire, after the Greek town of Byzantium on whose site Constantinople was founded.

Byzantine civilization represents a fusion of three elements: Roman government, Christian religion, and Greco-Oriental culture. From Rome, and most particularly

from the authoritarian Empire of Diocletian and Constantine, Byzantium inherited its administrative system and its legal principles. Byzantine autocracy was a direct outgrowth of the imperial philosophy of Diocletian, as Byzantine caesaropapism was a product of Constantine's Christian Empire. And the prevailing Byzantine mood, like the mood of the late Roman Empire, was one of defense—of self-preservation. The state was regarded as the ark of civilization in an ocean of barbarism—as the political embodiment of the Christian faith—and as such it had to be preserved at all costs. The appropriate virtues in such a state were entrenchment, not expansion; caution, not daring.

Bureaucrats; Armies; Heretics

This defensive, conservative mood is evident in both the Byzantine bureaucracy and the Byzantine army. The bureaucracy, huge and precedent-bound, preferred to take as few risks as possible. Resisting the policies of Byzantium's few vigorous and imaginative emperors, it gave cohesion to the state during the reigns of incompetents and thereby made its important contribution to the endurance of the Empire. The army, small and highly effective, also clung to a policy of few risks. Its generals, who were often men of remarkable skill, usually pursued policies of cunning and caution. They understood only too well that the preservation of their Empire might depend heavily on the survival of their armies.

The Byzantine emperors drew invaluable strength from the loyalty of their tax-ridden but fervent Christian subjects. The orthodox Christians within the Empire regarded their ruler as more than a mere secular sovereign; he was God's vice-regent, the protector of the Holy Church, and as such he merited their unquestioned allegiance. Thus, Byzantine armies fought not merely for the Empire but for God. The Byzantine warrior was not merely a soldier; he was a crusader. Christianity served as a potent stimulus to patriotism, and the Byzantine Emperors enjoyed popular support to a degree quite unknown in the pagan Rome of old.

But the emperor's central position in Byzantine Christianity was a source of weakness as well as of strength. Religious controversy was a matter of imperial concern, and heresy became a grave threat to the state. The fifth and sixth centuries were singularly rich in doctrinal disputes, and in the end these religious conflicts cost the Empire dearly. The most widespread heresy of the age was Monophysitism, a doctrine which arose in Egypt and spread quickly into Syria and Palestine, creating a widespread mood of hostility against the orthodox emperors. The controversy between the orthodox and the Monophysites turned on the question of whether Christ's humanity and divinity constituted two separate natures (as the orthodox said), or were fused together into a single nature (the Monophysite position). It has been suggested that the Monophysite Christ, with a single nature in which divinity tended to supersede humanity, represents a return to the "spiritualism" of the ancient Near East which scorned human nature and the physical universe. However this may be, the orthodox-Monophysite quarrel raged long and bitterly and constituted a dangerous threat to the unity of the Byzantine Empire. The emperors, convinced that doctrinal unity was essential to the preservation of their state, followed one policy, then another—sometimes persecuting the Monophysites, sometimes favoring them, sometimes proposing compromise doctrinal formulas that they hoped would satisfy everyone but that in fact satisfied no one. Whatever policy the emperors might follow, the controversy remained an open wound in the body politic until the seventh century when the rich but disaffected Monophysite provinces were lost permanently to the expanding empire of the Arabs.

Byzantine Culture

Roman government, Christian religion, Greco-Oriental culture—these were the three pillars of Byzantine civilization. But all three were shaped—and to a degree transformed—by the experience of the fourth-century Christian Empire. As a consequence of that experience, Byzantium inherited Roman government in its late, authoritarian form. Byzantine Christianity was a direct outgrowth of the Christianity of the later Roman Empire—its theology tightened and defined by the Arian struggle, its ecclesiastical organization overshadowed by the caesaropapism of the emperors.

Byzantium's Greco-Oriental culture, too, was molded by the intellectual and cultural currents of the Roman Empire's final centuries. The Greek culture which Byzantium

Sancta Sophia: this great church, converted into a mosque after the fall of Constantinople in 1453, was intended to epitomize the glory of Byzantine ecclesiastical architecture. Built between 532 and 537, it remains one of the great monuments of Justinian and Theodora.

inherited was by no means the culture of Periclean Athens—with its sturdy, straightforward, superbly proportioned architecture, its profoundly human drama, its bold flights into uncharted regions of speculative thought, and its controlled, tensely muscular sculpture. This tradition had undergone successive modifications in the Hellenistic age, during the Principate, and above all during the third- and fourth-century Empire. The mood of otherworldliness that gradually seized Roman culture resulted in a momentous transformation of the classical spirit. The former emphasis on the tangible, the earthly, the concrete, gave way to a preoccupation with religious symbolism and matters of the spirit. Artists lost their interest in portraying physical perfection and sought instead to portray sanctity. A new Christian art arose which produced slender, heavily robed figures with solemn faces and deep eyes. Techniques of perspective, which the artists of antiquity had developed to a fine degree, ceased to interest the artists of the new age. Ignoring physical realism, the artists of the late Empire adorned their works with rich, dazzling colors which stimulated in the beholder a sense of heavenly radiance and deep religious solemnity. Such was the artistic·tradition which Byzantium inherited. It conformed so perfectly to the Byzantine spirit that the artists of the Eastern Empire were able to produce enduring masterpieces without ever departing far from its basic aesthetic presuppositions. Majestic domed churches arose in Byzantine cities—churches such as Sancta Sophia in Constantinople and St. Mark's in Venice—whose interiors shone with glistening mosaics on backgrounds of gold. Here was an art vastly different from that of Greek antiquity, with different techniques and different goals, yet in its own way just as successful, just as valid, as the art of the Athenian Golden Age.

In the transcendental environment of Byzantium, Greek culture was significantly

The spread of Byzantine ecclesiastical forms into Italy was impelled by the desire of Justinian and Theodora to create ecclesiastical monuments to commemorate their rule. Among the more famous of these monuments are the two Byzantine churches, San Vitale and San Apollinaire in Classe, at Ravenna, the last imperial capital of the Western Empire. Above is a section of mosaic from San Vitale depicting Justinian and his courtiers. The second picture (top, p. 197) is a section of mosaic also from San Vitale showing Theodora and her attendants. The third picture (bottom, p. 197) is the mosaic behind the altar of San Apollinaire which portrays symbolically the transfiguration and the twelve evangelists.

altered, yet Byzantine civilization remained Greek none the less. Greek was the language of most of its inhabitants, and despite their profound commitment to the Christian faith they never forgot their Greek heritage. Indeed, the transition from late Roman to Byzantine civilization is marked by an increasing dissociation with the Latin-Roman past and a heightened appreciation of the Hellenic legacy. As time went on, Byzantine intellectuals forgot their Latin; Greek replaced Latin as the language of the imperial court; and the Byzantine Church all but lost contact with the Roman pope. Greek philosophy and Greek literature were studied with undying enthusiasm by an intelligentsia that cherished its ties with the Hellenic past.

The extent to which the architecture of Byzantium continued to influence later generations even outside the Eastern Empire may be seen in these two illustrations of the interior and exterior of St. Mark's at Venice. Begun in 1063, this cathedral of the Venetian patriarchs is one of the most ornate of all Byzantine churches.

Reign of Justinian; Aftermath

Achievements

The Emperor Justinian was the key figure in the transition from late Roman to Byzantine civilization. In many respects Justinian stands as the last of the Roman emperors; in others, he was a Byzantine through and through. He spoke in the Latin tongue, and was haunted by the dream of reconquering the West and reviving the Roman Empire of old. It was under his direction that the vast heritage of Roman law was assembled into one coherent body. In all these respects he was a ruler in the great Roman tradition. On the other hand, his reign witnessed a Golden Age of Byzantine art and the climax of imperial autocracy and caesaropapism which typified Byzantine culture over the centuries that followed.

The spectacular achievements of Justinian's reign were a product not only of the genius of the Emperor but also of the wise and cautious rule of his predecessors who endured the worst of the barbarian invasions, nurtured the financial resources of the Empire, and gradually accumulated a sizable surplus in the treasury. Justinian was also fortunate in the fact that the Germanic kingdoms of the West, which he had

determined to conquer, were losing much of their early vigor. Theodoric, the great Ostrogothic king, died in 526, a year before Justinian ascended the Byzantine throne, and the Vandal monarchy of North Africa, once a cruel oppressor of its subject people, was now merely corrupt.

The opportunities were present, and Justinian was the man to seize them. He was a ruler of iron determination and boundless ambition, a prodigious administrator and organizer, and an able theologian. His tireless energy and daring represented a radical departure from Byzantine conservatism, but his vast plans, although largely successful in a limited sense, left the Em-

pire bankrupt and exhausted. He applied his theological knowledge to the difficult problem of reconciling the orthodox and the Monophysites, but his compromise formula was satisfactory to neither side. When a series of riots early in his reign resulted in the burning of much of Constantinople, he lavished imperial funds on the rebuilding of the capital on an unprecedented scale. One product of his rebuilding program was the church of Sancta Sophia—Byzantium's greatest work of art. Gold, silver, ivory, and dazzling mosaics adorned its interior, and a vast dome seemed almost to float on air above it. The total effect was such as to stun even Justinian; he is said to have exclaimed on its completion, "Glory to God who has judged me worthy of accomplishing such a work as this! O Solomon, I have outdone thee!"

It was at Justinian's bidding that a talented group of legists set about to assemble the immense mass of legal precedents, juridical opinions, and imperial edicts that constituted the legacy of Roman law. These materials were arranged into a vast, systematic collection known as the *Corpus Juris Civilis* — the "body of civil law." Justinian's monumental *Corpus* not only became the keystone of future Byzantine jurisprudence but also served as the vehicle in which Roman law returned to Western Europe in the twelfth century to challenge the age-long domination of Germanic legal custom. The appearance of the *Corpus Juris Civilis* in the twelfth-century West was of incalculable importance to the development of sophisticated and rational legal systems in the European states. Indeed, its effect is still very much apparent in the legal codes of modern nations. But the importance of the *Corpus Juris Civilis* extended even beyond this. In Justinian's hands, Roman law absorbed some of the autocratic flavor of the Byzantine state; in the West, during the twelfth century and thereafter, it became a powerful factor in the rise of royal absolutism — an effective counterpoise to the limited-monarchy notions of Germanic legal tradition. The monarchs of late medieval and early modern Europe found much to admire in Justinian's precept that the highest law was the ruler's will.

Historians are prone to criticize Justinian for lavishing the limited resources of his Empire on the chimerical policy of reconquering the West. In one sense they are quite correct: the reconquest did drain the treasury and prostrate the Empire, and the victories of Justinian's western armies proved in time to be largely ephemeral. Yet Justinian, with his keen sense of the Roman imperial tradition, could not rest until he had made one all-out attempt to recover the lost western provinces and to re-establish imperial authority in the city of Rome. His armies, small but well-led, conquered the worm-eaten Vandal kingdom of North Africa with astonishing ease in 533–534, and succeeded in wresting a long strip of the Spanish Mediterranean coast from the Visigoths. For 20 years his troops struggled against the Ostrogoths in Italy, crushing them at length in 555 but only after enormous effort and expense. The campaigns in Italy, which are known as the "Gothic Wars," devastated the Italian peninsula and left Rome itself in ruins. The Visigothic sack of 410 was nothing compared with the havoc wrought by Justinian's armies.

During the final decade of his reign Justinian ruled almost the entire Mediterranean coastline, but his vastly expanded empire was impoverished and bankrupt. A devastating outbreak of bubonic plague struck the Empire in 541–543 and recurred sporadically over the succeeding decades, taking a fearful toll of human lives and crippling the Byzantine economy. But even without the plague Byzantium would have found it exceedingly difficult to hold the immense territories which Justinian's armies had conquered. Justinian's greatest shortcoming was his inability to match ambitions to resources, and the swollen empire which he bequeathed to his successors was exhausted and dangerously vulnerable.

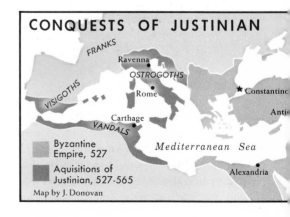

CONQUESTS OF JUSTINIAN

FRANKS

Ravenna

OSTROGOTHS

VISIGOTHS

Rome

★ Constantino

Carthage

VANDALS

Anti

Mediterranean   Sea

Byzantine Empire, 527

Aquisitions of Justinian, 527-565

Alexandria

Map by J. Donovan

Aftermath

In 568, three years after Justinian's death, a savage Germanic tribe known as the Lombards burst into Italy, compounding the devastation of that troubled land and carving out in the northern part of the peninsula an extensive kingdom which centered in the Po Valley. The Byzantines retained much of southern Italy and clung to Ravenna and other cities along the Adriatic coast, but their hold on Italy was badly shaken. Shortly thereafter the Visigoths reconquered the Byzantine territories in southern Spain, and eventually, in the 690s, Byzantine North Africa—the former Vandal state—fell to the Moslems. In the long run, therefore, Justinian's conquests were not lasting. His theological policies failed to reconcile the orthodox and Monophysites. His building program was magnificent but terribly expensive. In the field of law, however, his achievement was fundamental and permanent.

Justinian's successors were forced to abandon his daring policies and to face the hard realities of survival. Many of the newly won territories were abandoned as the Empire turned its back on the West to face more immediate threats from hostile peoples to the north and east. And as Byzantium concentrated more and more of its attention and energy on Eastern matters, its Latin heritage was gradually forgotten. Greek replaced Latin as the official court language; the emperor came to be known by the Greek title, *Basileus*, rather than the Latin *Caesar* or *Augustus*. The empire of Persia, which had been revived under a powerful new dynasty, began to press dangerously against Byzantium's eastern frontier, and a tribe of savage Asiatic nomads, the Avars, moved down from the north. In 626 Constantinople withstood a furious combined Persian-Avar attack and was able to defeat the Persian army only by summoning the last ounce of its strength. No sooner had the Persians been defeated than the Moslem armies exploded out of Arabia to wrest Syria, Palestine, and Egypt from the Empire and put Constantinople once again in grave danger. In 717–718 Constantinople was forced to defend itself against the full fury of the Moslem armies.

Evaluation of Byzantine Achievements

Yet in the face of all these dangers Constantinople held firm and Byzantium survived. And in later centuries the Byzantines were able to take the offensive once again, although never in so spectacular a fashion as under Justinian. Courageous Byzantine missionaries converted many of the Slavic peoples to Christianity and ultimately brought Russia herself within the fold of the Eastern Church. Constantinople remained Europe's eastern bastion against the Moslems until 1453. When nomadic tribes invaded the Balkans, the Byzantines, after generations of strenuous effort, finally brought them under control. In later centuries the Byzantine Empire underwent new Golden Ages of art and learning fully comparable to the Golden Age of Justinian. Indeed, at the very end of its long history, in 1453, Byzantium was in the midst of an impressive intellectual revival which drew its inspiration from the classical-humanist tradition of antiquity and which made a significant impact on the culture of Renaissance Italy.

To the end, Byzantium revered its classical heritage. As a great custodian of Greco-Roman culture the Eastern Empire provided an invaluable service to the emerging civilization of Western Europe. Roman law and Greek philosophy and literature were preserved and studied in Constantinople at a time when they were all but unknown in the West. Yet Byzantium's classical heritage—the inspiration of many of its greatest cultural triumphs—was in the long run a mixed blessing. Its government was never able to transcend the stifling autocracy of the late Roman Empire or the essentially defensive mood which it implied. Byzantium's creative impulses were all too often stunted by its remorse-less conservatism. The Byzantines opened new vistas in art and heresy but in little else. They expended so much of their energy on the survival of their Empire and the preservation of their cultural legacy that little was left for creative originality. They were, in short, prisoners of their own past.

THE WEST

Political, Economic, and Cultural Decline

The ignorance and savagery of the early medieval West stand in sharp contrast to the urbanity of Byzantium. Yet Western Europe had the inestimable advantage of a fresh start. It was inspired and enriched by the classical heritage, but unshackled by it.

Town and Country

In the aftermath of the Germanic inva-sions Western Europe found itself cut adrift from the government of the Roman Em-pire. The Church survived to carry on much of the old classical legacy. But Ger-manic kings and nobles were generally in-capable of preserving the political and economic institutions of the Roman past. Towns had been declining in Western Europe ever since the third century; by A.D. 600 they were shrunken phantoms of what they once had been. North of the Alps the municipal governments of antiquity had disappeared without a trace. But many of the towns themselves managed to endure, after a fashion, as centers of ecclesiastical administration. They remained the head-quarters of episcopal government and the sites of the bishops' cathedral churches. Many towns became important pilgrimage centers, for the more important cathedral churches possessed relics—bones of dead saints for the most part—which were re-garded as agents of spiritual and physical healing. The cathedral at Tours, for ex-ample, possessed the bones of the noted miracle-worker, St. Martin, which were said to heal any who touched them.

These episcopal centers played only a minor role in the culture and economy of the barbarian successor states. Far more important were the monastery, the peasant village, and the great farm or villa owned by some wealthy Roman or Germanic aristocrat and divided into small plots worked by semi-free tenant farmers. A small-scale luxury trade persisted, but by and large the economy of the sixth and seventh centuries was local and self-con-tained. Small agrarian communities pro-duced most of their own needs, for their life was meager and their needs were few.

Except in Britain and northeastern Gaul the barbarians tended to become absorbed into the older indigenous population. Pre-viously free Germanic farmers often de-scended into the ranks of the semi-servile *coloni*. But at the aristocratic level the pattern of life was set by the barbarian warrior nobility, and consequently the civility of the Roman villa gradually dis-appeared. The Roman and barbarian no-bility were fused through intermarriage into one class—hard-bitten and warlike—far more Germanic than Roman.

Government; Intellectual Life

With the exception of Theodoric, the barbarian kings proved incapable of per-petuating the Roman administrative tradi-tions which they inherited. They allowed the Roman tax system to break down com-pletely; they permitted the privilege of minting coins to fall into private hands. The power and wealth of the state declined ac-cordingly not because the kings were generous but because they were ignorant.

They lacked the slightest conception of responsible government and regarded their kingdoms as private estates to be exploited or alienated according to their whims. They made reckless gifts of land and public authority to nobles and churchmen and regarded what remained as their personal property, to be exploited for the sole purpose of their own enrichment. In brief, they succeeded in combining the worst features of anarchy and tyranny.

During the late Roman Empire Western Europe had been ruthlessly overgoverned; now it was radically undergoverned. The Germanic monarchs did precisely nothing to enliven the economy or ameliorate the general impoverishment. The Church strove to fill the vacuum by dispensing charity and glamorizing the virtue of resignation, but it was ill-equipped to cope with the chaos of the barbarian West. Its organization was confined largely to the defunct towns and walled monasteries. Only gradually were rural parishes organized to meet the needs of the countryside. Not until after the eighth century did the country parish become a characteristic feature of the Western Church. In the meantime a peasant was fortunate if he saw a priest once a year. The monarchy and the Church, the two greatest landholders in the barbarian states, were better known among the peasantry as acquisitive landlords than as fountains of justice and divine grace. Rural life was harsh, brutish, and short, and the countryside was politically and spiritually adrift.

The intellectual life of the barbarian West was almost as backward as its political and economic life. The culture of old Rome was rotting, and the new civilization of Western Europe had scarcely begun to develop. The intellectual level of the sixth and seventh centuries can best be appreciated by looking at a few leading scholars of the period. Bishop Gregory of Tours (d. 594), whose *History of the Franks* is our best source for the reigns of Clovis and his successors, must be counted one of the leading historians of his age. Yet Gregory's *History* is written in barbaric, ungrammatical Latin and is filled with outrageous and silly miracles. The world portrayed by Gregory of Tours was dominated by savage cruelty and naked force and beclouded by magic and superstitious fantasy. Both the story that he presents and the way in which he presents it attest to the radical decline of civilization in sixth-century Gaul.

Pope Gregory the Great (d. 604) was awarded a place alongside Ambrose, Jerome, and Augustine as one of the four Doctors of the Latin Church. But his writings, although marked by the profound practical wisdom and psychological insight of a potentially brilliant man, suffered from the cultural decadence of his age and are incomparably below the level of the fourth-century doctors in philosophical and scholarly sophistication. Pope Gregory's works had the effect of over-simplifying Augustinian theology and watering it down for the benefit of his own naive contemporaries. The lofty theological issues with which Augustine grappled are overshadowed in Pope Gregory's thought by a concentration on such matters as angels, demons, and relics.

Bishop Isidore of Seville (d. 636) was known as the foremost intellectual of his generation. His most impressive work, the *Etymologies,* was intended to be an encyclopedia of all knowledge. It was a valuable work for its time and was studied by many generations thereafter. But its value was vastly diminished by Isidore's remarkable lack of critical powers. He seems to have included every scrap of information that he could find, whether likely or unlikely, profound or absurd. It can perhaps be said that he was victimized by the credulity of the ancient writers on whom he depended, and left adrift by the weakness of the Roman scientific tradition. Nevertheless, as the greatest mind of his age he was astonishingly naive. On the subject of monsters, for example, he writes as follows:

The Cynocephali are so called because they have dogs' heads and their very barking betrays them as beasts rather than men. These are born in India. The Cyclopses, too, hail from India, and they are so named because they have a single eye in the midst of the forehead. . . . The Blemmyes, born in Lybia, are believed to be headless trunks, having mouth and eyes in the breast; others are born without necks, with eyes in the shoulders. . . . They say the Panotii in Sythia have ears of so large a size that they cover the whole body with them. . . . The race of the Sciopodes is said to live in Ethiopia. They have one leg apiece, and are of a marvelous swiftness, and . . . in summertime they lie on the ground on their backs and are shaded by the greatness of their feet.

Finally, in a burst of skepticism, Isidore concludes,

Other fabulous monstrosities of the human race are said to exist, but they do not; they are imaginary.

In fairness to Isidore it should be said that his treatment of monsters fails to show him to best advantage, and that it was drawn from earlier materials dating from the ancient world. But he combined and synthesized these materials with an intellectual abandon typical of his age. Even so he was the best his era could produce.

Western Europe in Early Post-Empire Centuries

The century between A.D. 500 and 600 witnessed important changes in the political structure of Western Christendom. In A.D. 500 Theodoric's Ostrogothic regime dominated Italy, the Vandals ruled North Africa, the Visigoths governed Spain, Clovis and his Franks were conquering Gaul, and the Anglo-Saxons were beginning their settlements in Britain. A century later, two of these states had been destroyed by Justinian's armies: North Africa was now Byzantine rather than Vandal, and the Ostrogothic kingdom of Italy had collapsed.

"Barbarian" Kingdoms

By 600 the Anglo-Saxon tribes had occupied much of Britain, enslaving many of the indigenous Celtic inhabitants and driving the rest into the western mountains of Wales. Anglo-Saxon Britain was now a confused medley of small, independent heathen kingdoms in which the process of Christian conversion was just beginning.

Gaul in 600 was thoroughly dominated by the Franks under the cruel and incompetent successors of Clovis, founder of the *Merovingian* dynasty.* This dynasty followed the Germanic custom of dividing the kingdom among the sons of a deceased ruler. Often the sons would engage in bitter civil war until, as it sometimes happened, one of them emerged as sole monarch of the Franks. He would then die, dividing the kingdom among *his* sons, and the bitter comedy would be repeated. Merovingian government was predatory and unenlightened; the Merovingian Church became disorganized and corrupt.

Corruption was also paralyzing Church and state in Visigothic Spain. The monarchy, converted in 589 from Arianism to Catholicism, was able at length to reconquer its Mediterranean shore from feeble Byzantium (*c.* 624). But the inept Visigothic kings allowed their power to slip little by little into the hands of a greedy and oppressive landed aristocracy. The worm-eaten regime was an easy prey for the conquering Moslems in the early 700s.

The century since Theodoric's reign had been a disastrous one for Italy. The horrors of Justinian's Gothic wars were followed by the invasion of the savage Lombards. By 600 the decimated peninsula was divided between the Byzantines in Ravenna and the south, and the Lombards in the north. The papacy, under nominal Byzantine jurisdiction, dominated the lands around Rome and sought to preserve its fragile inde-

* Named after Clovis' half-mythical ancestor, Merovech.

pendence by playing Lombard against Byzantine.

Creative Forces

Such was the condition of Western Europe in 600. At first glance one can see little to hope for in the all-prevailing gloom. Yet this was the society out of which Western civilization was born. This was the formative epoch—the age of genesis—in which apparently minor trends would one day broaden into the powerful traditions that would govern the course of European history. Even in 600 there were glimmerings of light in the darkness. Classical culture still survived, if only in a sadly vulgarized form. Isidore of Seville was no Augustine, but he was far more than a mere barbarian. The Church, although tainted by the ignorance and corruption of its environment, still retained something of its power to inspire, enlighten, and civilize.

Far to the north, Ireland had been won for Christianity by St. Patrick in the fifth century; by 600 it had developed an astonishingly creative Celtic-Christian culture. Irish scholars were familiar with both Greek and Latin literature at a time when Greek was unknown elsewhere in the West. By the later seventh century Irish artists were producing magnificent illuminated manuscripts in a flowing, curvilinear Celtic style. Irish Christianity, isolated from the continental Church by the heathen Anglo-Saxon kingdoms, developed distinctive customs of its own. It was organized around the monastery rather than the diocese, and its leaders were abbots rather than bishops. Irish monks were famous for their learning, the austere holiness of their lives, and the vast scope of their missionary activities. They converted large portions of Scotland to their own form of Christianity and by the early 600s were conducting missionary activities on the Continent itself.

Monasticism was the most dynamic and significant institution in the Early Middle Ages. The impulse toward monastic life is

EUROPE AROUND 600

not peculiar to Christianity but is found in many religions—Buddhism and Judaism, to name but two. The Essenes, for example, whose cult may have produced the famous Dead Sea scrolls, constituted a kind of Jewish monastic order. There have always been religious souls who longed to withdraw from the sinful world and devote their lives to uninterrupted communion with God, but among Christians this impulse was particularly strong. Monasticism came to be regarded as the most perfect form of the Christian life—the consummate embodiment of Christ's own words: "And every man that has forsaken home, or brothers, or sisters, or father, or mother, or wife, or children, or lands for my name's sake, shall receive his reward a hundredfold, and obtain everlasting life" (Matt., XIX, xxix).*

* It may be noted that this is not the only interpretation to which these words lend themselves.

The spread of Celtic Christianity outward from Ireland in the 6th and 7th centuries is well illustrated by the Lindisfarne Gospels. *Lindisfarne was an Hiberno-Saxon monastic foundation in Northumbria whose monks had an enormous effect on the Christianization of northern England and Scotland.*

The impulse toward withdrawal and renunciation first affected Christianity in the later third century when the Egyptian St. Anthony retired to the desert to live the ascetic life of a godly hermit. In time the fame of his sanctity spread, and a colony of would-be ascetics gathered around him to draw inspiration from his holiness. Saint Anthony thereupon organized a community of hermits who lived together but had no communication with one another, like apartment dwellers in a large American city. Similar hermit communities soon arose throughout Egypt and spread into other regions of the Empire. Hermit saints abounded in the fourth and fifth centuries. One of them, St. Simeon Stylites, achieved the necessary isolation by living atop a sixty-foot pillar for thirty years, evoking widespread admiration and imitation.

In the meantime a more down-to-earth type of monasticism was developing. Beginning in early fourth-century Egypt and then expanding quickly throughout the Roman Empire, monastic communities, based on a cooperative rather than a hermit life, were attracting numerous fervent Christians who found insufficient challenge in the increasingly complacent post-Constantine Church. The holy individualism of the desert and pillar saints thus gave way to a more ordered monastic life. Still, the early communities remained loosely organized and continued to emphasize the ascetic practices of severe fasting, hair shirts, and purifying lashings, which had been pioneered by the hermits.

St. Benedict and His Rule

Saint Benedict of Nursia (*c.* 480–544) changed the course of Western monasticism, tempering its flamboyant holiness with common sense and realistic principles of organization. As a youth, St. Benedict fled corrupt Rome and took up the hermit life in a cave near the ruins of Nero's country palace. In time word of his saintliness circulated and disciples gathered around him. As it turned out, Benedict was more than a mere ascetic; he was a man of keen psychological insight—a superb organizer who slowly learned from the varied experiences of his youth how the monastic life might best be lived. Born of a Roman aristocratic family, he brought to task a practical genius and a sense of order and discipline that were typically Roman. He founded a number of monasteries which drew not only prospective saints but ordinary people as well—even the sons of wealthy Roman families. At length he established his great monastery of Monte Cassino atop a mountain midway between Rome and Naples. For centuries thereafter Monte Cassino was one of the chief centers of religious life in Western Europe. It became a model monastery, governed by a comprehensive, practical, compassionate rule. In the midst of Justinian's Gothic Wars St. Benedict died, but his rule survived to inspire and transform Western Europe.

Pope Gregory the Great described the Rule of St. Benedict as "conspicuous for its discretion." It provided for a busy, closely regulated life, simple but not over-severely ascetic. Benedictine monks were decently clothed, adequately fed, and seldom left to their own devices. Theirs was a life dedicated to God and to the attainment of personal sanctity, yet it was also a life that could be led by any dedicated Christian. It was rendered all the more attractive by the increasing brutality of the outside world. The monastic day was filled with carefully arranged activities: communal prayer, devotional reading, and work — field work, household work, manuscript copying — according to the needs of the monastery and the ability of the monk. The fundamental obligations were chastity, poverty, and obedience; the monk must be celibate; he must discard all personal possessions; he must obey his abbot. The abbot, elected by the monks for life, was unquestioned master of the monastery, but he was to consult the monks in all his decisions. He was strictly responsible to God and was instructed to govern justly in accordance with the Rule. He was cautioned not to sadden or "overdrive" his monks or give them cause for "just murmuring." Here especially is the quality of discretion to which Pope Gregory alludes and which doubtless has been the major factor in the Rule's success.

Contributions of the Benedictines

Within two centuries of Benedict's death the Rule had spread throughout Western Christendom. The result was not a vast hierarchical monastic organization but rather a host of individual, autonomous monasteries sharing a single Rule and way of life but administratively unrelated. Benedict had visualized his monasteries as spiritual sanctuaries into which pious men might withdraw from the world. But the chaotic and illiterate society of the barbarian West, desperately in need of the discipline and learning of the Benedictines, could not permit them to abdicate from secular affairs.

In reality, therefore, the Benedictines had an enormous impact on the world they renounced. Their schools produced the vast majority of literate Europeans during the Early Middle Ages. They served as a cultural bridge, transcribing and preserving the writings of Latin antiquity. They spearheaded the penetration of Christianity into the forests of heathen Germany and later into Scandinavia, Poland, and Hungary. They served as scribes and advisers to kings, and were drafted into high ecclesiastical offices. As recipients of gifts of land from pious donors over many generations they held and managed vast estates which became models of intelligent agricultural organization and technological innovation. With the coming of feudalism, Benedictine abbots became great vassals, responsible for political and legal administration and military recruitment over the large areas under their control. Above all, as islands of security and learning in an ocean of barbarism the Benedictine monasteries were the spiritual and intellectual centers of the developing classical-Christian-Germanic synthesis that underlay European civilization. In short, Benedictine monasticism became the supreme civilizing influence in the barbarian West.

The Benedictines carried out their great civilizing mission with the enthusiastic and invaluable support of the papacy. The alliance between these two institutions was consummated by the first Benedictine pope, Gregory the Great, who recognized immediately how effective the Benedictines might be in spreading the Catholic faith and extending papal leadership far and wide across Christendom.

We have already encountered Pope Gregory as a Dark Age scholar—a popularizer of Augustinian thought. His theology, although highly influential in subsequent centuries, failed to rise much above the intellectual level of his age. His real genius lay in his keen understanding of human nature and his ability as an administrator and organizer. His *Pastoral Care,* a treatise on the duties and obligations of a bishop, is a masterpiece of practical wisdom and common sense. It answered a need of the times and became one of the most widely read books in the Middle Ages.

Gregory loved the monastic life and ascended the papal throne with genuine regret. On hearing of his election he went into hiding and had to be dragged into the Roman basilica of St. Peters to be consecrated. But once resigned to his new responsibilities, Gregory bent every energy to the extension of papal authority. Following in the tradition of Pope Leo I, Gregory the Great believed fervently that the pope, as successor of St. Peter, was the rightful ruler of the Church. He reorganized the financial structure of the papal estates and used the increased revenues for charitable works to ameliorate the wretched poverty of his age. His integrity, wisdom, and administrative ability won for him an almost regal position in Rome and central Italy, towering over the contemporary Lombards and Byzantines who were then struggling for control of the peninsula. The reform of the Frankish Church was beyond his immediate powers. But he set in motion a process that would one day bring both France and Germany into the papal fold when he dispatched a group of Benedictine monks to convert heathen England.

The mission to England was led by the Benedictine St. Augustine (not to be confused with the great theologian of an earlier day, St. Augustine of Hippo). In 597, Augustine and his followers arrived in the English kingdom of Kent and began their momentous work. England was then divided into a number of independent barbarian kingdoms of which Kent was momentarily the most powerful, and Augustine was assured a friendly reception by the fact that the king of Kent had a Christian wife. The conversion progressed speedily, and on Whitsunday, 597, the King and thousands of his subjects were baptized. The chief town of the realm, "Kent City" or Canterbury, became the headquarters of the new Church, and Augustine himself became Canterbury's first archbishop.

During the decades that followed, the fortunes of English Benedictine Christianity rose and fell with the varying fortunes of the barbarian kingdoms. Kent declined, and by the mid-600s political power had shifted to the northernmost of the Anglo-Saxon states, Northumbria. This remote outpost became the scene of a deeply significant encounter between the two great creative forces of the age: Irish-Celtic Christianity moving southward from its monasteries in Scotland, and Roman-Benedictine Christianity moving northward from Kent.

Although the two movements shared a common faith, they had different cultural backgrounds, different notions of monastic life and ecclesiastical organization, and even different systems for calculating the date of Easter. At stake was England's future relationship with the Continent and the papacy; a Celtic victory might well have resulted in the isolation of England from the main course of Western Christian development. But at the Synod of Whitby in 664, King Oswy of Northumbria decided in favor of Roman-Benedictine Christianity and papal influence in England was assured. Five years later, in 669, the papacy sent the scholarly Theodore of Tarsus to assume the archbishopric of Canterbury and reorganize the English Church into a coherent hierarchical system. As a consequence of Northumbria's conversion and Archbishop Theodore's tireless efforts, England, only a century out of heathenism, became Europe's most vigorous and creative Christian society.

The Irish-Benedictine encounter in seventh-century Northumbria produced a significant cultural surge known as the Northumbrian Renaissance. The two traditions influenced and inspired one another to such an extent that the evolving civilization of the barbarian West reached its pinnacle in this remote land. Boldly executed illuminated manuscripts in the Celtic curvilinear style, a new script, a vigorous vernacular epic poetry, an impressive architecture—all contributed to the luster of Northumbrian civilization in the late 600s and the early 700s. This Northumbrian Renaissance centered in the great monasteries founded by Irish and Benedictine missionaries, particularly in the Benedictine monastery of Jarrow. Here the supreme scholar of the age, St. Bede the Venerable, spent his life.

Bede entered Jarrow as a child and remained there until his death in 735. The greatest of his many works, the *Ecclesiastical History of England*, displays a keen critical sense far superior to that of Bede's medieval predecessors and contemporaries. The *Ecclesiastical History* is our chief source for early English history. It reflects a remarkable cultural breadth and a penetrating mind, and establishes Bede as the foremost Christian intellectual since Augustine.

By Bede's death in 735 the Northumbrian kings had lost their political hegemony, and Northumbrian culture was beginning to fade. But the tradition of learning was carried from England back to the Continent during the eighth century by a group of intrepid Anglo-Saxon Benedictine missionaries. In the 740s the English monk St. Boniface reformed the Church in Frankland, infusing it with Benedictine idealism and binding it more closely to the papacy. Pope Gregory had now been in his grave for 140 years, but his spirit was still at

work. St. Boniface and other English missionaries founded new Benedictine monasteries among the Germans east of the Rhine and began the long and difficult task of Christianizing and civilizing these savage peoples, just as Augustine and his monks had once Christianized heathen Kent. By the later 700s the cultural center of Christendom had shifted southward again from England to the rapidly rising empire of the Frankish leader Charlemagne, whose career will be traced in the next chapter. Significantly, the leading scholar in Charlemagne's kingdom was Alcuin, a Benedictine monk from Northumbria.

The Church and Western Civilization

The barbarian West differed from the Byzantine East in innumerable ways, the most obvious being its far lower level of civilization. But even more important is the fact that the Western Church was able to reject Byzantine caesaropapism and to develop more or less independently of the state. Church and state often worked hand in hand, yet the two were never merged as they were in Constantinople and, indeed, in most ancient civilizations. The early Christian West was marked by a profound dichotomy—a separation between cultural leadership which was ecclesiastical and monastic, and political power which was in the hands of the barbarian kings. This dualism underlay the fluidity and dynamism of Western culture. It produced a creative tension which tended toward change rather than crystallization, toward an uninterrupted series of cultural climaxes, and toward ever-new intellectual and spiritual configurations. Like St. Augustine's two cities, the heroic warrior culture of the Germanic states and the classical-Christian culture of church and monastery remained always in the process of fusion yet never completely fused. The interplay between these two worlds governed the development of medieval civilization.

ISLAM

Background and Origins

Islam, Byzantium, and Western Christendom were Rome's three heirs, and of the three, Western Christendom remained for many centuries the most primitive and underdeveloped. Medieval Europe had much to learn from Islam and Byzantium, and its developing synthesis of classical, Christian, and Germanic traditions was shaped in many ways by its two neighboring civilizations. The influence of these neighbors was impeded, however, by Europe's profound hostility toward the "infidel" Moslems and the "effete, treacherous" Byzantines. In the eighth and ninth centuries Western Europe's contacts with Islam were limited largely to the battlefield. Only after the turn of the millennium did the West begin to draw upon the rich legacy of Moslem thought and culture.

Arabian Setting; Mohammed

Islam made its explosive debut early in the seventh century and developed with astonishing speed into a great, cohesive civilization extending from India to Spain. The birthplace of this compelling new faith was the Arabian peninsula—the modern Saudi Arabia. For countless centuries Arabia had harbored fierce nomadic tribes which emerged periodically into the rich civilized districts of Palestine, Syria, and Mesopotamia to the north. As we noted in a previous chapter many Semitic invaders of the Ancient Near East came originally from the Arabian Desert.* These peoples, as we have seen, quickly assimilated the ancient civilization of the Fertile Crescent and developed it in new, creative ways. But their kinsmen who stayed in Arabia remained primitive and disorganized.

* See Ch. 3.

In Mohammed's time most Arabians still clung to their nomadic ways and to their crude, polytheistic religion, but by then new civilizing influences were beginning to make themselves felt. A great caravan route running northward from southern Arabia served as an important link in a far-flung commercial network between the Far East and the Byzantine and Persian Empires. Along this route cities developed to serve the caravans, and with city life came a modicum of civilization. Indeed, the greatest of these trading cities, Mecca, became a bustling commercial center which sent its own caravans northward and southward and grew wealthy on its middleman profits. As the tribal life of Mecca and other caravan cities began to give way to commercial life, new, foreign ideas challenged old ways and old viewpoints. It was in Mecca, around the year 571, that the prophet Mohammed was born.

At Mohammed's birth the Emperor Justinian had been dead for six years. Mohammed's contemporaries include such men as Pope Gregory the Great and Bishop Isidore of Seville. When the Benedictine mission from Rome landed in Kent in 597 to begin the conversion of England, Mohammed was in his twenties, as yet quite unknown outside of his own immediate circle.

The future architect of one of the world's great religions was born of a poor branch of Mecca's leading clan. With little formal education behind him, he became a caravan trader; as such, his travels brought him into close contact with Judaism, Christianity, and Persian Zoroastrianism. A high-strung, sensitive man with a powerful, winning personality, he received God's call while in his late thirties and began to promulgate his new faith by preaching and writing. He won little support in Mecca apart from his wife and relatives and a few converts from the underprivileged classes. The Meccan commercial oligarchy seemed immune to the teaching of this low-born upstart. Perhaps they feared that his new religion would discredit the chief Meccan temple, the *Kaaba,* which housed a sacred meteoritic stone and was a profitable center of pilgrimages. Their belief that Mohammed's faith would ruin Mecca's pilgrim business was an ironic miscalculation, but their hostility to the new teaching forced Mohammed to flee Mecca in 622 and settle in the town of Medina, 280 miles northward on the caravan route.

The flight to Medina, known among the Moslems as the Hegira (He-jī-ra), was a momentous turning point in the development of Islam and marks the beginning date of the Moslem calendar. Mohammed quickly won the inhabitants of Medina to his faith, and became the city's political chief as well as its religious leader. Indeed, under Mohammed's direction religious and civil authority were fused so that the sacred community was at once a state and a church. In this respect it foreshadowed later Islamic civilization.

The Medinans made war upon Mecca, raiding its caravans and blockading its trade. In 630 Medina conquered Mecca and incorporated it into the sacred community. During the two remaining years of his life Mohammed, now an almost legendary figure in Arabia, received the voluntary submission of many tribes in the peninsula. By the time of his death in 632 he had united the Arabians as never before into a coherent political-religious group, well-organized, well-armed, and inspired by a powerful new monotheistic religion. The violent energies of these desert people were now channeled toward a single lofty goal: the conquest and conversion of the world.

Islamic Religion: Dynastic Developments

Faith was the cement with which Mohammed unified Arabia. The new faith was called *Islam,* the Arabic word for "surren-

der." Mohammed taught that his followers must surrender to the will of Allah, the single, almighty God of the universe. Allah's attributes of love and mercy were overshadowed by those of power and majesty, and the greatest good was therefore not to love God but to submit to his commands. Mohammed was not regarded as divine but rather as the last and greatest of a long line of prophets of whom he was the "seal." Among his predecessors, as recognized by Mohammed himself, were Moses, the Old Testament prophets, and Jesus.

Koran; Religious Obligations

Islam respected the Old and New Testaments and was relatively tolerant toward Jews and Christians—the "people of the book." But the Moslems had a book of their own, the *Koran,* which superseded its predecessors and was believed to contain the pure essence of divine revelation. The *Koran* is the comprehensive corpus of Mohammed's writings, the bedrock of the Islamic faith: "All men and jinn in collaboration could not produce its like." Moslems regard it as the word of Allah, *dictated* to Mohammed by the angel Gabriel from an original "uncreated" book located in heaven. Accordingly, its inspiration and authority extend not only to its meaning but also to its every letter (of which there are 323,621), making any translation a species of heresy. Every good Moslem must therefore read the *Koran* in Arabic. Thus as Islam spread, the Arabic language necessarily spread with it.

The *Koran* is perhaps the most widely read book ever written. More than a manual of worship, it was the text from which the non-Arabian Moslem learned Arabic. And since it was the supreme authority not only in religion but also in law, science, and the humanities, it became the standard text in Moslem schools for every imaginable subject. Mohammed's genius is vividly illustrated by his success in adapting a primitive language such as seventh-century Arabic to the sophisticated religious, legal, and ethical concepts that one encounters in his sacred book.

Mohammed offered his followers the assurance of eternal bliss if they led upright, sober lives and followed the precepts of Islam. Above all, they were bound to a simple confession of faith: "There is no god but Allah, and Mohammed is his prophet." The good Moslem was also obliged to engage in ritualistic prayers and fasting, to journey as a pilgrim to Mecca at least once in his lifetime, and to work devoutly toward the welfare and expansion of the sacred community. Holy war was the supremely meritorious activity, for service to the faith was identical with service to the state. Public law in Islamic lands had a religious sanction, and the fusion of religion and politics which Mohammed created at Medina remained a fundamental characteristic of Islamic society. There was no Moslem priesthood, no Moslem "Church" apart from the state; Mohammed's political successors, the caliphs, were defenders of the faith and guardians of the faithful. The creative tension between Church and state which proved such a stimulus to medieval Europe was thus unknown in the Moslem world.

Early Caliphs;
Civil War

Immediately after Mohammed's death the explosive energy of the Arabs, harnessed at last by the teachings of the Prophet, broke upon the world. The spectacular conquests that followed resulted in part from the weakness and exhaustion of its enemies. The Byzantines had just defeated the Persians, and both Byzantium and Persia were spent and enfeebled by their long and desperate conflict. And the Monophysites of Syria and Egypt remained deeply hostile to their orthodox Byzantine masters.

The Arabs entered these tired, embittered lands afire with religious zeal, lured by the wealth and luxuries of the civilized world. They had no master plan of conquest—most of their campaigns began as plundering expeditions—but unexpected victories resulted in an ever-accumulating momentum. Moving into Byzantine Syria they annihilated a huge Byzantine army in 636, captured Damascus and Jerusalem, and by 640 had occupied the entire land, detaching it permanently from Byzantine control. In 637 they inflicted an overwhelming defeat on the Persian army and entered the Persian capital of Ctesiphon, gazing in bewilderment at its opulence and wealth. Within another decade they had subdued all Persia and arrived at the borders of India. In later years they penetrated deeply into the Indian subcontinent and laid the foundations of modern Moslem Pakistan. The inhabitants of the Persian Empire gradually adopted the Islamic faith and the Arab language. In later years they were destined to play a central role in Islamic politics and culture.

Meanwhile the Moslems pushed westward into Egypt, capturing Alexandria in the 640s. With Egypt and Syria in their hands they took to the sea, challenging the long-established Byzantine domination of the eastern Mediterranean. They took the island of Cyprus, raided ancient Rhodes, and in 655 won a major victory over the Byzantine fleet.

Omayyad and
Abbasid Dynasties

In 655 Islamic expansion ceased momentarily as the new empire became locked in a savage dynastic struggle. The succession to the caliphate was contested between the Omayyads, a leading family in the old Meccan commercial oligarchy, late to join the Islamic bandwagon but no less ambitious for all that, and Ali, the son-in-law of Mohammed himself. Ali headed a faction that was to become exceedingly powerful in later centuries. His followers insisted that the caliph must be a direct descendant of the Prophet. As it happened, Moham-

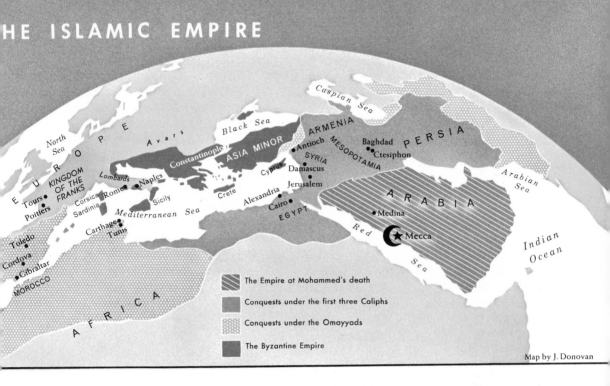

North Sea

EUROPE

Caspian Sea

Black Sea

Avars

Constantinople

ASIA MINOR

ARMENIA

MESOPOTAMIA

Antioch
SYRIA
Damascus

Baghdad
Ctesiphon

PERSIA

KINGDOM OF THE FRANKS

Tours
Poitiers

Lombards

Naples

Corsica

Rome

Sicily

Cyprus

Arabian Sea

Sardinia

Mediterranean Sea

Crete

Jerusalem

ARABIA

Toledo

Carthage

Alexandria

Cairo

Tunis

EGYPT

Medina

Indian Ocean

Cordova

Gibraltar

MOROCCO

Red Sea

Mecca

AFRICA

The Empire at Mohammed's death

Conquests under the first three Caliphs

Conquests under the Omayyads

The Byzantine Empire

Map by J. Donovan

med had left no surviving sons and only one daughter, Fatima, who married the Prophet's cousin, Ali.

In 661 the Omayyad forces defeated Ali in battle and initiated an Omayyad dynasty of caliphs that held power for nearly a century. But the legitimist faction that had once supported Ali persisted as a troublesome, dedicated minority, throwing its support behind various of the numerous progeny of Ali and Fatima. In time the political movement evolved into a heresy known as *Shi'ism* which held that the *true* caliphs—the descendants of Mohammed through Fatima and Ali—were sinless, infallible, and possessed of a body of secret knowledge not contained in the *Koran*. *Shi'ism* became an occult underground doctrine which occasionally rose to the surface in the form of civil insurrection. In the tenth century it gained control of Egypt and established a "Fatimid" dynasty of caliphs in Cairo. It inspired an infamous band of Moslem desperadoes known as the "Assassins" and survives to this day in the Ismaili sect led by the Aga Khan.

Omayyads

The intermission in the Moslem expansion ended with the Omayyad victory over Ali in 661. The capital of the growing Islamic Empire, which had been at Medina prior to the civil war, was now established at Damascus in Syria; but the old Arabian aristocracy continued to exert a firm control over Islam. Constantinople was now the chief military goal, but the great city on the Bosphorus threw back a series of powerful Moslem attacks between 670 and 680. The Byzantine defense was aided by a remarkable secret weapon known as "Greek Fire"—a liquid which ignited on exposure to air and could not be extinguished by water, but only by vinegar or sand. In 717–718 a great Arab fleet and army assaulted Constantinople in vain, and having expended all their energies and resources without success the Moslems abandoned their effort to take the city. Byzantium survived for another seven centuries, effectively barring inroads into southeastern Europe for the remainder of the Middle Ages.

213

In the meantime, however, Moslem armies were enjoying spectacular success in the West. From Egypt they moved westward along the North African coast into the old Vandal kingdom, now ruled by distant Byzantium. In 698 the Moslems took Carthage. In 711 they crossed the Straits of Gibraltar into Spain and crushed the tottering Visigothic kingdom at a blow, driving Christianity into the fastness of the Pyrenees Mountains. Next the Moslems moved into southern Gaul and threatened the kingdom of the Merovingian Franks. In 733, 101 years after the Prophet's death, the Moslems were halted at last at the battle of Tours * by a Christian army led by the able Frankish aristocrat, Charles Martel. The Christians at Tours were not the sort that one imagines when singing "Onward Christian Soldiers." They were semibarbarous Franks clad in wolf skins, their tangled hair hanging down to their shoulders. But they managed to halt the momentum of militant Islam in Western Europe, just as the Byzantines had stopped it in the East.

Abbasids

Seventeen years after the battle of Tours, in 750, the Omayyads were overthrown by a new dynasty known as the Abbasids. The new rulers were Arabian in family background but they supported a program of greater political participation for the highly civilized conquered peoples, now converting in large numbers to Islam. It was above all the Islamized Persian aristocracy whom the Abbasids represented, and shortly after the victory of the new dynasty the capital was moved from Damascus to Baghdad on the Tigris, deep within the old Persian Empire and a stone's throw away from the ruins of ancient Babylon.

Baghdad, under the early Abbasids, became one of the world's great cities. It was

the center of a vast commercial network spreading across the Islamic world and far beyond. Silks, spices, and fragrant woods flowed into its wharves from India, China, and the East Indies; furs, honey, and slaves were imported from Scandinavia, and gold, slaves, and ivory from tropical Africa. Baghdad was the nexus of a far-flung banking system with branches in other cities of the Islamic world. A check could be drawn in Baghdad and cashed in Morocco, 4000 miles to the west. The Abbasid imperial palace, occupying fully a third of the city, contained innumerable apartments and public rooms, annexes for eunuchs, harems, and government officials, and a remarkable reception room known as the "hall of the tree" which contained an artificial tree of gold and silver on whose branches mechanical birds chirped and sang. The wealth and culture of Baghdad reached its climax under the Abbasid caliph, Harun-al-Rashid (786–809), whose opulence and power quickly became legendary. Harun was accustomed to receiving tribute from the Byzantine Empire itself. When on one occasion the tribute was discontinued, he sent the following peremptory note to the emperor at Constantinople:

> In the name of God, the merciful, the compassionate.
> From Harun, the commander of the faithful, to Nicephorus, the dog of a Roman.
> Verily I have read thy letter, O son of an infidel mother. As for the answer, it shall be for thine eye to see, not for thine ear to hear. Salaam.

The letter was followed by a successful military campaign which forced the unlucky Byzantines to resume their tribute.

The era of Harun-al-Rashid was an age of notable intellectual activity in which the learned traditions of Greece, Rome, Persia, and India were absorbed and synthesized. Harun's son and successor founded a great intellectual institute in Baghdad—the House of Wisdom—which was at once a library, a university, and a translation

---

* The battle was fought between Tours and Poitiers; it is sometimes called the battle of Poitiers, and is traditionally, but incorrectly, dated 732.

center. Islamic culture had come of age with remarkable speed. At a time when Charlemagne was struggling desperately to civilize his semibarbaric Franks, Harun reigned over glittering Baghdad.

The rise of the Abbasids marked the breakdown of the Arabian aristocracy's monopoly on political power. Now the government was run by a medley of races and peoples, often of humble origin. As one disgruntled aristocrat observed, "Sons of concubines have become so numerous amongst us; Lead me to a land, O God, where I shall see no bastards." The Abbasid government drew heavily from the administrative techniques of Byzantium and Persia. A sophisticated and complex bureaucracy ran the affairs of state from the capital at Baghdad and kept in touch with the provinces through a multitude of tax-gatherers, judges, couriers, and spies. The government was enlightened up to a point, although no more sensitive to the demands of social justice than other governments of its day. The Abbasid regime undertook extensive irrigation works, drained swamps, and thereby increased the amount of land under cultivation. But the status of the peasant and unskilled laborer was kept low by the competition of vast numbers of slaves. The brilliance of Abbasid culture had little effect on the underprivileged masses who, aside from their fervent Islamic faith, retained much the same primitive way of life that they had known for the last two millennia.

The Abbasid Revolution of 750 was followed by a long process of political disintegration as one province after another broke free of the control of the caliph of Baghdad. Even in the palmy days of Harun-al-Rashid the extreme western provinces — Spain, Morocco, and Tunisia — were ruled by independent local dynasties. In the later ninth century the trend toward disintegration gained momentum as Egypt, Syria, and eastern Persia (Iran) broke free of Abbasid control. By then, the Abbasids were slowly losing their grip on their own government in Baghdad. Ambitious army commanders gradually usurped power, establishing control over the tax machinery and the other organs of government. The Abbasid dynasty endured until 1258 when Baghdad was ravaged by the Mongols, but by 950 the caliphs had become the pawns of the supreme military commander and the imperial guard.

Expansion, Conversion, Diffusion

Throughout this epoch of political disintegration the Moslem world remained united by a common tongue, a common culture, and a common faith. It continued to struggle vigorously and often successfully with Byzantium for control of the Mediterranean; for a time it managed to occupy the key islands of Crete, Sicily, Sardinia, and Corsica.

By now almost all the inhabitants of Syria, Egypt, and North Africa had converted to Islam, even though these lands had once supported enthusiastic and well-organized Christian churches. The Moslems did not ordinarily persecute the Christians; they merely taxed them, and it may well be that the prolonged tax burden was a more effective instrument of conversion than ruthless persecutions would have been.

The brilliant intellectual awakening of Harun-al-Rashid's day continued unabated. The untutored Arab from the desert became the cultural heir of Greece, Rome, Persia, and India, and within less than two centuries of the Prophet's death Islamic culture had reached the level of a mature, sophisticated civilization. Its mercurial rise was a consequence of the Arabs' success in absorbing the great civilized traditions of their conquered peoples and employing these traditions in a new and unique cultural synthesis. Islam borrowed, but never without digesting; what it drew from previous civilizations, it transmuted and made its own.

Interior of the sanctuary of the mosque of Cordova. Begun in 786, this structure offers an excellent example of the horseshoe arch, a peculiarly Moslem architectural form.

The political disintegration of the ninth and tenth centuries was accompanied by a diffusion of cultural activity throughout the Moslem world. During the tenth century, for example, Cordova, the capital of Islamic Spain, acquired prodigious wealth and became the center of a brilliant cultural flowering. With a population of half a million or more, Cordova became another Baghdad. No other city in Western Europe could even remotely approach it in population, beauty, or municipal organization. Its magnificent mosques, mansions, aqueducts, and baths, its bustling markets and shops, its efficient police force and sanitation service, its street lights, made Cordova the wonder of the age. Particularly remarkable was its splendid, sprawling palace, flashing with brightly colored tiles and surrounded by graceful minarets and sparkling fountains.

All across the Islamic world, from Cordova to Baghdad and far to the east, Moslem scholars and artists developed the fruitful legacy of past civilizations. Architects molded Greco-Roman forms into a brilliant and distinctive new style. Philoso-

phers studied and elaborated the writings of Plato and Aristotle despite the hostility of narrowly orthodox Islamic theologians. Physicians expanded the ancient medical doctrines of Galen and his Greek predecessors, describing new symptoms and identifying new curative drugs. Astronomers tightened the geocentric system of Ptolemy, prepared accurate tables of planetary motions, and gave Arabic names to the stars—names such as Altair, Deneb, and Aldebaran which are used to this day. The renowned astronomer-poet of Persia, Omar Khayyam, devised a calendar of singular accuracy. Moslem mathematicians borrowed creatively from both Greece and India. From the Greeks they learned geometry and trigonometry; from the Hindus they appropriated the so-called Arabic numerals, the zero, and algebra, which were ultimately passed on to the West to revolutionize European mathematics.

Islamic Culture— Limitations and Contributions

But the Moslem scholars and scientists, although masters of the knowledge of past cultures and diligent observers of the world around them, were by and large unsuccessful in going beyond their predecessors in any profound way. They tightened, they elaborated, they tinkered, but they produced few fundamental hypotheses; they created no new systems of rational thought to replace those of Aristotle, Plato, and Galen. They knew their Ptolemy backward, yet they produced no Copernicus.

This same inability to think creatively in large systematic terms characterizes Islamic literature. Arab prose is fragmentary and episodic; the individual anecdote takes precedence over the extended narrative. Moslem poets endeavored to perfect individual verses rather than to create long coherent poems. The quatrains of Omar Khayyam's *Rubiayat* actually seem to have been arranged in alphabetical order.

Even the chapters of the *Koran* were assembled in order of decreasing length without the slightest thought of structural unity.

Still, there is no denying Islam's immense achievement. The Arabs conquered their vast territories three times over: with their armies, their faith, and their language. In the end, the term "Arab" applied to every Moslem from Spain to India, regardless of his ethnic background. Within its all-encompassing religious and linguistic framework, Arab culture provided a new stimulus and orientation to the long-civilized peoples of former empires. With its manifold ingredients, the rich Islamic heritage would one day provide invaluable nourishment to the voracious mind of the reawakening West.

SELECTED READINGS

*St. Augustine, *The City of God*, V. J. Bourke, ed., Doubleday, Garden City, New York, 1958.
  A skillful abridgment.

*Bark, William C., *Origins of the Medieval World*, Doubleday, Garden City, New York.
  A provocative work which challenges the view that Rome's fall was a disaster.

*Baynes, N. H., and H. St. L. B. Moss, eds., *Byzantium, An Introduction to East Roman Civilization*, Oxford University Press, New York, 1948.
  An anthology of essays by scholarly specialists, organized topically.

*Bury, J. B., *History of the Later Roman Empire*, Dover, New York, 1957, 2 vols.
  The standard account, full and authoritative, by one of the distinguished historians of this century.

*Chambers, Mortimer, ed., *The Fall of Rome; Can It Be Explained?*, Holt, Rinehart and Winston, New York, 1963.
  Well-chosen excerpts from historical writings dealing with the decline of Rome provide a compact, illuminating survey of historical opinion on the subject.

Asterisk (*) denotes paperback.

*Cochrane, C. N., *Christianity and Classical Culture*, Oxford University Press, New York, 1944.
  An intellectual tour-de-force, sympathetic to the rise of the mystical point of view.

*Dawson, Christopher, *The Making of Europe*, Meridian, New York, 1946.
  A thoughtful, sympathetic analysis of early medieval culture which emphasizes the central role of the Catholic Faith.

Deanesly, Margaret, *A History of Early Medieval Europe—476–911*, Barnes and Noble, New York, 1960 (2nd ed.).
  An excellent, accurate, and detailed text.

*Dill, Samuel, *Roman Society in the Last Century of the Western Empire*, Meridian, New York.
  A brilliant, older work.

*Gibb, H. A. R., *Mohammedanism: An Historical Survey*, Galaxy, New York, 1953 (2nd ed.).
  A skillful, compact summary of Islamic civilization.

*Gibbon, Edward, *The Triumph of Christendom in the Roman Empire*, Harper, New York, 1958.
  Chapters XV–XX from Gibbon's late-eighteenth century masterpiece, *The Decline and Fall of the Roman Empire*. The entire work is available in a three-volume Modern Library Edition.

Gregory of Tours, *History of the Franks*, O. M. Dalton, Translator, Oxford University Press, New York.
  An important and interesting but not always trustworthy contemporary account of early Merovingian Gaul.

*von Grunebaum, G. E., ed., *Medieval Islam*, University of Chicago Press, Chicago, 1963 (2nd ed.).
  A learned and original work; the best on the subject.

*Havighurst, A. F., ed., *The Pirenne Thesis—Analysis, Criticism, and Revision*, Heath, Boston, 1958.
  An excellent approach to one of the central problems in early medieval history through excerpts from the writings of contending historians.

*Hitti, P. K., *History of the Arabs*, St. Martin's Press, New York, 1958 (6th ed.).

Broad, yet full; a monumental work. For a much shorter survey by the same author see *The Arabs: A Short History*, Gateway.

*Hussey, J. M., *The Byzantine World*, Harper, New York, 1961.

A brief, skillful summary of Byzantine civilization.

*Katz, Solomon, *The Decline of Rome and the Rise of Medieval Europe*, Cornell University Press, Ithaca, New York, 1955.

A short, perceptive, well-written introductory survey.

Laistner, M. L. W., *Thought and Letters in Western Europe, A.D. 500–900*, Methuen, London, 1936 (rev. ed.).

The best intellectual history of the period.

Latouche, Robert, *The Birth of Western Economy*, Barnes and Noble, New York, 1960.

A splendid up-to-date account of early medieval economic trends. The author stresses particularly the persisting importance of the small farm in the European countryside.

*Lot, Ferdinand, *The End of the Ancient World and the Beginnings of the Middle Ages*, Harper, New York, 1961.

A masterly study which places stress on the economic factors in the decline. A valuable introduction by Glanville Downey summarizes recent scholarship on the problem of "decline and fall."

*Moss, H. St. L. B., *The Birth of the Middle Ages 395–814*, Oxford University Press, New York.

A thoughtful survey running from the Principiate through Charlemagne.

Ostrogorsky, G., *History of the Byzantine State*, Rutgers University Press, New Brunswick, 1957.

Longer and more detailed than the surveys by Hussey and Baynes and Moss (above), this is the best single-volume history of Byzantium.

*Pirenne, Henri, *Mohammed and Charlemagne*, Meridian, New York, 1955.

The firmest statement by the great Belgian scholar of his controversial thesis that Roman civilization persisted in the West until the eighth century. This book should be read in connection with Havighurst (above).

*Wallace-Hadrill, J. M., *The Barbarian West 400–1000*, Harper, New York, 1962.

An intelligent condensation and popularization by England's leading authority on early-medieval Frankland. The account of the Carolingian Renaissance is particularly illuminating.

Wallace-Hadrill, J. M., *The Long-Haired Kings and Other Studies in Frankish History*, Barnes and Noble, New York, 1962.

A collection of illuminating essays on the Merovingian period.

9

Carolingian Europe and the New Invasions

THE RISE OF THE CAROLINGIAN EMPIRE

The Significance of the Carolingian Renaissance

In the course of the eighth century Western Christendom began to emerge as a coherent civilization. It did so under the aegis of the Carolingian Empire—a vast constellation of territories welded together by the Frankish king Charlemagne and his talented predecessors. Here for the first time the various cultural ingredients— classical, Christian, and Germanic—that went into the making of European civilization achieved a degree of synthesis. Charlemagne was a Germanic king—of that there could be no question—and he surrounded himself with Germanic warrior-aristocrats. But he also drew churchmen and classical scholars around him and took very seriously his role as protector and sustainer of the Western Church. Although his empire was fundamentally Germanic, its intellectual life, limited though it was, drew heavily from the classical-Christian tradition. The fusion of these cultural ingredients was evident in the life of the Carolingian court, in the rising vigor of the Carolingian Church, and in the person of Charlemagne himself.

Charlemagne's Frankland stood in vivid contrast to contemporary Byzantium and the Abbasid Empire of Islam. Baghdad and Constantinople were the centers of brilliant, opulent, mercantile civilizations. Charlemagne's Franks were a half-barbarized agrarian people struggling toward political and intellectual coherence. But eighth-century Western Europeans were steadily moving toward a life of larger meaning for themselves and for those who came after them. For the first time it began to dawn on a few that they were a people apart. It is hardly likely that they gave over to critical analysis their common heritage rooted in Athens and Jerusalem, Rome and Germany. But some sensed that they were participants in the creation of a new and distinctive civilization; that they were bound together, much as the Moslems, by a common faith and a common scholarly language.

The new Europe was aroused spiritually by the wide-ranging Benedictines and invigorated intellectually by the Bible. It was stirred by the writings of the Latin Doctors and their contemporaries, and by the surviving masterpieces of the Latin literary tradition. And it was bound together politically by a new dynasty of Frankish monarchs, the Carolingians.*

Carolingian Europe differed profoundly from the Western Roman Empire of old. It was a land without large cities, thoroughly agrarian in its economic organization, with its culture centered on the monastery, the cathedral, and the perambulatory royal court rather than the forum. And although Charlemagne extended his authority into Italy, the center of his activities and his interests remained in northern Frankland. In a word, the new Europe no longer faced the Mediterranean; its axis had shifted northward.

Agricultural Technology

The relative brightness of the Age of Charlemagne was the product of creative processes that had been at work during the preceding dark centuries. From the economic standpoint the most interesting and significant of these processes was the development of a new agrarian technology which increased the productivity of northern European farmlands beyond the level of the old Roman Empire.

The New Plow

By the opening of the eighth century the ineffective scratch plow of Roman times had been superseded throughout the northern districts of the barbarian West by a heavy compound plow with wheels, colter, plowshare, and moldboard which cut deeply into the soil, pulverized it, and turned it aside, thereby producing ridges and furrows. The development of this heavy plow was complex and gradual; the basic idea may perhaps have been brought into Western Europe by the Slavs in the sixth or seventh century. Its introduction into the West opened up vast areas of rich, heavy soil in which the older scratch plow was ineffective, and accentuated the tendency toward dividing fields into long strips cultivated by the eight-ox teams which the heavy plow required. Peasants now pooled their oxen and their labor in order to exploit the new plow; in so doing they laid the foundation for the cooperative agricultural communities of medieval Europe with strong village councils to regulate the division of labor and resources.

The Three-Field System

The upsurge in productivity brought about by the introduction of the heavy compound plow made possible a fundamental change in the method of rotating crops. By the Carolingian age parts of Northern Europe were beginning to adopt the three-field system in place of the two-field system typical of Roman times. Formerly a typical farm had been divided into two fields, one of which was planted each year and allowed to lie fallow the second year. But it was found that the rich northern soils, newly opened by the heavy plow, did not require a full year's rest between crops. Instead, they were often divided into three fields, each of which underwent a three-year cycle of autumn planting, spring planting, and fallow. The shift from two fields to three had an important impact on the European economy, for it increased food production significantly and brought a degree of prosperity to Northern Europe. It is possible that the heavy plow and the

---

* Whose family name is derived from that of their most illustrious representative — Charles the Great, or Charlemagne.

three-field system, which could not be employed efficiently in the light, dry soils of the Mediterranean South, contributed to the northward shift in the economic and cultural orientation of Carolingian Europe.

Mechanization

The Age of Charlemagne also profited from a trend toward mechanization. The water mill, which was used occasionally in antiquity for grinding grain, had now come into widespread use and was a typical feature of the Carolingian farm. During the centuries following Charlemagne's death the water mill was put to new uses— to power the rising textile industry of the eleventh century, and to drive triphammers in forges. Thus, the technological progress of Merovingian and Carolingian times continued into the centuries that followed. By A.D. 1000 the development of the horseshoe and a new, efficient horse collar, both apparently imported from Siberia or Cen-

tral Asia, made possible the very gradual replacement of the ox by the more energetic horse as the chief draught animal on the farms of Northwestern Europe. And in the twelfth century the windmill made its debut in the European countryside. These new advances resulted in still greater productivity and underlay the rich and prosperous civilization of Northern Europe in the High Middle Ages (c. 1050–1300). Slowly one of the chief economic bases of human slavery was being eroded as human power gave way more and more to animal and machine power.

Carolingian Europe gained much from the earlier phase of this drawn-out revolution in agrarian technology, but even so the peasants of the Carolingian age remained near the level of subsistence. A single bad year could ruin them. During a great famine of 791, for example, the peasants were driven to cannibalism and were even reported to have eaten members of their own

Illuminations from the Flemish Hours of the Virgin *(c. 1515): on the left, the month of July; on the right, the month of September. Note two examples of medieval technological achievement: the windmill and the compound plow with moldboard.*

family. Conditions may have been improving, but only very gradually.

Political and Religious Developments

Rise of the Carolingians

The dynasty of Clovis, the Merovingians, had declined over the centuries from bloodthirsty autocrats to crowned fools. By the later 600s all real power had passed to the aristocracy. Meanwhile, as a consequence of the Merovingian policy of dividing royal authority and crown lands among the sons of a deceased king, Frankland had split into several distinct districts, the most important of which were Neustria (Paris and northwestern France), Austrasia (the heavily Germanized northeast including the Rhinelands), and Burgundy in the southeast.*

During the seventh century a great aristocratic family, known to historians as the Carolingians, rose to power in Austrasia. The Carolingians became "mayors of the palace"; that is, they held the chief administrative post in the Austrasian royal household and made it hereditary. As the Merovingians grew increasingly feeble and inept the Carolingians became the real masters of Austrasia. The Carolingian mayor of the palace increased his power by gathering around him a considerable number of trained warriors somewhat in the tradition of the old Germanic *comitatus*.† These men became his vassals, placing themselves under his protection and maintenance and swearing fealty to him. Other aristocrats also had their private vassalic armies. But the Carolingians, with far the greatest number of followers, dominated the scene. In 687 a Carolingian mayor named Pepin of Heristal led his Austrasian army to a decisive victory over the Neustrians at Tertry, and the Carolingians thenceforth were the

leading family in all Frankland. With Neustria under their control they swung Burgundy into line. Thus when the Moslems moved into Gaul in the early 730s they faced a united Frankish people under the able leadership of Pepin of Heristal's son, the vigorous Carolingian mayor Charles Martel ("The Hammer," 714–741).

Charles Martel

This brilliant, ruthless warrior not only turned back the Moslems at the battle of Tours (733), he also won victory after victory over Moslems and Christians alike, consolidating his power over the Franks and extending the boundaries of the Frankish state. Like the Adams family in American history, the Carolingians of the seventh and eighth centuries had the good fortune to produce exceedingly able representatives over several generations. Martel's father, Pepin of Heristal, had conquered Neustria; Martel himself defeated the Moslems and, indeed, almost everybody he faced. His son, Pepin the Short, gained the Frankish crown, and his grandson, Charlemagne, won an empire.

Surprisingly, the Carolingians followed the same policy of divided succession among male heirs which had so weakened the Merovingians. But here too Carolingian luck played a crucial role in history. For as it happened, the Carolingian mayors and later kings over several generations had only one long-surviving heir. Frankish unity was maintained not by policy but in spite of it. When Charles Martel died in 741 his lands and authority were divided among his two sons, Carloman and Pepin the Short. But Carloman ruled only six years, retiring to a Benedictine monastery in 747 — leaving the field to his brother Pepin. Carloman represented a new kind of barbarian ruler, deeply affected by the spiritual currents of his age, whose piety foreshadowed that of numerous saint-kings of later centuries. Christian culture and Germanic political leadership were beginning to draw together.

* See map, p. 227.

† See p. 190.

Missions from Northumbria

The fusion of these two worlds was carried still further by Pepin the Short (741–768) who supported a Benedictine Christian revival in Frankland and consummated an alliance of far-reaching consequences between the Frankish monarchy and the papacy. By the time of Charles Martel's death in 741 English Benedictine monks had long been engaged in evangelical work among the heathen Germanic peoples east of the Rhine. The earliest of these missions was directed at the Frisians, a maritime people who were settled along the coast of the Netherlands. The first of the Benedictine evangelists were monks from Northumbria who brought to the Continent not only the strict organizational discipline and devotion to the papacy that had been characteristic of the Northumbrian Benedictines but also the peripatetic missionary fervor which the Celtic monks had contributed to the Northumbrian revival. So it was that Benedictine monks such as Wilfrid of Ripon and Willibrord left their Northumbrian homeland during the later 600s to evangelize the heathen Frisians. The transference to Frankland and Germany of the vital force of Northumbrian Christianity, with its vibrant culture, its Roman-Benedictine discipline, and its profound spiritual commitment was of immense significance in the development of Western civilization. Wilfrid of Ripon, Willibrord, and their devoted followers represent the first wave of a movement that was ultimately to infuse the Frankish empire of Charlemagne with the vibrant spiritual life that had developed in Anglo-Saxon England during the century following St. Augustine's mission. The dynamic thrust of Roman-Benedictine Christianity, having leapt from Rome to Kent and thence to remote Northumbria, was returning to the Continent at last.

Saint Boniface in Germany

The key figure in this crucial cultural movement was St. Boniface, an English Benedictine from Wessex. Reared in Benedictine monasteries in southern England, Boniface left Wessex in 716 to do missionary work among the Frisians. From that time until his death in 754 he devoted himself above all other tasks to the tremendous challenge of Christianizing the heathen Germanic peoples. Boniface was a man of boundless energy and considerable learning, a wise and charismatic leader of men. He worked in close cooperation with both the papacy and the Anglo-Saxon Church; a great number of his letters survive, many of which request support from his compatriots in Wessex and advice from Rome. On three occasions he visited Rome to confer with the pope, and from the beginning his work among the heathens was performed under papal commission. In 732 the papacy appointed him archbishop in Germany. Some years later he was given the episcopal see at Mainz as his headquarters. Throughout his career he was devoted to the Anglo-Saxon Church, the Benedictine Rule, and the papacy. As he put it, he strove "to hold fast the Catholic faith and Unity, and to yield submission to the Church of Rome as long as life shall last for us."

Boniface also worked with the backing of the Frankish mayors—Charles Martel, Carloman, and Pepin the Short. Armed with the Christian faith and the Benedictine rule, and supported by England, Frankland, and Rome, Boniface labored among the Germanic tribes in Frisia, Thuringia, Hesse, and Bavaria. There he won converts, founded new Benedictine monasteries in the German wilderness, and erected the organizational framework of a disciplined German Church. There were moments of discouragement, as when he wrote to an English abbot, "Have pity upon an old man tried and tossed on all sides by the waves of a German sea." Yet Boniface accomplished much, and the monasteries which he established—particularly the great house of Fulda in Hesse—were to become centers of learning and evangelism which played a great role in converting and civilizing the peoples of Germany.

Reform of the Frankish Church

During the decade following Charles Martel's death in 741 Boniface devoted much of his energy to Frankland itself, for the Frankish Church of the early eighth century stood in desperate need of reform. On the whole it was corrupt, disorganized, and ignorant—the product of several centuries of Merovingian misrule. Many areas of Frankland had no priests at all; numerous Frankish peasants were scarcely removed from heathenism. Priests themselves are reported to have sacrificed animals to the gods and shared their homes with concubines. Charles Martel, although willing enough to support Boniface's missionary endeavors among the Germanic heathens, had no taste for ecclesiastical reforms within his own Frankish Church. Indeed, he weakened the Church by confiscating a considerable amount of ecclesiastical property and granting it to his military vassals. Carloman and Pepin, however, encouraged Boniface to work toward the reform of the Frankish Church, and beginning in 742 he held a series of synods for that purpose. Working in close collaboration with the papacy, Boniface remodeled the Frankish ecclesiastical organization on the disciplined pattern of Anglo-Saxon England and papal Rome. He reformed Frankish monasteries along the lines of the Benedictine Rule, saw to the establishment of monastic schools, encouraged the appointment of dedicated prelates, and worked toward the development of an adequate parish system to bring the Gospel to the country folk. This great missionary and ecclesiastical statesman laid the groundwork for both the new Church in Germany and the reformed Church in Frankland. In doing so, he served as one of the chief architects of the Carolingian cultural revival.

The Franco-Papal Alliance

Carolingian Motives

Boniface's introduction of Roman discipline and organization into the Frankish Church was followed almost immediately by the consummation of a fateful political alliance between Rome and Frankland. It may well have been at Boniface's prompting that Pepin the Short, mayor of the palace, sought papal support for his seizure of the Frankish crown. Though their family retained the enormous prestige always enjoyed by a Germanic royal dynasty, the Merovingians had long been shadowy, do-nothing kings. Even so, if the Carolingians hoped to replace the Merovingians on the Frankish throne, they would have to call upon the most potent spiritual sanction available to their age: papal consecration. In supporting Boniface and his fellow Benedictines the Carolingian mayors had fostered a notable upsurge of papal influence in the Frankish Church. Now, seeking papal support for a dynastic revolution, Pepin the Short could reasonably expect a favorable response in Rome.

Papal Motives

For their part, the popes had been seeking a strong and loyal ally against the untrustworthy Byzantines and the aggressive Lombards who had long been contending for political supremacy in Italy. The Carolingians, with their policy of aid to the Benedictine missionaries and their support of Boniface's reform measures, must have seemed strong candidates for the role of papal champion. And by mid-eighth century a papal champion was desperately needed. Traditionally the papacy had followed the policy of turning to Byzantium for protection against the fierce Lombards who, although they had by now adopted trinitarian Christianity, remained an ominous threat to papal independence. By 750 the popes could no longer depend upon Byzantine protection for two reasons: (1) the Byzantine emperors had recently embraced a doctrine known as *iconoclasm* which the papacy regarded as heretical; (2) Lombard aggression was rapidly becoming so intense that the Byzantine army could no longer be counted on to defend the papacy.

The iconoclastic controversy was the chief religious dispute of the Christian world in the eighth century. It was a conflict over the use in Christian worship of statues and pictures of Christ and the saints. These icons — statues and pictures — had gradually come to assume an important role in Christian worship. Strictly speaking, Christians might venerate them as symbols of the holy persons whom they represented, but in fact there was a strong tendency among the uneducated to worship the objects themselves. A line of reform emperors in Constantinople, beginning with Leo the Isaurian (717–741), sought to end the superstitious practice of worshiping images — vigorously fostered by the numerous itinerant monks of the Eastern Empire — by banning icons altogether. Such a radical decree was offensive to a great many Byzantines, image worshipers and intelligent traditionalists alike. In the West little or no support was to be found for the policy of iconoclasm; the papacy in particular opposed it as heretical and contrary to the Christian tradition. Though it ultimately failed in the Byzantine Church, iconoclasm in the 750s was a vital issue and a storm center of controversy which aroused intense enmity between Rome and Constantinople.* The papacy was deeply apprehensive of depending on the troops of an heretical emperor for its defense.

Even without the iconoclastic controversy it was becoming increasingly doubtful that the papacy could count on the military power of Byzantium in Italy. For by 750 the Lombards were on the rampage once again, threatening not only Byzantine holdings but also the territories of the pope himself. In 751 the Lombards captured Ravenna, which had long served as the Byzantines' Italian capital, and the papal position in Italy became more precarious than ever. If Pepin the Short needed the

support of the papacy, the papacy needed Pepin's support even more.

Pepin the Short

Accordingly the alliance was struck. Pepin sent messengers to Rome with the far from theoretical question, "Is it right that a powerless ruler should continue to bear the title of king?" The pope answered that by the authority of the Apostle Peter, Pepin was king of the Franks, and ordered that he should be anointed into his royal office at Soissons by a papal representative. The anointing ceremony was duly performed in 751. It had the purpose of buttressing the new Carolingian dynasty with the strongest of spiritual sanctions. Not by mere force, but by the supernatural potency of the royal anointing was the new dynasty established on the Frankish throne. Appropriately, this ceremony — the symbolic junction of the power of Rome and Frankland — was performed by the aged Boniface.

With Pepin's coronation the last of the Merovingians were shorn of their long hair and packed off to a monastery. Three years thereafter Boniface, now nearing 80, returned to his missionary work in Frisia and met a martyr's death. In the same year, 754, the Pope himself traveled northward to Frankland where he personally anointed Pepin and his two sons at the royal monastery of Saint-Denis, thereby conferring every spiritual sanction at his disposal upon the upstart Carolingian monarchy. At the same time he sought Pepin's military support against the Lombards.

Pepin obliged, leading his armies into Italy, defeating the Lombards, and donating a large portion of central Italy to the papacy. This "Donation of Pepin" was of notable historical significance. It had the immediate effect of relieving the popes of the ominous Lombard pressure. In the long run, it became the nucleus of the Papal States which were to remain a characteristic feature of Italian politics until the later nineteenth century. For the moment, the papacy had been rescued from its peril. It

* That is, it failed in its extreme form. Eventually a compromise was reached which permitted flat representations of holy persons but not their representation in the round.

remained to be seen whether the popes could prevent their new champion from becoming their master.

Charlemagne

Pepin the Short, like all successful monarchs of the Early Middle Ages, was an able general. As the first Carolingian king he followed in the warlike traditions of his father. Besides defeating the Lombards in Italy he drove the Moslems from Aquitaine and left Frankland larger and better organized than he had found it. Pepin was a great monarch, but he was overshadowed by his even greater son. Charlemagne (768–814) was a phenomenally successful military commander, a statesman of rare ability, a friend of learning, and a monarch possessed of a deep sense of responsibility for the welfare of the society over which he ruled. In this last respect he represents a tremendous advance over his Merovingian predecessors whose relationship to their state was that of a leech to his host.

The Man

Charlemagne towered over his contemporaries both figuratively and literally. He was 6'3½" tall, thick-necked and pot-bellied, yet imposing in appearance for all that. Thanks to his able biographer, Einhard, whose *Life of Charlemagne* was written a few years after the Emperor's death, Charlemagne has come down to posterity as a remarkably three-dimensional figure. Einhard used the Roman historian Suetonius as his model, lifting whole passages from the *Lives of the Twelve Caesars* and adapting many others to his own purposes; yet there is much in Einhard's *Life* that represents his own appraisal of Charlemagne's deeds and character. Reared at the Monastery of Fulda, Einhard served for many years in Charlemagne's court and so gained an intimate knowledge of the Emperor. Einhard's warm admiration for Charlemagne emerges clearly from the biography, yet the author was able to see Charlemagne's faults and foibles as well as his virtues:

Charles was temperate in eating and particularly so in drinking, for he hated drunkenness in anybody, particularly in himself and those of his household. But he found it difficult to abstain from food, and often complained that fasts injured his health. . . . His meals usually consisted of four courses not counting the roast, which his huntsmen used to bring in on the spit. He was fonder of this than of any other dish. While at the table he listened to reading or music. The readings were stories and deeds of olden times; he was also fond of St. Augustine's books, and especially of the one entitled *The City of God*. So moderate was he in the use of wine and all sorts of drink that he rarely allowed himself more than three cups in the course of a meal.

Einhard provides full accounts of Charlemagne's military and political career; but the most fascinating passages in the biography deal with the Emperor's way of life and personal idiosyncrasies which reveal him as a human being rather than a shadowy hero of legend:

While he was dressing and putting on his shoes, he not only gave audience to his friends, but if the Count of the Palace told him of any suit in which his judgment was necessary, he had the parties brought before him forthwith, considered the case, and gave his decision, just as if he were sitting on the judgment seat.

Einhard was also at pains to show Charlemagne's thirst for learning. He portrays the Emperor as a fluent master of Latin, a student of Greek, a speaker of such skill that he might have passed for a teacher of eloquence, a devotee of the liberal arts, and in particular a student of astronomy who learned to calculate the motions of the heavenly bodies. Einhard concludes this impressive discussion of Charlemagne's scholarship with a final tribute which unwittingly discloses the Emperor's severe scholastic limitations:

He also tried to write, and used to keep tablets and blanks in bed under his pillow so that in his leisure hours he might accustom his hand to form the letters; but as he did not begin his efforts at an early age but late in life, they met with poor success.

Charlemagne could be warm and talkative, but he could also be hard, cruel, and violent, and his subjects came to regard him with both admiration and fear. He was possessed of a strong, if superficial, piety which prompted him to build churches, collect relics, and struggle heroically for a Christian cultural revival in Frankland. But it did not prevent him from filling his court with concubines and other disreputable characters. In short Charlemagne, despite his military and political genius, was a man of his age, in tune with its most progressive forces yet by no means removed from its barbaric past.

Military Career

Above all else Charlemagne was a warrior-king. He led his armies on yearly campaigns as a matter of course. When his magnates and their retainers assembled around him annually on the May Field the question was not whether to go to war but where to fight. Traditionally the Franks had fought on foot; but the epoch of Charles Martel and Pepin the Short had

This contemporary illustration which shows how the stirrup was used by Carolingian warriors is from the Golden Psalter of St. Gall.

witnessed the rise of cavalry as the elite force in the Frankish army. This momentous shift, which amounted in effect to the birth of medieval knighthood, was perhaps associated with the coming of the stirrup to Frankland in the earlier 700s. For the stirrup gave stability to the mounted warrior and made possible the charge of cavalrymen with lances braced against their arms which was such an effective feature of later feudal warfare. In any case, the conquering armies of Charlemagne were built around a nucleus of highly trained horsemen. Such warriors were still something of a novelty in the age of Charlemagne, and under his masterful leadership they struck fear in their foes and acquired a reputation for invincibility.

Italy and Spain

It was only gradually, however, that Charlemagne developed a coherent scheme of conquest built on a notion of Christian mission and addressed to the goal of unifying and systematically expanding the Christian West. At the behest of the papacy Charlemagne followed his father's footsteps into Italy. There he conquered the Lombards completely in 774, incorporated them into his growing state, and assumed for himself the Lombard crown. Thenceforth he employed the title, "King of the Franks and the Lombards."

Between 778 and 801 Charlemagne conducted a series of campaigns against the Spanish Moslems which met with only limited success. He did succeed in establishing a frontier district, the "Spanish March," on the Spanish side of the Pyrenees. In later generations the southern portion of Charlemagne's Spanish March evolved into the country of Barcelona which remained more receptive to the influence of French institutions and customs than any other district in Spain. A relatively minor military episode in Charlemagne's Spanish campaign of 778 — an attack by a band of Christian Basques against the rearguard of Charlemagne's army as it was withdrawing across the Pyrenees into Frankland — became the inspiration for one of the great epic poems of the eleventh century: the *Song of Roland*. The unknown author or authors of the poem transformed the Basques into Moslems and made the battle an heroic struggle between the rival faiths. Charlemagne was portrayed as a godlike conqueror, phenomenally aged, and Roland, the warden of the Breton March and commander of the rearguard, acquired a fame in literature far out of proportion to his actual historical importance.

The Eastern Frontier

Charlemagne devoted much of his strength to the expansion of his eastern frontier. In 787 he conquered and absorbed Bavaria, organizing its easternmost district into a forward defensive barrier against the Slavs. This East March or *Ostmark* became the nucleus of a new state later to be called Austria. In the 790s Charlemagne pushed still farther to the southeast, destroying the rich and predatory Avar state which had long tormented Eastern Europe. For many generations the Avars had been enriching themselves on the plunder of their victims and on heavy tribute payments from Byzantium and elsewhere. Charlemagne had the good fortune to seize a substantial portion of the Avar treasure; it is reported that 15 four-ox wagons were required to transport the hoard of gold, silver, and precious garments back to Frankland. The loot of the Avars contributed significantly to the resources of Charlemagne's treasury and broadened the scope of his subsequent building program and patronage to scholars and churches. Indeed, it placed him on a financial footing comparable to that of the Byzantine emperors themselves.

Charlemagne's greatest and most prolonged military effort was directed against the heathen Saxons of northern Germany. With the twin goals of protecting the Frankish Rhinelands and bringing new souls into the Church, he campaigned for some thirty years (772–804), conquering the Saxons repeatedly and baptizing them by force, only to have them rebel when his armies withdrew. In a fit of savage exasperation he ordered the execution of 4500 unfaithful Saxons in a single bloody day in 782. At length, however, Saxony submitted to the remorseless pressure of Charlemagne's soldiers and the Benedictine monks who followed in their wake. By about 800, Frankish control of Saxony was well established, and in subsequent decades Christianity seeped gradually into the Saxon soul. A century and a half later Christian Saxons were governing the most powerful state in Europe and were fostering a significant artistic and intellectual revival that was to enrich the culture of tenth-century Christendom.

Charlemagne's Empire

Imperial Coronation

Charlemagne's armies, by incorporating the great territories of central Germany into the new civilization, had succeeded where the legions of Augustus and his successors had failed. No longer a mere Frankish king, Charlemagne, by 800, was the master of the West. A few small Christian states such as the principalities of southern Italy and the kingdoms of Anglo-Saxon England remained outside his jurisdiction, but with these relatively minor exceptions Charlemagne's political sway extended throughout Western Christendom. He was, in truth, an emperor, and on Christmas Day, 800, his immense accomplishment was given formal recognition when Pope Leo III placed the imperial crown upon his head and acclaimed him "Emperor of the Romans." From the standpoint of legal theory this dramatic and epoch-making act reconstituted the Roman Empire in the West after an interregnum of 324 years. In another sense it was the ultimate consummation of the Franco-Papal Alliance of 751.

The imperial coronation of Charlemagne is difficult to interpret and has evoked heated controversy among historians. According to Einhard, Pope Leo III took Charlemagne by surprise and bestowed upon him an unwanted dignity. Charlemagne had such an aversion to the titles of Emperor and Augustus, so Einhard reports, "that he declared he would not have set foot in the Church the day that they were conferred, although it was a great feast day, if he could have foreseen the design of the pope."

Modern historians have tended to be skeptical of this assertion. It has been argued that Charlemagne was much too powerful—much too firmly in control of events—to permit a coronation that he did not wish. More likely the imperial coronation of 800, like the royal coronation of Pepin the Short in 751, represents a coalescence of papal and Carolingian interests. For some years Charlemagne had been attempting to attain a status comparable to that of the Byzantine emperors. In 794 he had abandoned the practice, traditional among Germanic kings, of traveling constantly with his court from estate to estate, and had established his permanent capital at Aachen in Austrasia. Here he sought, though vainly, to create a Constantinople of his own. Aachen was called "New Rome," and an impressive palace church was built in the Byzantine style—almost literally a poor man's Sancta Sophia. Even though Charlemagne's "Mary Church" at Aachen was a far cry from Justinian's mas-

Interior of the "Mary Church" at Aachen. The Byzantine arches and the structural formation are very similar to Justinian's basilica of San Vitale at Ravenna.

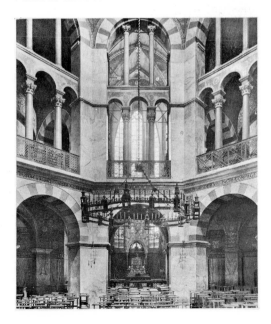

terpiece, it was a marvel for its time and place and made a deep impression on contemporaries. Einhard describes it as a beautiful basilica adorned with gold and silver lamps, with rails and doors of solid brass, and with columns and marbles from Rome and Ravenna. It was evidently the product of a major effort on Charlemagne's part—an effort not only to create a beautiful church but also to ape the Byzantines. The coronation of 800 may well have been an expression of this same imitative policy.

Papacy and Empire

The papacy, on the other hand, must have regarded the coronation as a priceless opportunity to regain some of the initiative it had lost to the all-powerful Charlemagne. To be sure, the Carolingians had been promoted from kings to emperors; but their empire thenceforth bore the stamp, "Made in Rome." In later years the popes would insist that what they gave they could also take away. If the papacy could make emperors it could also depose them. Indeed, it was only shortly before this that the papal chancery had produced a famous forged document called the "Donation of Constantine" * in which the first Christian emperor allegedly resigned all his authority to the pope and received it back as a kind of papal commission. The popes believed that the emperors ought to be papal stewards wielding their secular political authority in the interests of the Roman Church. So convincing was this theory of papal supremacy in the eyes of the papacy that it justified the use of any documentation to support its case. The "Donation of Constantine," therefore, was not an effort to rewrite history but an attempt to buttress what the papacy regarded as historical truth.

Though Charlemagne always respected the papacy he was unwilling to cast himself in the subordinate role which papal theory demanded of him. He was careful to retain the title, "King of the Franks and the Lombards" alongside his new title of "Emperor"; when the time came to crown his son emperor, Charlemagne excluded the pope from the ceremony and did the honors himself. In these maneuvers we are witnessing the prologue to a long, bitter struggle over the correct relationship between empire and papacy which reached its crescendo in the eleventh, twelfth, and thirteenth centuries. At stake was the ultimate mastery of Western Christendom.

But during the reign of Charlemagne the struggle remained latent for the most part. Charlemagne's power was unrivaled, and the popes were much too weak to oppose him seriously. Indeed, the warm Carolingian-papal relations of Pepin's day continued, and the papacy was nearly smothered in Charlemagne's affectionate embrace.

Carolingian Theocracy

At no time since has Europe been so nearly united as under Charlemagne. And never again would Western Christendom flirt so seriously with theocracy. The papal anointing of Pepin and Charlemagne gave the Carolingian monarchy a sacred, almost priestly quality with which Charlemagne merged his immense authority to govern not only the body politic but the imperial Church as well. The laws and regulations of his reign, which are known as *capitularies,* dealt with both ecclesiastical and secular matters. Though he did not claim to legislate on Church doctrine he felt a deep sense of responsibility for purifying and systematizing ecclesiastical discipline. He was a far greater force in the Carolingian Church than was the pope. He summoned a number of ecclesiastical synods and even presided over one of them. Indeed, the significant intellectual revival known as the "Carolingian Renaissance" was mostly a product of Charlemagne's concern for the welfare of the Church and the perpetuation of ecclesiastical culture.

* Probably sometime in the 740s.

The Carolingian Renaissance

The term "Carolingian Renaissance" is dangerously misleading. Charlemagne's Age produced no lofty abstract thought, no original philosophical or theological system, no Leonardo da Vinci. If we look for a "renaissance" we are bound to be disappointed. The intellectual task of the Carolingian age was far less exalted, far more rudimentary: to rescue continental culture from the pit of ignorance into which it was sinking.

As with so many other aspects of the era the Carolingian Renaissance bears the stamp of Charlemagne's will and initiative. It was he who saw the desperate need for schools in his kingdom and sought to provide them. There could be no question of establishing institutions of higher learning. None existed north of the Alps, and none would emerge until the High Middle Ages. It was for the Carolingians to build a system of primary and secondary education, and even this was an immensely difficult task. Frankland had no professional class of teachers either lay or clerical. The only hope for pedagogical reform lay with the Church, which had an almost exclusive monopoly on literacy. Accordingly, Charlemagne endeavored to force the cathedrals and monasteries of his realm to operate schools which would preserve and disseminate the rudiments of classical-Christian culture. A capitulary of 789 commands that

In every episcopal See and in every monastery, instruction shall be given in the psalms, musical notation, chant, the computation of years and seasons, and grammar, and all books used shall be carefully corrected.

A curriculum of the sort described in this capitulary can hardly be described as intellectually sophisticated or demanding, yet it is clear enough that many Carolingian monasteries and cathedrals fell considerably short of the standards which it sought to establish. Still, Charlemagne succeeded in improving vastly the quantity and quality of schooling in his empire. There was even an attempt to make village priests provide free instruction in reading and writing. Only a minute fraction of Charlemagne's subjects acquired literacy. But those few provided an all-important learned nucleus which kept knowledge alive and transmitted it to future generations. It was above all in the monastic schools that learning flourished—in houses such as Fulda, Tours, and Reichenau. During the turbulent generations following Charlemagne's death many of these monastic schools survived to become seedbeds of the far greater intellectual awakening of the eleventh and twelfth centuries. In sum, Charlemagne's pedagogical reforms insured that learning in Europe would never again descend to the pre-Carolingian level.

The Carolingian Scholars

As an integral part of his effort to raise the intellectual standards of his realm and sustain Christian culture Charlemagne assembled scholars at his court from all over Europe. One such scholar was the Emperor's biographer, Einhard, from eastern Frankland. Another was the poet-historian, Paul the Deacon, from the great Italian Benedictine house of Monte Cassino. Paul the Deacon's *History of the Lombards* provides an invaluable account of that Germanic tribe and its settlement in Italy. From Spain came Theodulf, later bishop of Orleans and abbot of Fleury, a tireless supporter of Charlemagne's pedagogical reforms as well as a poet of considerable talent. The most important of these Carolingian scholars was the Northumbrian Alcuin of York, a student of a student of Bede's and the last important mind to be produced by the Northumbrian Renaissance. Alcuin, along with his fellow countrymen of an earlier generation—Wilfred of Ripon, Willibrord, and Boniface—represents the vital connecting link between the vigorous Christian cultural life of seventh- and eighth-century England and the intellectual upsurge of Carolingian Frankland.

Alcuin performed the essential task of

Writing of the eighth century, from a Capitulary of Charlemagne addressed to Pope Adrian I in 784.

preparing an accurate new edition of the Bible purged of the scribal errors which had crept into it over the centuries, thereby saving Christian culture from the hopeless confusion arising from the corruption of its most fundamental text. For many years the chief scholar in Charlemagne's court school, Alcuin spent his final years as abbot of St. Martin of Tours. He was extraordinarily well educated for his period, and his approach to learning typified the whole philosophy of the Carolingian Renaissance: to produce accurate copies of important traditional texts, to encourage the establishment of schools, and in every way possible to cherish and transmit the classical-Christian cultural tradition (without, however, adding to it in any significant way). Alcuin and his fellow scholars were neither intellectual innovators nor men of conspicuous holiness. Drawn by Charlemagne's wealth and power and enriched by his patronage, they struggled to improve the scholarly level of the Carolingian Church; but they showed little concern for deepening its spiritual life or exploring uncharted regions of speculative thought. They had the talents and inclinations — and the limitations — of the schoolmaster. At best they were scholars and humanists; in no sense could they be described as philosophers or mystics.

Accordingly, Alcuin, Theodulf, Einhard, Paul the Deacon, and others like them purified and regularized the liturgy of the Church and encouraged the preaching of sermons. They carried on some of the monastic reforms begun by Boniface and saw to it that every important monastery had a school. It was a question not of producing new Aristotles and Augustines but

of preserving literacy itself. A new, standardized script was developed — the Carolingian minuscule — which derived in part from the Irish and Northumbrian scripts of the previous century. Thenceforth the Carolingian minuscule superseded the heterogeneous and often illegible scripts earlier employed on the Continent. Throughout the realm monks set about copying manuscripts on an unprecedented scale. If classical-Christian culture was advanced very little by these activities it was at least preserved. Above all, its base was broadened. In the task they set themselves, these Carolingian scholars were eminently successful.

Carolingian Renaissance after Charlemagne

It is characteristic of the powerful theocratic tendencies of the age that this significant cultural-pedagogical achievement was accomplished through royal rather than papal initiative. Germanic monarchy and classical-Christian culture had joined hands at last. With the breakdown of European unity after Charlemagne's death the momentary fusion of political and cultural energies dissolved; yet the intellectual revival continued. A deeply spiritual movement of monastic reform and moral regeneration began in Aquitaine under the leadership of the ardent and saintly Benedict of Aniane. Soon the influence of this movement took hold at the court of Charlemagne's son and successor, Louis the Pious. Louis gave St. Benedict of Aniane the privilege of visiting any monastery in the Empire and tightening its discipline in whatever way he chose. And in 817 a significantly elaborated and modified version of the old Benedictine Rule, based on the strict monastic regulations of Benedict of Aniane, was promulgated for all the monasteries of the Empire and given the weight of imperial law. Benedict of Aniane's reform represents a marked shift from the spiritually superficial monastic regulations of Charlemagne's day to a deep concern for the Christ-centered life. The elaborate Benedictine Rule of 817 lost its status as imperial law on Louis the Pious' death in 840, but it remained an inspiration to subsequent monastic reform movements in the centuries that followed. Thenceforth the Benedictine life *par excellence* was based on Benedict of Aniane's modification of the original Rule.

While Carolingian spiritual life was deepening in the years after Charlemagne's death, Carolingian scholarship continued to flourish in the cathedral and monastic schools. A vigorous controversy over the question of free will and predestination testifies to the vitality of Carolingian thought in the early and middle decades of the ninth century. And in keeping with the Carolingian intellectual program of preserving the classical-Christian tradition, learned churchmen of the Carolingian Renaissance's "second generation" devoted themselves to the preparation of encyclopedic compilations of received knowledge, unoriginal but important none the less in the significant process of cultural transmission. For example, Raban Maur (d. 856), abbot of the great monastery of Fulda, provided an elaborate encyclopedia on the pattern of Isidore of Seville's *Etymologies,* entitled *De Universo.* He also carried forward the Carolingian pedagogical tradition by writing a handbook on the instruction of the clergy—*De Clericorum Institutione*—which had a significant influence on the operation of monastic schools.

John Scotus

The most interesting scholar in this "second generation" was the Irishman, John Scotus Erigena, who stands as the one original thinker of the whole Carolingian age. John Scotus or John the Scot (the "Scots" in his days were inhabitants of Ireland rather than Scotland) served for years in the court of Charlemagne's grandson, Charles the Bald. Not only a brilliant speculative thinker, he was also a rather precocious wit, at least if we can give credence to the later legend of a dinner-table conversation between John the Scot and King Charles the Bald. The King, intending to needle his court scholar, asked the rhetorical question, "What is there that separates a Scot from a sot," to which John is alleged to have replied, "Only the dinner table."

John Scotus was a profound student of Neoplatonism and the only Western European scholar of his age who was a master of the Greek tongue. He translated into Latin a crucially important Greek philosophical treatise, *On the Celestial Hierarchy,* written by an anonymous late-fifth-century Christian Neoplatonist known as the Pseudo-Dionysius. This author was incorrectly identified in the Middle Ages as Dionysius the Areopagite, the first-century Athenian philosopher who is described in the *Acts of the Apostles* as being converted to Christianity by St. Paul. Accordingly, the writings of the Pseudo-Dionysius, even though tinged with pantheism, passed into the Middle Ages with the powerful credentials of an early Christian author who was a Pauline convert. In reality, the importance of the Pseudo-Dionysius lay in his providing a Christian dimension to the philosophical scheme of Plotinus and other pagan Neoplatonists. The unknowable and indescribable Neoplatonic god—the center and source of the concentric circles of reality—was identified with the God of the Christians. Such a god could not be approached intellectually but only by means of a mystical experience; hence, the Pseudo-Dionysius became an important source of inspiration to later Christian mystics.

Stimulated by the work of the Pseudo-Dionysius which he translated, John Scotus went on to write a highly original Neoplatonic treatise of his own, *On the Division of Nature,* which, in its merely shaded distinction between God and the created world, reflected the Neoplatonic tendency toward pantheism. The work was condemned as heretical in the thirteenth century, but it made little impact on contemporaries who lacked both the interest and the background to understand it. John Scotus is a lonely figure in intellectual history, without any immediate predecessors or successors. He founded no schools of thought and carried on no real philosophical dialogue with his contemporaries who were scholars, poets, and pedants rather than abstract thinkers. He figures as the supreme intellect in the West between St. Augustine and the philosophers of the High Middle Ages, yet being neither the direct product of earlier intellectual currents nor the cause of subsequent ones, he played a surprisingly minor role in the evolution of thought. He remains, nevertheless, the one interesting philosopher of the Carolingian epoch.

Historical Significance of Carolingian Renaissance

The intellectual revival instigated by Charlemagne reverberated down through subsequent generations. John Scotus' Neoplatonism may have been generally ignored and quickly forgotten. Yet in the monasteries and cathedrals of the ninth and tenth centuries, particularly in the German districts of Charlemagne's old empire, documents continued to be copied, schools continued to operate, and commentaries and epitomes of ancient texts continued to appear. By the eleventh century Europe was ready to build soaring and original intellectual edifices on her sturdy Carolingian foundations.

The Carolingian State

Charlemagne's Empire was an ephemeral thing, arising from a chaotic past and disintegrating in the turbulent age that followed. It is far easier to understand why the Empire broke up than to explain how such a vast, primitive, amorphous state was able to coalesce even briefly. The answer to this puzzle is to be found above all in the person of Charlemagne himself. It was Charlemagne who held his immense empire together, and he did so by the quality of his leadership and the strength of his personality. In an era of primitive roads and wretched communications he was obliged to depend heavily on the competence and loyalty of the counts, dukes, and margraves who administered his provinces. He kept some control over these great lords by sending pairs of inspectors known as *missi dominici* (envoys of the lord) from his court into the provinces to insure the implementation of his will. These *missi dominici*, consisting normally of one churchman and one layman, typified the theocratic trend of Charlemagne's Age. They seem to have been moderately effective in binding the empire together, but only because they were received respectfully in the provinces as representatives of a mighty, fear-inspiring monarch. The allegiance of Charlemagne's counts and dukes was mostly a product of their respect for Charlemagne himself. They obeyed his commands and submitted to his capitularies not out of patriotism to his state but because of their devotion to his person. In sum, the administrative institutions of the Carolingian Empire were grossly inadequate to the needs of a great state. Beneath the imposing military and cultural veneer Carolingian Europe was still semi-barbaric. Alcuin was yielding to illusion when he told Charlemagne, "If your intentions are carried out, it may be that a new Athens will arise in Frankland, and an Athens fairer than of old, for our Athens, ennobled by the teachings of Christ, will surpass the wisdom of the Academy." Alcuin's vision was a pathetic mirage; the Carolingian state remained a land of rude, untutored warriors and peasants just emerging from barbarianism.

Charlemagne's "Roman Empire" was an almost ludicrous parody of that of Augustus, yet one can only admire this dogged Carolingian who could do so much with so little; who could make such an effort to transcend his own barbaric past; who as an adult struggled vainly to learn how to write; who sought bravely but hopelessly to master the lofty subtleties of Augustine's *City of God*. The historian Christopher Dawson caught the spirit of Charlemagne's achievement perfectly when he wrote, "The unwieldly empire of Charles the Great did not long survive the death of its founder, and it never really attained the economic and social organization of a civilized state. But, for all that, it marks the first emergence of the European culture from the twilight of prenatal existence into the consciousness of active life." [1]

1. C. Dawson, *The Making of Europe*, Meridian Books, 1957, p. 187.

THE NEW INVASIONS

Tentative though it was, the economic and cultural revival under Charlemagne might conceivably have developed steadily in the direction of a prosperous and sophisticated civilization had it not been for the devastating new invasions that followed Charlemagne's death in 814. Until then the Carolingian realm had enjoyed at least relative peace. Intellectual life, although still rudimentary, was in the process of reawakening, and with the stimulus of the second silver coinage which Charlemagne issued, commerce quickened. One historian has recently gone so far as to suggest that under the bracing influence of Charlemagne's economic policy towns were beginning to grow and flourish once again. But these hopeful signs proved to be a false dawn. For during the ninth and tenth centuries Europe was obliged to fight for its life against the triple thrust of alien invaders—the semi-nomadic Hungarians from the East, the piratical Saracens (Moslems) from the South, and the wide-ranging Vikings from the North. As a result, the maturing of a higher civilization was delayed for another two centuries.

The Later Carolingians

Louis the Pious

It would be wrong to ascribe the political fragmentation of the Carolingian Empire entirely to these outside pressures, for Charlemagne himself, in keeping with Frankish tradition, planned to divide his state among his several sons. As it happened, however, Charlemagne outlived all but one of them. But the luck of the Carolingians was still running, and when the great conqueror died in 814 his realm passed intact to his remaining heir, Louis the Pious (814–840).

Though Louis was by no means incompetent, his military and political talents were distinctly inferior to those of his father Charlemagne, his grandfather Pepin the Short, and his great-grandfather Charles Martel. Carolingian unity continued but Carolingian leadership showed signs of faltering. Louis the Pious was well named. He ran Charlemagne's minstrels and concubines out of the imperial court and replaced them with priests and monks. Far more than his hard-headed father, Louis committed himself to the dream of a unified Christian Empire—a City of God brought down to earth. Yet he was far less suited than Charlemagne to the Herculean task of maintaining unity and cohesion in the immense, heterogeneous empire which the Carolingians had won. He was the first of his line to conceive the notion of bequeathing supreme political authority to his eldest son and thereby making the unity of the kingdom a matter of policy rather than chance. Ironically, he turned out to be the last Carolingian to rule an undivided

Frankish realm. His bold plan for a single succession was foiled by the ambitions of his younger sons who rebelled openly against him and plunged the empire into civil war.

Treaty of Verdun

When Louis the Pious' unhappy reign ended in 840, his three surviving sons struggled bitterly for the spoils. The eldest of the three, Lothar, claimed the indivisible imperial title and hegemony over the entire realm. The other two sons, Louis the German and Charles the Bald, struggled to win independent royal authority in East and West Frankland respectively. In the end, Lothar was obliged to yield to the combined might of his younger brothers. The controversy was settled by the momentous Treaty of Verdun in 843 which permanently

divided the empire and foreshadowed the political structure of modern Europe. Lothar was permitted to keep the imperial title, but was denied any sort of superior jurisdiction over the realms of Louis the German and Charles the Bald. Louis ruled East Frankland which became the nucleus of the modern German state. In a very real sense, he was Germany's first king. Charles the Bald became king of West Frankland which evolved into modern France. The Emperor Lothar retained a long, narrow, heterogeneous strip of territory which stretched for some thousand miles northward from Italy through Burgundy, Alsace, Lorraine, and the Netherlands, embracing considerable portions of western Germany and eastern France. * This Middle Kingdom included the two "imperial capitals"— Rome and Aachen—but its long exposed

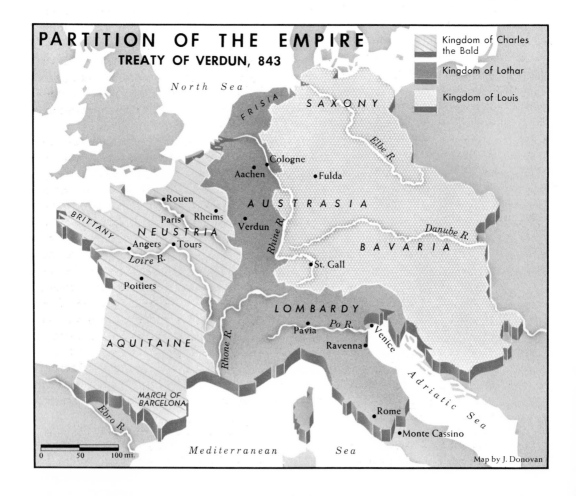

PARTITION OF THE EMPIRE
TREATY OF VERDUN, 843

Kingdom of Charles the Bald
Kingdom of Lothar
Kingdom of Louis

North Sea
FRISIA
SAXONY
Elbe R.
Cologne
Aachen
•Fulda
•Rouen
AUSTRASIA
BRITTANY
Paris• Rheims
Verdun
NEUSTRIA
Rhine R.
Danube R.
Angers •Tours
BAVARIA
Loire R.
•St. Gall
•Poitiers
LOMBARDY
Po R.
AQUITAINE
Rhone R.
Pavia
Venice
Ravenna•
Adriatic Sea
MARCH OF BARCELONA
•Rome
Ebro R.
•Monte Cassino
0   50   100 mi.
Mediterranean   Sea
Map by J. Donovan

frontiers were virtually impossible to defend, and it was utterly lacking in unity. At Lothar's death in 855 it was subdivided among his three sons, one of whom inherited Carolingian Italy and the increasingly insignificant imperial title. From the ninth century to the twentieth, fragments of Lothar's middle kingdom have been the source of endless bitter territorial disputes between Germany and France.

The struggles among Charlemagne's grandsons occurred against a background of Viking, Hungarian, and Saracen invasions which accelerated and vastly increased the tendency toward political fragmentation brought about by internal weaknesses. But even without the invasions, and without the Frankish tradition of divided succession, it was unlikely that Charlemagne's huge, unwieldy empire could have long remained intact once his iron hand had been removed from control. As it turned out, even the more modest political units arising from the Treaty of Verdun were too large—too far removed from the desperate realities of the countryside to cope successfully with the lightning raids of Viking shipmen or Hungarian horsemen. During the ninth and tenth centuries Carolingian leadership was visibly failing. The incapacity of the later Carolingians was nowhere better illustrated than in their names: Charles the Fat, Charles the Simple, Louis the Child, Louis the Blind.

CAROLINGIAN CHRONOLOGY

687: Pepin of Heristal, Carolingian mayor of Austrasia, defeats Neustria; Carolingian hegemony established.
714–741: Rule of Charles Martel.
733: Arabs defeated at Tours.
741–768: Rule of Pepin the Short.
751: Pepin crowned king of the Franks. Merovingian Dynasty ends.
754: Death of St. Boniface.
768–814: Reign of Charlemagne.
772–804: Charlemagne's Saxon Wars.

800: Charlemagne crowned Roman Emperor.
814–840: Reign of Louis the Pious.
843: Treaty of Verdun.

Impact of Invasions

The Saracens, Hungarians, and Vikings, who plundered the declining Carolingian state, were in part drawn by the growing political vacuum, and in part impelled by forces operating in their own homelands. Europe suffered grievously from their marauding, yet it was strong enough in the end to survive the invasions and absorb the invaders. And they were the last that Western Christendom was destined to endure. From about A.D. 1000 to the present the West has had the unique opportunity of developing on its own, sheltered from alien attacks that have so disrupted other civilizations over the past millennium. As the historian Marc Bloch has said, "It is surely not unreasonable to think that this extraordinary immunity, of which we have shared the privilege with scarcely any people but the Japanese, was one of the fundamental factors of European civilization. . . ."[2]

Yet in the ninth and tenth centuries Europe's hardpressed peoples had no way of knowing that the invasions would one day end. A Frankish historian of the mid-ninth century wrote in a tone of anguish: "The number of ships grows larger and larger; the great host of Northmen continually increases; on every hand Christians are the victims of massacres, looting, and incendiarism—clear proof of which will remain as long as the world itself endures. The Northmen capture every city they pass through, and none can withstand them." In southern Gaul people prayed for divine protection against the Saracens: "Eternal Trinity . . . deliver thy Christian people from the oppression of the pagans." To the

---

* See map on facing page.

2. Marc Bloch, *Feudal Society,* translator L. A. Manyon, Chicago, 1961, p. 56.

north they prayed, "From the savage nation of the Northmen, which lays waste our realms, deliver us, O God." And in northern Italy: "Against the arrows of the Hungarians be thou our protector."

Saracens

The Saracens of the ninth and tenth centuries, unlike their predecessors in the seventh and early eighth, came as brigands rather than conquerors and settlers. From their pirate nests in Africa, Spain, and the Mediterranean islands they preyed on shipping, plundered coastal cities, and sailed up rivers to carry their devastation far inland. Saracen bandit lairs were established on the southern coast of Gaul from which the marauders conducted raids far and wide through the countryside and kidnapped pilgrims crossing the Alpine passes. Charlemagne had never possessed much of a navy, and his successors found themselves helpless to defend their coasts. In 846 Saracen brigands raided Rome itself, profaning its churches and stealing its treasures. As late as 982 a German king was severely defeated by Saracen bandits in southern Italy; but by then the raids were tapering off. Southern Europe, now bristling with fortifications, had learned to defend itself and was even beginning to challenge Saracen domination of the western Mediterranean.

Hungarians and Vikings

The Hungarians or Magyars, fierce nomadic horsemen from the Asiatic steppes, settled in the land now known as Hungary. From the late 800s to 955 they terrorized Germany, northern Italy, and eastern Gaul. Hungarian raiding parties ranged far and wide seeking defenseless settlements to plunder, avoiding fortified towns, outriding and outmaneuvering the armies sent against them. In time, however, they became more sedentary, gave more attention to their farms, and consequently lost much of their nomadic savagery. In 955 King Otto the Great of Germany crushed a large Hungarian army at the battle of Lechfeld and brought the raids to an end at last. Within another half century, the Hungarians had adopted Christianity and were becoming integrated into the community of Christian Europe.

The Vikings, or Norsemen, were the most fearsome invaders of all. These redoubtable warrior-seafarers came from Scandinavia, the very land that had, centuries before, disgorged many of the Germanic barbarians into Europe. Thus the ninth century Vikings and the Germanic invaders of Roman times had similar ethnic backgrounds. But to the ninth-century European—the product of countless Germanic-Celtic-Roman intermarriages, tamed by the Church and by centuries of settled life—the Vikings seemed a hostile and alien people.

Then, as now, the Scandinavians were divided roughly into three groups: Danes, Swedes, and Norwegians. During the great age of Viking expansion in the ninth and tenth centuries the Danes, who were brought cheek to jowl with the Carolingian Empire by Charlemagne's conquest of Saxony, focused their attention on Frankland and England. The Norwegians raided and settled in Scotland, Ireland, and the North Atlantic. The Swedes concentrated on the East—the Baltic shores, Russia, and the Byzantine Empire. Yet the three Norse peoples had much in common, and the distinctions between them were by no means sharp. It is therefore proper to regard their raids, their astonishing explorations, and their far-flung commercial enterprises as a single great international movement.

Though the breakdown of Carolingian leadership doubtless acted as a magnet to Viking marauders, their raids on the West began as early as Charlemagne's Age. The basic causes for their great outward thrust must be sought in Scandinavia itself. Since pre-tenth-century Scandinavia is almost a closed book to historians, their explanations for the Viking outburst are little more than educated guesses. It is likely, however, that the Scandinavian population, once sharply reduced by the outward migrations of Roman times, had increased by the later 700s to a level which the primitive Norse agriculture was scarcely able to support. The pressure of overpopulation was probably aggravated by growing centralized royal power which cramped the more restless spirits and drove them to seek adventures and opportunities abroad. A third factor was the development of improved Viking ships, eminently seaworthy, propelled by both sail and oars, and capable of carrying crews of 40 to 100 warriors at speeds up to ten knots. In these long ships the tall, muscular, reddish-haired Viking warriors struck the ports of Northern Europe. They sailed up rivers far into the interior, plundering the towns and monasteries of Frankland and England, sometimes stealing horses and riding across the countryside to spread their devastation still further.

Attacks against England

England was the first to suffer from Viking attacks. About 789 three long ships touched the Channel coast in Dorset and Vikings poured out of them to loot and sack a nearby town. Thenceforth the Anglo-Saxon kingdoms were tormented by incessant Viking raids. In 794 Norse brigands annihilated the Northumbrian monastery of Jarrow, where Bede had lived and died. Other great monastic cultural centers of Northumbria suffered a like fate.

In 842 the Danes plundered London, and a few years thereafter they began to establish permanent winter bases in England which freed them from the necessity of returning to Scandinavia after the raiding season. By the later 800s they had turned from simple piracy to large-scale occupation and permanent settlement. One after another the Anglo-Saxon kingdoms were overrun until at length, in the 880s, only the southern kingdom of Wessex remained free of Danish control—and even it came within a hair of falling before the Danish onslaught.

Attacks against the Continent

To mariners such as the Vikings the English Channel was a boulevard rather than a barrier, and their raiding parties attacked the English and Frankish shores indiscriminately. They established permanent bases at the mouths of great rivers, and sailed up them to plunder defenseless monasteries and sack towns. Antwerp was ravaged in 837, Rouen in 841, Hamburg and Paris in 845, Charlemagne's old capital at Aachen in 881. Europe was truly under siege.

But if some Europeans were driven to helpless resignation others fought doggedly to protect their lands and their heritage. King Alfred the Great of Wessex saved his kingdom from Danish conquest in the late 870s and began the arduous task of rolling back the Danish armies in England. King Arnulf of East Frankland won a decisive victory over the Norsemen in 891 at the battle of the Dyle and thereby vastly decreased the Viking pressure on Germany—although it was at this very moment that the Hungarian raids began. West Frankland continued to suffer for a time, but in about 911 King Charles the Simple created a friendly Viking buffer state in northern France by concluding an epoch-making treaty with a Norse chieftain named Rollo. The Vikings in Rollo's band had been conducting raids from their settlement at the mouth of the Seine River. Charles, less simple than his name would imply, believed that if he could make Rollo his ally the Seine settlement might prove an effective barrier against further raids. Rollo became a Christian, married Charles the Simple's daughter, and recognized at least in some sense the superiority of the West Frankish monarchy. Thus his state acquired legitimacy in the eyes of Western Christendom. Expanding gradually under Rollo and his successors it became known as the land of the Northmen or "Normandy." Over the next century and a half the Normans became as good Christians as the Franks.

ICELAND

Vikings

NORWAY

SWEDEN

DENMARK

Dnieper R.

Kiev

Aachen
Paris

Rhine R.

Hungarians

Tours

Danube R.

Marseilles

CORSICA   Rome

Constantinople

SARDINIA   Naples

Moslems   *Mediterranean Sea*

INVASIONS

→ Vikings
- - → Moslems
➤ Hungarians

0   300   600 mi.
Map by J. Donovan

established temporary settlements on the northern coasts of North America itself in the eleventh century, thereby anticipating Columbus by half a millennium.

Russia

To the east, Swedish Vikings overran Finland and penetrated far southward across European Russia to trade with Constantinople and Baghdad. The Byzantine emperors took inordinate pride in the tall Norse mercenaries who served in their imperial guard. In Russia a Swedish dynasty established itself at Novgorod in the later ninth century, ruling over the indigenous Slavic population. In the tenth century a Norse ruler at Novgorod captured the strategic Russian city of Kiev which became the nucleus of a powerful, well-organized Russian state. Deeply influenced by the culture of its subjects, the dynasty at Kiev became far more Slavic than Scandinavian. It adopted Byzantine Christianity around the turn of the millennium, and looked to Constantinople rather than to the West for its religious and cultural inspiration. Altogether, the Norsemen showed that they could build kingdoms as well as destroy them.

Twilight of the Viking Age

The development of centralized monarchies in Denmark, Norway, and Sweden ultimately resulted in taming the Viking spirit. As Scandinavia became increasingly civilized its kings discouraged the activities of roaming independent warrior bands, and its social environment gave rise to a somewhat more humdrum, sedentary life. Far into the eleventh century England continued to face the attacks of Norsemen but these invaders were no longer pirate bands; rather, they were royal armies led by Scandinavian kings. The nature of the Scandinavian threat had changed profoundly; by the late eleventh century the threat had ceased altogether.

They adopted French culture and the French language, yet retained much of their old energy. In the eleventh century Normandy was producing some of Europe's most vigorous warriors, Crusaders, administrators, and monks.

Ireland, Greenland, North America

France, England, and Germany formed only a part of the vast Viking world of the ninth and tenth centuries. By the mid-800s Norwegians and Danes had conquered the greater part of Ireland, and between 875 and 930 they settled remote Iceland. There a distinctive Norse culture arose which for several centuries remained only slightly affected by the main currents of Western civilization. In Iceland the magnificent oral tradition of the Norse saga flourished and was eventually committed to writing. The Icelandic Norsemen were perhaps the greatest sailors of all. They settled on the coast of Greenland in the late 900s, and

Around the year 1000 Christianity was winning converts all across the Scandinavian world. In Iceland, in Russia—even in the kingdoms of Scandinavia itself—the ferocious Northmen were adopting the religion of the monks who had once so feared them. Scandinavia was becoming a part of Western European culture.

Even at the height of the invasions the Norsemen were by no means pure barbarians. They excelled at commerce as well as piracy. They were the greatest seafarers of the age. They introduced Europe to the art of ocean navigation and immeasurably enlarged the horizons of Western Christendom. In a word they injected a spirit of enterprise and cosmopolitanism into the conservative, parochial outlook of Carolingian civilization.

EUROPE SURVIVES THE SIEGE

Response to the Invasions: England

The invasions of the ninth and tenth centuries wrought significant changes in the political and social organization of Western Europe. Generally speaking, political authority tended to crumble into small local units as cumbersome royal armies failed to cope with the lightning raids. This was the case in France, but it was less true in Germany where the monarchy, after a period of relative weakness, underwent a spectacular recovery in the tenth century. In England, paradoxically, the hammer blows of the Danes had the ultimate result of unifying the several Anglo-Saxon states into a single kingdom.

In the later eighth century, on the eve of the Viking invasions, England was politically fragmented, just as it had been ever since the Anglo-Saxon conquests. But over the centuries the several smaller kingdoms had gradually passed under the control of three larger ones: Northumbria in the north, Mercia in the Midlands, and Wessex in the south. The Danish attacks of the ninth century, by destroying the power of Wessex's rivals, cleared the field for the Wessex monarchy and thereby hastened the trend toward consolidation that was already under way. But if the Danes were doing the Wessex monarchy a favor neither side was aware of it during the dark days of the later ninth century. England suffered grievous devastation, and for a time it appeared the Danes might conquer Wessex itself.

King Alfred

At the moment of crisis a leader rose to the Wessex throne who was perhaps the most remarkable king England has known: Alfred the Great (871–899). Alfred did everything in his power to save his kingdom from the Vikings. He fought ferocious battles against them. He even resorted to bribing them. In the winter of 878 the Danes, in a surprise attack, invaded Wessex and forced Alfred to take refuge, with a handful of companions, in a remote swamp on the isle of Athelney. As it turned out, Athelney was England's Valley Forge. In the following spring Alfred rallied his forces and smashed a Danish army at the battle of Edington. This victory turned the tide of the war; the Danish leader agreed to take up Christianity, to withdraw from the land, and to accept a "permanent" peace. Wessex was never again seriously threatened.

But other Danes under other leaders refused to honor the peace, and Alfred, in his later campaigns, conquered Kent and

ENGLAND
ABOUT 885

Scots

Picts

North Sea

ENGLISH NORTHUMBRIA

Lindisfarne

Picts

•Whitby

•York

Irish Sea

IRELAND

DANELAW

WALES

ENGLISH MERCIA

EAST ANGLIA

London•

SURREY   Canterbury

DEVON   *WESSEX*   SUSSEX   KENT

CORNWALL

English Channel

0   40   80 mi.

Map by J. Donovan

most of Mercia and captured London—even then England's greatest city. In the 880s a new peace treaty gave Wessex most of southern and southwestern England. The remainder of England—the "Danelaw"—remained hostile, but all non-Danish England was now united under King Alfred.

Like all successful leaders of the age Alfred was an exceedingly able warrior. But he was far more than that. He was a brilliant, imaginative organizer who systematized military recruitment and founded the English navy, seeing clearly that Christian Europe could not hope to drive back the Vikings without challenging them on the seas. He filled his land with fortresses which served both as defensive strongholds and as places of sanctuary for the agrarian population in time of war. And gradually, as the Danish tide was rolled back, new fortresses were built to secure the territories newly reconquered. Alfred clarified and rationalized the laws of his people, enforced them strictly, and ruled with an authority such as no Anglo-Saxon king had exercised before his time.

Intellectual Revival

This remarkable monarch was also a scholar and a patron of learning. His intellectual environment was even less promising than Charlemagne's. The great days of Bede, Boniface, and Alcuin were far in the past, and by Alfred's time, Latin—the key to classical Christian culture—was almost unknown in England. Like Charlemagne, Alfred gathered scholars from far and wide—England, Wales, the Continent—and set them to work teaching Latin and translating Latin classics into the Anglo-Saxon language. Alfred himself participated in the work of translation, rendering such works as Boethius' *Consolation of Philosophy,* Pope Gregory's *Pastoral Care,* and Bede's *Ecclesiastical History* into the native tongue. In his translation of Boethius, Alfred added a wistful comment of his own: "In those days one never heard tell of ships armed for war." And in his preface to the *Pastoral Care* he alluded with nostalgia to the days "before everything was ravaged and burned, when England's churches overflowed with treasures and books." Alfred's intellectual revival, even more than Charlemagne's, was a salvage operation rather than an outburst of originality. He was both modest and accurate when he described himself as one who wandered through a great forest collecting timber with which others could build.

Alfred's task of reconquest was carried on by his able successors in the first half of the tenth century. Midway through the century all England was in their hands, and the kings of Wessex had become the kings of England. Great numbers of Danish settlers still remained in northern and eastern England—the amalgamation of Danish and English customs required many generations—but the creative response of the Wessex kings to the Danish threat had transformed and united the Anglo-Saxon world. Out of the agony of the invasions the English monarchy was born.

Renewal of Danish Attack

For a generation after the conquest of the Danelaw, from about 955 to 980, England enjoyed relative peace and prosperity. English flotillas patrolled the shores, the old fortresses began to evolve into commercial centers, and dedicated churchmen addressed themselves to the task of monastic reform. But the Danish inhabitants of northern and eastern England remained only half committed to the new English monarchy, and with the accession of an incompetent child-king, Ethelred the Unready (978–1016), Danish invasions began anew.

The new invasions evolved into a campaign of conquest directed by the Danish monarchy. The English defense was characterized by incompetence, treason, and panic. In 991 Ethelred began paying a tribute to the Danes, known thereafter as "danegeld." In later years the danegeld evolved into a land tax which was exceedingly profitable to the English monarchy, but at the time it was a symbol of a profound humiliation. In 1016 Ethelred fled the country altogether, and in the following year King Canute of Denmark became the monarch of England (1017–1035).

Canute

Canute has been described as very nearly a dwarf and nearly a genius. He conquered Norway as well as England, and joining these two lands to his kingdom of Denmark, he became the master of a vast, heteroge-

neous empire centering on the North Sea. A product of the new civilizing forces at work in eleventh-century Scandinavia, Canute was no bloodthirsty Viking. He issued law codes, practiced Christianity, and kept the peace. Devoting much of his time to England, he cast himself as an English king in the old Wessex tradition. He respected and upheld the ancient customs of the land and gave generously to the monasteries. Despite his Danish background, he was a far better English monarch then Ethelred. In a very real sense his reign was a continuation of the past, adding luster to the crown which Alfred's dynasty had forged. English religion and culture prospered as before: "Merry sang the monks of Ely as Canute the king rowed by."

Canute's immense Danish-Norwegian-English empire was hopelessly disunited and failed to survive his death in 1035. When the last of his sons died in 1042 the English realm fell peacefully to Edward the Confessor, a member of the Old Wessex dynasty who had grown up in exile in Normandy.

The Aftermath

Though a poor general and a mediocre administrator Edward the Confessor was a man of genuine piety who won the love of his people despite his political ineptitude. His pious insistence on his own virginity insured a disputed succession upon his death in 1066 and set the stage for the Norman Conquest. When William the Conqueror, duke of Normandy, invaded England and won its crown in 1066, he inherited a prosperous kingdom with strong and well-established political and legal traditions—a kingdom still divided by differences in custom, but with a deep-seated respect for royal authority. Ethelred the Unready notwithstanding, the Wessex dynasty had done its work well. With the timber that Alfred collected his successors had built an ample and sturdy edifice.

Response to the Invasions: French Feudalism

In England the invasions stimulated the trend toward royal unification; in France they encouraged a shattering of political authority into small local units. This paradox can be explained in part by the fact that France, unlike England, was far too large for the Vikings to conquer. Although many of them settled in Normandy, the chief Norse threat to France came in the form of plundering expeditions rather than large conquering armies. Distances were too great, communications too primitive, and the national territorial army too unwieldy for the king to take the lead in defending his realm. Military responsibility descended to local lords who alone could hope to protect the countryside from the swift and terrible Viking assaults. The French Carolingians became increasingly powerless until at length, in 987, the crown passed to a new dynasty—the Capetians. During the twelfth and thirteenth centuries the Capetian family produced some of France's most illustrious kings, but for the time being the new dynasty was as powerless as the old one. After 987, as before, the nobles overshadowed the king. About all one can say of the French monarchy in these dark years is that it survived.

Benefice and Vassalage

The Viking Age witnessed the birth of feudalism in France. In a very real sense feudalism was a product of France's response to the invasions. Yet in another sense the Franks had long been drifting in a feudal direction. The roots of feudalism ran deep: one root was the honorable bond of fidelity and service of a warrior to his lord—which characterized the lord-vassal relationship of late-Merovingian and early-Carolingian times, and the still earlier *comitatus* of the Germanic barbarians. Another root was the late-Roman and early-medieval concept of land-holding in return for certain services to the person who granted the land. An estate granted to a tenant in return for service was known as a *benefice*.

Charles Martel took an important step toward feudalism by joining the institutions of benefice and vassalage. He undertook heavy confiscations of Church property and granted the appropriated estates to his military vassals. There were several reasons for this step. For one thing money was in very short supply throughout the Early Middle Ages so that it was almost impossible for a ruler to support his soldiers with wages. Often the vassals of an important Frankish lord were fed and sheltered in his household. Indeed, the "household knight" persisted throughout the feudal age. But as their military importance grew these warrior-vassals exhibited an ever-increasing hunger for land. Their lords were therefore under considerable pressure to grant them estates—benefices—in return for their loyalty and service.

This tendency was associated with a profound revolution in Frankish military tactics which occurred around the 730s. Previously the Franks had been foot soldiers for the most part. Thereafter, cavalry became increasingly important; within a century and a half it had become all-important. The Frankish warrior *par excellence* was now the armored, mounted knight, far more effective than the infantrymen, but also far more expensive to support or maintain. The knight needed a fine mount, heavy armor and weapons, several attendants, and many years of training. Hence the tendency for a lord to support his knightly vassals by granting them estates in return for their service. The knight did not, of course, labor on his own fields; rather he administered them and collected dues, chiefly in kind, from his peasants.

The Carolingian military vassal was typically a knight. As knightly tactics came more and more to dominate warfare the custom of vassalage spread widely. The great Frankish magnates of Charlemagne's time pledged their allegiance to their emperor and thereby recognized that they were his vassals and he their lord. Moreover, these royal vassals had vassals of their own who owed primary allegiance to their immediate lords rather than to the emperor. Charlemagne himself approved of this practice and encouraged the free men of his realm to become vassals of his magnates. In time of war these vassals of vassals (or subvassals) were expected to join their lords' contingents in the royal army. The centrifugal tendencies implicit in such an arrangement are obvious. Yet Charlemagne, lacking a coherent civil service or adequate funds to hire a professional army of his own, was obliged to depend on this potentially unstable hierarchy of authority and allegiance.

With the removal of Charlemagne's commanding personality, and under the pressure of the invasions, the rickety hierarchy began to crumble into its component parts. Charlemagne's old territorial officials, the dukes, counts, and margraves, backed by their own vassals, tended increasingly to usurp royal rights, revenues, and prerogatives. They administered justice and collected taxes without regard for the royal will. In time, they built castles and assumed all responsibility for the defense of their districts. Nominally these feudal magnates remained vassals of the kings of France, but they soon became much too powerful to be coerced by the crown. Their authority was limited chiefly by the independence of their own vassals who began to create subvassals or sub-subvassals of their own. At the height of the feudal age the lord-vassal relationship might run down through some ten or twenty levels; there was scarcely a vassal to be found who was not the lord of some still lower vassal.

The ultimate consequences of these developments have been described as "feudal anarchy." In a sense the term is well chosen but it should not mislead us into thinking of feudalism simply as a "bad thing." Given the instability of the Carolingian Empire and the desperate plight of France in the Viking era, feudalism emerges as a realistic accommodation to the hard facts of the age. It should never be forgotten that whereas Roman Europe succumbed to barbarian invasions, Feudal Europe survived its invaders and ultimately absorbed them.

The Fief

French feudalism reached its height in the tenth and eleventh centuries. Its key institution was the military benefice, the estate granted by a lord to his vassal in return for allegiance and service—primarily knightly military service. This military benefice was commonly known as a *fief* (rhyming with beef). It was a logical response to the desperate requirements of local defense, the perpetuation of at least some degree of political authority, and the scarcity of money which necessitated the paying for service in land rather than wages. A great lord would grant an estate—a fief—to his vassal. The vassal might then grant a part of the estate—another fief—to a vassal of his own. And so on and on, down and down, the process of enfeoffment went. The result was a hierarchically organized landed knightly aristocracy. Each knight gave homage and fealty—that is, the pledge of his personal allegiance—to his immediate lord; each lived off the labor and dues of a dependent peasantry which tilled the fields that his fief embraced; each administered a court and dispensed justice to those below him.

Feudalism Defined

Such were the essential ingredients of feudalism. The term is extremely difficult to define and has been frequently abused and misunderstood. If we wish to put the whole institution in a nutshell we can do no better than repeat the definition—or description—of medieval feudalism's greatest modern scholar, the French historian Marc Bloch: "A subject peasantry; widespread use of the service tenement (that is, the fief) in-

13th century seal showing Raimond de Mont-Dragon kneeling before the archbishop of Arles, his suzerain. This is an act of faith and homage.

stead of a salary, which was out of the question; the supremacy of a class of specialized warriors; ties of obedience and protection which bind man to man and, within the warrior class, assume the distinctive form called vassalage; fragmentation of authority — leading inevitably to disorder; and in the midst of all this, the survival of other forms of association, family and state . . . — such then seem to be the fundamental features of European feudalism." [3]

With this description in mind it may be helpful to emphasize some of the things that feudalism was not. It was not, for one thing, a universal and symmetrical system. Born in northern France in the Viking age it took on many different forms as it spread across Europe. In northern France itself it varied widely from one region to another. It by no means encompassed all the land, for even at its height many landowners owed no feudal obligations and had no feudal ties. The feudal hierarchy or feudal "pyramid" was riddled with ambiguities: a single vassal might hold several fiefs from several lords; a lord might receive a fief from his own vassal, thereby putting himself in the extraordinary position of being his vassal's vassal. The degree of confusion possible in feudalism can best be appreciated by examining a typical document of the age:

"I, John of Toul, affirm that I am the vassal of the Lady Beatrice, countess of Troyes, and of her son Theobald, count of Champagne, against every creature living or dead, excepting my allegiance to Lord Enjourand of Coucy, Lord John of Arcis, and the count of Grandpré. If it should happen that the count of Grandpré should be at war with the countess and count of Champagne in his own quarrel, I will aid the count of Grandpré in my own person, and will aid the count and countess of Champagne by sending them the knights whose services I owe them from the fief which I hold of them."

So much for feudal order!

Feudalism was not, in its heyday, associated with the romantic knight errant, the many-turreted castle, or the lady fair. The knight of the ninth, tenth, and eleventh centuries was a rough-hewn warrior. His armor was simple, his horse was tough, his castle was a crude wooden tower atop an earthen mound, and his lady fair was any available wench. Chivalry developed after a time, to be sure, but not until the foundations of the old feudal order were being eroded by the revival of commerce and a money economy, and the stronger monarchies. Only then did the knight seek to disguise his declining usefulness by turning to elaborate shining armor, lace and ruffles, courtly phrases, and wedding-cake castles.

Feudalism was not entirely military. The vassal owed his lord not only military service but a variety of additional obligations as well. Among these were the duty to join his lord's retinue on tours of the countryside; to serve, when summoned, in his lord's court of justice; to feed, house, and entertain his lord and his lord's retinue on their all-too-frequent visits; to give money to his lord on a variety of specified occasions; to contribute to his lord's ransom should he be captured in battle. Early in its history the fief became hereditary. The lord, however, retained the right to confiscate it should his vassal die without heirs, to

3. Bloch, *op. cit.*, p. 446.

supervise and exploit it during a minority, and to exercise a power of veto over the marriage of a female fiefholder. In return for such rights as these the lord was obliged to protect and uphold the interests of his vassals. The very essence of feudalism was the notion of reciprocal rights and obligations. Consequently the feudal outlook played a key role in steering medieval Europe away from autocracy.

Political Feudalism

Feudalism was both a military system and a political system. With military responsibility went political power. As the central government of West Frankland demonstrated an ever-increasing incapacity to cope with the invasions or keep peace in the countryside, sovereignty tended to descend to the level of the greater feudal lords. Although nominally royal vassals these magnates were in effect powers unto themselves, ruling their own territories without royal interference and maintaining their own courts and administrative systems as well as their own armies. In the days of the Viking raids many of these magnates had extreme difficulty in controlling their own turbulent vassals; feudal tenants several steps down in the pyramid were often able to behave as though they had no real superiors. Sub-vassals and sub-sub-vassals with their own courts and armies were frequently in a position to defy their lords. Accordingly, it is difficult to identify the real locus of political power in early feudal France. Sovereignty was spread up and down the aristocratic hierarchy, and a lord's real power depended upon his military prowess, his ambition, and the firmness of his leadership.

Specialists in medieval history are inclined to limit "feudalism" to the network of rights and obligations existing among members of the knightly aristocracy—the holders of fiefs. Although it rested on the labor of peasants the feudal structure itself encompassed only the warrior class of lords and vassals. There was, in other words, a world of difference between a vassal and a serf. Beneath the level of the feudal warrior class, 80 or 90 per cent of the population continued to labor on the land, producing the food that sustained society. Yet the peasantry was disdained by the nobility and largely ignored by the chroniclers of the age.

The feudal chaos of the ninth and tenth centuries, with its extreme fragmentation of sovereign power and its incessant private wars, gradually gave way to a somewhat more orderly regime. Great territorial magnates such as the counts of Anjou and Flanders and the duke of Normandy extended their frontiers at the expense of weaker neighbors and tightened their control over their own vassals and subvassals. But it was not until the twelfth century that the French monarchs began to rise above the level of their great feudal magnates and assert real authority over the realm. Indeed, the high noon of feudalism was a period of virtual eclipse for the French crown.

Response to Invasions: Germany

"Tribal" Duchies

Different peoples responded differently to the invasions of the "new barbarians." In England they brought royal unification; in France, feudal particularism. The response of Germany differed from those of both England and France, owing to the special character of the invasions which Germany faced and the unique conditions prevailing in Germany itself. Though the east Frankish kingdom—which evolved directly into the medieval German state— was subject to Viking attacks, the real threat came from the Hungarian horsemen of the East. The late Carolingian kings of Germany—the successors of Louis the German who was granted East Frankland at the Treaty of Verdun—proved incapable of coping with the Hungarian raids. As in France, real authority descended to the great magnates of the realm. But these magnates were not the dukes and counts of Carolingian officialdom. Most of Germany had remained outside Frankish control until the Carolingian conquests of the eighth century; consequently the Frankish system of local administration was but imperfectly established there. Moreover, the ancient tribal consciousness of Saxons, Bavarians, and Swabians was still strong. In the critical decades of the late ninth and early tenth centuries ambitious aristocrats exploited this tribal patriotism by grasping leadership over the old tribal districts. These men of the hour assumed the title of duke and the regions that they ruled came to be known as tribal duchies.* The "tribal" dukes sought to dominate the local ecclesiastical organizations, to seize the royal Carolingian estates in their duchies, and to usurp royal powers. It was they who stood up to the Hungarian thrust.

In the early tenth century there were five important tribal duchies: Saxony, Swabia, Bavaria, Franconia, and Lorraine. Saxony, Swabia and Bavaria had been incorporated only superficially into the Carolingian state, whereas the western duchies of Franconia and Lorraine were much more strongly Frankish in outlook and organization.

The five "tribal" dukes might well have become the masters of Germany. Their ambitions were frustrated by two closely related factors: (1) their failure to curb the Hungarians, and (2) the reinvigoration of the German monarchy under an able new dynasty. The Carolingian line came to an end in Germany in 911 with the death of King Louis the Child. He was succeeded first by the duke of Franconia and then, in 919, by the duke of Saxony—the first of a remarkable and illustrious line of kings who based their royal power on their domination of the powerful Saxon duchy.

* Otherwise known as stem duchies.

Otto I

The Saxon kings struggled vigorously to assert their authority over the tribal duchies. With the duchy of Saxony under the authority of the monarchy the Saxon kings quickly won direct control over Franconia as well. But the semi-independent dukes of the two southern duchies, Swabia and Bavaria, presented problems. The real victory of the Saxon monarchy occurred in the reign of the second and greatest of the Saxon kings, Otto I (936–973).

Otto I, or Otto the Great as he is often called, devoted his considerable talents to achieving three goals: (1) the defense of Germany against the Hungarian invasions, (2) the establishment of royal power over the remaining tribal duchies, and (3) the extension of German royal control to the crumbling, unstable Middle Kingdom which the Treaty of Verdun had assigned to Emperor Lothar back in 843. We have already seen how this heterogeneous Middle Kingdom began to fall to pieces after Lothar's death. By the mid-tenth century it had become a confused political shambles. Parts of it had been taken over by Germany and France but its southern districts—Burgundy and Italy—retained a chaotic independence. The dukes of Swabia and Bavaria both had notions of seizing these territories. Otto the Great, in order to forestall the development of an unmanageable rival power to his south, led his armies into Italy in 951 and assumed the title "King of Italy."

From 951 onwards events developed rapidly. Otto the Great was obliged to leave Italy in haste to put down a major uprising in Germany. His victory over the rebels enabled him to establish his power there more strongly than ever. In 955 he won the crucial battle of the age when he crushed a large Hungarian army at Lechfeld. In this one blow he terminated forever the Hungarian menace. Lechfeld served as a vivid demonstration of royal power—a vindication of the monarch's claim that he, not the "tribal" dukes, was the true defender of

Germany. With the Hungarians defeated Germany's eastern frontier now lay open to the gradual penetration of German-Christian culture. The day of the tribal duchies was over; the monarchy reigned supreme. Otto the Great now towered over his contemporaries as the greatest monarch of the West and the most powerful ruler since Charlemagne. The invasions of Germany, which had begun by uplifting the tribal duchies, ended by contributing to the revival of royal authority.

Revival of the Empire

After Lechfeld there remained for Otto I one important piece of unfinished business. Since his departure from Italy a usurper had seized the Italian throne and was harassing the pope. In response to a papal appeal — which conveniently dovetailed with his own interests — Otto returned to Italy in force, conquered the usurper, and recovered the Italian crown. In 962 the pope hailed Otto as Roman Emperor and placed the imperial crown on his head. It is this momentous event, rather than the coronation of Charlemagne in 800, that marks the true genesis of the medieval institution known as the Holy Roman Empire. Although the events of 962 are reminiscent of those of 800 Otto's empire was vastly different from Charlemagne's. Above all, Otto and his imperial successors made no pretensions of universal jurisdiction over France or the remainder of Western Christendom. The medieval Holy Roman Empire had its roots deep in the soil of Germany, and most of the emperors subordinated imperial interests to those of the German monarchy. From its advent in 962 to its long-delayed demise in the early nineteenth century the Holy Roman Empire remained fundamentally a German phenomenon.

The German orientation of Otto's empire is illustrated dramatically by the fact that neither he nor the majority of his successors over the next two centuries made any real effort to establish tight control over Italy.

THE HOLY ROMAN EMPIRE IN 962

Slavs

SAXONY

LORRAINE

FRANCONIA

Bohemia

Rhine R.

Elbe R.

SWABIA

Lechfeld

BAVARIA

Danube R.

Hungarians

Rhone R.

KINGDOM OF BURGUNDY

——— The Holy Roman Empire

Rome

The five Stem Duchies

0   100   200 mi.

Map by J. Donovan

Only when they marched south of the Alps could they count on the obedience of the Italians; when they returned to Germany they left behind them no real administrative structure but depended almost solely on the fickle allegiance of certain Italian magnates. The medieval German emperors were never really successful in straddling the Alps.

In Germany conditions were quite different. There the coming of feudalism was delayed for more than a century after Otto's imperial coronation. The great magnates, to be sure, became vassals of the king. But they normally had no vassals of their own. The chief tool which Otto and his successors employed in governing their state was the Church. In an era of a weak papacy the German kings dominated the Church within their realm and kept close control over important ecclesiastical appointments.

Otto had successfully wrested control of the Church in the various tribal duchies from the defunct dukes, and in a very real sense the great bishops and abbots of Germany were the king's men. They made ideal royal lieutenants. They could not make their estates hereditary for when a bishop or abbot died his successor was hand-picked by the king. Thus the loyalty and political capacity of the churchly royal administrators was assured. After 962 the German monarchy was even moderately successful in appointing popes. There would come a time when churchmen would rebel at such high-handed treatment; but in Otto's reign the time was still far off.

Otto's lofty claims to proprietorship of the imperial Church were supported by both tradition and theory. Otto was regarded as far more than a mere secular monarch. He was *rex et sacerdos,* king and priest, sanctified by the holy anointing ceremony which accompanied his coronation. He was the vicar of God—the living symbol of Christ the king—the "natural" leader of the Church in his empire. In the closing years of his reign his actual political power over Church and state came close to matching his exalted pretensions.

The Ottonian Renaissance

Otto's remarkable reign provided the impulse for an impressive intellectual revival which reached its culmination under his two successors, Otto II (973–83) and Otto III (983–1002). This "Ottonian Renaissance" produced a series of able administrators and scholars, the greatest of whom was the brilliant churchman Gerbert of Aurillac—later Pope Sylvester II (d. 1003). Gerbert visited Spain and returned with a comprehensive knowledge of Islamic science. This event marked the beginning of the infiltration of the intellectual legacy of Arab civilization into Western Christendom. Gerbert had an encyclopedic, though unoriginal, mind. A master of classical literature, logic, mathematics, and science he astonished his contemporaries by teaching the Greco-Arab doctrine that the earth was spherical. There were widespread rumors that he was some kind of wizard in league with the Devil—rumors somewhat dampened by his elevation to the papacy. Rather than a wizard Gerbert was the advance agent of a momentous intellectual awakening that Europe was about to undergo—a harbinger of the High Middle Ages.

Although successors of Otto the Great were no longer troubled by the tribal duchies or the Hungarians, they were obliged as all men are to cope with new problems and devise new solutions. In 1024 the Saxon dynasty died out and was replaced by a Franconian family known as the Salian dynasty (1024–1125). The "tribal" dukes gave way to a new, particularistic aristocracy whose impulse toward independence taxed the ingenuity of the emperors. Still, the early Salian kings were generally successful in maintaining their power. Working hand in glove with the German Church, the Salians improved and elaborated royal administration and ultimately came to exercise even greater authority than Otto I had known. In the mid-eleventh century the mightiest of the Salian emperors, Henry III (1039–1056), ruled unrivaled over Germany and appointed popes as effortlessly as he selected his own bishops. In 1050, at a time when France was still a medley of feudal principalities and England, under Edward the Confessor, was relatively small and more-or-less isolated, the German Emperor Henry III dominated Central Europe and held the papacy in his palm.

Europe on the Eve of the High Middle Ages

During the centuries between the fall of the Roman Empire in the West and the great economic and cultural revival of the later eleventh century, the foundations were built on which Western civilization rose. Kingdoms were forming, distinctive customs and institutions were developing, and a classical-Christian intellectual tradition was gradually being absorbed, adapted, and broadened. And at the bottom of the social order, the peasant had become firmly attached to the soil, hedged about with various obligations, and trained from childhood in a variety of traditional techniques.

To discuss the typical medieval manor is as difficult as to discuss the typical American business. Medieval agrarian institutions were almost infinitely diverse; medieval agriculture exhibited countless variations. Nevertheless some features of agrarian life recur throughout much of the more fertile and more-heavily populated portions of Northern Europe. Certain generalizations can be made about medieval agrarian institutions if we bear in mind that numerous exceptions to any of them can always be found.

Village and Manor

Any discussion of medieval husbandry must begin by distinguishing between two fundamental institutions: the village and the manor. The village, the basic unit of the agrarian economy, consisted of a population nucleus ranging from about a dozen to several hundred peasant families living in a cluster. In some of the poorer or more isolated districts, peasant families lived in separate farms or hamlets; but village life was the norm in medieval agriculture.

The manor, on the other hand, was an artificial unit—a unit of jurisdiction and economic exploitation controlled by a single lord. The lord might be a king, a duke or count, a bishop or abbot, or a great baron. He might and commonly did have numerous manors under his control. Or he might be a simple knight, at the bottom of the feudal pyramid, with only one or two manors at his disposal. The manor— the unit of jurisdiction—was often coterminous with the village; but some manors embraced two or more villages and, on occasion, a village might be divided into two or more manors. In any case the agrar-

ian routine of plowing, planting, and harvesting was based on the village organization, whereas the peasants' dues, obligations, and legal and political subordination were based on the manor.

Let us discuss these two institutions— the village and the manor—in turn. The ordinary village consisted of a grouping of peasants' huts surrounded by open fields. There would normally be either two or three such fields. Two was the traditional number but, as we have seen, the agrarian economy had been shifting in many districts of Northern Europe from a two-field to a three-field system of rotation. The peasants of a three-field village would plant one field in the spring for fall harvesting, plant one field in the fall for early summer harvesting, and let the third field lie fallow throughout the year. The next year the fields would be rotated and the process repeated.

The arable lands surrounding the village were known as *open fields* because they were unfenced. They were divided into strips of about 220 yards in length separated from one another by furrows. Each peasant possessed several strips scattered throughout the fields, but the peasant community labored collectively, pooling their plows, their draught animals, and their toil. Collective husbandry was necessary because plows were scarce and had to be shared and because no one peasant owned sufficient oxen or horses to make up a plow team of eight beasts which was necessary to draw the heavy plow. The details of this collective process were usually worked out in the village council and were guided by immemorial custom.

The shape, contour, and method of cultivation of the open fields was determined by the topography of the region and the fertility of the soil. It therefore varied enormously from place to place. The strips themselves were products of the heavy plow and the necessity of reversing the eight-ox team as infrequently as possible. The length of the strips was determined by the distance a team could draw the plow without rest. A group of four strips, the plowing of which constituted a normal day's work, became the basis of our modern acre.

The open fields were the fundamental element in the village economy and, indeed, the entire agrarian economic system of the Middle Ages. But there was more to the village community than the cluster of peasants' huts and the encircling fields. Besides his scattered strips in the fields, a peasant ordinarily had a small garden adjacent to his hut where vegetables and fruits could be raised and fowl kept to provide variety to his diet. The village also included a pasture where the plow animals might graze, and a meadow from which hay was cut to sustain the precious beasts over the winter. Some village communities kept sheep on their pasture as a source of cheese, milk, and wool. Indeed, certain districts, particularly in Flanders and northern England, took up sheep raising on a scale so large as almost to exclude the growing of grains.

Attached to most village communities was a wooded area that served as a source of fuel and building materials. It also served as a forage for pigs, which provided most of the meat in the peasants' diet. There was commonly a stream or pond nearby which supplied the community with fish, a water mill for grinding grain, and a large oven which the community used for baking bread. By the eleventh century most village communities were organized as parishes. Each parish possessed a village church supervised by a priest who was drawn from the peasant class and who had land of his own scattered among the strips of the open fields.

The village community has often been described as a closed system, economically self-sufficient, capable of sustaining the material and spiritual needs of the villagers without much contact with the outside world. From the foregoing discussion it should be clear enough why this was so.

We need further to note that the economy of the Early Middle Ages, lacking a vigorous commercial life and a significant urban population, failed to provide villages with much incentive to produce beyond their immediate needs. There was only the most limited market for surplus grain. Accordingly, village life tended to be uneventful, tradition-bound, and circumscribed by the narrowest of horizons. On the other hand, gradual but profound changes were occurring in medieval civilization which eventually made a deep impact upon the village. The medieval innovations in agrarian technology already discussed significantly increased agricultural efficiency and productivity. Moreover the commercial and urban revival of the High Middle Ages provided an ever-expanding market for surplus grain. These developments in turn eroded village parochialism, freed the village economy from its self-sufficiency by incorporating it into a far vaster economic system, and provided enterprising peasants with a means of acquiring considerable money. They also encouraged a tremendous expansion of villages and fields through the clearing of forests and wilderness and the draining of marshes. Timeless though it might have seemed, the village economy was changing; its dynamic elements must never be overlooked.

In the foregoing summary of the village economy one essential element has been deliberately excluded: that of private lordship. Superimposed on the economic structure of the village was the political-juridical structure of the manor. The average peasant was bound to a manorial lord. Some agrarian laborers were outright slaves, although slavery was in decline throughout the Early Middle Ages and had practically disappeared by the end of the eleventh century. Some peasants, on the other hand, were of free status, owing rents to their lord but little or nothing more. A few were landless laborers working for a wage. But the great middle stratum of the medieval peasantry consisted of serfs—

men of unfree status, bound to the land like the Roman *coloni* and possessed of strips of their own in the open fields. They owed various dues to their manorial lord, chiefly in kind, and were normally expected to labor for a certain number of days per week—often three—on the lord's fields.

The lord drew his sustenance from the dues of his peasants and from the produce of his own fields. The lord's fields were strips scattered among the strips of the peasants, and were known collectively as the lord's demesne. Theoretically, then, the fields of the manor were divided into two categories: the lord's demesne (perhaps one-fourth to one-third of the total area) and the peasants' holdings—known as tenements. But in fact the demesne strips and the peasants' strips were intermixed. The demesne was worked by the peasants who also paid their lord a percentage of the produce of their own fields and rendered him fees for the use of the pasture, the woods, and the lord's mill and oven. Such were some of the more common and more important peasant obligations on many manors. It must however be understood clearly that such obligations were exceedingly diverse, varying from district to district and from manor to manor.

The lord also enjoyed significant political authority over his peasants—an authority which flourished and grew in proportion to the disintegration of sovereign power which occurred in late Carolingian times. The administrative nexus of the manor was the manorial court, usually held in the lord's castle or manor house. Here a rough, custom-based justice was meted out, disputes settled, misdeeds punished, and obligations enforced. Since most lords possessed more than one manor, authority over individual manors was commonly exercised by an agent of the lord known as a bailiff or steward. It was he who supervised the manorial court, oversaw the farming of the demesne, and collected the peasants' dues. In addition to the peasants' agrarian obligations, the lord was also entitled to certain payments deriving from his political and personal authority over his tenants. He might levy a tallage—an arbitrary manorial tax which was theoretically unlimited in frequency and amount but was in fact circumscribed by custom. He was normally entitled to payments when a peasant's son inherited the holdings of his father, and when a peasant's daughter married outside the manor.

In general the serfs had no standing before the law. The lord was prevented from exploiting them arbitrarily only by the force of custom. But custom was exceedingly strong in the Middle Ages and protected the serf in many different ways. He was by no means a chattel slave. He could not be sold, nor could his own hereditary fields be taken from him. After paying his manorial dues he was entitled to keep the produce of his own fields. Hardly enviable, his situation could have been worse.

The Medieval Agrarian System: Conclusions

Although drawing from Roman and Germanic traditions the manor and the village were typically medieval. One broad generalization concerning manorial and agrarian institutions is that they showed endless variations—evolving in time and differing significantly from place to place. In the eleventh century the manorial regime was only incompletely established in England and was scarcely evident at all in Scandinavia and in parts of northern Germany and southern France. Although the two-field system was common in Southern Europe and the three-field system in the north, many northern villages had only two fields. Others had four or five or even more, all subjected to complex rotation arrangements. Vital, diverse, and on the whole healthy, medieval agriculture proved itself capable of expanding sufficiently to support the soaring new economy and the rich civilization of the High Middle Ages.

The Church

The existence of parish churches in the villages of the eleventh century illustrates the deeply significant fact that the process of Christianizing Europe was reaching the point of successful completion. Whatever were the intellectual and moral shortcomings of the village priests, they were at least representatives of the international Church operating at the most immediate local levels throughout the European countryside. At a rather more elevated level was the work and influence of the Benedictines. They offered prayers to God, copied manuscripts, taught in their schools, supplied knights to secular armies, and served as prelates and counsellors under counts, dukes, and kings. While continuing their traditional spiritual activities they played, even more so than in early Carolingian times, a major role in lay political life.

The greatest Benedictine house of the later tenth and earlier eleventh centuries was Cluny in Burgundy. Founded in 910 by the duke of Aquitaine, Cluny was free of local episcopal jurisdiction, subject to the pope alone, and blessed with a series of remarkably able and long-lived abbots. Cluny followed Benedict of Aniane's modifications of the original Benedictine Rule. Its monks, shunning field work, devoted themselves to an unusually elaborate and magnificent sequence of daily prayers and liturgical services, and a strict, godly life. This strictness was relative, falling far short of the austere regimes of several of the more ascetic orders of the High Middle Ages. Yet the Cluniacs were successful in avoiding the abuses and corruption that flourished in many monasteries of their day. Richly endowed, holy, and seemingly incorruptible, Cluny became famous and widely admired. In time it began to acquire daughter houses. Gradually it became the nucleus of a great congregation of reform monasteries extending throughout Europe —all of them obedient to the abbot of Cluny. In the mid-eleventh century the Congregation of Cluny was both powerful and wealthy. Its high ideals were tempered by a sense of dignity—and perhaps also by a comfortable feeling of spiritual success and social acceptance. Enriched and supported by the lay aristocracy, it was by no means in radical opposition to secular society; rather it tended on the whole to accept and uphold the social system of its day and to worship the Lord God without disparaging the lords of men.

Cluny's attitude typified that of the entire Church in the earlier eleventh century. As the lay world became more and more exposed to Christianity, as pious kings such as Edward the Confessor in England and Henry III in Germany demonstrated their concern for the welfare of their churches, the Church itself tended increasingly to come to terms with lay society. Through the ceremony of anointing, kings became virtual priest-kings. Indeed, contemporary political theory taught that the Church and the world were one—a single, God-oriented organism in which churchmen and lay lords each had appropriate roles to play.

Apart from Cluny, the monasteries and bishoprics of eleventh-century Europe tended to be under lay control. They were dependent on lay patronage and were often subsumed under the feudal system. Their prelates were appointed by lay lords in much the same way that village priests were chosen and controlled by manorial lords. Although not free, the Church was wealthy, respected, and comfortable, and few churchmen were inclined to challenge the situation. Those few, however, were to undertake in the later eleventh century a political-spiritual revolution which severely undermined the long established Church-state entente.

Summary

By 1050 both England and Germany were comparatively stable, well-organized kingdoms. The French monarchy was still weak, but within another century it would be on its way toward dominating France. Meanwhile feudal principalities such as

Normandy, Flanders, and Anjou were well on the road to political coherence. Warfare was still endemic, but it was beginning to lessen as Europe moved toward political stability. Above all, the invasions were over—the siege had ended. Hungary and the Scandinavian world were being absorbed into Western Christendom, and Islam was by now on the defensive. The return of prosperity, the increase in food production, the rise in population, the quickening of commerce, the intensification of intellectual activity, all betokened the coming of a new era. Western Civilization was on the threshold of an immense creative upsurge which was destined ultimately to transform the world.

SELECTED READINGS

*Barraclough, Geoffrey, *The Origins of Modern Germany,* Capricorn, 1963.
A general account of German constitutional history that places particular emphasis on the medieval period. The interpretations of Otto I and Otto III are particularly noteworthy.

*Bloch, Marc, *Feudal Society,* L. A. Manyon, translator, University of Chicago Press, Chicago, 1961, 2 vols.
A masterly work, challengingly written and boldly original in its conclusions. Bloch interprets feudalism in an exceedingly broad sociological sense.

*Cantor, Norman F., ed., *The Medieval World,* The Macmillan Co., New York, 1963.
A good recent collection of medieval sources.

*Einhard, *Life of Charlemagne,* translator, S. E. Turner, Ann Arbor Paperbacks, University of Michigan, 1960.
A short, reasonably trustworthy biography by Charlemagne's secretary.

*Fichtenau, H., *The Carolingian Empire,* Harper, New York, 1963.
The best English-language work on the subject, but some of the interpretations are controversial.

*Ganshof, F. L., *Feudalism,* translator, P. Grierson, Harper, New York, 1961 (2nd ed.).
A short, somewhat technical, and authoritative survey of medieval feudal institutions.

Loyn, H. R., *Anglo-Saxon England and the Norman Conquest,* St. Martin's Press, New York, 1963.
An authoritative recent work emphasizing economic and social history.

*Painter, Sidney, *French Chivalry,* Cornell University Press, Ithaca, New York, 1957.
Short, witty, and perceptive.

Sawyer, P. H., *The Age of the Vikings,* St. Martin's Press, New York, 1962.
A rather technical, highly-significant reappraisal of the Viking age.

Stenton, F. M., *Anglo-Saxon England,* Oxford University Press, New York, 1947 (2nd ed.).
A massive masterpiece.

*Stephenson, Carl, *Medieval Feudalism,* Cornell University Press, Ithaca, New York, 1956.
Brief, semipopular, and lucid; a well-organized account, broader and less detailed than Ganshof's.

*White, Lynn, *Medieval Technology and Social Change,* Oxford University Press, New York, 1962.
An important and provocative pioneering work, beautifully written and opulently annotated, which stresses the significance of technological progress to the development of medieval civilization.

Asterisk (*) denotes paperback.

10

The High Middle Ages: Economic, Territorial, and Religious Frontiers

ECONOMIC FRONTIERS

The High Middle Ages: Periodization, Characteristics

History, it has often been said, is a seamless web. But the human mind can only cope with the flow of historical reality by dividing it into arbitrary chronological units, forcing it into compartments of the historian's own making. In this sense every historical "period" is a kind of falsehood—an affront to the continuity of human development. Yet unless we concoct historical epochs, unless we invent ages, unless we force the past into some relatively tidy chronological framework, we cannot make history intelligible to the human mind. Thus the historian speaks of "Classical Antiquity," "The Early Middle Ages," "The

Renaissance," etc. These are all historiographic artifices, to be sure, but they are necessary ones. Without them the past would have little meaning. But we should never forget that they are inventions of our own; we should never lose sight of their limitations.

The term *High Middle Ages* has been applied to the great cultural upsurge of the later eleventh, twelfth, and thirteenth centuries. Yet no spectacular event occurred in 1050 to signal the advent of the new era; no cataclysm occurred in 1300 to mark its end. The transition from Early Middle Ages to High Middle Ages was gradual and uneven. It might be argued that the High Middle Ages came to Germany as early as the tenth century under the Ottos, or that it was delayed in France until the twelfth century when the Capetian monarchy rose from its torpor. Ever since the waning of the Viking, Hungarian, and Saracen invasions, many decades prior to 1050, Europe had been pulsing with new creative energy. Broadly speaking, however, the scope and intensity of the revival did not become evident until the later eleventh century. By the century's end, Europe's lively commerce and bustling towns, her intellectual vigor and political inventiveness, her military expansion, and her heightened religious enthusiasm left no doubt that vast new forces were at work—that Western Christendom had at last become a great creative civilization. As the historian would say, a new age had dawned.

The causes of an immense cultural awakening such as occurred in the High Middle Ages are far too complex to be identified precisely or listed in order of importance. One essential element was the ending of the invasions and the increasing political stability that followed. We know that in the eleventh century Europe's population was beginning to increase significantly and that her food production was rising. Whether increased productivity led to increased population or vice-versa is difficult to say. But productivity could not have risen as it did without the revolutionary developments in agricultural technology: the three-field system which spread across much of Northern Europe, the windmill, the water mill (by 1086 there were over 5000 water mills in England alone) the heavy, wheeled plow, the horseshoe and improved horse collar which transformed horses into efficient draught animals, and the tandem harness which made it possible to employ horses and oxen in large teams to draw plows or to pull heavy wagons. These and numerous related inventions came to the West gradually over the centuries, but they had a powerful cumulative influence on the great economic boom of the High Middle Ages.

Towns and Commerce

Nature of Medieval Towns

The rise in productivity and population was accompanied by a great commercial revival and a general reawakening of urban life. In turn, the new towns became the foci of a brilliant, reinvigorated culture. The intimate human contacts arising from town life stimulated European thought and art. The cathedral and the university, perhaps the two greatest monuments of high medieval culture, were both urban phenomena; the Franciscan order, possibly the loftiest and most dynamic monastic institution that the new age produced, devoted itself primarily to evangelical work among the new urban population. Yet the towns were also, and above all, centers of commercial and industrial enterprise. The European economy in the High Middle Ages remained fundamentally agrarian, but the towns were the great economic and cultural catalysts of the era.

There had been towns in Europe ever since antiquity. The administrative-military town of the Roman Empire gave way in time to the far humbler cathedral town of the Early Middle Ages. But both had one crucial thing in common: both were economic parasites living off the blood, labor and taxes of the countryside; both consumed more than they produced. The towns of the High Middle Ages, on the other hand, represented something radically new to Western Europe. With few exceptions, they were true commercial entities who earned their own way, living off the fruits of their merchant and industrial activities. Small, foul, disease-ridden, and often torn by internal conflict, they were nevertheless Western Europe's first cities in the modern sense of the word.

Commercial Growth of Towns

These commercial towns arose in rhythm with the upsurge of international commerce and the development of vigorous markets for local agrarian products. Often they began as suburbs of older cathedral towns or as humble settlements outside the walls of some of the many fortresses that had arisen in ninth- and tenth-century Europe. These fortresses were generally known by some form of the Germanic word *burgh,* and in time the term came to apply to the town itself rather than the fortress that spawned it. By the twelfth century a *burgh* or *borough* was an urban commercial center, inhabited by *burghers* or *burgesses,* who constituted a new class known later as the *bourgeoisie.*

In the later eleventh century towns were developing rapidly all over Europe. They were thickest in Flanders and northern Italy where the immense opportunities of international commerce were first exploited. The greatest Italian city of the age was Venice, long a Byzantine colony but now an independent republic, whose merchants carried on a lucrative trade with Constantinople and the East. Other Italian coastal towns—Genoa, Pisa, and Amalfi—soon followed Venice into the profitable markets of the eastern Mediterranean, and the ramifications of their far-flung trade brought vigorous new life to the towns of interior Italy, such as Milan and Florence. During the High Middle Ages the Moslems were virtually driven from the seas and Italian merchants dominated the Mediterranean.

Meanwhile, the towns of Flanders were growing wealthy from the commerce of the North—from trade with northern France and the British Isles, the Rhineland and the shores of the Baltic Sea. Flanders itself was a great sheep-growing district; her towns became centers of woolen textile production. In time, the towns were processing more wool than Flemish sheep could supply so that from the twelfth century onward Flemish merchants began to import wool on a huge scale from England. By then, Flanders was the great industrial center of Northern Europe, and its textile industry the supreme manufacturing enterprise of the age.

Seal of the town of Dunwich (thirteenth century). Many towns used commercial symbols on their seals.

Urban Privileges

The rise of towns and commerce injected a vigorous new urban class into a society that had heretofore been almost exclusively agrarian. The merchant class was drawn from vagabonds, runaway serfs, avaricious minor noblemen, and, in general, the surplus of a mushrooming population. At an early date these ambitious traders began to form themselves into merchant guilds in order to protect themselves against confiscatory tolls and other exactions levied by a hostile landed aristocracy. A town was almost always situated on the territories of some lord—sometimes a duke or even a king—and the merchants found that only by collective action could they win the privileges essential to their calling: personal freedom from serf-like status, freedom of movement, freedom from inordinate tolls at every bridge or feudal boundary, the rights to own property in the town, to be judged by a town court, to execute commercial contracts, and to buy and sell freely. By the twelfth century, a number of lords, recognizing the economic advantages of having flourishing commercial centers on their lands, were issuing town charters which guaranteed many of these rights. Indeed, some farsighted lords began founding and chartering new towns on their own initiative.

At first the urban charters differed greatly from one another, but in time it became customary to pattern them after certain well-known models. The charter granted by the king of England to Newcastle-on-Tyne, and that of the French king to the town of Lorris, were copied repeatedly throughout England and France. In effect, these charters transformed the commercial communities into semi-autonomous political and legal entities, each with its own local government, its own court, its own tax-collecting agencies, and its own customs. These urban communes paid well for their charters and continued to render regular taxes to their lord. But — and this is all-important — they did so as political units. Individual merchants were not normally subject to the harassments of their lords' agents. These townsmen enforced their own law in their own courts, collected their own taxes, and paid their dues to their lord in a lump sum. In short, they had won the invaluable privilege of handling their own affairs.

One should not conclude, however, that the medieval towns were even remotely democratic. It was the prosperous merchants and master craftsmen who profited chiefly from the charters, and it was they who came to control the town governments, ruling as narrow oligarchies over the towns' less exalted and less fortunate inhabitants. Some towns witnessed the beginnings of a significant split between large-scale producers and wage-earning workers. It can be said, in fact, that the medieval town was the birthplace of European capitalism. For as time progressed towns tended to become centers of industry as well as commerce. Manufacturing followed in the footsteps of trade. And although most industrial production took place in small shops rather than large factories, some enterprising businessmen employed considerable numbers of workers to produce goods, usually textiles — on a large scale. Normally, these workers did not labor in a factory but rather in their own shops or homes. Since the entrepreneur sent his raw materials out to his workers, rather than bringing the workers to the materials, this mode of production has been called the "putting-out system." As a direct antecedent of the factory system, it was a crucial phase in the early history of capitalism.

Craft Guilds

The more typical medieval manufacturer worked for himself in his own shop, producing his own goods and selling them directly to the public. As early as the eleventh century, these craftsmen were organizing themselves into craft guilds, as distinct from merchant guilds. In an effort to limit competition and protect their market, the craft guilds established strict admission requirements and stringent rules on prices, wages, standards of quality, and operating procedures. A young craftsman would learn his trade as an apprentice in the shop of a master craftsman. After a specified period, sometimes as long as seven years, he ended his apprenticeship. With good luck and rich parents he might then become a master himself. Normally, however, he had to work for some years as a day laborer — a journeyman — improving his skills and saving his money, until he was able to demonstrate sufficient craftsmanship to win guild membership and accumulate enough money to establish a shop of his own. Toward the end of the High Middle Ages, as prosperity began to wane and urban society became more crystallized, it became increasingly common for journeymen to spend their whole lives as wage earners, never becoming masters at all. Accordingly, the town became the scene of bitter class feeling which erupted from time to time into open conflict.

Commerce and Money Economy

There were many who made their fortunes in commerce and manufacturing. Europe was astir with new life; for a clever, enterprising man the possibilities were vast. In the twelfth and thirteenth centuries, merchants were moving continuously along the roads and rivers of Europe. Italians crossed the Alps bringing spices and luxury goods from the Near East and the Orient to the aristocracy of France and Germany. French, Flemish, and German merchants carried goods far and wide across the continent, "buying cheap and selling dear." A series of annual fairs along the overland trade routes provided the long-distance merchants with excellent opportunites to sell their goods. As large-scale commerce grew, credit and banking grew along with it, and by the thirteenth century several banking families had amassed immense fortunes. It may seem paradoxical that the period which is often regarded as the supreme age of faith witnessed the rise of large-scale commerce and a money economy. Yet it was money that built the Gothic cathedrals and supported the Crusades, that financed the pious charities of St. Louis and gave zest to the magnificent religious culture of the thirteenth century — money and, of course, an ardent faith. In time, faith itself would fall victim to the acquisitive spirit which was evolving in the towns, but during the High Middle Ages the townsmen, by and large, exhibited a piety that was far more vibrant and intense than that of the peasantry and the aristocracy. Indeed, the powerful upsurge of lay piety among the European townsmen became a crucial factor in the evolution of medieval Christianity.

Decline of Feudalism

Feudalism, based as it was on hereditary land tenure in return for service, was a characteristic product of a money-poor society which could not afford to pay wages to its warriors. With the rise of a money economy in Europe, the basic feudal relationship began to dissolve. The deep impact of feudal custom on the European mind is demonstrated by the various ingenious ways in which the aristocracy sought to adapt feudalism to the new economic realities. Indeed, during the eleventh and twelfth centuries the feudal system spread from France into England, Germany, and the Crusader States of the Holy Land. At the same time, however, kings and dukes were resorting increasingly to the hiring of mercenaries for warfare and professional judges and civil servants for the administration of their realms. As the twelfth century progressed the feudal vassal was, oftener than not, asked to pay a tax in lieu of his personal service in the feudal army. With the income from this tax, which was sometimes called *scutage,* a monarch could hire professional warriors who were better trained, better disciplined, and more obedient than the landed knights. The feudal aristocracy retained its lands and much of its power for centuries to come, and even continued to produce warriors. But the knights of the new age expected to be paid. They no longer served at their own expense in return for their fiefs. Once the paying of taxes had replaced personal service as the vassal's primary obligation — and this was the case almost everywhere by the thirteenth century — feudalism had lost its soul.

Evolution of Agrarian Life

Changes in Peasant Life

The new social and economic conditions of the High Middle Ages wrought a profound transformation in the European countryside. Doubtless the most spectacular change was the immense expansion of arable land. The great primeval forest of Northern Europe was reduced to isolated patches, swamps and marshes were drained, and vast new territories were opened to cultivation. This prodigious clearing operation was stimulated by the soaring population and the rising money economy. Agricultural surpluses could now be sold to townsmen and thereby converted into cash. Consequently, the peasant was strongly motivated to produce as far in excess of the consumption level as he possibly could. Every new field that could be put into operation was likely to bring a profit.

A second change, no less significant than the first, was the elevation of the peasant. Slavery, which was rare in Carolingian times, had virtually disappeared from Europe by the eleventh century. The tillers of the land were chiefly freemen and serfs. Often the freeman owned his own small farm, but the serf was generally to be found on a manor. Normally, it will be remembered, the manor included the peasants' fields and the lord's fields (demesne) the produce of which went directly to the lord. Among the obligations which the serf normally owed his lord was labor service for a stipulated number of days on the lord's demesne. In Carolingian times, manorial lords had augmented the part-time serf labor on their demesne fields by using slaves. As slavery gradually died out, the lord was faced with a severe labor shortage on his demesne.

As a result of this problem, and in keeping with the trend toward transforming service obligations into money payments, the lords tended to abandon demesne farming altogether. They leased out their demesne fields to peasants and, in return for a fixed money payment, released their serfs from the traditional obligation of working part-time on the demesne. At about the same time they translated the serf's rent-in-kind from his own fields into a money rent. By freeing the serf of his labor obligation they transformed him, in effect, into a tenant farmer, thereby improving his status immensely. The obligations of the serf, like those of the feudal vassal, were gradually being placed on a fiscal basis.

The abandonment of demesne farming was a slow and uneven trend which progressed much more rapidly in some areas than in others. In thirteenth-century England, a counter-trend developed whereby many lords successfully reclaimed and enlarged their demesnes. But on the continent the demesne gradually disappeared and, in quite a literal sense, the peasant inherited the earth.

When the lords transformed the dues and services of their serfs into fixed money rents, they failed to reckon with inflation. The booming economy of the High Middle Ages was accompanied by an upward spiral of prices and a concomitant decline in the purchasing power of money. Hence, the real value of the peasants' rents steadily diminished, and many lords of the later Middle Ages came to regret the bargains their ancestors had made.

Inflation ruined more than one lord, but it was a godsend to the medieval peasantry. The lords could do little to recoup their losses; indeed, they were often obliged to improve the condition of their peasants still more in order to keep them from fleeing to the towns or to the newly cleared lands. The peasant was in great demand, and the enterprising land developers who were engaged in turning woods and marshes into fields competed for his services. As a consequence, the High Middle Ages witnessed the elevation of innumerable peasants from servile status to freedom. Rural communes emerged — peasant villages whose lords had granted them charters closely paralleling those of townsmen. One should be careful not to idealize the lot of the thirteenth-century peasant — it was still impoverished and brutish by present standards — yet it compared very favorably with peasant life in the Roman Empire or the Early Middle Ages. The terrifying peasants' rebellions of Early Modern Europe were products of a later and different era when the expansion and prosperity of the High Middle Ages had given way to an epoch of recession and closed frontiers.

TERRITORIAL FRONTIERS

European Expansion

The open, expanding frontier is one of the most characteristic aspects of the High Middle Ages. The clearing of forests and draining of swamps represents the conquest of a great internal frontier. It is paralleled by an external expansion all along the periphery of Western Christendom which brought vast areas of the Arab, Byzantine, and Slavic worlds within the ballooning boundaries of European civilization and added wealth to the flourishing economy.

Western Europe had been expanding ever since Charles Martel repelled the Arabs in 733. Charlemagne had introduced Frankish government and Christianity into much of Germany and had established a Spanish bridgehead around Barcelona. The stabilization and conversion of Hungary and Scandinavia around the turn of the millennium pushed the limits of Western Civilization far northward and eastward from the original Carolingian core. Now, in the eleventh, twelfth, and thirteenth centuries, the population boom produced multitudes of landless aristocratic younger sons who sought land and military glory on Christendom's frontiers. And the ever-proliferating European peasantry provided a potential labor force for the newly conquered lands. While the Christian warrior of the frontier was carving out new estates for himself, he was also storing up treasures in heaven, for as a result of his aggressive militancy Christendom was everywhere expanding at the expense of the heathen Slavs of Eastern Europe and the infidel Moslems of Spain, Sicily, and Syria. Land, gold, and eternal salvation—these were the alluring rewards of the medieval frontier.

Spain

Reconquest from the Moors

So it was that knightly adventurers from all over Christendom—and particularly from feudal France—flocked southwestward into Spain during the eleventh century to aid in the reconquest of the Iberian Peninsula from Islam. The powerful Moslem Caliphate of Cordova had broken up after 1002 into a kaleidoscope of small, warring Moorish states, thereby providing the Christians with a superb opportunity. Unfortunately, the Christians were themselves divided into several kingdoms which consumed more energy fighting one another than fighting the Moors. Taking the lead in the reconquest, the Christian kingdom of Castile captured the great Moslem city of Toledo in 1085. In later years Toledo became a crucial point of contact between Islamic and Christian culture. Here numerous Arab scientific and philosophical works were translated into Latin and then disseminated throughout Europe to challenge and invigorate the mind of the West.

Early in the twelfth century the Spanish Christian kingdom of Aragon contested the supremacy of Castile and undertook an offensive of its own against the Moors. In 1140 Aragon was greatly strengthened by its unification with the county of Barcelona—the Spanish March of Charlemagne's time. During the greater part of the twelfth century Aragon, Castile, and the smaller Christian kingdoms exhausted themselves in fighting one another and the reconquest momentarily stalled. But in 1212 the powerful Pope Innocent III proclaimed a crusade against the Spanish Moslems, and the king of Castile advanced from Toledo with a powerful pan-Iberian army, winning a decisive victory over the Moors at the battle of Las Navas de Tolosa. Thereafter

RECONQUEST OF SPAIN

1000

FRANCE
NAVARRE / BARCELONA
LEON
Ebro R.

CALIPHATE
OF
CORDOVA

Moslem possessions
Mediterranean   Sea

1100

LEON AND
BARCELONA
ARAGON
CASTILE
PORTUGAL
Lisbon
MOORISH STATES
Balearic Is.
Guadalquivir R.

0   50   100 mi.
Map by J. Donovan

1212

•Compostella
NAVARRE
LEON
ARAGON
Saragossa
PORTUGAL
CASTILE
CATALONIA
Toledo
Valencia•
Lisbon
Guadiana R.
Cordova   •Las Navas
de Tolosa
Seville   •Granada

1300

GALICIA
NAVARRE
LEON AND
ARAGON
Barcelona•
PORTUGAL
CASTILE
Toledo
Valencia•
Cordova   •
Seville•
GRANADA
To Castile 1492

Moorish power was permanently crippled. Cordova fell to Castile in 1236, and by the later thirteenth century the Moors were confined to the small southern kingdom of Granada where they remained until 1492. Castile now dominated central Spain, and the work of re-Christianization proceeded apace as Christian peasants were imported *en masse* into the reconquered lands. Aragon, in the meantime, was conquering the islands of the western Mediterranean from the Moslems and establishing a powerful maritime empire.

Thus, the High Middle Ages witnessed the Christianization of nearly all the Iberian Peninsula and its organization into two powerful Christian kingdoms and several weaker ones. The long crusade against the Moslems was the chief factor in the molding of Spanish life in the Middle Ages, and its ultimate result was to produce the intense blend of piety and patriotism which inspired the saints, soldiers, and *conquistadores* of Spain's sixteenth-century Golden Age.

Southern Italy and Sicily

The Normans in Southern Italy

Probably the most vigorous and militant force in Europe's eleventh-century awakening was the warrior-aristocracy of Normandy—largely Viking in ancestry but now thoroughly adapted to French culture. These Norman knights, French in tongue,

Christian in faith, feudal in social organization, plied their arms across the length and breadth of Europe: in the reconquest of Spain, on the Crusades to the Holy Land, on the battlefields of England and France, and in southern Italy and Sicily. Normandy itself was growing in prosperity and political centralization, and an ever-increasing population pressure drove the greedy and adventurous Norman warriors far and wide on distant enterprises. The impression which they made on contemporaries is suggested by a passage from an Italian chronicler:

> The Normans are a cunning and revengeful people; eloquence and deceit seem to be their hereditary qualities. They can stoop to flatter, but unless curbed by the restraint of law they indulge in the licentiousness of nature and passion and, in their eager search for wealth and power, despise whatever they possess and seek whatever they desire. They delight in arms and horses, the luxury of dress, and the exercise of hawking and hunting, but on pressing occasions they can endure with incredible patience the inclemency of every climate and the toil and privation of a military life.

Early in the eleventh century the Normans began to try their luck in the chaotic politics of southern Italy. Here, Byzantine coastal cities—a legacy of Justinian's conquests—struggled with old Lombard principalities and rising seaport republics such as Naples and Amalfi. The great offshore island of Sicily was controlled by the Moslems—or rather it was divided among several mutually hostile Moslem princes who had been compounding the confusion of southern Italy by mounting raids against it. The whole area was a bewildering mixture of at least four peoples: Greek, Lombard, Latin-Italian, and Arab—and the three major religions: Roman Catholic, Eastern Orthodox, and Islamic—in addition to which there existed an important and vigorous Jewish minority. It was, in short, a chaotic melting pot, politically unstable and, from the standpoint of the Normans, enormously promising.

First hiring themselves out as mercenaries to one side or another, the Norman adventurers quickly began to found states of their own. During the 1030s and 1040s a group of eight brothers, sons of a relatively insignificant Norman lord named Tancred d'Hauteville, began wandering into southern Italy and gradually assumed leadership in the movement of conquest. These eight d'Hauteville brothers illustrate vividly the dynamism engendered in Europe by the adventurous enterprises of landless younger sons of the Northern European nobility. For although they were nobodies in Normandy the d'Hauteville's rose to supreme power in southern Italy. In the early 1040s the district of Apulia was thrown into chaos by a Lombard insurrection against Byzantine control; when the dust had cleared, it was found that most of Apulia was dominated by neither Byzantines nor Lombards but by three of Tancred d'Hauteville's sons, bearing the formidable names: William Iron-Hand, Humphrey, and Drogo.

The papacy, fearing the ominous rise of Norman power to the south of the Papal States and spurred on by stories of Norman atrocities, mounted an army against the Normans and engaged them in battle at Civitate in 1053. The Normans defeated the army, captured the pope himself, and, after paying him due reverence, obliged him to confirm their conquests and become their lord—in short, to legitimize them. No longer free-booters, the Normans now enjoyed the status of respectable landholders and vassals of St. Peter.

Robert Guiscard

In the meantime the greatest of the d'Hauteville brothers, Robert Guiscard (the Cunning), had arrived in the area and had carved out a patrimony for himself in the southern province known as Calabria. Robert was proud, ambitious, ruthless, calculating, and dishonest—possessed, in other words, of all the qualities of the successful statesman and empire builder. As master of Calabria he lived like a brigand, inviting distinguished guests to dinner only to have them robbed. In 1054 he won control of Apulia and thereby rose to a position of dominance in Norman Italy. A treaty which he executed with the papacy in 1059 gave him the title, "By the grace of God and St. Peter, duke of Apulia, Calabria, and hereafter Sicily." This last phrase was in effect a papal suggestion that Robert and his fellow Normans might well direct their energies to the conquest of the Sicilian Moslems.

Robert Guiscard's newly conquered duchy was wealthy and powerful by the standards of the age. It included an important center of medical studies at Salerno and several thriving commercial cities such as Amalfi which carried on an extensive trade with Africa, Arabia, and Constantinople. But the Normans, who "despise whatever they possess and seek whatever they desire," were not satisfied with dominion over Apulia and Calabria. In 1060 Guiscard, taking up the papal challenge, landed with a Norman army in Sicily. Shortly afterward he turned the enterprise over to his brother Roger, the youngest of the d'Hautevilles. In later years Guiscard, although hard pressed to suppress the incessant revolts of his Apulian nobles, found time to launch a major attack against Byzantine lands and to come to the papacy's rescue by driving a hostile Holy Roman emperor from Rome.* His death in 1085 terminated a career that reflected in full measure the limitless confidence, enterprise, and ambition of his age.

Conquest of Sicily

While Robert Guiscard was occupied in his farflung projects, his brother Roger was proceeding with the subjugation of Sicily. The Norman conquest of the island was difficult and prolonged, but in 1072 the rich Sicilian city of Palermo, with one of the finest harbors in the Mediterranean, fell to the Normans. By 1091 the conquest was

* See p. 297.

completed and Roger d'Hauteville stood as undisputed master of Sicily.

By now the entire area of Sicily and southern Italy was in Norman hands, yet it remained for a time politically divided. Robert Guiscard's heterogeneous, rebellious state passed first to his son, then to his grandson who died without direct heirs in 1127. Under these two successors, southern Italy became ever more turbulent. Sicily, on the contrary, was much less prone to rebellion. Roger d'Hauteville wisely instituted a policy of toleration which placated the Sicilian Moslems and won their support for the new Norman dynasty. When Roger died in 1101 he passed on to his heirs a well-organized state and a sophisticated administration which combined Moslem, Byzantine, and feudal elements and was backed by an obedient Saracen army.

In 1105 Sicily passed to Roger d'Hauteville's son, Roger II or Roger the Great (d. 1154), a brilliant administrator and empire builder of a rather different type than Guiscard. Roger the Great was able, ambitious, tolerant, and cruel—less the adventurous feudal warrior than his predecessors had been, and far more sophisticated than they. In 1127 Roger undertook a campaign for the mastery of southern Italy, and by 1129 he assumed control of all the Norman domains, Apulia and Calabria as well as Sicily. In the following year he was elevated to royal status by papal coronation and the lands won by the Normans were thereby fused into a kingdom.

The Kingdom of Sicily

Although Roger the Great's new realm embraced both Sicily and southern Italy it was called simply the Kingdom of Sicily; it would later be called the Kingdom of the Two Sicilies. Roger ruled strongly but tolerantly over the assorted peoples of his realm with their variety of faiths, customs, and languages. The Sicilian capital of Palermo, with its superb harbor and magnificent palace, its impressive public buildings and luxurious villas, was at once a great commercial center and a crucial point of cultural exchange. Known as the city of the threefold tongue, Palermo drew its administrators and scholars from the Latin, Byzantine, and Arabic cultural traditions.

The legal structure of the kingdom included elements from Justinian's *Corpus Juris* and subsequent Byzantine law, from Lombard law, and from Norman feudalism. The royal court or *curia* was the core of an efficient, centralized bureaucracy with special departments of justice and finance. The administration profited from the inclusion of an important non-noble professional class, devoted to the king and to the efficient execution of its duties. Drawing on the long experience of Byzantium and Islam, Roger's government was far in advance of the other states of Latin Christendom.

The kingdom's splendid and varied architecture was similarly multicultural in inspiration. The Capella Palatina (Palace Church) at Palermo, built on a marble foundation and opulently decorated with mosaics, was a source of wonder and admiration. Not far from the capital, the magnificent cathedral at Monreale, begun several decades after Roger's death, synthesizes Italian, Norman-French, Moslem, and Byzantine artistic traditions with wonderful artistry. The nave of the

The Capella Palatina at Palermo; note the mosaics on the inside of the arches and on the floor.

Mosaic of Christ from the cathedral at Monreale.

cathedral is built on the pattern of the Italian basilica, but the building is enlivened with rich Islamic and Byzantine decorations. It contains a remarkable set of brass doors executed in the Byzantine style, and its interior sparkles with some 70,000 square feet of Byzantine mosaics. This remarkable structure, the cathedral church of the archbishop of Sicily, remains today in an excellent state of preservation. It epitomizes in stone the multiform civilization of twelfth-century Norman Sicily.

Under Roger and his successors the kingdom enjoyed a vital and diverse intellectual life. Its history was well chronicled by talented contemporary historians—in particular, Hugo Falcandus who produced an illuminating biography of Roger the Great. The Moslem scholar Idrisi, the greatest geographer of his age, produced a comprehensive geographical work which drew from classical and Islamic sources. Characteristically, Idrisi dedicated his masterpiece to Roger the Great, and the work bears the title, "The Book of Roger." Sicily, like Spain, became a significant source of translations from Arabic and Greek into Latin. The Sicilian translators provided Western European scholars with a steady stream of texts drawn from both classical Greek and Islamic sources, and these texts, together with those passing into Europe from Spain, served as the essential foundations for the impressive intellectual achievements of thirteenth-century Christendom.

In many ways Norman Sicily was Western Europe's most interesting and fruitful frontier state. Having been carved out partially at Moslem expense, it was representative of twelfth-century Europe's advancing territorial frontier, and as a vibrant center of cultural interplay it demonstrated that the frontier was not only advancing but also open. Europe besieged had given way to a new Europe—buoyant, expanding, and exposed to the invigorating influences of surrounding civilizations. And nowhere was this stimulating cultural contact more intense than in Norman Sicily. East and West met in Roger the Great's glittering, sun-drenched realm, and worked creatively side by side to make his kingdom the most sophisticated European state of its day.

The Crusades

Background and First Crusade

The Crusades to the Holy Land were the most spectacular and self-conscious acts of Western Christian expansionism in the High Middle Ages, although by no means the most lasting. They arose in response to a major political crisis in the Near East. During the eleventh century a new warlike tribe from Central Asia, the Seljuk Turks,

swept into Persia, took up the Islamic faith, and turned the Abbasid caliphs of Baghdad into their pawns. In 1071 the Seljuk Turks inflicted a nearly fatal blow upon the Byzantine Empire, smashing a Byzantine army at the battle of Manzikert and seizing Asia Minor, the essential reservoir of Byzantine manpower. Stories began filtering into the West of Turkish atrocities against Christian pilgrims to Jerusalem, and when the desperate Byzantine emperor, Alexius Comnenus, swallowed his pride and appealed to the West for help, Europe, under the leadership of a reinvigorated papacy, was only too glad to respond.

The Crusades represented a fusion of three characteristic impulses of medieval man: sanctity, pugnacity, and greed. All three were essential. Without Christian idealism the Crusades would be inconceivable, yet the pious dream of liberating Jerusalem and the Holy Land from the infidel was reinforced mightily by the lure of new lands and unimaginable wealth. The Crusades provided a superb opportunity for the Christian warrior aristocracy to perform their knightly skills in the service of the Lord—and to make their fortunes in the bargain.

It was to Pope Urban II that Emperor Alexius Comnenus sent his envoys asking for military aid against the Turks, and Urban II, a masterful reform pope, was quick to grasp the opportunity. The Crusade presented many advantages to the Church. It enabled the papacy to put itself at the forefront of an immense popular movement and to grasp thereby the moral leadership of Europe. Moreover, the Church may well have seen in the Crusade a partial solution to the problem of endemic private warfare in Europe—a means of drawing off many of the more warlike and restive members of the European nobility and turning their ferocity outward against the Moslems rather than inward against each other. And as a rescue mission to Byzantium, the Crusade opened the possibility of reuniting the Eastern and Western

Churches which had been in schism for more than a generation. Finally, Urban shared with many other Europeans of his day the beguiling dream of winning Jerusalem for Christendom.

Accordingly, in 1095 Pope Urban II summoned the European nobility to take up the Cross and reconquer the Holy Land. He delivered a powerful, epoch-making address to the Frankish aristocracy at Clermont-Ferrand, calling upon them to emulate the brave deeds of their ancestors, to avenge the Turkish atrocities (which he described in gory detail), to win the Biblical "land of milk and honey" for Christendom and drive the infidel from the holy city of Jerusalem. Finally, he promised those who undertook the enterprise the highest of spiritual rewards: "Undertake this journey for the remission of your sins, with the assurance of the imperishable glory of the kingdom of Heaven."

The response was overwhelming. With shouts of "God wills it!" Frankish warriors poured into the crusading army. By 1096 the First Crusade was under way. A great international military force—with a large nucleus of feudal knights from central and southern France, Normandy, and Sicily—made their way across the Balkans and assembled at Constantinople. Altogether the warriors of the First Crusade numbered around twenty-five or thirty thousand, a relatively modest figure by modern standards but immense in the eyes of contemporaries. Emperor Alexius was gravely disturbed by the magnitude of the Western European response. Having asked for a certain amount of military support, he had, as he put it, a new barbarian invasion on his hands. Cautious and apprehensive, he demanded and obtained from the Crusaders a promise of homage for all the lands they might conquer.

From the beginning there was friction between the Crusaders and the Byzantines. They differed in temperament and also in aim, for the Byzantines wished only to recapture the lost provinces of Asia Minor whereas the Crusaders were determined on nothing less than the conquest of the Holy Land. Alexius promised military aid, but it was never forthcoming, and not long after the Crusaders left Constantinople they broke with the Byzantines altogether. Hurling themselves southeastward across Asia Minor into Syria, they encountered and defeated Moslem forces, captured ancient Antioch after a long and complex siege, and in the summer of 1099 took Jerusalem itself. Urban II, who had remained behind, died just before the news of Jerusalem's fall reached Rome.

The Crusaders celebrated their capture of Jerusalem by plundering the city and pitilessly slaughtering its inhabitants. As a contemporary eyewitness describes it,

If you had been there you would have seen our feet colored to our ankles with the blood of the slain. But what more shall I relate? None of them were left alive; neither women nor children were spared. . . . Afterward, all, clergy and laymen, went to the Sepulcher of the Lord and His glorious temple, singing the ninth chant. With fitting humility they repeated prayers and made their offering at the holy places that they had long desired to visit.

With the capture of Jerusalem, after only three years of vigorous campaigning, the goal of the First Crusade had been achieved. No future crusade was to enjoy such a notable success as the first, and during the two centuries that followed, the original conquests were gradually lost. For the moment, however, Europe rejoiced at the spectacular success of its Crusaders. Some of them returned to their homes and received heroes' welcomes. Others remained in Latin Syria to enjoy the fruits of their conquests. A long strip of territory along the eastern Mediterranean shore had been wrested from Islam and was now divided, according to feudal principles, among the Crusader knights. These warriors consolidated their conquests by erecting large and elaborate castles whose ruins still excite the admiration of travelers.

The conquered lands were organized

THE CRUSADER STATES

SULTANATE OF ROUM

COUNTY OF EDESSA

KINGDOM OF ARMENIA

Edessa

BYZANTINE EMPIRE

Tigris R.

Euphrates R.

Antioch

PRINCIPALITY OF ANTIOCH

CYPRUS

Tripolis

COUNTY OF TRIPOLIS

Mediterranean Sea

Damascus

Acre

Sea of Galilee

KINGDOM OF JERUSALEM

Jerusalem

Jordan R.

Dead Sea

Arabian Desert

EMIRATE OF CAIRO

Cairo

Red Sea

0   50   100 150 mi.

Map by J. Donovan

into four Crusader States: the County of Edessa, the Principality of Antioch, the County of Tripolis, and the Kingdom of Jerusalem. This last was the most important of the four states, and the king of Jerusalem was theoretically the feudal overlord of all the crusader territories. In fact, however, he had difficulty enforcing his authority outside his own kingdom. Indeed, the feudal knights who settled in the Holy Land were far too proud and warlike for their own good, and the Crusader States were characterized from beginning by dangerous rivalries and dissensions.

Second Crusade

Gradually, over the years, the Moslems began to reconquer their lost lands. In 1144 the County of Edessa fell before Islamic pressure, and the disaster gave rise to a renewal of crusading fervor in Europe. The renowned twelfth-century abbot, St.

Bernard of Clairvaux, preached the crusade across Europe, and described the enthusiastic response to his preaching as nothing less than miraculous. The Second Crusade (1147–48) was led by King Louis VII of France and Emperor Conrad III of Germany. Louis transported his army by sea while Conrad's forces took the land route. They met in Jerusalem and at once encountered friction with the established Christian residents who had learned to live alongside the Moslems, who imitated their dress and customs, and who lacked the zeal of the newly-arrived warriors. This contrast in mood between established residents and new crusaders was to be a recurring problem in the Holy Land.

Rather than moving on Edessa, the Crusaders decided to besiege the great inland caravan center of Damascus. It was a wise plan, in theory, for possession of Damascus would have added much to the strategic and commercial stability of the Crusader States, but Damascus proved impregnable and the siege failed. The Crusaders returned to Europe empty-handed, prompting St. Bernard to describe the campaign as "an abyss so deep that I must call him blessed who is not scandalized thereby."

The 1170s and 1180s witnessed the rise of a new, unified Islamic state centered in Egypt and galvanized by the skilled leadership of a Kurdish warrior-prince named Saladin. Chivalrous as well as able, Saladin at first engaged in a truce with the Crusader States, but the rise of his new principality was nevertheless an ominous threat to Latin Syria. The truce was broken by a Christian robber baron, a typical product of the feudal environment, who persisted in attacking Moslem caravans. Saladin now moved on Jerusalem, and in 1187 he captured it. It was not to be retaken by a Christian army for the remainder of the Middle Ages.

Third Crusade

This new catastrophe resulted in still another major crusading effort. The Third

Scene from an English Coronation Ordo, ca. 1272–1325. In medieval England a coronation was a sacred rite symbolizing the tie between church and state. In this illumination, the Archbishops of Canterbury (left) and York (right) each grasp the crown. The king holds a globe topped by a cross, symbolizing the triumph of Christianity over the world. The crude sketches of the commoners at the rear suggest their lowly place in the social order. (Master and Fellows of Corpus Christi College, Cambridge)

Harbor at Classe, *before* A.D. *547. The great north Adriatic seaport of Classe was founded by the Roman Emperor Augustus at the time of Christ to serve the city of Ravenna. Five centuries later, under the Byzantine Emperor Justinian, Ravenna was made an outpost of the Eastern Empire. Classe then became the receiving center for a flow of Byzantine materials, artwork, builders, and craftsmen, which transformed the Italian city into the "Byzantium of the West." (S. Apollinare Nuovo—Scala)*

The Battle of Hastings, *from the* Bayeux Tapestry, ca. *1073–83. In 1066 the Norman Duke known to us as William the Conqueror defeated and killed King Harold of England. This portion of a tapestry made within living memory of the Battle of Hastings shows the Normans temporarily overcome. The Norman Conquest ultimately transformed England into a major European power and infused English life with French culture and language, since then a permanent part of the English heritage. (European Art Color Slides)*

Convent scenes, miniature from La Sainte Abbaye, *ca. 1300. The rise of monasticism in the Middle Ages reflected the importance of religion in medieval life. The top of this illuminated page from a manuscript on "the holy convent" shows French nuns celebrating the Mass; at the bottom they walk in procession with the priest and his assistants. The borders which enclose the scenes symbolize the walls of the convent, for nuns of that period were forbidden to leave their sanctuaries. (British Museum, London)*

The Building of the Tower of Babel, *detail from the* Maciejowski Old Testament, ca. *1250. This page represents a Biblical subject as if it were happening in the artist's time. Peasant artisans, like the French stonemasons shown here, were employed in the construction of the great cathedrals and castles of the Middle Ages. As early as the eleventh century, guilds—the ancestors of today's trade unions—were formed for the mutual aid and protection of specialized craftsmen. (Pierpont Morgan Library, New York)*

Scenes of Student Life, detail from the Ordonnances de l'Hotel du Roy, *14th century. The Middle Ages saw the development of many great centers of higher learning. These illustrations of student life at Ave Maria College in Paris show the ceremonial accounting of library books (top), the ringing of the morning bell by the first boy to wake (bottom left), and the feeding of the goldfinches, birds which held a religious significance in medieval France. (Nationales Archives, Paris—Photographie Giraudon)*

Crusade (1189–92) was led by three of medieval Europe's most illustrious monarchs: Emperor Frederick Barbarossa of Germany, King Philip Augustus of France, and King Richard the Lion-Hearted of England.* Frederick Barbarossa had a long and successful career behind him as Holy Roman Emperor; Philip Augustus was later to become the architect of the great thirteenth-century Capetian monarchy in France; and Richard the Lion-Hearted was already a warrior of immense renown on the battlefields of Europe. Yet for all that, and notwithstanding the abundant growth of legend and romance that has sprung up around the Third Crusade, the enterprise can hardly be described as successful. Frederick Barbarossa never reached the Holy Land at all. He drowned while crossing a river in Asia Minor and the greater part of his army returned to Germany. Philip and Richard, who had been enemies at home, were hostile toward one another from the beginning. They joined forces in besieging and capturing the important coastal city of Acre, but shortly thereafter King Philip returned to France to plot against Richard. There followed a series of encounters between the forces of Saladin and Richard during which the two chivalrous antagonists developed a degree of mutual admiration. Richard won several battles but failed to retake Jerusalem, and in the end he settled for a pact with Saladin, granting Christian pilgrims free access to the holy city. It was, all in all, a miserably disappointing conclusion to such an immense undertaking. As an ironic postscript, King Richard fell into hostile hands on his return journey and became the prisoner of Frederick Barbarossa's son, Emperor Henry VI, who released his royal captive only after England had paid the immense sum of 100,000 pounds—quite literally, a king's ransom.

Fourth Crusade

Within another decade Europe was ready for still another attempt on Jerusalem. Al-though lacking the distinguished royal leaders of the previous campaign, the Fourth Crusade (1201–4) had as its instigator the most powerful of the medieval popes: Innocent III. Like the First Crusade, it was led by great feudal lords rather than kings. The most important of its leaders was Baldwin IX, count of Flanders. It was, withal, the oddest of the Crusades. It never reached the Holy Land at all, yet in a certain sense it was successful.

The Crusaders resolved to avoid the perils of overland travel by crossing to the Holy Land in Venetian ships. The doge of Venice, a Christian but also a man of business, demanded as payment for the service of his ships a sum of money greater than the Crusaders could afford. He agreed, however, to take what money the Crusaders had and to transport them to the Holy Land if in return they would do him an errand on the way. They were to capture for Venice the port of Zara which had recently been taken by the king of Hungary. Pope Innocent III was infuriated by this bargain which diverted the crusading army against a king who was a Christian and a papal vassal. He repudiated the entire enterprise and excommunicated the Crusaders.

Nevertheless, the warriors went doggedly ahead. Capturing Zara in 1202, they were then diverted still again by a political dispute in Constantinople involving the succession to the Byzantine throne. One of the two claimants having been driven into exile, his son contacted the Crusaders and begged their support, promising them immense wealth, aid against the Moslems, and reunion of the Eastern and Western Churches under Rome. Rising to the challenge, the Crusaders moved on Constantinople. Entering the city through the treachery of parties friendly to the exiled claimant, the Crusaders installed him in power only to have him die. As a consequence of his death, they were obliged to flee the city. Having expended considerable

* All three of these monarchs will be encountered in the next chapter.

effort in what was apparently a fruitless cause, the Crusaders resolved to take the city for themselves, to elect a new Byzantine emperor from their own ranks, and to divide the Eastern Empire among themselves. Accordingly, they besieged Constantinople and took it by storm in 1204. The impregnable Byzantine capital had fallen at last to enemy conquerors; the Crusaders had succeeded where hordes of Moslems, Persians, and barbarians had failed. Count Baldwin IX of Flanders became emperor, and he and his heirs ruled in Constantinople for over half a century. A nucleus of the old Byzantine state held out in Asia Minor, gathering its strength, until in 1261 the Latin Empire was overthrown and Greek emperors reigned once again in Constantinople. But the Fourth Crusade had succeeded in delivering a blow from which Byzantium never entirely recovered.

The wealth of Constantinople permanently diverted the warriors of the Fourth Crusade from the Holy Land. The Eastern and Western Churches were temporarily reunited, however, and under the circumstances Pope Innocent III belatedly recognized the remarkable achievements of the Crusaders and readmitted them to communion. The Crusaders, for their part, returned to Europe with immense booty from Constantinople — precious gems, money, and gold such as few of them had imagined, but the greatest prize of all was the immense store of relics which the Westerners liberated from the Byzantine capital and brought to their homeland. Bones, heads, and arms of saints, the crown of thorns, St. Thomas the Apostle's doubting finger, and many similar treasures passed into Western Europe at this time. Perhaps more important, the West was given additional access to the intellectual legacy of Greek and Byzantine civilization during the decades of the Latin Empire.

Later Crusades

The later Crusades require less discussion than the early ones. During the thirteenth century crusading fervor gradually waned. Crusades against the Moslem Near East were generally unsuccessful, and the papacy weakened the crusading ideal by calling for repeated crusades not only against the Moslems in the Holy Land but also against the Moslems in Spain, the Albigensian heretics of southern France, and even the Holy Roman Emperor. In 1212 a visionary and ill-organized enterprise known as the "Children's Crusade" ended in utter disaster as thousands of boys and girls — gripped by religious fervor and convinced that the Mediterranean would dry up before them and provide them a miraculous pathway into the Holy Land — flocked into the ports of Southern Europe. Many of them were obliged to abandon the enterprise and return home disillusioned; the remainder were sold into Moslem slavery.

The next major effort against the Moslems of the Near East, the Fifth Crusade (1217–1221), was directed not at the Holy Land but against the real center of Moslem power: Egypt. The Crusaders captured the important Egyptian port of Damietta in 1219 and refused a Moslem offer to trade Jerusalem for it. But dissension within the crusader ranks and an abortive attack against Cairo in which the Crusaders were caught between a Moslem army and the flooding Nile, resulted in military disaster, the abandonment of Damietta, and the failure of the Crusade.

Three additional crusades of importance were undertaken in the thirteenth century. The first of these, led by the brilliant emperor Frederick II, was at once the most fruitful and least edifying of the three. Frederick negotiated with the sultan of Egypt rather than fighting him, and in 1229 obtained possession of Jerusalem by treaty. The triumph was ephemeral, however, for Jerusalem fell into Moslem hands once again in 1244. And because of the lack of fighting, Frederick II's crusade was never dignified by being given a number.

The Sixth and Seventh Crusades were led by the saint-king of France, Louis IX. One was undertaken against Egypt in 1248, the other against Tunisia in 1270. Both these crusades failed, and the second of them cost St. Louis his life. Crusades continued to be organized and mounted in subsequent generations, but as the thirteenth century closed it was obvious that crusading enthusiasm was waning and the movement dying out. In 1291, the fall of Acre — the last Christian bridgehead on the Syrian coast — brought an end to the Crusader States in the Holy Land.

Significance of the Crusading Movement

Yet the Crusades were more than simply a splendid failure. During the greater part of the High Middle Ages Christian lords ruled portions of the Holy Land. Their activities caught the imagination of Europe and held it for two centuries, uniting Western Christendom in a single vast effort. At the same time, European merchants established permanent bases in Syria and enormously enlarged their role in international commerce. Knights and barons who participated in the Crusades broadened their perspective through contacts with other civilizations. The effect of such contacts in dissolving the provincial narrow-mindedness of the European nobility is incalculable.

The Crusades gave rise to several semi-monastic orders of Christian warriors bound by monastic rules and dedicated to fighting the Moslems and to advancing the crusading cause in every possible way. One such order was that of the Knights Hospitallers which drew chiefly on the French for its membership. Another was the Knights Templars, an international brotherhood that acquired great wealth through pious gifts and intelligent estate management, and gradually became involved in far-flung banking activities. A third order, the Teutonic Knights, was composed chiefly of men from Germany. In the thirteenth century the Teutonic Knights transferred their activities from the Holy Land to northern Germany where they devoted themselves to the eastward thrust of German-Christian civilization against the heathen Slavs. Orders of a similar sort arose on other frontiers of Western Christendom. The Knights of Santiago de Compostella, for example, were dedicated to fighting the Moslems in Spain and aiding in the Christian reconquest of the Iberian Peninsula. These crusading orders, bridging as they did the two great medieval institutions of monasticism and knighthood, represented the ultimate synthesis of the military and the Christian life.

The German Eastward Expansion

Eastern Germany was still another of medieval Europe's expanding territorial frontiers. The German expansion eastward was not a product of active royal policy but rather a movement led by enterprising local aristocrats and, in particular, the dukes of Saxony. It was a slow movement with a great deal of momentum behind it which succeeded, over a long period running from *c.* 1125 to 1350, in pushing the eastern boundary of Germany from the Elbe River past the Oder to the Vistula at Slavic expense. The gains were consolidated by the building of innumerable agrarian villages and a massive eastward migration of German peasants. Consequently, the new areas were not only conquered; they were in large part Christianized and permanently Germanized. As a by-product of the movement, the Slavic kingdom of Poland was converted to Catholic Christianity and incorporated into the fabric of Western Christendom.

The later phases of the German push were spearheaded by the Teutonic Knights

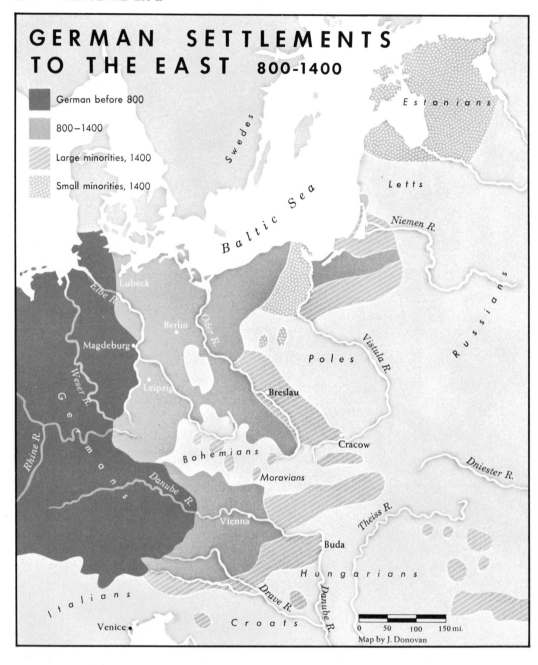

GERMAN SETTLEMENTS
TO THE EAST 800-1400

- German before 800
- 800–1400
- Large minorities, 1400
- Small minorities, 1400

Swedes

Estonians

Letts

Baltic Sea

Niemen R.

Lubeck

Elbe R.

Berlin

Oder R.

Magdeburg•

Weser R.

G e r m a n s

Leipzig

Breslau

Vistula R.

Poles

R u s s i a n s

Cracow

Dniester R.

Rhine R.

B o h e m i a n s

Moravians

Danube R.

Vienna

Theiss R.

Buda

H u n g a r i a n s

I t a l i a n s

Drave R.

Danube R.

C r o a t s

Venice•

0   50   100   150 mi.

Map by J. Donovan

who penetrated temporarily far northward into Lithuania, Latvia, and Estonia, and even made an unsuccessful bid to conquer Byzantine Russia. During the fourteenth and fifteenth centuries the Teutonic Knights were forced to forfeit many of their conquests, but much of the great German expansion proved to be permanent.

The epoch between 1125 and 1350 witnessed the conquest and Germanization of what ultimately became the eastern two-fifths of modern Germany.*

In the later thirteenth and early fourteenth centuries the great European expansion was clearly coming to an end. The in-

* Prior to World War II.

ternal frontiers of forest and swamp had by then been won, and the external frontiers were everywhere hardening, sometimes even receding as in the Holy Land. The closing of the frontiers was accompanied by diminishing prosperity and a drying up of high medieval culture. For the brilliant cultural achievements of the High Middle Ages were products of a buoyant, expanding, frontier society, fired by a powerful faith, driven by immense ambitions, and captivated by a world in which, so it seemed, anything was possible.

CHRONOLOGY OF THE EUROPEAN TERRITORIAL FRONTIER MOVEMENT

Spain	Sicily	Holy Land
1002: Breakup of Caliphate of Cordova	1016: Norman infiltration begins	
	1060–91: Sicily conquered	
1085: Capture of Toledo	1085: Death of Robert Guiscard	1095: Calling of First Crusade
1140: Aragon unites with Catalonia	1130: Coronation of Roger the Great	1099: Crusaders take Jerusalem
	1154: Death of Roger the Great	
		1187: Crusaders lose Jerusalem
1212: Christian victory at Las Navas de Tolosa		1204: Crusaders take Constantinople
1236: Castile takes Cordova		1291: Crusaders driven from Holy Land

RELIGIOUS FRONTIERS

The Church in the High Middle Ages

The expansion of civilization during the High Middle Ages has been viewed thus far as a series of advancing economic and territorial frontiers. In fact, however, frontiers of all sorts were being explored and extended in this dynamic epoch. Scholars were pioneering in new intellectual frontiers, artists and writers were adding ever-new dimensions to Western culture. Administrators were pushing forward the art of government. And underlying all these phenomena — which will be explored in the next two chapters — was an intense deepening of the religious impulse which manifested itself in many different ways: in the rise of a vigorous papacy dedicated to reform and the creation of a Christian world order,* in the development of new and different monastic orders, in the rapid expansion of ecclesiastical administration and Church activities, in the intensification of lay piety, and in the growth of religious heterodoxy.

Medieval religion followed many dif-

* See pp. 291–299.

ferent paths. It could be devoutly orthodox, it could be anticlerical, and it could be openly heretical. Yet its basic institutional expression was the Catholic Church, and the most obvious thing that the preponderant majority of Western Christians had in common was the fact of their being Catholics. Nationalism was scarcely yet alive, and the allegiance of Europeans tended to be either local or international. In the twelfth and thirteenth centuries the majority of Europeans were still intensely local in their outlook, only vaguely aware of what was going on beyond their immediate surroundings. But alongside their localism was an element of cosmopolitanism—a consciousness of belonging to the great international commonwealth of Western Christendom, fragmented politically, but united culturally and spiritually by the Church.

The Church in the High Middle Ages was a powerful unifying influence. It had made notable progress since the half-heathen pre-Carolingian era. A flourishing parish system was by now spreading across the European countryside to bring the sacraments and a modicum of Christian instruction to the peasantry. New bishoprics and archbishoprics were formed, and old ones were becoming steadily more active. The papacy never completely succeeded in breaking the control of kings and secular lords over their local bishops, but by the twelfth century it was coming to exercise a very real control over the European episcopacy, and the growing efficiency of the papal bureaucracy evoked the envy and imitation of the rising royal governments.

The Sacraments

The buoyancy of high medieval Europe is nowhere more evident than in the accelerating impact of Christian piety on European society. The sacraments of the Church introduced a significant religious dimension into the life of the typical European layman: his birth was sanctified by the sacrament of *baptism* in which he was cleansed of the taint of original sin and initiated into the Christian fellowship. At puberty, he received the sacrament of *confirmation* which reasserted his membership in the Church and gave him the additional grace to cope with the problems of adulthood. His wedding was dignified by the sacrament of *marriage*. If he chose the calling of the ministry, he was spiritually transformed into a priest by the sacrament of *holy orders*. At his death, he received the sacrament of *extreme unction* which prepared his soul for its journey into the next world. And throughout his life he could receive forgiveness from the damning consequences of mortal sin by repenting his past transgressions and humbly receiving the comforting sacrament of *penance*. Finally, he might partake regularly of the central sacrament of the Church—the *eucharist*—receiving the body of Christ into his own body by consuming the eucharistic bread. Thus, the Church, through its seven sacraments, brought God's grace to all Christians, great and humble, at every critical juncture of their lives. The sacramental system, which only assumed final form in the High Middle Ages, was a source of immense comfort and reassurance: it brought hope of salvation not simply to the saintly elite but to the sinful majority; it made communion with God not merely the elusive goal of a few mystics but the periodic experience of all believers. And, of course, it established the Church as the essential intermediary between God and man.

Evolution of Piety

The ever-increasing scope of the Church, together with the rising vigor of the new age, resulted in a deepening of popular piety throughout Europe. The High Middle Ages witnessed a profound shift in religious attitude from the awe and mystery characteristic of earlier Christianity to a new emotionalism and dynamism. This shift is evident in ecclesiastical architecture, as the stolid, earthbound Romanesque style gave way in the later twelfth century to the tense, upward-reaching Gothic.* A parallel change is evident in devotional practices as the divine Christ sitting in judgment gave way to the tragic figure of the human Christ suffering on the Cross for man's sins. And it was in the High Middle Ages that the Virgin Mary came into her own as the compassionate intercessor for hopelessly lost souls. No matter how sinful a person might be, he could be redeemed if only he won the sympathy of Mary, for what son could refuse the petition of his mother? Indeed, a legend of the age told of the devil complaining to God that the tender-hearted Queen of Heaven was cheating Hell of its most promising candidates. In this atmosphere of religious romanticism, Christianity became, as never before, a doctrine of love, hope, and compassion. The God of Justice became the merciful, suffering God who died in agony to atone for the sins of men and to bring them everlasting life.

Like all other human institutions, the medieval Church fell far short of its ideals. Corrupt churchmen were in evidence throughout the age, and certain historians have delighted in cataloguing instances of larcenous bishops, gluttonous priests, and licentious nuns. But cases such as these were clearly exceptional. The great shortcoming of the medieval Church was not gross corruption but rather a creeping complacency which resulted sometimes in a shallow, even mechanical attitude toward the Christian religious life. The medieval Church had more than its share of saints, but among much of the clergy the profundity of the Faith was often lost in the day-to-day affairs of the pastoral office and the management of far-flung estates.

The Crisis in Benedictinism

The drift toward complacency has been a recurring problem in Christian monasticism. Again and again, the lofty idealism of

a monastic reform movement has been eroded and transformed by time and success until, at length, new reform movements arise in protest against the growing worldliness of the old ones. This cycle has been repeated countless times. Indeed, the sixth-century Benedictine movement was itself a protest against the excesses and inadequacies of earlier monasticism. St. Benedict had regarded his new order as a means of withdrawing from the world and devoting full time to communion with God. But Benedictinism, despite Benedict's ideal, quickly became involved in teaching, evangelism, and ecclesiastical reform, and by the tenth and eleventh centuries the whole Benedictine movement had become deeply immersed in wordly affairs. Benedictine monasteries controlled vast estates, supplied significant contingents of knights in their service to feudal armies, and worked closely with secular princes in affairs of state. Early in the tenth century the Cluniac movement, which was itself Benedictine in spirit and rule, arose as a protest against the worldliness and complacency of contemporary Benedictine monasticism, but by the later eleventh century the Congregation of Cluny had definitely come to terms with the secular establishment and was beginning to display traces of the very complacency against which it had originally rebelled. Prosperous, respected, and secure, Cluny was too content with its majestic abbeys and priories, its elaborate liturgical program, and its bounteous fields to support the radical transformation of Christian society for which many Christian reformers were now struggling.

St. Benedict had sought to create monastic sanctuaries in which Christians might retire from the world, but the High Middle Ages witnessed an endeavor to sanctify society itself. The new goal, pioneered by the reform papacy of the eleventh century, was not *withdrawal* but *conversion*. Rather than making Christians safe from the world,

* See pp. 342–346.

the world would be made safe for Christianity. During the eleventh and twelfth centuries, these two contrary tendencies—withdrawal and conversion—both had a profound impact upon monastic reform.

In the opening decades of the High Middle Ages the Benedictine movement was showing signs of exhaustion. During the long, troubled centuries of the Early Middle Ages, Benedictine teachers and missionaries, scribes and political advisers, had provided indispensable services to society. Benedictine monasteries had served as the spiritual and cultural foci of Christendom. But in the eleventh and twelfth centuries, the Benedictines saw their pedagogical monopoly broken by the rising cathedral schools and universities of the new towns. These urban schools produced increasing numbers of well-trained scholars who gradually superseded the Benedictine monks as scribes and advisers to princes. In other words, the great urbanizing impulse of the High Middle Ages drastically diminished the traditional Benedictine contribution to the functioning of society.

Still, the Benedictines retained their great landed wealth. The Benedictine monastery was scarcely the sanctuary from worldly concerns that St. Benedict had planned. Nor was it any longer the vital force it once had been in Christianizing the world. Twelfth-century Benedictinism followed neither the path of withdrawal nor the path of conversion, and even in the arena of secular affairs it was losing its grip. The Benedictine life was beginning to appear tarnished and unappealing to sensitive religious spirits caught up in the soaring piety of the new age.

The New Monasticism

Carthusians

The monastic revolt against Benedictinism followed the two divergent roads of uncompromising withdrawal from society and ardent participation in the Christianization of society. The impulse toward withdrawal pervaded the Carthusian order which arose in eastern France in the later eleventh century and spread across Christendom in the twelfth. Isolated from the outside world, the Carthusians lived in small groups, worshiping together in communal chapels but otherwise living as hermits in individual cells. This austere order exists to this day and, unlike most monastic movements, its severe spirituality has seldom waned. Yet even in the spiritually-charged atmosphere of the twelfth century it was a small movement, offering a way of life for only a minority of heroically holy men. Too ascetic for the average Christian, the Carthusian order was much admired but seldom joined.

Cistercians

The greatest monastic order of the twelfth century, the Cistercian, managed for a time to be both austere and popular. The mother house of the order, Cîteaux, was established in 1098 on a wild, remote site in eastern France. The Cistercian order grew very slowly at first, then gradually acquired momentum. In 1115 it had four daughter houses; by the end of the century it had 500.

The spectacular success of the Cistercians demonstrates the immense appeal of the idea of withdrawal to the Christians of the twelfth century. Like Cîteaux, the daughter houses were deliberately built in remote wilderness areas. The abbeys themselves were stark and primitive in dramatic contrast to the elaborate Cluniac architecture. Cistercian life was stark and primitive too—less severe than that of the Carthusians but far more so than that of the Cluniacs. The Cistercians sought to resurrect the strict, simple life of primitive Benedictinism, but in fact they were more austere than Benedict himself. The numerous Cistercian houses were bound together tightly, not by the authority of a central abbot as at Cluny, but by an annual council of all Cistercian abbots meeting at Cîteaux. Without such centralized control it is unlikely that the individual houses could have clung for long to the harsh, ascetic ideals on which the order was founded.

Saint Bernard of Clairvaux

The key figure in twelfth-century Cistercianism was St. Bernard, who joined the community of Cîteaux in 1112 and three years later became the founder and abbot of Clairvaux, one of Cîteaux's earliest daughter houses. St. Bernard of Clairvaux was the leading Christian of his age — a profound mystic, a brilliant religious orator, and a crucial figure in the meteoric rise of the Cistercian order. His moral influence was so immense that he became Europe's leading arbiter of political and ecclesiastical disputes. He persuaded the king of France and the Holy Roman Emperor to participate in the Second Crusade. He persuaded Christendom to accept his candidate in a hotly disputed papal election in 1130. On one occasion he even succeeded in reconciling the two great warring families of Germany: the Welfs and Hohenstaufens. He rebuked the Pope himself: "Remember, first of all, that the Holy Roman Church, over which you hold sway, is the mother of churches, not their sovereign mistress — that you yourself are not the lord of bishops but one among them. . . ." And he took an uncompromising stand against one of the rising movements of his day: the attempt to reconcile the Catholic faith with human reason which was led by the brilliant twelfth-century philosopher, Peter Abelard. In the long run Bernard failed to halt the reconciliation of faith with reason, but he succeeded in making life miserable for the unfortunate Abelard and in securing the official condemnation of certain of Abelard's teachings.*

Above and beyond all his obvious talents as a leader and persuader of men, St. Bernard won the devotion and admiration of twelfth-century Europe through his reputation for sanctity. He was widely regarded as a saint in his own lifetime, and stories circulated far and wide of miracles that he performed. Pilgrims flocked to Clairvaux to be healed by his touch. This aspect of St. Bernard's reputation made his admittedly skillful preaching and diplomacy even more effective than it would otherwise have been. For here was a holy man, a miracle worker, who engaged in severe fasts, overworked himself to an extraordinary degree, wore coarse and humble clothing, and quite obviously devoted himself totally to the service of God. By contemporary standards he was relatively tolerant: he opposed the persecution of Jews, and urged that heretics — "the little foxes that spoil the vines" — should be won over to the truth "not by force of arms but by force of argument." But if a heretic should prove immune from persuasion, "he should be driven away or even a restraint put upon his freedom, rather than that he should be allowed to spoil the vines." Coming from an age in which heresy was regarded as repugnant, an offense to God, and a grave threat to Christian society, Bernard's views on the subject must be regarded as moderate and restrained.

The great Cistercian saint impressed Europe deeply with his nobility of nature and his genuine charity and humility. His religion was essentially Christ-oriented; Christ was at the center of his devotional life, with the Virgin Mary and the saints occupying a very important but fundamentally subordinate position. Humble and prayerful though he was, he could also overawe men with his energy and iron will. On one occasion, for example, he commanded Duke William of Aquitaine to reinstate certain bishops whom the Duke had driven from their sees. When, after much persuasion, the Duke proved obdurate, St. Bernard celebrated a high mass for him. Holding the consecrated host in his hands, Bernard advanced from the altar

* See pp. 356–357.

toward the Duke and said, "We have besought you, and you have spurned us. The united multitude of the servants of God, meeting you elsewhere, has entreated you and you have scorned them. Behold! Here comes to you the Virgin's Son, the Head and Lord of the Church which you persecute! Your Judge is here, at whose name every knee shall bow. . . . Your Judge is here, into whose hands your soul is to pass! Will you spurn him also? Will you scorn him as you have scorned his servants?" The Duke threw himself on the ground and submitted to St. Bernard's demands.

Bernard's career demonstrates vividly the essential paradox of Cistercianism. For although the Cistercians strove to dissociate themselves from the world, Bernard was drawn inexorably into the vortex of secular affairs. Indeed, as the twelfth century progressed, the entire Cistercian movement became increasingly worldly. Like the later Puritans, the Cistercians discovered that their twin virtues of austere living and hard work resulted in an embarrassing accumulation of wealth and a concomitant corrosion of their spiritual simplicity. Their efforts to clear fields around their remote abbeys placed them in the vanguard of the internal frontier movement. They became pioneers in scientific farming and introduced notable improvements in the breeding of horses, cattle, and sheep. The English Cistercians became the great wool producers of the realm. Altogether the Cistercians exerted a powerful, progressive influence on European husbandry and came to play a prominent role in the European economy. Economic success brought ever-increasing wealth to the Order. Cistercian abbey churches became steadily more elaborate and opulent, and the primitive austerity of Cistercian life was progressively relaxed. In later years there appeared new offshoots, such as the Trappists, which returned to the strict observance of original Cistercianism.

Monasticism in the World

The Cistercians had endeavored to withdraw from the world, but despite their goal they became a powerful force in twelfth-century Europe. At roughly the same time, other orders were being established with the deliberate aim of participating actively in society and working toward its regeneration. The Augustinian Canons, for example, submitted to the rigor of a rule, yet carried on normal ecclesiastical duties in the world, serving in parish churches and cathedrals. The fusion of monastic discipline and worldly activity culminated in the twelfth-century Crusading orders—the Knights Templars, the Knights Hospitallers, the Teutonic Knights, and similar groups—whose ideal was a synthesis of the monastic and the military life for the purpose of expanding the political frontiers of Western Christendom. These and other efforts to direct the spiritual vigor of monastic life toward the Christianization of society typify the bold visions and lofty hopes of the new, emotionally-charged religiosity that animated twelfth-century Europe.

Heresies and the Inquisition

Rise of Heresy

The surge of popular piety also raised serious problems for the Church and society, for it resulted in a flood of criticism against churchmen. It was not that churchmen had grown worse, but rather that laymen had begun to judge them by harsher standards. Popular dissatisfaction toward the workaday Church manifested itself in part in the rush toward the austere twelfth-century monastic orders. Yet the majority of Christians could not become monks, and for them, certain new heretical doctrines began to exert a powerful appeal.

The heresies of the High Middle Ages flourished particularly in the rising towns of Southern Europe. The eleventh-century urban revolution had caught the Church unprepared; whereas the new towns were the real centers of the burgeoning lay piety, the Church, with its roots in the older agrarian feudal order, seemed unable to minister effectively to the vigorous and widely literate new burger class. Too often the urban bishops appeared as political oppressors and enemies of *burghal* independence rather than inspiring spiritual directors. Too often the Church failed to understand the townsmen's problems and aspirations or to anticipate their growing suspicion of ecclesiastical wealth and power. Although the vast majority of medieval townsmen remained loyal to the Church, a troublesome minority, particularly in the south, turned to new, anticlerical sects. In their denunciation of ecclesiastical wealth, these sects were doing nothing more than St. Bernard and the Cistercians had done. But many of the anticlerical sects crossed the boundary between orthodox reformism and heresy by preaching without episcopal or papal approval; far more important, they denied the exclusive right of the priesthood to perform sacraments.

Waldensians, Albigensians, and the Inquisition

One such sect, the Waldensians, was founded by a merchant of Lyons named Peter Waldo who, *c.* 1173, gave all his possessions to the poor and took up a life of apostolic poverty. He and his followers worked at first within the bounds of orthodoxy, but gradually their anticlericalism and their denial of special priestly powers earned them the condemnation of the Church. Similar groups, some orthodox, some heretical, arose in the communes of Lombardy and were known as the *Humiliati*. Naturally these groups proved exceedingly troublesome and embarrassing to the local ecclesiastical hierarchies, but generally they escaped downright condemnation unless they themselves took the step of denying the authority of the Church. Many of them did take that step, however,

and by the thirteenth century heretical, anticlerical sects were spreading across northern Italy and southern France, and even into Spain and Germany.

The most popular and dangerous heresy in southern France was sponsored by a group known as the *Cathari* (the pure) or the Albigensians—after the town of Albi where they were particularly strong. The Albigensians represented a fusion of two traditions: (1) the anticlerical protest against ecclesiastical wealth and power, and (2) an exotic theology derived originally from Persian dualism. The Albigensians recognized two gods: the god of good who reigned over the universe of the spirit, and the god of evil who ruled the world of matter. The Old Testament God, as creator of the material universe, was their god of evil; Christ, who was believed to have been a purely spiritual being with a phantom body, was the god of good. Albigensian morality stressed a rigorous rejection of all material things—of physical appetites, wealth, worldly vanities, and sexual intercourse—in the hope of one day escaping from the prison of the body and ascending to the realm of pure spirit. In reality this severe ethic was practiced only by a small élite known as the *perfecti;* the rank and file, who were called *credentes* (believers), normally begat children, and participated only vicariously in the rejection of the material world—by criticizing the affluence of the Church. Indeed, their opponents accused them of gross licentiousness, and it does seem to be true that certain Provençal noblemen were attracted to the new teaching by the opportunity of appropriating Church property in good conscience.

However this may be, Albigensianism was spreading rapidly as the thirteenth century dawned and was becoming an ominous threat to the unity of Christendom and the authority of the Church. Pope Innocent III, recognizing the extreme gravity of the situation, tried with every means in his power to eradicate Albigensianism. At length, in 1208, he responded to the murder of a papal legate in southern France by summoning a crusade against the Albigensians—the first crusade ever to be called against European Christians. The Albigensian Crusade was a ruthless, savage affair which succeeded in its purpose but only at the cost of ravaging the vibrant civilization of southern France. The French monarchy intervened in the Crusade's final stages, brought it to a bloody conclusion, and thereby extended the sway of the Capetian kings to the Mediterranean. The Albigensian Crusade was an important event in the development of French royal power, and it succeeded in reversing the trend toward heresy in Southern Europe. It also disclosed the brutality of which the Church was capable when sufficiently threatened.

In the years immediately following the Albigensian Crusade, there emerged an institution that will always stand as a grim symbol of the medieval Church at its worst: the Inquisition. The Christian persecution of heretics dates from the later fourth century, but it was not until the High Middle Ages that heterodox views presented a serious problem to European society. Traditionally, the problem of converting or punishing heretics was handled at the local level, but in 1233 the papacy established a permanent central tribunal for the purpose of standardizing procedures and increasing efficiency in the suppression of heresies. The methods of the Inquisition included the use of torture, secret testimony, conviction on the testimony of only two witnesses, the denial of legal counsel to the accused, and other procedures offensive to the Anglo-American legal tradition but not especially remarkable by standards of the times. Indeed, many of these procedures—including torture—were drawn from the customs of Roman Law. In defense of the Inquisition it might be said that convicted heretics might escape death by renouncing their "errors," and that far from establishing a reign of terror, the Inquisition seems to have enjoyed popular support.

Some historians have adduced other arguments in an attempt to defend an indefensible institution. Let us say here merely that the Christian faith was far more important to the people of medieval Europe than national allegiance—that the medieval Church, with its elaborate charitable activities, its hospitals and universities, and its other social services, performed many of the functions of the modern state, and that therefore medieval heresy was analogous to modern treason. To the medieval Christian, heresy was a hateful, repugnant thing, an insult to Christ, and a source of contamination to others. Today, when political and economic doctrines are more important to most people than religious creeds, the closest parallel to medieval Waldensianism or Albigensianism is to be found in the communist and Nazi parties in modern America. In examining popular opposition toward extremist groups such as these, perhaps we can gain an inkling of the state of mind that produced the medieval Inquisition.

Mendicantism

The thirteenth-century church found an answer to the heretical drift in urban piety which was far more compassionate and effective than the Inquisition. In the opening decades of the century two radically new orders emerged—the Dominican and the Franciscan—which were devoted to a life of poverty, preaching, and charitable deeds. Rejecting the life of the cloister, they dedicated themselves to religious work in the world—particularly in the towns. Benedictines and Cistercians had traditionally taken vows of personal poverty, but the monastic orders themselves could and did acquire great corporate wealth. The Dominicans and Franciscans, on the contrary, were pledged to both personal and corporate poverty, and were therefore known as mendicants (beggars). Capturing the imagination of thirteenth-century Christendom, they drained urban heterodoxy of much of its former support by demonstrating to the townsmen of Europe that Christian orthodoxy could be both relevant and compelling.

The Dominicans

St. Dominic (1170–1121), a well-educated Spaniard, spent his early manhood as an Augustinian canon at a cathedral in Castile. In his mid-thirties he traveled to Rome, met Pope Innocent III, and followed the Pope's bidding to preach in southern France against the Albigensians. For the next decade, between 1205 and 1215, he worked among the heretics, leading an austere, humble life, and winning considerable renown for his eloquence and simplicity. For the most part the Albigensians seem to have been unaffected by Dominic's preaching; they respected him but did not follow him.

The Dominican Order evolved out of a small group of volunteers who joined Dominic in his work among the Albigensians. Gradually, Dominic came to see the possibility of a far greater mission for his followers: to preach and win converts to the faith throughout the world. In 1215, Dominic's friend, the bishop of Toulouse, gave the group a church and a house in the city, and shortly thereafter the papacy recognized the Dominicans as a separate religious order and approved the Dominican Rule. The congregation founded by Dominic was to be known as the Order of Friars Preachers. It assumed its permanent shape during the years between its formal establishment in 1216 and Dominic's death in 1221 by which time it had grown to include some 500 friars and 60 priories organized into eight provinces embracing the whole of Western Europe. The Dominicans stood in the vanguard of the thirteenth-century upsurge of piety. Their order attracted men of imagination and unusual religious dedication, men who could not be satis-fied with the enclosed and tradition-bound life of earlier monasticism but who were challenged by the austerity of the Dominican Rule, the disciplined vitality of the order, and the stimulating goal of working toward the moral regeneration of society rather than withdrawing from the world.

The Dominican Rule drew freely from the earlier rule of the Augustinian Canons which Dominic had known in his youth, but added new elements and provided a novel direction for the religious life. The order was to be headed by a minister-general, elected for life, and a legislative body that met annually and consisted sometimes of delegates from the Dominican provinces, sometimes of priors from all the Dominican houses. The friars themselves belonged not to a particular house or province but to the order, and their place of residence and activity was determined by the minister-general. Their life, strictly regulated and austere, included such rigors as regular midnight services, total abstinence from meat, frequent fasts, and prolonged periods of mandatory silence. And the entire order was strictly bound by the rule of poverty which Dominic had learned from his contemporary, St. Francis. Not only should poverty be the condition of individual Dominicans as it was of individual Benedictines, it was to be the condition of the order itself. The Dominican order was to have no possessions except churches and priories. It was to have no fixed incomes, no manors, but was to subsist through charitable gifts. It was, in short, a mendicant order.

The Dominican order expanded at a phenomenal rate during the course of the thirteenth century. Dominican friars carried their evangelical activities across the length and breadth of Europe and beyond, into the Holy Land, Central Asia, Tartary, Tibet, and China. Joining the faculties of the rising universities they became the leading proponents of Aristotelian philosophy and included in their numbers such notable scholars as St. Albertus

Magnus and St. Thomas Aquinas. Dominic himself had insisted that his followers acquire broad educations before undertaking their mission of preaching and that each Dominican priory include a school of theology. Within a few decades after his death his order included some of the most brilliant intellects of the age.

The Dominicans were, above all, preachers, and their particular mission was to preach among heretics and non-Christians. Their contact with heretics brought them into close involvement with the Inquisition, and in later years their reputation was darkened by the fact that they themselves became the leading inquisitors. The grand inquisitor of Spain, for example, was customarily a Dominican. They acquired the ominous nickname, *"Domini canes"*—hounds of God—by their willingness to supplement St. Dominic's policy of persuasion with the easier and crueler policy of force.

The Dominican order still flourishes. The rule of corporate poverty was softened increasingly and finally, in the fifteenth century, dropped altogether, for it was recognized that full-time scholars and teachers could not beg or do odd jobs or be in doubt as to the source of their next meal. But long after their original mendicant ideals were modified, the Dominicans remained faithful to their essential mission of championing Catholic orthodoxy by word and pen.

St. Francis

Dominic's remarkable achievement was overshadowed by that of his contemporary, St. Francis (*c.* 1182–1226)—a warm and appealing man who is widely regarded as Christianity's ideal saint. Francis was a true product of the medieval urban revolution. He was the son of a wealthy cloth merchant of Assisi, a northern Italian town with an influential Albigensian minority. As a youth he was generous, high-spirited, and popular, and in time he became the leader of a boisterous but essentially

harmless "teen-age gang." He was by no means a rake or a dissolute young man but rather, as one writer has aptly expressed it, he "seems altogether to have been rather a festive figure."

In his early twenties, St. Francis underwent a profound religious conversion which occurred in several steps. It began on the occasion of a banquet which he was giving for some of his friends. After the banquet Francis and his companions went out onto the town with torches, singing in the streets. Francis was crowned with garlands as king of the revellers, but after a time he disappeared and was found in a religious trance. Thereafter he devoted himself to solitude, prayer, and service to the poor. He went as a pilgrim to Rome where he is reported to have exchanged clothes with a beggar and spent the day begging with other beggars. Returning to Assisi, he encountered an impoverished leper and, notwithstanding his fear of leprosy, he gave the poor man all the money he was carrying and kissed his hand. Thenceforth he devoted himself to the service of lepers and hospitals.

To the confusion and consternation of his bourgeois father, Francis now went about Assisi dressed in rags, giving to the poor. His former companions pelted him with mud, and his father, fearing that Francis' incessant almsgiving would consume the family fortune, disinherited him. Undaunted, Francis left the family house gaily singing a French song. He spent the next three years of his life in the environs of Assisi, living in abject poverty, ministering to lepers and social outcasts, and continuing to embarrass his family by his unconventional behavior. It was at this time that he began to frequent a crumbling little chapel known as the Portiuncula. One day, in the year 1209, while attending mass there, he was struck by the words of the Gospel which the priest was reading: "Everywhere on your road preach and say, 'The kingdom of God is at hand.' Cure the sick, raise the dead, cleanse the lepers, drive out devils. Freely have you received; freely give. Carry neither gold nor silver nor money in your girdles, nor bag, nor two coats, nor sandals, nor staff, for the workman is worthy of his hire." (Matt. X. 7–10). Francis at once accepted this injunction as the basis of his vocation and immediately thereafter—even though a layman—began to preach to the poor.

Disciples now joined him, and when he had about a dozen followers he is said to have remarked, "Let us go to our Mother, the Holy Roman Church, and tell the pope what the Lord has begun to do through us and carry it out with his sanction." This may have been a naive approach to the masterful, aristocratic Pope Innocent III, yet when Francis came to Rome in 1210, Innocent sanctioned his work. Doubtless the Pope saw in the Franciscan mission a possible orthodox counterpoise to the Waldensians, Albigensians, and other heretical groups who had been winning masses of converts from the Church by the example of their poverty and simplicity. For here was a man whose loyalty to Catholicism was beyond question and whose own artless simplicity of life might bring erring souls back into the Church. Already Innocent III had given his blessing to movements similar to that of Francis. An orthodox group of *Humiliati* had received his sanction in 1201, and in 1208 he permitted a converted Waldensian to found an order known as the "Poor Catholics," which was dedicated to lay preaching. In Francis' movement the Pope must have seen still another opportunity to encourage a much-needed wave of radical reform within the orthodox framework. And it may well be that Francis' glowing spirituality appealed to the sanctity of Innocent himself, for the Pope, even though a great man of affairs, was a genuinely pious person. However this may be, thirteenth-century Europe deserves some credit for embracing a movement which in many other ages would have been persecuted or ridiculed. Rome crucified Christ, but high-

This painting, ascribed to the thirteenth-century Italian artist Cimabue (c. 1240–1302), is taken from a series of frescoes in the upper church of the Basilica di S. Francesco in Assisi. Although the fresco was executed about two generations after St. Francis's own time, some historians believe that it may possibly be a fairly reasonable likeness. It is, in any event, the earliest known painting of the saint.

medieval Europe took Francis to its heart and made him a saint.

Immediately after the papal interview Francis and his followers returned to the neighborhood of Assisi. They were given the Portiuncula as their own chapel, and over the years it continued to serve as the headquarters of the Franciscan movement. Around it the friars built huts of branches and twigs. The Portiuncula was a headquarters but not a home, for the friars were always on the move, wandering in pairs over the country, dressed in peasants' clothing, preaching, serving, and living in conscious imitation of the life of Christ. During the next decade the order expanded at a spectacular rate. Franciscans were soon to be found throughout northern Italy; by 1220 Franciscan missions were active in Germany, France, Spain, Hungary, and the Holy Land, and the friars numbered in the thousands. The immensely attractive personality of Francis himself was doubtless a crucial factor in his order's popularity, but it also owed much to the fact that its ideals appealed with singular effectiveness to the highest religious aspirations of the age. Urban heresy lost some of its allure as the cheerful, devoted Franciscans began to pour into Europe's cities, preaching in the crowded streets and setting a living example of Christian sanctity.

The Franciscan ideal was based above all on the imitation of Christ. Fundamental to this ideal was the notion of poverty, both individual and corporate. The Franciscans subsisted by working and serving in return for their sustenance. Humility was also a part of the ideal; Francis named his followers the "Friars Minor" (little brothers). Preaching was an important part of their mission, and it answered an urgent need in the rising cities where the Church had hitherto responded inadequately to the deepening religious hunger of townsmen. Perhaps most attractive of all was the quality of joyousness, akin to the joyousness that Francis had shown prior to his conversion, but directed now toward spiritual ends. Contemporaries referred to Francis affectionately as "God's own troubadour."

Pious men of other times have fled the world; the Albigensians renounced it as the epitome of evil. But Francis embraced it joyfully as the handiwork of God. In his "Song of Brother Sun," he expressed poetically his holy commitment to the physical universe:

> Praise be to Thee, my Lord, for all thy creatures,
> Above all Brother Sun

> Who brings us the day, and lends us his light;
> Beautiful is he, radiant with great splendor,
> And speaks to us of Thee, O most high.
> Praise to Thee, my Lord, for Sister Moon and for the stars;
> In heaven Thou hast set them, clear and precious and fair.
> Praise to Thee, my Lord, for Brother Wind.
> For air and clouds, for calm and all weather
> By which Thou supportest life in all Thy creatures.
> Praise to Thee, my Lord, for Sister Water
> Which is so helpful and humble, precious and pure.
> Praise to Thee, my Lord, for Brother Fire,
> By whom Thou lightest up the night.
> And fair is he, and gay and mighty and strong.
> Praise to Thee, my Lord, for our sister, Mother Earth.
> Who sustains and directs us,
> And brings forth varied fruits, and plants and flowers bright. . . .
> Praise and bless my Lord, and give Him thanks,
> And serve Him with great humility.

Crisis and Aftermath

Early Franciscanism was too good to last. The order was becoming too large to retain its original disorganized simplicity. Francis was a saint rather than an administrator, and well before his death the movement was passing beyond his control. In 1219–1220 he traveled to Egypt in an effort to convert its Moslem inhabitants — a hopeless task, but Francis was never dismayed by the impossible — and while he was away it became apparent that his order required a more coherent organization than he had seen fit to provide it. Many perplexing questions now arose. With thousands of friars invading the begging market, what would become of the poor common tramp? Would Europe's generosity be overstrained? Above all, how could these multitudes of friars be expected to cleave to the ideal without an explicit rule and without Francis' personal presence to inspire and guide them? In short, could the Franciscan ideal be practical on a large scale? For the movement was proliferating at a remarkable rate. Besides the Friars Minor themselves, a Second Order was established—a female order directed by Francis' friend, St. Clare—known as the Poor Clares. And there was a peripheral group of part-time Franciscans, known as Tertiaries, who dedicated themselves to the Franciscan way while continuing their former careers in the world. The little band of Franciscan brothers had evolved into a vast and complex body.

On his return from the Near East, Francis prevailed upon a powerful friend, Cardinal Hugolino—later Pope Gregory IX—to become the order's protector. On Hugolino's initiative a formal rule was drawn up in 1220 which provided a certain degree of administrative structure to the order. A novitiate was established, lifetime vows were required, and the rule of absolute poverty was mitigated. In 1223 a shorter and somewhat laxer rule was instituted, and over the years and decades that followed, the movement continued to evolve from the ideal to the practical.

St. Francis himself withdrew more and more from involvement in the order's administration. At the meeting of the general chapter in 1220 he resigned his formal leadership of the movement with the words, "Lord, I give thee back this family that Thou didst entrust to me. Thou knowest, most sweet Jesus, that I have no more the power and the qualities to continue to take care of it." In 1224, St. Francis underwent a mystical experience atop Mt. Alverno in the Apennines, and legend has it that he received the stigmata * on that occasion. It is not entirely clear how St. Francis reacted to the evolution of his order, but in his closing years his mysticism deepened, his health declined, and he kept much to himself. At his death in 1226 he was universally mourned, and the order which he had founded remained the most powerful and attractive religious movement of its age.

As Franciscanism became increasingly modified by the demands of practicality it also became increasingly rent with dissension. Some friars, wishing to draw on Francis' prestige without being burdened with his spiritual dedication, advocated an exceedingly lax interpretation of the Franciscan way. Others insisted on the strict imitation of Francis' life and struggled against its modification. These last, known in later years as "Spiritual Franciscans," sought to preserve the apostolic poverty and artless idealism of Francis himself, and by the fourteenth century they had become vigorously anti-papal and anti-clerical.

The majority of Franciscans, however, were willing to meet reality halfway. Although Francis had disparaged formal learnings as irrelevant to salvation, Franciscan friars began devoting themselves to scholarship and took their places alongside the Dominicans in the thirteenth- and fourteenth-century universities. Indeed, Franciscan scholars such as Roger Bacon in thirteenth-century England played a crucial role in the revival of scientific investigation, and the minister-general of the Franciscan order in the later thirteenth century, St. Bonaventure, was one of the most illustrious theologians of the age. The very weight and complexity of the Franciscan organization forced it to compromise its original ideal of corporate poverty. Although it neither acquired nor sought the immense landed wealth of the Benedictines or Cistercians, it soon possessed sufficient means to sustain its members. It is interesting to see how the minister-general Bonaventure, a holy man and also a brilliant philosopher, instituted and

---

* The stigmata, which has been attributed to several saints, consists in a person receiving, by divine grace, wounds on his hands, feet, and side corresponding to the wounds of Christ.

justified some of the changes that the order underwent in the thirteenth century. Although an intense admirer of St. Francis, Bonaventure was not himself a beggar by nature, nor a wandering minstrel, nor a day laborer, but a scholar-administrator burdened with the task of adapting a way of life designed for a dozen friars living in huts of twigs to an international order of many thousands. Contrary to Francis, Bonaventure encouraged scholarship as an aid to preaching and evangelism. St. Francis had urged his followers that "manual labor should be done with faith and devotion." Bonaventure, after demonstrating the superiority of contemplation over manual labor, concluded that Franciscans were under no compulsion to engage in physical work, though if any wished to do so he should by all means do it, "with faith and devotion."

Necessary though they were, these compromises robbed the Franciscan movement of a good measure of the radical idealism that Francis had instilled in it. In the progress from huts of twigs to halls of ivy something very precious was left behind. The Franciscans continued to serve society, but by the end of the thirteenth century they had ceased to inspire it.

The Passing of the High Middle Ages

The pattern of religious reform in the High Middle Ages is one of rhythmic ebb and flow. A reform movement is launched with high enthusiasm and lofty purpose, it galvanizes society for a time, then succumbs gradually to complacency and gives way to a new and different wave of reform. But with the passing of the High Middle Ages one can detect a gradual waning of spiritual vigor. The frontiers were closing as the fourteenth century dawned. Western political power was at an end in Constantinople and the Holy Land, and the Spanish reconquest had ground to a halt. The economic boom was giving way to an epoch of depression, declining population, peasants' rebellions, and debilitating wars. And until the time of the Protestant Reformation, no new religious order was to attain the immense social impact of the thirteenth-century Franciscans and Dominicans. Popular piety remained strong, particularly in Northern Europe where succeeding centuries witnessed a significant surge of mysticism. But in the south a more secular attitude was beginning to emerge. Young men no longer flocked into monastic orders; soldiers no longer rushed to crusades; papal excommunications no longer wrought their former terror. The electrifying appeal of a St. Bernard, a St. Dominic, and a St. Francis was a phenomenon peculiar to their age. By the fourteenth century, their age was passing.

CHRONOLOGY OF HIGH MEDIEVAL MONASTICISM AND HETERODOXY

        910: Founding of Cluny
       1084: Establishment of Carthusian Order
       1098: Establishment of Citeaux
  1112–1153: Career of St. Bernard of Clairvaux
             as a Cistercian.
       1128: Original rule of Knights Templars.
    c. 1173: Beginning of Waldensian sect.
       1208: Innocent III calls Albigensian
             Crusade.
       1210: Innocent III authorizes Franciscan Order.
       1216: Dominican Rule sanctioned by papacy.
       1226: Death of St. Francis.
       1233: Inquisition established.

SELECTED READINGS

Bettenson, Henry, translator, *Documents of the Christian Church,* Oxford University Press, New York, 1963 (2nd ed.).
   A useful collection running from antiquity to the present.

Cantor, Norman F., *Medieval History,* The Macmillan Co., New York, 1963.

A recent, highly interpretive textbook, particularly strong on ecclesiastical history.

*Heer, Frederick, *The Medieval World*, Mentor, New York, New American Library, 1964.
The author contrasts twelfth-century expansion with thirteenth-century stabilization.

Knowles, David, *The Monastic Order in England*, Cambridge University Press, New York, 1963 (2nd ed.).
A brilliant scholarly study of monasticism in England from the mid-tenth century to 1216.

Knowles, David, *The Religious Orders in England*, Cambridge University Press, New York, 1948, 1955, 1959, 3 vols.

*Painter, Sidney, *Medieval Society*, Cornell University Press, Ithaca, New York, 1951.
A short introductory essay.

*Pirenne, Henri, *Economic and Social History of Medieval Europe*, Harvest, New York, 1956.
A compact, richly interpretive survey by a great scholar.

*Pirenne, Henri, *Medieval Cities*, Anchor, Garden City, New York, 1956.
Brief, lucid, and highly original.

*Ross, J. B. and M. M. McLaughlin, eds., *The*

Portable Medieval Reader, Viking, New York, 1946.
Like Cantor's *Medieval World*, a useful, well-chosen collection of medieval sources in translation.

*Runciman, Steven, *A History of the Crusades*, Harper, New York, 1951, 1952, 1954, 3 vols.
Comprehensive and authoritative.

Sabatier, Paul, *St. Francis of Assisi*, Charles Scribner's Sons, New York.
A warm and deeply sympathetic older study.

*Sherley-Price, L., translator, *The Little Flowers of St. Francis*, Penguin, Baltimore, Md.
A fascinating collection of sources relating to the life of St. Francis.

*Southern, R. W., *The Making of the Middle Ages*, Yale University Press, New Haven, Connecticut, 1953.
A brilliant, sympathetic treatment of the eleventh and twelfth centuries.

Villehardouin and de Joinville, *Memoirs of the Crusades*, Sir Frank Marzials, translator, Everyman.
Excellent contemporary accounts of the Fourth Crusade and the crusading exploits of St. Louis.

Asterisk (*) denotes paperback.

11

Church and State in the High Middle Ages

EMPIRE AND PAPACY

The Background of the Struggle

Papacy and Church in the Mid-Eleventh Century

The role of the papacy in the changing religious configurations of the High Middle Ages was scarcely touched upon in the previous chapter, for although it was fundamental to the spiritual development of the period it was also closely associated with the politics of empire and kingdom which is the central topic of this chapter. Therefore, we must go back to the mid-eleventh century, the age when Cluny still stood in the vanguard of European monasticism, when Cîteaux was yet an untouched wilderness and the mendicant movement lay in the distant future. With the dawning of the High Middle Ages there emerged a newly invigorated papacy, dedicated to ecclesiastical reform and the spiritual regeneration of Christian society. Almost at once the reform papacy became involved in an epic struggle with the Holy Roman Empire — a tragic conflict which dominated European politics for more than two centuries. On the eve of the conflict Germany was the mightiest monarchy in Western Christendom and the German king or Holy Roman emperor held the papacy in his palm. By 1300 the Holy Roman Empire was reduced to a specter of its former greatness and the papacy, after 250 years of political prominence, was exhausted, battle-scarred, and on the brink of a prolonged decline.

Prior to the beginnings of papal reform in the mid-eleventh century, a chasm existed between the papal theory of Christian society and the realities of the contemporary Church. The papal theory, with a venerable tradition running all the way back to the fifth-century pope Leo the Great, envisaged a sanctified Christian commonwealth in which lords and kings accepted the spiritual direction of priests and bishops who, in turn, submitted to the leadership of the papacy. The popes claimed to be the successors—the vicars—of St. Peter. Just as St. Peter was the chief of Christ's apostles, they argued, the pope was the monarch of the apostolic Church. And as eternal salvation was more important than earthly prosperity—as the soul was more important than the body—so the priestly power was greater than the power of secular lords, kings, and emperors. The properly ordered society, the truly Christian society, was one dominated by the Church which, in turn, was dominated by the pope. In the intellectual climate of the High Middle Ages this view had great pertinence and caught the imagination of many thinking men. It provided the papacy with a dynamic, convincing, almost irresistible intellectual position.

The reality of mid-eleventh-century society was far different. Almost everywhere the Church was under the control of aristocratic lay proprietors. Petty lords appointed their priests; dukes and kings selected their bishops and abbots. As we have seen, the Holy Roman emperors used churchmen extensively in the administration of Germany. In France, the Church provided warriors from its estates for the feudal armies, clerks for the feudal chanceries, and shrewd political advisers for the feudal princes. The Church played a vital role in the operation of tenth- and early-eleventh-century society but it was always subordinate to the lay ruling class. Its spiritual and sacramental role was compromised by its secular administrative responsibilities. As was bound to happen under such conditions, the Church tended to neglect its sacred mission. From the lay standpoint it was an effective administrative tool, but from the spiritual standpoint it was inadequate and often corrupt. Monasteries all too frequently ignored the strict Benedictine Rule.

Some priests had concubines, and a great many had wives, despite the canonical requirement of priestly celibacy. Lay lords often sold important ecclesiastical offices to the highest bidder, and the new prelate customarily recouped the expense of buying his office by ruthlessly exploiting his tenants and subordinates. This flourishing commerce in ecclesiastical appointments was known as *simony*. It was regarded by some contemporary reformers as the arch sin of the age.

Ecclesiastical corruption was nowhere more evident than in Rome itself. The papacy of the earlier eleventh century had fallen into the soiled hands of the Roman nobility and had become a prize disputed among the several leading aristocratic families of the city. In 1032 the prize fell to a callow, sensual young man, Pope Benedict IX, whose outrageous pontificate was scandalous even by contemporary Roman standards. Pope Benedict sold the papacy, then changed his mind and reclaimed it. By 1046 his claim to the papal throne was challenged by two other claimants; the papacy had degenerated into a three-way schism.

Ecclesiastical Reform

Such were the conditions of the European Church as the mid-eleventh century approached. A Church dominated by lay proprietors had long existed in Europe and had long been accepted. But with the powerful upsurge of lay piety that accompanied the opening of the High Middle Ages, the comfortable Church-state relationship of the previous epoch seemed profoundly wrong to many sensitive spirits. This was the epoch in which Christians were beginning to join hermit groups such as the Carthusians; they would soon be flocking into the new, austere Cistercian order. Such men as these were responding to the spiritual awakening of their age by following the path of withdrawal from worldly society. Others chose the more novel and adventurous approach of *con-*

version and took up the onerous task of reforming the Church and the world. The dream of sanctifying society, which was later to find such vivid expression in the career of St. Francis, was shared by many Christians of the High Middle Ages. During the second half of the eleventh century it manifested itself in a powerful movement of ecclesiastical reform which was beginning to make itself felt across the length and breadth of Western Christendom. At the heart of this movement was the reform papacy.

In general, the reformers fell into two groups: (1) a conservative group which sought to eliminate simony, enforce clerical celibacy, and improve the moral calibre of churchmen, but without challenging the Church's traditional subordination to the lay aristocracy — a subordination which had been sweetened by countless generous gifts of lands and powers to submissive prelates, and (2) a radical group which sought to demolish the tradition of lay control and to rebuild society on the pattern of the papal monarchy theory. The radical reformers struggled to establish an ideal Christian commonwealth in which laymen no longer appointed churchmen — in which kings deferred to bishops and a reformed papacy ruled the Church. The conservative reformers endeavored to heal society; the radicals wished to overturn it.

Henry III and Leo IX

The Congregation of Cluny, firm in its spiritual rectitude yet at peace with the existing social order, was one of the chief centers of conservative reform in the eleventh century. Its ideals were shared by several of the more enlightened rulers of the age, among them, Emperor Henry III, the powerful Salian monarch of Germany. Shocked by the disgraceful antics of Pope Benedict IX and the three-way tug-of-war for the papal throne, Henry III intervened in Italy in 1046, arranged the deposition of Benedict and his two rivals, and drastically improved the quality of papal leadership by appointing the first of a series of reform popes. The ablest of these imperial appointees, Pope Leo IX (1049–54), carried on a vigorous campaign against simony and clerical marriage, holding yearly synods at Rome, sending legates far and wide to enforce reform, and traveling constantly himself to preside over local councils and depose guilty churchmen. Leo IX's reform pontificate opened dramatically when, at the Roman Synod of 1049, the bishop of Sutri was condemned for simony and promptly fell dead in the presence of the whole assembly — a victim, it was assumed, of the divine wrath.

Leo IX labored mightily for reform, and his pontificate constitutes the opening phase in the evolution of the dynamic high-medieval papacy. His concern for a secure territorial position in central Italy prompted him to lead an army against the enterprising Norman adventurer to the south, Robert Guiscard, but being defeated and captured at Civitate he was forced to recognize the Normans and give them the status of papal vassals.* His insistence on a vigorous assertion of papal authority led him into a conflict with the Eastern Orthodox Church, and in 1054 the conflict culminated in a permanent schism between the two communions. More than anything else, Leo struggled to enforce canon law and to purge the Church of simony and incontinence. In all his enterprises, he could count on the general support of Emperor Henry III. In these early years empire and papacy worked hand in glove to raise the moral level of the European Church.

But however successful this reform movement might have been, there were those who felt that it was not going far enough. The real evil, in the view of the radical reformers, was lay supremacy over the Church, and Henry III's domination of papal appointments, however well-intentioned, was the supreme example of a profound social sin. A number of ardent reformers were to be found among the car-

* See p. 266.

dinals whom Pope Leo IX appointed and gathered around him. These new men, who dominated the reform papacy for the next several decades, came for the most part from monastic backgrounds. Many of them were deeply influenced by the strong piety surging throughout the towns of eleventh-century northern Italy: a piety that was stimulating a widespread revival of hermit monasticism.

Damiani, Humbert, and Hildebrand

One such man was St. Peter Damiani, a leader of the northern-Italian eremitic movement before he was brought to Rome by Leo IX and made a cardinal. Zealous and saintly, Damiani was deeply respected by his contemporaries. He was a mystic and, like St. Bernard after him, a vigorous opponent of the growing tendency among Christian intellectuals to elucidate the Faith by means of reason and logic. Damiani served the reform papacy tirelessly, traveling far and wide to enforce the prohibitions against simony and incontinence and to reform the clergy. Yet he drew back from what seemed to him the irresponsible efforts of his more radical brethren to challenge and destroy the contemporary social order. Aflame with the new piety and deeply dedicated to the papacy, Damiani was nevertheless one of the less extreme of Leo IX's new cardinals.

The real leaders of the radical group were Humbert and Hildebrand. Both were cardinals under Leo IX; both had, like Damiani, left monastic lives to join the Roman curia. Humbert was a German from Lorraine, probably of aristocratic background, who used his subtle, well-trained intellect to support papal reform in its most radical form. He was the author of a bitter, closely reasoned attack against the lay-dominated social order, *Three Books Against the Simoniacs,* in which he extended the meaning of "simony" to include not merely the buying or selling of ecclesiastical offices but any instance of lay interference in clerical appointments. In Humbert's view, the Church ought to be utterly free of lay control and supreme in European society.

Hildebrand, an Italian probably of humble origin, lacked the originality and intellectual depth of Humbert but had a remarkable ability to draw ideas from the minds of others and formulate them into a clearly articulated program. Intellectually, Hildebrand was a disciple of Humbert, but as a leader and man of action he was second to none. Contemporaries described him as a small, ugly, potbellied man, but they also recognized that a fire burned inside him—a holy or unholy fire depending on one's point of view, for Hildebrand was the most controversial figure of his age. Consumed by the ideal of a Christian society dominated by the Church and a Church dominated by the papacy, Hildebrand served with prodigious vigor and determination under Pope Leo IX and his successors. At length he became pope himself, taking the name of Gregory VII (1073–85). His was to be one of the greatest and most tragic pontificates of the Middle Ages.

The Papal Election Decree

So long as Henry III lived, radicals such as Humbert and Hildebrand remained in the background. But in 1056 the Emperor died in the prime of life, leaving behind him a six-year-old heir, Henry IV, and a weak regency government. His death was a catastrophe for the Empire and a godsend to the radicals who longed to wrest the papacy free from imperial control. At the death of Henry III's last papal appointee in 1057, the reform cardinals began electing popes of their own choosing. In 1059, under the influence of Cardinals Humbert and Hildebrand, they issued a daring and momentous declaration of independence known as the *Papal Election Decree* which stated that thenceforth emperors and Roman laymen would merely give formal approval to the candidate whom the cardinals elected. In the years that followed, this revolutionary proclamation was challenged by both the Empire and the Roman aristocracy, but in the end the cardinals won out. The papacy had broken free of lay control and was in the hands of the reformers. For now the cardinals elected the pope * and the pope appointed the cardinals. The Decree of 1059 created at the apex of the ecclesiastical hierarchy a reform oligarchy of the most exclusive sort.

The Investiture Controversy

The next step in the program of the radical reformers was infinitely more difficult. It involved nothing less than the annihilation of lay control over the entire Church. At a time when the Church possessed untold wealth, including perhaps a third of the land in Europe, the total realization of such a goal would cripple secular power and revolutionize European society. Yet only by its realization, so the radical reformers believed, could a true Christian commonwealth be achieved.

Reform in Milan

One of the first arenas of conflict was the ancient city of Milan with its proud archbishopric renowned since St. Ambrose's time. Milan was in the grip of the new commercial revival and, like many other Lombard towns of the eleventh century, was seething with activity. The Lombard towns of this era were, as a rule, dominated by their bishops—who were inclined to cooperate with the Holy Roman Empire—and by an élite group of landed noblemen. As a group, the Lombard bishops tended to ignore the new wave of reform, and some were themselves guilty of simony. Throughout Lombardy, and in Milan in particular, the rule of the nobles and episcopacy was being challenged by the vigorous and grow-

ing lower classes of artisans, day workers, and peasants. In Milan and elsewhere, this revolutionary lower-class group was called, by its enemies, the *patarenes* (ragpickers). Deeply hostile to the domination of the traditional ruling group and fired by the new piety, the patarenes made common cause with the reform papacy against their unreformed and oppressive masters. The reformers in Rome had no sympathy for the Lombard bishops and were especially hostile to the archbishop of Milan who was, in effect, an imperial agent and who, by condoning simony and incontinence among his clergy, symbolized the old proprietary Church at its worst.

In 1059 Cardinal Peter Damiani journeyed to Milan to enforce reform. Backed by the patarenes and the authority of Rome, he humbled the archbishop and the higher clergy, made them confess their sins publicly, and wrung promises of amendment from them. Thus, the Milanese church, despite its traditional cooperation with the Empire and independence of Roman authority, was made to submit to the power of the papacy. Over the next decade and a half the conflict flared up anew. The struggle between the patarenes and the noble-ecclesiastical ruling group continued, and the city was torn by murder and mob violence. When, in 1072, the young Emperor Henry IV ordered the consecration of an anti-reformer as archbishop of Milan, he was at once faced with the combined wrath of the papacy and patarenes. The patarenes rioted and the pope excommunicated Henry IV's counsellors. The most significant aspect of this entire affair is the way in which it typifies the close alliance between radical urban piety and papal reform. During the second half of the eleventh century the papacy managed to place itself at the forefront of the new piety and to draw upon the vital energy of the revolutionary social-spiritual movement that was sweeping across Europe. At odds with much of the traditional ecclesiastical establishment, the radical reformers in

---

* Strictly speaking, the Decree of 1059 provided that the pope should be elected not by all the cardinals but by the cardinal bishops alone. The other cardinals—cardinal priests and cardinal deacons—were empowered to participate in papal elections by a decree of the twelfth century.

Thirteenth-century bishop. The episcopal ring and staff were traditionally conferred by lay lords against whose right of investiture medieval reformers struggled fiercely from the pontificate of Gregory VII onward.

Rome were nevertheless in tune with the most vigorous spiritual forces of the age.

The Ban against Lay Investiture; Its Consequences

The immense struggle over lay control of ecclesiastical appointments broke out in earnest in 1075 when Hildebrand, now Pope Gregory VII, issued a proclamation banning lay investiture. Traditionally, a newly chosen bishop or abbot was invested by a lay lord with a ring and a pastoral staff, symbolic of his marriage to the Church and his duty toward his Christian flock. Pope Gregory VII attacked this custom of lay in-

vestiture as the crucial symbol of lay authority over churchmen. Its prohibition was a momentous challenge to the established social order. It threatened to compromise the authority of every ruler in Christendom, and none more than the Holy Roman Emperor himself, for the administrative system of the Empire was particularly dependent on the emperor's control of the German Church. By Gregory VII's time, Henry IV had grown to vigorous manhood and was showing promise of becoming as strong a ruler as his father, Henry III. Refusing to accept the decree against lay investiture, Henry IV sent a flaming letter of defiance to Gregory VII in which he asserted his right as a divinely appointed sovereign to lead the German Church without papal interference and challenged Gregory's very right to the papal throne. The letter was addressed to Gregory under his previous name, "Hildebrand, not pope but false monk." It concluded with the dramatic words, "I, Henry, king by grace of God, with all my bishops, say to you: 'Come down, come down, and be damned throughout the ages'."

Henry's letter was in effect a defense of the traditional social order of divinely ordained priest-kings ruling over a docile church. Gregory VII's view of society was vastly different: he denied the priestly qualities of kings and emperors, suggested that most of them were gangsters destined for Hell, and repudiated their right to question his status or his decrees. Emperors had no power to appoint churchmen, much less depose popes, but the pope, as the ultimate authority in Christendom, had the power to depose kings and emperors. Accordingly, Gregory VII responded to Henry IV's letter with a startling and unprecedented exercise of spiritual authority which was, nevertheless, perfectly in accord with his conception of Christian society: he excommunicated and deposed Henry IV. It was for the pope to judge whether or not the king was fit to rule, and Gregory had judged. His judgment was nothing less than revolutionary, however, for in banning lay investiture and deposing the king of Germany he was putting into practice the papal theory in its most radical form and striking at the very bedrock of the traditional order.

Canossa: Background and Aftermath

Radical though it was, the deposition was effective. Under the relatively calm surface of Salian monarchical authority in Germany, a powerful aristocratic opposition had long been gathering force. Subdued during the reign of the powerful Henry III, local and regional particularism asserted itself during the long regency following Henry III's death, and Henry IV, on reaching maturity, had much ground to recover. In 1075 he succeeded in stifling a long and bitter rebellion in Saxony and seemed to be on his way toward reasserting his father's power when the investiture controversy exploded. Gregory VII's excommunication and deposition—awesome spiritual sanctions to the minds of eleventh-century Christians—unleashed in Germany all the latent hostility that the centralizing policies of the Salian dynasty had evoked. Many Germans, churchmen and laymen alike, refused to serve an excommunicated sovereign. The great German aristocrats took the revolutionary step of threatening to elect a new king in Henry's place, thereby challenging the German tradition of hereditary kingship with the fateful counterdoctrine of elective monarchy. The elective principle, which so crippled the later-medieval and early-modern German monarchy, had its real inception at this moment.

Desperate to keep his throne, Henry IV crossed the Alps into Italy to seek the Pope's forgiveness. In January 1077, at the castle of Canossa in Tuscany, the two men met in what was perhaps medieval history's most dramatic encounter—Henry IV humble and barefoot in the snow, clothed in rough, penitential garments; Gregory VII torn between his conviction that Henry's change of heart was insincere

and opportunistic, and his priestly duty to forgive a repentant sinner. Finally, Pope Gregory VII lifted Henry's excommunication and the monarch, promising to amend his ways, returned to Germany to rebuild his authority.

Down through the centuries Canossa has symbolized the ultimate royal degradation before the power of the Church. Perhaps it was. But in the *immediate* political context it was a victory, and a badly needed one, for Henry IV. It did not prevent a group of German nobles from electing a rival king, nor did it restore the powerful centralized monarchy of Henry III; but it did save Henry IV's throne. Restored to communion, he was able to rally support, to check for a time the forces of princely particularism, and to defeat the rival king.

As his power waxed, Henry ignored his promises at Canossa and resumed his support of lay investiture. In 1080 Gregory VII excommunicated and deposed him a second time, only to find that these potent spiritual weapons were losing their strength through overuse. In the early 1080s Henry IV returned to Italy, this time with an army. Gregory VII summoned his vassal and ally, the Norman Robert Guiscard, to rescue him from his situation, but Robert's boisterous Normans, although they frightened Henry IV away, became involved in a destructive riot with the Roman townspeople. The commoners of Rome had always supported Gregory, but now they turned furiously against him and he was obliged, for his own protection, to accompany the Normans when they withdrew to the south. In 1085 Gregory died at Salerno, consumed by bitterness and a conviction of failure. His last words were these: "I have loved justice and hated iniquity; therefore I die in exile."

The Investiture Controversy after Gregory VII

Although Gregory VII failed to transform Europe into what he conceived to be a proper Christian society, his theory of papal monarchy retained its potency. The reform papacy soon fell into the able hands of Urban II (1088–99), a former prior of Cluny, who seized the moral leadership of Europe by calling the First Crusade. Pope Urban steered a more moderate course than Gregory had done, yet he and his successors continued to make life miserable for the unlucky Henry IV, stirring up rebellions in Germany and eroding the power of the imperial government. In 1106 Henry IV died as unhappily as had Gregory VII. In the end, Henry's own son and heir, Henry V, led an army of hostile aristocrats against his father. As Henry IV died, the German Empire seemed to be collapsing in ruins around him.

Henry V (1106–1125) enjoyed a happier reign than his father's, but only because he foresook his father's struggle to recover the fullness of imperial power as it had existed in the mid-eleventh century. The independence-minded aristocracy consolidated the gains it had made during the preceding era of chaos, and Henry V could do nothing about it.

Toward the end of his reign, Henry V worked out a compromise settlement with the Church which brought the Investiture Controversy to an end at last. Already the controversy had been settled by compromise in England and France where the Church-state struggle had been considerably less bitter than in Germany. As time progressed both papacy and Empire tended to withdraw somewhat from the extreme positions they had taken during Gregory VII's pontificate. At length they reconciled their differences in the Concordat of Worms of 1122. Henry agreed that the investiture ceremony would no longer be performed by laymen, but the pope conceded to the emperor the important privilege of bestowing on the new prelate the symbols of his *territorial* and *administrative* jurisdiction. Bishops and abbots were thenceforth to be elected according to the principles of canon law, by the monks of a monastery or the canons of a cathedral, but the emperor had the right to be present at such elections and to make the final decision in the event of a dispute. These reservations enabled the emperor to retain a considerable degree of *de facto* control over the appointment of important German churchmen. The reconciliation of royal control and canonical election is illustrated in a delightful twelfth-century charter of King Henry II of England to the monks at Winchester: "I order you to hold a free election, but nevertheless I forbid you to elect anyone except Richard, my clerk, the archdeacon of Poitiers."

Consequences of the Investiture Controversy

There was no real victor in the Investiture Controversy. The Church had won its point—lay investiture was banned—but monarchs still exercised very real control over their churches. The theory of papal monarchy over a reconstituted Christian society remained unrealized.

Still, the papal-imperial balance of power had changed radically since the mid-eleventh century. The papacy was now a mighty force in Europe, and the power of the emperor had declined sharply. During the chaotic half-century between the onset of the Investiture Controversy in 1075 and Henry V's death in 1125, feudalism came to Germany. In these decades of civil strife a powerful new aristocracy emerged. Ambitious landowners rose to great power, built castles, extended their estates, and usurped royal rights. They forced minor neighboring noblemen to become their vassals and, in some instances, forced free peasants to become their serfs. The monarchy was helpless to curb this ominous process of fragmentation.

The Investiture Controversy resulted in the crippling of imperial authority in northern Italy. The fierce patarene struggle of Milan was repeated throughout Lombardy, and in the anarchy wrought by the papal-imperial conflict the pro-imperial Lombard bishops lost the wide jurisdictional rights that they formerly had exercised over their cities and the surrounding countryside. For everywhere the pious and vigorously independent Lombard townsmen took up the cause of papal reform, rebelled against the control of nobles, bishops, and emperor alike, and established quasi-independent communes or city states. By 1125, Milan and her sister cities were free urban communes and imperial authority in Lombardy had become virtually nominal.

In Germany and Italy alike, imperial power was receding before the whirlwind of local particularism, invigorated by the Investiture Controversy and the soaring popular piety of the age. Well before the Concordat of Worms, the downfall of the medieval Empire had begun.

The Age of Frederick Barbarossa

Welfs and Hohenstaufens

The Salian dynasty died out with the passing of Henry V in 1125. During the next quarter century Germany reaped the bitter harvest of princely particularism. The great nobles ignored the principle of hereditary royal succession and reverted to the elective principle which they had asserted at the time of Canossa. Their choice always fell to a man of royal blood but never to the most direct heir. In the turbulent decades between 1125 and 1152 a great rivalry developed between two powerful families who had risen to power in the anarchic era of the Investiture Controversy: the Welfs of Saxony and the Hohenstaufens of Swabia. In 1152 the princes elected as king a powerful and talented Hohenstaufen, Frederick Barbarossa (the Red-Bearded), duke of Swabia, who took as his mission the revival and reconstruction of the German monarchy.

Policies of Frederick Barbarossa

Emperor Frederick Barbarossa recognized fully that the mighty imperial structure of Henry III was beyond recovery. His goal was to harness the new feudal forces of his age to the royal advantage. He actually encouraged the great princes of the realm to expand their power and privileges at the expense of the lesser lords, but at the same time he forced them to recognize his own feudal lordship over all the kingdom. In other words, he succeeded in establishing the leading feudal magnates as his vassals—his tenants-in-chief. He was the supreme overlord at the apex of the feudal pyramid.

But as the sorry state of the early French monarchy well illustrates, feudal overlordship was an ephemeral thing if the royal overlord lacked the power and resources to support his position. Therefore, Frederick Barbarossa set about to increase his revenues and extend the territories under his direct authority. A strong feudal monarchy required a substantial territorial core under exclusive royal control—an extensive royal demesne to act as a counterweight to the great fiefs of the chief vassals of the realm. Frederick enlarged his demesne territories, most of which were concentrated in Swabia, by bringing many of the new monasteries and rising towns under imperial jurisdiction. The crux of his imaginative policy was the reassertion of imperial authority over the wealthy cities of Lombardy. With Lombardy under his control and its revenues pouring into the imperial treasury, no German lord could challenge him.

Barbarossa's Lombard policy earned him the hostility of the papacy which had always feared the consolidation of imperial power in Italy, and of the intensely independent Lombard cities which were determined to give up as little of their wealth and autonomy as they possibly could. And should he become too deeply involved in Italy, Barbarossa exposed himself to re-

bellion on the part of the German aristocrats and high nobility—in particular, the
Welf family which was vigorously represented at the time by Duke Henry the Lion
of Saxony.

Hadrian IV and Arnold of Brescia

The papacy of the mid-twelfth century
was having problems of its own. Pope
Hadrian IV (1154–59), who was to become one of Frederick Barbarossa's most
ardent foes, was faced at the beginning of
his pontificate with the problem of maintaining the papacy's hold on Rome itself. A
gifted man of humble origins, Hadrian IV
was the one Englishman ever to occupy the
papal throne. Rome was turbulent during
his years, for the patarene movement had
reached the Holy City and had turned
violently anti-papal. The revolutionary
social forces that had earlier allied with the
papacy in breaking the power of an archbishop in Milan were now challenging the
Pope's authority over Rome. In the 1140s
the city was torn by a lower-class rebellion
whose leaders struggled to drive out the
Pope and dreamed of reestablishing the
ancient Roman Republic. Very quickly this
anti-papal communal movement spread to
other cities in the Papal States, and for a
time the papacy itself was forced into exile.
Before long, the Roman rebellion fell under
the leadership of Arnold of Brescia, a
gifted scholar and spiritual revolutionary,
whose goal it was to strip the Church of its
wealth and secular authority. Suppressed
by the Norman troops of Roger the Great
in the 1140s, Arnold of Brescia's revolution reasserted itself under Hadrian IV,
and the Pope was driven to the desperate
expedient of placing Rome under interdict,
ordering the suspension of church services
throughout the city. The interdict proved
an effective weapon; among other things, it
severely curtailed the influx of pilgrims and
thereby had an adverse effect on Rome's
economy. The revolution collapsed and
Arnold of Brescia was driven from the city.

Hadrian and Barbarossa joined forces to
hunt him down, and no sooner had he fallen
into their hands than he was hanged,
burned, and thrown into the Tiber (1155).
Thus, Arnold was emphatically eliminated
and his relics were put out of the reach of
any future admirers. But his movement persisted as an anti-clerical heresy—an early
example of the opposition to ecclesiastical
wealth and power that was soon to find expression among the Waldensians and
Albigensians and, by implication, among
the Franciscans.

The growing split between the papacy
and the Roman townsmen was an ominous
indication that papal leadership over urban
reform movements was at an end. The
papacy was no longer able to make common cause with the explosive forces of
popular piety as it had done in the age of
Gregory VII, but was now beginning to
suppress them. Pope Hadrian IV actually
had little choice but to defend himself in
whatever way possible against Arnold of
Brescia, yet, in laying Rome under interdict, he was following a path that would
lead within a century to the Albigensian
Crusade and the Inquisition. This tragic
schism between papal leadership and popular piety was a factor of no small importance in the ultimate downfall of the later
medieval papacy.

Barbarossa and the Lombard League

Hadrian IV and Frederick Barbarossa
first met on the occasion of the imperial
coronation in Rome in 1155. The two men
had collaborated against Arnold of Brescia,
but thereafter they became enemies. At
their initial encounter, Hadrian insisted that
Frederick follow ancient tradition and lead
the papal mule.* At first Frederick haugh-
tily refused to humble himself in such a

---

* The tradition of the ceremonial mule-leading seems
to have originated in the eighth-century forgery, the
"Donation of Constantine."

manner, but when it appeared that there would be no coronation at all he grudgingly submitted. This small conflict was symbolic of far greater ones, for Hadrian IV and his successors proved to be implacable opponents of Frederick's drive to win control of the Lombard cities.

The Lombard struggle reached its climax under the pontificate of Alexander III (1159–1181), Hadrian's successor. Wise, shrewd, and learned, Alexander III was the greatest pope of the twelfth century and Frederick Barbarossa's most formidable opponent. Whereas most of the early reform popes had been monks, Alexander III and many of his successors were canon lawyers. Hildebrand himself had urged the study of canon law and the formulation of canonical collections in order to provide intellectual ammunition to support papal claims to authority. During the later eleventh and twelfth centuries the study of canon law was pursued vigorously in northern Italian schools, particularly the great law school at Bologna, and a good number of twelfth and thirteenth century popes were products of these schools. Alexander III was one of the ablest of them.

Determined to prevent Frederick Barbarossa from establishing himself strongly in northern Italy, Alexander III rallied the Lombard towns which had long been engaged in intercity warfare but now combined forces against the Empire. They formed an association called the Lombard League and organized a powerful interurban army to oppose Frederick. The Emperor had meanwhile thrown his support behind a rival claimant to the papal throne, and Alexander III responded by excommunicating and deposing Frederick. There followed a bitter, prolonged struggle involving Alexander III, Frederick Barbarossa, and the Lombard League, which ended in the total victory of the Lombard army at the battle of Legnano in 1176. Barbarossa submitted as graciously as he could, granting *de facto* independence to

THE HOLY ROMAN EMPIRE IN 1190

Map by J. Donovan

the Lombard cities in return for their admission of a vague imperial overlordship. Pope and Emperor tearfully embraced; Barbarossa led Alexander's mule and promised thereafter to be a dutiful son of the Roman See.

Barbarossa's Triumph

Barbarossa had lost a battle, but he had by no means lost the war. Leaving Lombardy severely alone, he shifted his operations southward to Tuscany, establishing administrative control over this rich province immediately to the north of the Papal States. At the same time he arranged a fateful marriage between his son and the future heiress of the Norman Kingdom of southern Italy and Sicily—a marriage which ultimately brought that opulent kingdom within the imperial fold. The papacy had been outwitted and was in grave danger of being encircled and stifled by the Empire. In 1180 Barbarossa consolidated his power in Germany by crushing the greatest and most hostile of his vassals, Henry the Lion, the Welf duke of Saxony. After Alexander III's death in 1181, the papacy ceased for a time to be a serious threat, and the far-sighted Emperor was at the height of his power in 1190 when he died while leading his army toward the Holy Land to participate in the Third Crusade.

Barbarossa had taken pains to circumvent the princely policy of elective monarchy by forcing the princes, prior to his death, to elect his son, Henry VI. In 1190 Henry VI succeeded to the German throne without difficulty, and in 1194 he made good his claim to the Kingdom of Sicily. The Papal States were now an island completely surrounded by Holy Roman Empire, and the papacy was powerless to alter the situation. The bounteous revenues of southern Italy and Sicily fattened the imperial purse. The territories under imperial rule had never been so extensive.

But for an age in which the emperor had to remain ever vigilant against the centrifugal forces of local particularism and, above all, against the ambitions of the great German vassals, the imperial frontiers had become dangerously overextended. It remained ominously uncertain whether a single man could rule Italy and Germany concurrently. Whether Henry VI could have accomplished this task we shall never know, for he died prematurely in 1197 leaving as his heir his infant son, Frederick II. The problems the Empire faced in 1197 would have taxed the ablest of leaders, yet at this crucial moment imperial leadership failed. The papacy had its opportunity at last.

The High Noon of the Medieval Papacy

During the twelfth century, the papacy lost much of its former zealous reform spirit as it evolved into a huge, complex administrative institution. Revenues flowed into its treasury from all the states of Western Christendom; bishops traveled vast distances to make their spiritual submission to the Roman pontiff; the papal curia served as a court of last appeal for an immense network of ecclesiastical courts. Papal authority over the European Church had increased immeasurably since the mid-eleventh century. As the dream of a papal monarchy came ever nearer to realization, the traditional theory of papal supremacy over Christian society was increasingly magnified and elaborated by the canon lawyers. These subtle ecclesiastical scholars were beginning to dominate the papal curia, and, like Alexander III, to occupy the papal throne itself.

Pontificate of Innocent III

Innocent III (1198–1216), the greatest of all the lawyer popes, came to power in the year following Emperor Henry VI's death. It was he who seized the opportunity offered by the succession of an infant to the throne of the overextended Empire. Innocent III was history's most powerful pope—a brilliant, astute diplomat, an imperious, self-confident aristocrat who, although genuinely pious, was distinctly aloof from the surging religious emotionalism of the humbler folk of his age. He had the wisdom and sensitivity to support the Franciscans, and the ruthlessness to mount the Albigensian Crusade.*

Animated by the theory of papal monarchy in its most uncompromising form, Innocent III forced his will on the leading monarchs of Europe, playing off one king

* See pp. 281–282, 285.

against another with consummate skill. In the course of a long struggle with King John of England over the appointment of an archbishop of Canterbury, Innocent laid John's entire kingdom under interdict, threatened to depose John himself, and endeavored to persuade King Philip Augustus of France to send an army against him. The struggle ended with John's complete submission, the installation of Innocent's man in the archbishopric of Canterbury, and the establishment of papal lordship over England. Innocent had earlier clashed with Philip Augustus over the King's refusal to repudiate an uncanonical second marriage and return to his first wife. After laying France under interdict and excommunicating Philip, Innocent obtained his submission.* It has already been shown how Innocent instigated the Fourth Crusade, which was aimed at Jerusalem but ended in Constantinople, and how he mounted crusades against the Albigensians and the Spanish Moors. These diverse activities illustrate clearly the unprecedented political and moral sway which Innocent exercised over Christendom.

A mighty force in the secular politics of his age, Innocent III also dominated the Church more completely than any of his predecessors had done. In 1215 he summoned a general Church council in Rome — the Fourth Lateran Council — which produced a remarkable quantity of significant ecclesiastical legislation: clerical habit was strictly regulated, a moratorium was declared on new religious orders, the ancient Germanic legal procedure of the ordeal † was condemned, fees for the administration of sacraments were forbidden, cathedral churches were ordered to maintain schools and to provide sermons at their chief services, and all Catholics were bound to receive the sacraments of penance and the

eucharist at least once a year. The efficient organization of the Fourth Lateran Council, and the degree to which Pope Innocent dominated and directed it are clearly illustrated by the fact that the churchmen in attendance — more than 1200 bishops, abbots, and priests — produced their important new legislation in meetings that lasted a total of only three weeks. By contrast, the fifteenth century Council of Basel met off and on for 18 years and the Council of Trent for 19 years.

The Disputed German Succession

The range of Innocent III's activities was seemingly boundless, but throughout his pontificate one political issue took precedence over all others: the problem of the German imperial succession. It was a marvelously complex problem which taxed even Pope Innocent's diplomatic skill. Involved in it were the questions of whether or not the kingdom of Sicily would remain in imperial hands, whether the imperial throne would pass to the Welfs or the Hohenstaufens, and whether an accommodation could be achieved between the traditionally hostile forces of papacy and Empire. The German succession problem also touched the interests of the French and English monarchies: the Welf claimant, Otto of Brunswick, was a nephew of King John of England and could usually count on his support, whereas the Hohenstaufens enjoyed the friendship of the French king, Philip Augustus.

The direct Hohenstaufen heir was the infant Frederick, son of the late Henry VI. But since a child could hardly be expected to wage a successful fight for the throne in these turbulent years, the Hohenstaufen claim was taken up by Frederick's uncle, Philip of Swabia, brother of the former emperor. The young Frederick remained in Sicily while Philip of Swabia and the Welf, Otto of Brunswick, contended for the imperial throne. Innocent recognized the principle that the German princes had the right to elect their own monarch, but, as

---

* Philip Augustus' submission was less complete, however, than might have been wished. His controversial second wife had died — conveniently but naturally — and his reconciliation with his first wife was a mere formality.

† See p. 190.

it happened, Philip and Otto had both been elected, each by a different group of German nobles. In the case of a disputed election such as this, Innocent claimed the right to intervene by virtue of the traditional papal privilege of crowning the emperor. He delayed his decision considerably, and in the meantime, civil war raged in Germany. At length he settled on Otto of Brunswick. Otto had promised to support the papal interests in Germany and to abandon almost entirely the policy of imperial control of the German Church which had been spelled out in the Concordat of Worms of 1122. Further, a Welf emperor would have no claim on the Hohenstaufen Kingdom of Sicily, and Otto's coronation would therefore realize the papal goal of separating the two realms.

Despite Innocent's decision, the civil was continued in Germany until, in 1208, Philip of Swabia died. Otto was crowned emperor in 1209, but now, having no rival to oppose him, he repudiated his promises to Innocent III, asserted his mastery over the German Church, and even launched an invasion of southern Italy. Innocent responded to this breach of faith by deposing and anathematizing Otto and throwing his support behind the young Frederick. From the beginning, the kingdom of Sicily had been, at least nominally, a papal vassal state, and Innocent III, as overlord, claimed the feudal privilege of guardianship over its minor king. Frederick, in other words, was Innocent's ward. Before undertaking to back Frederick, Innocent wrung a number of promises from him, making him swear to abdicate as king of Sicily and sever the Sicilian kingdom from the Empire, to go on a crusade, to follow the spiritual direction of the papacy, and in general to confirm the promises that Otto of Brunswick had made and later repudiated.

Innocent's decision in favor of Frederick resulted in a revival of the Hohenstaufen cause in Germany and a renewal of the civil war. Innocent employed all his diplomatic skill and leverage to win over German nobles to Frederick's cause. He was supported in these maneuverings by King Philip Augustus of France, now on friendly terms with the papacy, traditionally sympathetic to the Hohenstaufens, and hostile to the English and their Welf allies.

The complex currents of international politics in Innocent's pontificate reached their climax and their resolution in 1214; King John invaded France from the west while Otto of Brunswick led a powerful army against Philip Augustus from the east—an army heavily subsidized by England and consisting of the combined forces of pro-Welf princes from Germany and the Low Countries. John's invasion bogged down and accomplished nothing; Otto's army met the forces of Philip Augustus in pitched battle at Bouvines and was decisively defeated. The battle of Bouvines of 1214 was an epoch-making engagement. Philip Augustus emerged as Europe's mightiest monarch, Otto's imperial dreams were demolished, and Frederick became emperor in fact as well as in theory. Bouvines was a triumph not only for Philip Augustus and Frederick but also for Innocent III. His ward was now emperor-elect and was pledged to sever the kingdom of Sicily from Germany and free the German Church of imperial control.

Germany itself was in a state of chaos. The solid achievements of Frederick Barbarossa, which might have served as the foundation for a powerful revival of imperial power, were compromised by the subsequent imperial involvement in the affairs of the Sicilian kingdom and were demolished by 19 years of civil strife during which the German princes usurped royal privileges and royal lands on a vast scale. By the time of Innocent III's death, the imperial authority that Barbarossa had achieved was all but unrecoverable.

Achievements of Innocent III: an Appraisal

The policies of Innocent III were everywhere triumphant. Yet Innocent, by the very range and breadth of his political activities, had involved the papacy in secular affairs to such a degree that its spiritual authority was becoming tarnished. Innocent had won his battles, but he had chosen a dangerous battlefield. His successors, lacking both his skill and his luck, could do little to arrest the gradual decline of papal political authority during the middle and later decades of the thirteenth century and over the centuries that followed. For papal power was based ultimately on spiritual prestige, and the thirteenth-century popes, despite their piety, despite their continuing concern for ecclesiastical reform, were lawyers, administrators, and diplomats rather than charismatic spiritual leaders. The papacy was a mighty force in the world of the thirteenth century, but it was failing more and more to satisfy the spiritual hunger of devoted Christians. Piety remained strong, but many of the pious were coming to doubt that the papal government, with its vast wealth and bureaucratic efficiency, was indeed the true spiritual center of the apostolic Church and the citadel of Christ's kingdom on earth. The popes were doing what they had to do, and in playing the game of international politics they continued to dream of a regenerated Christian society led and inspired by the Church. But as time went on they dreamed less and, perhaps understandably, permitted their political means to overshadow their spiritual ends.

The impressive diplomatic success of Innocent III's pontificate ended abruptly with his death in 1216. Once Innocent was gone, his former ward and candidate, Frederick II, now a grown man, made it clear that he would ignore his promises as completely as Otto of Brunswick had earlier done. Frederick ruled exactly as he pleased, and as his reign progressed he became the medieval papacy's most ferocious adversary. In choosing Frederick and supporting his candidacy to the imperial throne, Innocent III had made a fearful miscalculation.

Frederick II (1211–1250)

Frederick II, whose Sicilian childhood exposed him to several faiths, grew up to be a brilliant, anticlerical skeptic, more concerned with his harem and his exotic menagerie than with his soul. He dazzled his contemporaries and earned the name *Stupor Mundi*, the "Wonder of the World." His dream of unifying all Italy and making it the nucleus of the Empire won him the undying hatred of the papacy. Indeed, some churchmen regarded Frederick quite literally as the incarnate Anti-Christ.

Frederick II was a talented, many-sided man—perhaps the most flamboyant product of an intensely creative age. He was a writer of considerable skill and an amateur scientist, curious about the world around him, but in some matters deeply superstitious. After much delay he kept his promise to lead a crusade (1228), but instead of fighting the Moslems he negotiated with them, and did so with such success that Jerusalem itself came into his hands for a time. The amicable spirit of Frederick's crusade against the infidel struck many churchmen as unholy, and its success infuriated them. That this irreverent skeptic should win the crown of Jerusalem was almost more than they could stand.

Sicily and Italy

Frederick II ruled his kingdom of Sicily in the autocratic but enlightened manner of a Renaissance despot, establishing a uniform legal code, tightening and broadening the centralized administrative system of his Norman-Sicilian predecessors, encouraging agriculture, industry, and commerce, abolishing interior tariffs and tolls, and founding a great university at Naples. He had promised Innocent III that he would cut Sicily off from his Empire, but he made no effort to keep his promise. He had always preferred his urbane, sunny Sicilian homeland to the cold forests and gloomy castles of Germany. Although he tried to follow Frederick Barbarossa's policy of strengthening the royal demesne and enforcing the feudal obligations of his great German vassals, he did so half-heartedly. To him, Germany was important chiefly as a source of money and military strength with which to carry out his policy of bringing all Italy under his rule.

As it happened, this policy proved disastrous to the Holy Roman Empire. Frederick's aggressions in Italy evoked the opposition of a revived Lombard League and the implacable hostility of the papacy. He gave up lands and royal rights in Germany with an almost careless abandon in order to keep the peace with the German princes and win their support for his persistent but inconclusive Italian campaigns. In the end, he was even obliged to tax his beloved Sicily to the point of impoverishment in order to support his endless wars. Brilliant lawyer-popes such as Gregory IX and Innocent IV devoted all their diplomatic talents and spiritual sanctions to blocking Frederick's enterprises, building alliances to oppose him and hurling anathemas against him. In 1245 Pope Innocent IV presided over a universal council of the Church at Lyons which condemned and excommunicated the Emperor. Frederick II was deposed, a rival emperor was elected in his place, and a crusade was called to rid the Empire of its ungodly tyrant. Revolts now broke out against Frederick throughout his Empire. The royal estates in Germany slipped more and more from his grasp, and his Italian holdings were ridden with rebellion. Against this unhappy background Frederick II died in 1250.

The Decline of the Medieval Empire

Germany

In a very real sense, the hopes of the medieval Empire died with him. His son succeeded him in Germany but died in 1254 after a brief and unsuccessful reign. For the next 19 years, Germany endured a crippling Interregnum (1254–1273) during which no recognized emperor held the throne. In 1273 a vastly weakened Holy Roman Empire re-emerged with papal blessing under Rudolph of Hapsburg, the first emperor of a family that was destined to play a crucial role in modern European history. Rudolph attempted to rebuild the shattered royal demesne and shore up the foundations of imperial rule, but it was much too late. The monarch's one hope had been to strengthen and extend the crown lands, gradually transforming them into the nucleus of a modern state. This was the policy on which the medieval French monarchy had risen to a position of dominance in France; it was the policy that Frederick Barbarossa had pursued so promisingly in Germany. But it was a policy that aroused the unremitting opposition of the great princes who had no desire to see their own rights and territories eaten away by royal expansion. On the contrary, they longed to extend their own principalities at the expense of the crown.

The civil strife during Innocent's pontificate, the Italian involvements of Frederick II, and the Interregnum of 1254–1273 gave the princes their opportunity, and by 1273 the crown lands were hopelessly shrunken and disorganized. Germany was now drifting irreversibly toward the loose confederation of principalities and the anemic elective monarchy which characterized its constitutional structure from the fourteenth to the later nineteenth century. The tragic failure of the medieval Empire doomed Germany to 600 years of agonizing disunity—a bitter heritage which may well have contributed to her catastrophic career in the twentieth century.

Italy

Italy, too, emerged from the struggles of the High Middle Ages hopelessly fragmented. The Papal States continued to divide the peninsula, but they were torn with unrest and disaffection, and the papacy had trouble enough maintaining its authority over the turbulent inhabitants of Rome itself. North of the Papal States, Tuscany and Lombardy had become a chaos of totally independent warring city-states — Florence, Siena, Venice, Milan, and many others — whose rivalries would form the political backdrop for the Italian Renaissance.

The Kingdom of Sicily, established by the Normans and cherished by the Hohenstaufens, passed shortly after Frederick II's death to his illegitimate son, Manfred. The papacy, determined to rid Italy of Hohenstaufen rule, bent all its energies toward securing Manfred's downfall. At length it offered the Sicilian crown to Charles of Anjou, a cadet member of the French royal house, with the intention that Charles should drive Manfred out of the Sicilian kingdom. Charles of Anjou, a dour, cruel man of enormous ambition, defeated and killed Manfred in 1266 and established a new, French dynasty on the throne of the kingdom.

The inhabitants of the realm, particularly those on the island of Sicily, had become accustomed to Hohenstaufen rule and deeply resented Charles of Anjou. They looked upon his French soldiers as an army of occupation. When, on Easter Monday, 1282, a French soldier mishandled a young married woman on her way to evening services in Palermo, he was struck down, and on all sides was raised the cry, "Death to the French." The incident resulted in a spontaneous uprising and a general massacre of the French which quickly spread

throughout the island. When the French retaliated, the Sicilians offered the crown to Peter III of Aragon, Manfred's son-in-law, who claimed the Hohenstaufen inheritance and led an army to Sicily.

There resulted a long, bloody, indecisive struggle known by the romantic title, "The War of the Sicilian Vespers." For twenty years, Charles of Anjou and his successors, backed by the French monarchy and the papacy, fought against the Sicilians and Aragonese. In the end, southern Italy remained Angevin and its kings ruled from Naples, while Sicily passed under the control of the kings of Aragon. The dispute between France and Aragon over southern Italy and Sicily persisted for generations and was an important factor in the politics of the Italian Renaissance. The chaotic and destructive strife of the thirteenth century destroyed the prosperity of the region. Once the wealthiest and most enlightened state in Italy, the kingdom of Sicily became backward, pauperized and divided — a victim of international politics and of the ruthless struggle between Church and state.

The Papacy After Innocent III

Signs of Weakness

To judge by the disintegration of the Holy Roman Empire in the thirteenth century, one would conclude that the papacy had won an overwhelming victory. But the victory was an empty one. For as popes like Innocent III, Gregory IX, and Innocent IV became increasingly involved in power politics, their spiritual role was more and more obscured. In the thirteenth century the papacy's international religious mission was being steadily subordinated to its local political interests. Slowly, almost imperceptibly, it was losing its hold on the heart of Europe. Papal excommunication, after several centuries of overuse — often for political purposes — was no longer the terrifying weapon it once had been. To call

The collection of tithes on wine (fifteenth century). The Church's growing need for larger revenues during the High Middle Ages continuously thrust ecclesiastical functionaries deeper into the economic life of society with serious consequences for relations between the Church and state.

a crusade against Frederick II was doubtless an effective means of harassing that troublesome emperor, but the crusading ideal was debased in the process. The time would come when a pope would call a crusade and nobody would answer.

As the papacy became a great political power and a big business, it found itself in need of ever-increasing revenues. By the end of the thirteenth century the papal tax system was admirably efficient, with the result that the papacy acquired an unsavory reputation for boundless greed. As one contemporary observer complained, the supreme pastor of Christendom was supposed to lead Christ's flock but not to fleece it. Ironically, the fiscal and political cast of the later medieval papacy came as a direct consequence of its earlier dream of becoming the spiritual dynamo of a reformed Christendom. Rising to prominence in the eleventh century upon the floodtide of the new popular piety, the papacy became in the twelfth and thirteenth centuries increasingly insensitive to the deep spiritual aspirations of European Christians as it became more and more absorbed in the external problems of political power.

Boniface VIII

The papacy humbled the Empire only to be humbled itself by the rising power of the new centralized monarchies of Northern Europe. By the end of the thirteenth century a new concept of royal sovereignty was in the air. The kings of England and France were finding it increasingly difficult to tolerate the existence of a semi-independent, highly privileged, internationally controlled Church within their realms. By endeavouring to bring these ecclesiastical "states within states" under royal control, the two monarchies encountered vigorous papal opposition. The issue of papal versus royal control of the Church was an old one, but the ancient controversy now took on a new form. The growing monarchies of the late thirteenth century found themselves increasingly in need of money. This was particularly true after 1294 when England and France became locked in a series of costly wars. Both monarchies adopted the novel policy of systematically taxing the clergy of their realms, and Pope Boniface VIII (1294–1303) retaliated in 1296 with the papal bull *Clericis Laicos* that expressly forbade this practice. Once again, Church and state were at an impasse.

Boniface VIII was another lawyer-pope — a man of ability but not of genius — proud and intransigent, with a vision of absolute papal power that transcended even the notions of Innocent III, but with a fatal blindness to the momentous implications of the new centralized monarchies of late thirteenth-century Europe. His great weakness was his inability to bend his stupendous concepts of papal authority to the hard realities of contemporary European politics.

In King Philip the Fair * of France (1285–1314), Boniface had a powerful and ruthless antagonist. Philip ignored the

* Fair in the sense of "handsome." See pp. 330–331.

papal bull prohibiting clerical taxation; he set his agents to work spreading scandalous rumors about the Pope's morals, and exerted serious financial pressure on Rome by cutting off all papal taxes from his French realm. Boniface VIII was obliged to submit for the moment, and Philip taxed his clergy unopposed. But a vast influx of pilgrims into Rome in the Jubilee year of 1300 restored the Pope's confidence. He withdrew his concession to Philip the Fair on clerical taxation and in 1302 issued the famous bull *Unam Sanctam* which asserted the doctrine of papal monarchy in uncompromising terms: ". . . we declare, announce, affirm, and define that for every human creature, to be subject to the Roman pontiff is absolutely necessary for salvation."

CHRONOLOGY OF THE PAPAL-IMPERIAL CONFLICT

1039–1056: Reign of Henry III
   1046: Henry III deposes 3 rival popes, inaugurates papal reform movement.
1049–1054: Pontificate of Leo IX
1056–1106: Reign of Henry IV
   1059: Papal Election Decree
1073–1085: Pontificate of Gregory VII
   1075: Gregory VII bans lay investiture.
   1076: Gregory VII excommunicates and deposes Henry IV.
   1077: Henry IV humbles himself at Canossa.
   1080: Second excommunication and deposition of Henry IV.
1088–1099: Pontificate of Urban II
1106–1125: Reign of Henry V
   1122: Concordat of Worms
1152–1190: Reign of Frederick I "Barbarossa"
1154–1159: Pontificate of Hadrian IV
   1155: Execution of Arnold of Brescia
1159–1181: Pontificate of Alexander III
   1176: Lombards defeat Barbarossa at Legnano.
   1180: Barbarossa defeats Duke Henry the Lion of Saxony.
1190–1197: Reign of Henry VI
   1194: Henry VI becomes king of Sicily.
1198–1216: Pontificate of Innocent III

1211–1250: Reign of Frederick II
   1214: Philip Augustus defeats Otto of Brunswick at Bouvines.
   1215: Fourth Lateran Council
1227–1241: Pontificate of Gregory IX
1243–1254: Pontificate of Innocent IV
   1245: Council of Lyons
1254–1273: Interregnum
1273–1291: Reign of Rudolph of Hapsburg
1282–1302: War of the Sicilian Vespers
1294–1303: Pontificate of Boniface VIII
   1302: Boniface VIII issues *Unam Sanctam.*
   1303: Boniface VIII humiliated at Anagni.
1305–1314: Pontificate of Clement V. Papacy moves to Avignon.

Philip the Fair now summoned an assembly of the realm and accused Pope Boniface of every imaginable crime from murder to black magic. A small French military expedition crossed into Italy in 1303 and took Pope Boniface prisoner at his palace at Anagni with the intention of bringing him to France for trial. Anagni, the antithesis of Canossa, symbolized the humiliation of the medieval papacy. The French plan failed—Boniface was freed by local townsmen a few days after his capture—but the proud old Pope died shortly thereafter, outraged and chagrined that armed Frenchmen should have dared to lay hands on his person.

Decline and Fall

The great age of the medieval papacy was now at an end. In 1305 the cardinals elected the Frenchman Clement V (1305–1314) who pursued a policy of timid subservience to the French throne. Clement V submitted on the question of clerical taxation, repudiated *Unam Sanctam,* and abandoned faction-ridden Rome for a new papal capital at Avignon on the Rhone. Here the popes remained for the next several generations, their independence often limited by the power of the French monarchy and their spiritual prestige continuing to decline.

It is easy to criticize the inflexibility of a Boniface VIII or the limpness of a Clement V, but the waning of papal authority in the later Middle Ages did not result primarily from personal shortcomings. Rather it stemmed from an ever-widening gulf between papal government and the spiritual hunger of ordinary Christians, combined with the hostility to Catholic internationalism on the part of increasingly powerful centralized states such as England and France. It would be grossly unfair to describe the high medieval papacy as "corrupt." Between 1050 and 1300 men of good intentions and high purposes sat on the papal throne. Not satisfied merely to chide the society of their day by innocuous moralizing from the sidelines, they plunged boldly into the world and struggled vigorously to transform and sanctify it. Tragically, perhaps inevitably, they soiled their hands.

ENGLAND IN THE HIGH MIDDLE AGES

The Anglo-Norman Monarchy

England and France

While empire and papacy were engaged in their drawn-out struggle, England and France were evolving into centralized states. Strong monarchy came earlier to England than to France, yet in the long run it was the English who were the more successful in imposing constitutional limitations on the crown. French royal absolutism and English parliamentary monarchy are both rooted in the High Middle Ages.

The Anglo-Saxon period of English history came to an end when Duke William of Normandy won the English crown with his victory at Hastings in 1066. In the centuries that followed, England was more closely tied to the Continent than before; her rulers dominated both England and significant portions of France. As kings of England they were masterless, but they held their French territories as vassals of the king of France. England's territorial involvement in France continued from 1066 until the mid-sixteenth century. It was a source of cultural enrichment to the English, but it also led to centuries of hostility and warfare between the two monarchies.

The Anglo-Saxon Background

The English kingdom that William the Conqueror won was already centralized and well-governed by the standards of mid-eleventh-century Europe. Its kings enjoyed the direct allegiance of all their subjects. Its army was subject only to the commands of the king or his representatives; private armies and private war were virtually unknown. A royal council of nobles and household officials known as the *witenagemot* advised the king on important matters and approved the succession of new kings. The chief officers in the royal household were gradually coming to assume important administrative responsibilities: issuing writs that carried royal commands to local officials in the countryside, administering the royal treasury, and performing other governmental functions. Although the late-Saxon royal household was constantly on the move, traveling around England from one royal estate to another, the treasury had become fixed permanently at Winchester in Wessex.

England in 1066 had long been divided into regional units known as shires, each with its own shire court and administered by a royal officer called a "shire reeve" or sheriff. The sheriff presided over the shire court, the membership of which was drawn from important men of the district. The customs and procedures of the shire courts were rooted in the traditions of the locality rather than in royal mandates. In operation as in membership, the shire courts were local phenomena and are often described, quite accurately, as folk courts. The sheriff, too, was usually a local figure whose sympathies were apt to be divided between his native shire and the king. The subtle interplay between local initiative and royal authority—a significant characteristic of Anglo-Saxon government—persisted over the post-conquest centuries to give medieval England a political balance lacking in many contemporary states.

The English shires were subdivided into smaller administrative units known as hundreds—deriving perhaps from the early days of the barbarian invasions when such a district might provide settlements for a hundred warriors. Each hundred had its own court which handled less important cases than those brought to the shire courts. Like the shire courts, the hundred courts were local in membership and legal custom yet were presided over by royal officials. By 1066 a number of hundreds had passed into the hands of private lords—lay or ecclesiastical—in which case the royal official was replaced by an official of the lord.

The sheriff was responsible for administering the unique Anglo-Saxon land tax, the danegeld, which varied somewhat in amount but in most instances provided the crown with about 10 pounds from each hundred. It was also the sheriff's task to assemble the shire's contingent when the king summoned the army—the *fyrd* as it was then called. Our evidence suggests that by 1066 it had become customary for each hundred to provide about twenty armed men for the fyrd and to supply their sustenance during their period of duty.

The Norman Conquest and Settlement

Such were some of the more important institutions which William the Conqueror inherited when he won the English crown. He came to England not as an open aggressor but as a legitimate claimant to the throne, related (distantly) to the Anglo-Saxon royal family and designated—so he claimed—by King Edward the Confessor who died childless early in 1066. On the Confessor's death, the *witenagemot* had chosen an able warrior, Earl Harold Godwinson of Wessex, to succeed him, but William had always regarded Harold as a usurper, and when Harold was killed at Hastings and his army put to flight, William took the position that he was passing into his rightful inheritance. Although another five years were required to put down the last vestiges of English resistance, William was crowned king of England in London on Christmas Day, 1066, and turned at once to the problem of governing his new realm.

Taking up his role as Edward the Confessor's proper successor, William promised to preserve the laws and customs of Edward's day. Indeed, it was to his advantage to do so, since many of these customs were exceedingly beneficial to the monarchy. He maintained the danegeld, as well he might, continued to summon the fyrd whenever he needed it, perpetuated the folk courts of shire and hundred, and drew needed strength from the Anglo-Saxon custom of general allegiance to the crown.

The Conqueror preserved much, but he also built energetically on the system that he inherited. The changes and additions that he introduced were products in part of the customs that he had known in Normandy, in part of his own creative imagination, and in part of his unique position as unquestioned master of a conquered land. If the government of Anglo-Saxon England was remarkably strong, the government of Norman England was far stronger, and its strength was, in large measure, a consequence of the political genius of William the Conqueror.

Establishment of Feudalism

In the years immediately following the Conquest, William divided much of England among the leading warriors of his victorious army, thereby introducing into the kingdom a new, knightly, French-speaking aristocracy. He established a feudal regime in England more-or-less on the Norman pattern, but more rationally organized and more directly subordinate to the royal will. Most English estates, both lay and ecclesiastical, were transformed into fiefs, held by crown vassals in return for a specified number of mounted knights and various other feudal services. He was careful to reserve about one sixth of the lands of England for his own royal demesne, so that he and his successors would never be mere nominal overlords like the early Capetians and the later Hohenstaufens.

The crown vassals, or tenants-in-chief, in order to raise the numerous knights required by the monarchy, subdivided portions of their fiefs into smaller fiefs and granted them to knightly subvassals. In other words, the process of subinfeudation proceeded in much the same way that it had centuries earlier on the Continent. As a natural byproduct of the establishment of feudalism in England, scores of castles were quickly erected across the land by the king and his barons.

Feudalism in England was by no means accompanied by political disintegration as it had been in Carolingian Frankland. With the resources of their vast royal domain on which to draw, the Norman kings of England were firmly established at the apex of the feudal pyramid and were generally successful in keeping their vassals under tight rein. Their authoritative position in the Anglo-Norman feudal structure owed much to the centralizing traditions of the Anglo-Saxon monarchy. The new barons estab-

lished feudal courts, as had been their custom in Normandy, but alongside these baronial courts there persisted the far older courts of shire and hundred. The new feudal army could be an effective force, but when it proved inadequate or when barons rebelled against the monarchy, the Old English fyrd could be summoned or mercenaries could be hired. Feudal particularism was attenuated by the Anglo-Saxon custom of general allegiance to the crown, which enabled the Norman kings to claim the direct and primary loyalty of every vassal and subvassal in the English feudal hierarchy. A knight's allegiance to his lord was now secondary to his allegiance to the crown. Private war between vassals was prohibited, and private castles could be built only by royal license. In brief, the new institution of feudalism was molded by the powerful Anglo-Saxon tradition of royal supremacy into something far more centralized—far less centrifugal—than the feudalism of the Continent.

Anglo-Norman Administration

On the Conqueror's death, his kingdom passed in turn to his two sons, William II (1087–1100) and Henry I (1100–1135). Both were strong, ruthless men, but Henry I was the abler of the two. A skillful general and brilliant legal and administrative innovator, Henry I rid England of rebellion and exploited the growing prosperity of his day by a policy of severe taxation. He was not a kindly man, but his was an age in which firmness and military skill were the chief requisites to successful rule and excessive geniality was a grave weakness. His great service to his English subjects was his pitiless enforcement of the peace.

The reigns of William the Conqueror and his sons witnessed a significant growth in royal administrative institutions. The unique survey of land holdings known as Domesday Book—the product of a comprehensive census of the realm undertaken by royal order in 1086—testifies eloquently to the administrative vigor of William the Conqueror. Between 1066 and 1135 royal administration became steadily more elaborate and efficient. By Henry I's reign, royal justices were traveling around England, hearing cases in the shire courts, and thereby extending the king's jurisdiction far and wide across the land. The baronial courts and the ancient folk courts of the counties and hundreds continued to function. But the extension of royal jurisdiction under Henry I was the initial step in a long and profoundly significant process whereby folk justice and baronial justice were gradually overshadowed and finally superseded by the king's justice.

Administrative efficiency and royal centralization were the keynotes of Henry I's reign. Royal dues were collected systematically by local noblemen in the king's service—the sheriffs—who passed the money on to a remarkably effective accounting agency known as the exchequer. A powerful royal bureaucracy was gradually coming into being. The growing efficiency of the exchequer and the expansion of royal justice were both motivated chiefly by the king's desire for larger revenues. For the more cases the royal justices handled, the more fines went into the royal coffers; the more closely the sheriffs were supervised, the less likely it was that royal taxes would stick to their fingers. The Norman kings discovered that strong government was good business.

The Anglo-Norman Church was ornamented by two leaders of exceptional ability: Lanfranc (d. 1089) and St. Anselm (d. 1109). Both were brilliant theologians, both, in different ways, were deeply involved in the politics of their day, and both were Italians who migrated to the great Benedictine monastery of Bec in Normandy.

William the Conqueror drew Lanfranc from Bec to become archbishop of Canterbury and primate of the English Church. William and Lanfranc were contemporaries of Hildebrand and could not help but become involved in the raging con-

troversy over ecclesiastical reform. The King and the archbishop were both sympathetic to reform, but neither was receptive to the Gregorian notions of an independent Church and a new social order. William was more than willing to work toward the reform of the Anglo-Norman Church, and Lanfranc supported him vigorously in this endeavor, but when Gregory VII demanded that William become his vassal, the Conqueror flatly refused: "I have not consented to pay fealty nor will I now, because I never promised it, nor do I find that my predecessors ever paid it to your predecessors."

Gregory VII had his hands full with the Holy Roman Emperor and could not afford to alienate William who was, after all, friendly toward reform. Accordingly, the specific issue of lay investiture did not emerge in England until after Gregory's death. It was raised by St. Anselm, who had followed Lanfranc as abbot of Bec and was chosen in 1093 to succeed him as archbishop of Canterbury. Lanfranc and William the Conqueror had worked in close cooperation with one another, but St. Anselm's relations with the Norman monarchy were turbulent indeed. Already advanced in years when he reluctantly assumed the archbishopric, Anselm was the greatest theologian of his age and was, perhaps, the most profound philosopher that Western Christendom had produced since St. Augustine's time. He was also deeply devoted to the Gregorian notions on ecclesiastical independence, lay investiture, and papal monarchy.

These notions no Norman king could accept, and Anselm came into bitter conflict with both William II and Henry I. He spent much of his tenure as archbishop in exile, and it was not until 1107 that a compromise on the investiture issue was hammered out between Henry I, Anselm, and the papacy. As in the later Concordat of Worms, the agreement of 1107 prohibited lay investiture as such, but permitted the king to retain a certain control over important ecclesiastical appointments. Ecclesiastical tenants-in-chief were to continue their traditional practice of rendering homage to the king. More important than the settlement itself is the fact that Anselm died two years thereafter, and the powerful Henry I, rid at last of his troublesome saint, dominated the English Church through pressure and patronage. Anselm had won a point, but the Church remained generally subservient to the Norman monarchy.

The Disputed Succession: Stephen and Matilda

Henry I's death in 1135 was followed by a period of unrest brought on by a disputed royal succession. Henry was survived by a daughter, Matilda, who was wed to Geoffrey Plantagenet, count of Anjou. Henry I had arranged the marriage with the hope of healing the bitter rivalry between the two great powers of northern France: Normandy and Anjou. Shortly before Henry I's death, his daughter Matilda bore him a grandson, Henry Plantagenet, who was destined ultimately to inherit a vast territory including Anjou, Normandy, and England. But when the old King died, his grandson was still an infant, and the English crown was seized by Henry I's nephew, Stephen of Blois (King of England 1135–1154). For two turbulent decades Stephen and Matilda struggled for control of England while the English barons, often shifting their allegiance from one side to the other, threw up unlicensed castles and usurped royal rights. English churchmen and commoners, tormented by the endemic warfare of the period, looked back longingly toward the peaceful days of Henry I.

Henry II

His Accession

During Stephen's troubled reign Henry Plantagenet grew to vigorous manhood and established control over Anjou and Normandy. A marriage with Eleanor of Aquitaine, the heiress of that large, heterogeneous southern duchy, extended still further the territories under his jurisdiction. And at King Stephen's death in 1154 Henry peacefully acquired the English throne and became King Henry II of England (1154–89). He now held sway over an immense constellation of territories north and south of the English Channel which has been called the Angevin Empire. On the map, the Angevin Empire dwarfed the modest territory controlled by the King of France. But Henry II and his sons who succeeded him had difficulty in keeping order throughout their vast, diverse territories. The Angevin Empire was doubtless a source of power and prestige to the English monarchy, but it was also a grave burden.

Henry II was an energetic, brilliant, exuberant man—short, burly, and redheaded. Named after his grandfather, he ruled in Henry I's imperious tradition and consciously imitated him. In many respects he was a creature of his age—a product of the great intellectual and cultural outburst of twelfth-century Europe. He was a literate monarch who consorted with scholars, encouraged the growth of towns, and presided over an age of economic boom. A chaos of feverish activity pervaded his court which was constantly on the move and, in the opinion of one of Henry's court scholars, was "a perfect portrait of Hell."

Policies and Administration

Henry II's chief goals were the preservation of the Angevin Empire, the strengthening of royal authority, and the increasing of his revenues. He began his reign by ordering the destruction of a great many unlicensed baronial castles that had been thrown up during the previous anarchic period, and was exceedingly cautious thereafter in permitting new private castles to be built. At once he began to recover the royal privileges that had been eroded during Stephen's reign and, in some cases, to expand them considerably. During the 35 years of his rule the royal administration grew steadily in complexity and effectiveness. The maturity of Henry II's exchequer is illustrated not only by a series of annual financial accounts — known as Pipe Rolls — but also by a comprehensive detailed treatise on the exchequer's organization and methods — the *Dialogue of the Exchequer* — which was written by one of the king's financial officers. The royal secretarial office — the chancery — was similarly increasing in efficiency and scope. Indeed, the entire royal administration was growing more specialized, more professional, and more self-conscious. Separate administrative departments were evolving, and public records became fuller and more extensive. Many Englishmen were delighted at the return of peace and order; others were uneasy over the steady rise of "Big Government."

Throughout the twelfth century commerce was becoming ever more vigorous and the circulation of money was rapidly increasing. Under the pressure of royal ambition and the growing money economy, the older feudal relationship of service in return for land was giving way to wage service. By the time of Henry II it had become commonplace for feudal tenants-in-chief to pay scutage to the crown in lieu of their military-service obligation. Dues from the royal demesne estates were being collected in coin rather than in kind, and royal troops, servants, and administrators customarily served for wages. These trends can be traced back to the reign of Henry I and beyond, but under Henry II they were clearly accelerating. The feudal hierarchy remained powerful, but feudal obligations were being translated into fiscal terms. Both the economy and the administration were steadily increasing in complexity and sophistication.

Of necessity, the authority of the king and the efficiency of his central administrative system depended upon an effective

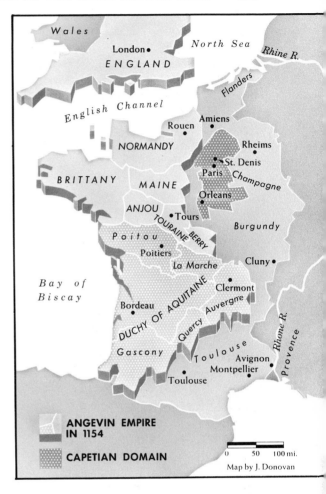

ANGEVIN EMPIRE
IN 1154

CAPETIAN DOMAIN

0   50   100 mi.

Map by J. Donovan

local government and the maintenance of strong bonds between court and countryside. The two were linked under Henry II, as under Henry I, by the activities of sheriffs and itinerant royal justices. Henry II seems to have broadened the scope of these itinerant justices and increased their organizational efficiency, thereby making royal justice more available to ordinary Englishmen than ever before. Now, itinerant royal justices made periodic circuits of the countryside, bringing the king's law to considerable numbers of Englishmen who had previously been untouched by it.

The sheriffs were bound to enforce the king's orders which continued to issue from the chancery in the form of writs. It was also the sheriff's duty to collect royal dues and fines and to render a periodic accounting of them to the exchequer. Thus, the sheriffs were subordinated to the central administration and subjected to royal control. Nevertheless, most sheriffs were powerful local nobles with wide estates of their own and were by no means completely dependent on the royal favor. Many of them abused their power and displayed a degree of independence such as to challenge the king's authority. In 1170 Henry II ordered a searching investigation of his sheriffs' behavior—the Inquest of Sheriffs —and subsequently replaced most of them with new and more tractable men.

Expansion of Royal Justice

Henry II has been called the father of the English common law. Like his predecessors, he favored the extension of royal jurisdiction chiefly for its financial rewards to the crown, and in his quest for ever-greater judicial revenues he was able to advance the powers of the royal courts well beyond their former limits. His *Assize of Clarendon* of 1166 widened the scope of royal justice to include the indictment and prosecution of local criminals. It provided that regional inquest juries should meet periodically under royal auspices to identify and denounce notorious neighborhood criminals whose guilt or innocence was then to be determined by the ordeal of cold water.* The inquest jury was more akin to the modern grand jury than to the modern trial jury, for its duty was to investigate and indict rather than to judge guilt. Inquest juries had been used before: they were assembled under William the Conqueror to provide information for the Domesday survey; there is a reference to one such jury in the records of late Anglo-Saxon times, and bodies of a similar nature were employed in the administration of Carolingian Frankland. Never before, however, had they been used in such a systematic fashion.

Henry II also extended royal jurisdic-

tion over the vast and turbulent field of land disputes, employing local juries to determine the rightful possessors or heirs of disputed estates. The most important of Henry's "possessory assizes," the *Assize of Novel Disseisin,* was designed to curb local violence by providing a legal action against forcible dispossession of an estate. Regardless of whether the plaintiff had a just claim to the estate in question, if he was driven from his land by force he was entitled to purchase a royal writ commanding the sheriff to assemble a jury to determine the facts of the case. If the jury concluded that the plaintiff had indeed been violently dispossessed, the sheriff, acting with full royal authority, would see that the estate in dispute was restored to the plaintiff. Another of the new legal actions provided by Henry III—the *Grand Assize*—used a similar procedure of purchased writ and jury to determine not whether the plaintiff had been dispossessed but whether he had, in fact, the best title to the land in question.

These and similar assizes carried the king's justice into an area that had formerly been dominated by the feudal courts which usually settled questions of land possession by the crude procedure of trial by battle. Previous kings had intervened in territorial quarrels, but never in a consistent, systematic way. Now, Englishmen learned to turn to Henry II's courts for quick, modern, rational justice. Feudal law, with its archaic and time-consuming procedures, had little chance in the competition. Gradually the patchwork of local laws and customs which had so long divided England gave way to a uniform royal law—a *common law* by which all Englishmen were governed. The *political* unification of the tenth century was consummated by the *legal* unification under the Angevin kings.

The Controversy with Becket

Predictably, Henry II also sought to expand royal justice at the expense of the ecclesiastical courts. At least since the reign of William the Conqueror, a separate

* See p. 190.

system of ecclesiastical jurisdiction had been in effect, distinct from the various secular courts—local, feudal, and royal. The ecclesiastical court system can be regarded as one manifestation of the vast and complex government of the international Church which—as it grew steadily more elaborate—came increasingly into conflict with the proliferating governmental structures of England and other secular states. The two governments, royal and ecclesiastical, were both expanding in the twelfth century, and conflicts between them were bound to occur. The first great conflict centered on St. Anselm, the second on St. Thomas Becket.

In 1162 Henry II sought to bring the English Church under strict royal control by appointing to the archbishopric of Canterbury his chancellor and good friend, Thomas Becket. But in raising Becket to the primacy, Henry had misjudged his man. As chancellor Becket was a devoted royal servant, but as archbishop of Canterbury he became a fervent defender of ecclesiastical independence and an implacable enemy of the King. Henry and Becket became locked in a furious quarrel over the issue of royal control of the English Church. In 1164 Henry issued a list of pro-royal provisions relating to Church-state relations known as the Constitutions of Clarendon, which, among other things, prohibited appeals to Rome without royal license and established a degree of royal control over the Church courts. Henry maintained that the Constitutions of Clarendon represented ancient custom; Becket regarded them as novel encroachments on the freedom of the Church.

At the heart of the quarrel was the issue of whether churchmen accused of crimes should be subject to royal jurisdiction after being found guilty and punished by Church courts. The king complained that "criminous clerks" were often given absurdly light punishments by the ecclesiastical tribunals. A murderer, for example, might simply be defrocked and released, and the Constitutions of Clarendon provided that such a person should then be remanded to a royal court for punishment. Becket replied that no man should be put in double jeopardy. In essence, Henry was challenging the competence of an agency of the international Church, and Becket, as primate of England, felt bound to defend Catholicism against royal encroachment. Two worlds were in collision.

Henry turned on his archbishop, accusing him of various crimes against the kingdom, and Becket, denying the king's right to try an archbishop, fled England to seek papal support. Pope Alexander III, who was at that time in the midst of his struggle with Frederick Barbarossa, could ill afford to alienate Henry II; yet neither could he turn against such an ardent ecclesiastical champion as Becket. The great lawyer-pope was forced to equivocate—to encourage Becket without breaking with Henry—until at length in 1170, the King and his archbishop agreed to a truce. Most of the outstanding issues between them remained unsettled, but Becket was permitted to return peacefully to England and resume the archbishopric. At once, however, the two antagonists had another falling out. Becket excommunicated a number of Henry's supporters; the King flew into a rage, and four overenthusiastic knights of the royal household went to Canterbury Cathedral and murdered Becket at the high altar.

This dramatic crime made a profound impact on the age. Becket was regarded as a martyr; miracles were alleged to have occurred at his tomb, and he was quickly canonized. For the remainder of the Middle Ages Canterbury was a major pilgrimage center and the cult of St. Thomas enjoyed immense popularity. Henry II, who had not ordered the killing but whose anger had inadvertently prompted it, suffered acute embarrassment. He was obliged to do penance by walking barefoot through the streets of Canterbury and submitting to a flogging by the Canterbury monks.

The dramatic impact of Becket's murder on the mind of medieval Europe is illustrated in this crudely graphic illumination from a thirteenth-century psalter.

But his campaign against the ecclesiastical courts was delayed only momentarily. Although forced to give in on specific matters such as royal jurisdiction over criminous clerks and unlicensed appeals to Rome, he obtained through indirection and subtle maneuvering what he had failed to get through open conflict. He succeeded generally in arranging the appointment to high ecclesiastical offices of men friendly to the crown, and by the end of his reign royal justice had made significant inroads on the authority of the Church courts. The monarchy had succeeded in bringing the English Church under tight rein. Here, as elsewhere, Henry II was remarkably successful in steering England toward administrative and legal centralization.

The Angevin Empire

Throughout his reign Henry had to divide his time between England and the other territories of the Angevin Empire. Strictly speaking, these territories did not constitute an "empire" in any real sense of the word. For they were in fact a multitude of individual political units, each with its own customs and its own administrative structure, bound together by their allegiance to Henry Plantagenet. The French monarchy did what it could to break up this ominous configuration, encouraging rebellions on the part of Henry's dutiless sons and his estranged wife, Eleanor of Aquitaine. Henry put down the rebellions one by one, relegated Eleanor to comfortable imprisonment, and sought to placate his sons. It did little good. The rebellions persisted, and as Henry neared death in 1189 his two surviving sons, Richard and John, were in arms against him. In the end the aged monarch was outmaneuvered and defeated by his offspring and their French allies; he died with the tragic statement, "Shame, shame on a conquered king."

Richard and John

Richard

Although Henry's final days were saddened by defeat, the Angevin Empire remained intact, passing into the capable hands of his eldest surviving son, Richard the Lion-Hearted (1189–1199). This illustrious warrior-king devoted himself chiefly to two great projects: defending the Angevin Empire against the French crown and crusading against the Moslems. He was a superb general who not only won immense renown on the Third Crusade but also foiled every attempt of the French monarchy to reduce his continental territories. He was far less impressive as an administrator and, indeed, spent less than six months of his ten-year reign in England. During his protracted absences, the administrative system of Henry II proved its worth; it governed England more-or-less satisfactorily for ten kingless years. Meanwhile Richard was engaging in his romantic but fruitless adventures in the Holy Land, and campaigning along the frontiers of the

Angevin Empire against the remorseless pressure of King Philip Augustus of France.

John and the Loss of the Angevin Empire

The fortunes of the Angevin Empire veered sharply with the accession of King John (1199–1216), Richard the Lion-Hearted's younger brother. John was an enigmatic figure — brilliant in certain respects, a master of administrative detail, but a suspicious and unscrupulous leader. He trusted nobody, and nobody trusted him. Consequently his subjects never supported him more than halfheartedly in moments of crisis.

In Philip Augustus of France (1180–1223) John had a shrewd and unremitting antagonist. Philip took full advantage of his position as feudal overlord over John's continental possessions. In 1202 John was summoned to the French royal court to answer charges brought against him by one of his own Aquitainian vassals. When John refused to come, Philip Augustus declared his French lands forfeited and proceeded to invade Normandy. The duchy quickly fell into Philip's hands (1203–4) as John's demoralized vassals defected, one after another, and John himself fled ignominiously to England. In the chaos that followed Philip Augustus was able to wrest Anjou and most of the remaining continental possessions of the Angevin Empire from John's control. Only portions of distant Aquitaine retained their connection with the English monarchy. King John had sustained a monstrous political and military disaster.

For the next ten years John nursed his wounds and wove a dextrous web of alliances against King Philip in hopes of regaining his lost possessions. His careful plans were shattered by Philip's decisive victory over John's Flemish and German allies at the battle of Bouvines in 1214.* With Bouvines went John's last hope of reviving the Angevin Empire.

* See above, pp. 304, 327.

John and Innocent III

In the decade between the loss of Normandy and the catastrophe at Bouvines, John engaged in a bitter quarrel with Pope Innocent III. At stake was royal control over the appointment of an archbishop of Canterbury. According to canon law and established custom, a bishop or archbishop was to be elected by the canons of the cathedral chapter. The Investiture Controversy notwithstanding, such elections were commonly controlled by the king who would overawe the canons into electing the candidate of his choice. Canterbury differed from most other cathedrals in that a body of monks performed the functions that were ordinarily the responsibility of cathedral canons; it was the monks who customarily elected the archbishop, but they, no less than canons, were usually susceptible to royal control. In 1205, however, the monks of Canterbury declined to wait for royal instructions and elected one of their own number as archbishop, sending a delegation to Rome to obtain Pope Innocent III's confirmation. John responded vigorously. Going personally to Canterbury, he forced the monks to hold another election and to select his own nominee. In the course of events several delegations went from England to Rome, and Innocent, keenly interested in the enforcement of proper canonical procedures, quashed both elections. He ordered those Canterbury monks who were then in Rome — quite a number by this time — to hold still another election, and under papal influence they elected Stephen Langton, a learned Englishman who had spent some years as a scholar in Paris.

Furious that his own candidate should have been passed over, John refused to confirm Langton's appointment or to admit him into England. For the next six years, 1207–1213, John held to his position while Innocent III used every weapon at his disposal to make the King submit. England was laid under interdict; John retaliated by confiscating all ecclesiastical revenues. John was excommunicated, and Innocent even threatened to depose him. This threat, together with the danger of a projected French invasion of England with full papal backing, forced John to submit at last. In 1213 he accepted Stephen Langton as archbishop and, evidently on his own initiative, conceded to Innocent the overlordship of England. John would hold his kingdom thenceforth as a papal fief and would render a substantial annual tribute to Rome. Having lost the battle, John was anxious to transform his antagonist into a devoted friend, and his concession of the overlordship had precisely that effect.

Magna Carta

John had won the papal friendship, but many of his own barons were regarding him with increasing hatred and contempt. The Bouvines disaster of 1214, coming at the end of a long series of expensive and humiliating diplomatic failures, destroyed what remained of John's royal prestige. It paved the way for the epoch-making English baronial uprising that culminated on the field of Runnymede in 1215 with the signing of Magna Carta. John's barons had good reason to oppose him. He had pushed the centralizing tendencies of his Norman and Angevin predecessors to new limits, and was taxing his subjects as they had never been taxed before. The baronial reaction of 1215 may be regarded both as a protest against John and as an effort to reverse the trend toward royal authoritarianism of the past 150 years.

Magna Carta has been interpreted in contradictory ways: as the fountainhead of English constitutional monarchy, and as a reactionary, backward-looking document designed to favor the particularistic feudal aristocracy at the expense of the enlightened Angevin monarchy. In reality, Magna Carta was both feudal and constitutional: both backward-looking and forward-looking. Its more important clauses were designed to keep the king within the bounds of popular tradition and feudal custom. Royal taxes not sanctioned by custom, for example, were to be levied only by the common council of the kingdom. But implicit in the traditional feudal doctrine that the lord had to respect the rights of his vassals — and in the age-old Germanic notion that the monarch had to adhere to the customs of his people — was the profound constitutional principle of government under the law. In striving to make King John a good feudal lord, the barons in 1215 were moving uncertainly, perhaps unconsciously, toward constitutional monarchy. For this was the crucial moment when the English nobles were just beginning to represent a national viewpoint. In the past, baronial opposition to royal autocracy had taken the form of a selfish insistence on local aristocratic autonomy. But one finds in Magna Carta the notion that the king is bound by traditional legal limitations in his relations with all classes of free Englishmen. It would be misleading to lay too much stress on the underlying principles of this intensely practical document which was concerned primarily with correcting specific royal abuses of fuedal custom, but it would be equally misleading to ignore the momentous implication in Magna Carta of an overarching body of law which limited and circumscribed royal authority.

The chief constitutional problem in the years following Magna Carta was the question of how an unwilling king might be forced to stay within the bounds of law. A series of royal promises was obviously insufficient to control an ambitious monarch who held all the machinery of the central government in his grasp. Magna Carta itself relied on a committee of 25 barons who were empowered, should the king violate the Charter, to call upon the English people "to distrain and distress him in every possible way." Thus, the monarch was to be restrained by the crude sanction of baronial and popular rebellion — a desperate and unwieldy weapon against an unscrupulous king.

John himself seems to have had no intention of carrying out his promises. He repudiated Magna Carta at the first opportunity, with the full backing of his papal overlord, Innocent III. At his death in 1216 England was in the midst of a full-scale revolt. John's death ended the revolt, and the crown passed to his nine-year-old son, Henry III (1216–1272) who was supervised during his minority by a baronial council. In the decades that followed, Magna Carta was reissued many times, but the great task of the new age was to create political institutions capable of limiting royal autocracy by some means short of rebellion. The ultimate solution to this problem was found in Parliament.

Henry III and Edward I

Henry III was a petulant, erratic monarch: pious without being holy, bookish without being wise. Surrounding himself with foreign favorites and intoxicated by grandiose, impractical foreign projects, he ignored the advice of his barons and gradually lost their confidence.

Beginnings of Parliament

Ever since its beginning, the English monarchy had customarily arrived at important decisions of policy with the advice of a royal council of nobles and officials. In Anglo-Saxon times, this council was called the *witenagemot;* after 1066 it was known as the *curia regis.* Its composition had always been vague, and it had never possessed anything resembling a veto power over royal decisions, but many Englishmen, particularly noblemen, put much importance in the fact that royal policies were framed in consultation with the barons.

Traditionally, English royal councils were of two types. Ordinary royal business was conducted in a small council consisting of the king's household officials and whatever barons happened to be at court at the time. But in moments of crisis, or when some important decision was pending, the kings supplemented their normal coterie of advisers by summoning the important noblemen of the realm to meet as a great council. It was this great baronial council that eventually evolved into Parliament.

A key factor in the evolution from great council to Parliament was the trend in the thirteenth century toward including representatives of the county gentry and the townsmen alongside the great barons. This notable development resulted from the royal policy, particularly evident after Magna Carta, of summoning the great council for the purpose of obtaining approval for some uncustomary tax. As wealth gradually seeped downward into the sub-baronial classes, the king found it expedient to obtain the consent of these lesser orders to new royal taxes by summoning their representatives to the great council.

Henry III and the Barons

The vigorous baronial opposition to Henry III arose from the fact that he summoned the great council not for the purpose of consulting his magnates on policy matters but chiefly for the purpose of obtaining their consent to new taxes. The barons resented being asked to finance chimerical foreign schemes in which they had not been consulted and of which they disapproved. They might well have chosen as their motto, "No taxation without consultation." They responded to Henry III's fiscal demands with increasing reluctance, until at last, in 1258, the monarch's soaring debts brought on a financial crisis of major proportions. In order to obtain desperately needed financial support from his barons, King Henry submitted to a set of baronial limitations on royal power known as the Provisions of Oxford.

These Provisions went far beyond Magna Carta in providing machinery to force the king to govern according to good custom and in consultation with his magnates. The great council was to be summoned at least three times a year and was to include, along with its usual membership, 12 men "elected" by the "community"—in other words, chosen by the barons. These 12 were empowered to speak for the magnates in the great council, so that even if heavily outnumbered their authority would be great. The Provisions of Oxford also established a Committee of Fifteen, chiefly baronial in composition, which shared with the king control over the royal administration. Specifically, the Council of Fifteen was given authority over the exchequer and was empowered to appoint the chancellor and other high officers of state.

The Provisions of Oxford proved premature, and the governmental system which they established turned out to be unworkable because of baronial factionalism. Their importance lies in the fact that they disclose clearly the attitude of many mid-thirteenth-century barons toward the royal administration. These magnates had no thought of abolishing the enlightened administrative and legal achievements of the past two centuries or of weakening the central government. Their interests were national rather than parochial, and they merely sought to exert a degree of control over the royal administration. Most of them acted as they did, not on the basis of theoretical abstractions, but because they thought it necessary to curb an incompetent, arbitrary, spendthrift king.

With the failure of the Provisions, Henry III resumed exclusive control over his government and returned to the arbitrary policies that his barons found so distasteful. At length, baronial discontent exploded into open rebellion. The barons, led by Simon de Montfort, defeated the royal army at Lewes in 1264 and captured Henry himself. For the next 15 months Simon ruled England in the King's name, sharing authority with two baronial colleagues and a committee of magnates similar to that of the Provisions of Oxford. The rule of Simon de Montfort and his committee was augmented periodically by meetings of the great council—now commonly called "parliaments." Simon's government was a product of the same philosophy that underlay

the Provisions of Oxford, and like the government of the Provisions, it was weakened and ultimately brought to ruin by baronial factionalism.

In 1265 the monarchy rallied under the leadership of Henry III's talented son, Edward, defeated a baronial army at Evesham, and crushed Simon de Montfort's faltering rebellion.

Further Evolution of Parliament

But the effect of the uprising proved to be lasting. England had undergone an interesting experience in baronial government and, far more important, a significant step had been taken in the development of Parliament. For earlier in 1265 Simon de Montfort had summoned a great council—a parliament—which included for the first time all three of the classes that were to characterize the parliaments of the later Middle Ages. Simon de Montfort's parliament included, in addition to the barons, two knights from every shire and two burghers from every town. Simon's chief motive in summoning this parliament was probably to broaden the base of his rebellion, but in later years parliaments were summoned for many purposes: to sit as a high court of law, advise the king on important matters of policy, declare their support in moments of crisis, and give their consent to the ever-increasing royal taxes.

The English Parliament was built upon a sturdy foundation of local government, and all three of the major parliamentary orders—barons, burghers, and shire knights—brought with them a wealth of local political experience. The burghers in Parliament were usually veterans of town government. The shire knights had long been involved in the administration of the counties and the county courts. Intermediate between the baronial nobility and the peasantry, these men constituted a separate class—a country gentry—rooted to their shires and their ancestral estates, experienced in local government, and well suited to represent their counties in Parliament.

In 1272 Henry III was succeeded by his son, Edward I (1272–1307), a far wiser man than his father. Edward I was a monarch of strong will and independence, but he had the sagacity to take the barons into his confidence and he was successful by and large in winning their support. Although he, like his father, regarded parliaments chiefly as means of winning approval for new taxes, he used them for many other purposes as well. He summoned parliaments frequently and experimented endlessly in their composition. In the later years of his reign the inclusion of shire knights and townsmen became customary. It was not until the fourteenth century, however, that the knights and burghers began meeting separately from the barons, thereby giving birth to the great parliamentary division into Lords and Commons.

As the thirteenth century closed, the actual powers of parliaments remained exceedingly vague and their composition was still fluid. At best, they might bargain discreetly with the king for concessions in return for financial aid. Still, a beginning had been made. The deep-rooted medieval concept of limited monarchy had given rise to an institution that would develop over the centuries into a keystone of representative government. There was obviously nothing remotely democratic about the parliaments that Edward I summoned. He regarded them as instruments of royal policy, and used them to aid and strengthen the monarchy rather than limit it. Yet ultimately, Parliament was to be the crucial institutional bridge between medieval feudalism and modern democracy.

Edward I

The reign of Edward I witnessed the culmination of many trends in English law and administration that had been developing throughout the High Middle Ages. Edward was a great systematizer, and in his hands the royal administrative structure and the common law acquired the shape they were to retain in future centuries.

The four chief agencies of royal government under Edward I were the chancery, the exchequer, the council, and the household. Chancery and exchequer were by now both permanently established at Westminster. The chancery remained the royal secretarial office, and its chief officer, the chancellor, was the custodian of the great seal by which royal documents were authenticated. A staff of professional chancery clerks prepared the numerous letters and charters by which the king made his will known, and preserved copies of them for future reference. The exchequer, headed by a royal official known as the treasurer, continued to serve, as it had for nearly two centuries, as the king's accounting agency. By now it supervised the accounts not only of sheriffs but of many other local officials who were charged with collecting royal revenues.

Unlike the chancery and exchequer, the council and household accompanied the king on his endless travels. Since meetings of the great council were coming more and more to be referred to as "parliaments," the "council" in Edward's government is to be identified with the earlier "small council." It was a permanent group of varied and changing membership, consisting of judges, administrators, and magnates, who advised the king on routine matters. In the Provisions of Oxford the barons had endeavored to dominate the council, but under Edward it was firmly under royal control. The household was a royal government in miniature, with its own writing clerks supervised by the keeper of the privy seal and its own financial office known as the "wardrobe." By means of his household administration the king could act quickly, that is, govern on the move, without the necessity of routing all his business through Westminster.

Royal government in the countryside continued to depend on sheriffs and itinerant justices, whose duties and responsibilities were defined and regularized as never before. But now other royal servants were working alongside them: coroners, who were charged with investigating felonies; keepers of the peace, whose duty it was to apprehend criminals; assessors, tax collectors, customs officials, and others— local men, for the most part, who were responsible for serving the king in their native districts.

The royal legal system was also taking permanent and coherent form. Cases of singular importance were brought before the king himself, sitting in Parliament or surrounded by his council. Less important cases were handled by the king's itinerant justices or by one of the three royal courts sitting at Westminster. These three were the courts of the *king's bench*, which heard cases of particular royal concern; *exchequer*, which, besides its fiscal responsibilities, heard cases touching on the royal revenues; and *common pleas*, which had jurisdiction over most remaining types of cases. These three courts were all staffed with highly trained professionals—lawyers or, in the case of the exchequer, experienced accountants. There could be no question but that by Edward I's day the royal judicial system had come of age.

Like his predecessors, Edward worked toward the expansion of royal justice over private justice. From the beginning of his reign he issued numerous writs of *quo warranto* (by what warrant) which obligated noblemen who claimed the right of private legal jurisdiction to prove their claims. They might do so either by producing royal charters granting such jurisdictional privileges or by demonstrating that they and their predecessors had exercised such rights since before the reign of Richard I. In 1290 Edward issued the statute of *Quo Warranto* which quashed all private jurisdictions unsupported by royal charter, no matter how ancient such jurisdiction might be. By means of these policies, Edward eliminated a good number of private jurisdictional franchises, and, perhaps more important still, made it clear that all remaining private franchises were exercised

through royal license and royal suffrance. The absolute supremacy of royal jurisdiction was at last established beyond question.

Edward's reign was marked by the appearance of a great many royal statutes— issued by the king in Parliament—which elaborated and systematized royal administrative and legal procedures in many different ways. Law had formerly been regarded as a matter of custom; the king might interpret or clarify it, but did not have the right to make a new law. As ancient Germanic tradition had it, the king was bound by the customs of his people, that is, he was under the law. It is, of course, not always possible to distinguish between the act of clarifying or elaborating old law and making new law, and many of Edward's predecessors had been lawmakers whether they admitted the fact or not. But only in the later thirteenth century did Englishmen begin to recognize that their government had the power to legislate. Even in Edward's day, original legislation was such a novel and solemn affair that the king issued his statutes only with the approval of the "community of the realm" as expressed in his parliaments. Edward dominated his parliaments, and his statutes were unquestionably products of the royal initiative, but it is nevertheless highly significant that in his reign the role of parliaments in the making of law was clearly established. In the course of the fourteenth century, Parliament employed its power of approving royal taxes to win control of the legislative process itself.

Thus, Edward I was a crucial figure in the development of English law. He completed the great work of his predecessors in creating an effective and complex royal administrative system, bringing feudal justice under royal control, and building a comprehensive body of common law. More than that, he solidified the concept of original legislation and nurtured the developing institution of Parliament, thereby setting into motion forces that would have an immense impact on England's future.

Edward was also a skillful and ambitious warrior. He brought to a decisive end the centuries-long military struggle along the Welsh frontier by conquering Wales altogether in a whirlwind campaign of 1282–83. He granted his eldest son the title, "Prince of Wales," which male heirs-apparent to the English throne have held to this day. By a ruthless exploitation of the traditional English overlordship over the Scottish realm he came very near to conquering Scotland and was foiled only by the dogged determination of the great Scottish hero-king, Robert Bruce. His war with Philip IV of France was expensive and inconclusive, but it did succeed in preserving English lordship over Gascony which had been seriously threatened by French aggression. These wars gradually exhausted the royal treasury, and during the latter portion of his reign, Edward was faced with growing baronial and popular opposition to his expensive policies. But the King was able to ride out this opposition by making timely concessions: reissuing Magna Carta and recognizing Parliament's right to approve all extraordinary taxation. At his death in 1307, Edward left behind him a realm exhausted by his prodigious foreign and domestic activities but firmly under his control. Edward's England was still, in spirit, a feudal kingdom rather than a modern nation, but feudalism was clearly waning and the initial steps toward nationhood had been taken.

The most significant of all Edward's contributions was, in the long run, his policy of developing Parliament into an integral organ of government. It is ironic, therefore, that King Edward looked upon Parliament as a source of strength to the crown and a useful instrument for raising the necessary revenues to support his far-flung projects. He would have been appalled to learn that his royal descendants would one day be figurehead kings and that Parliament was destined to rule England.

FRANCE IN THE HIGH MIDDLE AGES

The Capetians

Weakness of the First Capetians

When William of Normandy conquered England in 1066, the French monarchy exerted a feeble control over a small territory around Paris and Orléans known as the Île de France and was virtually powerless in the lands beyond. To be sure, the French kings had as their vassals great feudal magnates such as the dukes of Normandy and Aquitaine and the counts of Anjou, Flanders, and Champagne, but vassalage was a slender bond indeed when the king lacked the power to enforce his lordship. In theory the anointed king of the French, with his priestly charisma, with the sovereign power traditionally associated with royalty, and with the supreme feudal overlordship, was a mighty figure indeed. But in grim reality he was impotent to control his great vassals and unable to keep order even in the Île de France itself.

Since 987 the French crown had been held by the Capetian dynasty. The achievement of the Capetians in the first century or so of their rule was modest enough. Their one triumph was their success in keeping the crown within their own family. The Capetians had gained the throne originally by virtue of being elected by the magnates of the realm, but from the first they sought to purge the monarchy of its elective character and to make it hereditary. This they accomplished by managing to produce male heirs at the right moment and by arranging for the new heir to be crowned before the old king died. They may have been aided by the fact that the crown was not a sufficiently alluring prize to attract powerful usurpers.

Capetian Policy

In the early twelfth century the Capetians remained weaker than several of their own vassals. While vassal states such as Normandy and Anjou were becoming increasingly centralized, the Capetian Île de France was still ridden with fiercely insubordinate robber barons. If the Capetians were to realize the immense potential of their royal title they had three great tasks before them: (1) to master and pacify the Île de France, (2) to expand their political and economic base by bringing additional territories under direct royal authority, and (3) to make their lordship over the great vassals real rather than merely theoretical.

During the twelfth and thirteenth centuries a series of remarkably able Capetian kings pursued and achieved these goals. Their success was so complete that by the opening of the fourteenth century the Capetians controlled all France, either directly or indirectly, and had developed an efficient and sophisticated royal bureaucracy. They followed no hard and fast formula. Rather their success depended on a combination of luck and ingenuity—on their clever exploitation of the powers which, potentially, they had always possessed as kings and feudal overlords. They were surprisingly successful in avoiding the family squabbles that had at times paralyzed Germany and England. Unlike the German monarchs, they maintained comparatively good relations with the papacy. They had the enormous good fortune of an unbroken sequence of direct male heirs from 987 to 1328. Above all, they seldom overreached themselves: they avoided grandiose schemes and spectacular strokes of policy, preferring instead to pursue modest, realistic goals. They extended their power gradually and cautiously by favorable marriages, by confiscating the fiefs of vassals who died without heirs, and by dispossessing vassals who violated their feudal obligations toward the monarchy. Yet the majority of the Capetians had no desire to absorb the territories of all their vassals. Rather they sought to build a kingdom with a substantial core of royal domain lands surrounded by the fiefs of loyal, obedient magnates.

Philip I and Louis VI

The first Capetian to work seriously toward the consolidation of royal control in the Île de France was King Philip I (1060–1108), a bloated, repugnant man who grasped the essential fact that the Capetian monarchy had to make its home base secure before turning to loftier goals. Philip's realistic policy was pursued far more vigorously by his son, Louis VI, "the Fat" (1108–1137). Year after year, Louis the Fat battled the petty brigand-lords of the Île de France, besieged their castles one after another, and at last reduced them to obedience. At his death in 1137 the Île de France was relatively orderly and prosperous, and the French monarchy was beginning to pull abreast of its greater vassals.

Louis the Fat received invaluable assistance in the later part of his reign from Abbot Suger of the great royal abbey of Saint Denis. This talented and dedicated statesman served as chief royal adviser from 1130 to 1151, and labored hard and effectively to extend the king's sway, to systematize the royal administration, and, incidentally, to augment the wealth and prestige of Saint Denis.

Louis VII

Suger provided an invaluable element of continuity between the reigns of Louis the Fat and his son, Louis VII (1137–1180), who pursued his father's goals with less than his father's skill. Pious and gentle, Louis VII was, in the words of a contemporary observer, "a very Christian king, if somewhat simple-minded." When Abbot Suger died in 1151, Louis VII was left to face unaided a new and formidable threat to the French monarchy. The Angevin Empire was just then in the process of formation, and in 1154 the ominous configuration was completed when Henry Plantagenet, count of Anjou and duke of Normandy and Aquitaine, acceded to the English throne as King Henry II. Louis VII sought to embarrass his mighty vassal by encouraging Henry's sons to rebel, but his efforts were too halfhearted to be successful. Still, Louis VII's reign witnessed a significant extension of royal power. Indeed, as one historian has aptly said, it was under Louis VII that "the prestige of the French monarchy was decisively established." * The great vassals of the crown, fearful of their powerful Angevin colleague and respectful of Louis VII's piety and impartiality, began for the first time to bring cases to the court of their royal overlord and to submit their disputes to his judgment. Churchmen and townsmen alike sought his support in struggles with the nobility. These developments resulted not so much from royal initiative as from the fundamental trends of the age toward peace, order, and growing commercial activity. Frenchmen in increasing numbers were turning to their genial, unassuming monarch for succor and justice, and, little by little, Louis VII began to assume his rightful place as feudal suzerain and supreme sovereign of the realm.

Philip Augustus, Louis VIII, and St. Louis

Philip Augustus and the Angevin Empire

The French monarchy came of age under Louis VII's talented son, Philip II "Augustus" (1180–1223). By remorseless insistence on his feudal rights, and by a policy of dextrous and ruthless opportunism, Philip Augustus enlarged the royal territories enormously and, beyond the districts of direct royal jurisdiction, transformed the chaotic anarchy of the vassal states into an orderly hierarchy subordinate to the king.

Philip Augustus' great achievement was the destruction of the Angevin Empire and the establishment of royal jurisdiction over Normandy, Anjou, and their dependencies. For two decades he plotted with dissatisfied members of the Angevin family against King Henry II and King Richard the Lion-Hearted, but it was not until the reign of King John (1199–1216) that his efforts bore fruit. Against John's notorious faithlessness and greed, Philip was able to play the role of the just lord rightfully punishing a disobedient vassal. And when Philip Augustus moved against Normandy in 1203–4, John's extreme unpopularity played into his hands. The prize which Philip had sought so long fell with surprising ease, and, once Normandy was his, John's remaining fiefs in northern France fell like dominoes. Ten years later, in 1214, Philip extinguished John's last hope of recovering the lost territories by winning his decisive victory over John's German allies at Bouvines.† Settling for good the fate of Normandy and Anjou, Bouvines was also a turning point in the power balance between France and Germany in the High Middle Ages. For thereafter the waxing Capetian monarchy of France replaced the faltering kingdom of Germany as the great continental power in Western Europe.

Capetian Government

Under Philip Augustus and his predecessors significant developments were occurring in the royal administrative system. The *curia regis* had assumed its place as the high feudal court of France and was proving an effective instrument for the assertion of royal rights over the dukes and counts. Hereditary noblemen who had traditionally served as local administrators in

---

* R. Fawtier, *The Capetian Kings of France*, Macmillan, London, 1960, p. 23.
† See above, pp. 304, 319.

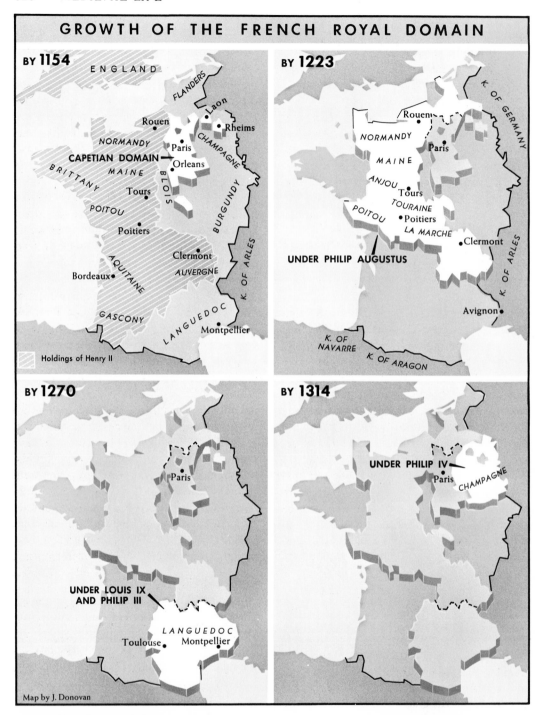

GROWTH OF THE FRENCH ROYAL DOMAIN

BY **1154**

ENGLAND

FLANDERS

Rouen

Laon

Rheims

NORMANDY

Paris

CHAMPAGNE

CAPETIAN DOMAIN →

Orleans

BRITTANY

MAINE

BLOIS

Tours

BURGUNDY

POITOU

Poitiers

AQUITAINE

Clermont

AUVERGNE

Bordeaux

K. OF ARLES

GASCONY

LANGUEDOC

Montpellier

Holdings of Henry II

BY **1223**

K. OF GERMANY

Rouen

NORMANDY

Paris

MAINE

ANJOU

Tours

TOURAINE

POITOU

Poitiers

LA MARCHE

Clermont

UNDER PHILIP AUGUSTUS

K. OF ARLES

Avignon

K. OF NAVARRE

K. OF ARAGON

BY **1270**

Paris

UNDER LOUIS IX AND PHILIP III

LANGUEDOC

Toulouse   Montpellier

Map by J. Donovan

BY **1314**

UNDER PHILIP IV

Paris

CHAMPAGNE

the royal territories were gradually replaced by salaried officials known as *baillis*. These new officials, whose functions were at once financial, judicial, military, and administrative, owed their positions to royal favor and were therefore fervently devoted to the interests of the crown. Throughout the thirteenth century the *baillis* worked tirelessly and often unscrupulously to erode the privileges of the feudal aristocracy and extend the royal sway. This intensely loyal and highly mobile bureaucracy, without local roots and without respect for feudal or local traditions, became in time a powerful instrument of royal absolutism. The *baillis* stood in sharp contrast to the local officials in England—the sheriffs and the shire knights—who were customarily drawn from the local gentry and whose loyalties were divided between the monarch whom they served and the region and class from which they sprang.

Louis VIII

The closing years of Philip Augustus' reign were concurrent with the savage Albigensian Crusade in southern France, called by Philip's great contemporary, Pope Innocent III, against the supporters of the Albigensian heresy which was spreading rapidly through Languedoc and northern Italy.* Philip Augustus declined to participate personally in the crusade, but his son, Prince Louis, took an active part in it, and when the Prince succeeded to his father's throne in 1223 as Louis VIII (1223–1226) he threw all the resources of the monarchy behind the southern campaign. The crusade succeeded in eliminating the Albigensian threat to Western Christendom, but only by devastating large portions of southern France and exterminating the brilliant culture that had previously flourished there. Thenceforth southern France tended to be dominated by northern France, and the authority of the French monarchy was extended to the Mediterranean.

It may perhaps be surprising to discover that Louis VIII, who inherited a vastly expanded royal jurisdiction from his father and extended it still further himself, gave out about a third of the hard-won royal territories as fiefs to junior members of the Capetian family. These family fiefs, created out of the royal domain, are known as *appanages*. Their emergence should

serve as a warning that the growth of the Capetian monarchy cannot be understood simply as a linear process of expanding the royal territories. The Capetians had no objection to vassals so long as they were obedient and subject to royal control. Indeed, given the limited transportation and communication facilities of twelfth- and thirteenth-century France, the kingdom was far too large to be controlled directly by the monarchy. The new vassals, bound to the crown by strong family ties, played an essential role in the governance of the realm and strengthened rather than weakened the effectiveness of Capetian rule.

Character of St. Louis

Louis VIII died prematurely in 1226, leaving the land in the capable hands of his stern and pious Spanish widow, Blanche of Castile, who acted as regent for the boy-king Louis IX (1226–1270), later St. Louis. Even after St. Louis came of age in 1234 he remained devoted to his mother, and Queen Blanche continued for years to be a dominant influence in the royal government.

St. Louis possessed both his mother's sanctity and his mother's firmness. Unlike many saint-kings, he was a strong monarch, obsessed with the obligation to rule justly and firmly and to promote moral rectitude throughout the kingdom of France. His sanctity, although thoroughly genuine, was perhaps too orthodox—too conventional. He persecuted heretics and crusaded against the Moslems. He once remarked that the only possible response for a Christian toward Jews who blasphemed was "to plunge his sword into their bellies as far as it would go." Still, in asserting these attitudes he was only mirroring his age. His reign was far different from that of Philip Augustus, for he oriented his life not toward political ends but toward what he conceived to be religious ends. He believed in war against the infidel, but he believed just as fervently in peace among Christian rulers. Accordingly, he arranged treaties with Henry III of England and with the king of

* See pp. 281–282.

Aragon which settled peacefully all out-standing disputes. He played the role of peacemaker among Christian princes and was even called upon to arbitrate between King Henry III and his barons.

Administration and Cultural Life

St. Louis was content, in general, to maintain the royal rights established by his predecessors. His *baillis* and other officials were actually far more aggressive than he in extending the royal power. As one modern historian puts it, "in this reign monarchical progress was the complex result of the sanctity of a revered ruler, and the patient and obstinately aggressive policy of the king's servants." Indeed, St. Louis went to the length of establishing a system of itiner-ant royal inspectors—*enquêteurs*—who re-ported local grievances and helped keep the ambitious local officials in check.

In France under Louis IX medieval cul-ture reached its climax. Town life flourished under St. Louis' rule, and in the towns magnificent Gothic cathedrals were being erected. This was the great age of the medieval universities, and at the most dis-tinguished university of the age, the Univer-sity of Paris, some of the keenest intellects of medieval Europe—St. Bonaventure, St. Albertus Magnus, St. Thomas Aquinas— were assembled concurrently. The universi-ties produced brilliant and subtle theolo-gians, but they also produced learned and ambitious lawyers—men of a more secular cast who devoted their talents to the king and swelled the ranks of the royal bureauc-racy. The Capetian government became steadily more complex, more efficient and, from the standpoint of the feudal nobility, more oppressive.

Philip the Fair
(1285–1314)

Philip III and Philip IV

St. Louis died in the midst of his second crusade. Under his successors the bureauc-racy pursued its ruthless centralizing poli-cies without restraint. The saint-king was succeeded by his inept son, Philip III (1270–1285) and his frigid, unscrupulous grandson, Philip IV, "the Fair" or "the Handsome" (1285–1314). Philip the Fair was a mysterious, silent figure, conven-tionally pious, but with a real flair for choos-ing able, aggressive and thoroughly un-principled ministers—chiefly middle-class lawyers from southern France—who de-voted themselves with remarkable single-mindedness to the exaltation of the French monarchy.

Policies of the Reign

The reign of Philip the Fair was an age of unceasing royal aggression against the terri-tories of neighboring states, against the papacy, and against the traditional privi-leges of the French nobility. Philip waged an indecisive war against King Edward I of England over Edward's remaining fiefs in southern France. He made a serious ef-fort to absorb Flanders, imprisoning the Flemish count and ruling the district di-rectly through a royal agent, but he was foiled by a bloody uprising of Flemish nobles and townsmen who won a stunning victory over him at Courtrai in 1302. He pursued a successful policy of nibbling aggression to the east against the Holy Roman Empire. He suppressed unscrupu-lously the rich crusading order of Knights Templars, ruined their reputation by an astonishingly modern campaign of vitu-perative propaganda, and confiscated their wealth. We have already seen how he struggled with Pope Boniface VIII, how his agents held Boniface captive for a brief time, and how he finally engineered the election of the pliable French Pope Cle-ment V who took up residence at Avignon.* Against his nobles he pursued a rigorously anti-feudal policy. He short-circuited the feudal hierarchy and demanded direct al-legiance and obedience from all French-men. All these activities were manifesta-

* See pp. 308–309.

tions of the prevailing political philosophy of his reign: that the French king was by rights the secular and spiritual master of France and the dominating figure in Western Europe. We encounter this same philosophy in ambitious French statesmen of succeeding centuries: in Cardinal Richelieu; in Louis XIV; and, stripped of its monarchical trappings, in Napoleon and De Gaulle.

Administrative Developments

Throughout the thirteenth century the French royal bureaucracy had been developing steadily. The royal revenues came to be handled by a special accounting bureau, roughly parallel to the English exchequer, called the *chambre des comtes.* The king's judicial business became the responsibility of a high court known as the Parlement of Paris which was to play a highly significant political role in later centuries. Under Philip the Fair the bureaucracy became an exceedingly refined and supple tool of the royal interest and its middle-class background and fanatical royalism gave the king a degree of independence from the nobility that was quite unknown in contemporary England.

Still, the king could not rule without a certain amount of support from his subjects. Philip's victory over the papacy on the issue of royal taxation of the clergy and his rape of the Knights Templars brought additional money into his treasury, but the soaring expenses of government and warfare forced him to seek ever-new sources of revenue and as in England, to secure his subjects' approval for extraordinary taxation. But instead of summoning a great assembly — a parliament — for this purpose, he usually negotiated individually with various tax-paying groups.

The Estates-General

Nevertheless, it was under Philip the Fair that France's first great representative assemblies were summoned. Beginning in 1302, the "Estates-General" was assembled from time to time, primarily for the purpose of giving formal support to the monarchy in moments of crisis — during the height of the struggle with Pope Boniface VIII, for example, or in the midst of the Knights Templars controversy. The assembly included members of the three great social classes or "estates": the clergy, the nobility, and the townsmen. It continued to meet occasionally during the succeeding centuries, but it never became a real organ of government as did Parliament in England. Its failure resulted in part from a premature and unsuccessful bid for power during the fourteenth century in the midst of the Hundred Years' War. But even under Philip the Fair the Estates-General lacked the potential of the contemporary parliaments of England. It had no real voice in royal taxation and was therefore not in a position to bargain with the king through increasing control of the purse strings. It was not, as in England, an evolutionary outgrowth of the royal council, but rather an entirely separate and therefore somewhat exotic body. There was no real opportunity for the bourgeoisie and the gentry to join ranks as in the English House of Commons; lacking the important responsibilities in local government which fell on the English shire knights, the knights of France remained an inarticulate and subordinate part of the aristocratic class. Above all, the French nobility and bourgeoisie lagged far behind the English in developing a national consciousness or a feeling of cohesion. Late-thirteenth-century France was too large, too heterogeneous, and too recently consolidated under royal authority for its inhabitants to have acquired a meaningful sense of identification as a people; their outlook remained provincial.

Yet despite the significant differences between the English Parliament and the French Estates-General, the two institutions had much in common. Both were products of a European-wide evolution out of feudal monarchy and out of the vague but pervading medieval notion of government under the law or government by the consent of the realm. Similar representative institutions were emerging concurrently all over Western Christendom: in the Christian kingdoms of Spain, in Italy under Frederick II, in the rising principalities of Germany, and in innumerable counties, duchies, and communes across the length and breadth of Europe. Of these many experiments, only the English Parliament survives today. But Parliament was not merely the outgrowth of an isolated English experience; it was one particular manifestation of a broad and fundamental trend in European civilization during the High Middle Ages.

CHRONOLOGY OF THE ENGLISH AND FRENCH MONARCHIES IN THE HIGH MIDDLE AGES

ENGLAND

1066: Norman Conquest of England
1066–1087: Reign of William the Conqueror
1087–1100: Reign of William II
1100–1135: Reign of Henry I
1135–1154: Disputed succession:
         King Stephen
1154–1189: Reign of Henry II
1189–1199: Reign of Richard the
         Lion-Hearted
1199–1216: Reign of John
1203–1204: Loss of Normandy
1215: Magna Carta
1216–1272: Reign of Henry III
1258: Provisions of Oxford
1264–1265: Simon de Montfort's rebellion
1272–1307: Reign of Edward I

FRANCE

987–1328: Rule of the Capetian Dynasty
1060–1108: Reign of Philip I
1108–1137: Reign of Louis VI, "the Fat"
1137–1180: Reign of Louis VII
1180–1223: Reign of Philip II, "Augustus"
1214: Battle of Bouvines
1223–1226: Reign of Louis VIII
1226–1270: Reign of St. Louis IX
1270–1285: Reign of Philip III
1285–1314: Reign of Philip IV, "the Fair"

SELECTED READINGS

*Bagley, J. J., *Historical Interpretation,* Penguin, Baltimore, Md.
A collection and evaluation of contemporary sources in English history between 1066 and 1540.

Barraclough, Geoffrey, *Medieval Germany, 911–1250,* Blackwell, 1961, 2 vols.
Volume I is a valuable introductory essay by Barraclough; Volume II consists of specialized studies by German scholars in English translation.

Brook, Christopher, *From Alfred to Henry III,* Thomas Nelson & Sons, New York.
Accurate, up-to-date, and interestingly written.

*Cam, Helen M., *England Before Elizabeth,* Hillary, New York, 1950.
Very brief but excellent, with a strong emphasis on political history.

Douglas, David, *William the Conqueror,* University of California Press, Berkeley, Calif., 1964.
This splendid and beautifully written work of scholarship is perhaps the best single-volume account of a medieval English king. Due attention is given to William's background and achievements in Normandy.

*Fawtier, Robert, *The Capetian Kings of France,* St. Martin's Press, New York, 1960.
A short, masterful treatment, highly recommended.

Kantorowicz, Ernst, *Frederick II,* Ungar, New York, 1957.
An excellent biography. Kantorowicz's conclusions should be compared with those of Barraclough in his *Origins of Modern Germany* (Capricorn paperback).

*Kelly, Amy, *Eleanor of Aquitaine and the Four Kings,* Vintage, New York, 1957.
Sound and entertaining.

Otto of Freising, *The Deeds of Frederick Barbarossa,* C. C. Mierow and R. Emery, translators, Columbia University Press, New York, 1953.

Asterisk (*) denotes paperback.

A good example of medieval historical writing.

Petit-Dutaillis, *The Feudal Monarchy in France and England*, E. D. Hung, translator, Routledge & Kegan Paul, London.
A sound, thoughtful comparative study.

Poole, A. L., *From Domesday Book to Magna Carta 1087–1216*, Oxford University Press, New York, 1955 (2nd ed.).
This book, like F. M. Stenton's *Anglo-Saxon England*, is a volume in the monumental Oxford History of England. Poole's volume, covering the period from 1087 to 1216, is more genial in style than many of its companions.

*Powell, J. M., ed., *Innocent III, Vicar of Christ or Lord of the World*, D. C. Heath & Co., Boston, Mass., 1963.
Essays by historians representing diverse viewpoints.

Powicke, F. M., *The Thirteenth Century 1216– 1307*, Oxford University Press, New York, 1953.
This volume of the Oxford History of England is full, authoritative, and highly detailed.

Tellenbach, Gerd, *Church, State and Christian Society at the Time of the Investiture Contest*, Humanities, New York, 1940.
The finest analysis of the Investiture Controversy in English.

Ullmann, Walter, *The Growth of Papal Government in the Middle Ages*, Barnes and Noble, New York, 1962 (2nd ed.).
An intellectual history of the medieval papal ideology.

William of Malmesbury, *Chronicle of the Kings of England*, J. A. Giles, translator, Bohn.
Written in the first half of the twelfth century, this is the major work of one of medieval Europe's greatest historians. The translation is less than satisfactory.

12

Literature, Art, and Thought in the High Middle Ages

THE DYNAMICS OF HIGH MEDIEVAL CULTURE: LITERATURE AND ART

Thirteenth-century Paris has been described as the Athens of medieval Europe. It is true, of course, that a vast cultural gulf separates the golden age of Periclean Athens from the golden age of thirteenth-century France, but it is also true that these two golden ages had something in common. Both developed within the framework of traditional beliefs and customs which had long existed but were being challenged and transformed by powerful new forces. The socio-religious world of the Early Middle Ages, like the socio-religious world of the early Greek polis, was parochial and tradition-bound. As the two cultures passed into their golden ages, the values of the past were being challenged by new intellectual currents, and the old economic patterns were breaking down before a sharp intensi-

fication of commercial activity. Yet, for a time, these dynamic new forces resulted in a heightened cultural expression of the old values. The Parthenon, dedicated to the venerable civic goddess Athena, and the awesome Gothic cathedral of Notre Dame (Our Lady) are both products of a boundless new creativity harnessed to the service of an older ideology. In the long run, the new creative impulses would prove subversive to the old ideologies, but for a time, both ancient Greece and medieval Europe achieved an elusive equilibrium between old and new. The results, in both cases, were spectacular.

Thus, twelfth- and thirteenth-century Europe succeeded by and large in keeping its vibrant and audacious culture within the bounds of traditional Catholic Christianity.

And the Christian world view gave form and orientation to the new creativity. Despite the intense dynamism of the period, it can still be called, with some semblance of accuracy, an Age of Faith.

Europe in the High Middle Ages underwent a profound artistic and intellectual awakening which affected almost every imaginable form of expression. Significant creative work was done in literature, architecture, sculpture, law, philosophy, political theory, and even science. By the close of the period, the foundations of the Western cultural tradition were firmly established. The pages that follow will provide only a glimpse at a few of the remarkable achievements of this fertile era.

Literature

Latin Literature

The literature of the High Middle Ages was abundant and richly varied. Poetry was written both in the traditional Latin—the universal scholarly language of medieval Europe—and in the vernacular languages of ordinary speech that had long been evolving in the various districts of Christendom. Traditional Christian piety found expression in a series of somber and majestic Latin hymns, whose mood is illustrated—through the clouded glass of translation—by these excerpts from "Jerusalem the Golden" (twelfth century):

> The world is very evil, the times are waxing late,
> Be sober and keep vigil; the judge is at the gate. . . .
> Brief life is here our portion; brief sorrow, short-lived care.
> The life that knows no ending, the tearless life, is there. . . .
>
> Jerusalem the Golden, with milk and honey blessed,
> Beneath thy contemplation sink heart and voice oppressed.
> I know not, O I know not, what social joys are there,
> What radiancy of glory, what light beyond compare.

At the opposite end of the spectrum of medieval Latin literature one encounters poetry of quite a different sort, composed by young, wandering scholars and aging perpetual-undergraduate types. The deliberate sensuality and blasphemy of their poems is an expression of student rebelliousness against the ascetic ideals of their elders:

> For on this my heart is set, when the hour is neigh me,
> Let me in the tavern die, with a tankard by me,
> While the angels, looking down, joyously sing o'er me . . . etc.

One of these wandering-scholar poems is an elaborate and impudent expansion of the Apostles' Creed. The phrase from the Creed, "I believe in the Holy Ghost, the Holy [Catholic] Church . . ." is embroidered as follows:

> I *believe* in wine that's fair to see,
> And in the tavern of my host
> More than *in the Holy Ghost*
> The tavern will my sweetheart be,
> And *the Holy Church* is not for me.*

These sentiments should not be regarded as indicative of a sweeping trend toward agnosticism. Rather, they are distinctively medieval expressions of the irreverent student radicalism that all ages know.

Vernacular Literature: the Epic

For all its originality, the Latin poetry of the High Middle Ages was overshadowed both in quantity and in variety of expression by vernacular poetry. The drift toward emotionalism, which we have already noted in medieval piety, was closely paralleled by the evolution of vernacular literature from the martial epics of the eleventh century to the delicate and sensitive romances of the thirteenth. Influenced by the sophisticated and somewhat feminine romanticism of the southern troubadour tradition, the bellicose spirit of northern France gradually softened.

* Our italics.

In the eleventh and early twelfth centuries, heroic epics known as *chansons de geste* (songs of great deeds) were enormously popular among the feudal nobility of northern France. These *chansons* arose out of the earlier heroic tradition of the Teutonic north that had produced such moody and violent masterpieces as *Beowulf.* The hero Beowulf is a lonely figure who fights monsters, slays dragons, and pits his strength and courage against a wild, windswept wilderness. The *chansons de geste* reflect the somewhat more civilized and Christianized age of feudalism. Still warlike and heroic in mood, they often consisted of exaggerated accounts of events surrounding the reign of Charlemagne. The most famous of all the *chansons de geste,* the *Song of Roland,* tells of an heroic and bloody battle between a horde of Moslems and the detached rearguard of Charlemagne's army as it was withdrawing from Spain. Like old-fashioned Westerns, the *chansons de geste* were packed with action, and their heroes tended to steer clear of sentimental entanglements with ladies. Warlike prowess, courage, and loyalty to one's lord and fellows-in-arms were the virtues stressed in these heroic epics. The battle descriptions, often characterized by gory realism, tell of Christian knights fighting with almost superhuman strength against fantastic odds. The heroes of the *chansons* are not only proud, loyal and skilled at arms, but also capable of experiencing deep emotions — weeping at the death of their comrades and appealing to God to receive the souls of the fallen. In short, the *chansons de geste,* and the *Song of Roland* in particular, mirror the bellicose, masculine spirit and sense of military brotherhood that characterized the feudal knighthood of the eleventh-century Europe:

> Turpin of Rheims, his horse beneath him slain,
> And with four lance wounds he himself in pain,
> Hastens to rise, brave lord, and stand erect.

He looks on Roland, runs to him, and says
Only one thing: "I am not beaten yet!
True man fails not, while life in him is left."
He draws Almace, his keen-edged steel-bright brand
And strikes a thousand strokes amid the press. . . .

Count Roland never loved a recreant,
Nor a false heart, nor yet a braggart jack,
Nor knight that was not faithful to his lord.
He cried to Turpin — churchman militant —
"Sir, you're on foot, I'm on my horse's back.
For love of you, here will I make my stand,
And side by side we'll take both good and bad.
I'll not leave you for any mortal man. . . ."

Now Roland feels that he is nearing death;
Out of his ears the brain is running forth.
So for his peers he prays God call them all,
And for himself St. Gabriel's aid implores.

Roland's rearguard is slain to a man, but the Lord Charlemagne returns to avenge him, and a furious battle ensues:

> Both French and Moors are fighting with a will.
> How many spears are shattered! lances split!
> Whoever saw those shields smashed all to bits,
> Heard the bright hauberks grind, the mail rings rip,
> Heard the harsh spear upon the helmet ring
> Seen countless knights out of the saddle spilled,
> And all the earth with death and death-cries filled,
> Would long recall the face of suffering!

The French are victorious, Charlemagne himself defeats the Moorish emir in single combat, and Roland is avenged:

> The Moslems fly, God will not have them stay.
> All's done, all's won, the French have gained the day.

Minstrels playing the harp, the flute, and the pipe and tabor.

The Lyric

During the middle and later twelfth century the martial spirit of northern French literature was gradually transformed by the influx of the romantic troubadour tradition of southern France. In Provence, Toulouse, and Aquitaine, a rich and colorful culture had been developing in the eleventh and twelfth centuries, and out of this vivacious society came a lyric poetry of remarkable sensitivity and enduring value. The lyric poets of the south were known as *troubadours*. Many of them were courts minstrels, but some, including Duke William IX of Aquitaine himself, were members of the upper nobility. Their poems were far more intimate and personal than the *chansons de geste*, and placed much greater emphasis upon romantic love. The wit, delicacy, and romanticism of the troubadour lyrics betoken a more genteel and sophisticated

nobility than that of the feudal north—a nobility that preferred songs of love to songs of war. Indeed, medieval southern France, under the influence of Islamic courtly poetry and ideas, was the source of the romantic-love tradition of Western civilization. It was from southern France that Europe derived such concepts as the idealization of women, the importance of male gallantry and courtesy, and the impulse to embroider relations between man and woman with potent emotional overtones of eternal oneness, undying devotion, agony, and ecstacy. One of the favorite themes of the lyric poets was the hopeless love—the unrequited love from afar:

> I die of wounds from blissful blows,
> And love's cruel stings dry out my
>   flesh,
> My health is lost, my vigor goes,
> And nothing can my soul refresh.
> I never knew so sad a plight,
> It should not be, it is not right. . . .
>
> I'll never hold her near to me
> My ardent joy she'll ever spurn,
> In her good grace I cannot be
> Nor even hope, but only yearn.
> She tells me nothing, false or
>   true,
> And neither will she ever do.

The author of these lines, Jaufré Rudel (flourished 1148), unhappily and hopelessly in love, finds consolation in his talents as a poet, of which he has an exceedingly high opinion. The poem from which the lines above are taken concludes on a much more optimistic note:

> Make no mistake, my song is fair,
> With fitting words and apt design.
> My messenger would never dare
> To cut it short or change a line. . . .
>
> My song is fair, my song is good,
> 'Twill bring delight, as well it
>   should.

Many such poems were written in southern France during the twelfth century. The recurring theme is the poet's passionate love for a lady. Occasionally, however, the pattern is reversed, as in the following lyric poem by the poetess Beatritz de Dia (flourished 1160):

> I live in grave anxiety
> For one fair knight who loved me so.
> It would have made him glad to know
> I loved him too — but silently.
> I was mistaken, now I'm sure,
> When I withheld myself from him.
> My grief is deep, my days are dim,
> And life itself has no allure.
>
> I wish my knight might sleep with me
> And hold me naked to his breast.
> On my own form to take his rest,
> And grieve no more, but joyous be.
> My love for him surpasses all
> The loves that famous lovers knew.
> My soul is his, my body, too,
> My heart, my life, are at his call.
>
> My most beloved, dearest friend,
> When will you fall into my power?
> That I might lie with you an hour,
> And love you 'til my life should end!
> My heart is filled with passion's fire.
> My well-loved knight, I grant thee grace,
> To hold me in my husband's place,
> And do the things I so desire.

Not all the lyric poems of southern France took love or life quite so seriously. In some, one encounters a refreshing lightness and wit. The following verses, by Duke William IX of Aquitaine (1071–1127), typify the vivacious spirit of the South and contrast sharply with the serious, heroic mood of the *chansons de geste:*

> I'll make some verses just for fun,
> Not of myself or anyone,
> Nor of great deeds that knights have
>   done
> Nor lovers true.
> I made them riding in the sun,
> My horse helped, too.
>
> When I was born, I'm not aware,
> I'm neither gay nor in despair,
> Nor stiff, nor loose, nor do I care,
> Nor wonder why.
> Since meeting an enchantress fair,
> Bewitched am I.

> Living for dreaming I mistake,
> I must be told when I'm awake,
> My mood is sad, my heart may break,
> Such grief I bear!
> But never mind, for heaven's sake,
> I just don't care.
>
> I'm sick to death, or so I fear,
> I cannot see, but only hear.
> I hope that there's a doctor near,
> No matter who.
> If he can heal me, I'll pay dear,
> If not, he's through.
>
> My lady fair is far away,
> Just who, or where, I cannot say,
> She tells me neither yea nor nay,
> Yet I'm not blue,
> So long as all those Normans stay
> Far from Poitou.
>
> My distant love I so adore,
> Though me she has no longing for,
> We've never met, and furthermore —
> To my disgrace —
> I've other loves, some three or four,
> To fill her place.
>
> This verse is done, as you can see,
> And by your leave, dispatched 'twill be
> To one who'll read it carefully
> In far Anjou.
> Its meaning he'd explain to me
> If he but knew.

These verses, only a brief sampling of the fascinating lyrics of southern France — and distorted by translation — may provide some feeling for the rich and delightful civilization that flourished there in the twelfth century and disintegrated with the savage horrors of the Albigensian Crusade.

The Romance

Midway through the twelfth century, the southern tradition of courtly love was brought northward to the court of Champagne and began to spread rapidly across France, England, and Germany. As its influence grew, the northern knights discovered that more was expected of them than loyalty to their lords and a life of carefree slaughter. They were now expected to be gentlemen as well — to be courtly in manner and urbane in speech, to exhibit delicate and refined behavior in feminine company, and to idolize some noble lady. Such, briefly, were the ideals of courtly love. Their impact on the actual behavior of knights was distinctly limited, but their effect on the literature of Northern Europe was revolutionary. Out of the convergence of vernacular epic and vernacular lyric there emerged a new poetic form known as the romance.

Like the *chanson de geste*, the romance was a long narrative poem, but like the southern lyric, it was exceedingly sentimental and imaginative. It was commonly based on some theme from the remote past: the Trojan War, Alexander the Great, and, above all, King Arthur—the half-legendary sixth-century British king. Arthur was transformed into an idealized twelfth-century monarch surrounded by charming ladies and chivalrous knights. His court at Camelot, as described by the great French poet,

Lancelot and Guinevere, an early depiction of the Arthurian legend. The widespread influence of this legend and its continuing popularity attest to its importance as one of the major literary creations of the Middle Ages.

Chrétien de Troyes, was a center of romantic love and refined religious sensitivity where knights worshiped their ladies, went on daring quests, and played out their chivalrous roles in a world of magic and fantasy.

In the *chanson de geste* the great moral imperative was loyalty to one's lord; in the romance it was love for one's lady. Several romances portray the old and new values in direct conflict. An important theme in both the Arthurian romances and the twelfth-century romance of *Tristan and Iseult* is a love affair between a vassal and his lord's wife. Love and feudal loyalty stand face to face, and love wins out. Tristan loves Iseult, the wife of his lord, King Mark of Cornwall. King Arthur's beloved knight Lancelot loves Arthur's wife, Guinevere. In both stories the lovers are ruined by their love, yet love they must—they have no choice—and although the conduct of Tristan and Lancelot would have been regarded by earlier standards as nothing less than treasonable, both men are presented sympathetically in the romances. Love destroys the lovers in the end, yet their destruction is romantic—even glorious. Tristan and Iseult die together, and in their very death their love achieves its deepest consummation.

Alongside the theme of love is the medieval romances, and standing in sharp contrast to it, is the theme of Christian purity and dedication. The rough-hewn knight of old, having been taught to be courteous and loving, was now taught to be holy. Lancelot was trapped in the meshes of a lawless love, but his son, Galahad, became the prototype of the Christian knight—pure, holy, and chaste. And Perceval, another knight of the Arthurian circle, quested not for a lost loved one but for the Holy Grail of the Last Supper.

The romance flourished in twelfth- and thirteenth-century France and among the French-speaking nobility of England. It spread also into Italy and Spain, and became a crucial factor in the evolution of vernacular literature in Germany. The German poets, known as Minnesingers, were influenced by the French lyric and romance, but developed these literary forms along highly original lines. The Minnesingers produced their own deeply sensitive and mystical versions of the Arthurian stories which, in their exalted symbolism and profundity of emotion, surpass even the works of Chrétien de Troyes and his French contemporaries.

Aucassin et Nicolette; the Romance of the Rose

As the thirteenth century drew toward its close, the French romance tended to become conventionalized and drained of inspiration. The love story of *Aucassin et Nicolette,* which achieved a degree of popularity, was actually a satirical romance in which the hero was much less heroic than heroes usually are, and a battle is depicted in which the opponents cast pieces of cheese at each other. Based on earlier Byzantine material, *Aucassin et Nicolette* makes mortal love take priority over salvation itself. Indeed, Aucassin is scornful of Heaven:

For into Paradise go only such people as these: There go those aged priests and elderly cripples and maimed ones who day and night stoop before altars and in the crypts beneath the churches; those who go around in wornout cloaks and shabby old habits; who are naked and shoeless and full of sores; who are dying of hunger and of thirst, of cold and of misery. Such folks as these enter Paradise, and I will have nothing to do with them. I will go to Hell. For to Hell go the fair clerics and comely knights who are killed in tournaments and great wars, and the sturdy archer and the loyal vassal. I will go with them. There also go the fair and courteous ladies who have loving friends, two or three, together with their wedded lords. And there go the gold and silver, the ermine and all rich furs, the harpers and the minstrels, and the happy folk of the world. I will go with these, so long as I have Nicolette, my very sweet friend, at my side.

Another important product of thirteenth-century vernacular literature, the *Romance of the Rose,* was in fact not a romance in the ordinary sense but an allegory of the whole courtly love tradition in which the thoughts and emotions of the lover and his lady are transformed into actual characters. Thus, Love, Reason, Jealousy, Fair-Welcome, and similar personifications all have their roles to play. Begun by William of Lorris as an idealization of courtly love, the *Romance of the Rose* was completed after William's death by Jean de Meun, a man of limited talent and bourgeois origin. Jean's contribution was long-winded and encyclopedic, and the poem as a whole lacks high literary distinction, yet it appealed to contemporaries and enjoyed a great vogue.

Fabliaux and Fables

Neither epic, lyric, nor romance had much appeal below the level of the landed aristocracy. The inhabitants of the rising towns had a vernacular literature all their own. From the bourgeoisie came the high medieval *fabliaux,* short satirical poems, filled with vigor and crude humor, which devoted themselves chiefly to ridiculing conventional morality. Priests and monks were portrayed as lechers, merchants' wives were easily and frequently seduced, and clever young rascals perpetually made fools of sober and stuffy businessmen.

Medieval urban culture also produced the fable, or animal story, an allegory in the tradition of Aesop in which various stock characters in medieval society were presented as animals—thinly disguised. Most of the more popular fables dealt with Renard the Fox and were known collectively as the *Romance of Renard.* These tales constituted a ruthless parody of chivalric ideals in which the clever, unscrupulous Renard persistently outwitted King Lion and his loyal but stupid vassals. Thus, paradoxically, the medieval town, which produced such powerful waves of piety, was responsible for literary forms characterized chiefly by secularism, immorality, and the ridiculing of customs and conventions. To balance the impression conveyed by the *fabliaux* and fables one must consider the great Romanesque and Gothic cathedrals, the *Song of Brother Sun* composed by that illustrious son of a medieval merchant, St. Francis of Assisi, and the deeply religious poetry of the Florentine Dante.

Dante

Vernacular poetry matured late in Italy, but in the works of Dante (1265–1321) it achieved its loftiest expression. Dante wrote on a wide variety of subjects, sometimes in Latin, more often in the Tuscan vernacular. He composed a series of lyric poems celebrating his love for the lady Beatrice, which are assembled, with prose commentaries, in his *Vita Nuova* (*The New Life*). Dante's lyrics reflect a more mystical and idealized love than that of the troubadours:

> A shining love comes from my lady's eyes,
> All that she looks on is made lovelier,
> And as she walks, men turn to gaze at her,
> Whoever meets her feels his heart
>   arise. . . .
> Humility, and hope that hopeth well,
> Come to the mind of one who hears her
>   voice,
> And blessed is he who looks on her a while.
> Her beauty, when she gives her slightest
>   smile
> One cannot paint in words, yet must
>   rejoice
> In such a new and gracious miracle.

Firmly convinced of the literary potential of the Tuscan vernacular, Dante urged its use in his *De Vulgari Eloquentia,* which he wrote in Latin so as to appeal to scholars and writers who scorned the vulgar tongue. And he filled his own vernacular works with such grace and beauty as to convince by example those whom he could not persuade by argument. In his hands, the Tuscan vernacular became the literary language of Italy.

Dante was no mere disembodied writer,

but a man deeply immersed in the politics of his age. His experience brought him to the opinion that Italy's hope for peace lay in imperial domination and in divorcing the papacy from politics. Although rather futile and anachronistic in view of the Empire's impotence in Dante's time, these views were expressed forcefully in his great political essay, *On Monarchy*.

Dante's masterpiece was the *Divine Comedy*. Written in the Tuscan vernacular, it is a magnificent synthesis of medieval literature and thought. It abounds in allegory and symbolism, and encompasses in one majestic vision the entire universe of medieval man. Dante tells of his own journey through hell, purgatory, and paradise to the very presence of Almighty God. This device permits the poet to make devastating comments on past and contemporary history by placing all those of whom he disapproved—from local politicians to popes—in various levels of hell. Virgil, the archetype of ancient rationalism, is Dante's guide through hell and purgatory; the lady Beatrice, a symbol of purified love, guides him through the celestial spheres of paradise; and St. Bernard, the epitome of medieval sanctity, leads him to the threshold of God. The poem closes with Dante alone in the divine presence:

> Eternal Light, thou in thyself alone
> Abidest, and alone thine essence knows,
> And loves, and smiles, self-knowing and
>   self-known. . . .
>
> Here power failed to the high fantasy,
> But my desire and will were turned—as
>   one—
> And as a wheel that turneth evenly,
> By Holy Love, that moves the stars and
>   sun.

Architecture

From Romanesque to Gothic

The High Middle Ages is one of the great epochs in the history of Western architecture. Stone churches, large and small, were built in prodigious numbers: in France alone, more stone was quarried during the

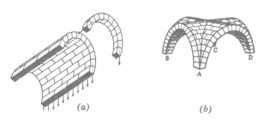

(a) Barrel Vault   *(b) Cross Vault*

High Middle Ages than by the pyramid and temple builders of ancient Egypt throughout its 3000-year history. Yet the real achievement of the medieval architects lay not in the immense scope of their activities but in the splendid originality of their aesthetic vision. Two great architectural styles dominated the age. The Romanesque style evolved in the eleventh century, rose to maturity in the early twelfth, and during the latter half of the twelfth century gave way gradually to the Gothic style. From about 1150 to 1300 the greatest of the medieval Gothic cathedrals were built. Thereafter, the Gothic style lost some of its inspiration as it became overly elaborate and increasingly showy, but during the High Middle Ages it constituted one of humanity's most audacious and successful architectural experiments.

High medieval architecture was deeply affected by two of the basic cultural trends of the period. First, the great cathedrals were products of the urban revolution and the rise of intense urban piety. Second, the evolution from Romanesque to Gothic closely parallels the shift which we have already observed in literature and piety toward emotional sensitivity and romanticism. Romanesque architecture, although characterized by an exceeding diversity of expression, tended in general toward the solemnity of earlier Christian piety and the uncompromising masculinity of the *chansons de geste*. Gothic architecture, on the other hand, is dramatic, upward-reaching, and even somewhat feminine. A vast number of Gothic cathedrals were dedicated to Notre Dame—Our Lady.

343

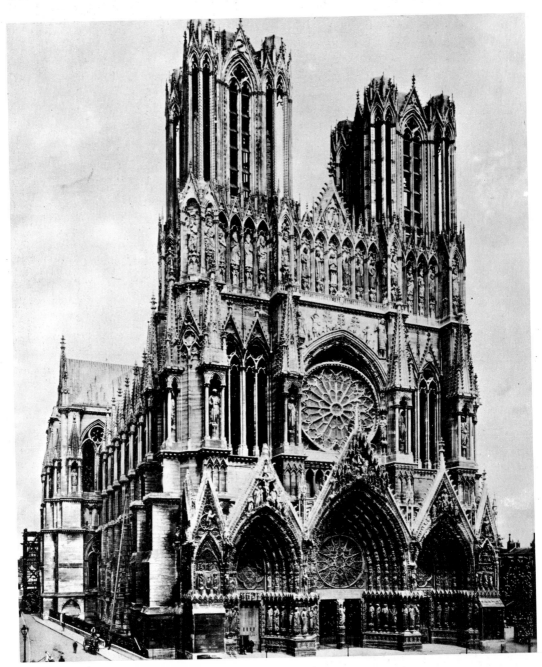

Above: Rheims Cathedral (1211–1290), exterior. Top left, p. 345: Chartres Cathedral (rebuilt 1194–1260), interior. These two cathedrals are classic thirteenth-century examples of the French Gothic architectural achievement. Gothic church structures were peculiarly French in origin—more specifically northeastern French. The prototype of all Gothic churches is the Abbey Church of St. Denis, seven miles north of Paris. Most of the earliest Gothic cathedrals were built in the area of France lying within a 75-mile radius of Paris. From this region, the Gothic form spread throughout Western and Northern Europe.

The flying buttresses of Notre Dame in Paris.

Visitation, *from the west portals of Rheims Cathedral. These statues are splendid illustrations of Gothic naturalism.*

The development from Romanesque to Gothic can also be understood as an evolution in the principles of structural engineering. The key architectural ingredient in the Romanesque churches was the round arch. Romanesque roof design was based on various elaborations of the round arch, such as the barrel vault and the cross vault. These heavy stone roofs required thick supporting walls with windows that were necessarily few and small. A church in the fully developed Romanesque style conveys a powerful feeling of unity and earthbound solidity. Its massive arches, vaults, and walls, and its somber, shadowy interior give the illusion of mystery and otherworldliness while suggesting the steadfast might of the universal Church.

The Gothic Style

Midway through the twelfth century, Abbot Suger, the chief adviser of the French crown, became a pioneer of the new

Gothic style by introducing significant novel elements into the construction of his abbey church at St. Denis. The key features of the Gothic style, which now spread rapidly outward from the Île de France, were the pointed arch and the flying buttress. These and related structural devices resulted in a totally new aesthetic experience. The pointed arch, as the accompanying illustration makes clear, permitted the cathedral roof to soar upward. Churches now lost their earthbound quality and began to reach toward the sky. In the simplest terms, the Romanesque round arch resulted in a structure whose lines were chiefly horizontal, whereas the Gothic pointed arch emphasized the vertical. From the aesthetic standpoint, this shift in orientation made an immense difference.

The flying buttresses were devices to relieve the church walls of the outward and downward thrust of the roof. By so doing, they rendered the walls structurally superfluous and permitted the architects to design huge windows, usually filled with brilliant stained glass, which flooded the interior of the Gothic church with light and color. The Gothic exterior was richly ornamented with sculptural representations of plants and animals, saints and statesmen. Gothic sculpture often sought to tell a story—to reproduce scenes and episodes from the Bible or from the lives of saints. Sometimes this was done in a straightforward way, sometimes through religious symbolism. And sometimes the Gothic sculptors had no further wish than to portray the variety of the natural world in stone. In many instances they succeeded in reproducing plants, animals, and humans with a remarkable degree of realism.

The Gothic cathedral was a functional and closely unified work of art. Its soaring silhouette dominated the town in which it stood, and its lofty, richly illuminated interior created a dramatic effect that must have overwhelmed the medieval worshipers whose piety it so superbly reflected. After the physical and spiritual ravages of seven centuries its spell still holds.

THE DYNAMICS OF HIGH MEDIEVAL CULTURE: EDUCATION, MEDICINE, AND LAW

The Rise of Universities

The University Defined

Like the Gothic cathedral, the university was a product of the medieval town. The urban revolution of the eleventh and twelfth centuries brought about the decline of the old monastic schools which had done so much to preserve culture over the previous centuries. They were superseded north of the Alps by cathedral schools located in the rising towns, and in Italy by semi-secular municipal schools. Both the cathedral schools and the municipal schools had long existed, but it was only in the eleventh century that they rose to great prominence. Many of these schools now became centers of higher learning of a sort that Europe had not known for centuries. Their enrollments increased steadily and their faculties grew until, in the twelfth century, some of them evolved into universities.

In the Middle Ages, *university* was an exceedingly vague term. A university was simply a group of persons associated for any purpose. The word was commonly applied to the merchant guilds and craft guilds of the rising towns. A guild or university of students and scholars engaged in the pursuit of higher learning was given the more specific name, *studium generale.* When we speak of the medieval university, therefore, we are referring to an institution that would have been called a *studium generale* by a man of the thirteenth century. It differed from lesser schools in three significant respects: (1) the *studium generale* was open to students from many lands, not simply those from the surrounding districts; (2) the *studium generale* was a large school with a number of teachers rather than merely one omnicompetent master; (3) the *studium generale* offered both elementary and advanced curricula. It offered a basic program of instruction in the traditional "seven liberal arts": astronomy, geometry, arithmetic, music, grammar, rhetoric, and dialectic; and also instruction in one or more of the "higher" disciplines: theology, law, and medicine. Upon the successful completion of his liberal arts curriculum, the student could apply for a license to teach, but he might also wish to continue his studies by specializing in medicine, theology, or—most popular of all —civil or canon law. Legal training offered as its reward the promise of a lucrative administrative career in royal government or the Church.

Fundamentally, the medieval university was neither a campus nor a complex of buildings, but a guild—a privileged corporation of teachers, or sometimes of students. With its classes normally held in rented rooms, it was a highly mobile institution, and on more than one occasion, when a university was dissatisfied with local conditions it won important concessions from the townsmen simply by threatening to move elsewhere.

University Organization and Student Life

In the thirteenth century, flourishing universities were to be found at Paris, Bologna, Naples, Montpellier, Oxford, Cambridge, and elsewhere. Paris, Oxford, and a num-

The corporate permanence of a great medieval university is symbolized by this fourteenth-century seal of the University of Paris.

ber of others were dominated by guilds of instructors in the liberal arts. Bologna, on the other hand, was governed by a guild of students which managed to reduce the exorbitant local prices of food and lodgings by threatening to move collectively to another town, and which established strict rules of conduct for the instructors. Professors had to begin and end their classes on time and to cover the prescribed curriculum; they could not leave town without special permission. This, surely, was student government run rampant. It is important to point out, however, that Bologna specialized in legal studies and that its pupils were older professional students for the most part—men who had completed their liberal arts curriculum and were determined to secure sufficient training for successful careers in law.

The students of the medieval universities were, on the whole, rowdier and more exuberant than students of American universities today, more imaginative in their pranks, and more hostile toward the surrounding towns. Thus, the history of medieval universities is punctuated by frequent town-gown riots. New students were hazed unmercifully; unpopular professors were hissed, shouted down, and even pelted with stones. Most of the students were of relatively humble origin—from the towns or the ranks of the lesser nobility—but they were willing to spend their student days in abject poverty if necessary in order to acquire the new knowledge and prepare themselves for the rich social and economic rewards that awaited many graduates.

Despite the enormous differences between medieval and modern university life, it should be clear that the modern university is a direct outgrowth of the institution that came into being in high medieval Europe. We owe to the medieval university the concept of a formal teaching license, the custom—unknown to antiquity—of group instruction, the idea of academic degrees, the notion of a liberal arts curriculum, the tradition of professors and students dressing in clerical garb (caps and gowns) on commencement day, and numerous other customs of university life. Even the letters written by medieval students to their parents or guardians have a curiously modern ring:

This is to inform you that I am studying at Oxford with the greatest diligence, but the matter of money stands greatly in the way of my promotion, as it is now two months since I spent the last of what you sent me. The city is expensive and makes many demands; I have to rent lodgings, buy necessities, and provide for many other things which I cannot now specify. [A fuller elaboration here would have been illuminating.] Wherefore I respectfully beg your paternity that by the promptings of divine pity you may assist me, so that I can complete what I have well begun. For you must know that without Ceres and Bacchus, Apollo grows cold.

Medicine and Law

Medicine

The chief medical school of medieval Europe was the University of Salerno. Here, in a land of vigorous cultural intermingling, scholars were able to draw from the medical heritage of Islam and Byzantium. In general, medieval medical scholarship was a bizarre medley of cautious observation, common sense, and gross super-

stition. In one instance we encounter the good advice that a person should eat and drink in moderation. But we are also instructed that onions will cure baldness, that the urine of a dog is an admirable cure for warts, and that all one must do to prevent a woman from conceiving is to bind her head with a red ribbon. Yet in the midst of this nonsense, important progress was being made in medical science. The writings of the great second-century scientist Galen, which constituted a synthesis of classical medical knowledge, were studied and digested, as were the important works of Arab students of medicine. And to this invaluable body of knowledge European scholars were now making their own original contributions on such subjects as the curative properties of plants and the anatomy of the human body. It is probable that both animal and human dissections were performed by the scholars of twelfth-century Salerno. These doctors, their crude and primitive methods notwithstanding, were laying the foundations on which western European medical science was to rise.

Civil Law

Medieval legal scholarship addressed itself to two distinct bodies of material: civil law and canon law. The legal structure of early medieval society was largely Germanic in inspiration and custom-based, particularly in Northern Europe where Roman law had disappeared without a trace. Customary law remained strong throughout the High Middle Ages: it governed the relationships among the feudal aristocracy and determined the manorial obligations of the medieval peasantry. It limited the feudal prerogatives of kings, and underlay Magna Carta. But from the late eleventh century on, Roman law was studied in Bologna and other European universities. Christendom was now exposed to a distinctly different legal tradition—coherent and logical—which began to compete with Germanic law, to rationalize it, and in some instances to replace it.

The foundation of medieval Roman law was the *Corpus Juris Civilis* of Justinian which was unknown in the West throughout most of the Early Middle Ages but reappeared at Bologna in the last quarter of the eleventh century. Italy remained the center of Roman legal studies throughout the High Middle Ages, for the traditions of Roman law had never entirely disappeared there, and the Italian peninsula therefore provided the most fertile soil for their revival. From Italy, the study of Roman law spread northward. A great school of law emerged at Montpellier in southern France, and others flourished at Orleans, Paris, and Oxford. But Bologna remained the most notable center of Roman legal scholarship. There, able scholars known as "glossators" wrote analytical commentaries on the *Corpus Juris,* elucidating difficult points and reconciling apparent contradictions. Later on they began to produce textbooks and important original treatises on the *Corpus* and to reorganize it into a coherent sequence of topics. Eventually such an extensive body of supplementary material existed that the glossators turned to the task of glossing the glosses — elucidating the elucidations. Around the mid-thirteenth century the work of the earlier glossators was brought to a climax with a comprehensive work by the Bolognese scholar Accursius, the *Glossa Ordinaria,* which was a composite synthesis of all previous commentaries on the *Corpus Juris.* Thereafter the *Glossa Ordinaria* became the authoritative supplement to the *Corpus Juris* in courts of Roman law.

The impact of the glossators was particularly strong in Italy and southern France where elements of Roman law had survived as local custom. By the thirteenth century Roman law was beginning to make a significant impact in the north as well, for by then civil lawyers trained in the Roman tradition were achieving an increasingly dominant role in the courts of France, Germany, and Spain. These men devoted themselves wholeheartedly to the royal service

and used their legal training to exalt their monarchs in every possible way. Although the Roman legal tradition had originally contained a strong element of constitutionalism, it inherited from Justinian's age an autocratic cast which the court lawyers of the rising monarchies put to effective use. Thus, as Roman law gained an increasingly firm hold in the states of continental Europe, it tended to make their governments at once more systematic and more absolute. In France, for example, civil lawyers played an important part in the gradual transformation of the early Capetian feudal monarchy into the royal autocracy of later times. And the development and durability of the parliamentary regime in England owed much to the fact that a strong monarchy, founded on the principles of Germanic law with its custom-based limitations on royal authority, was already well established before Europe felt the full impact of the Roman law revival.

Canon Law

Canon law developed alongside Roman law and derived a great deal from it. Methods of scholarship were quite similar in the two fields — commentaries and glosses were common to both — and the ecclesiastical courts borrowed much from the principles and procedures of Roman law. But whereas Roman law was based on the single authority of Justinian's *Corpus Juris,* canon law drew from many sources: the Bible, the writings of the ancient Church fathers, the canons of Church councils, and the decretals of popes. The *Corpus Juris,* although susceptible to endless commentary, was fundamentally complete in itself; popes and councils, on the other hand, continued to issue decrees, and canon law was therefore capable of unlimited development.

Canon law, like civil law, first became a serious scholarly discipline in eleventh-century Bologna and later spread to other major centers of learning. The study of canon law was strongly stimulated by the Investiture Controversy and subsequent

Church-state struggles, for the papacy looked to canon lawyers to support its claims with cogent, documented arguments and apt precedents. But the medieval scholars of canon law were far more than mere papal propagandists. They were grappling with the formidable problem of systematizing their sources, explaining what was unclear, reconciling what seemed contradictory—in other words, imposing order on the immense variety of dicta, opinions, and precedents upon which their discipline was based.

The essential goal of the canon lawyers was to assemble their diverse sources—their canons—into a single coherent work. It was up to them, in short, to accomplish the task that Justinian had performed for Roman law back in the sixth century. The civil lawyers had their *Corpus Juris Civilis;* it was up to the canon lawyers to create their own "Corpus Juris Canonici." The first attempts to produce comprehensive canonical collections date from the Early Middle Ages, but it was not until the eleventh-century revival at Bologna that serious scholarly standards were applied to the task. The definitive collection was completed around 1140 by the great Bolognese canon lawyer, Gratian. Originally entitled *The Concordance of Discordant Canons,* Gratian's work is known to posterity as the *Decretum.*

Gratian not only brought together an immense body of canons from a bewildering variety of sources; he also framed them in a logical, topically organized scheme. Using scholarly methods that were just beginning to be employed by scholastic philosophers and logicians, he raised questions, quoted the relevant canons, endeavored to reconcile those that disagreed, and thereby arrived at firm conclusions. The result was an ordered body of general legal principles derived from particular passages from the Bible, the fathers, and papal and conciliar decrees. The *Decretum* became the authoritative text in ecclesiastical tribunals and the basis of all study in canon law.

As time passed, and new decrees were issued, it became necessary to supplement Gratian's *Decretum* by collecting the canons issued subsequent to 1140. The first collection was made in 1234 under the direction of the lawyer-pope Gregory IX, another in the pontificate of Boniface VIII, and still others in later generations. Together, the *Decretum* and the supplementary collections were given the title, *Corpus Juris Canonici,* and became the ecclesiastical equivalent of Justinian's *Corpus.* These two great compilations, ecclesiastical and civil, symbolize the parallel growth of medieval Europe's two supreme sources of administrative and jurisdictional authority: Church and monarchy.

THE DYNAMICS OF HIGH MEDIEVAL CULTURE: PHILOSOPHY AND SCIENCE

Philosophy

Background of High Medieval Philosophy

It is only to be expected that an age which witnessed such sweeping economic and political changes and such vigorous

creativity in religious and artistic expression would also achieve notable success in the realm of abstract thought. Medieval philosophy is richly variegated and marked by boundless curiosity and heated controversy. Although every important philosopher in the High Middle Ages was a churchman of one sort or another, ecclesiastical authority did not stifle speculation. Catholic orthodoxy, which hardened noticeably at the time of the Protestant Reformation, was still relatively flexible in the twelfth and thirteenth centuries, and the philosophers of the age were far from being timid apologists for official dogmas. If some of them were impelled by conviction to provide the Catholic faith with a logical substructure, others asserted vigorously that reason does not lead to the truth of Christian revelation. And among those who sought to harmonize faith and reason there was sharp disagreement as to what form the logical substructure should take. All were believers—all were Catholics—but their doctrinal unanimity did not limit their diversity or curb their adventurous spirit.

The high medieval philosophers drew nourishment from five earlier sources. (1) From the Greeks they inherited the great philosophical systems of Plato and Aristotle. At first these two Greek masters were known in the West only through a handful of translations and commentaries dating from late Roman times. By the thirteenth century, however, new and far more complete translations were coming into Christendom from Spain and Sicily, and Aristotelian philosophy became a matter of intense interest and controversy in Europe's universities. (2) From the Islamic world came a flood of Greek scientific and philosophical works which had long before been translated from Greek to Arabic and were now translated from Arabic into Latin. These works came into Europe accompanied by extensive commentaries and original writings of Arab philosophers and scientists, for the Arabs had come to grips with Greek learning long before the advent of the High Middle Ages. Islamic thought made its own distinctive contribution to European science; in philosophy it was important chiefly as an agency for the transmission and interpretation of Greek thought. (3) The early Church fathers, particularly the Latin Doctors, had been a dominant influence on the thought of the Early Middle Ages and their authority remained strong in the twelfth and thirteenth centuries. St. Augustine retained his singular significance, and was, indeed, the chief vessel of Platonic and Neo-platonic thought in the medieval universities. No philosopher of the High Middle Ages could ignore him, and some of the most distinguished of them were conscious and devoted Augustinians. (4) The early medieval scholars themselves contributed significantly to the high medieval intellectual revival. Gregory the Great, Isidore of Seville, Bede, Alcuin, Raban Maur, John the Scot, and Gerbert of Aurillac were all studied seriously in the new universities. The original intellectual contributions of these men were less important, however, than the fact that they and their contemporaries had kept learning alive, fostered and perpetuated the classical tradition in Europe, and created an intellectual climate that made possible the reawakening of philosophical speculation in the eleventh century. Although stimulated by contacts with other civilizations, the intellectual surge of the High Middle Ages was fundamentally an internal phenomenon with roots in Ottonian, Carolingian, and pre-Carolingian Europe. (5) The high-medieval philosophers looked back beyond the scholars of the Early Middle Ages, beyond the fathers of the early Church, to the Hebrew and primitive Christian religious traditions as recorded in Scripture. Among medieval theologians the Bible, the chief written source of divine revelation, was quite naturally the fundamental text and the ultimate authority.

Nature of Scholasticism

Such were the chief elements—Greek, Islamic, Patristic, early medieval, and scriptural—which underlay the thought of the scholastic philosophers of the High Middle Ages. Narrowly defined, "scholasticism" is simply the philosophical movement associated with the high medieval schools—the cathedral and monastic schools, and later the universities. More basically it was a movement concerned above all with exploring the relationship between rationalism and theism—reason and revelation. All medieval scholastics were theists, all were committed, to some degree, to the life of reason. Many of them were immensely enthusiastic over the intellectual possibilities inherent in the careful application of Aristotelian logic to basic human and religious problems. Some believed that the syllogism was the master key to a thousand doors, and that with sufficient methodological rigor, with sufficient exactness in the use of words, the potentialities of human knowledge were all but limitless.

The scholastics applied their logical method to a vast number of problems. They were concerned chiefly, however, with matters of basic significance to human existence: the nature of man, the purpose of human life, the existence and attributes of God, the fundamentals of human morality, the ethical imperatives of social and political life, the relationship between God and man. It would be hard to deny that these are the most profound sorts of questions that philosophers can ask, although many thinkers of our own day are inclined to reject them as unanswerable. Perhaps they are, but the scholastics, standing near the beginning of Europe's long intellectual journey and lacking the modern sense of disillusionment, were determined to make the attempt.

Relationship of Faith and Reason

Among the diverse investigations and conflicting opinions of the medieval thinkers, three central issues deserve particular attention: (1) the degree of interrelationship between faith and reason, (2) the relative merits of the Platonic-Augustinian and the Aristotelian intellectual traditions, and (3) the reality of the Platonic archetypes or, as they were called in the Middle Ages, "universals."

The issue of faith *versus* reason was perhaps the most far-reaching of the three. Ever since Tertullian in the third century, there had been Christian writers who insisted that God so transcended reason that any attempt to approach him intellectually was useless and, indeed, blasphemous. It was the mystic who knew God, not the theologian. Tertullian had posed the rhetorical questions,

What has Athens to do with Jerusalem? What concord is there between the Academy and the Church? . . . Let us have done with all attempts to produce a bastard Christianity of Stoic, Platonic, and dialectic composition! We desire no curious disputation after possessing Christ Jesus, no inquisition after enjoying the Gospel!

Tertullian had many followers in the Middle Ages. St. Peter Damiani, standing at the fountainhead of the new medieval piety, rejected the intellectual road to God in favor of the mystical. Damiani had insisted that God, whose power is limitless, cannot be bound or even approached by logic. He was followed in this view by such later mystics as St. Bernard, who denounced and hounded his brilliant rationalist contemporary Peter Abelard, and St. Francis, who regarded intellectual speculation as irrelevant and perhaps even dangerous to salvation. A later spiritual Franciscan, Jacopone da Todi, expressed the anti-intellectual position in verse:

Plato and Socrates may oft contend,
And all the breath within their bodies
   spend,
Engaged in disputations without end.
What's that to me?
For only with a pure and simple mind
Can one the narrow path to heaven find,
And greet the King; while lingers far
   behind,
Philosophy.

The contrary view was just as old. Third-century theologians such as Clement and Origen in the school of Alexandria had labored to provide Christianity with a sturdy philosophical foundation and did not hesitate to elucidate the faith by means of

Greek — and particularly Platonic — thought. The fourth-century Latin Doctors, Ambrose, Jerome, and Augustine, had wrestled with the problem of whether a Christian might properly use elements from the pagan classical tradition in the service of the Faith, and all three ended with affirmative answers. As Augustine expressed it,

If those who are called philosophers, and especially the Platonists, have said aught that is true and in harmony with our faith, we must not only not shrink from it, but claim it for our own use from those who have unlawful possession of it.

Such is the viewpoint that underlies most of high medieval philosophy — that reason has a valuable role to play as a servant of revelation. St. Anselm, following Augustine, declared, "I believe so that I may know." Faith comes first, reason second; faith rules reason, but reason can perform the useful service of illuminating faith. Indeed, faith and reason are separate avenues to a single body of truth. By their very nature they cannot lead to contradictory conclusions, for truth is one. Should their conclusions ever *appear* to be contradictory, the philosopher can be assured that some flaw exists in his logic. Reason cannot err, but man's use of it can, and revelation must therefore be the criterion against which reason is measured.

This, in general, became the common position of later scholastic philosophers. The intellectual system of St. Thomas Aquinas was built on the conviction that reason and faith were harmonious. Even the arch-rationalist of the twelfth century, Peter Abelard, wrote: "I do not wish to be a philosopher if it means resisting St. Paul; I do not wish to be Aristotle if it must separate me from Christ." Abelard believed that he could at once be a philosopher and a Christian, but his faith took first priority.

Among some medieval philosphers the priorities were reversed. Averroës, a profound Islamic Aristotelian of twelfth-century Spain, boldly asserted the superiority of reason over faith. He affirmed the truth

The enormous respect that medieval man had for the intellectual powers of the classic philosophers may be seen in this thirteenth-century illustration which naively credits Socrates with the power to foretell the sex of an unborn child.

of several propositions which were logical byproducts of Aristotle's philosophy but were directly contrary to Islamic and Christian doctrine. Averroës taught, for example, that the world had always existed and was therefore uncreated — that all human actions were determined — that there was no personal salvation. In the thirteenth century a Christian philosophical school known as Latin Averroism became active at the University of Paris and elsewhere. Latin Averroists such as Siger of Brabant took the position that reason and revelation led to radically contrary conclusions. As Christians they accepted the teachings of the Church as ultimate truth, but as scholars they insisted that the conclusions of Aristotle and Averroës, being logically air-tight, were "philosophically necessary." This position came to be called the doctrine of the "two-fold truth."

The Latin Averroists shared with anti-intellectuals such as Damiani the belief that reason did not lead to the truth of revelation; they shared with Anselm and Aquinas the conviction that ultimate truth was revealed truth. Yet unlike most scholastics they abandoned altogether the effort to harmonize reason and revelation, and unlike the anti-intellectuals they did not reject philosophy but made it their profession. As believers they conceded the supremacy of dogma; as philosophers they insisted on the supremacy of reason. And although Siger of Brabant and most of his contemporaries appear to have held this awkward position in full sincerity, some of their successors became outright religious skeptics and only paid the necessary lip service to Christian doctrine. The fourteenth-century Latin Averroist John of Jaudun, for example, never lost an opportunity to poke subtle fun at any Christian dogma that seemed to him contrary to reason. On the subject of the Creation, John points out that according to reason the world has always existed. He concludes — with tongue in cheek — that as Christians we must nevertheless believe that God created the world; "Let it be added that creation very seldom happens; there has been only one, and that was a very long time ago."

Platonism-Augustinianism versus Aristotelianism

Thus, medieval thought produced a diversity of views on the proper relationship of reason and revelation. The same is true of the other two issues that we are to consider: the rivalry between Platonism and Aristotelianism, and the controversy over universals. The conflict between the intellectual systems of Plato-Augustine and Aristotle did not emerge clearly until the thirteenth century when the full body of Aristotle's writings came into the West in Latin translations from Greek and Arabic. Until then, most efforts at applying reason to faith were based on the Platonic tradition transmuted and transmitted by Augustine to medieval Europe. St. Anselm,

for example, was a dedicated Augustinian, as were many of his twelfth-century successors. The tradition was carried on brilliantly in the thirteenth century by the great Franciscan, St. Bonaventure. Many thoughtful Christians of the thirteenth century were deeply suspicious of the newly recovered Aristotelian writings, and the rise of Latin Averroism served to deepen their apprehensions. They regarded Aristotle as pagan in viewpoint and dangerous to the Faith. Other thirteenth-century intellectuals, such as St. Thomas Aquinas, were much too devoted to the goal of reconciling faith and reason to reject the works of a man whom they regarded as antiquity's greatest philosopher. St. Thomas sought to Christianize Aristotle much as Augustine had Christianized Plato and the Neoplatonists. In the middle decades of the thirteenth century, as high medieval philosophy was reaching its climax, the Platonic and Aristotelian traditions flourished side by side, and in the works of certain English scientific thinkers of the age they achieved a singularly fruitful fusion.

The Conflict over Universals

The contest between Platonism and Aristotelianism carried with it the seeds of yet another controversy: the argument over archetypes or universals. Plato had taught that terms such as "dog," "man," or "cat" not only described particular creatures but also had reality in themselves — that individual cats are imperfect reflections of a model cat, an archetypal or universal cat. Similarly, there are many examples of circles, squares, or triangles. Were we to measure these individual figures with sufficiently refined instruments we would discover that they were imperfect in one respect or another. No circle in this world is absolutely round. No square or triangle has perfectly straight sides. They are merely crude approximations of a perfect "idea." In "heaven," Plato would say, the perfect triangle exists. It is the source of the concept of triangularity that lurks in our minds and of all the imperfect triangles that we see in the phenomenal world. The heavenly triangle is not only perfect but *real*. The earthly triangles are less real, less significant, and less worthy of our attention. To take still another example, we call certain acts "good" because they partake, imperfectly, of a universal good which exists in heaven. In short, these universals—cat, dog, circle, triangle, beauty, goodness, etc.—exist apart from the multitude of individual dogs, cats, circles, triangles, and beautiful and good things in this world. And the person who seeks knowledge ought to meditate on these universals rather than study the world of phenomena in which they are only imperfectly reflected.

St. Augustine accepted Plato's theory of universals but not without amendment. Augustine taught that the archetypes existed in the mind of God rather than in Plato's abstract "heaven." And whereas Plato had ascribed our knowledge of the universals to dim memories from a prenatal existence, Augustine maintained that God puts a knowledge of universals directly into our minds by a process of "divine illumination." Plato and Augustine agreed, however, that the universal existed apart from the particular and, indeed, was *more real* than the particular. In the High

The continuing influence of Augustine. These two fifteenth-century illustrations portray the admiration of later generations of the faithful for the great Bishop of Hippo. In the portrait, Augustine is wearing the dress of his order under his episcopal cape, surrounded by monks to whom he is giving the books of prayer. At his feet lies Aristotle whose doctrine of the eternity of matter Augustine was believed to have satisfactorily refuted. The other is a miniature of the "City of God" from Augustine's work of that name. The upper enclosure is inhabited by saints who have been received into heaven; the lower enclosures each surround a group of people who are either preparing themselves for the heavenly kingdom by exercising Christian virtues or excluding themselves from it by committing one or another of the seven capital sins.

Middle Ages, those who followed the Platonic-Augustinian approach to universals were known as realists—they believed that universals were real.

The Aristotelian tradition brought with it another viewpoint on universals: they existed, to be sure, but only in the particular. Only by studying particular things in the world of phenomena could men gain a knowledge of universals. The human mind drew the universal from the particular by a process of abstraction. The universals were real, but in a sense less real—or at least less independently real—than Plato and Augustine believed. Accordingly, medieval philosophers who inclined toward the Aristotelian position have been called *moderate realists.*

Medieval philosophers were by no means confined to a choice between these two points of view. Several of them worked out subtle solutions of their own. As early as the eleventh century the philosopher Roscellinus declared that universals were not real at all. They were mere names that men gave to arbitrary classes of individual things. Reality was not to be found in universals but rather in the multiplicity and variety of objects which we can see, touch, and smell in the world around us. Those who followed Roscellinus in this view were known as *nominalists*—for them, the universals were *nomina*—"names." Nominalism remained in the intellectual background during the twelfth and thirteenth centuries but was revived in the fourteenth. Many churchmen regarded it as a dangerous doctrine, since its emphasis on the particular over the universal seemed to suggest that the Church was not, as Catholics believe, a single universal body but rather a vast accumulation of individual Christians.

St. Anselm

Having examined the great issues of high medieval philosophy—the relationship of reason to revelation, the relative validity and relevance of the Platonic-Augustinian

and Aristotelian systems of thought, and the problem of universals—we shall now see how they developed in the minds of individual philosophers between the eleventh and fourteenth centuries.

The scholastic philosophers first made their appearance in the later eleventh century and were products of the general reawakening that Europe was just then beginning to undergo. The earliest important figure in scholastic philosophy was St. Anselm (*c.* 1034–1109), the Italian intellectual who came to Bec in Normandy and later, as archbishop of Canterbury, brought the Investiture Controversy into England. During his eventful career he found time to write profoundly on a variety of philosophical and theological subjects.

As an Augustinian, Anselm took the realist position on the problem of universals. It was from Augustine, too, that he derived his attitude on the relationship of faith and reason. He taught that faith must precede reason, but that reason could serve to illuminate faith. His conviction that reason and faith were compatible made him a singularly important pioneer in the development of high medieval rationalism. He worked out several proofs of God, and in his important theological treatise, *Cur Deus Homo,* subjected the doctrines of the incarnation and atonement to rigorous logical analysis.

Anselm's emphasis on reason, employed within the framework of a firm Christian conviction, set the stage for the significant philosophical developments of the following generations. With Anselm, Western Christendom regained at last the intellectual level of the fourth-century Latin Doctors.

Abelard

The twelfth-century philosophers, intoxicated by the seemingly limitless possibilities of reason and logic, advanced boldly across new intellectual frontiers at the very time that their contemporaries were pushing forward the territorial frontiers of Europe. The most brilliant and audacious of these twelfth-century Christian rationalists was Peter Abelard (1079–1142), an immensely popular teacher, dazzling and egotistical, whose meteoric career ended in tragedy and defeat.

Abelard is perhaps best known for his love affair with the young Heloise, an affair that ended with Abelard's castration at the hands of thugs hired by Heloise's enraged uncle. The lovers then separated permanently, both taking monastic vows, and in later years Abelard wrote regretfully of the affair in his autobiographical *History of My Calamities*. There followed a touching correspondence between the two lovers in which Heloise, now an abbess, confessed her enduring love and Abelard, writing almost as a father confessor, offered her spiritual consolation but nothing more. Abelard's autobiography and the correspondence with Heloise survive to this day, providing modern students with a singularly intimate and tender picture of romance and pathos in a society far removed from our own.

Abelard was the supreme logician of the twelfth century. Writing several decades prior to the great influx of Aristotelian thought in Latin translation, he anticipated Aristotle's position on the question of universals by advocating a theory rather similar to Aristotle's moderate realism. Universals, Abelard believed, had no separate existence, but were derived from particular things by a process of abstraction. In a famous work entitled *Sic et Non* (*Yes and No*), Abelard collected opinions from the Bible, the Latin fathers, the councils of the Church, and the decrees of the papacy on a great variety of theological issues, demonstrating that these hallowed authorities very often disagreed on important religious matters. Others before him had collected authoritative opinions on various theological and legal issues, but never so thoroughly or systematically. Abelard, in his *Sic et Non*, employed a method of inquiry that was developed and perfected by canon lawyers and philosophers over the next several generations. We have already seen how the canonist Gratian, in his *Decretum*, used the technique of lining up conflicting authorities. But Abelard's successors sought to reconcile the contradictions and arrive at conclusions, whereas Abelard left many of the issues unresolved and thereby earned the enmity of his more conservative contemporaries. Abelard was a devoted Christian, if something of an intellectual show-off, but many regarded him as a dangerous skeptic. Thus he left himself open to bitter attacks by men such as St. Bernard who were deeply hostile to the Christian rationalist movement which he so flamboyantly exemplified. The brilliant teacher was hounded from one place to another. At length, his opinions were condemned by an ecclesiastical council in 1141. He died at Cluny, on his way to Rome to appeal the condemnation.

Peter Lombard and Hugh of Saint-Victor

But twelfth-century rationalism was far more than a one-man affair, and the persecution of Abelard failed to halt its growth. His student Peter Lombard (*c.* 1100–1160), for example, produced an important theological text, the *Book of Sentences*, which set off conflicting opinions on the pattern of the *Sic et Non*, but which, like Gratian's *Decretum*, took the further step of reconciling the contradictory authorities. Lombard's *Book of Sentences* remained for centuries a fundamental text in schools of theology.

The Augustinian tradition was best represented in Abelard's time at the school of Saint-Victor in Paris, and in particular by the distinguished scholar, Hugh of Saint-Victor (d. 1141). Hugh was a Christian rationalist, but he believed that reason was only the first step in man's approach to God. Beyond reason lay mysticism, and God could not be circumscribed by logic alone. Hugh and his school emphasized the subordination of the material to the spiritual, and—drawing on the ancient tradition of Biblical allegory—interpreted the entire natural world as a vast multitude of symbols pointing to spiritual truths.

John of Salisbury

The intellectual mood of the twelfth century was one of immense excitement at the possibilities of logic or dialectic. In this atmosphere, the remaining liberal arts—and especially the study of humanistic disciplines such as Latin literature—began to lose out in the competition. The cathedral school of Chartres was an important center of literary studies in the eleventh century and remained so throughout much of the twelfth. But as the century closed it began to fade before the onslaught of dialectic and the shift of students to the urban universities. The accomplished twelfth-century English scholar, John of Salisbury (c. 1115–1180), had studied under Abelard and also under the masters at Chartres. A scholar of Greek and a well-trained logician, John of Salisbury was above all a humanist—a student of classical literature. He approved of dialectic but regretted the fact that it was growing to the exclusion of all else; he complained that the schools were tending to produce narrow logicians rather than broadly educated men.

In his *Policraticus* (1159), John of Salisbury made a notable contribution to medieval political philosophy. Drawing on the thought of Classical Antiquity and the Early Middle Ages, he stressed the divine nature of kingship but emphasized equally its responsibilities and limitations. The king drew his authority from God, but was commissioned to rule for the good of his subjects rather than himself. He was bound to give his subjects peace and justice and to protect the Church. If he abused his commission and neglected his responsibilities, he lost his divine authority, ceased to be a king, and became a tyrant. As such he forfeited his subjects' allegiance and was no longer their lawful ruler Under extreme circumstances, and if all else failed,

John of Salisbury recommended tyrannicide. A good Christian subject, although obliged to obey his king, might kill a tyrant. Apart from the highly original doctrine of tyrannicide, the views expressed in the *Policraticus* reflect the general political attitudes of the twelfth century—responsible limited monarchy and government in behalf of the governed. These theories, in turn, were idealizations of the actual feudal monarchies of the day which were deterred from autocracy by the power of the nobility, the authority of the Church, and ancient custom.

The New Translations

In the later twelfth and early thirteenth centuries the movement of Christian rationalism was powerfully reinforced by the arrival of vast quantities of Greek and Arabic writings in Latin translation. Significant portions of the philosophical and scientific legacy of ancient Greece now became available to European scholars. Above all, the full Aristotelian corpus now came into the West through the labors of translators in Spain, Sicily, and the Latin Empire of Constantinople.

These translations were by no means fortuitous. They came in answer to a deep hunger on the part of Western thinkers for a fuller knowledge of the classical heritage in philosophy and science. The introduction of certain new Aristotelian works provoked a crisis in Western Christendom, for they contained implications which seemed hostile to the Faith. And with them, as we have seen, came the skeptical and intellectually impressive works of the Spaniard Averroës which gave rise to the corrosive doctrine of the "twofold truth." For a time it seemed as though reason and revelation were sundered, and the Church reacted in panic by condemning certain of Aristotle's writings. It was one of the major goals of St. Thomas Aquinas to refute the Latin Averroists—to rescue Aristotle and, indeed, reason itself for Western Christianity.

The Shape of Thirteenth-Century Thought

The thirteenth century—the century of St. Thomas—differed sharply in spirit from the twelfth. The philosophers of the twelfth century were intellectual pioneers undertaking a great adventure, advancing across new frontiers into virgin soil. They were daring, original, and often radical; their mood was one of youthful exploration. The thirteenth century, although by no means lacking in intellectual originality, was preeminently an age of consolidation and synthesis. Its scholars digested the insights and conclusions of the past and cast them into great comprehensive systems of thought. The characteristic products of the age were encyclopedias and summas. Vincent of Beauvais (d. 1264), attempted in his *Speculum Majus* to bring together all knowledge of all imaginable subjects into one immense compendium. At a much higher level, theologians such as Alexander of Hales (d. 1245), Albertus Magnus (1193–1280), and Thomas Aquinas (1225–1274) produced great systematic treatises on theology known as summas in which they gave majestic structure and unity to the theological speculations of their own and past ages.

St. Bonaventure

The thought of Aristotle loomed large in the thirteenth-century schools, but the Platonic-Augustinian tradition was well represented, too. There was a tendency for the Dominican scholars to espouse Aristotle, and the Franciscans to follow Plato and Augustine. Thus, the outstanding thirteenth-century exponent of Platonism-Augustinianism was the Franciscan St. Bonaventure (1221–1274), an Italian of humble origin who rose to become a cardinal of the Church and minister-general of the Franciscan order.

Bonaventure was at once a philosopher and a mystic. Following in the Augustinian tradition, he was a realist on the matter of universals and a rationalist who stressed the subordination of reason to faith. He accepted the nature symbolism of Hugh of Saint-Victor, and visualized the whole physical universe as a vast multitude of symbols pointing to God and glorifying Him. For example, he regarded everything in the natural world that could possibly be divided into three parts as a reflection of the Holy Trinity. Bonaventure's universe was eternally reaching upward toward the Divine Presence.

Bonaventure, like many of his intellectual predecessors and contemporaries, regarded the cosmos as an immense series of transparent concentric spheres. At its periphery, beyond the range of mortal eyes, were the nine spheres of angels. According to medieval theology, the angels were divided into nine ranks arranged hierarchically into three major groups, each containing three subgroups. As might be imagined, Bonaventure interpreted these three angelic triads as multiple symbols of the Trinity. Inside the spheres of angels was the sphere of stars which whirled daily round the earth. Within the stellar sphere were the spheres of the planets, sun, and moon. Such, in essence, had been Plato's conception of the universe, and Bonaventure remained faithful to it.

At the center of all the celestial spheres was the earth itself, and on the earth was man—the ultimate reason for the physical universe. Man was a creature of immense dignity and importance—the lord of the earth, the master of all lower creatures. The cosmos was created for man—to sustain him and, through its myriad symbols, to lead him to God. Indeed, it was for man that God himself died on the cross.

Man was at the fulcrum of creation. His body gave him kinship with beasts; his soul gave him kinship with the angels. The human soul was created in the image of the Trinity, with three components: intellect, will, and memory. Man perceived the physical universe through his senses, but he knew the spiritual world—the world of universals—through the grace of divine illumination. The road to God and to truth, therefore, lay in introspection, meditation, and worship, not in observation and experiment.

Bonaventure's philosophy is not coldly intellectual but warm, emotional, and deeply spiritual. His discussion of God's attributes becomes a litany—an act of worship. His emphasis is less on knowledge than on love, and his entire system of thought can be regarded as a prayer in praise of God.

The New Aristotelianism; St. Albertus Magnus

While Bonaventure was bringing new dimensions to traditional Platonism-Augustinianism, several of his contemporaries were coming to grips with the great Aristotelian-Averroistic challenge to orthodox Christian rationalism. The conflicting intellectual currents of the age were brilliantly represented by philosophers and theologians on the faculty of the University of Paris. There, teaching concurrently, were the Augustinian Bonaventure, the Latin Averroist Siger of Brabant, and the orthodox Aristotelians Albertus Magnus and Thomas Aquinas.

Albertus and his student, Thomas Aquinas, were both Dominicans, and both devoted themselves wholeheartedly to the reconciliation of reason and faith through the fusion of Aristotelianism and Christianity. They sought to confound the Latin Averroists by demonstrating that reason and revelation pointed to one truth, not two. A product of Germany, Albertus Magnus was a scholar of widely ranging interests who made important contributions to natural science—especially biology—as well as to philosophy and theology. He was a master of Aristotelian philosophy and a summa writer, whose goal was to purge Aristotle of the heretical taint of Averroism and transform his philosophy into a powerful intellectual foundation for

Christian orthodoxy. This audacious goal was brilliantly achieved, not by Albertus Magnus himself but by his still more gifted student, Thomas Aquinas

St. Thomas Aquinas

St. Thomas was born of a Norman-Italian noble family in 1225. His family intended him to become a Benedictine, but in 1244 he shocked them by joining the radical new Dominican Order. He went to the University of Paris in 1245 and spent the remainder of his life traveling, teaching, and writing. Unlike Augustine he had no youthful follies to regret. Unlike Anselm, Bernard, and Bonaventure, he played no great role in the political affairs of his day. His biography is agonizingly dull except possibly for an incident late in his life in which he abandoned his theological work, asserted that all his writings were worthless, and devoted his remaining days to mysticism. Shortly before his death he is reported to have risen off the ground while in a mystical trance. This act of levitation, if we can accept it, was a particularly noteworthy miracle in view of St. Thomas' marked corpulence during his later years. At his death, the priest who heard his final confession described it as being as innocent as that of a five-year-old child.

From the standpoint of intellectual history St. Thomas is a figure of singular interest and significance. In his copious writings—particularly his great comprehensive work, the *Summa Theologica*—he explored all the great questions of philosophy and theology, political theory and morality, using Aristotle's logical method and Aristotle's categories of thought but arriving at conclusions that were in complete harmony with the Christian faith. Like Abelard, St. Thomas assembled every possible argument, pro and con, on every subject that he discussed, but unlike Abelard he drew conclusions and defended them with cogent arguments. Few philosophers before or since have been so generous in presenting and exploring opinions contrary to their own, and none has been so systematic and exhaustive.

St. Thomas created a vast, unified intellectual system, ranging from God to the natural world, logically supported at every step. His theological writings have none of the fiery passion of St. Augustine, none of the literary elegance of Plato; rather, they have an *intellectual* elegance, an elegance of system and organization akin to that of Euclid. His *Summa Theologica* is organized into an immense series of separate sections, each section dealing with a particular philosophical question. In part I of the *Summa,* for example, Question II takes up the problem of God's existence. The *Question* is subdivided into three Articles: (1) "Whether God's existence is self-evident" (St. Thomas concludes that it is not), (2) "Whether it can be demonstrated that God exists" (St. Thomas concludes that it can be so demonstrated), and (3) "Whether God exists" (here St. Thomas propounds five separate proofs of God's existence).

In each article, St. Thomas takes up a specific problem and subjects it to a rigorous formal analysis. First, he presents a series of *Objections (Objection I, Objection II,* etc.) in which he sets forth as effectively as he possibly can all the arguments *contrary* to his final conclusion. For example, *Question II, Article III,* "Whether God exists," begins with two *Objections* purporting to demonstrate that God does not exist. One of them runs as follows:

Objection I. It seems that God does not exist, because if one of two contraries can be infinite, the other would be altogether destroyed. But the name "God" means that He is infinite goodness. Therefore, if God existed there would be no evil discoverable; but there is evil in the world. Therefore God does not exist.

After presenting the *Objections,* St. Thomas then turns to the second step in his analysis, the appeal to authority. This appeal is always introduced by the phrase,

The power of the Summa Theologica. *St. Thomas Aquinas, flanked by Plato and Aristotle, holds the* Summa *in his hands. The brilliant rays of its truth have struck down the heretical Averroës who lies at St. Thomas's feet.*

On the contrary, followed by a quotation from Scripture or from some authoritative patristic source which supports St. Thomas' own opinion on the subject. In the *Article* on God's existence, the *Objections* are followed by the statement, "On the contrary, It is said in the person of God: 'I am Who I am' (Exodus, iii, 14)." Having cited his authority, St. Thomas next appeals to reason and subjects the problem to his own logical scrutiny, beginning always with the formula, *I answer that.* ... For example, "I answer that, The existence of God can be proved in five ways," followed by a presentation of the five proofs of God:

The fifth way is taken from the governance of the world. We see that things which lack knowledge, such as natural bodies, act for an end, and this is evident from their acting always or nearly always in the same way, so as to obtain the best result. Hence it is clear that they achieve their end not only by chance but by design. Now whatever lacks knowledge cannot move toward an end unless it be directed by some being endowed with knowledge and intelligence, as the arrow is directed by the archer. Therefore some intelligent being exists by whom all natural things are directed to their end; and this being we call God.

The analysis concludes with refutations of the earlier *Objections*:

Reply to Objection I. As Augustine says, "Since God is the highest good, He would not allow any evil to exist in His works unless His omnipotence and goodness were such as to bring good even out of evil." This is part of the infinite goodness of God, that He should allow evil to exist, and out of it to produce good.

Having completed his analysis, St. Thomas then turns to the next *Article* or the next *Question* and subjects it to precisely the same process of inquiry: *Objections, On the contrary, I answer that* and *Reply to Objections*. And as in Euclidian geometry, so in Thomistic theology, once a problem is settled the conclusion can be used in solving subsequent problems. Thus the system grows, problem by problem, step by step, as St. Thomas' wide-ranging mind takes up such matters as the nature of God, the attributes of God, the nature and destiny of man, human morality, law, and political theory. The result is an imposing, comprehensive intellectual edifice embracing all major theological issues.

As the Gothic cathedral was the artistic embodiment of the high medieval world, so the philosophy of Aquinas was its supreme intellectual expression. Both were based on clear and obvious principles of structure. St. Thomas shared with the cathedral builders the impulse to display rather than disguise the structural framework of his edifice. Like the boldly executed Gothic flying buttress, the Thomistic *Questions,*

Articles, and Objections allowed no doubt as to what the builder was doing, where he was going, or how he was achieving his effects. The scholastics were nothing if not systematic—they loved to exhibit the underlying principles of their organization—and none carried this tendency farther than St. Thomas. It is not without reason that the *Summa Theologica* has been called a cathedral of thought.

As a devoted Christian and Aristotelian, Aquinas contended against both the Augustinians, who would reject Aristotle altogether, and the Latin Averroists, who would make a heretic of him. St. Thomas distinguished carefully between revelation and reason, but endeavored to prove that they could never contradict one another. Since human reason was a valid avenue to truth, since Christian revelation was undoubtedly authoritative, and since truth was one, then philosophy and Christian doctrine had to be compatible and complementary. "For faith rests upon infallible truth, and therefore its contrary cannot be demonstrated." This was the essence of St. Thomas' philosophical position. This was the conviction that separated him so radically from the Latin Averroists.

As against the Augustinianism of St. Anselm, Hugh of Saint-Victor, and St. Bonaventure, Aquinas emphasized the reality of the physical world as a world of things rather than symbols. Embracing the moderate realism of Aristotle, he declared that universals were to be found in the world of phenomena and nowhere else— that knowledge came from observation and analysis, not from divine illumination. Whereas Augustine, following Plato, had emphasized the *duality* of matter and spirit, earth and heaven, body and soul, Aquinas emphasized the *unity* of God's creation. He asserted the unity of ideas and phenomena —the universal was not outside the particular but within it—and thus he shared with St. Francis and others the notion that the physical world was deeply significant in itself, that matter mattered. He affirmed the unity of intellectual knowledge and sensation, maintaining that knowledge is acquired by a gradual ascent from things to concepts, from the visible to the invisible world. He stressed the unity of man, declaring that a human being was not a soul using a body or a spirit imprisoned in flesh, as the Platonists suggested, but an inseparable composite of body and soul. The human body, although a source of temptation, was good in itself and was an essential part of man.

Likewise, the state, which previous Christian thinkers had commonly regarded as a necessary evil — an unfortunate but indispensable consequence of the Fall of Adam — was accepted by Aquinas as a good and natural outgrowth of man's social impulse. He echoed Aristotle's dictum that "Man is a political animal," and regarded the justly governed state as a fitting part of the Divine Order. Like John of Salisbury, St. Thomas insisted that kings must govern in their subjects' behalf and that a willful, unrestrained ruler who ignored God's moral imperatives was no king but a tyrant. Just as the human body could be corrupted by sin, the body politic could be corrupted by tyranny. But although the Christian must reject both sin and tyranny, he should nevertheless revere the body, the state, and indeed all physical creation as worthy products of God's will, inseparable from the world of the spirit, and essential ingredients in the unity of existence.

Such was the Thomistic vision. In binding together matter and spirit, the concrete and the abstract, body and soul, God and man, Aquinas was seeking to encompass the totality of being in a vast existential unity. At the center of this majestic system was God, the author of physical and spiritual creation, the maker of heaven and earth, who himself assumed human form and redeemed mankind on the Cross, who discloses portions of the truth to man through revelation, permits him to discover other portions through the operation of his intellect, and will lead him into all truth through salvation. Ultimately, truth is God Himself, and it is man's destiny, upon reaching heaven, to stand unshielded in the divine presence — to love and to know. Thus the roads of St. Thomas, St. Bonaventure, St. Bernard, and Dante, although passing over very different terrain, arrived finally at the same destination. It is not so very surprising, after all, that in the end St. Thomas rejected the way of the philosopher for the way of the mystic.

Critics of St. Thomas: Duns Scotus

To this day there are men of keen intelligence who accept the philosophy of St. Thomas. On the other hand, many of his own thirteenth-century contemporaries rejected it in whole or in part, and it remained a source of intense controversy in the centuries that followed. Franciscan intellectuals such as Bonaventure were particularly suspicious of the intellectual *tour de force* of this gifted Dominican. Bonaventure was a rationalist, but in a far more limited sense than was Aquinas, and Bonaventure's Franciscan successors came increasingly to the opinion that reason was of little or no use in probing metaphysical problems. The Scottish Franciscan, Duns Scotus (d. 1308), undertook a rigorous and subtle critique of St. Thomas' theory of knowledge. Although he by no means rejected the possibility of supplementing and elucidating revealed truth through reason, he was more cautious in using it than Aquinas had been. Whereas St. Thomas is called "The Angelic Doctor," Duns Scotus is known as "The Subtle Doctor," and the almost tortured complexity of his thought prompted men in subsequent generations to describe anyone who bothered to follow Duns' arguments as a "dunce." The sobriquet is unfair, for Duns Scotus is an important and original figure in the development of late scholasticism. Nevertheless, one is tempted to draw a parallel between the intricacies of his intellectual system and the overly elaborate late-Gothic churches. A Christian rationalist of the most subtle kind, he nevertheless made the first move toward dismantling the Thomist synthesis and withdrawing reason from the realm of theology.

William of Ockham

In the field of philosophy, as in so many other areas, the synthesis and equilibrium of the High Middle Ages began to disintegrate with the coming of the fourteenth century. In the hands of the brilliant English Franciscan, William of Ockham (c. 1300–1349), reason and revelation were divorced altogether. Christian doctrine, Ockham said, could not be approached by reason at all but had to be accepted on faith. The Thomist synthesis was a mirage. Reason's province was the natural world and that alone. Thus, Ockham was a pietist on matters of faith—a firm Christian believer—but a man who employed his keen philosophical mind to emasculate reason and challenge the whole Christian rationalist position of the High Middle Ages. There was no metaphysics; there was no rational theology. God could neither be proved nor defined but only accepted. Reason could not be elevated beyond the world of the senses.

Science

Robert Grosseteste

The Ockhamist position represents a distinctive combination of empiricism and mysticism. Both these elements had been present among the Franciscans of the thirteenth century. The mysticism of a Bonaventure represents one pole of Franciscan thought. At the other pole stands a group of important scientific thinkers who applied their logical tools to the humble but significant task of investigating the natural world. Thirteenth-century Oxford became the leading center of scientific investigation, and it was here that western European science came of age.

The key figure in the development of medieval science was the great English scholar, Robert Grosseteste (1168–1253), who, although not a Franciscan himself, was chief lecturer to the Franciscans at Oxford. Grosseteste was on intimate terms with Platonic and Neoplatonic philosophy, Aristotelian physics, and the rich scientific legacy of Islam. At bottom, he was a Platonist and an Augustinian, but he wrote important commentaries on the scientific works of Aristotle and was able to draw on both traditions. From Plato he derived the notion that mathematics is a basic key to understanding the physical universe; the fundamental importance of numbers is very much in keeping with the Platonic realist interpretation of universals, and Plato himself had once asserted that "God is a mathematician." From Aristotle he learned the importance of abstracting knowledge from the world of phenomena by means of observation and experiment. Thus, bridging the two great traditions, Grosseteste brought together the mathematical and experimental components that together underlie the rise of modern science. More than that, drawing on the suggestive work of his Islamic predecessors he worked out a far more rigorous experimental procedure than is to be found in the pages of Aristotle. An outstanding pioneer in the development of scientific method, he outlined a system of observation, hypothesis, and experimental verification that was elaborated by his successors into the methodological technique which modern physical scientists still employ.

Like other pioneers, Grosseteste followed many false paths. He was better at formulating a scientific methodology than in applying it to specific problems, and his explanations of such phenomena as heat, light, color, comets, and rainbows were rejected in later centuries. But the experimental method which he formulated was to become in time a powerful intellectual tool. The problem of the rainbow, for example, was solved by the fourteenth-century scientist Theoderic of Freiburg who employed a refined version of Grosseteste's experimental methodology. The great triumphs of European science lay far in the future, but with the work of Robert Grosseteste the basic scientific tool had been forged. Grosseteste's career illustrates not that science was born in the thirteenth century but rather that scientific thought evolved gradually from antiquity to modern times, and that the High Middle Ages contributed markedly to its development.

Roger Bacon

Grosseteste's work was carried further by his famous disciple, the Oxford Franciscan Roger Bacon (*c.* 1214–1294). The author of a fascinating body of scientific sense and nonsense, Roger Bacon was more an advocate of experimental science than a consistent practitioner of it. He dabbled in the mysteries of alchemy and astrology, and his boundless curiosity carried him along many strange roads. He led a turbulent life, at times enjoying the friendship of the papacy, at other times imprisoned by his own Franciscan order which suspected him of practicing magic. Roger Bacon was critical of the deductive logic and metaphysical speculations that so intrigued his scholastic contemporaries: "Reasoning," he wrote, "does not illuminate these matters; experiments are required, conducted on a large scale, performed with instruments and by various necessary means."

At his best, Roger Bacon was almost prophetic:

Experimental science controls the conclusions of all other sciences. It reveals truths which reasoning from general principles would never have discovered. Finally, it starts us on the way to marvelous inventions which will change the face of the world.

One such marvelous invention, the telescope, was not to be invented for another three centuries, yet Roger Bacon described it in astonishing detail:

We can give such figures to transparent bodies, and dispose them in such order with respect to the eye and the objects, that the rays will be refracted and bent toward any place we please, so that we will see the object near at hand or at a distance, under any angle we wish. And thus from an incredible distance we may read the smallest letters, and may number the smallest particles of dust and sand, by reason of the greatness of the angle under which we see them. . . . The sun, moon, and stars may be made to descend hither in appearance, and to be visible over the heads of our enemies, and many things of a like sort which persons unacquainted with such matters would refuse to believe.

The Medieval Intellectual Achievement

Thus, the intense intellectual activity of the thirteenth century produced both the supreme synthesis of Christian rationalism in the philosophy of St. Thomas and the genesis of a new method of scientific inquiry in the thought of Robert Grosseteste and his successors. In the realm of the intellect, as in so many others, the thirteenth century was both synthetic and creative.

With the coming of the fourteenth century, the growth of scientific thought was accompanied by the gradual erosion of the Thomist synthesis. Universal systems such as that of St. Thomas have seldom been lasting, but for a few brief years Thomism represented, for many, the perfect fusion of intellect and belief. As such, it takes its place alongside the Gothic cathedral, the *Divine Comedy* of Dante, and the piety of St. Francis as a supreme and mature expression of high medieval culture.

Conclusion

The world of the High Middle Ages is described in some outworn textbooks as stagnant, gloomy, and monolithic. At the other extreme, it has been portrayed as an ideally constituted society, free of modern fears and tensions, where men of all classes could live happily and creatively, finding fulfillment in their service to the common good. In reality, it was an age of vitality, of striking contrasts, of dark fears and high hopes, of poverty that was often brutal yet gradually diminishing. Above all, it was an age in which Europeans awoke to the rich variety of possibilities that lay before them. A thirteenth-century poet, in his celebration of springtime, captured perfectly the spirit of this awakening:

> The earth's ablaze again
> With lustrous flowers.
> The fields are green again,
> The shadows, deep.
> Woods are in leaf again,
> And all the world
> Is filled with joy again.
> This long-dead land
> Now flames with life again.
> The passions surge,
> Love is reborn,
> And beauty wakes from sleep.

SELECTED READINGS

*Copleston, F. C., *Medieval Philosophy,* Harper, New York, 1961.
　　A popular introduction by a leading scholar.

*Haskins, C. H., *The Renaissance of the Twelfth Century,* Meridian, New York.
　　An epoch-making book, particularly strong in the area of Latin literature.

*Haskins, C. H., *The Rise of the Universities,* Cornell University Press, Ithaca, New York, 1957.
　　Short, highly competent, and a pleasure to read.

*Knowles, David, *The Evolution of Medieval Thought,* Vintage, New York.
　　A lucid survey of medieval intellectual history, sympathetic, judicious, and readable.

*Leff, Gordon, *Medieval Thought,* Penguin, Baltimore, Md.
　　A good survey which emphasizes the development of metaphysics.

*Lewis, C. S., *The Allegory of Love: A Study in Medieval Tradition,* Oxford University Press, New York, 1936.
　　An illuminating, beautifully written study of courtly love and the medieval Romance.

McIlwain, C. H., *The Growth of Political Thought in the West,* The Macmillan Co., New York.
　　The classic one-volume account of medieval political theory.

*Milano, Paolo, ed., *The Portable Dante,* Viking, New York.
　　Good translations of *The Divine Comedy* and other works.

*Panofsky, Erwin, *Gothic Architecture and Scholasticism,* Meridian, New York.
　　A challenging study which endeavors to demonstrate lines of connection between these two great medieval enterprises.

Pegis, Anton C., translator, *Introduction to St. Thomas Aquinas,* Modern Library, New York.
　　Intelligently chosen selections together with a stimulating introduction.

Rashdall, Hastings, *The Universities of Europe in the Middle Ages,* F. M. Powicke and A. B. Emden, editors, Oxford University Press, New York, 1936, 3 vols.
　　This is the great, definitive treatment of the subject.

*Sayers, D. L., translator, *The Song of Roland,* Penguin, Baltimore, Md.
　　A good new translation of the famous medieval epic.

Southern, R. W., *St. Anselm and his Biographer,* Cambridge University Press, New York, 3 vols. (revised).
　　A splendid study of St. Anselm and his contemporary biographer, Eadmer of Canterbury, which casts much light on monastic thought and life in the great age of Benedictinism.

*Ullmann, Walter, *A History of Political Thought: The Middle Ages,* Penguin, Baltimore, Md.
　　A short synthetic work which stresses the ideology of the papal monarchy and points to the medieval background of modern political thought.

*Waddell, Helen, *Medieval Latin Lyrics,* Penguin, Baltimore, Md., 1963.
　　Sensitive translations of lyric poems.

Asterisk (*) denotes paperback.

D

CENTURIES OF CRISES

13

The Renaissance 1300–c. 1520

Why We Use the Word, Renaissance

Literally, "Renaissance" means rebirth. Its usage for the fourteenth and fifteenth centuries stems from Italian humanists who believed that the centuries following the fall of Rome had been dominated by "barbarians." By way of contrast, their own age marked a wonderful revival of classical learning and art. Around 1435, Palmieri of Florence was thanking God for being "born in this new age, so full of hope and promise." Not all of this optimism proved sustainable, for events betrayed part of it. But Italian humanists had created the concept of historical periods subsequently adopted by Western educators. Modern authors who have shared the humanists' disdain for the Middle Ages extended the concept of rebirth to apply to almost all phases of human activity during

this era. In 1860, a German-Swiss historian, Jacob Burckhardt, popularized this view in a famous book, *The Civilization of the Renaissance in Italy.* He wrote that the Renaissance was a "golden age" of beauty and individualism, when aesthetic considerations so dominated the minds of men that even making war or building a state became a work of art. Burckhardt's followers insisted that the Renaissance was a crucial turning point in Western history, that a new civilization no longer medieval but recognizably modern came into being. Their influence on historical writing has been so strong that even those who think that the modern world was not born so early usually use the term, Renaissance, as a matter of convenience.

Romantics who idolize the Middle Ages and many modern scholars have tried to deny that a rebirth actually occurred. Especially since the 1920s, historians have been trying to disprove Burckhardt's interpretation. Upon close examination, they say, the break with the Middle Ages was not so sharp as the humanists and Burckhardt thought. Some have even found a preponderance of traditional darkness—or at least tradition—during the Renaissance. And they have made their point. Medieval ways and institutions had great staying power. For example, the aristocracy which had dominated medieval institutions proved resilient enough to overcome the challenge of the urban middle classes. But to prevail, the aristocracy had to adopt new ways and to rely on new, more authoritarian governments which themselves were novelties. Thus the Renaissance was an age of transition, and some of its changes anticipated more recent events.

In order to study that transition we shall examine in turn the changes that occurred in three important areas. First, we shall trace in some detail the major developments in learning and the arts, those parts of civilization that are the most malleable to man's hand, where changes are highly visible. It is only in this area that we can apply the concept, Renaissance. Humanists and artists self-consciously used classical models to express new attitudes toward learning, man, society, and nature. Second, we shall study the great secular institutions and activities, the Renaissance states, politics, societies, and economies. Changes in this area during the two centuries concerned were gradual and, for the most part, very slight. Third, we shall examine the grave problems affecting the Church, for conditions leading to a religious explosion, the Reformation, were created during the Renaissance.

Learning

The revival of classical philosophy, law, and science had made substantial advances in the Late Middle Ages. During the Renaissance, revival also spread to rhetoric, poetry, and especially to history.

The medieval revival of classical studies had been carried out by Churchmen. The vastly broadened revival that took place during the Renaissance was mainly the work of laymen. Humanists propagated classical, moral, and aesthetic standards as the code of an educated and social elite. The strongest lay influence, however, came not from humanists but from officials of the territorial and dynastic states who were trained in law. These officials also censored the new printing press, which, had it been free of political and religious controls, might have extensively democratized literary culture.

Vernacular Literature and Literary Naturalism

The cultural unity of medieval Europe rested upon the use of a common language of learning, administration, and liturgy —ecclesiastical Latin. Vernacular dialects —usually the language of political administration and royal courts—achieved written stature as competitors with Latin in the thirteenth and fourteenth centuries. In the Spanish kingdoms, Castilian—a blend of Germanic, Latin, and some Moorish elements—gained ascendancy as the language of affairs. English, a composite of Anglo-Saxon and Norman French as spoken in Middlesex, was required in the courts and used in most official documents by the middle of the fourteenth century.

The most influential late medieval vernacular was Parisian French. Although local dialects vied with it, as the language of the French court it became the literary pacesetter and the language of much business as well. Later Tuscan, the spoken Latin of the Italian peninsula and the language of the most advanced commercial areas of the Middle Ages, began to set literary standards. German was slower to crystallize. High Saxon was used by most local princely courts after the middle of the fourteenth century. Except for a temporary period of Czech religious and political agitation during the late fourteenth and fifteenth centuries, the Slavic and Ural-Altaic languages of Eastern Europe failed to achieve literary status until the nineteenth century.

In Italy, the great poet Dante (1265–1321) made a remarkable use of the Tuscan dialect as a literary language. His life span and his works are often seen as bridging the Middle Ages and the Renaissance. His greatest work, the *Divine Comedy*, was medieval in that it was a religious allegory and relegated natural science (and many Florentine businessmen) to the Inferno. But he put Boniface VIII there too. And he gave expression to the notion that feminine beauty and goodness could exercise a regenerative influence. It was an idealized woman, Beatrice, who led him into Paradise – a far cry from the monastic ideal and the Fall of Man.

Dante's claims to fame were advertised and the Tuscan tongue further developed by Francesco Petrarch (1303–1374) and Giovanni Boccaccio (1313–1375). Though both were humanists dedicated to classical learning, their principal literary impact came from Petrarch's poetry and Boccaccio's *Decameron*. Petrarch continued Dante's theme of feminine inspiration (Laura), to whom his sonnets, which became classic models imitated in Italy and Europe, were dedicated. The uneasiness he felt in breaking with traditional ascetic norms was not shared by his friend, Boccaccio. The Paris-born illegitimate son of a Florentine merchant, Boccaccio flaunted traditional respectability in his frankly naturalistic and hedonistic *Decameron*. Returning to Florence from the sophisticated, cosmopolitan court of Naples (where his subsequent feminine literary inspiration, Fiametta, had been his mistress), Boccaccio witnessed the horrors of the Black Death which provided indirectly for the *Decameron's* setting. Seven fashionable young men and women from Florence pass their

time in a secluded refuge relating tales which Boccaccio culled from popular lore. Satirical, witty, full of situations involving artful defenses of virtue and more frequent yieldings to infidelity, Boccaccio's "Human Comedy" set down the realism, actual or touched-up, of Florence. In common with other bourgeois literati of the times, he pilloried the clergy and the Church for their hypocrisy. In one tale the idea of the equal validity of Christianity, Judaism, and Mohammedanism is introduced. In another a Jew returning from a trip to Rome is converted to Christianity on the grounds that any institution so degenerate could only have survived so long with divine assistance! Like other urban anticlerics, Boccaccio made no formal break with the Church; later he regretted the *Decameron's* tone. Nevertheless it struck popular fancy by artfully handling subjects more often discussed than written. His naturalistic tone was echoed throughout Europe in the writings of Chaucer, Rabelais, and many others. Meanwhile, as Italian society became more aristocratic, Northern feudal themes found expression in popular literature. When influential Italian reappeared in the early sixteenth century, it was dominated by crusade adventures, Italianized versions of the French *Song of Roland* (Ariosto's *Orlando Furioso*, for example), and manuals of the art of being a proper courtier.

Italian served as a model for subsequent Northern vernacular naturalism. In the Middle English of London and the court, Geoffrey Chaucer (1340–1400) drew upon a busy life of affairs, French and Italian literary contacts, and late medieval lore to produce *The Canterbury Tales*. Chaucer initiated the first tradition of vernacular English realism, a tradition which culminated in Shakespeare in the sixteenth century.

French chronicles and poetry tended to be chivalric and medieval in subject matter. But secular elements of love, anticlericism, and even the debunking of crusades and fraudulent relics were represented. After the Hundred Years' War, François Villon (1432–1463) left a great and a small *Testament* of the world of thieves and harlots, of sickness and want, of death, dungeons, and the expectation of execution. A century later such lower class naturalism had yielded to the aristocratic learning of court and learned letters, represented by Marguerite of Navarre and François Rabelais (1490–1553).

By the sixteenth century the vernacular languages had established themselves as the media of creative literature, while Latin remained the language of learning. Vernacular languages helped emphasize political boundaries; Latin was international. In its revived classical form, Latin was the medium of expression of the humanists.

Italian and Spanish Humanism

Consistent with the belief that their age marked a new departure from the medieval past was the heralding by Italian humanists of a "revival of learning." By learning they meant largely the Roman—later also some Greek—classics whose content and attitudes had flourished in an earlier urban culture. Classical humanism rapidly became a movement. Its contagiousness grew among the many educated laymen who hungered for a secular, practical ethic. Medieval scholars had also used the classics widely, but they had subordinated them to theology and scholastic philosophy or had borrowed legal and scientific data from them as final statements of an eternal universal order. Humanists whose manuscript discoveries immensely expanded the body of available classical writings approached them with a different intent and purpose. The "revival of learning" was thus not so much the rediscovery of a new set of authorities as a different appreciation of the meaning and usage of pagan antiquity.

Generally recognized as the first to give classical studies a new turn was Petrarch, a notary living in the Florentine colony at papal Avignon. In classical literature,

especially in Cicero's writings, he found his model of literary style and moral philosophy. Noting that Cicero had been at once an active statesman and a recluse Stoic philosopher, Petrarch turned his attention to "civic humanism." Here he made a lasting contribution to the moral philosophy of involvement in political affairs.

Conceiving of religion as moral philosophy rather than knowledge of doctrine, he saw no conflict between Cicero and Christ. But his quest for fame and his exaltation of ideal womanhood in his vernacular sonnets brought him into conscious conflict with traditional ascetic ideals. He set down the tensions generated by this conflict in his *Soul's Secret,* a hypothetical exchange of letters with St. Augustine, who himself had abandoned classical wisdom for doctrinal and institutional Christianity. Petrarch agreed with the great other-worldly theologian on many points, but he insisted upon living in one world at a time.

There is a certain justification of my way of life [he wrote to Augustine]. It may be only glory that we seek here. . . . Another glory awaits us in heaven and he who reaches there will not wish to even think of earthly fame. So this is the natural order, that among mortals the care of things mortal should come first; to the transitory will then succeed the eternal; from the first to the second is the natural progression.[1]

Although Petrarch affirmed the validity of contemplative ideals his successors, inflamed by his enthusiasm for classical studies, put increasing weight on the saint's "earthly city" as against his "heavenly city."

But it was via Boccaccio that Cicero's civic humanism and standards of style were transmitted to Florence, where they found their fullest development between 1375 and 1450. After Boccaccio's death in

---

1. Quoted by John Herman Randall, Jr., *The Making of the Modern Mind,* Rev. ed., Houghton Mifflin Co., Cambridge, Mass., 1940, pp. 118–119.

1375, leading Florentines formed study groups to re-examine the classics. They collected libraries and manuscripts, and, beginning with Coluccio Salutati (1331–1406), installed a succession of distinguished humanist chancellors. This venture in civic humanism served as a rationale for the Florentine elite to use their talents and leisure for the advancement of the common weal of the republic. For the most part, their ideals were culled from their study of classical history and moral philosophy. Preeminent among them was the development of well-rounded men of universal accomplishments, strength of character in adversity, possession of fortune or luck's favor, and the ability to wield power.

Florentine civic humanism became most secular and utilitarian at the hands of Leonardo Bruni (1370–1444). As chancellor he promoted educational practices designed to create citizens rather than scholars. For patriotic purposes he wrote a legend-purged and naturalistic history of the city. However worthy such efforts as these were, they could flourish only in a republic. Eventually the institutional basis of their ideology atrophied when Florence became a Medicean principality. Sixteenth-century Venice, whose leading families belatedly adopted humanism, preserved some aspects of its outlook. But for the most part civic humanism was a transient phenomenon of the Renaissance confined to one city, Florence, and even there it lasted for less than a century.

While activist republican humanism was running its course, classical scholarship matured in knowledge and method to the point where it became a potentially explosive cultural and intellectual force. Boccaccio contributed to a deeper knowledge by compiling biographies of famous men and women, a genealogy of the gods, and a classical geography. With all the enthusiasm of prospectors caught up in the fervor of a gold rush, traveling scholars combed monastic libraries and Eastern cities for the manuscripts of classical authors. Some devoted their energies to inscriptions, archeology, architecture, and coinage. Visiting Eastern Orthodox Church dignitaries taught Italians Greek language and philosophy, especially Platonic philosophy. In addition to learning Latin and Greek in their ancient styles, humanist scholars, the better to cope with deviating texts and copyist errors, developed historical philology and a respect for pure sources. Unlike the scholastics who used multiple allegorical meanings for passages picked out of historical context, they learned to rely upon a single literal, historical meaning within a specific context.

Enamored with the clarity and forcefulness of ancient expression as compared with contemporary "barbarous" Latin, the humanists became zealous advocates of pure style. But the implications of their methodology and knowledge reached much deeper than the training of stylists. The career of Lorenzo Valla (1405–1457) illustrates this. As a young teacher, rhetorician, and philologist, he was employed in 1433 by King Alfonso of Naples who, like many another prince, was an enemy of the pope. Before he had been long in his job, Valla conclusively demonstrated from internal evidence that the Donation of Constantine, a purported cession of central Italy to the papacy in the fourth century, was in fact a fabrication of the ninth century. This exposé Valla followed with a demonstration that the Apostles' Creed originated in Nicean rather than apostolic times.

Valla's method of going to the sources armed with philological and historical erudition undercut much traditional authority not only by unmasking errors but also by inculcating a sense of historical perspective. For the new literary historical method introduced the novel idea of *anachronism,* something utterly foreign to previous thought which had dealt with timeless universals and authority. To the idea of going back to pure sources was also linked the idea of return to a period of previous ecclesiastical or ethical purity as a standard or norm.

In addition to the employment of a revolutionary method, Italian humanists differed from traditional theologians and scholastics in posing a different set of significant questions. Most of them totally eschewed metaphysics, formal theology, and preoccupation with death. Rather they were concerned with practical questions of human relationships. Because they ignored theology they found no conflict between ancient pagan philosophers and Christianity. Though they taught rational restraint, they considered nature good— worthy of enjoyment and artistic imitation. Religion was a part of nature. All but a few denounced monasticism or monastic vows, but rarely did a humanist abjure the Church. They found divinity less in sacrament or priest than in worldly or classical beauty. To most Northern humanists as well as later religious reformers, whether Catholic or Protestant, the aesthetic, political, and social morality of Italian humanism appeared pagan.

Italian humanists made their greatest impact as educators. If they were mistrustful of logic and abstract philosophy, they were downright scornful of law and science. For these disciplines they substituted rhetoric, grammar, poetry, history, and purified classical languages. Mathematics, physical education, and music also received attention. The emphasis upon classical language and perfected style tended to make humanist scholarship a cult with high admission requirements, particularly as they began to look down upon vernacular languages. As late as the nineteenth century, classical education was a mark of achievement and status in Western countries.

Obviously not all products of humanist schools became scholars. The fact that humanism became a movement of general social importance is probably best explained by the availability of positions open to men trained in style and rhetorical persuasion. Most boys with classical educations found employment with the Church, princes, or aristocracy. Many were employed as the equivalents of modern press agents to present their employers' cases persuasively. As historians, they frequently wrote commissioned and biased accounts, or graced their patron's heroic deeds with impossible classical orations.

The nature of patronage and educational opportunities helped shape the course of late Italian humanism. As republics declined, civic humanism waned or adjusted to courtly surroundings. In Florence, Lorenzo de Medici founded a formal school of philosophy, the Platonic Academy headed successively by Ficino and Pico della Mirandola. Though both espoused free will and the dignity of man, both exalted a contemplative over an active life. Rising despotism and a feeling of helplessness in the face of foreign invasion after 1494 made faith in man's ability to use institutions for human improvement difficult to sustain. Witchhunts and Savonarola's rise to power in 1490 (he was a puritanical Dominican who attacked humanism as sheer paganism) demonstrated how slight a hold the humanists had on Florence. As Florentine republicans became disillusioned cynics, the typical ideal which emerged from the Italian Renaissance was the refined, well-rounded courtier, witty in repartee, appreciative of feminine beauty, and adept at arms. Count Baldassare Casti-

A spellbinder: Savonarola preaching, 1496.

glione (1478–1529), a product of the polished courts and diplomatic service of Milan and Mantua, gave classic and much imitated expression to the new courtly ideal of the secularly and classically educated chivalric gentleman in *The Courtier* (written 1508, published in 1529).

In Spain tradition blunted the impact of secular humanism. There, philological and linguistic studies which spread rapidly during the reign of Ferdinand and Isabella were strictly subordinated to theology. This diluted brand of humanism culminated in the career of Ximenes, head of the Spanish Inquisition, and regent upon Ferdinand's death. Ximenes was responsible for the founding and reform of several universities, notably Alcala. The faculties in these schools devoted a third of their instructional time to language and literature as auxiliaries to theology. Ximenes' crowning philological achievement was a Polyglot Bible. To allow textual comparison, the Scriptures were presented in original languages set up in parallel columns. Other Spanish humanists such as Juan Luis Vives (1492–1540) proved more receptive to the advanced doctrines of Erasmus of Rotterdam. But under Inquisition pressures to conform to scholastic tradition, they either emigrated or were silenced. As political master of Italy during the Catholic Reformation, Spain effectively stifled secular Italian humanism.

Northern Humanism

The force of contemplative, religious, and chivalric humanism was felt, by the end of the Italian Renaissance, in the more aristocratic and religiously oriented parts of Northern Europe. But Northern humanism did not become a carbon copy of Italian models. Local traditions and the vagaries of individual humanists filtered and modified their impact. Nor was Northern humanism more of one temper than Italian humanism. In general, it was less aesthetic and secular; in particular, philology and the content of the classics were more subordinated to religion and metaphysics. Northern humanists were also less antagonistic toward scholasticism and the study and practice of Roman law.

Ultimately France, the hearth of medieval scholasticism, responded creatively to Italian humanism, especially after the French invasion of Italy in 1494. The royal court of Francis I and especially of his sister, Marguerite of Navarre, patronized the "new learning" most of whose early devotees sought a fusion of traditionalism, religious mysticism, and classical forms. Prominent among these were Lefèbvre d'Étaples, Guillaume Briçonnet, bishop of Meaux, and Guillaume Budé, all of whom flourished around the turn of the sixteenth century. They spurned secularism and devoted their energies to religion based upon the classics and Scripture. In particular, they de-emphasized the sacraments and exalted conduct as the essence of Christianity. In phrases such as salvation by "faith alone," they seemed to anticipate Protestantism. Actually, their fundamental assumptions concerning human dignity and free will were quite different from the premises of depravity and bondage held by Luther and Calvin.

Alongside this strain of French thought ran the secular naturalism of François Rabelais, physician and humanist, whose *Gargantua and Pantagruel* pilloried scholasticism and proposed an ideal coeducational "monastery" system in which universal learning and disciplined will power would set all rules. Stoicism, which identified virtue with happiness and wisdom with prudence, was also widespread in French humanist circles.

German humanism had roots in a variety of institutions: the imperial court of the fifteenth century, the schools of the Brethren of the Common Life, and the elite families of the imperial cities. Colored by romantic cultural nationalism it refuted the Italian charge that Northern barbarians, by exalting Germanic heroes, had ruined classical culture during the Middle Ages. Some

VTOPIAE INSVLAE FIGVRA

Title page from More's Utopia, *a place where all's well because all men are good.*

England also developed a strain of religious humanism that drew inspiration from the late Italian Renaissance. John Colet returned from Italy to lecture (1496) on the Scriptures, particularly the letters of St. Paul. Of greater fame was another English townsman, Thomas More (1478–1535), a lawyer and classically educated layman who served the first two Tudor monarchs, Henry VII and Henry VIII. An ascetic more devoted to redemptive religion than to the classics, More published a mocking satire on contemporary England, *Utopia,* which was also a sketch of an ideal society. In this and other writings More advocated limited tolerance, a warm sympathy for the lower classes, and a concept of limited government. As an official his practice did not always correspond to his theoretical views. He was ultimately caught between loyalty to Henry VIII as head of the English church and loyalty to the Roman Church. Opting for the latter, he became a martyr, and was canonized in the twentieth century.

Erasmus

Far overshadowing the reputations and influence of all other contemporary Northern and Italian humanists, with most of whom he kept in one or another kind of contact, was the cosmopolitan "prince of the humanists," Erasmus of Rotterdam (1467?–1536).

An orphaned illegitimate son of a priest, educated at the Deventer school of the Brethren of the Common Life, Erasmus was sent by guardians to a monastery. Thereafter he became an episcopal secretary, a theology student at the University of Paris, and a nomadic scholar. Attracted early by the classics and the works of Lorenzo Valla, he rejected contemporary scholasticism (though not Thomas Aquinas) and spent the remainder of his life outside cloister walls. A trip to England in 1500 resulted in lasting patronage contacts and friendship with Thomas More and John Colet, who encouraged him to follow a

German humanists upheld scholasticism and were trained in civil or canon law or both. Most were primarily interested in religious reform. Although they usually defined religion more as deeds than creeds, they rejected the "paganism" of the Italian Renaissance. The most accomplished German humanist was Johann Reuchlin (1455–1522), a jurist and professor who mastered not only Greek and Latin but also Hebrew literature.

Reuchlin's works touched off a celebrated controversy between advocates of "good letters," and traditionalists who indicted him (unsuccessfully) before the Inquisition. In his defense, Erfurt humanists satirized the ignorance, credulity, and petty doctrinal preoccupations of Reuchlin's monkish opponents in the *Letters of Obscure Men,* two series of which appeared in 1515 and 1517. The Reuchlin affair fractured German humanism, soon to become even more splintered by the credal religious controversies of the Reformation.

career of religious scholarship. When he returned to the Continent he began a prolific publishing career, editing the early church fathers beginning with St. Jerome, and a Greek edition of the New Testament. Textbook selections for style and reference from the classics, works of satirical criticism, personal letters, and paraphrases from the New Testament followed and attained wide popularity. Mostly they dealt with literary history and a pacific educational reform program, very little with formal theology and philosophy.

Among his publications were the *Adages,* a selection of classical quotations, and the *Colloquies,* a reader much used in schools. From inspired pagans who anticipated Christianity he sought to gain knowledge of all that was known of the arts of peace and war, poetry, writing, speech, and, nominally, science. "Good letters" were essential to virtue, for love without knowledge he held to be blind. For him classical scholarship was never an end in itself. Although he constantly revised his immense personal correspondence to achieve literary excellence, he attacked "Ciceronian" stylistic purists and Italian "paganism." Indeed he subordinated classical scholarship to a broad educational and religious reformation which was to be rooted in the New Testament and the early Church Fathers.

Although Erasmus wrote on theological subjects he de-emphasized rites, doctrines, and external observances in favor of a Christian ethic defined by the epistles of Paul and the Sermon on the Mount which he described as "the philosophy of Christ." He worked to reform Christianity so that it rested on texts, institutions, and practices purged of corruption. His "social gospel" involved a drastic social transformation, but his method was marked by gradualism and nonviolent education rather than by force. His publication of critical editions of the Greek New Testament (1516 ff.) was intended as the basis for vernacular translations which he hoped

eventually would be read and sung by the simplest laymen, male and female. Most of his publishing efforts were devoted to the printing of the early Church Fathers' writings. They appealed to him not only because they represented uncorrupted Christianity, but because they differed sharply from one another on doctrines which had become hardened orthodoxy in the medieval Church. Toward controverted or undocumented dogmas, Erasmus was tolerantly skeptical; for his classic moral Christianity, they were beside the point.

Erasmus became known to posterity primarily as a satirical critic who tried to take an independent course through the confessional wrangles of the early Reformation. Best known has been *The Praise of Folly,* a tract in which Folly, a laconic woman, twits the foibles of society, clergy, businessmen, and—so alive and honest was his sense of humor—even scholars. In other writings, Erasmus associated war with savagery and held that it should be circumvented among Christians by judicious princes—a rare lot, he said, for, like fools, princes needed only to be born!—and arbitration. His satirical criticism extended to relics, indulgences, domination of clerical posts by nobles, the invocation of saints, pilgrimages, and sundry other aspects of external popular piety then current. His satire and his pacific humor were intolerable to both doctrinal Protestants and traditionalist Catholics; for Erasmus they were a means to laugh his opponents out of court, much preferred to reliance upon force. The latter course he accurately predicted would lead to generations of religious warfare rather than to peace and unity under reformed existing institutions.

Always writing in Latin (with the exception of the Greek New Testament) Erasmus believed in a cosmopolitan aristocracy of talent which should practice and develop a social as well as an individual moral gospel. To others he left the tasks of translating and implementing his humanistic reform program. After 1517, however, its

A late fifteenth-century printing press. The man at the right is a compositor selecting the letters. Printing was big business, and skilled help was hard to find.

fate became inextricably intertwined with the confessional controversies of the Reformation, a consequence we shall consider in the following chapter.

The Impact of Printing with Movable Type

The Renaissance printing press with movable metallic type produced a revolution in the quantity of and pace of disseminating the written word. Heretofore all forms of thought and expression had been dependent upon handwritten manuscripts and "books" printed with carved wooden blocks. But now editions or printings of a single work or broadside could easily amount to 20,000 or more copies, and governments could rapidly circularize laws, decrees, and instructions to their officials and subjects.

Technologically, printing brought together the skills and inventions of craftsmen—goldsmiths and silversmiths, metal-lurgists, paper makers, etc.—and artists who had developed oil-based paints suitable for pressurized applications to paper. Transition from wood block printing to movable type may have been developed simultaneously in two or more cities, but the first printing shop known to the book trade was that of Johann Gutenberg. He set it up in Mainz slightly before 1450. From Mainz, printing establishments spread rapidly. By 1500 the Low Countries had at least 50, Venice and Paris each had over 150. England had only two, but the number rapidly increased. Presses were also found in all the large towns of Spain and in some towns of Eastern Europe outside of Russia.

Most early printed books (called *incunabula* up to 1500) were traditional in content. The great majority of them were religious devotionals or treatises. Books on the art of dying, apocalyptic themes, and prophecy had greater circulation than reports of new geographical discoveries or business techniques, especially in Germany.

Churchmen and political authorities quickly realized the power of the press to influence public opinion—educated opinion. They moved early to control heresy and sedition, particularly after the religious schism of the sixteenth century. Where this control was weak, as in parts of pre-Reformation Germany, large numbers of popular tracts gave impetus to social revolutionary movements. Throughout Europe, including all of Germany after 1525, censorship became a constant function of government. Only in periods of tension did censorship break down (as in England during the 1640s or in France during the religious wars of the second half of the sixteenth century). Then large quantities of critical materials circulated in the vernacular. They were preludes to revolution. Potentially, mass-produced books meant the democratization of culture. Now, for example, the goal of Erasmus and Martin Luther to have Biblical texts in the hands of the simplest layman was possible.

The Fine Arts

Renaissance thinkers were self-consciously certain that their age had broken sharply with the medieval past. They could point not only to the revival of classical literature and philosophy but also to vast accomplishments in the fine arts. In his *Lives of the Painters, Sculptors, and Architects* Giorgio Vasari revelled in this decisive break. He wrote of the "rebirth" of naturalism and classicism, describing how they gained ascendancy over post-Roman "barbarian" and Christian philosophies. While his generalizations would not apply to many areas of fourteenth and fifteenth-century life, his judgment in aesthetic expression (he might have included literature) has been upheld. Without question, there was a "renaissance" in art.

Gothic Realism

In its naturalism, Renaissance art was partly an outgrowth of Gothic art. Medieval artists had used allegorical symbols and had not imitated nature. But the same spirit of "naturalism" which came to prompt new forms of literature, new methods of philosophy, and new views of theology, also eventually worked changes in art. Gothic painters and sculptors began to portray individuals rather than types. They started, in northern France in the thirteenth century, to master the techniques of realistic detail. Their realism is evident in the late statuary on the Cathedral of Chartres. At the Burgundian court, the Low-Country sculptor Claus Sluter (d. 1406) achieved flesh-like verisimilitude with painted stone. The van Eyck brothers, especially Jan (1370?–1440), painted almost photographic altar pieces with oil paint, a new medium permitting greater detail. Though they achieved marked realism, northern Gothic artists, like the architects of Gothic cathedrals, multiplied picturesque details without achieving consistency of form. Nor did they master the portrayal of natural space. Though lay patrons

Flemish realism: The Crucifixion *by Hubert van Eyck, early fifteenth century. Historical scenes were translated into contemporary settings. Note that perspective is not yet well developed.*

commissioned some works from them, these artists did mostly death and crucifixion scenes for traditional, didactic purposes.

379

This Gothic realism became universal during the Renaissance. It was *the* art form of the era. Prior to 1500 only Italy produced an ascendant competing style. And there, too, the plastic arts had been dominated by Gothic realism until the fifteenth century. But during the Quattrocento (1400s) Italy became the hearth of scientific realism, and Italian artists turned to classical expression.

Scientific Naturalism and Classicism in Italy

Science and classicism often merged in the careers of fifteenth-century artists. The work of Brunelleschi, architect and sculptor, is illustrative. He was the first both to work out mathematical laws of linear perspective and to influentially emulate classical styles of building. Disliking Gothic, he studied in Rome, a veritable museum of ancient, earth-bound architecture. Commissioned to remodel Florence he introduced round columns, rounded arches, pilasters, and domes. He refrained, however, from copying buildings of antiquity. Another architect and theorist, Leone Battista Alberti (1405–1471) soon developed a more imitative classicism and proposed to make architecture a mathematical science of balance and proportion as well as the most utilitarian of the arts.

Donatello (d. 1466), who excelled in obtaining balance between scientific realism and classical models, cast a bronze *David* designed to stand alone in a garden. A

An engineering and architectural triumph—Brunelleschi's Dome, Cathedral of Florence—still the dominating structure in that city. Giotto's campanile is free standing. Note the pronounced horizontal lines and the classical influences. The cathedral was begun about 150 years before Brunelleschi added the cupola, 1420–1436.

combination of grace, reserve, mathematically conceived proportions, and naturalism, *David* was presumably chosen to kill the giant because of his natural perfection, not because of his piety. In another feat of symmetry and balance, Donatello cast at Padua one of the first equestrian statues since antiquity (*Gattamelata*). In this work, the movements of the horse and rider were in perfect harmony. Other sculptors, such as Verrocchio, equalled or surpassed Donatello on specific projects, but at his best Donatello came closer than any to achieving perfection as it was then defined.

As an art for which no antique models were extant, painting was slow to respond to classical stimulation. But Masaccio, who died in 1428 at the age of 27, introduced mathematical laws of perspective. He was realistic without being Gothic. Imitating nature rather than his masters, he worked out the perspective of the human body. His figures exist in three-dimensional space, so that the viewer feels able to touch them. In the expressions of two lifelike nudes, *Adam and Eve*, he portrayed the pathos of man's expulsion from the Garden of Eden. Before Masaccio Florence had been the fountainhead of Renaissance sculpture and architecture. Now it became also the center of painting's "rebirth."

Realism in painting made the canvas a transparent windowpane with nature on the other side. "That picture is most praiseworthy," wrote Leonardo da Vinci, "which most clearly resembles the thing to be imitated." [2] No paintings better conformed to this dictum than his own. His service as a military and civil engineer for Cesare Borgia and others took precedence over his artistic work. So did his research into anatomy, physiology, botany, geology, and mechanics. But these pursuits were also closely related to his art. In whatever he did he sought rational mathematical laws from empirical reality. He noted hitherto unob-

Classical realism at its peak: Donatello's David *(c. 1440). The first nude statue since antiquity.*

served color and line aberrations in ocular perception. He combined these with the use of light and shade to secure a better illusion of perspective. His adherence to imitation was selective. He tempered his realism with a classical sense of decorum, carefully picking elements of ideal beauty from his environment. Classical repose and dramatic tension coexist in the few paintings he completed, which include *St. John the Baptist, St. Jerome, The Madonna of the Rocks,* and especially *The Last Supper.* Even when scientifically conceived, Italian realism was usually selective and strove for an ideal form.

As contemporary humanists sought to describe a perfect literary style, artists fused realism with classical balance, harmony, proportion, and decorum. While

2. Quoted by Erwin Panofsky, *Renaissance and Renascences in Western Art,* Russack and Company, Copenhagen, 1961, p. 162.

da Vinci. The Madonna of the Rocks (*1508*).

northern artists concentrated on stark scenes of death and crucifixion, Italian artists, painting both secular and religious works, dealt with life, natural beauty, and the spectrum of human emotions. At the peak of classical realism, man became the measure of all things; his dignity, perfection, or fame replaced metaphysical principles as the measuring rod of values. His struggles with himself replaced the struggle between heaven and hell as the chief concern of artist and humanist. The enjoyment of life, which art enhanced, was more divine than the contemplation of death and salvation. In tracts on architecture, sculpture, painting, mathematics, natural science, family life, law, and religion, the civic humanist and universally accomplished Florentine, Leone Battista Alberti, summed up this blend of humanism and realism.

During the second half of the fifteenth century artists began to draw more upon classical literature than upon contemporary life. The realistic imitations of da Vinci and Alberti gave way to Graeco-Roman gods, heroes, battles, and myths painted by such artists as Mantegna and Piero de Cosimo. Other painters such as Botticelli were influenced by the philosophy of Neoplatonism. His *Allegory of Spring* and *Birth of Venus* combine a command of scientific realism with a return to allegorical symbolism (classical rather than religious). They depict hierarchies of spirits, types of soul, and forms of love. Following Botticelli, artists of the High Renaissance no longer considered themselves recorders of external nature. Rather they were creative geniuses inspired by divine spirit. Having developed the ability to reproduce nature photographically, they began to look away from their immediate environment for new themes with which to experiment.

The High Renaissance

Idealized classical form rather than fidelity to empirical nature characterized the art of the High Renaissance, a short period of two or three decades following 1500. Compared to the youthful realism of the previous century, High Renaissance art emphasized grandeur, perfection of form, and self-assurance. Now artists often worked in greater-than-life proportions. They were encouraged in this by the patronage of monarchs in Rome, northern Italy, and France, successful bidders for the greatest artistic skills. Increasingly art's purpose was to glorify these ruling patrons and attain immortal fame for both them and the artist. By 1500 the major artists were no longer respected guildsmen. They were highly rewarded individuals of great prestige and affluence who traveled from one court to another, at least until Spanish influence reduced the status of most of them.

The most ambitious patron of the High Renaissance was Pope Julius II. He called Bramante, Raphael, Michelangelo, and others to Rome. Bramante was a student of Roman architecture who brought principles

Botticelli's return to mystical allegory: The Birth of Venus (c. *1483–1484*).

of mathematics and physics to bear upon his work. Julius commissioned him to build St. Peter's church in the capital of Christendom, a grandiose project whose completion required over a century. Raphael also worked on the design of St. Peter's. But his fame rests primarily upon paintings of idealized madonnas—for example, his *Sistine Madonna*—and of various classical themes. Generally, his madonnas were more human than pious in appearance, but they conveyed an abstract humanity of grace and dignity rather than individuality. Like other late Renaissance painters, Raphael drew on philosophical and classical themes in the *School of Athens,* an assemblage of savants of the past, and in *Parnassus,* an anachronistic combination of classical antiquity, the classical present, and inventive imagination.

The crowning jewel of Julius' assemblage of talent was Michelangelo, a Florentine-trained sculptor. The pope set him to work from 1508–1512 on frescoes of the Sistine

Religious naturalism and quizzical cherubs: Sistine Madonna *by Raphael.*

A giant to kill a giant: Michelangelo's David *(1504).*

Chapel and later on the plans of St. Peter's. Working on his back for four years to paint 300 figures on wet plaster on the Sistine Chapel ceiling, Michelangelo displayed both dependence on and independence of Florentine scientific naturalism. Departing from mathematical laws of perspective, he consciously used distortion to awaken a heightened sense of perspective and to convey a feeling of power. Ideal beauty he found in the nude human form, which he used in his depictions of creation and of man's early Biblical history. He included no crucifixion or judgment scenes until Paul II pressed him into doing a wall on the chapel entitled the *Last Judgment* (1535–1541).

Primarily Michelangelo was a sculptor rather than a painter or an architect. For the Medici he built tombs portraying the family head as a victor in greater-than-life size and flanked by moot, symbolical figures. His most classical work was *David,* a relaxed and serene but powerful giant who could self-assuredly kill his Biblical opponent without miraculous intervention. For Julius II's tomb he carved another giant, *Moses,* in a psychological state of restrained rage. In sculpture as in painting, Michelangelo relied upon his own subjective standards and produced art for art's sake. His inner tranquillity was shaken by political and religious crises after 1527, however. And this is reflected in his art. Rome was sacked in 1527. Italy was conquered by the Emperor in 1530. Advocates of force replaced Catholic humanists in the papacy in 1541. As his optimistic world of the Renaissance crumbled, Michelangelo turned more and more to mysticism and pious resignation. The full range of his work is impossible to classify under a single heading. His art styles chronicle successive changes from classical realism to subjective and imitative "mannerism" to, finally, baroque.

In quantity of works and in grandeur of restrained style the High Renaissance far surpassed the early Italian Renaissance. It was no longer primarily a Florentine or even exclusively an Italian phenomenon. Venice rivaled Rome as a center of High Renaissance art. There a school of painters developed whose members relied more upon color and oil-painted texture than upon light and shade. At the very same time when Italian art began to influence all of Europe, its own foundations of classical and scientific naturalism were disintegrating.

By 1500 an Italian journey had become a necessity for northern men of culture and learning, and Italian artists were summoned to the northern courts. Still, High Renaissance influence was uneven outside of Italy. France proved receptive to both its art and letters, but Spain and Germany remained primarily Gothic and religious in a doctrinal sense. Albrecht Dürer (1471–1528) of Nurnberg and Hans Holbein (d. 1543), primarily a portrait painter, did utilize Italian techniques of perspective. But neither they nor other northern artists would adopt the secular aesthetic content of the Italian Renaissance; symbolism and mannerism eventually proved easier for them to absorb.

States, Economies, and Societies

Traditionally, Renaissance politics has been conceived of as a continuation of efforts by medieval kings, aided by townsmen, to centralize their kingdoms into "national states." But the framework of politics remained decidedly dynastic and aristocratic. Most exceptional were the city states of northern Italy which served as laboratories for the development of a territorial state run by officials wielding absolute power over all subjects within its confines. The same states also pioneered the use of modern diplomatic machinery for foreign affairs. Dynastic rulers imitated the Italians' diplomacy and occasionally forged part of their possessions into consolidated territorial states also. We shall see how different areas of Europe developed during the fourteenth and fifteenth centuries after considering Renaissance theories of the state.

Four Approaches to the Renaissance State

Four concepts of the state were formulated during the late Renaissance: the Roman law or absolutist conception, the divine right theory, the humanistic idealism of Erasmus, and the political realism of Machiavelli.

Roman law was revived around 1100 when Irnerius of Bologna began teaching the subject to mature students. Those who became authorities in the Roman civil law commanded more prestige and power than any other intellectuals. They seemed to possess the secrets of the "mysteries of state." Consulted by princes and rich townsmen, they often had high positions in governments. What did men find in the Roman law? In part of it they found that it provided legal support for absolute property rights and the contractual obligations basic to a commercial, capitalistic society. Other parts were used by kings as a rationale for centralizing power in the hands of state officials, rather than delegating it to feudal tenants.* This was important for effecting the transition from decentralized feudalism to the centralized, absolute state of the late Renaissance. Furthermore, the Roman law principle, "The will of the prince has the force of law," sanctioned the growing authoritarianism of Renaissance rulers.

Clergymen reinforced and extended this concept with the doctrine of the divine right of kings: kings were accountable to God alone; resistance to them was a cardinal sin. As the pope had been exalted by canonists, divine right princes were now exalted above law and representative assemblies. Their courts, councils, and officials combined legislative, executive, and judicial functions. Still, in practice they shared authority with the Church. By the beginning of the sixteenth century, all wielders of power—magisterial, ecclesiastical, patrimonial—constituted a separate "estate," a privileged status group within the traditional social hierarchy. The members of this estate were too numerous and often too obscure to mention here by name.

Quite different from Roman lawyers and theological theorists of divine right monarchy were the contemporary political viewpoints of the Erasmian humanists. For Thomas More and Erasmus, the ruler was neither possessor of the kingdom nor above the law. Rather he was a steward subject to deposition by "freemen"—that is, by the aristocracy. In his *Institution of a Christian Prince* Erasmus treated

---

* Often, however, royal officials exploited these powers to benefit themselves rather than their ruler.

politics as a branch of ethics as defined by the New Testament. The prince's first duty was to care for the common weal of his subjects. He ought to tax the luxuries rather than the necessities of life, and promote peace, education, and the practical arts. In matters of taxation and peace, Erasmus was advocating nothing less than a complete reversal of current political trends. His critique of princes frankly implied republicanism.

The humanist concept of government as existing for the common weal was very widespread on the eve of the Reformation. But then religious controversies restored the notion that Christian magistrates must secure the salvation of souls by enforcing doctrinal purity. That enforcement need not coincide with the mundane general welfare. Erasmian influences remained strongest in republican towns, the Low Countries, and in England.

The most significant approach to politics during the Renaissance was Machiavelli's realism. Niccolo Machiavelli (1469–1527), became one of the most celebrated political theorists in history. Born into a prominent family and given a gentleman's education (which included the Roman classics), Niccolo entered public service in 1498 while the Medici were in exile. After serving as secretary of the secret committee for military affairs, the chancery, and the highest council, he was sent as a diplomatic agent to France, Germany, Switzerland, and various parts of Italy. His letters show that he was particularly impressed with Ferdinand of Spain, Cesare Borgia, Julius II, and the armed citizenry of the Swiss Confederation. When the Medici returned in 1512, he was recruiting peasant subjects for a "citizens' army" with which to recover rebellious Pisa.

Politically suspect to the restored Medici, Machiavelli spent the remainder of his life writing political commentaries, history, satirical drama, and even a religious devotional. Apart from his *Art of War,* which advocated the restoration of a citi-

zens' army, his most significant political works were *The Discourses on Titus Livy* and *The Prince.* His writing reflected secular humanism. But he included topics most humanists omitted: conspiracies, assassinations, the calculated use of terror. His announced intention was to create a science of statecraft based on classical learning. With instructive examples and maxims drawn from the repetitiveness of history— a record forever marked by the depravity of man—perhaps men could foresee events and prevent future errors. With classical examples related to the Italian milieu he illuminated contemporary problems. Many critics consider him the first empiricist in modern political science.

Machiavelli followed earlier civic humanists in refuting religious justification for the state and in advocating a secularized state religion. He conceived the state as having its own rules apart from social or individual morality and from divine or natural law. In a wicked world, moral rulers failed. State-building required force, fraud, and deceit to advance the common weal. In both foreign and domestic policies "Reason of State"—concern exclusively for the security of the state—should determine political action. Machiavelli's state is not irreligious, however. Princes and heads of republics should uphold religion, keep their people pious, and exalt the importance of miracles as a means of enhancing their own authority and of keeping the state well-ordered and united. But ultimate human values should be defined to guarantee the preservation and growth of the state. "I love my native city more than my own soul," he wrote. Thus he chastized the existing church for making men soft, indolent, and unfit for battle. As did most officials and diplomats of the period, Machiavelli advocated state supremacy over the church.

In Machiavelli's age society was rigidly stratified and gentility highly honored. But in his scheme the heroic virtues would supplant gentility. For extraordinary crises he advocated despotic tyranny. In *The Prince* we find the ideal nature of his autocrat. He should be both feared and loved, but mostly feared. By concentrating cruelties in short periods and extending well-advertised liberality over longer times, he could maintain an aura of goodness. He should kill opponents rather than confiscate their property, for heirs will be grateful for the inheritance and not permanently alienated as dispossessed persons. He should keep faith—when it served his interest to do so.

The Prince lends itself to varying interpretations. A few scholars say it is a tongue-in-cheek satire. They argue that his republican contemporaries could not have sanctioned the despotic Prince. However, many Italian classical republicans did sanction temporary tyrannies in unusual circumstances. Whatever Machiavelli intended, *The Prince* offered a rationale for monarchical power politics. Often, however, Machiavelli was condemned as immoral by statesmen and clergy who subordinated religion to the secular ruler and who approved similar tactics when it advanced their own confessional point of view.

Having seen how men approached politics theoretically, we shall now examine the actualities of Renaissance political life.

The States of Italy, 1300–1527

Italy was a region of many different states. In the extreme south, Sicily belonged to the house of Aragon, which also claimed Naples. The former seat of Frederick II's centralized, cosmopolitan, and secular imperial headquarters, Naples was dominated by local feudal barons. Central and parts of northern Italy were controlled by the Papal States whose local noble families gained dominance during the popes' absence in Avignon after 1305.

Distinctly different in political evolution were the towns of the Tuscan and Lombard plains where town life and Roman law had never completely disappeared. Venice held a commercial empire in the Mediterranean retained from her continued contacts with the Byzantine Empire. Starting like other medieval towns, as republican communes, the Lombard and Tuscan towns leagued together and, allied with the papacy, threw off the authority of the Holy Roman Emperor in the twelfth century. Titular imperial governors presided over several of their councils, but thenceforth they retained *de facto* independence. Bankers from Lombardy and Tuscany dominated financial affairs in late medieval courts, fairs, and the Crusades. Two Italian cities, Florence and Venice, gave their stable units of money to the early modern

ITALY, c. 1490

Map by J. Donovan

Republic

0   60   120   180 mi.

commercial world, the florin and the ducat. Commercial rivalry between these towns led to naval and land wars in which the stronger city-states swallowed their weaker neighbors. In Tuscany, Florence extended her territory over Arezzo (1384), Pisa (a port city which had previously reduced her neighbors to submission in 1406), and others. In Lombardy, Milan was the principal expansionist state, but Venice also pushed her holdings landward to control the commercial routes extending northward across the Alps. By the middle of the fifteenth century, Italy consisted of five major states locked in a relative equilibrium of power maintained by shifting alliances: Naples, the Papal States, Venice, Florence, and Milan.

Constant factional strife and turbulence affected constitutional development within ruling cities. When the Emperor was the principal enemy, the Ghibellines, or imperialists, were proscribed and their property confiscated. Where they triumphed, the Guelfs, or papalists, formed one-party states; but their ruling factions, which were based on family groupings, were broken apart by family rivalries. Newly enriched families tried, by revolution if necessary, to break into the ruling oligarchies. In Venice such efforts were curbed by the creation of a permanent committee of public safety which preserved the old oligarchy in uneasy power. Florentine guildsmen came to power in 1282 and proscribed, exiled, or executed their patrician foes. Warfare gave this factionalism another dimension. Military defeats were the most frequent causes for revolution or the outbreak of civil war. But victory also had its dangers. For town councils, fearing to arm their own subjects, often hired troop captains to conduct wars on land. These captains, in Milan and other towns, seized power and set up hereditary dynastic tyrannies, marking a general trend away from oligarchical representative government.

Both republics and despotisms had established territorial states whose law and administration were sovereign within their borders. Establishment of that sovereignty required the smashing of both noble and clerical privileges and jurisdictions. Once the authority of the Emperor was removed the aristocracy, which tended to be urban and favorably disposed toward commerce anyway, was brought under city law. Similarly the Church was more thoroughly subordinated to secular government in the Italian city-states than in any monarchy, even though the towns had achieved their independence as allies of the papacy. A Visconti of Milan once summed up his powers to an archbishop as follows: "Do you not know, you fool, that here I am pope and emperor and lord in all my lands, and that no one can do anything in my lands save I permit it — no, not even God." [3]

Considerations of power rather than dynastic claims regulated the relationships between the Italian city states. In the interest of territorial aggrandizement Milan originated the practice of sending resident diplomatic agents to neighboring states. Their chief tasks were to acquire intelligence, to mask aggressive intentions with pacific eloquence, and to secure allies. Other Italian states soon adopted the practice. Neither mercenary armies nor diplomats were inspired by either religious zeal or modern nationalism, but solely by the desire to gain expansive domains and political power.

By the middle 1400s the states of the whole peninsula had achieved a "balance of power" by means of constantly shifting alliances in which yesterday's enemy became tomorrow's ally. As each state strove to tip that balance in its own favor, individual Italian states sought allies among the great northern monarchies, two of which, France and Spain, had conflicting claims to Naples and Milan. Once these relative giants intervened, no individual Italian state could turn them back. In the early sixteenth century the papacy shifted alliances to prevent

3. Quoted by Denys Hay, *The Italian Renaissance in its Historical Background*, University Press, Cambridge, England, 1961, p. 105.

either Habsburg or Valois dominance. But by 1527 the Spanish Habsburgs were in effective control of the peninsula, except for Venice.

More than any other court, the Spanish Habsburgs developed an Italian type of diplomatic corps and supported it with immense resources. In this way the secular diplomacy of the Italian city states was grafted onto the leading divine right of kingship of sixteenth-century Europe.

The Iberian Kingdoms

The Christian reconquest of Spain from the Moors was a long, fervent crusading effort that gave a strong chivalrous bent to the Spanish nobility who came to rule a decentralized land. Among them, honor, religious faith, and arms rather than knowledge and mastery over the material environment became the basis of a noble-borne "individualism." For all its pious character this code cheerfully allowed renunciation of obedience to authority and defrauding of the government at every opportunity. In the Middle Ages considerable tolerance, cultural exchange, and intermarriage marked the contacts between Christians, Moors, and Jews. But as the Iberian Christians obtained unquestioned military ascendancy they turned their sense of divine mission into the achievement of empire, total uniformity, and "racial purity."

Another sequel to the attainment of relative military security was the outbreak of endless dynastic feuds and civil wars in the fourteenth and fifteenth centuries. Royal weakness provided an opportunity for local estates (*Cortes*) to consolidate their power. This occurred in the kingdoms combined under the crown of Aragon, where the diets remained the watchdogs of noble, clerical, and urban privileges rather than becoming legislative chambers responsive to the common welfare. Resumption of royal authority in Castile was easier because the Castilian *Cortes* atrophied due to the abstention of the clergy and nobility. Despite the fact that

leagues of townsmen usually fought for kings against noble lawlessness, the principal beneficiaries of the disorders were the nobility who gained lands at the expense of the royal domains. Towns, under royal officials who severely taxed their commerce (the Castilian *alcabala*), began to decline in the fourteenth century.

Ultimately the joint reign of Ferdinand in Aragon (1479–1516) and Isabella in Castile (1474–1504) produced order out of chaos by means of monarchical absolutism. The Catholic sovereigns enforced domestic peace and set up a system of royal councils, courts, and administration that overrode the political claims of towns, nobles, and clergy. All towns in Castile were brought under firm royal control in 1480. Gentry (*hidalgos*) were placed in half their offices, town leagues were broken up, and the guild system was made kingdom-wide under royal auspices. Ferdinand attempted similar measures in Aragon against fairly effective opposition by the local *Cortes*. Individual townsmen continued to serve in the royal administrations, especially as Roman law jurists; but politically the towns' autonomy was broken and their future prosperity undermined by royal taxation and social policies.

Ferdinand and Isabella also stripped the nobility of autonomous political power. Their social policy, however, was much more favorable to the nobility than to the townsmen. Royal police enforced order, duelling and private warfare were forbidden, baronial castles were torn down, and the crown regained part of the lands previously seized from the royal domain. The monarchs relied upon councils and courts rather than the *Cortes*, which they seldom called. The use of churchmen and townsmen in the royal administration further reduced the political role of the nobles, as did royal control of the army and the Church. With power to appoint high civil, military, and clerical officials, Ferdinand and Isabella dominated the nobility and won loyal support by their policies of

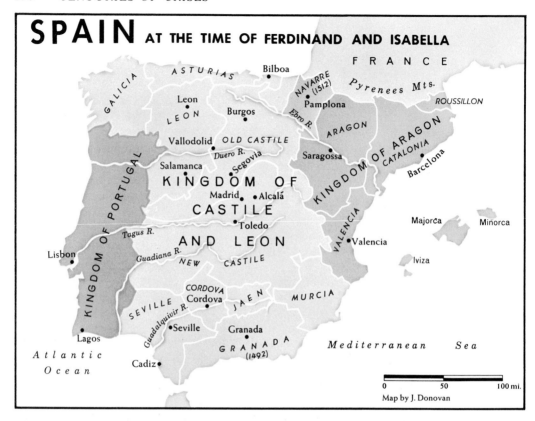

SPAIN AT THE TIME OF FERDINAND AND ISABELLA

Map by J. Donovan

patronage. Churchmen were not unhappy to have monarchs who demanded religious uniformity. The Spanish Inquisition, established by a papal bull in 1478, became a symbol of terror to Jews, Moors, and deviationist Christians, but gained the support of the powerful clerics, such as Cardinal Ximenes, the great humanistic churchman who became regent after Ferdinand's death. The only nagging problem of the monarchs was the shortage of money. The Church agreeably fed some of its tithes into the royal treasury, but royal costs, especially to maintain the splendid army and the big diplomatic corps, were like a bottomless pit. To get more money more quickly, the monarchs resorted to unwise fiscal policies which damaged the long-run strength of the economy by inhibiting the development of capitalism and enterprise. Expulsion of the Jews in 1492 was hardly compensated for by the discoveries of Columbus, and New World gold and silver did not begin to flow to Spain regularly until the 1540s. Because wool sold well abroad, the monarchs favored the corporation of sheepherders (the Mesta) with privileges, despite the injuries to peasant agriculture caused by the sheep drives to distant summer pastures. Loans from German and Italian bankers eased the financial needs of the monarchs and showed that the credit of the Spanish crown was very high. By 1519, when Charles I, Spain's new monarch, became Holy Roman Emperor and began to drag Spain into continental affairs, the Spanish crown was master of an obedient population and, at least in Castile, of a unified state. The sixteenth was to be the Spanish century.

England and France: The Hundred Years' War and After

Because English kings held large sections of France (as vassals of the French kings) English power was a constant threat to the security of the French throne. After 175 years of feudal warfare between the French Capetians and their "overmighty" English royal vassals, the direct male Capetian line died out in 1316. Thereafter English kings claimed the French throne itself. Anglo-French conflicts went deeper, however, than feudal and dynastic rivalries. France supported Scotland, England's perennial enemy. It also sought to acquire Flanders, the principal market for English wool. Seamen of both countries engaged in piracy and mutual coastal raids. When war broke out in 1338 popular passions contributed to wanton destruction, pillage, and the killing of prisoners and noncombatants. Large parts of France were denuded of people and economic resources.

The opening phases of the war demonstrated the superiority of English ships and the ability of yeomen armed with longbows to win battles, such as Crécy (1346), Poitiers (1356), and Agincourt (1415). But sufficient resources to conquer France were lacking. Over the half century after 1360 the French recovered from early defeats. But in 1415 Henry V, using siege guns, launched a new major invasion. Once again the French rallied, this time under the inspired leadership of Joan of Arc whom the English burned at the stake in 1431. Finally in 1453 the English made peace, retaining only the port of Calais.

The Hundred Years' War left deep marks on France's constitutional and political development. Until about 1440 Charles VII, financially assisted by Jacques Coeur, attempted to centralize the monarchy under royal authority. The King emerged from the war with independent tax powers, a small standing army, control over the French Church, and, for the period, a substantial bureaucracy.

Charles' successor, Louis XI (1461–1483), established a reputation for resuming political centralization by forceful suppression of the nobility. But for their loss of autonomous political power, Louis compensated them with sufficient pensions and

Early field gun and gunmaster. Cannoneers became very devout before firing these temperamental monsters.

emoluments to make him one of their principal benefactors socially and economically. French constitutional development after the Hundred Years' War was marked by tension between centralized royal authority and the provincial law courts and estates which upheld local autonomy. At the level of central government Louis and his immediate successors (Charles VIII, Louis XII, and Francis I) pushed aside the Estates-General and ruled absolutely. Nevertheless French commoners found "government" and aristocracy to mean very much the same; provincial authorities maintained their rights in vigorous local estates. Thus French "absolutism" was still far from absolute.

English kings had no paid bureaucracy comparable to that of the French monarchy. They depended rather on newly created Justices of the Peace paid by fees and drawn from leading local families. Thereafter they became the local governors of England, though they were subject to parliamentary statutes applicable to the whole kingdom. Neither Parliament nor

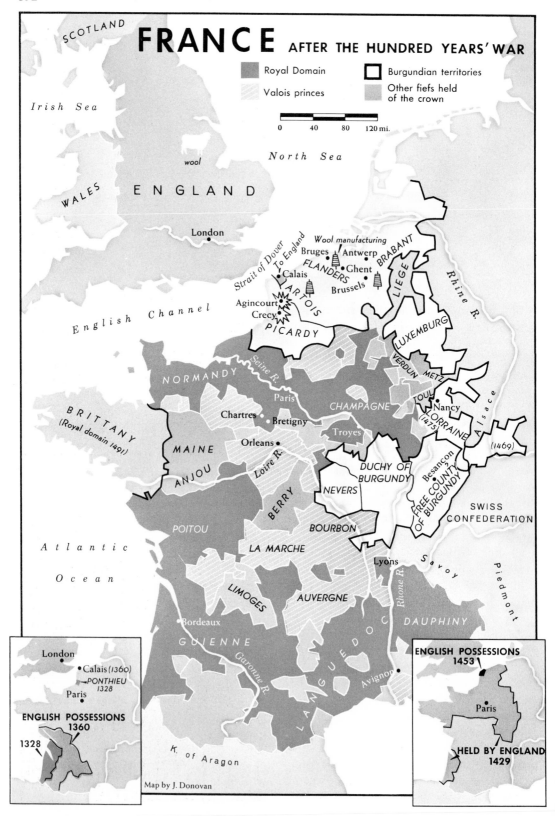

FRANCE AFTER THE HUNDRED YEARS' WAR

Royal Domain

Valois princes

Burgundian territories

Other fiefs held
of the crown

0   40   80   120 mi.

SCOTLAND

Irish Sea

WALES

ENGLAND

London

North Sea

wool

English Channel

Strait of Dover
To England

Wool manufacturing

Bruges Antwerp BRABANT
FLANDERS Ghent
Calais Brussels LIEGE

Rhine R.

Agincourt ARTOIS
Crecy PICARDY

LUXEMBURG

NORMANDY

Seine R.

Paris

VERDUN METZ

TOUL Nancy

CHAMPAGNE

LORRAINE
(1475)

Alsace

Chartres Bretigny

Troyes

(1469)

BRITTANY
(Royal domain 1491)

MAINE

ANJOU

Orleans

Loire R.

DUCHY OF
BURGUNDY

NEVERS

Besancon

FREE COUNTY
OF BURGUNDY

BERRY

SWISS
CONFEDERATION

Atlantic

POITOU

BOURBON

LA MARCHE

Ocean

Lyons

Savoy

Piedmont

LIMOGES

AUVERGNE

Rhone R.

DAUPHINY

Bordeaux

GUIENNE

LANGUEDOC

Avignon

Garonne R.

K. of Aragon

Map by J. Donovan

London

Calais (1360)
PONTHIEU
1328

Paris

ENGLISH POSSESSIONS
1360

1328

**ENGLISH POSSESSIONS
1453**

Paris

**HELD BY ENGLAND
1429**

the Justices of the Peace represented the interests of the peasantry or the lower urban classes. Following the Black Death, the Statute of Laborers (1351) charged Justices of the Peace with the checking of wage increases. Riled by egalitarian preaching of the "Lollards" or "poor priests" and reacting to severe poll taxes, peasants and townsmen revolted in 1381. Disarmed by the king's false promises, the revolt was easily suppressed; but its failure did not check the gradual release of English leaseholders from compulsory services, a process completed in the sixteenth century.

Following the Hundred Years' War, England was plagued by feuds between private armies maintained by the nobility in "livery and maintenance," and finally by the dynastic Wars of the Roses. From these wars the first Tudor monarch, Henry VII, emerged victorious in 1485. Fearful of further disorders Henry established a popular absolutism favorable to the commercial interests and intent upon the reduction of the nobility. His use of the judicial proceedings in the prerogative court of the Star Chamber,* his administrative organization, and his taxation policies were extraordinarily effective. They established order, removed potential competitors for the throne, and cowed the old nobility whose ranks had been thinned by the dynastic wars. Henry retained Parliament as a part of the sovereign power of the state; before his accession it had been reduced to an echo of temporarily victorious military factions. By working with Parliament, which represented the major vested interests of the kingdom, Henry wielded greater power than his French counterparts, even though it continued to control taxation and to deny the King a standing army. Thrust off the Continent by the Hundred Years' War, Englishmen applied their energies increasingly to commerce, industry, and mercantile expansion.

---

* A court made up of certain councillors who met in secret and decided cases more or less arbitrarily.

Flanders and Burgundy

Coveted by both France and England was Flanders, the most industrialized, urbanized, and richest area of northern Europe. The great textile industries in the cities of Ghent, Ypres, and Bruges brought together an artisan class that contested the power of the local patricians. To prevent that rich area from falling to the English who were eager to secure their Flemish wool markets, the French King agreed to let Burgundy control Flanders. That control was not happy. Taxing the rich Flemish cities, the Duke of Burgundy used his enormous revenues for display. Burgundian court life was dazzling. The dukes collected libraries and patronized historians whose writings upheld the chivalric values practiced there. That court was also the major patron of Northern Renaissance music, drama, sculpture, painting, and poetry. Universities were established to train officials and laws were codified. The

Burgundian defense of a beseiged town, obviously a wealthy city worth defending.

common people in both Burgundy and Flanders chafed under this costly, chivalric culture.

Eventually the ambitious, expansionist Duke, Charles the Rash, 1467–1477, overreached himself and suffered military defeats in 1476 that weakened his power. Without a male heir, he arranged a marriage between his daughter Mary and Maximilian, son of the Holy Roman Emperor, a marriage that led to the joining of Burgundy and Flanders with Spain and the Holy Roman Empire. Their son, Philip, married Joanna, daughter of Ferdinand and Isabella. Charles (b. 1500) the son of Philip and Joanna, inherited not only Flanders and Burgundy, but having become the King of Spain in 1516, as Ferdinand's grandson and heir, united the richest territories of Europe under one crown. These lands remained the basis of his military and financial power when he became Holy Roman Emperor in 1519 and began playing the extraordinary role of trying to bring unity to Europe.

The Holy Roman Empire

The area of the Holy Roman Empire was probably too large and too diversified to be organized under one administration. The elective principle, codified in the Golden Bull of 1356, also acted against centralization because no single imperial family could count on its territory remaining the center around which to build a state, as the French Capetian kings had done. Geography also worked against centralization. Consequently, the local governments of the numerous German principalities and free cities were the effective ones, and the Emperor's authority did not reach into local territories. The German princes contested the authority of the Emperor, who was never powerful enough to impose his will on all of them at once. The Imperial Reichstag (Parliament) was impotent because the Emperor had to get the approval of the electors, the seven churchmen and princes who elected the Emperor,

before he could convene it. The Emperors managed to get various constitutional reforms through the Reichstag in 1495 and 1512, including the banning of private warfare, controlling monopolistic banking and trading companies, creating local "circles" for defense, and obtaining an administrative council. With a weak imperial army, the Emperor was unable to enforce these reforms and the German nobility continued to go their own way. When Charles I became Emperor in 1519, with his powerful Spanish army and his vast financial resources, the German princes met their match. However, the vexing issue of the Reformation and Charles' many world commitments prevented him from unifying the Holy Roman Empire.

The Eastern Frontiers

During the fourteenth and fifteenth centuries Eastern Europe absorbed in small measure the culture of the West. Through royal courts, colonization, and commerce Western sociopolitical institutions filtered into parts of the area—Poland-Lithuania, Bohemia, Hungary, and Novgorod. But the torch was lit. The vast distance that separated many areas of Eastern Europe from the commercial centers of the West retarded the development of a flourishing town life. So did endemic warfare and the hostility of princes and noblemen. In the main, therefore, the political and social life of Eastern Europe was slanted away from the culture of the West. East of the Elbe River in Germany, peasants began to lose their legal status as independent yeomen. By the seventeenth century many had become formally bound to soil and master. Critical for the political evolution of all of Eastern Europe was the rise of two aggressive, non-Western military autocracies, Muscovy and the Ottoman Empire.

On the far northeastern fringes of Europe the princes of Muscovy built a more lasting autocratic state, almost totally outside the reach of Western influence. Most of old Kievan Russia had been incor-

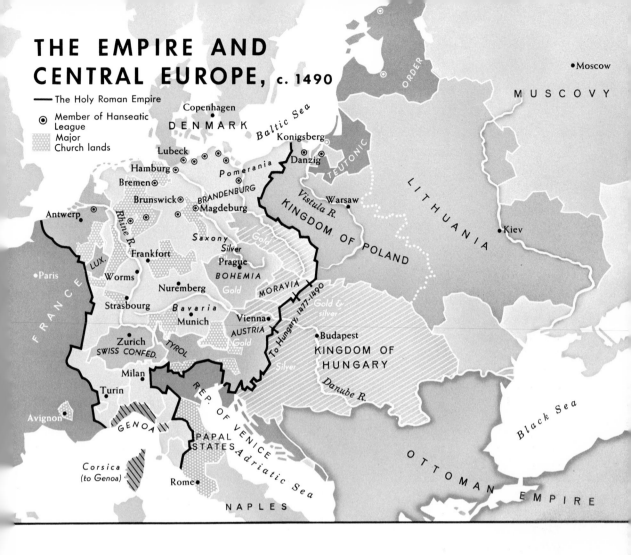

Moscow

MUSCOVY

Copenhagen

DENMARK

Baltic Sea

Konigsberg

Lubeck

Danzig

Pomerania

TEUTONIC ORDER

Hamburg

Bremen

BRANDENBURG

Brunswick

Magdeburg

Antwerp

Rhine R.

Warsaw

Vistula R.

KINGDOM OF POLAND

LITHUANIA

Kiev

LUX.

Paris

Worms

Frankfurt

Saxony

Silver

Gold

Prague

BOHEMIA

Gold

MORAVIA

To Hungary 1477-1490

Strasbourg

Bavaria

Nuremberg

Munich

Vienna

AUSTRIA

Gold

Silver

Gold & silver

Zurich

SWISS CONFED.

TYROL

Budapest

KINGDOM OF HUNGARY

Milan

REP. OF VENICE

Turin

Danube R.

Avignon

GENOA

Black Sea

Corsica (to Genoa)

PAPAL STATES

Adriatic Sea

Rome

OTTOMAN EMPIRE

NAPLES

FRANCE

porated into Lithuania. The rest fell under the suzerainty of the Mongol-led Tartars (1238) until Muscovite princes threw off the "Tartar Yoke" and substituted their own authority for it. Under the Mongols these princes gained ascendancy by collecting tribute and helping to suppress revolts. They also made Moscow the seat of the Russian Orthodox Church. The latter's repudiation of both Rome and Constantinople made it easy to identify the divine mission of Moscow—the "Third Rome"—with the Muscovite state.

With full religious support, Ivan III and Vasili III pushed Muscovite frontiers to the Baltic Sea and the Ural Mountains by purchase, treaty, and war. Noteworthy

victims of their military autocracy were the city-states of Novgorod (1478) and Pskov (1510), whose institutional and social developments had closely paralleled those of the city-states of Italy. The tsars rooted out their republican institutions and exiled their leading citizens into remote areas. Henceforth lacking a native middle class, Russia failed to develop a diet or parliament comparable to the Renaissance kingdoms of the West. Most Russians remained peasants on the estates of the military aristocracy. For the next two centuries the general trend was toward a uniform level of serfdom.

Muscovite expansion cut off Western trade routes and isolated Russia more than

EXPANSION OF MUSCOVY TO 1533

Map by J. Donovan

in the Balkans and in the eastern Mediterranean. Then Europe received a respite until 1520; but between 1515 and 1519 the sultans doubled their empire in the Near East by conquering Persia, Mesopotamia, Syria, and Egypt. These victories put the Ottomans in control of the trade routes to the Far East, a commercial advantage weakened by Portugal's earlier establishment of a cheaper, all-water route to the Indies around Africa.

Summary of Political Evolution

Everywhere except in northern Italy territorial authority was incompletely centralized. But all of these states legislated economic and social controls and curbed the autonomous power of the Church, nobility, and town corporations. Their authoritarianism imposed a greater degree of order and social stability. In international affairs, however, internal consolidation was a prelude to dynastic warfare on an unprecedented scale. European culture transmitted through the Roman Catholic Church no longer held universal sway.

A Century of Depression

Renaissance culture is inconceivable apart from late medieval commercial expansion. But recent economic studies conclusively demonstrate that it came not on the crest of growing prosperity but in the slough of a century-long depression. The commercial depression from about 1350 to about 1450 may have been due in part to previous overexpansion. But its timing suggests that famine, plague, war destruction, and domestic turmoil were principal causes.

Following severe famines, the Black Death (or bubonic plague) killed more than a quarter of Europe's population between 1348 and 1350; in Mediterranean towns 35 to 65 per cent may be a more accurate estimate. Thereafter the plague recurred generation after generation. Population decline retarded both commerce and industry. Decreased opportunities for profit demoral-

before from the West. But the other Eastern autocracy, the Ottoman Empire, thrust itself into Western affairs by direct land and sea invasion. Originally mercenaries of the Seljuk Turks from Asia Minor, the Ottomans took possession of Anatolia and turned it into a base for imperialism. Heading the government, the army, and the Church was the sultan, who relied upon slaves as administrators and foot soldiers. His military machine was further served by fief-holding cavalrymen and the development of effective artillery. By 1333 the Ottomans had reached the Dardanelles; thereafter they moved into the Balkan peninsula, overrunning Greeks, Serbs, and Bulgarians. Thus they encircled Constantinople, whose empire had degenerated into feudal factions and civil war. In 1453 the old capital of the Eastern Roman Empire fell. Until 1480, when the Sultan Mahomet died, the Turks pressed their advantage ized entrepreneurs and cut the rise of newly enriched merchants competing for positions of power and influence. Concentrated financial power gravitated into the hands of a few great banking families or individuals such as the Medici of Florence, the Fuggers of Augsburg, or Jacques Coeur of France. Though outstanding as great "individualists" of the age, their total resources were less than those previously held by a greater number of earlier merchant capitalists. And these "few great" increasingly tied their resources to leading ruling dynasties and the papacy.

In Western Europe, the Hundred Years' War (1338–1453) between France and England disrupted trade routes and laid waste to considerable parts of France. After the war, England was beset by feuds and a dynastic civil war. Similarly, endemic warfare in Italy, Spain, Scandinavia, and Eastern Europe disrupted trade and destroyed wealth. Invasion of Eastern Europe by the Ottoman Turks made Eastern trade more difficult. About 1340 the Mongol Empire which had policed trade routes from Poland to Korea began to disintegrate, and Europeans were barred from China by the nativist Ming dynasty. As trade and industry declined, Italian banks, often involved in financing military ventures, began to fail.

Recovery from the depression was uneven. Some formerly thriving towns, especially those in Eastern Europe, never recovered from the combination of misfortunes that befell them in the fourteenth and fifteenth centuries. Other towns such as the German centers of Augsburg and Nuremberg did not reach their former levels of population and economic activity until after 1450. The mining of precious metals expanded in Central Europe, facilitating both recovery and inflation. But the cloth industries of the same areas were unable to compete with the cheap cloth produced in England and Flanders.

The development of the compass, astro-labe, and stout clinker-built ships, capable of tacking against the wind, made long sea voyages feasible, and gave the Atlantic seaboard an economic advantage over Italian and German cities. Portuguese probes down the coast of Africa after 1420 brought new, exotic products and Negro slaves. By 1520, the effects of reviving commerce were noticeable and Antwerp was becoming the hub of international trade.

Aristocratic Recovery and Decline of the Peasantry

Seen as a whole, the Renaissance marked an unprecedented prominence of townsmen in government. Monarchs recognized the importance of wealthy bourgeoisie by drawing them into diets or by employing them as officials. But urban officials usually used their talents to secure admission into the aristocracy, whose social traditions they aped. Instead of contributing to the rise of the middle class, the shifting of the most talented townsmen from business to royal service weakened the impact of towns on early modern European institutions. Urban influence was further weakened by depression and the social-political revolutions which followed in its wake almost everywhere. Princes and nobles took advantage of these conflicts to secure control over the towns. In short, the Renaissance concluded with an aristocratic recovery.

For a time the traditional aristocracy was demoralized by several important innovations. One was the new means of warfare which they could not afford, that is, expensive guns and mercenary infantry. Another was the commutation of peasant obligations into fixed money payments whose value was cut by inflation. Still another was the competition of burghers for state and church offices. Even so, considerable evidence indicates that the aristocracy proved resilient enough to maintain its social dominance. In Eastern Europe the ascendancy of the aristocracy and gentry is unquestioned; they dominated towns, peasants, and kings. Elsewhere noblemen and gentry found compensation for their losses in tighter estate management, remunerative church positions, and posts, sometimes as sinecures, at princely courts. They made it difficult for commoners to marry into noble families or to otherwise gain noble status. At the same time they saw to it that their sons secured educations to outbid commoner competitors. Noblemen responded to the creation of infantry armies, financed by kings, by becoming royal officers.

In strong monarchical states rulers helped the nobility to preserve the caste system. Although monarchs curbed the nobles' political powers, royal courts shared their social outlooks and culture and gave them grants and preferences once their political rebelliousness was tamed. Thus the traditional nobility, the gentry, and a new service aristocracy (particularly jurists drawn from the bourgeoisie) proved to be the most dynamic elements of Renaissance society.

The lower urban and peasant classes, which constituted the great bulk of the population, were even more unsuccessful than the bourgeoisie in their bid for social and political recognition. Peasant revolts were endemic during the Renaissance; but only in areas where town life remained active did the peasants' *legal* position improve. *Economically* their gains, if any, were not so clear. New taxes, court fees, and requisitions by new state officials for civil and military purposes — when added to traditional obligations to church and manorial lords — took the greater part of their income. And in Eastern Europe (outside the Ottoman Empire) both the legal and economic status of the peasant deteriorated as the German-Slavic frontier became less an area of relative freedom and more an area of nascent serfdom.

Crisis in the Church

For the Roman Catholic Church the Renaissance was a period of unprecedented crisis. Although its institutional machinery had never been more centrally organized, the areas of its jurisdiction and effective obedience were shrinking. Popular piety may not have been declining, but ecclesiastical influence on culture and secular activities clearly was. Part of the problem concerned the inability to meet the spiritual needs of a great many Europeans; another part grew out of the old Church-State disputes of the High Middle Ages.

Babylonian Captivity, Great Schism, and Conciliarism

Already around 1300, the local interests of the territorial state came into conflict with the universal interests of the Church. Philip the Fair, King of France, was, like other European monarchs, eager to control his own bishops and abbots as well as to tap the wealth tied up in the Church. Countering this royal desire, Pope Boniface VIII issued two papal bulls, *Clericis laicos* (1296) and *Unam sanctam* (1302), in which he advanced the claim that the wealth of the Church is not taxable without papal authorization, and reaffirmed the old claim of papal supremacy in the most resounding language ever used by a pope. Infuriated, Philip responded to the second of these claims with a boldness and brutality that indicated how little regard monarchs felt for the moral authority of the pope. Philip's henchman, the great lawyer Nogaret, went to Italy and invaded the little town of Anagni where the pope was staying, with the object of dragging him to France to depose him. The townsfolk prevented that, but Boniface died soon after from shock and humiliation.

French interests, however, did not suffer because in 1305, the pope moved the papal see to the little enclave of Avignon within France. Here French influence predominated until 1378, when Europeans clamored for the release of the Church from its "Babylonian Captivity."

During the years of the Babylonian Captivity, the Avignon popes developed an effective administration. The chancery, courts, and diplomatic service of the Church excelled those of any contemporary government. Particularly elaborate was the pope's revenue collection. Because some of the traditional sources of income such as tithes had fallen to lay collectors, other resources were developed. In addition to various smaller obligations, the papal curia levied a tax on the clergy's net income which drew tremendous amounts from great prelates unprotected by their rulers. New offices were created and sold (a practice called simony) and fees were set for dispensations, absolutions, legal cases, and document services. The sale of indulgences also became a major source of income. The Avignon papacy marked the Church's adjustment to a world of commercial wealth.

In 1378 papal prestige and influence with certain powerful states plunged lower when part of the College of Cardinals seceded and elected a second pope. Thereafter rival popes at Rome and Avignon, both claiming divine sovereignty, exchanged anathemas, sponsored polemical propaganda, erected competing administrative and tax systems, and vied for the support of local hierarchies. For the most part, foreign policy considerations determined alignment behind one or the other pope. More than the "Babylonian Captivity," the Great Schism invited total rejection of the ecclesiastical system and the subordination of local hierarchies to secular rulers.

To end the Great Schism, one of the two popes would have to step down. To bring this about, leading thinkers urged the adoption of conciliarism. This doctrine held that Church councils, which princes as well as popes could summon, possessed divine authority equal to or greater than papal authority. One recalls that many councils were held since the first one at Nicea in 325 A.D. in order to resolve fundamental problems. After an abortive council at Pisa in 1409, which produced not one but three popes, the Emperor Sigismund convened a great council in 1414 at Constance, which successfully concluded the Schism by 1417. It also anathematized the dead John Wycliffe and added to the dead by burning John Hus and Jerome of Prague.

The conciliar doctrine continued to be dominant for a time as councils met to determine Church policy. The popes considered these councils subversive of their sovereignty, and by skillful diplomacy they managed to bypass the councils and gain the support of European monarchs. In 1460, Pius II was in a strong enough position to threaten to excommunicate all who appealed to conciliar authority over the pope. From this point onward, papal authority was complete. Resistance to conciliarism remained very strong, and the problems a council should have resolved were not attacked until some time after the Protestant part of Europe had been lost.

Heresy, Mysticism, and Reform Agitation

Christian teachings had led Europeans to believe that the hallmark of the Church was spiritual purity and Christian solicitude. What they actually saw was something quite different. The vows of poverty, chastity, and obedience were violated with impunity. Wealth was visibly used for the self-gratification of high churchmen, but parishes were poor. Many prelates held several benefices at the same time (pluralism), enjoyed their extra incomes, and were rarely if ever seen in their benefices (absenteeism). Meanwhile, poverty was the lot of the vicar who substituted for the absentee churchman. Nepotism, simony, and concubinage were openly practiced. The interests of the aristocracy and wealthy townsmen were given priority by bishops and abbots over those of the poor. Mendicant friars, such as the Spiritual Franciscans who held to apostolic poverty, stimulated popular dissatisfaction with the

Church by their denunciations of the world-liness of the secular clergy. It should be understood that anticlericalism was a protest against the intolerable secularism of the clergy; it was not a sign of disbelief in Christianity.

The erosion of confidence in the Church was shown in many ways, but the causes were not altogether the worldliness of the clergy. The Black Death, 1347–1350, was a traumatic event, a spiritual crisis. Occurring during the Babylonian Captivity, the early years of the Hundred Years' War, and the general retrenchment of Europe, it seemed to some a terrible judgment on wayward Christianity. Millennialism, self-flagellation, apocalyptical prophecies, social revolt, violence, and dwelling on scenes of death, such as the "dance of death" cartoons with their grinning skeletons,

St. Dominic Burning Books — *painted while the Spanish Inquisition was at its height: Civilization paying a high price for purity of thought.*

were some of the manifestations of a deep fear, fear bordering on hysteria, and a spiritual dislocation that endemic plagues only deepened. Here were ample psychological conditions for a diversity of religious expression. A kind of religious epidemic swept across Europe.

Of the major heresies of the Middle Ages, Albigensianism had been reduced to impotent fragments. But Waldensianism was still active in parts of France, Italy, and Germany. It proclaimed the priesthood of all believers, denied the efficacy of sacraments performed by priests in states of mortal sin, and used the Bible as authority in opposing the hierarchy's demand for obedience. During the Hundred Years' War, John Wycliffe of Oxford, a popular preacher, writer, and scholar who assisted in the preparation of the government's anti-papal enactments of the 1350s, initiated a similar heretical movement in England. Wycliffe relied upon the Bible for authority and, asserting the competence of inspired laymen to understand it, stimulated its translation into English. Disdaining the hierarchical Church at Avignon, he taught that the true Church consisted of all who were predestined to salvation. He denied the miracle of the mass, in which the priest transformed bread and wine into the flesh and blood of Christ, and from the exercise of which the priest secured his elevated status. In addition, he denounced the temporal possessions and temporal authority of churchmen. He also encouraged poor wandering priests, or "Lollards," to preach throughout the country.

Although Wycliffe taught absolute obedience to secular authority even when it was tyrannical, the court eventually had second thoughts about his religious orthodoxy and secured his retirement to a country estate. Wycliffe's teachings continued at Oxford, however, eventually permeating all classes of society. When they reached the lower classes through the Lollards, they became intertwined with demands for secular and social reforms. The "Peasants' Rebellion" of 1381 compromised religious radicalism, causing a conservative reaction to set in. A half century of persecution by the authorities of Church and state, during which the burning of heretics was first introduced into England, sufficed to extinguish Lollardy. By the end of the Hundred Years' War, it had all but disappeared.

In Bohemia, John Hus (1369–1415) drew upon the teachings of Wycliffe to attack clerical immorality, scholastic philosophy, simony, sale of indulgences, and reverence for relics and saints. Excommunicated by the local archbishop, his case came before the Council of Constance, where he was burned at the stake.

Instead of ending the Bohemian heresy, Hus's betrayal and execution fanned national and religious resistance to the Church and to the German emperor who inherited the Bohemian crown in 1419. Nobles and knights drew up a reform program; and the emperor was turned away from Prague's gates by force. Between 1420 and 1436 a series of Bohemian wars, at once civil and foreign, devastated Central Europe as the Czechs turned back repeated German and papal crusades and raided neighboring territories. Internally, the Hussites split between moderate nobles and militant egalitarian radicals (Taborites) who sought the destruction of noble and clerical privileges. Although the Taborites were ultimately defeated, the Church was obliged to yield to doctrinal deviations which it could not stamp out by force of arms.

More successful in avoiding official condemnation were the mystical Upper Rhenish "Friends of God" who produced a popular devotional treatise entitled *The German Theology*. Others formed lay brotherhoods in the Netherlands called the Brethren of the Common Life. The latter was founded in the wake of the Black Death by Gerard Groote (1340–1384), a scholar priest from a leading Deventer family. The Brethren organized lay men and women who dedicated themselves to devotionals, education, and preaching in the vernacular without taking irrevocable vows. As mystics, they held the complexities of scholastic theology in low esteem and emphasized a simple ethic of humble imitation of the life of Christ. The Brethren scored great success in educating the townspeople of the lower Rhine. (Deventer became the center of Northern humanism; one Brethren pupil, Erasmus, became the leading humanist of Renaissance Europe.) Despite their criticism of the clergy they escaped excommunication during the fifteenth century. In the early part of the Reformation period many of the people influenced by them apparently became "Sacramentarians," that is, persons who denied any divine miracle in the sacraments. On the other hand, Ignatius Loyola, founder of the Society of Jesus during the Catholic Reformation, was significantly influenced by their writings.

The Papacy of the High Renaissance

In the absence of ecclesiastical reform the papacy of the High Renaissance was powerless to check the erosion of its influence. It did move, however, to regain its hold on culture and, at least in Italy, on political affairs. Popes and prelates became foremost patrons and often practitioners of classical arts and letters. Humanism they made "safe" by drawing it into the service of religious education and scholarship. Many high churchmen became more concerned with aesthetics, learning, and luxurious living than with religious doctrines and administration. Understandably, they alienated fundamentalists preoccupied with salvation, self-denial, and the traditional ideals of the Church. As social conservatives, they also frustrated social as well as religious reform. Thus although the higher clergy came to terms with Renaissance arts and letters, they risked social and doctrinal revolts against their authority.

It was the tragedy of the papacy to be

Julius II, detail from the Mass of Bolsena *by Raphael. He was a determined, powerful, princely pope.*

drawn into inescapable political situations which caused it to lose further prestige as a spiritual force. During the Great Schism noble families, mercenary captains, and nearby princes and republics carved up the papal states into local domains or dependencies. With the restoration of a single line of popes in Rome, the task of recovery began. Lacking reliable officials, Renaissance popes distributed offices among their own relatives, a nepotistic device which soon produced scandalous conditions. Alexander VI (1492–1503), for example, attempted to establish his son, Cesare Borgia, at the head of a conquered personal family principality. Military efforts to reconquer the Papal States reached a peak under Julius II (1503–1513). This "warrior pope," a patron of Michelangelo, Bramante, and Raphael, personally led his troops in the field.

Invasion of Italy by France and Spain after 1494 further complicated papal politics. For the popes, fearing domination of Italy and the papacy by either France or Spain, organized "holy leagues" against whichever one was most threatening at the moment. Thus papal diplomacy became indistinguishable from the secular diplomacy of the Italian city-states, and its spiritual weapons of interdict and excommunication lost all effectiveness. Eventually the papacy failed to prevent the domination of the

peninsula by Spain; thereafter papal fortunes were wed to the secular power of the Spanish Habsburgs who superintended much of the Catholic Reformation of the sixteenth century. Meanwhile the expenses of war, papal patronage of the arts, and clerical luxury alienated non-Italians on whom fell heavy financial burdens. Particularly roused were the Germans who had little sympathy with the purposes to which papal revenues were put.

Conclusion

Seen as a whole, the Renaissance was not a solo of subsequent modernity. Composed and performed by diverse creators, it was a dissonant symphony of contradictory voices. Nor were its ideals always novel. Often they accommodated rather than undermined chivalric tradition. The "universal man," for example, had by its close become a well-born gentleman. His highest values were still medieval: military valor, honor, and the thirst for fame and glory.

Many would measure the Renaissance by the ideals of a few of its shining lights: Lorenzo de Medici, Leonardo da Vinci, and Erasmus. They epitomized the ideals of the Renaissance. Still, they did not set the tone of the succeeding age. But the humanistic world view, Renaissance aesthetics, and concepts of state and society survived the passions of the Reformation. Combined with new scientific discoveries, they inspired the secular society of the Age of Reason, thus helping to shape the world view of modern man.

SELECTED READINGS

The Renaissance 1300–1520

*Berenson, Bernard, *Italian Painters of the Renaissance,* Meridian Books, New York, 1957.
    Vivid interpretations of individual painters, especially those who made two-dimensional

Asterisk (*) denotes paperback.

canvasses "windowpanes" through which appeared the illusion of an external, objective reality.

*Blunt, Anthony, *Artistic Theory in Italy 1450–1600,* Clarendon Press, Oxford, 1962.
Sketches with illustrations the purposes for which art was intended from the middle ages through the Catholic Reformation.

Brucker, Gene A., *Florentine Politics and Society 1343–1378,* Princeton University Press, Princeton, 1962.
Portrays factional turbulence of Renaissance town life within the machinery of a "one-party" state.

Burckhardt, Jacob, *The Civilization of the Renaissance in Italy,* many English editions.
Discovers the spirit of the Renaissance in the union of the classics and the genius of the Italian people. An extremely influential romantic interpretation of the nineteenth century now controversial.

Bush, Douglas, *The Renaissance and English Humanism,* Oxford University Press, London, 1962.
Lectures which emphasize religious traditionalism in English humanism.

Calmette, Joseph, *The Golden Age of Burgundy,* W. W. Norton, Inc., New York, 1963.
A cultural and political account of Burgundy's blending of northern Europe's richest urban culture, dynastic aggrandizement, and sumptuous chivalric display at court.

Carsten, Francis L., *The Origins of Prussia,* Clarendon Press, Oxford, 1954.
Traces the transition of the German-Slavic frontier from freedom to serfdom. The account carries on to the seventeenth century.

Chabod, Federico, *Machiavelli and the Renaissance,* Harvard University Press, Cambridge, 1960.
Essays assessing Machiavelli's realism as a political reporter and theorist; concludes with a keen analysis of what was new in the Renaissance.

*Cheyney, Edward P., *The Dawn of a New Era 1250–1453* (Rise of Modern Europe series), Harper & Row, New York and Evanston, 1962.
Comprehensive summary stressing the emergence of national cultures and concluding with an extensive annotated bibliography.

Ferguson, Wallace K., *Europe in Transition 1300–1520,* Houghton Mifflin Co., Boston, 1962.
New standard textbook account which makes the middle of the fifteenth century a turning point from depression and internal disorder to economic improvement and dynastic consolidation.

Ferguson, Wallace K., *The Renaissance in Historical Thought: Five Centuries of Interpretation,* Houghton Mifflin Co., Boston, 1948.
Chronicles changing attitudes toward the Renaissance; as informative on later generations as on the Renaissance itself.

*Gilmore, Myron P., *The World of Humanism 1453–1517* (Rise of Modern Europe series), Harper & Row, New York and Evanston, 1962.
General history of all Europe and its contacts with other civilizations.

Hays, Denys, *The Italian Renaissance in Its Historical Background,* Cambridge University Press, Cambridge, 1961.
Readable survey based upon the most recent scholarship.

*Hexter, J. H., *Reappraisals in History,* Harper & Row, New York and Evanston, 1961.
Collection of articles on early modern European history provocatively challenging such commonly accepted clichés as "the rise of the middle class."

*Huizinga, Johan, *The Waning of the Middle Ages,* Doubleday & Co., Garden City, n.d.
Perceptive cultural history based on the Low Countries which fails to find evidence of revolutionary changes during the Renaissance.

*Lucki, Emil, *History of the Renaissance 1350–1550,* University of Utah Press, Salt Lake City, 1963–1965.
Textbook arranged according to subject in five small volumes; emphasizes continuity rather than change.

Mariéjol, J. H., *The Spain of Ferdinand and Isabella,* Rutgers University Press, New Brunswick, N.J., 1961.
Translation of a nineteenth century French account still fresh and valuable.

Martines, Lauro, *The Social World of the Florentine Humanists 1390–1460,* Routledge and Kegan Paul Ltd., London, 1963.

> A sociologist investigation of the leading Florentine humanists and their family connections which places them among the ruling elite.

Mattingly, Garrett, *Renaissance Diplomacy,* J. Cape, London, 1955.

> Masterful combination of institutional analysis and political events which traces the origin and spread of the sending of diplomatic envoys and characterizes Renaissance politics as dynastic rather than national.

*Mollat, G., *The Popes at Avignon 1305–1378,* Harper & Row, New York, 1965.

> Detailed classical French account of the church's "Babylonian Captivity."

*Pirenne, Henri, *Early Democracies in the Low Countries,* Harper & Row, New York, Evanston, and London, 1963.

> Opinionated but rare treatment of conflicts leading to the loss of urban autonomy in the Netherlands.

The Renaissance: Six Essays, Harper & Row, New York and Evanston, 1962.

> Interpretative essays by representative authorities on politics, economics, art, literature, science and religion. Ferguson on the Renaissance state, and Panofsky on art are outstanding essays in this collection.

Smith, Preserved, *Erasmus,* Frederick Ungar Publishing Co., New York, 1962.

> Sympathetic biography of the "prince of the humanists" which finds in him roots of a twentieth century non-dogmatic religion.

Taylor, Henry O., *Thought and Expression in the Sixteenth Century,* Vol. I, Frederick Ungar Publishing Co., New York, 1959 (2nd rev. ed.).

> Literary history which, despite its title, begins with the early Italian humanists of the fourteenth century.

14

The Confessional Age: The Reformations of the Sixteenth Century

THE PROTESTANT REVOLT

The founders of new religious movements in the sixteenth century were primarily theologians occupied with new interpretations of old authorities revered by their Roman Catholic opponents. For this reason the historian must consider divergent schools of theology as critically important. Harder to assess but omnipresent and equally critical were the religious passions of the common people. In addition to the ultimate terror of death, their lives were made doubly uncertain by new diseases, large-scale warfare, famine, and plague — scourges for whose partial control they lacked the science and institutions of more recent, less religiously oriented men. Whether Catholic, Protestant, or sectarian Anabaptist, they sought solace in supernatural salvation along paths prescribed by

revelation and tradition. Religious faith was the principal focus of their loyalties and concerns, the standard of value for which most were willing to kill as instruments in the hands of God.

Thus theology and popular faith were constant ingredients of the Reformation era. But they alone do not satisfactorily explain the success or failure of specific religions in specific areas. Social, economic, and especially political movements became inextricably a part of both the religious controversies and their eventual outcomes. Except among sectarians, religious thinkers of the sixteenth century did not conceive of a separate church and state. Indeed, most theologians used religious principles to buttress the existing social order.

But changes in that *status quo* inevitably

Illustrations from a German tract of 1508, prophesying disasters to come. Many Germans were ready for a religious change.

meant changes in the administration if not the doctrine of the Church. Conversely, reform programs which coincided with the existing power structures, particularly those of nascent "absolutist" princes and councils, received political and military support. By the same token, sectarians and humanists who opposed existing power structures suffered general persecution and frequently extirpation. How well a given government could suppress religious dissidents depended upon how much support it had. And a significant degree of that support was determined by the success or failure of its military and diplomatic ventures.

The German Reformation

Secular Background

Exceptionally great power was exercised by the Church in the Holy Roman Empire. Not only did the papacy draw far more revenues from it than the emperor, but certain clerical states, chiefly the electorates of Mainz, Cologne, and Trier, as well as numerous principalities of bishops, abbots, and commanders of the Teutonic Knights, were provokingly prominent in public affairs. The lack of an effective central government in the Empire left the Church stronger there than in the territorial states of Italy or the more centralized monarchies of France and England.

Germans at all social levels resented the Church. The great princes tried to control the Church and prevent revenues from flowing to Rome. The guildsmen and merchants resented the tax exemptions of the Church and the economic competition with churchmen in milling, craft production, and retail sales. The peasants resented the immoral behavior of clerics, the paying of tithes, and the ecclesiastical support of the nobility that was oppressing them.

Economic hardships hit Germany hard around 1500. Commercial and industrial enterprises were losing ground, because centers of trade and industry shifted to the Atlantic seaboard. The nobles were able to remain fluid by exacting heavier dues and services from the peasants, who had less and less wherewithal. The small traders, money lenders, and mine operators were being crowded out by the monopolies of the great merchants who were involved in international commerce and finance, and who in some cases served as bankers for

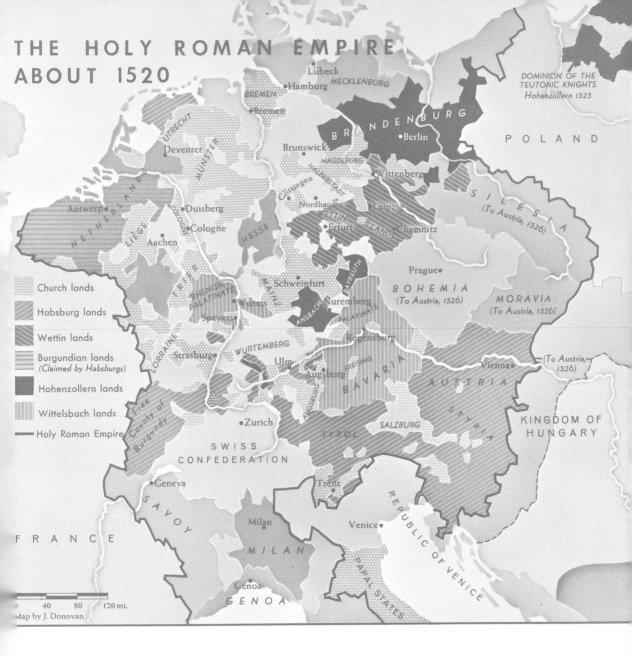

THE HOLY ROMAN EMPIRE ABOUT 1520

DOMINION OF THE
TEUTONIC KNIGHTS
Hohenzollern 1525

Lübeck
Hamburg
MECKLENBURG
BREMEN
Bremen
POLAND
BRANDENBURG
Berlin
Deventer
MÜNSTER
Brunswick
MAGDEBURG
Wittenberg
HALBERSTADT
SILESIA
(To Austria, 1526)
Antwerp
Göttingen
COLOGNE
Duisberg
Nordhausen
WETTIN
LANDS
Leipzig
LIÈGE
Cologne
HESSE
Erfurt
Chemnitz
Aachen
Prague
BOHEMIA
(To Austria, 1526)
TRIER
Schweinfurt
BAYREUTH
MORAVIA
(To Austria, 1526)
RHENISH
PALATINATE
Worms
MAINZ
ANSBACH
Nuremberg
Speyers
LOWER
PALATINATE
Strasburg
LORRAINE
WURTEMBERG
Regensburg
Ulm
FREISING
Vienna
(To Austria, 1526)
Augsburg
AUGSBURG
BAVARIA
AUSTRIA
Free County of Burgundy
Zurich
STYRIA
KINGDOM OF
HUNGARY
TYROL
SALZBURG
SWISS
CONFEDERATION
Geneva
Trent
SAVOY
REPUBLIC OF VENICE
Milan
Venice
FRANCE
MILAN
PAPAL
STATES
Genoa
GENOA

	Church lands
	Habsburg lands
	Wettin lands
	Burgundian lands (Claimed by Habsburgs)
	Hohenzollern lands
	Wittelsbach lands
—	Holy Roman Empire

40 80 120 mi.
Map by J. Donovan

the papacy. Governmental taxes, invariably falling on those least able to bear them, were becoming intolerable. Economic misery affected the majority of Germans, except the Church and the upper levels of society. Social discontent and resentment of the Church reinforced each other.

Meanwhile, popular leaders sought to overcome German woes by leading revolts against the Church and the princes, and against landlord nobility in the country and patrician oligarchy in the cities. In the towns there was conflict between guildsmen and patricians. Revolutionaries attacked officials for improper behavior. They demanded an end to alleged financial corruption, nepotism, and government by secret manipulation. They sought to prevent the legal system from making justice too expensive for common people to obtain. Above all they protested the increasing indirect taxation on items of consumption and commerce. Between 1509 and 1512 many towns experienced revolts.

At the same time, in the southern countryside, peasant uprisings occurred. These

A Bundschuh *rebel, as pictured by a hostile tract of 1513. The* Bundschuh *was still found in radical pamphlets of World War I as a symbol of rebellion.*

Bundschuh revolts (named after the thonged peasant boot which they adopted as their banner) were sometimes directed toward a return to communal autonomy and old custom.* Sometimes they aimed at establishing a standard of divine justice which would render serfdom unchristian. These revolts failed.

Emergence of Luther

Temporarily the different levels of German discontent were knit together by the activities of Martin Luther (1483?–1546) in Saxony and Ulrich Zwingli in Zurich. Though their principal appeal was religious, their early attack on the *status quo* was sufficiently broad to bring together divergent, even contradictory, bodies of dissent under common slogans.

Born a younger son of a copper-smelting family of peasant stock, Luther grew up while his family's fortunes were rising. Educated in urban schools, he obtained a bachelor's and a master's degree in liberal arts at Erfurt University. At his parents' urging he began the study of Roman law,

---

* Although that "old custom" certainly had not been based on equality and justice, many felt it was a far easier kind of oppression to live under.

the most promising path to power and prestige. Fulfilling a vow taken in a moment of terror, young Martin suddenly switched his career, broke with his father, and joined an Augustinian cloister at Erfurt in 1505.

Zealous but unsatisfied as a monk, Luther was directed by his superiors to obtain a doctorate in theology at the new university founded by Elector Frederick the Wise of Saxony at Wittenberg. Here, as a professor of theology, Luther resolved his personal longings for certainty in the course of preparing his lectures. Despairing of ever meriting grace from an angry, incomprehensible, and predestining God by his own works, he found an escape from eternal damnation in St. Paul and St. Augustine. Salvation was not to be found in pious acts or ethical behavior but in a God-implanted faith which alone served to justify man, who remained immutably and impotently depraved. Authority for this doctrine of "faith alone" he found not in the papacy or tradition of the church but in the Scripture or Word of God.

Luther began his career of reform with the curriculum of the University. At Wittenberg he met and befriended Melanchthon, an accomplished classical scholar and a nephew of Reuchlin. Melanchthon became Luther's lifetime ally and systematizer of his doctrine. Together they excluded the traditional scholastic disciplines from Wittenberg's course of study. This gave Luther a reputation as an Erasmian. But his theology opposed that line of thought as much as it opposed scholasticism. Erasmian humanists were preoccupied with replacing ignorance by reason and with encouraging men to behave ethically. Luther was preoccupied with religious justification and with opening people to the experience of faith. For him reason and ethics were serviceable only under the direction of that faith; otherwise reason was the "devil's harlot" and ethical conduct was a lure to heresy. Luther's changing subjective moods made him a volatile and sometimes inconsistent theologian; but whatever position he took in a given situation he was confident that it represented faith in an objective, revealed creed which anyone not blinded by the Devil could find for himself in Scripture.

The Wittenberg monk became a public figure in 1517 when he posted Ninety-Five Theses attacking abuses in the sale of indulgences. The Theses were for an academic debate that never occurred, but they were translated, printed, and circulated throughout Germany. Luther did not attack the principle of indulgences until 1520, but in the meantime he attacked the Church in tracts and debates. He went so far as to call for a new general Church council. Later he questioned the infallibility of past councils. Pope Leo X tried to curb Luther's attacks, but political complications—namely Leo's efforts to prevent the powerful Charles of Spain from becoming Emperor in 1519—delayed decisive action. Meanwhile the monk ignored papal rulings. Finally in 1520 Leo X issued a papal bull excommunicating Luther and his associates.

Because Luther placed Scripture over the authority of tradition, he came into conflict with the Church. Debating John Eck at Leipzig in 1519, Luther had declared both popes and councils fallible. He elaborated upon this declaration in a series of tracts the following year. His *Address to the Christian Nobility of the German Nation* was directed to the princes. It called upon them to reform the Church if the clerics would not. Luther further argued for the "priesthood of all believers." With this principle (introduced earlier by Waldensians and others) he could justify state intervention: princes were also priests. In the same tract he advocated congregational control of pastors and Church property. *The Babylonian Captivity of the Church* Luther addressed to the clergy in Latin. In this tract he argued that only baptism, the Lord's Supper, and perhaps penance were based on Scripture. All other so-called sacraments had been added

by papal Anti-Christs and deserved destruction. A third "little book," *On the Freedom of a Christian,* was intended for both the papacy and the general populace. In it Luther—who had already denounced the merit of all good works—developed more fully his concept of the priesthood of all believers. He set freedom apart from the secular world, defining it as wholly internal and spiritual. In the wake of these three tracts followed a great wave of popular publications, many of them anonymous. Their authors saw a relationship between spiritual freedom from papal authority on the one hand and physical freedom from political, social, and economic oppression on the other. They insisted that the Gospel was about brotherhood and justice. Basic reform, they believed, meant the transformation not just of the Church but of society as well.

The Diet and Edict of Worms

Charles V had become Emperor in 1519, and was the greatest dynast Europe had yet beheld. He called an imperial diet at the city of Worms in 1521 primarily to secure tax grants and a new military organization to defend his vast holdings against the Turks, France, and internal enemies. Luther's hearing was secondary. The German princes, fearful of Charles' power, refused his tax and military demands. Since many of them were also aggrieved with the papacy, some of them refused to enforce Luther's condemnation. After some delegates had departed, the Emperor and Aleander, the papal legate, pushed through an edict outlawing Luther, his books, and his followers, after they had prevented him from arguing the details of his position.

Meanwhile Luther had been spirited away for safekeeping to Wartburg Castle by agents of Frederick the Wise. Under Frederick's protection Luther continued to work. He translated the New Testament into idiomatic German from Erasmus' Greek New Testament and continued to pen influential tracts. In one particularly powerful piece he appealed to monks and nuns to leave their cloisters. Luther's revolt was characterized by considerable personal courage, but for its success depended upon the simultaneous revolt of the German princes and city councils against the Emperor and Rome.

Pamphlets, Agitation, and Revolts

Luther had attributed German woes solely to clerical greed, sophistry, and obscurantism. But fellow pamphleteers, such as Martin Bucer, combined social and religious reform into a "social gospel," an anticipated reorganization of society based upon divine justice and Scriptural text. An influential anonymous tract probably written by Martin Bucer went further in urging the peasants—whom these pamphlets venerated as superior in religious judgment to Romanist clerics—to "use their flails" to coerce authorities into accepting reform without overt revolution. In Zurich, Ulrich Zwingli denounced tithes and called for resistance to ungodly governments. In Saxony, Thomas Muentzer preached revolution against princes who barred the Gospel's path. All these had revolutionary implications, but agreement on the path to reform was lacking, especially in territories ruled by clerical or aggressively Catholic princes.

After 1521 the slogans of the major reformers penetrated the lower classes. Often led by former monks, urban masses attacked the old regime and the partial reforms of authorities adhering to Luther. In widespread areas peasants began to withhold tithes, dues, and services.

After a poor harvest in 1524 the peasant and urban lower classes of southwestern Germany were raw with deprivation and discontent. Their hostility, which clerical and secular rulers had nurtured by trying to enforce the Edict of Worms, spilled over into what is known in German history as the "Great Peasants' War." Revolutionary townsmen of the major cities adopted articles condemning clerical and peasant economic competition. But most of these revolts were inspired by a common program of reform, *The Twelve Articles of the German Peasantry,* which swept northward through the clerical states of central Germany. In 1525 they joined another center of revolt in Saxony. The articles were written in the form of a contract to which local rebel "hosts" sought to secure their lords' assent. The contract, assuming that society and politics should rest upon Scripture unadulterated by human invention, stipulated that congregations should have the right to elect and depose their own clergy. Common people would have hunting and fishing rights. Serfdom would be abolished. Tithes not mentioned in the Bible would be forgotten. And the legal system would be revamped. Counting upon divine assistance, rather than overt revolution, the rebels sought to enforce these contracts by withholding dues from the authorities.

The initiative taken by the rebellious lower classes, their demand for civic equality or brotherhood, and their ecclesiastical congregationalism collided squarely with the existing order. Amid charges of anarchy and communism, local leagues of princes organized loyal nobles, townsmen, and mercenary troops into an aggressive counteroffensive. They determined to make sanguinary examples of those who dared revolt. After the merciless slaughter of about 100,000 peasants, the revolt collapsed. The peasants had assumed that they were acting in accord with Luther's wishes. But in the closing days of the revolt Martin Luther preached a crusade of extermination against them. Terrified by the anarchical implications of their uprising, he came to believe that they had perverted the spiritual Gospel for secular gain.*

* Later Luther took credit for the suppression of the revolt even though his tract, *Against the Robbing and Murdering Bands of Peasants,* did not appear until the eve of the peasants' rout at Frankenhausen in Thuringia, one of the last encounters of the revolt. Similarly he attributed the whole uprising to his arch-foe in Saxony, Thomas Muentzer, an opinion which documentary evidence fails to substantiate.

The Shattering of Reformation Unity

Luther's premise that Scriptural authority would produce a single, objectively revealed creed which every person could quickly discover for himself soon ran into trouble. Erasmian humanists abhorred his incitement to violence and repudiated his Augustinian predestinarian doctrines as subversive of morality. Radical evangelicals and humanists opposed his social and political authoritarianism. The rebels of 1525 learned the hard way that they and Luther held different concepts of Scriptural authority and Christian brotherhood. What appeared to be a common assault on the Catholic Church soon dissolved into a number of competing creeds and organizations seeking consolidation and control over local areas.

Zwinglian Reform in Zurich

Ulrich Zwingli (1484–1531) became a public reforming figure in Zurich about the same time that Luther became famous in Saxony. Theologically Zwingli had much in common with Luther, from whom he derived some of his doctrines. They agreed on the absolute sovereignty and inscrutability of God from whom fallen man was separated by a gulf unbridgeable except by divine grace. Though both affirmed the principle of Biblical authority, Zwingli treated the Lord's Supper as a memorial service rather than a supernatural sacrament. And he offended Luther's followers by justifying revolution. Zwingli established a state church in Zurich, a republican state controlled largely by the guilds from whom Zwingli drew most of his political support. In this, too, he differed from and antagonized Luther, who leaned heavily upon princely support. "Sacramentarians," as Zwinglians were called, were soon proscribed by Saxon laws. Theologically and politically the basis for cooperative efforts between northern and southern reformers was lacking. Philip of Hesse, an energetic early Protestant prince, brought Luther and Zwingli together at Marburg in 1529; but Luther refused to discuss what he considered to be Zwingli's use of reason in matters of revelation. Shortly thereafter Zwingli was killed in a war between Zurich and Swiss Catholic cantons which resisted Zwinglian proselytism.

Sectarians and the Radical Reformation

Whatever their differences on other questions, both Luther and Zwingli, like the Roman Catholics they opposed, relied upon secular coercion to secure their religious authority. Both established state churches binding upon all members of the political community. In Zurich the state church was directed by a city council which heard debates and legislated new doctrine and rites. Working through it, Zwingli reinstated infant baptism and tithes, and made state intervention in religious affairs common practice. Rejection of the state's authority in enforcing the Gospel, Zwingli denounced as sedition and blasphemy.

Certain radical reformers soon proved "blasphemous." Like the Erasmian humanist, they insisted that doctrine must be judged by its adherents' behavior. A creed was acceptable only if following it meant living by New Testament ethics. They also insisted that the priesthood of all believers required voluntary religious participation and tolerance. In 1524 Conrad Grebel, a Zurich humanist, led a secession from Zwingli's ranks. He and his followers refused to obey government regulations on religion. They insisted that only adult or adolescent converts had the faith requisite for baptism. Converts from older confessions were baptized a second time. Joined by other dissenters from established churches (whether Protestant or Catholic) they thus launched the Radical Reformation. Quite naturally it was denounced by all established clergy as sedition, heresy, and blasphemy. The very name applied to them, Anabaptists (rebaptizers), reflects this animosity, for under the Justinian Code rebaptism was a death-penalty offense.

The Anabaptists found their model in the early persecuted church recorded in the Book of Acts. For them, the true church was not an invisible body or the political community at large. It was a voluntary association of baptized believers whose purity of conduct was maintained through admonition and expulsion. Their measuring rod for both creed and society was the New Testament, especially the Sermon on the Mount. Most Anabaptists refused to take oaths and disavowed the taking of human life by any state or individual. The ruling concerns of their common life were Christian brotherhood and the distribution of alms. They were not much preoccupied with distinctions of rank and sex. Those who fled to Bohemia for sanctuary practiced a form of consumption communism, or communitarianism. Though humanists and persons of high social status occasionally joined or led their congregations, most Anabaptists were petty craftsmen and peasants. From the Anabaptist point of view, the state-church Reformation offered "no improvement" over the previous order. Their ranks in Germany rapidly swelled after the suppression of the Peasants' Revolt. Protestant and Catholic churchmen viewed them as a revolutionary threat to established society and subjected them to bloody persecution. As persecution removed their leadership, their adversity tended to encourage their belief that the end of the world was at hand. The Dutch Mennonites, (so-called after the Anabaptist leader, Menno Simons) who became prominent in business and agriculture, obtained tolerance in 1572. But they were an exception.

Consolidation of Lutheran Territorial Churches

After the Peasants' Revolt several German princes prominent in its suppression — Landgrave Philip of Hesse, Elector John

of Saxony, and Margrave Casimir of Brandenburg — had become converts to Lutheranism. They found it more effective than Catholicism in maintaining public order. Several imperial cities also adopted Lutheranism or a modification of it. The Diet of Speyer, over which the Emperor had little control, resolved to leave each prince free until a general council was called, to interpret the Edict of Worms.

Philip of Hesse seized this opportunity to install Lutheran clergymen in the towns and to confiscate all Church property and endowments. His precedent in establishing princely control over a territorial church was soon followed in Saxony, Brandenburg, Prussia, Denmark, Sweden, Württemberg, and other principalities. Everywhere the chief beneficiaries were the privileged orders of town and country and the "Christian magistracy" — usually a prince or king, considered by Lutherans as the father of an extended family. To him as head of the family — or to the city council — the Lutheran Church taught passive obedience as the first requirement of piety. The clergy relied on him to root out all remnants of Roman Catholicism and all new heresies, especially Anabaptism. New state-appointed clergy undertook the strict enforcement of credal uniformity.

The German magisterial reformers emphasized that their reform was purely spiritual and uncorrupted by material motives. Most of their changes were confined to doctrine and liturgy. They reduced the number of sacraments to two, baptism and the Lord's Supper. Monasticism they suppressed. In worship but not in scholarship they used the vernacular language. Also, to church services they added more sermons and congregational singing. Otherwise they followed tradition.

For a generation these changes took place without imperial intervention. The Emperor was not strong enough to oppose them and wanted a political compromise. But in 1529 Charles had won a war with Francis I, and could attend to the Lutheran

EUROPE IN 1526

DYNASTIC POWER RIVALS

- France (Valois)
- Dominions of Charles V (Habsburg)
- Holy Roman Empire
- Ottoman Empire

K. OF SCOTLAND

IRELAND

North Sea

K. OF DENMARK

Baltic Sea

K. OF ENGLAND
(Tudor)

London

Antwerp

NETHERLANDS

Münster

Wittenberg

THE EMPIRE
(Habsburg)

Worms

Speyer

Prague

BOHEMIA

SILESIA

KINGDOM OF POLAND
(Jagellon)

GRAND DUCHY
OF LITHUANIA
(Jagellon)

Paris

KINGDOM
OF
FRANCE

Atlantic
Ocean

Zurich

SWISS CONFED.

Geneva

MILAN

Pavia
1525

Venice

Vienna

AUSTRIA

HUNGARY

Mohács
1526

Transylvania

Moldavia

Wallachia

Danube R.

Black Sea

REP. OF VENICE

OTTOMAN EMPIRE

Genoa

Florence

PAPAL
STATES

K. OF PORTUGAL

KINGDOM OF

Madrid

SPAIN

Aragon

Balearic Is.

Granada

Corsica

Rome

KINGDOM OF
NAPLES

SARDINIA

Mediterranean

K. OF SICILY

Sea

Crete (Venice)

---

problem. A decree issued at the second Diet of Speyer in 1529 forbade any further extension of Lutheranism. The Lutheran princes and 14 imperial cities *protested* formally, hence the name Protestant.

In 1530 the Emperor, freshly strengthened by the defeat of the Turks at Vienna, attended the Diet of Augsburg in person. Failing to get a compromise between the Lutherans (for whom Melanchthon drew up the conciliatory Augsburg Confession) and the Catholics, and profiting from the doctrinal divisions separating northern from southern Protestants, Charles ordered their return to the traditional faith. Led by Philip of Hesse, the Lutheran princes organized a Schmalkaldic League for defense against a Catholic League and the Emperor.

Hostilities remained limited, since Charles was much too preoccupied with the defense of his inheritance against the Turks and the French to have much opportunity to fight the Lutherans, who took advantage of the Emperor's troubles to continue to expand. It was not until 1546 that Charles could launch a strong military and diplomatic offensive against the Protestant princes and cities. When his campaigns proved inconclusive, Charles gradually adopted a policy of toleration. That policy became permanent in 1555 in the Peace of Augsburg, in which the Emperor granted the Protestant princes equal rights within the Empire. He accepted the principle that each prince has the right to choose between

413

Lutheranism and Catholicism, and that the prince's religion would be the religion of his subjects, or they could emigrate.

Exhausted and disillusioned with the task of ruling his vast dynastic empire, Charles retired as a private person to a monastery in 1556. He abdicated the Spanish crown to his son Philip and the eastern Habsburg lands to his brother Ferdinand, who became the new Emperor. Relations between Lutherans and Catholics in the Empire remained tense, but, strange to say, there followed the longest period of peace since the German Reformation. The major German wars of religion did not break out until 1618.

England Secedes from Rome

The English Reformation was an act of state; initially religious doctrine had little to do with it. The issue of papal supremacy was sometimes debated as a theological question, and there were doctrinal disputes over the English translation of the Bible. Mainly the Reformation was a change of administration. Because papal authority in England had long been checked by secular controls over the church, this change seemed at first more an evolutionary mutation than a clean break with the past.

Henry VIII and the Succession Crisis

In 1527, Henry VIII filed a plea for a papal annulment of his marriage to Catherine of Aragon, in order that he might remarry with the hope of begetting a male heir. Since Pope Clement VII was a prisoner of Emperor Charles V, who was Catherine's nephew, he denied Henry's petition. Henry then set about getting the annulment on his own by separating the English Church from allegiance to Rome so that his own churchmen could annul the marriage. The revenues that had been flowing to Rome would naturally remain in England.

By a series of measures during the years 1529–1534, Henry gained control of his clergy and became head of the Anglican Church. He named a new Archbishop of Canterbury, Thomas Cranmer, whose devotion to royal supremacy made him the ideal ecclesiastic to acquire the authority to nullify Henry's marriage. That was accomplished in 1533. In 1534 a succession act required all subjects to swear to the legitimacy of Henry's new marriage and made dissenters guilty of high treason.

Secession from Rome was formalized in 1534 by the Act of Supremacy which declared the King head of the church. No authority outside England was henceforth recognized. No doctrinal issue except papal supremacy was at stake, but Henry enforced this administrative revolution with statutes of treason. The executions of Bishop John Fisher and Sir Thomas More served as a warning of the penalties that resistance entailed.

Reformation Settlement of Henry VIII and Edward VI

Henry VIII's break from Rome proved to be an entering wedge of further changes. In 1535 Henry commissioned Thomas Cromwell, who replaced Wolsey as Lord Chancellor, to investigate the cloisters. These monasteries were no longer playing a major social or economic role in society. They merely served as inns and centers of alms distribution. In 1539 Parliament sanctioned the dissolution of all cloisters. The redistribution of property which followed was more far-reaching than any since the Norman Conquest. The recipients of this property, local gentry families and royal favorites, now had a vested interest in Henry's Reformation which his Roman Catholic daughter, Mary, would later be unable to shake when she temporarily returned England to Roman jurisdiction.

In breaking with Rome, Henry VIII had no intention of bringing England into conformity with continental Protestant doctrines. He worked to repress the influence

Andrea Mantegna, Gonzaga Family, *1474. The diversity of Italian Renaissance culture was due in large part to the rise of powerful city-states ruled by local aristocratic families. The noble Gonzagas of Mantua were outstanding patrons of the arts. This fresco, painted on a wall of their castle, presents a forceful characterization of each of the Gonzagas. The head of the family, Ludovico, holds a letter announcing that his son Francesco has been made a cardinal. (European Art Color Slides)*

Pierre Desceliers, World Map, *1550. Renaissance mapmakers had an amazingly accurate conception of the world. Voyages of exploration made between about 1450 and 1600 by Columbus, Magellan, Vasco da Gama, and others provided information about parts of North America, South America, Africa, and Indonesia. Only Scandinavia, parts of Asia, and Australia are inaccurately represented here. Meant to be placed on a table to be read, the map is lettered in opposing directions. (British Museum, London)*

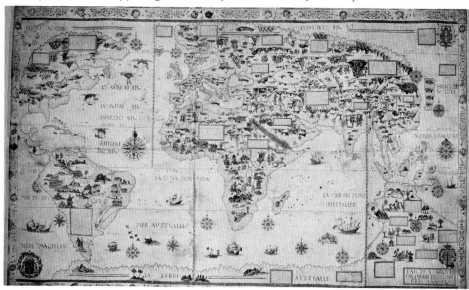

Hieronymus Bosch, The Peddler (The Prodigal Son?), ca. *1510. Under the influence of the Reformation, artists painted didactic pictures meant to serve as moral guides to Christians. This painting of an itinerant peddler, thought to be the Biblical prodigal son, clearly postulates the dual nature of man. Torn between evil and good, the peddler-prodigal looks back with regret at a house of ill fame as he walks toward his father's fields, the way of righteousness. (Museum Boymans-van Beunigen, Rotterdam)*

Quentin Metsys, The Moneylender and His Wife, 1514. *In contrast to the Bosch work above, Metsys' painting depicts the prosperous side of Flemish life in the sixteenth century. A jewelry merchant counts his gold as his wife idly turns the pages of a splendid Book of Hours. Along with other rich accessories, this is a sign of their wealth, for only the well-to-do could afford such books. The phlegmatic expressions on the couple's faces suggest the tranquility and the tedium of prosperity. (Musée du Louvre, Paris)*

TEMPLE DE LYON, NOMME PARADIS.

Jean Perrissin, Lyon's Church Named Paradise, 16th century. Because they were well organized and relatively wealthy, the Huguenots, French Calvinists, largely escaped the persecution meted out to other early Protestant groups until 1572, when thousands of Huguenots were massacred on St. Bartholomew's Eve. The austere setting depicted here illustrates the Protestant preference for simple, unadorned places of worship. (Bibliotèque Publique et Universitaire, Geneva)

Ambrogio Lorenzetti, The Effects of Good Government, *1338–40. These panoramic views of fourteenth-century Siena are part of a huge fresco cycle in Siena's city hall depicting the effects of good and bad government on the life of the people. The painting above presents communal life in a well-ordered city-state. The city is filled with bustling activity—dancing girls, merchants plying their trades, artisans at work. The Tuscan countryside (below), looking much as it does today, is patterned with fields and vineyards carefully tended by peasant farmers. The people are prospering, the land is yielding, and life is good. These ideal scenes may represent wishful thinking on the part of the artist, for Siena in the fourteenth century was not only involved in frequent warfare with Florence but was also afflicted by continuous struggles between popular and aristocratic elements within the city. According to the Renaissance historian Commines, Siena was "all divided and governed more madly than any town in Italy." Yet Siena managed to retain her independence until well into the sixteenth century. (Palazzo Pubblico, Siena—Scala)*

of William Tyndale, whose Protestant-oriented translation of the New Testament the bishops absorbed into the official English translation of the Bible. The Six Articles of Faith passed by Parliament in 1539, for which the King was primarily responsible, upheld clerical celibacy, private masses for the dead, auricular confession, and the transubstantiation of the bread and wine in the Lord's Supper into the body and blood of Christ. Lutherans he sent to the stake in the latter part of his reign.

Henry was succeeded by Edward VI, a boy of ten whose regency was dominated until 1550 by his uncle the Earl of Hereford (then Duke of Somerset). Somerset allowed the English Reformation to veer more toward continental Protestantism. He relaxed the heresy and treason laws and permitted the clergy to marry. In 1549 Parliament proclaimed an Act of Uniformity introducing the first Book of Common Prayer. It failed to affirm transubstantiation, and it contained Protestant prayers by Archbishop Cranmer. Opposition to the Prayer book rose in Devonshire and Oxfordshire, but the activities of Protestant mobs destroying relics and images indicated that Protestant doctrines were reaching into the general population.

Social Tension, Revolt, and Reaction

Under the regents governing for young Edward VI, England was a land of misery for many poor and of opportunity for the rich. Debasement of the coinage, further confiscations of church properties, rising prices, and the advance of the enclosure movement benefited the gentry and the royal treasury but deepened the distress of the poor. When Robert Kett of Norfolk led a rebellion in the summer of 1549 against the policies of the government and the enclosures of great tracts of land, thousands of peasants joined his cause. Somerset sympathized with the peasants, but his enemy, the Earl of Warwick, led professional troops out to crush "Kett's

Henry VIII in Parliament. When he wanted advice he asked for it.

Mary Tudor, portrait by Antonio Moro. How stiff and heavy was her gold-embroidered clothing!

Rebellion," slaying 3000 peasants. Somerset was the next victim of this ruthless man. Warwick took Somerset's place early in 1550 and executed him in 1552. He pursued a harsh policy toward the poor and moved England further toward Protestantism. When Edward died in 1553, the new queen, Mary Tudor, the Catholic daughter of Henry VIII and Catherine, imprisoned Warwick and other Protestant leaders.

Mary (1553–1558) achieved gradual but only partial success in restoring Catholicism. Her first Parliament returned to the religious *status quo* at the end of Henry VIII's reign, but it refused to persecute non-Catholics, or restore confiscated church properties. Against her will, the Queen remained head of the English Church until she secured a more pliant parliament. She also failed to gain support for her alliance with Spain (sealed by her marriage with Philip II, son of her cousin, Charles). Finally, a parliament was returned which restored papal authority and enacted laws against Protestant heretics. Under persecution, which led more than 300 to the stake, Protestant resistance stiffened. Its exiles to the Continent imbibed deeply of a more strident Protestantism with which they returned after her death. When she died in 1558 the Catholic cause in England was lost. Her successor, Elizabeth, daughter of Anne Boleyn, was necessarily Anglican, for in Catholic eyes she was illegitimate. A single short reign by a Catholic monarch proved insufficient to reverse the English religious revolution.

The Calvinist Reform

Except among the sectarians, most religious revolutionists were not interested in engaging in missionary attempts to universalize their faith. The reformation initiated by John Calvin (1509–1564), however, constituted an aggressive "international" movement which threatened existing governments with armed revolution and Roman Catholicism with a "visible,"

disciplined, rival church whose ideal state-church relationship closely resembled church-state relations during the papacy of Innocent III. As militant Roman Catholics became aware, Calvin's combination of the moral zeal of the sectarians with the conscious use of political and military power in carrying out "the will of God" made Calvinism the most serious threat to the religious *status quo* of Europe during the sixteenth and seventeenth centuries.

John Calvin, Would-Be Reformer of France

John Calvin (Jean Cauvin) was born into a rising middle class family of artisan ancestry in the cathedral city of Noyon. Destined for the priesthood, John was sent to the College of Montaigu in Paris, the school whose harsh discipline had repelled Erasmus. His father later changed his mind, and sent John to pursue the study of Roman law at Orleans and Bourges. Both schools had come under the influence of humanist philology and historical interpretation of the Justinian Codes. Calvin pursued law only so long as his father lived. With the elder Calvin's death in 1531 he returned to Paris and the study of the classics. For these languages, and later Hebrew, he had the best teachers in France — teachers who also happened to be Protestant in outlook. His first book, a commercial failure, was a humanist commentary upon Seneca's Stoicism. It emphasized morality and a sense of sin, but was quite different in tone from the Biblical and theocentric theology to which he devoted his life after 1533. Although his study of the law was brief, marks of the legalist remained strong in his systematic theology and in his refutations of opponents.

Unlike Luther, Calvin left few detailed personal reminiscences about his conversion to Protestantism. Probably it occurred in or before 1533. It is certain that he considered his conversion the work of a sovereign God who directed all of his subsequent actions and whose honor was at stake whenever he, Calvin, was criticized or contradicted.

Unsafe as a Protestant, Calvin wandered about France and then fled early in 1535 to Basel, a Protestant but humanist city. There he drafted the first edition of *The Institutes of the Christian Religion,* the most influential handbook of Protestant doctrine produced in the sixteenth century. To the *Institutes* Calvin appended a prefatory letter to Francis I. It exonerated French Protestants from charges of anarchy and attributed such charges to malicious rumors. His plea failed to secure tolerance for French Protestants, but it projected its author, an exile, into leadership of the French Reformation. Before the *Institutes* appeared in print in Basel, Calvin wandered to Geneva on the way to Strassburg. Asked to remain in Geneva by William Farel, reformer of Bern and Geneva, Calvin acquired a fortuitous base for the implementation of his ideas.

The *Institutes,* repeatedly revised and enlarged and eventually published in French as well as Latin, contained few novelties, but its clarity and precision made it the cutting edge of expanding Protestantism. In asserting the absolute sovereignty of a predestining God and the total, immutable depravity of man, Calvin was in agreement with Luther, upon whom he depended heavily. His doctrine of predestination can be understood only by seeing it as a necessary outcome of the attributes of an exalted, omnipotent God. Rather than gloom or uncertainty, predestination served to give the parishioner confidence of salvation by divine election and to stimulate a communal feeling of "God-chosenness." Men need not live as doomed reprobates predestined to eternal Hell. In Calvin's system all aspects of life—economic activity, politics, worship services, and family relationships—were subordinated to the absolute standard of Scriptural revelation. All morality should serve the advancement of the kingdom of God on earth.

John Calvin.

For authority, Calvin used the Scripture, but he interpreted it more narrowly than Luther. The church should be governed as the early church was, by pastors, elders, and deacons whose duties were spelled out in the text. He agreed with Luther in reducing the sacraments to two, but he denied the effective physical presence of the body and blood of Christ in the Lord's supper, a denial which precipitated acrimonious exchanges with various Lutherans. Calvin's scripturalism cut away more of the supernatural and magical tradition of Christianity than Luther's.

In theory, Calvin, like Luther, advocated the Christian's freedom from binding laws. Like Bucer, however, he reconstituted in practice both laws and enforcement procedures which regulated private life minutely. Though he did not impose celibacy, dietary regulations, or formal works of grace, Calvin tried to establish a universal monastic standard. Legislation of morals was equally stringent in Lutheran, Anglican, and Calvinist areas. But Calvin and his followers enforced their laws with special zeal, by excommunication and by sending teams of elders and clergymen into all homes annually to ferret out any religious or moral nonconformists. Unlike the Anglican and Lutheran establishments, the Calvinist church was not subservient to the secular authority. Calvinism adopted a system of synods representing clergy and elders. Through them the state was to serve as handmaiden of the church, its primary task the prevention of blasphemy. Far from introducing a separation of church and state, Calvin sought to reassert the authority of the clergy and elders over the sociopolitical order.

Politically a sharp difference separated Calvinism from the Anglican and Lutheran churches. Both of the latter taught obedience to the existing authorities as a matter of conscience. Declaring doctrinal orthodoxy the only legitimate basis of government, Calvin proselytized against hostile secular authorities. Faced with royal suppression of his gospel in France, he abandoned the obedience originally proffered Francis I and justified resistance to that French monarch by the "lesser magistrates"—nobles, town councilors, and jurists. In France and other areas, Calvin attracted powerful political forces of dissidence. Potentially, they constituted alternate governments. Thus his followers laid the groundwork for the civil and international wars of the second half of the century.

The Holy Commonwealth of Geneva

Calvin never succeeded in converting more than a small minority of his French countrymen. But following his accidental appearance in Geneva—which he interpreted as an act of Divine Providence—he turned that city into his own religious kingdom.

The Ecclesiastical Ordinances enacted by the councils of Geneva in 1541 were basically his. But the city magistrates retained their right to confirm appointments of pastors, teachers, elders, and deacons, and only they could name the elders who met every Thursday with the "Venerable Company" of ministers. And they jealously guarded the city's authority in legal affairs by denying the clergy the power to pronounce civil penalties. Although the secular authorities retained these legal prerogatives, the clergy still gained considerable autonomy of action.

Calvin's political power, absolute by 1555, derived from two sources: an unshakable belief in his own righteousness accompanied by unquenchable zeal, and the numerical strength of his following. He was unalterably determined to overcome all obstacles to the execution of God's will. All opponents, personal and political, he denounced as enemies of God. An influx of refugee pastors and other exiles contributed significantly to his following. His ranks outnumbered those of the divided Genevan opposition. In 1551 the Genevans countered Calvin's ascendancy by making a 25-year residence requirement for citizenship. Two years later, however, in the events surrounding the burning of Michael Servetus, Calvin's opposition was routed and subsequently broken. "Holy terror" thus served to consolidate the reformer's position. Theological critics who attacked Calvin's predestination doctrine on the grounds that it made God a tyrant were tortured and banished.

The Calvinist "International"

Often identified as a forerunner of modern nationalism, Calvinism was in fact the most international of the major Protestant reformations. Its adherents accepted a common doctrine, performed the same liturgy, and organized their churches according to the Genevan model. Everywhere Calvin's *Institutes,* clarified and extended by his personal correspondence, were the guide. Missionaries and pastors were trained almost exclusively in Geneva, and their orthodoxy was assured before they were allowed to fill teaching or pastoral posts. In some instances, the work of missionaries

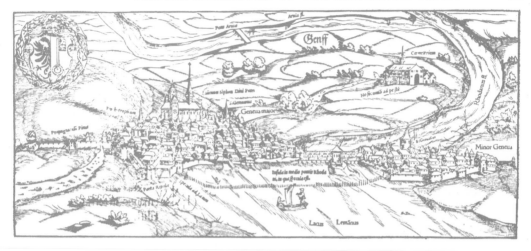

View of Geneva, the Calvinist Mecca, from which streamed propaganda and trained cadres of ministers to carry the reformed religion to France and other parts of Europe.

was kept under surveillance. Most of the Genevan students were from other lands: France, Scotland, England, Germany, etc. In 1559 the Genevan consistory * established a college headed by Theodore Beza, Calvin's eventual successor, to enlarge and systematize the training of the Calvinist clergy.

This uniform and well-controlled Calvinism spread widely in Europe. Under conditions of relative tolerance, Calvinist missionaries gained followings in Bohemia, Hungary, Poland, and Transylvania. Calvinism also grew in the Low Countries where it was less under Genevan control. Trained at Geneva, John Knox returned to Scotland and carried out a political-religious revolution there. Calvinist influences became perceptible too, in England during and after the reign of Edward VI. Radical, armed Calvinist reformers were striving for total control over the machinery of state, and thus precipitated violent reactions from kings and traditionalist religious opponents. Except where they were in full control or too weak to challenge existing authority, the growth of their influence was the prelude to civil war.

* A court composed of ministers and elders.

The Humanist between Confessional Fronts

After religious wars had taken heavy tolls Erasmians gained influence on both sides; but at the outset they were despised all around. To traditional Catholics their appeals for reform were heresy. Their opposition to schism and vituperation also alienated them from the Protestants. In the midst of brutality and authoritarianism they and a few humane but powerless sectarians stood alone for diversity, tolerance, and for a humanitarianism which placed the commonweal above religious differences.

The Break between Luther and Erasmus

As Luther and Erasmus became more familiar with each other's reform programs, they recognized unbridgeable gulfs between them. In Luther's theology of predestination the human will was totally without merit; free exercise of it led to sin. Without divine grace, that is, without professing Luther's creed, the doer of good works was doomed to become a mortal sinner. To Erasmus, preoccupied with ethics and the overcoming of ignorance and vio-

RELIGIONS, 1560

Map by J. Donovan

Legend:

R	Roman Catholic
A	Anabaptist & Sectarian
L	Lutheran
C	Calvinist
	Anglican

lence, Protestant denial of free will weakened man's sense of morality and made God a tyrant who kept men bound to evil. This reënactment of the classic quarrel between St. Augustine and Pelagius * pitted Luther, the theologian, against Erasmus, the moralist. The moralist de-emphasized the sacraments and was skeptical of the theologian's "revealed" and absolute dogmas. In 1525 the two exchanged polemical pamphlets on the human will. Erasmus upheld the dignity and capabilities of man. Luther asserted man's total immutable depravity and denied that he had a free will. As this quarrel grew heated, Erasmian humanists drew back from Luther. Erasmi-

ans found Geneva no more hospitable than Wittenberg. Theodore Beza, Calvin's successor, frankly wrote that he preferred tyranny to religious individualism and that "the freedom of conscience is the devil's principle of faith." Eventually such humanists did influence Protestantism, especially in England, the Netherlands, and to a lesser extent in southern Germany. But the Protestants who opened themselves to their influence were not the major continental reformers of the sixteenth century.

Expulsion of Humanists from Catholic Reform

Meanwhile Catholic traditionalists attacked Erasmus and his followers for aiding and abetting the Protestant enemy.

---

* See p. 188 for St. Augustine on predestination and original sin. Pelagius, a contemporary British monk, denied both and was declared a heretic.

They argued that unconditional obedience was due to the papal Church whatever its shortcomings, because it was commissioned by God. Nonconforming humanists and their books were burned in the Low Countries as early as 1522 and 1523. Erasmus complained of being "stoned by both sides."

Actually, the humanists had a strong influence in the Catholic Church until 1542, but their irenic approach was always in competition with the uncompromising approach of religious zealots. In Italy some reformers followed the Venetian nobleman, Gasparo Contarini, an apostle of conciliation. Others supported Giovanni Pietro Caraffa, equally dedicated to changes, but by inquisitional methods. As both of these men were appointed by Pope Paul III to successively higher posts, they came to epitomize the two conflicting trends in the Catholic Reformation.

Contarini equated Christianity with freedom. He denied the theory of absolute papal authority and refused to exalt the papal monarch above canon law. He also pursued a course of conciliation with the Protestants. At the Imperial Diet of Regensburg (Ratisbon) in 1541, he followed a very liberal interpretation of Catholic dogma in order to seek agreements with Bucer and Melanchthon, the doctrinally more flexible Protestant reformers. In so doing he overrode Catholic traditionalists and exceeded his instructions from the Pope. He also failed to reach a general agreement with the Protestants. The Colloquy at Regensburg, the last attempt to heal the religious schism, fell apart, and negotiators on both sides were denounced in their respective camps as heretics. Rapidly losing influence, Contarini died in 1542. His demise marked a milestone in the disappearance of Erasmian influence upon the Catholic reformation.

Humanism was narrowed and restricted by the competing orthodoxies it tried to temper, reform, or stand against. In the late sixteenth and early seventeenth centuries after surviving the religious wars, it became a rallying point for many who were weary of fanaticism and violence.

THE CATHOLIC REFORMATION

Roman Catholic Resurgence

Instead of submitting to a rout, the Roman Catholic Church began to muster forces to check the Protestant tide and, in subsequent decades, to regain lost or wavering territories. Following the lead of the Society of Jesus a host of new orders emphasizing education, social welfare, and pastoral work labored to counteract heresy and to inculcate piety. These were most effective in mobilizing the emotional religious passions of the masses behind tradition and ingrained patterns of religious life. These passions provided Catholic sovereigns with the popular support to meet Protestantism by force.

After 1544, the influence of the Spanish in Catholic reform increased. The wars between the Habsburgs and Valois became less frequent after 1544 and they ceased altogether by the Treaty of Cateau-Cambrésis in 1559. That was also the year in which the last anti-Spanish pope, Paul IV, died. Thereafter, the French were rent by wars of religion while united, powerful Spain became the model for the institutions and procedures of the Catholic Reformation.

New Religious Orders

The Church had always gained new strength whenever new monastic orders were founded. This was especially true in

Woodcut showing the "true" Roman Church surrounded by heretical devils.

Ignatius of Loyola, an old soldier who did not fade away.

the sixteenth century when several orders appeared and spearheaded the reform movement in the Church. The Oratories of Divine Love, the Theatines, and the Barnabites of Italy were composed of clergy and lay aristocrats who combined strict, ascetic, pious religious practices with secular activism. The Ursulines and Capuchins arose from the common people and ministered to the masses.

Far exceeding the other new orders in total efforts and effectiveness was the Society of Jesus, the "shock troops of the Counter Reformation," founded by a disabled Spanish soldier, Ignatius of Loyola (1491–1556). A young nobleman serving in the Habsburg-Valois wars, Loyola was wounded while campaigning in Navarre in 1521. While recuperating, he experienced a mystical religious conversion equal in impact to Martin Luther's revelation of salvation by faith alone. From chivalry he turned to "spiritual knighthood." In 1523 he set out on a pilgrimage via Rome and Venice to the Holy Land. Back in Barcelona in 1524, he decided he lacked sufficient education to be an efficient instrument of God. With the city's school children he attended grammar school. Thereafter he attended the universities of Alcala, Salamanca, and Paris. At Paris he gathered around him ten disciples who became the Society's early nucleus. He demanded of them a disciplined will and unconditional obedience to higher authority. He strongly encouraged their higher education and urged that they foster the zeal to work (in the words of his personal motto) "to the greater glory of God."

Upon the recommendation of Contarini, the Pope made the Jesuits an order in 1540, and the members took permanent vows of poverty, chastity, and obedience to the papacy. They were commissioned soldiers of God to propagate doctrine and faith by public preaching, acts of charity, and especially public education. The new order expanded rapidly, especially in the Iberian kingdoms and their colonial empires. The

Jesuits' zeal for missionary work proved as intense as that of the Franciscans and Dominicans. One of the original ten founders, Francis Xavier (1506–1552), was credited with hundreds of thousands of converts in India, China, Malaya, and Japan.

The Jesuits also moved into those areas of Europe jeopardized by Protestantism. Many parts of western and southern Germany were recovered for the Roman Church. Supported by the rulers of Bavaria and Poland during the second half of the century, the Jesuits almost totally restored religious conformity there by both persuasion and force.

Among primitive peoples the Jesuits usually worked for little more than acceptance of the sacraments *en masse*. But in Europe their goals were political and power-oriented. Their methods, both admired and feared by their enemies, were highly sophisticated. Aside from pastoral work, Jesuits devoted great attention to higher education. They founded colleges to train and indoctrinate the elite of both Church and state. These colleges and their faculties became an integral part of the Catholic resurgence.

The Council of Trent (1545–1563)

After disastrously long delays, prelates, theologians, canonists, generals of the mendicant orders, and papal legates assembled with other dignitaries of the Roman Church at the city of Trent. This council faced the serious business of refuting Protestantism and purifying the Church of those abuses which had helped the Protestant influence to spread.

The problem of organizing a council was political as much as religious. The Emperor's overriding concern was for peace in the Empire. Since he could not crush the Protestants militarily, as the papacy wished, he urged that the two religions compose their differences by working out some doctrinal formula that they could agree on. This would have meant treating the Protestants as equals, not as heretics.

The papacy was hardly in favor of doing that.

When the Council of Trent opened in 1545, it was controlled by the legates that had been instructed by the Pope. In its first sessions (1545–1547), the council achieved some reforms in addition to its approval of traditional doctrine, and the council members certainly debated fundamental issues.

The debate on original sin, the longest of the entire council, drove the members inexorably to grapple with Luther's fundamental doctrine of unmerited salvation by faith alone. The council avoided rigid personal predestination and asserted the necessity of human free will to opt for salvation through the sacraments, which had to be supplemented by faith, love, hope, and good works. In emphasizing the sacraments, it denounced the Anabaptists as well as the Protestants. Logically this position required another decree which affirmed the seven sacraments, the major part of which Protestants had denounced as human inventions.

The council took major steps to restore the authority of bishops over their dioceses and to produce a more competent clergy. Another decree attacked the central problems of administrative disorder: absenteeism, pluralism, the use of offices as sinecures, and exemptions from episcopal visitation. With few exceptions, the council ordered heavy penalties for absentee prelates. Meanwhile in other moves hard on the prelates' affluence, the Pope suspended the sale of indulgences and cut back the sale of offices and favors.

The Emperor's disappointment with the uncompromising results of the first session led him to proclaim a religious settlement of his own, the "Interim" of 1548. This failed to bridge the confessional gap. Protestant representatives were invited to the second session of the council (1551–1552), but they were adamant in sticking to their own doctrines. When no compromise followed, the Emperor concluded the Peace of Augsburg (1555), which asserted the principle that the ruling German prince would decide what religion his territory would have. Pius IV convened the third session in 1562 and the council finished its work in 1563. It amplified and extended previous decisions, creating the basic legislation for the subsequent government of the Church. This session greatly improved the moral tone of the Church. It abolished dispensations, special privileges, indulgences, and moral laxity. Thomas Aquinas was declared the authoritative interpreter of Christianity.

To inculcate the approved doctrines, the council ordered that clerical and popular catechisms be prepared. The common prayers (*Breviary*), the official lives of the saints,

and the *Missal* were also to be revised. Charles Borromeo, archbishop of Milan and director of the final session at Trent, supervised these tasks.

Implementation of Catholic Reform

Most European monarchs resisted the new rulings of the Council of Trent because they regarded any demands emanating from Rome as foreign intervention in their affairs. These monarchs merely vetoed whatever rulings they did not wish to adopt. No secular government, least of all the Most Catholic King of Spain, fully accepted the administrative reforms of the Council of Trent. Outside the clerical archbish-

Didactic Reformation art: Seven Deadly Sins *by Hieronymous Bosch, an earlier Flemish artist (d. 1516). Bosch's works were widely reproduced, especially in Spain.*

oprics few German principalities ever adopted them.

Catholic reformers relied heavily upon persuasion, but the popes had at their disposal two instruments of coercion initiated by Cardinal Caraffa, the Inquisition and the *Index of Prohibited Books*. Since most secular governments preferred their own tribunals or autonomous inquisitions, the Roman Inquisition in practice functioned little outside Italy. Efficient machinery for its enforcement was set up, including a system of pre-publication censorship. The *Index*, a powerful tool of thought control during the Reformation, proved to be a permanent institution; but more recent revisions have restricted its scope — no works of Erasmus appear in the latest compilation, for example. And the list of specific works for which permission to read must be secured has been confined to matters relating solely to faith and morals.

Catholic resurgence was a reality, but the locus of power remained not in the papacy or Church councils but in the hands of secular rulers who had broken from Church control prior to the Reformation. For them religion was subordinate to the interests of power.

Eastern Europe and the Reformation

By the mid-1500s the Protestant Reformation had spread into Central Europe where it became entangled in the political conflicts within Bohemia, Hungary, and Poland-Lithuania. But the Balkan countries, Greek Orthodox by tradition and ruled by Mohammedans, were impervious to its creeping influence. So was Muscovy, the only independent principality with an Orthodox population. Muscovite Orthodoxy, isolated from developments in the West by barriers of both geography and tradition, remained devoted to anti-intellectualism, monasticism and an authoritarian political state. In fact, the Reformation never went beyond Western and Central Europe.

Covetousness (detail from Seven Deadly Sins).

In Habsburg Bohemia, first Lutheranism and then Calvinism became important to movements of political and religious revolt. There the native Hussite tradition was dominant. The Hussites were divided between conservative Utraquists, who had gained the Church's recognition for extending communion to the laity in both bread and wine, and the more radical Czech Brethren, who had replaced revolutionary fervor with pacifist pietism. Persecution of the Czech Brethren between 1548 and 1552 failed to check religious dissent, and Maximilian II (1564–1576) permitted extensive toleration.

Compared to Bohemia, Hungary's experience of the Reformation was much more chaotic. After 1526 the Ottoman Turks held the eastern two-thirds of that kingdom, and the Habsburgs occupied the remainder. Against these two powers, Transylvanian nobles led a movement for Hungarian autonomy. Denouncing the authority of the Church as well as the state, they espoused Calvinism and Lutheranism. After 1560, Anti-Trinitarianism also became an important force in their revolt. In 1564 all three new religions were recognized equally beside Catholicism by law. Unlike Roman resurgence in Poland and Bohemia, the Catholic Reformation in Habsburg Hungary never suppressed religious dissent, especially Calvinism, entirely.

When the Ottoman Turks conquered Asia Minor and the Balkans in the late fourteenth century, they brought almost all Greek Orthodox peoples, except the Muscovites, under Mohammedan rule. But even the shock of conquest and government by the foreign infidel created no more than temporary ties between Eastern and Western Christianity. The sultans moved the Patriarch of Constantinople out of Sancta Sophia, which was converted into a mosque, and deposed refractory patriarchs. But they did not disestablish the popularly supported Greek Orthodox clergy. Instead they profited from selling high church offices to the highest bidder. By the sultan's religious toleration, political stability was fostered.

The Ottomans, often as allies of Francis I, made repeated invasions along the Danube. Their forays distracted the German Emperor and kept him from working on domestic religious uprisings. Their influence in eastern trade was considerable, too. They imposed tolls and transfers, all to the commercial advantage of the Atlantic seaboard states. Traders from these states had opened all-sea routes to the Indies. After 1566 the efficiency of Ottoman rule declined. But up to then the Turks made a distinctive impact upon events in Western Europe.

THE REFORMATION AND THE MODERN WORLD

The Reformation is a lasting part of the Western heritage. Many historians, Protestant and secular, have discovered the roots of the modern world in the Reformation. We can assess its role in shaping the modern world by examining some of its consequences or alleged consequences.

Individualism

Since Luther proclaimed every man to be his own priest, the Protestant Reformation has been widely interpreted as a major step toward the recognition of individual judgment or conscience. In theory, the assertion of a direct relationship between man and God was a powerful fillip to the idea of individuality. Nothing was further from the reformers' minds, however, than the submission of divine revelation to private judgment or interpretation. For Holy Church they substituted Holy Writ, which each reformer in his own way held to be concretely and objectively revealed. To assert that the individual took any initiative in his own salvation was to derogate the absolute sovereignty of God. Faith came from hearing or reading the Word, but its re-

ception was a divine miracle for which the individual person was totally unworthy.

The Catholic Reformation, especially the Council of Trent, had no such ambiguities as the "priesthood of all believers" to deal with. It categorically denounced religious individualism and substantially narrowed the tolerable range of diversity in thought. Like the Protestants, but to a lesser degree, the Catholic reformers also curbed individual expression in the arts.

Toleration

Because they believed in predestination—that a sovereign God had selected the elect and the damned before earthly time began—the Protestant reformers, unlike the Roman Inquisitors, could not justify persecution on the grounds that it could lead to the heretic's salvation. They found sufficient other bases for it, however. One was Scriptural authority. Another was their concept of the origin of heresy. Deviations from their own version of divine revelation could only be the work of Satan. Persecution of Satan's legions, the heretics, upheld the honor of God and protected the faithful who were incapable of recognizing the Devil's snares. Still another justification was political. The reformers shared the traditional Roman Catholic belief that it was the magistrate's commission from God, from whom all legitimate authority flowed, to maintain the morality and orthodoxy of his subjects. The alternative, they believed, was civil war. Until religiously pluralistic states survived in peace and demonstrated that coexistence was possible the secular premises of religious persecution went unchallenged except among sectarians, radical humanists, and state-church minorities who were not in power.

Rather than an outgrowth of Protestantism, toleration was more often the result of religious, civil and diplomatic wars. People came to choose diversity over the devastation and turmoil of war.

Political Ramifications

Clergymen cast reforming princes as Old Testament ruler-priests, agents of an inscrutable deity to whom alone they were accountable. This divine warrant did not give Protestant rulers absolute control over religious affairs, however. They were subject to the Word. If they transgressed this limitation, Lutheran and Anglican divines sanctioned passive resistance against them. According to Romans XIII, however, active resistance was no less than resistance to God.

Thus many Protestant churches encouraged the notion of divine right kingship. Defending the old order, Roman Catholic spokesmen also advocated rule by divine right as well as passive obedience to constituted authority. But the aggressive Calvinists actively defied traditional governments. In France, for example, Calvinists sanctioned revolution led by "lesser magistrates," whereas Jesuits appealed to the majority of the population. Both viewpoints reflected a broader appeal to people than in the past. To this degree, the Reformation released forces which were "democratic."

Anti-Catholic intolerance of Henry VIII: the beheadings of John Fisher (Cardinal-Bishop of Rochester), Thomas More, and the Countess of Salisbury are included in one illustration.

But it was not liberal in the sense of protecting individual rights or of establishing constitutional processes for government by persuasion.

Social and Economic Repercussions

Protestants made drastic changes in the status and role of the clergy. They removed its prestige as agents in transforming the bread and wine into the body and blood of Christ in the Eucharist.

In dress, social status, and political obligations, the Protestant clergy became less distinguishable from ordinary subjects. Exemptions of clergy from secular justice and from taxes, tolls, and guild regulations usually lapsed. Costly projects such as relief, education, and building now required *state* support or administration. The Protestant and Catholic reformations paralleled one another in the gradual creation of an educated clergy charged with preaching, teaching, and pastoral care. Both also curtailed commercialized religion and the sale of offices.

According to some historians the Protestant reformers not only secularized society and weakened clerical influence over it but they also played a major role in advancing modern capitalism. At the end of the nineteenth century, Max Weber, a German sociologist, published a classic thesis, *The Protestant Ethic and the Spirit of Capitalism,* to demonstrate this connection. He argued that the positive attitude of Protestants, especially Calvinists and sectarians, toward hard work, self-denial, and the holiness of secular callings was *one factor* in the development of the spirit of capitalism. He defined that spirit not as the desire for unlimited accumulation of wealth but as the rational organization of men and material to produce recurrent profits. Paradoxically he found that the practice of ascetic otherworldiness, which repudiated the aristocracy's flaunting displays of wealth, contributed to constructive social and individual economic success.

Weber's thesis is not immune from serious criticism in several details. Before the Reformation capitalism flourished in Italy and Flanders. In the nineteenth century, Catholic Belgium industrialized rapidly while a distinctly medieval economic organization persisted in large parts of Lutheran Germany. Furthermore the fact that Calvin sanctioned the taking of interest does not mean that he was a pioneer of an unregulated economy. The five per cent interest which he approved was below rates already current. Finally, orthodox Calvinist sermons from seventeenth-century England and the Netherlands, the two areas of greatest economic development and the period from which Weber drew much of his evidence, indicate that on-going capitalism eventually influenced Calvinist doctrines rather than *vice versa.*

Nevertheless certain Protestant and sectarian practices had undeniable significance for economic growth where resources and other requisites were present. The creation of a literate laity is one case in point, though, of course, it was not achieved by all Protestants. The devotion of nonconformists to productive economic activity and to the building of reputations for business integrity is another.

Asterisk (*) denotes paperback.

As in other aspects of life, the Protestant assault on tradition, which varied widely from confession to confession, helped open the path to innovations which the reformers themselves did not intend or necessarily promote.

SELECTED READINGS

*Bainton, Roland, *Here I Stand, A Life of Martin Luther,* Abingdon Press, New York, 1950.

Leading critical but sympathetic biography with excellent bibliography. Unlike many biographies of Luther it includes details on his later life.

*———. *The Travail of Religious Liberty,* Harper & Brothers, New York, 1951.

Series of biographical sketches treating victims and practitioners, Catholic and Protestant, of religious persecution. In effect it presents the Reformation as a highly intolerant age.

Brandi, Karl, *The Emperor Charles V,* J. Cape, London, 1954.

Lengthy standard political biography concerned mainly with Charles' government of the Holy Roman Empire.

Breen, Quirinus, *John Calvin: A Study in French Humanism,* Wm. B. Eerdmans Publishing Co., Grand Rapids, Mich., 1931.

Excellent for Calvin's humanist background and the basis for his break with the humanists. Provides references to other biographies of Calvin and their points of view.

*Burns, Edward McNall, *The Counter Reformation,* D. Van Nostrand Co., Princeton, New Jersey, 1964.

A recent short critical account with major documents in an appendix.

Butterfield, Herbert, *The Whig Interpretation of History,* G. Bell and Sons, London, 1931.

A devastating critique of nineteenth century liberal-national history which rebuts popular Protestant interpretations of the Reformation.

*Chadwick, Owen, *The Reformation,* Penguin Books, Baltimore, Md., 1964.

An excellent non-partisan survey concentrating on religious developments; especially good for the Reformation's impact on the clergy as a social class.

*Elton, Geoffrey R., *Reformation Europe, 1517–1559*, Meridian Books, Cleveland, 1964.
One of the author's many works on the Reformation emphasizing the role of politics in determining its outcome.

Franklin, Julian H., *Jean Bodin and the Sixteenth Century Revolution in the Methodology of Law and History*, Columbia University Press, New York and London, 1963.
Traces French humanist origins of new comparative and empirical methods in sixteenth century studies of society. Basic for understanding differences between humanist and religious approaches to society and politics.

Gelder, Herman Arend Enno van, *The Two Reformations in the 16th Century*, The Hague, Martinus Nijhoff, 1961.
Develops the controversial thesis that the major reformation of the sixteenth century was not Protestant but humanist.

Grimm, Harold J., *The Reformation Era 1500–1650*, The Macmillan Co., New York, 1954.
Factual, standard textbook treating all aspects of the period.

Hillerbrand, Hans J., ed., *The Reformation; A Narrative History Related by Contemporary Observers and Participants*, Harper and Row, New York, 1964.
Collection of vivid sources related to major personalities and events.

Holborn, Hajo, *A History of Modern Germany*, Vol. I, *The Reformation*, Alfred A. Knopf, New York, 1959.
Definitive political, cultural, and religious history of Germany from about 1500 to 1648.

*Hughes, Philip, *A Popular History of the Reformation*, Doubleday & Co., Garden City, N.Y., 1960.
Balanced summary by a Roman Catholic authority on the English Reformation.

Jedin, Hubert, *A History of the Council of Trent*, B. Herder Book Co., St. Louis, 1957–1961, 2 vols.
Exhaustive unfinished account of the Church councils of the Renaissance and Reformation by a German Catholic scholar. These volumes reach only the first session at Trent.

Janelle, Pierre, *The Catholic Reformation*, Bruce Publishing Co., Milwaukee, 1949.
Catholic version which treats the Catholic Reformation as a spontaneous movement and omits reference to the Inquisition.

Kidd, B. J., *The Counter-Reformation 1550–1600*, SPCK, London, 1958.
Emphatically Protestant; reverses the interpretation of Janelle.

McNeil, John T., *The History and Character of Calvinism*, Oxford University Press, New York, 1957.
Sympathetically and comprehensively relates the origins, nature, and spread of Calvinism.

*Mosse, George L., *The Reformation*, Holt, Rinehart and Winston, New York, 1953.
Short balanced account of the entire Reformation; excellent as an introduction.

Philips, Margaret Mann, *Erasmus and the Northern Renaissance*, Hodder and Stoughton, London, 1949.
Presents Erasmus as the formulator of an independent religious and secular reform movement. Publication of Erasmus' later correspondence has forced modification of this interpretation at least for the older Erasmus.

Schapiro, Jacob S., *Social Reform and the Reformation*, Columbia University Dissertation, 1909.
The only collection of documents on the German Peasants' Revolt in English; includes penetrating commentaries which find the origins of liberalism within the revolt rather than among the reformers.

Tavard, Georges H., *Holy Writ or Holy Church; the Crisis of the Protestant Reformation*, Harper and Brothers, New York, 1960.
Describes the differing bases of authority used by sixteenth-century Catholics and Protestants and traces the origins of the latter.

*Tawney, Richard H., *Religion and the Rise of Capitalism*, New American Library, New York, 1950, and *Weber, Max, *The Protestant Ethic and the Spirit of Capitalism*, Charles Scribner's Sons, New York, 1958.

Advance the classic thesis in vulnerable forms that Protestantism, especially Calvinists and sectarians, stimulated capitalism by fostering ascetic renunciation of luxury and dedication to secular work.

Nelson, Benjamin N., *Idea of Usury,* Princeton University Press, Princeton, New Jersey, 1949. Restates the thesis for Calvinism by investigating the psychological background of prohibiting usury and provides rare detail on the anti-capitalistic attitudes of the early German Reformation.

Williams, George Hunston, *The Radical Reformation,* Westminster Press, Philadelphia, 1962. Makes heavy use of recently published documents on the Anabaptists and other sectarians to reevaluate the defamed radicals of the Reformation. Heavily theological in tone.

15

The Century of Crises—
1560–1660

Facing new realities with old ideas, Europeans passed through a century of terrible crises, 1560–1660. It was not a simple matter for Europeans to adjust to the new religious and political pluralism, the recent intellectual, spiritual, and social upheavals, and the enormous new geographical world. Their traditions and experiences had not taught them how to cope with ideological ferment on such a colossal scale, or a new conception of the world that shattered their familiar Biblical view of three continents inhabited by the three races of men, descendants of Shem, Ham, and Japheth. Europeans became global men for the first time, and immediately projected their internal conflicts upon a world stage. As population growth outstripped subsistence at home, they fought for the world's wealth which could be fed into the engines of war to give an advantage to one side or the other. Seething with religious hatreds, Europeans fought one bloody ideological war after another among themselves until they were forced by sheer exhaustion, after the

Thirty Years' War (1618–1648), to try to reorganize their civilization as a coexisting family of nations. By 1660, Europeans had learned to accept their cultural pluralism and globalism, and were beginning to find that it might not be so bad after all to have different ideas about sin and salvation or to be borne at great speed around the sun, offensive as that was to common sense. At least Europeans were on top of the world of men, with a divine mandate to transform the world in their own image.

Europe's Territorial Expansion

Why should European expansion have entered such a dazzling phase in the sixteenth century? The answer is partly that European military and naval technology was so superior to what non-Western people possessed that Europeans were easily able to dominate commerce and control any coastal areas.

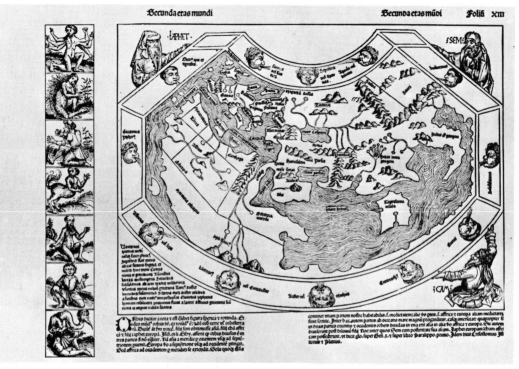

German map of the world, 1493. The three sons of Noah, founders of the three races of men who would inhabit the three continents, occupy the corners of the map. Jerusalem, the holy city, is near the center.

Because of the political weakness and tribal hostilities prevailing in large areas such as the Americas and parts of Africa, Europeans found it a relatively simple matter to push into the interior of continents. Their strong drive for dominance was, moreover, strongly supported by the Christian religion. Europeans believed that they had a divine mandate to subjugate and convert God's enemies. Expansion seemed both necessary and right for Europeans.

Portugal's Commercial Empire

The little kingdom of Portugal led the way to Europe's overseas empires. From 1418 to 1460, Prince Henry "the Navigator" directed explorations down the coast of Africa. The bold voyage of Diaz in 1488 around the southern tip of Africa was followed by the notable voyage of Vasco da Gama in 1498 to India to return laden with riches. In 1509, a naval victory over the Arabs and Egyptians, off the west coast of India, put the Portuguese in a position to monopolize the spice trade with Europe. From Goa, their base in India, the Portuguese flung out a series of trading stations: Java and Sumatra in 1511, the Moluccas in 1512, Formosa in 1542, Japan and later

Confrontation of Europeans and Indians in Mexico.

Macao on the coast of China. The Portuguese empire in the Far East was strictly commercial; spices were its main commodity. The Portuguese did not even market the spices in Europe; rather they turned that business over to an Antwerp monopoly. In the vast Portuguese empire only Brazil—which was of little economic significance before the establishment of sugar plantations using African slaves—was to become a major colonial settlement. The Portuguese empire was mainly commercial.

Spain's Bid for Colonial Wealth

The Spaniards were at first disappointed with Columbus' West Indies, but they found compensation for being cut off from the profitable Eastern trade in the gold and silver treasures of the Aztecs and Incas and the mines of South America that rapidly yielded phenomenal wealth. In 1545 the richest mine of all, the Potosí mine in Peru, was brought into production; in 1600 precious metals comprised 90 per cent of all European imports from Spanish America. Meanwhile Magellan's voyage around South America in 1519 had opened a route to the Far East, but the Pacific crossing was so hazardous that, except for trade with the western coast of South America, the new route was of little commercial value. Content to rule the Philippines indirectly through Mexico, the Habsburgs left the Portuguese commercial monopoly in the Far East undisturbed.

Spaniards tried but largely failed to transplant their institutions in American soil. Fortune-hunting noblemen were superb conquerors but inept administrators. When the rulers of Spain replaced Columbus, Pizzaro, Cortes, and other *conquistadores* with royal appointees, the New World affairs passed into the hands of men who were seldom capable and usually uninterested. Many mistakes were made. Castilians tried to harness Indian labor, but the natives died so rapidly from European diseases (such as smallpox) that by 1600 their population had dwindled from an estimated 11 million to 2 million. The Spaniards imported African slaves, but they too were subject to disease. After 1576 the history of the Spanish Empire is a history of economic depression and the disintegration of order. Colonial officials lost control over the hinterlands of the empire. Cattlemen on the continent and buccaneers on the islands defied their authority.

Empire Building by the Dutch

At first the Dutch were far more successful as empire builders than the English and the French. By organizing the East India stock company they eliminated competition among themselves and, in the first years of the seventeenth century outbid Portuguese merchants in the East Indies, Formosa, and Japan. Like the Portuguese before them, the Dutch monopolists carefully controlled supplies for the European spice market. They also dealt in silk, chinaware, sugar, coffee, tea, cocoa, precious metals, Japanese copper, and Indian cloth. Even more lucrative was the local Far Eastern carrying trade which shipped cargoes from India, around Malaya and the East Indies to Japan. They set up posts in Indonesia.

Closer to home, in the carrying trade from the Baltic Sea where they displaced the Hanseatic League and on the Mediterranean where they dislodged the Italians, the Dutch were immensely successful. Still, overseas trade made only a small contribution to the general prosperity of the Netherlands, which depended on local trade in fish, Baltic grains, salt, Scandinavian timber, and French wine. Thriving Dutch commerce benefited from adopting advanced techniques in industry, finance, and technology. Especially rewarding was the development of an unarmed sailing ship called the flute (*fluit*) that required few men and offered little resistance to wind and water. By the end of the sixteenth century the Dutch merchant marine had an estimated 10,000 ships.

Arctic

Hudson
Bay

ICELAND

Frobisher 1576-1578

Hudson 1609

Cabot 1497

60°N

NORTH
AMERICA

Cartier 1534-35

FRAN

40°N

PORTUGAL

SPAIN

1607

Cabot 1493

Azores Is.

Verrazano 1524

BARBARY

Tropic of Cancer

20°N

Drake 1579

San Salvador

Columbus 1492

A F

MEXICO

CUBA

Vera Cruz

Caribbean

ESPANOLA

Route of Spanish Fleet

Cape Verde Is.

Sea

Spanish Main

Magellan 1519

Diaz 1486-87

Isthmus of
Panama

Magell

Equator

Pizarro 1532

SOUTH
AMERICA

Da Gama

Pacific   Ocean

Drake 1578

Atlantic
Ocean

Cuzco

20°S

Potosi

Magellan 1521

Cabral 1500

Tropic of Capricorn

40°S

Strait of Magellan

Cape Horn

60°S

TO SPAIN
Treaty of Tordesillas 1494 ▶

TO PORTUGAL
◀ Papal Division 1493

LINE OF DEMARCATION

160°   140°   120°   100°   80°   60°   40°   20°W

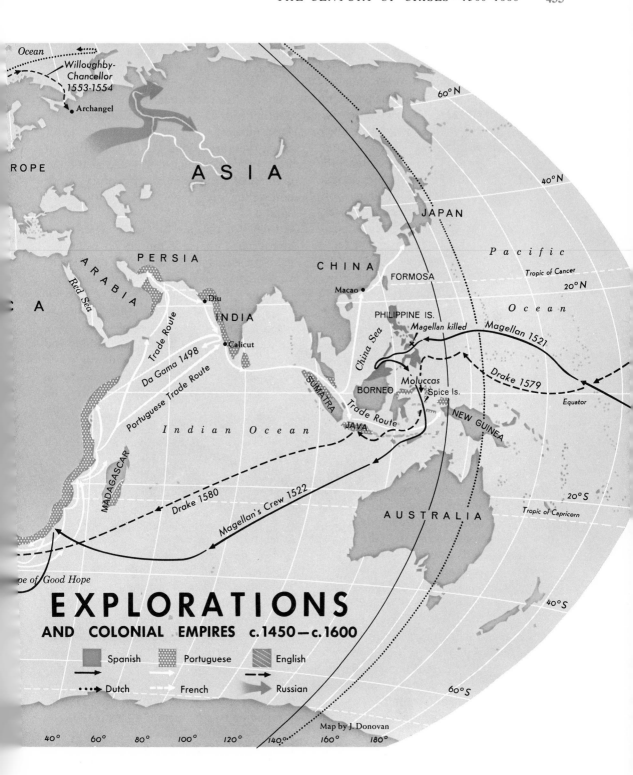

Ocean

Willoughby-
Chancellor
1553-1554

• Archangel

ROPE

A S I A

PERSIA

ARABIA

Red Sea

Trade Route

• Diu

INDIA

• Calicut

Da Gama 1498

Portuguese Trade Route

SUMATRA

Indian Ocean

MADAGASCAR

Drake 1580

Magellan's Crew 1522

pe of Good Hope

CHINA

• Macao

China Sea

BORNEO

JAVA

Trade Route

FORMOSA

JAPAN

PHILIPPINE IS.

Magellan killed

Moluccas
• Spice Is.

NEW GUINEA

AUSTRALIA

Pacific

Tropic of Cancer

20° N

Ocean

Magellan 1521

Drake 1579

Equator

20° S

Tropic of Capricorn

60° N

40° N

40° S

60° S

EXPLORATIONS

AND COLONIAL EMPIRES c.1450—c.1600

	Spanish		Portuguese		English
⟶		⟹		⇢	

•••• Dutch   — — French   ⟹ Russian

Map by J. Donovan

40°   60°   80°   100°   120°   140°   160°   180°

The Course of Economic Change

The establishment of empires overseas was only one facet of Europe's radically changing economic shape in the sixteenth century. The astonishing growth in volume, variety, and value of its long distance trade was another. Also the centers of commerce were shifting, for states along the Atlantic seaboard now held the economic initiative and were speedily gaining control. The fruits of European economic expansion were, however, unevenly divided. While the Dutch, English, and French reaped the profits of imperial trade, eastern and southern Europe were depressed. Even the more prosperous states faltered during the century's crisis. To provide for subsistence, trading opportunities, social stability, and military strength most territorial governments enlarged their regulation of economic activity.

The Joint-Stock Company

One of the most significant commercial innovations during our period was the development of the joint-stock company, a method of conducting trade in which Dutch and English merchants soon excelled. The joint-stock company was an outgrowth of the regulated company, a trading organization which had come down from the Middle Ages. Particularly well suited to enterprises that required heavy capital, the joint-stock company appeared first in mining. The investors in the joint-stock company used their money to purchase shares in the company and, by virtue of their status as share-holders, elected directors who were responsible for managing paid company employees. The joint-stock company bore more resemblance to the corporation as we know it today than to the old regulated companies. Shares could be converted to cash. The death of a shareholder in no way disrupted the company's operations or affected its continuity as would death

in a partnership. Naturally, the earliest joint-stock companies were rather crudely organized. At first, the capital invested as well as the profits realized on each specific venture were distributed among shareholders after each undertaking. The idea of continuity took a while to develop, but by 1660 managers of both great pioneer joint-stock ventures (the Dutch and English East India Companies, founded at the beginning of the seventeenth century) were controlling permanent aggregations of capital.

Joint-stock trading companies were often chartered with great powers to wage aggressive economic warfare for the expansion of depressed trade. The directors received legal and political powers to exclude all competitors outside the company. Against foreign rivals they were empowered to wage war with their own ships and troops. Frequently they waged war while home governments were at peace. Some of these chartered companies such as the English East India Company gained immense power in domestic politics and continued to function as colonial governments until the nineteenth century.

The Organization of Production

Since the late Middle Ages the cloth dealers who met the needs of large markets had sought to employ cheap labor and evade the stringent quality controls imposed by the urban guildmasters. The usual method was to distribute raw materials among suburban and rural laborers who bought or rented their own hand-operated machines. After the various steps of production were completed, the entrepreneur (or merchant-capitalist) collected the finished cloth and stored it in a "factory" for further shipment or sale. (Thus he was often known as a "factor.") This method of organizing production revolved about the merchant-capitalist. His main role was to coordinate the various functions of production and distribution, and his knowledge of

Domestic carding, spinning, and weaving.

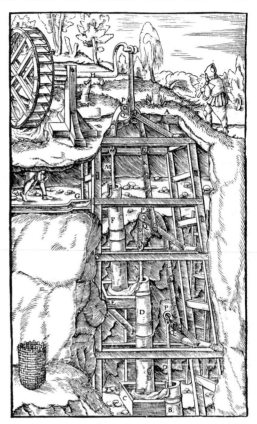

German mine water-pump linkage of the sixteenth century. The big problem was to keep the mines from flooding, hence the big, expensive pumps.

market conditions was crucial for success or failure. The "domestic system," which required that little fixed capital be tied up in productive machinery, allowed merchant-capitalists to adjust output to the demands of rapidly fluctuating markets.

Occasionally the entrepreneurial system brought together some finishing process at a single place resembling a modern factory. But centralized production calling for heavy capitalization was required in only a few industries like mining, shipbuilding, cannon-founding, and printing. The invention of hand-operated machines like the stocking frame (1589) or the ribbon loom (1621) foreshadowed the machine age. Even these primitive machines contributed to economic growth, notably

in England and the Netherlands. Coal, Europe's cheap fuel supply, also figured in the expansion of industry before 1660. Coal was used in brewing, distilling, sugar refining, glass and soap making, and the production of salt, gunpowder, and alum. Ships, windmills, and water wheels came into impressive prominence as Europeans learned to harness nature.

Agricultural expansion was still constrained by traditional techniques and the lack of new arable land. Productivity increased in England, in the Netherlands, and in the vicinity of commercial centers. Elsewhere output per acre was limited by the peasants' ignorance of replenishing the fertility of the soil by any means but letting land lie fallow. Until seed grasses for hay were introduced, the scarcity of forage dictated that few cattle could be kept alive over the winter, and in turn the scarcity of cattle signified a shortage of manure for fertilizer. Good weather brought bountiful harvests, but poor weather meant famine, soaring grain prices, starvation, and weakened resistance to disease. Until Europeans were able to supply enough food for all and to control plagues, famine and disease would be endemic and would invariably upset production and distribution.

The Price Revolution

Famines struck primarily at the lower classes, but a general inflation of prices cut across all economic developments and affected all social classes in the period from 1450 to about 1650. At first gradual, this acceleration of prices—often called the "price revolution"—was most rapid in Western Europe between 1500 and 1600. During these hundred years prices roughly doubled, especially the prices of foodstuffs, hay, and wood.

Few contemporaries could offer a rational explanation of the inflation, but modern economic historians attribute it largely to population growth that created shortages of products whose supply was inelastic or declining. The influx of precious metals from the mines of Central Europe and New Spain as well as the debasing of coinage also stimulated inflation.

As usual, inflation benefited debtors and reduced the value of fixed incomes. Many petty nobles (*hidalgos* in Spain, *hobereaux* in France, *Rittern* in western Germany), who were bound by long-term rent contracts with their peasants, eventually lost their estates to peasants and townsmen. These newly landless men, together with vagabonds, were ready recruits for mercenary armies. Those English gentry, on the other hand, who were able to raise their rents, often prospered. During the era of inflation the largest fortunes were, on the whole, amassed by merchants, bankers, investors in commerce, cour-

tiers, officials, lawyers, and commanders of mercenary troops.

State Economic Policies

In their efforts to secure order in society and maintain the flow of tax revenues into the coffers of the state, early modern governments intervened directly and participated extensively in economic life. Such active intervention was based upon a theory, since called mercantilism.

While mercantilism varied from state to state, all states shared certain fundamental assumptions which constituted the core of "mercantilist" thought. Mercantilists took it for granted that state intervention was necessary to secure prosperity and power, which they believed went hand in hand. They lived in an age of scarcity and thus readily assumed that the world's wealth was relatively static. It seemed obvious to them that one state's gain was another's loss. Hence even in those states where merchant prosperity was identified with the general welfare, a powerful state—or at least a powerful navy—was considered indispensable to maintain and extend prosperity. In the agrarian continental monarchies, state intervention during this period served to preserve the traditional framework of society more often than it advanced commerce and industry. The kind of "mercantilism" practiced in the absolute monarchies often hewed to traditional regulations; their rulers did not yet subscribe to Thomas Mun's belief that expanding exports was the surest way to national prosperity. A director of the East India Company, Thomas Mun (1571–1641), wrote *Discourse on England's Treasure by Forraigne Trade* (1664), published posthumously, in which he stressed the idea that good economic policy is to sell more abroad each year than is imported. In the long run, a favorable balance of trade would bring wealth and power to the state.

To insure maximum gains, the carrying trade should be in the hands of native shippers. In response to this assumption, the

English passed the Navigation Act of 1651 to exclude Dutch competition. The effect was a significant increase in the British maritime fleet. The colonies, too, were integrated into the mercantilist system. They provided sources of raw materials for home industries as well as markets for finished goods.

Trade, however, was only the most visible aspect of mercantilism. Equally important in mercantilist policies was the maintenance of the traditional social order. Entrepreneurs hiring rural labor were regulated by being brought under the production codes of urban guildmasters. Regulating them restricted the growth of unstable working classes dependent on wages and liable to revolt during times of unemployment and scarcity.

In England, the Poor Law (1601) represented an effort to provide relief and employment for the indigent and hungry who seemed to be growing more numerous. Elizabeth's leading counselor, Lord Burghley, encouraged English industry; patents were granted for new industries, searches for mineral deposits were sponsored, skilled artisans were imported from the Continent, and the production of gunpowder and naval stores was fostered. Similar efforts were made in other European states.

The Dominance of the Spanish Habsburgs

Philip of Spain (1527–1598) wielded the preponderant power in Europe for over forty years (1556–1598). He identified his own dynastic ambitions with the will of God, which he took to mean that all Europe must be restored to Roman Catholicism. Extraordinary events followed from his extraordinary delusions.

Philip's father, the Emperor Charles V, had bequeathed him a vast but scattered empire: the Spanish kingdoms, territory in Italy, the Low Countries, the so-called Free County of Burgundy, Spain's possessions in Central and South America, the

Bust of Philip II. The most powerful monarch of Europe, why should he seem troubled?

West Indies and the Philippine Islands. In 1580 Philip came closest to satisfying his hunger for empire when he succeeded to the Portuguese throne. The Portuguese were to govern themselves and to continue the direction of their commercial empire. But while Philip was technically only an administrator, the territories he "administered"—the Azores, the Canaries, the Madeiras, Cape Verde, posts on the eastern and western African coasts, trading stations in Sumatra, Java, Ceylon, Burma, China, and Japan—comprised the second greatest world empire in the sixteenth century.

The Government of Philip II

Philip could draw on dynastic traditions to found his empire and could support it by military might. But the practical problems of ruling such extensive lands eventually overwhelmed him. He was unable to maintain communication with his far-flung outposts. And he could hardly pursue policies that served the conflicting interests of all his subjects.

Only in the kingdom of Castile and in the Castilian empire did Philip have an efficient bureaucracy as well as the power to impose

Burning of heretics (auto-da-fé) *by the Spanish Inquisition.*

his will. Outside Castile, he ruled through his viceroys and regents who were obliged to bend to local customs and representative assemblies. Philip's empire was a federation of provinces and kingdoms. In most of them a separate royal council sat in the capital. No single council, not even the Supreme Tribunal of the Spanish Inquisition, was capable of exerting authority throughout the king's possessions.

Philip had been educated by a bishop and was deeply devout. He placed full confidence in his confessors and theologians, all of whom were advocates of absolute monarchy. But he was not in any way a servant of the papal hierarchy. He ruled the Spanish Church quite as authoritatively as Henry VIII ruled the Church of England. His proclamation of "one king, one faith" was perfectly in keeping with all other measures — fiscal, military, political — that he took to preserve the Habsburg power.

King and Church shared all property confiscated from "heretics" condemned by the Spanish Inquisition. By the end of the sixteenth century the Church controlled half of the revenues of the kingdom, but from this it made substantial contributions to the crown. Although the flow of bullion imported from America increased, Philip never established a firm structure of fi-

nance. Direct taxes levied on Castile were his main source of revenue, but because the aristocracy and clergy were exempt from direct taxation, almost the entire weight of the tax system fell on peasants and townsmen. Only with the imposition of the *alcabala,* a tax of ten (later 14) per cent on every commercial transaction as well as a heavy excise (*millones*), were the other social classes forced to contribute to the costs of the state. Still, revenues always failed to cover expenditures, and the monarchy negotiated new loans, debased the coinage, sold state offices, and disposed of its shares in privileged monopolies.

Defense of the Mediterranean

Philip's European hegemony involved him in expensive wars. It fell to his lot to drive Ottoman power from the western Mediterranean. This was at a time when Ottoman naval power was at peak strength under Suleiman the Magnificent (1520–1566). After initial defeats, Philip took the offensive in 1565 with new ships that the papacy helped to subsidize, and drove the Turks from Malta. A great victory at Lepanto in 1571 under Don Juan, Philip's brother, broke the power of the Ottoman Turks, and a truce was signed in 1580.

The Revolt of the Low Countries

The Low Countries comprised the 17 richest provinces of Philip's Burgundian territory. His father, the Emperor Charles V, had crushed the independence of the towns and executed thousands of religious dissenters. But in the time of Philip the Low Countries still persisted in their defiance of Habsburg absolutism.

Philip became ruler of the Low Countries in 1556. Three years later, when he took up residence in Spain, he appointed a regent, his natural sister, Margaret of Parma. She at once pressed for heavy new taxes and demanded ecclesiastical reorganization, measures that were fiercely resented by the Dutch aristocrats as well as the urban oligarchs.

The regency was determined to halt the spread of Calvinism and bring the Church under its control. This proved to be a thorny task. In the French-speaking Walloon provinces, Calvinist preachers set to organizing armed congregations. When the nobility resisted all attempts to reorganize the Church, the regency, acting on its own authority, resorted to means of persecution more violent than those practiced by the Inquisition in Spain.

When the nobles forced Margaret to yield to their demands for moderation, Philip replaced her as regent in 1567 with the brutal Duke of Alva who brought his mercenaries to destroy opposition to Habsburg rule. The Dutch responded by organizing military resistance behind William of Orange. While privateers (called "sea beggars") disrupted Spanish shipping and captured coastal towns, the Dutch resistance movement frustrated the Duke of Alva's sanguinary goals. Requesens replaced Alva in 1573 and tried the policy of gaining Catholic support by moderation while smashing the hard core Calvinist opposition. But even loyal Catholics rebelled when unpaid Spanish troops in 1576 murdered six thousand inhabitants of Antwerp (the Spanish Fury). They joined with the Calvinists to force an end to military oppression by the terms of the "Pacification of Ghent."

With the Spanish troops dispersed, the problem of settling religious differences in the Netherlands led to a territorial solution. In 1579, the Calvinists banded together in the Union of Utrecht, and the Catholics in the League of Arras. These combinations created the division into the Calvinist United Provinces, and the Catholic Spanish Netherlands, today's Belgium.

In their revolt the Dutch broke away from the tradition of "one king, one faith." They established the first pluralistic society in

Flemish protest in Biblical allegory: Pieter Brueghel the Elder, Massacre of the Innocents.

DIVISION OF THE NETHERLANDS

1579-1609

to Spain 1580

GRONINGEN

FRIESLAND

DRENTHE

UNITED PROVINCES

OVERYSSEL

Zuider Zee

Zwolle

MÜNSTER

North Sea

Haarlem — • Amsterdam

• Deventer

Leyden

UTRECHT   GELDERLAND

The Hague —

HOLLAND

Rotterdam

CLEVES

ZEELAND

• Breda

Final boundary 1648

GELDERLAND

B R A B A N T

• Antwerp

COLOGNE

Rhine R.

Boundary of provinces in revolt

• Bruges

Ghent   *Scheldt R.*

JÜLICH

SPANISH NETHERLANDS

• Maestricht

FLANDERS   • Brussels

LIÈGE

Liège

A R T O I S

to Artois

H A I N A U T   NAMUR

to Liège

• Cateau-Cambrésis

LUXEMBURG

TRIER

F R A N C E

Meuse R.

L O R R A I N E

0   20   40   60 mi.

Map by J. Donovan

This map illustrates the territorial solution to the religious problem of the Low Countries. The Calvinists gained control in the seven northern provinces, the Catholics in the ten southern provinces. Note how favorably Antwerp is located for commercial greatness and how Holland dominates the great river traffic on the Rhine. With their fortunate location on the sea, the Dutch built a strong, wealthy, activist mercantile society in which freedom and toleration were natural consequences of the preoccupation with business.

Western Europe with reluctant but actual toleration of religious and secular heterodoxy. To justify their revolt against a God-anointed king, leaders and publicists invoked traditional rights and contractual obligations of princes to their subjects. Democratic ideas made a hesitant appearance, but were rapidly submerged when urban patricians and the landed aristocracy took over the direction of the rebellion. Although Dutch society remained in their control, they were too divided to impose a new absolutism.

Philip II and Tudor England

After Elizabeth restored Protestantism to England, Philip's religious hostilities significantly, but not completely, determined his policy toward that land. His emissaries were implicated in a Catholic uprising in northern England in 1569. On the Continent his government helped support Catholic colleges for training emigrés who were to bring about a Catholic restoration in England. But the King of Spain refrained from committing himself completely against England so long as Mary Queen of Scots was alive. Prospective ruler of a Catholic England, she belonged to the Valois family. Philip had no intention of securing the island kingdom for another dynasty.

Once Mary Queen of Scots was executed Philip decided that the best and most economical way to protect the coast, colonies, and shipping trade of Spain was to invade England. After many delays, the supposedly "invincible" Armada was dispatched in 1588. It consisted of 130 ships, an imposing number, but they were ill-equipped. Philip's plan called for transporting troops from the Netherlands to conquer England. While the Armada waited at anchor for troops that never came, an English fleet combined of private vessels and governmental warships attacked from the windward side. The English, who were outnumbered, effectively deployed fire ships and artillery, and the elaborate but inflexible formations of the Armada were broken.

English medal struck to celebrate victory over the Armada of 1588.

The crippled ships which survived were forced northward around Scotland; on the way back to Spain the damaged fleet suffered severe losses from storms.

Philip received the bad news impassively and announced that he would build a still larger armada. And he did. New convoy tactics and increased naval construction made Spanish sea power stronger than ever before. Drake and Hawkins had predicted that Philip's supply of the world treasure would be cut off. But for the next 15 years bullion flowed to Spain at an unprecedented rate, and new fortifications of colonial bases made them less vulnerable to piracy.

The defeat of the Armada had more significance in European politics. It proved to spectators all over Europe that the Habsburgs were not omnipotent and that they had no special claim to the blessings of Divine Providence. Protestant England had escaped being made a Catholic kingdom within the Habsburg empire. No longer could Spain be seen as the instrument that would enforce a uniform Catholic peace upon Europe.

Elizabethan England

Religious and naval rivalry with Spain cast England in the role of a leader of Europe's Protestant forces. Many Englishmen thought of their beleaguered island

443

kingdom as a city set on a hill and their Virgin Queen as the true Christian monarch guarding the faith. Domestic affairs reflected England's religious position.

The Elizabethan Religious Settlement

Elizabeth's policies concerning religion were tailored to fit political expediency. She sought only one measure from her first parliament of 1559 to overturn Mary's restoration of Catholicism: the reassertion of royal supremacy over the English church. But many of her subjects took their religion far more seriously. A strong group in the House of Commons sympathized with the Marian exiles (laymen and clergymen who had fled England under the persecution of "Bloody Mary"). During their residence in Geneva and the cities of Germany these exiles had absorbed Protestant doctrines as well as techniques of propaganda. Their militant supporters in the House of Commons pressed for a return to the religious settlement of Edward VI. They further demanded harsh measures against Catholics and retribution from various persecutions. Elizabeth compromised. She agreed to an act of supremacy and an act of uniformity. Nevertheless the compulsory prayer book which she had published under the act of uniformity was ambiguous enough in theology to accommodate many diverse opinions.

Compromise between Queen and Commons laid the basis for a middle way, and what emerged in England was a state church whose strict hierarchy was traditional, but whose doctrines were flexible.

Elizabeth's middle way was not agreeable to the Puritans. They attacked what they considered popish survivals in the services authorized by the Elizabethan settlement: the wearing of vestments by ministers, and the Queen's leniency toward Catholics. During the latter part of her reign clashes in the House of Commons between Elizabeth and the Puritans laid bare those issues which would later ignite the civil wars of the seventeenth century.

Society, Politics, and Constitutional Development

The gentry whose power and influence grew during the sixteenth century constituted one of the most important classes in Elizabethan society. They were landed gentlemen whose estates were a main source of income. Membership in this social class was extremely fluid. From below, their ranks absorbed yeomen, wealthy lawyers, officials, and merchants who purchased country estates. In their turn the gentry—who had no titles—were anxious to narrow the gap between themselves and the titled nobility.

In local government, the gentry monopolized the important positions of Justices of the Peace. Many JPs were also members of the House of Commons where they helped make the laws which they enforced in the counties. Administering the Poor Law became their largest single task. Recruited from the gentry to serve in their own neighborhoods, they set compulsory tax rates and appointed and supervised the overseers of the poor in each parish. They also served as judges and sheriffs, searched out and penalized Catholic recusants, set wages and prices, enforced craft and trade regulations, and maintained waterways. Familiarity with the law helped them to secure their own lands as well as carry out their official functions. The gentry thus exerted enormous power, for fundamental to Elizabethan government was the fact that the government had no chance of implementing any policies to which the gentry was opposed.

During Elizabeth's reign the House of Commons expanded and developed new vigor. No tax measure, nor any other bill, could be passed without its assent. Since many new towns were chartered and privileged to send two burgesses to Parliament, the size of the house increased.

French Civil and Religious Wars

While England united under Elizabeth against Spain, France floundered in civil wars; between 1562 and 1598 there were eight. Had a strong monarch been at the helm in France as long as Elizabeth ruled in England, these wars might have been avoided. Instead a succession of weak boy-kings undermined the power of the throne. The unsteady control of Catherine de Medici over her royal sons and the extinction of the Valois male line subjected the kingdom to bitter feuds among aristocratic factions and allowed a Calvinist minority to establish an alliance with highly placed dissidents who were bidding for power.

Prelude to Religious Revolution

Between 1536 and 1559 French Calvinists, or Huguenots, became strong enough to challenge the unreformed French church. Though Francis I considered them anarchists, his alliance with the German Protestants at first forced him to be lenient. After 1540, however, his government began systematically to uproot heresy. His more bigoted successor, Henry II (1547–1559), established a special court in the Parlement of Paris (the *chambre ardente,* or "hot box") where summary justice was handed down to Protestants. The Huguenots defied persecution and even increased in numbers, especially in the southern provinces. At Paris in 1559 they held a clandestine "national synod" which drew up a uniform confession of faith. The Huguenot organization in effect provided an alternate government capable of raising money and troops.

Most of the early Huguenots were people of little political significance. After 1559, however, highly placed noblemen joined their ranks, and when these powerful men flocked to the movement, resignation gave way to armed resistance. Thus Protestantism became involved in the power struggles of the top echelons of the French state.

A Generation of Religious Hatred and War (1562–1588)

Calvinism grew into a significant political force at a time when the two oldest and most powerful feudal families were arrayed against each other. The Bourbon faction was headed by Anthony of Navarre who held vast territories in south central France. The Guise family from Lorraine, whose cardinal-patriarch administered (among other benefices) the sees of Rheims, Metz, and Verdun and the rich abbeys of St. Denis and Clery, led the other faction. Members of the third surviving great family, the Montmorencys, divided their loyalties between Bourbon and Guise.

Queen Catherine de Medici tried various expedients to bring peace to divided France. A religious colloquy to which she invited leading Calvinists from Geneva failed to bring any agreement, and the edict of toleration that the Queen promulgated a few months later, early in 1562, was ignored. Neither compromise nor toleration suited the hostile factions. A decade of intermittent but bloody war was followed by the massacre of St. Bartholomew's Eve, an event partly engineered by the Queen who hoped to eliminate the leading Huguenots, Admiral Coligny and Henry of Navarre, in order to break the back of Huguenot power and end the war.

In August 1572, a large number of prominent Huguenots gathered in Paris for the wedding of Henry of Navarre and Margaret of Valois, the sister of King Charles IX. Urged on by the Guises, an impassioned mob slaughtered thousands of Huguenots in Paris and other towns. Coligny was among the victims, but Henry of Navarre escaped by embracing Catholicism for the time being. It was a dreadful event.

Although the massacre decimated the Huguenots' leadership, it did not impair their military capacity sufficiently to enable the Guise faction, despite help from the Spanish, to defeat them decisively. Factional leadership in the mid-1580s passed

The Massacre of St. Bartholomew's Eve (*August 23–24, 1572*) (*Francois Dubois*).

into the hands of King Henry III, Henry, Duke of Guise, and Henry of Navarre. Their brief conflict has been labelled "The War of the Three Henrys."

The End of the French Wars of Religion

The religious wars dragged on to a ragged conclusion when King Henry III, disillusioned with the aggressiveness and domineering character of the Guises, had their leaders, Henry and Louis the Cardinal, murdered; then he himself was assassinated by a fanatical monk in 1589.

These acts of violence enabled Henry of Navarre to become King Henry IV. Because he was a Huguenot, he was not admitted to the first city of France until he acted on Montmorency's advice and announced himself a Catholic. "Paris is worth a mass," he is reported to have said. Henry's attitude that the welfare of the country was more important than a dogmatic creed enabled France to gain religious peace. In this attitude he was powerfully supported by a faction of moderates called *politiques*

who "preferred the safety of their country to the salvation of their own souls," as religious zealots put it.

Following *politique* doctrines, Henry made toleration an official and enforceable policy when he issued the Edict of Nantes in 1598. By its terms the Huguenots were authorized to conduct private and extensive public worship. They could attend schools and universities, establish a limited number of colleges, and hold public office. To guarantee their security amid the Catholic majority, they were given complete control over 200 towns including the seaport of La Rochelle. These walled towns were garrisoned at royal expense and they boasted more troops than the King himself maintained. No matter; Frenchmen were grateful for peace.

One other concept had high priority in the *politiques'* program: the establishment of a strong national monarchy. Henry helped make that concept a political reality. He made himself master of his subjects by politic dealings with the nobility and by refusing to share sovereignty. Centralization became more effective when his principal minister, the Duke of Sully, introduced a new official called the *intendant,* who was a direct agent of the crown in the provinces.

With domestic peace and some government aid French peasants and tradesmen could recoup from the extensive destruction of the wars. The Duke of Sully promoted agriculture, introduced new silk and glassware industries, and built highways and canals. As the economy rapidly recovered taxes decreased and the royal treasury grew fat. Unfortunately for France, Henry was assassinated in 1610, and once again a boy-king and his mother ruled the country.

Four Decades of War and Revolution (1618–1660)

At the beginning of the seventeenth century, Europe had a respite from general conflict. Henry IV pacified France, and in 1598 made a settlement with Spain. Spain and England came to terms in 1604; Spain and the Dutch in 1609. But this fragile peace was only a temporary interlude and was nearly shattered by Henry IV. Only a few years later, in 1618, a Bohemian revolt against the Habsburgs embroiled every Western and Central country in a series of general wars which lasted until 1660. Only England, which underwent its own civil wars in isolation, kept aloof.

The Opening and Spread of the Thirty Years' War

The Thirty Years' War involved many powers and was fought over many issues. In Germany it was a civil and religious war. For France and Sweden it was a war of imperialist expansion. Between the Habsburgs and the Bourbons it was a confrontation of dynasties; between the Habsburgs and the Dutch, a naval and colonial conflict. The war passed through several stages. The Bohemian revolt—a religious war—spread into a general conflict between the Catholic

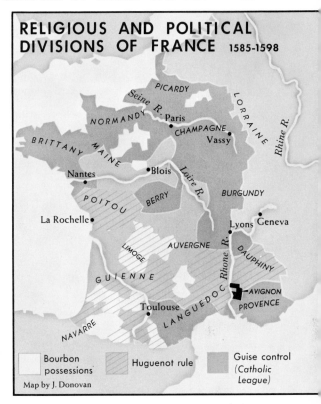

RELIGIOUS AND POLITICAL DIVISIONS OF FRANCE 1585-1598

Map by J. Donovan

Henry IV, 1589–1610.

and Protestant powers of Europe. In its final stages, that conflict became a political power struggle between France on the one hand and the houses of Habsburg on the other.

Religious tensions building in the domains of the German Habsburgs provided the fuel for the fires of war. The Peace of Augsburg (1555) had recognized only Lutherans and Catholics in the formula that whosoever reigns shall determine the religion of his territory. Since 1555, Calvinism made a strong appeal to activist noblemen, especially in Bohemia, where the Hussite tradition persisted. While Emperors were tolerant, the changes in religious affiliation did not cause much trouble. After 1600, however, the Protestants desired acquiescence in their gains, while Catholics pressured the Emperor to nullify the prerogatives of the Protestants. Rival armed leagues sprang up, the Protestant Union in 1609 and the Catholic League immediately thereafter.

Conflict centered in Bohemia, where in 1618 insurrectionary Bohemian nobles chose a Calvinist as their King. He was Frederick V, the son-in-law of James I of England, and Palatine Elector. This act, following upon the notorious "Defenestration of Prague," when Bohemian noblemen threw the imperial governors bodily out of a palace window about sixty feet above the ground (they landed in a manure pile), was occasion enough for war.

Under the brilliant command of Baron Tilly, the Catholic forces routed the Bohemian rebels in 1620 at the battle of the White Mountain, not far from Prague. The Habsburgs confiscated the extensive lands of the fleeing rebels which they distributed among their followers, such as Albert of Wallenstein.

The collapse of Bohemia spelled doom for Austrian Protestantism. Austria was subjected to a rigorous counter-reformation, as was Silesia; between 1622 and 1628, Protestants throughout the Habsburg provinces were shorn of all their rights.

Meanwhile Spain gained possession of important Alpine passes, enabling her to move her forces without depending on sea lines of communication to the Netherlands. Since the 12-year truce with Holland had expired and was followed by renewed warfare, this was a crucial gain.

Between 1624 and 1629 the German Protestants were routed, and Ferdinand II gained a control over the imperial domains more complete than any emperor had held for centuries. Tilly and Wallenstein (whose large private army was now paid by booty and was run for profit) won victory after victory as Central Europe became one great theater of war. During the so-called Danish period, 1625 to 1629, King Christian IV of Denmark led the Protestants. Christian's aim in the war was to gain bishoprics and power in northern Germany. The forces of Tilly and Wallenstein defeated him. They went on to conquer Holstein and to occupy the German Baltic coast as far east as Stralsund.

Swedish and French Intervention, 1630–1648

His Baltic possessions threatened, King Gustavus Adolphus of Sweden entered the war at the head of the most advanced army of Europe. In 1630 he landed in Pomerania and proclaimed himself the deliverer of the German Protestants. Heavy subsidies from Cardinal Richelieu and some assistance from the Dutch aided his invasion the following year. The Swedish invasion quickly turned the military situation about. Near Leipzig in Saxony, Gustavus Adolphus' forces met and annihilated nearly half of the imperial army under Tilly. At Lützen in Saxony in 1632 the Swedes defeated Wallenstein, but in the battle the "snow king" of Sweden was killed. Wallenstein was assassinated in 1634 for conducting unauthorized negotiations with the Swedes and French. Despite his loss, imperial strength increased and Richelieu felt it necessary to commit French forces to stop the Habsburgs.

Since 1624 Richelieu had been building up France's military and diplomatic power in anticipation of a showdown with the Habsburgs; now he brought France directly into the Thirty Years' War. While Gustavus Adolphus invaded Germany French troops made major gains in Alsace. Richelieu died in 1642, but French strength continued to grow. After the Dutch cut Spanish lines of communication with the Netherlands, French troops were able, for the first time in over a century, to defeat Spanish military formations in open country. Thus the victory in 1643 at Rocroi in the Low Countries was highly significant in the history of European power politics.

The Outcome of the War in Central Europe

Serious peace talks began in 1644, but the complexities of the war were so great that four years passed before negotiators could arrive at a generally acceptable solution. Westphalia was the first general peace conference in history; no body of accepted rules as yet existed by which precedence and rank could be determined. Since the papacy could not sanction concessions to Protestants, the negotiators were obliged to meet at two different Westphalian cities — Protestants at Osnabrück, Catholics at Münster. The separation, combined with poor communications between Westphalia and distant Spain, slowed the pace of the talks.

A compromise on the question of Church property and official recognition of three religions, Lutheranism, Calvinism, and Catholicism, resolved the religious wars in Germany. Religious boundaries hardened into a pattern little disturbed until the mass migration of Germans after 1945.

Sweden, France, and France's protegé, Brandenburg, left Westphalia with substantial territorial gains. France retained the Alsatian bishoprics of Metz, Toul, and Verdun, and sovereign though vaguely defined authority over all of Alsace. Sweden received western Pomerania and territory

(towns, bishoprics, or islands) near the mouth of every major river flowing from the Empire into the Baltic; these were remunerative toll stations. With French support the Hohenzollerns of Brandenburg increased their scattered holdings, gaining Eastern Pomerania, Minden, Halberstadt, Cammin, and inheritance rights to Magdeburg. Westphalia also recognized the independence of Switzerland and the United Provinces.

Westphalia began the final breakup of the Holy Roman Empire and sealed the decline of the papacy as a force in international affairs. Though modified by subsequent treaties, it laid the foundation of the European state system which prevailed until the days of the French Revolution. Nationalists would eventually lament that Westphalia divided Germany, but at its inception the treaty was generally hailed as a diplomatic success and a keystone of European order and peace. This settlement implied that states, no matter how they differed in might, were — in theory at least — equal members of a community of sovereign states. The medieval ideal of universal rule by pope and emperor thus gave way to a new order.

After hostilities were ended, Central Europe faced an immense task of reconstruction. Although we do not have accurate population statistics, the Empire as a whole probably lost one third of its population. Some areas in Saxony were barely touched; others, like Henneberg along the Main River, may have lost four-fifths of their people. Depopulation on this scale resulted not so much from military losses, as from the plagues that swiftly followed armies and swept through the towns where civilians sought refuge from marauding troops. Under normal conditions, human beings are generally able to recover from such losses within a generation, but conditions in post-war Germany were severely abnormal. Germany grew more parochial and sluggish than it had been during the Middle Ages.

CENTRAL EUROPE AFTER 1648

North Sea

Vistula R.

KINGDOM OF POLAND

HITHER POMERANIA To Sweden
FARTHER POMERANIA

BREMEN To Sweden
•Hamburg
VERDEN
Stettin

UNITED NETHERLANDS

BRANDENBURG
MAGDEBURG

Osnabrück•
MINDEN

•Münster

WESTPHALIA *Weser R.*
HALBERSTADT
Breitenfeld
LUSATIA

•Cologne
Lützen
•Leipzig
SAXONY

SILESIA

Oder R.

SPANISH NETHERLANDS

PALATINATE
White Mountain •Prague
BOHEMIA

MORAVIA

Rocroi
FRANCE
•Paris

VERDUN
METZ
To France
TOUL

PALATINATE
Nördlingen Donauworth

Rhine R.
Breisach Spanish

BAVARIA

AUSTRIA
Danube R.
Vienna

KINGDOM OF HUNGARY

FRANCHE COMTÉ (Spanish)

TYROL

STYRIA

CARNIOLA

OTTOMAN EMPIRE

SWITZERLAND
(Independent of the Empire, 1648)

Church lands

Habsburg lands

Wettin lands

Hohenzollern lands

Wittelsbach lands

Holy Roman Empire

Land ceded by Westphalia

VENETIAN REPUBLIC

Adriatic Sea

0   50   100 mi.

Map by J. Donovan

Aside from their peace with the Dutch, the Spanish gained nothing from Westphalia. Reluctant to concede that their imperial star had fallen, the Spanish continued the war with France until the Peace of the Pyrenees in 1659. For a hundred years Spain had lived with delusions of grandeur. Her medieval, chivalric, noble, crusading ideals inspired a period of expansion and imperial confidence. But the world changed and the Spanish did not. Clinging to their ideals long after they had lost their meaning, the Spanish lived in two worlds and suffered a kind of schizophrenia that Cervantes captured so poignantly in *Don Quixote*. The Spanish dream

of regaining by war the solid strength that the realistic Dutch, English, and French were daily consolidating by sweaty industry and vigorous commerce was shattered by the reverses of the Thirty Years' War. After 1659 Spain remained a peripheral kingdom.

Richelieu, Mazarin, Revolution, and Peace in France

Louis XIII did not prove to be a strong ruler, but his selection in 1624 of a first minister made up for his deficiencies. Though trained for the clergy and championed by zealous Catholics, Cardinal Richelieu was a *politique* whose ruling passion was to build the authority of the French monarchy at home and extend French influence abroad. In 1626 he destroyed the fortresses of the great nobles, and removed them from positions of command of his new navy. In the meantime the Huguenots, who made common cause with the aristocracy, rebelled. By 1628 they were crushed and their political and military rights were withdrawn. They retained only religious toleration. Richelieu further subordinated France to royal authority by extending the power of the *intendants,* bureaucrats who came from the middle class. Gradually they assimilated the judicial and financial functions that had once belonged to the aristocratic governors of the provinces. Richelieu followed a typical mercantilist policy. He built a navy, expanded the army, founded trading companies and colonies, and let the increasing burden of taxes and services be laid on the lower classes.

Both Louis XIII and his chief minister, Richelieu, died before the end of the Thirty Years' War (Richelieu in 1642, Louis in 1643); but French policy changed little. The new king, Louis XIV, was only five years old; the state was controlled by his first minister Cardinal Mazarin. Mazarin was hand-picked by Richelieu, and if Richelieu was unpopular with the nobility, Mazarin was even more so. The French nobility and upper classes hated him. Not only was he a foreigner building a private fortune at state expense, but also he refused to recognize the aristocracy as tax exempt.

Disaffected jurists of the Parlement (high law court) of Paris and members of royal councils initiated a revolution (the *Fronde*), in 1648. The *Fronde* was a revolt against the whole financial-administrative system of Richelieu and Mazarin. The leaders of the *Fronde* were primarily concerned with protecting ennobled officeholders from taxation and freeing them from the supervision of administrative officials. Such aims were too narrow to sustain an effective revolt. By 1653 Mazarin's foreign mercenaries

Three of the many sides of Cardinal Richelieu —a triple portrait.

had defeated the nobles. He then reneged on all his previous concessions to them and set about in earnest to actualize Louis XIV's ambitions to rule absolutely.

Before Mazarin died in 1661, he negotiated the Peace of the Pyrenees and, by aligning German princes along the Rhine with French foreign policy, laid the groundwork for future French expansion. He also left Louis XIV the corps of officials who made the French monarchy a model of dynastic absolutism. An outstandingly efficient bureaucracy in the service of the crown was one outcome of the seventeenth-century crisis in France.

Crisis in Eastern Europe

The Swedish invasion of Germany from 1630 to 1648 was only one part of a larger and longer Eastern power struggle. This struggle, mainly instigated by Sweden's imperial ambitions, was a contest for control of the territories adjoining the Baltic Sea. Between 1655 and 1660 all of Europe was concerned about its outcome. Sweden's rise to power in Europe was impressive, but she did not maintain for very long her role as a leading state. By the

Treaty of Oliva (1660), Sweden lost her wartime conquests with the exception of Livonia (now part of Latvia and Estonia), and the Baltic was opened to the ships of all states.

The peace terms of Oliva proved transitory, but the northern war left lasting marks on the societies of the Baltic states. Like the Thirty Years' War, it provoked an agrarian crisis which helped rivet the status of serfdom onto the peasants of east-central Europe. It also cleared new ground in which authoritarianism could take root. The principality of Brandenburg, for example, was so dismayed at its vulnerability to foreign invaders that Frederick William ("the Great Elector") had little trouble building a standing army and instituting military despotism there. The outstanding exception to the despotic social orders that took root in the wake of these wars was Sweden. Unlike peasants and townsmen in Poland and Germany, the commoner Swedes had well-established legal rights and sent representatives to a diet which possessed considerable vitality. The nobles made impressive gains in power, but the lower orders in the diet—in coalition with lower-ranking officials—were able to check them. In this respect, Swedish social and constitutional development resembled that of England more than the rest of the Continent.

Civil War in Stuart England

After building up their opposition for two generations, Puritans in the House of Commons launched a full scale assault on the Stuarts' claim to absolute authority in state, church, and economic life. The assault ended in a nation controlled by Puritans, but that control lasted less than 20 years. Still, the Puritan Revolution left its mark. Although the Stuart dynasty regained the powers of the crown, those powers no longer included prerogative courts and arbitrary taxation.

Stuart Kings and Parliaments, 1603–1641

Elizabeth had always managed the House of Commons very diplomatically, but James departed from this policy and asserted that its members owed him obedience as a matter of right and principle— an obedience he claimed from all his subjects.

Between 1611 and 1621 James only called Parliament once: in 1614. But a serious depression in the cloth trade from 1620 to 1624 so strained the already flagging royal revenues that James was forced in 1624 to seek new grants of taxes. The House of Commons not only failed to comply, but reasserted some of its ancient prerogatives. In that same year Parliament attacked trading company monopolies, which many independent merchants held responsible for the depression. Now Parliament was no longer staging a defensive struggle against the King; it was claiming the right to initiate legislation and to appoint committees to supervise the execution of the laws it enacted.

James' successor, Charles I (1625–1649), had been a popular young prince because he opposed his father's pro-Spanish policy. But once on the throne he soon came into conflict with the same institutions and doctrines that had confronted James I. When Charles requested money, Parliament proceeded to proclaim its rights anew and to attack his favorite minister. In his desperate search for new forms of revenue, the King exacted forced loans from his subjects and revived archaic feudal dues. In 1628 Parliament firmly responded with the Petition of Right, a landmark in the history of constitutional government. It declared that no taxation should be levied without parliamentary consent, that no troops should be billeted in private homes, that martial law should not be imposed in peace time, and that no man should be imprisoned without the cause being shown. As it reaffirmed personal liberty, attacked royal control over a standing army, and posited the right of Parliament to approve taxation, the Petition of Right significantly challenged the fundamental bases of royal absolutism.

The struggle against the King had religious as well as political roots. Puritan religious and social ideals, so hostile to royal high church policies, were propagated by the press and pulpit, and by the Puritan members of the House of Commons. Puritanism established an aristocracy of the predestined elect, "the Godly people," who were known by their moral code and their religious devotion. Puritan doctrines placed a high premium on individual thought and action and set commitments derived from personal experience above rulings handed down from church hierarchies. Moral responsibility counted for more than formal religious observance. In rituals and traditions of priestly privilege, Puritans saw the embodiment of the devil and superstitious idolatry. They identified their enemies as God's enemies, deserving bitter invective, persecution, and, ultimately, death. They did not conspire to create a revolution. But as they tried to achieve the reforms dictated by their consciences, they followed a course that led, gradually but inexorably, to the overthrow of the monarchy. After 1630 it seemed all too apparent to Puritans that royal policy offered them only the choices of emigration, conformity, or struggle. Some did emigrate; eventually most of them took to arms.

In 1629 when the House of Commons disobeyed Charles' command and discussed religious issues, the King locked the chamber and arrested eight of its leaders. Charles then ruled without Parliament from 1629 to 1641, but the conflict did not abate.

When Charles called Parliament in 1641 to ask for money it refused to be dissolved. The "Long Parliament" did not end its first session until it had brought about a constitutional revolution. Charles was forced to assent to an act that authorized

Parliament to meet once every three years whether or not summoned by the crown (the Triennial Act). He was also made to abolish such unpopular prerogative courts as High Commission and Star Chamber and to eliminate all feudal revenue measures. His two closest ministers, Strafford and Archbishop Laud, were impeached; a parliamentary statute was passed demanding Strafford's execution, and the King assented to it. In spite of all his concessions a majority of the members of the House of Commons did not trust Charles with control of the army. Parliament voted — by a narrow majority — to assume command of the militia, an act that precipitated civil war, the first England had known since the Wars of the Roses in the fifteenth century and her last to date.

The Civil Wars

Ever since the seventeenth century men have offered various explanations of the civil war, and historians still argue about

ENGLISH CIVIL WARS

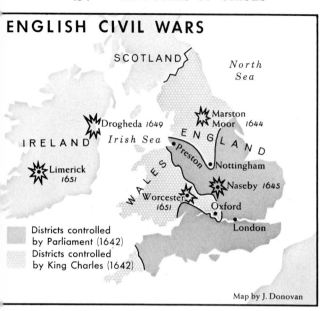

SCOTLAND

North Sea

Drogheda 1649

Marston Moor 1644

IRELAND   *Irish Sea*   E N G L A N D

Preston

Limerick 1651

Nottingham

W A L E S

Naseby 1645

Worcester 1651

Oxford

London

Districts controlled by Parliament (1642)
Districts controlled by King Charles (1642)

Map by J. Donovan

how and why loyalties were divided into warring factions. One thing, however, is certain; every major faction of the revolution drew its leadership from men of the gentry. Whether a man chose the side of the King or the side of the Parliament, his decision was probably influenced by his religious feelings and his connections—or lack of connections—at court.

Because of the structure of economic life in early seventeenth-century England, men who had friends and could wield power at court and in administration were likely to prosper. It was only natural, therefore, that merchants and members of the gentry who had no or only weak court connections blamed their economic difficulties on the court, on the monopolies, and, finally, on the crown itself.

In every English county there was a contest for loyalty between the King and the revolutionary parliamentarians. Opposing armed camps of "Roundheads" (parliamentarians) and "Cavaliers" (royalists) were slowly and reluctantly formed. War preparations were interspersed with negotiations.

Until 1642 the conflict was confined to the members of the ruling aristocracy who

feuded among themselves, but once conflict developed into full-scale hostility, the door was opened to the more radical Puritan minorities. Paramount among these were the so-called Independents, or Separatists, who demanded autonomy for the religious congregations and (since it would benefit them) advocated tolerating other Puritan sects. These aims could only be achieved by the King's defeat and, as Oliver Cromwell emerged as the leader of the radical Puritans, the civil war began in earnest.

When Oliver Cromwell (who came from a minor gentry family) took command of what would become the nucleus of the national army, the "New Model," he picked his men for their fighting zeal, a quality that apparently went hand in hand with radical religious views. Under Cromwell and his men the war became an enthusiastic crusade to defeat "papist" royalists and to secure toleration for sectarian Puritanism. Cromwell's army, "Ironsides," backed by the resources of the wealthier southeastern part of England (now taxed by excises never conceded to the Stuart kings) destroyed the main Cavalier army at the decisive battle of Naseby in 1645. The Royalist cause was crushed and Charles I surrendered to the Scots.

Once the King was defeated, the Puritans in Parliament set about the religious and political reconstruction of the nation, a task that was at once complicated by the sharp disputes that arose between conservative Presbyterians and more radical Independents. The Independents drew their support from the victorious army whose members were every day growing more vociferous in their demands. Parliament sought to disband the army although the soldiers' pay was seriously in arrears. Led by Cromwell, the army seized power in 1647, and established its hold on the nation; Presbyterians were banished from Parliament and, in 1649, Charles Stuart was executed.

The relative freedom of thought and expression permitted under the earlier Cromwellian government was fully exploited by political and social reformers. A significant group were the Levellers—a name given to them by their opponents who feared that the extension of the franchise they advocated (though this was by no means universal manhood suffrage) would lead to an assault on property rights and the ultimate leveling of all social distinctions. The Levellers based their political programs on the doctrine of natural rights. They demanded legal equality, a written constitution, annual parliaments, a single-chambered legislature, separation of church and state, the abolition of tithes and excise taxes, and intensive reform of common law that would among other things do away with imprisonment for debt, arbitrary imprisonment and compulsory self-incrimination. The Levellers were a small minority, and even within the army they had no real opportunity to achieve their objectives. Although Cromwell and his Independents were willing to go along with part of their program, they saw in the most advanced of the Levellers' ideas a threat to public order and an attack on the rights of property.

The Commonwealth and the Protectorate

The kingship was abolished from 1649 to 1660. Under the Commonwealth England conducted her only experiment in republican government. The real power of the state was in the hands of the parliamentary commander, Oliver Cromwell, who accepted his military victories as evidence that he was now the chosen instrument by which England would become a truly "Godly" society. Despite his severe leadership, Cromwell failed to unify England behind him. The Instrument of Government of 1653 (England's last written constitution) represents an attempt to restore a balance between the executive and Parliament that was not very different from what Englishmen had known under the Stuarts. Cromwell too found that Parliament was intolerant, oligarchical, and uncooperative.

The Independents never obtained their

Oliver Cromwell, a contemporary portrait.

constitutional and religious goals. Cromwell eventually resorted to ruling by a military system, but he was never able to induce or force Englishmen to accept toleration and Puritanism. He was subjected on all sides to criticism—from radicals and sectarians on the left, and on the right by monarchists for whom Charles I had become a beloved martyr. Cromwell died in 1658 leaving as his designated heir his son Richard, but Richard was completely ineffectual. It was General George Monk who gained control of the armed forces. Under his direction the crown was restored to Charles II. Although a Stuart was once again on the throne, the crown was stripped of prerogative courts, extraordinary powers of raising revenue, feudal rights, and rule by royal edict.

The Art and Literature of Crisis

Humanists and artists of the Italian Renaissance had emulated a classical tradition. They had aimed for perfect form and style, proportion, naturalism, tempered emotion, and decorous serenity. But the model of classical simplicity was supplanted by the colossal grandeur, metaphysical allegory, and emotional subjectivity we characterize

Bernini, Colonnade of St. Peter's.

Detail from Bernini's Ecstasy of St. Theresa.

as baroque. Baroque artists retained classical themes, but adapted them to portray power, spirit, suffering, emotion, and sensuality.

To view most Renaissance works with maximum effect, the eye rests on definite planes and within fixed boundaries. But the baroque characteristically required a visual sweep which knew no bounds and suggested something beyond. In both art and literature, baroque artists revived the use of allegory and metaphysical symbolism that had been dominant in the Middle Ages.

Baroque art was a product of the militant Catholic Reformation. Outside Italy, the baroque had its greatest appeal in Habsburg Europe. There crown, nobility, and Church exploited it to celebrate victories, exalt noble families, and satisfy the emotional hunger of a people beset by war, famine, epidemics, and the oppression of a rigid social hierarchy. Baroque art flourished in Spain, Portugal, southern Germany, Flanders, Bohemia, Hungary, Poland, and, to a lesser extent, France. The Iberian kingdoms carried it to their American colonies, where some of its most exotic expressions can still be found today.

Sculpture and Architecture

The most versatile and influential baroque artist was Giovanni Bernini (1598–1680). After 1629 he was the architect of St. Peters in Rome. Together with his famous contemporary, Borromini, he worked under papal patronage to make Rome the fittingly ornate capital of a rejuvenated Catholicism. Bernini grew famous as the only worthy successor of Michelangelo. Louis XIV, the English court, and other high powers sought him out for commissions. And he was paid a personal visit by the pope. Although he thought his genius lay in painting, Bernini is best known today for such architecture as the Plaza and Colonnade of St. Peters and such sculptures as *Daphne and Apollo, Bust of Louis XIV,* and the *Ecstasy of St. Theresa.* He also drew plans to rebuild the Louvre in Paris, but royal ministers rejected them as too expensive. Most of his career was spent in Rome, where he and his large staff of assistants were employed by a series of pontiffs.

Bernini and his Italian contemporaries profoundly influenced architecture and sculpture in Catholic Europe, particularly churches, palaces, and villas, which were usually as large as funds permitted. Ba-

An example of Borromini's work in Rome: S. Carlo alle Quattro Fontane. This is highly representative of Baroque church architecture in the Latin countries.

roque buildings were characterized by curved exterior walls with recesses, twisted columns, massive facades, ornate and sometimes grotesque statuary both inside and out. Their rooms were often oval-shaped, and interiors were heavily laden with paint-

ings, tapestries, and massive carved decorations. Ceilings sometimes took on the appearance of infinite sky, an impression floating figures were designed to convey. Statuary, including altar pieces (Bernini's *Ecstasy of St. Theresa* was designed as an

Eerie otherworldliness: El Greco's View of Toledo. *In the threatening
sky, the sense of foreboding, and the mystical qualities in this painting,
El Greco captured the spiritual agonies of a medieval society in decline.*

altar piece), expressed movement and dynamic emotion. Twisted figures were shown in diagonal positions, and the figures were partially shrouded in blowing drapery to magnify the sense of grandeur or movement.

Not all statuary and architecture in Catholic countries were baroque, and the baroque influence outside Catholic boundaries was limited. Traditional classicism and simple functionalism predominated in England, the United Provinces, and, to some degree, in France. In classical architecture the simple lines and pillars of the Venetian architect Andrea Palladio (1518–1580) were widely imitated.

Painting

Baroque painting reflected the same emotionalism found in baroque statuary, and techniques were as parallel as the different media allowed. Baroque painters covered a wide range of subjects. They frequently portrayed the great, religious themes (saints and martyrs were particularly popular), mythological episodes, and grotesque or disfigured persons from the lower classes. Mysterious or eerie lighting effects often gave their works an otherworldly aura. The plethora of canvasses produced in the baroque era defies any attempt to discuss individual examples. We shall limit our study here to representative groups. Italians of Rome and Venice produced most of the baroque art of the seventeenth century, but important baroque painters also appeared in Spain during the reign of Philip IV (El Greco, Velásquez, Murillo, José Ribera), and in Flanders (Rubens and Van Dyck). Classicism and realism were intermingled with the baroque in France by Poussin, Lorrain, and the Le Nain brothers.

That baroque techniques also penetrated the Dutch provinces is demonstrated by the later works of Rembrandt van Rijn (1606–1669), the greatest of the Northern masters. He was not alone in portraying religious themes infused with anguish, pity, or passion. But as he became more drawn to these themes—after his famous *Night Watch* of 1641—his commissions declined, and he (and other painters), long dependent on a highly competitive dealer-dominated market, fell into poverty. Perhaps as many as 2000 painters were working in the Netherlands. Most of them employed some baroque techniques, but they catered to urban middle-class patrons who preferred art that was less gaudy and not so metaphysical. The works of Hobbema, van Ruisdael, Vermeer, and Hals were painstakingly realistic. Baroque art had little opportunity to flourish in the Netherlands. A landowning aristocracy did not dominate society. The Dutch did not have a monarch bent on glory and grandeur. And Catholicism, which provided the imagery and emotional content in baroque works, was not a force there.

Literature

The baroque literature of the century between 1560 and 1660 is ornate, dramatic, and tense. Baroque writers, playwrights, and poets were influenced by chivalric romance of the late Renaissance, by elaborate treatises on courtly behavior, and by mythology, as well as by the Judeo-Christian religious tradition revived during the Reformation. They repudiated the skeptical humanism and robust earthiness of writers like Montaigne, Cervantes, and Shakespeare. Baroque writers saw life governed by two irreconcilable bodies of law: strict secular laws of vengeance and personal honor, and absolute moral laws of obedience to divine commands. Running through their works were themes of violent conflict: in politics, between the rewards and penalties of power; in morality, between the norms of society and the teaching of religion; in art, between the rigid formal rules to which they bowed, and the ornateness and complexity of expression which often led them to pile words upon words in great profusion. The best examples of baroque literature are the works of Spanish poets and dramatists like Góngora (1561–1627), Lope de Vega (1562–1635), Calderón (1600–1681), and the priest-dramatist Molina (1571–1648). Unlike Cervantes, whose *Don Quixote* was written at the beginning of the seventeenth century, their works have seldom been translated because of their ponderous formal style, emphasis upon aristocratic virtues and dilemmas, and complicated allusions to classical mythology and geography. They are, therefore, little appreciated today.

To some degree baroque forms did appear in England, France, and the Low

Countries. Although his particular genius defies any simplified labeling, Shakespeare shared the emotionalism of the baroque writers and often seems to echo their conclusion that secular life is only an empty illusion. For Macbeth, life is "a tale Told by an idiot, full of sound and fury Signifying nothing," and in *The Tempest*, Prospero tells us that

> We are such stuff
> As dreams are made on; and our little life
> Is rounded with a sleep.

The dominant literary and artistic form developing in Northern and Western Europe, however, was neoclassicism adapted to meet the needs of aristocratic society in those areas. Neoclassicists uncovered and tried to honor the formal canons of simplicity, serenity, conciseness, emotional restraint, and brevity which defined the classical tradition. They sponsored campaigns to standardize the spelling and form of vernacular languages and were supported in such efforts by royal literary societies.

The Roots of Crisis

Historians look to concrete social and technical data in order to understand the disorders of this period. But contemporaries had only their own immediate experiences, their intuitive feelings, and their traditions to draw upon to explain and confront the dilemmas of their age. Despite their differing approaches, the search by contemporaries for more ordered societies reinforces the conclusion of modern historians that this century was one of either a general crisis or a series of individual crises.

A theme that runs throughout most histories of this period is the theme of dynastic and religious war. Rulers sought to achieve security from invasion, to eliminate warfare that was conducted only for private profit, and to effectively control all military forces within their realms. By 1660 European monarchs had generally adopted disciplined standing armies whose activities were sponsored and supported almost exclusively by the state. At sea, however, private warfare was still accepted as a normal means of conducting hostilities.

Religious hatreds bred by the schisms of the Reformation also inspired the use of unrestrained force and represented an important threat to life, property, and domestic tranquillity.

Economic crises were less susceptible to rational solutions than military and religious problems. Agriculture and commerce were unable to support the growing population.

Political and religious wars called forth new political and religious thought. The *politiques* formulated the notion of state sovereignty and proposed that the sovereign state, responsible to the common weal, tolerate religious dissent too strong to be crushed. Kings continued to demand unconditional obedience from their subjects—"by divine right"—and to control the established churches, but their international activities reflected increasingly secular policies. The humanist, Hugo Grotius, who wrote in the Netherlands during the Thirty Years' War, outlined a theoretical system of international politics that was independent of any theology. To this jurist goes the credit for founding the science of international law. Under his system the sovereign state, in its own self-interest, had to accept certain rational restraints on the conduct of war. The often disastrous interaction of religion and power politics helped to discredit Reformation doctrine in certain religious circles. Pietists in Germany and Quakers in England, as well as many other sectarian groups, cultivated religions which set personal morality above formal creeds. As religious wars bred increasing disillusionment, secular doctrines of natural law based on science and humanitarianism took form. But they would not attract widespread attention until after 1660.

SELECTED READINGS

Ashley, Maurice, *The Greatness of Oliver Cromwell*, Hodder & Stoughton, 1957.

An outstanding apologetic biography by the leading English authority on Cromwell's career.

Ashton, Trevor, ed., *Crisis in Europe 1560–1660*, Basic Books, New York, 1965.

Articles from *Past and Present*, an English journal of "scientific history." The contributors agree that a general crisis existed but fail to find a single common cause.

Cipolla, Carlo M., "The Decline of Italy," *Economic History Review*, 2nd series, V (1952–1953), 178–187.

One of many recent articles in that journal whose conclusions sharply modify older general histories of early modern Europe.

* Clark, George N., *The Seventeenth Century*, Oxford University Press, New York, 1961 (2nd ed.).

Perceptive analytical chapters arranged by subject and particularly useful for early modern institutions.

Clough, Shepard B., *The Economic Development of Western Civilization*, McGraw-Hill, New York, 1959.

Several chapters incorporating recent research are pertinent to this period.

Davies, D. W., *A Primer of Dutch Seventeenth Century Overseas Trade*, Martinus Nijhoff, The Hague, 1961.

Basic discussion of the commerce of Europe's dominant trading state.

Elliott, J. H., *Imperial Spain 1469–1716*, St. Martin's Press, New York, 1964, and Lynch, John, *Spain Under the Habsburgs*, Vol. I, *Empire and Absolutism 1516–1598*, Oxford University Press, New York, 1964.

Two recent in-depth accounts of Spanish institutions and policies by recognized authorities.

*Friedrich, Carl J., *The Age of the Baroque 1610–1660* (Rise of Modern Europe series), Harper & Row, New York and Evanston, 1962.

Excellent factual account which finds baroque art the prevailing symptom of the era's tensions.

Geyl, Pieter, *The Revolt of the Netherlands*, Barnes and Noble, New York, 1958, and

———, *The Netherlands in the 17th Century, 1609–1648*, Vol. 1 of 2, Barnes and Noble, New York, 1961 (rev. ed.).

Replace the classic account of the Dutch Republic by John L. Motley with a fundamental re-evaluation and de-emphasis of the role of Calvinism in determining the outcome of the Dutch revolt.

Hamilton, Earl J., *American Treasure and the Price Revolution in Spain 1501–1650*, Harvard University Press, Cambridge, 1934.

Demonstrates that inflation was related to bullion imports but in this and other writings Hamilton exaggerates the role of bullion in producing the "price revolution" and economic growth.

Heckscher, Eli F., *Mercantilism*, 2 vols., Allen & Unwin, London; The Macmillan Co., New York, 1955, 2 vols. (2nd ed.).

Much-criticized attack on mercantilism but provides basic facts on economic policies and conditions in the continental monarchies.

Lea, Henry C., *A History of the Inquisition of Spain*, The Macmillan Co., New York and London, 1906–1907, 4 vols.

A heavily documented indictment of the Spanish Inquisition; Volume IV pertains to this period.

Mattingly, Garrett, *The Armada*, Houghton Mifflin, Boston, 1959.

Good literature and excellent history which assesses the significance of England's naval victory over Spain.

Merriam, Roger B., *Six Contemporaneous Revolutions*, Clarendon Press, Oxford, 1938.

A study of the revolutions at the end of the Thirty Years' War; a pioneer in the comparative history of revolutions.

Mosse, George L., *The Holy Pretense*, Basil Blackwell, Oxford, 1957.

Demonstrates that English Puritans condemned Machiavelli's principles but implemented them under religious terms.

Neale, John E., *The Age of Catherine de Medici*, J. Cape, London, 1943.

Asterisk (*) denotes paperback.

Particularly valuable on Calvinism as an international revolutionary movement.

——, *Elizabeth I and Her Parliaments 1559–1581,* St. Martin's Press, New York, 1958.
Outlines Elizabeth's relations with Puritans in Parliament and the compromises behind the "Elizabethan Settlement."

*Neff, John U., *Industry and Government in France and England 1540–1640,* Cornell University Press, Ithaca, New York, 1957.
Comparative history of mercantilist industrial regulations and their enforcement emphasizing England's lack of a centralized bureaucracy as a major factor in the decline of English mercantilism.

*Ogg, David, *Europe in the Seventeenth Century,* A. and C. Black, London (6th rev. ed.), and a Collier paperback.
Old, useful survey which does not consider England part of Europe.

Palm, Franklin C., *Politics and Religion in Sixteenth-Century France,* Ginn and Co., Boston, 1927.
A political biography of Montmorency-Damville, a leader of the *politiques.*

Redlich, Fritz, *De Praeda Militari, Looting and Booty 1500–1815,* Franz Steiner Verlag, Wiesbaden, 1956.
Legal study which provides reasons why mercenary warfare was economically deleterious.

Reynolds, Robert L., *Europe Emerges. Transition Toward an Industrial World-Wide Society 600–1750,* University of Wisconsin Press, Madison, 1961.
Basic for the expansion of early modern Europe, Europeans' advantages over non-Europeans, and economic policies.

Roberts, Michael, *The Military Revolution 1560–1660,* Boyd, Belfast, 1956.
Lecture on military adoption of firearms, new tactics, and discipline by the leading biographer of Gustavus Adolphus.

Rowse, Alfred L., *The England of Elizabeth: The Structure of Society,* The Macmillan Co., New York, 1950.
Exceedingly well-written social history.

Simpson, Alan, *The Wealth of the Gentry 1540–1660,* University of Chicago Press, Chicago, 1961.
Most definitive attack on Tawney's thesis that the gentry was rising economically. Simpson finds that the law and office holding were more remunerative than agriculture.

Supple, B. E., *Commercial Crisis and Change in England 1600–1642,* Cambridge University Press, Cambridge, 1959.
Derives "mercantilism" from government efforts to remedy specific commercial crises rather than from an ideology of power.

Tapié, Victor-L., *The Age of Grandeur, Baroque Art and Architecture,* Grove Press, New York, 1960.
Stimulating art history which relates baroque artistic tastes to the social, political, and religious milieu of the Catholic Reformation.

Tawney, Richard H., *The Agrarian Problem in the Sixteenth Century,* Longmans, Green & Co., London and New York, 1912.
One of several works in which Tawney presents economic arguments for the rise of the English gentry.

Unwin, G., *Industrial Organization in the Sixteenth and Seventeenth Centuries,* Clarendon Press, Oxford, 1904.
Old but useful analysis based on England.

Wedgwood, Cicely V., *Richelieu and the French Monarchy,* English Universities Press, London, 1949.
A short political biography.

——, *The Thirty Years' War,* J. Cape, London, 1938 *et seq.*
Standard English account from the emperor's point of view supplanted in part by untranslated German works.

THE SHAPING
OF THE
MODERN WORLD

16

Governments and Societies in the Age of Absolutism

Out of the crises of both the Renaissance and Reformation emerged authoritarian governments that claimed to be arbiters of society and thought. By 1660 divine-right kings were trying to obtain absolute control over military, political, legal, economic, and cultural affairs—hence, the label "absolutism" has often been used to describe this type of regime. These kings—with their standing armies, their bureaucracies, and their control over established churches—attempted to impose domestic order and to extend their hereditary domains.

Strengthened by the new powers surrendered to them, they attempted to reshape their society, making it dependent upon their personal will. But, in doing this, they jeopardized their alliance with the old aristocracy by elevating commoners to the highest offices. After 1660 the most effective monarchs—Louis XIV of France, Frederick William I of Prussia, Leopold I of Austria, and Peter the Great of Russia—had to deal with an alienated nobility. Their successes and failures are our main concern in this chapter.

Other monarchs claimed but did not attempt to wield this kind of unlimited authority. They cooperated with the privileged orders whose political and social claims they respected. We shall refer to their kingdoms, which remained firmly in the grip of custom, as "aristocratic monarchies."

Only a few seventeenth-century states were outside the political mold of monarchical authoritarianism. These included oligarchic Venice, the Imperial Free Cities of Germany, and the Swiss Confederacy; the two most important ones were the Dutch Republic and England. The Dutch fought off absolutism in the "Eighty Years' War" against Spain (1576–1648). England escaped it in 1688 by revolution. These two states went furthest in developing new constitutions, but their revolutions were still far from complete at the beginning of the eighteenth century.

THE NATURE OF ABSOLUTISM

The All-Powerful Monarchy in Theory and Practice

The theory of royal absolutism has an interesting history. It begins with the late Middle Ages when royal publicists, some clergymen, and civil lawyers began to claim autocratic powers for kings with a long pedigree. They interpreted the relationship between the king and his people as a lord-subject relationship based on the sovereign authority of the ruler. In contrast, the feudal lord-vassal relationship was based on mutual rights and obligations spelled out in a contract. One should watch the concept of contract, for it became a revolutionary weapon in the hands of Locke and Jefferson. These two men derived their political theories ultimately from the feudal idea of a contractual relationship between ruler and ruled. But royal absolutists looked to a much older tradition, the imperial Roman law, in which they found the precept that "The will of the Prince has the force of law." Well buttressed by Roman law, kings were able to delegate some of their sovereign powers to personal officials, set up personal courts to enforce their will, and exclude all but themselves and their favorites from the "mysteries of state." Late medieval and Renaissance monarchs also were believed to possess sacral qualities. In their capacity as anointed kings they could heal disease and many a sufferer knelt in line for the king's touch, expecting a miraculous cure.

It was only a short step from such an exalted and sacramental view of kingship to the divine right doctrine that became prevalent by 1600.

Roman Catholic and Protestant clergy appointed by kings cited Scripture, especially the Old Testament and Romans XIII, to prove that kings were direct agents of God, that their power was subject to no limitation except Him and His revelation, and that resistance to a divinely ordained ruler was a cardinal sin. If these kings ruled tyrannically, they were only punishing human wickedness for God. A few monarchist propagandists, such as Bishop Bossuet in France, added still another—a secular and modern—argument for authoritarian rule. They accepted the premises of Jean Bodin and Thomas Hobbes that complete centralization of state authority was rational, necessary, and natural. But this theory was frowned upon as being too secular until the "enlightened despots" of the eighteenth century made it their own. Seventeenth-century advocates of royal absolutism depicted their kings as ruling in the image of God, simultaneously manifesting traits of feudal and classical heroes.

Absolute monarchs built royal supremacy into the machinery of their governments. Their new standing armies provided security from invasion and put in royal hands the only armed forces permitted within their states. In domestic affairs, however, absolutism was more often a superficial façade than a reality. No absolute monarch had as much control over his subjects as did the king and Parliament of England, both of which exacted only semivoluntary obedience.

A backward technology was a major curb on royal absolutism; slow transport and communications limited its range to the vicinity of capitals and provincial administrative centers. Still more important in limiting royal authority were the vested interests of the privileged classes and the strong hold of custom among the masses; no monarch could completely eliminate these restraints.

The Brakes of Custom, Privilege, and Poverty

Strikingly absent from the configuration of absolutist society were the large commercial middle classes—bankers, merchants, and entrepreneurs—comparable to those in England and the Dutch Republic. The rest of Europe remained primarily agrarian. Only France had an extensive professional and commercial middle class, and even its ambitions were set by the aristocracy. In Brandenburg-Prussia, Poland, Russia, and the Habsburg Danubian monarchy, no such class existed except for officials.

Formal division of society into the estates of the late Middle Ages—nobles, clergy, and commoners—lasted until the French Revolution. Besides maintaining their traditional social ties with the monarchy, the nobles became officers of the royal army and held the most prestigious offices in the state and the church, thus sharing power with titled and privileged officials, themselves on the way to becoming nobles. In these ways absolute monarchy remained basically, although not entirely, a conservative social force. At the apex of the social pyramid stood the king. He alone had the power to promote limited numbers of men of ability or wealth.

In the simplest kind of hierarchy, as for example in France, the established clergy retained its preeminent position among the estates. In Roman Catholic kingdoms the clergy retained its prestige as the first estate and continued to educate the nobility's offspring, but its ranks were staffed at the top by noblemen or commoners elevated by the king. Protestant churchmen were more likely to come from professional ranks, especially the sons of clergy.

Among the privileged laymen, highest honors and preferment went to the nobility, itself a hierarchy of ranks. Law and custom recognized two different types of noble patents—titles inherited from

The English nonconformist minister could be a Presbyterian, Congregationalist, Baptist, Quaker, and later also a Methodist, or Unitarian. Socially inferior to Anglicans, he was also politically inferior until 1828.

knightly or military ancestors and titles acquired by service and made hereditary by purchase or gratuitous royal grant. Despite rivalries between them, hereditary and service nobles shared common traits: they held landed estates, rights to local milling and baking monopolies, tolls, and legal jurisdictions over peasants; they were exempt from common taxes and believed that acts of manual labor or trade in goods not produced on their own estates were demeaning.

On the fringe of privileged ranks in Western Europe lived the upper bourgeoisie. Aspiring to attain nobility, these professionals, bankers, and great merchants acquired offices and land with manorial rights. They received tax exemptions and other privileges from royal and municipal offices

A merchant and his accounts. Here is the rational, calculating spirit that so happily unites intellect with acquisitiveness.

A master silversmith's shop, about 1700. Old guild traditions and ideals of fine craftsmanship persisted into the nineteenth century.

Concluding an arranged marriage, or how to live happily ever after.

and sometimes patents of nobility from the king. Like nobles, they disdained and avoided manual labor.

A hierarchy also existed within the bourgeoisie. It ranged from scholars and councillors at the top down through officials, notaries, and merchants (wholesale and retail) and masters of corporate guilds. These master craftsmen inherited their status but were considered less respectable if they actually worked with their hands.

Journeymen, apprentices, domestic workers, day workers, and agriculturists who lived within town walls constituted an unprivileged majority subject to excise and other taxes. They were forbidden to band together for mutual political or economic advantage, even if they had desired to do so. For them, rapid social ascent was difficult if not impossible.

In the hierarchies of all classes the hereditary family, not the individual, was the unit of society. Families sought marriage alliances to increase their fortunes or status. Since private and public rights were not sharply separated, dowries and legacies included offices of church and state, profitable legal jurisdictions, and manorial dues, as well as lands and securities. Money enough to give a daughter a large dowry or a son an education was the principal means of social ascent. At the middle level of the townspeople, guild masterships passed almost exclusively by inheritance and marriage. By voluntary or compulsory systems similar to the nobility's entails, even landholding peasants prevented the division of estates among heirs. Normally, the individual's status was determined for life by the position of the family into which he was born, and the social order strengthened family control over him.

Upward of 80 per cent of Europe's population was rural; usually it was over 90 per cent. Even where personal movement was not legally prohibited, most village people lived, worked, and died without leaving the same villages that their ancestors had inhabited since time immemorial. Tradition ordered their daily lives much the same as it had the lives of their forebears, and it made novelty an object of fear. The peasantry lived on the brink of famine not only because its obligations to state, church, and lord took the greater part of its productivity, but also because agriculture was bound by tradition to backward methods.

No year of Louis XIV's seventy-two-year reign was without famine in some province. Starvation or malnutrition brought death first to the weaker members of the lower classes: children, women, old persons, and beggars. (Half the children died before the age of one.) Average longevity was probably not more than twenty-five, certainly not over thirty. Peasant women were weathered and old at that age. At forty, village men were often gray-beards. Upper-class persons who reached adulthood lived longer, averaging perhaps fifty. Paradoxically country folk suffered more than townspeople from food shortages. Town governments stocked grain in warehouses, but even so famine caused

There was no happier occasion for the well-to-do peasant than the time of working beside his neighbors to gather in another bountiful harvest.

deprivation and unemployment within their jurisdictions.

Basic poverty thus curtailed the absolute ruler's credit and revenues. It also set limits upon his militarism. Louis XIV could muster the largest army in Western Europe since the Roman Empire, but its range was limited by a lack of fodder and oats for its horses. And this was true even though the French monarch geared his policy for power rather than his subjects' welfare.

THE EFFECTIVE ABSOLUTIST REGIMES

The pace-setter for authoritarianism in all of Europe was Louis XIV. The Austrian Habsburgs, the Hohenzollerns, and some smaller German princes charted courses similar to his. Eastern Europe also boasted its great autocrat, Peter the Great, who thrust Russia into European affairs and built up his power at home by borrowing technology and institutions from the West.

The France of Louis XIV

The King's Personal Monarchy

In attempting to fulfill and improve on Mazarin's paternalism, Louis XIV resolved to have no prime minister. Reacting against

the civil wars of the 1640s, he was determined to exclude the nobility from making high-level decisions. When queried by a Church official as to whom he should address himself on questions of public affairs after Mazarin's death, Louis replied, "To myself." Like his Bourbon predecessors, he considered the state his private inheritance.

Kings [he wrote] are absolute *seigneurs* [lords], and from their nature have full and free disposal of all property both secular and ecclesiastical, to use it as wise dispensers, that is to say, in accordance with the requirements of their State.[1]

In administering the state Louis proved to be diligent and industrious. After formal court rituals in the morning, he met in the afternoons with his high councillors. Unfortunately for France and Europe, he pursued glory and power for their own sake. He built a bureaucracy of elevated commoners who owed their positions to the monarch alone. It excluded the nobility and high clergy. He set up special courts to discipline nobles, but his greatest thrust at their political power was indirect. At Versailles, a former hunting lodge just outside Paris, Louis constructed a huge palace built at tremendous expense and staffed by nearly fifteen thousand servants. Apart from the palace's role in setting the court and art fashions of Europe, it served Louis' purpose of gathering the greater nobility around the court. In return for personal services exalting the monarchy, he gave them pensions and made them financially dependent upon his favor.

The Machinery of State

Louis' administration of France became a model for absolutism in other parts of Europe. In deciding matters of high policy the King attended three councils in person — War, Finance, and Foreign Affairs. They were made up of ministers of state. Lesser councils dealt with justice and internal administration. Officials did the work, but the King personally made decisions, which were then communicated to his diplomats and military commanders. For domestic affairs they were directed to the provinces through the *intendants* whose authority was absolute, at least in theory. ("The *intendant*," Louis wrote, "is the king present in the provinces.") In practice, however, they were often thwarted by provincial institutions, especially the *parlements* (high law courts).

Early in Louis' reign Mazarin appointed

1. Quoted by Jean Longnon, ed., *A King's Lessons in Statecraft: Louis XIV: Letters to His Heirs,* translated by Herbert Wilson, A. & C. Boni, New York, 1925, p. 149.

and put at the sovereign's disposal a number of outstanding officials: de Louvois over the army, de Lionne over foreign affairs, and particularly Jean Baptiste Colbert (1619–1683). An ennobled draper's son who had been manager of Mazarin's personal fortune, Colbert became Controller of France in 1665. His efforts to strengthen France's economic capacity for war became so familiar that one form of mercantilism is usually designated by his name. His successes and failures graphically illustrate the gulf between the aims and accomplishments of the royal government.

"Colbertism"

As finance minister Colbert worked assiduously to increase tax revenues, expand commerce, and reduce debts and corruption. Under his direction, the government took the initiative in encouraging industry — notably silk, lace, drapery, luxury goods, forestry, sugar refining, iron, and glassware. It sponsored colonial trading companies to build an empire in North America and India. To make the quality of French exports uniform and acceptable, Colbert promulgated minutely detailed industrial production codes drawn up by guildmasters. These codes, which specified minimum standards for manufacture, were enforced over the whole of France by the *intendants*. To stimulate trade and commerce Colbert built roads and canals. He proposed abolition of the provincial tariffs and grain trade regulations that hindered the flow of goods. Foreign goods, especially Dutch merchandise, he sought to exclude by heavy protective tariffs in 1664 and 1667. He strove to make France self-sufficient in grain by prohibiting the export of wheat. Finally he tried to standardize the legal procedures of the royal courts.

Few basic reforms were implemented. The system of farming taxes to private contractors continued to plague the kingdom until the Revolution of 1789. Private French capital failed to support Colbert's industries and trading companies, going instead to state bonds (*rentes*). His industrial production codes stifled technological innovations and encouraged craftsmen to maintain the *status quo*. Nor did Colbert's attempted revision of the legal system give real unity to France, for approximately 400 different "systems" still existed in 1789, and extreme confusion over conflicting weights, measures, and tolls left the country an economic hodgepodge until the Revolution swept them away at the end of the eighteenth century.

Although Colbert is often depicted as an opponent of Louis' aggressive wars, he advocated economic warfare: exclusionist tariffs, colonial struggles waged by private companies, and the seizure of Dutch wealth. Moreover he was dedicated to the splendor of Louis — "For the king's glory, no sacrifice was too great," he wrote — and his fiscal measures financed his monarch's campaigns. Most of the revenue came from the *taille,* a headtax on the peasantry. In the recently acquired border provinces that retained their estates it was moderate, but in the older provinces it was particularly burdensome. The *gabelle* or government salt monopoly likewise varied according to province. As the pressure of war intensified after Colbert's death, taxes were extended to include marriages, births, and deaths. Even in some of the richer areas the peasantry was in a state of semistarvation during Louis' wars.

Royal military espenditures exceeded the kingdom's taxable wealth, especially during famines. But without Colbert's management the consequences would have been graver. From the *intendants* he solicited detailed and precise tax lists and information on business activity, population, and the temper of the people. Collated in government archives, the *intendants'* reports constituted a large store of information necessary to policy-making.

The State and the Arts

In charge of royal buildings, Colbert was in a position to regiment architecture and

Colbert, Controller of France, 1665–1683, one of the most enlightened administrators in French history. Louis XIV was lucky to have him.

plastic arts as well as the economy of Europe's most influential state. At the Gobelins royal factory he assembled an army of painters, sculptors, engravers, weavers, cabinet makers, and other artists under the leadership of the painter Charles Lebrun. But Versailles was Colbert's principal artistic concern. As an effort of major construction, it is matched only by the architect Christopher Wren's rebuilding of London after the Great Fire of 1666.

Colbert wielded his influence to tame baroque elaborateness with classical simplicity. The Catholic Reformation that had inspired baroque emotionalism was over. Classical baroque was dedicated not to an otherworldly religion but to a secular hero, Louis XIV. The Royal Academy of Sculpture and Painting set the tone of official taste, returning to the principles of Aristotle

Versailles and its classical gardens, about 12 miles from Paris, where the King could live with the people—nobles, diplomats, relatives, artists, musicians, actors, cronies, administrators, guards, messengers, French chefs—that made the hard work of ruling a great country efficient and somewhat endurable.

and of the Italian High Renaissance. Versailles' exterior was classical; its gardens were rigidly symmetrical and geometrical. Its interior, however, was classical baroque, done in themes drawn from the ancient world but laden with allegorical rather than literal meaning. Versailles was designed not for comfort or utility but for magnificence. It was the culmination in grandeur of the courts of the late Renaissance. It set the norm for courtly architecture and furnishings to such a degree that other monarchs felt obliged to imitate it. Likewise its operas, ballets, and plays set Europe's standards of entertainment.

One King, One Church

The Church as well as the arts felt the steely grip of royal absolutism. For a time it appeared that Louis, like the Protestant rulers of Germany, would try to create a national (Gallican) Church. The Concordat of Bologna (1516), which the Council of Trent had not nullified, empowered French kings to make most high Church appointments. Louis' appointees supported him against the papacy, but he still lacked the power to name prelates in parts of southern France. During the 1670s he determined to bring these posts under royal sway. This extension of government power precipitated a sharp quarrel with the pope who refused to confirm the King's appointments. During the deadlock that ensued, many Church offices fell vacant, and the monarchy collected their revenues. In 1682 a national Church council led by Bishop Bossuet supported the King. It reiterated the position of the Gallican Church that the pope's spiritual powers were limited to those confirmed by a council. After protracted conflict that cost Louis the diplomatic support of the papacy, he and the pope reached a compromise.

At this point, Louis' personal life and the tone of his court were changing. His shapely, vivacious mistress, Madame de Montespan, "as wicked as the devil himself," gave way in royal favor to Madame de Maintenon, governess of the royal bastards. With the advent of de Maintenon, whom the King married secretly in 1684, puritanical winds blew through the royal corridors. Comedy was banned at court, and the atmosphere at Versailles became sober and stiff. During the same years the King turned to persecuting the Huguenots.

Here, too, he yielded to the pressure of the clergy and his advisors, who after 1655 demanded the complete elimination of Protestantism. Noble families of "political Huguenots" went back to the Roman Church. Financial inducements were offered to apostates, while church closures canceled their privileges and narrowed the range of toleration. Then dragoons were stationed in Huguenots' homes to harass them. Royal troops forced nominal conversions in the public squares of southern towns. Finally on the specious argument that there were few dissenters left in France, the King revoked the Edict of Nantes in 1685.

Louis forbade the Huguenots to emigrate, but over 200,000 of them escaped the kingdom. Their numbers included skilled artisans, scholars, merchants, soldiers, and professional men. Their talents enriched Prussia, the English colonies, and other new Protestant homelands.

Louis XIV and Europe

The France of Louis XIV epitomized aggressive diplomacy during a century in which warfare decisively influenced institutions. As personal ruler, Louis lavished resources and attention upon the army. Under de Louvois the army adopted improved artillery, bayonets, and a quicker-firing muzzle-loading handgun. Soldiers donned uniforms and were given a serious military education. Their administrators centralized command and devoted great attention to supply. Marshal de Vauban, an engineering genius, devised scientific ways

to reduce fortresses that were precise enough to predict the time of capitulation. Nobles filled the officer corps, whereas commissioned recruiting captains, often corrupt, hired or impressed the common soldiery. By 1678 the standing army reached 279,000 men, a formidable and expensive force, and it continued to grow.

Louis sought first to conquer those territories in the Spanish Netherlands that had escaped Mazarin's grasp during the Thirty Years' War. When the queen's father, the king of Spain, died in 1665, Louis claimed the Spanish Netherlands as her inheritance. Catching Spain diplomatically isolated, French armies under de Condé and de Turenne swept through a series of Flemish forts and Franche-Comté in 1667 and 1668. With his diplomats neutralizing the alliances formed against him, Louis prepared for the next onslaught.

Without a declaration of war, French armies invaded Lorraine and Holland in 1672. Desperation and fear of defeat brought William of Orange to power in the Dutch Republic. The Dutch opened dikes and flooded fields to stop the invasion. William enlisted foreign assistance, and the war became a stalemate. At the peace made at Nimwegen in 1678, the Spanish ceded Franche-Comté to France and France returned territory conquered from the Dutch.

Having acquired Franche-Comté, France was mistress of her eastern frontier. Now Louis XIV's ambition, heightened by success, extended to the Rhine itself. He paved the way with clever diplomacy and inflated legal claims. The Peace of Westphalia had ceded ambiguous rights to France in Alsace in 1648. Now French jurists laid claim to full sovereignty before specially constituted "Chambers of Reunion," courts set up in frontier cities. As the courts consistently rendered decisions favorable to France, the French army occupied their territorial awards. Theoretically, by taking advantage of outdated feudal relationships, the Chambers

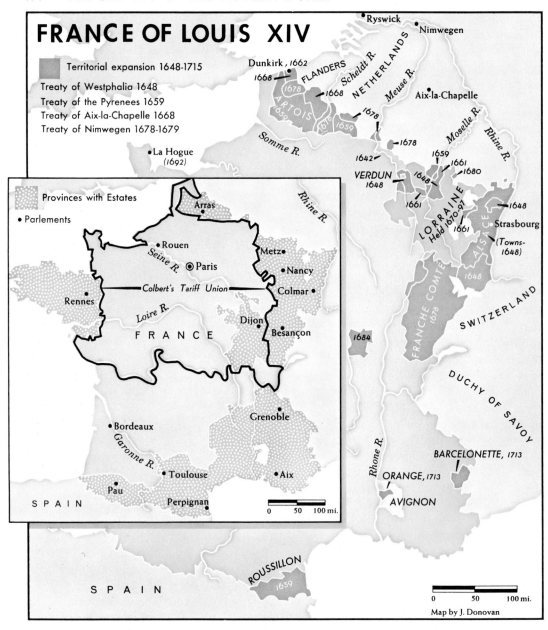

FRANCE OF LOUIS XIV

■ Territorial expansion 1648-1715

Treaty of Westphalia 1648
Treaty of the Pyrenees 1659
Treaty of Aix-la-Chapelle 1668
Treaty of Nimwegen 1678-1679

Provinces with Estates

• Parlements

Ryswick
Nimwegen
Dunkirk, 1662
1668
FLANDERS
Scheldt R.
NETHERLANDS
Meuse R.
ARTOIS 1659
1668
1678
1659
Aix-la-Chapelle
1678
1678
Moselle R.
Rhine R.
1642
1659
1661
VERDUN 1648
1648
1680
1648
1661
LORRAINE Held 1670-97
1661
1648
Strasbourg (Towns-1648)
ALSACE
FRANCHE COMTÉ 1678
1648
1684
SWITZERLAND
Somme R.

La Hogue (1692)

Arras
Rouen
Metz
Seine R.
⊙ Paris
Nancy
Colbert's Tariff Union
Colmar
Rennes
Loire R.
Dijon
Besançon
FRANCE
Rhine R.

Grenoble

Bordeaux
Garonne R.
Toulouse
Aix
Pau
Perpignan

SPAIN

0   50   100 mi.

DUCHY OF SAVOY

Rhone R.
BARCELONETTE, 1713
ORANGE, 1713
AVIGNON

ROUSSILLON 1659

SPAIN

0   50   100 mi.

Map by J. Donovan

of Reunion could have pushed French claims progressively across most of Germany.

Meanwhile French diplomacy—which was setting the language and procedures, open and secret, for all of Europe—was disarming German resistance to this creeping expansion. The French King posed as the protector of the "liberties" of German princes against the emperor; by 1683 Louis himself had hopes of being elected emperor. By the same date he had reconstructed an alliance system consisting of Sweden, Poland, Turkey, Brandenburg, Saxony, Bavaria, and Hungarian leaders in revolt against the Habsburgs. When the Turks laid siege to Vienna in 1683, Louis played a waiting game hoping to save Europe from the Turks at Austrian expense. But he miscalculated; the Habsburgs drove the

Turks from Vienna. Then they purchased temporary peace in the West by recognizing the work of the Chambers of Reunion. They used the time thus gained to turn the Turkish retreat into a rout. Belgrade fell in 1688. Louis, fearing the loss of his Turkish ally, invaded and devastated the Palatinate. Louis was also still hopeful of gaining territories along the Rhine River.

To counter this latest expansionist move, William of Orange, who became King of England in 1688, organized the League of Augsburg. The exhausting War of the League of Augsburg (1689–1697) was the first major European struggle to extend to the rest of the world; in the English colonies of North America it was known as King William's War. The League turned back French expansion. At Ryswick in 1697 peace terms substantially restored prewar boundaries. It gave Emperor Leopold peace in the West again, thus allowing him to drive the Turks eastward until, suspicious once again of France, he called a halt in 1699.

The War of Spanish Succession

Louis made peace in 1697 because he could not risk being at war with Spain when the feeble, childless Charles II died. Otherwise he might forfeit his claims to Charles' empire. By accidents of birth and death, there were three dynastic claimants to this, the largest European empire—the French Dauphin, the duke of Bavaria, and Emperor Leopold I. Consulting with the English and the Dutch, Louis decided that the Empire ought to be divided in such a way that no single dynasty would monopolize power in Europe. A balance-of-power principle was substituted for the strict system of legitimate succession. In accordance with this principle, successive partition treaties were drawn up in 1698 and 1699. But Charles II destroyed these well-intentioned plans. Just before his death in 1700, Charles II drew up a will, a "crop of dragon's teeth," which bequeathed the entire empire to Louis' grandson Philip. If he and his younger brother refused the inheritance, all of Charles' domains would then go to an Austrian archduke. A more devastating threat to peace could scarcely have been contrived. Louis was now faced with the most difficult choice of his reign.

Louis chose to take the inheritance and, in the bargain, he also chose to provoke the English and the Dutch by seizing Dutch-controlled forts in the Spanish Netherlands and by issuing a series of decrees regulating Spanish colonial trade—at the expense of the English and the Dutch. These actions led to a grand coalition against Louis and a long war to prevent French hegemony over Europe.

The brilliant victories that the Duke of Marlborough won at Blenheim (1704), Ramillies (1706), and other battles and campaigns never led to a French defeat because Louis with his large population was able to call up additional reserves. The French, however, were driven out of Italy and the Spanish Netherlands, while the English gained Gibraltar and Minorca enabling them to have a fleet in the Mediterranean all year. The war spread to the American colonies where it was called Queen Anne's War.

In 1711 the Austrian claimant to Spain died, and his rights reverted to the Habsburg emperor. England found herself fighting to unite the Spanish and Austrian thrones. This union would upset the balance of power as much as if Louis would seize the whole domain. Weary of war, concerned about commerce, and fearful of Austrian Habsburg dominance, a peace party—the Tories—took charge in England and negotiated a separate peace with France. Two treaties—Utrecht (1713) and Rastatt (1714), known together as the Peace of Utrecht—halted the devastating war. Louis' grandson Philip retained possession of Spain and her colonies on the condition that the French and Spanish thrones would never be joined. The Austrian Habsburgs received Naples, Sardinia,

Milan, and the Spanish Netherlands, where the Dutch were granted the right to garrison forts in order to forestall any new French invasion. The house of Savoy received Sicily and the status of kingdom. The Hohenzollern rulers of Prussia were also allowed to call themselves "king," and they received a small territory (Guelderland) along the lower Rhine. The lion's share of the spoils of war went to England. She retained Gibraltar, Minorca, Newfoundland, Acadia, St. Kitts, and Hudson Bay. In Spain's American colonies British merchants gained a limited right to trade, which served as an entrée for large-scale smuggling. The South Sea Company also obtained a monopoly of the Spanish colonial slave trade (*Asiento*). In subsequent decades Spain was to upset the peace arrangements in Italy, and France was to obtain Lorraine (1739). Despite these changes, however, the Peace of Utrecht stands as one of the most important territorial settlements in modern European history.

Habsburg and Hohenzollern

In the Old Regime, dynastic state boundaries were set by births, deaths, and marriages within ruling families as well as by conquest. Ruling families inherited diverse territories with a variety of laws, customs, and constitutions. Provincial diets usually put provincial interests first and tried to prevent outsiders from holding local positions of power and privilege. This particularism was especially notable in the provinces of Central Europe held by the Habsburgs and Hohenzollerns. Compared to them, Louis XIV's territories were contiguous and relatively homogeneous. Hohenzollern lands were scattered from the Rhine to the Niemen rivers, whereas the Habsburgs ruled peoples of diverse languages along the Danube. Despite the disunity of their holdings, these two families tried to administer them as coherent states. Thus they laid the basis for future rivalry over the control of German affairs.

Absolutism in the Habsburg Danubian Monarchy

The Peace of Westphalia (1648) left the Habsburg emperors of the Holy Roman Empire with an empty title. It admitted their rivals, France and Sweden, to direct participation in German affairs. Their authority was further diluted by the growing independence of the larger German principalities — Bavaria, Brandenburg-Prussia, Saxony, and Hanover — which had their own armies and foreign dynastic ties. Against the strength of his competitors, Leopold I (1658–1705) had no chance of recovering imperial authority.

Leopold I admired the power and prerogatives of Louis XIV and tried to imitate them by being his own first minister. Like his opposite number in France, he made the higher nobility dependent on the court for its honors and privileges. His central government was compartmentalized into a privy council, a war council, an imperial treasury, and an imperial chancery. But these were considerably weaker than the institutions of France. The German provinces retained their privileged estates. In order to raise money and troops, Leopold had to negotiate with each diet, which then supervised its own levies. The privy council remained an advisory rather than an executive body, and the imperial treasury's revenue was limited to mineral rights and indirect taxes.

In the chancery a group called the "cameralists" stood ready to assert the authority of the crown more rigorously than Leopold himself. But at the outset of his reign their authority was effective only in Bohemia, which had been reduced after 1620 to a hereditary monarchy directly under the Viennese court. Leopold summoned the Magyar estates to Pressburg in 1687 to

WESTERN EUROPE AFTER UTRECHT, 1721

NORTH AMERICA

BRITISH

FRENCH

BRITISH

ACADIA AND NEWFOUNDLAND
(To Britain, 1713)

SPANISH

FRENCH

TREATY ADJUSTMENTS 1713-1721

To Prussia

To Hapsburgs

To England

To Savoy

× Barrier Fortresses

K. OF GREAT BRITAIN

★ London

(To Hanover, 1719) Hamburg
BRANDENBURG
UNITED NETHERLANDS *(1702-1707)* *(1720)*
HANOVER Berlin ★
PRUSSIA

Utrecht

Guelderland
(To Prussia, 1713)

AUSTRIAN NETH.
(1714)

K. OF POLAND

SAXONY

HOLY ROMAN EMPIRE
AUSTRIA

Paris ★

• Rastatt

BAVARIA Vienna ★

K. OF HUNGARY

K. OF FRANCE
(House of Bourbon)

SWITZERLAND

VENETIAN REPUBLIC

SAVOY

MILAN
(To Hapsburgs, 1714)

PIEDMONT

R. OF GENOA

TUSCANY

PAPAL STATES

K. OF PORTUGAL

K. OF SPAIN
(House of Bourbon)

★ Madrid

Balearic Is.

Minorca
(To Britain, 1713)

CORSICA Rome •

SARDINIA
(To Hapsburgs, 1714)
(To Savoy, 1720)

K. OF NAPLES
(To Hapsburgs, 1714)
(To Bourbons, 1735)

Gibraltar
(To Britain, 1713)

Mediterranean   Sea

SICILY
(To Savoy, 1714)
(To Hapsburgs, 1720-1735)

Map by J. Donovan

ratify an absolutist constitution which abolished their rights to elect and resist the king. It equated Protestantism, long associated with political dissent, with treason and was meant to stamp it out.

Unlike the Bohemian nobles, the turbulent, ungovernable Magyars were not displaced. For one thing the monarchy lacked a middle class from which to draw loyal bureaucrats. In the eastern part of the Habsburg realm only Transylvania was ruled directly from Vienna. Hungary's administration remained in the hands of

the nobility, although its finances were subject to central control. The nobles were confirmed in their privileged rule over an enserfed peasantry, and in order to enforce this settlement, Austria was obliged to garrison the kingdom with 30,000 troops during the War of Spanish Succession. After the war Leopold's successors Joseph I (1705–1711) and Charles VI (1711–1740) won over individual rebel leaders. Charles VI's Pragmatic Sanction of 1713 proclaimed as an established fact that his German, Bohemian, and Hungar-

ian possessions were administratively unified. In the German provinces a centralized state with officials comparable to *intendants* did not take form until the reign of Maria Theresa after 1740. But in the eastern, non-German parts of the monarchy, absolutism was firmly entrenched during the reign of Leopold I.

The Rise of Brandenburg-Prussia

Hohenzollern lands were even more scattered than those of the Habsburg patrimony, but within a few decades the rulers of Brandenburg, who had the title "Elector of the Holy Roman Empire," instituted a more effective absolutism. After the Thirty Years' War the Hohenzollerns ruled Cleves, Mark, Ravensburg, Halberstadt, Cammin, Minden, Magdeburg, Brandenburg, Eastern Pomerania, and Prussia—all as separate principalities. Each had its own diet or assembly and its own customary law. But these diets were still wed to parochial interests and privilege, and Frederick William, the Great Elector who acceded to power in 1640, was forced to cooperate

RISE OF BRANDENBURG-PRUSSIA

- BEFORE 1648
- 1648-1680
- 1713-1720

Map by J. Donovan

with them temporarily.

Between 1653 and 1688 the Great Elector became one of Europe's most powerful rulers; his standing army and its administration made this development possible. At the end of the Thirty Years' War the Privy Council had been the highest legal and administrative body for both military and civil matters, but in 1660 it lost control of military affairs to the War Commissariat. This organization had originally been responsible for assembling, equipping, provisioning, and financing the army. Steadily it encroached upon civilian affairs. It stripped local diets of fiscal power, and its agents extended their authority over guilds, town government, and courts. It also came to control taxes, trade, settlement of the Huguenots, and numerous other matters.

The Hohenzollerns guaranteed to the Junker class control over both rural and urban affairs, a guarantee that proved very costly. Taxes per capita were probably double those of France. These heavy taxes drained potential capital from the economy, thus undercutting the Great Elector's mercantilist policies, which were designed to stimulate economic growth. They actually crippled the growth of towns, commerce, and industry.

Under the Great Elector's successors, Frederick (1688–1713) and Frederick

William I (1713–1740), Prussian absolutism became increasingly centralized. The military bureaucracy grew as the Hohenzollerns struggled to contain Louis XIV along the Rhine and to assume supremacy in the Baltic area. In 1723 the General Directory was formed, uniting civil and military chains of command. Created to save the state from near bankruptcy, it became the nucleus around which the power of the eighteenth-century Prussian state was built.

Frederick William I devoted special attention to the army. Indeed Prussia was sometimes referred to as "an army with a state." At great expense he recruited giants from all over Europe for his palace guard

Frederick William I reviewing his "giant guards." He liked these men so well that he couldn't bear to lose any; he was a peaceful monarch and a very paternal one.

at Potsdam. To Frederick II, who succeeded him in 1740, he bequeathed a large army (80,000 men) and a centralized bureaucracy. The one great chink in the absolutist armor was the power and degree of independence that aristocratic officials enjoyed. Furthermore, the nobles resented the tax that Frederick William I imposed on them in order to help support his army. As the nobility had risen up in France after the death of Louis XIV, so the nobility of Prussia renewed its bid for power when Frederick William died.

The Emergence of Russia as a European Power State

By the eighteenth century Russia came to resemble Brandenburg-Prussia as a society composed of serfs and lords and governed by a military bureaucracy. Since English and Dutch traders had made contact with Russia in the sixteenth century, Russian rulers had borrowed technology from the West to undergird their military power. Peter the Great (1682–1725) accelerated this Westernization and by territorial expansion brought Russian power to bear upon Western and Central Europe. Absolutism in Russia, however, rested upon political, social, religious, and intellectual traditions quite different from those of any Western or Central European state.

The Muscovite Tradition

Forged by the grand dukes of Moscow, the Russian state never experienced that feudal decentralization which vested nobles, churchmen, and town councils in the West with legal and political autonomy. No diets defended the vested interests of privileged Russians. Still, the nobles represented a potential threat to the grand dukes and the tsars.

Ruling an agrarian state and short of money, they were obliged to reward their servants with land and privileges that became hereditary. To undermine the growing influence of the hereditary nobles (the *boyars*), Ivan IV (the first tsar) called a representative advisory assembly, the *zemski sobor,* but this body never achieved the status of a Western diet.

The Russian Orthodox Church was another potential rival to the tsar. Russian Christianity stemmed from Constantinople (Byzantium) where caesaropapism—the subordination of the Church to secular rulers or caesars (hence czars or tsars)— was well established. During Moscow's wars of expansion, Russian churchmen nationalized Orthodoxy into the doctrine that the tsar was the only Christian king and Moscow, the "Third Rome," the only capital of pure Christianity on the face of the earth. This messianic doctrine made holy crusades of Moscow's wars. And the hold that religious leaders assumed over the Russian masses threatened the secular ruler who aimed to concentrate all power in himself.

The Early Romanovs

From 1605 to 1613 Russia was beset by a "Time of Troubles"—bitter faction, fighting, foreign invasion, internal brigandage, and famine. Swedish and Polish troops entered Moscow and vied to make their candidates tsar. Finally in 1613 the *zemski sobor* selected Michael Romanov, who secured order and drove out the Poles and Swedes. His dynasty lasted until another time of troubles and social disintegration in 1917.

Michael's son Alexis waged wars of expansion and followed policies that foreshadowed the social regimentation completed by his son, Peter the Great. Popular resistance failed to check Alexis' progressive oppression of the peasantry and the Church.

Peter the Great (1682–1725)

Peter transformed Russia from an isolated, landlocked state into a major European power. Petrine Russia adopted Western technology, built a navy, and entered into diplomatic relations with Western chanceries. At Peter's death it extended from the Baltic Sea to the Kurile Islands north of Japan. These rapid changes were mainly the work of the eccentric giant who became tsar in 1682. A drunken tutor from the bureaucracy gave him a meager formal education, but he learned mainly from experiences that left him disrespectful of the conventions of Russian society and gave him the tastes of an artisan proud of his calluses. At the outset of his reign his elder half-sister and half-brother intrigued with the palace guard, the *streltsy,* to purge his relatives and many old *boyars.* His half-sister, Sophia, became regent over both boys as co-tsars, but when she made a second bid for power in 1689, Sophia was confined to a convent. Little impressed with the *streltsys'* contribution to order, Peter set out to consolidate all power in his own hands.

Peter soon recognized the vital role that technical knowledge plays in gaining and holding political power. In order to acquire that knowledge, he went incognito on a "Grand Embassy" to the West (1697–1698), where he amassed an astonishing amount of knowledge and spoke with learned men. In the Netherlands he discussed the Quaker religion with William Penn. But his mission was to acquire technical knowledge, to sate his catholic curiosity. In England he visited factories, arsenals, and shipyards, taking copious notes; in the Netherlands he even served as a shipwright carpenter. In Vienna, where he stopped to negotiate an alliance against the Turks, news reached him that the *streltsy* had revolted again. Stopping only to negotiate with Augustus, Elector of Saxony and King of Poland, Peter hastened home.

Peter's ferocity in putting down the *streltsy* and the radicalness of his new reform edicts expressed his determination to imitate Western European absolutism. In quelling the revolt, he punished the innocent with the guilty in order to break the

Peter the Great.

guards' power permanently. The Tsar then ordered courtiers to shave their beards and adopt Western dress; peasants and priests could escape the order only by paying a special tax.

Peter's Foreign Policy

Constant warfare filled the rest of Peter's reign, and military demands became the primary motive for the subsequent reforms that are so closely linked to his name. He fought on all frontiers, making Russia an empire. But his overriding goal was to gain unimpeded access to the Baltic and Black seas. In order to gain these objectives, Peter had to learn how to be successful in war. His first encounter with Charles XII of Sweden in 1700 at Narva was a disaster for his large but untrained army.

The Tsar spent the years between 1700 and 1709 feverishly training a new peasant army with which he conquered Ingria and Livonia, the two Swedish possessions nearest Russia. These territories gave him access to the Baltic and provided the site for the city of St. Petersburg, the Tsar's window on the West, founded on a barren moor in 1703. Built by forced labor at a tremendous sacrifice of life, St. Petersburg

EXPANSION OF PETRINE RUSSIA

Acquisition of Alexis, 1667
Acquisition of Peter the Great
Invasion route of Charles XII
Shipyard
Iron & armaments — Under Peter the Great
Textiles

SWEDEN

White Sea

FINLAND

KARELIA

Viborg

ESTHONIA

Narva
1700

INGRIA

St. Petersburg

Dvina R.

Ural Mts.

R U S S I A

Ekaterinburg

Riga

LIVONIA

Novgorod

Pskov

Volga R.

Smolensk

Moscow

Volga R.

Ural R.

POLAND

Caspian Sea

Kiev

Dnieper R.

Poltava
1709

OTTOMAN

Bender

Ochakov

EMPIRE

Don R.

Azov
1696-1711

Sea of Azov

Crimea

Caucasus Mts.

Black Sea

0   100   200   300 mi.

Map by J. Donovan

became the capital of Russia, a monument to Peter's Western orientation.

By 1708 Charles XII moved into the Ukraine on an ill-fated expedition. In vain he sought alliances with dissident Cossacks and Turks. At Poltava in 1709 the Tsar's larger army decisively defeated the Swedes. While Peter was unsuccessful in holding his Black Sea gains, he was highly successful in the Baltic. After the death of Charles

XII in 1718, England prevented Russia from overrunning Sweden. But the Treaty of Nystad in 1721 forced the Swedes to cede most of their Baltic empire to Russia. Although this treaty restored Finland to Sweden, it recognized Russian possession of the Baltic coast from Riga to Viborg. Peter had acquired not one but nine ports and bases on the Baltic. Russia seemed about to become a major naval and maritime power, but after Peter's death the fleets deteriorated rapidly.

Russian Administrative Absolutism

Keeping the war machine going on all frontiers took immense manpower and money and necessitated administrative reorganization. In order to maintain his huge standing army the Tsar conscripted the enserfed subjects of his nobles. (His recruiting system, with its twenty-five-year term of enlistment, lasted until 1874.) His campaigns also required conscript labor, whose losses often equaled those of the army. Peter relied upon nobles and foreign adventurers to lead the army and bureaucracy, forcing the nobility to share preferment with newcomers.

In a country lacking commercial capital and banking institutions the raising of money to finance administration and wars was a major undertaking. Because the treasury had no credit, all expenses had to be met currently. Tax revenues trebled during Peter's reign. His government established monopolies to raise revenue on such items as salt, tobacco, cod liver oil, potash, and coffins. It also commandeered monastic revenues and debased the coinage again. The levy on households, which had been the principal source of revenue, began to dry up as householders evaded it, fled, or were conscripted. The government replaced it with a head or "soul" tax, applicable to all male peasants. The backbone of the revenue structure until 1886, this tax was collected by the lords of the village communes. Since

Satirical cartoon of Peter's order to clip beards.

anyone enrolled on their tax registers was automatically a serf, this tax system helped spread serfdom.

Peter's effort to introduce Western mercantilist policies fared no better than his tax reforms. In order to encourage industry, mining, and commerce under paternal direction of the state, he enacted high protective tariffs and leased state-built factories to private individuals on favorable terms. Entrepreneurs who copied Western technology were given tax exemptions, interest-free loans, and the coveted privilege of owning serfs. Peter also sent technicians abroad for training and wooed skilled immigrants. Overall, Peter's program of economic development failed, even though the country became self-sufficient in some industrial lines and exported iron and sailcloth. Capitalists, distrustful of officials and regulations, failed to meet his expectations. Rather than increasing revenues, his mercantilism added to state expenditures.

Repeated attempts to reorganize the central administration also failed. In prac-

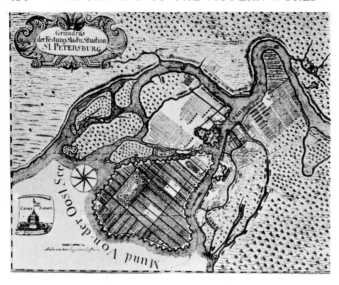

Layout of St. Petersburg in 1738. Peter chose this swampy site at the mouth of the Neva River because it provided access to the Baltic and Europe. Capital of Russia, 1713–1918, this city was built at great cost and symbolized Peter's westernizing effort.

tice the central government was more often represented by military commanders than by civil authorities. In most of Russia the local nobles constituted the only government. Neither military rule, savage punishments, decentralization, nor secret informers eliminated the bribery and corruption that riddled the bureaucracy from top to bottom.

However, Peter did succeed in bringing the Orthodox Church, the largest organization in Russia, under secular control. When the current patriarch died in 1700 he named no successor. Several years later the Holy Synod, a collegiate board headed by a lay procurator, assumed control of the Church. The state thus silenced, to some extent, clerics who opposed such reforms as secular education, limited toleration, and the Julian calendar. The subordination of the Church to the state served Russian autocracy until 1917.

By dynastic marriage and intrigue, the Romanov dynasty became basically German. The petrine state assumed a lasting place in the European state system. Nevertheless Peter's Westernization was selective. Mainly it modified and strengthened existing institutions that resisted deep penetration by Western culture. The army was modernized, but it remained the basic tool for administration. Serfdom was extended and riveted into law and practice by the state. Some of the higher nobles eventually accepted Westernization, but over the larger society of enserfed peasants and boorish lords it lay as a shallow veneer. A question remains whether Peter really wanted to Westernize or whether he borrowed European technology to defend Russia against Western encroachment. In either case his experience indicated the limitations of absolutism even in a state where organized opposition was not possible.

Peter's impact upon Russian society and government was decisive and long-lived. Despite its failings, in practice the structure he built held firm until the nineteenth century, much of it until 1917.

ARISTOCRATIC MONARCHIES

Alongside the divine-right kingdoms that we have discussed stood other monarchies whose rulers laid equal claim to unlimited authority but whose effective power was too weak to be considered absolute at all. Some of them had been Europe's leading states but were now in decline. None of them had the strength to hold its own in the dynastic power struggles of the second half of the seventeenth century. In all of them the trend of political development was toward decentralization, away from absolutism.

Spain, Italy, and Poland

There was a close relationship between the rising star of France in Western Europe and the falling star of the Spanish Habsburg empire. Spain emerged from the Thirty Years' War and the Bourbon-Habsburg conflict with an immense empire, still Europe's largest, and great imperial pride. But her men and materials had been overcommitted and overexpended during a previous century of warfare. The efforts of Philip IV's war minister, de Olivares, to revitalize Spain and shunt some of the burdens of empire onto kingdoms other than Castile had come to naught. To put down revolts against de Olivares' "Castilianization" the King was forced to confirm the territorial privileges of the Catalans. The Portuguese, whose revolt in 1640 opened a second front in the Iberian Peninsula until peace was signed with France in 1659, slipped away completely. Thereafter Louis XIV denied the exhausted Habsburgs any respite from his encroachment upon the Spanish Netherlands and along France's eastern frontier.

The postwar government of Philip V momentarily arrested Spain's decline. To some degree he imitated Louis XIV in subordinating the Church and the nobility to central control. He restored authority and commerce in the empire. Yet he could not fundamentally cure the hardening of Spain's social and political arteries. Schemes of reform failed without exception. By and large the empire remained impervious to contemporary commercial change, rationalized government, secular science, and speculative thought. And failure to cope with these developments hastened its relative decline.

Like Spain, whose decaying and corrupt authority still dominated the peninsula, Italy was caught in a midcentury depression. Her cities, population, and trade continued to decline, until, by 1700, most Italian principalities were completely agrarian. Venice, still a maritime state independent of Spain, was beset by a long series of wars with the Turks, and her capital resources flowed steadily from commerce to land. Commercial life still flickered in Lombardy, Tuscany, and Piedmont, but their societies were dominated by the routine of petty courts. Intellectual life and even the arts, save for music and baroque architecture, were in a state of decay. Italy was a major stopping point on the "grand tour" of every young European aristocrat, but it had become a museum for the greatness of the past rather than a showplace of vitality for the present.

Poland furnished the classic case of aristocratic decentralization. Extending from the Baltic almost to the Black Sea in the fifteenth and sixteenth centuries, she was now surrounded by aggressive neighbors who took advantage of her internal weakness to invade her repeatedly. An exceedingly numerous nobility, the only class represented in the local and central diets, crushed town interests, the peasantry, and the authority of the elective monarchy. Political life centered around the conflicts of a few great noble families, behind which the lesser nobles arrayed themselves in factions. By the middle of the seventeenth century decisive action by the central government was hardly possible. The diet kept the army ridiculously small. Foreign-sponsored candidates (Augustus the Strong of Saxony was one "successful" example) contested for the empty honor. By the infamous *liberum veto* any delegate to the central diet could, and on critical occasions did, rise to end further deliberations. Only the inability of her foes to cooperate preserved Poland from dismemberment until the late eighteenth century.

THE MARITIME STATES: ENGLAND AND THE DUTCH REPUBLIC

In both England and the Dutch Republic, authoritarian Roman law yielded to the political demands of aristocratic and commercial groups whose strength lay in trade, finance, industry, and rationalized agriculture. By their wealth and credit they created more military resources than any impoverished absolutism ever enjoyed. Significantly geography partially guaranteed both countries against foreign invasion. England was protected by the sea, the Dutch Republic by its system of rivers, canals, and floodable fields. Thus they could escape from the two primary instruments of absolutism: a permanent standing army and extraparliamentary taxation to finance it. England and the Dutch Republic, along with the English colonies of North America, became the seedbeds of those liberal and humanitarian heresies that flowered during the eighteenth-century Enlightenment.

The Dutch Republic

Constitutionally the Dutch Republic was a confederation of disparate provinces whose diets sent instructed delegates to the common States General. In Guelderland feudal nobles ruled over subsistent tenant farmers. In Utrecht authority was vested in Protestant canons who had replaced electors of the former Roman Catholic bishop. The richest and most powerful provinces were the commercial states of Zeeland and Holland, ruled by tight republican oligarchies of regents. Led by the Grand Pensionary of Holland, Jan De Witt, the regents coordinated the Republic's affairs from 1650 to 1672, defending its aristocratic, decentralized constitution. Humanistic Calvinists or Arminians, the regents had the tacit support of both Roman Catholics and the sectarians whom they protected from Calvinist persecution.

Jan De Witt was locked in a political tug of war with the House of Orange, which traditionally had filled the chief executive, judicial, and military office of stadtholder in each province. Behind the Orange faction stood the orthodox Calvinist clergy, the discontented urban poor, and most of the local authorities in the rural provinces. To check Orangist monarchical ambitions, De Witt in 1670 secured acceptance in all seven provinces of an eternal edict barring the young William of Orange from the stadtholderates. But failures in foreign policy brought down De Witt and the regents' government. When the French invaded in 1672 he was murdered during an Orangist revolution. Though he did not become a monarch and establish a court, William of Orange, dealing through favorites, directed Dutch affairs as King of England until his death in 1702.

Experimenting with a compromise between liberty and order, the Dutch Republic of the seventeenth century became a haven of personal freedom in absolutist Europe, a laboratory of liberalism. But as its commerce declined, its political evolution followed the earlier course of Venice. Dutch greatness had filled the interim between Spanish and French hegemony on the Continent. After 1650 its economy ceased to expand.

The Triumph of the English Parliament

Fed up with the rule of Puritan saints, the people of England restored the Stuart court in 1660. An able monarch coming to the throne on a wave of religious and political reaction against the Puritan revolution, Charles II posed a serious challenge to parliamentary authority. But the Restoration proved to be only an interlude before Parliament took control of the royal succession and ultimately of most of the powers of the crown itself.

The Stuart Restoration

Charles II had great political abilities; had he lived longer, he might have been able to put Stuart concepts of government into effect. The Restoration Settlement was moderate enough not to create large numbers of foes for him. Crown and church lands were restored, but confiscated Cavalier estates that had been resold often remained in Cromwellian hands. Only about twenty persons, who had not been quick enough to declare for the Stuarts, were executed for their part in the civil wars. The least moderate part of the Settlement was a series of laws designed to break Puritan power forever, the Clarendon Code. These laws removed Puritan clergymen from their benefices, barred Puritans from political activity, and prohibited nonconformist teaching and worship assemblies. But the Clarendon Code was the work of the "Cavalier Parliament," not the King.

The most irreconcilable issue between

Jan De Witt and the mob that lynched him.

King and Parliament was religion. Charles had pro-Catholic proclivities and a French Catholic queen. His brother and heir apparent, James, Duke of York, was an open Catholic. Suspicion that the King had bound himself to Louis XIV in order to restore Catholicism in England was founded in fact; the secret Treaty of Dover (1670) had just such stipulations. By exempting Catholics and Protestant dissenters from the penalties of law, Charles aroused religious ire and the constitutional objection that he was setting himself above the law. Parliament rebuffed him with the Test Act of 1673. It required officeholders to denounce the Roman Catholic form of communion and to take the Anglican sacrament annually. Anglicanism became the necessary badge for political privilege and advancement.

Bills to exclude the Duke of York from succeeding to the throne failed in Parliament, but they became the issue around which political factions formed. The Whig party — composed of progressive landlords, merchants, and Protestant dissenters — originated these bills. The Whigs' opponents were the Tories, a court party whose religious views were High Anglican and whose viewpoints represented the more conserva-

James II, an unwelcome king.

tive landed gentlemen. Committed as a matter of religious conscience to the passive obedience of subjects to legitimate kings, the Tories supported Charles II and received offices and favors from him. Radical republican and Whig plotters pushed conservative Whigs into the King's camp also.

James II and the "Glorious Revolution"

James II inherited the throne, Charles' revenues, and his brother's conflicts. His accession was contested by the Duke of Monmouth, Charles II's illegitimate son. Counting upon Whig support, Monmouth led an insurrection against James. Bloodily suppressed by James, the revolt put a standing army at his disposal. In violation of the Test Act he appointed Roman Catholic officials and revived the Court of High Commission to deal with religious offenders. He acted rapidly to remove recalcitrant judges, maintain his standing army, and force suspension of legal penalties against Catholics and Protestant dissenters. These actions opened old and tender sores, but Englishmen would probably have put up with him

if he had had no male heir. In 1688, however, the queen bore a son.

Threatened with an eventual Roman Catholic succession, prominent Whigs and Tories cooperated in inviting William of Orange and his wife, Mary, James' Protestant daughter by an earlier marriage, to the throne.

The Revolutionary Settlement and After

The "Glorious Revolution" of 1688 established the constitutional supremacy of Parliament. The Bill of Rights in 1689 confirmed Parliament's past demands against Stuart kings. It limited royal authority over a peacetime standing army to a specific number of years. It defined treason more narrowly, thus making this crime more difficult to prove in court. James II's bid for support from religious dissenters had forced Anglicans to promise them toleration, though not political and civic rights. An act of 1689 exempted all except Roman Catholics and Unitarians from punitive penalties. Formal censorship, but not stringent libel laws, lapsed in 1695.* The crown, whose succession Parliament now determined, retained considerable powers. After the judiciary's independence was confirmed by an act of 1701, the English constitution had a balance and division of executive, legislative, and judicial powers. But royal prerogatives gradually dwindled. Queen Anne (1702–1714) was the last English monarch to wield a royal veto. During the eighteenth century executive and legislative functions began to merge in the cabinet, a committee standing between king and Parliament.

Clearly Parliament was replacing the court as the source of both favor and corruption, an unmistakable indication that power had shifted. But Parliament was an oligarchy, part of the same oligarchy from which local justices and jurists were drawn.

---

* The press became freer in England's American colonies because libel was much more narrowly construed.

To a degree, individual rights were protected by the division of the oligarchy into factions of Whig and Tory. But when they were in solid agreement, as upon economic and social policy, their sympathies were distinctly aristocratic. Parliament, not the people, was sovereign, and its two houses were substantially under the control of the same coterie of agrarian and commercial interests.

Having men of means involved in politics marshaled unexpected power behind the English government. As distrust dissolved between king and Parliament, the latter's purse strings loosened. Royal debts became state debts and after 1694 were handled by the Bank of England.

Thus in cooperation with the central government, men experienced in trade, finance, and administration were laying the basis for England's colonial and commercial supremacy during the eighteenth century. Unlike trade and production in the Dutch Republic, British commerce continued to expand until the end of the eighteenth century, when it became the basis for urban industrialization.

SELECTED READINGS

Ashley, Maurice, *Louis XIV and the Greatness of France,* English Universities Press, London, 1957.
> A very readable, short account of the "Sun King's" reign in the Teach Yourself History series.

*Beloff, Max, *The Age of Absolutism 1660– 1815,* Hutchinson University Library, London, 1954, and Harper Torchbook.
> Interpretation that considers societies rather than governments decisive in the age of absolutism.

Boxer, Charles R., *The Dutch Seaborne Empire 1600–1800,* Alfred A. Knopf, New York, 1965.
> A social history of both the Dutch Republic and the Dutch Empire in the series, The

Asterisk (*) denotes paperback.

History of Human Society, edited by J. H. Plumb.

Carsten, Francis L., ed., *The Ascendancy of France 1648–88,* Volume V, *The New Cambridge Modern History,* University Press, Cambridge, 1961.
> Exhaustively thorough for Europe in the age of Louis XIV, useful for reference.

Clark, G. N., *The Later Stuarts, 1660–1714,* Clarendon Press, Oxford, 1949.
> A dispassionate scholarly account in the Oxford History of England.

Cole, Charles W., *French Mercantilism 1683– 1700,* Columbia University Press, New York, 1943.
> One of the author's several detailed works on French mercantilism, especially informative on the industrial production codes after Colbert.

Davies, R. Trevor, *Spain in Decline, 1621– 1700,* Macmillan, London; St. Martin's Press, New York, 1957.
> A rambling posthumous work useful in assessing the causes of decay in the aristocratic monarchy of Spain.

Fay, Sidney B., *The Rise of Brandenburg— Prussia to 1786,* H. Holt, New York, 1937.
> A short, classic description of the consolidation of Prussian military absolutism which needs to be supplemented by the works of Francis L. Carsten (see Selected Readings, Chapter 8).

Figgis, John N., *The Divine Right of Kings,* University Press, Cambridge, 1922 (2nd ed.).
> An analysis of the major ideology of royal absolutism.

Holborn, Hajo, *A History of Modern Germany 1648–1840,* Alfred A. Knopf, New York, 1966.
> A lucid treatment based on recent scholarship which is part of the author's projected three-volume History of Modern Germany.

King, James E., *Science and Rationalism in the Government of Louis XIV, 1661–1683,* Johns Hopkins Press, Baltimore, 1949.
> A detailed interpretation of the reign of Louis XIV which links efficient government with the rational viewpoint of contemporary science.

*Lewis, W. H., *The Splendid Century, Life in the France of Louis XIV,* Doubleday Anchor Books, Garden City, N.Y., 1957.

Aspects of French society, omitting institutions that the author considers tedious to write about.

Lough, John, *Introduction to Seventeenth Century France,* Longmans, Green & Co., London, 1960.

A literary approach to the period that is well illustrated but carries key points, unfortunately, in French.

Maland, David, *Europe in the Seventeenth Century,* St. Martin's Press, New York, 1966.

New, exceptionally well-balanced textbook of the period by a British scholar.

*Nussbaum, Frederick L., *The Triumph of Science and Reason 1660–1685,* Harper & Brothers, New York, 1953, and Harper Torchbook.

A general account emphasizing intellectual developments and recognizing absolutism as a façade of aristocratic society.

Petrie, Charles, *Earlier Diplomatic History 1492–1713,* Hollis & Carter, London, 1949.

Short manual of exceedingly complex diplomatic relationships; the second half is applicable to this chapter.

Rosenberg, Hans, *Bureaucracy, Aristocracy and Autocracy, The Prussian Experience 1660–1815,* Harvard University Press, Cambridge, 1958.

A sociological investigation of the Prussian bureaucracy and its rivalry with the monarchy and the aristocracy.

Schevill, Ferdinand, *The Great Elector,* Chicago University Press, Chicago, 1947.

A political and institutional biography of Frederick William, the founder of Prussian absolutism.

Sumner, B. H., *Peter the Great and the Emergence of Russia,* English Universities Press, London, 1956.

Another short, moving account in the Teach Yourself History Series; it emphasizes the military basis of Peter's administration.

Trevelyan, G. M., *The English Revolution, 1688–1689,* Butterworth, London, 1938.

A well-written study in the Home University Library by the author of several well-known works on the Stuarts.

*Wolf, John B., *The Emergence of the Great Powers 1685–1715,* Harper and Brothers, New York, 1951, and Harper Torchbook.

An account of the power struggles in which seventeenth-century absolutism culminated; a volume in the Rise of Modern Europe series.

See also the works by J. H. Elliott, Eli Heckscher, David Ogg, and George N. Clark in Selected Readings, Chapter 15.

17

The Secularization of Thought—the Seventeenth and Eighteenth Centuries

Secularization first penetrated deeply those areas of northwestern Europe where the pursuit of wealth and comfort were primary social goals. Although England and the Dutch Republic retained established churches, they did not forcibly impose religious uniformity the way most absolutist states did. The fact that different religious groups could live together peacefully bred tolerance.

The seventeenth century produced a more secular humanism than that of the Renaissance. The "new" humanism was more involved in the problems raised by scientific developments than in the ideas of classical literature. Hence it, too, contributed to the secularization of thought.

More than any other single factor, the demonstrable success of seventeenth-century science brought past authority into doubt and provided the intellectual foundation for new world views. Science did not openly undermine tradition until philosophical conclusions were drawn from its discoveries and methodology. When this happened, however, by the second half of the eighteenth century, popularized science and secular humanism merged into the qualified optimism of the Enlightenment. Popular writers of the Enlightenment competed with the clergy in defining morality, religious doctrine, and the goals of society. Theirs was a new secular gospel, which they hoped to spread through national systems of education oriented toward natural sciences, modern languages, economics, and modern history. This goal was not to be realized for over a century, and then only where industrialization and urbanization were firmly rooted.

The "Scientific Revolution"

By breaking with the prevalent Western intellectual tradition, science became a revolutionary force. But this break did not come about suddenly, nor was it always

The Ptolemaic system. In 1660, when Newton was 18, Andreas Cellarius engraved this traditional Ptolemaic-Aristotelian view of the universe. Note the four elements in the sub-lunar world—fire, air, water, earth. The planets, sun, and moon were believed to be composed of a fifth element, the quintessence.

overt. Indeed no clear distinction existed between natural science and natural philosophy before the end of the seventeenth century. The study of nature had been cultivated for centuries by isolated scholars. Fourteenth-century schoolmen in England and France had already questioned Aristotle's explanation of motion. During the Italian Renaissance the University of Padua had become a center for Aristotelian scientists seeking natural causes for natural phenomena. Meanwhile literary humanists were rediscovering Greek and Hellenistic scientific works, including parts of the writings of Euclid and Archimedes; in 1543 the publication of Archimedes' theories contributed significantly to the revival of science.

Copernicus' Challenge to Ptolemaic Astronomy

The discoveries in astronomy illustrate how slowly early modern science progressed. Prevailing traditions in 1500 stemmed from Aristotle and Ptolemy, who asserted that a stationary earth occupied the center of the universe. According to them, stars, sun, planets, and the moon

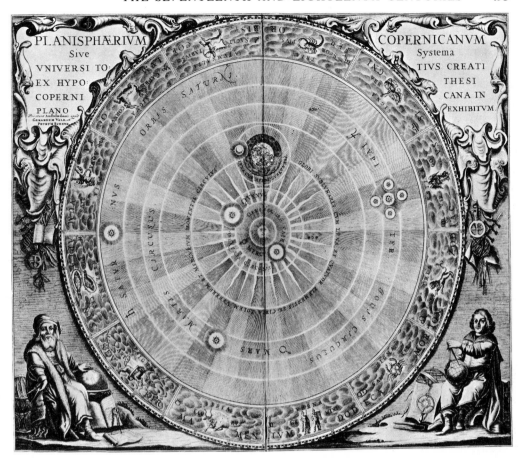

The Copernican system. Cellarius made this engraving of the new conception of the universe in 1660. Rays from the sun spread out to sweep the planets and moon around in orbits. Now only air surrounds the earth. Note the term "hypothesi"; it is applied to both world pictures. Men could take their choice of these two hypotheses and several others as well. In 1687 Newton transformed this Copernican hypothesis into what men accepted as the true picture of the universe.

were held in circular orbits around the earth by crystalline spheres. The source of motion was an alleged "prime mover" identified with the Christian God. In the heavens, where Dante and lesser men had located Paradise, perfection was expressed in circular motion and immutability, and it reigned as the supreme law. On earth, at whose center Hell was popularly pictured, imperfection was expressed in irregular vertical and horizontal motion and degeneration. But the low prestige of earth was redeemed by theology. According to the Christian epic, earth was the stage for the unique drama of Creation, Incarnation, and Redemption, which gave cosmic significance to human life. Thus physics, astronomy, and theology were integrated into a consistent cosmology or description of the universe. As Copernicus and other early astronomers learned, any effort to reformulate this cosmology was not only difficult but also dangerous.

Nicholas Copernicus (1473–1543), a Polish-German churchman, had probably come to doubt Ptolemaic astronomy as a student in Italy. He made few observations, and these were without the aid of a telescope. Instead he assembled older observations and arguments in favor of a simplified and more symmetrical scheme in which the planets, including the earth, revolved around the sun. To explain the observed retrograde motion of the planets, Copernicus regarded the fixed stars as stationary and enormously distant. He published his description of the universe, *On the Revolutions of the Heavenly Orbs,* in 1543, the year of his death. The preface, written anonymously by a Lutheran clergyman, described Copernicus' conclusions as merely mathematical hypotheses, which they were.

Astronomers could not long avoid the issues that Copernicus had raised. The heavens themselves enlivened the cosmological debate in 1572 when a new star appeared and again in 1618 when a new comet came into view. In the past, comets had been interpreted as divine signs of impending doom. So was this one. But it also caused astronomers to question the existence of crystalline spheres supporting the planets and to doubt the sharp distinction held to exist between the immutable heavens and the mutable earth.

Vindication for Copernicus' sun-centered hypothesis awaited the accumulation of observations by Tycho Brahe (1546–1601), the improvement of his theory by Johannes Kepler (1571–1630), the invention of the telescope, and the later achievements of Isaac Newton (1642–1727) and his generation.

In the thirty-year course of accumulating a mass of exceedingly accurate observations with the naked eye, the Danish astronomer Tycho Brahe proposed a mathematical theory of the solar system that still put the earth at its center. Kepler obtained Brahe's great store of recorded observations.

Inspired by scientific zeal, astrology, and fantasies of the aesthetic orderliness of the universe (which he related to the harmonies of the musical scale), Kepler energetically worked out a series of laws describing planetary motion. Kepler discovered that

the planets' paths are elliptical. That discovery is his first law of planetary motion. This may seem an uninspired law, but we must keep in mind the unwillingness of all astronomers, even Kepler, to abandon the idea of circular motion. The data of Mars' orbit, observed night after night, forced Kepler to admit that its path traced out an ellipse with the sun at one focus. Because planets speed up as they approach the sun and slow down as they move farther away in their elliptical orbits, a mathematical relationship to describe that fact had to be discovered. That discovery was Kepler's second law—that a line from the sun to the planet sweeps out equal areas of the ellipse in equal times. Finally, he showed in his third law that the distances of the planets from the sun and their orbital speed are mathematically related, distance cubed being proportional to the square of the time of making a complete revolution. We can check the truth of these laws from present-day figures. While these laws laid the foundations for Newton's astronomy, their importance to Kepler was that they proved the underlying mathematical harmony of the universe, and delighted his fine mystical soul.

Galileo's Contributions to Modern Science

While Kepler worked in Prague, Galileo Galilei (1546–1642) and his successors pursued another line of scientific development in Italy. Here knowledge of Hellenistic scientists, notably Archimedes, had been revived, and Italian science seemed destined to succeed to the glory of Italian art. An industrious student and mathematical genius, Galileo started his career in physics and mechanics in opposition to Aristotelian teachings. By mathematical description and analysis he worked out laws of ballistic trajectories, pendulum movements, and uniform acceleration. He worked at a highly abstract level, considering neither causal theories nor observable effects of resistance. His conclusion that the velocity of a body falling freely in a vacuum was proportional to the square of the elapsed time of fall laid the foundations for mechanics, the field of natural phenomena that was most productive of seventeenth-century scientific methodology. His studies of motion and falling bodies were directly related to controversies over Copernican astronomy. Anti-Copernicans argued that if the earth were in motion and turning on its axis, terrestrial motion would be distorted. In meeting their objections, Galileo partially formulated the concept of inertia. He carried his astronomy much further, however, with a new instrument, the telescope. Learning of its invention in the Netherlands, he built such an instrument for his own use. With it he detected sunspots, saw the four satellites of Jupiter, followed the phases of Venus, studied the mountains and valleys on the surface of the moon, and noted that the Milky Way was a dense cluster of stars. All these observations were new. In 1610 he published the *Message of the Stars*. This work demonstrated that the same laws applied both to the earth and the heavens and that Aristotelian natural philosophy was as unreliable in astronomy as in mechanics.

Galileo's fame spread, but he aroused intense opposition in the universities and churches. Scholars who had devoted their lives to examining nature within an Aristotelian framework rejected his conclusions and even refused to look through his telescope. By 1616 a board of inquiry appointed by the Roman Inquisition had enjoined him to make only hypothetical statements concerning cosmology. Even so, in 1632 he published in Italian for a lay audience the *Dialogue on the Two Principal Systems of the Universe, the Ptolemaic and the Copernican.* Technically the Aristotelian, Simplicio, won the debate with the Copernican, but his victory was undeserved from the evidence used by his opponent. The *Dialogue* revealed that Galileo possessed remarkable literary talents as a propagandist for the new science. While he had support

within the Church, clearly Galileo's criterion for scientific truth was not the authority of the Church. For defying its authority he was summoned before the Inquisition in 1632, forced to retract his conclusions, and put under house arrest for the remainder of his life. Spectacular as Galileo's accomplishments were, he merely initiated the broad lines of inquiry that were left to a new generation to follow up.

The Organization of Science: Scientific Societies

Men of disparate interests who shared a common enthusiasm for the "new philosophy" banded together in informal groups that evolved into formal scientific societies. Galileo himself belonged to the new Roman *Accademia dei Lincei*, which sponsored his reports on sunspots in 1613. When that society disappeared, it was temporarily replaced by the *Accademia del Cimento* (Academy of Experiments), which flourished in Florence under Medici patronage only from 1657 to 1667.

More permanent and important were the societies given official sponsorship in France and England. The French *Académie des Sciences* founded in 1666 received financial support from the French crown. And in 1662 Charles II of England chartered, but did not subsidize, the Royal Society of London for the Promotion of Natural Knowledge. Other scientific societies were founded later in Russia and in a few German states.

These societies varied somewhat in their organization, but they performed similar functions. Their members experimented individually and in groups with new instruments. Duplicating experiments of others, they verified or corrected previous findings. Through corresponding secretaries and by publishing monographs and journals they disseminated detailed reports of their work to foreign scholars, irrespective of political or sectarian boundaries. The *Accademia del Cimento,* for example, working with the first physical

Louis XIV at the Paris Observatory, 1662, a scientific establishment that the great monarch subsidized.

was open to men of accomplishment without regard to birth. They encouraged clarity and precise objective description, choosing to avoid philosophical speculation beyond what was observable and definable in the world of nature.

Scientific Instruments

The rapid expansion of scientific knowledge depended in part on the invention and elaboration of instruments that extended the senses. For aid in building such instruments, scientists turned to skilled craftsmen. In the seventeenth century these craftsmen and scientists developed the telescope, the microscope, the thermometer, the barometer, the air pump, and the clock; in the eighteenth century they built electrometers and delicate scales, which helped to open new fields of physical and chemical research.

In many ways the clock became the most expressive symbol of new mechanistic concepts of the universe and society. Popularizers of the new science described the universe as a gigantic clockwork whose operations were regular, repetitive, and predictable. They reduced God to the position of the master clockmaker who had designed and set it in motion. Later the clock would assume a central role in the organization of complex industrial societies.

laboratory in Europe, repeated and extended Galileo's experiments, employed the barometer invented by Torricelli, studied vacuums, computed the velocity of sound, and engaged in unproductive studies of the digestive processes of animals. The French society succeeded in computing the approximate speed of light, measuring the length of a degree of latitude, and applying the telescope to angular measurement in surveying. The Royal Society of London reached a high level of prestige as Isaac Newton and his contemporaries completed the mathematical synthesis of seventeenth-century astronomy and physics. Although the scope of the societies' interests extended to natural history and medicine, their greatest achievements during the early years lay in the field of physics; here their advances eventually carried them beyond the point where amateurs could make contributions.

Seeking to formulate universal natural laws, the scientific societies set secular, often utilitarian goals. Their membership

Mathematics and the Completion of the Copernican Revolution in Astronomy

To solve problems of motion, European mathematicians learned to apply the algebra they had borrowed from the Arabs to geometry; René Descartes * led the way in this field. Equally indispensable for the study of motion, and hence for the Newtonian theories in celestial mechanics, was the invention of the calculus, achieved concurrently by Newton and by Gottfried Wilhelm von Leibniz (1646–1716). Leibniz' system of notation was adapted for general use outside of England.

* See pp. 500–501.

Mathematics and the experimental work of astronomers and physicists after Galileo and Kepler laid the basis for a more systematic explanation of the solar system. Both men had given impetus to the notion of an orderly, mechanistic universe, but neither one had provided answers to fundamental questions. What kept the planets in motion? What held them in their orbits? Or, assuming some gravitational force as Kepler did, what kept them from plummeting to its center? Many men furnished partial answers to these questions. Credit for mathematically demonstrating the operation of gravity in the solar system belonged to Isaac Newton, a genius among the giants of the Royal Society.

Newton was born and trained at the very time when mathematics and physics were ready for a synthesizer of his ability. After graduating from Cambridge, Newton spent a momentous year in the country (1664–1665). During this time he formulated the calculus, discovered the compound nature of white light, and arrived at the essentials of the law of gravitation. In 1687 he finally published his magnum opus, *Philosophiæ Naturalis Principia Mathematica* (*The Mathematical Principles of Natural Philosophy*).

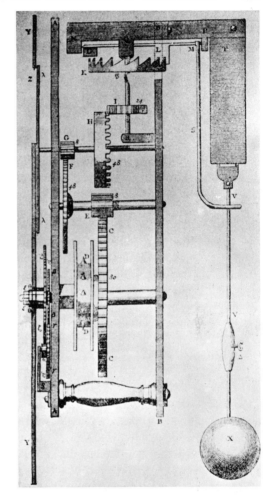

Exact time: Huygens' clock.

This complex treatise explained natural mathematical principles of matter in motion but cautiously refrained from speculation on ultimate causes. The best known part of it described the celestial mechanism in terms of mass, attraction, and the laws of motion. It incorporated Kepler's laws of planetary motion into a general mathematical model. Newton's model for matter in motion was to remain "valid" until challenged in the late nineteenth and early twentieth centuries by the theory of relativity. So sweeping was his concept of the constitution of the "World Machine" that intellectuals soon found themselves in a universe from which animistic spirits seemed to have been banished.

Newton believed that his investigation supported religion. His last scientific pub-

Newton and his classic third edition.

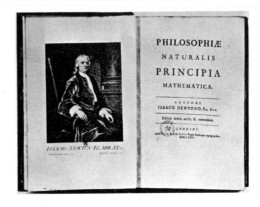

lication suggested hypotheses to explain the phenomena of light, gravitation, and the composition of matter. Upon his death he received honors previously reserved to royalty.

The Birth of Modern Chemistry

Traditional natural philosophy did not recognize physics and chemistry as separate studies. All earthly things were considered imperfect compounds of four elements — earth, air, fire, and water — each of which had inherent propensities for movement. Alchemy, the esoteric art of changing one substance into another, thus seemed a reasonable pursuit to most men of learning. In their trial-and-error pursuit of new remedies, doctors sometimes worked with a different set of assumptions. So did metallurgists. Gradually there developed the basis for a pure science of chemistry.

Robert Boyle (1627–1691), one of the first members of the Royal Society, wrote a book, *The Sceptical Chymist* (1661), which showed the untenable character of previous chemical theories. He worked with the Galilean, Cartesian ideas that phenomena must be explained in terms of two ultimate realities: matter and motion. Matter is composed of ultimate particles (corpuscles), which move into different configurations accounting for chemical properties and changes. He laid the basis for an experimental program, but not for a general scheme of chemistry.

A conception that correlated a number of the phenomena of combustion and behavior of gases was the "Phlogiston theory," developed between 1703 and 1730 by Stahl in Germany. Phlogiston, he believed, is an actual substance, the principle of fire, which is released when something burns. Anything that will burn has phlogiston in it. A candle under a jar goes out when the air becomes so saturated with phlogiston released in combustion that it can absorb no more. This theory reflected the lack of knowledge about the active chemical role of gases. This subject was pursued with success in England and Scotland by Henry Cavendish (1731–1810), Joseph Black (1728–1799), and Joseph Priestley. They succeeded in producing and differentiating gases such as oxygen and hydrogen, and their discoveries concerning the active chemical role of gases seriously undermined the old theory.

The French chemist Antoine Laurent Lavoisier (1743–1794) finally overthrew the phlogiston theory. In contact with Priestley and others, by 1778 Lavoisier developed the new theory of oxidation. He explained that weight gained by the residue of an "oxidized" object was due not to an elusive fluid but to the fixation of oxygen during the process. Meanwhile Cavendish analyzed the ratio of hydrogen and oxygen in water (1782), thus adding to the emphasis placed upon quantitative measurement by Lavoisier. In 1787 Lavoisier gave his theory a new and lasting terminology for the known elements. His work indicated great progress, but in certain aspects of metallurgy and applied technology, procedures that as yet had no scientific explanation were still being used.

Biology

Biology was even slower than chemistry in responding to new scientific concepts. At the beginning of the modern era it too was enmeshed in methods and concepts that explained little and resisted change. Its inheritance included the fixity of species, animistic concepts of the "soul" of plants, and the belief that certain animals represented moral virtues and vices, concepts as firmly rooted as the stability of the earth in the center of the universe. Early modern biologists were primarily catalogers of types of plants and animals, but they lacked an overall system of classification that would give order to their catalogs.

With the microscope, investigators extended their range of knowledge concerning the complexity of living things. Marcello Malpighi, an Italian anatomist, used this new instrument to examine body tissues. Anton van Leeuwenhoek's unexcelled microscopic work revealed the existence of protozoa, bacteria, and red corpuscles of the blood. The Englishman Nehemiah Grew, a contemporary of Malpighi and Leeuwenhoek, observed the sexual reproduction of plants.

Medicine and Public Health

Renaissance artists sometimes practiced dissection illicitly and achieved far greater detail than anatomists. Their realism was reflected in Andreas Vesalius' *On the Fabric of the Human Body,* which was published in 1543, the same year that Copernicus' major work appeared. Vesalius, a Fleming who had worked at Paris, Padua, Bologna, and Pisa threw his work together

Empirical anatomy: Vesalius. This famous frontispiece shows Vesalius demonstrating the structure of the body.

Hooke's compound microscope, 1665. Note the method of focusing light on the specimen.

hastily without any intention of assaulting Galen's authority. But his attempt to describe human anatomy part by part, layer by layer, inadvertently piled up evidence against Galen. Facing a hostile reception, Vesalius suspended his work to become court physician to Charles V. Nevertheless anatomy was the earliest medical science to be emancipated from speculative philosophy and the authority of the ancients.

William Harvey (1578–1657) demonstrated—insofar as he could without a microscope—the circulation of the blood. Inspired by analogies between mechanics and the operation of valves in the veins, he described the heart as a mechanical pump forcing blood through the arteries whence it returned through the veins. Thus he replaced Galen's postulate that the two types of blood—one emanating from the liver, the other from the heart—ebbed and flowed within the veins and arteries. Harvey worked on this hypothesis for ten years prior to publishing his conclusions in 1628. Another generation or two passed before medical scientists accepted it. Not until Malpighi used a microscope to discover capillaries connecting arteries and veins in the tissues of a frog's lungs was Harvey's thesis of circulation empirically confirmed.

Public health remained primarily a local and humanitarian concern. Isolated doctors produced descriptions of epidemics and treatises on occupational diseases. Local governments ordered the cleaning of streets and the provision of water (usually by undersupervised private companies), but in neither case were the standards used nor the level of enforcement sufficient to eliminate the continued threat of epidemics. Control of rats by 1720 brought the end of bubonic plague epidemics except in the jails, but other urban epidemics, including diseases totally new in Western Europe, still took heavy tolls. Humanitarian reformers, especially the Quakers in England, concerned themselves with "jail fever," the treatment of the mentally ill, and high infant mortality; they built hospitals, some of them specialized. With all its shortcomings improved public health probably accounted in part for Europe's rapid increase of population after 1750.

Once bubonic plague was curbed, progress in the control of smallpox began. After 1722 upper-class Englishmen began to use inoculation—a practice of long standing in the Near and Far East—to give the patient a mild case as a means of achieving immunity.

The Methodology of Science

"We are to admit," Newton wrote, "no more causes of natural things than such as are both true and sufficient to explain their appearances." This statement seemed to contain the essence of scientific methodology.

But scientific spokesmen did not speak with one voice in defining scientific methodology. The English philosopher Francis Bacon saw it primarily as empiricism, the use of inductive logic to give meaning to direct observations. But René Descartes, author of a classic essay on method, emphasized the necessity of first having a set of hypotheses, even a completely new metaphysics, before empirical testing could take place.

Between the extremes of Bacon's empiricism and Descartes' rationalism stood experimentalism, an approach that represented scientific methodology at its best. Setting up a hypothesis of how nature might behave and planning an experiment to test it, is a rational process. Performing the experiment and collecting verifiable data from it, is an empirical matter. Galileo, Boyle, and Newton were great exponents of experimentalism. This method yielded so much reliable knowledge about nature that it became a model for scientific inquiry.

Behind the superficial chaos of observable natural phenomena, science presupposed regularity rather than supranatural intervention. Mathematically regular "natural laws" came to be set in opposition to arbitrary miracles. Although scientists like Newton specifically disavowed this conclusion, it was inherent in their mechanistic approach to nature. They justified their probing into this world as the unveiling of a "second scripture" or laying bare the handiwork of God.

Scientific Philosophy and the New Humanism

Scientific philosophers who followed the new models of natural philosophy were unanimous in repudiating, even scoffing at, Aristotelianism. They used concepts, terms, and problems produced by contemporary science. But they failed to agree on conclusions drawn from these common roots.

The Cartesian Revolution

René Descartes (or des Cartes, hence Cartesian) (1596–1650) was the first person since Aristotle to start afresh in building a philosophical system. A budding mathematical genius disgusted with the authorities taught in the universities, Descartes in 1619 developed the notion of applying mathematics to all nature. In the following decade he worked to found a complete metaphysics based on the premise that ultimate reality would have to be explained theoretically before meaningful experimentation could take place. The starting point for his new system was the one reality he could not refute by systematic doubt: "I think, hence I am." Although he advocated experimentation, he preferred the ultimate certainty of such "clear and distinct" ideas arrived at by introspection and deduction to the chaotic complexities of experience. From his central single axiom he proceeded to deduce the existence of God and of a material world in motion. Beside this material world and sharply separated from it was the realm of the mind. The human mind obtained real knowledge of the external world by innate ideas such as the concept of God, the axioms of mathematics, and common notions of space, time, and motion. Mind and matter did not interact in Descartes' universe save in the human brain. Accepting Galen's erroneous statement that only man had a pineal gland, Descartes concluded that it was the cosmic meeting point of mind and matter. The supernatural intervention of God was required to hold this dualistic universe together. Descartes' dogmatic system thus saved the prestige of man and insulated religion, politics, and moral affairs from empirical study.

Empiricists: Bacon and Locke

Along with the rationalists like Descartes, the men we call empiricists also condemned prejudices, passion, and tradition, but they disputed the existence of innate ideas in the mind. For them the mind was not a storehouse of such master ideas but, in John Locke's phrase, it was a *blank tablet* on which experience wrote. The mind was a device that sorted and associated the data of experience derived from the senses. In fact, however, seventeenth-century empiricists did not maintain this view consistently. Instead they started with nonempirical assumptions and made room for the compelling authority of what was "clear and distinct" or "self-evident," even while consciously rejecting innate ideas. Boundaries separating rationalists from empiricists were geographical as well as methodological. On the Continent, Cartesianism swept the field. But an empirical tradition maintained itself in revolutionary seventeenth-century England.

An early spokesman of English empiricism was James I's Lord Chancellor, Francis Bacon (1561–1626). Bacon called for a new science that would establish man's dominion over nature. Isolated writers since the Renaissance had hailed and lauded new inventions, but Bacon optimistically predicted that if the universities were over-

Title page of Bacon's Novum Organum. *Just as the explorer was on the broad sea of discovery after sailing past the Pillars of Hercules, so the scientific investigator would be on his way to new discoveries by using Bacon's new logic.*

hauled and scientific societies for cooperative research were founded, the mysteries of the universe could be unveiled. As a first step he set out to dispel the "idols" or harmful mental habits that had perverted reason and led to the repetition of error in the past. He spoke against the Idol of the Tribe, the desire of men to see only what they wanted to believe. Another snare was the Idol of the Cave, the transformation of personal prejudices and limited personal experience into universal principles. In labeling the Idol of the Market Place, Bacon referred to confusion resulting from different meanings of words. Lastly he denounced the Idol of the Theater, stubborn commitment to particular schools of thought that had become untenable.

In order to become free of these idols Bacon said that men had to disentangle science from theology for the mutual benefit of both. He denied that nature was Satan's bailiwick; the created world was, he affirmed, a second Scripture whose study would reinforce religion. "It is . . . most wise to render unto faith the things that are faith's," he wrote in the *New Logic,* but it was apparent that he left it to the scientist, not the theologian, to define the boundary between science and religion.

John Locke (1632–1704) applied the new empiricist and materialist doctrines to develop a revolutionary and historically significant psychology.

A member of the Royal Society, Locke was a physician and the secretary of the Earl of Shaftesbury, a radical Whig who led the fight against James II's accession. From discussions within these radical intellectual circles, Locke concluded that conflicts over terminology and contradictory assertions arose because men carried their inquiries beyond the mind's possible experience.

After considering the origins and validity of human knowledge for twenty years, Locke published *An Essay Concerning Human Understanding* in 1690. In it he states that the mind derives its ideas from sensory data. They are recorded as on a blank sheet of paper, and their range is limited to areas of human sensation and experience. No room was left for Platonic universal ideas. Moreover, valid sensations were not sensible qualities such as color but the mathematical, physical primary qualities of solidity, extension, form, and motion. Yet Locke did not maintain that the mind was wholly passive. He accorded it the ability to originate ideas through active reflection, repeating, comparing, and uniting sensations in a practically infinite variety of ways. It could not formulate metaphysical realities. Knowledge of these might be obtained from Christian revelation, subject always to the test of reason.

In *An Essay Concerning Human Understanding* Locke accepts the compelling validity of "clear and distinct" or self-evident ideas. Among these were the natural rights that justified revolution in his political philosophy. He also anticipated the development of a system of mathematically demonstrable ethics. In contrast to Hobbes, who wanted the state to enforce uniformity of opinion, Locke wanted an exchange of ideas, which required limited religious toleration.

The Politics of Reason

Political philosophers of the seventeenth century demonstrated that their new premises could be used to support revolution, confederation, or absolute states. But even those who advanced absolutism were at variance with traditional concepts.

To prevent further civil warfare of the kind he had witnessed in England and France, Thomas Hobbes (1588–1679) prescribed a thoroughgoing absolutism. Convinced that men would never cease warring against one another in a state of nature, he proposed in his *Leviathan* of 1651 to make the state a "mortal god" with the unlimited power to set all moral and religious values. It would be contractual, rational, and utilitarian in origin. Once entered into, the contract between state and people was irrevocable. In international relations, however, Hobbes foresaw no contract that might curtail wars. Rather he believed that the nations were trapped in a state of nature and would carry out an insatiable struggle for power that would cease only in death.

A concept of government based on natural law emerged in the Dutch Republic and the Empire. In rebelling against Spain in the sixteenth century, the Dutch had appealed to both natural law and chartered rights. Government in the Dutch Republic became a confederation recognizing individual and corporate rights.

The Dutch humanist Hugo Grotius (1583–1645) asserted that associations might limit central governments. He conceived of the state as an agreement among individual holders of rights, whose autonomous associations could coexist within it. But his concept of revolution did not go beyond the *fait accompli* represented by the Dutch Republic. Grotius' main concern, however, was with international relations, a field in which he exerted considerable influence. Reacting against the religious wars, he tried to detach politics from theology. His major work, *On the Law of War and Peace,* set down the principle that relations between sovereigns should be governed by reason and natural law; their own self-interest and preservation dictated restraint. Grotius considered natural law to be as self-evident and as self-enforcing as the axioms of geometry.

In England John Locke made natural law a revolutionary doctrine. Prior to his writing, English colonists in North America had demonstrated their ability to institute government by voluntary compact, an accomplishment that contradicted the premises of contemporary authoritarianism. In England itself Locke's radical circle worked against the Catholic Stuart absolutism of James II, and Locke wrote a justification for the Revolution of 1688. Like Hobbes, the English philosopher assumes an initial "state of nature." But to him natural man was neither fallen, as theological politics assumed, nor

Title page of Hobbes' Leviathan, *1651. "This is the birth of that great LEVIATHAN, or rather . . . of that mortal God to which, under the Immortal God, we owe our peace and defense."*

brutish, as Hobbes had said. Instead Locke agreed with Harrington that man possessed a certain sociability. To guarantee certain natural rights—life, liberty, and property—men in a state of nature entered a social contract. Locke could not demonstrate empirically either the existence of these rights or the formation of a contract. Nevertheless, they furnished the basis for asserting that natural rights were anterior to government. Government was instituted, Locke argued, by a second contract with a ruler. Should the ruler flagrantly transgress upon individual rights, the ruled might revoke the contract, that is, revolt. In this way Locke provided a justification for overturning James II. In so doing, he shifted the emphasis of political theory from the indefeasible right of rulers to the inalienable rights of subjects.

Locke appropriated from Hobbes the ideas of a state of nature and a contractual government, but he used them to refute Hobbes' absolutism. Rather than a monolithic state, Locke advocated a balance of social and political powers. From the revolutionary thinkers of the Puritan Commonwealth he borrowed the notion of a separation and balance of executive and legislative powers, which was as prominent a part of his political theory as the right of revolution.

This idea of a "balanced government" whose primary function was the protection of property, the only natural right that Locke discussed at length, was far more congenial to the thought of the eighteenth century than his rationale for revolution. It was forgotten that he defined property as life, liberty, and the fruit of labor. His precepts of balanced government were invoked on behalf of the English constitution as a perfect balance of aristocracy, monarchy, and democracy. But his doctrines could also serve the cause of revolution, as American colonists demonstrated in 1776.

Natural law theorists were primarily concerned with domestic rather than international politics. They left foreign affairs in a state of nature regulated only by the doctrine of rational self-interest. Increasingly that doctrine was supplemented by the notion of a balance of power, a phrase borrowed from physics. The Peace of Utrecht (1713) deepened Western Europe's commitment to a balance of power and weakened the tradition of inheritance by divine right. Subsequent to that treaty the Western powers intervened diplomatically in other wars in order to prevent any one state from gaining hegemony.

Rational Religion

Rational religion has many historical roots. The religious wars taught men that internal peace is more important than confessional partisanship. Contacts with more and more of the world's religions broadened points of view, and Christian merchants found trade with heretics to be beneficial.

Humanists discovered general moral precepts behind the variety of religious practices.

Thus in many parts of Europe conditions were ripe for a redefinition of doctrines that would include humanism, a secular ethic, and the new world view of science and scientific philosophy. That redefinition led to religious formulations that gradually transformed faith in revelation into faith in reason or piety. It was the humanists of the seventeenth and eighteenth centuries who led that transformation.

In 1627 Hugo Grotius proposed an Erasmian Christianity based on piety rather than doctrine alone. His *Concerning the Truth of the Christian Religion* adhered to Scripture but interpreted it according to its environment at the time of its composition. An Englishman, Edward Herbert of Cherbury (1583–1648), went further in the direction of universality. Through the study of comparative religion and through introspection he set out to find the universal religious principles on which all rational men could agree. He eliminated the sacraments and the concept of God-chosenness whether of nation or the predestined "elect." His emphasis fell instead upon the worship of a Supreme Being, conscience, and piety. In the Netherlands Spinoza arrived at similar conclusions. Later in the century Pierre Bayle (1647–1706) began publishing from the Netherlands the *Historical and Critical Dictionary* in the same year that Louis XIV revoked the Edict of Nantes (1685). The *Dictionary* lashed out against superstition, intolerance, and dogmatic assertions. It appealed to the primacy of moral conscience over all Scripture that seemed to command violent behavior. At the same time Locke was reconciling faith and reason in his *Reasonableness of Christianity*. Locke defined reason as "natural revelation," which served as a check upon recorded miracles. According to him, those who had not been exposed to Christianity could learn moral law by the light of nature. In Germany Johann Semler (1725–1791) followed a similar course in biblical criticism, treating the Scriptures as historical evidence rather than literal, inspired injunctions.

As the new science and philosophy spread, the premises of religious rationalism became increasingly those of scientific natural law. Locke and others had set the main lines of Deistic thought, but it came more into vogue and became more secular as Newton's concepts of a mechanistic universe were popularized.

Newtonian science provided the two principal Deistic arguments for the existence of a Supreme Being: (1) that He was necessary as the first cause of the universe, and (2) that the flawless order of that universe presupposed an intelligent creator. Since the laws of the universe were uniform and universal, the Deists rejected miracles and relegated prophecy and rites to superstition. They professed a faith in immortality primarily as a sanction for ethics, since the focus of their interest was on this world. They examined traditional Christianity for ethical utility and humanitarianism and found it seriously lacking in both. Their faith was set upon the existence of a Supreme Being who seldom intervened in the affairs of men but also upon man's capacity to reform.

All proponents of rational religion pressed in the direction of universality, minimized dogma, and emphasized morality.

The Enlightenment

In the eighteenth century the effort to popularize science and the new humanism and to use these new outlooks as a basis for improving the political and social order was known as the Enlightenment.

The Prominence of the French Philosophes

Among the publicists of the Enlightenment the most prolific were the *philosophes* of France. Writers elsewhere wrestled with the same problems, often making basic contributions, but it was such men as Montesquieu, Voltaire, Condillac, Diderot, and Condorcet who set the Enlightenment's basic tone. Unlike previous continental intellectuals, they depended for their livelihood not on patronage of church and state but on a reading public of middle classes, clergy, and aristocrats.

Without being consciously revolutionary, the *philosophes* took positions squarely at odds with inherited institutions. According to them, the reform of society required that freedom of thought replace authoritarian censorship and indoctrination by the Church. They condemned the priesthood for using coercion and manipulating popular hopes and fears. They attacked clerical obscurantism as the most serious threat to social progress. They provided no blueprint, but it was clear that the French Church, made vulnerable by doctrinal warfare between Jesuits and Jansenists, would have to be remodeled. Some *philosophes* wanted its conflicting doctrines replaced by a universal natural Deism without sacraments and rites. All of this "reformism" meant that they rejected the doctrine of the depravity of man. By education, at least the upper echelons of society could be transformed. Education, a key part of the *philosophes'* program, should pass from the Church to the state and be oriented toward citizenship, science, practical arts, and modern languages.

All of the *philosophes* denounced arbitrary government and the violation of rights of property and person. They also opposed economic regulations, clerical influences, and systems of forced labor. Their ideal enlightened ruler would legislate according to the dictates of natural law or social utility to advance the arts, the sciences, and the general welfare. Against the divine prerogatives of the monarchy and the Church, they appealed to nature and the natural goodness of man.

Along with "reason," the word "natural" became their touchstone for testing institutions. Unfortunately that word was (and still is) used in a variety of confusing and contradictory ways. Among other things it meant (1) the ideal determined by reason, what ought to be, (2) the customary or usual, what was or was done, (3) the worldly as opposed to the supernatural, thus making miracles unnatural, and often (4) the primitive or untarnished original state of nature inhabited by the "noble savage" and reported by travel literature. Thus the repeated proposition that man should discover the laws of nature and conform to them was ambiguous. The *philosophes* believed that "nature," unmolested by arbitrary authority, would operate harmoniously as a unifying force.

Most of the *philosophes* considered "social science" an instrument of progress. Past history made some of them pessimistic; Voltaire, for example, believed that progress would always be limited. Condorcet, however, postulated perfectibility as an inexorable law of nature replacing divine Providence. In either case the golden age for man was to be found in the future rather than in revelation or in a past era of excellence. (As Fontenelle had explained earlier, moderns were really the ancients, for they had at their disposal the experience of those who had gone before them.)

The *philosophes* assumed that knowledge of nature would make men virtuous, but as another part of their program for progress, they called for sweeping humanitarian reforms. Following in the footsteps of the Quakers, they attacked slavery, torture, secret accusations, arbitrary imprisonment, cruel and unusual punishments, treatment of the insane as criminals, and the inferior status of women. Many also attacked war and militarism. Although they advocated a state in which the individual had a stake in property and civic rights, their patriotism was cultural and not based upon emotional hatred or disparagement of foreigners. As a means of curtailing warfare they relied upon enlightened self-interest working through a balance of power. Rarely did a *philosophe* think that reason should be supplemented by institutions to resolve international conflicts. They were cosmopolitans rather than internationalists.

Montesquieu and Historical Empiricism

Rational criticism of the existing regime in France had begun during the reign of Louis XIV, but it first obtained wide currency and general significance with Montesquieu. During the aristocratic resurgence following the death of Louis XIV, Baron de Montesquieu (1689–1755) opened an era with *The Persian Letters* (1721). This satire placed caustic remarks on French government, religion, and manners in the mouth of a visiting oriental. Then, after many years of research and travel, Montesquieu published in 1748 *The Spirit of the Laws*. Here, by inductive methods, he tried to go behind the apparent diversity of governmental systems and find a natural law of constitutional and social structure. His sources were both ancient and contemporary. In the England of his own time he found a political freedom that contrasted with the "tyranny" of Louis XIV. That freedom, he concluded, was guaranteed by a separation of the executive, legislative, and judicial powers and by the maintenance of the hereditary nobility with a veto over legislation. Everywhere he found constitutions conditioned by climate and environment to which wise legislators were obliged to adjust specific enactments.

The Spirit of the Laws, although blemished with naïve associations of cause and effect and with rambling formlessness, remained a fountainhead of constitutions that embodied the principle of a separation of powers and systems of checks and balances among those powers. At the same time it served as a sharp criticism of the tyranny of monarchs ruling without the nobility and other intermediate orders of society.

Whereas Montesquieu represented the enlightened nobility, Jean François Marie Arouet—better known as Voltaire (1694–1778), the undisputed prince of *philosophe* letters—expressed the anti-aristocratic viewpoint of the middle class. A political realist who praised English constitutionalism and considered absolutism appropriate for Russia, Voltaire differed sharply from Montesquieu about what was best for France. There he championed an enlightened despotism that would curb the nobility. A promising poet who was twice imprisoned in the Bastille at a nobleman's instigation, Voltaire crossed the Channel and imbibed English philosophy, literature, science, and Deism. Returning for fifteen years to the Duchy of Lorraine on the French frontier, he popularized Newton, Locke, and the whole English social system as sharp contrasts to contemporary French thought and institutions. A star of the salons and a confidante of princes, notably Frederick the Great of Prussia, Voltaire finally settled in 1758 at Ferney, an estate on the French-Swiss frontier, where he spent most of the remainder of his life writing, supervising his estates and factories, and entertaining guests who made their pilgrimage to him. He produced a flood of plays, histories, essays, satires, letters, and deistic sermons, today filling nearly ninety volumes of collected works. His work conveyed the Enlightenment's message of free thought, common sense, and hatred of fanaticism, ignorance, persecution, and war. He took up individual cases of injustice under the aegis of his sharp and witty pen. Hostile to revolution and aloof from democratic sentiments, at least until his old age, he urged rulers to enact the *philosophes'* program of civil rights and freedoms for their citizens.

Voltaire displayed a humanitarian rage toward intolerance and inhumanity. In this vein his name is most closely linked with criticism of organized Christianity. *Écrasez l'infâme*—"crush the infamous thing" (namely intolerance)—he wrote. He held the organized church largely responsible for the ignorance, superstition, servility, and fanaticism of the masses. He deplored its role in perverting justice and supporting cruelties. Purged of its evils, however, the church could serve a useful social purpose.

The Enlightenment's Problem of Knowledge

By denying divinely implanted innate ideas as the source of truth, the leaders of the Enlightenment proceeded to secularize thought drastically. Distrusting rationalist systems of all kinds, they followed Locke's empiricism in setting limits on human knowledge by excluding innate ideas. According to Voltaire, "Locke has set forth human reason just as an excellent anatomist explains the parts of the human body."

But by the middle of the eighteenth cen-

Voltaire (Houdon). Without his high sense of humor he would have found the follies of mankind unbearable.

tury fundamental dilemmas appeared in the *philosophes'* empirical doctrine of knowledge. Locke had acknowledged the disparity between sensory data, which could be misleading, and what he took to be the external reality of extension, motion, weight, and so forth. But did these Lockean categories actually conform to reality in the external world? Or were they entirely subjective forms imposed by the mind or human passions?

David Hume, a Scottish philosopher in revolt against all rationalist systems, adhered to a thoroughgoing empiricism; he questioned all knowledge except individual sensory experience. He assigned supernatural knowledge insufficiently attested by miracles to the realm of subjective hopes and fears. At the same time he doubted the reality of cause-and-effect relationships as mental habits. Likewise he attacked self-evident propositions, rational religion based on the assumption of a universal human nature, and rational morality. No man, Hume said in effect, had ever observed a "state of nature." Hence, assumptions drawn from such an idea were unverifiable. In order to discover human nature, he urged the study of psychology, history, and anthropology. Since reason was a slave to the passions, sound human relations could not be based on it. They could rest only on an ethic of moral sentiment or on the ability to put oneself into the "shoes" of another. Hume thus divorced "reason" from "nature" and substituted an alliance between "nature" and "feeling."

Diderot and the Encyclopedists

Not all the *philosophes'* work was individual; their crowning collective achievement was the seventeen-volume *Encyclopédie* published from 1751 to 1780 under the principal editorship of Denis Diderot (1713–1784). It had no less a purpose than to "bring together all the knowledge scattered over the face of the earth, to lay its general system before the men with whom

we live . . . so that our children will know more, and so that they may at the same time be greater in virtue and in happiness. . . ." Its contributors included such men as Montesquieu, Turgot, Rousseau, d'Alembert, Holbach, Voltaire, and especially Diderot. In order to pass the scrutiny of the censors, the political and religious articles were orthodox, but its columns carried the Enlightenment's assault on existing institutions and values in unsuspected places. The *Encyclopédie* was much more than a philosophic compilation; it became the outstanding work popularizing the Newtonian revolution and Bacon's ideas of inductive science on the Continent. Its technical articles and plates, drawn to reproducible specifications, provided a storehouse of skills, for technology's future social significance was not lost on Diderot and his collaborators. The *Encyclopédie* was too large, too unwieldly a work to be as effective as Voltaire's tracts. Nevertheless, as a vehicle for spreading the Enlightenment, it reinforced the activities of the salons, the Masonic lodges, an increasing number of scientific societies, newspapers, and public libraries and museums which appeared both in Europe and America.

The Encyclopedists carried faith in empiricism and in the overwhelming influence of environment to its limits. Diderot explained human conduct entirely in natural terms, and occasionally he concluded that environment determined it. On a similar basis Claude Helvétius built up a morality based upon people's aversion to pain and attraction to pleasure. His political doctrine was utilitarianism—the greatest good for the greatest number. These ideas were later expanded in England by philosophic radicals led by Jeremy Bentham.

In stressing the emotions as wellsprings of human behavior, these *philosophes* sought to redirect antisocial feelings into useful paths. In so doing they put natural forces above an abstract deity as a basis for morality.

Rousseau and the Emancipation of Passions

The idea of harnessing the emotions or passions to useful ends was shared by many writers of the Enlightenment and was brought to a climax by Jean Jacques Rousseau (1712–1778), Genevan born and self-educated wanderer. A plebeian misfit in the exaggerated refinement of Parisian salons, Rousseau became the prophet of revolt against the *philosophes'* rationalism and materialism. In 1749 he bounded into fame by winning an essay contest on the question, "Has the Restoration of Sciences and Arts Tended to Corrupt or Purify Morals?" By charging that luxury and cities had corrupted man, he attacked the cherished assumption of many *philosophes* that increased knowledge automatically brought progress. In the *Discourse on Inequality* (1755) he broadened his criticism to indict the morally corrupting influence of society and rule by and for the rich, thereby questioning the existence of a natural harmony between self-interest and society. According to Rousseau, a moral revolution was the first prerequisite for progress.

Rousseau sketched the path this moral revolution should take in his *Social Contract* (1762). If existing society corrupted natural man, then government ought to be transformed into an expression of popular will. For Rousseau, only the "general will" could legitimately bind men to law and government. Therefore the *Social Contract* could be construed as a call for popular revolution against monarchical and aristocratic governments. Perfect democracy, however, could only exist in small states such as his native Geneva. For large states such as France, he proposed a sovereign restrained from tyranny through forced submission to periodic local assemblies in each province. Rousseau's chief concern was to maintain civic spirit and curb materialistic self-interest. To this end he wanted citizens to be indoctrinated with group pride and civic religion. This proposal

Business, politics, and coffee: Lloyd's in the eighteenth century.

seemed to contradict his commitment to the individual's moral autonomy. It also conflicted with his contemporary tract on education, *Émile,* which advocated a natural spontaneous education of youth apart from artificial social contacts.

Rousseau's *Confessions* provides a possible key to his thought and personality. In this autobiographical sketch he portrayed at length his moods, reveries, and feelings. His ideal norm for human societies is the better but unrealized nature of Jean Jacques himself, tortured by his own shortcomings to preach social virtues. His idea that a moral revolution must precede progress gave unity to his thought. His intuitive approach, his denial of natural harmony, his refusal to equate virtue with knowledge, and his uncompromising conclusion that contemporary society and its spokesmen were corrupt made a break between him and the *philosophes* inevitable.

Rousseau's approach admirably suited the tastes of those who wanted governments responsive to their peoples and who sought immediate solutions to practical problems that the Enlightenment's intellectualism failed to provide. As a diverse and fertile writer, he stands as the fountainhead of such nineteenth-century movements as the religious revival, democracy, romanticism, socialism, and especially nationalism. For the divine right of kings, he substituted the natural right of peoples.

This principle called the legitimacy of all existing governments into question, but it contributed less to effective representative government than Montesquieu's constitutionalism.

Economic Thought of the Enlightenment

The first "scientific" school of political economy, the Physiocrats, arose in France among the followers of François Quesnay (1694–1774), who claimed to have discovered the self-evident laws regulating the flow of money. Apart from government regulation of interest rates, the Physiocrats advocated leaving the economy to the natural laws of supply and demand and to man's enlightened self-interest (*laissez faire*). Government, which they would vest in an absolute monarchy, should guarantee the natural and limitless rights of property, security, and (economic) liberty. The Physiocrats agreed with many mercantilists that internal trade barriers were intolerable, but the bulk of their outlook was a reaction against the policies of Colbert. They denounced restrictive industrial production codes, guild regulations, protective tariffs, commercial wars, and the mercantilist emphasis upon industry and foreign commerce. Sympathetic to estate holders, they publicized their new agricultural techniques and accorded full rights over communal property to them. Only agriculture and extractive industries, they asserted, produced wealth; manufacturing and the professions were "sterile." As a substitute for forced peasant labor and the cumbersome tax structure of the times, they advocated a single tax on the net product of the land. This reform would have swept away many administrative cobwebs and inequalities.

Prior to the French Revolution the Physiocrats' influence was small. In 1776 Turgot, Louis XVI's reforming minister of finance, was dismissed for championing their views. In that same year, Adam Smith, who had praise as well as criticism for them, published a more comprehensive explanation of economic phenomena, *An Inquiry Concerning the Wealth of Nations*.

In this classic treatise Smith (1723–1790) shared the Physiocrats' optimistic faith in the natural harmony of the economic mechanism, provided that men recognized their true self-interests. But in contrast to the Physiocrats, Smith emphasized trade and labor, especially the division of labor, as principal sources of wealth. To government he assigned three tasks: (1) national defense, (2) the administration of justice with the purpose of protecting each member of society against oppression by any other member, and (3) the construction and maintenance of essential public utilities. Traditionally Smith's name has become more closely identified with *laissez-faire* economics than that of any other man. Yet his criticism of certain business practices on moral grounds sets him apart from many later adherents and practitioners of *laissez faire* who used this principle to justify such practices. Smith's edifice rested upon the premise that the greatest social benefits would result when each individual was allowed to pursue his own rational self-interest. Despite his moral strictures he insisted that natural economic processes need be guided only by the "invisible hand" of natural law. Although he did not break completely with the mercantilists on navigation acts and tariffs, he warned against the political dangers of high protective tariffs, and he roundly criticized monopolistic corporations, such as the East India Company, that exercised governmental powers.

Popular Religious Reactions to Science and Reason

As "world views"—explanations of the universe and man's place in it—rationalism, Deism, and sceptical empiricism satisfied only part of the educated classes. The conservative rationalism that upheld the social hierarchy and taught resignation to the *status quo* as "the best of all possible worlds" did penetrate the established Protestant churches. But rationalists chastened by the religious wars to decry "enthusiasm" in all forms could not hold the loyalty of those who craved a "religion of the heart," an emotional experience of conversion, and a humanitarian morality.

The English civil wars of the seventeenth century spawned several new religious sects that sponsored secular reforms, but the Society of Friends—or Quakers—was at the same time the most spiritualistic and worldly among them. Rejecting a professional clergy—whom they identified as "hirelings of princes"—tithes, sacraments, and the external paraphernalia of worship, the Quakers emphasized a private faith for living that transcended the boundaries of creed, nationality, race, and social class in the same way that natural law did for scientists and secular philosophers. Although a small sect, the Quakers included an inordinate number of wealthy businessmen who devoted much time and money to the relief of poverty, unemployment, alcoholism, slavery, scandalous prison conditions, and inadequate medical facilities.

Pietism formed the basis for an emotional religious revival that spread over the Protestant world during the eighteenth century. Against the mechanistic world view of Deism the Protestant revival asserted "fundamentalism,"—that is, absolute faith in the literal meaning of the Bible. The number of dogmas inherited from the Reformation was pared down to a few basic ones, but those that were retained reasserted the active intervention of divine spirit in human affairs. Unlike traditional orthodoxies that checked emotion and denied all conscience except that sworn to their own doctrines, the eighteenth-century revivalists emphasized piety and taught that salvation depended not upon predestination or sacraments but upon the individual's religious and moral rebirth.

Evangelism in a home: John Wesley. People did not mind hearing from him what great sinners they were!

In England and British North America, Methodism challenged the drift toward rationalism. This new revivalist sect was organized by George Whitefield and the Wesley brothers, John (1703–1791) and Charles. Calling passionately for personal conversion, these early Methodists revived fundamental doctrines of man's utter depravity, of the Atonement, and of divine intervention. They revived Puritanism in England, particularly among the industrial workers and miners. Neglected by the established church, these urban laborers were inoculated by their religion against revolutionary doctrines of natural rights.

Protestant revivalism in Europe recruited principally from those members of the middle and lower classes who were at odds with their theologically liberal but socially conservative establishments. To some extent it was, like the Enlightenment, subversive of the *status quo*. It pressed for humanitarian reforms, the extension of

A witchcraft trial in Massachusetts, 1692. One of the last outbreaks of this form of an old epidemic.

Scene from a slave ship. Slave quarters were rarely so spacious and airy.

literacy among the lower classes, and a combination of self-help and mutual assistance. These ascetic fundamentalist movements promoted dedication to hard work and disciplined labor; they were also vehicles of religious nationalism, which was ultimately to threaten the legitimacy of princely continental states.

One form of protest against the secularization of thought in religious circles was a renewed belief in witchcraft, especially during the seventeenth century. In a sense this response was a desperate reassertion of the continued intervention of supernatural spirits in human affairs. John Wesley, among others, would assert that he who disbelieves in witchcraft disbelieves in God.

But the days of *religious* witchcraft proceedings in the Western world were dying out; to later, more secular Europeans educated in science, they seemed hopelessly benighted. They were an integral part of the older spiritual view of the universe which even Protestant fundamentalism could not maintain on the basis of biblical authority alone.

The new thought of the seventeenth and eighteenth centuries deserves emphasis because of its overwhelming importance for the future. Yet it left a varied and confused legacy, no more providing a unifying ideology than the religious authoritarianism that had preceded it. There was no common standard of values. Many scientific philosophers were certain that a self-evident standard of ethics was not only possible but immediately forthcoming. But no such standard appeared, and voices like Hume's soon raised to question the validity of the quest. Nevertheless, humanitarianism gained wider currency than in any previous period of Western history. Indifferent toward heaven and convinced that life on earth could be improved, the publicists of the Enlightenment popularized reform as a social goal.

Although humanitarianism was professed more widely than before, secularized thought had not yet deeply penetrated European society. It remained the property of a narrow, albeit powerful, elite. Even in France the *philosophes* converted only a minority of the clergy, nobles, and literate middle classes. Literate Frenchmen apparently read more in works that reconciled traditional religious doctrines with popularized science than in the *Encyclopédie*. Dissatisfied peasants knew nothing of the *philosophes*. In Eastern and Southern Europe, the Enlightenment was hardly felt at all. In fact, most Europeans had little reason to take an optimistic view toward this world. Optimism was generally the prerogative of those who benefited from commerce or royal patronage. And even among them deep pessimism was common.

The fate of the *philosophes'* "search for humanity" was to be determined by foreign and domestic struggles in their own and subsequent centuries; again and again reactionaries were to attack their goals and values. In the twentieth century these conflicts were to be fought with unheard of violence as fascists mobilized traditionalists to banish the Enlightenment's influence from Western society.

SELECTED READINGS

*Becker, Carl L., *The Heavenly City of the Eighteenth-Century Philosophers*, Yale University Press, New Haven, 1932.

A popular series of essays propounding the dubious thesis that the *philosophes* were reconstructing medieval philosophy with more up-to-date materials.

Beer, Max, *An Inquiry into Physiocracy*, G. Allen and Unwin, London, 1939.

An analysis of the doctrines of early *laissez-faire* economists that links them to practices of the medieval towns and exposes weaknesses in their method.

Brinton, Howard, *Friends for 300 Years, the History and Beliefs of the Society of Friends since George Fox Started the Quaker Movement*, Harper, New York, 1952.

A brief sketch of the Quaker organization, doctrines, and social action. Chapter 8, "The Meeting and the World," is especially pertinent.

*Bronowski, J., and Mazlish, B., *The Western Intellectual Tradition from Leonardo to Hegel*, Harper, New York and Evanston, 1962.

Brilliant intellectual history of Europe from the Renaissance to the early nineteenth century particularly sensitive to the impact of science.

*Bury, J. B., *The Idea of Progress, An Inquiry into Its Growth and Origin*, Dover Publications, New York, 1955.

An older discussion, with some omissions, of early advocates of the idea of progress.

*Butterfield, Herbert, *The Origins of Modern Science, 1300–1800*, The Free Press, New York.

A history of the "scientific revolution" by an author who considers science the most influential force making the modern world.

*Cassirer, Ernst, *The Philosophy of the Enlightenment*, Beacon Press, Boston, 1955.

A classic account that rehabilitates the *philosophes* as serious thinkers.

*————, *The Question of Jean-Jacques Rousseau*, Columbia University Press, New York, 1954, and a Midland Book.

A probe of Rousseau's fundamental ideas which confirms his claim that all of his works had a consistent theme; indispensable for distinguishing Rousseau from the French *philosophes*.

Cobban, Alfred, *In Search of Humanity, the Role of the Enlightenment in Modern History*, George Braziller, New York, 1960.

A sympathetic account and an appeal for a return to the Enlightenment's humanitarian principles.

*Feuer, Lewis S., *Spinoza and the Rise of Liberalism*, Beacon Press, Boston, 1958.

One of the few detailed works in English relating seventeenth-century Dutch thought to its environment.

Gay, Peter, *The Party of Humanity, Essays in the French Enlightenment*, Alfred A. Knopf, New York, 1964.

Interpretive essays rescuing the *philosophes*, especially Voltaire, from charges of frivolity and utopianism and dissociating them from the rhetoric of the revolution.

*Gierke, Otto, *Natural Law and the Theory of Society, 1500 to 1800*, Beacon Press, Boston, 1957.

A detailed exposition of early modern social and political theory by a German critic of rational natural law.

*Hall, A. R., *The Scientific Revolution 1500–1800, The Formation of the Modern Scientific Attitude*, Beacon Press, Boston, 1954.

A narrative manual of scientific developments organized according to subject.

*Koyré, Alexandre, *From the Closed World to the Infinite Universe*, Harper, New York, 1958.

Traces the destruction of the conception of

Asterisk (*) denotes paperback.

the cosmos as an earth or man centered, finite, hierarchically ordered whole by the new philosophy and science of the seventeenth century.

*Kuhn, Thomas S., *The Structure of Scientific Revolutions,* University of Chicago Press, Chicago and London, 1962.

An attempt to acquaint nonscientists with scientific methodology, particularly helpful in emphasizing the role of conceptual models in scientific advances.

*Lovejoy, Arthur O., *The Great Chain of Being, A Study of the History of an Idea,* Harper, New York, 1960.

Traces a basic assumption of classical and medieval thought through the rationalism of the seventeenth and eighteenth centuries.

*Manuel, Frank E., *The Eighteenth Century Confronts the Gods,* Harvard University Press, Cambridge, 1959, and Atheneum paperback.

Explores explanations by the men of the Enlightenment of popular religious beliefs, especially deification of gods in the past.

More, Louis T., *Isaac Newton, a Biography,* Charles Scribner's Sons, New York and London, 1934.

Factual biography of the leading scientist of the period.

Morley, John, *Diderot and the Encyclopedists,* Macmillan Company, London, 1923.

Old account of the Encyclopedists by a Victorian Liberal who also wrote on Voltaire and Rousseau.

Palmer, R. R., *Catholics and Unbelievers in Eighteenth-Century France,* Cooper Square Publishers, Inc., New York, 1961.

Sympathetically examines religious opponents of the *philosophes* showing areas of agreement as well as disagreement.

Pinson, Koppel S., *Pietism as a Factor in the Rise of German Nationalism,* Columbia University Press, New York, 1934.

A study of the political implications of emotional fundamentalism in the German states.

*Robbins, Caroline, *The Eighteenth-Century Commonwealthman,* Harvard University Press, Cambridge, 1959, and Atheneum paperback.

An in-depth examination of the transmission of English radical thought from the civil wars through the eighteenth century.

*Santillana, Giorgio de, *The Crime of Galileo,* University of Chicago, 1955.

An investigation of the quarrel between the Church and Galileo, with an eye to political measures taken in the United States after World War II against outspoken scientists.

Schapiro, J. Selwyn, *Condorcet and the Rise of Liberalism,* Harcourt, Brace, New York, 1934.

Sympathetic biography of the only *philosophe* who lived to participate in the French Revolution; a study in activism.

*Smith, Preserved, *The History of Modern Culture,* Volume II, *The Enlightenment,* Holt, New York, 1934, and Collier paperback.

Detailed comprehensive account that neglects the continued force of tradition.

Vyverberg, Henry, *Historical Pessimism in the French Enlightenment,* Harvard University Press, Cambridge, 1958.

A necessary corrective to the notion that unqualified optimism dominated the thought of the Enlightenment.

*Willey, Basil, *The Seventeenth-Century Background; Studies in the Thought of the Age in Relation to Poetry and Religion,* Columbia University Press, New York, 1952, and an Anchor paperback; and

*————, *The Eighteenth-Century Background; Studies on the Idea of Nature in the Thought of the Period,* Columbia University Press, New York, 1953, and a Beacon paperback.

Lucid works based on England that show drastic changes in the meanings of the slogans "reason" and "nature" and that emphasize conservative uses of rationalism.

*Wolf, A., *A History of Science, Technology and Philosophy in the Sixteenth and Seventeenth Centuries,* G. Allen and Unwin, London, 1950, and a Harper Torchbook.

Standard detailed account useful for reference.

See also the relevant sections of the volumes by Friedrich, Nussbaum, Wolf, Roberts, and Gershoy in the Rise of Modern Europe series edited by W. L. Langer.

18

The Decline of Absolutism, 1720 to 1787

The era of 1720 to 1787 encompasses what we call the Old Regime. It was a period of the fulfillment of what the traditional monarchic, aristocratic society had to offer before it was consumed in the fires of democratic revolutions. The aristocratic character of society gave this era of about seventy years a distinctive stability and an aura of fine living. The surface of society appeared orderly: everyone was in his proper place in the social pyramid; power emanated from kings and aristocrats; established churches as well as new sects guarded the faith; enlightenment was spreading; and Europe was expanding and prospering. "Whatever is, is right," seemed an appropriate commentary on the age.

But that was only on the surface; beneath it, ominous tremors and far-off rumblings could be detected. Those who read *Candide,* the *Persian Letters, Tom Jones, Nathan the Wise,* or *On Crimes and Punishments* could sense that not all was well. Those who watched the growing insolence of the resurgent nobility; the militarism; the competitiveness among states and the imperial rivalries that plunged the Western world into a Seven Years' War; the restlessness of the poor; the growing population; the flight to the frontiers; the dissatisfaction with aristocracy and the spreading of egalitarian sentiments—those who watched these events and trends with intelligent interest might concur with Louis XV, "After us, the deluge."

It is the full flowering and incipient decay of the old order, and the gathering together of the forces of the liberal, democratic order that we shall study in this chapter.

The Competitive State System, around 1720 to 1740

After Louis XIV failed to create a personal European empire, negotiators at Utrecht restored the balance of power. Ignoring a plan for a federation of states, the major powers agreed instead to consult regularly in diplomatic congresses. This machinery for the peaceful settlement of international disputes was stillborn, however. It failed to replace the competitive system in which each state pursued its own interests individually or collectively. On the other hand, in the years following Utrecht, several major powers did work in a concert based on alliances to preserve the general peace.

That peace and concert, which successfully prevented general war until 1740, rested on a minor diplomatic revolution, an alliance between recent foes, Britain and France. An understanding between these two powers, each of which had been of pivotal importance in their earlier hostile alliances, was considered a sure guarantee of general peace. The architect of the alliance was Lord Stanhope, a belligerent Whig soldier who involved Britain everywhere in continental affairs. The agreement secured both dynasties which were momentarily weak, and Stanhope extended the alliance to include other major powers.

Diplomacy that recognized or adjusted dynastic claims and commercial rights, such as forcing the disbanding in 1731 of Austria's Ostend Company which encroached on English and Dutch trade in the Far East, succeeded in maintaining a period of relative stability in European international affairs. This stability undergirded a generation of reconstruction, which laid the foundations of aristocratic dominance until the nineteenth century.

The Politics of Oligarchy and Stability, 1720 to 1740

Against efficient absolute monarchs, aristocrats reacted by reasserting claims to positions of enhanced honor and power. Many of the aristocrats involved in this movement were not of the old feudal nobility, who could trace their titles to past centuries. Rather, the bulk of them were office holders, magistrates, and councillors whose aristocratic lineage was recent and, in many cases, purchased. Drawing incomes from manorial revenues, loans to the state, and

the emoluments of public office, these oligarchies were the backbone of a "cult of stability" in domestic affairs.

This cult predominated in a world half modern, half medieval, and the interests of both central governments and commoners were sacrificed to it. Entrenched bureaucratic power led such men as Voltaire in France and John Adams in America to conclude that a strong executive was necessary to defend the interests of the many against the few.

France

When Louis XIV died at the end of the War of the Spanish Succession, the nobles of the sword—those who claimed medieval lineage—made a bid for power. On no matter did they founder worse than in handling the king's debts. Accounts were chaotic, and there was no budget. Nor was there a centralized institution such as the Bank of England. However, a Scottish adventurer, John Law, who was an able financial planner, came to France with a plan to centralize and pay off the debt. Establishing a central, note-issuing bank in 1716, he then financed it. The trading company (Mississippi Company) that he set up absorbed all French chartered companies, gaining a monopoly of French colonial trade. To extinguish the royal debt, Law then had the company exchange its shares for certificates of debt, which it planned to pay off through trading profits and by acquiring a monopoly on the collection of internal indirect taxes.

The scheme was not a total failure. Law's bank notes stimulated trade as promised. But the purchase of shares in the Company became a speculative mania, in which the price of shares skyrocketed to many times their real worth. In 1720 the "Mississippi Bubble" broke, taking many investors from paper riches to rags. In the disillusionment which followed, the Parlement of Paris canceled Law's charters. Only his original trading company survived and continued to prosper. The French government, however, continued to be plagued with fiscal problems, which neither the aristocracy nor the court found the means to alleviate.

Unlike Louis XIV, the new French monarch had no taste for affairs of state. After he came of age in 1726, Louis XV turned them over to the seventy-two-year-old Cardinal Fleury. A cautious administrator who avoided offending vested interests, Fleury worked for retrenchment and recovery. He stabilized the coinage, provided security for highways, and built better roads than England's. Tax farming was not abolished, but the Cardinal kept taxes down by avoiding the expenses of war. Fleury worked for stability at home and abroad, but his policies did not check the growing power of the nobility of the robe, whose obstructionism eventually crippled the central government and made "French absolutism" a misnomer.

Nobles of the robe, who now filled numerous judicial and other official positions in the monarchy, had been considered a part of the bourgeoisie a century before. After 1715 their ascent was indicated by their social merger with the older nobility. In their religion, they supported Jansenism, a puritanical Catholicism which opposed papal centralism, the Jesuits, and a state-directed church. Supported by the *parlements* against the central government, the Jansenists engaged in doctrinal brawls with the Jesuits that discredited the French Church and made it vulnerable to attacks by the *philosophes* of the Enlightenment. By portraying themselves as defenders of liberty against arbitrary government, these nobles, who constituted the membership of the *parlements,* also discredited the monarchy. But at the same time, they blocked reforms. More than any other group, the nobles of the robe protected the provincial and social privileges that made France's nominal absolutism a contradiction in terms. But prior to 1789 their refurbished feudalism could offer no substitute for it.

In a distinctly separate compartment of French life, but coincident with the aristo-

Cardinal Fleury, first minister of France, 1726–1743. Under his policies of promoting peace abroad and orderly government at home, France recovered from the wars of Louis XIV.

cratic resurgence, was the development of an overseas empire and colonial trade. In Martinique, Guadeloupe, and Santo Domingo, French planters had the most productive sugar islands of the West Indies. French traders vied with English companies for illicit trade with the Spanish empire. They encroached upon the decrepit Portuguese empire in India and increasingly came into hostile contact with the English East India Company. Marseilles was a prosperous port for trade with the Levant, which French merchants made virtually their own. As a result of the War of Spanish Succession, France had lost part of North America to Britain. French efforts to build a self-sustaining society in Canada and Louisiana failed, but merchants traded with the Indians and returned a profitable supply of furs. French commerce thrived during the first half of the century, but it affected a lesser proportion of the population than was the case in England.

British press gang at work. Englishmen did not often relish the thought of seeing the world on board a British man-of-war.

Britain

In addition to being a constitutional kingdom dominated by the gentry, England was fast displacing the Dutch Republic as Europe's principal entrepôt of colonial trade. Merchants as well as "improving landlords" had social respectability and influence. Younger sons of the aristocracy entered trade and married heiresses of mercantile fortunes. Thus the aristocracy was attentive to trade and harkened to publicists such as Daniel Defoe, who attributed England's manifest wealth to commerce.

> . . . Trade is the Wealth of the World [Defoe wrote]; Trade makes the Difference as to Rich and Poor, between one Nation and another; Trade nourishes Industry, Industry begets Trade; Trade dispenses the natural Wealth of the World, and Trade raises new Species of Wealth, which Nature knew nothing of; Trade has two Daughters, whose fruitful Progeny in Arts may be said to employ Mankind; namely
>
> MANUFACTURE
> and
> NAVIGATION.[1]

With respect to both commerce and industry, Defoe was not wide of the mark. Better balanced and protected than French

1. Quoted by J. H. Plumb, *England in the Eighteenth Century* (Penguin Books, Baltimore, 1950), p. 21.

commerce, British overseas trade increased rapidly during the century. The growth of western ports such as Liverpool, Bristol, and Glasgow reflected this expansion and Britain's strategic advantage over both the Dutch Republic and France. In North America, Britain had a unique series of moderately populous agricultural colonies. They supplied raw materials and markets, but they did not fit well into the mercantilists' mold. Their lines of commerce gravitated more naturally toward the French and Spanish West Indies and to other parts of Europe than to Britain. More congenial to British strategic interests, as mercantilists saw them, were Jamaica and the Barbados, producers of sugar, tobacco, and dyestuffs.

Unlike France, England had a large central financial institution, the private Bank of England, founded in 1694. This bank handled exchange, issued notes, and floated the public debt. In the last role it funneled private savings to public use and tied the moneyed classes to the existing system of government. Their representation in Parliament gave assurance that the debt would not be repudiated, that it would be considered a national, not just a royal, obligation.

This was a new and unusual concept in financial responsibility for an age that regarded the debts of the government as the king's personal obligation, as they had been in the Middle Ages. But despite the Bank's effective mobilization of capital for the War of Spanish Succession, its facilities were partially bypassed in 1720 by political leaders confronted with the difficulties of paying for the war. It was the same sort of difficulty that had beset the French governing oligarchy after the War of the Spanish Succession, and it was met in nearly the same way with about the same disastrous results. But it brought a great leader, Robert Walpole, to power.

Walpole had established a sinking fund to retire part of the debt at reduced rates of interest. Its bonds became prized securities among investors. But in 1720 directors of the South Sea Company obtained authority

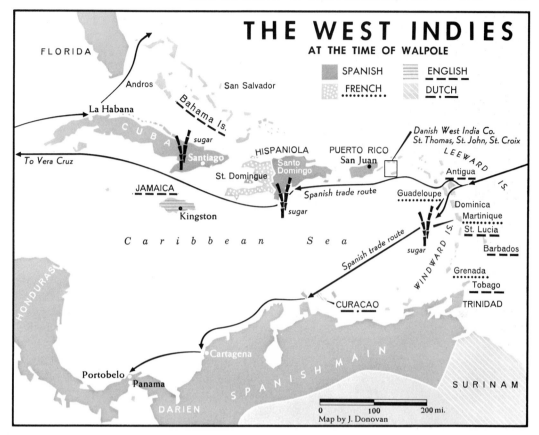

THE WEST INDIES
AT THE TIME OF WALPOLE

SPANISH   ENGLISH
FRENCH   DUTCH

FLORIDA

Andros   San Salvador

La Habana

Bahama Is.

CUBA

sugar

To Vera Cruz

Santiago

St. Domingue

HISPANIOLA

Santo Domingo

Spanish trade route   sugar

PUERTO RICO
San Juan

Danish West India Co.
St. Thomas, St. John, St. Croix

LEEWARD IS.

Antigua

JAMAICA

Kingston

Guadeloupe

Dominica
Martinique
St. Lucia

Barbados

Grenada
Tobago

TRINIDAD

C a r i b b e a n   S e a

Spanish trade route   sugar

WINDWARD IS.

HONDURAS

CURACAO

SURINAM

Cartagena

Portobelo
Panama

SPANISH MAIN

DARIEN

0   100   200 mi.

Map by J. Donovan

to take over other parts of the debt, exchanging its stock for bonds. Walpole opposed the scheme, but the directors liberally plied leading politicians and the king's mistresses with stock. The company got its way, and a mania of speculation in its shares followed. In 1720 the "Bubble" broke into a financial panic. No general depression of commerce occurred, but Parliament reacted by restricting the incorporation of banks, a measure that eventually became a serious obstacle to Britain's industrial expansion. Uncompromised by the scandal, Walpole served as a "screen" to save the dynasty and drove the implicated Whigs from office.

A landed gentleman who had married into a family trading in Baltic timber, Walpole was a representative of the cult of stability, not of Stanhope's radical Whiggery. "I am no Saint," he wrote, "no Spartan, no Reformer." He considered the nobility an indispensable element of any free government. Preferring to "let sleeping dogs lie," he cautiously avoided offending any great interest except those who pressed for war.

But Walpole's reluctance to confront great opposition must not be misunderstood: he dominated British politics more thoroughly than any previous minister. He is often considered Britain's first prime minister working with a cabinet. Following the scandal of the Bubble, he joined the inner circle of the Privy Council, the precursor of England's modern cabinet. This early committee of ministers was responsible to both Parliament and the king. Meetings were informal, often at dinner, and no records were kept. One man, Walpole, acted to secure the king's assent to measures they agreed upon collectively.

Cabinet session at the time of Walpole (1721–1742).

In tying his policies to powerful vested interests, Walpole failed to respond to new problems brought by social changes. At the top, British society was remarkably stable and uniform. At the bottom of the social pyramid riots, looting, vagabondage, unpaid debts, drunkenness, and ever-present death and crime were festering. Officials responded with penalties more and more severe. They filled prisons and constantly employed the gallows, but they failed to get at the roots of poverty and unrest. Politically, however, the lower segments of society were inarticulate and impotent.

The Prevalence of Aristocratic Stabilization

France and Britain furnish only two examples, albeit major ones, of stabilization under aristocratic oligarchies between 1720 and 1740. Nearly everywhere else in eighteenth-century Europe, a similar aristocratic consolidation was also taking place. These oligarchies were almost everywhere ineffi-cient, often irresponsible and, in the case of Poland, ungovernable as well. Only in Prussia did the monarch dominate the aristocracy and integrate them into the state apparatus.

The Renewed Struggle for Power, 1740 to 1763

The War of Austrian Succession

The politics of stability ended in 1740 when Maria Theresa ascended the throne of the Habsburg inheritance. The succession of a woman to so high a position seemed peaceful enough, having been approved in advance by all major European powers. But Frederick II shattered the peace by moving quickly to take Silesia from the young princess. By 1741 France, Bavaria, Spain, Prussia, and Saxony had agreed to partition the Habsburg empire, leaving Maria Theresa only her eastern Austrian and Hungarian provinces. Meanwhile the war for overseas trade and empire, which Britain initiated in 1739 with the War of Jenkins' Ear, merged with the continental dynastic struggle. There fol-

The state of the urban poor: "Beer Street and Gin Lane" by William Hogarth.

EUROPE c. 1763

Map by J. Donovan

lowed a series of wars lasting until 1748, collectively known as the War of Austrian Succession.

In 1748 financial exhaustion, or fear of it, brought both the dynastic and imperial conflicts to an end in the Peace of Aix-la-Chapelle. This peace restored boundaries as they were before the war except that Frederick II retained Silesia. It did nothing to assuage the imperial antagonisms between Britain and France, nor did it reduce Maria Theresa's resolve to retake Silesia at the first favorable moment. For these reasons, Aix-la-Chapelle endured only as a truce, not as a lasting pacification.

The Seven Years' War, 1756 to 1763

Hostilities first began again in the race for overseas empire. In both Britain and France, publicists ascribed prosperity to the rapid increase in colonial trade. The port cities and planters of both kingdoms displayed the wealth of colonial commerce; and they echoed the conviction that greater wealth and security were to be had by eliminating the competition represented by the other. The Anglo-French conflict now encircled the globe; it focused on West Indian plantations, slave-shipping stations in Africa, trading "factories" in India, and control of the North American continent. The plantations produced a cash crop of great economic importance—sugar. They imported foodstuffs, clothing, and, because the life-expectancy of slaves was short, an ever-increasing amount of "black gold." In India conflict grew out of expansionist policies by rival East India companies.

Hostilities broke out in North America two years before the main war began in Europe, and, unlike India, they involved government troops of both countries. In North America the issue was not so much markets or prized colonies as it was a strug-

Shipbuilding at Toulon, headquarters of the French Mediterranean fleet. The French built better ships than the English did during the 18th century; they did not always sail them as well.

gle for strategic locations for an empire.

Working out from their small Canadian settlements, the French built a line of forts north and south to block off the British advance into the Ohio River valley. There, they would have competed with the British for trade, Indian loyalties, and land. In the first clashes of 1754 and 1755, the French and Indians drove off the British and their Indian allies. Then both home governments committed themselves to a greater collision by reinforcing their respective colonial claims. When pro-war forces in Britain were able to promote raids against French shipping in 1755, maritime hostilities became inevitable. In part, then, the world war which followed was a struggle for control over the American mainland east of the Mississippi River and north of Florida.

The war spread to the European continent, but not because the English or French wanted that to happen. It was the growing strength of Prussia that frightened the Austrians into a diplomatic alliance with France in 1756, a diplomatic revolution that put Habsburgs and Bourbons into the same camp. Count von Kaunitz who engineered this diplomatic switch also negotiated a subsidiary treaty with Russia. Faced with powerful enemies, Frederick II hastened to align himself with the Hanover-

ian king of England, George II. Furthermore, aware that Russia and Austria were planning to reduce Prussia, he seized Saxony, from which he drew revenues during the general war that followed.

The destruction of Prussia was less an aim of France, however, than of Austria and Russia; and only narrowly did they miss achieving it. Together they put Frederick's military prowess to its supreme test. The allied sovereigns' failure to cooperate, however, allowed him for a time simply to defeat each in turn. But his position became so precarious, due to the massive demands on manpower, money, and supplies, that he actually contemplated suicide early in 1762. Russia's sudden withdrawal from the war saved him. Peter III, who succeeded the Prussophobe Empress Elizabeth in January 1762, admired Frederick very much and switched from foe to ally. Catherine II, Peter's wife and successor (she had her imbecilic husband done away with after only a few months of his reign) did not resume the war against Prussia, thus enabling Frederick to survive.

Meanwhile, rallied by William Pitt the Elder, British forces swept away most of the French colonial empire. By 1760 Canada fell to Britain and her Colonists; parts of the French West Indies were lost; and French forces in India yielded to British sea power and the resourcefulness of the East India Company's agent, Robert Clive. Though saddled with heavy war debts, Britain prospered while French shipping, commerce, and credit suffered disastrously.

Attrition and Russian withdrawal from the war made peace necessary. In Europe the Peace of Paris of 1763 restored prewar boundaries and therefore did not resolve the rivalry between Austria and Prussia. France was driven from the North American continent, retaining only two offshore islands and fishing rights. To placate Spain for the loss of Florida to Britain, France ceded Louisiana to her. The French West Indies were restored, but in India France retained only unfortified trading stations. Her political power there was definitely broken.

France's humiliation and the discrediting of her Bourbon monarchy were not the only legacies of the Seven Years' War. Its scope and intensity challenged the *philosophes'* optimistic antimilitarism, because it demonstrated that within the competitive state system enlightened self-interest was insufficient to stop wars. Rather, reason had become an adjunct of *raison d'état,* a tool of predatory states. The war also demonstrated that Britain's parliamentary regime, antimilitaristic at home but the largest spender on arms, had proved more than a match for declining absolutism in France.

Imperial Rivalry and the War of the American Revolution

As we shall soon see in greater detail, the American Revolution was simultaneously a civil war and a national revolt against Britain. But its success was also the result of renewed imperial rivalry that aligned France and the other major powers against Britain. Whetting the long knife of revenge, the French court stood ready to give the rebellious Colonists immediate covert aid. As soon as the Colonists' victory over Burgoyne at Saratoga demonstrated their resolve to pursue independence seriously with force, France concluded a permanent alliance and a commercial convention with the new republic in 1778.

French aid was the foreign mainstay of the American Revolution, but it was not the only assistance the Colonies received. When Spain joined France against Britain in 1779, but not as an ally of the Colonists, Britain lost control over the seas. At great loss to its trade, the Dutch Republic made loans to the Continental Congress and became an active, but ineffective, belligerent in 1780. Russia and several other continental states in 1780 formed the League of Armed Neutrality, designed to stop British search and seizure on the high seas. Only

Lord Clive (after a Gainsborough portrait). He helped establish England in India.

the general hostility toward Britain within the context of continental rivalries can fully explain the paradox of the aid given by Europe's absolute and aristocratic states to this republican revolution.

Eastern Power Struggles and the Partition of Poland

Poland's misfortune was to be the buffer between the three great Eastern powers. Because of internal weakness, Poland, territorially the third largest state in Europe, incited the appetites and mutual distrust of her stronger neighbors. Prior to their actual partition of the kingdom, they worked to preserve the nobles' "freedoms," that is, they maintained the constitutional anarchy that virtually disarmed the kingdom and made it subject to their manipulation.

Catherine II installed Stanislas Poniatowski, a former lover, on the Polish throne in 1763 to assure virtual control over Poland. In 1768 she invaded the Ottoman Empire to take the northern shores of the Black Sea. Frederick II was sure this move would arouse Habsburg fears of Russian power and would divert Austria while he took West Prussia. Hoping thus to consolidate his eastern territories into a single block, Frederick proposed the partition of Poland to Catherine in 1772. To pacify Maria Theresa, she, too, would share the spoils. Catherine reluctantly agreed. The plan shocked Maria Theresa, but as Frederick noted cynically, "The more she wept for Poland, the more she took of it." Frederick got his land bridge, Catherine took White Russia, and Maria Theresa annexed Galicia. A revolutionary act, the first partition of Poland had only *raison d'état* to justify it. In no way could monarchical legitimacy, which in theory underlay absolutism itself, be invoked in its defense.

Continuing her advance into Turkish territory, Catherine acquired Azov in 1774 and completed an important aim of Russian expansionism: to have Russian ships sailing on the Black Sea. By repeated power plays, Prussia, Russia, and Austria entirely absorbed Poland in two further partitions, 1793 and 1795. Poland disappeared from the map until Napoleon put it back on.

Enlightened Despotism

The idea that society should be managed by philosopher-kings was as old as Plato, but eighteenth-century rulers had a rather specific program of enlightened policies in mind. First and foremost was the centralization of administration and justice in separate, parallel institutions. Thereby, all subjects would be under the same laws, taxes, and officials. Among other things, local uniformity entailed adjusting the serfs' status to make them to a greater extent legal personalities subject more directly to the state than to their lords and, incidentally, subject also to conscription. Made uniform within, the state would also use its power to simplify its boundaries, making its territory compact and thereby rationally manageable. Clerical orders such as the Jesuits, who spurned natural reason and tran-

scended the state's boundaries, had to be abolished or subordinated to secular authority. Enlightened domestic policy also required that the established churches relinquish control over censorship, education, welfare, and family affairs. Under secular officials there would be intellectual freedom except in politics, and freer exchange of goods. Compared to absolutism of the past, enlightened rulers placed more emphasis on humanitarianism and economic well-being. All initiative, however, lay with hereditary monarchs. Enlightened despots would do everything *for* the people; nothing would be done *by* the people except under royal supervision.

Maria Theresa and Joseph II

Charles VI's Pragmatic Sanction securing Maria Theresa's succession bound all Habsburg territories permanently under a single ruler for the first time. Nevertheless, it was still more appropriate to speak of a Habsburg dynasty than a Habsburg state. A congeries of duchies and kingdoms gathered together by dynastic marriage and the fortunes of war, the Habsburg empire was inhabited by Germans, Hungarians, Czechs, Slovenes, Slovaks, Croats, Flemings, Walloons, Italians, and, by the end of the century, Poles and Ruthenians also. Unlike their Hohenzollern rivals in Prussia, the Habsburgs had retained provincial diets that shared executive powers with the cosmopolitan court in Vienna.

To strengthen her power, the first female Habsburg ruler taxed the nobility, limited nobles' jurisdictions over and dues from the peasantry, laid plans for a system of state education, and had the laws codified in a more humane, orderly, and secular direction. Above all, she reorganized the army in order to cope with Prussia.

Maria Theresa was too pious to sympathize with the secular *philosophes*. Never could her attitude be described as "enlightened." But Joseph II, her son and co-ruler from 1765 to 1780, took over the reins of government and was determined to make "philosophy" the legislator of the empire. Joseph undertook to reduce the power of the clergy, nobles, and chartered towns throughout the empire. This assault on privilege was the reflection both of his personal enlightenment and of his desire to increase the state's vitality and power. Deliberately bypassing the provincial diets, the defenders of privileged interests, he divided the realm into administrative districts supervised directly from Vienna. He had the civil and penal laws codified for application to all subjects alike. In conformity with the Enlightenment's humanitarianism, these codes substantially reduced the number of capital offenses.

The Habsburg dynasty had identified itself with an intolerant Roman Catholicism. Joseph turned this traditional policy upside down.

In general he sought to bring the Church under state control. The Jesuits, who operated directly under papal authority, were expelled. Papal bulls now required the approval of the emperor, and the clergy had to take an oath of allegiance to him.

To Protestants and Jews, Joseph extended toleration of private worship, but his enlightenment was not sufficient to tolerate Deists and atheists. Revenues taken from the Church were assigned to a system of free compulsory state education, to charity, and to newly founded medical facilities at Vienna. Catholic reaction to "Josephism" was severe; in the Austrian Netherlands it was the core of a revolution designed to frustrate the Emperor's policies.

In order to protect her source of taxes from the peasantry, Maria Theresa had curbed the nobility's power to increase their receipts from the peasants. Joseph went much further. He tried to emancipate all peasants from the remnants of serfdom. Surveys by his officials indicated that peasants had been paying about 73 per cent of their gross incomes to Church, landlord, and state. Joseph proposed reducing it to 30 per cent. But when he attempted to implement these reforms, the privileged

PARTITIONS OF POLAND

orders resisted with force. He utterly failed to free the peasants under noble and clerical lords.

The Emperor's policy toward the peasantry was part of a more comprehensive general economic reform, which entailed restriction of the guilds, reduction of industrial controls, and the removal of internal trade barriers.

As a theory of government, enlightened despotism was predicated on the prince's absolute sovereignty, his ability to alter society by edict. To execute his reforms, Joseph needed an immensely larger bureaucracy than he possessed, and one more committed to his goals than were the aristocrats who filled most of the important official posts of his government. No supply of such men existed. Even had they been available, it is unlikely that they would have succeeded, for the Emperor simply lacked the power and public support to decree and implement the overturn of existing privileges and property relationships. In 1790 he died a disillusioned man. His adminis-

The "revolutionary emperor," Joseph II.

trative reorganization, legal codification, emancipation of the peasants on the royal domains, and his stimulus to medical research in Vienna survived the aristocratic counterattack that followed. But his brother-successor, Leopold II, former enlightened despot of Tuscany, was forced to cancel most of Joseph's other changes.

Frederick II, 1740 to 1786

Frederick II of Prussia was more the heir than the builder of an efficient bureaucratic absolutism. Most of his "enlightened" reforms were simply continuations of his predecessors' policies. This is not to say, however, that he was not a child of the Enlightenment.

From the French Enlightenment Frederick appropriated a completely secular at-

titude toward life. Neither religious nor political passions had a legitimate place. Revealed religion he held to be an "absurd system of fables," but his Protestant state was tolerant rather than anticlerical. Moreover, he also denied that the state was the personal property of the dynasty; rather, it was something above and beyond both king and people, something to which they owed their lives and fortunes.

Reason was to order state, church, society, economics, and high policy. But for Frederick the rule of reason was severe, a deterministic providence that made statesmen and soldiers stoic marionettes. Their duty was not to humanity in general but to the concrete historical state. Self-interest, not international agreements, determined the relationships between these states. "The fundamental principle of great states at any time," he wrote, "is to subordinate all in order to expand their own power without ceasing." In 1740, therefore, he felt secure in invading Silesia without diplomatic preparations or alliances, because he calculated that the self-interests of the other states would force them either to join him or to accept the outcome. State power, not individual well-being, was his overriding concern, though he tended to see the latter as realizable only through the former. In a real sense, his enlightened ideas were secularizations of the religious doctrines of church, state, and society that had prevailed during the religious wars. The one great exception was his hostility to enthusiasm and emotional passion. His regime was founded on a rational royalism; violence was to be constrained by reason, the reason of state.

He distrusted and despised all men as hopelessly depraved. Only the nobility was partially redeemed by virtue of its military valor and relative detachment from selfish worldly concerns.

Frederick's redefinition of enlightened values did not prevent him from collecting leading European intellectuals at Sans Souci, his palace at Potsdam, in an attempt

Jean-Honoré Fragonard, The Swing, *1766–69. Bored by a surfeit of elegance, the courts of Louis XV and XVI amused themselves by pretending to emulate the simple lives of ordinary folk. Thus this lady, costumed as a shepherdess, floats in her velvet-cushioned swing above a mock-rustic landscape. But such frivolous play bore little resemblance to peasant life, and not even the life of the aristocrat was always so idyllic in prerevolutionary France. (Scala, Courtesy of the Wallace Collection, London)*

Tapestry designed by Charles Le Brun, Entrevue de Louis XIV et de Philippe IV dans l'Ile des Faisans, *1665–80. The monarchs of France and Spain, accompanied by their entourages, meet just before the marriage of Louis XIV (at the left) to Princess Marie Thérèse of Spain, a union contracted under a peace treaty between their two countries. The pomp of this gathering underlines the remoteness of the nobility from the lives of the populace in the Age of Absolutism. (Luc Joubert, Courtesy of Collection Mobilier Nationale, Paris)*

Anacète Lemonnier, The Salon of Madame Geoffrin, 1814. *In the Age of Enlightenment, French intellectuals often gathered in the drawing rooms of socially prominent or accomplished women, like Mme. Geoffrin, to discuss current ideas and events. Here the actor Le Kain reads before an audience including Rousseau and Diderot, a group in sharp contrast to the one above in its devotion to humanitarianism, freedom, and reason. (Giraudon, Courtesy of Musée des Beaux Arts, Rouen)*

Jan Vermeer, A Little Street, *1655–60. Stimulated by her recently won independence from Spain, Holland in the Baroque period developed a solid, prosperous middle class. The house shown in this peaceful view of a street in Delft has been identified as a hostel for old women, one of many such institutions established by the civic-minded burghers. Paintings like this were often produced for sale to wealthy bourgeois who wished to display their new-won prosperity. (Rijksmuseum, Amsterdam)*

Joseph Wright of Derby, The Orrery, *ca. 1765. In an age noted for its scientific achievements, eighteenth-century England made great strides in astronomy and physics. Here a group spanning several generations regards a model of the solar system. Perhaps the children represent a new generation which will penetrate the mysteries of outer space. Or perhaps the viewers are meant to symbolize the ages of man, of momentary duration when compared with the life of the planets. (Derby Art Gallery, Derby)*

Louis Le Nain, Return from Hay-making, *1641. The simple rural life so frivolously play-acted by the French nobility was in truth a hard existence, with much poverty and few pleasures. In this portrait family groups, in a moment of relaxation after the day's work, appear joyless, yet have a serenity and wholesomeness lacking in their upper-class imitators. Their lives were soon to be transformed by the Industrial Revolution. (Musée du Louvre, Paris)*

A Coal Mine in the 1790's, *artist unknown. As a result of heavy concentrations of coal mines and iron foundries, the Industrial Revolution brought blight to much of the pastoral countryside of western and northern England. The placid landscape shown here is already undergoing destructive changes. The huge scale of the machinery in relation to the human figures suggests the difficulty of man's struggle against domination by the machine. (Walker Art Gallery, Liverpool)*

to make his court the literary and scientific center of Europe. His closest intellectual ties were with the continental rationalists, but for forty years he maintained contact with Voltaire. Although punctuated with quarrels, his patronage of the great *philosophe* enhanced his reputation, for Voltaire gave him favorable publicity as a beacon of light in the midst of clerical obscurantists.

The king displayed phenomenal energy as he conducted journeys of inspection (often incognito) and issued reports and instructions that flowed down to every level of his bureaucratic machine.

In economic policy, Frederick made no breach in the mercantilistic tradition of his predecessors. His main concern, like theirs, was to raise revenues for the army. He retained the tightly administered system of exploiting revenues from the royal domains, which in Prussia were very extensive. But his wars consumed far more revenues than the Hohenzollern lands produced.

In addition to military industries, the state threw its weight behind the production of luxuries such as silk and porcelain. In 1765 the government founded a bank to finance new industries. Monopolies were established for colonial products that were particularly in demand, such as coffee and tobacco. The acquisition of Silesia added a territory rich in textiles, iron, lead, and coal. Some of these industries, especially luxuries, continued to grow. By 1783 Prussia was exporting about one third of its manufactures.

Prussian agriculture did not undergo an "agricultural revolution" comparable to that of England in the eighteenth century. Customary methods of farming and land tenure were little touched.

Because revenues continued to flow into the treasury and because Prussia became an exporting state, Frederick's mercantilism has generally been considered a marked success. The growth of population from about 2 million to 6 million, partly as a result of conquest, is often cited to demonstrate the point. There is, however, another side to the coin, one which indicates that Prussia was headed toward a major social-economic crisis.

State capitalism and bureaucratic paternalism crowded out individual enterprise at every level. Because state taxes were heavy and the landed aristocracy was largely exempt, peasant and urban incomes were sharply reduced by taxes, which left little capital for productive investment. Frederick proposed the emancipation of the peasants, whom he sympathetically described as "the beasts of burden of human society," but like Joseph II he could free only those on the royal domains.

Probably sustained by high-priced colonial commodities such as sugar and the cultivation of potatoes, the population, however, increased rapidly. Between 1757 and 1805 births are estimated to have exceeded deaths by 30 per cent. Silesia grew especially fast in spite of major famines during the 1770s. Pressure of youth upon "places" in society hit all classes. Those in positions of power within the bureaucracy responded to this population pressure by forcefully maintaining the traditional social order. But Prussia's disinherited "surplus population," which plagued other states of the Old Regime also, provided one of the dynamic social forces behind the revolutionary and romantic assault on reason in the following generation.

Unlike Joseph II, Frederick did not attempt to alter the distribution of wealth, power, and privilege. On the contrary, he gave the nobility more authority in the bureaucracy than it possessed under his predecessors. The law code he ordered compiled preserved intact the social order of three estates. The nobles' accrual of power within the bureaucracy enabled them to resist basic reforms. When Frederick died childless and with no one trained to succeed him, decay set in. The reign of Frederick William II (1786–1797) was one of reaction against the Enlightenment. Fundamental reform awaited the shock of Napoleonic invasions.

Catherine II: despot, enlightened or otherwise.

Russian peasant family at the time of Catherine the Great.

Catherine II

After Peter the Great's death, Western influences had continued to affect the narrow intellectual circles at the court, the nobility, and the bureaucracy. Through foreign travel, tutors, and literature they became attached to French culture, rococo art, and the writings of the *philosophes*. On no one did the Enlightenment seem to make a deeper impression than on the obscure German princess who became the slighted wife of Peter III. Upon his removal and murder in 1762, she became Catherine II, Empress of Russia.

The climax of her enlightened idealism came in setting forth an Instruction for a convention called in 1767 to prepare the way for a new codification of Russian law. Justifying autocracy but adopting the principle that "people do not exist for the ruler, but the ruler for the people," the Instruction borrowed most of its contents from Montesquieu and Beccaria. Among other things, it advocated equality before and freedom under the law. It denounced torture and serfdom and criticized the concentration of ownership of large estates in a few hands.

This convention, the first real Russian deliberative assembly, represented all social classes except serfs under private landlords, which were about half the population. But as a vehicle for translating Catherine's intentions into concrete proposals, it was a dismal failure. Long sessions repeatedly failed to achieve agreement on particulars. Noble delegates construed "freedom" to authorize their extension of power over the peasantry and denounced critics of serfdom as "traitors to their class." Townsmen interpreted "equality" to mean their equality with nobles in sharing privileges such as the holding of serfs. In 1768, long after she herself had ceased to take it seriously, its sessions were suspended. By 1774 its committees ceased to meet. Apart from stirring up discussion of controversial subjects, the convention had no practical significance.

To portray Catherine as a faithful executrix of the Enlightenment would be to distort the major weight of her reign's significance for Russian development. She was more concerned with an aggressive foreign policy than with the worsening condition of most of her subjects' lives. As avidly enthusiastic for Machiavelli as for the *philosophes,* she adopted the traditional Russian political system of intrigue among favorites. Had she been sincerely and primarily devoted to enlightened principles, it is difficult to see how she could have carried out reforms and kept power. As a matter of practical politics, she was dependent upon an ascendant nobility for provincial and local government.

Instead of ameliorating the deep social ills of Russian society, Catherine legitimized and extended them. The nobles secured confirmation of their gains during the previous half century in a Letter of Grace of 1785. It constituted them henceforth as "an estate . . . separated by its rights and privileges from the rest of the people." Exempted from military service, personal taxation, and corporal punishment, they were confirmed in their rights to buy and sell land freely, to trade, and to operate mines and factories. To the hereditary nobility was given the exclusive privilege of owning serfs, a privilege which was becoming the foundation of Russian society and its chief curse.

Despite the state's interest in the serf as the principal source of taxes, the serf became almost a chattel slave. Not only was the lord his overseer, tax collector, and landlord, to whom he owed undefined amounts of labor and fees, but the lord (or his bailiff) also served as policeman, judge, jury, and sometimes (as a result of beatings) executioner. With this boundless power, lords eroded peasants' rights to the use of the land. While exactions in labor and fees were increased, peasants' appeals to the government were forbidden by law. Individual lords were forbidden to emancipate their serfs, who on occasion were detached from their land and sold at increasing prices at public auction.

If the peasants believed that rebellion would lead to amelioration, the complete failure of the massive and powerful Pugachev Rebellion (1773–1775) taught them otherwise. Pugachev's suppression firmly reestablished noble superiority and snuffed out all further thought of reform. As servitude was riveted on the peasants, the social distance between peasant and noble increased. And as social dualism increased, this Frenchified nobility lost its sense of reality. Unproductive administrators, often living in towns as absentee landlords, they denied social improvement or migration to the serfs and by their economic and trading privileges hindered the growth of the tiny indigenous middle class. At Catherine's death, the urban population constituted not more than 4 per cent of the total population. The path of gradual change was thus virtually closed on the eve of the gigantic population increase that was to come during the nineteenth century.

Enlightened Despotism in the Lesser States

The major states had no monopoly of enlightened despots. Indeed, the chances for their success seemed to have been greater in smaller states that had neither the resources nor the desire to become embroiled in major wars. A notable instance is Charles III of Spain.

From 1759 to 1788 he made Spain the seat of a reform movement designed to revive Spanish power. Hindering both centralization of secular authority and reform were the Inquisition and the Roman Catholic clergy. Charles curbed both, centralized his administration in a council of state, proclaimed economic reforms, and attempted, with only small success, to break the landholding monopoly of nobles

Flogging of a Russian peasant.

William Pitt the Elder (Earl of Chatham), 1708–1778. Haughty, autocratic, ambitious, high-minded, he presided over England's rise to fortune and victory over France, 1756–1761.

and clergy. But Charles did revitalize Spanish power in Europe and the New World. In Germany the dukes of Baden and Saxe-Weimar followed such formulas, giving some slight roots to German liberalism and the basis for a cultural renaissance, involving such important literary figures as Johann Gottfried von Herder and Johann Wolfgang von Goethe.

The Collapse of Absolutism and the Rise of Democratic Movements in the Maritime States

Enlightened despotism was one of two major responses to the resurgent aristocracy during the eighteenth century. With varying degrees of success, enlightened despots contended with aristocrats in agrarian kingdoms whose commerce and industry were relatively backward. In the more commercially developed societies, espe-cially in the Atlantic maritime states, a different evolution led to the second response: demands for the democratization of political institutions and the social structure. In Britain's older North American Colonies, where semidemocratic institutions were indigenous, this movement became overtly revolutionary after the Seven Years' War. In Britain itself, democratic elements sought means short of revolution to reverse the growing oligarchical trend of British institutions, especially the English and Irish parliaments. There were also democratic movements that led to open revolution in Geneva and the Low Countries. Except for the American Revolution, whose success was due partly to the diplomatic alignment of Europe, all of these movements failed. As events proved, however, France had developed the potential for the most significant of the revolutionary democratic movements.

The Failure of the Democratic Movement in Great Britain

Walpole's fall in 1742 brought no change in the methods he had used to manage Parliament. Backed by the Duke of Newcastle, his successors disposed of proposed reforms as easily as he had done. Charges of corruption were widespread, but no reform in the parliamentary system occurred until after the Seven Years' War.

This delay came in part because discontented elements pinned their faith on William Pitt, a prophet of empire, and on war with France, all of which detracted from interest in reform. As early as 1746 Pitt considered proposals to conquer Canada and to ruin French commerce. Under his direction in the Seven Years' War, Britain carried the day in one theater of war after another: North America, India, North Africa, and on the seas in general. The trade and the industry that supplied Britain flourished as the victories mounted. While British debts, taxes, and nationalistic fervor grew, Pitt would not make peace. After his resignation in 1761 over the question of the conduct of the war, that task was undertaken by Newcastle on terms that Pitt denounced as too lenient. Although the peace was unpopular in London, it gave the small but vocal movement for parliamentary reform a new impetus.

Further impetus came from the dissatisfaction of the people with the long period of government weakness and embarrassment in foreign affairs from the early 1760s to the late 1780s. The British were divided on the justice of the war with the colonists, a war that England entered without allies. This situation resulted in the temporary coincidence of two separate reform movements which produced a near revolution in Britain in 1780. One, largely within Parliament, sought to strip the crown of its control over "placemen" (that is, those who enjoyed the benefits of government patronage) in the House of Commons, while making no concessions to democratic control over the House. The other, mainly outside of Parliament, aimed to make the House of Commons more representative of the population.

The extraparliamentary movement was led by radicals from the new industrial bourgeoisie. Many of them were religious dissenters who were being discriminated against under the present system. While the decadent universities were firmly wed to things as they were, dissenting academies taught science, economics, and history, as well as rational religion and more modern approaches to new social problems. Joseph Priestley, chemist and founder of modern Unitarianism, and Richard Price, later to be a target of Edmund Burke's polemics for teaching the doctrine of natural rights, were among their teachers and leaders. Literate men, whose practical and political interests were not served by parliamentary representation as then constituted, also formed technical societies, clubs, and workingmen's associations, which joined in the campaign to democratize Parliament.

Early popular discontent with Parliament's oligarchy centered around the personality of John Wilkes, a townsman of recent wealth who founded a newspaper, the *North Briton*, in 1762. When it attacked Bute's "ministerial despotism" with a more than merely implied slap at the king himself, the crown tried to suppress it by arresting Wilkes, a member of Parliament, and the paper's staff. The courts declared the general warrants on which Wilkes and his associates were arrested illegal, but Parliament expelled him.

The townsmen continued to reelect Wilkes to Parliament, but it was not until he had been elected mayor of London and had put Parliament under public scrutiny by publishing (for the first time and with the city's support) the debates of Parliament that he was finally seated. His bill for universal manhood suffrage failed, but his effort was symbolic of the trend toward democracy.

British democrats saw in the American Revolution many of the same elements of the fight they were waging at home. One Major Cartwright, for example, refused to serve in America and proposed home rule for the Colonies and thorough democratization of Parliament. When the popular reform movement organized local "associations" and called for a national General Association, a representative body that might rival and perhaps even displace Parliament, it alarmed parliamentary Whigs and country gentlemen alike. In 1780 the Association Movement, which had its counterpart among Protestants in Ireland, was badly compromised by the Gordon riots in London.* Ignited by mild but extremely unpopular parliamentary concessions to Roman Catholics and by lower class frustrations, these riots destroyed sections of unpoliced London. More destructive of property than any single episode during the

---

* Named after an eccentric Scotsman, Lord George Gordon, the riots followed his presentation of a petition to the House of Commons protesting reduction of penalties against Roman Catholics.

Mob firing Newgate Prison during the Gordon Riots.

French Revolution in Paris, the Gordon riots revealed the latent violence at the bottom of Britain's social order. It also demonstrated the gulf between the lower classes themselves and the would-be reformers of Parliament, for Priestley's house was destroyed and Wilkes tried to quiet the disturbance.

After the Association Movement petered out, bills to reform Parliament also failed. Between 1782 and 1785 the younger Pitt introduced a series of bills to redistribute parliamentary seats and to broaden the suffrage. They failed without exception.

The only successful reform was the parliamentary one for which Edmund Burke was spokesman. And its success weakened the executive still further. He introduced bills that reduced some corruption by barring certain placemen and contractors from sitting in Commons. These measures weakened the executive but did not democratize the legislature. Threatened by a new and radical urban society, Whig and Tory lords drew together to preserve their own power. But they relied upon their own control of Parliament, not on the authority of an absolute monarch, to secure that goal. Burke himself, although sympathetic to the American Revolution, now turned to defending the existing British constitution as perfection itself.

The American Revolution

Meanwhile the thirteen mainland colonies of Great Britain in North America succeeded in breaking free from the Empire. Only those colonies which had been most successful in transplanting European populations and civilization overseas were involved. In 1700 they had a population of 200,000. By mid-century there were nearly two million in these thirteen colonies. Over two thirds of them were native-born, and their birth rate was prodigious. In Philadelphia, New York, and Boston they possessed commercial cities of significance. In the middle and northern Colonies shipbuilding, distilling, and commerce, including the slave trade, flourished.

The growing Colonial self-confidence assured that if the Empire were to remain a harmonious body, constitutional means of resolving divergent interests within it would have to be found. Before 1775 Americans had based their resistance to unpopular British enactments on their rights as Englishmen guaranteed by local charters and grants. Thus they defended themselves as part of the corporate structure of the British constitution.

Within the colonies a struggle developed between debtors and creditors, orthodox and nonconformists, and frontier and tidewater interests. For reasons that varied in different colonies, discontented elements challenged the commercial, family, and religious oligarchies whose control over government and its spoils mitigated the democratizing effect of broad suffrage. During the decade of discontent that preceded the American Revolution, part of the Colonial leadership (the radicals or patriots) came to espouse separation from Britain as a necessary step in the realization of their own goals.

The Colonial Rift with Britain, 1763 to 1775

As a result of the experience of the Seven Years' War, the British policy of "salutary neglect" gave way to a "new imperial policy." The financial needs of England had multiplied so radically as a consequence of the war that Parliament demanded that the colonists share the administrative and military expenses of the Empire. Regulations and revenue collections were now strictly enforced after a long period of laxity. Money was in short supply just as taxes and customs were raised; the lucrative trade with the West Indies was curtailed, further aggravating the money shortage; the colonists were not allowed to print or mint money to alleviate the shortage of specie; troops, stationed on the Indian frontier, were to be financed by the colonists; and with the French cleared out beyond the Appalachians, the colonists' access to the frontier was restricted by British Indian policies. While the Americans did not actually suffer financially, since some of the new taxes were simply evaded, the many revenue schemes of Parliament were taken as occasion for loud complaint and for serious constitutional debates. The Stamp Act Congress denounced "taxation without representation." Pressure was put on the English by means of boycotts of English trade. Resistance (mainly nonviolent but occasionally violent) angered some British, impressed others. It was the angry response of the British government to Colonial harassments that touched off the war for American Independence.

In 1775 the radicals gained control of the Second Continental Congress, which met to organize Colonial resistance. Within individual Colonies they carried out revolutions that produced state constitutions curtailing executive authority, curbing existing oligarchies, and providing bills of rights. Their campaign for independence was reinforced by the writings of Thomas Paine, a recent radical immigrant from England who there had agitated unsuccessfully for reform of the British constitution. The success of the radicals became clear when the Second Continental Congress opened American ports and adopted the Declaration of Independence. The Declaration, drafted by Jefferson, invoked a natural universal right of revolution whenever existing governments persistently trampled on the natural rights of the governed to life, liberty, and the pursuit of happiness. To demonstrate the Revolution's legitimacy, the Declaration attributed to George III a long list of tyrannical acts. In reality, Parliament was primarily responsible for them. Those abusive acts represented a breach of contract and justified the American rebellion.

Powers accorded to the Revolutionary Congress reflected the radicals' opposition to any central government, British or American, possessing power to tax or regulate commerce. The same was true of the Articles of Confederation, which operated as the first American constitution between 1781 and 1789. The radicals devoted their

A Colonial antidote for Loyalists.

attention largely to the state governments whose failure to cooperate fully had made the Continental Congress' task of prosecuting the war reminiscent of Britain's experience during the French and Indian War.

The Achievement of American Independence

After the revolutionary fervor abated, state constitutions were rewritten more in accordance with the British past. They incorporated stronger executive power and devices to insulate part of the government from direct popular control. The states' failure to restore confiscated Loyalist estates in accordance with treaty commitments seemed a dangerous precedent for property relationships. In several states, sharp conflicts between factions of debtor-farmers and creditor-merchants broke out. By 1787 conservative and national forces joined hands to replace the Articles of Confederation with a new constitution, which provided for a federal government wielding the power of taxation, controlled

Louis XV's influential mistress, the Marquise de Pompadour, by Boucher.

commerce, and protected property from expropriation in the future without due process of law.

Although the drafters of the Constitution of 1787 were obliged to compromise with advocates of a bill of rights defining individual and states' rights against the central government, the new instrument represented a mild resurgence of conservatism. Nevertheless, American conservatism had been weakened by the permanent exclusion of the Loyalists, who found new homes in Canada, England, or elsewhere. Finally, the Constitution's espousal of popular sovereignty made it a distinctly radical document. It was, after all, the product of a democratic revolution, a precedent that soon inspired other revolutions.

The Failure of French Absolutism, 1743 to 1786

The difficulties of the British government at home and abroad were matched by a more gradual, but in the long run even more serious, disorganization of royal government in France. After the competent but superannuated Fleury died in 1743, Louis XV took personal charge of the government but without giving it direction. Affairs of state drifted during the decades from 1743 to the early 1770s. For the king, these were years of growing unpopularity. His personal lassitude and disinterest in governmental and administrative affairs introduced a creeping paralysis into the central government, and he was particularly vulnerable to the charge that his mistress, the Marquise de Pompadour, an upstart commoner, was manipulating decisions and appointments behind the scenes. His administration was obstructed by the *parlements* while their members, armed with Montesquieu's aristocratic arguments, raked him for tyranny. In such attacks they appealed to the nation over and above the king and presented themselves as its true representatives. In actuality, they represented the old hierarchical and corporate structure of the privileged orders of French society, which commercialization was steadily undermining and whose legal safeguards Louis' ministers were beginning to dismantle.

Louis XVI (1774–1793), an affable man, had the good sense to appoint able ministers of finance, such as Turgot, Necker, and Calonne, but not the wisdom to keep them. Turgot, a Physiocrat, tried from 1774 to 1776 to abolish the exemptions of the clergy and nobility from a new single tax on land and to curb the waste and corruption that allowed half the revenues collected to find their way into private hands. The steps he was taking might have saved the situation in the long run if Louis had been strong enough to resist the offended privileged orders and to keep Turgot in office. His successor, Necker, before being dismissed in 1781, published an explanation of the budget, *Account Rendered to the King,* which tried to be optimistic about the government's finances, but actually damaged the monarchy by revealing to the public the tremendous sums spent by the king on gifts and pensions to the parasitic court nobility. His successors, notably Calonne, tried various expedients to save the government of Europe's richest state from bankruptcy. Failing to secure consent to increased but also more equitable taxation from the *parlements,* clergy, and nobility, their efforts were doomed. The rapidly deepening financial crisis proved to be the undoing of the Bourbons' nominal absolutism, for it enabled the ascendant privileged orders to make a revolutionary assault on royal authority in the years after 1786.

For the years ahead, both the American Revolution and the phenomenon of enlightened despotism presented alternative solutions to the problems of eighteenth-century political and social life. In their different ways, both had the same objective: the strengthening of the secular power of the state to overcome the power of tra-ditional corporate "intermediate bodies" between the state and the individual.

Eighteenth-century experience indicated that without fundamental alterations in the nature of society itself, something which enlightened despots were unwilling to consider, governments had little ability to legislate basic changes in the distribution of power and prestige.

But in contrast to enlightened despotism, the parliamentary reform movement in England and the American Revolution were on courses that would reconcile greater individual liberty and initiative with stronger government based on legal equality and the active consent of the governed.

SELECTED READINGS

Anderson, M. S., *Europe in the Eighteenth Century 1713–1783,* Holt, Rinehart, and Winston, New York, 1961.

  Up-to-date textbook written as comparative history.

*Barber, Elinor G., *The Bourgeoisie in Eighteenth-Century France,* Princeton University Press, Princeton, 1955. Paperback, 1967.

  An analysis of social stratification of pre-revolutionary France. Good for indicating bourgeois imitation of the nobility but becomes prisoner of its preconceived social theories.

Blum, Jerome, *Lord and Peasant in Russia from the Ninth to the Nineteenth Century,* Princeton University Press, Princeton, 1961.

  An authoritative history of the Russian peasant in the bondage that reached its apogee in the eighteenth century.

*Brunn, Geoffrey, *The Enlightened Despots,* Holt, New York, 1929.

  Brief, comprehensive summary well suited for the beginning student.

*Dorn, Walter L., *Competition for Empire, 1740–1763,* Harper and Brothers, New York and London, 1940, and a Harper Torchbook.

Asterisk (*) denotes paperback.

Comprehensive account of the renewed power struggle; well balanced between colonial and continental rivalries; also excellent on the thought of the Enlightenment.

*Ford, Franklin L., *Robe and Sword, the Regrouping of the French Aristocracy after Louis XIV,* Harvard University Press, Cambridge, 1953, and a Harper Torchbook.
Demonstrates the growing community of interest between the two major branches of the French nobility during the eighteenth century.

*Gershoy, Leo, *From Despotism to Revolution, 1763–1789,* Harper and Brothers, New York, 1944, and a Harper Torchbook.
One of the best accounts in English; part of the Rise of Modern Europe series.

*Gipson, Lawrence H., *The Coming of the Revolution 1763–1775,* Harper and Brothers, New York, 1954.
Presents the origins of the American revolution from the point of view of the British Empire.

Gooch, George P., *Maria Theresa and Other Studies,* Longmans, Green, London and New York, 1951.
One of the author's several biographical studies of the period, which tend to be rather old-fashioned.

*Goodwin, Albert, ed., *The European Nobility in the Eighteenth Century,* A. and C. Black, London, 1953, and a Harper Torchbook.
Studies of the nobility in each of the major states showing that "enlightened despots" in Eastern Europe actually favored the nobility.

Kluchevsky, V. O., *A History of Russia,* translated by C. J. Hogarth, 5 volumes, Russell and Russell, New York, 1960.
Volume V relates to the reign of Catherine II; particularly clear in establishing serfdom as the basic social institution of Russia.

Lindsay, J., ed., *The Old Regime, 1713–1763,* Vol. VII, *The New Cambridge Modern History,* Cambridge University Press, Cambridge, 1957.
Thorough reference work particularly good for diplomatic and general military developments.

Link, Edith M., *The Emancipation of the Austrian Peasant 1740–1798,* Columbia University Press, New York, 1949.
Critical for an understanding of peasant conditions in Central Europe and for the aims of Joseph II.

Namier, Lewis B., *England in the Age of the American Revolution,* 2nd ed., St. Martin's Press, New York, 1961, and

———, *The Structure of Politics at the Accession of George III,* 2nd ed., Macmillan, London; St. Martin's Press, New York, 1957.
Detailed analyses of British political life that focus on the personal connections of its factions.

*Ogg, David, *Europe of the Ancien Régime 1715–1783,* Harper and Row, New York, 1965.
A new conventional history distinguished by its recognition of geographic factors in political and economic developments.

Palmer, Robert R., *The Age of the Democratic Revolution, A Political History of Europe and America 1760–1800,* Vol. I, *The Challenge,* Princeton University Press, Princeton, 1959.
Sets forth lucidly the consolidation of aristocratic power against which both democrats and enlightened despots contended.

Pares, Richard, *War and Trade in the West Indies, 1739–1763,* F. Cass, London, 1963.
The standard account of the subject.

Petrie, C. A., *Diplomatic History, 1713–1933,* Hollis and Carter, London, 1946.
A manual of diplomatic events that sketches the balance of power in the eighteenth century.

*Plumb, J. H., *England in the Eighteenth Century,* Penguin Books, Baltimore, Md., 1950.
A social, cultural, and technological summary by the leading biographer of Robert Walpole and the elder Pitt.

Priestley, Herbert I., *France Overseas through the Old Regime: A Study of European Expansion,* Appleton-Century-Crofts, New York and London, 1939.
A survey from the beginning of the French empire through Napoleon.

Reddaway, W. H., *et al.,* eds., *The Cambridge History of Poland,* Vol. II, The University Press, Cambridge, 1941.

The major large-scale study of Poland in the English language edited by a major contributor to the history of the eighteenth century.

*Roberts, Penfield, *The Quest for Security, 1715–1740,* Harper and Brothers, New York, 1947, and a Harper Torchbook.
    A basic study of the oligarchical politics of stability in the Rise of Modern Europe series.

Thomson, Gladys Scott, *Catherine the Great and the Expansion of Russia,* The Universities Press, London, 1959.
    Short, readable and scholarly treatment of Russia under an "enlightened despot" in the Teach Yourself History series.

Williams, Basil, *The Whig Supremacy, 1714–1760,* Clarendon Press, Oxford, 1936.
    A competent survey in the Oxford History of England series.

Wilson, A. M., *French Foreign Policy during the Administration of Cardinal Fleury, 1726–1743,* Harvard University Press, Cambridge, 1936.
    A monographic study, one of the few modern scholarly histories of the reign of Louis XV.

See also the works by Boxer, Holborn, and Rosenberg listed at the end of Chapter 16 and the great work on mercantilism by Elie Heckscher cited at the end of Chapter 15.

NATIONALISM, INDUSTRIALISM, SCIENTISM

19

A Generation of Revolution,
1787 to 1815

We saw in Chapter 18 that the second half of the eighteenth century was characterized by a three-way division of contending forces. Kings and ministers, in the best tradition of enlightened despotism, sought to preserve their deteriorating positions and even to deprive the opposition of its grievances by reform programs. Broader in base, and relying on historic claims to an exalted place in the constitution were the aristocratic groups. These "constituted bodies" sought not only to dominate reform movements, but also to protect their privileges against despot and democrat alike. The third party was composed of democrats in the political sense only—men usually of relatively high social standing (lawyers, bureaucrats, journalists, teachers, businessmen) who sought to broaden existing political institutions. Although these "democrats" were not all middle-class, they usually came from the elite of the Third Estate, which was below the ranks of clergy and nobility. In France and elsewhere, they suffered from inexperience in politics, but enjoyed high expectations of participation.

From the vantage point of 1815, it is difficult to assess the exact roles of these three great factions. The subjugation of the most expansionist and revolutionary power (France) by a congress of states dedicated to Christian, legitimate monarchy (Austria, Prussia, Russia, and England) would seem to indicate that counterrevolution had triumphed. Yet within each nation the revolutionary virus had left an infection. Below the level of courts and ministers, institutions had changed, especially the bureaucracies and the military establishments. The map of Europe, particularly of Germany, had been redrawn. A new spirit of national self-determination and pride in lingual and cultural achievement had arisen to shatter the easy cosmopolitanism of the eighteenth century.

The French Revolution, 1787 to 1792

Few events have so greatly disturbed mankind or so fired the imagination as has the French Revolution. Since its occurrence, men have tried in various ways to account for it. Conservative writers have usually argued that the Revolution represented the seizure of power by conspirators who were inspired by evil geniuses such as Rousseau and Voltaire. Radicals have also attributed the Revolution to the deliberate action of a few men. Since 1917, for example, leftists have argued that social leaders, precursors of Lenin, tried to seize power in behalf of the downtrodden masses.

Today, scholars on both sides of the Atlantic hold the deteriorating economic and social conditions in France from about 1770 responsible for the popular unrest that characterized the revolutionary situation. In the 1930s, beginning with the work of such influential professors as Ernest Labrousse and Georges Lefebvre in Paris, historians came to recognize the picture of a nation that was overpopulated for its food supply, in an era of erratic harvests and poor communications, and subject to inflated prices, and in which the relations between landlord and tenant, producer and consumer were strained. After 1786, a full-scale depression set in. By the winter of 1788 to 1789, the landless peasantry was fleeing unemployment in the countryside to join the relief projects of the city,_ while working-class families in Paris were spending almost nine tenths of their budget on bread. The wealthier classes also suffered after 1786. The overt break with the past occurred when Louis XVI and his Finance Minister Calonne tried to forestall the impending crisis with a thorough set of reform measures. Within three years, factions of the nobility and of the common estate were to force their own versions of reform on the nation.

The Revolt of the Nobility

As 1786 came to a close, Louis XVI and his ministers realized that they could no longer ignore the growing state deficit which was well over 100 million livres, almost one fourth of the yearly revenue. The old tax structure, which put the burden so heavily on peasant income and on consumer goods, would stand no further increase in a time of depression. The interest on short-term loans already accounted for almost one half of the royal treasury's payments.

Calonne, the Controller General, proposed a reformation of the tax system very much like that urged by Turgot ten years earlier. The privileged interests had loudly opposed Turgot's reforms. Would Calonne's proposals fare any better? Louis decided to test the matter with the Assembly of Notables, a special advisory group of nobles, Churchmen, and magistrates of the *parlements*. Apparently Louis was willing to undertake reforms if they were approved by the aristocracy. Sympathetic to a certain amount of reform, the Assembly of Notables approved almost all of Calonne's proposals, and the King acted on some of them at once by cutting the army pension list and the queen's expenses. Calonne, however, was dismissed for addressing the Parisian populace on the evils of privilege. The Assembly also discussed other serious reform measures which led to the granting of civil status to Protestants and edicts reforming the *parlements*. A limited revolution was underway, but one that in no sense endangered the privileged system or the traditional order.

While this much was not enough for liberal nobles like Lafayette, it was too much for the members of the *parlements*, who refused to register the new tax edicts. Instead, they called for an Estates General as the only acceptable vehicle for reform.

Hoping to rule without the recalcitrant *parlements*, Louis XVI replaced them in May 1788 with a plenary court that was well-laced with notables. But in the ensuing months the parlementarians had the last word. When the treasury was admitted to be empty in August, 1788, the disgrace of the ministerial solution was complete. The plenary court was abandoned and the *parlements* reinstated. Along with this admission of defeat, the King agreed to call a meeting of the Estates General in May

1789. Traditionalism seemed to have won. If there was to be reform, it would come through the action of a traditional body, the Estates General. This body was composed of representatives of the three estates or status groups: Clergy, Nobility, and Third Estate. Although the Estates General had not met since 1614, the first two of the three represented orders expected to dominate the proceedings as they had done previously. One could therefore expect that the measures agreed upon by that body would express the wishes of the aristocracy.

The Emergence of the Third Estate

The Estates General as the historic form of a national representative body was only a fiction in terms of the French population in 1789. Nobility and clergy totaled about 750,000 members. In previous Estates, each of these orders had enjoyed one of the three votes. Their delegates combined had outnumbered those of the Third Estate. By 1789, the single vote accorded to the commoners was to represent 25,000,-000 men and women. Although the ranks of the nobility and clergy included rich and poor alike, the variation of social classes within the Third was staggering. It may be argued that the sharecropper accepted the judgment of his clerical or noble landlord, and that the wholesale merchant often sought to imitate the titled nobility. Yet bourgeois lawyers, journalists, and other professionals were highly critical of noble privilege and of the venality of the 130 bishops, all of whom were noblemen in 1789. Many businessmen and independent farmers were ambitious for a role in the reform movements in their own localities and within their own Estate.

In the autumn of 1788, Parisian and provincial lawyers attacked the pretensions of the *parlements* and urged the "doubling of the Third," so that the number of commoners' delegates would equal those of

the first two orders together. Press censorship was suspended to allow the nation to advise the King, and a flood of petitions from the cities convinced Louis XVI to accept the principle of double representation.

Elections to the Estates took place in the spring of 1789. Each electoral assembly, even at the lowest levels of guild and country parish, drafted a "notebook of grievances," or *cahier*. In these *cahiers* one finds what the French people wanted on the eve of their great revolution. For this reason the "notebooks of grievances" are among the most important documents of the French Revolution. From their contents we learn that there was broad agreement among the orders on the need to guarantee civil rights and impose fiscal equality. However, the nobility, which elected only a small minority of liberals among its 270 delegates, demanded a return to archaic social practices and the protection of seigneurial (manor lords') rights. The clergy was more clearly divided, because the parish priests outnumbered the bishops five to one. The notebooks of grievances produced by the Third Estate's assemblies, in which the humbler citizens had little influence, displayed great variety in discussing local economic conditions. The commoners occasionally used phrases borrowed from the *philosophes,* went further in their demands for civil liberties and constitutional government, and demanded the surrender of ancient privileges conveyed by birth. Two thirds of the 648 deputies to the order were lawyers or former royal bureaucrats. Only one in seven was a businessman, and one in ten was a country dweller.

When the Estates General met at Versailles on May 5, 1789, the deputies were given little indication that they were to participate in decisions. No reform program was offered to them. The commons found themselves treated as inferiors, left to deliberate as a separate assembly without assurance that they might later

The Oath of the Tennis Court, *by Jacques Louis David. The scene was worth recording, for the decision of these men on June 20, 1789, to stay and face the real issue of making a new government and not to let themselves be intimidated by the King, was a revolutionary act.*

vote by head. For five weeks the commoners urged members of the nobility and clergy to join them in one great assembly. The commoners' determination soon split the clergy, some of whom crossed over to join the Third on June 15. Two days later this already mixed group assumed the title of National Assembly, representing the nation as a whole. If the King were to dissolve their new Assembly, the deputies declared, no taxes would be valid. With this step the constitutional history of France took a new and profound turn. On June 20 the Assembly, finding itself locked out of its hall, retired to the royal tennis court where they took a solemn oath not to disperse until the constitution of the realm should be on a firm foun-

dation. The first great symbolic act of the Revolution was thus consummated; it is immortalized on David's canvas.*

The King did not realize that it was too late to settle the crisis on his own terms. The Third Estate claimed parliamentary immunity and refused to leave the hall. On the next day the majority of the clergy defected, and on the following day almost fifty noblemen walked out on their order. On June 27, Louis reluctantly ordered the remnants of the other orders to merge with the National Assembly. An English traveler who knew France well was moved to write in his diary that "the whole busi-

* Jacques Louis David (1748–1826) was the most famous artist of the Revolution.

ness now seems over, and the revolution complete."[1]

Completion of the Bourgeois Revolt

But the third phase of revolution, that of the politically aware Third Estate, was far from complete. The court party began at once to move troops (including Swiss and German regiments) into the vicinity of Paris, probably not so much to occupy the city as to prepare to dissolve the Assembly. Meanwhile, within the city itself, the electors of the Third Estate remained sitting as an informal new government for Paris, while more daring journalists sought to win over the French Guards from the court. Finally, the city lay in readiness for a typical eighteenth-century urban riot; food prices soared, and the lives of grain merchants and bakers were endangered.

The crisis broke on July 11. At Versailles, Necker was dismissed. In Paris, customs posts were systematically demolished and documents burned. On July 12, the insurrection became more general when groups of marchers forced the royal garrison to withdraw from Paris. The electors quietly took over the city hall and tried unsuccessfully to control the ferment by announcing the formation of a National Guard, a militia for the respectable bourgeoisie. On the morning of July 14, the shortage of arms and gunpowder led the crowds first to an arsenal, where they removed 30,000 muskets, and then across the city to the Bastille. The old fortress for state prisoners was said to be another arms depot. There in the east end of Paris the first bloody act of the Revolution was played out when the governor refused to open the gates. Ninety-eight of the civilian attackers—laborers and master craftsmen for the most part—died at the Bastille. Seven of the defenders were murdered after the

governor capitulated; his head and the mayor's were paraded through the city on pikes.

The Bastille became "the shot heard 'round the world" of 1789. The National Assembly was saved. Louis XVI even journeyed to Paris to recognize the electors as a municipal council, Lafayette as Commander of the National Guard, and the tricolor as the symbol of the new regime in Paris. Necker was recalled, and many ultras of the court, including the two royal brothers, fled the country.

In much of France political power in the cities changed hands in the summer of 1789. The provincial bourgeoisie responded first to Necker's dismissal and then to the Bastille. Although the timing of these urban revolts varied, in most cases a civilian National Guard effectively held the military balance, while a political elite of merchants and lawyers took control. In a few cities the old corporation merely expanded its ranks. Other cities, including Bordeaux, replaced their old governments with the electors of the Third, as Paris had done. Many cities (Dijon, Rouen) installed men new to politics. The primary effect of these changes was to drive out royal officials and weaken the King's authority.

In the countryside, starting in the fall of 1788, there had been sporadic violence and protest against game laws, royal taxes, and feudal dues. After the Bastille fell, waves of rumor affected much of the country. The peasantry envisaged imaginary oppressors—brigands, Poles and Spaniards, aristocrats. The exact relationship between this "Great Fear" and the economic condition of the peasantry is unclear. But it is clear that manorial records and houses were the principal targets of peasant action in 1789. Perhaps the peasants believed that they were carrying out the King's reform program in attacking the seigneurial privileges of the nobility.

Lacking the power to suppress the peasant uprising, the Assembly was obliged to

---

1. Arthur Young, *Travels in France,* London, 1909, p. 182.

Cartoon showing a French peasant holding up the privileged orders. This abuse had to stop.

consider peasant grievances. In an emotional session on the night of August 4, 1789, the liberals led the Assembly in renouncing personal services, hunting rights, seigneurial justice, venality of office, and plural benefices. The National Assembly declared that it had destroyed the entire "feudal system." Its resolutions put an end to the principle of aristocratic privilege in France.

Later in August, the Assembly turned to more positive principles in a virtual preamble to the forthcoming constitution. On August 26, 1789, the Assembly proclaimed the Declaration of the Rights of Man and Citizen. Basically a document of the Third Estate, the Declaration made private property "a sacred and inviolable right" along with freedom of conscience, freedom of press, and freedom of the citizen from arbitrary arrest. Equality in the Declaration meant equality before the law and in eligibility for office. Economic equality and state obligation to the poor were not mentioned. Citizens were invited to take part

in lawmaking, but no specific rights of suffrage were granted. The Declaration was expressed in good eighteenth-century universals. Law was held to be "the expression of the general will," and there were marked similarities to the American Declaration of 1776. For those who idealize history, the French Declaration reads as strong philosophy. For its authors, it prepared a nation for the constitutional changes to come.

The King refused to assent to the August decrees and to the Declaration of the Rights of Man and the Citizen. He refused to change his conception of his role as defender of privilege. But royal obstructionism was dramatically modified after October 5th when a large group of Parisian women marched to Versailles and brought the King and Queen to Paris the next day. Lafayette and the National Guard rode gallantly beside the royal coach. Ten days later the National Assembly joined the royal family in Paris. The revolution was moving swiftly.

The Constitutional Monarchy, 1789 to 1792

The National Assembly

Paris became a city teeming with ideas as the National Assembly worked on the constitution and laws that would codify revolutionary gains and lay the foundations of a bourgeois society. Burgeoning journals of opinion covered the aristocratic (the Swiss Mallet du Pan's *Mercure de France*), the patriotic (Brissot's *Patriote Français*), and the democratic (Marat's *L'Ami du Peuple*). Political clubs, which had sprung up in the cafés of Versailles, now dotted the neighborhood of the Assembly.

Often taking their names from the vacated monasteries and convents in which they met, the clubs reviewed the agenda of the Assembly and sought favorable legislation through petitions. These clubs also covered the political spectrum. The Feuillants were conservative and charged high dues; the Cordeliers were radical and had low dues; between them was the influential Society of the Friends of the Constitution, the famous Jacobin Club, which had nominal dues, an upper-middle-class membership, and about 400 provincial affiliates. A young provincial lawyer who had become a Parisian journalist, Maximilian Robespierre, belonged to this group.

More than 200 clergy and 50 nobles sat in the National Assembly. Nevertheless, the electoral arrangements were, at least on first glance, quite liberal. Citizens were divided into "actives" and "passives." The vote in primary assemblies was reserved for active citizens—males of age 25 or over who were domiciled for a year and paid a direct tax equivalent to three-days' wages. This primary electorate of about 4¼ million, or two thirds of the adult males, was by far the largest in Europe.

In economic policy, the Assembly's bourgeois character was more evident. The landlord's dues were upheld, unless the peasant could disprove their validity with documents. The redemption price of dues was high, at least twenty times the annual cash payment. Most sharecroppers and landless laborers remained unaffected, and probably a majority of peasant leaseholders simply refused to pay any compensation. The establishment of unitary metric weights and measures and the abolition of internal customs and monopolistic trading companies suited private commerce. The prohibition of all forms of association by employers and employees in June 1791 (the Chapelier Law) was designed to prevent political agitation, but such zealous liberalism pleased manufacturers more than workingmen. The end of the corporate regime was most clearly signaled by the abolition of titles and hereditary nobility.

The National Assembly revealed its concern for rationality more than its class interests in redrawing the map of France.

Eighty-three departments, which were approximately equal in size and were named after natural phenomena, replaced the unequal historic provinces. Each department was subdivided into districts, but the real foundation of local government lay in the communes, in which active citizens voted directly for councils. France became a federation, in which village and town politics played an especially important part in training men for national life.

Following the suggestions of Montesquieu and the precedent of America, the Assembly separated the judiciary from the executive. *Parlements* and seigneurial courts disappeared and were replaced by tribunals at municipal and departmental levels. Magistrates were compensated for the loss of their offices. Justice was free and equal, and judges and criminal juries were elected.

The replacement of the old fiscal system with a new land tax and income taxes had failed to produce the revenue to meet old debts and current expenditures. The left wing of the Third Estate and many reforming clergymen had singled out the lands of the Catholic Church, estimated now at about 10 per cent of the country's surface, as a potential national resource as early as August 1789. With clerical members leading the way, it was decided in December to sell crown lands and Church property to obtain 400,000,000 livres. These assets would secure an issue of interest-bearing bonds or *assignats*, with which the state could pay off the holders of the long-term debt. The solution proved so attractive that by June of 1790 all Church holdings of rural and urban property were readied for the auction block, while the *assignat* became legal tender. Historians are still tracing the sales of Church property, but it seems evident that the bourgeoisie bought more lands and houses than the peasantry or former nobility. As for the *assignat*, it relieved a currency shortage in 1790, but by the end of 1791 had lost one third of its nominal value. Afterward it depreciated more rapidly.

The Assembly and the Church

The Assembly granted freedom of worship to Protestants and Jews. But lay and clerical members of the Assembly fell into fundamental conflict over the ratification of the new Civil Constitution of the Clergy, which was approved by the King in August 1790. The clergy could not accept the redistribution of parishes and dioceses, the reduction of bishops from 130 to 83 to correspond with the departments, and popular election of bishops and curés without the approval of the Pope or of a national Church synod. When, by November 1790, no such approval seemed possible, the National Assembly declared the Civil Constitution of the Clergy to be in force and required a loyalty oath to the nation from bishops and priests. The confrontation of spiritual and temporal authority was all the more tragic in a nation that was not noted for its religiosity. Only seven bishops took the loyalty oath, and in some parts of the country, especially in Brittany and in Alsace, up to 90 per cent of the priests would not join the new state Church. Pope Pius VI condemned the arrangement in the spring of 1791. The newly elected constitutional clergy was regarded by the devout as blasphemous, and the "nonjurors" or refractory priests were considered by the patriotic to be potential counterrevolutionaries. The refractory priests often led their congregations into deep hostility toward the new regime.

Seeds of Counterrevolution

Other signs of danger had appeared by 1791. Across the border on the east there lived small groups of noblemen including many army officers, who had emigrated from France and were bitterly hostile to the Revolution. The *émigrés* at Turin (Savoy) and Coblentz and Worms (west of the Rhine) were seeking foreign support and even beginning to form a counterrevolutionary army.

It was treason of Louis XVI that broke the precarious balance. The King chose the night of June 20–21, 1791, to flee Paris and to attempt to join up with the *émigré* garrisons over the northeastern frontier. The royal family was detected at Varennes, close to the frontier, and brought ignominiously back to Paris. The King could no longer be seen as a weak monarch with good intentions. His repudiation of the regime very nearly produced his suspension. Varennes had an international effect, too, because the rulers of Austria and Prussia joined in the Declaration of Pillnitz on August 27, 1791, threatening the restoration of the old order in France.

Elsewhere in Europe, the Revolution gained an ambiguous image. Kant, Herder, Wordsworth, Priestley, and the liberal Polish nobility hailed the Revolution with enthusiasm. But those who lamented the confiscation of Church property, the curtailing of royal power, and emigration became bitter enemies. The most famous of these unfriendly observers was the British statesman, Edmund Burke. He was genuinely afraid for the fate of the court and of the clergy by the time he published his *Reflections on the Revolution in France,* in November 1790. Burke's opposition to change in France rested on grounds that have made him one of the pillars of European conservatism. The French experiment was dangerous, irreligious, and bound to fail because it proceeded from abstract principles, he argued. Politics is not a manipulation of contracts, but the indissoluble partnership of succeeding generations in eternal society. The "Rights of Man" were a blind substitution for the experience of the landed, ruling classes. Burke's *Reflections* opened a great debate on the French Revolution, for he was challenged in 1791 by the Anglo-American pamphleteer, Thomas Paine. There were soon self-styled counterrevolutionaries and revolutionaries in Europe.

The Legislative Assembly and the Constitution of 1791

In September 1791, the constitution was presented to the King for his assent, and elections to the new government took place. The unicameral Legislative Assembly, like its predecessor, overrepresented urban areas.

The political elite that was most in evidence was a loose coalition of provincial deputies, known to posterity as the Girondins from the river of their native Bordeaux. Their principal spokesman was the impulsive journalist Brissot. Their inspiration was the imaginative Madame Roland, who yearned to make of revolutionary France another, more virtuous Rome. Brissot and the other Girondins rapidly moved to secure strong measures against refractory clergy and *émigrés,* including death sentences for nobility who assembled against the nation. But it was as war hawks that the Girondins left their mark on revolutionary politics.

The Girondins and the Outbreak of War

Brissot and his friends viewed the idea of a war against France's eastern neighbors, Prussia and Austria, as a crusade to spread revolution against wicked kings. On April 20, 1792, France declared war on Austria. The Emperor's Prussian ally joined him, and Catherine the Great of Russia promised to send troops. As Prussian forces advanced, fear grew and Parisians rioted against rising costs. The King tried to stem the rush of events by using his veto against the plan to bring 20,000 National Guards to Paris to celebrate the "Federation Day" on July 14. Ignoring the royal veto, the Assembly summoned the provincial National Guards to Paris in July. The Marseilles battalion arrived singing a battle hymn that had been written for a northern regiment, but was soon to become a stirring national anthem.

Lafayette as Commander of the National Guard.

In Paris, the National Guards found a militant atmosphere. Poverty began to be equated with virtue, and vice became the inevitable trait of the wealthy. A ringing phrase that summed it up for many Parisians by the summer of 1792 was the famous negative appellation, sans-culotte, that is, he who went without the knee breeches of the upper class. The term was first applied to intransigents after Varennes. It implied contrast with the high bourgeoisie as well as with the nobility. A type of the sans-culotte was the artisan who had no classical education and who saw issues in blacks and whites. He was not represented politically because of the distinction between active and passive citizens, although he was often in attendance at the meetings of the Paris sections, or wards.

By the end of July, 47 of the 48 sections of Paris had come out for the abdication of the King. The Prussian commander only strengthened the Parisians' will when he published a manifesto that threatened summary treatment after he took the city. On the night of August 9–10, 1792, deputies from the sections took over the city government while the Legislative Assembly stood by, paralyzed. Early the next morning, the insurgents marched on the Tuileries (Royal Palace), while the royal family fled to the Assembly.

The Revolution Revolutionized

The August insurrection turned the Parisian government into a revolutionary Commune, which proceeded to imprison many liberal noblemen and clergy as suspects and to assume direction of the war. The Legislative Assembly was shattered when more than half of its members fled Paris. Louis XVI, in reality a condemned man, was suspended by the Assembly's rump and turned over to the Commune for imprisonment. Following Robespierre's aims, the rump announced a National Convention, the deputies to be elected by universal male suffrage. As Lenin was to say many years later after the second upheaval of 1917, the events of August 10, 1792, revolutionized the Revolution. This was the beginning of the violent phase of the Revolution when the scepter passed into the hands of men capable of using terror and of introducing radical changes in the name of protecting the Revolution from its enemies.

In the six weeks before the Convention assembled, the implications of August 10 became clear. The deportation of refractory priests was declared. Emigré property was to be sold off by the state. Landlords lost all their dues without compensation unless they could prove title. The egalitarian form of address, "Citizen," was adopted. A distinguished group of foreign intellectuals, including Tom Paine, was given honorary citizenship. By the end of the month, the enemy had taken Verdun, only 150 miles away. Thousands of Parisians marched off to the front, as the Commune combed the city for arms and for suspects. On September 2, the mood of patriotic frenzy turned to paranoia against the supposed enemy within. Violent mobs

raged through Paris for the next five days to liquidate presumed enemies. They emptied the prisons, administered hasty trials, and executed between 1100 and 1400 prisoners. Thus, after August 10, 1792, a fourth force had thrust itself into the arena where "democrat" had already triumphed over aristocrat and monarch.

The Republic of the Convention, 1792 to 1795

The Republic and the War

The Convention celebrated its first session on September 21, 1792, by replacing the monarchy with a republic. The occasion was a triumphant one, for news had arrived of the first clear French victory in the field, which had halted the Prussian advance at Valmy, in the Argonne Valley to the north. In the next six weeks, the French armies "liberated" Savoy, crossed the Rhine to take Frankfurt, and overran Belgium, after a true victory at Jemappes, where 40,000 sans-culottes overwhelmed the enemy while chanting the "Marseillaise."

By mid-November 1792, the Convention was in a position to promise "aid and fraternity to all peoples wishing to recover their liberty." The simple formula was tested in occupied Belgium, where oligarchical Statists and Democrats disputed the right to organize the new regime. The Convention announced the confiscation of noble and princely property to pay for the occupation. The Convention followed the requests of Democrats and annexed Belgium in February 1793.

Politics, however, became the great divisive issue in the new Republic. The Girondins had aroused the opposition of a small group of deputies from Paris even before the war. Now the Girondins, who were basically men of the provinces, found their opponents from Paris clustered high on the benches of the Assembly and taking for themselves the name of the Mountain.

Both groups were approximately of the same social class, and there was rough agreement on anticlericalism and economic liberalism. The Mountain, however, could accuse the ministers of federalist tendencies, and they were less afraid of an alliance with the sans-culottes. The rapid train of events exaggerated ill feeling between the two groups. The harmony of the first days of the Republic soon faded before the question of the King. The fate of Louis XVI marked a clear break between the two factions. It was Robespierre who had to remind the Convention early in December that either Louis XVI was guilty of treason or they were. After debating the issue of the King's fate for over a month, the Assembly voted 361 to 321 for the death penalty, with the Mountain voting for and the Girondins against regicide. Louis XVI was guillotined on January 21, 1793. The real victors were the Mountain and their friends in the Jacobin clubs.

The war entered a new phase with France declaring war on England and Holland in February 1793, while the Russians and Prussians moved into Poland to crush the year-old liberal regime and to take more territory. This Second Partition of Poland was the greatest victory of the counterrevolution.

Internal Crises

The coming together of social unrest, political agitation, and unfavorable foreign entanglements had marked the crises of May–June 1789 and July–August 1792. Now, late in February of 1793, another rapid series of events left the legislative body torn asunder.

High commodity prices and intense suspicion of hoarding and speculation touched off enforced sales at prices that were set by the crowds, often women. An atmosphere of emergency now covered France, but especially Paris, as a major insurrection led by nobles and clergy broke out in March in the Vendée, and French forces were driven from the Rhineland.

The government responded to these events with coercive measures. The Convention organized an army recruitment program, appointed some of its deputies as special agents called "representatives on mission" to serve as political commissars to the army, set up a revolutionary tribunal to judge political cases and refractory priests, imposed a maximum price on flour and bread to appease the sans-culottes, and created a Committee of Public Safety to supervise the executive functions of the state. France began to behave like a besieged city which had to mobilize its resources while making sure that no enemies remained within to endanger the survival of the community.

The conflict between the Girondins and Jacobins reached a crisis in May, 1793. A rough coalition of sectional leaders, Jacobin Club members, and sans-culotte National Guards put an end to the crisis, purging the Convention of 29 Girondin leaders from May 31 to June 2, 1793. Paris had experienced its third great revolutionary day, but the pattern of conflict between aristocrat and democrat had been left behind. The summer of 1793 was to be the summer of the sans-culottes.

During the summer of 1793 crises mounted. The *assignat* fell from 36 per cent of value in June to 22 per cent of value in late August. Bread shortages were constant. The war went very badly on both northern and southern fronts; the handing over of Toulon and half the navy to the British was the cruelest loss of all. Not until September did the Convention turn back rebel power in the Vendée, and then only with seasoned troops. The argument between historians of plot and of circumstances may never end, but the atmosphere of treason, defeat, and assassination in the summer of 1793 prepared for the period of the Terror that followed.

The Convention triumphed over the sans-culottes with great difficulty in the autumn of 1793. The crisis—still another dramatic turning point—came on September 4 and 5,

Marie Antoinette led to execution, by Jacques Louis David. The artist sketched the Queen as she joggled past him in the wagon.

when crowds of workingmen surrounded the city hall and penetrated to the floor of the national legislature, demanding more bread and a revolutionary army. The day was narrowly saved by a promise to pay indigent sans-culottes for attendance at the sections. Before the end of September, the Convention moved to set up a wide system of price controls on more than forty necessities. Wages as well as foodstuffs, fuel, and clothing were affected. With large-scale requisitions of raw materials and labor, city control of the grain trade, and prices set by the districts, government intervention in economic life was complete.

The Terror and the Republic of Virtue

An even more profound legacy of the struggle for control of the Revolution was the routinization of Terror in the fall of 1793. A law regarding suspects listed many vague categories of enemies who were to be imprisoned for the duration of the war. The Committee of Public Safety, which Robespierre joined in July, now received two extremist Parisian deputies. On October 10, the new mood of the Committee was expressed by its youngest member, Saint-Just. In a speech justly famous, he defined the principles of the Terror. Not only treachery but indifference would be punished. The Republic has but two parties — the people and their enemies. Justice is reserved for the former and iron for the latter. The Constitution of 1793 was to be suspended (to which the Convention assented) and the "provisional government of France" was to be "revolutionary until the peace."

Saint-Just justified the startling transition in dangerously abstract terms, citing the sovereign will of the people. Neither he nor Rousseau thirty years earlier meant a majority rule when they used the term. The sovereign will expresses the fundamental truth of a community; it must always be just and reasonable. To the men who governed France in the winter of 1793 to 1794, the regime had to be absolutely virtuous. To those who so believed, the seeds of totalitarianism remained hidden.

Police power lay with the Committee of General Security, which also presided over the political trials. In mid-October, Marie Antoinette went to the guillotine; the scene, with her proud figure seated in the tumbrel, was caught on canvas at the right moment by the artist David. Two other well-known women followed her — a mistress of the old regime (Madame Du Barry) and one of the new (Madame Roland). Twenty-one Girondin leaders were executed in November.

The Committee of Public Safety, although temporarily immune from review by the Convention, was opposed on the "Right" by a group that gathered around Danton and on the "Left" by the revolutionary militia and by more radical clubs that were inspired by Hébert, one of history's great yellow journalists. The Committee of

Twelve owed their power in 1793 to 1794 far more to circumstances than to cohesion and genius. Their reign after December rested on victory in the civil war in the west and the southeast and on the expulsion of the enemy from French territory. The *assignat* regained some of its purchasing power by 1794. Through the representatives on mission, the Committee was associated with the widespread anticlericalism that became a veritable campaign for the dechristianization of France. A Republican calendar in which months were named after the seasons had already replaced the Christian year. History began with the year I, on the day of the declaration of the Republic. Sunday became a workday and every tenth day became a lay holiday. Churches were stripped of their ornaments and vessels. By the end of 1793, Parisian churches were closed and a Festival of Reason had taken place in Notre Dame. The ultimate effect of dechristianization was to alienate further small communities and the Church from the Revolution.

The apparent rule of the Committee lasted only a few months. By April 1794, it had brought about the trial and execution of Hébert on the Left and Danton on the Right. Robespierre and Saint-Just were crying of a "foreign plot," but were prosecuting domestic enemies. Some measures of social justice were passed—free medical care for the aged, free compulsory primary education, the end of slavery—but Robespierre and Saint-Just were increasingly preoccupied with moral absolutes. Terror deepened and executions increased after a law of 22nd *Prairial* (June 10, 1794) allowed the accused no counsel and only one verdict—acquittal or death.

By July, 1794, the emergency ended as well-led French armies swept into Belgium again. The crisis that had sustained Virtue and Terror ceased to exist and men indulged their fatigue and personal animosities. As a result, Robespierre, Saint-Just, and others were executed on July 28th (10th *Thermidor*), 1794. The Terror came to an end; France had prevailed over its enemies and the Revolution no longer needed friends like Robespierre.

"Paris in the Terror" still symbolizes a people caught up in moral oppression. Death on the guillotine weighed heavily on men's minds, but equally dominating was the realization that the state demanded complete devotion. Until the enemy without and the enemy within should be vanquished—and only the state could say when that might be—every citizen had to show his dedication. For a few brief months in the Year Two of the Revolution, men and women suspended their ordinary interests and changed their civic symbols, their dress, and even their names. Robespierre, in his most important speech, declared that a popular revolutionary government must have both virtue and terror. What he could not realize in the spring of 1794 is that very few ordinary men shared his profound belief that the Revolution could substitute morality for egotism, principle for habit, and right reason for tyrannical custom.

The Reaction of Thermidor

The Republic of the Convention hung on for more than a year after Robespierre's death, but the infamous *Prairial* law survived Robespierre by only three weeks.

Procession headed by the Goddess of Reason. Dechristianization did not end the need for a religion.

Robespierre, spokesman for the Republic of Virtue.

The Convention negotiated a peace with the rebels of the Vendée and returned their firearms and their clergy. The puritanism of the Republic of Virtue gave way to a cynical press and theater, to the revival of the salon, and to revealing dress. Price controls ended in December, yet requisition for war continued. The popular phase of the Revolution came to an end, leaving bourgeois democrats solely in command.

Great success on the military front characterized the year after *Thermidor*. The army of occupation in Belgium swept into the Ruhr. The Palatinate fell, and Prussia withdrew from the war in April 1795, leaving the left bank of the Rhine to France. Spain withdrew from the coalition in the summer of 1795, and French troops gained the Italian Riviera. They also crossed into the Low Countries where they supported the native Dutch Jacobins in the creation of the Batavian Republic, the first of the "sister republics." The Dutch democrats were the first to combine in a motto the three key words, "Liberty, Equality, Fra-

ternity." Of the First Coalition, only Britain at sea and Austria on land still challenged France.

Late in the summer of 1795 the Thermidoreans produced a new, more bourgeois constitution, which specified the duties as well as the rights of man and reinstated the system of a qualified electorate. Fear of centralized power led to a bicameral legislature and a five-man executive, the Directory.

The Republic of the Directory, 1795 to 1799

The Bourgeois Republic and Its Enemies

The sans-culottes and their cry for "bread and the Constitution of 1793" had been defeated in 1795. Under the new constitution, the vote was restricted as it had been in 1791. Property qualifications for members of the two houses (Council of Five Hundred and Council of Ancients) were higher than before.

The period of the Directory is interesting because it represents the kind of bourgeois republic that many Frenchmen had set out to create in 1789. The rich and powerful controlled the government. The members of the assembly included speculators, many businessmen, 158 regicides, and an equal number of royalists. Enemies to the left were routed when the "Conspiracy of the Equals," led by François Babeuf, was defeated in May, 1796. Babeuf believed that a just regime was impossible so long as the protection of private property continued to dominate politics. Enemies on the Right also threatened this bourgeois regime, and the Directors relied on the generals and on the loyalty of the troops to their officers in the cause of the great purges of royalism after the yearly elections to the legislatures (1795–1799).

The Directory also decreed elite secondary schools, and a National Institute for scientific research. Strict accounting procedures were introduced in the administration of relief to the poor and in the preparation of the national budget. This era favored the upper-middle class, the bourgeoisie.

The "Grande Nation"

The latent power of the military rested on the great accomplishment of the Directory — the expansion of France and her revolutionary institutions. This expansion was prepared by the many young generals who had been promoted so rapidly after 1792, by the Jacobin sympathizers who acted as commissars to the armies, and by the hundreds of thousands who served in the ranks. Almost one million men had been mobilized by 1796, and about 450,000 were in service when the Directory began.

It was in northern Italy that the French army proved that its aims went far beyond simple conquest. There an opportunist who knew how to mix politics with his military career, Napoleon (1769–1821), conducted a swift and brilliant campaign, taking Milan and neutralizing the entire peninsula. He was active in aiding middle class revolutionaries establish the Cisalpine Republic, and sending home bullion and art treasures to impress the Directory. But he was even more impressive in ignoring instructions and negotiating the Treaty of Campo Formio in October, 1797. It confirmed French possession of Belgium and sacrificed the ancient Republic of Venice to the Austrians, who withdrew from the war.

The year 1798 has been called "the high tide of revolutionary democracy." Sister republics in Holland, Switzerland, northern Italy, Genoa, Rome, and Naples, had constitutions similar to that of the Directory in France. Each contained a declaration of the rights of man, and most specified citizens' duties as well. Each republic was divided into departments and had two legislatures and a five-man Directory. The republics had been founded with the aid of local patriots, and the citizenry voted in primary and electoral assemblies. In 1798, Frenchmen were speaking of the *"Grande Nation"* and the "natural frontiers" of the French people, which included the left bank of the Rhine. On the fourth anniversary of Robespierre's fall, a procession wound through Paris honoring Liberty and proudly showing the imperial scope of the Republic.

Defeat and Coup d'état

All historians are agreed that French military power was at its height in 1798, the year of the Jourdan law that established universal military service. But military success indirectly brought down the Republic. The actual plot to unseat the Directors and expel the legislators came from within and was carried out by two old clerics who were wise in diplomacy, Sieyès and Talleyrand, and a former Jacobin terrorist, Fouché. The French expansion, however, had driven into a Second Coalition some of the old allies (England, Austria, Russia, Turkey, Sweden). In 1799, Austrian forces drove the French from Switzerland and Germany, while the Russian general Suvorov liberated northern Italy.

Meanwhile, Napoleon had gone his own way by taking an expeditionary force to Egypt to challenge British power in the Near East. He actually lost most of his fleet, failed to conquer Syria, and barely got back to France through Nelson's fleet after abandoning his army. But this fiasco was overlooked by Frenchmen and the conspirators who needed Bonaparte as their "man on horseback" to put down the Republican Councils. The General presided over the events of the 19th *Brumaire* (November 10, 1799) when the two Councils were summoned in special sessions and then dissolved at sword's point, although he needed the help of his younger brother, Lucien, to regain his nerve in front of the lower house. Within three weeks, the bourgeois Republic had come to an end and Napoleon was First Consul under a Caesarean constitution. Ten years of history had come to a close when the Consuls proclaimed the Revolution to be ended.

The Revolution Stabilized, 1799 to 1804

Early Napoleonic Government

The civilian instigators of the *coup* of 1799 sought a more powerful executive who shared their fears of popular government. In Napoleon, a second choice, they thought they had found a man of order without a compromising political past who would be content to name generals and ambassadors and who would be responsible to the Senate, a kind of constitutional jury. Sieyès' proposed constitution called for a tripartite executive with an equal voice in decisions for each of the three consuls.

From the outset Napoleon intended to exercise full command in France, as he had done in Italy and Egypt. He argued successfully that the First Consul was to have final decisions in all matters, although he took care at first to give the appearance of deferring to his legislature and his advisors.

The legislature, consisting of a Tribunate and Legislative Corps, was virtually meaningless, since it could only discuss proposed legislation but could not initiate measures. The Senate chose the legislators. The Council of State revived the old royal council with its expert ministers. The Council drafted laws and administrative rules. Napoleon worked hard with this group of advisors and received long periods of service from them.

In local administration, Napoleon built upon Jacobin centralization. He appointed prefects in charge of each department, sub-prefects for the *arrondissements,* and mayors in the communes. The First Consul even had a crude semaphore telegraph system; he was determined to know the mood of his nation as well as he prided himself on knowing his troops. Napoleon financed his state through rational assessment of taxes and more stringent collection, rather than through loans. Between 1800 and 1802, Napoleon set up committees to codify civil, criminal, and commercial law. The lawyers combined revolutionary legislation with the ordinances of Louis XIV and produced succinct and well-defined documents. Napoleon attended the meetings often enough to affix his name to the codes collectively in 1807, but the Civil Code of 1804 especially drew its strength from the Revolution. Napoleon leaned on Roman law to tighten procedures on marriage and divorce, but the granting of absolute property rights, the freedom to bequeath a portion of one's property at will, and the abolition of all servitude were legacies of the 1790s. Although the codes enforced social conformity, especially the rights of husband over wife and father over children, they were sufficiently adaptable to have influenced the law of Italy, Egypt, Canada, Louisiana, and Japan.

Both old-regime authority and revolutionary equality pervaded Napoleon's social and economic policy. He required workers to carry a passbook, thus hardening the law of 1791 against trade unions. In place of the Directory's secondary schools, with their permissive curricula, he established 45 *lycées* with state scholarships to train boys for civil service, the professions, engineering, and the army. With the characteristic statement that girls should believe, not think, Napoleon left their education to religious orders. Napoleon conceived of the national economy more in Colbert's terms than those of Adam Smith. He sought a favorable balance of trade with protective tariffs and excluded English goods. The most obvious attempt to strike a balance between old and new was the Legion of Honor, founded in 1802. The First Consul genuinely sought to bestow distinction, without regard to social rank, on individuals for civic achievement.

Yet Napoleon also sought a captive institution named by himself, a kind of republican service nobility.

For reasons of state Napoleon effected a reconciliation with the Church. Bonaparte's own religious attitudes were tolerant and skeptical, and it was for political and social gains that he negotiated with the Pope in 1800. As he so often did, Napoleon had the better of the bargain. The Catholic clergy would be named by the bishops, who in turn were nominated by the First Consul and instituted by the Pope. The distinction between refractory and constitutional clergy came to an end, and the clergy became once again salaried servants of the state. The Pope was persuaded to accept the dispossession and sale of Church lands. Roman Catholicism was declared to be "the religion of the great majority of the citizens." The Concordat was published in April 1801. In the long run, the bishops rather than the Pope or the Consul came to control the French Church, but in 1802 Napoleon won his gamble that the legislatures and men of liberal opinion everywhere would accept this charter.

The Pacification of Europe

Napoleon fulfilled the popular trust that he had come to power to make an honorable peace. After he had won some hard-fought battles in 1800 at Marengo, Zurich, and Hohenlinden, Napoleon signed the Peace of Lunéville with the Emperor in 1801. By this peace treaty, France gained what she had historically desired: the left bank of the Rhine from Switzerland to Holland, her so-called "natural frontiers." Thirteen months later, England made peace with France at Amiens. This peace was only a respite as far as Napoleon was concerned.

Termination of the Revolution

Napoleon's contempt for parliamentary government emerged in 1802. Counting on the gratitude of the nation for the Peace of Amiens, the First Consul again used a plebiscite to force his plan on the government. He became Life Consul, able to nominate most senators, to declare war and make treaties, and to designate his successor. Ominously, his profile appeared on coinage for the first time.

By 1804, Napoleon had broken openly with the revolutionary past. His arbitrary arrest and murder of the Bourbon Duc d'Enghien, who was kidnapped from the neutral territory of Baden, shocked European opinion and discredited Napoleon more than any other act.

In May 1804, by proclamation of the private council, Napoleon Bonaparte became "Emperor of the French." The populace was given its third (and most meaningless) plebiscite to approve the proposition that "the Imperial dignity is hereditary." Bonaparte planned to assume the title in a manner calculated to remove any question of Bourbon legitimacy and to humiliate the Habsburgs. He summoned Pope Pius VII north of the Alps for a coronation rite intended to recall that of Charlemagne. The Emperor crowned himself, bringing to a close the period in which the Revolution in France might have continued.

Coronation of Napoleon *by David, artist of the revolution. About 1004 years after Charlemagne became Emperor.*

The Grand Empire, 1804 to 1815

Napoleon's admirers see the turning point of his career in the military disasters of the three years beginning with the invasion of Russia in 1812. The new Emperor's treatment of France and the republics abroad, however, indicated from the start that he cared little for the pattern of change from the 1790s. A desire to legitimize his family's claim, while he himself had no children to inherit the throne, prompted Napoleon to install his relatives in new monarchies that had once been sister republics. Three of his four brothers were installed as rulers in Holland, Naples, and Rhenish Prussia, while his stepson was made ruler in Venice. Eager to have an heir, Napoleon divorced Josephine in 1809 when she was 46 and past child bearing. Austria supplied the new Empress, Marie Louise, who bore Napoleon a son within a year. An Imperial court of about 3500 dukes, counts, barons, and chevaliers formed the backdrop for the Empire. Old revolutionary officials and generals as well as relatives received Italian, Spanish, and Portuguese estates as Imperial fiefs. Using the discipline of the Jesuit order as an analogy, Napoleon placed an Imperial University over the entire structure of education. Modern scholars have seen in all of these public actions a private anxiety over the succession. Contemporaries merely saw a man who was insensitive not only to the true meaning of 1789, but even to the aristocratic amenities of the old regime.

French Expansion

The first three years of the Empire produced stunning victories on the Continent and a stalemate on the seas. The invasion fleet assembled at Boulogne in the summer of 1805 never sailed, having failed to secure the Channel. While Napoleon turned eastward with his Grand Army in the autumn of 1805, the British Admiral, Nelson, crippled the Spanish and French fleets at Trafalgar (October 21, 1805), off the southern coast of Spain.

What Napoleon gave up at sea in 1805, he gained on land, in the Habsburg Empire. The Austrians and Russians still believed that they could defeat Napoleon in a pitched battle, and foolishly engaged him at Austerlitz in Moravia. On the first anniversary of his coronation, the Emperor cut the allied force in half, thus gaining his greatest victory.

In the Peace of Pressburg that followed, Francis II gave up Venetia and the Tyrol and recognized Bavaria, Württemburg, and Baden as independent kingdoms. In 1806, the Holy Roman Empire came to an end, and Napoleon reorganized further German territory in the Confederation of the Rhine, taken from Prussia's western provinces. Frederick William II of Prussia, convinced that Napoleon would soon break the truce and expecting Russian aid, mobilized his army. In three weeks and two swift battles (Jena and Auerstadt), Napoleon humiliated the Prussians and went on to Berlin, where he decreed that all continental ports under his protection were closed to British ships. In the spring of 1807, Napoleon's army advanced toward the Baltic and defeated Alexander I of Russia at Friedland. The Emperor and the Tsar met at Tilsit in July 1807 to divide Europe into two spheres of influence, Alexander being particularly eager to set his own course against Sweden and Turkey. Prussia lost her Polish districts to a new French satellite, the Grand Duchy of Warsaw. The campaigns of 1805 and 1807 sealed Napoleon's reputation as a field commander, but it was the failure of the allies to place military cooperation ahead of individual interest that opened the Continent to France.

The "Continental System"

After Tilsit, the Emperor was convinced that his conquests would reinforce the blockade against the British Isles—a blockade that was changing from one of protection to that of economic warfare. By 1810 the Atlantic, the Baltic, and even the Adriatic had become untenable for neutral ships caught between French Decrees and British Orders in Council. The Continental System, as some perhaps too-rational historians have called it, hurt British exports to Europe, but new markets in Latin America appeared. Although Britain suffered from inflation, bad harvests, and mass unemployment in 1811, the blockade probably did less damage than monetary instability, and Britain never lost her continental grain supply. France, too, suffered from a commercial and industrial depression in 1811. Above all, her neighbors' trading interests were damaged, and the Empire began to mean heavy taxes and customs duties.

Napoleon's military reversals also began as a result of the blockade system. He needed the Iberian Peninsula to seal off trade with the enemy, and set out to occupy Portugal in 1807, but the Emperor's ambitions were drawn to Spain itself. In 1808 he secured the abdication of the Bourbon Spanish king, replacing him with his brother, Joseph, who was transferred from Naples. The Spanish peasantry, which was little affected by the Enlightenment, reacted to French rule as a threat to Church and society as well as a violation of nationality. Guerrilla forces drove Joseph from Madrid and defeated two French divisions in the field at Baylen, in July 1808. Supplied by the Duke of Wellington's British base in Portugal, local militia and juntas fought the savage occupation in scenes that were immortalized by Goya. Until Wellington cleared the Peninsula in 1813, the French were forced to commit many thousands of troops to the occupation. "The Spanish ulcer," Napoleon later wrote, "destroyed me."

The Empire at Its Height

Between 1810 and 1812, the Grand Empire reached its height. A total of 131 departments and about 44 million inhabitants

The result of Spanish resistance to the French: The Third of May, 1808, by Goya. As Rousseau put it, you have to force people to be free.

fell under French rule. Napoleon's son, the infant King of Rome, ruled directly over a long stretch of the Mediterranean coast and over the Illyrian provinces. The Low Countries and the coastal plain of Germany, including Hamburg, were French territory. Napoleon's relatives in Italy ruled principalities that conformed to older boundaries. Political lines had been redrawn, however, in Germany and in Poland. His youngest brother, Jerome, ruled over a Kingdom of Westphalia which was pieced together from Hanover, Brunswick, Hesse-Cassel, and the Prussian Rhenish provinces. Prussia was in fact the great victim of the Empire's growth, in both West and East, and she was demilitarized between 1806 and 1813.

The Grand Empire never achieved complete unity, but all its parts shared the authoritarian order that was seen in France after 1804. The Emperor allowed religious toleration and internal free trade, but he restricted electoral rights everywhere. He tried to use the Civil Code to destroy the old social order in the Empire by secularizing marriage and education and abolishing feudal dues and corporate bodies. His attack on monasteries and his search for administrative unity recalled the enlightened despotism of Joseph II. Wherever the Directory and Consulate had already

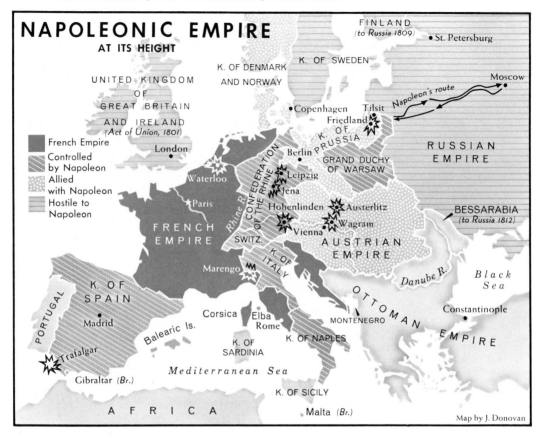

NAPOLEONIC EMPIRE
AT ITS HEIGHT

French Empire
Controlled by Napoleon
Allied with Napoleon
Hostile to Napoleon

Map by J. Donovan

touched an educated middle class with these proposals, the Napoleonic regime evoked no great opposition. The assimilation was incomplete in the areas across the Rhine and south of Rome. The price of the French mission—taxes, tariffs, recruitment, loss of political liberty—was not fully apparent until after the fateful invasion of Russia in 1812.

Collapse of Napoleonic Europe

By 1810 the accord that had been reached between Napoleon and Alexander at Tilsit, the cornerstone of French expansion, had worn thin. French and Russian ambitions collided in the Balkans. Napoleon's reconstitution of Poland as the Grand Duchy of Warsaw was intolerable to Alexander. On the last day of 1810, he renounced the Continental System and began preparations for war. In 1811, the Emperor retaliated by assembling in Po-

land a polyglot "grand army" of almost 600,000 men. He recognized the campaign as his greatest gamble, but, as usual, he counted on a short war, that would be won in a great single encounter.

In June of 1812, the grand army crossed the Niemen to start the invasion. Napoleon entered Moscow in mid-September, but he found the city deserted and soon in flames. Alexander still refused to negotiate or to engage in a decisive battle. On October 1812, Napoleon gave the order to retreat.

Both armies had wasted away tremendously, but the French retreat through the bitter northern winter finished the destruction of the grand army. About 100,000 were killed, another 100,000 imprisoned, and perhaps 200,000 perished of disease, cold, and famine. Napoleon hurried back to France where he might have made peace with the allies, but chose instead to invade Germany. For this purpose he put together an army of 150,000 men. But 1813 was in no way like 1806. German nationalism had been awakened from the Rhine to the Oder by the message of the Civil Code, by the example of what an authoritarian administration could do, and especially, as Jerome Bonaparte put it in Westphalia, by "the crushing burden of taxation."

The reaction to Jena in 1806 had been further cultural nationalism, led by professors and liberal bourgeoisie, but the building of an army to face the French was the work of Prussian ministers. In 1807, Barons Stein and Hardenberg abolished serfdom and feudal obligations, ended the restrictive allocation of professions and vocations by social rank, and tried to build up a bureaucracy that would be free of privilege. Hardenberg summed up his program as "democratic rules of conduct in a monarchical administration." [2] The most effective reforms took place in the Prussian army, where Scharnhorst and Gneisenau relaxed barbarous punishments, retired incompetent officers, and made universal military service a patriotic duty. Using a rotating reserve to avoid Napoleon's limit on the size of the army, Prussia trained 150,000 men by 1812.

In February 1813, Prussia allied with Russia and declared war on France. Napoleon gained enough time to field 450,000 men by August, but the Prussian *Landwehr,* or civilian militia, had also become available by that time. Austria broke off negotiations and declared war, and the Swedes sent British-subsidized troops. On October 16–19, 1813, in the "Battle of the Nations" at Leipzig, Napoleon was decisively beaten and driven across the Rhine into France.

Napoleon's opponents at first failed to agree on war aims, Metternich being particularly distrustful of Russia. The promise of British subsidy, however, brought the four major powers together at Chaumont

2. Quoted in Geoffrey Brunn, *Europe and the French Imperium, 1799–1814,* Harper and Brothers, New York, 1938, p. 174.

in March 1814, binding them to a twenty-year alliance against Napoleon and establishing a cordon of independent states around France. Meanwhile, Wellington's armies had crossed the Pyrenees into France, and the Dutch had recalled their stadtholder. Napoleon had already precluded any repetition of the nationalist crusade of 1793 with his recruitment (a million men were drafted in 1812–1813), requisitions, taxes, and repression of popular movements. The civilian population took the defeat at Leipzig passively and offered little resistance to the allied troops. In Paris, the Senate and legislature prepared to restore Louis XVIII, who promised a liberal charter. Napoleon abdicated on April 6, 1814, retiring with his dignity intact to the island of Elba, while the allies granted pensions to the entire Bonaparte family.

The Treaty of Paris of May 1814 was generous to France. She kept her frontiers of 1792, losing Belgium, Italy, and the left bank of the Rhine, but there was no occupation, no disarmament, and no indemnity. Talleyrand, the versatile Foreign Minister, was to join the discussion of Europe's fate at the Congress of Vienna. Meanwhile, Louis XVIII's Charter had guaranteed the election of two houses by the new nobility and the wealthy bourgeoisie, and had assured the rights of land purchasers, bondholders, army officers, and religious dissenters. The Charter threatened the return of *émigré* nobility, while the King's brother, the Count d'Artois, pressed for full restoration of noble privilege and properties.

But before Louis XVIII could erect a stable new government, Napoleon left Elba, returned to France in March 1815, and resumed his military preparations after the King fled. With 125,000 troops he met Wellington and Blücher at Waterloo (June 16, 1815) and was defeated. A Prussian escort returned Louis XVIII to France and Napoleon was carried to the remote South Atlantic Island of Saint

EUROPE, 1815
AFTER THE CONGRESS OF VIENNA

KINGDOM OF SWEDEN
AND NORWAY

St. Petersburg

Moscow

UNITED KINGDOM
OF
GREAT BRITAIN
AND IRELAND
London

K. OF
DENMARK

RUSSIAN
EMPIRE

K. OF THE
NETHERLANDS

Hanover

PRUSSIA

Warsaw

K.
OF
Berlin

POLAND
(to Russia)

Saxony

Paris

Baden

Bavaria

German Confederation

K. OF
FRANCE

Wurttemberg

Vienna

SWITZ.

AUSTRIAN EMPIRE

Turin

Danube R.

Black
Sea

K. OF
PORTUGAL

Madrid

K. OF
SPAIN

K. OF
SARDINIA

TUSCANY
(Austria)

PAPAL STATES

Rome

Naples

MONTENEGRO

OTTOMAN EMPIRE

Constantinople

K. OF THE
TWO SICILIES

Gibraltar
(Br.)

Mediterranean Sea

Ionian Is.
(Br. 1815)

Athens

Map by J. Donovan

Helena where he died in 1821. The second Treaty of Paris (November 1815) deprived France of Savoy and the Saar, declared an occupation of three to five years, and set an indemnity of 700 million francs.

The Congress of Vienna

Before Waterloo, the diplomats at Vienna had already agreed on the territorial settlement in Europe. The Congress had nearly disbanded over the question of Poland in January 1815. Russia and Prussia were suspected of designs on Poland and Saxony. The issue was settled by one of the great principles of the Treaty of Vienna (June 1815)—mutual compensation. Prussia received the Rhineland, part of Saxony, and Swedish Pomerania; Alexander I was entrusted to oversee a constitutional monarchy in "Congress Poland" and was guaranteed his conquests in Bessarabia and in

Finland. Sweden was compensated for the loss of Finland by Norway, which was taken from Denmark, Napoleon's ally. Austria received Lombardy, Venetia, and Dalmatia, as well as the presidency of a German Confederation of thirty-nine lay states. Holland gained Luxembourg and the Austrian Netherlands. Great Britain's colonial territories were increased by Mauritius, Tobago, Saint Lucia (taken from France), Malta (from the Knights of St. John), and Ceylon and the Cape Colony (from Holland).

Restoration of prerevolutionary dynasties also helped to destroy the Grand Empire. Bourbons were returned in France, Spain, and the Kingdom of the Two Sicilies. The Pope was guaranteed his estates in central Italy and a safe residence in Rome. The Braganzas, who had fled to Brazil, were reinstated in Portugal. The Congress powers respected national self-determination no more than Napoleon had.

Eventually the Norwegians, Poles, and Belgians were to gain their independence, and Venetians were to become Italian citizens. Other provisions of the Treaty have remained more acceptable to modern sensibilities: suppression of the international slave trade and piracy and establishment of freer international waterways.

The Hundred Days of Napoleon's reign after his return changed the orientation of the Congress. The four conquering powers entered a Quadruple Alliance, pledging themselves to prevent a Napoleonic restoration, to enforce the second Treaty of Paris, and to provide contingents to occupy France. Castlereagh then bound all five participants at Vienna to a "Concert of Europe," which was not only to protect the settlement, but also to provide machinery to settle disputes without recourse to war. Yet Britain steadfastly refused to support armed intervention in the internal affairs of other states, and it was unclear from the start whether the Congress System would act against nationalist and democratic uprisings after 1815. Soon liberals began to identify the Congress System with the counterrevolution.

The Revolution of the 1790s had apparently been overturned at Vienna. Expansionist France was contained, self-determination was denied, and secular ways of thought were refuted—such was the message of the dynastic restoration. Yet the revolutionary generation left a legacy of profound change in European history. The nature of that change was visible to Napoleon in exile, when he cultivated the legend that the Empire had been founded on principles of liberalism, nationalism, and religious toleration.

Liberalism, in its classic sense of the right to make free choices, especially in politics, broadly characterized the hopes of the Constituent Assembly in 1789. The Constitution of 1795 and the Civil Code were perhaps the two most widely imitated documents of the period. Although they

Counterrevolution triumphant: The Congress of Vienna. Here are Metternich, Talleyrand, and the boys. Today we study with respect a pacification of Europe that lasted nearly 100 years.

promised no great downward redistribution of power in society, each of them was concerned with the protection of inalienable rights. The idea of a career open to talent entered European thinking about administration. Ecclesiastical and seigneurial justice yielded to national courts within the Empire. But monarchy was the system of government that was most trusted in Western Europe in 1815.

Of great consequence to the future was the conversion of warfare after 1792 from the use of mercenaries and lower-class conscripts under aristocratic officers to the idea of the nation in arms. The emigration of noble officers and the *levée en masse* of 1793 set a pattern for a classless mass army, although no other nation achieved a base of conscription so broad as that of France in 1805. For scholars who see a humanitarian concern in eighteenth-century ideas, the wars of the Revolution have been called "the frustration of the Enlightenment."

Nationalism cannot be attributed directly to the revolutionary generation, although after 1808 the reaction against the Empire was also a reaction against the French. Nationalist German and Italian historians consider the national awakenings in their countries, which had their roots in native soil but were nevertheless influenced by the French example, as part of a European-wide phenomenon of the 1790s.

Napoleon was unable to appreciate the passing away of two aspects of the generation. Guided by his own star, he could not have realized that aristocratic privilege received its deathblow between 1787 and 1815. It seems clear that the constituted noble bodies lost much of their personal privilege, if not their political power or their lands, by 1815.

Bourgeois society, defined in terms of economic activity, especially trade and manufacturing, was retarded by the wars. When considered in terms of the "democrats" of the Jacobin clubs or the civil servants of Prussia, bourgeois society undoubtedly enjoyed greater prestige in 1815 than in 1787.

Written constitutions and declarations of rights became living organisms in France and America by 1791, and most Western societies still venerate these documents more than any other civic artifact except the flag. The use of force by France to achieve legitimate ends became blessed with success too many times to allow Europeans to disregard the history of the period. Terror itself became legitimized in 1793, and every major revolution since then has seen the rationalization—and even glorification—of violence.

SELECTED READINGS

*Amann, Peter, *The Eighteenth-Century Revolution, French or Western?*, Heath, Boston, 1963.
   An introduction to a current debate on the scope and nature of the revolutionary movement(s).

*Brinton, Crane, *A Decade of Revolution, 1789–1799*, Harper & Brothers, New York, 1934; also a Harper Torchbook.
   A competent general survey in the Rise of Modern Europe series; the revised paper-

Asterisk (*) denotes paperback.

back edition furnishes differing interpretations of the revolution.

———, *The Jacobins*, Macmillan, New York, 1930.
   Describes the organization and activities of the dominant revolutionary republican faction.

———, *The Lives of Talleyrand*, Norton, New York, 1936.
   Sympathetic biography of a celebrated opportunist who served many phases of the revolution and the restored Bourbons.

*Bruun, Geoffrey, *Europe and the French Imperium, 1799–1814*, Harper & Brothers, New York, 1938; also a Harper Torchbook.
   A volume in the Rise of Modern Europe series which treats Napoleon as an enlightened despot.

Cobban, Alfred, *The Social Interpretation of the French Revolution*, Cambridge University Press, Cambridge, 1964.
   Historiographical essays on the social history of the revolution raising fundamental questions about all historical writing.

———, *Edmund Burke and the Revolt against the Eighteenth Century*, Barnes & Noble, New York, 1961 (2nd ed.).
   Sets forth the reversal of Locke's philosophy by Burke and the early romantic poets.

Gershoy, Leo, *The French Revolution and Napoleon*, Appleton-Century-Crofts, New York, 1964.
   A standard textbook with an excellent annotated bibliography.

Geyl, Pieter, *Napoleon, For and Against*, Yale University Press, New Haven, 1949.
   A collection of judgments passed on Napoleon.

Godechot, Jacques, *France and the Atlantic Revolution of the Eighteenth Century*, translated by Herbert H. Rowen, The Free Press, New York; Collier-Macmillan, London, 1965.
   Develops fully the controversial theme that a general "Atlantic revolution" encompassed the Western World.

Goodwin, Albert, *The French Revolution*, Hutchinson University Library, London and New York, 1953.

A short, factual account, especially useful for beginning students.

Herr, Richard, *The Eighteenth-Century Revolution in Spain,* Princeton University Press, Princeton, 1958.
 Discovers a belated Spanish Enlightenment produced by the French Revolution between 1792 and 1801.

Hobsbawm, E. J., *The Age of Revolution, Europe 1789–1848,* Weidenfeld and Nicolson, London, 1962.
 With Marxist overtones, presents the thesis that two revolutions, one industrial and one political, remade Europe with global consequences.

Hyslop, B. F., *A Guide to the General Cahiers of 1789,* Columbia University Press, New York, 1936.
 Discusses the formulation and content of the "notebooks of grievances" compiled by the upper electoral assemblies at the outset of the French Revolution.

*Kaplow, Jeffry, ed., *New Perspectives on the French Revolution, Readings in Historical Sociology,* John Wiley & Sons, New York, 1965.
 A collection of articles on the social and economic pressures behind the revolution, especially those making the lower classes revolutionary.

*Lefebvre, Georges, *The Coming of the French Revolution,* translated by R. R. Palmer, Alfred A. Knopf, New York, 1957.
 Superlative short analysis of the events and background of the revolutionary movements of the year 1789.

———, *The French Revolution,* Routledge and Kegan Paul, London; Columbia University Press, New York, 1962–1964, 2 vols.
 Translation of the author's influential work in *Peuples et Civilisations,* an interpretation friendly to the revolutionaries of 1789.

Markham, F. M. H., *Napoleon and the Awakening of Europe,* Macmillan, New York, 1954.
 An easy-to-read account in the Teach Yourself History series.

*Nicolson, Harold, *The Congress of Vienna, A Study in Allied Unity: 1812–1822,* The Viking Press, New York, 1965.

A short treatment of the wartime treaties and the peace settlement.

Palmer, Robert R., *The Age of the Democratic Revolution, A Political History of Europe and America, 1760–1800,* II, *The Struggle,* Princeton University Press, Princeton, 1964.
 Recounts the revolutionary conflicts; especially informative on revolutions outside of France.

———, *Twelve Who Ruled: The Committee of Public Safety during the Terror,* Princeton University Press, Princeton, 1941.
 An analysis of the men and policies of the Terror, which emphasizes military considerations and treats Robespierre as one—not the most powerful—of the Twelve.

*Rudé, George, *The Crowd in History, A Study of Popular Disturbances in France and England 1730–1848,* John Wiley & Sons, New York, 1964.
 Analyzes the origin, composition, and motives of preindustrial crowds; the central chapters deal with the French Revolution.

———, *Revolutionary Europe 1783–1815,* Harper & Row, New York, 1964.
 A new general history, which disputes the Palmer-Godechot thesis of a general Atlantic revolution.

Soboul, Albert, *The Parisian Sans-Culottes and the French Revolution 1793–4,* Clarendon Press, Oxford, 1964.
 Shows differences between the urban lower-class movements and the Jacobins in power.

Stewart, John Hall, *A Documentary Survey of the French Revolution,* Macmillan, New York, 1951.
 A comprehensive collection of the most significant documents up to 1799.

*Thompson, James M., *The French Revolution,* Oxford University Press (Galaxy Books), New York, 1966.
 Solid summary by a biographer of Robespierre and Napoleon.

Van Deusen, Glyndon G., *Sieyès: His Life and His Nationalism,* Columbia University Press, New York, 1932.
 Biography of an outstanding French nationalist who urged expansion and engineered Napoleon's *coup d'état.*

20

Reaction and Revolution, 1815 to 1850

Tumult Revisited: Multitude versus Elite

Challenged by revolution, the old elite had produced a counter-ideology of conservatism or traditionalism. Traditionalists asserted that the rights, privileges, and powers that they had acquired in the past were indispensable in governing depraved men. Social and political reorganization, natural rights, progress, popular sovereignty, French dominion—these concepts must be repudiated.

Aristocratic repression precipitated a renewed struggle with the bourgeoisie, dissatisfied intellectuals, urban workers and, eventually, the peasantry. Liberals demanded constitutional, parliamentary government which would provide civic freedoms to the many and political rights to those who held property. Most liberals were convinced that such a regime was possible only when a single nationality constituted the body politic. For their part, socialist intellectuals and urban workingmen were not primarily interested in individual liber-

ties or the securing of property rights. Rather they sought the creation of a regime that would guarantee social justice and distribute more widely the fruits of industrial productivity. For these purposes they naturally believed democratic government was best suited. Peasants also were more interested in economic justice than in individual liberties. When liberal-nationalist revolutionaries proved unsympathetic to their economic problems, the peasants—still the great bulk of Europe's people—staged their own autonomous revolutions, especially in 1848.

By mid-century the bourgeoisie had gained power in most of Western Europe. Only in Britain and France were the middle classes seriously challenged by urban labor. In Southern, Central, and Eastern Europe, however, military establishments usually came to the aid of the traditionalists and kept them in power.

Superficially these nineteenth-century struggles appear to be between partisans of traditional society on the one side and heirs of the Enlightenment and the French

Revolution on the other. Though this generalization contains a large kernel of truth, it is much too simple, because both sides—and shades of opinion between them—were deeply imbued with romanticism.

Before turning to the renewed struggle of the liberals to remake Europe and the actions of the traditionalists to prevent it, we must, therefore, give some detailed attention to the admittedly confusing, indeed often baffling, romantic impulse.

The Romantic Impulse

The Many Faces of Romanticism

In its broadest sense romanticism meant reliance upon the emotions or intuitive feelings as a test of truth. It appealed especially to intellectuals who found the "cold rationalism," scientific analysis, and material environmentalism of the Enlightenment unsatisfying. It attracted a generation torn by revolution, a generation that had failed to find simple, precise, rational solutions to pressing problems.

Romanticism as a respectable approach to life had literary origins in the late eighteenth century. As early as 1756, Edmund Burke strengthened the revolt against neoclassical forms with his *Philosophical Inquiry into the Origin of Our Ideas on the Sublime and Beautiful.* Burke took the position that man's deepest, most sublime emotions were not aroused by proportion, unity, serenity, and decorum. Rather, they were stimulated by disintegration, dissolution, and distortion, awakening horror and incomprehensibility. Instead of rules and reason, the early romantics turned to genius, intuition, and emotions that stirred the soul intensely.

Romantics self-consciously repudiated the Deists' mechanistic world view that conceived of God as a detached author of mathematical, mechanical laws operating the same everywhere. Instead, they viewed the universe as a gigantic organism infused with and directed by spirit—a "World Spirit." Instead of a finished product of

past creation they conceived of the cosmos as a "growing world" in which ever-increasing diversity expressed the essence and divinity of nature.

If nature's essence were spiritual and organic, it could not be perceived by analysis and mathematical laws. Nature could be fully understood only by intuition. The individual's feelings enabled him to grasp the spirit dwelling within nature.

Self-made worlds were no longer consigned to childhood fantasies; they, too, were part of experience and added to the spirit's diverse manifestations. By dreaming themselves into the utopian future or the idealized past—usually the Middle Ages—romantics could vent the frustration and anguish they felt for their contemporary world. In denouncing materialism they asserted the power of will or character over the material environment. Man's material creations, instead of being man's glory, appeared somehow degenerate to the romantics.

More than a specific ideology, romanticism was a method of confronting the universe and of answering questions of all kinds. In politics and social theory, romanticism cut across every ideology and gave particular force to varying kinds of nationalism, the identification of self with the nation, the greater whole. Anarchists who proclaimed the iniquity of every restraint on natural freedom were romantics, it is true, of one particular sort. But so were collectivists who started with the premise that the individual possessed no reality apart from—or no higher duty than to—the nation. Between these two poles there were humanitarian liberals who would divide loyalties among state, church, family, inherited rights, and the individual's separate identity.

The Romantic Break from the Classical Mold: Art and Music

Romantic individualism reigned most freely in the creative arts. Here it took the form of the revolt of genius against re-

Classicism in painting: Jacques Louis David, The Death of Socrates.

strictive rules of composition and form imposed by neoclassicism, a revolt which culminated—in the nineteenth and twentieth centuries—in impressionism and expressionism. This romantic impulse was strongest in music and literature. Some neo-Gothic architecture appeared—the British Houses of Parliament, for example. "Wild" landscape painting flourished; painters such as Goya and Delacroix depicted the idealized writhing emotion of civil war and atrocities.

The compositions of Ludwig Beethoven (1770–1827), notably his *Eroica* or Third Symphony of 1804, initiated a break from "classical form" to meet the demands of expressing such psychological qualities as heroic strength and vitality, fear, horror, terror, grief, and endless longing. Other modes of musical feeling were created—the adaptation by Franz Schubert of lyric poetry to art songs, and the tone and symphonic poems of Felix Mendelssohn (1809–1847), Robert Schumann, and Fred-

eric Chopin. This generation used a wide variety of new devices to explore tone and color. Their experiments, coupled with the adoption of folk sagas as operatic themes in Germany, opened an era of romanticism for the following generation.

Literature

English romantic poets evoked emotions ranging from childhood memories to the far-off mistiness of Kubla Khan in Xanadu (Coleridge). Theirs was an attempt to communicate directly and intuitively with nature through inner spirit. At the hands of Sir Walter Scott (1771–1832), history was transformed from the *philosophes'* record of the follies, vices, and manners of mankind to the idealized and legendary local color of King Arthur's court. In America, which lacked the grandeur of a medieval past, James Fenimore Cooper attempted to penetrate the imagined inner soul of the American Indian, presenting him as the truest son of unspoiled nature.

The attraction of Gothic and unspoiled nature: John Constable, Salisbury Cathedral.

German literary romantics revolted against the petty, cramped court society of local princes, against French cultural dominance in aristocratic circles, and against the stringent rationalism of pulpit and university. Nowhere else had the classical ideal become such a fetish as in Germany. Fed by Rousseau, English romanticism, and a revival of baroque literature, the German poets and dramatists turned to transcendental, creative poetry to express an unrequited yearning for the "Absolute." From poetry and drama they turned to folktales and history, especially the history of the Middle Ages. Eschewing scientific detachment, they made history witness to the manifestations of a World Spirit in successive "spirits of the time" (*Zeitgeiste*) and to the working out of be-

neficent purpose behind the violence and bloodshed which marked their own time. In rejecting the Enlightenment, they praised all it had condemned: religious fanaticism, the Middle Ages, the baroque, and spirited faith.

Romantic Politics and Philosophy

Germany was the fountainhead of not only the literature but also the social philosophy of romanticism. Johann Gottfried Herder (1744–1803) developed a cultural nationalism that laid the foundations for subsequent nationalist politics.

Herder conceived of each nationality as a living organism with its own peculiarities and myths. Each had its own divine revelation from the World Spirit in its primitive stages—to its "founding fathers." Germany's national spirit or genius (its *Volksgeist*) had its origins in late medieval folk poetry according to Herder. He was a cosmopolitan who conceived of each genius living side by side with every other in harmony, each with the duty of developing its own peculiar spirit. Accordingly, he popularized early Slavic as well as German literature, laying a basis for Slavic cultural nationalism. But his premises could also be turned into a bigoted creed at the hands of traditionalists and nationalists.

German evolutionary philosophy was expounded in most classic form by Georg Wilhelm Friedrich Hegel (1770–1831). He depicted an evolving World Spirit, which human reason could "understand" or contemplate but not fathom, directing human affairs. Historical experience was the unfolding of a dialectical clash between opposites, a thesis and an antithesis, which, in collision, would produce a synthesis. This synthesis would, in turn, be a new thesis generating a new opposite or antithesis, and the dialectical process would be repeated. The younger Hegel saw this conflict primarily between economic and social classes which only a reign of absolute law could quell. Later he saw it more as one between states, each bound to assert its peculiar genius against others. Therefore in this spiritual clash it was military leaders who made the real stuff of history. Hegel's contemporary Prussian rulers puzzled over whether to consider him as a revolutionary or an absolutist. In one breath he identified the Prussian autocratic monarchy with perfection. In another, because the present was imperfect, his scheme indicated that change was both necessary and inevitable. His system was sufficiently ambiguous to serve those whose sentiments ranged from radicalism to reactionarism.

The Religious Revival and the Restoration

After reaching the nadir of demoralization during the Enlightenment, the Roman Catholic Church revived during the revo-

lutionary wars. Then it regained prestige even in Protestant countries as a bulwark against revolution. From previously fashionable scepticism, most of the aristocracy returned to the fold of the Church. Restored Catholic monarchs, who showered churchmen with favors, proclaimed the union of Throne and Altar as the only legitimate basis for secular authority. The Jesuits were re-established, and in Rome and Spain the Inquisition and *Index of Prohibited Books* were resurrected. Moreover romantics who repudiated liberalism and the revolution were attracted by the Church's symbolic rites, art, traditions, and organic social doctrines.

The reactionary and obscurantist side of the Church remained to inhibit its resurgence. As the century progressed, the spread of science and industry undermined the Catholic resurgence because high churchmen found it difficult to come to

Johann Gottfried von Herder promoted cultural nationalism by his history writing.

Friedrich Schleiermacher, prophet of religious nationalism.

terms with modern, urban society.

Political consequences flowed from religious revivalism in Protestant countries. German Pietism, in particular, merged with romanticism and nationalism. This merger became especially explicit in the writings of Friedrich Schleiermacher (1768–1834), one of the most influential theologians of his era. Schleiermacher separated religion from dogma and from the fear of God — who could be dispensed with in the pure contemplation of the universe. Religion was an intuition, a *feeling* that answered a deep need in man. The Enlightenment's search for a universal religion was all wrong. "If you want to grasp the idea of religion as a factor in the infinite and progressive development of the World Spirit, then you must give up the vain and empty desire for one religion." [1] Cosmopolitanism would disfigure the uniqueness of the individual and

his national group. Christianity commands attachment to the nation, and Schleiermacher would make the nation-state the mediator between God and man.

Like the Pietists, the English Wesleyans identified themselves with English nationalism and repudiated the French Revolution's philosophy of natural rights. But provisions in the peace arrangements to eradicate the slave trade were included largely at their instigation.

Postwar Politics

Immediately after the Napoleonic wars, the peacemakers' concern was to contain future French aggression. The Concert of Europe, created by the Quadruple Alliance of Britain, Prussia, Austria, and Russia had maintained that purpose. But by 1818 Bourbon France had demonstrated her monarchical respectability. Thereafter the concern of the Concert changed from the containment of France to the repression of liberal and national revolts. French entry into the Alliance — now the Quintuple Alliance — clearly signified that change.

Conforming to the principle of a balance of power, the international settlement at Vienna had been moderate. It laid the basis for a lasting peace. There was no major war before 1854, and no general war until 1914. Headed by Austria, the Concert worked to keep in power restored regimes that were reactionary and often vindictive at home.

Moreover, reaction had broad acquiescence if not popular support. For a generation the prestige of having beaten Napoleon put halos around the triumphant aristocratic leaders. Most people on the Continent were still peasants disinterested in politics. Except in Western Europe, liberal and national revolutionary leaders could count on little popular support.

"Austria Over All"

The pivot of diplomacy on the Continent was the Habsburg Empire. This multi-national conglomeration was held together

1. Quoted by Koppel S. Pinson, *Pietism as a Factor in the Rise of German Nationalism*, Columbia University Press, New York, 1934, p. 73.

by its sovereign, the well-intentioned but inflexibly reactionary Francis I. He presided over an uncoordinated central bureaucracy that relied heavily on the army and a secret police network. From Joseph II's reign and the revolutionary wars, the directors of this "absolutism tempered with inefficiency" concluded that reform did not pay. Francis I sounded the dominant note of the court when he wrote:

> I do not want any novelties; all that needs to be done is to apply the laws in a fair way; they are good and satisfactory. The present is no time for reforms. The nations are dangerously wounded. We must avoid provoking them by touching their wounds.[2]

He rejected administrative reforms proposed by Metternich, although Metternich himself was not committed to any basic social change beyond strengthening the landed aristocracy. Concessions to rapid economic growth, liberalism, and nationalism threatened the structure of the Empire. Hence Metternich's foreign policy (as well as Austrian domestic policy) was intended to squelch their emergence anywhere for fear that they might spread.

Unrest in Germany

As elsewhere, the war left behind depression and stagnation. But Germany's economic problems were aggravated by traditionally anarchical standards for money, weight, measurement, and tolls. Articulate agitation for national unification, constitutional government, and economic reform came primarily from the urban middle classes. Some university professors and students, and a few nobles and government officials also worked for these reforms.

Student societies (the *Burschenschaften*) and patriotic societies such as the *Tugendbund* and *Turnverein* led the nationalist agitation. Despite their meager following, they aroused the fears of the existing authorities.

2. Quoted by Hans G. Schenk, *The Aftermath of the Napoleonic Wars,* Kegan Paul, Trench, Trubner and Co., London, 1947, p. 69.

In 1817 the Jena student society led a rally at the Wartburg Castle near Eisenach to celebrate Luther's break from Rome as a great national act. The celebration—the first public protest against the settlement of 1815—ended with the burning of the Napoleonic Code and the symbols of restoration society. In 1819 student radicals caused still greater fears when one of them assassinated a tsarist agent.

Local monarchs reacted sharply and invited the Confederation to intervene. It enacted the Carlsbad decrees of 1819, which banned the student and patriotic societies. It also established rigid newspaper censorship, prevented "objectionable" professors from being employed, and put informers in lecture rooms and some churches.

Austria dominated the German Confederation, and guaranteed the sovereignty of its princes. But the more liberal monarchies such as Baden, Württemburg, and Saxe-Weimar were restive under Austrian

Prince Metternich, diplomat of stability and reaction, the "Coachman of Europe" till 1848.

hegemony, and by 1819 Prussian officials had already started a customs union, the *Zollverein*. By eliminating local tolls between Prussia and her neighbors, the *Zollverein* facilitated commerce and eventually political unification.

Repression in Italy

In Italy the peace replaced French ascendancy with Austrian ascendancy. Secret police and troops under Austrian control secured political conformity, but economically and administratively the peninsula was as divided as before. In northern Italy enlightened despots and French rule had removed the last remnants of manorial and noble jurisdictions. Ferdinand I (restored Bourbon ruler of the largest state, the southern Kingdom of Two Sicilies) committed himself to respect French reforms. But he also secretly pledged to Austria that he would allow no further constitutional changes. As in the rest of southern Italy, aristocrats and clerics continued to wield great power. Corruption, inefficiency, censorship, and restored clerical power alienated the middle classes and the army. Throughout the peninsula political reaction, and clerical and papal resurgence marked the postwar years.

Bourbon Spain

With the possible exception of Russia, no European kingdom had been less influenced by the *philosophes* and revolutionary thought. But Ferdinand VII proceeded against political dissent as though it were a tremendous threat. Clerics and nobles not only tried to erase effects of the revolutionary epoch but also all changes of the eighteenth century. The government identified itself with the Jesuits and the Inquisition. Only two newspapers were authorized, and they were devoted to the weather and religious subjects.

Restoration France

Even though Louis XVIII shared the clergy's belief in divine-right kingship and the union of Throne and Altar, he proved to be the most circumspect and practical of the restored monarchs. In 1814 he granted a constitutional charter that created an upper House of Peers and an elected Chamber of Deputies. With this machinery he tried to promote a constitutional royalist movement. He drove the republicans and liberals underground, but his greatest opposition came from recalcitrant nobles and clerics, leaders of the Ultras.

Headed by the King's brother, the Count d'Artois, the Ultras possessed the only open political organization besides the King's. During the first elections, the Ultras inaugurated a bloody white terror against revolutionists, Bonapartists, and Protestants. They thereby secured an irreconcilable assembly "more royalist than the king and more Catholic than the pope." They denounced legal equality as blasphemy against God. They attacked Louis XVIII as "a crowned Jacobin" because of his royal constitutionalism. In their vindictive attack on the Revolution and all its works, they pushed through the Chamber of Deputies laws for administrative arrest and detention, and military courts removed from royal clemency.

When Louis XVIII died in 1824, making way for the Count d'Artois as Charles X, the Ultras' leader held the throne.

Russia

The institutions of the Old Regime remained more vitally alive in Russia than in any other state. Alexander I (1801–1825) tried to introduce new ideas.

Educated by a Swiss Jacobin tutor, Alexander was a late product of the Enlightenment and of religious pietism. Disliking class privilege, he ordered the drafting of a constitution, set about reorganizing the government, and laid plans for serf emancipation and education. He fostered intellectual and religious freedom, and founded three universities and many urban public schools. He also encouraged manufacturing and commerce, and forced serf holders to humanize peasant labor conditions. Theoretically the Tsar wielded unlimited powers but, in practice, Alexander was repeatedly frustrated. Nine tenths of the people were illiterate serfs, turbulently dissatisfied, but not demanding constitutional change. Townsmen, a potential source of discontent, were few in number, for Russia had only two cities of note, Moscow and St. Petersburg. That part of the aristocracy, bureaucracy, and army which had been exposed to European ideas and institutions was reform-minded. But the Tsar was dependent upon irreplaceable administrators who detested reform and were subject to pressure from like-minded landed nobility. Understandably, perhaps, Alexander came to the conclusion that liberty in Russia depended upon unquestioned obedience to royal will. Upon his death an uprising of liberal nobles and soldiers—the Decembrist Revolt—utterly failed to gain popular support or to shake the foundations of the autocracy.

Conservatism in Britain

In spite of her long tradition of concern for the rights of citizens, England also endured civic repression during and after the war. Almost unbroken warfare from 1793 to 1815 enabled the Tories to dominate the government, identifying domestic reformers with external revolutionary foes. To encourage this identification of reform with traitors, the ministry employed *agents provocateurs,* newspaper subsidies, packed juries, and cultivated conservative clergymen to crush the English "Jacobins." Parliamentary reform was thus postponed until 1832, and the English model of Montesquieu and Voltaire became an effective tyranny in ways that war alone did not explain.

The Tory government, basking in the prestige of victory but faced with intense postwar problems, continued repression after Waterloo. Unemployment was especially severe. During the depth of the crisis from 1816 to 1817, there were strikes, bread riots, machine-breaking demonstrations, and rural incendiarism. Cheap newspapers, reaching the lower middle classes for the first time, occasionally used revolutionary language. But, in Parliament, Whig critics went no further than to complain about using secret agents. Fear, whipped by the ministry's investigation reports, gripped the upper classes.

All opposition outside Parliament was repressed, and a crowd illegally assembled at the new industrial city of Manchester was charged by cavalry. Following this "battle of Peterloo," the government passed Six Acts, most of which were intended to be permanent. They further curbed public meetings, provided drastic punishments for offenses against public order and libel laws, and authorized broad powers of search and seizure.

During the 1820s new men began to form an opposition group in Parliament. They attacked slavery, the abusive care of orphans, and conditions in factories, mines, and prisons. These measures and the reform of parliamentary representation were probably the fundamental reason that Britain escaped the wave of revolutions that swept the Continent in 1830.

A Generation of Dissent, 1820 to 1848

Between 1820 and 1848, three revolutionary waves hit Western society. In each one, men tried to complete what the French Revolution had begun. Using that revolution as their model, liberals planned and led revolts to destroy Old Regimes and inaugurate modern, liberal societies. Economic dislocations, social aspirations, and the inadequacies of traditional governments were their allies, while liberalism and romantic nationalism gave them direction. Although liberal goals were only partly achieved, widespread social and constitutional changes appeared by the end of that revolutionary generation.

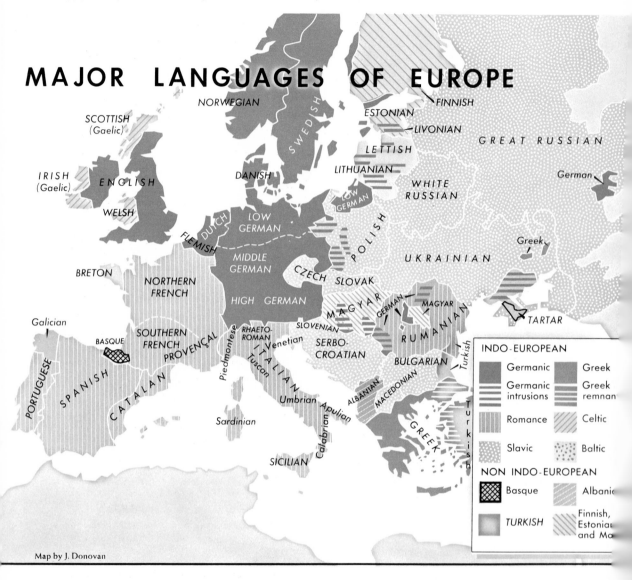

MAJOR LANGUAGES OF EUROPE

Map by J. Donovan

The Resurgence of Liberalism and Nationalism

The liberals' watchword was individual freedom — under law enacted by representative, constitutional government. Nationalism was the belief that ultimate authority should be accorded to the nation-state. The nation — a new word in the century's vocabulary — was defined by language, cultural kinship and, above all, by a subjective feeling of "we-ness." Liberals and nationalists shared some common assumptions such as self-determination of peoples.

Historical circumstances joined them in opposition to the Concert of Europe which forcefully represented monarchical legitimacy, the divine right of kings. But further experience has amply demonstrated that nationalism has combined with far more ideologies than liberalism. By 1848 several European nationalist movements had proved incompatible with liberalism. Nevertheless the revolts between 1820 and 1848 were sufficiently interfused with the two "isms" to be categorized as "liberal-national" affairs.

The Many Mansions of Liberalism

Liberalism presupposed the individual's rationality. It aimed at a rationally directed social-constitutional structure without legal curbs on individual development or on the disposition of labor and property. Within the environment of traditional authoritarianism its first tasks were to secure free speech, a free press, religious toleration, and the removal of legal restraints on economic activity. This required changing to a constitutional monarchy or a republic whose legislative authority would be lodged in a representative assembly of those who were capable of independent thought—that is, those who were economically independent of others. Where representative assemblies already existed, liberalism was reformist and evolutionary. Where king, noble, and priest jealously guarded their monopoly of power, it was necessarily revolutionary and anticlerical. Once in power, liberalism's formula was civic rights for all who accepted its constitutional order and political rights for those capable of rational, independent decisions.

Early nineteenth-century liberalism was preeminently the outlook of the bourgeoisie who lived from investments, professional services, large-scale farming, or industrial management. Hence it is usefully called "bourgeois liberalism" to differentiate it from the "democratic liberalism" put in practice during the second half of the century and from the "social liberalism" of the twentieth century. Most bourgeois liberals feared and withheld the franchise from the urban lower classes and the peasantry. The conservatives among them, like François Guizot of France, considered democracy inherently socialist. Radicals like Jeremy Bentham, on the other hand, envisaged a democratic republic based upon an educated electorate. In effect, power in their state would fall to leaders of commerce, industry, and the professions, which they held to be the vivifying elements of society.

At least in the realm of economic production, bourgeois liberals considered all governments necessary evils at best. The state's authority should be limited to justice, defense, and a minimal number of public utilities. Above all, it should protect property.

In theory, liberals wanted a weak, narrowly limited government, unlike the harsh, arbitrary Old Regimes. But, actually, the liberal state was legally more "absolute," although not more arbitrary, than "absolute" monarchies. It would abolish the legal jurisdictions of the aristocracy and clergy over commoners, outlaw the guilds, and centralize the economy to an unprecedented degree. It would allow no institution except the state to command the ultimate loyalties of the individual. And it could rely on the consent of the governed to a much greater degree. But its reputation as a "watchman state"—Thomas Carlyle dubbed it "anarchy plus the constable"— proved transitory. Wherever liberal economic objectives were achieved, greater and greater centralization of power occurred.

Major liberal theorists—Jeremy Bentham, Benjamin Constant, and François Guizot—flourished where parliamentary government already existed and the bourgeoisie already had economic and political power. In Southern, Central, and Eastern Europe the liberals' only available channels were secret societies, conspiracies, and the use of force—which contradicted and weakened their own adherence to constitutional procedures. Also in Central and Eastern Europe existing governments were multinational. In this setting romantic nationalism, propagated by literary figures rather than experienced political leaders, came to overshadow liberalism.

Nationalism

Nationalism was ethnocentric and demanded self-sacrifice. In Herder's footsteps, most nationalist theorists before 1850 professed a cosmopolitan humanitarianism which would be advanced as each nationality put its own house in order. Some even viewed the achievement of national unity as a stepping-stone to international federation. But others cherished the prospect of exerting their collective military power as the supreme moral good. Either way, the romantic nationalists shared with Giuseppe Mazzini (1805–1872), leader of the Italian unification movement after 1831, the view that the nation was "the God-appointed instrument for the welfare of the human race." Thereby each particular nationality was the messianic agent for redeeming mankind.

The European Revolts of 1820 and 1821

The first wave of revolution occurred in the Mediterranean peninsulas, the old Latin and Greek area, and its extension in Latin America. The pattern was similar in each case. Small liberal minorities were able to capture the government, but lacked support from any sizeable portion of the population. Armies determined whether the revolutions failed or succeeded. Opposed by French and Austrian armies, the revolutions in Italy and the Iberian peninsula were crushed; supported by foreign armies, the Greek revolt succeeded. The Latin

Giuseppe Mazzini, cosmopolitan Italian nationalist. His writings on national self-determination and a world of free nations made an impression on President Woodrow Wilson.

Americans forged their own armies, while the British prevented outside intervention.

In 1820, the small but active liberal element in Spain was able to get the support of angry soldiers who were rebelling against going to South America to crush the revolts there. From Madrid and other major cities came men to join the rebellion that overthrew the government of Ferdinand VII. A copy of the French Constitution of 1791 provided the framework of government. Would a liberal regime be able to organize and hold a largely illiterate and traditionalist population? Hardly. The provisional government's actions quickly stirred opposition among nobles, clergy, and peasants. They denounced freedom of the press and legal equality. When the new civilian authorities suppressed the Inquisition, confiscated some Church lands, and abolished some monasteries, they met

UPRISINGS OF THE 1820s

St. Petersburg 1825

RUSSIAN EMPIRE

K. OF PRUSSIA
★Berlin

Paris★
FRANCE

Troppau
★Vienna
EMPIRE OF AUSTRIA
•Laibach

PIEDMONT
1821

SERBIA
1815-1826

1821

PORTUGAL

1820
★Madrid
K. OF SPAIN

1820
NAPLES

SICILY
1820

GREECE
1821-1829
(Successful)

Map by J. Donovan

greater resistance than they could manage. French soldiers, acting in the name of the Concert of Europe, restored Ferdinand. In the name of religion and stability, he suppressed the rebels ruthlessly.

Meanwhile, in 1820, a revolt in Portugal overturned the Braganza's regency council, which was dominated by a British officer. The rebels persuaded John VI to return from Brazil and proclaimed a constitution and laws similar to those in Spain. John accepted this revolution, but counterrevolutionary forces soon gained the upper hand.

News of the Spanish revolt set off a similar one near Naples among discontented military detachments. They were joined by the militia and members of the *Carbonari,* a secret society of clandestine "charcoal burners." Most of the *Carbonari* were well-to-do landholders, professionals, liberal nobles, and judges. The successful Neapolitan revolt sparked a rebellion in the Two Sicilies. The moderate, inexperienced new rulers faced insuperable obstacles, which brigandage and an empty treasury only aggravated. In 1821 an Austrian army brought the king back to Naples and a terror purged the rebels. The Austrian army also kept the restored Bourbon rulers in power in the Two Sicilies. The Neapolitan revolt had been liberal. It was local rather than national, but the mode of its suppression could not have been better calculated to turn reform aspirations into nationalist, anti-Austrian channels.

In the Piedmont, insurgents composed of liberal aristocrats, army officers, intellectuals, and students revolted in 1821. Their aim was to unite all of Italy under a liberal government. But they failed to coordinate their efforts with the Neapolitan rebels. Austrian armies stopped the revolt.

One area where major powers countenanced revolution was the Ottoman Empire in Europe. Its institutional decay and political disintegration invited outside interference. Russia, France, Britain, and Austria were all interested parties.

Greek nationalism had been fostered by Greek merchants whose wartime prosperity was reduced by the Viennese peace. The merchants, who had little in common with the illiterate, economically backward, clerically led peasantry, had imbibed revolutionary European ideas. They revived Greek linguistic culture in their schools and founded a secret society, the *Hetaira Philike,* which spread among the Greek mercantile colonies of the Black Sea and Aegean ports. The society's aim was to oust the Ottomans from the Balkans and resurrect the Greek medieval empire. Greek leaders proclaimed a constitutional government whose separate existence Britain recognized in 1822. Jealousies between leaders vying for political and economic spoils split the revolution into factions. In 1825 it began to collapse before Turco-Egyptian forces. At this point, the interested governments cited above, especially Britain, supported by Philhellenic movements sentimentally attached to Greece's cause for her glorious past, sent military and naval units that defeated Turco-Egyptian forces and compelled the Sultan to concede Greek independence. It was the first triumph of the principle of nationality in Europe since 1815.

Before Greek independence was finally recognized, most of Latin America had successfully broken from Europe. Expulsion of Spanish authority was largely the work of Bolivar in the north and José San Martin in the south. After 1815 Bolivar's fortunes declined sharply, but when the Spanish Revolution broke out in 1820 he drove Spanish garrisons from present-day Venezuela. By 1824 Spanish America had driven out its European officials, and Brazil had become an independent empire under a younger son of the Portuguese monarch.

Latin America became independent with the aid of Britain, who reaped commercial rewards for her efforts. British freebooters and veterans gave San Martin provisions, men, and direction. Meanwhile, British trade and investments flowed into

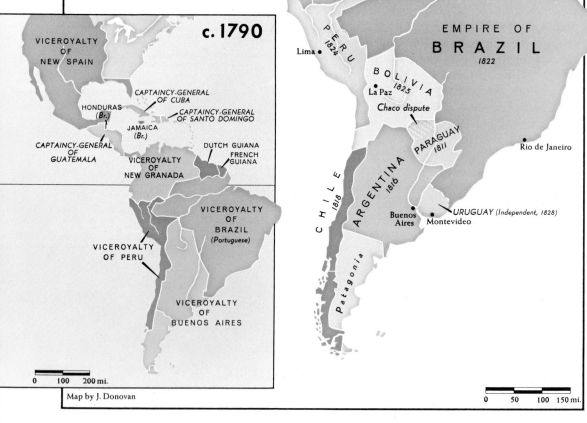

LATIN AMERICAN INDEPENDENCE
c. 1824

TEXAS

Gulf of Mexico

MEXICO

Mexico City

Atlantic Ocean

Havana CUBA (Sp.)

DOMINICAN REPUBLIC

BRITISH HONDURAS

HAITY   PUERTO RICO (Sp.)

GUATEMALA   HONDURAS   *Caribbean Sea*
SALVADOR
NICARAGUA

Panama   Caracas   TRINIDAD (British)

CENTRAL AMERICA
Independent, 1821
Divided, 1838   COSTA RICA   VENEZUELA 1830   BRITISH GUIANA
DUTCH GUIANA
FRENCH GUIANA

Pacific   Ocean   Bogotá   GREAT COLOMBIA 1819-1830

Equator

ECUADOR 1830   Quito   *Amazon R.*

PERU
Lima 1824

EMPIRE OF BRAZIL 1822

BOLIVIA 1825
La Paz

Chaco dispute

PARAGUAY 1811   Rio de Janeiro

CHILE 1818   ARGENTINA 1816

Buenos Aires   URUGUAY (Independent, 1828)
Montevideo

Patagonia

c. 1790

VICEROYALTY OF NEW SPAIN

CAPTAINCY-GENERAL OF CUBA

HONDURAS (Br.)   CAPTAINCY-GENERAL OF SANTO DOMINGO

JAMAICA (Br.)

CAPTAINCY-GENERAL OF GUATEMALA   DUTCH GUIANA
FRENCH GUIANA

VICEROYALTY OF NEW GRANADA

VICEROYALTY OF BRAZIL (Portuguese)

VICEROYALTY OF PERU

VICEROYALTY OF BUENOS AIRES

0   100   200 mi.

Map by J. Donovan

0   50   100   150 mi.

the whole Ibero-American area. At first the new states' independence was recognized only by Great Britain and the United States, who engaged in weak competition with one another for the area's trade.

The Collapse of the Quintuple Alliance

The revolutions of 1820 and 1821 tested the resolve of the Quintuple Alliance of 1818 to keep Europe peaceful and conservative. What that resolve actually meant was spelled out at the meeting of the Alliance at Troppau in 1820 in a statement: the Troppau Protocol. Austria, Russia, and Prussia agreed to the Troppau Protocol justifying intervention against liberal-national revolutions:

States which have undergone a change of government due to revolution, the results of which threaten other states, *ipso facto* cease to be members of the European Alliance, and remain excluded from it until their situation gives guarantees for legal order and stability. If owing to alterations, immediate danger threatens other states, the powers bind themselves, by peaceful means, or if need be by arms, to bring back the guilty state into the bosom of the Great Alliance.[3]

Created to provide political stability by crushing liberal revolutions, the Quintuple Alliance could not long survive on purely negative purposes. The crushing of the Spanish Revolution in 1823 was the Concert's last victory. The members became more concerned about checking one another's expansionist ambitions than about acting collectively for the common good. In 1823, when President Monroe announced the doctrine of mutual noninterference (later called the Monroe Doctrine, a policy statement that virtually nullified the Troppau Protocol), many statesmen welcomed the return to a situation of "every nation for itself and God for us all,"

as George Canning, the new foreign minister of England put it. The Greek revolt showed how conflicting the interests of the great powers actually were. From that point they easily slid back to traditional diplomacy and power politics.

Tremors of Change, 1830 to 1832

None of the risings of 1820 and 1821 had survived without foreign assistance, and the Italian and Spanish revolutions had collapsed when met with force. But, by 1830, conditions had begun to change perceptibly. The Concert of Europe was in disarray. Ecclesiastics no longer presented a solid counterrevolutionary front. Romantic liberals and nationalists were gaining converts through an expanding press, education, and the popularization of causes such as Greek independence. Expanding commerce and industry bred discontent among businessmen and guildsmen. In 1830 only France sustained a revolution without foreign aid, but the revolts of 1830 and the peaceful constitutional changes that occurred in Britain, some Swiss cantons, and a few German states by 1832 indicated a much broader liberal-national base of support than in 1820 and 1821.

France Initiates a New Round of Revolution, 1830

France (or, more specifically, Paris) was the epicenter of the revolutionary quake beginning in 1830. Charles X, whose accession Louis XVIII prophetically feared as the doom of the Bourbon dynasty, could not keep a moderate ministry working under the Charter of 1814. The court, ministries, and legislators were under Ultra influence. At all events, the attempt to return France to conditions of society like those of the Old Regime created a powerful response from the people.

Liberal opposition (fanned by journalists) mounted as influential bankers, journalists, and intellectuals joined in denouncing the government. The poor workers suffered from low wages, unemployment,

3. Quoted by W. Allison Phillips, *The Confederation of Europe*, 2nd ed., Longmans, Green & Co., London and New York, 1920, pp. 208–209.

Barricades romanticized: Delacroix's Liberty Leading the People (*1830*).

and the high price of bread. They were not interested in constitutional issues as the liberals were, but with their fundamental grievances they were in a fighting mood.

Charles X believed he could distract Frenchmen from their problems and appeal to their nationalism by invading Algiers, but the voices of dissent only grew louder. As a result, he issued the repressive July Ordinances. They dismissed an elected assembly before it met, forbade further publications without prior government authorization, reduced the electorate, and placed Ultras in high office.

The revolt began when employers freed their workers to take up arms. The republicans made the first show of force, but they were promptly stranded when Lafayette, their political idol, attached himself to the dominant revolutionary faction: the consti-

tutional monarchists. Their candidate for the throne was Louis Philippe of Orleans, who had participated in the early stages of the French Revolution and who now accepted its symbols.

Louis Philippe, replacing the fleeing Charles X, gave up royal power to issue decrees, recognized Catholicism as the religion of the majority (personally he was a Deist), made civil liberties more firm, and slightly lowered voting qualifications. As in England in 1688, divine-right monarchy was replaced by the rule of an elite defined primarily by wealth. Louis epitomized the ideals of his principal supporters—thrift, investments, and dedication to order. The ideological spokesman for the July or "Bourgeois" Monarchy was a historian— François Guizot—who held office during most of Louis' reign. Guizot's histories and policies identified the interests of the bourgeoisie as the golden mean, the *juste milieu,* between royal absolutism and democracy, which he considered as a stepping-stone to socialism. But his policies alienated the republicans, Bonapartist advocates of power politics, and urban workingmen to whom the government made few concessions.

The revolt excited both conservatives and liberals across Europe. Metternich, a constant prophet of doom, judged it as being the end of his life's work. Of course it was not, and it had far more important repercussions than posing a threat to Metternich's career. For one thing, it led very quickly to a rebellion of the Belgians against the Dutch, with whom they had been forcibly united in 1814. The Belgian provisional government, set up in the summer of 1830, had the most liberal constitution in Europe in 1831. The deed was done, though William of Orange would have loved to undo it. England and France would not permit that, and he accepted Belgian independence in 1839.

Poland, too, felt the exhilarating breeze blowing in from Paris. In reaction to the repressive policies of Nicholas I, nationalism flared in "Congress Poland" among the aristocracy, army, and intellectuals. The Polish Diet declared Tsar Nicholas deposed. But those aristocrats who feared the radical nationalists and their social program negotiated with the Tsar. Russian troops suppressed the revolt in the spring of 1831 and inflicted reprisals on the insurgents. The intellectual elite emigrated, and Poland's loss was America's gain. In their new homelands they helped paint Russia's image as the major suppressor of human liberties.

In northern Italy, local revolts challenged Austria's hold on the land, particularly in Parma, Modena, and the northeastern Papal States. Symbols of Italy's past greatness, such as Dante and Machiavelli, were revived to stimulate resistance to Germanic people. But the Austrians found no powerful foe here and crushed the *Carbonari* and their followers in 1831.

The reaction that followed was significant for both Italy and Europe. The papacy, in whose states revolts had occurred, condemned liberalism unconditionally in 1832. Liberal Catholics were denounced for supporting freedom of conscience, freedom of the press, separation of church and state, and "other harmful errors of those who possessed by an undue love for liberty, do their utmost to undermine authority." This position sharpened the cleavage between liberalism and the Church, and it encouraged nationalists to uphold their creed as a rival religion.

The Great English Reform Bill

England's Reform Bill of 1832 was the main nonrevolutionary constitutional change in Europe. By 1830, when the first bill to alter Parliament was introduced, industrialization had drastically altered Britain's economic, social, and demographic structure, while the basis for representation to the House of Commons was still that of the seventeenth century. Wealthy landed persons, sometimes a single family in a "rotten borough," elected members to the House of Commons while populous industrial cities like Manchester were totally unrepresented or industrial counties like Yorkshire had only its two old seats. Conservative defenders of the existing constitution claimed that under the old

Polish revolutionary forces, 1831.

A Union Jack for the Reform Movement, 1832.

system all Englishmen were "virtually" represented by men of wisdom. Tory repression, however, failed to check pressures for reform.

Agitation for reform, led by the newspapers, by the articulate and intelligent utilitarians, and by influential men like Canning and Robert Peel, continued until Lord Grey, Whig Prime Minister, introduced a reform bill to Parliament. The older Tories and churchmen in the Parliament did not like the bill at all and the House of Lords blocked the bill in 1831. There was enormous clamor over this piece of obstruction, and England came close to civil war. The Lords then agreed to let the bill pass, after considering the King's threat to pack the House of Lords with new peers.

The reform bill cut away some of the worst abuses of the old system without a thorough revision of the electoral machinery. It took seats from smaller boroughs and transferred them to the industrial towns and counties of the north and west. It extended suffrage to the upper middle classes. Landed and commercial wealth still dominated the House of Commons. But the admission of wealthy in-

dustrialists to political power challenged the Tories and established a balance of power that utilitarian radicals and humanitarians exploited to secure reform. Both Whigs and Tories considered the Great Reform Bill "final"—its sharing of power between aristocracy and middle classes provided the axis of politics known as the "Victorian Compromise." Instead of being final, however, it had broken the principle that only landed property holders could participate in politics.

The General Revolutionary Sweep of 1848 to 1850

Constitutional changes between 1830 and 1832—by evolution and revolution—drew a boundary between a liberal West and an absolutist East and Center. It was in the East and Center where the worst economic and social conditions (famine, cholera epidemic, high prices, and persisting feudal dues and services) were to be found. The populace was stirred only in part by the burgeoning liberalism and nationalism of the middle classes and intelligentsia.

The liberals' apparent power was illusory and temporary because they represented only a small segment of the forces working to sustain the revolution. The peasants lost interest in it once they secured release from their old manorial and feudal dues and services. The liberal leaders of the revolutions found that they had very little in common with either the peasants or the urban workingmen; and this was as true in the east of Europe as in Germany or France. The liberals did not know how to take the masses into the mainstream of the revolution. The consequence was defeat.

French Revolution and Counterrevolution, 1848 to 1850

Since 1846, restiveness caused by the economic depression was general. But Paris, a nonindustrialized city of over one

MAJOR REVOLUTIONS AND REFORMS
1848-1849

IRELAND

UNITED KINGDOM
OF
GREAT BRITAIN

K. OF SWEDEN
AND NORWAY

DENMARK

K. OF THE NETHERLANDS

1850 Berlin

German Confederation

RUSSIAN EMPIRE

POLAND

London

K. OF PRUSSIA

BELGIUM

SAXONY

Prague

Paris

Frankfurt-am-Main

PALATINATE

BADEN

Vienna
AUSTRIA

HUNGARY

TRANSYLVANIA

MOLDAVIA

FRANCE

1847

SWITZERLAND

PIEDMONT

Milan

Budapest

AUSTRIAN

EMPIRE

WALACHIA

Turin

PARMA

Custozza

MODENA

TUSCANY

Florence

PAPAL
STATES

SERBIA

OTTOMAN

EMPIRE

SPAIN

K. OF
SARDINIA

Rome

MONTENEGRO

Naples

Constitutional
reforms

Revolutions

Mediterranean   Sea

KINGDOM
OF THE
TWO SICILIES

GREECE

100   200   300 mi.

Map by J. Donovan

million people which had increased by one third since 1830, again set off the revolutionary powder train.

Louis Philippe's government had lost the support of one major segment of the population after another. François Guizot, his principal minister from 1840 to 1848, found it difficult to maintain the loyalty of the minute electorate which consisted of 3 per cent of the adult males, whose unpaid representatives he manipulated by appointments to remunerative government posts.

This narrow bourgeois government not only aroused traditional opposition but also—by a callous policy toward urban labor—contributed to the rise and influence of socialist intellectuals.

Unable and unwilling to harmonize the diverse interests in France, the government of Louis Philippe had thoroughly alienated most Frenchmen by the beginning of 1848. Even political meetings were forbidden. Supporters of opposition deputies began holding banquets with political

Procession of Napoleon's ashes at the Arc de Triomphe, 1840. Disappointed with the bourgeois liberalism of Guizot and Louis Philippe, Frenchmen were happy to have Napoleon with them again.

toasts and long speeches. They planned a massive banquet and demonstration in Paris on February 22, 1848. By ordering the banquet canceled, the government provoked rioting. Students and workers clashed with the police, and rioting inspired by martyrs continued for several days. Louis Philippe, reluctant to provoke further bloodshed, successively dismissed Guizot, called off military suppression and, after barricades were thrown up in the working class districts, abdicated.

Republicans and socialists (mostly journalists from two capital newspapers) joined together in proclaiming a provisional government. The advanced program of the new government—freedom of the press, universal manhood suffrage, ten hour work day, guaranteed right to work at livable wages, and an employer-worker council—aroused bitter hostility. Republicans, monarchists, and clericals, who gained a majority in the elections for the constituent assembly in April, were determined to wipe out concessions to urban labor. To enforce

their antilabor measures, the constituent assembly utilized the National Guard—a bourgeois "honor society." The aggrieved working people, 100,000 of them, crying "bread or lead," took to the barricades and fought for four bloody days in June against the well-equipped troops of General Cavaignac. The workers could not prevail against artillery. The military, judicial, and social defeat of the working classes was complete and the "specter of communism" was, for the time being, exorcised. The 1848 revolution ended in social repression worse than France knew before it began.

The victory of the clerical and monarchist element, completely reversing the earlier victory of the radicals, was consummated by the election in December of Louis Napoleon, the nephew of the Emperor. He was not only a symbolic hero to the masses of peasants but an apostle of authority and order, and a disciplinarian of labor pleasing to the reactionary clerical monarchists. By overreacting against radicalism, the French produced another man on horseback and destroyed a republic. On December 2, 1851, Louis Napoleon obtained by plebiscite the authority to write his own constitution. A year later he was Emperor.

Habsburg Paralysis: The Viennese Revolt

The fifty-odd revolutions of 1848 to 1849, whose font was Paris, brought to a climax and exhausted the ideology of the French Revolution in Central Europe. Probably the most significant revolt of the series was the one that toppled the Habsburg bulwark of counterrevolution in Central Europe.

The goals of the revolutionaries in France were simple. The middle classes wanted a broad, liberal republic; the working classes and their socialist spokesmen wanted a democracy. By contrast, the revolutionary aims in central and eastern Europe were terribly complicated and difficult to achieve. Austrian rebels were faced with four problems: (1) the task of solving a peasant problem, (2) liberalizing the government, (3) satisfying the separatist aspirations of a dozen different nationalities, and (4) giving attention to Italian rebellion against Austrian rule. Let us look at these problems in turn.

The Austrian peasants, four fifths of the population, were caught in a gigantic squeeze. Church, state, and landlord took as much as 70 per cent of the labor of peasant families. Landholders in the 1840s were introducing scientific agriculture and needed an efficient supply of hired labor in place of inefficient forced labor. To get such labor they called for emancipation of the peasants from feudal jurisdictions. The peasants were eager for emancipation, but balked at paying for their land, and for their release from labor, dues, and fees, as the landholders wished. The bureaucracy refused to consider emancipation, fearing bands of idle peasants.

The liberalizing trend actually began under Emperor Ferdinand who was under pressure during March to grant liberal concessions. First, the court dismissed Metternich, symbol of the era just past. He took refuge in Britain. Then the Emperor promised a constitutional convention, agreed to revolutionary Hungarian laws, and promised administrative autonomy to the Bohemians, Croats, Serbs, Slovaks, Czechs, Moravians, Galicians, and Rumanians, who, stirred by nationalism and liberalism, were demanding constitutional rights and local autonomy. Late in April the Emperor promulgated a centralized constitution based on the Belgian constitution of 1830. But the Emperor did not fulfill all his promises, and he was suspected of being insincere. Rioting in Vienna grew until the imperial court left the capital in May. A popular government took the place of the imperial authorities. Victory seemed easy. Yet, during the summer and fall, the liberal-national tide began to ebb as rapidly as it had risen.

Dissipation of pent-up emotional energies, the ruinous impact of political uncertainty upon the economic crisis, and liberal fears of urban lower-class movements partly explained the debacle that began during the summer. More important were the consequences of the peasant problem, the nationalities movements, and the administrative inefficiency of the liberals.

In July of 1848 the revolutionary constituent assembly, composed mainly of urban liberals, proclaimed emancipation of the peasants but postponed a decision on indemnities. The peasantry, the greatest social force behind the whole revolutionary movement, had no interest in constitutions or liberal government. Thinking that the victory was won, they withdrew support from the revolution, leaving the liberals and nationalists to fight their own battles. The liberals alienated the peasants by passing a law in September 1848 that required the peasants to pay for the release from old obligations in kind, labor, and cash.

Two approaches to the nationalities prob-

Louis Kossuth in the Hungarian Diet.

lem were offered: the Hungarian solution (Magyar) and the Pan-Slavic solution. The Hungarian solution would have led to independent nations, such as Hungary was striving to be, and as she became for a short time in 1849. The Pan-Slavic solution would have meant a federated empire of equal nationalities. The Hungarians had been semi-independent, with their own Diet. A liberal movement involving the gentry was successful in 1847, and when revolutions swept Europe in 1848, Louis Kossuth (1802–1894) secured royal approval of the liberal reforms. But narrow and aggressively intolerant nationalism asserted itself as the minority of Magyars imposed their language, culture, and rule upon the entire kingdom. This alienated the Croatian and Rumanian majority in Hungary. When Habsburg power revived, the Croatians helped the Habsburgs and the Russian armies to crush Kossuth's newly proclaimed Hungarian Republic in 1849.

The Pan-Slavic movement was led by Francis Palacky, a Czech historian, who organized a Pan-Slav Congress in Prague in June 1848. When riots broke out among the city's people who wanted democracy and national autonomy for the Czechs, the Habsburg general in Prague, Prince Windischgrätz, destroyed the revolutionary movement before the month of June ended. The counterrevolution had begun. The Pan-Slav Congress came to an end.

In Italy, hatred of Austrian rule had become a religion for the angry young men who lacked wealth and social position. Some of them heeded Mazzini's plans for achieving a united republic by guerrilla warfare; others followed Gioberti's scheme of federating under the papacy; and another group hoped that Charles Albert of Piedmont-Sardinia would lead a crusade for unity. Charles Albert appeared to be the best bet, since he had an army, and had just put in force a *Statuto* with limited liberal provisions, which became the constitution of united Italy a dozen years later. The insurgents in Italy scored early successes. The Austrian troops were driven out of the land to their fortifications in far northern Italy. In June and July, the old Austrian general, Radetzky, counterattacked and regained control of one city after another, defeating the armies of Charles Albert, along with others. Apart from the Piedmont Constitution, no positive vestige of the revolution survived the vengeful reaction which again reigned in Italy.

The counterrevolution led by Radetzky in Italy coincided with the victories of Windischgrätz in the older Habsburg domains. Prince Schwarzenberg, Radetzky's favorite, gained control of the Habsburg government and secured the accession of Francis Joseph (1848–1916), who was not committed to the liberals by any promises. A constitution that granted peasant emancipation and equality of subjects (*not* citizens!), coupled with a modernized bureaucracy, laid the basis for a restored Habsburg Empire. After the Hungarian Republic was crushed in 1849 with Russian help, the Habsburgs were again masters in their house of many national mansions.

The Liberal-National Miscarriage in Germany, 1848 to 1850

Like Italy, Germany lacked an existing central government which liberal-national forces could take over. The Diet of the German Confederation represented Austrian influence and illiberal local German states. Liberal-nationalists were therefore obliged to pursue three different goals: (1) to liberalize the various German monarchies and oligarchies, which would eventually become parts of a unified German nation; (2) to create a central, parliamentary government which would become the government of the unified German nation; and (3) to determine whether to include Austria and other German-speaking areas in the unified German nation. These goals would prove to be difficult to achieve in a country that had never been united under a common government.

Prussia was the critical factor since it embraced one third of all Germans and had an awesome army. The Prussian kings had not been hospitable to liberalism, and Prussian pride might not permit integration of Prussia into a larger state. King Frederick William IV (1840–1861), a somewhat romantic figure, eased fears of Prussian authoritarianism when he conceded some liberties to the press and in 1847 called Prussia's first General Diet, even though he only did so to request a loan for a railroad for his eastern Prussian aristocracy. When the citizens of Berlin revolted in March 1848, he did not attack his "dear Berliners," who he supposed had been misled by foreign agitators. Thus, much to the army's chagrin, he ordered its withdrawal, made repeated liberal promises, and embraced the national cause by declaring that "Prussia will henceforth be merged into Germany." Agitation by workmen and guildsmen,* however, scared the intellectuals and middle classes, who left the capital in droves. A constituent assembly and parliament assembled to prepare a constitution and to govern, just as was happening in Vienna at the same time. But this inexperienced group passed only eight laws, could not arouse peasant interest in its constitutional objectives, and was unable to control taxation and the army.

Following the army's recapture of Berlin and the proclamation of martial law in December 1848, the king proclaimed his own constitution. This constitution, lasting until 1918, prevented the Diet from controlling the ministry and tax collection, which left true power in the hands of the king.

Abortive Unification at Frankfurt

While the local German revolutions ran their course from early success to triumphant reaction, the first all-German parliament in history met at Frankfurt-am-Main. Its purpose was to formulate a constitution and to take direction of German affairs. Dubbed "the professors' parliament" by its detractors because it represented a plethora of scholars to the exclusion of seasoned statesmen, its membership was almost exclusively middle-class lawyers, administrators, judges, and professors. There was a slight sprinkling of landowners and still fewer businessmen. The Assembly lacked more than experience; it lacked a machinery of government and a populace obedient to it. It tried to establish a provisional executive, an army, and a navy, but the dynastic states (whose forces it commissioned for specific tasks) followed its direction at their own discretion. As a government, the Frankfurt Assembly functioned in a vacuum. After the revolutionary movement had receded, a narrow majority

---

* The industrial workers' organizations were national in scope. Besides political democratization they demanded unemployment insurance, consumer cooperatives, free secular schools with free books and elected teachers, housing, income taxes, a ten-hour day, a ministry of labor, and equality for women. Guildsmen, who also began to organize nationally during the summer, wanted a return to a restricted number of guilds and guildmasters—that is, a return to their guaranteed position of the past. Neither organization agitated for the liberal demands of a free press, an armed militia, or commercial reforms.

The Frankfurt Assembly in session. These men talked a lot, wrote a little, and went home.

tried to enlist Prussian support by making the Prussian King the constitutional monarch of Germany. But Frederick William refused to accept "a crown of filth and mud"—that is, one based on popular sovereignty. Mortally wounded by this rejection, the Assembly disbanded after an existence of eleven months.

Even more difficult for the deputies at Frankfurt was the question of the inclusion or exclusion of the Austrian Germans. The Greater German (*grossdeutsch*) radicals would have disrupted the Habsburg Empire by annexing it with its Czech subjects. The Smaller German (*kleindeutsch*) party favored the exclusion of Austria altogether. For the time being the question was settled by the failure of both the German and Austrian revolutions, but the basic issue remained.

In later eras, the *kleindeutsch* approach dominated Bismarck's unification of Germany around Prussia in 1871, while the *grossdeutsch* solution triumphed with Hitler's annexation of Austria to Germany in 1938 and the incorporation of the *Sudetenland* in 1939.

On social issues the members assumed typical nineteenth century liberal-conservative positions. Neither the constitutional monarchists nor the republicans favored working-class programs. The Assembly re-

jected a government-guaranteed right to work and called upon Prussian and Austrian troops to put down a national organization of trade unionists at whose headquarters in Frankfurt disorders designed to influence the Assembly broke out.

Germany remained as before, a loose confederation of thirty-eight states. As a result of these failures in 1848, nationalists became disillusioned with pacific parliamentary procedures. In the next decade most of them became "realists," ready to follow Bismarck in unifying Germany by "blood and iron."

At both the national and local dynastic levels, the German revolutions of 1848 and 1849 utterly failed to transfer political initiative from kings and their ministers to parliamentary assemblies dominated by the middle classes. No dynasty was unseated. Whatever constitutional changes that followed were granted by sovereigns. They usually allowed the nobility and upper classes a strong voice, although more in an advisory capacity than as directors of affairs. At the same time, programs of workingmen received no recognition whatsoever.

A Summing Up

In theory, Western liberalism held a concept of collective status—the self-determination of nationalities—which it would substitute for the dynastic state. Where national cultural boundaries and the dynastic state approximately coincided, self-determination could be achieved by the evolutionary or revolutionary transformation of existing governments. In Germany and Italy, national unity required the expulsion of Habsburg power and the elimination of existing petty states. Within the Habsburg Empire, self-determination meant either federation of equal, autonomous nationalities (the Pan-Slav approach) or the total disruption of the Empire into separate states (the radical Hungarian position). In this environment, collectivist romantic nationalists gained the upper hand.

During and following the revolutions of 1848, tough-minded nationalists jettisoned all pretense of universal humanitarianism. Reaping a harvest of disillusionment from parliamentary failures of 1848, they became willing allies of radical conservatives and "national liberals," who subordinated the goals of individual liberty and responsible government to the cause of unification by "blood and iron"—power politics abroad, and forced uniformity at home. The liberal catastrophe of 1848 marked the end of an era in which publicists envisaged nationalism as a stepping-stone to international cooperation. Free, unrestrained nationhood had become the highest good.

SELECTED READINGS

*Artz, Frederick B., *Reaction and Revolution, 1814–1832*, Harper & Brothers, New York, 1934, and a Harper Torchbook.

   A general account in the Rise of Modern Europe series, revised in detail by more recent research.

Babbitt, Irving, *Rousseau and Romanticism*, Houghton Mifflin Co., Boston and New York, 1919.

   Root and branch assault on the premises and methodology of the romantic thought attributed to Rousseau and his successors.

Barzun, Jacques, *Classic, Romantic and Modern*, Secker and Warburg, London, 1962.

   A romantic who believes that twentieth-century critics have vilified his tradition rehabilitates romanticism, narrowly defined.

Blum, Jerome, *Noble Landowners and Agriculture in Austria, 1815–1848: A Study in the Origins of the Peasant Emancipation of 1848*, Johns Hopkins University Press, Baltimore, 1948.

   Sets forth the agricultural changes which caused peasant grievances and moved many secular landowners toward a form of emancipation.

Asterisk (*) denotes paperback.

Brinton, Crane, *Political Ideas of the English Romanticists*, Oxford University Press, London, 1926.

   Demonstrates parallels between German romanticism and the English romantic poets.

*Bruun, Geoffrey, *Revolution and Reaction 1848–1852, A Mid-Century Watershed*, D. Van Nostrand Co., Princeton, N.J., 1958.

   A short introduction to the impact and sequel of Europe's most general revolution of the nineteenth century.

Bury, J. P. T., ed., *The Zenith of European Power, 1830–1870*, X, *The New Cambridge Modern History*, Cambridge University Press, 1950.

   An exhaustive work useful for reference.

*Butler, Eliza M., *The Tyranny of Greece over Germany*, University Press, Cambridge, 1935, and a Beacon paperback.

   Portrays the rigid idealized classicism which dominated German aesthetics and against which an exaggerated romanticism was in revolt.

Englebrecht, H. C., *Johann Gottlieb Fichte, A Study of His Political Writings with Special Reference to His Nationalism*, Columbia University Press, New York; P. S. King and Son, London, 1933.

   A monograph which sketches Fichte's drastic change from romantic individualism to collectivist nationalism in response to the French invasion of Germany.

Ergang, R. R., *Herder and the Foundations of German Nationalism*, Columbia University Press, New York, 1931.

   A basic work on the fundamental formulator of modern nationalism.

Evans, David Owen, *Social Romanticism in France 1830–1848*, Clarendon Press, Oxford, 1951.

   Traces origins of republican socialism in France, especially in literary circles.

Halévy, Elie, *A History of the English People in the Nineteenth Century*, E. Benn, London, 1949–1952, 6 vols. (2nd rev. ed.).

   A celebrated study by a perceptive French scholar.

Hayes, Carleton J. H., *The Historical Evolution of Modern Nationalism*, R. R. Smith, New York, 1931.

A study which identifies and describes several different kinds of nationalism.

Herring, Hubert C., *A History of Latin America from the Beginnings to the Present*, Alfred A. Knopf, New York, 1962 (2nd rev. ed.).
A standard textbook excellent for the revolutionary period.

Hovell, Mark, *The Chartist Movement*, Longmans, Green and Co., New York and London, 1918.
Presents an account purely factual and descriptive.

Kissinger, Hans A., *A World Restored, Metternich, Castlereagh and the Problems of Peace 1812–1822*, Houghton Mifflin, Boston: The Riverside Press, Cambridge, 1957.
Both a general theoretical and historical account which finds much to admire in the balance of power established at Vienna.

Marcuse, Herbert, *Reason and Revolution, Hegel and the Rise of Social Theory*, The Humanities Press, New York, 1954 (2nd ed.).
An attempt to absolve Hegel of fascist implications, interpreting him as a rational critic of the *status quo.*

*May, Arthur, *The Age of Metternich 1814–1848*, Henry Holt, New York, 1933.
A good short summary in the Berkshire Studies in European History designed for beginning students.

*Namier, Lewis B., *1848: The Revolutions of the Intellectuals,* Doubleday & Co., Garden City, N.Y., 1964.
Finds evidence that nationalism was overcoming liberalism in Germany.

*Robertson, Priscilla, *Revolutions of 1848: A Social History,* Princeton University Press, Princeton, 1952, and a Harper Torchbook.

A general study which finds social class lines often more significant than economic and political categories.

*Ruggiero, Guido de, *The History of European Liberalism,* translated by R. G. Collingwood, Beacon Press, Boston, 1959.
A detailed historical analysis.

*Schapiro, J. Salwyn, *Liberalism: Its Meaning and History,* D. Van Nostrand Co., Princeton, N.J., 1958 (an Anvil Book).
Excellent for differentiating different strains of bourgeois, democratic, and social liberalism.

Schenk, Hans G., *The Aftermath of the Napoleonic Wars, the Concert of Europe — an Experiment,* Kegan Paul, Trench, Trubner and Co., London; Oxford University Press, New York, 1947.
Deals with postwar difficulties, including economic problems, briefly and well.

Schroeder, Paul W., *Metternich's Diplomacy at its Zenith, 1820–1823,* University of Texas Press, Austin, 1962.
Uses archival evidence to demonstrate the exploitative nature of Austrian dominance in Italy, thus refuting apologies such as the one which follows.

*Viereck, Peter, *Conservatism Revisited,* Collier Books, New York, 1962 (revised and enlarged ed.).
A vindication of Metternich whose argument turns upon an undefined and misleading usage of the word "constitution."

Walzel, Oskar, *German Romanticism,* translated by A. L. Lussky, G. P. Putnam's Sons, New York and London, 1932.
A comprehensive survey covering political views as well as literature.

21

The Industrialization
of Society

French observers, comparing England's rapid pace of change with their own revolution of the eighteenth century, coined a phrase that took permanent root in popular usage by the end of the nineteenth century: "the industrial revolution." Noting that food production also expanded rapidly, other observers added the concept of an accompanying "agricultural revolution." Because trade increased more than at any past time, some historians would also apply the term "the commercial revolution" to the industrial epoch. But sober economic historians distrust these "revolutions" as oversimplifications of the complicated process of economic growth. Certainly, the steam-powered factory represented a threshold more than a completed "revolution." With industrialization came organized efforts to develop new technology—the "invention of invention." Economists are inclined to view "the industrial revolution" as a phase of rapid economic growth made possible by a favorable interaction of people, resources, technology, institutions, and international trade patterns at

given times and places. Our appreciation for this complex interaction of factors may be sharpened by studying not only cases of successful industrialization but also those "underdeveloped areas" whose population growth has outstripped the accumulation of capital and the use of inanimate energy for power—frequently with disastrous political and economic results.

England by the last half of the eighteenth century possessed some basic requirements for industrialization: productive agriculture; capital for investment in mechanized production and distribution; coal and iron in abundance; inventiveness; skilled labor and a reservoir of unskilled workers capable of being trained; a great transportation system connecting with the ports of the world and reaching inland through canals and waterways; a temperate climate; no internal barriers; laws favorable to property and production; political power of the commercial classes; a work ethic augmented by the dissenting religions; and a growing awareness of the social good to be derived from a better standard of living. The dream of Francis Bacon of using the knowledge of nature for human welfare was capable of being realized in England. By 1850, England had earned the reputation of being the "workshop of the world" and inspirer of the industrialization of the Western world.

Commercial Capitalism as a Prelude to Industrialization

The states along the Atlantic seaboard were the chief beneficiaries of an all-sea route to the Indies, exploitation of the New World, and Europe's carrying trade. Britain emerged as the unchallenged mistress of the seas, arbiter of the world's most lucrative trade, and principal center of finance. She thus secured, through war and diplomacy, markets barred formerly by mercantilist regulations.*

Accumulation and Use of Commercial Capital

By the end of the eighteenth century Britain, the Dutch Republic, and—to a lesser degree—France and a few German cities possessed large accumulations of capital. Successful merchants, investors, and "adventurers" multiplied their assets from shipping, ground rents, the slave trade, and colonial plantations. They also profited from foreign sales and inflation as prices outdistanced wages. They refined and expanded the fund of inherited techniques and institutions for mobilizing capital: stock markets; stock companies for mines, utilities, and colonization; insurance companies; mortgage credit; banks handling state loans, issuing bank notes, and discounting commercial paper. Yet English financial institutions were inade-

quate to meet the demands of agriculture and large-scale industry. English and Dutch bankers did make loans to industrial entrepreneurs, but the bulk of the capital invested in industry during the early stages of mechanization seems to have been raised by individual proprietors and partners. They struggled competitively for survival and those with viable, adequately financed businesses won out. In England, commercial capitalists first invested significantly in industrial production during the Napoleonic wars.

Capital investments in transportation also supported industry. Better ships, equipped with chronometers for determining longitude, facilitated overseas trade. Their crews could remain hardy thanks to a method of controlling scurvy discovered in England. Better transportation also served home markets that were economically more significant than colonial trade. Britain, in the eighteenth century supplemented river improvements with large-scale canal building and the rapid extension of a network of turnpike roads, some of which were macadamized or hard surfaced. Because of these advances, coal as a fuel could be more easily substituted for wood; grain could be shipped to famine areas; and agriculture entered a market economy.

Commercialization of Agriculture and Land Redistribution

The "agricultural revolution" broke the cycle of endemic famine and diminishing returns from soil exhaustion, the consequences of traditional methods of agriculture. New crops from the New World played a significant role in increasing productivity as their adoption spread. Maize or Indian corn increased cereal production as much as tenfold. Even in poor soils the "Irish" potato had a similar capability of augmenting food supplies. But the heart of this "revolution" was the reorganization of traditional agriculture to use

---

* Whatever their stimulus to the economy, the same wars harmed economic growth by destroying capital, raising interest rates, drawing investment money into state loans, dislocating industrial production, causing financial panics, and drawing potential consumption into postwar taxes.

the land more intensively and to maintain or build its fertility. New techniques for this purpose were introduced in Italy and the Low Countries during the sixteenth and seventeenth centuries. England imported and improved upon them in the eighteenth and nineteenth centuries. Since they hinged upon new crop cycles and the enclosure of lands, they required the reorganization of rural institutions and the system of land tenure.

This reorganization of agriculture introduced seed grasses and root crops such as clovers, lucern, alfalfa, and turnips into the crop rotation cycles. The legumes among these served the dual purpose of increasing animal nutrition (and thereby manure) and a rebuilding the chemical composition of the soil. By the judicious rotation of crops — such as turnips to barley to grasses to wheat popularized in England by Lord Townshend — no land lay fallow. By including hayfields in the rotation cycle, the farmers could dispense with their permanent common meadow. They could reclaim many wastes with proper (and expensive) drainage, fertilization, and cultivation. Robert Bakewell publicized selective breeding of livestock to improve gaunt and bony cattle with results indicated by the following table.

Robert Bakewell (1725–1795) promoted selective breeding of livestock.

AVERAGE WEIGHT (POUNDS) OF CATTLE SOLD AT SMITHFIELD[1]

	1710	1795
Oxen	370	800
Calves	50	150
Sheep	38	80

In 1731 Jethro Tull published a work urging adoption of horse-drawn "hoes" and drills — the drills to replace inefficient broadcast sowing. These gentlemen farmers cre-

ated a popular movement for agricultural change. King George III identified himself with their cause, and in 1793 Arthur Young, an unsuccessful farmer but a brilliant publicist and observer, was named secretary of a new Board of Agriculture. Young advocated new techniques and the redistribution of landholding by enclosures, which he described as "sensibly dividing the country among opulent men." As on the Continent before the revolution of 1848, commercially minded landlords led the campaign against the inherited system of cultivation and tenure.

Enclosure — the consolidation of arable strips and common lands and their redistribution as compact parcels of private, fenced lands — spread progressively in eighteenth-century England. Enclosures were initiated by large holders either by voluntary agreement or in compliance with private acts of Parliament. Parliamentary enclosure acts reached their apogee between 1791 and 1801, the same years in which machine industry was being introduced. By 1851 the process of consolidation and redistribution was nearly complete.

1. Adapted from J. H. Plumb, *England in the Eighteenth Century*, Penguin Books, Baltimore, Md., 1965, p. 82.

London slums, a source of upper-class fears (by Gustave Doré).

Enclosures had profound but controversial effects. Older historical accounts consider enclosures responsible for destroying small holders and the leasing yeoman class and driving them to industrial cities to work as propertyless laborers. Recent studies of land-tax statistics suggest, however, that in most areas the number of landholders on newly enclosed lands actually increased. But after wartime demands ceased in 1814, only large estates and small, family-worked plots increased in number. Holders of middle-sized farms, backed by insufficient capital, could not sustain themselves. Enclosures brought hardship for unknown numbers of cottagers and small tenants who had no legal title to their plots and pasturage on the commons. Losing access to land they became dependent solely on wages and charity.

It has usually been assumed that enclosures drove people from the country to take urban jobs. But demographic research indicates that industrial labor forces were recruited chiefly from natural population increases in the cities themselves. Large-scale migration from country to city apparently awaited the coming of the railroads and agricultural mechanization.

Providing an increasing population with a constant supply of food, "the agricultural revolution" relieved the country of serious famines and stabilized the economy as a whole. In the past, general economic crises were often rooted in food shortages. By remedying this depression cycle, "the agricultural revolution" undoubtedly assisted industrialization.

Population Growth, Subsistence, and Industrialization

Before 1750 famine and disease in Western Europe had checked population growth and held average life expectancy down to thirty years or less. But in the following century these barriers to demographic expansion crumbled, and rates of population growth and longevity shot upward. Because statistics are sparse and faulty, there is little hope of unraveling the precise relationship between this development and industrialization. But one thing is certain. This demographic "takeoff" is every bit as phenomenal as the increase wrought in industrial productivity by steam-powered factories.

Many ills that were later attributed peculiarly to industrialization were commonplace long before 1750: long hours at low pay, occupational diseases, unemployment, dearth during financial panics, and hard labor for women and children. With certain logic, mercantilists had recommended employment of children since it enabled them to survive in impoverished households. Crime and drunkenness were rampant.

Late seventeenth-century observers asserted that over one half of the English people was dependent upon charity, relief, or thievery to bridge the gap between income and subsistence costs. Accumulated capital may have provided the means to alleviate these conditions in certain preindustrial cities, but most of these commercial centers suffered health hazards similar to those in army encampments. Deaths usually exceeded births. Predominantly urban civilization was impossible until cities became more wholesome places in which to live.

Cleanliness was the principal development of urban sanitation. As magistrates in England and on the Continent began to heed the advocates of cleanliness, they copied London's vermin-resistant brick and paved streets. Although usually pumping from polluted sources, they enlarged their water supplies. People began to wash with soap, killing lice, and they replaced woolen clothing—often worn until it rotted—with cheap, washable cottons. Urban leaders had sewer drains installed. They prohibited garbage dumping in the streets and hired street cleaners. Water-closet privies were introduced. Still, water supplies polluted by sewage left the cities vulnerable to cholera and typhoid fever.

By twentieth-century standards medicine during England's early industrialization was primitive. Nevertheless, doctors made significant breakthroughs. They identified and largely eliminated nutritional deficiencies as the cause of scurvy and rickets. Probably more than anything else their practice of quarantine checked epidemics of plague by preventing reinfection from abroad. They had malarial swamps drained, checked typhus by fumigation and other means, and controlled smallpox by isolation, inoculation and, after 1805, vaccination. A physician's report of 1813 indicates the significance of controlling just smallpox:

. . . I found that not more than half of the human species died before they were ten years of age and that of this half more than a third part died of Small Pox so that nearly one fifth of all that were born alive perished by this dreadful malady.[2]

Doctors and patrons of charity (frequently

London's Foundling Hospital.

the same persons active in other humanitarian causes) established hospitals, dispensaries, and foundling homes—institutions that rarely received public assistance. Efforts to improve midwifery, a traditional craft which the English government did not regulate until the twentieth century, helped reduce infant mortality. Greater survival of children increased the proportion of young people in the total population during the years of industrialization. During the "Hungry Forties" an extraordinary wave of young adults entered the labor market and contributed to strains upon living standards.* Departing sharply from past trends, England's population increased from an estimated 7.5 million in 1751, to 16.5 million in 1831, to 21 million in 1851, and to more than 37 million in 1901.

As industrialization occurred or was anticipated, public servants and commentators became acutely conscious of relationships between population size, economic development, and standards of living. For the first time governments took comprehensive censuses of people, manufactures, resources, and commerce, and used this information in making administrative decisions. They supplemented general censuses with special inquiries into conditions of health, poverty, housing, unemployment, and various other facets of economic and social life. England completed her first survey in 1801. Before England did so, Sweden

2. Quoted by M. C. Buer, *Health, Wealth and Population in the Early Days of the Industrial Revolution* (George Routledge and Sons, London, 1926), p. 182. It may be added that many who survived smallpox were blinded or otherwise incapacitated.

* It was also undoubtedly involved in causing the wave of revolutions of 1848.

and the United States instituted regular census taking, and French *intendants* had carried out local tabulations within their generalities. It was becoming clear that demographic conditions need not be left to Providence. They were a legitimate object of legislation.

Machines, Factories, and the "Energy Revolution"

New agriculture and public health were essential to the transition from agrarian to urban industrial society. At the core of this transition was the general adoption of mechanical energy as a source of motive power. The steam engine made a decisive divide in Western economic history — between "low-energy society" dependent for power upon man, beast, wind, and flowing water and "high-energy society" that gave its population the equivalent of many slaves per capita.

Technological Developments in Textiles

Except in a few instances prior to the later eighteenth century, England imitated rather than initiated new technology. But for a time thereafter her chemists, clockworkers, carpenters, locksmiths, iron masters, farmers and others took the lead in inventiveness. Innovations were particularly significant in the cotton textile industry where a long series of inventions culminated in the replacement of spinning wheels and manual looms with power-driven machines.

The inventions that mechanized English cotton mills were called forth by production problems which many persons had sought to solve. In 1733 John Kay, a clockmaker, patented a "flying shuttle" for throwing the woof across the warp in broadloom weaving, thus eliminating one of the two loom operators. It was not gen-

erally used until 1760, but as it spread and as the marked demand increased, both wool and cotton yarn became scarce. The cotton yarn shortage was relieved after 1770 when Samuel Crompton patented a "mule" which, combining features of James Hargreave's "jenny" (1767) and Richard Arkwright's "water frame" (1769), produced a fine, strong thread. Cotton production soared thereafter. The amount of raw cotton imported in this period can be used as an index to this increased production. In 1751 raw cotton imports were less than 3 million pounds. In 1784 they were nearly 11.5 million and by 1800 the figure exceeded 50 million. For raw cotton, English and Scottish mills depended upon the Near East, India, South America, and the United States. After 1793, when Eli Whitney invented the cotton gin to separate seeds from fibers, the American South, relying on slave labor and "soil-mining" agriculture, became the principal supplier of raw cotton. Ironically Great Britain, which had abolished slavery in its Empire in 1833, helped rivet that same institution upon the United States.

By 1860 difficulties in mechanizing the wool industry had been overcome. At the same time, sewing machines — invented in the United States — had further speeded and refined the production of clothing. The power-driven factory system now extended to all manufacturing except that of raw materials and the final operations of clothes-making.

Spread of the Factory System

Factories had prototypes, with the specialized division of labor, in arsenals, shipyards, mines, ore and metal processing establishments, paper and glass plants, breweries, and finishing sheds for wool and linen cloth. But the factory system did not spread among the textile and other mechanized industries until water- or steam-driven machinery was adopted. Hence, the early textile mills were concentrated along the rivers in northern and western England and southern Scotland where commercial outlets, coal fields, and proper degrees of humidity were also present.

Factories that were established to make use of mechanized power were institutions for the supervision and discipline of labor. Bells or whistles announced the beginning and end of the work sessions, and machines set the pace of operatives' work. Manufacturers were frequently called "captains of industry" and their organizations were compared to disciplined armies. Owners of highly capitalized interdependent factory operations would not tolerate irregularity or independence in their workers. A doctor disillusioned with the "debilitating consequences of uninterrupted toil" in Manchester described this regularity as follows:

While the engine runs, the people must work —men, women and children are yoked together with iron and steam . . . chained fast to the iron machine, which knows no suffering and no weariness.[3]

Textile manufacturers recruited labor from the countryside, from Ireland, and particularly from women and children who were least prone to organized resistance.

Factory production completed the destruction of traditional craft organizations. The minority of craftsmen who were put in competition with machinery felt their distress and loss of status so much that they sometimes engaged in machine-breaking riots. They tended to look backward to the old secure guild system and petitioned Parliament to enforce old Elizabethan statutes. Parliament responded by not only abolishing the laws supporting the guild structure but by enacting laws against collective action by journeymen and factory laborers so they could not combine against their masters. British laws helped to make the laborers disciplined adjuncts of the factories.

3. Quoted from Dr. James Kay by J. T. Ward, *The Factory Movement 1830–1855*, St. Martin's Press, New York, 1962, p. 65.

Workmen destroying their mechanized competition, in this case a spinning jenny. In periods of depression, such as in 1811 and 1816, workmen attacked machinery, sometimes to force higher wages.

Mule spinning in an English textile mill.

Once it was perfected, mechanized industry served well. But machines were adopted so slowly as to render inaccurate the phrase "industrial *revolution*." In 1831 the "typical Englishman" was still a countryman and the "typical worker" a handicraftsman; only one in eighty was employed in a textile mill. Even in textiles, domestic production continued to coexist with machines, and handicraftsmen prevailed in the metal trades until after the middle of the century. Although the momentum of the factory system spurred the entire economy, as late as 1851 nonmechanized workers outnumbered machine hands three to one.

Newcomen's atmospheric steam-engine pump. Atmospheric pressure pushed the piston down into the cylinder C in which the condensation of steam had created a partial vacuum.

Watt's double-acting steam engine. Note that now the cylinder is closed and steam can be admitted on each side of the piston alternately by a valve arrangement. A flywheel makes for smooth motion.

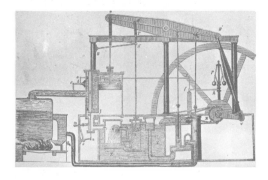

Coal and Iron

Iron and coal, hitherto little related to one another, became the keys to the new economic era. Making good iron was a problem. An English Quaker family of ironmasters experimented for three generations until they were able in the 1750s to produce a high grade cast iron with a coke-burning furnace. By using compressed air for higher temperatures, later innovators like Henry Cort (1784) produced iron with fewer impurities. Cort's rolling mill replaced hammers for shaping the iron. Thereafter Britain's annual iron production soared to 750,000 tons in 1830, 3 million tons in 1855, and over 6 million tons in 1870. Except for fine Swedish iron and steel Britain's imports of foreign iron ceased, and her cheaper, plentiful iron products dominated markets wherever inexpensive transportation facilities existed. Although the metal trades were mechanized only slowly, they opened a new era.

Iron production and steam power made coal the basis of nineteenth-century industrialization. Coal deposits were most advantageous when coking-grade coal lay near the surface in the immediate vicinity of low phosphorus iron ore. The unusual proximity of such coal and iron in many places gave Britain an initial advantage over other countries and encouraged the decentralization of her metal industries.

The Harnessing of Steam

Generations of technical and scientific progress preceded James Watt's patent of 1769. Scientists had noted the expansive power of steam and the partial vacuum created by its condensation. In 1698 an Englishman patented a steam pump using both the expanding and condensing properties of steam to expel water from mines. It was replaced in 1705 by a "fire engine" patented by the locksmith and blacksmith Thomas Newcomen. For power, Newcomen's pump relied entirely on atmospheric pressure on a piston in a cylinder below which steam was condensed. It wasted fuel and was incapable of producing regular rotary motion, but its largest model generated nearly 75 horsepower. In the development of the steam engine, science influenced technology more than any other invention (with the possible exception of chemical dyes and bleaches). It is romantic fantasy to attribute Watt's ideas to his watching his mother's teapot as a boy. As the son of an architect and ship-builder, Watt grew up in a scientific environment, became a builder of apparatus for experiments in astronomy and physics at the University of Glasgow, studied chemistry and latent heat under the eminent chemist, Joseph Black, and kept abreast of scientific developments on the Continent. Setting out consciously to improve the university's Newcomen engine, Watt developed ideas for a separate condensing chamber to save heat. He also determined how the expansive power of steam could be used on both sides of the piston, and how regular rotary power could be transferred to machines.

His initial patent was for a concept, not for a completed engine. The building of an actual engine led to further refinements and required heavy financial support. Watt was first financed by John Roebuck, but Matthew Boulton, another entrepreneur, took over when the failure of Roebuck's other businesses forced him to withdraw. Boulton obtained the major share of Watt's patent rights which Parliament extended from 1775 to 1800. Watt's exclusive rights barred the field to men more technologically advanced than he was, and until 1800 all steam-engine designs were marketed by him and Boulton. Technical problems such as the production of minutely engineered cylinders, pistons, and automatic valves were more influential than patent rights in retarding early widespread adoption of the engine, however.

Machine Tools and Engineering

Industrialization could not advance until it became possible to produce precisely engineered machine tools. For industry in general the invention of new lathes, borers, and screw-threading machines was a *sine qua non* for the transition from wood to iron. James Wilkinson in 1776 developed a process for boring cannons, a technique applicable to steam

engine cylinders. Smooth valve facings and true cylinders and pistons could be built with the improved lathes made by Henry Maudsley. Wilkinson became the principal builder of Watt's engines.

The inventors and designers of industrial tools formed a new engineering profession. Their increasingly versatile and complex creations propelled industrialization along a path of continuing technological advance. Drop forges, die stamps, and pattern turning were used to make interchangeable parts in clock- and watch-making, rifle manufacture, and (particularly in the United States) the production of sewing machines and reapers. Hydraulic machinery for lifting of all kinds appeared before the middle of the nineteenth century. Eventually, the machine-tool or capital-goods industry became a critical nerve center of technology whose expansion and contraction economists use to predict economic trends.

Transportation and Communications

Transportation was not mechanized in England until late in the history of her industrialization because a long series of technological inventions had to appear first. Nations industrializing later, however, could transform their transportation systems first. Until the decade of the 1840s Englishmen relied primarily on coastal ship-

Stephenson's Rocket *locomotive, 1829. Not much to look at but it started a trend.*

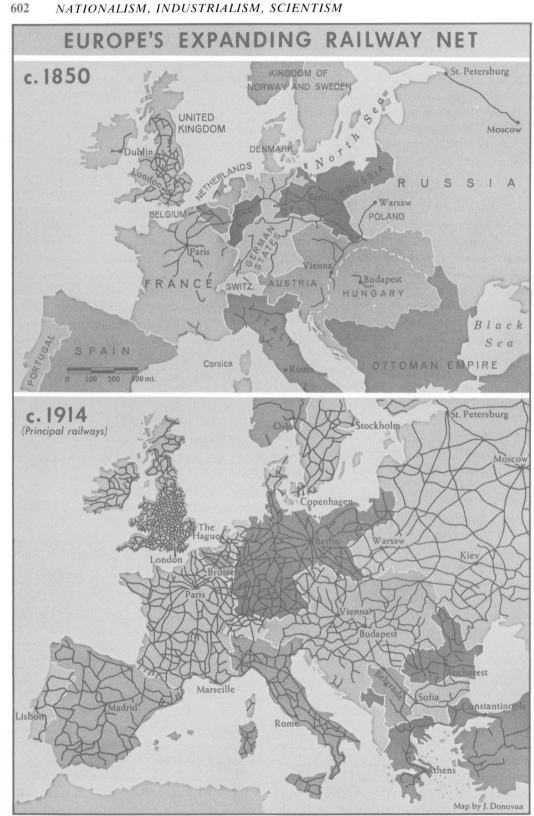

EUROPE'S EXPANDING RAILWAY NET

c.1850

c.1914
(Principal railways)

Map by J. Donovan

ping, canals, roads, and horses. The steam locomotive was made practical by a colliery worker, George Stephenson, whose *Rocket* locomotive demonstrated its superiority over stationary pulling engines in 1829. The first trains were only capable of the (then) sensational and frightening speed of twenty miles per hour, but they progressively reduced the cost of transporting heavy bulk fuel, raw materials, and products over terrain not accessible to the still cheaper waterways.

Railways proved to be profitable investments, and railroad construction was a priority item for British financiers. By 1838, Britain had 500 miles of track, almost 5000 by 1848, and 16,700 miles by 1886. Britain supplied the initial rolling stock, capital, and the rails to start railroads in other parts of the world, whose tracks totalled 4000 miles in 1840. In 1880 the figure had jumped to 200,000. Now Europeans could more thoroughly dominate the world.

Railways tied provincial economies together. Rapid bulk transport made industrial centers less dependent upon local agriculture. Within a few years, railroad links between town and country changed rural life more drastically than many successful political revolutions.

As the railway displaced stagecoaches, canal boats, and freight wagons on land, the steamboat later pushed other transportation aside at sea. Commercial sailing ships actually enjoyed their greatest vogue after the invention of both the railroad and the steamboat, but British marine engineering developments during the 1840s and 1850s ultimately sealed their doom. Screw propellers, better marine engines, and iron hulls — soon replaced by lighter steel ones — gave British liners and merchantmen the lion's share of the world's commerce.

The new "commercial revolution" advanced mightily around 1820 when steam-powered cylindrical printing presses, introduced by the *London Times,* began turning out thousands of newspapers per hour,

Opening of the Suez Canal in 1869, the year the Transcontinental Railroad was completed.

which were then distributed rapidly by rail and steamship. Studies of electricity by Faraday and others led to the perfection of telegraphic communication, first demonstrated in the United States in 1844. Within a generation the continents were linked together by lines and underwater cables, which relayed information about world markets, kept railroads properly scheduled, and expedited the dispatch of fleets and troops. Technologically and economically the world was becoming a single unit, but political attitudes by no means reflected this wholeness.

The Organization of Industrial Society

By 1850 the British began to realize that industrialization had effected drastic changes within their country. Not just their technology, but their basic institutions, their culture, and their very ways of life were taking new form. Many nineteenth-century observers claimed that industrialization was dividing society into two antagonistic new classes: capitalists and laborers dependent entirely upon wages. Labor had organized to oppose the expanding power of the capitalists, and their organizations had gained legal recognition. But the British census of 1861 revealed that the notion of two antagonistic classes was oversimplified. Both industrial classes were diverse in composition. Moreover merchants, miners, and especially professionals in law, medicine, teaching, and recreation were increasing more rapidly than other segments of the population. At the same time a declining proportion of the people was absorbed into factory labor.

Entrepreneurs and Financial Organization

Industrialization was an economic as well as a technological process. To fully exploit machinery and natural resources, capitalists had to invest more heavily than before in plants, mines, and transportation. They then had to reinvest a still higher proportion of profits in capital goods, if the ventures they supported were to become self-sustaining. No new enterprise could survive without long-term credit for capital goods and short-term credit for operations, wages, raw materials, and warehousing. In addition to the entrepreneurs an enlarged, specialized, and increasingly powerful financial community grew up as co-organizers of industrial society.

The characteristics of early entrepreneurs have been the subject of interminable controversies. Nineteenth-century portraits of them ran the gamut of description from greedy oppressors to honest men of thrift, frugality, and adaptability, whose tragic flaw was that they could not control the market forces upon which their lives depended. As a total group, entrepreneurs were diverse. Some, especially the Quakers, combined intense competitiveness with equally intense humanitarianism. But while their humanitarianism deserves emphasis, for many "average employers" it may well have stopped short of the factory gate. The entrepreneurs claimed absolute control over production and distribution as the prerogative of ownership. Only mavericks among them welcomed state intervention on behalf of health, safety, and welfare. On the other hand, the entrepreneurs were struggling against unbridled competition, within

an imperfect financial framework, subject to the dislocations of war and to adverse fiscal policies of their government.

Industrialization expanded the range of adjustments made through the price mechanism of the market, but it failed to eliminate the trade cycles that affected entrepreneurs, merchants, and labor. To remain profitable, heavily capitalized production normally required continuous operation, but sharp commercial crises in 1772, 1792, 1814–1816, 1825, 1839, and 1847 suspended operations sufficiently to remove marginal operators. The causes of these fluctuations are still controversial. England's worst crisis in the nineteenth century occurred after the Napoleonic wars. The crisis can be attributed in part to the aftermath of these wars, in part to Parliament's deflationary taxation and monetary policies. But "boom and bust" cycles recurred in industrial society, and governments were eventually moved to attempt their correction.

Labor and Workingmen's Organizations

To generalize about living standards in England prior to 1850 is difficult. Skilled labor was generally well rewarded, but women, children, and the unskilled suffered. Few historians doubt that the *average* standard of living was increasing even during the trying years between 1820 and 1850, but its distribution to the lowest classes is questionable. Poverty has continued in industrialized societies. Only a few "welfare states" of the twentieth century—Sweden is a notable example—have eliminated slums and poverty, and their success has been accompanied in each case by the general adoption of birth control and the avoidance of war.

Whether working conditions worsened during industrialization or whether humanitarian sentiments had made old practices less tolerable is another moot question. The conditions of industrial labor were probably no worse than the former environments and, in some respects, were better. At least the factory, mill, or enlarged mine was a unit more open to public exposure and was brought under public regulation more easily than individual homes.

Investigations demanded by evangelical Tories and Utilitarian reformers revealed unsavory conditions in mines and mills. Young children and women were in some cases mercilessly driven for long days in unventilated mills or dark narrow mines. These horror stories provoked legislation such as the Health and Morals of Apprentices Act of 1802 limiting work for pauper children to twelve hours, or the Act of 1819 banning employment of children under nine years of age in cotton mills. But it was not until the shocking disclosures of Michael Sadler's investigating committee of 1831 had stirred the public conscience that an enforceable Factory Act was passed in 1833. It provided four paid inspectors to help local magistrates enforce the act. High death rates, heavy welfare costs, and cholera epidemics brought further probing of mines and factories in the 1840s. An act of 1844 introduced the first safety regulations in cotton mills and stripped Justices of the Peace, who had obstructed enforcement of previous acts, of their jurisdiction. In 1847 the workday for women and children was reduced to ten hours, but until the 1860s the scope of these acts was limited to cotton mills and mines. Nevertheless the basis for the systematic factory code of 1901 was being built.

Apart from special laws applicable to dangerous trades, adult males were left to their own devices. Collective bargaining was illegal until 1824 and 1825, and after 1825 English courts still did not recognize unions as legal personalities. After 1848, highly paid craftsmen led by the engineers succeeded in organizing unions that had sufficient discipline and funds to survive strikes and depressions. But their legal position was insecure until the 1870s. The lower ranks of labor did not organize successfully until prosperity declined in the

Carting coal from the mines, 1842. It was this kind of misery that gave the Industrial Revolution a bad name.

1880s. Then they furnished recruiting grounds for socialist unions who sought political redress and a reorganization of the power structure of English industrial society.

The Impact of Urbanization

If the full complexity of industrial society was obscure to contemporaries, at least one trend was unmistakable—urbanization.

As the pioneer of industry, England was also first to face the problems of city life. In 1851 her inhabitants were roughly half urban, half rural. By comparison her degree of urbanization in 1881 was not reached by Germany until 1910 or by the United States until 1960.

Urbanization told heavily against traditionalism and passive acceptance of previous conditions. Ties of kinship—especially the patriarchal family structure—lost their hold, and the rural-oriented, tithe-supported church alienated the working districts. The traditional social order based on birth, status, and wealth was being eroded further and replaced by a new hierarchy in which wealth predominated.

Urbanization was part of a process that produced sharp political struggles between town and country and between different urban classes. New towns—and hence the centers of population—were located in the industrial Midlands, in the North, and in the West. Landed classes unresponsive to urban problems retained political power during this population shift. Justices of the Peace, for example, obstructed execution of social legislation. Slowly and belatedly local vested interests were overridden by officials of the central government, and between 1832 and 1885 parliamentary districts were redrawn to conform more closely to the distribution of the population. English adaptation to urbanization was slow; still it was rapid enough that the lower classes were not alienated from constitutional procedures. In 1867 the majority of city dwellers obtained the suffrage, and significant laws favoring their interests soon followed.

The Integration of Industrial Society

English liberals held in 1850 that *laissez faire* caused industrialization. As yet no other economic system had fostered industrial growth to shed doubt on this opinion. Defenders of paternalism and the traditional social hierarchy held that the forces changing their society were forces of anarchy. So did many humanitarian and religious critics of *laissez faire*. Disapprovingly they agreed with its economists that the price mechanism had become the arbiter of religious, moral, and human values. But both sides were ignoring strong indications that industrial society in Britain was becoming far more integrated and producing conditions far more uniform than the Old Regime.

When power became concentrated in the hands of employers, the central government began in an unprecedented fashion to extend its administrative control. This was true not only in England but in every subsequent highly urbanized industrial state. Rapid communications and transportation facilitated the centralized supervision of local affairs, while the increasing complexity of an industrial economy made local control impossible. No longer could families, parishes, counties, towns, or even to some degree national states regulate their own financial affairs. Unable to escape the effects of rapid and far-reaching transportation and communication systems, they were now part of a larger, interrelated community. And an unprecedented number of international institutions were created between 1850 and 1914.* Still none of them created a lasting alternative to the system of competition among sovereign states.

An "Open-Ended 'Revolution' "

The economic transformation which Britain had pioneered proved "open-ended" in a double sense. Changes in technology and economic institutions continued to accelerate and to produce further social changes. Meanwhile other parts of the world adopted power-driven machinery. British exports of capital, men, and machines stimulated industrialization elsewhere.

* In 1914 these included a Universal Postal Union, a Universal Telegraphic Union, copyright conventions, a Parliamentary Union, the socialists' Second International, The Hague Court, the Rotary Club, the Boy Scouts, about thirty scientific societies, many church groups, and about 160 peace organizations with a permanent international headquarters.

The history of industrialization in these other nations was similar to, but not exactly the same as, that in Britain. Nor did it conform to the predictions of Adam Smith and other classical economists. Smith and his immediate successors foretold an interdependent world divided into zones of specialized production that would contribute to peace as well as to the wealth of nations. But nearly every country supported its industrialists with high tariffs that restricted imports and protected domestic monopolies. After 1875 agrarian interests secured tariffs and restrictions against products shipped from America and various colonies by railroad and steamship. Growing trade between industrialized states clearly demonstrated their interdependence, but imperialists and economic nationalists rebelled against it. The most striking sequel to industrialization within the competitive state system was not the creation of new economic mechanisms for international peace or the dominance of economics over political passions, but intensified power differentials, rivalries, and the advent of total war. Industrialization not only changed the tools of war but it also revamped the balance of power and involved entire citizenries in the conduct of hostilities. Since World War II Europeans have looked in many directions—toward the United Nations, the European Economic Community, and in some areas toward Communist parties—for an escape from mutual annihilation.

Energy Conversion and Power Transmission

The development of steam turbines between 1840 and 1880, a feat of mathematics and alloy metallurgy, provided much more speed, power, and fuel economy than the reciprocating steam engine. Used to propel newly invented dynamos, the turbines greatly increased coal's potential as a source of power. Electricity permitted industrial centers to branch out and set up regional enterprise.

Inside the Crystal Palace, the first World's Fair, 1851. Marvels, such as the electric motor, excited the imagination.

An early assembly line of the Ford Motor Company. Industrial history owes something to Henry Ford; but history, he said, "is the bunk."

Although coal remained the key industrial fuel, other sources of energy came to rival it in the twentieth century. Hydroelectricity and natural gas are comparatively insignificant ones. Far more important were petroleum and the internal combustion engine. It took Western technicians less than twenty years after Gottlieb Daimler built a road-worthy motor car in 1885 to adapt the versatile internal combustion engine to boats, airplanes, and land vehicles.

The impact of motorized transport has been far more revolutionary than anything the railroad age dreamed of. Besides

Bessemer process of making steel.

Marconi and his wireless apparatus, 1897.

permitting the physical emancipation of millions from narrow localities, it has reduced the rural-urban differential; and motorized mechanization has enabled a few farmers to feed a vast population. The end of this revolution is not yet in sight.

Contemporaries who feel themselves part of the atomic age may protest the omission of atomic energy from this list of power sources, but *at present levels of technology* the input of electrical energy into refined atomic fuel exceeds its economic potential for most uses. So far the "atomic age" terminology relates primarily to military preparations where economic considerations cease to govern human activities.

Metallurgy and Heavy Industry

Although the greater advantages of steel were known, iron remained the basic structural metal until after 1860 because no means for the mass production of steel were

at hand. With a thunderous roar and a shower of sparks from burning silicon and carbon, Henry Bessemer provided such a method in 1859. The Bessemer process oxidizes impurities by injecting an air blast into molten pig iron. While his converter was being improved, the Martin-Siemens open-hearth method was discovered on the Continent. The new processes increased steel production sharply. But the major known iron deposits outside Britain, the United States, and Spain contained ruinous phosphorus. It had to be eliminated by chemical means discovered finally in 1878 by two Londoners, Sidney Gilchrist Thomas and Percy Gilchrist. The Thomas-Gilchrist process was widely adopted on the Continent within a single year. It made the large deposits of iron ore in Lorraine, Luxembourg, and northern Sweden the most valuable in all of Europe. Technology thus helped erase Britain's initial advantage in usable resources, since regions on the Continent were better endowed for the age of steel.

In the twentieth century a large array of chemical processes and the use of electricity and natural gas as sources of heat have encouraged some plants to decentralize and establish sites near larger markets. Culminating after World War II in a "straight-through" converter eliminating almost all hand labor, mechanization ("automation") has preserved the advantages of integration for the largest producers.

New Industries

Alongside established trades technology has produced a proliferating series of new industries. Chemicals—notably heavy industrial acids and alkalis, fertilizers, dyes, explosives, photographic materials, pharmaceutical products, plastics, and cosmetics—advanced most rapidly at first in Germany where chemical knowledge and resources were superior. Basic research in electricity continued to yield practical results. At the end of the century Guglielmo

Marconi perfected wireless telegraphy. Knowledge of electromagnetism underlay the electronic industries of the twentieth century which have integrated local and regional societies more thoroughly than any previous means of communication and transportation. But with the exception of motion pictures, intercontinental mass communications remain severely limited by cultural, economic, political, and some technical barriers. The military may be the most predominant users of this field of communications.

Scientific and Mechanized Agriculture

Although farming continued to be a major source of wealth in Britain, other countries took the lead in agricultural technology. Germany and to a lesser extent the United States excelled in the application of science — notably chemistry, microbiology, genetics, and veterinary medicine — to agriculture. Temperate parts of the British Empire and the United States, whose agricultural resources far exceeded their own consumption needs, led in the introduction of labor-saving machinery. New milling machines, refrigerated railway cars and steamships, steel cans, and other means of food preservation facilitated the transport of surpluses to Europe. In the twentieth century mechanized scientific farming has extended into Southern and Eastern Europe.

The Evolution of Financial Capitalism

Only heavy capital investment could support the mass production industries and their proliferating technology. Often individual proprietors, partners, and family businesses were incapable of such investment. About the middle of the nineteenth century, Western states enacted general incorporation laws permitting the formation of limited liability stock companies. Shareholders in these corporations were liable only to the extent of their investments —

hence, they were "limited." At the end of the century only Russia and the Ottoman Empire still required special grants of incorporation. Limited liability corporations permitted the raising of large amounts of capital and provided the machinery to make ownership easily transferable. The rate at which these corporations were chartered became an index of economic activity. They also provided lines of financial control over economic activity far beyond the capability of small individual entrepreneurs. By the end of the century the bulk of capital investment, production, and employees was under corporate management in every industrial country. In negotiable shares ownership was distributed among many investors. But blocks of stockholders, corporate banks, investment banking firms, or other corporations usually held the real powers of management. In financial institutions that directed the flow of credit (the very lifeblood of capitalist economy), economic power was most centralized. Thus, by corporate organization, an economy dominated by financial institutions supplanted the early capitalism of entrepreneurs.

The dominant financiers made agreements among themselves to curb unrestricted competition and to form combinations through which they could control the

An early steam threshing machine. Obviously better than chasing bulls around to trample out the grain.

markets. To secure the collective monopoly they usually sought and obtained high tariffs. Their first, simplest, and least enduring form of combination was normally an agreement to fix prices or, in the case of the railroads, to establish pools for the prearranged sharing of traffic or profits. Overstocked participants were, of course, tempted to reduce prices and break the agreement. Several devices were used to remedy this defect. German bankers and producers formed cartels or incorporated associations that operated through common sales agencies at high fixed domestic prices and allotted production quotas. The government granted them tariff protection, sales assistance, transportation bounties, and colonies. In return they put their economic power at its disposal to back its foreign policy and to prevent unwanted democratization.

Outside Germany other devices were more common than cartels. High tariffs, major resources concentrated in a few areas, and general dependence upon the railroad fostered the growth of monopolies. In America as in Germany they were held together by major investment banking firms. Their tendency was not toward common sales agencies or cartels but toward the corporate merger or coordination of management in the form of trusts, holding companies, and interlocking directors named by investment bankers who supplied credit. Monopolists improved or—as in the aluminum industry—perfected their control by obtaining exclusive rights to raw materials, by assuming transportation advantages, by absorbing their competitors, or by reaching informal agreements. At the beginning of the twentieth century heavy industry, transportation, fuel, and finance were generally controlled by the apex of a corporate pyramid.

Industry in Belgium and France

The first countries to industrialize rapidly after Britain were Belgium and France. Until after 1814 the Napoleonic wars absorbed

the Continent's resources and isolated the Continent from Britain's early industrial technology. After the peace, British products undersold their competitors, further delaying economic growth on the Continent. Both Belgium and France had a history of technical skills and commerce, and in both countries the French Revolution had swept traditional institutions away and left behind economic unity. Together with Luxembourg, Belgium and France shared the mineral resources of an international region whose deposits extended eastward into the Prussian Ruhr Valley. Because they lacked credit and cheap overland transportation, their economies developed only slowly at first, but eventually they overcame these scarcities.

Belgium was first to introduce the railways, coke-burning furnaces, machine tools, mechanized textiles, and new banking institutions that made her the gateway of continental industrialization. By mid-century Belgium was keeping pace with England, and its self-sustaining economy was as much admired as its liberal constitution. But toward the end of the nineteenth century, when Belgium's population was the densest in the world, its deep mines failed to produce sufficient coal and iron for domestic use. Belgium then became a net importer of both materials, yielding economic leadership to areas having superior resources. Capital and engineers flowed out of Belgium into other parts of Europe.

Industrialization in nineteenth-century France was rapid, slow, or hardly existent depending on the area in question. After 1815 Alsatian cotton textiles kept pace with leading British centers. For a brief period before 1870 France—much of whose technology was superior to England's—became a leading producer of iron. But on the whole the country's industrialization was slow before 1895 and not spectacularly fast thereafter. At the beginning of the twentieth century France remained a land of small preindustrial workshops and tiny, inefficient, nonmechanized farms.

Tardy industrialization did not result from a shortage of capital or top-level engineering skills, since France supplied these to other areas of Europe and the world. But the quality, quantity, and geographical location of her mineral resources were major drawbacks. She lacked large deposits of quality coking coal and rich nonsulfurous iron ore. Domestic or imported coal could reach the major iron deposits of Lorraine and the northern departments only by rail. And political disputes and rivalries among promoters delayed completion of a railway network until 1870.

Although their achievements at home were limited, French capitalists and engineers promoted industrialization on the rest of the Continent. They founded foreign investment firms, constructed railway networks, opened mines, built factories, and established utilities and commercial businesses. By 1914 French foreign loans amounted to about fifty billion francs (ten billion dollars). French capital and engineers also built the Suez Canal of 1869, over which the British gained control.

German Industrial Preeminence in Europe

Few other early nineteenth-century areas appeared less favored for large-scale industry than Germany. As a battleground divided among thirty-nine mercantilist states, its economy was primitive. Most Germans were peasants bound to the soil or were entering a century-long process of compensated emancipation. Capital was lacking and commercial banking was nonexistent outside a few commercial cities and princely courts. In few areas of Europe had traditionalist lords and clerics succeeded so well in preserving a medieval economy.

But several breaches were opened in this economy during the first half of the nineteenth century. French occupation had its most lasting effects in the Rhineland, the areas where most German resources were later discovered. After 1835 individual German states and investors began to construct railroads at a pace more rapid than that of the French. Prussia sponsored a customs union (the *Zollverein*) that in 1844 imposed a tariff on British iron. In the quarter century between 1850 and 1875 German political unification created the largest effective single market in Europe.

By 1875 Germany was producing more iron and coal than Belgium and France. By 1910 it was the greatest industrial producer in Europe and the second trading nation in the world (Britain was the first). Change occurred so rapidly in the German Empire that her rulers had to cope with remnants of peasant emancipation and pressing urban-social problems simultaneously. From the beginning her industrialists adopted the latest technology. That her people were literate and knowledgeable, adaptable, and subject to discipline partially explains her dazzling rate of growth. But nineteenth-century industry was founded on coal and iron, and the German Empire probably possessed as much of these resources as the remainder of Western Europe put together. Furthermore, she had easy access to the rich ores of Sweden after 1890. As John Maynard Keynes observed with little exaggeration, "The German Empire has been built more truly on coal and iron than blood and iron." [4] In addition, the Empire possessed rich chemical resources and deposits of nonferrous metals.

Rapid industrialization quickly brought new social and political problems to the fore. Between 1871 and 1910 Germany's population increased from just over forty-five to nearly sixty-five million. Although industrial workingmen suffered fewer hardships than displaced artisans, they organized more thoroughly in Germany than in France or Britain. The dissatisfied labor movement, the most literate of Europe at the time, turned to socialism after the depression of 1873. After failing to destroy

4. *The Economic Consequences of the Peace*, Harcourt, Brace & Howe, New York, 1920, p. 81.

the socialist movement with coercion, Bismarck sought after 1880 to undermine it with the most comprehensive social insurance system of the century. The Socialist party, supported by about four fifths of organized labor, had become the largest political party in Germany by 1910. But German labor proved loyal to the regime at the outbreak of World War I.

The United States' Rise to World Industrial Preeminence

The United States was abundantly endowed for industrialization, and its deficiencies proved remediable. Agricultural and industrial resources were sufficient to sustain the impression for over a century that they were unlimited. Over Europe and contemporary "underdeveloped countries" America had the cardinal advantage of no population pressures. Despite an influx of cheap immigrant labor there was a labor shortage. That shortage helped bolster a per capita purchasing power higher than any other market in the world. It also furnished incentives for mechanizing farm and factory without producing the serious side effects of technological displacement. In Europe industrialization alleviated problems of subsistence, social immobility, and poverty, but in America, industrialization was popularly associated with the first appearance of these problems.

America's continental resources and her great potential attracted foreign capital, as well as droves of European workers with skilled and willing hands. Great tracts of free land were available to reward agricultural immigrants and the enterprisers who risked building the superb railroad network that tied east and west into one gigantic market. By 1870 that network was tied in with steamship lines on both oceans so that the commerce of the world could flow in from both Asia and Europe.

Richly endowed with resources and the entrepreneurial and labor skills to exploit them, the United States forged ahead rapidly after 1861 under the umbrella of a government that was responsive to the needs of industry, finance, and agriculture. Loans were available for great enterprises; protective tariffs gave industries every opportunity to grow by guaranteeing a large noncompetitive market; with no large military establishment to support after 1865, taxes were kept low; and court decisions favorable to industry and commerce were handed down. Hardly has a government responded with so many benefactions for its business community. Few governments have been as zealous in helping business interests maintain a position of unchallenged supremacy in the community.

Courts, police, and military troops stood ready to suppress any challenge to the system from labor. Entrepreneurs and financiers influenced every level of government. Corporation lawyers on the Supreme Court bench reinterpreted the Constitution. Senators were identified by their business interests rather than by their states. The same government that championed capitalism at home strove for imperial expansion abroad. As long as prosperity was widespread and opportunities open, voices of dissent were scattered and divided.

At the end of the nineteenth century agrarian dissent in the prairie states signalled the beginning of a vast revolt against business interests and values. Farmers and local merchants revolted against business and monetary policies. But farm revolts were often anti-urban, anti-Negro, anti-Catholic, and prohibitionist. They rejected the city and often blocked urban attempts at reform. Successful labor organizations, on the other hand, frankly accepted laborer status and pitted their economic power against the collective power of their employers. Professionals and older "patrician" families also rose in protest. They wanted more democracy—at least until the present rulers had been replaced.

Further expansion and urbanization ended in the crash of 1929, which provoked

THE INDUSTRIALIZATION OF SOCIETY

social legislation comparable to that in Britain and Germany at the turn of the century. Political power, however, continued to reside disproportionately with the rural minority until after World War II.

Three Latecomers: Sweden, Russia, and Japan

Technical advances enabled some qualified areas to industrialize more rapidly than all their predecessors. Probably the most sensational and least socially painful case was Sweden. Sweden had immensely rich iron deposits, an active commercial community, and a highly skilled, literate population, but she lacked coal and capital. Imports and electricity made up for the coal. Officials borrowed capital abroad. Democratization occurred at the outset, and politics passed quickly from a liberal to a welfare stage. The Social Democratic party, practically unknown in 1890, secured one third of the parliamentary seats in 1910 and lasting control during the world depression of the 1930s. Approximately 92 per cent of Sweden's economy remains privately owned. But welfare-oriented officials working with one of the world's most stable populations have gained a wide reputation for eliminating slums and dire poverty through social legislation, monetary controls, and a pacific foreign policy. Sweden has shared with Switzerland the highest standard of living in twentieth-century Europe.

In sharp contrast stands the Russian Empire whose industrialization was rapid, jerky, and uneven. Russian resources were immense and only partially known, but her institutions were primitive. Illiterate, emancipated, tradition-bound peasants constituted all but a narrow segment of the population. A landed aristocracy that was only a little more progressive than the peasantry dominated society. As late as 1900 about 80 per cent of the population derived its income from the soil.

Industry, science, and mechanization

Stockholm, a city without slums.

came too late to prevent massive famines that probably carried away between two and three million people between 1892 and World War I. Further famines during the 1920s followed the upheavals of war and revolution.

The Tsarist government, defeated militarily and diplomatically by industrial powers in 1856 and 1878, threw its full weight behind railway construction after 1857 and behind heavy industry after 1880. Coming late, Russian industry utilized the largest production units in all of Europe. Emphasis fell on heavy industry rather than on consumer goods. The period from 1906 to 1914 was one of spectacularly rapid investment and growth.

The Tsarist government pressed industrialization at huge social costs. Like other Eastern autocratic regimes, the bureaucracy mistakenly assumed that industrialization would lessen political and social discontent. Grain was exported even during famine to secure foreign exchange. Instead of supporting the weakened *status quo*, however, the government's revolutionary economic policy produced unwanted social, political, religious, and intellectual effects which the bureaucracy tried to suppress.

Labor organizations were forbidden until 1904, and secret police infiltrated their ranks. After a revolution in 1905 the government attempted agrarian reforms, but it lost the race between subsistence and catastrophe. Population pressures and resultant land hunger left the peasantry unappeasable.

Japan emerged rapidly from feudalism and world isolation. During the 1860s a young Japanese warrior class appealed to nationalist sentiments, adopted European military science and economy, united the islands under the emperor, and set out to modernize Japan from above. Eclectically borrowing from advanced nations, the government sponsored industry and commerce. It avoided financial dependence on foreign investors. Despite serious shortages of raw materials, industry — especially electrically powered heavy industry — grew extraordinarily after 1890. Subsidized industry and commerce, combined with low labor costs, enabled Japanese businessmen to expel foreign competitors at home and to undersell them in Asia. By Asian standards the Japanese attained a high standard of living, but the greater portion of their gains in productivity went to maintain a growing military establishment and to support a population that increased from about thirty million in 1850 to seventy million in 1940. A new educational system and the Shinto religion inculcated militant nationalism.

Industry and International Rivalry

Industry was convertible to military power. Hence, uneven economic development increased power differentials between industrialized and nonindustrialized peoples and drastically altered the balance of power among those who were technologically advanced. Germany's superior industry as much as her large population was responsible for her emergence as the strongest military power in Europe. French armies had overrun the Continent at the beginning of the nineteenth century. But now against a united and industrialized Germany the French were incapable of standing alone. Recognizing this fact, their leaders not only made foreign alliances but also sank investments in Russia and Eastern Europe hoping to develop a counterbalance. The United States, up to this time preoccupied on the North American continent, began to build a navy during the 1880s and to penetrate distant areas politically and economically. In the Far East, an industrialized Japan defeated China in 1895 and Russia in 1905, annexing territory in each case. While Occidental industrial states were engaged in World War I, Japan established her hegemony in the Far East. In each region dominated by an industrialized power, nominally sovereign but economically backward states lost their self-determination.

As major power rivalries became tense, military expenditures rose and absorbed productive energies that, if directed elsewhere, might have raised stagnating living standards. These developments climaxed in the year of 1914. The disciples of Adam Smith, relying upon *economic* laws to produce a harmonious world, had not foreseen industrialized warfare. Their postulate of interdependence was real enough, but unless international organization was a utopian dream their rejection of political institutions was naïve. The world wars of the twentieth century produced economic dictatorships that provided the first working models of economies completely controlled and planned by states bent on aggrandizement.

Industrialized Warfare

Industrialization has offered vast scope for applying ingenuity to efficient killing. Contemporaries need no reminder that the end product of industrialized warfare, radioactive thermonuclear energy, threatens the continuation of the very society that produced it.

While high-energy technology multiplied the radius of human killing power, industrialized warfare took on another dimension. Now that societies could produce more, they could expend more — in men and resources — for the battlefield without endangering domestic subsistence standards.

In World War I, for example, Britain mobilized 5.7 million men with scant decline in her total production despite shortages and losses. Thus, industrialization quietly reduced material limitations that had restrained past warfare and laid the foundations for "total wars" in the twentieth century. Total war has drawn every able civilian adult into the production of war materials or into essential civilian goods and services. And it has destroyed their immunity from direct military attack. In both World Wars I and II civilian deaths exceeded military deaths. New long-range guns, aircraft, and rockets aimed at industrial complexes were used to create these casualties. Nationalism—fostered by mechanized transport, mass communications, and education—is equally, if not more, responsible for total war than industrialization. With emotional propaganda, national mass media gear the psychology of their populations to war. With their hate-fed civilians behind them, it is not surprising that the governments of industrialized countries have lacked moderation at peace tables or that some defeated powers have turned to totalitarianism to overturn unfavorable peace treaties.

Compared to the warriors of earlier periods, today's military powers justify their deeds by secular rather than religious ideologies. What is decisively new is their access to unprecedented control over technological knowledge including the means of mass communications.

Long before the implications of this "open-ended 'revolution'" became apparent, industrialization began to affect the popular ideology and politics of Western societies.

Mechanized warfare, 1966: jet aircraft on a napalm bombing run.

ping, exchange, and labor during the early period of industrialization emphasizing continuity rather than revolutionary developments.

————, The Industrial Revolution, 1760–1830, Home University Library, London, 1949, and a Galaxy Book.
A lucid short treatment of early English industrialization sympathetic to the plight of entrepreneurs and emphasizing the role of credit and banks.

Bowden, Witt, Michael Karpovich, and A. P. Usher, *An Economic History of Europe Since 1750,* American Book Co., New York, 1937.
An old account well balanced and still useful.

Buer, M. C., *Health, Wealth and Population in the Early Days of the Industrial Revolution,* Routledge, London, 1926.
Indispensable for the subjects of subsistence and longevity.

Cameron, Rondo E., *France and the Economic Development of Europe 1800–1914,* Princeton University Press, Princeton, 1961.
Traces the use of French capital on the Continent, especially to build railways, and its impact in spurring industrialization there.

Chambers, Jonathan D., *The Workshop of the World: British Economic History from 1820 to 1880,* Home University Library, London, 1961.
An analysis of the British economy during

SELECTED READINGS

Ashton, Thomas S., *An Economic History of England: The Eighteenth Century,* Barnes & Noble, New York, 1955.
Describes the structure of population, agriculture, transportation, manufacturing, ship-

Asterisk (*) denotes paperback.

its period of world leadership in industrial production.

*Cipolla, Carlo, *Economic History of World Population*, Penguin Books, Baltimore, Md., 1962.
A very brief history of world population which puts in sharp focus the ability of industrial society to sustain large populations.

Clapham, John, *An Economic History of Modern Britain*, University Press, Cambridge, 1951–1959, 3 vols.
Detailed running account from the railway age after 1820 to the organization of big business, labor, and government in the twentieth century.

————, *The Economic Development of France and Germany, 1815–1914*, University Press, Cambridge, 1955 (4th ed.).
A standard descriptive account.

Clough, Shepard B., *The Economic Development of Western Civilization*, McGraw-Hill, New York, 1959.
An excellent up-to-date economic history.

*Cottrell, William F., *Energy and Society*, McGraw-Hill, New York, 1959.
Describes the introduction of energy-conversion machines using natural fuels as the basic divide separating "low energy" past and present societies from industrialized societies having "high energy" consumption per capita.

Deane, Phyllis, *The First Industrial Revolution*, University Press, Cambridge, 1965.
Based on research by others, this study analyzes the factors of economic growth in the British economy between 1750 and 1850.

Deane, Phyllis and W. A. Cole, *British Economic Growth 1688–1959, Trends and Structure*, University Press, Cambridge, 1962.
Using the oldest industrial economy, the authors marshal available long-term quantitative data for the testing of theories of economic growth.

Dunham, Arthur L., *The Industrial Revolution in France 1815–1848*, Exposition Press, New York, 1955.
A topic-by-topic survey that provides much detail but it is not easy reading.

Fuller, John F. C., *The Conduct of War 1789–1961, A Study of the Impact of the French, Industrial and Russian Revolutions on War and Its Conduct*, Eyre, Spottiswoode, London, 1961.
A caustic critique of modern total warfare by a British general who finds much of its origins in technological developments beginning with the railroad.

George, M. Dorothy, *England in Transition: Life and Work in the Eighteenth Century*, Penguin Books, London, 1953.
A masterly survey of the social process of early industrialization which destroys romantic myths concerning subsistence and working conditions in preindustrial England.

Griffith, G. T., *Population Problems of the Age of Malthus*, University Press, Cambridge, 1926.
Critical for the early debate on the relationship of population to subsistence.

Habakkuk, H. J. and M. Postan, eds., *The Cambridge Economic History of Europe*, Volume VI, *The Industrial Revolution and After: Incomes, Population and Technological Change* (*I*), University Press, Cambridge, 1965.
Disjointed discussions of income, world population, technological changes in agriculture and industry, and the industrialization of the United States, Russia, and the Far East.

Henderson, William O., *The Industrial Revolution in Europe: Germany, France, Russia, 1900–1914*, Quadrangle Books, Chicago, 1961.
A pioneering and none too successful effort to relate the industrial development of the Continent.

Hobson, J. A., *The Evolution of Modern Capitalism: A Study of Machine Production*, Allen & Unwin, London; Macmillan, New York, 1954 (4th ed.).
A basic study with important observations on trading patterns.

Knowles, Lilian C. A., *Economic Development in the Nineteenth Century, France, Germany, Russia, and the United States*, Routledge, London, 1932.
A general summary that includes information on tariffs and trade policies, domestic and foreign.

*Mantoux, Paul, *The Industrial Revolution in the Eighteenth Century,* Harper & Row, New York, 1962.

A reprint of an old but sound discussion of English industrial mechanization.

Mumford, Lewis, *Technics and Civilization,* Harcourt, Brace & World, New York, 1934.

Insight-filled associations between machines, the culture they arose from, and the problems they present.

Pounds, Norman J. G. and William N. Parker, *Coal and Steel in Western Europe,* Indiana University Press, Bloomington, Indiana, 1957.

Historical geography of the basic industrial resources emphasizing disparities between their distribution and political boundaries.

Rosen, George, *A History of Public Health,* MD Publications, New York, 1958.

Discusses improvements in sanitation and their relationship to population growth.

*Toynbee, A., *The Industrial Revolution,* Beacon Press, Boston, 1956.

The classic that crystallized the term "industrial revolution" in English usage.

*Usher, Abbott P., *A History of Mechanical Inventions,* Beacon Press, Boston, 1959.

Superbly illustrated account of which Chapters XI through XV apply to the era of power machinery.

Ward, J. T., *The Factory Movement 1830–1855,* St. Martin's Press, New York, 1962.

Chronicles the public agitation to secure regulation of factories in England during the first half of the nineteenth century.

22

Intellectual and Ideological Ferment in the Age of Realism and Science

Nineteenth-century thinkers attempted to discover natural or scientific laws operating in society. Industrialization persistently and irrepressibly made economic considerations a part of their raw materials. Rapid social change created crises for those who believed in an unchanging, divinely ordained order, and static metaphysics gave way before evolutionary theory and speculative, historical sociology. Social theorists now sought to explain the principles that govern social change itself.

Most "social scientists" worked with a set of precepts borrowed from evolutionary philosophy or from physics and biology. Dominant among these various "scientific" ideologists were the various types of Darwinists whose views of nature were taken from evolutionary biology. Significantly, this model had little resemblance to the harmonious Newtonian world of natural laws beneficent to the individual. Rather, it portrayed nature as a sanguinary jungle of natural antagonisms and a struggle to the death for survival in which the species or collective group, not the individual, counted.

Reflecting contemporary social and political antagonisms, evolutionary social doctrines split into several "scientific" ideologies. In industrialized countries conservative "Social Darwinism" provided a rationale for giving all initiative to the industrial and financial elite. Although it was formulated in England, its assumptions more accurately fit conditions in preindustrial societies. Meanwhile, "reform" Social Darwinism provided a new basis for progressive liberalism. Also rising to oppose conservative Social Darwinism was the uncompromising class-conscious socialism of Karl Marx. Marx, who was steeped in Hegel's philosophy of evolutionary progress through conflict, immediately recognized similarities between his advocacy of class warfare and Darwin's natural selection of species. But the most common form of evolutionary ideology was still a different application of Darwinism—the nationalist and imperialist argument that warfare regenerated human society. Thus realism, an old and recurrent aspect of Western thought, gave cynical, deterministic, and "scientific" connotations to the thirst for bloodshed. By the end of the nineteenth century, "spiritual" Darwinist nationalists were locked in conflict with "materialistic" evolutionary socialists, both of them claiming to have absolute scientific truth.

Their dogmatic clash created a crisis for the whole idea of a social science, because some observers considered this conflict proof that no objective study of society was possible. Romantic realists cast further doubts on the objectivity of any social science by probing the role of instincts and unpredictable, irrational environmental influences in the determination of individual behavior. Mathematicians of "relativity," although they believed in a fixed objective reality, inadvertently gave impetus to the antiscientific revolt by questioning popularly accepted physical "laws of nature." Among the youth of the generation just before World War I, mystical cults of irrationality took root. Nationalist and religious historians everywhere had long been following the subjectivist approach, and now German philosophers and historians were making subjectivism into a formal system. Separating physical science sharply from social studies, they considered social truth to be entirely relative to the investigators' value systems. To these challenges of irrationality and subjectivism, chastened rationalists and empiricists replied with sociological and psychological methods that claimed only tentative and hypothetical validity. Their concessions to irrationality were sufficient, however, to question the basic assumptions of rationality on which classic liberalism rested.

Responses to Industrialization

Both of the new urban industrial classes —capitalists and workers—faced novel problems to which traditional institutions responded slowly or negatively, and initially both were critical of existing political and religious creeds. Middle-class intellectuals formulated new ideologies for each of them. For entrepreneurs and financiers they elaborated a most congenial tenet from the doctrines of Adam Smith: *laissez faire* or nonintervention by public authority in the management of production and distribution.

Those intellectuals who were sympathetic to labor's conditions or critical of economic instability, supplied various alternatives to private *laissez-faire* capitalism in the form of state intervention, cooperatives, or state ownership.

The Evolution of Liberal Economics

In Britain, the hearth of classical liberal economics, Thomas Malthus dampened Adam Smith's humanitarian optimism with a cold shower of economic realism. In his *Essay on the Principles of Population* (1798), Malthus rejected the idea of progress and predicted gloom. If unchecked, he said, men multiply by a geometric ratio and thus outstrip subsistence, which increases only by an arithmetic ratio. Grossly excess numbers would be removed, luckily, by war, famine, and plague; misery and vice would continue to operate as checks on the multiplication of the poor. Although they blame institutions, the niggardliness of nature, or others for their plight, poor people are responsible for their own want. Government intervention, higher wages, and charity would not relieve it. The only remedy that Malthus sanctioned was moral restraint—late marriages and chastity. In this and other works, Malthus, a clergyman by training, established himself as the leading early professional economist.

To contemporaries who disagreed with him, he was the pessimistic architect of the "dismal science" of economics. Classical economists and Charles Darwin considered that Malthus had contributed an enduring element, foreign to Adam Smith's optimism: an inexorable struggle for survival as the basic law of nature.

As economic conditions changed, the economic doctrines of liberalism changed and broke into divergent streams. One was the conservative liberalism of Herbert Spencer (1820–1903), who coined the phrase, the "survival of the fittest." Spencer adjusted the doctrine of *laissez faire* to guard against governmental intervention while corporations and combinations of capital — in some cases monopolies — were replacing individual proprietorships and partnerships in heavy industry. He described all state intervention — public charity, state banking, sanitation and housing inspection, health and safety codes — as "socialism." His social science demonstrated the impossibility of conscious change, at least for the poor or unfit. Such people should be eliminated to make way for a new human nature in a coming era of peace and industry.

Herbert Spencer, prophet of Social Darwinism. He hated government so much that he carried his letters across town to avoid having to use postal facilities.

The poverty of the incapable, the distresses that come upon the imprudent, the starvation of the idle, and those shoulderings aside of the weak by the strong, which leave so many "in shallows and in miseries," [he wrote] are the decrees of a large far-seeing benevolence. It seems hard that an unskillfulness, which with all his efforts he cannot overcome, should entail hunger upon the artisan. It seems hard that a laborer incapacitated by sickness from competing with his stronger fellows, should have to bear the resulting privations. It seems hard that widows and orphans should be left to struggle for life and death. Nevertheless, when regarded not separately, but in connection with the interests of universal humanity, these harsh fatalities are seen to be full of the highest beneficence. . . .[1]

1. Herbert Spencer, *Social Statics; or, the Conditions Essential to Human Happiness,* Appleton and Co., New York, 1886, pp. 353–354.

Accompanying Spencer's gospel of resignation for the unfit was his emphasis on the importance of business success for the elite, whose philanthropy should help those who are capable of survival to help themselves. He gathered most of his following from the "self-made men" who built personal industrial and financial empires.

"Bourgeois liberalism," which in Europe sought to maintain property restrictions on suffrage and to limit education to those who could afford it, had its culmination in Spencer. Breaking with the bourgeois liberals in Western Europe were "democratic liberals" who, looking to the United States as a model, advocated universal manhood suffrage, primary education at public expense, and some modifications of *laissez faire* to recognize labor organizations and to permit state intervention in matters of health and safety. Motives for this break were probably many. In Britain they were partly poli-

Robert Owen's New Lanark. This model industrial community was a financial success, which suggested that industrialists could be good to their workers and still make a profit.

tical. Liberals were competing with Disraeli's "Tory Democracy" for the political loyalty of the working classes. Evangelical churchmen were cultivating a social consciousness that held society, not just individual shortcomings, responsible in some measure for the squalor and poverty of the poor. This moral impulse, which impelled many to go beyond liberalism to socialist politics, Christian socialism, and a "social gospel," was reinforced by the Utilitarians whose intellectual leader at mid-century was John Stuart Mill.

The Utilitarians inherited from Jeremy Bentham a tradition of legal reform, empirical methodology, a crude materialistic rational psychology, and the premise that the purpose of government was the greatest good for the greatest number. At first they had been vociferous advocates of *laissez faire*. At the same time, however, they adhered to the use of reason, law, education, eventual manhood suffrage, and the restriction of births as a means of mitigating social conditions. John Stuart Mill (1806–1873) went further in search of a balance between social justice and property rights. Although he remained a democratic liberal, he reluctantly became sympathetic to certain socialist points of view. He rejected the Calvinist attitude that poverty was the result of individual moral faults and instead advocated reliance on institutions, leadership,

and a secular education that would teach youth a sense of social justice. Thus he contributed to the "social gospel" movement, which at the end of the century brought segments of British liberalism, socialism, and religious reform movements together in a common cause.

"Utopian Socialism"

Various categories of socialists sought to substitute association and cooperation for competition, to put the ownership of the means of production and distribution in the hands of collective associations or the state, and to bring productive processes and the ups and downs of the business cycle under rational control for a broader distribution of industrial wealth. Socialist objections to the economic and political inequalities of both the Old Regime and industrial society were moral and ideological as well as economic. Ideologically they represented an extension of "liberty, equality, and fraternity" from the legal to the economic realm. Socialists denounced liberal individualistic morality on the grounds that economic freedom of the entrepreneurs amounted to the freedom of the working classes to starve amidst increasing plenty. Moreover, the propertyless classes bore the brunt of depression and unemployment.

Initially, few socialists had broad support from the working classes in whose cause or name they worked. Because most of them relied on persuasion rather than force or on altruism rather than interest, Karl Marx branded them "Utopians," a label that conservatives have also adopted and made general.

Disillusioned with the course and outcome of the revolution of 1789, French liberals inaugurated criticism of *laissez-faire* capitalism. One disillusioned liberal was Henri de Saint-Simon (1760–1825). Saint-Simon concluded that revolution had failed to do away with one cardinal privilege—unearned or inherited wealth. His solution was leadership by an elite—bankers, engineers, industrialists—who should

Baron Gros, Napoleon at Eylau, *1808. Gros, an eyewitness of Napoleon's battles, has here shown the Emperor comforting the wounded on the battlefield of Eylau, in east Prussia. Although this battle, fought in 1807 against the allied Prussian and Russian forces, was indecisive, within a few months Napoleon had resoundingly defeated the allies at Friedland, negotiated the Tilsit treaty with Czar Alexander, and gained a hold over large parts of eastern Europe. (Musée du Louvre, Paris)*

Honoré Daumier, The Uprising, *ca. 1848. In this painting Daumier has captured the spirit of the Paris mob during the uprising of 1848. Throughout Europe, general unrest and dissent erupted in a series of revolutions and counter-revolutions from about 1815 to 1850. In France the middle and upper classes disputed nationalist and constitutional issues, but urban workers revolted for the familiar economic reasons—low wages, high prices, and lack of work. (Phillips Collection, Washington)*

Georges Seurat, A Sunday Afternoon on the Grande Jatte, *1884–86. Although France's political turmoil did not end with the defeat of the uprising of 1848, there were periods of tranquility for all classes. This painting shows a group of Parisians enjoying their leisure on an island in the Seine. A working-class man reclines on the grass at the left; a well-dressed couple, the lady with her pet monkey, strolls at the right, while nursemaids, mothers, children, and lovers also enjoy their outing. (Art Institute of Chicago)*

Otto Bollhagen, Friedrich Krupp Steel Foundry, *1873. Thanks to her huge deposits of coal and iron and to the energy and application of her people, the German Empire achieved rapid and spectacular success in industry. By the 1880's, the Krupp steelworks at Essen, the largest foundry in Europe, employed 20,000 workers. It was the first foundry to manufacture steel artillery, and the first to use the Bessemer process. (Friedrich Krupp Gemeinshaftsbetriebe)*

Vincent van Gogh, The Loom, *1884. In marked contrast to the flourishing industrial society of Germany, Holland was slow to make the transition from handicraft to mechanical production. Peasant life in many small villages and rural areas was virtually unchanged through much of the nineteenth century. Weaving, a traditional domestic craft in northern Europe, continued to be a "cottage industry." Compare this worker, in intimate relation to his product, with the modern industrial laborers shown above. (Rijksmuseum Kröller-Müller, Otterlo, Holland)*

Claude Monet, La Gare St. Lazare, *1877. The symbol of the Age of Industry was the rail-road, the "Iron Monster," which brought raw materials to the producer and finished goods to the consumer. Although France was quick to embark on industrialization, she lagged behind Germany and England, in part because her railway network was not completed until 1870. Iron and glass—a combination popular in the nineteenth century—were used to roof St. Lazare and many other railway stations. (Art Institute of Chicago)*

Peasants' living room, from F. Hempel, Tableaux Pittoresques de L'Empire Russe, *n.d. Until Czar Alexander II freed the serfs in 1861, Russia's agrarian economy depended on the virtual slave-labor of peasants. This page from a book of "picturesque scenes" shows the crowded conditions under which the serfs were forced to live. Industrialization had little effect on the Russian economy or the life of the people until the twentieth century. (Anne S. K. Brown, Military Collection, Courtesy American Heritage Publishing Co., Inc.)*

rule according to scientific and humanitarian principles. This elite would promote efficiency and assure a more just distribution of wealth. It would also furnish the high priests of a renovated, this-worldly religion, the "New Christianity," which would reinforce humanitarianism. Saint-Simon did not envisage a classless society. Rewards were to be distributed on the basis of performance. To achieve that end more equitably, society should provide productive tools from a "social fund," establish a state bank to exercise a monopoly of credit, and abolish inheritance rights. Saint-Simon's technocratic doctrines secured their greatest following among youthful engineers, many of whom became the leading builders and managers of French foreign and domestic enterprise. Bankers and businessmen also welcomed his emphasis on a managerial elite, but they rejected his "New Christianity."

British Utopianism, which was cultivated during the wars of the French Revolution in the anticlerical natural-rights philosophy of Thomas Paine and the anarchism of William Godwin, took a socialist course under the leadership of Robert Owen (1771–1858), manager of a well-known cotton factory in New Lanark, Scotland. Owen broke with fellow managers, turned New Lanark into a model community, and led agitation for labor organization and factory legislation. He accepted mechanized industry and private property, but argued that both should be used to promote general human welfare. He shared with other socialists the Enlightenment's faith in human perfectibility, progress, and the development of a science of society. Convinced that human nature was largely the product of environment, he sought to change that environment to produce greater happiness and morality. His humanitarian environmentalism brought him in direct conflict with the Christian doctrine of the depravity of man, and, as he experimented with communitarian settlements on the American frontier, he became sharply anticlerical.

Both his labor organization and communitarian experiments eventually failed. Although only a cooperative store movement that he started has endured, some observers consider him a precursor of twentieth-century "scientific management."

Marxian Socialism—an Ambiguous Legacy

The transition from "Utopian" to "scientific" socialism, which was introduced by Karl Marx (1818–1883) and Friedrich Engels (1820–1895) in the *Communist Manifesto* of 1848, was part of a general switch of the intellectuals to "realism." Realism meant a recognition of force and violence in achieving social and national goals.

A realistic thinker, Karl Marx put together a broad synthesis of economics, history, philosophy, politics, prophetic moral judgments, and sociology, which offered a total world view. Hegelian philosophy taught him to derive the key law of nature from historical evolution, but, unlike Hegel, Marx concluded that the purpose of philosophy was not to explain and contemplate evolution, but to change the world. The extent to which change could be accomplished depended on circumstances, particularly on the prevailing "mode of production" or the ownership, control, and organization of the means of production. He traced the evolution of successive modes of production from primitive communal societies through master-slave, lord-peasant, and capitalist-laborer relationships to a future classless, socialist state.

For Marx and Engels the meat of history was a struggle between classes. In 1848, as they saw it, that struggle involved the two classes that were engaged in industrial production: the upper middle class (the bourgeoisie), who owned the means of production and distribution (factories, mines, ships, etc.), and the proletariat, or the propertyless workers. The bourgeoisie, Marx and Engels pointed out, had played the leading historical role in modernizing the world. That class had, in the course of centuries, destroyed feudalism, expanded production, created a world market, and set up modern representative governments. That much was good. But by 1848, they believed, the bourgeoisie were no longer creating freedom; they were creating wage slavery. They were using their control of the economy to destroy the artisan, the peasant, and the weaker capitalists. They were using their absolute ownership of industrial and commercial property to exploit the workers. And they were using their political power to pass laws assuring their ascendancy over other classes.

Marx borrowed valuable ideas about the labor theory from the classical economists to show why capitalism could not avoid exploiting the workers. Any object that man produces has a certain value which is created by working up raw materials into a finished product. While the worker puts forth the labor to make something, he receives in wages only a fraction of the value of what he has created. The owner gets the remainder of its value in profits. The surplus value represented by profits should go to the man who puts in the labor that creates value; instead, it goes to the owner, who piles up capital while the worker gets barely enough for subsistence. This capitalistic economic system alienates the worker from what he makes, alienates him from the owner, alienates him from the government in which he may not participate because he has no property, and alienates him from the legal, educational, and religious system which supports the capitalist arrangement. Marx indicted the evil of a divided society with economic arguments which seemed to show that there was only one way to overcome that evil — by public ownership of the means of production and distribution. The private property that would have to become state-owned was therefore not personal property such as one's house, garden, chicken, or buggy, but large-scale property having an obvious social character, such as railroads, factories, banks, or large estates. In such profit-making property men can be and are exploited. This argument appealed to urban industrial populations. For the peasants and aristocracy, whom he thought obsolescent, Marx had nothing to say. Marx tried to make the workers acutely aware of their situation (class consciousness), so they would revolt and destroy the roots of class antagonism.

Marx proclaimed his basic objectives in 1848, but he offered no detailed blueprint for society after the revolution had occurred. For the most advanced countries, the *Communist Manifesto* called for the abolition of private landed property and the right of inheritance; a graduated income tax; the centralization and control of credit, communications, transportation, and the means of production in the hands of the state; equal obligation of all to work; abolition of distinctions between industry and agriculture; and free public education for children freed from child labor. In highly industrialized countries where democratic channels were open, Marx believed, his program could be obtained peacefully.

Actually, Marx believed important changes would come both by evolution and revolution. *Das Kapital* (*Capital*), his last major work, sought to demonstrate that capitalism, beset by inherent, internal contradictions, would fall of its own weight. Centralization and concentration of capital would force small capitalists into the burgeoning ranks of the proletariat, and periodic depressions would bring intolerable pressures to bear on industrial urban classes. With capitalist appropriation of surplus labor value unchecked, the working classes would become increasingly miserable. Moreover, as the rates of domestic profit declined capitalism must inevitably expand in imperialism or die.

Before Marx's death in 1883, political parties had begun to organize on the Continent that were composed primarily of nonrevolutionary trade-union members but were led by Marxian intellectuals. After

1889, these parties were coordinated by the loosely confederated Second International Workingman's Association, within which the best-organized and dominant group was the German Social Democratic party. Party platforms spoke of a coming revolution, but simultaneously demanded comprehensive democratization and social-welfare programs, whose implementation would ultimately diminish revolutionary fervor. Attacked by Bismarck's government, the party became the largest in the German Reichstag, but its members were rigorously excluded from the civil service and from universities. The leadership was undermined by the rise of "revisionist" platforms that were formulated, with individual differences, by Eduard Bernstein in Germany, Jean Jaurès in France, and their counterparts elsewhere. Bernstein attacked fundamental Marxist tenets. His *Evolutionary Socialism* (1898) concluded that, in fact, the middle classes were not decreasing under capitalism, that the law of increasing worker misery was inoperative, and that depressions left behind a higher standard of living than had existed before. Revisionism opened a breach in Marxist orthodoxy through which flowed humanitarian idealism, patriotism, and, as long as the entire population profited from it, imperialism.

Christian Socialism, Fabian Socialism, and the Social Gospel

"Christian socialism" as a response to industrialization first appeared among Evangelical Anglicans, led by Charles Kingsley (1819–1875), a novelist, historian, priest, and social critic. Kingsley preceded Marx in denouncing merely creedal Christianity as an opiate for the lower classes, and he attacked an economy based exclusively on self-interest as a repudiation of Christian principles. Although he considered socialism a Christian heresy, his practical program was limited to the establishment of cooperatives that were financed at low interest rates by wealthy and pious Christians. His immediate impact was

slight, but the "social gospel" continued within Anglicanism, spread to lower-class Non-Conformists, and in the twentieth century espoused more radical proposals with respect to private property.

Evangelical Christian socialism applied such medieval ideals as the "just price" and social solidarity to conditions of farm and urban labor. More secular, usually less romantic, but also imbued with a social-gospel concept were the gradualists who became known as the Fabian socialists. The Fabian Society, whose ultimate goal was the nationalization of the means of production and distribution, included such diverse, independent people as George Bernard Shaw, H. G. Wells, and the husband-wife combination of Sydney and Beatrice Webb, who founded the London School of Economics and Political Science in 1895. Because the Fabians dominated English social thought at the outset of the twentieth century, they wielded influence disproportionate to their numbers, especially within the new Labour party.

After a period of suppressing liberals and modernists, the Roman Catholic hierarchy under Pope Leo XIII (1878–1903) moved to grope with the social problems of industrialization. Following the revolutions of 1848, his predecessor, Pius IX, had repudiated his former concessions to liberalism, cemented the union of Throne and Altar, and extended clerical education in a series of concordats. In 1864, Pius IX turned his back on liberalism, "modern civilization," and progress in the *Syllabus of Errors*. During the 1870s, the Papacy lost its extensive territories in central Italy to the new Kingdom of Italy, anti-clerical governments came to power in France and Germany, and secular ideologies were depriving the Church of working-class allegiance. Leo XIII conciliated the modernist Catholics and in 1891 issued a bull, *Rerum Novarum* (*Concerning New Things*), for which he was called in some quarters "the workingman's pope." The bull castigated abuses of economic power

Pope Leo XIII, "the workingman's pope." He wished to see harmony prevail.

and advocated the formation of Catholic trade unions, but it made no concessions to either economic liberalism or socialism. Instead, it advocated under the term "corporatism" medieval ideals of a corporate society of estates, each with mutual moral ties, responsibilities and obligations. The state had an obligation to protect the workers from greedy owners. The Church would provide the moral framework for all society.

Anarchism and Anarcho-Syndicalism

While Socialists believed in using a powerful state to achieve reforms, the anarchists believed in having no state at all. Every state, they said, exercises coercion by means of armies, police, and laws, particularly to protect property. The use of· coercion makes men vicious. Their basic premise was that the individual, liberated from repressions, would be vir-

tuous and cooperative. An ideal society could be built on a system of federated economic groups. Men who are engaged in the primary concerns of life—production of goods and services—would be naturally orderly; they would not need an expensive state apparatus to harass them and force them into line.

Anarchism had a wide appeal among people who lacked confidence in the integrity of state officials, especially in Latin and Eastern Europe. One man whose ideas gained considerable attention was Pierre Joseph Proudhon (1809–1865) of France. He contributed the vision of a future stateless, classless society, which would operate under the motto "From each according to his ability, to each according to his need." Despite such opinions and despite his celebrated catch phrase "Property is theft," Proudhon was not a socialist. By "property" in this context he meant unearned income—interest, rents, and promotional profits. Otherwise, he considered private property a bulwark against a strong state and against lower-class socialism. Proudhon, a self-educated printer who was too poor to secure a formal education, formulated a lower-middle-class revolt against both financial capitalism and organized labor. To achieve an ideal society, small property holders and workmen should combine within federations of producers and consumers. Proudhon despised government, including democratic government, but when he thought that Napoleon III would follow his program as a dictator, he welcomed him.

Opposed to political parties, anarcho-syndicalists proposed to rely on syndicates of corporate economic structures, particularly industrial trade unions, which would use direct action such as sabotage or general strikes to weaken and overturn the capitalist order. The principal theorist of anarcho-syndicalism, Georges Sorel (1847–1922), a French engineer, believed that violence was a beneficial, purifying agent which alone could emotionally unite the revolutionary proletariat. Sorel, a self-trained sociologist who explored irrational social motivations, was a principal popularizer of the general strike, with which Russian revolutionaries experimented in 1905 and which fascinated European socialist unions for a time thereafter.

Major Nineteenth-Century Sciences

Major syntheses in nineteenth-century physics and biology proved as corrosive of traditional certainties and as productive of ideological changes as the transformation of the social order by industrialization. These syntheses were rational constructs that explained the apparently contradictory phenomena of nature in terms of the operation of inexorable natural laws. These laws not only satisfied curiosity by explaining the world, but also proved valuable in medicine and technology. At the expense of philosophers and theologians, scientists gained more and more prestige as wielders of the only method of acquiring reliable knowledge.

Physics

Physics and chemistry probed significantly and deeply into the seen and unseen nature of matter and motion. Physicists formulated a new unifying concept—energy—to relate heat to motion. The Englishman Joule expressed heat in mathematical symbols that indicated its mechanical work potential. The German Ludwig Helmholtz added a general law of the conservation of energy to the already accepted premise that matter was indestructible. The universe's store of force, Helmholtz wrote, "cannot in any way be increased or diminished. . . . The quantity of force in Nature is just as eternal and unalterable as the quantity of matter."[2] In the new field of electricity,

2. From "The Conservation of Energy," *Classics of Modern Science,* Alfred A. Knopf, New York, 1927, p. 286.

from which a whole new technology flowed, energy equivalents were also reduced to mathematical description. Heat produced by chemical reactions was also integrated into the unifying concept of energy. Theories concerning the composition of matter eventually coalesced around John Dalton's atomic theory that all matter was composed of a basic number of elements, and their combining weights were tabulated. Spectrum analysis, assisted by photography, aided the identification of these elements in laboratory and observatory. With the discovery of radium at the end of the century, the number of known elements rose from an initial twenty to more than eighty. Eventually, electrons rather than atoms appeared to be the smallest units of matter, and many physicists believed, erroneously, that the atom operated as a small replica of the Newtonian solar universe.

Physics and chemistry until near the end of the century seemed to be filling in details of an absolutely known Newtonian universe. Mathematicians working with three-dimensional space began to conclude, however, that mathematical description yielded only a *symbolic* and incomplete representation of reality. Moreover, minute experimentation convinced Albert Einstein and others that Newtonian concepts were inadequate. In the early twentieth century, Einstein achieved a still broader synthesis in physics, which encompassed mass, energy, light, time, space, and electromagnetism within the same basic formula. But the physics and mathematics of relativity were not a philosophical relativism; they were based, rather, on rigorous experimentation and on the assumption of a fixed objective reality. Man's apprehension of this reality, however, was subject to limits and modifications because of his relative position within cosmic space and time.

Biology

Biological research tended to move in two independent directions that seldom converged. One dealt with biochemistry,

Charles Darwin.

physiology, and heredity. The other explored the origin of species as a product of environmental influences.

Within the first type of biological science, bacteriology as an adjunct of medicine made the largest popular impact. Foremost among early bacteriologists was Louis Pasteur (1822–1895), who concluded from studying fermentation and putrefaction that living organisms were responsible for certain chemical actions. Pasteur succeeded in controlling wine spoilage, a devastating silkworm disease, rabid hydrophobia, and the transmission of microorganisms in liquids and on surgical instruments. The germ theory of disease, to which Pasteur's work gave credence, was established by Robert Koch (1843–1910), who isolated and identified the bacilli causing tuberculosis and cholera and who identified rat-borne fleas as the transmitters of the bacilli causing bubonic plague. While other microbe hunters sought out and identified disease-causing "germs," surgery was transformed by the combination of chemical anesthesia and aseptic procedures that depended either on

Joseph Lister's use of carbolic acid or on Pasteur's more effective heat treatment. Biochemists also added to the security of life by discoveries that were useful in agriculture and nutrition, such as the nitrogen cycle of plant nutrition and the process of photosynthesis.

During the 1860s, unknown to the general scientific world, an obscure Austrian monk, Gregor Mendel, explored the mathematical distribution of inherited traits by crossing "sport" peas with peas whose ancestors were normal in appearance. Although allowances were made for variations and mutations, the application of mathematics to genetics made the study of heredity an increasingly exact science.

The dominant climate of opinion during the second half of the nineteenth century was less congenial to genetics than to the other major course of biological inquiry which reached a synthesis in the writings of Charles Darwin (1809–1882). Botanists, zoologists, and paleontologists had accumulated large quantities of descriptive data on species and varieties of life extant and extinct. Darwin took this data, together with the uniformitarian geological ideas of Charles Lyell (1797–1875), the ideas of Malthus relating food supply and population growth, his own researches carried out during a long voyage on H.M.S. *Beagle* (early 1830s), and his later researches, to produce a decisive breakthrough in evolutionary theory. He organized his material around the idea of natural selection as the mechanism bringing about changes in species. Darwin published in 1859 a work whose full title reveals its essence: *On the Origin of Species by Means of Natural Selection, or The Preservation of Favored Races in the Struggle for Life*. The *Origin* argued that more creatures were born than could survive, that both within and between species there was a struggle for life, that each creature differed slightly from its parents, and that in the struggle for life those most suited to cope with environment and internecine competition were naturally selected to survive and reproduce their traits. Ultimately, the accumulative preservation of differences produced new species. Thus Darwin's law of nature was not merely a demonstration of biological evolution; it offered a thesis to explain the mechanism that had produced different species and their variations during vast spans of geologic time. Progress and differentiation were rooted in nature where they were exempt from human or divine intervention and where they operated in an amoral "nature red in tooth and claw with ravin," as Tennyson had expressed it poetically before Darwin's *Origin* appeared. Yet on the fundamental point of natural selection, Darwin himself wavered. While it might explain survival of certain traits, it did not explain the origin of the variations preserved. Darwin suggested sexual selection as an auxiliary to natural selection, a theme that he elaborated in the *Origin of Man*. This work made explicit the earlier inference that man stemmed from ancestors common to other life.

Darwin's science drew fire from a variety of scientific, moral, and religious spokesmen, especially from those who considered his account of human origins irreconcilable with a literal reading of the Book of Genesis. Roman Catholics had less difficulty than Protestants in reconciling evolution with religion. Darwin's works were never placed on the *Index*. Even though some religious apologists insisted that fossils had been planted by God to test the faith of man, Protestant opposition was short-lived, especially in areas where "survival-of-the-fittest" economic doctrines were already prevalent. Protestant fundamentalists had more difficulty with the "death of Adam," but some of them found Social Darwinism quite scientific and acceptable. The clash between evolution and religion was sharp and, in the United States, prolonged; nevertheless, science scored a rapid victory. More critical than the conflict with traditional religions was the collision between proponents of the "survival of the fittest"

and humanitarians, religious or secular. Most "scientific" ideologies that advocated the use of force—nationalism, racism, class conflict, unrestrained economic competition—seized upon Darwin's biology to prove its agreement with natural law. Once applied, the doctrine that might makes right became a self-fulfilling prophecy, for force could be answered only in kind.

Social "Scientism" and Relativism

Nineteenth-century scientists, respectable social scientists, and ideologists believed that key natural laws of science were absolute parts of the universe's design. By the end of the century physicists, mathematicians, and sociologists had come to consider their laws useful and pragmatically valid but less than absolute. Those who lost their faith in "scientism" usually went to the opposite pole of total relativism, insisting that all beliefs and knowledge rested on faith alone or on a collectively held myth.

Positivism

Positivism was a highly characteristic intellectual attitude in the nineteenth century. Positivists believed that the natural laws governing society could be formulated from the facts of social life. This assumption guided the efforts of classical economists, Utilitarians, Marxists, anarchists, Socialists, and empiricists alike. While they discovered different social laws, they agreed that society had advanced through various stages of development and that a higher and happier stage could be reached by applying scientific knowledge of man and society to social life.

Positivism was more than an attitude. In the hands of August Comte (1798–1857) and his disciples, positivism became a way of life. Secretary to Saint-Simon as a young man, Comte absorbed the French Enlightenment and Utopian Socialism. Encyclopedic in his thinking, he presented a comprehensive social philosophy in his six-volume *Course of Positive Philosophy* (1830–1842) and other writings. He taught that mankind had evolved through theological and metaphysical stages of thought and was in the scientific or positivist stage in which a science of society (which he called sociology or social physics) had become possible. Positive knowledge is based on patterns, laws, or correlations of facts. Our job, he said, is to show *how* things happen, since we cannot answer the question *why*. Anything speculative, theological, miraculous, or metaphysical is to be rigorously excluded. Positivism meant a matter-of-factness, accepting as true only what could be verified by experience. Comte effectively captured a basic trend of modern civilization.

But he concluded that reason and science alone were too weak to insure order and to command the loyalties of men. Therefore, he set forth a Religion of Humanity, in which Humanity replaced God as the supreme being, and great benefactors of mankind like Gutenberg and Newton became the objects of veneration. Worship services with readings from the world's great literature and music by Mozart were performed wherever positivist societies sprang up. Disciples accepted Comte's belief that mankind evolves from selfishness to altruism. Empirical scientists like the physiologist Claude Bernard, scholars like the great dictionary compiler, Emile Littré, novelists like George Sand, and reforming civil servants such as the men who tried to modernize Mexico before 1910 were followers of Comte. Intellectuals in Russia, Latin America, or Italy were especially drawn to Comtean positivism, since humanitarian advocates of reform in authoritarian societies tended to be hostile to metaphysics and theology while accepting nothing incapable of scientific proof.

When positivists became convinced that they had discovered deterministic laws, their ideologies often became metaphysical, dogmatic, and religious. Social Darwinism — the belief that beneficent change was produced by the survival of the fittest individual, class, nation, or race — became the most dogmatic and widespread form of positivism.

Darwinian and Integral Nationalism

Darwinist nationalists glorified warfare as the agent of human progress. Only the ever-present threat of war could eradicate selfish materialism, comfortable softness, and indolence. But in purely biological terms, Darwinian nationalism could be attacked on the grounds that warfare eliminated the best physical specimens and destroyed the material basis of physical health. Although avowed materialists continued to be popular, Darwinian nationalism was decked out more and more attractively in romantic, spiritual, and religious clothes. Heinrich von Treitschke wrote:

> It is a false conclusion that wars are waged for the sake of material advantage. . . . Here the high moral ideal of national honor is a factor . . . enshrining something positively sacred, and compelling the individual to sacrifice himself to it.[3]

The late nineteenth century may have been a "generation of materialism," but it was dominated by a patriotic religion of force. In Renan's words, which were echoed eveywhere, the nation is a "soul, a spiritual principle." Warfare nurtured that soul and assured progress. "You may hope for a time when the sword shall be turned into the ploughshare," Karl Pearson, an English advocate of imperialism and national eugenics wrote, "but believe me, when that day comes mankind will no longer progress."[4]

3. Quoted by Franklin Le Van Baumer, *Main currents of Western Thought,* Alfred A. Knopf, New York, 1952, p. 547.

4. Quoted by Carleton J. H. Hayes, *A Generation of Materialism 1871–1900,* Harper and Row, New York and London, 1941, p. 340.

Between 1871 and 1914 there were no major wars to sate the Darwinists' thirst for bloodshed, but domestically "integral nationalists" sought to extirpate internal minorities and to discredit all forms of diversity. After the unification of Germany in 1871, the government placed heavy legal and economic pressures on Polish, Danish, and French minorities, and the imperial government tried to break down the internationalism of Roman Catholics and socialists. After the Hungarians achieved autonomy in 1867, their government attempted to "Magyarize" the Slavic peoples who constituted a majority of the population. Similar policies were applied in the Balkans, but the most extensive attempt to repress all national, religious, and social minorities occurred in Tsarist Russia, where Social Darwinism was less a newfangled ideology than an implicit, traditional policy. Applied most bloodily against the Jews, Russian integralism contributed to the revival of anti-Semitism in Western Europe by driving to it refugees who were less educated, wealthy, and adapted than the older Western Jewish families.

Whether in Russia, where they were in power, or in France, where they constituted an anti-Republican minority, integral nationalists held similar assumptions, objectives, and a burning faith in the uniqueness and God-chosen mission of their own particular nationality. Institutions that antedated the Enlightenment were the natural products of divine evolution, which formed the collective soul of their nation. This soul was most purely represented by the military and the peasantry; it was threatened by "rootless" capitalists, merchants, urban laborers, internationalists, nonconformist minorities, and especially by Jews, whose historical claims as the chosen people of God rankled advocates of other national messianisms. Be it German, French, Russian, Japanese, or American, nativist nationality was God-chosen, and God's chapel was the history classroom.

Racism and Racial Anti-Semitism

In the nineteenth century, "race" was a general but imprecise term that was often used interchangeably with "nationality," but racism was a "scientific" ideology that claimed to find *the* key to history within the racial compositions of societies past and present. In 1852, the Comte de Gobineau set down in "scientific" form the inherited right of the nobility, as descendants of Germanic conquerors, to rule the Gauls or French. Instead of progress in liberal equality, Gobineau predicted doom unless a new "Aryan" elite rose to replace the aristocracy. Gobineau's *Inequality of Human Races* gained little popularity until the late nineteenth century, when the middle classes as well as the traditional privileged classes felt that their positions were being jeopardized by new families rising through educational and economic opportunities. Although ultranationalists preached it, racism generally was an international elitist doctrine. Because it postulated inherent biological inequality, it also became current in the American South and in mixed European colonies around the world. Racial superiority was a constant rationale for imperialism. Domestically its principal manifestation was aggressive anti-Semitism.

Although Darwinism gave anti-Semitism a "scientific" basis, religious and economic sanctions against Jews had long existed in Europe. Sporadic mob murders, riots, inquisitional legal proceedings, segregated housing districts or ghettos, distinctly marked clothing, and exclusion from professions and landholding reach far back into medieval Europe. Romantic nationalists castigated their "rootlessness," their "materialism"—from which both capitalism and socialism were said to flow—and their lack of conformity to the romantics' peasant ideal.

Jews became the scapegoat for all social frustrations and failures. By inventing the fear that wealthy Jews—a minority—were

Charles Dickens writing, 1859.

conspiring to rule the world, anti-Semites justified counterconspiracy and violence. British Prime Minister Disraeli warned of such a conspiracy at mid-century, and Rightist critics of the French Republic kept the idea alive after the 1880s. Early in the twentieth century, *The Protocols of the Elders of Zion,* forged in Paris at the instigation of the Tsarist secret police, "proved" the charge. In this widely published proof of Machiavellian chicanery, the modern world had its equivalent to the Spanish Inquisition's charges that Jews habitually conspired with the Archdevil—now the capitalists—to control the world. Generally, Jews responded to persecution and defamation with intensified efforts to assimilate or fled to new homelands. A few turned to the Zionist movement, which aimed to restore a Jewish national state in Palestine.

Literature of Industrial Criticism

Responding to the harsh facts of industrialism and urbanization, romantic writers began to produce sociological criticism and "industrial novels." These depicted, in presumably scientific detail, the impact of mechanization and urbanization on humankind. They attacked the demoralization of rural crafts and derided the middle class for its "philistine" conventions and optimistic ideologies.

Romantic realists employed a new vocabulary generated by industrialization to portray the sufferings and social callousness of mid-century society. In Britain, the industrial novelists included Benjamin Disraeli, later Conservative Prime Minister; Charles Kingsley, a Christian socialist leader; and two notable women, Elizabeth Gaskell and George Eliot, who described lower-class conditions during the "Hungry Forties" and the fate of craftsmen forced to compete with machines. More popular was Charles Dickens, who like Gaskell and Eliot, abhorred revolutions and lower-class activism as well as middle-class acquisitiveness and self-satisfied smugness. Although the industrial novelists stirred up reform sentiments, their proposed remedies were remarkably limited. Principally, they sought "social" as distinct from "political" solutions, a change in the hearts of the possessing classes without the organization of pressure groups by those who were afflicted. They praised workingmen who spurned the Chartists or unions, and they denounced utilitarian reformers who would use "materialistic" data to construct coercive legislation or urge the restriction of births. In the final analysis, their individualism rested on *noblesse oblige.*

The French counterparts of British realists tended to be activist republicans and socialists. Women such as George Sand—who like George Eliot assumed a male name—were among them, but the leading early luminary was Victor Hugo (1802–1885). During the Orleanist monarchy, Hugo took up the cause of the unemployed and the wretched majority whom he contrasted with the selfish and corrupted governing classes.

Novels of Naturalism and Psychological Analysis

Even though sociological realists dipped deeply into sordid and hitherto unmentionable aspects of life, they were generally more optimistic than the naturalists and psychological novelists. The works of Émile Zola (1840–1902) illustrate the borderline between realism and naturalism. Dwelling upon natural science and heredity and attempting to reduce writing itself to a science, Zola joined with Hugo in defending individual liberties during the Third Republic and in sympathizing with the lower classes in mine, factory, and slum. His naturalistic realism contrasted somberly with the ardent optimism of earlier romantics. Yet he was ultimately optimistic in thinking that the environment itself could be changed.

Other naturalists seldom shared this faith. The English novelist and poet Thomas Hardy (1840–1928) also contributed novels such as *The Return of the Native* which dwelt upon the omnipotence of early environment, instinct, and heredity. As naturalism covered the Western literary world, Jack London, among others in America, experimented with it as a break from earlier realism and local color. Joining the sociological novel, the legitimate theater, partially freed from earlier legal and social restrictions, raised to international fame such playwrights as Henrik Ibsen and George Bernard Shaw, who worked over hypocrisy and respectability in shocking, but avidly attended, drama at the end of the century.

The most somber probing of the murky depths of irrationality was done by Fedor Dostoevsky (1821–1881), the Russian revolutionary turned conservative, conformist, and nationalist. Dostoevsky transformed Russian romantic tradition, established by Gogol and Turgenev, into pessimistic psychological realism. In *Crime and Punishment* (1866) he pilloried reason by making it responsible for the pointless and heinous crimes committed by his central figure, Raskolnikov, whose name literally means "the schismatic." Among the impoverished and none-too-respectable common people he found heroic qualities and virtue. Perhaps greater classical proportions were attained by Dostoevsky's Russian contemporary, Count Leo Tolstoi, who wrote deterministic realism in *War and Peace*. Confronted with the stern realities of Russian social and political life, Tolstoi turned toward radical Christian anarchism, whereas Dostoevsky became an aggressive Pan-Slav nationalist.

Philosophies of the Will and Neoromanticism

Realism and naturalism deeply influenced German literature, while German philosophy—subjectivism and aesthetics—rivaled and complemented Darwinism in attracting disillusioned idealists. Its theoretical roots antedated the psychological novelists, whose conclusions often pointed in the same direction.

Arthur Schopenhauer (1788–1860) published *The World as Will and Idea* shortly after the Congress of Vienna. In this long-obscure treatise Schopenhauer considered the will the fundamental metaphysical reality. Although he considered exercise of the will to be evil, his disciple Friedrich Nietzsche (1844–1900) exalted it as the sovereign origin of good. In denouncing equality, utilitarianism, and mechanized culture, Nietzsche had much in common with Carlyle, Sigmund Freud, and Matthew Arnold, the celebrated Victorian literary critic. Both Arnold and Nietzsche assailed the smugness and mediocrity of middle-class society, but Arnold was an emotionally restrained classicist whereas Nietzsche was an exuberant, "Dionysian" enthusiast. Nietzsche's interests were cultural; like Schopenhauer he was no nationalist, racist, or libertine, and he was aloof from politics. When twentieth-century Nazis in their revolt against bourgeois society plagiarized his terms for purposes of political propaganda, they radically perverted his meaning.

As an individualist who demanded that the elite exercise willpower to set standards above the common herd, Nietzsche inspired writers such as George Bernard Shaw. The idea of the primacy of the will also appeared in France in Henri Bergson's

Nietzsche with his mother.

evolutionary philosophy of an *élan vital* or life force and in America in William James' pragmatism. Outside formal philosophy, the Nietzschean mantle was re-tailored by continental neoromantics who took advantage of the ambiguity of his loose style, rambling metaphors, polemics against the ethics of the New Testament, and remarks that were probably due to incipient insanity, to make Nietzsche a patron saint of irrationality, nationalism, and racism. Richard Wagner (1813–1883) grafted Nietzsche's "will to power" and theories of tragic creativity onto romantic German nationalism and racism, thus personally alienating the philosopher. Wagner used his musical drama, a "total work of art," to inculcate the populace with primitivistic, pagan, and chivalric myths and to replace Nietzsche's pessimism with an apocalyptic faith in a future hero-deliverer. Thus transformed, Nietzscheanism became, for the youth of the generation preceding World War I, a nationalist cult that defied all social conventions.

Romantic Innovations in Art: Impressionism

Another outlet for the romantics' quest for reality was art, especially painting in France. Romantic realists excelled as social commentators. Their depictions of the

D'où Venons Nous . . . Que Sommes Nous . . . Où Allons Nous?, *by Paul Gauguin.*

pathos of French life were not to the liking of the conservative critics in the French Academy. A new generation of artistic innovators, the Impressionists, pursuing art for art's sake, were perhaps even less acceptable to the critics. These Impressionists—Monet, Renoir, Pissaro, Cézanne, and Manet, among others—came from varied backgrounds to form an artistic circle in Paris after 1860. For subjects they turned to the open air of coast, forest, and riverbank to catch transitory, fleeting personal or natural moods in unusual combinations of pure, often bright and sharply contrasting or blending colors. Using new knowledge of color perception by the human eye, they left sharp details to be filled in at a distance by the viewer.

Later Impressionists or "Postimpressionists" such as Gauguin went further in repudiating photographic reproductions of nature. Gauguin sought to find a primordial unifying link between man and nature antedating the artificiality of complicated modern societies. He found it in the lives of the unspoiled primitives of Tahiti, among whom he lived in conscious revolt against European social conventions. Other Postimpressionists expressed their rejection of bourgeois and industrial society by living as "bohemians" in Europe itself. Preoccupied with planes, geometric forms, and colors, the late Impressionists, especially Cézanne, opened a path to the abstract art of the twentieth century. Continuing in revolt against realistic naturalism, a field preempted by the photographic industry, descendants of the Impressionists have subsequently probed the irrationalities of individuals and society by using a wide range of symbols.

Late Nineteenth-Century Social Thought

The quest for a science to explain and control the immense political and social changes of the nineteenth century eventually reached a stage of crisis. Ideologies

Fishermen on the Seine, *by Claude Monet. The camera had come widely into use and the artist was doing something that no camera can do.*

that claimed absolute validity were hopelessly at odds with one another, and their collisions shattered faith in objectivity. Mathematicians themselves were attacking the absoluteness of physical laws, although not the objective reality of external nature. Darwin's natural selection was under fire from geneticists and those who, like Prince Kropotkin (1842–1912), argued that cooperation rather than internecine rivalry preserved species in nature. Romantics, although rejecting scientific methodology, had amassed evidence that unconscious motivation, myths, and social environment rather than reason dominated social life. German idealist philosophers, notably Wilhelm Dilthey, concluded that the social sciences or "nonphysical disciplines" were subjective and that the writing of history by the historian was an act of faith in his own ideals or traditional values.

These challenges and the rapid spread of liberal constitutionalism and socialism stimulated some continental intellectuals to reconstruct their premises and turn to sociology and psychology for guidance. They reasserted the validity of empiricism and reason as tools of social analysis against relativists and dogmatic ideologists. At the same time, however, they made vast concessions to the role of the irrational in human society. These concessions undermined the basic assumptions of liberal bourgeois society and provided the empirical data that its opponents would use to undermine it in the twentieth century.

Anthropology, Sociology, and Political Theory

Anthropologists opened new theoretical doors by delving into the role of myth (the personification of collective desires) and its dramatic counterpart, tribal rites — group conduct regulated by magician-rulers. Since the eighteenth century, utilitarian liberals had looked on myth as an irrationality foisted upon society by cunning priests, whereas collectivist romantics had envisaged it as the indispensable soul or personality of society itself. Among others, Edward Tylor (1832–1917), who held the first chair of anthropology at Oxford, saw no essential difference between the myths of primitive and civilized man, except in the materials with which each worked. Scholars disputed the origin and functions of myths, but they regarded them as persistent elements of society. Such theorists as Georges Sorel joined anthropology with sociology in an effort to inculcate in the irrational masses emotionally satisfying myths. Sorel, who was later claimed by the Fascists and who was personally attracted to Bolshevism, helped to formulate the tactics of those modern political movements which represent a return to "tribalism" — an instinctive aggregation of the group around an intuitive leader — which in practice nationalism and racism already anticipated.

After having been revamped to exclude physical and biological analogies, sociology no less than anthropology produced revisions in political thought. The impact of the new sociology was exclusively neither liberal nor authoritarian, but it did modify classical liberalism and socialism by casting

doubt on their basic premise: the rational self-interest of the individual or class.

Vilfredo Pareto (1848–1923) made apparent the authoritarian potentialities of anti-intellectual sociology. A *laissez-faire* economist who turned to historical sociology to refute Marx, Pareto was as convinced as Marx that a class struggle underlay historical events. But he denied that revolution would bring a classless society and that economic planning would be effective. Instead, he stressed exclusively the irrational, noneconomic factors in social motivation. Pareto saw social stability as dependent on inherited nonrational behavior patterns (not intellectually acquired creeds) which changed at an almost imperceptibly slow pace. The only certain way to curb irritating minority patterns was to extirpate the groups that follow them. Verbal ideologies only rationalized "illogical" actions and sentiments. Whatever its form, governmental power rested with an elite, which propagated its own myth for the whole society. Governing elites, he concluded, rule either like "foxes" by manipulative resourcefulness or like "lions" by force alone. Any elite that desisted from the use of force entirely would abdicate to a new armed elite in revolution. On the other hand, if the existing oligarchy should become closed and rely wholly on force, it would degenerate and fall. Thus the class struggle was inevitable; a social revolution would only install a new elite. Society might benefit from a measure of humanitarian ideals, but these could never be fully attained in practice.

As Pareto attacked socialism, he simultaneously laid theoretical grounds for an assault on liberalism. He demonstrated that the rationalism and humanitarianism of the Enlightenment had been a skin-deep affair on most of the Continent and urged existing elites to use force to maintain their power. When Mussolini, a "lion" and former "Leftist," rose to power at the head of the Italian "Right" after World War I, Pareto approved him as a spiritual regenerator of the nation. If Pareto's analysis of elites was correct, however, the terms "Right" and "Left" were no longer meaningful, for after the Bolshevik revolution both extremes were "lions" determined to root out liberal and socialist "foxes."

While Pareto provided continental traditionalists with the conceptual equipment for harnessing mass sentiments and prejudices to authoritarian purposes, the German sociologist Max Weber fought a losing battle to save sociology as an empirical discipline and the rational humanitarian values of the Enlightenment. He supported elitism and imperialism but opposed dogmatism in both its relativist and scientific forms. He popularized "ideal types"—models abstracted from social and political experience which were to be used as analytical tools. Rationally constructed, these models were considered valid only insofar as they rendered empirical data meaningful. Ideal types, often expressed in quantitative or diagrammatic form, have been adopted by the social and behavioral sciences of the twentieth century, especially economics, with considerable success. Weber did not regard his ideal types as absolute pictures of reality any more than contemporary mathematicians considered the "laws" of physics absolute, and even contradictory models could contain partial truths. Although Weber's historical writings traced the influence of religious ideas on economic development, he avoided the absolute dichotomy of "materialism" and "idealism" which characterized his German environment, and he found elements of value in Marxism. In comparing Western civilization with other civilizations, he concluded that rationalism in law, thought, science, and industrial organization was its distinguishing feature. Weber was a partisan for the unpopular values of the Enlightenment and feared the rise of a demagogic, charismatic leader who would exploit the mass sentiments that were latent in Germany.

The rational, autonomous individual who satisfies his own economic self-interest while benefiting society was no longer a tenable object of faith. Studies of mob psychology gave convincing evidence of irrationality, and economists began to incorporate subjective elements in the determination of economic values.

Psychology

While sociologists made a heavy impact on political theory, findings in the new field of empirical psychology implied a veritable revolution in man's conceptions of his own mental makeup. The most far-reaching speculation about the human mind and its relationship to the social environment emanated from a Viennese circle of psychologists. That circle was dominated by Sigmund Freud.

Freud, who began as a clinical psychologist treating abnormal behavior (neuroses), theorized that emotional disturbances were not purely physical, but rather psychic in their origins. He was principally concerned with the hitherto unrecognized subconscious activities of the mind. Fantasies, dreams, and apparently illogical elements elicited from the patient's "unconscious" became his raw material for analysis and treatment (psychoanalysis). Eventually, he developed a set of hypotheses about the structure of the mind. Psychic energy, he concluded, originated primarily in the *Id*—a bundle of biologically inherited instincts for food, drink, and especially sex, whose earliest manifestations appeared in infancy. Because unrestrained pursuit of pleasure or the gratification of these instincts would lead to self-destruction, self-preservation required the development of another "layer" of the mind (*Ego*) to mediate between a repressive external reality of scarcity and the desires of the *Id*. Curbed by the *Ego*, the *Id* then found expression in dreams and fantasies. Superimposed on both the *Id* and the *Ego* by parental and social authority was the *Superego* or conscience which imparted a sense of guilt. The function of all three—the *Id,* the *Ego,* and the *Superego*—became unconscious or automatic, but repressions based on early experience could thereafter cause emotional disturbances in adulthood. With this hypothetical construct, which he expected further clinical findings to modify, Freud attempted to reduce the irrational realm thrust forward in thought by the romantics to a rational, scientific, and utilitarian formula.

Although Freud eschewed formal philosophy, he diverted more and more attention away from clinical psychoanalysis to "metapsychology" or the speculative application of his theory to society and culture as a whole, especially after World War I. Because he was concerned with the deep, dark powers of the unconscious and instinctual endowment, Freud interpreted the war not as a fall from a previously attained plateau, but rather as the failure to have reached such a plateau at all. Civilization, he concluded, rests on the repression of instincts, particularly the libido and the aggressive impulse. Society and the individual mind are both arenas of a contest between *Eros*—the power of love and creativity— and *Thanatos,* the wish for death. The will to destroy usually exceeds the strength to create. Tighter social organization, he predicted, would increase repression and the prospects for greater rebelliousness. Religion was no escape, for, although Freud did not teach a break in Puritan ethics, he linked the need for religion and the origin of religious rites to primitive tribal acts of savagery. His social theory was generally pessimistic, but scattered in his works were guarded passages which speculated that the antagonism between repression and instincts would be gradually moderated. His own strivings were toward extending the application of reason. His analysis was mechanistic, but it was not deterministic; he sought a purely secular humanitarianism based on rationalism and realism.

Intellectual Currents on the Eve of World War I

In the first decades of the twentieth century, more than in the eighteenth century, science emerged as the criterion for truth. Nevertheless, in most "scientific" ideologies "science" was tantamount to a single-cause explanation deduced from absolute, and often empirically undemonstrable, cosmic laws. When absolutes were questioned or revised by further applications of scientific methodology, most dogmatists chose to look the other way. Others became disillusioned with scientific objectivity as a god that had failed. For them the succeeding years became an "age of anxiety," characterized chiefly by a metaphysical void.

The dogmatic myths of racism and idealistic nationalism were prepared to fill this void. Religiously tinged, these tribalisms became common on the Continent and among imperialist parties everywhere. Polemicists launched frankly irrational and fatalistic assaults on universal concepts of law and justice and proposed governments by special elites. While empirical sociologists, psychologists, and anthropologists bared the role of irrational behavior in organized society, unbending ideologists threatened to disrupt the institutional framework on which bourgeois society rested. In all of its manifestations, rational individualism was under attack.

To some degree, this disruption of bourgeois values came from within the middle classes. In frantic efforts to combat socialism, part of the bourgeoisie seized upon intellectual weapons that were equally destructive to liberalism, socialism's closest ideological relative. Subsequent experience indicated that well-rooted liberal institutions with lower-class support could survive assault and grave crises. But where they had only a recent and shallow hold, they fell before their combined foes during major crises. Because it precipitated such crises, World War I was the principal catalyst. To understand the political conditions that produced that war, it is necessary to turn to the domestic and international developments of the nineteenth and early twentieth centuries; they are discussed in the next three chapters.

SELECTED READINGS

*Barzun, Jacques, *Darwin, Marx, Wagner, Critique of a Heritage,* Doubleday Anchor Books, Garden City, New York, 1958.

> Finds a repugnant element of naturalistic determinism in the works of all three men.

*Benda, Julian, *The Betrayal of the Intellectuals,* Beacon Press, Boston, 1955.

> Written after World War I, this essay attacks intellectuals for betraying their mission by becoming propagandists for popular causes, especially national, racial, and class hatreds.

*Bentley, Eric, *A Century of Hero-Worship,* Beacon Press, Boston, 1957 (2nd ed.).

> Studies of Carlyle, Nietzsche, Wagner, and others who preached an antidemocratic doctrine of heroic vitalism, advocating that great men should rule and others revere them.

*Berlin, Isaiah, *Karl Marx, His Life and Environment,* Oxford University Press, New York, 1959.

> One of the best biographies of the founder of "scientific socialism."

*Brinton, Crane, *The Shaping of Modern Thought,* Prentice-Hall, Englewood Cliffs, New Jersey, 1963.

> An intellectual history especially useful for the development of anti-intellectualism in the early twentieth century.

Cole, G. D. H., *A History of Socialist Thought,* 5 vols., Macmillan, London; St. Martin's Press, New York, 1955–1961.

> Volumes I to III of this extensive work by a British socialist pertain to this period.

Asterisk (*) denotes paperback.

Gay, Peter, *The Dilemma of Democratic Socialism, Eduard Bernstein's Challenge to Marx,* Columbia University Press, New York, 1952.

> Sketches the life of the founder of revisionist socialism in Germany, his criticisms of Marxism, and the problems confronting democratic socialists in an increasingly bourgeois society.

*Halévy, Elie, *The Growth of Philosophic Radicalism,* Beacon Press, Boston, 1955.

> Classic analysis of the doctrines and the impact of the English Utilitarians.

*Himmelfarb, Gertrude, *Darwin and the Darwinian Revolution,* Doubleday Anchor Books, Garden City, New York, 1962.

> A critical biography showing the Malthusian origins of Darwin's basic theory which, applied to society and thought, had conservative as well as revolutionary implications.

Homans, George C., and Charles P. Curtis, *An Introduction to Pareto, His Sociology,* A. A. Knopf, New York, 1934.

> A basic summary of Pareto's sociology—his method, categories, and conclusions.

*Hook, Sidney, *Marx and the Marxists, The Ambiguous Legacy,* D. Van Nostrand Co., Princeton, New Jersey, 1955.

> Marx's basic ideas and the divergent strains of thought and politics which evolved from them set forth, with appended documents, by a philosopher.

*Hughes, H. Stuart, *Consciousness and Society, The Reorientation of European Thought 1890–1930.* A. A. Knopf and Random House, New York, 1958.

> A keen intellectual history that portrays a crisis in the search for an objective method to study society at the end of the nineteenth century.

*Irvine, William, *Apes, Angels, and Victorians,* Meridian Books, New York, 1959.

> Presents in popular form the careers, contrasting personalities, and writings of the two major evolutionists, Darwin and Huxley, and their relationships with other leading Victorians.

*Kaufmann, Walter, ed., *The Portable Nietzsche,* Viking Press, New York, 1954.

Collection of writings by a leading biographer of Nietzsche and historian of existentalism.

Laidler, H. W., *Social-Economic Movements: An Historical and Comparative Survey of Socialism, Communism, Coöperation, Utopianism,* Crowell, New York, 1949.
Delivers in summary form what the title promises.

*Lichtheim, George, *Marxism, An Historical and Critical Study,* Frederick A. Praeger, New York, 1962.
Shows modifications of Marxist doctrine as it conformed to differing local situations while spreading over Europe.

Manuel, Frank E., *The Prophets of Paris,* Harvard University Press, Cambridge, 1962.
Excellent for Saint-Simon, Fourier, and Comte, set in the environment of their heritage from the Enlightenment.

Mosse, George L., *The Culture of Western Europe, The Nineteenth and Twentieth Centuries,* Rand McNally & Co., Chicago, 1961.
An unusually perceptive intellectual history of modern Europe.

*Puner, Helen Walker, *Freud, His Life and His Mind,* Dell Books, New York, 1959.
A succinct account of Freud's background, his psychoanalytic hypotheses, and the divergent schools of his successors.

Rewald, John, *The History of Impressionism,* Museum of Modern Art, New York, 1955 (2nd ed.).
An illustrated discussion intelligible to non-artists.

Schapiro, Jacob S., *Liberalism and the Challenge of Fascism: Social Forces in England and France, 1815–1870,* McGraw-Hill, New York, 1949.
Makes distinctions between liberalism and certain strains of "utopian socialism" and authoritarianism whose similarities with fascism are overstated.

*Schweitzer, Albert, *The Quest for the Historical Jesus,* The Macmillan Co., New York, 1961.
Sketches a major aspect of nineteenth-century "higher criticism" of Biblical texts, including rational attempts to explain in human terms their recording of miracles and expectations of the end of the world.

Taton, René ed., *History of Science,* III, *Science in the Nineteenth Century,* Basic Books, New York, 1965.
Translation of a French collaborative manual, including medicine, useful for reference.

*Williams, Raymond, *Culture and Society 1780–1950,* Doubleday & Co., Garden City, New York, 1960.
Exposes romantic novelists who revolted against industrialism as paternalists sharing basic assumptions with traditionalists.

*Wilson, Edmund, *To the Finland Station,* Doubleday & Co., New York, 1953.
A sympathetic account of the socialist tradition before the Bolshevik Revolution.

See also works by Marcuse, Ruggiero, and Schapiro in Selected Readings, Chapter 20.

G

POLITICS OF THE NEW INDUSTRIALISM

23

The Politics of Emergent Industrial Society– About 1850 to 1914

During the decades between 1850 and 1914, the urban industrial type of society that Britain pioneered took root throughout the Western world. Everywhere it raised similar problems. A new industrial and financial elite challenged established elites, usually demanding constitutional changes that would admit them to power. Behind the industrial bourgeoisie came more numerous classes of urban working-men and intellectuals who sought to democratize political institutions and obtain economic security.

Governments were called upon to regulate conflicts within this new society, and between it and the old order. The growth of civil services with industrial jurisdictions was nearly as conspicuous a part of this transition as the extension of representative government. During these decades, some political leaders attempted to find compromises or accommodations between the preindustrial and industrial segments of society.

Patterns of adaptation to industrialism varied according to local conditions. The Western democracies were much better equipped to industrialize without revolution than were the autocratic states of Central and Eastern Europe. For Italy and Germany, unification cleared the path for large-scale industry. But the new German middle classes were uncertain of themselves and fell under the tutelage of the old military aristocracy and autocratic government. Together they blocked the political "reforms" that were so characteristic of the democratic countries. Thus, they produced a revolutionary situation. Both Austria-Hungary and Russia were beset by other, more serious problems. Nationalism, born of resistance to centralist pressures, threatened to break up both empires, especially Austria-Hungary, while Russia was engaged in a race with catastrophe between population growth and subsistence. By thwarting the liberalization of political life, the governments of these countries prepared their own destruction.

THE WESTERN DEMOCRACIES: BRITAIN, FRANCE, AND THE UNITED STATES

The Democratization of Great Britain, 1832 to 1914

Britain was both the industrial leader and the model of constitutional government in nineteenth-century Europe. She alone among Europe's states had a long-established parliamentary government with which to confront industrial problems. Unlike most continental systems which had many parties spread in a continuum from "Left" to "Right" and ruling in coalitions, British politics were based on a two-party structure—one party in power, the other in opposition. In the House of Commons both parties faced each other from opposing benches. Because the executive—the cabinet—depended upon a majority in Parliament, both the voters and the M.P.'s had the means of deposing a government. Neither of the two choices at the polls might be entirely satisfactory to the individual voter but, by assuring the victorious party the power to effect its program, Britain's political machinery provided stability. As an alternative or a "shadow" government, the opposition had to keep its program pragmatically in tune with political realities. Liberals and Conservatives, respectively, replaced the traditional Whigs and Tories, but both upheld the constitutional structure. At the outset, both were firmly committed to maintaining the "Victorian Compromise"—the sharing of power between the gentry and industrial capitalists effected by the first Reform Bill of 1832.

But the interplay of party politics in a changing social environment led to progressive democratization of the British constitution between 1832 and 1914.

Reform Under the Victorian Compromise

Far-reaching reforms began in earnest immediately after the first Reform Bill broke Tory dominance over the House of Commons. Colonial slavery was abolished by compensated emancipation in 1833. The first enforced factory act became law the same year. The Poor Law's administration was centralized and narrowed in scope in 1834 and, in 1835, oligarchies controlling municipal governments were replaced by elected councils. Political concessions to the laboring classes were denied the Chartists, however, in the 1830s and 1840s.

Britain's governing class suffered a good deal of anxiety during the 1830s and 1840s by the political agitation and street demonstrations of the Chartists. Chartism stemmed from lower-class disillusionment with the Reform Bill, resentment toward the Poor Law's curtailment of alms, religious dissent, and the displacement of domestic weavers by power looms. Representing Britain's first significant labor-in-politics movement, the Chartists aimed to democratize the state. Their petitions to Parliament (called charters) asked for manhood suffrage, vote by secret ballot, annually elected parliaments, equal electoral districts, abolition of property qualifications for voting, and payment to members of Parliament. During the economic crises of the 1840s, they sponsored a "Convention" to rival Parliament. A petition of 1848 contained nearly two million signatures—many of them bogus. However, excise tax reductions and repeal of the Corn Laws (agricultural tariffs) in 1846 combined with internal factionalism to eventually undermine their movement. It disappeared as an organized political force during the prosperity of the 1850s.

Seen as a whole, the reforms culminating in 1846 with the abandoning of agricultural protection were considerable and far-reaching. Besides the reforms discussed above, Parliament introduced police and penal reforms in 1829, which created the model force of unarmed London "Bobbies" and removed the death penalty for more than a hundred offenses. Effective policing methods soon spread to other cities and the counties. Respect for law and order increased with the security of the ordinary citizen. Grave-robbing ended when an Anatomy Act enabled the medical schools to have enough cadavers for the first time. When we include the Factory Acts discussed in Chapter 21 and many other acts not detailed here, we can see why the English gained a sense of living in an age of improvement. While these reforms were only a foretaste of the extensive reforms still to come, they were enough to satisfy the British ruling classes that they had, for the time being, solved England's most pressing internal problems. For the next twenty years, attention shifted to foreign affairs.

The Victorian Compromise generally held up, but in the case of the repeal of the Corn Laws in 1846 it broke down, and party realignments followed. Sir Robert Peel, the Tory leader, was convinced by the Irish famine that free trade would guarantee a cheaper loaf of bread. In the long run he was probably right, but his support of the repeal act split the Tory party. The "Peelites" became the nucleus of the new Liberal party for whom Lord John Russell,

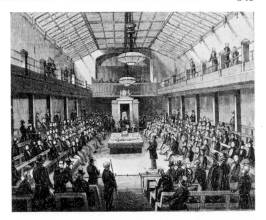

The House of Commons in session. Here one often heard persuasive oratory.

Lord Palmerston, and Gladstone provided competent leadership. The very wealthy Whigs sometimes left their party to join the socially more prominent Tories. The Conservative party, successor to the Tory party, enjoyed the brilliant leadership of Benjamin Disraeli.

Although their special interests differed, no great gulf separated the Conservatives from the Liberals. Entrenched in the House of Lords, the Conservatives—who came increasingly from the ranks of business—were still quick to defend the Anglican Church, agrarian economic interests, and the prerogatives of the nobility. The Liberals were an amalgam of Whigs, Dissenters, and former Conservatives who were as respectably upper class as their opponents. Except for some Utilitarian Radicals,* those who agitated for democratic reform were outside of Parliament and were politically impotent.

Russell and Palmerston's Liberal Nationalism

Liberals took credit for the rising standard of living between 1846 and 1865 under the governments of Lords John Russell and

* The Utilitarian Radicals were followers of Jeremy Bentham who advocated *laissez-faire* economic policies, comprehensive legal reforms, democratization with public education, and an empirical approach to social problems.

Gladstone, Liberal Reformer.

Palmerston. While prosperity sapped the impetus of reform, public attention focused on the personality, pronounced nationalism, and "spirited" foreign policy of Lord Palmerston. His chauvinism electrified the nation when, in 1850, he sent England's fleet to vindicate the claims of a single subject (Don Pacifico) whose property an Athenian mob had destroyed. In 1855 he became prime minister. His government successfully repressed the Sepoy Mutiny in India and, in 1857, started a war against China for commercial concessions. After 1860, his ministry succeeded in negotiating free-trade treaties with other European nations, beginning with France.

Extensive domestic reforms did not occur in the British Empire during the Liberal era, but a new policy toward Anglo-Saxon colonial settlements evolved. It pointed toward local autonomy for the colonies and looser ties with the mother country. In 1839 Lord Durham reported in favor of such a policy after he had been sent to North America to prevent a Canadian revolt from culminating in another American Revolution. The Canadians were granted a representative assembly where French-Canadian interests were subordinated to those of the English colonists. They secured the abolition of the Navigation Acts in 1849 and, in 1859, were able to introduce local tariffs. The Liberals' colonial policy remained in effect after they had fallen from power and, in 1867, the British North American Act granted Dominion status to Canada. Later, similar autonomy was extended to Australia, New Zealand, and South Africa. Britain's calculated loosening of ties with her white settlement colonies contrasted sharply, however, with her aggressive exploitation elsewhere.

Disraeli and Gladstone Break the Victorian Compromise

After Palmerston's death in 1865, Liberal leadership passed to the Eton-educated son of a wealthy Scottish merchant, William Ewart Gladstone (1809–1898). Gladstone began his long parliamentary career as a Peelite Conservative, dedicated to the preservation of the Anglican Church. Although he was abidingly devoted to a fundamentalist religion that denied Darwinian biology, he became a political reformer and eventually sponsored anticlerical legislation. Competing for leadership with Disraeli, he cast his lot with the Liberals, who accepted him as their "Grand Old Man" long after their younger members had abandoned his faith in *laissez-faire* capitalism. As the pendulum of power swung between Disraeli and Gladstone, reform revived. And often Disraeli's "Tory Democracy"—a system of social reform similar to that which Bismarck later developed in Germany—effected more radical change than Gladstone's Liberalism.

Between 1867 and 1885 a series of reforms extended and reorganized the House of Commons' electorate, dismantling the Victorian Compromise. In an effort to cement new voters to traditional institutions and to the Conservative party, Disraeli in 1867 sought to outbid the Liberals, "to dish the Whigs," with a greater extension of suffrage. The Liberals countered with amendments even broader in scope. The result was the second Reform Bill of 1867 that doubled the electorate by reducing property qualifications. Now all householders paying poor rates and all renters paying an annual rent of £10 could vote in borough elections. Because most urban workingmen had such means, the bill initiated democracy based on manhood suffrage in urban constituencies, but it failed to enfranchise agricultural laborers.

Electoral victory in 1868 went to the Liberals. Until 1874, Gladstone presided over a wave of reforms comparable to those following the first Reform Bill. To educate "our masters," as one member put it, the Parliament passed the Forster Education Act of 1870. It instituted the first public primary education system in Britain. In the same year, competitive examinations were introduced to open the Civil Service (except the Foreign Office) to all classes, and in 1871 religious qualifications that had barred Dissenters from the universities were removed. Before the reform impetus temporarily flagged, an army reorganization act introduced a reserve system, and stopped the practice of purchasing commissions. These measures made British society more competitive but, nonetheless, dominated by the privately schooled sons of the upper classes.

As democracy spread in England, national political parties were formed; leaders began to take issues to the country as a whole; and desires for more democracy were whetted. In 1874 Disraeli campaigned for extended imperialism and state intervention into the relations of capital and labor. He was elected, and his ministry consolidated and extended public health codes and initiated government housing for the urban poor. It also removed obstacles to labor organization by nullifying common-law doctrines that made contract-breaking a criminal offense and picketing a conspiracy.

The second Gladstone ministry (1880–1885) resumed parliamentary reform on a major scale. Gladstone introduced a bill in 1884 that reduced rural property qualifications sufficiently to enfranchise agricultural laborers. To allay Conservative objections that the bill did not abolish electoral inequalities, the Prime Minister secured passage of a second law in 1885 that based representation in the House of Commons on population instead of the traditional boroughs and counties. Within a decade, traditional county government by justices of the peace was replaced by elective councils similar to those introduced in the towns in 1835. Thus democratic procedures reached both the House of Commons and the countryside following the reforms of 1885.

The Dilemma of Ireland

In British politics no issue was more intractable to rational resolution than Ireland. By coercive laws and armed force, England had fastened a tithe-supported Anglican Church on Irish Roman Catholics and an exploitative colonization on the whole population of the island. Resistance to tithes and English rule had repeatedly

Disraeli, advocate of "Tory Democracy."

Irish tenants resisting eviction.

flared into open rebellion without gaining more than mild concessions. Supported by potato culture rather than industry and commerce, the Irish population almost doubled during the first half of the century only to be caught in massive famines between 1845 and 1847 when poor harvests and potato blight cut into the food supply. Ireland's tragedy contributed to the abandonment of the Corn Laws in 1846, but starvation and emigration combined to drive the population down from 8.2 million in 1841 to 6.5 million in 1851. Yet, landlords were able to raise rents and to deny their Irish tenants security of tenure and compensation for their improvements.

English political leaders ignored the Irish "sore" as long as possible, but after 1850 organized resistance made it inescapable. Boycotts were held against English landlords and merchants. A Land League coordinated demands for peasants' freedom to sell their rights, fixity of tenure, and fair rents—the "Three F's." Irish veterans of the American Civil War organized the Fenian Society that used American funds to instigate violence on the Canadian-American frontier, in English cities, and in the Irish countryside. After the Irish Reform Act of 1868 enlarged the electorate, the staunch Anglophobe, Charles Stewart Parnell, led an Irish Nationalist contingent in the British House of Commons that demanded Home Rule in a separate Irish parliament.

Until 1885, Gladstone and Disraeli tried to substitute various reforms for Home Rule, such as compensating peasants who were evicted arbitrarily, providing loans for those who wished to buy out their landlords, and exempting Roman Catholics from paying tithes to the Anglican Church. Since Ireland's submission was a Conservative article of faith, these measures had to be forced through Parliament by threats. The Irish Nationalists, for their part, resisted these reforms vigorously (even the land act of 1881 which granted the "Three F's") because they feared that the settlement of agrarian issues would jeopardize Home Rule. Because Gladstone needed the votes of the Irish M.P.'s, he took the fatal plunge in 1886 and offered a Home Rule Bill. Some of the Liberals thereupon split from the party, called themselves Unionists, and voted with the Conservatives against the bill. In 1892, Gladstone made a second attempt to offer Ireland Home Rule, only to have the House of Lords strike down his bill. The Irish Question remained a contentious issue for another generation.

The Rise of Social Liberalism and the Labour Party

The Liberal split over Ireland delivered power to Conservative governments under Lord Salisbury and Arthur Balfour until 1905. Their governments coincided with the waning of prosperity that had muffled radicalism during the middle of the century. Imports of duty-free agricultural goods after 1880 depressed English agriculture. As other states, such as Germany and the United States became technologically progressive industrial giants, Britain ceased being *the* workshop of the world. Her relative economic and political power in the world declined. During that decline, Gladstone's *laissez-faire* Liberalism came under fire from two sides. Conservatives and Unionists advocated imperialist expansion, closer ties with the Empire, industrial tariffs, and the reduction of organized labor's power. On the other side, younger Liberals (such as David Lloyd George) criticized imperialism and campaigned for free trade and greater social welfare.

During the decline, trade unions picked up marked strength, and Socialists obtained labor followings. When the House of Lords ruled in 1902 in the Taff Vale case that unions could be sued for losses resulting from strikes, the unions' continued existence was threatened. Finding Liberals too little concerned, labor leaders formed their own party and shared in the Liberal victory of 1906. The appearance of laboring men in Parliament as a separate party marked a fundamental divide in British politics.

The cabinets of Sir Henry Campbell-Bannerman and Herbert Asquith presided over another era of domestic reforms. For labor, the reforms made employers responsible for workingmen's accidents—but the Liberals were inactive when a court decision made union political contributions illegal. To the aged and indigent, new laws provided pensions. By 1909 a combination of social welfare costs and naval building appropriations required either large deficits or new sources of revenues. In the "People's Budget" of 1909 the Welsh Chancellor of the Exchequer David Lloyd George spurned the tariff lobby headed by Joseph Chamberlain and proposed heavier income and inheritance taxes. The budget also called for various levies on unearned capital gains. To the House of Lords it appeared to be a social revolution instead of a budget. Breaking precedents, the Lords rejected it overwhelmingly. Thereupon, Prime Minister Asquith took the budget, the issue of the Lords' veto, and—to get Irish support—Irish Home Rule before the electorate. Although weakened, his cabinet kept its majority and promptly challenged the right of the House of Lords to veto money bills and to delay other legislation for more than two years. Again the Liberals held their majority in a new election and, upon the threat that the new king, George V, would create enough peers to break the Lords'

opposition, they acquiesced in the Parliament Bill of 1911. By this act the democratically elected House of Commons (whose term was now limited to five years) imposed its will upon the hereditary and appointive House of Lords where the power of landed family estates still held sway.

Prewar Crises

Despite the great Liberal victory of 1911, Asquith's government lost prestige with sectors of the British public, who took to extralegal, extra-Parliamentary tactics to secure redress. One sector was labor, still caught by rising taxes and prices but confident of the growing power of the unions. In 1910 and 1911, a series of strikes erupted in response to economic deterioration. Parliament granted a minimum wage to miners in 1911, a move that pleased neither the miners nor the employers but that succeeded in decreasing the number of strikes.

Another sector was the militant suffragettes who wanted feminine equality, especially at the polls. Led by the redoubtable Mrs. Emmeline Pankhurst, the militant feminists created quite a public stir when they smashed windows, set fire to Lloyd George's house, and chained themselves to the railings of Buckingham Palace, then refused to eat when they were imprisoned. Still, Asquith's ministry refused to act on their demands.

The third sector, made up of uncompromising Conservatives and Unionists, who opposed Irish Home Rule, became overtly insurrectionary and threatened Britain with a civil war. Asquith redeemed his promise of Home Rule to the Irish Nationalists in return for their support in 1910 by introducing a bill in 1912 granting Ireland a bicameral parliament and continued representation in Westminster. The bill became law in 1914 over the opposition of the Lords. Meanwhile, Protestants in Ulster, faced with being subordinated in a parliament in Dublin, set about enlisting a large militia to resist Home Rule by force.

When World War I broke out, the problem of Ireland, now rebellious in frustration, awaited settlement.

France: From Empire to Republic

Louis Napoleon, whose watchword was order, became Emperor in 1852. He rode to power largely on his uncle's legendary reputation, but he labored constructively to reconcile French traditions with the promotion of industry and finance. When his personal regime foundered, it bequeathed a broader social base for modern legislation and an efficient bureaucracy to the Third Republic. This bureaucracy provided continuity and direction that the unstable ministries of the Third Republic could not. The strength of the Third Republic rested upon a stable French society that was not yet industrial in the sense that England or contemporary Germany were. For in the early twentieth century, French society still consisted mainly of small farmers and small shopkeepers.

Louis Napoleon and the Authoritarian Empire

Managing French affairs in the style of his uncle, Louis Napoleon gained a plebiscite in December 1851, to draw up a constitution. His constitution gave him unfettered control over foreign policy, the armed forces, and the administration. In November of 1852 a second plebiscite gave approval to Napoleon's conversion of the authoritarian presidency into a hereditary Empire, and ratified the Emperor's title, Napoleon III.

Lacking an organized political following of his own, Napoleon made concessions to factions that were too strong to destroy. Considering Roman Catholic support indispensable, he wooed churchmen with educational favors and foreign policies calculated to gain their support. Catholic leaders responded by calling the Emperor a heaven-sent blessing, and many Bourbon and Orleanist monarchists were impressed by his solicitude for the faith. As long as clerics and monarchists supported him, the Emperor gave them considerable freedom of press and expression. To solidify his authoritarian regime, Louis Napoleon initially repressed liberal constitutionalists, especially the republicans. For a decade summary judicial commissions broke up republican organizations by either imprisoning or exiling their leaders. Public meetings were banned. Newspapers had to be licensed by the government and run by carefully selected editors. By such acts, Napoleon III earned the lasting enmity of Republicans.

On the positive side, the Emperor's court sponsored banks, credit institutions, railway construction and consolidation, shipping, mining, and urban rebuilding. Remodeled, gaslit Paris, hosting a succession of international expositions, became the showplace of France's industrial progress. Gaiety reigned in the capital, where businessmen served an international clientele and catered to the tastes of the middle class who were displacing landed aristocrats in high society. There was little evidence of the "Moral Order" that the clergy had heralded.

The Liberal Empire and Its Fall

But before such social change had shaken his alliance with the conservatives, the Emperor's foreign policies had already alienated churchmen and had forced him to woo the moderates by liberalizing the Empire between 1860 and 1870. Victory in the Crimean War enhanced his prestige, but the result of his intervention in Italy — the creation of an anticlerical kingdom there — cooled clerical and nationalist ardors. Napoleon moved to repair the damage with the clerics by garrisoning Rome and guaranteeing it to the pope. In 1861 he began supporting an ill-fated project to turn Mexico into a conservative, clerical Empire under Emperor Francis Joseph's brother, Maximilian. These actions succeeded more in alienating Italy and the United States than in reenlisting Catholic support.

The Emperor's efforts to attract the support of moderates included laws calling for compulsory primary education and vocational training and permitting temporary labor organizations to strike for economic objectives.

These measures fell far short of establishing a liberal government responsible to an elected parliament, but they contributed to pressures for further change to which concessions were made in 1869 and 1870. Opposition in the Legislative Assembly grew. There was a rash of strikes. And radical Republicans—stimulated by the removal of censorship—revived their agitation. The liberal experiment collapsed when Napoleon III became a Prussian prisoner of war at Sedan in September 1870.

The Paris Commune and Aftermath

The new government, formed after the capture of Napoleon III, came into conflict at once with the citizens of Paris. The defeat of 1870 appeared to Parisian leaders to be a betrayal and an insufferable humiliation, especially since the government had permitted a triumphal German march through the city that had fallen to bombardment and siege in 1871. Armed Parisian guardsmen set up a *de facto* government—the Commune—that resisted the central government from March through May 1871. For one week in May of that year, fierce civil war flared as government forces besieged and captured the disorganized city. The casualties and massive revenge in blood exacted by the victors exceeded any single French loss in the Prussian war. In both conservative and Marxian lore, the Commune was portrayed as the first modern Communist experiment, but in fact was more a resurgence of urban Jacobinism.

Parisians buying cat and dog flesh during the German siege, 1871.

After making a vindictive example of Paris, the Thiers government, backed by oversubscribed public loans, quickly paid a war indemnity to Germany and secured the evacuation of German troops in 1873. Marshal MacMahon, loser to Prussia but conqueror of the Commune, replaced Thiers. Then constitutional disputes resumed in earnest. MacMahon's intended role was to preside over a monarchist restoration. This end seemed certain, but the Bourbons and Orleanists could reach no agreement. Symbolized by the Duke of Chambord's stubborn refusal to give up the *fleur de lis* flag (the inviolate symbol of divine right monarchy that was intolerable to the Orleanists), the Bourbons utterly refused to come to terms with modern society. Unable to turn their majority in the Assembly into a restoration, the divided monarchists extended MacMahon's term of office to seven years. Their default gave liberal constitutionalists and Republicans another opportunity.

Birth of the Third Republic

In 1875 the monarchist assembly passed a series of stopgap constitutional laws which indicated its fear of both a strong executive and the masses. Engrained by the

Empire, universal manhood suffrage was retained for the Chamber of Deputies, but most of the upper legislative house was indirectly elected by preponderantly rural voters. Elected by the Senate and the Chamber jointly, the president had no veto but could, with approval by the Senate, dissolve the Chamber. By a majority of only one vote, he received the title "President of the *Republic*." These constitutional laws became the constitution of the Third Republic—the most enduring constitutional structure that France has had since 1789.

Under the Third Republic, parliamentary committees overawed and brought down one cabinet after another. Because of the multiplicity of political parties the cabinets were necessarily coalitions of undisciplined deputies. But the Third Republic, steadied by established social patterns and its civil service, proved too stable to warrant comparing the changing of French ministers to the changing of the Royal Guard in Britain. While ministers changed frequently, their subordinates were permanent employees who carried out established routines independently. As long as French society did not change so as to call these routines into question, the subordinates gave regularity to French public life.

The Republic and Its Foes on the "Right"

Up until 1914 the Third Republic succeeded more than preceding regimes in uniting Frenchmen in imperialist expansion, economic development, and fear of the German Empire whose margin of power over France increased. Despite its achievements, it was buffeted by continued attacks from the "Right"—by traditionalists and authoritarians who used its extensive shortcomings and lack of grandeur as weapons against liberal, constitutional government

No ideological conflict was more fundamental than that between the defenders of Church schools and the Republicans who worked to displace them with compulsory, primary education that would be both secular and free. Under successive clerical governments, the regular clergy—the monastic orders—had regained most of the ground lost during the great Revolution of 1789, against which churchmen had sworn eternal enmity. Republicans, in turn, viewed the Church's hold on education as a threat to themselves and to France's ability to cope with the modern world. In 1880, Education Minister Jules Ferry (1832–1892) ordered the Jesuits and all unauthorized teaching orders to disband. The government used force when the Jesuits (whose graduates filled the army officer and diplomatic corps and judicial benches) ignored the decrees. But the clergy retained considerable influence as educators, both because Ferry's decrees were laxly enforced and because the government delayed building schools, especially for girls.

Another threat to the Republic was the Boulanger Affair. General Boulanger was a former commander in Algeria and a stately appearing figure on horseback. He became Minister of War in 1886 under the aegis of Georges Clemenceau, a Republican who appreciated his lack of aristocratic connections. Stirring public fancy by profuse statements of patriotism and demands for revenge on Germany—themes that Republicans were also wont to play—Boulanger built up a Napoleonic image and following. Clergy, monarchists, revolutionary socialists, and purely adventuresome opponents of the government all looked to him. Stripped of command and military status by apprehensive Republicans, he was elected as a martyrlike hero to the Chamber of Deputies by many constituencies. When the moment for his *coup d'état* arrived, Boulanger proved himself a poor Bonapartist. Threatened with arrest, he fled to Brussels with his mistress where, the following year (1891), he committed suicide. In this case, fortunate timing saved the Republic. Within a few years, however, the Republic lost prestige in the eyes of world opinion because of a serious judicial error in the court martial of Alfred Dreyfus.

Captain Dreyfus and the Eclipse of the "Right"

Anti-Semitism became a central theme of the Dreyfus case, which brought the Republic into conflict with the strongholds of monarchism—the army and the Church. Dreyfus, a Jewish intelligence officer employed in the General Staff, was arrested in 1894 for allegedly leaking military secrets to Germany. A secret court-martial overrode his plea of innocence, and he was condemned to life imprisonment. But in 1896 a new chief of the Intelligence Section, Georges Picquart, provided his superiors with evidence that the real culprit was Major Esterhazy, a Hungarian adventurer of the Foreign Legion with papal Zouave experience. For his efforts Picquart was transferred to the Tunisian frontier. The case was reopened when a respected senator publicly bared Picquart's findings, but a reluctant court-martial triumphantly acquitted Esterhazy. Emile Zola now joined the efforts of Dreyfus' family to clear his name, by writing the article *J'accuse* in Clemenceau's newspaper. Zola, who escaped to England, was tried and convicted in absentia for his attack on the army's justice. Then Esterhazy, discharged from the army for embezzlement, implicated a Colonel Henry who had become head of the Intelligence Section, but Henry committed suicide rather than testify. The mystery and murkiness of the case deepened when a second court-martial still found Dreyfus guilty but reduced his sentence to ten years. Dreyfus was pardoned in 1899 and fully exonerated in 1906 but, by 1899, his tortuous case had become the basic issue in a realignment of French politics.

From the outset, monarchists, vocal clerics, and all varieties of authoritarian nationalists had defended the army's action as a patriotic duty. Organized in the League of the French Fatherland, they held to a faith in the integrity of the army that made belief in Dreyfus' guilt imperative. They dismissed any other view as subversive and probably foreign-inspired. Mobs, which they urged on, rioted against Jewish shopkeepers and Dreyfusards. For Dreyfus' defenders, a principle vital to the Republic was at stake: impartial justice and a guarantee that the law would always protect individual rights. In opposition to the conservative league, they formed the League of the Rights of Man and, when socialists led by Jean Jaurès threw in their lot with defenders of the Republic, the "Right" lost exclusive control of the streets.

Parliament, dominated by radical Republicans, for the first time included a Socialist, Alexandre Millerand. Heretofore the narrow band of French Socialists had been hostile to the Republic and refused to cooperate in any "bourgeois" ministry, but now they rallied to save the Republic.

As a direct sequel to the Dreyfus Affair, the Radicals purged the two citadels of authoritarian opposition, the army and the Church. Henceforth, clerical conservatism, which had been a test for promotion in the past, became a disability for army officers. By building a system of informers and secret personnel files, the government was able to reward friends and punish enemies. Difficulties between the Church and the anticlerical government were inevitable, since the Concordat of 1801 had given the government the right to nominate or appoint prelates. In 1905 the government legislated almost complete separation of Church and state, and the law required local congregations to take over Church buildings. The papacy objected to both congregational autonomy and separation *per se*. In the ensuing deadlock, the "Right" again benefited from reactions to aggressive Republican anticlerical policies.

Despite ministerial instability, the Third

Republic achieved a stability that alienated the "other France" — the urban lower classes — at the same time that it broke the "Right's" bastions of power. And that stability faithfully represented the predominant sectors of French society — the landowning peasants, the professionals, the shopkeepers, the industrialists, and the financiers. Only further industrial urbanization could decisively shift the political center of gravity further from the traditional "Right" and more toward the radical "Left."

The Emergence of the Americas: The United States

The other major democratic Western state to industrialize during the second half of the nineteenth century was the United States. In America, as in Britain and France, there were struggles between pre- and postindustrial elites. But especially after the fall of the aristocratic South, the new republic had virtually no institutions comparable to the Old Regime which worked to curb economic opportunity, social mobility, freedom of expression, and the democratization of politics. America pulsed with economic activity, but its spread out over an agrarian empire with immense per capita resources also contained the seeds of sectional conflicts which disrupted the national government.

The Civil War

Confronting each other in the Civil War were two nationalist military states fighting for unconditional victory. For Lincoln, the struggle was not to emancipate slaves but to maintain the Union and to secure individual rights. Hopes of quick victory on both sides gave way to a long weary war of attrition. Failing to get expected assistance from Britain, the agrarian South was less able to fight a war successfully. Despite sharp divisions of opinion on the justice of the war, the North remained physically stronger.

Involving greater bloodshed than any previous modern war, the Civil War evoked a spirit of righteous vengeance with which the victors "reconstructed" the vanquished. The Fourteenth Amendment to the Constitution made citizenship explicitly national, sealing the war's verdict against the right to secede claimed by the southern states. Union victory also doomed the institution of slavery, which a constitutional amendment of 1865 terminated. But the outcome of the war also meant the victory of the Republican party which, relying upon the votes of freedmen to stay in power, made the prosperous North into a veritable hotbed for the development of commercial agriculture and large-scale industry.

The Postwar Consolidation of Business Dominance

Although interrupted by periodic depressions, the North's postwar boom made the United States the largest industrial and agricultural producer in the world by the end of the century. As railroads crossed the western plains and tied mining centers to the East, grain, meat, and precious metals flowed outward in exchange, and millions of immigrants made their way to burgeoning northern cities and farms. As the continental frontier drew to a close in 1890, American life began to assume an urban, industrial complexion. Although still a majority, the proportionate number of farmers in the population began to shrink, and by 1900 the value of iron and steel production exceeded that of the milling and meat-packing industries.

Industrial growth during the consolidation of business dominance produced a large labor force, but it, like the farmers, had difficulty organizing in a hostile environment. A constant flow of immigrants willing to work for low wages (according to American standards) sapped the ability of unions to negotiate, as did apathy, born of the feeling that labor was a step on "the way up," and that laborers were not part of a permanent working class. Business dominance meant that courts, officials, police, and the armed forces were hostile; the use of force in strikebreaking was commonplace. Although revolutionary ideologies made only slight inroads into the American labor movement, the United States had one of the most violent records of employer-employee relationships. Nevertheless the strongest labor organization (the craft unions assembled in the American Federation of Labor in 1881) did not try to found a separate political party. During the Progressive era, when it obtained some political concessions, its membership grew rapidly (from one-half million to two million, 1900–1914).

The Progressive Era, 1900 to 1914

By 1900 a new self-conscious urban, industrial society had emerged in America. But it was foreign to inherited agrarian traditions and ideology. It became increasingly popular to speak of America as a unique frontier society breeding individualism and ruggedness. Some, including Roosevelt, tried to keep the frontier spirit going by military expansion overseas. Still others, nativists, attributed all agitation over urban social and economic conditions to immigrants and foreign ideologies. In the name of order and the preservation of American Anglo-Saxonism they advocated the curtailment of immigration. Despite these diversions, however, a general reform movement under the label of "Progressivism" swept the country during the first decades of the twentieth century. It came from many quarters and in many guises. Trade unionists, Socialists, and advocates of the "social gospel" all put forward their own formulas for change. Alone, no one of these programs could succeed. The Progressive Movement, however, effected a combination of urban-rural, northern-southern, and labor-upper class reform elements, joined for the first time since the Civil War in a conscious effort to remold American institutions.

Progressives opposed the concentration of political, economic, and social power

Richmond, Virginia, after the Civil War.

that had developed since the Civil War. They made the traditional appeal for fair competition, equal opportunity, and democratic institutions. In doing this, they rejected the Darwinists' definition of liberty as an unrestrained struggle for existence. Like the social Liberals and Labourites of Britain, they appealed to a sense of social justice—a social conscience. Believing that legislation could affect man's environment, they pressed for laws based on statistical social and economic facts.

Reform swelled at the state and local levels. Expert city officials hired by elective councils supplanted the "bosses." City-owned utilities replaced many former franchises and contracts. At the state level more than 1500 constitutional amendments were adopted. Among other things, the amendments provided for more expert administrators, regulatory commissions, and more direct control by the electorate over legislators and judges. Most cities and states began to hold primary elections, and the states adopted an amendment making the election of United States Senators direct.

In some instances, American Progressivism paralleled the social legislation of Britain and Germany, but the United States was still overwhelmingly rural. Therefore, urban-based reforms were tenuous, since political power continued to reside in the countryside. Not until the 1930s did the United States secure a social security system, minimum wage legislation, and the prohibition of child labor. With respect to industrial social legislation, her development was closer to France than to the more urbanized, industrial societies.

THE CONSOLIDATION OF GERMANY AND ITALY AS NATION-STATES

Of the major countries comprising Europe's state system in 1914, two of them, Italy and Germany, did not exist in 1850, except as geographical and cultural entities. The unification of each state required breaking the Austrian predominance in Central Europe which had been established by the Congress of Vienna. After revolutions in 1848 failed to overturn that settlement, Count Cavour of Piedmont and Otto von Bismarck of Prussia united their states by means of calculated international war. From their respective capitals of Turin and Berlin they challenged Vienna for control of their own affairs and enlarged their states, which became the nuclei of united Italy and united Germany. Because they succeeded in triumphing over both existing domestic and international law, Cavour and Bismarck contributed more than any ideologist to the popular conviction that might—whether national, racial, or economic—was right.

The Diplomatic Prelude: The Crimean War, 1854 to 1856

Russian encroachment upon Turkey—the "Sick Man of Europe" * whose body lay athwart the straits between the Black and Mediterranean Seas—precipitated Europe's first major war since 1815. Meeting at London in 1840 and 1841 to maintain the balance of power, the major European states guaranteed Ottoman territorial integrity and closed the straits to all foreign warships in time of peace. But Nicholas I of Russia persisted in pursuing bold annex-

ation plans. Backed by France and Britain, the Turks resisted. When the Habsburgs also demonstrated their hostility, Russia stood almost alone. Only Prussia was sympathetic.

The Turks declared war in 1853, but Russian annihilation of their wooden Black Sea fleet indicated their inability to resist Russian pressures. After much diplomatic maneuvering, Britain and France came to Turkey's aid in 1854. While Austria kept troops stationed on her frontiers with Russia and while Piedmont-Sardinia sent token forces to the allies, British and French forces destroyed Russian bases along the Black Sea and conquered the fortress of Sevastopol on the Crimean Peninsula.

Notable for the introduction of ironclad warships, for the development of military nursing, and for negligence and inefficiency on both sides, the Crimean War was a shock to the agrarian Russian Empire. With the exception of the Caucasus front, the Russians were defeated on their own soil. The rift between Russia and Austria broke the conservative Eastern remnant of the Concert of Europe. No longer able to count on Russian support in Central Europe, Austria now faced the Germans and Italians alone.

Italy

Formation of the Kingdom of Italy

Before 1848, Count Cavour of Piedmont had agitated through his newspaper, *Il Risorgimento* (*The Resurrection*), for a constitution and liberal economic reform modeled upon French and British theory. After holding several cabinet posts, Cavour

---

* The phrase came to be used by European diplomats after the reforms of the late eighteenth- and early nineteenth-century sultans failed to check the Empire's steady disintegration.

became premier in 1852. Relying upon a center coalition hostile to clerical traditionalism on the "Right" and democracy and republicanism on the "Left," he built up a conscript army, negotiated tariff reductions, and fostered the expansion of commerce, industry, and transportation.

Cavour left his greatest mark in foreign affairs. He led Italy into the Crimean War as a virtual ally of Austria. But he turned discomfiture into success at the peace conference by publicizing Austrian wrongs in Italy. His pleas enticed Napoleon III, who was eager to regain the influence that France had lost in Italy in 1815. The two met secretly at Plombières in July 1858. In return for Nice and Savoy, Napoleon pledged aid in Piedmont's seizure of Lombardy and Venetia—provided that Cavour could goad Austria into declaring war.

Cavour baited Austria by conscripting Lombard refugees into the army. As he had anticipated, Austria declared a preventive war, but she found herself confronted unexpectedly by France. No sooner were the Habsburgs driven out of most of Lombardy

Count Cavour, unifier of Italy (1810–1861). He had a passion for politics and became a master in that difficult field.

than Napoleon reconsidered his actions. Under British diplomatic pressure, and distrustful of Cavour's intentions, he made a separate truce with Austria. Through Napoleon III, Piedmont obtained Lombardy, but not until Piedmont was allowed to annex four smaller principalities was Napoleon able to obtain Nice and Savoy. The annexation of Lombardy, Parma, Tuscany, Modena, and Romagna consolidated Piedmont's position in northern Italy and left it with nearly half of the peninsula's population.

In 1860 Cavour's direction of Italian affairs was threatened by Mazzini and his republican followers who instigated an autonomous revolution in Sicily. Cavour had suppressed Mazzini's newspaper and activities in Piedmont, but he had secretly supplied Giuseppe Garibaldi (1807–1882), the principal republican military leader, and had diverted him from attacking Nice to a campaign against Sicily. In Sicily the picturesque sea captain, who had learned

UNIFICATION OF ITALY

Map by J. Donovan

guerrilla warfare in exile in South America, led his "Thousand Redshirts" to unexpected victory. To cut off Garibaldi's projected march on Rome and Venetia, which would have involved war with France and Austria, Cavour's army invaded the Papal States to "save them from revolution" and brought Garibaldi under control in Naples. In the spring of 1861 plebiscites, conducted by the Piedmontese army, joined Sicily, Naples, and the Papal States (except Rome) to the newly declared Kingdom of Italy.

A few months after the Kingdom of Italy was proclaimed by Victor Emmanuel, Cavour died, leaving the tasks of organizing the expanded kingdom to contending cliques. Total unification awaited another series of wars in which Italy benefited from Prussian victories. In the Austro-Prussian War of 1866, Italy gained Venetia. Napoleon III, whose plans for Italy had been dashed by Piedmont, garrisoned Rome and prevented its seizure until the Franco-Prussian War of 1870. Thus, except for scattered "unredeemed Italians" along the Austrian frontier, the Kingdom of Italy realized the dream of national unification.

Italian Politics, 1871 to 1914

Before World War I, Italian nationalists' visions of greatness remained largely dreams. Italy failed to become a major political and industrial power after attaining national unity. Requisite economic resources such as coal and iron were lacking, and population growth exceeded agricultural and industrial expansion. Moreover, government revenues were insufficient to simultaneously develop commercial facilities, educate a largely illiterate population, and maintain the armed forces necessary to make Italy a great power. Because of internal tensions and marked regional differences, especially between the dominant commercial north and the undeveloped, agrarian, and disorderly south, unity was more an aspiration than a reality.

The Kingdom of Piedmont-Sardinia pro-

vided the constitutional apparatus, the early leadership, and the initial policies for the kingdom as a whole. The Ministry was responsible to Parliament—an upper house of appointed lifetime peers and a lower house elected by property holders comprising a little more than 2 per cent of the total population. Northern leaders, who were constitutional monarchists rather than republicans in outlook, initially guided the centralization of law, administration, finance, taxation, and the army. Local administration was organized on the French model, which managed affairs uniformly from the capital. Inevitably its policies of free trade and anticlericalism collided with the interests of southern Italians (who tended to look upon the government as an alien power) and with the papacy, most of whose territories had been seized during unification. Following Sardinian precedent, the Parliament enacted a Law of Papal Guarantees in 1871. It guaranteed to His Holiness certain rights and privileges, and an annual subsidy. Although the state retained Roman Catholicism as the established faith and paid its clergy, subsequent measures curbed Church control over education, property, and marriage. The Pope responded by declaring himself a "prisoner" in the Vatican (no pope left the city until 1929), by rejecting the subsidy, and by encouraging —later in 1886 requiring—loyal Catholics to be "neither electors nor elected." This breach inhibited the political development of the Italian people, who were in any case badly led by men more interested in imperialism than in reform. The opportunistic government of F. Crispi (1887–1896) collapsed when the French-supported Ethiopians defeated the Italians at Aduwa in 1896. Now Italy had another opportunity for liberal experimentation.

Both remarkable material progress and widespread social unrest characterized the period 1896 to 1914, when the dominant political personality was Giovanni Giolitti. Northern Italy industrialized rapidly at this time, even though her high production costs penalized her in foreign trade. Hydroelectricity was harnessed as a native source of power, and the government provided tariff protection. But, drained by costly attempts to become a major military power, Italy continued on the verge of bankruptcy. Her lower classes experienced little if any relief from hardship. Her population growth so outstripped the rate of emigration and economic development that she maintained one of the lowest standards of living in Europe. Socialists of various revisionist schools attempted to shore up the weakly supported liberal institutions of Italy.

Giolitti's government was able to proceed with much of the socialists' reform program. Progress in education sharply reduced illiteracy. His government encouraged the organization of industrial and agricultural labor organizations and, in 1912, the franchise was extended to almost all adult males. In addition, some social insurance was adopted, a weekly day of rest was guaranteed to labor, and the railroads were nationalized.

Giolitti's "Leftist" politics and an attempted general strike in 1904 provoked a conservative reaction. In 1905 the papacy lifted its ban on political activity and founded Catholic Action groups that advocated a corporatist economy. The Church proclaimed itself defender of the existing social order against both liberalism and socialism.

Germany

Otto von Bismarck and Austria's Expulsion from Germany

Bismarck was not an ordinary Prussian Conservative. His aims—the aggrandizement of Prussian power and the maintenance of rule by the Junkers—were orthodox enough, but his methods at home and abroad were radical. In international af-

fairs he respected only state egotism and power, not the principle of monarchical legitimacy. As Prussian emissary to the Diet of the German Confederation at Frankfurt he had treated Austria, the embodiment of international conservatism, as the paramount enemy. The cornerstone of his diplomacy was the maintenance by his great generals, Roon and Moltke, of the army in a constant state of readiness for the exploitation of international crises. This enabled Bismarck to mobilize last and to appear as the injured, defensive party. Unlike other Conservatives, Bismarck appealed directly to the populace with universal, direct manhood suffrage. The purpose was neither liberal nor democratic, however, for Bismarck would not surrender control of affairs of state to a popularly elected assembly. From the Liberals he appropriated the goal of national unity and secured the support of a majority of them without conceding parliamentary government. Bismarck's unification of Germany amounted to an extension of Prussian dominance over the whole Empire.

Bismarck used a crisis over Schleswig-Holstein to precipitate a war with Austria. When German nationalists had tried to annex the two duchies in 1848, the great powers intervened, proposing in 1852 that the duchies go to the Danish heir to the throne upon his accession, a solution contrary to their laws of succession. The death of the Danish king, therefore, created a crisis into which Bismarck quickly stepped. In 1864 he negotiated an alliance with Austria, and the two jointly conquered the duchies. Refusing to exchange Austria's share for southern territory, Bismarck secured their administrative division in 1865, with Holstein going to Austria. But it gradually became clear that Bismarck intended to annex both duchies. In direct violation of the constitution of the German Confederation, he negotiated a secret alliance with Italy for immediate war with

Austria. Already having Russian friendship, he secured French neutrality by dangling prospects before the French ambassador of annexing either the Rhineland or Belgium. In vain, Austria sought to avoid a two-front war. When the Confederation Diet spurned reform plans offered by Prussia, the Prussian armies marched on Austria's northern supporters: Hanover, Saxony, and Hesse. These acts and Prussian occupation of Holstein moved Austria to declare war on Prussia in the summer of 1866.

Instead of a protracted conflict from which Napoleon expected to profit by staying neutral, Prussia humbled Austria in seven weeks. Taking advantage of railroads and telegraphs for mobility and coordination, and using breech-loading rifles to fire from prone positions, Prussian forces defeated the main Austrian army, with heavy losses at Königgrätz (Sadowa), on July 3, 1866. In the peace negotiations that terminated the Seven Weeks' War, Bismarck's strategy dictated leniency to the startled Austrians, whose assistance he might need in the future. Although Germany still lacked political unity, the Seven Weeks' War had driven Austria from the German states.

The Franco-Prussian War

Prussia's consolidation of northern Germany sharply altered the European balance of power with respect to France and undermined Napoleon III's domestic prestige and influence. Fearing a future shaped by Germany's rapid industrial, population, and military growth, many editors and generals were calling for a preventive war. The ailing Emperor, who preferred to rely upon international conferences, did not accede to these demands nor did he succeed in gaining allies in the event war should occur. When the war came, it fully revealed the glaring, growing differential between French and German military power.

Bismarck was determined to instigate war with France, but the origins of the Franco-Prussian War of 1870 and 1871 were less the result of his calculations than of French emotional reactions to wounded national honor. The episode that led to war started with efforts of Spanish liberal revolutionaries to secure a new monarch after 1868. One of the few available candidates was Leopold of Hohenzollern, a Roman Catholic. Because it would place a Hohenzollern on France's southern frontier, Bismarck promoted his candidacy. After once rejecting the offer, William I, head of the house, eventually accepted it. But the dynastic secret leaked out prematurely in July 1870.

When French diplomacy secured Leopold's withdrawal, Bismarck's scheme was defeated — temporarily. But to vindicate French honor, Napoleon's foreign minister demanded a promise from William I that Leopold would never be a candidate again. At the resort city of Ems, the King firmly but courteously rejected this demand. In Berlin, Bismarck, who was dining with Roon and Moltke, received William's report of his interview with the French ambassador and altered it for publication to make it appear that the ambassador and the King had exchanged insults. Bismarck's "editing" of the "Ems dispatch" spurred Napoleon III to declare war.

Lacking allies, France fought alone. She believed that her military forces were superior, but poor generalship and other factors belied her faith. Augmented by southern German forces, Prussian armies broke through Lorraine, encircled major French armies at Metz and Sedan, and besieged Paris. The surrender of the encircled French armies was doubly significant for, at Sedan, Napoleon himself became a prisoner of war. Republican leaders hastily assembled new forces that staved off total defeat for six months, but the terms of peace in February 1871 were

UNIFICATION OF GERMANY

GERMAN EMPIRE 1871

Kingdom of Prussia to 1866

States annexed in 1866

United with Prussia to form
North German Confederation, 1867

United with North German Confederation
to form German Empire, 1871

Ceded by France, 1871

*(Austrian Dominions
excluded from German
Confederation, 1866)*

by J. Donovan

costly. In addition to a large indemnity
and German occupation at French expense
until it was paid, the new French government was obliged to cede Alsace and most
of Lorraine to the new German Empire.
The cession of Alsace-Lorraine, with its
textile and metallurgical industries, was a
heavy blow to France.

In addition to the territorial settlement,
the balance of power was further turned
against France by the formation of the German Empire, which was proclaimed in
Louis XIV's Hall of Mirrors at Versailles.
At the invitation of the German princes but
not at the behest of a parliament, the Prussian King became German Emperor.

Bismarck and the German Empire

In creating the German Empire, Bismarck took pains to alleviate fears that preponderant Prussia would dominate the
Empire's institutions. Yet those institutions
were so designed that Prussia did dominate
the Empire and its policies. As emperor the
Prussian king had sole initiative in foreign
and military affairs. Independent of parliamentary control, he appointed the chancellor (Bismarck until 1890) and federal

Bismarck and William II.

officials. In the two-house legislature the instructed delegates, sent by the constituent states to the Federal Council (*Bundesrat*), dominated the lower house (*Reichstag*). The *Reichstag* was elected at large by direct, secret ballot. It had to concur with the *Bundesrat* in the passage of laws and budgets.

At first, Bismarck found support in a coalition of middle-class National Liberals (who admired his success in unifying Germany), and the Prussian Junkers (the military aristocracy that was left in possession of its privileges and power). Believing that only propertied elements should influence affairs, he feared the proletariat as a revolutionary force bent on the Empire's destruction.

After Austria had been defeated in 1866, Bismarck continued the war against the Catholics by means of the "Falk Laws," the anticlerical National Liberals' legislation in Prussia. These laws launched a "struggle for cultural purity" (*Kulturkampf*) against Roman Catholics, Poles, and Germans alike. Among other things they barred Jesuits, restricted Church offices to Germans, put ecclesiastical education under state control, and made civil marriage compulsory. But instead of destroying Catholic opposition, the laws precipitated the rapid growth of a Roman Catholic opposition party: the Center party. They also moved Lutheran Conservatives to launch an intolerable attack upon Bismarck. By 1879 the *Kulturkampf* had manifestly failed.

Bismarck regrouped his political base by a compromise of 1879, which he labeled the "second founding" of the Empire. It reflected rapid socioeconomic changes. Caught in an economic depression, peasants turned to the Conservatives for leadership. They sought cheap credit, reduced taxes, higher agricultural prices, and tariffs. The anti-*laissez faire* Center also advocated tariffs, as did the great industrialists of the National Liberal party who were forming cartels and combines. In 1879 the tariff front provided the Chancellor with a new coalition. Despite the *Kulturkampf,* the Center became a supporter, although not entirely trusted, of Bismarck's new system. Domestically, it had a primary purpose in keeping the "red menace" under control.

After the depression of 1873, socialists began to make notable headway among the burgeoning laboring population. They were feared by all conservatives and most of the middle classes. Bismarck saw the growth of labor activism as a threat to his whole structure and resolved to meet it by repression. By falsely attributing attempts to assassinate the Emperor to socialist organizations, he secured laws disbanding their associations and suppressing their press. To check their growth Bismarck announced in 1881 his support of state intervention to prevent part of the population—the capitalists—from using their power to oppress the rest. Bismarck's social legislation of the 1880s, which began with insurance for sickness, accidents, and old age, became a model for other industrial states. It alienated the National Liberals, but it failed to curb the Social Democrats' growth. As Germany became more and more urban and industrial, the Social Democrats' threat to Bismarck's system (as feared) grew.

William II and the Failure of Democratization

Bismarck's entire edifice was predicated on a man of his abilities and judgment holding it together. Although never losing control of the army to him, William I had deferred to his judgment. But in 1888 William II, rash in displaying power in both foreign and domestic affairs, came to the throne. By 1890 he and Bismarck came to a parting of the ways. The Emperor broke with Russia, a course that Bismarck considered disastrous because it exposed Germany to the possibility of defeat in a two-front war, a defeat that would destroy the dominance of the Prussian Junkers. William and Bismarck disagreed when Bismarck wanted still more repression of the Social Democrats. The Emperor removed him as intermediary between himself and other ministers and finally dismissed him in 1890. Without Bismarck at the helm, imperial affairs drifted. Once his Napoleonic personality was gone there was no force capable of wringing concessions from the industrialists and the Prussian Conservatives. The Conservatives held on to their control of the army and civil service and successfully resisted progressive income taxes and death duties. Most significantly, they defeated all attempts to democratize the constitution.

The principal party that demanded democratization was the Social Democrats, who polled one third of the vote on the eve of World War I. Prior to World War I, elections were going against the government, and Parliament voted no confidence in the government on specific issues. But no party could confront the army officered by the Junkers until the military machine at the heart of the imperial system had been overwhelmed by war. But before the debacle of World War I, only a few Social Democrats (such as Friedrich Engels) had been willing to think in these terms.

THE EASTERN EMPIRES: AUSTRIA-HUNGARY AND RUSSIA

Both socially and economically the Eastern empires lagged far behind the more industrialized West. Smarting from the defeats in the Crimean War and the Seven Weeks' War, their bureaucracies pushed the construction of railroads and factories. But at the same time they were committed to the preservation of old institutions. Leading bureaucrats in both states mistakenly assumed that modernization would preserve the Old Regime. However, urbanization brought new social conditions irreconcilable with it. The Eastern empires' problems were also compounded by the ferment of nationalism which threatened to break them up into their constituent national parts.

The Hapsburg Empire, 1850 to 1914

Since the seventeenth century the Habsburgs had served the useful function of organizing the peoples of Eastern Europe. An apparent anomaly in the age of nation-states, the Empire survived until the cataclysm of World War I. Because of slow industrial development, its basic problem was not restive urban populations but the task of reconciling divergent nationalities under the same tradition-bound dynasty.

The Habsburg Empire included a congeries of peoples differing in national culture. Germans were concentrated in the Old Habsburg duchies along the Danube

River and were scattered elsewhere in towns and administrative centers. There were also Slavs (Czechs, Slovaks, Poles, Ruthenians [Ukrainians], Serbs, Croats, Slovenes), Rumanians, Magyars, and some Italians. They were held together by the army, the hierarchy of the Roman Catholic Church, a German-speaking bureaucracy, and the inertia of custom. After the revolutions of 1848 and 1849, Habsburg unity was tightened by legal and economic measures, including the building of railroads. But the principal bond that kept the domains intact was the Emperor Francis Joseph, who ruled from 1848 to 1916. He proved open to various proposals for reorganizing the empire, as long as his prerogatives were not sacrificed.

Federalism Versus Centralization

To run the state, Francis Joseph depended alternatively upon German administrators advocating absolutist efficiency and great aristocrats who favored provincial autonomy. After the victory of the bureaucracy and army over the revolutions of 1848 and 1849, power in Vienna passed to Alexander Bach, Minister of Internal Affairs. He carried out a policy of centralized German absolutism and extended the power of the Roman Catholic Church. As long as prosperity lasted and Bach was successful in foreign affairs, the Emperor retained confidence in him. But non-Germans were alienated. Bach's policies in Hungary required the garrisoning of 150,000 men there. Inefficiency, desertions, and finally military defeat in Italy in 1859 led the Emperor to drop Bach from office.

In 1861 he restored the German bureaucrats with a new patent, or constitution. It provided for a parliament representing the various nationalities proportionately. But by "electoral geometry"—the unequal weighting of votes in electoral colleges—it assured power to the Austrian-Germans. The Magyars boycotted it; Czechs and Poles were refractory; and financiers became wary of further state expenditures. Again, Francis Joseph switched policies and constitutions by making a Polish nobleman, Belcredi, his highest official. But his concessions to Slavic autonomy aroused German and Hungarian fears of losing control to the Slavs.

The Compromise of 1867

Prussia's lightning victory in 1866 brought Belcredi down and precipitated another major constitutional reorganization of the Empire—this one permanent. After his defeat the Emperor could no longer fend off Hungarian demands for autonomy. By the *Ausgleich* or Compromise of 1867, the Empire became the Dual Monarchy of Austria-Hungary. Francis Joseph retained the Hungarian crown, and common ministries sat for military, foreign, and financial affairs. Nominally these three ministries were responsible to a parliament composed of delegations from the Austrian and Hungarian parliaments. Otherwise the two kingdoms became separate entities.

At the core of the *Ausgleich* were the mutual desires of the Germans and the Magyars to prevent their Slavic majorities from challenging their dominance. Neither considered the Slavs fit to rule themselves or the Empire. Hungarian Count Julius Andrassy stated the Compromise's purpose succinctly: "You look after your Slavs and we will look after ours." Thus, by creating privileged groups, the Compromise made a federative empire based on equal national rights even more impossible.

Social and Nationality Problems After the Compromise

With political domination went economic and cultural domination. Peasant emancipation in 1848 did not break up the *latifundia* (estates owned by the Church or the nobility and worked by landless or small-holding peasants). Ownership and control of industry and transportation were concentrated in German, Viennese, and often Jewish banking hands. Only sporadically did a native middle class exist, and both agricultural and industrial labor was usually recruited from subject nationalities. Such widespread conditions could only exacerbate national animosities and rivalry.

The Magyar oligarchy went farthest with policies of repression. Under Counts Andrassy and Stephen Tisza the Hungarian government after 1875 pressed a vigorous campaign of Magyarization in the schools and administration. The following estimates for the year 1900 indicate its success in crowding out Slavic competition for positions of power: 96% of the judges, 95% of the state officials, 92% of the county officials, 90% of the college students, 89% of the doctors, and 80% of the newspapers were Magyar. Two or three families controlled each county, and sixty families and forty bishops reputedly controlled national affairs. The gentry, which desired further separation from Vienna, dominated the Diet, which 6.5% of the population elected. The more pressure that the Magyars applied to the Slavs, the more they feared Slav treason or separation. The aggressive Magyars attributed all disaffection among the oppressed Slavs to the nationalist agitation emanating from Serbia. At Magyar insistence, Serbian imports were blocked from the Empire. Year by year after 1906, Magyar officials called for the military destruction of Serbia.

In the Austrian half of the Empire, the *Ausgleich* of 1867 restored power to the German bureaucrats who professed liberal principles. In liberal fashion they curtailed the power of the Roman Catholic Church, but they had no desire to make the Emperor and his ministries responsible to Parliament, since he was their only guarantee against dominance by the Slavic majority.

Shifting from one faction to another,

Francis Joseph failed to discover an alternative to nationalist disintegration. In 1907 he granted universal, equal, and direct manhood suffrage in the Austrian half of the Empire. On the eve of World War I, the heir-apparent, Francis Ferdinand, was considering federation as a new basis for the Habsburg Empire. By this time the higher levels of the Dual Monarchy's government had resolved upon the destruction of Serbia as the only possible means of preserving the Empire.

Russian Autocracy on Trial

Although the Russian autocracy in theory had absolute power, it was not actually a free agent. It could use its meager resources to foster commercial agriculture and industrialization only by risking a thorough overhaul of society. Historically dependent upon the serf-owning nobility, the Old Regime had good reason to fear such an overhaul. Russian intellectuals were torn between the "Westerners" and the "nativists" — proponents, respectively, of adding Western ideas and institutions to the Russian heritage and of preserving that heritage unchanged.

Nicholas I and the Crimean War

The reign of Nicholas I (1825–1855) became synonymous with increasingly efficient despotism. Some of the Tsar's measures indicated an awareness of basic problems. His decrees limited the power of nobles over their serfs and instigated investigations of serfdom. He ordered the laws codified for the first time since 1649, and he introduced a gold-backed currency. But he was nevertheless preoccupied with asserting the Crown's absolute power over all dissent.

He faced opposition at home largely from Western and Slavophile intellectuals. Westerners such as Alexander Herzen (1812–1870), illegitimate son of a nobleman, and the commoner, Belinsky (1811–1848), were attracted by French Utopian

Tsar Alexander II, autocratic reformer.

Socialism. Herzen, like most Westerners writing in exile, thought Russia was peculiarly suited to socialism because it lacked Roman law, private property, and rational religion. Belinsky, who remained in Russia, could voice his criticism only indirectly in book reviews. The Slavophiles, whose center was Moscow, worshipped Russian traditions and resented railroads and industry. Russian intellectuals formed an impotent class apart from the power structure, Gaining no influence, they vented their frustration in increasing radicalism. Even when Nicholas' regime ran aground in the Crimean War, they were in no position to influence affairs.

The Franco-British victory over Russian forces on Russian soil and coastal waters dispelled the myth of invulnerability that had made traditional institutions sacrosanct after 1812. The new tsar, Alexander II (1855–1881), who ascended the throne at the end of the war, turned immediately to the peasant question, determined to secure action.

Alexander II, Tsar Emancipator

In one of the most complicated decrees in history, Alexander decreed the serfs' emancipation in 1861. Unlike the American slaves emancipated later, these former serfs were granted land. But only their houses and garden plots were their personal property. The remainder of the land was divided between the lords and peasant communes. And land that was ceded to the peasantry (in the decree nobles were recognized as the rightful former owners of the land) was not free nor did it go to individual proprietors. In each locality the elders of the collective village (*Mir* or, literally, "world") were placed in charge of periodic reallotments to families, indemnity payments to the state for forty-nine years, tax and military draft levies, and discipline. To the nobility went the "psychologically best lands," usually the major portion of the former estates. Bonds from the state compensated them for lands and peasant obligations that were lost. Because it favored the nobility, the decree aroused violent peasant resistance. The peasant had legal freedom but was subject to heavy communal supervision and could not accumulate capital when he had to make indemnity payments, most of which fell eventually into arrears. The nobility was no more successful in coping with the new conditions, since the majority of the bond recipients "lived up" their proceeds in luxury instead of using them to introduce scientific agriculture. Thus Russian emancipation stirred more disaffection among the serfs and undermined the nobility. It failed to meet the subsistence crisis produced by an extraordinary increase in population.

Peasant emancipation was part of a larger goal of legal equality announced by the Tsar at his accession. Together these two reforms necessitated a thorough revamping of the entire administrative and judicial machinery of the Russian state. To substitute its officials for local nobles the government had to expand its bureaucracy greatly. Beginning in 1864 it organized the *Zemstvos*, local elective councils representing nobles, townsmen, and peasants. Given jurisdiction over roads, bridges, local welfare, some police functions, and primary education, the *Zemstvos* served as schools for training local leaders. Beginning in 1870, similar reforms were introduced in municipalities.

Russia's old legal system was based on paternalism and was closely connected with the administrative departments of government. The Tsar replaced it with a new judiciary modeled on French and British practice. The new system provided for public jury trials (with significant political exceptions), legal equality (although peasants still had separate courts), and the separation of judicial from administrative functions. On paper the legal system was the most enlightened in Europe; in practice its impact was more gradual and tentative than revolutionary. More than the *Zemstvo* reforms, Alexander's legal innovations weakened the nobility. And they opened paths to prominence for lawyers who constituted potential opposition to the aristocracy and bureaucracy.

Reactionary and Revolutionary Polarization, 1863 to 1881

Stimulated by Alexander's reforms, a new generation of radicals, impatient for immediate, more drastic changes, held Russian institutions up to the light of Utopian Socialism and British Utilitarianism. With such spokesmen as Nikolai Chernyshevsky (1828–1889), they focused their attention on economics, economic history, and the exploitation of the lower classes by the upper classes. Dubbed "Nihilists" for their repudiation of traditional authority and institutions, the radical intelligentsia lacked power to effect changes unless they could secure popular—that is, peasant—support. Student sons and daughters of the "conscience-stricken" nobility and middle classes turned to the "dark people," the peasantry, as the potential regenerators of Russian society. A Populist movement (*Narodniki*) sought to educate the peasants to improve their lot, but the tradition-bound peasantry rebuffed them, often reporting them to the police. Stung by this rejection, the radical intelligentsia formed bands of revolutionary elites, which the authorities hunted down. Curbed from above and at least temporarily spurned from below, the revolutionary movements vented their discontent by anarchistic acts of assassination that, in turn, brought more repression.

While the Western-oriented radicals turned Nihilist, an aggressively nationalist nativist and imperialistic Pan-Slav movement gained momentum. In 1869, N. Y. Danilevsky, a biologist, published *Russia and Europe*, a Social Darwinist work that argued that only through war with the West could peace-loving Russians fulfill their messianic mission of rescuing civilization from alien control. Dostoevsky used his literary fame to spread the Pan-Slav idea of mission: that it was the duty of Russia to save her Orthodox Slavic brethren from the menace of the West. The one most significant convert to authoritarian reaction in these years was the highly educated civil servant, Constantine Pobiedonostsev (1827–1907), chief administrator and confidant of Tsars Alexander III (1881–1894) and (until 1905) Nicholas II (1894–1917), whom he also tutored.

Reaction After 1881

Liberalism had no more competent, consistent, or powerful foe than Pobiedonostsev, for he was mainly responsible for Russian domestic policy until the Revolution of 1905 unseated him. As lay administrator of the Holy Synod of the Russian Orthodox Church, he held superior cabinet rank. Anti-rational and anti-Western, Pobiedonostsev viewed political society as an organic, historic, and unconscious growth propelled by inertia. To take over parts of another society (to introduce English juries into Russia, for example) violated the uniqueness of the recipient. To separate church and state was to attempt an impossible dichotomy of body and soul. Pobiedonostsev dismissed parliamentary government as an unstable façade for the personal egotism of demagogues and plutocrats. He felt that popular sovereignty would only breed discontent. Secular education corrupted youth by teaching abstractions, and any babbler might start publishing where the press was free. The only laws justifying obedience derived from divine commandments, not from the inventions of man. Equality he found only in the Russian Orthodox Church, not at the ballot box. He believed that to preserve precious institutions and customs, the ruling elite should prevail—with confident righteousness—against the positivist and utilitarian deceptions of the Western world.

Spurred by him, the Interior Ministry enlarged the secret police and its corps of secret agents. They infiltrated revolutionary organizations and incited mobs against unpopular groups. National minorities such as the Finns, the Baltic peoples, the Poles, Asian tribes, and the Georgians were subject to systematic "Russification." Similar pressures were applied to religious minorities—the Roman Catholics, "Old Believers," Baptists, Mohammedans, Tolstoyites, and especially the Jews, who were victims of bloody pogroms. Secret agents were set to watch secret agents, and an espionage system was established within the church itself to ensure obedience. Thus did "holy terror" mark the policy of Holy Russia.

Many oppressed minorities responded to Pobiedonostsev's repression by joining revolutionary movements. But revolutionary pressures also mounted because of economic developments. In part, the government itself under Count Witte was responsible for these developments.* First as an administrator of state railways, then as Minister of Transport, and finally as finance minister between 1892 and 1903, Witte pressed for the expansion of Russian industry and transportation at an unprecedented pace. Building the trans-Siberian railways was his most sensational but not his most solid achievement. By erecting a prohibitive tariff wall, he attracted foreign capital. Industrialization, with few concessions to urban labor, created a large, discontented proletariat separated for the first time from agriculture. But the middle class, whose growth was stifled by state ownership of industry and by foreign capitalists, had little strength to voice their liberalism. Much more significant were the land-hungry peasants whose numbers almost doubled between emancipation and World War I and whose mutterings forbode revolutions. In these prewar years nearly one million peasants emigrated to Siberia, and land prices nearly trebled. But after 1880, starvation threatened about two thirds of the population. For millions, poor harvests in 1891 and 1892 made that threat a reality. Apart from denying the famine's existence, the government abolished poll taxes and reduced peasant indemnity payments. But prior to the Revolution of 1905, discussed below, it offered no policies to cope with the agrarian-population crisis. Agriculture remained collective and technologically backward.

---

* Unlike Pobiedonostsev, Witte never possessed the complete confidence of the Tsar, despite his orthodox absolutism. He was dismissed in 1903, but recalled temporarily in 1905 to negotiate peace with Japan and a large French loan that, in his phrase, "saved Russia." By this he meant that it saved tsarist rule from parliamentary limitations.

The Formation of Revolutionary Parties

The government's intolerable economic policies disaffected the peasantry from the autocracy, but they were not attracted to the programs of the revolutionary parties that organized at the turn of the century. The first party to form was the Marxian Social Democratic party whose appeal was to industrial labor and intellectuals. Not only did Marx, whose *Das Kapital* the censors allowed to circulate as a procapitalist work, offer an extreme answer to an extreme situation, but he also offered a philosophy of history and a prophetic future congenial to Russian patterns of thought. Recovering from an abortive start in 1883, the Russian Social Democratic party reorganized and persevered after 1898. Most of its leadership agitated for democracy, labor reforms, and industrialization, but at the party congress held in London in 1903, advocates of more extreme measures secured a majority and organized as Bolsheviks. Thereafter, their leader, Lenin, and his followers exchanged polemics with the Menshevik ("minority") faction which advocated evolutionary reforms.* The second and largest party to organize was the Social Revolutionaries. Drawn from *Narodnik* (Populist) sources, it was a rustic socialist party that advocated continued communal land ownership, the cultivation of traditional folk customs, and opposition to industry. Although the party supported democratization, part of its numbers engaged in acts of terrorism and assassinated several tsarist officials between 1902 and 1904.

Following the two major socialist parties, the first formal liberal party organized during the early phases of the Revolution of 1905. Its roots were in the *Zemstvo* councils and in professional unions of lawyers, doctors, and teachers. The *Zemstvo* men had first taken the initiative when they attempted to organize a famine relief in 1892. In 1904 they met in a national congress that was called to assist the flagging war effort and to resolve an economic crisis. In May 1905, they joined with the professionals in the Union of Unions led by Professor Pavel (Paul) Milyukov to demand parliamentary government, social reform, and civic rights.

All of the revolutionary parties acting as a "popular front" got their first opportunity to gain power not from large popular followings, which they lacked, but from the military and economic embarrassments of the government during the Russo-Japanese War of 1904 and 1905.

War and Revolution, 1904 and 1905

Russian defeat in Manchuria and Korea began at the outset of the Russo-Japanese War and continued until the Japanese sank units of the Baltic fleet sent around Africa to the Orient. Facing ridicule at home for these defeats, Nicholas lost more prestige

Bloody Sunday, 1905. Tsarist response to a peaceful petition.

---

* These names reflected Lenin's propaganda tactics rather than the relative strength of the factions in Russia. The Menshevik ("minority") faction had and maintained a larger following than Lenin right down to March 1917.

when his palace guards fired on a procession of petitioning workers led by a secret-agent and priest, Father Gapon, on "Bloody Sunday," January 22, 1905. Following strikes and widespread rural disorders, the Tsar began to make concessions which he extended after every fresh major setback. In October 1905, a general strike tied up the economy and forced the dismissal of Pobiedonostsev. Thereafter, Count Witte was restored to favor to promulgate a manifesto promising an elective Duma or parliament and a broad range of civil liberties. As intended, Witte's October Manifesto split the liberals: conservative monarchical Octobrists against liberal Constitutional Democrats, or Cadets, who favored parliamentary government, state education, drastic land reforms, and autonomy for border regions. The Manifesto did not satisfy labor or the socialist parties, however. A labor council (soviet) in St. Petersburg and the Social Democrats organized further strikes and precipitated a conservative reaction among the liberals. When the government arrested the members of the St. Petersburg soviet, Moscow workers led by the Bolsheviks took to the barricades in a short, bloody, and futile revolt. Thus the revolutionary coalition quickly broke into contending factions with differing interests.

The October Manifesto, a promise rather than a constitution, marked the high point of the Revolution of 1905. Counterrevolution began as soon as peace was obtained. Royal troops returning from the Far East were screened out and set upon rebellious areas. In the countryside, where constitutional issues made no impact, bands of "Black Hundreds," whose membership included the Tsar, high churchmen, and landlords, loosed private terror on rebellious or suspicious peasants. Most important, the Tsar negotiated with France the largest international loan up to that point in history. The loan enabled the Tsar to brush aside the first Duma, which the Cadets dominated. The Tsar consolidated his victory

on May 6, 1906, by announcing fundamental laws that reduced the elective Duma to a minor role. Nicholas II, who had not given up his divine-right claims, reserved for himself an absolute veto, decree powers, budgetary initiative, and full control over foreign affairs, the military establishments, the administration and judiciary, and further constitutional changes. Atop the Duma he established an Imperial Council, half appointed and half elected by privileged corporations. When the Duma criticized the government and introduced unacceptable laws for the compensated expropriation and sale of gentry, state, and church lands, he dissolved it. Although not all of its results were erased, the revolution was over.

Old Russia's "Golden Age," 1906 to 1914

According to aristocratic exiles from the Bolshevik Revolution of November 1917, Russia now entered a period in which her basic problems were being solved, at least until the outbreak of World War I. Actually, substantial progress was recorded. Labor conditions were mitigated, the number of schools increased by 50 per cent, universities were thrown open to the lower and middle classes, and the Russian industrialization rate was one of the most rapid in the world. Censorship relaxed, and persecution of minorities declined. For the first time, the government headed by Peter Stolypin (1862–1911) worked toward a promising program for the peasantry. Now peasant banks began to make effective loans to needy peasants for capital improvements, and population pressures were eased somewhat by settlements in Siberia. Stolypin's reforms not only served to change rural conditions, but they also provided the social mobility indispensable for Russia's industrialization. His radical policies aroused reactionary fears, and he was assassinated in 1911.

Progress might have continued with proper direction. But Nicholas II was a weak administrator, preoccupied with preserving his family's prerogatives. In 1907 he altered the election laws to make landowners predominant in the Duma and to sharply curtail the influence of peasants, industrial laborers, and minorities. While this law secured a cooperative, conservative Duma, its success encouraged Nicholas II to think in terms of further reductions of parliamentary government.

Between 1850 and 1914, when all Western societies were under the uneven impact of industrialization, every major state had or acquired some form of representative government. All of them had one or more parties committed to such institutions, and often to their democratization. But their powers and ability to respond to changing conditions varied widely.

After 1914 the unresolved problems that produced internal instability were temporarily submerged in World War I. How far the outbreak of that war reflected the desires of political leaders to turn attention from them to foreign war is a moot question. Certainly Austria-Hungary's attempt to crush Serbia in 1914 stemmed from the fear of nationalist disintegration. Both Russia and Germany were in revolutionary situations because entrenched power elites would not yield. And Britain's influence was weakened by the prospects of imminent civil war over Ireland. Polemics against socialists generally hit hardest at their internationalism. It is also certain that nationalism, the principal ideology behind the war, was cultivated to secure a feeling of unity despite conflicting interests. But it was most commonly expressed in the quest to rule over and "civilize" other peoples — imperialism. Schisms within industrial societies hardly account for the outbreak of World War I, but the role of imperialism in bringing that war about awaits assessment in the following chapter.

SELECTED READINGS

*Binkley, Robert C., *Realism and Nationalism 1852–1871,* Harper, New York, 1935, and Harper Torchbook.

A comprehensive history of politics, thought, and business in the Rise of Modern Europe series; particularly good on the foreign policy of Napoleon III.

Briggs, Asa, *Victorian People,* University of Chicago Press, Chicago, 1955.

Depicts Victorian England between the Great Exposition of 1851 and the Reform Bill of 1867 by a biographical approach to major events and institutional changes.

Brogan, Denis, *France Under the Republic, 1870–1939,* Harper, New York, 1940.

A solid attention-keeping account, the first seven books of which are relevant to this chapter.

Bury, J. P. T., *Napoleon III and the Second Empire,* English Universities Press, London, 1964.

A short up-to-date analysis, packed with information, in the Teach Yourself History Library by the author of a longer history of France from 1814 to 1940.

*Dangerfield, George, *The Strange Death of Liberal England 1910–1914,* Capricorn Books, New York, 1961.

A study in the breakdown of parliamentary methods among the suffragettes, labor groups, and conservative opponents of Irish Home Rule on the eve of World War I.

*Eyck, Erich, *Bismarck and the German Empire,* W. W. Norton, New York, 1958.

An incisive political biography in the form of lectures based on the author's three-volume life of Bismarck, in German.

*Hamerow, Theodore S., *Otto von Bismarck, A Historical Assessment,* D. C. Heath & Co., Boston, 1962.

A collection of widely different interpretations of Bismarck's career, with an extremely perceptive introduction.

*Hayes, Carleton J. H., *A Generation of Materialism 1871–1900,* Harper, New York and London, and Harper Torchbook.

Asterisk (*) denotes paperback.

A volume in the Rise of Modern Europe series that sees the end of the nineteenth century, although witnessing the rise of economic imperialism and totalitarian nationalism, as the climax of the Enlightenment.

Jászi, Oszkár, *The Dissolution of the Habsburg Monarchy,* University of Chicago Press, Chicago, 1929.

Emphasizes illiberal Hungarian policies as the basic disintegrating force in Austria-Hungary.

Kann, Robert A., *The Multinational Empire: Nationalism and National Reform in the Habsburg Monarchy, 1848–1918,* Octagon Books, New York, 1964, 2 vols.

Volume I records the growth of nationalism among the Empire's constituent peoples; Volume II surveys the proposals put forth after 1848 to resolve national conflicts within the Empire.

King, Bolton, *A History of Italian Unity 1814–1871,* Nisbet, London, 1924, 2 vols. (rev. ed.).

An old account that is still useful.

*Kitson Clark, George, *The Making of Victorian England,* Harvard University Press, Cambridge, 1962, and Atheneum.

A revisionist history emphasizing religion, the percolation of wealth downward, and the growth of rule by experts and officials motivated by humanitarianism behind the Victorian ideology of *laissez faire.*

*Pares, Bernard, *The Fall of the Russian Monarchy,* Alfred A. Knopf, New York, 1939, and Vintage Books.

A history of the reign of Alexander II and the first revolution of 1917 by an historian intimately acquainted with source materials and leading persons involved in the events described.

Pobiedonostsev, Konstantin Petrovich, *Reflections of a Russian Statesman,* translated by R. C. Fong, University of Michigan Press, Ann Arbor, 1965.

A frank exposition of counterrevolutionary traditionalism by Alexander III's most powerful adviser.

Robinson, Geroid T., *Rural Russia Under the Old Régime,* The Macmillan Co., New York, 1961.

Investigates the peasants' situation before and after the emancipation of 1861 and analyzes in detail the effects of the early twentieth-century reforms.

*Rosenberg, Arthur, *Imperial Germany, The Birth of the German Republic 1871–1918,* Beacon Press, Boston, 1964.

An excellent study based on a parliamentary investigation of the reasons for Germany's loss of World War I by a liberal dissenter who participated in that investigation.

*Schorske, Carl E., *German Social Democracy 1905–1917,* Harvard University Press, Cambridge, 1955, and Wiley Science Editions.

Traces the origins of the great schism between the union-based democratic Socialists and revolutionary Communists within the German Social Democratic party.

Simmons, Ernest J., ed., *Continuity and Change in Russian and Soviet Thought,* Harvard University Press, Cambridge, 1955.

A collection of papers by more than thirty contributors on various aspects of Russian thought before and after the Bolshevik Revolution, several of which are indispensable to Russian history in the nineteenth century.

Simpson, Frederick A., *Louis Napoleon and the Recovery of France,* Longmans, Green & Co., New York and London, 1930.

A worthy pioneering attempt to rescue the Second Empire from inattention, a labor that the author has failed to conclude beyond 1856.

Somervell, D. C., *Disraeli and Gladstone, A Duo-Biographical Sketch,* Garden City Publishing Co., Garden City, N.Y., 1926.

A joint biography based on the classic exhaustive biographies of both men.

Taylor, A. J. P., *The Course of German History,* Coward-McCann, New York, 1946; and *The Habsburg Monarchy, 1809–1918,* H. Hamilton, London, 1948.

Authoritative studies of the two principal powers of Central Europe, rather heavy reading for the beginner.

Thompson, J. M., *Louis Napoleon and the Second Empire,* Blackwell, Oxford, 1965.

Biography of the emperor, based on up-to-date scholarship, that treats the Second Empire as a natural transition to the Third Republic.

*Thomson, David, *England in the Nineteenth Century, 1815–1914,* Penguin Books, Baltimore, 1950.

Traces social changes, mental habits, and social organization during Britain's transition from an agrarian to an industrial society, finding the Victorians liberal enough to have distributed wealth, without bloodshed, throughout the community to an unprecedented extent.

Whyte, A. J. B., *The Making of Modern Italy,* Blackwell, Oxford, 1944.

One of the best accounts of Italian history in English.

*Williams, Roger L., *Gaslight and Shadow, The World of Napoleon III 1851–1870,* The Macmillan Co., New York, 1957, and a paperback under its subtitle.

Biographical sketches illuminating various aspects—including education, culture, and science—of Louis Napoleon's France.

For the United States, see the volumes emphasizing social history by Arthur Cole, Allan Nevins, Ida Tarbell, Arthur M. Schlesinger, and Harold U. Faulkner in *A History of American Life,* edited by Arthur M. Schlesinger and Dixon Ryan Fox. See also:

Link, Arthur S., *Woodrow Wilson and the Progressive Era, 1910–1917,* Harper, New York, 1954, and

Mowry, George E., *Theodore Roosevelt and the Progressive Movement,* University of Wisconsin, Madison, 1946.

Two recent authoritative works on the quest for social justice in industrial America.

24

The New Imperialism and the Posture of Aggression

Much controversy has developed in recent years over the nature, purposes, and consequences of the so-called new imperialism. The first part of this chapter presents most of the more common arguments that make up this controversy. Brief attention is then given to the salient features of the state and alliance systems, secret diplomacy, militarism, new personalities, and the aims of the powers. The concluding, and major, portion is devoted to a somewhat detailed examination of the global thrusts of the new imperialist surge.

The Web of Forces

Imperialism

Imperialism may be defined as the extension of control or influence by one people over another. Throughout history it has assumed different forms and exerted varying degrees of influence upon other events, depending upon circumstances and the spirit of the times. In one form it radiates from a power center to contiguous territories. In another it stretches over land and sea to weave itself into the affairs of distant peoples and places. And often it combines both activities.

Sometimes imperialism has been a dominant force, as the history of ancient Rome attests. Sometimes it has faded, in one form at least, to slight significance; for more than a generation after the Vienna settlement of 1815, its extra-European influence was negligible. Later it entered a new phase, of particular importance for our present study. For almost a half century (c. 1870–1914) the imperial thrust penetrated seas and continents remote from the heartland of Europe. Pacific isles and ports, almost the whole of Africa, and a large part of Asia came under some degree of imperial rule before the movement, merging with others (particularly nationalism and the attempt to establish a new balance of power), issued in World War I. Continental imperialism was also at work, as we shall see when we come to consider the activities of Pan-Germans and Pan-Slavs in Central and Eastern Europe.

THE WORLD'S PLUNDERERS.
"It's English, you know."

A Thomas Nast cartoon (1885) pokes at the European powers for their "grab" of the underdeveloped world.

Motivating Forces

It is difficult to determine precisely what motivations lay behind the so-called new imperialism. Those who practiced it professed different, sometimes contradictory, aims. And nothing approaching a consensus has been reached by latter-day scholars. Here we will settle for a summary examination of the chief claims of both groups.

Some imperialists believed that modern man was under obligation to share the benefits of his advanced culture with the "lesser breeds" of backward regions. In a sense they may be thought of as missionaries of materialism. To bring the benefits of civilization to his colored brothers, the white man, so proponents of this view argued, necessarily had to remake and manage the new societies. In short, the beneficiaries, "half devil and half child," had first to be tamed and then paternalistically governed by their benefactors. Many of them naturally would not understand the need for white control, still less the jus-

tifiable "exploitation" which the white man felt must accompany that control. No one knew how long the period of tutelage would last. For however long, both colored and white would probably be beset by wearisome strains and tribulations. But as Rudyard Kipling, the most celebrated exponent of this view, insisted, for the white man there was no choice; his was the challenge to take up, his the burden to bear.

The new imperialism also had a religious perspective. Progress in effective means of getting places and communicating with one another enabled Christians to envision mass conversion of the "pagan" world. The attempt to establish a Christian imperium is of course as old as Christianity. But the advent of the second phase of the industrial revolution — providing as it did relatively easy access to remote areas, reliable channels of communication, and many physical facilities that ameliorated harsh living conditions — multiplied missions around the world. Besides the Christian message, missionaries took with them the cultural accouterments of their own land. More often than not they were also offered and accepted help and protection from the home government; in effect, the flag tended to follow the Cross.

A third apologia of the new expansion of Europe (and later America) grew out of the findings of Charles Darwin as these came to be applied to social behavior. For many persons, "survival of the fittest" explained and justified man's ancient urge to exploit his fellow man. The industrial revolution had brought to white Western societies techniques and powers unknown to the colored masses of Africa, Asia, and Oceania. Refusal to use them was both unnatural and unreasonable.

Finally, for governments and citizens of the times, the simple desire to gain control over some area before others did was an operating factor in intensifying the imperialist scramble. Pride and prestige are hard to document as causative factors, but certainly among the ruling elites of that period color on the map was a highly sought status symbol.

Critiques of the New Imperialism

The impact and significance of the new imperialism upon both Western and Eastern societies early attracted and continues to attract the attention of many scholars. Again, only the more prominent of the various interpretations can be examined. One school of thought emphasizes the psychological underpinnings of the movement. Proponents of this view argue that the industrial revolution created a society characterized by boredom, loss of identity, and a store of random energies. Formerly men had physically toiled long hours, which drained them of energies that otherwise could have nurtured mental and spiritual needs. Modern industry had freed man from this exhausting grind but at a frightful price — monotonous attendance upon soulless machines. Out of this new thralldom man periodically sought escape in excitement and adventure. The world's governing elite depended on this reservoir of unchanneled energy and the yen for new experiences when the diplomacy of acquisition entered its final fighting stage.

The Socialist Critique

Probably the most influential critique of the new imperialism rested upon an elaborate analysis of economic practices. Worked out originally by John A. Hobson, a British liberal economist, it has since served as the classic anticapitalist exposition of the movement. Lenin called it an "accurate description of the fundamental economic and political traits of imperialism" and based one of his own major works upon it. The following paragraphs sketch its main argument.

Industrial society's newly amassed capital soon overflowed the areas of its origin. This did not mean that home investments vanished. On the contrary, they increased.

Even so, capital resources outran investment opportunities as mass consumption (for reasons noted immediately below) lagged behind production. Therefore, capital came to be increasingly invested in "backward" areas where its owners were also seeking markets. In time, as finance capital came to dominate the resources of industrial capital, financial magnates took over leading roles in imperialist ventures.

Moreover, by 1880 the machine, powered now by the dynamo as well as the steam engine, had begun a fundamental transformation of Western society. For the first time in history man had at his disposal tools, skills, and techniques adequate to provide him with not only the necessities of life but many of its conveniences and luxuries. The affluent society seemed in the making.

But society at large did not become affluent, although living standards rose markedly, especially in England, France, Germany, the United States, and Japan. Two circumstances accounted for this anomaly. One was the control of capital by a relatively small entrepreneurial class. Whether called trusts, as in America, or cartels, as in Europe, giant corporations exercised almost exclusive power to set prices, wages, hours of work, and the methods and amounts of production. For the most part they used this power primarily for their own aggrandizement.

A second circumstance militating against a general distribution of wealth was the almost universal adoption of high tariff policies. In each of the major industrial states during this period, entrepreneurs dominated the government. To protect price levels that would guarantee substantial profits they sought heavy duties on incoming goods, thus keeping foreign competition out of the domestic market.* In the main they were successful. As a consequence

---

* This was not true in England. Far in advance of other nations in industrial efficiency and know-how, she felt she could outproduce and undersell her competitors without tariff aids.

consumers, mostly made up of the working class, paid prices set by corporations for purchased goods or went without.

For a while the masses seemed to be content. They sensed that the machine was, at least potentially, the herald and instrument of abundance. Wages, compared to those of former days, were high. Men believed that prices would fall as the machine produced ever greater quantities of goods. Moreover, labor unions were slowly gaining strength, pointing to a promise of yet higher income levels. Altogether, their tomorrows seemed bright.

Actually, the gap between wages and prices was not closed. Corporate wealth continued to dominate governmental policies. Magnates and managers crushed the budding power of organized labor. Such practices, of course, secured the profits of big business; but they also prevented buying power from reaching levels commensurate with production.

So a search for new markets began, particularly in what were called the backward areas of the world. If the door at home seemed closed, perhaps an open one could be found abroad. Other needs produced by the industrial revolution strengthened the trend. Certain raw resources needed to keep the machines going were found only in foreign lands. Tin and tungsten, for example, are basic requisites in any mechanized society. But they were not available in a single one of the Western industrialized states. Obviously the rugged individualist of Europe and America needed to stake out claims abroad.

The Capitalist Critique

More recently a counterargument has gained wide acceptance among historians and economists. One of its basic postulates is that capitalism, far from prompting imperialist adventures, is fundamentally opposed to them. Depending as it does upon conditions which encourage economic freedom at home and free trade abroad, cap-italism naturally opposes war and aggressive expansion. The natural habitat of the businessman is the counting house, not the battlefield. Indeed, not only is he not a war monger, he is actively and genuinely interested in creating a warless world.*

With these and other arguments, opponents of the surplus profits theory of imperialism sought to disassociate it quite completely from capitalism. They did not, however, minimize the impact of the movement upon world events. According to Schumpeter a great portion of the whole human drama regrettably has been shaped by it. The ruling elites of all peoples are tempted to prostitute their power and eventually to exercise it "disfunctionally." He looked upon nineteenth-century imperialism as a cultural inheritance from ancient warrior societies. Then, as so often before, its primary aim was conquest for the sake of conquest, devoid of rational object and spurred by a "will for . . . forcible expansion, without definite, utilitarian limits. . . ."

Almost all treatments of the causes and course of the new imperialism reject the claim that colonies made money for the home country. With rare exceptions, colonial possessions proved to be economic liabilities. Abundant statistical evidence makes clear that every pre-World War I imperialist power spent far more in military and administrative upkeep than it received as profit from either trade or capital investment.

"Reluctant Imperialism"

Indeed, a recent interpretation of the promptings of the new imperialism in Africa holds that it had little or nothing to do with the desire to bring either peoples or markets there under imperial control.

* Joseph Schumpeter, chief exponent of this view, has expressed this opinion in the plainest of terms: ". . . modern pacifism . . . is unquestionably a phenomenon of the capitalist world; [and] wherever capitalism has penetrated, peace parties of such strength arose that virtually every war meant a political struggle on the domestic scene."

Rather, according to this thesis, the aristocratic makers of Victorian policy believed that Britain's existence as a world power depended upon her control of India, and upon her general strength in the East. This control, in turn, hinged upon her dominance of the sea lanes leading to and from the Suez Canal and partly upon control of the waters around the Cape Colony. For a time this dominance was assured through informal "influence" over the weaker and backward peoples of those areas (except in the Cape, of course, where Britons already directly ruled). But when local African governments, "sapped by the strains of previous Western influences," began to collapse and spawn political voids, Britain was forced to occupy and eventually govern territories she would otherwise have had little interest in. The key event that sparked the change in British policy, as proponents of this thesis see it, was the rapid disintegration of normal governmental processes in Egypt in 1882. As the British moved in — reluctantly, almost perforce — many powers grew envious and apprehensive. Thus began the race of the powers to divide up the Continent, a race that continued until there was practically nothing left to divide.

To summarize, a number of varying and sometimes contradictory theses have been offered by imperialists and by students of the movement to explain the rather sudden burst of expansionist activity that occurred during the late nineteenth and early twentieth centuries: the human yen to aggrandize self, family, clan, nation; the white man's urge to share with the non-white world (at a price) his "advanced" culture; the desire to make Christianity truly catholic; the belief in the natural right of the strong to subjugate the weak; the need of bourgeois capitalists to export their surplus wealth; the impulse to escape from boredom created by the industrialization of society; "objectless" conquest rooted in atavistic drives; and the necessity to "stabilize" areas close to vital sea lanes.

The State System and the Alliance Systems

Both nationalism and imperialism functioned within the sovereign state system. Given philosophic justification by the writings of Hugo Grotius and a kind of official sanction by the treaty of Westphalia (1648), state sovereignty came to be accepted as the only right form of municipal organization. Each state came to believe itself beyond accountability to any authority other than its own. Of course, mutually agreed upon arrangements and compromises were useful, even necessary, for normal intercourse among peoples. But each state jealously guarded its absolute sovereignty as a possession beyond price. By the end of the nineteenth century this outlook and practice had led to what some observers recognized as international anarchy, with war as the ultimate instrument of national policy. Some social scientists and moral philosophers sensed the time had come to set up a supranational organization to preserve international comity and peace; but they were few and without political power or influence. Thus, although by the beginning of our century an amorphous world community was emerging, there existed no "parliament of man" to legislate for it, no executive body to administer, or court system to adjudicate, world law.

The doctrine of state sovereignty logically implies unending conflict among discrete political divisions, a condition hardly compatible with the basic requisites of civilization. Therefore, the major states had long ago worked out, although fumblingly and inadequately, a pattern of behavior that honored this principle while at the same time mitigating the more intolerable effects of its practice. This compromise often took the form of a balancing of power, characterized either by the formation of alliance complexes or by an extraordinarily strong power ready to act simultaneously as umpire and potential ally of one of the groups. Since Waterloo, England had played this latter role. Throughout this period she had consistently labored to prevent any nation or combination of nations from gaining a predominant position in Europe. Actually, no nation had seemed particularly possessed of such an ambition.

But in the 1870s a combination of events created a new situation. The introduction of the dynamo as an important source of machine power coincided with the unification of Germany. Possessing a large free trade area, access to abundant supplies of coal and iron, and an alert, educated business elite, the new nation soon became a strong contender not only for world markets but, as one of the kaiser's ministers expressed it, a place in the sun. Germany's victory over France (1871) gave her increased military and political prestige at the same time it reduced France, at least temporarily, to the status of a second-class power; it also clearly marked the end of Habsburg domination in Central Europe. For England these changes ultimately came to add up to an ominous challenge. In short, Europe's balance of power had rather suddenly and quite significantly shifted. Hereafter the course of world politics and international diplomacy had necessarily to change as nations sought to adjust themselves as advantageously as possible to the new conditions.

Secret Diplomacy, Militarism, and Emergence of New Personalities

Secret diplomacy was an instrument commonly used by all the nations to reestablish a workable balance of power. Although this kind of diplomacy was no innovation, it deserves inclusion in a survey of the forces that shaped events preceding and leading to World War I. It served as a vehicle for a remarkable, and in its ramifications almost unexampled, exercise in international deceit. It kept hidden plans

and strategies that citizens might otherwise have refused to countenance. And it constituted a *modus operandi* without which the grand alignments of the period almost certainly would have been impossible.

By definition power politics ultimately depends upon military sanctions. If war is the ultimate extension of diplomacy—that is, the final arbiter of international "justice"—then a nation's war machine must always be ready, continually undergoing refinement of its striking power. During the period from 1870 to 1914, Europe's armies and navies exceeded in size and power anything the world had yet seen. For the most part they were based upon universal conscription and managed by professional militarists whose views, especially in times of crisis, came increasingly to influence the decisions of their civilian superiors. In other words, militarism constituted one of the primary forces that shaped events throughout the whole of this period.

Whether decisively or only casually, certain personalities also influenced Europe's larger affairs and concerns, as they have influenced group behavior at all times everywhere. Who would care to argue, for example, that the course of American history would have been substantially unaffected had Mr. Lincoln been assassinated a month after his first rather than his second inauguration? Or if the bullet which killed Mayor Cermak had instead killed Mr. Roosevelt? If it is foolish to believe that the drama of human existence is wholly determined by a few devils or saints, it is naïve to ignore the influence of strong personalities upon the evolution of that drama. Certainly they played a large role in shaping events soon to be considered.

The Aims of the Powers: England and Germany

Finally we need to note the overall aims of the great and lesser powers which framed the developing web of power politics and secret diplomacy. England wanted not only to keep the great empire she already possessed but also to add to it, especially when new markets, raw resources, investment opportunities, or strategic waterways were the prizes. Since her imperial home base was so small and her need for imported goods so great, she claimed a kind of special right to patrol and police the seas. As a "have" nation she preferred peace to war. But she was prepared to oppose by force any attempt to frustrate what she thought of as justifiable national and imperial aims. Although she considered no nation her natural enemy, she was nevertheless disturbed by the German thrust into world markets, by Germany's attempt to supervise continental affairs, and after 1900 Germany's challenge to her dominance on the seas.

During Bismarck's long rule as Chancellor (1871–1890), Germany's basic aim was to keep the peace. Unification had been achieved and France, according to German thought, had been taught a lesson. Also, although industry was expanding, its rate of growth was slow throughout Bismarck's tenure, a circumstance that naturally made him cautious. Moreover, he needed time and peaceful conditions to consolidate the empire he had created. So far as Bismarck was concerned, war could bring Germany only suffering. But he was conscious of France's yearning for revenge. He was aware, too, of imperialist and nationalist fermentations in the Balkans. So he sought to beguile France (but still keep her friendless), to forestall an Austro-Russian clash in the Balkans, and to woo England as cokeeper of the peace. After Bismarck was dropped, a new course, which we will examine later, was laid out by the Kaiser and his advisers.

France, Russia, Austria

France wanted to erase the humiliation of 1871 from the record and to regain her old status as an undisputed first-class power. She believed neither was possible so long as Alsace-Lorraine remained German. She knew she could not achieve her goals without strong help from friends. She also wanted to expand her republican empire; whatever the economic returns might be, the psychological gains would be gratifying.

Russia's basic aims may also be stated simply. She sought hegemony over the Straits, including Constantinople (Istanbul) and its environs. Not only would this port give Russia entry to important trade lanes, it would also allow her easier control of the strategic waterway connecting the Black and Mediterranean seas, control long held by the Ottoman Turk and used by him to bottle up at will the Russian Black Sea fleet. Russia also wanted to supervise affairs in the Balkans both because she considered this essential to sound and permanent control of the Straits and because she believed herself to be the natural leader of the Slavic peoples, who constituted the preponderant part of the Balkan populations. Finally, she wanted to expand in the East, particularly in northern China. For many years she was pulled by these polar attractions, unable to go all out for both and unwilling to fix upon just one for sustained concentration.

Across the centuries Austria had built up an empire of assorted peoples. She wanted to keep it from falling apart. With the strong tides of nationalism flowing around her she was not sure she could, particularly since the emperor and his bureaucratic courtiers seemed weary of imperial burdens. Nonetheless, if the danger was not too great she occasionally assumed a posture of offence to forestall action that threatened the *status quo*. At the turn of the century aggressive new leaders were to carry the role beyond posture, into actions that precipitated World War I.

Italy and the Balkans

Italy, poorest and weakest of the great powers, wanted credits, colonies, and any friends who could help her to get them.

Plagued by poverty, mass illiteracy, and endemic political corruption, she nevertheless nurtured great expectations. Haunted by memories of ancient grandeur and prompted by the urge to keep up with the growing greatness of other powers, throughout this period Italy spent much of her energy in expansionist schemes and in intricate diplomatic maneuvers designed to win friends and fortune.

The Balkan peoples wanted independence and the unification of their ethnic families into true political bodies. For example, Serbia insisted upon the "return" of Bosnia and Herzegovina, peopled mostly by Serbs but long ruled by alien empires. In a number of border areas, nationals were so mixed with other nationals that accurate boundaries were almost impossible to define, even apart from the constant meddling of imperial overlords. But such conditions had little or no effect upon patriotic agitators for national justice. Most Balkan leaders seemed to believe that the sorting-out problem was either inconsequential or negotiable after imperial shackles had been broken. More

unfortunately, they also nursed aggrandizing ambitions of their own; what was altogether wrong for Turks or Austrians often became quite legitimate in their own scheming.

The Web of Events: Imperialism

The Imperialist Thrust in Africa

Such were the general movements, conditions, postures, and aspirations that characterized Europe's political life from 1870 to 1914. Out of them evolved the concrete events we must now consider.

Scarcely more than a century ago almost all of Africa and most of Asia lay beyond the white man's control and some parts of these continents were even unknown to him. Before 1875 European powers possessed only these portions of Africa: Algeria (France), Cape Colony and Natal (Britain), the coastal regions of Angola and Mozambique (Portugal), and scattered trading areas along the western bend of the continent; in all, less than one tenth of the land. A generation later less than one tenth remained under native control. (See maps, pp. 682 and 708.)

The Congo and Egypt

Interest in Africa was quickened by the combined efforts of missionaries and explorers. In the 1850s and 1860s David Livingstone, a Scottish medical missionary, published two books that gave many Europeans their first understanding of the vast dimensions and resources of this continent. When, around 1870, the outside world lost contact with him as he searched for the headwaters of the Nile, public excitement reached such a pitch that an enterprising newspaper publisher subsidized a search party, headed by the journalist-explorer Henry Stanley. The dramatic meeting of the searcher and the sought stirred millions. Other explorers probed the continent and reported their findings to a reading and lecture-attending public, who were eager to enjoy vicarious encounters with cannibals,

Map by J. Donovan

jungle beasts, and natural wonders such as the Zambezi (Victoria) Falls and the Sahara's rolling oceans of desert. Many accounts described the potential markets and riches of the "new" world.

But it was Belgian royalty rather than British business which made the first significant thrust into Africa. Holding that to "open to civilization the only part of our globe where it has not yet penetrated — is a crusade . . . worthy of this century of progress," King Leopold II organized the International Association of the Congo and sent Stanley back to Africa (1879) to take up the white man's burden. Within a few years the royal crusade had succeeded in bringing under Leopold's personal control a territory about eight times larger than Belgium. Later the "Free State" was taken over by the Belgian government; but not before Leopold had accumulated a personal fortune of about $20 million.

Meanwhile other nations felt apprehension over Leopold's expansive designs. At their insistence (and encouraged by Bismarck) an international conference was held in Berlin (1885). Behind a façade of humanitarian concern over the exploitation of primitive peoples, the conference worked out guidelines intended to regularize the impending partition of Africa.

Britain's ventures in Africa spanned the years from 1882 to 1902. Measured in

According to Stanley's own account, this drawing of the famous Stanley-Livingstone meeting "is as correct as if the scene had been photographed." Livingstone appears as one of the few unarmed members of the group.

Stanley.

Livingstone.

square miles, her possessions grew to cover an area thirty-five times greater than the homeland. The first push was in Egypt whose ruler, when the American Civil War had cut off the South from its world markets and thus sharply increased the demand for Egyptian cotton, had developed an appetite for luxuriant living along with an unpayable bonded debt. Naturally, British and French creditors, backed by their governments, demanded measures that would allow them to put the Khedive's financial house in order. Another lure for the British was the newly completed Suez Canal, large blocks of whose stock the British government soon acquired.

When it became clear in 1882 that Egypt could not meet her obligations, British troops landed in Alexandria and took over the country (and later the Sudan). Egyptian dismay was shared by a number of European governments, though for different reasons. The coup menaced Russian plans to dominate the Straits. And it posed an added problem for Germany whose chancellor favored a vague scheme to divide the Balkans between Austria-Hungary and Russia, a scheme obviously unworkable if British power (at that time hostile to Russian expansion to the southwest) operated from a base so nearby. Put most simply, the eastern Mediterranean was not considered large enough to accommodate two great powers.

Meanwhile explorer-traders were active in the Kenya and Uganda regions, about 1500 miles to the south. In 1887 the British East African Association persuaded the sultan of Zanzibar to give it a leasehold over 225,000 square miles of Kenya territory south of Ethiopia.* Several years later the association wrung from the king of Uganda a treaty whose terms invested the company with control over that area which lay adjacent to Kenya and which comprised about 95,000 square miles. In

the mid-1890s, the Queen's government bought out the association and assumed full responsibility for affairs in both regions.

From Cairo to the Cape

By this time the imperialist surge had become strong. Spurred by the vision of its dominion extending from Cairo to the Cape of Good Hope, the British government was concerned when it learned that France was formulating plans to connect its holdings on the west coast with its Somaliland colony in the east, that is, to conquer and occupy the vast Sudan region south of Egypt. When public warning that a French move into the Sudan would be considered an "unfriendly act" failed to stop her rival, England sent an army under General Kitchener up the Nile where, at Fasoda (1898), it encountered a French contingent and forced it to withdraw. British control was thus extended over another million square miles of African territory.

In South Africa the imperialist thrust cut an equally wide swath. England, as we have seen, had taken over Cape Colony from the Dutch in early years of the nineteenth century. For almost seventy years the new rulers seemed to feel no urge to expand, although both the climate and the topography of the country to the north were inviting. It is true, many Dutch settlers—in their *patois,* Boers—had trekked north to escape British rule. Subduing native Bushmen and Hottentots, they had set up two independent republics: the Orange Free State and the Republic of South Africa (Transvaal). For forty or fifty years considerable strife marked relations between Cape Colony and the Dutch republics, but until the advent of the new imperialism a fairly steady, if uneasy, peace prevailed.

The migration in 1870 of a young Englishman—John Cecil Rhodes—to Cape Colony very much affected the shape of things to come. As he read it, his future would be marked by the amassing of a large fortune and the construction of an empire. His arrival coincided with the discovery of

* For these and subsequent references to African regions and territories, see map, p. 407.

the Kimberley diamond beds. Within fifteen years Rhodes had created a monopoly that assured abundant realization of his first ambition. The discovery of gold in 1886 in the Orange Free State gave further scope to his entrepreneurial genius. His methods were contemporary with those of the American monopolists — masterfully astute calculation, ruthless elimination of competition, and unscrupulous manipulation of political controls. His interest in empire building grew out of a sincere if naive belief that the Anglo-Saxon civilization was God's chosen instrument for the perfection of man. Out of his own funds and energy he outfitted expeditions, beguiled missionaries, and sponsored propagandistic publications. Eventually he spurred his government to such heroic action that, between them, the whole of South Africa came under British control.

The Boer War and Its Aftermath

When the Boers found their rivals pushing too hard they demanded removal of British troops from frontier regions. The war that followed rejection of the demand lasted over two years and cost both sides heavy casualties and great material losses. In the end the Boer Republic (Transvaal was joined by the Orange Free State when the fighting began) accepted British dominion but was allowed to retain cultural autonomy. Besides more "color on the map" Britain gained important economic advantages. But the price was higher than she then realized. During the long struggle most of the powers clearly showed their sympathy for the Boers and disgust at what they felt was British rapacity and unjustifiable brutality. What had once been a self-imposed "splendid isolation" took on ominous overtones. Moreover, the war gave tremendous impetus to Anglo-German naval rivalry. During the war several German merchant ships had been captured as prizes. They were later released but not before German wrath had given Germany's

A Punch *cartoon of 1892 shows Cecil Rhodes striding the continent from Cape Town to Cairo.*

big-navy advocates, led by Admiral von Tirpitz, an opportunity to launch their program of building a fleet so large that "war with the mightiest naval power would involve risks threatening that power's supremacy." For the next two decades the naval race, thus begun, played an important, sometimes decisive, part in weaving the web of events that enmeshed most of the major powers in war in 1914.

Further British Expansion

On a more modest scale British expansionists were active in west Africa, particularly in the Niger region. The Niger river is one of the largest in the world. It rises in Sierra Leone, curves northeastward for a thousand miles and then drops to the sea about another thousand miles from its source. For explorers, missionaries, traders, and empire builders, it served to lay before them for conquest a vast portion of the continent. It would have been strange indeed had the imperialist thrust neglected it.

Shortly after Stanley set out to trace an empire in the Congo, an enterprising British trader with good financial connections began to talk business with African chieftains along the Niger's lower course. Using trinkets and spirits as lure, he persuaded many tribal rulers to sign treaties with terms that allowed a wide range of interpretations. Soon a half-million-dollar corporation, the United African Company, began to show profits marketing cocoa kernels and oil. Its chief worry was the newly formed French Company of Equatorial Africa, whose agents had also collected a number of "treaties" from native rulers. In the rivalry that followed, the United African Company's larger capital resources enabled it to undersell the French company so effectively that the latter was finally forced to sell out. A later German effort fared no better. In 1886 the British company received from the crown a charter authorizing it not only to trade in the region but also to administer it politically. Renamed the Royal Niger Company, it served as merchant chief and ruler until 1900, when the government took over the colony as a protectorate. From the late 1880s through the 1890s, Britain rounded out its expansion in Africa when British Somaliland, Sierra Leone, and the Gold Coast, much smaller territories, were tucked into the Empire.

It would be tediously repetitive to detail the expansionist activities of the other powers. The same pattern characterized them—explorers were followed by missionaries and traders, native rulers were corrupted or coerced, treaties were signed, troops stationed, and whites assumed political control of the area. It will be enough for us simply to note who took what.

Within the period from 1870 to 1914 France acquired French West Africa, French Equatorial Africa, Senegal, French Somaliland, and Madagascar; Germany took German East Africa, German Southwest Africa, Kamerun, and Togoland;

Portugal held Mozambique and Angola; and Italy gained Eritrea, Italian Somaliland, and Libya. By the eve of World War I the entire continent, except for Liberia and Ethiopia,* had been partitioned among a half-dozen or so European powers.

The Imperialist Thrust: Asia

Most of these powers, and several others which had not participated in the great safari, found in Asia a further field for adventure and expansion. Long before the advent of the "new imperialism," English and French interest in the riches of India had led to strong rivalry and a series of clashes, which ultimately forced the French to withdraw (1761). Thereafter for about a hundred years most of India was ruled by the East India Company, a private trading corporation. During this period many Indian states were brought directly under the company's rule; others were left to native princes who kept their thrones by agreeing to take orders from it. The commercial nexus that bound together Britain and India was highly profitable for the British. The factories of Manchester, Birmingham, and other industrial areas hungrily absorbed the flow of raw cotton, wool, flax, leather, and other unprocessed resources that were channeled to the "home" country. The British also systematically exploited other valuable resources of the great subcontinent—timber, tea, silk, tobacco, precious metals, and gems. For the white man, the burden did not seem intolerable.

The Sepoy Rebellion and Aftermath

By about the middle of the nineteenth century India's masses had become re-

* In 1896 Italy invaded Ethiopia and suffered, in the battle of Aduwa, a crushing defeat. This surprising event, the first victory of a "backward" people over the colonial powers, probably saved Ethiopia from attacks from other powers during the "partition period." But it also served, as we shall later see, to invite a new and successful invasion in the next century.

belliously restive. Village communal lands had been divided up among select land-holders who were then held responsible for the collection of taxes. The feudal practice of escheat—"lapse," as it was popularly dubbed—was revived to allow the East India Company to claim provinces whose rulers had died without natural heir.

For millions of Indians the limit of toler-ance was reached when Indian troops were issued new rifles that used cartridges with greased ends that had to be bitten off before they could be fired. The sepoys (as the native soldiers were called) be-lieved the grease came from cows and pigs. Since Hindus held the cow sacred and Moslems considered the pig ceremo-nially unclean, religious sensibilities were touched off. Insurrections broke out in several provinces and quickly spread over much of north and north-central India (1857). Although called a mutiny by British officials, the widespread uprising was actually a rebellion, the crushing of which caused the British to resort to atrocities that are hard to match in the record of man's inhumanity to man.

After the "mutiny," colonial adminis-trative machinery was overhauled. The East India Government surrendered all governing powers to the crown. Local princes were treated so deferentially that they soon became an integral part of the overall ruling elite. Many roads and rail-roads were built. But the condition of the masses and middle classes remained oppressive.

Indian intellectuals, business classes, and the more literate portions of the masses continued to agitate for reform, some even for independence. In 1885 the Indian National Congress was reformed to serve as the voice of all dissident Indians, whether Hindus or Moslems. Its original demands were modest enough: partici-pation in making policy at the local level, the right to discuss, if not to decide, legis-lative measures that would affect all of

British justice: a photograph showing the exe-cution of Indian "mutineers" in the Sepoy Re-bellion of 1857.

India; the appointment of some Indians to the highest ranks of the civil service administration. Wherever the British could do it without weakening real control, they granted Congress' requests; but by the latter part of the nineteenth century virtu-ally all classes, even the most lowly, fully understood the implications of the strict color line Britain had drawn. Increasingly their leaders made racial equality the touch-stone of reform agitation. Unfortunately for the Indians their struggle for home rule was made extraordinarily difficult by the existence of a large Moslem minority. As Moslem leaders came to envision an India eventually freed from white control, they saw Hindu domination of the whole land, a spectre little if any more inviting to them. Indeed many Moslems began to collaborate with the British to slow down the Indian nationalist drive. In 1906 their leaders formed the Muslim League as a counter-weight to the Congress. Whether English imperialists fostered this fatal split is both debatable and irrelevant, but it is certain that they exploited it. After World War I, in which Indian troops made an impressive record, Britain held out vague promises of self-government, promises that, as we will see later, led to full independence in the 1940s. But India entered the twentieth century still politically dependent, socially segregated, economically exploited, and

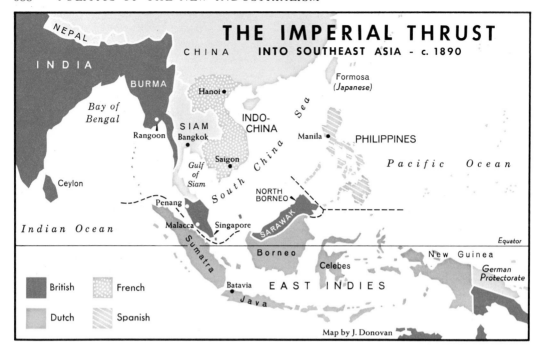

rent by religious strife. Certainly the imperialist thrust had not created all these unhappy conditions, but there is no doubt it consistently and seriously aggravated them.

In the late 1800s Britain brought other Asian lands and peoples under her control. By 1885 all of Burma, an ancient state lying east of India, was brought under the supervision of "white" India. To the south of Burma, in the bulge of the great peninsula into which Siam narrows, a melange of petty sultanates invited the attention of the British East India Company. The great archipelago stretching from Sumatra to New Guinea had already been conceded to its rival, the Dutch East India Company. But such strategic ports as Singapore, Malacca, and Penang (see map, p. 688) were potentially too valuable to pass over. Early in the nineteenth century they had become the Straits Settlements. Thereafter British merchants and marines worked their way north and east until, by the turn of the twentieth century, the whole bulge was under British control. Local sultans were allowed to keep their thrones and bureau-

cratic paraphernalia, but they were closely supervised by the British High Commissioner of the Federated Malay States. Ceylon, just off the tip of India, was occupied by the British in 1833. Until the invention of the automobile its chief resources were tea, coconuts, and pearls; since about 1900 the cultivation of rubber trees has made this island one of the world's foremost producers of latex.

Dutch Imperialism

Another great empire in southeast Asia was managed by the Netherlands. Like other corporations of its kind, the Dutch East India Company was interested in making profits from whatever lands and peoples lay open for exploitation. The lands and peoples it conquered, lost, and reconquered (in the early 1600s through early 1800s) probably constituted the most profitable colonial empire any European state has created in modern times. Geographically the colonies—Sumatra, Java, Borneo, Celebes, New Guinea, the Moluccas—encompass an area greater than all of Western Europe; and their combined population exceeded that of any Western European power except Germany.

Originally they were coveted for their spices, later for their sugar, rubber, tin, tobacco, coffee, tea, and petroleum. From about 1830 to 1870 their Dutch masters used what was called the "culture system." Natives were forced to set aside and to work, for the exclusive profit of their white rulers, 20 per cent of all land cultivated. The methods to keep native laborers producing were barbarous. Village chiefs, for example, were liable to hanging if quotas set for building roads were not met; and a number of chiefs were hanged. The system was abandoned when journalists published exposés that Dutchmen on the home front found hard to reconcile with even the loosest interpretation of the white man's burden. The new "free labor" system was somewhat, but not much, better. A poll tax was laid on all workers. To save enough from meager earnings to pay it demanded a fatiguing tempo of work. In addition, Dutch planters often tempted natives with long-term loans, which, since they were practically unpayable, bound them in virtual serfdom. Educational facilities were gradually extended throughout the islands. But the offering was especially designed to keep the natives content with their lot. When unrest developed nonetheless, repressive measures were used that made the line between savage and civilized hard to discern. In the 1940s much of this fabulously rich empire was wrested from the Dutch by Japan. Her defeat by the Allies in 1946 returned the archipelago to the Netherlands but only briefly. For by then a new mood was abroad among the so-called backward peoples of the world, a mood that ultimately led to the blunting and breaking of the imperialist thrust.

China's "Time of Troubles"

As the oldest, largest, and at that time the most civilized nation in Asia, China might have been expected to withstand Western expansion. In one sense she did. At no time throughout the period of rampaging imperialism was she wholly subdued or partitioned. But in another sense she fared little better than India or the East Indies. For a century after 1840, a number of foreign states pared down her size and sovereignty so steadily that it seemed, just before World War I, that she must certainly suffer the fate of Africa.

For many centuries China had been a world unto herself as a font of East Asian civilization and later as the "Middle Kingdom," around which other peoples moved and had their cultural origins. Since ancient times she had maintained contacts with the West, but under Manchu rule (established in the mid-1600s) they diminished in number and kind. By about 1800 the Middle Kingdom had become a hermit nation, living in a past almost wholly, and deliberately, cut off from the forces of life flowing around it. Not for centuries, if ever, had China's cultural and political life been so static, so moribund, nor her view of the outside world so illusory and distorted.

Since the West was simultaneously experiencing its heady thrust of power, a new and fateful meeting of East and West was hardly surprising. Its first manifestation was the so-called Opium War, 1839 to 1842. For a long time opium, much of it imported from India, had been supplied to an increasing number of Chinese by British and other foreign traders operating out of Canton. In 1839 the Peking government published a decree prohibiting its sale and use. British merchants ignored the decree. When Chinese officials disciplined them they called upon their government for succor. In the war that followed China experienced its first encounter with a military machine served by industrial technology. It was a humiliating experience. In the treaty that ended the uneven struggle, China was forced to legalize the opium traffic, open five ports to foreign trade, pay an indemnity, cede Hong Kong to Britain, reduce tariff duties on British goods to 5 per cent *ad valorem,* and to allow British

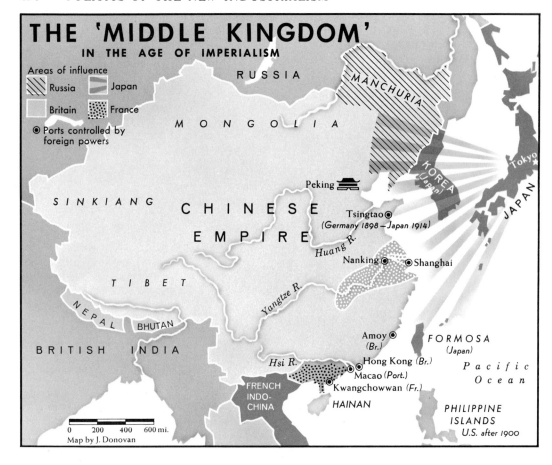

THE 'MIDDLE KINGDOM'
IN THE AGE OF IMPERIALISM

Areas of influence

Russia   Japan

Britain   France

● Ports controlled by foreign powers

RUSSIA

MANCHURIA

MONGOLIA

SINKIANG

CHINESE EMPIRE

Peking

Tsingtao●
(Germany 1898 – Japan 1914)

KOREA (Japan)

Tokyo ★

JAPAN

Huang R.

Nanking ● ● Shanghai

TIBET

Yangtze R.

NEPAL   BHUTAN

BRITISH   INDIA

Hsi R.

Amoy ● (Br.)

FORMOSA (Japan)

Hong Kong (Br.)
Macao (Port.)
Kwangchowwan (Fr.)

Pacific Ocean

FRENCH INDO-CHINA

HAINAN

PHILIPPINE ISLANDS
U.S. after 1900

0   200   400   600 mi.

Map by J. Donovan

citizens in the port cities to live under their own rather than Chinese law. Other nations soon forced China to extend the same trade, tariff, and extraterritoriality * provisions to them. A second war in 1857, in which France joined England to enforce observance of concessionary rights, ended in another victory for the Western powers; and more concessions.

Inner Turmoil; Spheres of Influence

Compounding China's troubles were internal stresses. The great kingdom had once exercised authority of one kind or another over an empire twice as large as itself— Mongolia, Sinkiang (Chinese Turkestan),

* This cumbersome term denominates the practice of allowing foreigners to live under the law and in accordance with the customs of their own country.

Tibet, Tongking, Korea, Taiwan (Formosa), and — with the coming of the Manchus, of course — Manchuria. By the mid-nineteenth century Outer Mongolia had become more or less autonomous, Sinkiang ruled by warlords, Tibet virtually independent, and the whole of Tonking absorbed by Annam. Moreover, most Chinese, especially those south of the Yangtze River, had never really reconciled themselves to Manchu rule. In the 1850s a series of uprisings occurred. The most serious and sustained was the T'ai Ping Rebellion, which at one point seemed to promise release from Manchu domination. But the government's importation of outside military leadership and the tendency of patriot generals to turn into self-seeking warlords caused the rebellion to fail, although the deep unrest that had motivated it persisted. In the end, inner decay and dissension paved the way for the new imperialist scramble to partition China.

Foreign control of tariff duties encouraged Western traders and industrialists, invariably backed by their governments, to block out spheres of influence where they could manage commerce and industry for their own aggrandizement. To tap China's mineral resources, mining concessions were demanded, and these demands too were backed up by force or the show of force. To connect market with market and markets with ports, the right to build and manage railroads was also insisted upon. By the mid-1890s the frantic struggle for East Asia was on, and within a decade large areas of China were parceled out among competing Western nations.

The Scramble for China

After absorbing Tonking and Annam into Cochin China-Cambodia, France occupied Laos (1893). As a base to protect and serve French Indochina, France "leased" the mainland port of Kwangchowan (1898). Fearful that France intended to push northward, Britain persuaded China to allow only British power to establish itself in the Yangtze Valley. Fearful too of Russian designs in the north, the British government negotiated a ninety-nine-year lease of Weihaiwei, in the Shantung peninsula. Although a late comer in the contest, Germany was determined to get her share. The best she could manage was a leasehold on Kiachow, a port strategically located in Shantung some 200 miles down the coast from the British base. Meanwhile Russia was busy consolidating her Siberian gains and devising ways to move into Manchuria.

Much of this pattern of imperial aggrandizement was determined by the outcome of the Sino-Japanese War, 1894 to 1895. Although nominally independent, Korea had been a Chinese dependency for many years. Japan desired Korea as a valuable possession in itself but also to use as a

springboard for penetration into southern Manchuria and as a strategic defense base. Russia's schemes and China's weakness spurred her to action. A Korean insurrection in 1894 set the stage. Acting under an earlier agreement, both China and Japan sent in troops to restore order. When the insurrection petered out, Japan demanded the removal of Chinese troops and the creation of an independent Korea. Sino-Japanese bickering over the terms of a settlement led to war in 1894. Again China suffered humiliating defeat. In the treaty of Shimonoseki (1895) Korea was recognized as an independent nation. China was forced to pay a large indemnity and to cede Taiwan, the Pescadores, and part of the Liaotung Peninsula to Japan. China also agreed to conclude a new and generous commercial treaty with Japan. Some of the edge was taken from the Japanese victory, however, when Russia, France, and Germany, fearing Japan's appetite would grow embarrassingly large after so much eating, concerted to force her to return the Liaotung cession to China.

China's defeat, the third in as many wars during the century, pitilessly laid bare her helplessness. From then on the expansionist powers pondered not whether China might be partitioned but when and how. Moreover, since by that time the imperialist thrust was cutting deeply around the world, the powers felt a sense of urgency. They also had gained some notion of

In this 1894 Judge cartoon, Japan is shown smashing the Chinese "wall" against the advance of Western civilization.

who wanted what. As we have already noted, Germany made haste to secure a foothold on the Shantung Peninsula before Japan, Russia, Britain, or some combination of them should preempt the whole of it. Britain's move into Weihaiwei was similarly motivated. Both Russia and Japan believed no time should be lost staking out their claims in Manchuria and Korea. Their rivalry led to war in 1904 and to the temporary withdrawal of Russian expansionism in the Far East when, for the first time in the modern era, an Asian state defeated a European power (1905). The treaty settlement opened the way for subsequent Japanese expansion in both Korea and southern Manchuria. Japan's surprising victory was due in part to many grave socio-political troubles with which Russia was struggling at the time, and the corruption and inefficiency that had long plagued her military establishment. But it was also partly due to the extraordinary, rapid, and multiform metamorphosis Japan had undergone after 1868.

The New Japan

Like China, Japan had for centuries nurtured a conservative, almost static, inner and institutional life. Bound by feudal patterns and practices and walled off from the white world to the West, she had not experienced the revolutionary impact of the Enlightenment, the advent of science, industrialism, and political liberalism, which had so profoundly remade that world. Theoretically her divine emperor ruled a united kingdom. Actually he was a figurehead. For centuries the kingdom was almost as much divided by provincial loyalties and institutions as it was bound together by common national sentiments and imperial bureaucratic machinery. At the national level the real ruler was the shogun, a hereditary official somewhat comparable to the early French Merovingian mayor of the Palace. At the provincial level considerable political power was held by the heads of great families.

From the 1600s on, the development of commerce—trade with China, Korea and a few Western outlets—and the flourishing of craft industry created a small but productive middle class that set the stage for the subsequent development of remarkable advances in economic modernization and the establishment of trade connections with Western nations. But Japan's remarkable metamorphosis, signalized by the overthrow of the shogunate and the restoration of imperial power, probably was caused more by political influence than economic developments. Two events were especially portentous. One was the power struggle between two strong feudal forces—on the one hand, barons who supported the shogunate and, on the other, the Satsuma and Chosu barons who sought to capture the shogunate for themselves. The other was the coincidental thrust of the West into the East. In 1853 Commodore Perry anchored an American naval force in Tokyo Bay. The Commodore's purpose was both plain and painful to the Japanese, that is, the opening of the island kingdom to Western trade and Western influence. What the white man had done to China and to other Asian states he now proposed to do to Japan. Pressure was at once put upon the shogun to resist. But the Japanese government was little better prepared to resist the foreigner than were the other Asian governments. Its bowing to the inevitable and the treaties and consuls that followed gave popular support to antishogun forces. Their success in 1868 ushered in the Meiji restoration.* Several years later (in 1877) an attempted reinstatement of the old regime failed. Thereafter imperial forces ruled supreme.

The New China

As we have seen, by 1900 great powers, old and new, had in one way or another moved into spheres of control in China: Britain, Russia, Japan, and Germany in

---

* That is, restoring political control to the imperial house.

the north; France in the south; and Britain in the Yangtze Valley. Few doubted that China could prevent or long postpone her complete partition. Nevertheless, there were restive stirrings in China that gave some hope of a brighter day. Two movements, unrelated to each other, roused enthusiasm. One sought quite simply to solve China's problems by ousting foreigners and all things foreign including, indeed especially, Christianity. It was organized in the northern provinces in the late 1890s. Formally the movement was designated the Society of Harmonious Fists. By Westerners its members were simply called Boxers. In the late spring of 1900 they staged uprisings in Hopei and nearby provinces. For a brief time they were successful. They "captured" Peking and a number of other cities in the north. Many foreigners were killed or captured; many fled before the fury of the Boxers. In Peking foreign officials, missionaries, and their families took refuge in the foreign legation and appealed to their home countries for help. It was promptly sent. Large and well-equipped contingents of foreign troops—German, Russian, Japanese, British, French, and American—landed in the region of the Taku Forts and soon invested the capital. Within a short time they had established themselves in Peking and had "pacified" the northern provinces.

In the settlement that followed, China suffered heavy penalties. Among them was an indemnity of $333 million apportioned among the powers; importation of arms and ammunition was prohibited for as long as the powers thought necessary; official decrees were published forbidding the expression of antiforeign sentiments; foreign powers were given the right to occupy certain cities lying between Peking and the sea. Moreover, the great and rich province of Manchuria was brought closer to alienation. The Boxer fiasco had again advertised China's disintegration and the government's inability to control provincial officials. Japan and Russia watched im-

Some of the Boxers captured during the rebellion of 1900.

perial authority fade. They looked at the chaos in Peking and the booty in Manchuria; and they made plans. The Boxer promise of a brighter tomorrow had not only failed, it led to yet darker days.

The 1912 Revolution

The other movement was broader in scope, more far reaching in consequence. For many years the Manchu regime had given increasingly clear evidence of its inability to cope with the forces of disintegration within and without. Concerned intellectuals and reformers—many of them influenced by study abroad and sensitive to the urgent necessity for drastic social, political, and economic changes based on the Western model—agitated for overthrow of the monarchy and the establishment of a dynamic, democratic, forward-looking regime. In the winter months of 1911 and 1912 revolutionary armies overthrew the Manchus and set up a republic. The most influential leader of the revolt was Dr. Sun Yat-sen, a Cantonese liberal who had been educated in American schools. Dr. Sun's program for rebuilding China was threefold: a government based upon the sovereign will of the people; the unification of all sections and areas into one

Dr. Sun Yat-sen, builder of the "New China," poses with his wife, a member of the famous Soong family.

Chiang Kai-shek, leader of the Chinese revolution after the death of Dr. Sun.

political body; and an equitable redistribution of the national wealth. Sun's "three principles" caught the imagination of millions and buoyed their hopes. Thus charted, the new China meant to shake off foreign shackles, create a new identity, and construct a national economy that served all citizens fairly.

But the demands of China's *risorgimento* were greater than China's capabilities to cope with them. For one thing, hundreds of millions of illiterate peasants could not overnight become sensitive, responsible citizens and voters. The government set up schools and launched a variety of educational campaigns. But chronic ignorance is a tenacious disease. Moreover, sectional strife had become so rooted that when the imperial façade was destroyed, local leaders, the famous warlords, sprang up almost automatically. Civil war became endemic. Also, European and Japanese holdings (of whatever kind) had by then become so secure that real popular sovereignty and national unity were out of the question. Finally, World War I, coming so soon after the revolution, heightened the atmosphere of violence, diverted the attention and energy of Chinese leaders, and sharpened imperialist tensions in China. Dr. Sun's death in 1925 passed leadership of the revolution to Chiang Kai-shek, one of his most trusted disciples. But the trinity of ignorance, sectional strife, and imperialist greed remained to plague the movement. Thirty years after the Sino-Japanese war, which so much influenced the shape of imperialist things to come, China, like most of Asia, was still in bondage.

The Imperialist Thrust: The Americas

During this period most of the nations of the western hemisphere also felt constraints imposed from without. Quite in line with the logic of geography, the main thrust came from the United States. Except for a few Caribbean dependencies, by the late 1820s all Latin peoples had set themselves up as independent states.* To shield them from European interference, the United States issued (in 1823) a pronouncement declaring the whole hemisphere henceforth beyond "future colonization by any European powers." Significantly, the declaration did not include a disavowal of future interference by the United States. No European government welcomed the announcement, of course; and Britain explicitly repudiated both its legality and propriety (although in practice her navy gave the "doctrine" probably its chief sanction).†

The French Fiasco in Mexico

Until the 1860s the new states were left relatively free from imperial harassments. The United States, it is true, carved off a substantial portion of Mexico (1848). But most United States officials and citizens seemed to view this not so much taking land from another people as finally claiming territory that had always been theirs by right of "manifest destiny."

The first new instance of large-scale exploitive imperialism occurred in 1863. Napoleon III, emperor of France, decided the time had come to interpose a Latin block to Anglo-Saxon expansion in the New World (and, some argue, to divert his people's attention from sagging morale at home). Involved in its own profound and protracted domestic strife, the United States could only reply to this violation of the Monroe Doctrine with paper protests. Believing the Union cause was lost, Napoleon landed an army in Mexico and installed a puppet regime. We cannot know

what the course of Latin American history might have been had Grant rather than Lee surrendered at Appomattox. Perhaps Napoleon's gamble would have led to the conquest of Latin America by the then dominant powers. Perhaps Mexican revolutionary forces eventually would have expelled the invaders from the land. Actually, Union victory in 1865 released federal troops for whatever action might be needed in Mexico. Unprepared to resist this kind of protest, Napoleon ordered his army home, and the puppet regime collapsed. Since then no European state has attempted to repeat the experiment.

Extension of U.S. Influence in Latin America

But Latin America was not thereby made secure from foreign interference. The emergence of big business (and the passing of the frontier) prompted American entrepreneurs, by then in control of the national government, to give serious thought to the markets and resources of our southern neighbors. By the opening of the new century, hundreds of millions of American dollars were invested in various enterprises in the so-called "banana republics" of the Caribbean area. Some European nations had made large loans to a number of Latin American governments. When these governments defaulted, as they did with disturbing regularity, foreign creditors turned to their own governments for help. Normally, as we have seen, foreign intervention almost invariably followed, but the United States felt bound by the Monroe Doctrine to intervene. It also felt, despite twinges of conscience, that it had the right to interpose its own control when Latin America's chronic political instability flared into unmanageable chaos. Thus in the latter decades of the nineteenth century and the early years of the twentieth, the United States came to exercise an imperial control in this hemisphere very similar to the kind it condemned in Europe and Asia. In 1895, for example, the United States Secretary of

---

* Their number and specific identity remained in flux for a long time. Periodically this or that independent unit became the province of another state or vice versa. Boundary disputes were (and are) seemingly endless.

† That is, British insistence on keeping the trade lanes to the South American markets open in effect kept Spain from pushing her plans to reconquer her one-time colonies.

State publicly announced that "the United States is practically sovereign on this continent, and its fiat is law upon the subjects to which it confines its interposition."

A far reaching act of "interposition" occurred in 1898 when the United States fought a war with Spain over Cuba. For years Cubans had tried to rid themselves of Spanish domination. Widespread uprisings in 1895 and for several years following attracted American attention. Spanish attempts to subdue the revolutionists were so savage that many Americans demanded United States intervention. Some American statesmen, such as the young Theodore Roosevelt and Henry Cabot Lodge, not only sympathized with the mistreated Cubans but saw in the overall situation a chance for America to expand in the Caribbean area. Other Americans, including many businessmen, although deploring Spanish ruthlessness, did not want to see the United States embark on what they thought of as martial adventures. But by 1898 the prevailing sentiment—shaped by sensational press releases, effective agitation by Roosevelt and his colleagues, the sinking of the battleship *Maine* in Havana harbor, and Spanish blunders—favored war with Spain. The conflict was brief and one-sided. By the Treaty of Paris in 1899, Spain relinquished not only its Caribbean possessions but the Philippine Islands and Guam as well. After a spirited debate, which figured prominently in the election campaign of 1900, the United States somewhat gingerly embarked on its first imperial enterprise. Cuba was granted nominal independence; in actual practice it became a quasi-protectorate. Puerto Rico, Guam, and the Philippines became colonial possessions. Hawaii, long desired by American sugar planters on the islands, was annexed in 1900 after the native ruler was overthrown and an interim "planter" republic set up in 1894.

Thereafter, although not consistently or steadily, the United States extended its control over various peoples and areas to the south. At times its motives were innocent enough, even altruistic. For example, in 1902 the United States saved Venezuela from at least temporary occupation by European powers. At that time Germany, Great Britain, and Italy were on the verge of landing troops to compel Venezuela's dictator to pay his government's overdue debts. At the insistence of the United States the matter was referred to an arbitration committee for settlement. But for the most part rather selfish, strategic, economic, and political interests dictated our actions in Latin America. In 1903 the United States asked Colombia to lease to it the isthmus of Panama for the construction of an interocean canal. When Colombia proved difficult to bargain with, Philippe Bunau-Varilla, a "Panamanian" personally interested in the construction of the canal, led a revolt against the Colombian government. To insure success for the revolution, President Theodore Roosevelt dispatched marines with orders to "interpose" themselves between the Colombian and rebel troops. Almost immediately Panama was given official recognition as an independent nation. Several weeks later it signed a treaty with the United States granting this country the right to build the projected canal.

The next year Santo Domingo was threatened by several European nations seeking to force payment of debts hopelessly in arrears. To forestall its occupation, Roosevelt announced that the United States (alone) would assume the responsibility of supervising the finances of any Latin American country which because of "chronic wrongdoing, or an impotence which results in a general loosening of the ties of civilized society, may . . . ultimately require intervention by some civilized nation." * As it turned out, such intervention led to dominant control over Haiti, Panama, El Salvador, Nicaragua, Honduras, and to a

---

* This is the essence of what has come to be called the Roosevelt Corollary to the Monroe Doctrine.

lesser extent Costa Rica. In the last, as well as in several other Latin American states, the United Fruit Company gained a virtual monopoly over their banana plantations. Other American business concerns acquired special rights, and of course special profits, in such diverse fields as sugar, oil, and banking. In Mexico a cooperative dictator, Porfirio Diaz, doled out railroad, land, oil, and mine concessions to a number of foreign nations, including a billion dollars' worth to Yankee capitalists.

The Meaning of Imperialism: A Summation

In summing up the meanings of these various imperial and colonial activities, we naturally note first the variegated abuse of the Afro-Asian and, to a lesser extent, South American peoples by the white-supremacist West. Economically, the nonindustrialized peoples were subjected to manipulations that kept standards of living low and local economies "subsidiaries to their Western masters. Malaya became a rubber plantation, Rhodesia a copper mine, Ceylon a huge tea plantation, Arabia an oil field." Psychologically, the imperialist thrust cleaved the world into snobbish tutors and sullen pupils. Even when it brought intrinsic good, that good often led to unexpected woe. A significant example is the introduction of Western medical knowledge and skills. Afro-Asians gladly accepted the balm of the healing arts, but by decreasing infant mortality and increasing adult life span, the population soon soared beyond production capacities. As a result, increasing millions suffered the miseries of subsistent, really sub-subsistent, living. Politically, the expansion of European power stimulated rivalries among the European imperialist powers that edged them nearer to crisis and conflict.

On the other hand, benign or potentially benign influences flowed out of the new imperialism. Without it, industrialism would have come even later to Asia and Africa. It also brought with it (although not by conscious design) many of the ideas of the Enlightenment and of the French and American revolutions. Particularly consequential were the concepts of nationalism and democracy and, however amorphously, a sense of movement and progress. Another contribution was the scientific method and attitude toward life. That these influences eventually led, as we shall see in a later chapter, to a sanguine confrontation of sahib and servant does not diminish their significance.

SELECTED READINGS

Hayes, Carlton J. H., *A Generation of Materialism, 1871–1900,* Harper & Brothers, New York, 1941.
One of the best accounts of the transformation of Western man's outlook and values that were shaped by the impact of the "second" industrial revolution. Emphasis is given to the secularization of society, the rise of the masses, and the genesis of totalitarian nationalism.

———, *Essays on Nationalism,* The Macmillan Co., New York, 1926.
A series of essays that deal with nationalism as a religion, its relationship to war, militarism, and intolerance, its basic nature and development. The author is one of the foremost authorities on this hard-to-handle subject. He deserves careful study.

———, *Nationalism: a Religion,* The Macmillan Co., New York, 1960.
A strictly historical approach to the study of what nationalism is and how it got to be what it is. The author takes a pessimistic view of the growing power of nationalist sentiment. He believes that it may be "moderated or watered down" only by the imperatives of the Christian faith.

Hobson, J. A., *Imperialism, a Study,* George Allen & Unwin, London, 1905.
Hobson considered imperialism a disease that society had to cure if it was to survive as a culture worthy of the name civilization. In spite of severe attacks, especially in the last 25 years, it remains one of the most il-

luminating studies the subject has yet received.

Kohn, Hans, *Prophets and Peoples,* The Macmillan Co., New York, 1946.

A study of five brands of nineteenth-century nationalism as it appeared to J. S. Mill, Michelet, Maini, Treitschke, and Dostoevsky in their times.

————, *The Age of Nationalism,* Harper & Brothers, New York, 1962.

In this work the author argues that in the third decade of our century a metamorphosis developed which is transforming the old state-rooted nationalism into a "garment for the globe." Ethnic bonds, he believes, have not and will not disappear, but over them is being superimposed a pan-nationalism that will make the relation of modern nations to a universal community similar to the old relation of family or clan to state-limited nationalism.

Langer, William L., *The Diplomacy of Imperialism, 1890–1902,* Alfred A. Knopf, New York, 1935, 2 vols.

Though written more than thirty years ago, this work is still of high value. All of the international clashes of the 12-year period stated in the title are given close examination—the struggle for the Nile, the "Armenian Question," the West's attempt to partition China, and the Boer War. The style is graceful; the temper is judicious; and the evidence is well used.

Lenin, V. I., *Imperialism,* Vol. V of his *Selected Works,* International Publishers, New York, 1943.

The classic Communist exposition of imperialism as the final stage of the capitalist economy.

Moon, Parker Thomas, *Imperialism and World Politics,* The Macmillan Co., New York, 1927.

Defining imperialism has become a kind of academic sport in recent years. There are now so many (and often contradictory) definitions that a student could hardly expect to immerse himself in them and come up with a unified concept. Moon does not concern himself with present-day abstractions. He treats the late nineteenth-century expansion of Europe and America as a strictly historical phenomenon. If only one book on imperialism is read, this could well be the one.

Shafer, Boyd C., *Nationalism, Myth and Reality,* Harcourt, Brace & Co., New York, 1955.

This is a brief examination of the origin, nature, and meaning of an institution that the author believes is the greatest force in the past 150 years. The concluding section is an eloquent diatribe against the evils inherent in the institution.

Thornton, A. P., *Doctrines of Imperialism,* John Wiley & Sons, New York, 1965.

Imperialism is considered as a force used by nations to gain power, wealth, and a position to exert their civilizing influences upon backward peoples. Although some of the examples used to develop his themes are not as clearly related to the themes as others he could have chosen, the author presents a sound account of the wide ranging forces of nineteenth-century European expansion.

Wilson, E. M., *The Pattern of Imperialism—A Study in the Theories of Power,* Columbia University Press, New York, 1947.

The author does not believe that capitalism necessarily issues in imperialism or that economic imperialism caused either of the great world wars. His examination of what happened in history and what caused these happenings leads him to conclude that imperialism and war are "political phenomena."

25

Power Politics, 1875 to 1914–
The Entangling Web

The Web of Events:
Nationalism, Alliances,
and the New Balance
of Power

In the preceding chapter we noted that other movements and forces besides imperialism helped mold the events of the period: nationalism, the sovereign-state system, militarism, strong personalities. We also noted that certain general conditions significantly bore upon these events: the shift in Europe's balance of power and the consequent development, abetted by secret diplomacy, of two great alliance systems. In this chapter we are concerned with particular European events produced by or made up of these movements and forces as they met and merged with the imperialist thrust. Because the multiple forces and movements are too interrelated for topical treatment, a simple chonological approach is used.

Special attention must be given to the nationalist impulse in the Balkans since, no

matter how paradoxically, Balkan affairs came to form the nexus of events that brought the imperial powers and their imperial schemes into bloody conflict in 1914. Until about 1830 the Balkan peoples were subjects of the sultan of Turkey (as they had been for about five hundred years). With the decline of Ottoman power they increased their agitation for ethnic unity and independence. In 1830 Greece won her independence, and Serbia and parts of Romania were granted autonomy. Bulgaria gained home rule in the 1870s; but like Greece, Serbia, and Romania, she complained that her true ethnic family had not been joined together.

Undoubtedly a kind of imperial aggrandizement motivated each of these victims of imperialism. But basically they sought the right to set up ethnic housekeeping for themselves. And they were determined to continue to do all they could to achieve it, whatever the difficulties, however great the sacrifices either to themselves or to others. By itself, the nationalist impulse that roiled throughout the whole Balkan region was

A CONSULTATION ABOUT THE STATE OF TURKEY.

This famous Punch *cartoon gave vogue to the reference to Turkey as the Sick Man of Europe. France and England are shown mulling over the possibilities that may develop if the Sick Man dies.*

likely to stir up trouble from time to time. If this Balkan nationalist impulse were to meet head on with the imperialism of the great powers (both "autocratic, continental," and "new" extracontinental), it was almost certain to create a thunderhead of turbulence that would sweep Europe into cataclysmic violence.

Balkan Embroglio, 1875 to 1878

In 1875 the oppressed peoples of Bosnia and Herzegovina revolted aginst their Turkish masters. The event in itself, one of dozens like it before, was hardly worth recording. But at this juncture the revolt touched the imperial interests of three great powers — Russia, Austria-Hungary, and Britain — and set off a chain of reactions that ultimately involved most of the nations of the world. It therefore deserves some detailed attention.

For several months in the summer of 1875 the Turks busied themselves with savage reprisals against the rebelling provinces and against whatever other Slavic groups supported them. For obvious reasons Serbia gave encouragement to the rebels. Russia, as their big Slav brother, was also sympathetic. Although Austria-Hungary was certainly not sympathetic to this or to any other kind of uprising, she was anxious for Turkey to call a halt to brutal repressions before they brought further reprisals against the already ailing power.

Of course, neither Russia nor Austria was motivated by altruism. Russia wanted control of the Straits, with Constantinople as her southern window on the sea. That meant kicking the Sick Man out of Europe. She was also strongly motivated by a complex of vague feelings subsumed under the term Pan-Slavism. Basically this movement aimed at uniting all peoples whose languages were Slavic, whose religion was Orthodox, and who claimed allegiance to a common historical heritage. Many of the champions of Pan-Slavism, such as Dostoevsky, sincerely believed that Eastern Europe was threatened with the same debauchery that befell the industrialized West. Others, including more than an occasional diplomat, used the movement simply as a stratagem to promote the interests of their nation or class. But no matter how it was used, Pan-Slavism was a force that shaped events, sometimes decisively.

Austria, in declining health herself, feared not so much Turkey's losing her European holdings as Russia's gaining them. But with the Ottoman Empire seemingly dissolving, and Austria unable to cope single-handedly with Russian designs, she found it expedient to collaborate with her rival.

Thus, when Turkey seemed on the verge of crushing the uprisings (1876), Russia, with Austria's reluctant blessing, sent her troops marching to the gates of Constantinople. At this point Turkey asked for an armistice and in March 1878 signed the treaty of San Stefano. This treaty created a large Bulgaria under covert Russian control. Since this violated earlier secret understandings between Austria and Russia, Austria objected. So did Britain, who saw Russia now in a position to threaten her own "lifeline" to the East. To implement her objection she sent a naval squadron into the Sea of Marmara where it anchored off the roadsteads of Constantinople.

The Congress of Berlin and Its Aftermath

Russia, knowing she could not cope with the combined forces of England and Austria, reluctantly agreed to a conference where the settlement might be reviewed. At Austria's suggestion (initiated by Bismarck), the meeting was held in Berlin in June 1878, and was attended by all the major powers. Chaired by Bismarck—who insisted he was acting only as an "honest broker"—the Congress of Berlin thoroughly revised the Russo-Turkish treaty. Bulgaria was divided and the pared-off portions were returned to the direct or indirect control of Turkey. Bosnia-Herzegovina was occupied by Austria; and Russian gains in Asiatic Turkey were cut down.

The reactions of the powers were what might have been expected. Many Russians were furious. They lamented the loss of both coveted territory and face, for which they chiefly blamed Bismarck who, they insisted, had favored Austria throughout the conference. England was satisfied—Russia's move toward the Straits had been blocked and an extra and unexpected plum, the island of Cyprus, had been gained. France, invited only because Bismarck hoped it would help her feel like a great power again and perhaps forget the rape of Alsace-Lorraine, was pleased by the Iron Chancellor's coy (and confidential) suggestion that Tunis probably needed her attention. Italy, also invited out of courtesy, felt some alarm at Austria's Balkan gains. All of the Balkan states grieved over their losses, and Serbia spoke ominously of a coming day of reckoning.

Before considering some of the events that flowed out of, impinged upon, or became connected with the decisions made at this conference, we may note its overall significance. The occupation of Bosnia-Herzegovina by Austria-Hungary was for that state a victory more seeming than real. Instead of consolidating imperial control in the Balkans, the occupation eventually led to crises which, as they culminated in World War I, led to the complete breaking up of the Austro-Hungarian Empire. The treatment accorded Russia by the Congress of Berlin and the treaty which came out of it contributed to the subsequent formation (1894) of an alliance between that nation and France. The strength thus gained by each encouraged England, in due time, to associate herself with both—and the Triple Entente was born. Because Russia was so seriously disaffected by the Treaty of Berlin, Bismarck believed that Germany should draw closer to Austria-Hungary; that, indeed, a formal alliance between the two should be effected. Italy's indignation at France's action in Tunis caused her to join France's principal enemy—and the Triple Alliance came into being. Thus, the Congress of Berlin re-created the alliance system of the pre-1815 period, and emphasized afresh the play of power politics. If it prevented a localized European war in 1878, as it almost certainly did, the Congress of Berlin sowed many of the seeds of a far greater conflict to come.

The Emergence of the Alliance System

After the Congress of Berlin many of the imperio-nationalist elements in Russia became convinced, quite understandably, that in spite of his honest-broker pose Bismarck intended to work more closely with Austria than Russian interests could tolerate. In these circumstances she made overtures to both France and Italy. To counter this development, Bismarck sought an alliance with Austria. Fearful of what Russia might attempt after her humiliation at Berlin, Austria was willing enough to join forces with the strongest military power in Europe. So, in 1879, the two empires joined in a secret, defensive military pact. This treaty, later expanded and renewed, became the cornerstone of the grand diplomatic edifice soon to be erected by Bismarck. The German Chancellor never tired of emphasizing the defensive nature of the pact, which he looked upon solely as a safeguard to be used only after conditions had already assumed threatening aspects. But obviously German interests called for the prevention, if possible, of the development of such conditions. In Bismarck's view this came down to the need to establish better relations with Russia; that is, to the re-creation of a former Austro-German-Russian league of friendship (the Three Emperors' League) which had dissolved amid the recriminations flowing out of the Berlin settlement.

Favoring this move was Russia's profound reluctance to ally herself with a republican regime. Clearly, her heart was not in the brief flirtation with France of the preceding year. England was out of the question because she considered the eastern Mediterranean to be her own special preserve. Italy was too weak to be of substantial help. But financial exigencies and military weakness precluded Russia's standing alone. Thus the logic of circumstances clearly pointed to Germany. Sensing this, Bismarck pressured Austria into agreement and a new pact was signed (1881). Its terms protected the interests of Germany by bringing Austria and Russia into peaceful collaboration. The pact protected the interests of Russia by insuring her partners' help if England should move against Russia through the Straits, and by fostering the peaceful union of Bulgaria and Rumelia. Austria's interests were protected by Russia's promise not to attempt to alter conditions in the Balkans without Austria's consent, and by Russia's agreement to an eventual absorption of Bosnia-Herzegovina into the Austrian empire. Thus, only three

years after Russia had vowed never to trust Germany again, she became her ally and, even more strangely, the ally of Austria whose influence in the Balkans she most feared.

In the meantime Italy had been busy readying plans to annex Tunisia. Before she could act, however, France occupied the territory (1881) with the covert support of England and Germany. Italy, thoroughly angered by this *fait accompli* and unaware of Bismarck's role in the affair, turned to him for comfort and aid. Although the terms of the Austro-German alliance were kept secret, the fact that an agreement of some kind existed was well known. Italy now offered to associate herself with the central powers.* Both Germany and Austria, although without enthusiasm, accepted the offer and thus, in 1882, the Triple Alliance was formed. Bismarck again made it plain that the pact was purely defensive. With tongue in cheek, Italy acquiesced. The secret treaty provided that Germany and Austria would give full support to Italy if she were attacked by France *without provocation;* that Italy would join with Germany if Germany were attacked by France without provocation; that all would join together if any one was attacked by two or more powers.

Meanwhile England continued to enjoy what she liked to think of as her "splendid isolation." Before sounding Austria in 1879, Bismarck had hinted of an alliance with Britain, but the cool response from across the Channel quickly discouraged him. The position of the island empire did indeed seem secure. Early ventures in industrialism had given England a substantial head start over other powers. Her empire circled the globe. On the high seas she was supreme; not only was her fleet more than double in size and effectiveness that of her nearest rival, France, but she controlled most of the strategic approaches

---

* Actually she desired an alliance with Germany alone but Bismarck made it clear that "the road to Berlin ran through Vienna."

to the sea lanes of the world. Control of Gibraltar and Suez, for example, allowed her to bottle up the Mediterranean whenever she wished (thus tending, incidentally, to make Italy an unofficial and subordinate ally). Squadrons stationed at the tip of South Africa watched over affairs at this juncture of two oceans. Waters washing the great subcontinent of India were policed by English ships. Singapore, Hong Kong, and Shanghai gave her not only entry to east Asian markets but the final word in disputes that might arise in that vast area. Ruling the seas, dominating the major trade areas, rich, secure, and at peace, England disdained entangling alliances. Within the span of a single generation, many of these conditions were to undergo marked change, and the splendor of isolation was to be lost. But at that time, as for so long before, she seemed unchallengeable.

New Pacts and Alliances

Renewed Balkan flareups, whose details cannot be described in a brief survey account, resulted in the collapse of the German-Russian-Austrian alliance. At the same time (1885–1887) the situation in France had become threatening when, under her chauvinistic minister of war, Georges Boulanger, France began beating the *revanche* drums which sounded menacingly like the drums of war.

In these circumstances Bismarck executed what many consider his subtlest diplomatic maneuver. In what came to be known as the Mediterranean Pacts (1887), he succeeded, in effect, in drawing England into an informal alliance without that nation quite understanding what had happened. Only its general features may be noted here. Italy and England agreed to work for the maintenance of the *status quo* in the Mediterranean (which eased Bismarck's apprehensions); Italy reaffirmed her approval of English domination of Egypt; England recognized that Italy had special interests in North Africa (particularly in Libya). In short, England, Italy,

and Austria (who adhered to the first pact and signed the second) were placed in combination to stave off French aggression in the western half of the Mediterranean and Russian aggression in the eastern half. The agreements were supposedly secret, but enough information was allowed to leak to give Russia pause in her Balkan schemes.

With the Triple Alliance and the Mediterranean agreements in force, Bismarck felt more optimistic about the preservation of peace. Only one link seemed missing — a close and formal tie with Russia. Rather surprisingly, Russia now suggested this herself. Two motives prompted this: rivalry between two factions of the ruling elite, and the menacing implications of the Mediterranean Pacts. For long, a struggle had been carried on between those who wanted to Westernize Russia and those who saw in Westernization the destruction of Russia's Slavic soul. At this time the Westernizers were in sufficient ascendancy to dictate foreign policy. A connection with Germany seemed to them both a good thing in itself, as well as a setback for Slavophile rivals.

So, in 1887, Russia's minister in Berlin indicated that although Russia could under no conditions consider a renewal of the Three Emperors' Alliance, she was quite willing to discuss a bilateral agreement. Bismarck responded at once. Out of the negotiations that followed there came what is commonly called the Reinsurance Treaty. It stipulated that Germany favored Russia's peaceful penetration of the east Balkans, particularly Bulgaria, and control of the Straits; and that each would observe neutrality toward the other if either became involved in war with a third power. Bismarck made it clear that this provision did not cover a *Russian-provoked* war with Austria and conversely agreed that it would not come into force in the event of a *German-provoked* war with France.

Thus, in the ten years following the Congress of Berlin, Bismarck's diplomacy seemed to have stilled the tempests raised by that conference, and to have laid the groundwork for pacific relations among the powers. The Triple Alliance appeared to insure that neither France nor Russia would quite dare to start big trouble in Europe. The Mediterranean agreements further shored up the forces working against violent modification of the Balkan *status quo;* they also gave ordered recognition to imperial ambitions in Africa. The Reinsurance Treaty brought Russia back within the German orbit without penalizing Russia's peaceful penetration to the south. Quite correctly, then, we may refer to this period as the "Bismarckian Era." Who else could have constructed a general peace within the framework of the politics of realism?

Weaknesses of Bismarckian Diplomacy

However, the substance of the Bismarckian achievement was more seeming than real. France, although active in Africa and Asia, had not forgotten the debacle of 1870 and 1871; she still yearned for revenge. For the most part she sought to follow Gambetta's advice — speak of it never, think of it always. She was convinced that her day would come. Russia was willing to *talk* of peaceful penetration. But, granted funds could be found to refurbish her ailing military machine, another kind and instrument of penetration was to be fashioned and held in reserve. As for what came increasingly to be called the Balkan Problem, Bismarck never really understood it. To him the ethnic groups of that region were pawns to be moved in the great game of power politics. He failed utterly to appreciate the dynamic, churning force of Balkan nationalism as a "wave of the future."

He also failed, though perhaps more understandably, to sense the demise of one era — his own — and the birth of another. Essentially he was a transitional figure. True, in the last days of his tenure he supported German industrialists in their efforts to exploit markets and resources in the so-

called backward areas of the world. But his support was reluctant and late. At no time did he seem to comprehend the ranging implications of the new industrial age. His own formative period had coincided with the flowering of the Manchester doctrine of free trade and anti-imperialism. Although he came to accept upward industrial tariff revisions and even eventually became somewhat enthusiastic over protection for agricultural produce, he remained basically insensible to the mercantilist, protectionist trend that was already working important changes in world affairs even before he left office. Almost by necessity his was, fundamentally, a static Germany and a static world. His boasted policy of "limited liabilities" served well enough the demands of *Europa-politik* (although he denied there existed such a thing as "Europe"). But the ingredients of the new age — industrialism, protectionism, colonies, big navies — called for a *Weltpolitik* beyond his ken. His passing from power in 1890 marked the transition from the steady-state world to a world of dynamic change.

New Paths and New Compacts

Beginnings of the "New Course"

Young, aggressive, and impressionable, the new emperor, William II (reigned 1888–1918), made it clear from the beginning that his royal hand was at the helm. He possessed talent without genius, intelligence without judgment, domineering ways without the capacity actually to dominate. Often he sought advice and almost as often failed to distinguish the sound from the unsound. Unlike Bismarck, he understood the need for a new concert of Europe functioning within the framework of *Weltpolitik*. Unfortunately, and illogically, he wanted a *dominated* concert, with Germany in the master role. Moreover, he worked simultaneously to set up a power system of alliances, a system obviously incompatible with his own projected concert. During his reign, therefore, Germany experienced the effects of a confused and ineptly directed foreign policy.

The year that Bismarck left office the Reinsurance Treaty came up for renewal. On advice from his advisers, William allowed the treaty to lapse. The excuse given by Chancellor Caprivi was that he could not keep five balls in the air at once, a reference to the diplomatic dexterity required to keep all of Germany's friends, some with conflicting aims, from breaking out of the orbits so adroitly set by Bismarck. Actually, the new leaders of Germany, managing what the Kaiser liked to call the "New Course," were afraid of what might happen if news of the treaty's terms should leak to Austria and England with whom the Kaiser-Caprivi government hoped to cement a grand new alliance of states.

The Franco-Russian Alliance, 1890 to 1894

Naturally Russia became alarmed and, feeling that she could no longer trust Germany and Austria, turned to France who welcomed the overture. As a gesture of friendship, French warships made a courtesy call at Kronstadt where the Tsar stood on the deck of the flagship with bared head as a band played the revolutionary *Marseillaise*. The next year the two governments, in an exchange of letters, promised to confer together when crises threatened. Not satisfied with this, the chiefs of staff in joint meetings framed a convention that stipulated mutual military obligations. But the Tsar felt that this was carrying the budding friendship too far, and, for the moment, he put it aside. But new French irritations with Britain and new Russian difficulties with Germany led the diplomats of both countries to press still harder for a pact with teeth in it. That such a pact was indeed approaching the draft stage was symbolized by the appearance, in 1893, of a Russian fleet in the French harbor of Toulon. Not only diplomats but the generals and ad-

A painting of the young Kaiser about two years after he became Emperor.

Czar Nicholas II is shown as he is about to embark at Cherbourg. The newspapers of both France and Russia made much of this royal visit.

mirals were obviously concerting to transform the *Entente* into a binding military agreement. The next year the alliance was signed. Its secret military clauses provided that Russia would come to the aid of France if France were attacked by Germany; that France would reciprocate if Russia were attacked by Germany; and that if one or more members of the Triple Alliance should order mobilization each of the contracting parties would do likewise.*

The significance of the treaty can hardly be overstated. By it Russia acknowledged finally that she was fully cognizant of Germany's practice of saying yes and meaning no; and that Austro-German aims were no longer compatible with her own. Further, the agreement revealed Russia's imperialist ambitions to be so strong that she could even agree to compromise her long-held monarchial principles. It tended, of course, to heighten the confidence of each partner and thus to prepare the ground for more ambitious ventures in foreign affairs. And naturally it prompted the central powers, particularly Germany, to become even more suspicious. In short, the treaty made possible a developing pattern of "trial by alliances" which would, within a brief score of years, bring on the first global war.

Milestones of the "New Course"

In 1890 Germany and England effected an exchange of territory. Heligoland, a British-owned island off the western approaches to the Kiel Canal (soon to be opened), was a natural base for defense of Germany's northern coast. To get it, Germany offered England Zanzibar, a rather sizable African territory. Normally, England did not give up island bases, no matter how remote or difficult to defend. That she now bargained away a European possession for an area to which she already had perhaps a better claim than the state who "offered" it seemed to some observers a hint that her imperial position was becoming more precarious than her vaunted boast of splendid isolation would have the world believe.

Three years later English and French ambitions clashed in Siam. For a while it ap-

peared that war could not be avoided. Officious and full of advice, William II accepted England's hints to mediate the quarrel, hoping by this gambit to draw her into the Triple Alliance. The incident closed peacefully when England agreed to a compromise. Once again the world took note of, if not an English retreat, at least a softening attitude. Germany in particular was impressed by the new British tendency to give ground when pushed. From early 1890s on, as colonial rivalry between England and Germany heightened, Germany increasingly pushed.

Two events occurred in 1898 that soon further strained relations between the rival empires. Von Tirpitz, newly appointed minister of marine, pushed a naval bill through the Reichstag which provided for a large high seas fleet. To win nationwide approval he set up a generously subsidized Navy League, with branches scattered throughout the Reich. From each of these units subsequently flowed an endless stream of noisy propaganda. The basis of the race for naval supremacy, soon to be begun in earnest, had been established.

This year also marked a change in Germany's attitude toward Turkey. Up to this time, affairs in the Ottoman Empire had but little interested Berlin officials. But Germany's rapid railroad development and her remarkable commercial expansion now combined with an upward thrust of national confidence to cause her to view Turkey, lying athwart two continents, in a new light. Seemingly limitless markets lay in the East. Could they not be tapped by a land route running from Berlin to Bagdad, thence by sea to India and China? To realize such a grand design, of course, Turkey's cooperation was necessary. Accordingly German diplomats began, as it were, to toast the health of the Sick Man of Europe, while German bankers held amiable discussions with Turkish officials.

Naturally Britain felt concern. For many years she had been Turkey's staunchest ally. While protecting her own lifeline to

---

* It is important to note that all military leaders at this time understood mobilization to mean war.

the East, she had kept the Ottoman Empire from falling apart and had prevented Russia from reaching the Straits. The proposed German railroad across Turkish territory, accompanied by generous loans to the Porte, thus constituted a triple threat to English interests. To meet it she reversed her position: perhaps it would be better if the Sick Man were allowed to die and his estate duly apportioned among the legitimate heirs.

Policy makers in Russia were also busy. The drive to the south had ground to a halt; meantime the Japanese had inflicted a crushing defeat upon China (1894–1895). Naturally this imperiled Russia's interests in the Far East, and she therefore decided to patch up an understanding with Austria-Hungary which would give her a free hand in the new trouble zone. Thus for the time being the fluid Balkan situation was "put on ice." By this agreement Austria gained a breathing spell and Russia gained a chance to block Japanese expansion. German prodding was behind Austria's rather reluctant cooperation. The dual monarchy had little faith in Russian promises, but the pressure exerted by the Kaiser and his advisers was too strong to resist.

In these ways the New Course revealed its fundamental aims: the creation of a powerful high seas fleet (conveniently based in the North Sea); a stubborn contesting of Britain's commercial supremacy; and a sustained effort to supervise European diplomacy in a manner befitting the Kaiser's coveted role as arbiter of continental affairs. Already William saw himself as a knight in shining armor, a new Siegfried. Thus accoutered he confidently cued the New Course into the world scene. As it turned out, neither confidence nor course was rooted in the realities of the age.

Emergence of England from Her Isolation

With international rivalries mounting, England found it necessary to reassess her own position. Almost overnight Germany,

The center figure is von Tirpitz, creator (with the Kaiser, shown left) of the "risk" navy, designed to keep Britain from interfering with German imperialist expansion.

France, Japan, and the United States had become industrial powers with expanding empires. Sprawled over the globe, the British Empire inevitably invited contests and conflicts. A generation earlier France was beaten and humbled; Germany was in its national infancy; Russia was recovering from the debacle of the Crimean War. Now conditions were changed, and the powers were talking back. Clearly splendid isolation was out of date. It was time to make some friends and share the world.

In 1902 England offered to join Japan in a formal alliance, hoping thereby to prevent Russia from running amuck—that is, from interfering with English interests in the East. Japan was next door to this source of possible friction; England was thousands of miles away. By itself, this geographic factor loaded the treaty in favor

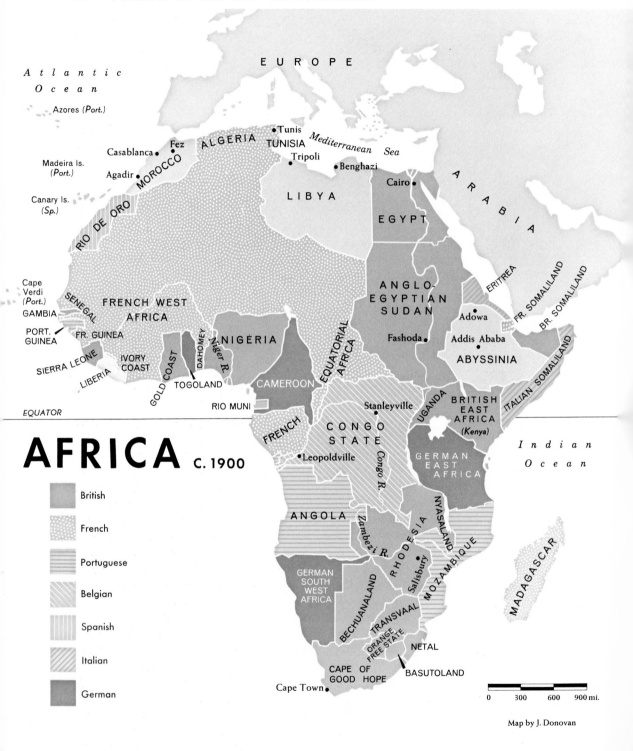

EUROPE

Atlantic Ocean

Azores *(Port.)*

Madeira Is. *(Port.)*

Canary Is. *(Sp.)*

Cape Verde *(Port.)*

GAMBIA

PORT. GUINEA

•Tunis
TUNISIA
Tripoli•

Mediterranean Sea

•Benghazi

Cairo•

LIBYA

EGYPT

ALGERIA

Fez•
Casablanca•
MOROCCO
Agadir•

RIO DE ORO

SENEGAL

FRENCH WEST AFRICA

FR. GUINEA

SIERRA LEONE
LIBERIA

IVORY COAST

GOLD COAST

DAHOMEY

TOGOLAND

NIGERIA

Niger R.

CAMEROON

RIO MUNI

EQUATORIAL AFRICA

ANGLO-EGYPTIAN SUDAN

Fashoda•

ERITREA

FR. SOMALILAND

BR. SOMALILAND

Adowa•

Addis Ababa•

ABYSSINIA

ITALIAN SOMALILAND

ARABIA

EQUATOR

FRENCH

CONGO STATE

Leopoldville•

Stanleyville•

Congo R.

UGANDA

BRITISH EAST AFRICA *(Kenya)*

GERMAN EAST AFRICA

Indian Ocean

AFRICA C. 1900

British

French

Portuguese

Belgian

Spanish

Italian

German

ANGOLA

Zambezi R.

GERMAN SOUTH WEST AFRICA

BECHUANALAND

RHODESIA

NYASALAND

Salisbury•

MOZAMBIQUE

MADAGASCAR

TRANSVAAL

ORANGE FREE STATE

CAPE OF GOOD HOPE

Cape Town•

NETAL

BASUTOLAND

0   300   600   900 mi.

Map by J. Donovan

of England; but Japan, flattered by the prospect of joining forces with a great Occidental power, agreed readily enough. In this year, then, England's famed isolation was formally abandoned. Of itself, the arrangement turned out to be relatively insignificant. But this break with her past made it easier for England to play the alliance game with others, especially in Europe where conditions were rapidly becoming unstable and unpredictable.

After briefly flirting with Russia and Germany, England turned to France. For a long time the Kaiser's advisers had insisted that such a combination was impossible; and their reasonong seemed quite sound. England and France had already fought two wars, each lasting a hundred years. Their overlapping imperial claims provoked mutual suspicion. Temperamentally they were poles apart. Almost any other partnership would seem to make more sense. What German diplomats failed to realize, however, was England's dawning understanding that, under the conditions of the new era, she could not "stay out of Europe." The exigencies of the new imperialism and the new nationalism clearly foreshadowed the day when she would either fight alone or ally herself in Europe, compromise her world position, and hope to preserve the peace and as much of her empire as she could.

France was willing to talk terms, especially after Fashoda. So in 1904, after the usual diplomatic preliminaries, the two nations reached an understanding in which it was agreed that France would give England a completely free hand in Egypt and the Sudan in return for English support of French interests in Morocco. The significance of the *Entente Cordiale,* as it came to be called, can hardly be exaggerated. It clearly implied that England, forced to choose between sharing naval and industrial supremacy on the one hand and colonial possessions on the other, would choose to share colonial possessions. It showed,

too, that France would compromise on colonial issues but not on Alsace-Lorraine or the day of revenge and that her alignments, in short, would always be aimed at Germany.

Formation of the Triple Entente

We have already noted that Russia, bogged down in her Balkan schemes, had decided to try her fortunes in north China. The same decision was reached by Japan at the same time. For the next several years each staked out its claims until in 1904 the expected collision occurred (see supra, p. 692). In the Treaty of Portsmouth which ended the war Russia ceded to Japan half of the island of Sakhalin, yielded up her foothold on the Liaotung Peninsula, and acknowledged special Japanese interests in Korea. Although Japan had been victorious, her financial and manpower resources had been so severely drained that she was willing to forgo demands regarding Manchuria, except those we have noted in an earlier section.

Russia, balked both in Europe and Asia, battered by war, and finally torn by revolution (see p. 669), looked about for means to recoup. England and France offered their services for a price. Both had been alarmed by the war. Linked to the rising Japanese power by the treaty of 1902, England was fearful that a too ambitious Japan might involve her in a large-scale war. France, quite understandably, wished to see her Russian ally unencumber herself in the East. Thus both worked to effect a *detente* between the late belligerents, a chore successfully concluded in 1907 when Russia and Japan signed an agreement acknowledging each other's spheres of influence in Manchuria. More by accident than design, then, the outlines of a Franco-Russo-English entente began to take shape. England had been remarkably friendly toward Russia in the Portsmouth negotiations. France was the ally of both. Why should not the friends of a friend themselves become friends? Logic and self-interest gave strong point to the question.

For years both nations had sought to establish hegemony over a sizable portion of the Middle and Far East—Persia, Afghanistan, and Tibet. Presumably, some kind of settlement there could prepare the way for the peaceful adjustment of general differences, both current and to come. A settlement of this type, moreover, could not but serve as a caution to Germany and Austria-Hungary. Under these benign promptings an agreement was formally concluded in June 1907. Persia was divided into three parts. The northern area was to be regarded as a Russian sphere of influence; the southern portion was "assigned" to Britain; a central section was to remain under Persian control as a buffer region. (In none of these decisions, incidentally, was the shah of Persia consulted.) Both states gave formal recognition to China's suzerainty over Tibet. Russia agreed to carry on all future negotiations between her government and Afghanistan through the good offices of the British.

Another wrench tightening the alliance system was the authorization given in 1907 to French and English military and naval officials to meet and work out joint plans of action. From these discussions there ultimately emerged a pattern of reciprocal responsibilities. For example, the French fleet was assigned exclusively to the Mediterranean, leaving British squadrons to guard the Atlantic coasts. In the famous Plan XVII (counterpart to Germany's von Schleiffen plan) the deployment of French troops was shifted away from the Channel ports from which incoming British forces were to fan out. Political authorities in both countries took pains to point out (to each other; the public knew nothing of them) that these arrangements had no binding political force, that both nations remained free to act as their interests dictated. But such disclaimers could hardly be taken seriously; nor were they when the great test came in 1914.

Mutual Distrust; "Alliance over All"

The juxtaposition of two great rival power blocs charged the European atmosphere with tense distrust. Entente diplomats increasingly feared what they thought of as the Machiavellian machinations of the Triple Alliance, particularly the schemes of Germany and Austria-Hungary. Germany's amazing industrial growth seemed to Britain a threat to her own supremacy, perhaps even to her security. Germany's claim to "a place in the sun," coupled with von Tirpitz's plans to build a formidable "risk" navy, heightened Britain's concern. Austria's refusal to heed her subject peoples' demands for self-rule gave further credence to the charge that the Triple Alliance was an unholy combination based upon medieval principles of autocracy and elitism.

Germany and Austria in turn looked upon the Triple Entente as an international instrument of evil. Again and again the Kaiser protested what he called the malicious encirclement of Germany. France, he complained, rebuffed all his efforts to reach a friendly understanding; England persisted in regarding the high seas, world markets, and a large portion of the globe as hers by a kind of divine right. Similarly, Austria-Hungary considered the Triple Entente a direct threat to her existence as an empire. Austrian officials argued that Russia (aided by France whose commitments to Russia gave her even greater confidence) would never rest until Serbs, Croats, Slovenes, Czechs, Slovakians, and other subject peoples were pried loose from the control of the dual monarchy, and until she had firmly established herself in the Straits.

These attitudes and circumstances naturally fostered mutual suspicion and recrimination. Of course, diplomatic niceties continued to be observed. From time to time the major powers published ringing affirmations of their respect for such commonly held ideals as peace, the territorial integrity and independence of all peoples, and international cooperation. But the bread-and-butter business of diplomacy was something else. Ministers of state could not bring themselves to believe that their counterparts in other lands could be expected to be any more forthright than they were themselves. And "national interests" seemed to require both calculated disingenuousness (if not deception) and when the pacts of "acquisitive diplomacy" failed, big guns and loyal allies.

An increasingly disquieting development was the growing tendency of each of the great powers to regard its individual destiny as intricately bound up with the power and prestige of the group to which it belonged. If the Triple Entente suffered a diplomatic setback, France (or England or Russia) felt it had been weakened. The same was true of members of the Triple Alliance. Eventually an absurd kind of diplomatic algebra was worked out. The triumphs of alliance T in conflicts 1 and 2 penalized alliance E by x number of points. If E in conflict 3 scored heavily enough, the balance might be righted or even tipped in its favor. If, however, either T or E consecutively lost y number of times, no future redress was possible. Admittedly these terms are somewhat fantastic. But they contain a hard core of truth, repeatedly revealed as European diplomacy unfolded its disastrous course in the opening years of the new century.*

Thus the imperialist thrust, the nationalist impulse, and the creation of a system of alliances designed to redress the balance of power had divided Europe into two armed camps before 1910. Piling armaments upon armaments each protested its horror of war and begged the other to mend its ways before a holocaust engulfed them all. Both met new, emergent crises with fear and fulmination and with an increasing conviction that compromise would only make matters worse. No one knew how many crises could occur before one of them would spark the conflagration. But each side hoped that the other would gain its senses long before that fatal fusing and call off its pyrotechnic displays of stubborn aggression.

The Tautened Web: Testing the New Balance of Power

The First Moroccan Crisis, 1905

Actually about fifteen more or less serious conflicts occurred in the period between 1904 and 1914. Each conflict added to the menace of the next and built up a cumulative tension. Several are worth examining in some detail: the first Moroccan crisis (1905); the so-called Buchlau Bargain and its aftermath (1908–1909); the second Moroccan crisis (1911); and the Balkan Wars (1912–1913).

The coming together of England and France in the "cordial understanding" of 1904 alarmed Germany. The Franco-Russian alliance was bad enough; the new entente, it was felt, would restrict Germany's freedom of action even more. German diplomats (especially von Bulow, the Chancellor, and Baron von Holstein, one of his chief advisers) therefore determined to break it up as quickly as possible.

Two developments conjoined to precipitate what has since been called the first Moroccan crisis. By 1904, even as Tirpitz had predicted, the German navy was well on its way to becoming the deterrent "risk" navy planned some years before. From now on English admirals would have to sing more softly. The second development evolved from a scheme of French Minister of Foreign Affairs Delcassé, one of the "new leaders" in European politics. Favoring an aggressive foreign policy Delcassé proposed, in 1905, to bring Morocco under French control. As a first move he asked England, Spain, and

* Consider, for example, the British Foreign Secretary's remark when Delcassé was forced to resign as French Foreign Minister at Germany's insistence in 1905: "The fall of Delcassé is disgusting and has sent the *Entente* down any number of points on the market."

Italy to join with him in demanding financial and political "reforms" in that Arab state. With their approval he sent off a note to the sultan which clearly indicated forthcoming French pressure. Holstein, who had been waiting for such an opportunity, urged Bulow to enter a vigorous protest. As it happened, the Germans had international law on their side. In the so-called Madrid Convention of 1880 all the major western European powers had underwritten the neutral status of Morocco.

Accordingly the Kaiser paid a visit to Tangier in 1905 where he bluntly announced Germany's intention to safeguard the independence and territorial integrity of the threatened Moslem state. The next month, in a Reichstag speech, Bulow deplored the French action and demanded an international conference to deal with the crisis. The challenge could scarcely have been put more bluntly: France could pull out or fight.

Believing the Germans were bluffing, and in any case supported by the British government, Delcassé called for a showdown. He got it, but not the kind he had anticipated; most of his own colleagues, including the premier, demurred. They argued that the Madrid Convention gave the Germans a strong case, that Bulow was not bluffing, and that in the event of war the English navy could hardly help in the defense of Paris. Delcassé, they insisted, must resign. When he did, the German press jubilantly hailed the event as the just desserts of a warmonger. Rouvier, the French premier, had hoped that by thus appeasing Germany the demand for an international conference would be dropped. But Bulow and Holstein were not satisfied; the conference must be held and the French action must be officially condemned.

Now both the French and English governments felt alarm. In a memorandum dated February 20, 1906, Sir Edward Grey, the newly appointed British Secretary of State for Foreign Affairs, wrote:

If there is a war between France and Germany, it will be very difficult for us to keep out of it. The *Entente,* and still more the constant and emphatic demonstrations of affection (official, naval, political, commercial, municipal and in the press) have created in France a belief that we should support her in war. . . . If this expectation is disappointed, the French will never forgive us.[1]

Germany, convinced that she held the trump cards, made it plain only an international conference would satisfy her. France yielded to this pressure. Meeting in Algeciras in January 1906, the powers debated the question for nearly three months. In the end, a compromise was reached. All nations, including of course Germany, were guaranteed the right of free trade in Morocco. A police force under international control, but supervised by France and Spain, was created to maintain internal order. Overall supervision of the execution of the agreement was entrusted to the Diplomatic Corps at Tangier.

In a sense the Entente powers had suffered a serious setback. Clearly France had begun something she could not finish. Virtually at Germany's dictation a French foreign minister had been forced to resign. International, not French, control was established in Morocco. But it was an empty victory for Germany and her allies, since out of it came an even closer drawing together of England and France. Each felt it had been ordered about by Germany for all the world to see. Each believed the Entente could not survive another such public humiliation. Both agreed to work together more closely in the future.

The "Buchlau Bargain": the Bosnian Crisis, 1908 to 1909

Several months after the Algeciras settlement, Count von Aehrenthal was made

1. Quoted in Luigi Albertini, *The Origins of the War of 1914,* translated by I. M. Massey, Oxford University Press, London, 1952–1957, 3 vols., Vol. I, p. 166.

Austria's minister for foreign affairs. He had long felt great dissatisfaction with his country's posture in world affairs. The Empire, he believed, suffered from two chronic deficiencies. One was failure of nerve, a refusal to risk all to save all. The other was a remarkable inability to understand its true interest in the Balkans. He believed that a bold venture, resolutely carried out, would serve a double purpose. A coup of this type would inject *élan* and confidence into the body politic and prepare the Empire for a resumption of its old leadership; and at the same time it would provide a means for regaining world respect. Moreover, if this venture were to have its locus in the Balkans, by that very fact an immense shoring up of the Empire's general European position would be effected. Many of its subject peoples were Slavs whose constant carping for unity and autonomy had kept the double state in continuous ferment. Especially troublesome were the Bosnians and Herzegovinians, forever clamoring for union with Serbia. If they were allowed to join their motherland, other ethnic groups would be encouraged to intensify their own nationalistic agitation. Surrender to one group would invite surrender to another, and another, until the Empire no longer existed. On the other hand, if Bosnia and Herzegovina were formally annexed and Serbia at the same time were dealt a crippling blow, prospects for the Empire's tomorrows would brighten.

Surprisingly, Austrian schemes were promoted by Russia who, rebuffed in the Far East as we have seen, now turned her attention again to the Straits. Izvolsky, minister of Foreign Affairs, believed Russia could afford to wink at Austria's annexation of Bosnia-Herzegovina in return for Austria's sympathetic neutrality toward Russian efforts to open the Straits to Russian warships. To this end he sought an exchange of views with Aehrenthal.

The meeting was held on Aehrenthal's Buchlau estate in the fall of 1908. Since no official record was kept of the discussions, it is hard to say precisely what agreements were reached. Subsequently both parties published full accounts of their conversations, but they differed widely in important details. According to Izvolsky, Aehrenthal approved of Russian expansion in the south in return for a free hand for Austria in Bosnia-Herzegovina. Neither, however, was to act until both were ready and had agreed upon the proper moment or, in other words, until Izvolsky had sounded out Italy, France, and England and had obtained their consent. Aehrenthal later agreed that they had sympathetically discussed reciprocal support but denied any timetable arrangements.

The Bubbling Balkan Cauldron

In any case, before the Russian minister could make his rounds of the capitals, Austria annexed Bosnia-Herzegovina and a new crisis faced the powers. Serbia called for war and, knowing nothing of the "bargain," Russian help in fighting it. Izvolsky was caught in a dilemma. The Russian half of the Buchlau bargain depended upon Anglo-French cooperation, the groundwork for which had not yet been laid. Moreover, he had plotted the affair without fully informing Tsar Nicholas or Prime Minister Stolypin of its details, particularly of the all-important commitment to Austria's annexation of Bosnia and Herzegovina. Deciding to brazen it out, Izvolsky called upon his *Entente* colleagues to demand an international conference. But Austria, strongly backed by Germany, stubbornly refused to agree to a conference. When Serbia ordered partial mobilization, Aehrenthal made it clear that Austria was not bluffing.

Serbia's adamant stand presented Russia with the choice of backing her up or calling her off. When England and France shied away from all-out support for their ally, Russia was forced to accept a compromise solution offered by Germany. In essence the proposal was this: Germany would send notes to all the interested powers asking whether they would agree to Austria's annexation of the provinces. Affirmative responses would make an international consultation. Acceptance of the "compromise" ended the crisis; but it edged Europe closer to the great showdown of 1914.

The one-sided settlement prompted Serbian leaders, assisted by Russia, to form a secret terrorist organization (the *Narodna Obrana* — "National Defense") to prepare for the day of reckoning. It also prodded the quarreling Balkan states to put aside their ancient rivalries and create a united front. The aims of the Balkan League were to prepare for a favorable moment for a combined attack against Turkey, eject the Sick Man from Europe, and divide the spoils among themselves. Naturally Russia supported the League (indeed, she helped to set it up). As its protectress and benefactor she could expect to share in the gains of the general settlement. France was also affected by the League's aims and activities because by this time she had come to rely heavily upon Russian support vis-à-vis a future showdown with Germany. France had also increasingly invested in Balkan commercial and industrial ventures. England was less directly interested in the plots and counterplots of Eastern Europe, but her commitments to France bound her much more intimately to Balkan affairs than her statesmen cared to admit.

The Second Moroccan Crisis

The interdependence of ally upon ally was further shown in the second Moroccan crisis (1911). As signatory to the Act of Algeciras, France had publicly affirmed her recognition of Moroccan independence. But her intention to make that Arab state part of her African empire was as strong as ever. In 1911 she occupied Fez, the capital city, prompting another German protest.

The pieces of the now-familiar pattern of challenge-counterchallenge again fell into place. Each power bloc charged the other with making unreasonable demands and of acting aggressively. Each fed its newspapers chauvinistic propaganda. Each feared that giving in to the other would deal its own prestige a serious, perhaps fatal, blow. To fend off another *Entente* defeat, the British Prime Minister authorized Lloyd George (then Chancellor of the Exchequer) to publicly warn Germany of the risk she was running. In his famous "Mansion House" address, the British leader bluntly declared:

> I believe it is essential in the highest interests, not only of this country, but of the world, that Britain should *at all hazards* maintain her place and prestige amongst the Great Powers of the world. . . . If a situation were to be forced upon us in which peace could only be served by the surrender of the great and beneficent position Britain has won by centuries of heroism and achievement, by allowing Britain to be treated when her interests were vitally affected as if she were of no account in the Cabinet of Nations, then I say emphatically that peace at *that price would be a humiliation intolerable for a great country such as ours to endure.*[2]

The challenge created a furor in Germany and brought Europe to the brink of war. At one point Grey himself believed hostilities might break out in a matter of hours. In a meeting with Lloyd George and Winston Churchill he said, "The Fleet might be attacked at any moment. I have sent for McKenna [First Lord of the Admiralty] to warn him." But, in the end, Germany moderated her demands and agreed to a treaty that assigned certain African territories to Germany and the "protection" of Morocco to France. War was averted, but again at the price of increased international tension and bitterness.

Balkan Wars, 1912 to 1913

In 1912 and 1913 another crisis occurred which brought Europe to the abyss that, a

2. Albertini, *op. cit.,* pp. 330–331 (italics added).

year later, engulfed it and eventually a large part of the rest of the world. The new crisis was a Balkan war deliberately precipitated by the newly formed League.

The League was made up of Serbia, Bulgaria, Greece, and Montenegro. After Turkey's defeat by Italy in a brief war, 1910–11, these states believed their hour had come. By 1912 the great powers were so delicately balanced in their alignments that no single member dared to act unilaterally to prevent a Balkan flare-up. Russia and Austria, not yet ready for a showdown between themselves, warned the Balkan states not to attack Turkey. But the warning was ignored. Weakened by her recent war with Italy, and torn by internal dissention and chronic maladministration, Turkey was beaten on all fronts and capitulated in May 1913. Almost all of her European territory was taken from her by the victorious Balkan states. After more than four hundred years of foreign domination, the peoples of southeastern Europe could call their land their own. For the moment, nationalism had won over imperialism. But this was only for a moment because fresh quarrels broke out almost immediately among the victors. What land belonged to whom? Where did Bulgaria leave off and Greece begin? What were the "true" boundary lines of Serbia, Romania, and Montenegro? A new state, Albania, had been created by the treaty settlement. What were to be its boundaries, fixed at whose expense? Bulgaria, having made larger gains than the others, was the special object of recriminatory charges. In an effort to redress the balance Serbia, Greece, and Montenegro concerted to force a rewriting of the treaty. When Bulgaria refused to negotiate, the three states promptly sent their armies marching against their erstwhile ally. Romania joined them, soon followed by Turkey. In this second Balkan war, Bulgaria was unable to stand against attackers who completely ringed her. In August 1913, she agreed, in the Treaty of Bucharest, to a sharp whittling

The powers of both alliance systems were apprehensive over inter-Balkan squabbles in 1912 and 1913, as this German cartoon suggests.

down of her original demands. Naturally this intra-Slav bitterness dissolved the Balkan League, which, in turn, led to further complications.

The Aftermath of the Balkan Wars

Several of the Balkan states emerged from the war against Turkey with sharpened tastes and tempers. Extreme Serbian nationalists, for example, formed the Union of Death (more commonly known as the Black Hand Society), a secret organization dedicated to effecting the early "return" of Bosnia-Herzegovina to the motherland. Their methods were frankly terroristic. Covertly supported by Russian agents, the Society sought to convince Austria that the retention of the provinces was not worth an endless future of bombings and assassinations. The Serbian government did not support, or even favor, such sanguine activities. Nevertheless, it continued to agitate for satisfaction of its irredentist claims. So both officially and unofficially Serbia stepped up its pressures on

Austria-Hungary. Similarly, other Balkan states nurtured territorial ambitions and made preparations for the next round.

Although not a direct outcome of the Balkan wars, a French army bill that was passed in 1913 further heightened the atmosphere of crisis in European chancelleries. This bill lengthened the term of conscript service from two to three years. Alliance powers denounced it as clear evidence of Entente aggressive designs. Naturally Russia saw nothing but good in it. Inspired perhaps by the Tsar's minister of war, an article in a Russian newspaper put it bluntly: "Russia is prepared; France too must be so." Maurice Paléologue, an influential French ambassador to Russia when World War I broke out and a close friend of Poincaré, repeatedly stressed the need for an army build-up if the Entente powers hoped to stand up to their rivals. Urging passage of the bill in 1913, Paléologue argued "that the probability of war with Germany, or more exactly, of a great European conflict, increases from day to day. . . . We must make ourselves strong without delay." One year later he told a colleague, "I have the inward conviction that we are moving towards the storm. At what point on the horizon and on what date it will break I am unable to say, but war is now irrevocable." [3]

Derived from whatever sources and shaped by whatever purposes, the ambassador's conviction proved terribly true.

Assessment of the Effect of the Alliance System

It is arguable whether or not the entangling web of interlacing forces and events had so caught up the powers of Europe in the Alliance system that that system automatically, as it were, prescribed and prefixed the responses and postures of the committed nations. We have seen that as crisis succeeded crisis the range of choice seemed to narrow almost to zero and the

direction of movement seemed to point irreversibly toward war. But historians are not agreed that this was quite the situation. What appears to some latter-day historians as the "eve of war" may not, others hold, have appeared so to many statesmen and citizens of that time. It cannot be disputed that alliance confronted alliance. But the "interpenetration of alliances" was also a fact beyond dispute. For example, in late 1912 Austria and Russia worked together in an attempt to prevent a flare-up in the Balkans. When it occurred in spite of this inter-alliance pressure, Austria opposed letting the Serbs gain access to the Adriatic. Here German support for her ally was both reluctant and qualified. As another example of flexibility within the seemingly inflexible alliance system, Germany, as late as 1913, insisted upon a Balkan policy requiring Austrian reconciliation with Serbia, Romania, and Greece quite consonant with Russian and French interests but decidedly opposed by the Austrians.

Thus the Alliance system, marked in its actual workings by elements of both flexibility and inflexibility, should not be thought of as a monolithic structure inescapably driving the world to war. Still, it would be inexcusable casuistry to underestimate the tug toward war that was so manifestly a feature of that system. In the opening section of the next chapter we will note the alliance system's relative position among the causes of World War I.

SELECTED READINGS

Albertini, L., *The Origins of the War of 1914*, translated by I. M. Massey, Oxford University Press, London, 1952–1957, 3 vols.

The most recent study of this much written about subject. Except for important new material on Italy's behavior and position in — and outside of — the politics of the Triple Alliance, there is little in these volumes that is not found in Fay, cited below.

---

3. Albertini, *op. cit.*, pp. 554–555.

Angell, Norman, *The Great Illusion*, G. P. Putnam's Sons, New York, 1913.

An eloquent argument on the incompatibility of war and modern civilization. The author treats the economic, moral, psychological, and biological conditions that argue against war in a way that is so convincing that the book became a classic in a remarkably short time but, as its publication date suggests, it was not convincing enough to prevent or even postpone the 1914 to 1918 reenactment of "the great illusion."

Brandenburg, Erich, *From Bismarck to the World War*, translated by Ann Adams, Oxford University Press, London, 1927.

Another study, this time from the German point of view, of the coming of World War I. For those who have read Fay or Sontag, this work is chiefly interesting for the opportunity it offers to evaluate the force of national bias in historical narration.

Coolidge, Archibald Cary, *Origins of the Triple Alliance*, Charles Scribner's Sons, New York, 1926.

This is a good short treatment of the subject. The "Notes" section in which the author makes use of material not available to him when the book first appeared in 1917 is particularly interesting. Students thus have the rather rare opportunity of noting how a competent professional historian revises his material, recognizes and corrects original misinterpretations, and integrates new data into a previously written account.

Dickinson, G. L., *The International Anarchy*, The Century Co., New York, 1926.

Based on the belief that the absence of world government produced World War I and will continue to produce world wars, this book examines the general condition of the great powers after the Franco-Prussian War, the formation of the Triple Alliance and the Triple Entente, and the long series of crises, beginning with the Moroccan crisis of 1905 and 1906, which culminated in World War I. It is one of the most effective polemics that that has been written against the sovereign-state system since that system was established.

Fay, Sidney B., *The Origins of the World War*, The Macmillan Co., New York, 1929, 2 vols.

Written nearly 40 years ago, this is still the best general account of the diplomatic background of World War I. It divides responsibility among the powers of both alliance systems. Although the author warns against assigning guilt according to any definite formula, he nevertheless ends up giving the reader a fairly clear feeling of which powers are more to blame than other powers for the coming of the war, and why they are blameworthy. All of the crises cited in this and the succeeding chapter are treated in detail. Excellent character sketches of the statesmen of the period (1870–1914) are woven into the narrative. Volume I deals with the background causes of the war; Volume II deals with the immediate causes.

Gooch, G. P., *Recent Revelations of European Diplomacy*, Longmans, Green & Co., London, 1928.

This is a book about people and the books they wrote dealing with, justifying, condemning or, too rarely, apologizing for events that led to World War I. Almost all of the foremost statesmen of the time either wrote of their roles themselves or were made the subjects of the accounts of others. In addition to being a significant contribution to an understanding of why the war came, the book is highly readable as a literary work.

Langer, William L., *European Alliances and Alignments, 1871–1890*, Alfred A. Knopf, New York, 1931.

Concerned with "the fundamental forces and broad currents that influenced the relations of states to each other" in the twenty-year period following the Franco-Prussian War. Among these forces are religion, Balkan nationalism, colonial activity, and Bismarck's efforts to keep both the peace and Prussia's new position of power in Germany and Europe. Although it covers much of the same ground as the first volume of Fay's book, its approach is different. Fay writes to explain why the war came; Langer is more interested in examining the developments for their own sake.

Manhart, George B., *Alliance and Entente, 1871–1914*, F. S. Crafts & Co., New York, 1932.

One of the *Landmarks in History Series*, this little work (of less than 100 pages) offers a taste of source material that stimulates the appetite. Pertinent portions of most of the basic diplomatic agreements are presented — the first treaty between Austria, Germany, and Italy; the First Mediterranean Pact; the Dual Alliance; the naval convention between France and Russia; and about thirty other treaties, conventions, or statements by leading diplomats of the period.

Medlicott, W. N., *Bismarck, Gladstone, and the Concert of Europe,* The Athlone Press, London, 1956.

The author develops the thesis that from the late 1870s until the early 1880s the more basic features of European politics were fixed by the contest between Gladstone and Disraeli in which Gladstone tried to revive the old Concert of Europe and Disraeli worked to set up a system of close alliances.

————, *The Congress of Berlin and After,* Methuen and Co., London, 1938.

Useful for those who have not read the author's *Bismarck, Gladstone, and the Concert of Europe,* cited above.

Mowat, R. B., *The Concert of Europe,* Macmillan and Co., London, 1930.

A general account of the main developments in international affairs in the period from 1870 to 1914.

Nicolson, Harold, *Portrait of a Diplomatist,* Harcourt, Brace & Co., New York, 1930.

A study of the "old diplomacy" as portrayed in the assumptions and behavior of a genteel Englishman — the author's father — whose nineteenth-century patriotism is held up as a sad example of what was wrong with the civilization that produced World War I. Good for details of the first Moroccan crisis and the Anglo-Russian entente.

Pribram, Alfred Franzis, *The Secret Treaties of Austria-Hungary, 1879–1914,* Harvard University Press, Cambridge, 1920–1921, 2 vols.

Since the dual empire was significantly involved in most of the political affairs of Central and Eastern Europe as these touched international relations, this carefully researched work is of high importance. Although the author was an Austrian, he has kept his bias well within bounds in both his selection of documents and his comments upon them.

Renouvin, Pierre, *The Immediate Origins of the War,* translated by Theodore Carswell Hume, Yale University Press, New Haven, 1928.

This is an extended treatment of the diplomatic and military activity of the great powers and Serbia during the fateful six weeks that followed the assassination of Archduke Franz Ferdinand. Despite claims of objectivity for the book, the reader must leave it feeling that Germany and Austria-Hungary were culpable beyond any stubbornness or shortsightedness shown by Britain, France, and Russia. As an exercise in comparative historiography, interested students should compare this account with that of Fay or Brandenburg.

*Rosenberg, Arthur, *Imperial Germany, The Birth of the German Republic 1871–1918,* translated by Ian F. D. Morrow, Beacon Press, Boston, 1964.

The first two chapters discuss the social forces at work under Bismarck and the politics of conflict in Kaiser William II's Germany. These chapters are perhaps the best account in brief compass that can be found. The rest of the book (about 200 pages) presents the futile struggle for victory and peace, in a conceptual framework and in an economy of words which deserve careful study.

Schmitt, Bernadotte E., *The Coming of the War, 1914,* Charles Scribner's Sons, New York, 1930, 2 vols.

The chief advantage of this book over Fay's and Sontag's is its great amplitude of detail. For example, almost eighty pages are devoted to the Austro-Hungarian note of 1914, and Serbia's reply to it. The author's readable style is an advantage. It has two other less desirable features. It deals only (except for the first two chapters) with the immediate coming of the war; and its bias is distinctly pro Entente powers.

Seton-Watson, R. W., *Sarajevo,* Hutchinson & Co., London, 1925.

An intensive and illuminating study of the "Eastern Question," whose ramifications brought on World War I.

Asterisk (*) denotes paperback.

Sontag, Raymond James, *European Diplomatic History, 1871–1932,* The Century Co., New York, 1933.

The author's main concern is to present a study of how Europe's diplomats tried, in the period stated in the title, to effect "desirable changes in the international *status quo,"* and how to prevent "undesirable changes . . . without recourse to war." He tries to hold in abeyance postwar judgments as he tells the story of prewar diplomacy, and to view postwar developments in the light in which he believes the diplomats themselves saw them. If Fay's two volumes cannot be read, this one should be.

Taylor, A. J. P., *The Struggle for Mastery in Europe, 1848–1918,* Oxford University Press, Oxford, 1954.

Lively, provocative, highly readable. The author certainly has a thorough command of the facts; his interpretation of some of them makes this one of the most controversial of all of the works dealing with this period. It deserves thorough study, but it should not be the only reference used.

Tyler, Mason Whiting, *The European Powers and the Near East, 1875–1908,* University of Minnesota, Minneapolis, 1925.

A detailed study of the conflicting forces at work in the Balkans in the generation before World War I. If the works of neither Langer, Sontag, nor Fay are read, see this study.

FROM WAR TO WAR

26

World War I and Its Settlement

Why the War Came

Imperialism and the Alliance System

It was once rather generally believed that the "new" imperialism was the basic cause of the war, and a few scholars still hold this view. For a generation after 1870, as we have seen, most of the great states and some of the lesser ones brought ever-widening portions of Africa, Asia, and America under some kind of control or influence. In the process, international tensions and occasional threats of war resulted. However, a closer and more critical study of these recurring crises has convinced most historians that overseas expansion was not the main cause of the war. They argue that statesmen seemed to sense that their peoples were not of a mind to go to war over color on the map. They point to the effective dampening of the flame of each crisis, however high it might flicker for a time, as proof of their thesis that issues that are consistently the subject of successful com-

promise can scarcely be considered causes of war. Nevertheless, they all agree that the new imperialism accentuated and conditioned the drift toward war.

The system of counterpoised alliances which formed after the Congress of Berlin (1878) certainly allowed their members to indulge in a more venturesome and even reckless outlook and posture than they would otherwise have done. It is quite impossible, for example, to believe that Austria-Hungary would have annexed Bosnia-Herzegovina in 1908, had she not been convinced that Germany would stand between her and an outraged Russia. Or that France would have allowed herself to become so deeply committed to Russian schemes in the Balkans after 1912, had she not felt that she could count heavily on British help in case of serious trouble. We should not, of course, confuse the alliance system with the many threatening conditions that caused its creation. By itself, the alliance system was harmless; as a contributory agent, it had influence that must not be overlooked or underestimated.

Secret Diplomacy;
Pan-Slavism and Pan-Germanism

The same is true of secret diplomacy. If the peoples of the world had known the details of the bargains and commitments made by their political leaders in the half century before the war, possibly neither leaders nor commitments would have long survived. But diplomacy, secret or open, is a procedure; it is not a goal, a hope, a vision, or any of the other things men fight over and for.

The collective forces labeled Pan-Slavism and Pan-Germanism fed aspirations and excited passions that gave an ominous cast to certain critical decisions. Russia's return to the troubled Balkans after her defeat by Japan in 1905 cannot be explained without acknowledging such aspirations and passions. Germany's thrust through the Balkans and into Mesopotamian lands, necessitated by her Berlin-to-Bagdad railroad project (see *supra*, p. 706), would have been highly unlikely in the absence of close ties with the Teutonic ruling elite of Austria, which was interested in developing hegemony over lands to the east. The force of ethnic feelings cannot, of course, be calibrated by any tool at the historian's disposal, but its deep and abiding influence is an evident fact of life. Even so, Pan-Slavism and Pan-Germanism encouraged rather than caused the drift to war.

Domestic Unrest;
Anglo-German Economic Rivalry

In recent years there has been a revival of interest in the idea that domestic conditions played a crucial role in the coming of the war. It is true that in each of the great states, including the United States, labor unrest and, in some countries, socialist agitation gave the ruling classes considerable concern in the years before the war. It is reasonable to suppose, at least for the autocratic regimes of Germany, Austria-Hungary, and Russia, that conservative rulers may have wondered whether a grand, patriotic rally might not divert the working man's attention from home conditions. The force of this argument is somewhat weakened, however, by available documentary evidence. In 1914 less than 10 per cent of the French labor force belonged to unions. In England, strikes were substantially fewer than they had been in the four years immediately preceding 1914. The same general situation prevailed in Germany and Russia. Many industrialists and their political spokesmen, moreover, believed that a war, far from dampening labor unrest and agitation, might turn them into a real revolution. Nevertheless, domestic unrest as a condition fostering international war should be kept in calculation in any serious assessment of the forces that brought on World War I.

Anglo-German economic rivalry played a large part in bringing on the world conflict. From 1898 to 1913, Germany made enormous export gains over England. For example, in this period England barely doubled her exports to the United States; Germany increased hers five times over. Figures for other areas show the same trend: English exports to India increased a little more than twofold, while Germany's increase was sixfold; England tripled her exports to Argentina, Germany quintupled hers; English exports to China increased about 100 per cent, German exports increased nearly 200 per cent. Germany's rate of increase exceeded England's in the construction of merchant ships by about 400 per cent. Naturally, both British industrialists and merchants and British statesmen were deeply troubled by this situation. On the other hand, as the clouds of war gathered in 1914, British industrial and financial concerns almost frantically implored the government to save the peace. Still, it is hard to believe that this rivalry did not incline England toward some kind of drastic solution to preserve her favorable balance of trade, and that in Germany it did not foster a heightened determination to gain what its merchants and indus-

EUROPE, 1914

The Triple Entente

The Triple Alliance

NORWAY

SWEDEN

FINLAND

• St. Petersburg

Christiana ★
(Oslo)

★ Stockholm

Moscow ★

GREAT BRITAIN

North Sea

Baltic Sea

RUSSIA

AND IRELAND

DENMARK

• Copenhagen

Liverpool •

• Hamburg

• Warsaw

• Kiev

London   The Hague
★   ★

★ Berlin

GERMANY

BELGIUM
★ Brussels

LUX.

Seine R.

Paris ★

Loire R.

Rhine R.

Vienna

AUSTRIA   HUNGARY

Budapest •

*Atlantic
Ocean*

FRANCE

★ Bern
SWITZ.

Munich •

Danube R.

RUMANIA

Bucharest •

Black Sea

Bordeaux •

Rhone R.

Po R.

Venice •

MONTENEGRO

Belgrade •

SERBIA

Sofia •

BULGARIA

Constantinople

Marseilles •

CORSICA

ITALY

Adriatic Sea

ALBANIA

OTTOMAN
EMPIRE

Madrid ★

Rome •

• Naples

Valone •

GREECE

Aegean

• Lisbon

PORTUGAL

SPAIN

Balearic Is.

SARDINIA

Valone

Athens ★

Sea

Mediterranean

SICILY

CRETE

SP. MOROCCO

• Gibraltar (Br.)

Algiers •

• Tunis

Sea

0   150   300 mi.

MOROCCO

ALGERIA

TUNISIA

Map by J. Donovan

trialists considered their fair share of the world's wealth.

Militarism and Nationalism

The strong emphasis in the prewar years on military buildup was a substantial force in the creation of the conditions that caused the war. The formation of large conscript armies and the massive stockpiling of armaments naturally developed in both the leaders and the people an outlook that was conducive to an easy acceptance of war as an instrument of national policy. The influence of chiefs of staff and other military leaders became so decisive in the crucial weeks of 1914 that it dominated all other influences. All the evidence indicates that most of the civilian leaders of the Alliance and Entente powers wanted to find a way to avoid war in the summer of 1914; however, as we shall see, generals, not diplomats and political leaders, had the last word.

There can be no doubt that nationalism was a prime cause of the war, both the "my-country-right-or-wrong" variety and the kind that aimed to free ethnic groups from foreign influence or dominance. The five-thousand-year record of civilization makes it clear that all peoples, of whatever race, language, or habitat, have, at least potentially, the same general virtues and vices. In spite of this, ethnic groups—large or small, advanced or backward, rich or poor —tend to fall victim to a universal illusion. Each group thinks of itself as a kind of sacred community, a special God-touched breed whose "national interests," to use the current phrase, must take precedence over all other interests within or without that sacred community. When this emotion is whipped up by either outside circumstances or inside political machinations, its force is incalculable.

Nevertheless, it was ethnic nationalism that directly precipitated the war. In the next section we shall discuss pertinent details of the surge of nationalism in the Balkans, which directly led to wholesale declarations of war among the great powers of Europe. Here our purpose is best served, perhaps, by noting the judgment of a longtime student of the war crisis:

We should ask not *who,* but *what,* was responsible for the three declarations of war [of the Central Powers against Serbia, Russia, France]; and the answer should be: "The rotten condition of the Austro-Hungarian Empire, the fact that the revolutionary principle of nationality was at work within its limits, and that it was about to break up into a number of independent states." [1]

The War

Sarajevo

By 1914, Franz Josef, Emperor of Austria, had ruled his sprawling Empire for nearly seventy years. His apparent successor-to-be, Archduke Franz Ferdinand, quite understandably had long been pre-

1. Elie Halévy, *The Era of Tyrannies,* translated by R. K. Webb, Anchor Books, Doubleday and Co., New York, 1965, p. 234.

paring for the day when he would become the Empire's royal master. Of special interest to him was the thorny Bosnian question, which he planned to solve by changing the Dual Monarchy into a Trial Monarchy in which Bosnia-Herzegovina would enjoy an autonomous status. To Serbian nationalists the proposal, if put into effect, would destroy all hope of creating a united Serbia. They were, therefore, determined to abort it at any cost.

The Archduke's visit to Bosnia on an inspection tour in June, 1914, gave Serbian conspirators a rare opportunity to combine terror with the elimination of the architect of the hated trialist program. On the day of the visit the official motorcade had scarcely entered Sarajevo, Bosnia's capital, when a bomb was thrown at the Archduke's car. It rolled off the hood and wrecked the next car behind it. A second attempt was successful when an assassin stepped from the curb and fired directly into the royal carriage. Both the Archduke and his wife (an accidental victim) were killed. More literally than those celebrated by Emerson in the *Concord Hymn,* these shots were heard round the world. Exactly thirty-eight days after the fateful shooting most of the major nations of Europe were involved in a war which, before its bloody end, encompassed the world.

Diplomatic Prelude to War

Austria's immediate reaction belied her real intentions. The government was determined to exploit the crime so effectively that Serbia would be destroyed as an independent power. Such drastic action would put an end, once for all, to the insidious Slavic agitation that for so long had eaten away at the foundations of the Empire. In short, the sword must finish in 1914 what Austrian diplomacy had begun in 1908. But secret preparations had first to be worked out in detail. One requisite was the gaining of German support. A special emissary sent to Berlin convinced the

Kaiser that without that support the Empire was finished and, with it, Germany's efforts to fend off encirclement auspicious. Hungary's consent, at first withheld, was bought by the promise of compensations.

After these diplomatic roadblocks had been removed, Austrian officials set themselves to composing an ultimatum that was deliberately designed to be unacceptable. On July 23, 1914, it was presented to Serbia, who was given forty-eight hours in which to reply. Anticipating such a note, Serbia had earlier consulted her Russian ally. If Serbia resisted, would Russia support her? Convinced that France by now was too intricately and irrevocably involved in Russia's Balkan commitments to yield again to German pressure, Russia counseled Serbia to stand firm against humiliating demands. The position of England was more obscure. But France believed that her ally across the Channel would not permit the Central Powers to destroy the *Entente*.

When Serbia refused those demands which infringed on her sovereignty, Austria mobilized. Russia announced her intention to stand by Serbia and accordingly mobilized against Austria. Because Russia was certain that Germany would enter the war on Austria's side, mobilization along the German border was also ordered. The great showdown was at hand.

The Coming of the War

The specific events that put the armies in motion may be briefly summarized. On July 28, 1914, Austria-Hungary declared war on Serbia and the next day bombarded its capital, Belgrade. On July 30, Russia ordered general mobilization. On July 31, England asked France and Germany to respect the neutrality of Belgium. Germany declined to commit herself; France readily agreed. At the same time Germany dispatched warning notes to Russia and France. On this day, too, Austria ordered mobilization along the Russian border. On August 1, Germany, receiving an unsatisfactory reply from Russia, declared war against her. The next day the English cabinet authorized Sir Edward Grey to inform the French ambassador that "if the German fleet comes into the Channel or through the North Sea to undertake hostile operations against the French coast or shipping, the British fleet will give all the protection within its power." Belgium received notification from Germany that German troops must be granted right of free passage across her territory. When this was refused, August 3, Belgian fortifications were attacked. The German government also declared war against France when that nation, in reply to the German ultimatum, refused to promise neutrality. On August 4, England sent an ultimatum to Germany demanding the evacuation of Belgium. When Germany ignored it, England declared war against her.

Italy refused to join her partners on the ground that Austria was the aggressor. Her real purpose in staying out was to bargain for territory. Because her irredentist claims were directed against Austria, only one outcome was possible. In May 1915, after concluding a secret treaty with the Entente powers, who promised her nearly all that she wanted, Italy entered the war against her former ally. Other states had become involved even earlier. Turkey and Bulgaria joined the Central Powers in the Fall of 1914 in the hope of participating in the partition of Serbia. Japan declared war against Germany at about the same time. Her aim was simple— to take over German interests in the Far East. All together, before the guns fell silent four years later, over sixty nations were actively or passively involved in the war.

Western Stalemate

Germany's plans called for a holding action against Russia, which would permit her main forces to execute an overpowering thrust into France. According to the

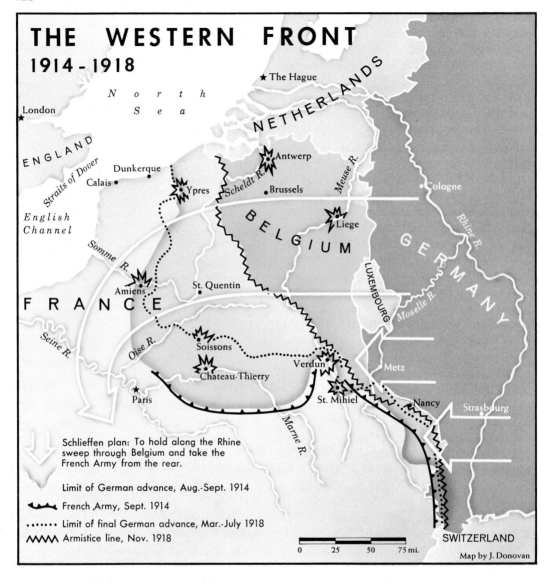

THE WESTERN FRONT
1914-1918

Schlieffen plan: To hold along the Rhine sweep through Belgium and take the French Army from the rear.

Limit of German advance, Aug.-Sept. 1914

French Army, Sept. 1914

Limit of final German advance, Mar.-July 1918

Armistice line, Nov. 1918

0   25   50   75 mi.

Map by J. Donovan

German timetable,* about six weeks would be needed to crush the French and Allied armies, encircle and occupy Paris, and force the Western powers to sue for peace. The holding action against Russia would then be turned into an all-out offensive. Altogether four or five months of serious fighting should bring the war to a victorious close. For their part, the French planned to launch an attack in the Metz-Strasbourg area (south of the German at-

tack), break through into· Germany, and join the Russians in Berlin. To hold and later encircle the German thrust through Belgium, French and Belgian troops were scheduled to link up with the British forces that would filter down from the Channel ports. The Allies also counted on a sharp, short war. Both plans miscarried as the war turned first from one of thrust and movement into one of position and, finally, of attrition.

Seven German armies participated in the assault against France. The three southern-

* Based on the famous Schlieffen Plan. Von Schlieffen was chief of the German general staff, 1891–1905.

most groups, which stretched from Luxembourg's southern border to Strasbourg, had two responsibilities—to turn back French invaders and to serve as anchor weights for the wide-sweeping armies to the north. As the northern armies moved scythe-like through Belgium and France, French armies drove northeastward into Germany (in the manner, as a recent writer has expressed it, of two persons simultaneously entering and leaving a revolving door). The French offensive was based on the belief that Germany had thrown so many men into the great northern movement that her Southern Front could not stand against a strong attack. Actually, German manpower in this sector was equal to that of the invaders. Moreover, the Germans had the advantage of fighting in fortified positions which nestled on wooded and hilly terrain. Within a fortnight after launching their "march to Berlin," the French suffered a severe mauling that sent them staggering back to their own fortifications.

Meanwhile, the German scythe had cut a broad swath through Belgium. By the end of August, Allied armies had retreated to the Marne. Everything seemed to be going according to plan, with Allied collapse imminent. At this juncture the Allies decided to risk all on a massive counteroffensive. Accordingly, on September 6, Allied armies were ordered to make a general turnabout and drive against their attackers. To meet the new situation, the German Command ordered the troops that constituted the point of the sweeping scythe to break off their encircling movement and turn south to avoid widening a gap that had developed under the blows of the counterattack. In effect, the whole line fell back to preserve itself as a line. The Allies made repeated assaults against this line in vain. But from a point near the Marne River (less than twenty miles from Paris) the Germans had retreated about forty miles to a position north of the River Aisne. Here they dug in and settled down to trench warfare. The Battle of the Marne, as it came to be

Hindenburg (left) and Ludendorff, the military team that shaped Germany's war plans and programs, 1916 to 1918.

called, thus ended the German offensive and, as it turned out, all hope of a short war.*

Action on the Two Fronts

The stalemate in the west did not have its counterpart in the east. There the soon-to-become famous team of Ludendorff and Hindenburg was sent to stop a surprising Russian advance.† While the German offensive was slowly grinding to a bloody halt along the Marne, a series of mauling attacks in East Prussia broke the back of the Russian effort and ended in a decisive German victory. Soon the German Command in the east called on the General Staff for reinforcements with which, they were con-

---

* For a detailed account of the many and intricate engagements lumped together as "the Battle of the Marne," see Barbara W. Tuchman, *The Guns of August,* The Macmillan Company, New York, 1962.

† Erich Ludendorff, appointed Quartermaster General of the Army in 1916, developed into Germany's most brilliant strategist. Paul von Hindenburg, called from retirement in 1914, efficiently executed Ludendorff's plans and became Germany's foremost field commander.

Trench warfare in World War I. Here, a German outpost is going into action against a British advance.

vinced, they could knock Russia out of the war. However, the strategy makers in Germany believed that the conditions in the west were too unsatisfactory to allow the front there to be weakened. So no reinforcements were sent to Ludendorff, and the knockout blow was postponed. Although entrenchment and stalemate did not develop, the commitment of German armies in the east prevented a grand unification of German might and thus indirectly contributed to the stalemate in France.

Stalemate did not necessarily mean inaction. On the contrary, each side periodically mounted gigantic offensives. Usually these assaults were opened with earthshaking artillery barrages, which were intended to force the enemy to abandon its entrenched forward positions. They were followed by an attacking infantry, which used bayonets, rifles, machine guns, grenades, and often, after the spring of 1915, poison gas. In most of these offensives the killed, mutilated, and captured numbered in the tens of thousands; in some cases they numbered in the hundreds of thousands. For example, in February 1916, the Germans launched an attack in the Verdun region. For more than four months the two armies grappled in a indescribable embrace of death and destruction. On July 11, the Germans gave up the attack. The ground gained was slight, hardly to be measured in acres.

German casualties numbered about 300,000; French losses were even higher. The next month the Allies (mainly the British) opened an offensive of their own in the Somme sector. It ground on for about five months. In November it "gradually ran out in mud and rain." For a net advance of about six miles, the British and French sacrificed about 600,000 lives. The German loss was around 500,000.

English Action in Turkey, and on the Sea

Two developments led England to open a new front: the deadlock in the west (which the entrance of Italy on the side of the Allies hardly affected) and the inability of Russia to do much more than keep her armies in the field. As we have seen, Turkey had come into the war on the side of the Central Powers. In 1915, England decided to attack the "soft underbelly of Europe" and, hopefully, to gain Turkey as a base. From Turkey she might strike a decisive blow against Austria-Hungary as well as threaten Germany from the east. Naval action began in February, followed in April by the landing of about 75,000 troops on the Gallipoli peninsula. The tempo of the offensive was so slow, however, that Turkish battalions were given time to occupy defensive positions from which they could not be driven. Another attempt was made in the fall with the same result. In the end the thrust from the south came to nothing.*

On the sea another kind of deadlock developed. England's Grand Fleet, although in control of the seas, was vulnerable to mines and torpedoes. Germany's High Seas Fleet, which had been built into an instrument of tremendous power by von Tirpitz, looked forward to the day of battle. But *der Tag* had to be carefully chosen; the en-

* Before the war ended, many other "fronts" were opened—in Mesopotamia, in the Balkans, in Africa, in Asia. These must be passed over in a brief study such as ours. For accounts of the fighting in these areas, see appropriate titles in the bibliography at the end of this chapter.

counter, that is, must wait for a time when the British navy had already been seriously weakened by mines and torpedoes. Britain's naval strategy was simply to keep the world's sea-lanes open; the destruction of the German fleet, although always something for British Sea Lords to dream about, was a secondary consideration.

Consequently, neither German nor British naval commanders were eager to rush into battle. Indeed, they were so cautious that only one major encounter occurred during the entire war. On May 31, 1916, the two fleets met not far off the Norwegian coast. In the Battle of Jutland, as it is called, each side took care not to expose itself to unnecessary risks. From late afternoon until darkness fell, they "groped towards each other, touched, broke away, touched again." Tonnage loss was greater for the British, but the Germans retreated to home waters, never to offer battle again. Britannia, it seemed, continued to rule the waves.

But not quite. If England was supreme on the seas, Germany was supreme under them. Cruising beneath the waters of the world's major sea-lanes, her submarines increasingly made Allied shipping a hazardous business. By the fall of 1915, U-boat activity had assumed serious proportions. And by the last months of 1916 Germany was sinking an average of 300,-000 tons a month, much more than the Allies could replace. England was especially vulnerable to the submarine menace because she literally lived on imported food, of which she could normally carry only a two-months' supply. For her a tight and continuing submarine blockade spelled certain defeat. In retaliation the British government announced its intention to step up seizure of all "contraband" goods. In practice this meant that England would decide who might send what produce to whom.

As Britain's definition of contraband became increasingly arbitrary and all-embracing, her relations with the United States became strained almost to the breaking point. It is pointless to conjecture what the result might have been, because a German action in May 1915 reversed the situation. A large English passenger liner (with a partial cargo of munitions) sailed from New York bound for England. Before its departure, German officials publicly warned American would-be passengers that the liner (the *Lusitania*) would be traveling in what the German government considered a war zone. Several hundred Americans nonetheless booked passage, presumably in the belief that the Germans were bluffing. They were not. On May 7, the *Lusitania* was torpedoed just off the Irish coast. More than 1000 passengers lost their lives, including about 130 Americans. Pres-

This notice appeared in New York newspapers just before the Lusitania *sailed for England. Few people took the warning seriously.*

NOTICE!

TRAVELLERS intending to embark on the Atlantic voyage are reminded that a state of war exists between Germany and her allies and Great Britain and her allies; that the zone of war includes the waters adjacent to the British Isles; that, in accordance with formal notice given by the Imperial German Government, vessels flying the flag of Great Britain, or of any of her allies, are liable to destruction in those waters and that travellers sailing in the war zone on ships of Great Britain or her allies do so at their own risk.

IMPERIAL GERMAN EMBASSY

WASHINGTON, D. C., APRIL 22, 1915.

ident Wilson, in a series of strong notes (so strong that his secretary of state resigned), demanded not only reparation but an official declaration that such action would not be repeated. Warned by its ambassador in Washington that the President was preparing to break off relations, the German government finally announced that there would be no more sinkings without warning. It also promised that when vessels were sunk care would be taken to rescue noncombatants.

War-Weariness

After two years of trench warfare the belligerents seemed locked in a Laocoön embrace that could be neither broken nor ended. Offensives and counteroffensives on the Western Front killed and wounded hundreds of thousands of men without changing the fundamental position of either side. On the Eastern Front, Germany consistently defeated but could not destroy Russian forces. On the sea, Allied navies remained unchallenged, but by late 1916 English and French shipping again began to suffer losses that seriously weakened the *Entente's* home and fighting fronts. More states continued to be drawn into the struggle (for example, Rumania and Greece on the Allied side in the fall of 1916), at the same time that a spreading war-weariness made itself felt among all peoples. Political changes reflected the growing discontent. Lloyd George replaced Asquith in December 1916. In France, Briand succeeded Viviani (October 1915) and was himself succeeded by Ribot, Painlevé, and finally (November 1917) Clemenceau. In Italy, Salandra gave way to Boselli, who was replaced by Orlando (October 1917). In other countries the same somewhat frantic search went on for leaders who might bring the bloody impasse to an end. The German Chancellor, Bethmann-Hollweg, was forced to resign (1917) when he objected to the ever-increasing interference in national policy-making by Lu-

dendorff. His successors were Ludendorff's puppets who danced to the General's strident, martial tunes.

American Involvement

In 1916 President Wilson sent his most trusted adviser, Colonel Edward M. House, to Europe in an attempt to sound out the powers. However, neither *Entente* nor Alliance leaders showed a willingness to state terms that were clear of ambiguous qualifications or reservations. Unknown at the time to both Wilson and House, secret treaties had been concluded among the Allies, which provided for the virtual partition of the Austro-Hungarian and Ottoman Empires. (Before the war ended, Wilson had learned of the existence of these treaties and some of their provisions.) Later in the year the President tried again. This time he publicly requested the belligerents to announce negotiable terms. In January 1917, the Allies replied with demands so extreme that Wilson himself could not accept them. The German government entered into confidential conversations with the President which revealed that government's unreasonable claims. Anyway, before practicable reconciliation could be seriously attempted, the German High Command forced a policy on its government that not only ended the negotiations but brought America into the war.

For some time Ludendorff and his staff had believed that only unrestricted submarine warfare could bring German victory. Civilian authorities opposed resumption of such warfare on the grounds that it would at once make the United States a belligerent. Ludendorff argued that this consideration, even though true, was irrelevant since unrestricted use of the submarine meant certain English capitulation within six or eight weeks, long before the United States could mobilize or make her influence felt on the Continent. And with England out of the war, France could not endure. The Chancellor and his civilian advisers were anything but enthusiastic about the proposal, but they were not in a position to counter it for, by then, Ludendorff had assumed virtually dictatorial powers.

Thus on January 31, 1917, the German government announced resumption of unrestricted submarine warfare. Three days later the United States broke off diplomatic relations with Germany. President Wilson indicated that he would not ask Congress for a declaration of war until the Germans had actually put their policy into practice. When they did—and they did it promptly and energetically—the President, on April 6, 1917, asked a willing Congress to declare that a state of war existed with Germany.

German troops cutting barbed wire in no-man's-land.

Allied Resurgence

The first results of Germany's resumption of unrestricted submarine warfare seemed to prove the soundness of Ludendorff's strategy. In April 1917, U-boats destroyed nearly one million tons of Allied shipping. English food supplies were, by the government's own (later) admission, sufficient to feed the country for only six weeks.

About this time the French, attempting a grand offensive, suffered a crushing defeat in what is called the Third Battle of Champagne. Their repulse was so complete and their losses so heavy that whole regiments of troops mutinied. The British admiralty was forced to yield to Lloyd George's demand for immediate adoption of the convoy system, which was simple in concept and, from the beginning, highly effective—the assignment of destroyers, torpedo boats, and other warcraft to guard merchant ships on their Atlantic and Channel crossings. Sinkings continued, of course, but not on the scale required by Germany's great gamble.

On the other hand, the Allied blockade of Germany became so severe that in 1917 food riots broke out in Berlin. The encirclement of Germany, which had formed the subject of so many of the Kaiser's harangues, assumed a new and crippling form. German armies were still in France and were still winning victories, but the victories brought neither bread nor fuel to the home front. Nor did they seem to promise a decisive change in the overall military situation. The feeling grew that the war was a kind of cosmic curse—ceaseless and, beyond the bloody and monotonous capture and recapture of villages and stretches of no-man's-land, senseless. In July 1917, the Reichstag, by an almost 2:1 vote, passed a resolution that called on the government to work for "a peace of understanding and the permanent reconciliation of the people," innocent of "forced acquisitions of territory and political . . . oppressions."

In the meantime, the immense resources of America were steadily being funneled into France and Britain. The first contingent of American troops, under General John J. Pershing, landed in France two months after Congress had declared war. Within a year two million American soldiers were in Europe.

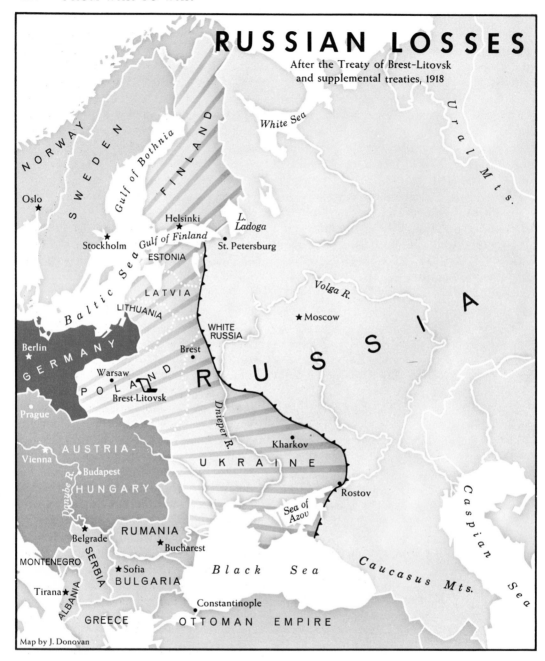

RUSSIAN LOSSES

After the Treaty of Brest-Litovsk
and supplemental treaties, 1918

Map by J. Donovan

Withdrawal of Russia: Brest Litovsk

In the spring of 1918, Russia and Rumania signed treaties of peace with the Central Powers. In the Treaty of Brest Litovsk, Russia suffered immense territorial losses. She was forced to recognize Poland as an "independent" nation. The Ukraine, Russia's vast breadbasket, was set up as a "sovereign" republic. The independence of Finland and the Baltic States—Estonia, Latvia, and Lithuania—was conceded. In the Caucasus region, generous territories were ceded to Turkey. The harsh treaty clearly foretold what was in store for the Allies if they should lose the war. The Treaty of Bucharest was also definitely punitive. The whole of Dobruja was sliced off and given to Bulgaria. Under terms of a ninety-year lease Germany took over all of Rumania's oil wells. Territory adjacent to Transylvania was given to Austria-Hungary.

On the surface it appeared that the position of the Central Powers had been greatly strengthened. But the gains were more illusory than real. The number of troops required to garrison the eastern areas, as finally determined by the German High Command, turned out to be so large that the Western Front received far fewer divisions than had been hoped for. Food and supplies were indeed siphoned off from the east, but they did not make up the enormous losses inflicted by the blockade. Any uplift in German and Austro-Hungarian morale was more than countered by the stiffening of Allied will provoked by the harsh terms of the treaties and by the substantial change that they effected in Wilson's attitude toward the German and Austro-Hungarian peoples.

Two months before the Brest Litovsk Treaty was signed, President Wilson laid before Congress his proposals for a just peace—the famous Fourteen Points.* His timing was motivated by twin hopes: that Russia could be persuaded to remain in the war, and that the German people could be weaned from allegiance to their power-mad warlords. In Point Six the President said: "The treatment accorded Russia by her sister nations in the months to come will be the acid test of their good will, of their comprehension of her needs as distinguished from their own interests. . . ." Speaking of Germany, in Point Fourteen he said: "We have no jealousy of German greatness. . . . We do not wish to injure her or to block in any way her legitimate influence or power. . . . Neither do we presume to suggest to her any alteration or

* For a summary of the "points," see *infra*, p. 737.

modification of her institutions." Brest Litovsk changed all that. A few months after its signing the President announced what amounted to a fifteenth Point. In a public address delivered at Mount Vernon in July 1918, he declared, in effect, that the Central Powers must substitute democratic institutions for autocratic institutions before peace terms could be discussed. We cannot know whether President Wilson would have been able to bring his colleagues at the peace conference to a moderate reasonableness, if there had not been a Brest Litovsk Treaty. It is certain that because of it, the President's new attitude encouraged a harsher interpretation of his original peace terms.

Germany's Last Throes

By the end of 1917, the German General Staff had become convinced that submarine warfare could not force a decision. Two alternatives remained: capitulation to the Allies before the military strength of the Central Powers was shattered, thus (hopefully) assuring good peace terms; or a final all-out assault to force Allied capitulation. Ludendorff, now the real ruler of Germany, chose the second alternative and, during the winter of 1917 to 1918, prepared for a last grand offensive. The offensive opened in March 1918 with a ferocity that sent the Allies reeling. In less than a week the British, who bore the brunt of the initial attack, were forced to retreat about forty miles. A second attack on another sector of the British line was also successful. Made desperate by impending catastrophe, the Allies finally gave the supreme command of their combined forces to Marshal Ferdinand Foch, who immediately coordinated holding operations along the whole of the Western Front. Shortly thereafter, he mounted a massive counteroffensive that broke the back of the German effort.

In September, a multinational army under the command of General Franchet d'Esperey opened a new front in Greece.

The Chicago Daily Tribune's *front-page story of the end of World War I.*

Overwhelmed by Allied forces, Bulgaria, the smallest of the Central Powers, asked for an armistice (September 29) and dropped out of the war. With Allied armies now pouring in the back door of Austria-Hungary, a negotiated peace was out of the question. On November 3, the Dual Monarchy laid down its arms and accepted Allied terms.

A few days before the capitulation, the crews of the High Seas Fleet, which was ordered by the German command to put to sea in the desperate hope of somewhere gaining a victory, had mutinied. As though awaiting this kind of signal, sporadic revolution broke out in Germany. On November 8, Foch received German representatives to discuss armistice terms. On November 9, the abdication of the Kaiser was announced. Two days later German commissioners were received again by Foch in a railroad coach in Compiegne Forest. With the scraping of pen on armistice papers, on November 11, 1918, the four years of fighting ended.

Consequences of the War

What had the Great War wrought? For the Austro-Hungarian Empire, it brought not vigor and stability but complete destruction. For Russia, not the key to the Straits but defeat and revolution. For Germany, not a place in the sun but humiliation, a huge indemnity, partition of its empire, and the collapse of its monarchical regime. For Italy, the satisfaction of some (although by no means all) of its irredentist claims, economic chaos, and political disruption. For Turkey, imperial demise and political upheaval. For England, continued control of the seas, more color on the map, temporary confirmation of her claim to leadership in the balance-of-power system, a colossal burden of debt, and a new rival (the United States) in the exploitation of the world's markets. For France, Alsace-Lorraine, revenge, ravaged earth, and the haunting knowledge that she had been rescued from defeat and German domination by the combined might of England and America. For the United States, vindication of neutral rights, the overthrow of German military autocracy, assured rank as a world power, emergence as the world's creditor, and a great weariness of everything European. For the Balkan peoples, the war brought nationhood, independence, and new quarrels over boundary lines gained or lost.

A German victory would have fastened the yoke of militarism and autocracy upon Europe. However, Allied victory did not prevent the ultimate spread of both throughout the world. Four years after the war that Wilson had hoped would make the world safe for democracy, Fascism was in power in Italy. Even earlier, in Russia one kind of autocracy had been substituted for another. Although ethnically united and free, most of the new—as well as the old—Balkan and Baltic states were run by military "strong men," as was the new Poland. Moreover, national armaments and reliance on them as instruments of national policy increased rather than decreased.

Perhaps the most significant conse-quence of World War I was that it brought to a climax the process of the West's changing value patterns. In the century before the war, two divergent *Weltan-schauungen* anomalously cradled the de-veloping events and purposes of Western society. One general outlook was charac-terized by political and economic liberal-ism, hopeful striving for universal peace, and general optimism regarding the "hu-man condition." The other stressed the in-evitability, even desirability, of heroic vio-lent force in the solution of human prob-lems, chauvinistic nationalism, and the need to keep in sharp focus the refractory nature of the human animal. The war gave strong impetus to the second outlook.

For four years much of the world had lived in a feverish atmosphere of hate. To the Allies, the Germans were inhuman Huns; to the Germans, England was per-fidious Albion. Long before the war was over, hate had become the great morale builder, the fundamental and indispensable ingredient of patriotism, and the basic force that would determine who should "win" the war. On November 11, 1918, at the stroke of a pen, the slaughterhouse was abandoned. Guns were stacked, armies were demobilized; humankind was ex-pected to resume the ways of peace. But the inner life of man is not so quickly changed. A year after the armistice was signed and "peace" had returned, William Butler Yeats gave expression to this di-lemma:

> Now days are dragon-ridden, the nightmare
> Rides upon sleep: a drunken soldiery
> Can leave the mother, murdered at her door,
> To crawl in her own blood, and go scot-free;
> The night can sweat with terror as before
> We pieced our thoughts into philosophy,
> And planned to bring the world under a rule,
> Who are but weasels fighting in a hole.[2]

In 1922, Sigmund Freud said of the war: "No event ever destroyed so much of the heritage of mankind . . . or so thoroughly debased what is highest." Thirty years later an American historian, Peter Viereck, put it even more bluntly: "World War I is the worst single catastrophe in human history."

The Unsettling Settlement

Writing the "Peace"

Against this variegated background of old-world hates and new-world ignorance and indifference, of dissolving empires and emerging states, of greedy hopes of the victors and the sullen bitterness of the van-quished, the Peace Conference opened at Paris on January 18, 1919. Twenty-seven Allied and Associated powers were repre-sented by seventy delegates. Ostensibly, they met to translate the Wilsonian pro-gram, on the basis of which the Germans had surrendered, into a treaty of peace. The points of this program may be paraphrased as follows:

1. The renunciation by all powers of the practice of secret diplomacy.

2. Freedom of the seas, "alike in peace as in war."

3. Equality of trade conditions among the powers.

4. Reduction of national armaments.

5. The settlement of colonial claims ac-cording to the wishes of the colonial peo-ples, as well as "the equitable claims of the government whose title is to be deter-mined."

6. The evacuation of all Russian territory by Germans and Austrians, and recognition of the right of Russia to determine inde-pendently her own political development.

7. Restoration of Belgium.

8. Evacuation of French territory and the return to her of Alsace-Lorraine.

9. Ethnic readjustments of the frontiers of Italy.

10. Self-determination of the peoples

2. M. L. Ronsenthal, ed., *Selected Poems of William Butler Yeats,* The Macmillan Company, New York, 1962, p. 109.

who made up the former Austro-Hungarian Empire.

11. Evacuation of the Balkan States, and international guarantees to strengthen their political and economic independence and territorial integrity.

12. Self-determination of the non-Turkish populations of the Ottoman Empire.

13. An independent Polish state, with secure access to the sea.

14. Creation of a League of Nations to protect the political independence and territorial integrity of all states, large and small.

Before agreeing to accept this program as the basis of a general settlement, England stipulated that "freedom of the seas" must not be understood to restrict her naval supremacy—a reservation which, of course, canceled this "point." The Allied powers also reserved the right to demand and secure reparations for war damages caused by Germany. Germany was informed of these reservations and, perforce, accepted them.

The actual treaty that finally emerged contained many provisions that were contrary to the terms of surrender. Clearly Allied statesmen had originally agreed to Wilson's Fourteen Points only because they were hard pressed on all battlefronts and because their peoples sympathized with the spirit and provisions of the Wilsonian program. (By the same token, Germany and her allies welcomed the program when the fortunes of war had turned against them.) For four months, until the treaty was put in final form in early May, Wilson fought with his colleagues over its terms. The provisions stipulating the creation of a League of Nations were given prompt attention. Working closely with Lord Robert Cecil, Wilson and other members of the committee selected to draft the League's Covenant spent weeks devising an instrument which would point the way to a warless world. Some old-world diplomats (including Clemenceau) gave assent to the venture merely to please Wilson and to expedite what they considered the real business of the Conference. In its final form the Covenant provided for a world organization made up of a General Secretariat, an Assembly, and a Council. All members of the League were admitted to representation in the Assembly. The five major powers— England, France, Italy, Japan, and the United States—were given permanent seats in the Council with instructions to elect four lesser powers to share term representation. The main business of the League was to prevent the outbreak of aggressive war. To this end, it was given the power to investigate quarrels that were likely to lead to war and to recommend settlements. If any League member went to war in violation of the Covenant's provisions and of the Assembly's and Council's procedures, it was considered, *ipso facto,* to have made war on all members of the League. Only the Council could decide whether and when military sanctions were to be used against an aggressor state, and then only after unanimous agreement (unless the designated aggressor was itself represented on the Council).

In the main, Wilson was pleased with both the Covenant (or constitution) of the League and its general structure. It was, however, the only major achievement of the Conference that did please him. At England's insistence he was forced to concede British control of the seas. The harsh French demands appalled him—partial dismemberment of Germany, astronomical indemnities, annexation of the Saar basin with its rich coal mines, and long-term occupation of the defeated country. He considered Italian claims equally extravagant, including those that called for cession of large areas of the Austro-Hungarian Empire, which had never been part of Italy and which contained only a minority of her nationals. Japan demanded control of Shantung as well as virtual overlordship of all of China (which, ironically, was one of the "victorious" Allies).

In the end a series of compromises saved the Conference from falling apart. Many of them cost the President spiritual agony. He agreed to indemnity provisions that went beyond what he believed to be either just or payable. He accepted Italy's Dalmatian claims and Japan's take-over of Shantung. Other provisions to which he reluctantly agreed were French exploitation of the Saar basin, Allied occupation of Germany, and the cession of certain German territories to Poland (some of which clearly contained a majority German population). Although Wilson was convinced that Germany deserved to be punished, he felt that the treaty spelled out a Punic peace. Nevertheless, he hoped that a strong League of Nations would ultimately rectify what he considered the treaty's grossest wrongs.

Several other major provisions of the treaty should be noted. Article 231 stated that Germany and her allies were solely responsible for causing the war. All German colonies were ceded to the Allies (as "mandated" territories, ostensibly under the supervision of the League). The German army was limited to 100,000 men; her navy was restricted to six warships, none of them larger than 10,000 tons, and a number of smaller vessels. Construction of military planes, tanks, heavy artillery, and submarines was forbidden. The Rhineland was to be demilitarized in perpetuity. Reparation charges were to include payment for all damages to Allied civilians and to their property (the total bill finally came to about $33,000,000,000). In addition, Germany was charged with all expenses incurred by the occupying troops. A corridor of land ceded to Poland divided Germany into two parts. All merchant ships of 1600 tons or more were surrendered to the Allies. Danzig was detached from Germany and made an international "free" city.

The final draft was presented to the Germans in May. Shocked at the severity of its terms, they refused to sign; Count von Brockdorff-Rantzau, chairman of the delegation, protested that the treaty was a cruel caricature of the Fourteen Points. To insist that Germany alone was responsible

for the war would be the vilest lie, he said. Germany was defeated; she was not, however, so weak as to sign away her honor. But the victors would make no substantial concessions. Faced with a resumption of hostilities for which it was in no way prepared, the government appointed a new commission which, on June 28, 1919, signed the treaty under the most solemn protest.

America Rejects the Treaty

Alone of the Great Powers represented at the Conference, the United States refused ratification. According to the American Constitution, no treaty is valid unless approved by two thirds of the United States Senate. On two occasions the Versailles Treaty was submitted to this body for ratification. In each instance the treaty was approved, but not by the necessary two-thirds majority. Because the League Covenant was inextricably bound up with other terms of the treaty, the United States rejected the world organization for whose creation its President had done so much.

For this failure, the President and certain Republican senators bear mutual responsibility. When Mr. Wilson went to Paris, he was advised by his own friends to take with him several Republican leaders, or at least one outstanding Republican senator. The President refused. The Republicans, he felt, would try to make political capital out of both what went on at the Conference and what came out of it. His own great objective, he believed, was above partisan machination. Thus seemingly disassociating the Republicans from the "Common Conscience" (and implicitly identifying it with the Democratic conscience!), the President blundered badly. Two outstanding Republicans, Elihu Root and former President William Howard Taft, had actually collaborated with Wilson in his early work on the Covenant. Others, such as Charles Evans Hughes, Mr. Wilson's opponent in the 1916 election, were certainly sympathetic to the idea of a world association of nations.

By deciding to head personally the American delegation in Paris, the President opened himself to another, perhaps more debatable, charge. Had he stayed home, it was argued, he would have preserved the world's picture of him as the great impartial arbiter. By entering the arena as a contestant, he perforce lost this advantage. Finally, the President's personality undeniably contributed to the Senate's repudiation of the treaty. Often high-handed and even haughty in dealing with his own associates and colleagues, he alienated many who genuinely wished to collaborate with him. Those who opposed him, or whom he suspected (but not always correctly) of opposing him, soon learned how nakedly autocratic the great democrat could be.

On the other hand, a number of Republican senators must share responsibility for America's rejection of the treaty. This was especially true of Henry Cabot Lodge, whose intense personal dislike of Wilson amounted to a kind of irrational hatred. As chairman of the powerful Senate Committee on Foreign Relations, Lodge was in a particularly strategic position to strike at Wilson. He took full advantage of the opportunity. At his instigation fourteen amendments, some of them needlessly crippling, were tacked onto the treaty as the price of Senate approval. Wilson indignantly refused to pay the price.

In a last effort to force the Republican-dominated Senate to ratify the work of the Peace Conference, the President "went to the people." In early September 1919, he set out on a whistle-stop campaign designed to let the country know what the treaty was all about and in what danger it was. Before he had completed his tour, he suffered a physical breakdown and was hurriedly brought back to Washington. Democratic leaders, knowing that the treaty as Wilson wanted it was doomed, begged the President to accept a half loaf rather than none. Turning his face sternly away from this plea, he demanded all or

nothing. When the vote was taken in November of 1919, more than twenty Democratic senators bolted and voted for the treaty as revised. All together there were 55 ayes against 39 noes, seven votes short of the required two-thirds majority. The Senate had spoken. The treaty was dead. Not until nearly two years later did the United States sign a separate, "covenantless" peace with Germany (July 1921). Ironically, the Versailles Treaty, undergirded by a Covenant that was largely the work of Wilson, was promptly signed by the Allied powers which originally had so critically viewed that Covenant.

Other Treaties

Treaties with the remaining belligerent powers, named after the suburbs of Paris in which they were signed, were concluded in the period of September 1919 to August 1920. Austria signed the Treaty of St. Germain (September 10, 1919), which officially dissolved the old Austro-Hungarian Empire. The new so-called succession states of Czechoslovakia and Yugoslavia were granted recognition by Austria, as was a reconstituted Poland. Although Austria desired organic union with Germany, she was expressly forbidden this privilege by the treaty (except by permission of the League Council—an unlikely development). Of all the peace settlements, this one made the least sense. Granted that the old Empire had been an amalgam of discontented peoples, it had at least provided the Austrians, as corulers of it, with a political excuse for being. As a great free-trading area, the Empire had also afforded Austria an economic base for existence. The St. Germain settlement, by forbidding union with Germany while (in effect) ringing the newly shorn state (now about the size of South Carolina) with formidable tariff barriers, doomed Austria to political and economic frustration.

The Hungarians experienced similar treatment. By the Treaty of Trianon (July 4, 1920), Hungary too became a truncated state, retaining only one fourth of her old territories and one third of her prewar population. Cessions to Italy and Yugoslavia completely deprived her of access to the sea. Although the old Empire no longer existed, the new Hungary was forced to assume a portion of the Empire's debts in addition to reparations payments. Her army was reduced to 35,000 men.

By the terms of the Treaty of Neuilly (November 27, 1919), Bulgaria (the only defeated nation to remain a monarchy) lost her Mediterranean outlet, assumed a reparations debt of nearly one half billion dollars, and was forced to recognize the independence of Yugoslavia, to which she also ceded some territory. Her army was limited by the treaty to 20,000 men.

The original settlement with Turkey (the Treaty of Sèvres, 1920) completely destroyed the Ottoman Empire. Palestine and Mesopotamia were mandated to Britain, and Syria to France. Other areas of the Empire were either granted independence (Armenia, for example), or occupied until a future decision by plebiscite about its disposition, or given outright to the victors (for example, Rhodes and other Dodecanese islands were given to Italy, and Thrace passed to Greece). The Straits were demilitarized and placed under international control. However, nationalist forces in Turkey, under the leadership of Mustapha Kemal, refused to accept the settlement. In the civil war that followed, Kemal's revolutionary armies overthrew the Sultanate and set up a Republic. Acting in the name of the Allies, Greek forces invaded Anatolia. Two years of fighting ended with the Greeks being driven into the sea. Allied and Turkish representatives then sat down to rewrite the terms of peace. The biggest problem was the question of what to do with the large Turkish population in Thrace and the substantial Greek settlements in western Turkey. It was finally agreed to resettle each group in its original land—a massive exchange of population unparalleled in modern times.

In July 1923, a new settlement was reached in the Lausanne Treaty. The Allies agreed to evacuate all Turkish territories; in return Turkey relinquished its claim to non-Turkish territories occupied by the Allies during the war. It is not without significance that the Lausanne Treaty, the only truly negotiated treaty to come out of the war, proved to be the most durable one.

Consequences of the Settlements

Some of the changes effected by the peace settlements contributed toward a healthier European community and even toward a potentially healthier world community.

The new League of Nations was a loose association of sovereign states, which was designed principally to provide a forum for the discussion of world problems and, hopefully, an apparatus to adjudicate international disputes. It was made up of three main bodies: the Assembly, composed of delegates from all member states; the Council, whose membership included representatives from the Great Powers on a permanent basis and (eventually) eleven representatives of smaller powers elected periodically by the permanent members; a Secretariat, made up of a Secretary-General and a host of civil servants to man its many bureaus. Under terms of the Covenant, the League was empowered to deal with any threat to the peace and to take "any action that may be deemed wise and effectual to safeguard the peace of nations." Its supporters hoped that the discussion of controversies in open meetings of the Assembly or Council would lead to their peaceful settlements. If it did not, "sanctions" could be voted against recalcitrant states—economic, political, and, if needed, military. In later chapters we shall note how the new "parliament of man" functioned in several specific and significant tests of its strength.

The destruction of the Austro-Hungarian, German, Russian, and Ottoman Empires meant that their subject peoples could set up national housekeeping for themselves. Poland was reborn. Yugoslavia was formed by the union of Serbians, Croatians, and Slovenes. Bohemians and Slovakians (and, less felicitously, Ruthenians) united to create Czechoslovakia. Albania, born of the Balkan wars, was recognized as an independent state. The movement for national self-determination did not come to perfect fruition, of course. Czechoslovakia's three million German Sudetenlanders were none too happy in a non-German state. Other Germans, in the Tyrol, violently objected to their forced transmutation into Italian citizens. Russians in Bessarabia protested their being turned into Rumanians. Such discontent was shared by other ethnic minorities which had been swept into this nation or that by the treaty makers. Other unfortunate features also developed out of the application of the nationality principle. Austria, for example, became a head without a body. Cut off from her economic trunk, she became, within three or four years, practically bankrupt. In the old days of the Empire, she had imported relatively little coal and iron, livestock, and grains. With Czechoslovakia, Yugoslavia, and especially Hungary set up as separate nations, Austria now found herself in the unenviable position of requiring huge imports without a fraction of the funds necessary to pay for them. To a lesser, but still serious degree, the same plight was experienced by Hungary. Even the newly freed nations found that the economic price of freedom came high. If the old Empire had been a kind of ethnic prison, it had at the same time been a great free-trading area, which had brought a prosperity that they now found hard to come by.

The democratic movement also made some progress, at least for a time. Germany, Russia, Austria-Hungary, and Turkey all lost their crowned heads. Almost frantic attention was given to the writing (or rewriting) of constitutions. At least in theory, the doctrine of government by consent of the governed flourished in areas where for centuries autocracy or absolutism had been accepted as the natural order of things. And, of course, the League of Nations gave flesh, grafted and weak as it was, to the once utopian concept of the Parliament of Man. Not even the Roman Empire in its most "democratic" phase gave so much promise of realizing man's universal political brotherhood.

Seeds of Trouble

However, the unsettling features of the Great Settlement were ominous. As we have seen, Germany was forced to admit that she and her allies were solely responsible for the war. The injustice and hypocrisy of the charge, freely (although always privately) confessed by Allied statesmen, created mounting resentment among all Germans. Damning documents of *Entente* diplomatic maneuvering, published by the Bolshevik regime, gave added point to their bitter protests.

Moreover, reparations charges, as finally reckoned by the Allies, came to more than thirty billion dollars. This accounting was so unrealistic that a number of Allied economists entered strenuous objections to it. One third of this amount, they argued, was the most that Germany could be expected to pay and still remain solvent; some believed that even this figure was far too high. To meet annual payments, the Germans were forced to use funds that they otherwise could have used to liquidate their huge internal debt and to develop a normal peacetime economy. The attempt to meet both external and internal demands led the government to an extravagant use of printing-press money. Within a few years, spiraling inflation brought the nation into almost complete bankruptcy, with effects that we shall consider later.

The creation of an independent Poland, with "secure access to the sea," resulted in a geographically divided Germany. The thrusting Polish Corridor, which separated East Prussia from the rest of Germany, proved a source of endless friction between the two states. In addition to the transit problem, the division caused serious ethnic dislocations. Throughout various regions of the Corridor there were scattered large pockets of settlers whose "Germanness" was rooted in the soil and in the centuries. Now they had suddenly become Polish citizens. Both they and their compatriots on the other side of the Corridor naturally looked forward to a day of reunion—and of reckoning.

Other grievances aggravated Europe's postwar discontents. The Allies had promised to set up and carry out a general disarmament program, consonant with their professed aim of building a warless world. This, indeed, was their justification for insisting that the military establishments of their former foes should be drastically reduced. But the victors showed little inclination to act upon this promise. Pleading her insular needs, England continued to maintain a powerful navy. France kept a large conscript army poised along the Rhine.* On the other side of Germany, Poland, which was soon to become an ally of France, raised an army more than twice as large as that of Germany. Disarmament, it seemed, was for the defeated. More than ever Germans came to believe that the Wilsonian program, heartily endorsed by the Allies when the going was rough, was a sham, a trick to achieve by the pen what they never could have gained by the sword.

The Russian government also found certain parts of the Great Settlement anything but satisfactory. The Allies, it was true, had forced Germany to disavow the infamous Treaty of Brest Litovsk. But they had also concerted to detach from Russia large territories along her western frontier and to set them up as buffer states—Finland, Estonia, Latvia, and Lithuania. The chief complaint of the Bolsheviks was not that these states

should become independent units. Indeed, at that time (say, 1917) the Soviet government was leaning over backwards to honor the principle of self-determination. What disturbed it were Allied motivations and purposes. Clearly, the Allies considered Bolshevism a disease that must be kept from spreading. The new small states in reality served as agents of quarantine, as a *cordon sanitaire.*

Nor did treaty settlements give satisfaction to Italy. Always the poorest of the Great Powers, she came out of the war with colossal new debts piled onto the old ones. Like all other belligerents, she had floated loans to buy implements of war that literally were made for destruction. All of the warring powers, of course, had suffered economic losses. But Italy, retarded industrially and lacking the resources to meet new burdens, found herself quite unable to redeem her debts or to provide adequate employment for her people. Politically she was little better off. Launched on at least a quasi-liberal course by the statesmen of the *risorgimento,* her poverty and lack of liberal traditions had combined to transmute incipient democracy into a political wasteland of corruption and factional parties. Although she came out of the great conflict on the "winning" side, she did not feel like a winner. And even though her territorial acquisitions were substantial, they did not measure up to what her ambitious politicians had led her to expect. Out of these circumstances came bitterness, festering frustrations—and *Il Duce.*

War as Revolution

In the opening section of this chapter we noted a strong prewar revolutionary ferment at work in various countries. During the early years of the war, this force was largely dissipated by the charged emotions of nationalism. But it was not destroyed. As the war turned from movement to stalemate, patriotic passions subsided and the discontents of the prewar years revived. In

---

* Justified by France by the failure of the United States to join with Britain in a guarantee of France's territorial integrity.

a later chapter we shall examine in some detail the Russian revolution of 1917, which was the most dramatic explosion of these discontents. Here we merely note the revolution as both a foretoken and a catalyst of the politico-economic storms that were to buffet Europe at the end of the war and for a long time afterward. In England the so-called "forces of movement"—that is, forces that desired the overthrow of established vested interests in favor of a liberal "establishment"—gained some influence and power. In France the Socialist party "took courage and before long became the nucleus of a united front of all parties and factions of movement."[3] In Germany the Social Democratic party became vocal and demanded, for example, a reexamination of the whole question of German war aims.

Radical or liberal leaders were not alone in giving expression to the feeling that much more than military decisions were involved in the great struggle. Men of the old order also sensed that the war had unleashed forces that seemed likely to change much of the fabric of Western civilization. Count Czernin, a leading Hungarian statesman, predicted that "the coming generation [would] not call the drama of the last five years the World War, but the world revolution which it [would] realize began with the world war." The German conservative leader Gustav Stresemann "saw the war as part of a world revolution which would profoundly stir all aspects of life [and] predicted that the revolution was destined to continue long after the formal end of hostilities."[4]

It would be a serious misreading of history to see World War I exclusively as one act in a continuing drama of collectivist revolution; our detailed examination of its background should save us from this elementary misjudgment. Nevertheless, unless we understand that from 1917 on the war assumed strong revolutionary overtones, we cannot hope to make sense out of the cataclysmic events that followed it: Communism in Russia; Fascism in Italy, Spain, and a number of central European states; Nazism in Germany; faltering socialism in Britain and France; Gandhism in India; New Dealism in the United States. Throughout the nineteenth century, the forces of industrialism and nationalism worked changes in the Old Order—in class structures, political systems, and the stability of empires. The war gave impetus to the tides of change. State planning in the production and distribution of industrial goods, foretaste of the affluent society for those on the home front, growing recognition of the bungling and vincibility of ruling classes—these merged with renascent restiveness in the later years of the war to make the strife that circled the globe both war and revolution.

SELECTED READINGS

Bailey, Thomas A., *Woodrow Wilson and the Lost Peace,* The Macmillan Co., New York, 1944.

A critical interpretation of the Paris Peace Conference, which was written just before the end of World War II to "educate American public opinion to its responsibilities in future peacemaking." Wilson is treated fairly, although, at times, severely. As usual, the author's style makes for easy reading.

Bonsal, Stephen, *Unfinished Business,* Doubleday, Doran & Co., New York, 1944.

The author served as interpreter for Wilson and House at many conferences during the period of peace-writing in Paris after World War I. The book is made up of journal entries that constitute important source material.

Churchill, Winston S., *The World Crisis, 1911–1918,* Odharns Press Ltd., London, 1939, 2 vols.

A close-up view of the coming and the course of the war as seen by a gifted statesman

---

3. Arno J. Mayer, *Political Origins of the New Diplomacy, 1917–1918,* Yale University Press, 1959, p. 5.
4. *Ibid.*

whose rhetoric is compelling, sometimes too much so. But if read with one's guard up, this work is not only one of the most interesting accounts of the great crisis, but one of the most enlightening.

Esposito, Vincent J., ed., *A Concise History of World War I,* Frederick A. Praeger, New York, 1964.
A reprint of various articles on the war published in the 1962 edition of the *Encyclopedia Americana.*

*Halévy, Elie, *The Era of Tyrannies,* translated by R. K. Webb, Anchor Books, Doubleday & Co., New York, 1965.
A reissue of a book originally published in 1938. It is a collection of thought-provoking essays on sociopolitical changes in our century. The section entitled "The World Crisis of 1914–1918" is especially recommended.

Hart, B. H. Liddell, *The Real War, 1914–1918,* Little, Brown & Co., Boston, 1930.
A short, lucid description of the great battles of World War I. The author uses memoirs, diaries, and autobiographical material to correct, as he sees it, the "essentially superficial" history that comes out of a study of formal, official documents.

Mantoux, Etienne, *The Carthaginian Peace, or the Economic Consequences of Mr. Keynes,* Charles Scribner's Sons, New York, 1952.
A savage attack on the "dogmas" of Keynes' *The Economic Consequences of the Peace.*

May, Ernest R., *The World War and American Isolation, 1914–1918,* Harvard University Press, Cambridge, 1959.
A well-organized study of America's tortuous drift toward war. If longer works on the subject cited elsewhere are not used, this one should be.

Mayer, Arno J., *Political Origins of the New Diplomacy, 1917–1918,* Yale University Press, New Haven, 1959.
A long and effectively constructed argument based on the thesis that any worthwhile study of the basic forces at work among the warring powers must give due cognizance to "domestic political determinants" and must deemphasize the traditional "international" war aims of those powers.

Nicolson, Harold, *Peacemaking, 1919,* Harcourt, Brace & Co., New York, 1939.
There is probably no other work on the Paris Conference that is more interesting and scintillating. Moreover, it offers an amplitude of facts, as well as a broad survey of opinions held by the men who made the peace. Yet it must be read with great caution. The author's opinions — especially his view of Woodrow Wilson — need the corrective of broad reading in other works such as James T. Shotwell, *At the Paris Peace Conference,* Macmillan Company, New York, 1937, and Stephen Bonsal, *Unfinished Business* (cited above).

*Smith, Daniel M., *The Great Departure, The United States and World War I, 1914–1920,* John Wiley & Sons, New York, 1965.
A good brief account of how America became involved in the war despite her long tradition of neutrality, and why Americans repudiated the Wilsonian peace.

Tuchman, Barbara W., *The Guns of August,* The Macmillan Co., New York, 1962.
An extraordinarily well-written account of the plans, performances, and blunders of both Allied and German military leaders in the first month of World War I.

Wheeler-Bennett, John, *The Forgotten Peace,* William Morrow Co., New York, 1939.
The only extended study in English of the "Tilsit Peace" made between Germany and Soviet Russia in 1918. It is probably more revealing and more meaningful today than when it was first published.

Asterisk (*) denotes paperback.

27

In the Wake of War:
1919 to 1930s

International Relations, 1919 to 1929

The Troubled Years, 1919 to 1924

Despite the grand stacking of arms and the signing of peace treaties, conflict and anguish harassed the peoples of Europe throughout the early 1920s. For France the taste of victory soon turned sour. In June 1919 she had signed a defensive treaty with England and the United States which aimed to secure her against a future day of German reckoning. Less than six months later the United States Senate, reflecting America's isolationist mood, refused to ratify the treaty. Because Britain's promise of assistance was contingent upon American participation, France naturally felt new fears and frustrations, indeed, became obsessed with the urge to protect her precarious security. To this end she persistently used the League of Nations as an instrument to preserve the new status quo created by the peace treaties. She tried, unsuccessfully, to detach portions of West

Germany and to set them up as puppet states. She concluded pacts with Poland and the states of the Little Entente— Czechoslovakia, Yugoslavia, Rumania— aimed to keep Germany from shaping the potentials of aggression. To the degree that these efforts were effective, German rancor and recalcitrance understandably increased. This reaction, in turn, stimulated new French efforts to keep the defeated nation down, and so the vicious circle went on.

The flaring of a number of little wars increased European tensions. In 1919 Poland and Russia fought over the possession of Vilna, a strategically located city south of the Gulf of Riga. Ultimately the League of Nations intervened and arranged for a plebiscite. When Poland opposed this solution, strained relations and much military bustle developed afresh. The result of an irregularly contrived plebiscite finally gave the city to Poland in 1922.

In 1919 and 1920 conflict spread to the Teschen area, claimed by both Czechoslovakia and Poland. When heavy fighting broke out between the contestants, members of the Allied Council sought to end the struggle by authorizing plebiscitary procedures. But neither side would agree to a ballot decision, and intermittent clashes continued throughout the early months of 1920. A conference of ambassadors finally succeeded in persuading the contestants to divide the territory. Nevertheless, ill will continued to mark relations between the two states up to the outbreak of World War II. In the belief that the Soviet regime was tottering and temporary, the Poles attempted to wrest from Russia the whole of the rich Ukraine. In the spring of 1920, they thrust through the heart of the region and captured Kiev. But the Red Army rallied and launched a counterattack which penetrated deeply into Polish territory. Aided by France, Poland stopped the Russian advance and again pushed to the east. When it finally became apparent that neither side could hold gains beyond its own borders, a compromise peace was negotiated in the Treaty of Riga (1921).

Greece and Turkey had long quarreled over their minorities in Anatolia and Thrace. In March 1921, a Greek thrust threatened Ankara, the nationalist capital. When it was finally halted by the determined Turks (aided by Soviet Russia) the Allies sought to bring the fighting to an end and to rewrite the Treaty of Sèvres. But a counterthrust by the Turks defeated the Greeks and forced a conference that ultimately satisfied most of their demands (1923; see the Lausanne Treaty, *supra*, p. 741).

In the same year Greece ran afoul of Italy and its prestige-minded Duce. During boundary negotiations between Greece and Albania, several Italian commissioners were killed by Greek terrorists. Mussolini immediately ordered the occupation of the Greek-controlled island of Corfu. For a time it seemed that a new war would break out. But again the League intervened and successfully mediated a settlement, despite continuing Italo-Greek tensions.

Reparations Troubles

For a number of years after the armistice, European conditions remained troubled by quarrels between victor and vanquished over the payment of war costs. As we have seen, Allied commissioners finally fixed (1921) the reparations sum at about 33 billion dollars. When Germany protested, she was told to accept the obligation or suffer extensive occupation of her Rhineland cities. Since the defeated nation simply did not have the resources to meet such demands, France (supported by Belgium but *not* by Britain) occupied the rich Ruhr valley in 1923. All German officials and many industrial leaders were removed from their positions and were replaced by Frenchmen and Belgians. To make certain that disturbances did not arise, the whole area was placed under strict military control. The elaborate effort proved quite futile. Some German laborers slowed down to an unproductive tempo; most of them simply left their jobs. To support their idle citizens, the German government printed money which was hardly off the presses before it lost most of its buying power. With the mark thus inflated beyond practical use (see *infra*, p. 764), the whole German economy teetered on the brink of bankruptcy. Meanwhile, British protests, coupled with mounting discontent in France and the appearance of a German statesman, Gustav Stresemann, who promised honest cooperation to the limit of Germany's ability, led to the abandonment (in 1924) of the fateful experiment.

In the interests of general stabilization and pacification, England and the United States sponsored the creation of a committee to reassess the reparations problem. Headed by an American, the former Vice-President Charles Dawes, the committee worked out a settlement satisfactory to all parties. By its terms, the German government set up a workable budget on a new unit of currency. Beginning in late 1924, she undertook to make progressively larger reparations payments (from one billion gold marks in 1924 to five billion in 1929). To stabilize international exchange and to "prime the pump" for Germany, the United States and certain European nations agreed to grant her substantial loans (800 million gold marks). This reasonable program — commonly referred to as the Dawes Plan — ushered in what has been called "the era of fulfillment."

This German bank note for 10,000 marks, issued in 1922, would not cover the price of a pair of shoes.

The Years of Hope, 1924 to 1929

The seemingly endless "little wars," interallied quarrels, and the reparations debacle had given warnings too large to be ignored. Clearly, a new temper and a new approach were imperative if world collapse was to be averted.

Under the aegis of the League, a comprehensive plan of compulsory arbitration was drawn up to permit the peaceful settlement of future disputes or, alternatively, to allow the mobilization of power against a would-be aggressor so as to deter or quickly overcome him. A fundamental feature of the Protocol for the Pacific Settlement of International disputes (1924; popularly called the Geneva Protocol) was its definition of an aggressor. Throughout the ages, nations and their leaders had been plagued by their inability to agree on criteria which would clearly demarcate aggressors from the victims of aggression. The Protocol provided a simple solution — an aggressor was any nation which refused to submit its claims to arbitration. The Protocol also provided detailed machinery of arbitration and, in the event of recalcitrance, a set of sanctions designed to coerce the refractory state. If the nations of the world had accepted the Protocol and had implemented it in the spirit of its designers, war necessarily would have disappeared as an instrument of national policy. But certain components of the British Commonwealth of Nations, particularly Canada, India, Australia, and New Zealand, were unsympathetic to the treaty. The fall of the British Labour government at this time, which had been one of the sponsors of the treaty, also militated against its general acceptance. But its defeat stimulated further efforts.

Even before the formal rejection of the Protocol by Great Britain in March 1925, Germany had persuaded her to support a Rhineland Mutual Guarantee Pact. Seemingly reconciled to the Versailles Rhineland settlement, Germany offered voluntary assent to the Rhineland provisions in return fur mutual assurances by France, Belgium, and Germany that international disputes involving this region would be settled by arbitration. Out of this suggestion came the Locarno Pacts, which seemed to herald a new era in international relations (for the provisions and significance of the Pacts, see *infra,* p. 760). In the fall of 1925, French troops were withdrawn from several Rhineland cities, further promoting amicable relations between the two long-time enemies.

Other events of hopeful augury followed. Germany had long complained that the victor states could not hope for the realization of world peace until they, as well as the vanquished, disarmed. In the spring of 1926, a preparatory commission for world disarmament was set up and began lengthy deliberations. The next year the Inter-

EUROPE, 1929

Map by J. Donovan

Allied Commission of Military Control in Germany was disbanded in favor of League supervision. In 1929 a new reparations commission was established under the chairmanship of Owen D. Young, an American banker. The new plan liberalized Germany's payments and returned to her domestic economic controls that had long been held by the Allies. In short, vexing political and economic problems seemed finally to be yielding to a new spirit of good will and understanding.

The Democracies After the War

Britain: Domestic Affairs — Economic Troubles

For a brief period after the Armistice, economic conditions in Britain were good, mostly because the war had created a backlog of orders the filling of which gave the country an economic boost.

By 1920, however, the troubles that were to harass Britain for the next twenty years had begun to appear. The postwar boom had inflated prices nearly 100 per cent (between early 1919 and 1920). This unsustainable price level led to a sudden collapse which brought on, in 1921, the worst depression that Great Britain had ever encountered. Moreover, much of the nation's overall economy depended on the production and exportation of coal. France's takeover of large German coal beds naturally depressed that industry and thus the whole economy. To make matters worse, oil was increasingly used in place of coal. Throughout the interwar period, Britain's economy never recovered its former stability and strength.

The roots of the trouble lay in conditions that we have already noted in an earlier chapter: serious maldistribution of wealth and the adamant refusal of the entrepreneurial class to allow the worker to develop effective bargaining strength. Already before the war these conditions had given shape to a revolutionary spirit which in autocratic countries, such as Russia and Turkey, had led to the overthrow of reactionary governments and the institution of radically new regimes. In Britain the democratic tradition blunted the edge of this thrust and offered alternative courses of action. Nevertheless, the war had given workers on the home front an added taste of power and a new determination to gain a greater share of the nation's resources.

Besides the sickness in the coal industry, several other serious economic ailments plagued the country. Britain had been forced to liquidate many of its overseas holdings to help finance the war; its capital investments in America, for example, were practically wiped out. The old, established patterns of trade, moreover, had necessarily been neglected during the war. It was expected that with the return of peace they would be reestablished. They were, but only in part. The United States had quietly taken over many former British markets, especially in South America; Japan had happily busied herself in the same manner in the East.

To finance the war Britain had borrowed heavily at home and abroad. By 1918 she had borrowed from the United States alone well over two billion dollars. Bonded indebtedness to her own citizens reached unprecedented levels. Without an ample supply of investment capital and without a healthy trade balance, it was difficult to

This Low cartoon, drawn some years after the first postwar coal strikes, depicts the spirit of workers and enterprisers as Britain drifts deeper into depressed conditions.

GOING BACK

meet the huge obligations. Compounding this difficulty was the "unrationalized" state of British industry. In the United States, Germany, and even Japan new machines and new methods of production were devised (for example, Ford's assembly-line process). These countries thus could and did produce the goods that people wanted more cheaply and in greater quantity. No one doubts that the British were as innately capable of creating new instruments and designing efficient production methods as any other nation in the world. The fact is that they did not. This, of course, further restricted domestic buying power, which inevitably led to curtailed production and layoffs of more workers.

Political Problems

In the postwar years, the overall political situation was marked by fluidity, change, and not a little confusion. Of the three parties, the Liberal party was in the most precarious position. It had long been the champion of economic and social reform. In the decade before the war it effected, as we have seen, a substantial change in the sociopolitical structure of British life. Paradoxically, its successes were also its undoing. The feeding of the workingman by the Liberal party had increased the worker's appetite beyond what the party believed it could reasonably tolerate. Thereafter the working class increasingly gave its support to Labour, although neither overwhelmingly nor irreversibly.

The Labour party was not without problems of its own. The tendency of many Englishmen to see the party simply as a cadre of dangerous revolutionaries quite insensible to the English way of life had to be overcome. There was also a lack of political and administrative experience among its leaders. Perhaps the most serious problem was the tendency of party members to split off into doctrinaire groups and to waste strength in intramural fighting, a practice which continued for many years.

Strikes, Strife, and "Baldwin Security"

As a wartime leader, Lloyd George was bold, imaginative, and effective. But his handling of the many postwar problems alienated most of his one-time supporters. In 1922, the Conservatives withdrew their support from the Coalition government and demanded new elections from which they emerged with a clear majority. The Liberals, indeed, suffered such a thumping defeat that the Labour party became the "loyal opposition." The new Prime Minister, Bonar Law, was an able man, but in failing health. Within a few months he withdrew from politics in favor of Stanley Baldwin. More than any other statesman in the interwar period, Baldwin came to sense the troubled spirit and serve the deeper yearnings of the British electorate. This is not to imply that either spirit or yearnings were marked by vigor or vision. A mood had found a man; from time to time each bickered with and wearied of the other, but for nearly two decades the two were, for better or worse, really one.

The First Labour Government

The first postwar Conservative government failed to bring Britain out of her doldrums. Higher tariffs were levied in an attempt to give home industries a boost. The dole was decreased to keep the budget in balance. This resulted in higher prices and lower buying levels which caused, hardly surprisingly, increased distress among the masses. A year of Conservative management convinced the electorate that a change was needed. In January 1924, Baldwin yielded to Ramsay MacDonald and a Labour government (the first in Britain's history). But Labour's representation in Parliament was too small to give MacDonald the strength and scope to maneuver. To win the necessary support from Liberal members, he dropped his demand for a capital levy and the immediate nationalization of basic industries. Tariff duties were reduced, however, and large estates were heavily taxed. Russia was given *de jure* recognition, and soon thereafter the two governments agreed to a resumption of commercial relations. To many Britons this seemed little short of treason, and a campaign was begun to throw out the socialist government before it could, as the Conservatives thought of it, subvert the nation to Communism. The Conservative party returned to power with an overwhelming majority (1924), denounced the recognition of Russia, abrogated the trade treaties, and again laid tariff duties on certain imports. Thus England returned to about the same condition that she had found so intolerable only two years before.

The General Strike of 1926

In the meantime, the United States and Japan had consolidated and expanded the trade gains that had been made earlier at Britain's expense. To meet the new competition, British industry further depressed wages, while the government, hoping to work some kind of financial magic, restored the pound sterling to its high prewar level. Both measures reduced domestic buying power, which in turn created greater unemployment. Particularly hard hit was the coal industry. In the spring of 1926 the miners were given substantial wage cuts. Supported by the General Council of the Trade Union Congress, they refused to accept reduction of their already low earnings and went on strike. Dock and transport workers joined in sympathy strikes, and were themselves soon joined by workmen from other unions. Within a week, one sixth of all union laborers had left their jobs — printers, iron and steel workers, construction laborers — in all, some three million of them. Prime Minister Baldwin declared that the general strike "threatened the basis of ordered government" and directed the workers to return to their jobs. The main thrust of the government forces came from Winston Churchill, who was at that time Chancellor of the Exchequer. Churchill and a few extremist Conservative leaders wanted to discipline labor and make it amenable to the command of England's financial industrial leaders. To this end, the government, in complete command of the news outlets that remained, played up the "insurrectionary" threat and succeeded in enlisting the wholehearted support of Britain's middle and upper-middle classes. Within a fortnight the strike had collapsed and all workers had returned to their jobs, with the exception of the miners. The miners stayed out for six months, but eventually near-starvation drove them back to work, at reduced wages. The next year the government passed a bill outlawing certain strikes and lockouts.

Coalition Governments

For a time the crackdown on labor created a calm without effecting any improvement in economic conditions. Unemployment increased and trade lagged. In the general elections of 1929, the Labour party regained power and Ramsay MacDonald returned as Prime Minister. During the campaign the Labourites again promised to nationalize and modernize Britain's "unrationalized" basic industries, to effect reforms in the tax laws, and generally to bring the nation out of its depression. The antistrike laws were repealed and greater relief was extended to the unemployed. A new trade treaty was negotiated with Russia which, it was hoped, would stimulate the export of British goods. However, no real improvement in general economic conditions resulted. For one thing, the Labourite majority was too small to prevail against Liberals and Conservatives who joined forces in order to block the nationalization of the coal and steel industries. Also, by the time the Labour government had pushed its abbreviated program through Parliament, the whole world was bogged down in depression. In this impasse the government resigned as a Labour government (1931) and reformed with power resting in a National Coalition made up of Conservatives, Labourites, and Liberals. As Prime Minister, MacDonald called on his party to support the coalition for the duration of the economic crisis. But most of his colleagues indignantly refused to accept this repudiation of Labour's program. Instead, they read their leader and the few who remained loyal to him out of the party and went into opposition.

MacDonald remained Prime Minister until 1935, but from 1931 until after World War II the government was dominated by Conservatives. Deteriorating economic conditions forced them to adopt a number of measures hardly compatible with their principles. To support sagging farm prices, the government passed legislation that guaranteed a minimum price for some grains; farm credits were also extended. Other legislation shored up the wages of industrial workers and stabilized price levels of various manufactured goods. For a time, unemployment was halted and better times seemed on the way. General elections, held in 1935, increased the Conservative majority. Although a pretense of multiparty management was maintained for a while, the replacement of MacDonald by Baldwin in June 1935 marked the end of the coalition. In the meantime the Labour party, reorganized under the leadership of Arthur Henderson, renewed its bid for national leadership. By this time the Nazi menace had grown so threatening that Britain felt forced to undertake extensive rearmament. Moreover, in the spring of 1935 the government introduced military conscription. The combined effects of removing tens of thousands of young men from the ranks of the unemployed and the stimulus given to industry by the rearmament program brought a degree of prosperity that no previous postwar government had been able to create. Naturally, the Labour party

lost voter appeal. The prosperity, of course, was artificial. Britain's basic economic and political problems were salved over rather than solved, as the years of the aftermath of another world war were to make plain. But for the time being the nation seemed content to make do with current solutions, no matter how contrived. In 1937, wearied by the compounding of governmental chores and physical ailments, Baldwin retired as Prime Minister and was succeeded by Neville Chamberlain.

Imperial Affairs: Ireland

In addition to domestic problems, imperial issues also plagued Britain during the postwar years. Even before the end of the war a serious crisis had developed in Ireland. In the spring of 1916, bands of Irish nationalists organized a rebellion that opened a period of turbulence and violence which lasted for more than twenty years. The English at first sought to woo their restive subjects by granting amnesty to the rebel leaders, including Eamon de Valera, leader of the nationalist Sinn Fein ("We Ourselves") party. But the rebels would not be wooed. Throughout the next three years relations between governors and governed remained strained. When the Sinn Feiners finally resorted again to widespread terrorism, the English decided to retaliate in kind. For several months in 1920 both sides perpetrated atrocities that neither one of them likes to remember. The carnage was ended when the British Parliament passed the Government of Ireland Act, which gave southern (as well as northern) Ireland its own governing body. By this time, however, many southern Irish were not of a mind to settle for dominion status, and demanded complete, unqualified independence. But others were willing to accept the Act's settlement. Fighting soon broke out between the two factions and continued for over fifteen years. Tension and troubles also continued between Irishmen and Englishmen. Eventually, the harassments became unendurable and brought all parties to negotiations. In 1938, Britain recognized Eire (as the nationalists insisted on calling their land) as completely independent, and Eire agreed to pay about $30 million that was owed to former English landlords. Complete harmony between the two states and between Irish moderates and extremists was hardly to be hoped for, but a reasonably workable peace was achieved.

Egypt

Nationalists in Egypt were also busy in the postwar period. As we have seen, England had occupied Egypt in 1882, nominally acknowledging Turkish sovereignty. With the outbreak of World War I, Britain denounced all Turkish claims and to pacify restive Egyptians promised to defend the land without calling up native conscripts. Before the end of the war, however, conscription was introduced. Egyptian representatives tried to bring their cause before the Paris Peace Conference, but were prevented by the British. For several years opposition of various kinds, ranging from flaring violence to passive resistance, agitated relations between the two peoples. In 1922 England dramatically — and unilaterally — declared Egypt independent. Egyptian nationalists repudiated the action on the grounds, which soon proved to be sound, that the independence was bogus. England reserved the right to intervene in Egyptian foreign affairs, to control communications, especially as they affected the Suez Canal, and to station troops in strategic areas. The next year a constitution was promulgated and elections were held. The nationalist party, the Wafd, gained a majority of seats in the new legislature and proceeded to work for complete independence. In the main their efforts were blocked by British military might and by lavish bribes that kept the native court at odds with its Egyptian subjects. To keep Egypt in line, Britain forced the Egyptian parliament to dissolve for three years, decreed suspen-

sion of certain civil rights, particularly free speech and free assembly, and enlarged its military establishment. When the Labourites returned to power in England, Egyptian nationalists hoped that new negotiations would lead to independence. Unfortunately, the deepening world depression created in both lands internal problems, which first slowed and finally scuttled negotiations. When the Wafdists swept the 1936 elections, Britain agreed to a treaty that gave Egypt a large measure of true independence. Most of the exploitative economic privileges enjoyed by foreign nations were abolished; Egypt was admitted into the League of Nations; Egyptian control was reinstated in the Sudan. Still, the existence of some English troops in the canal zone, together with the maintenance of mixed courts, kept relations between the two states strained. In a later chapter we shall note the drastic revisions of the 1936 treaty and the eventual creation of a fully independent Egyptian republic.

India

More than one million Indian troops had fought on the side of the Allies during World War I. Their sizable contribution to the war effort and fair words from their British overlords gave Indians strong hope that self-government would soon be granted. British procrastination, combined with serious crop failures (and a crippling influenza epidemic), stirred Indian nationalists to radical agitation in 1918 to 1919. To teach their wards a lesson, Parliament passed the Rowlatt Acts, which stripped Indians accused of sedition of the right of trial by jury. Hindus, Moslems, and Sikhs promptly abandoned the fighting among themselves and united in opposition under the leadership of Mohandas K. Gandhi (popularly called the Mahatma — the Holy One). Gandhi's tactics were unusual. Believing that truth is God and that love is the strongest force in the world, the sainted leader urged his

Gandhi at his spinning wheel. For Gandhi the spinning wheel was a symbol of both the "non-machine" way of life and India's capabilities of economic self-sustenance.

people to meet all wrongs with nonviolent resistance. Millions enrolled under his banner. But his straight way was hard to follow, and sometimes the passions of his devotees burst the bonds imposed by the Mahatma. To effect the repeal of the Rowlatt Acts, Gandhi had ordered a massive campaign of peaceful civil disobedience. At Amritsar, British troops fired into a crowd of demonstrators, killing hundreds. India seethed at this act of arrogant brutality and lashed back with violence of its own. To bring the situation under control, Gandhi called off the disobedience campaign and began an expiatory fast. This was to be the Mahatma's basic approach to the solution of India's problems in the years that followed: exhortation of his followers to the use of the love-force (*satyagraha*), trust in its efficacious effect on the British, occasional demonstrations of civil disobedience, fasting and self-sacrifice when either Indians or Englishmen spurned the way of love.

In 1920, Gandhi led the Congress party * in a renewed campaign for home rule. He urged Indians to boycott British businesses, to make their own homespun garments, and to refuse participation in any governmental affairs until complete home rule

* See *supra*, p. 687.

was granted. British officials reacted vigorously against what they considered insufferable insubordination. At the same time, serious friction developed between native Hindu and Moslem populations. To increase the pressure on the British, Gandhi launched a wide-spread civil disobedience program. In spite of the Mahatma's insistence on peaceful resistance, violence spread throughout the land, culminating in the discontinuance of the civil disobedience campaign and the arrest of Gandhi. For several years general confusion marked Indian affairs. Many Indian moderates followed Gandhi in his fight for dominion status but, with their leader in jail, they could make little progress. Other Indians looked to Jawaharlal Nehru for leadership that promised complete independence, but they constituted a minority of the restive masses.

After his release from jail in 1924, Gandhi adopted a policy of watchful waiting. Parliament appointed another commission to restudy the problem (1926), but nothing came of its work except increased Indian restlessness. In 1928 strikes broke out in a number of textile establishments and soon spread to the railroads. A new round of violence seemed imminent. At this point Gandhi appealed to the masses for order and discipline, and to the British government for a speedy working out of arrangements that would lead to dominion status. When the London government, by this time plagued by a deepening depression at home, gave Gandhi nothing to hope for, he inaugurated another campaign of civil disobedience (1930). To dramatize the struggle, he organized a great "march to the sea" where, in violation of a British law forbidding the manufacture of untaxed salt, he and hundreds of his followers crudely refined heaps of salt along the shores. Gandhi was again arrested, and another wave of violence spread across the land. Moderates in both India and England insisted that a final resolution of the protracted conflict somehow be found.

Several imperial conferences — "Round Tables" — were held. But clearly the white man was not ready to shed his burden, for the meetings produced no policies that had not already been tried.

In 1935, a new Government of India Act was passed by a still hopeful Parliament. Burma and Aden were separated from India and made crown colonies. An increased number of citizens were given the franchise. Extensive control over provincial affairs was granted. But the Act satisfied neither moderates nor radicals. As always, the British government reserved for itself the final word in foreign affairs and defense matters. And, as always, the imperial ministers could decree even local laws if an emergency required it. From then on Gandhi, despairing of partway measures, demanded complete independence. Strife continued between Hindus and Moslems, castes and untouchables, and princes and the people, so that Britain could and did argue that she could not withdraw until factional quarrels were settled. But by the outbreak of World War II it was clear that regardless of internal difficulties, a final reckoning could not be long delayed.

Palestine

As part of the Peace settlement, Britain had been given mandatory control over Palestine. The assignment turned out to be a thirty-year imperial headache. The land was inhabited by two peoples, Jews and Arabs, each claiming the right to the whole territory. Each had strong arguments to support its claims. For nearly two thousand years, from the time of Moses to the Moslem conquest, Palestine had been the homeland of the Jews, as well as the Holy Land for Hebrews everywhere. But certain Moslem tribes had conquered it in 638 and ruled it for well over one thousand years. They had multiplied in greater numbers than the Jews (by 1900 they outnumbered Jews seven to one), and to them, too, Jerusalem was a holy city. Historic and religious ties thus bound both to the land.

In these circumstances any mandatory power would have found governing the territory a frustrating ordeal. British interests in the region added further complications. Because of the advent of Communist Russia, England feared eventual Red control of the eastern Mediterranean, which would naturally threaten her lifeline to the East. In addition, some of the great oil conduits that tapped the resources of Iraq and Arabia had their outlets in the Palestinean area. The possession of these pipelines by an enemy could severely penalize Britain's economic interests.

Added to these vexations were the contradictory promises that England had made to the Jews and Arabs when she needed the support of both during World War I. To the Jews she had promised, in the famous Balfour Declaration, help in founding a national homeland. To the Arabs she had given strong hints that she would help them establish independent states. Both peoples called for redemption of these promises after the war. Both charged bad faith and imperial perfidy when England formally took over control of the whole region (including Transjordan) in 1922.

In the years that followed England found herself hung on the horns of a seemingly unresolvable dilemma. Concessions to one group brought anguished protests from the other. Specific Arab complaints included a Jewish immigration policy that threatened ultimately to destroy Arab numerical dominance, allocation of the best land to the Jews, and improper administration of sacred sites in Jerusalem. On the other hand, the growing Jewish population unceasingly lamented Britain's failure to implement the Balfour Declaration. No program seemed acceptable to both groups. In 1937, Britain tried to divide the territory into Jewish and Arab parts. Neither side would agree to the boundaries, nor even to the idea that there should be a division. Later we shall note how, eventually, partition and a precarious peace were effected; for the time being, however, Britain continued to bear a burden that had almost no Kiplingesque compensations.

France

Before turning to postwar events in France, we should note some general considerations. The war inflicted greater physical damage on France than on any other nation. Here most of the four-year fighting along the Western Front took place. Over twenty thousand factories were demolished, nearly one hundred thousand homes and farms were destroyed, almost one half of France's male population between the ages of 22 and 34 were slain.

The war also inflicted a psychic trauma on the nation. Without outside help France would surely have been overrun, and Frenchmen knew it. Clemenceau also admitted that the grandeur of victory was clouded not only by the indescribable misery that had won it but also by haunting fears that a new day of revenge awaited France, as once they had haunted Germany.

France suffered also from chronic political instability. Part of the nation—most of the workers and some intellectuals—clung to the liberal heritage of the Revolution and looked forward to a society truly grounded in liberty, equality, and fraternity. Another part, made up mostly of peasants, petite bourgeoisie, and the industrial elite, feared radical reforms as the prelude to anarchy. Proportional representation was another divisive force. Under it no single party could expect to seat a majority in the Assembly. Consequently, that body was normally made up of a number of blocs whose leaders were forever jockeying for domination of a coalition which only rarely lasted as long as two years and often broke up after several months or even weeks. Twenty different prime ministers, for example, held office during the twenty-year truce between the wars. Undersecretaries, it is true, gave some continuity to both domestic and foreign affairs, but too much

has been made of the influence of these civil servants.

For a while the nation enjoyed economic health. Unlike Britain, France produced a large part of the foodstuffs that she needed. The balance between agriculture and industry (the ratio was about 40 to 60) meant less dependence on the vagaries of world trade and exchange, hence greater internal economic stability. Even so, the margin was too close to guarantee sustained prosperity, should the world economy suffer severe depression. Even before this calamity occurred, huge war debts and the falling value of the franc presented grave problems that harried the ever-changing governments.

By 1924 it was clear that German reparations could not be depended on to pay for the nation's immense rebuilding projects. Plunging deficits, coupled with the chronic tendency of French citizens to evade taxes, sent the exchange rate of the franc down to about two cents, one tenth of its prewar value. When Republican and Leftist parties showed no sign of being able to handle the burgeoning financial crisis, the nation turned to the strong man of the Rightists, Raymond Poincaré (1926). Forming a National Union ministry (which included six former premiers of all parties to the right of the Socialists), Poincaré pushed through a Spartan program of governmental economies and increased taxes. About four fifths of the national debt was repudiated—in effect a capital levy on the rentier class. The nation groaned but suffered the ordeal, realizing that the melancholy choice was between individual belt-tightening and national bankruptcy. The franc was pegged at four cents, and the budget was brought into balance. For the next six or seven years economic conditions improved, although bitter memories of the cost remained to haunt and hamper future ministries.

Class Struggle

The working classes came out of the war with a new spirit and lively ambitions. They were conscious of their contribution to the great victory. They were impressed by the gains made by labor in other countries, as well as emboldened by the cumulative effect of the preachments of radical doctrinaries, from their own to those of the Russian Revolution. Some of them joined the Communist party to work for the overthrow of the whole capitalist establishment. Many others became active members of the Socialist party which, in 1920, joined the Communist-dominated Third International.

So long as prosperity lasted, the conflict between labor and capital remained minimal and sporadic; when the Great Depression spread to France (1931–1932), dissension became acute. Serious enough in itself, the conflict was aggravated by other, and in some cases quite irrelevant, issues. For example, in 1933 and 1934 the nation seethed with confused anger over the exposure of corruption in high places. A certain Serge Staviski, an imaginative rogue with political connections, had overplayed his hand in the promotion of a fraudulent bond issue. He was killed, it was alleged, resisting arrest. Leaders of royalist and quasi-fascist organizations charged the government with deliberately murdering a criminal whose public trial would have embarrassed a number of highly placed officials, including a Cabinet member or two. It finally led to the resignation of the Cabinet. The full facts of the case never became known, nor are they important in our context. For us the Staviski affair is significant because of the impetus that it gave to anti-Republican fulminations against "the system" and to the growing doubts among French citizens about the ability of democracy to deal with problems of modern industrial life.

Members of the working-class parties gradually came to realize that they could not continue to fight among themselves and still hope to stand against reactionary pressures. Therefore, in the face of growing unemployment, public confusion, and Rightist agitation, the chief parties of the

Left drew together in what came to be called the Popular Front. In the spring of 1936 it gained a majority in the Assembly and, under the leadership of Léon Blum, sponsored a wide-ranging program of social reform. The forty-hour week was introduced; arbitration of labor disputes was made compulsory; workers were granted vacations with pay; the munitions industry, one of the largest in the country, was nationalized; and the Bank of France was brought under strict governmental control. For a while France's "new deal" seemed to work. The laboring masses rejoiced in their new rights and in the crippling blow that had been dealt to the so-called ruling two hundred families. Unemployment, never as high as in other industrialized countries, fell. But the Popular Front's "new deal" lacked resources that its American model possessed—potentially abundant supplies of capital to be tapped for public works, a reasonably stable currency, and a geographic isolation which allowed it to concentrate on domestic problems. Within a year, Blum was forced to devalue the franc still further while calling in vain for popular subscription to large and badly needed bond issues. Developments in the savage civil war in Spain also contributed to his declining popularity. Most of his supporters favored giving assistance to the Spanish Republic, but Blum felt the need to stay in line with his British ally which was then (1937) slowly moving toward its appeasement stance. Thus harassed at home and abroad, Blum resigned, bringing to an end the attempted grand breakthrough of socialist reform.

Fear of Germany

From the end of World War I to the outbreak of World War II, national security constituted France's biggest worry. In the period of 1924 to 1927, she linked herself with the three powers of the Little Entente, thus effecting an almost complete encirclement of the German Republic. In this same period *de jure* recognition was given to

Soviet Russia, which was followed, with the advent of Nazism, by a formal military alliance (1935) aimed at discouraging Hitler from attempting power plays in the east.

All of these arrangements were motivated by a frankly acknowledged apprehension of revived German power, with little concern, to understate it, with the cultivation of good relations between herself and her defeated foe. One consequential undertaking, however, had precisely this concern as its objective. In 1925 Stresemann, Germany's foreign minister, asked France to concert with Germany in finally dissipating the abiding fear of another war between the two states. Peace-minded Briand happened to be France's premier at the time. He accepted the offer with the proviso that Britain, Belgium, Italy, Poland, and Czechoslovakia be invited to participate in a broad, general settlement of all outstanding issues. Stresemann agreed, and the conference was held at Locarno in the closing months of 1925. Out of it came agreements between France and Germany promising that their facing frontiers were never to be changed by force; that certain areas of the Rhineland (as provided by the Versailles Treaty) were to remain demilitarized in perpetuity; and that neither of them would ever aggressively attack or invade the other. The pacts were greeted with general acclaim. At Versailles, Germany had been forced to sign away Alsace-Lorraine and to accept demilitarization of the Rhineland. At Locarno she accepted these settlements voluntarily. One great trouble spot, it seemed, had been erased from the European map forever. Cautious critics pointed out that the question of the Polish Corridor, an eastern Alsace-Lorraine, remained unsettled, for Germany refused to make any pledges concerning the boundaries in the east. But the world seemed too happy over the "Locarno miracle" to feel much concern.

To reinsure herself, France began the construction of an elaborate system of fortifications along the German border (1929). The Maginot Line (so called after the name of its chief engineer) was built in such depth and strength that most military experts considered it impregnable. Some skeptics, it is true, professed to see in the costly, complicated works a symbol of the state of the French psyche—an elaborate admission of the nation's loss of vitality and venturesomeness. For most Frenchmen, however, the Line seemed to guarantee the kind of security that they were seeking.

The United States

Later we shall take up in some detail certain conditions and policies which significantly marked life in America after the war—inflation, depression, and the New Deal.* Here we briefly note the condition of the public mind and certain events which developed out of it.

The attitude is associated with a deceptively simple word—normalcy. World War I had sickened America of things European. Casualty lists, governmental restraints, the hypertension of global conflict (to say nothing of strange geographic place names and foreign ways of life)—all had generated in many Americans, perhaps most Americans, a deep longing for disengagement from a world that they did not understand and for an unencumbered opportunity to resume the acquisition and enjoyment of the good things of life. Thus in the campaign of 1920, Harding's call for a "return to normalcy" struck responsive chords. Actually, the phrase was as little grounded in historic reality as it was in grammatical usage. The war had in part shaped and in part revealed America as a world power. Technology had made that world, if not one, at least so interpenetrated and interdependent that no nation could stand alone or even measurably aloof; try as it might, America could never "go home again." Moreover, the forces of modern times had wrought changes internally as well as externally.

* See *infra*, pp. 813–819.

The American worker had tasted economic affluence; the American entrepreneur had multiplied millions beyond precedent. Although bewitched by the lure of Harding's call, neither would complacently return to the conditions of an earlier day. Furthermore, both were weaned, at least to some degree, from traditional moral restraints and from what came increasingly to be regarded as the naïve demands of a Victorian conscience. Not all Americans became Main Street Babbitts; but the breed multiplied abundantly. Even though Christian America did not disavow its Sunday trinity, it jubilantly made room for a secular workaday worship of nationalism, isolationism, and materialism.*

The "Red Scare," High Tariffs, and the Klan

One manifestation of overcharged nationalism was the "Red scare" which swept the country in 1919 and 1920. Attorney General A. Mitchell Palmer ordered wholesale arrests of aliens who were connected, however slightly, with socialist or liberal groups in this or their own country. A number of states passed laws so stringent that the display of a red flag, for example, was sufficient cause for imprisonment. A visiting English journalist wrote:

No one who was in the United States, as I chanced to be, in the autumn of 1919 will forget the feverish condition of the public mind at that time. It was hagridden by the spectre of Bolshevism. . . . Property was in an agony of fear, and the horrid name "Radical" covered the most innocent departure from conventional thought with a suspicion of desperate purposes.[1]

---

* For a different view, see David A. Shannon, *Between the Wars; America, 1919–1941,* Houghton Mifflin Co., Boston, 1965. The whole work is a provocative treatment of these times, but see especially pp. 6–7 and 47–57.

---

1. A. G. Gardiner, *Portraits and Portents,* New York, 1926, p. 13, quoted in Preston Slosson, *The Great Crusade and After,* Macmillan Co., New York, 1930, p. 79.

In 1922 Congress passed the Fordney-McCumber Tariff Act. Its basic purpose, which was frankly stated in the act itself, was to increase the costs of foreign goods to whatever extent was necessary to equalize them with the costs of American-produced goods. The record that it set in producing the highest schedules in our history stood only eight years. In 1930 the Smoot-Hawley Act increased the rates on some raw materials by as much as 100 per cent. More than one thousand professional economists petitioned President Hoover to veto the new bill, but the President, although voicing some apprehensions, signed it into law. Naturally, other nations retaliated, thus penalizing world trade at a time when its expansion was urgently needed.

In 1924 Congress turned its attention to protecting American workers from the competition offered by immigrants. A law passed in that year reduced the quotas of all countries to 2 per cent of the number of their nationals admitted in 1890. Later the act was amended (it became effective in 1929) so as to put a ceiling of 150,000 to the number of immigrants admitted in any one year. It also prohibited all Japanese from entering the United States except as students or visitors. While Congress was keeping aliens out by law, millions of Americans were busy denigrating non-American cultures. In the early 1920s, a revived Ku Klux Klan launched a sustained attack on all groups beyond the Wasp (White, Anglo-Saxon, Protestant) pale. Ethnic minorities, such as Italians and peoples from the Slavic countries of Europe, were denounced as parasites sucking America of its life blood. Catholics were pilloried as conspiratory agents of a nefarious power. Orientals were branded as unassimilable coolies, Negroes and Jews, not surpisingly, were especially singled out as objects of harassment and, occasionally, of outright brutality. By the mid-1920s, the Klan had become strong enough to impose its rule on many local communities and on at least one state.

Despite police orders to the contrary, Klansmen parade through the streets of Tulsa, Oklahoma (1923) in their campaign to keep Tulsa "white, free and 100% American."

A typical speakeasy bar of the 1920s.

Corruption and "Speakeasies"

Corruption in the higher echelons of national public service also marked the early postwar years. In the Department of Justice, of all places, plundering rascality took over. Before Attorney General Harry M. Daugherty was removed from office in 1924, he and his cronies had turned its bureaus and sections into agencies of personal profit and aggrandizement. Thomas W. Miller, alien-property custodian, was sentenced to a prison term in 1927 for illegal dealings with the American Metals Company. Colonel Charles Forbes, appointed head of the Veterans Bureau, used this office to enrich himself and his friends until a Senatorial investigation revealed the looting to the public. Secretary of the Interior Albert Fall secretly leased the Teapot Dome Oil Reserve to Harry F. Sinclair for an undisclosed consideration; he similarly leased the Elk Hill Reserve to oilman E. L. Doheney who, as later investigations disclosed, had "loaned" the Secretary $100,000 without either interest or security.

Paradoxically, these were also the years when America attempted an experiment, "noble in purpose," which was designed to rid the land of the evil influences of intoxicating drink. In 1920 Congress passed the National Prohibition Act which forbade the manufacture and sale of all beverages that had an alcoholic content greater than one half of 1 per cent. But from the first the law was flouted. "Speakeasies" replaced saloons, and racketeers briskly stepped into the business of illegally supplying a demand for this commodity which Americans had legally banned. Thus in its drinking habits, as in its economic and political life, the public gave clear evidence of its desire to "return to normalcy."

Our brief review of America's postwar mood and some of the events shaped by it should not lead us to conclude that the country became a carnival of violence and vice. Many of America's millions seriously sought to understand their country's new role in world affairs. Many favored, if not the League as it was, some kind of workable world association of nations. Most Americans were puzzled and saddened by the hate orgies and extremism of the superpatriots; most of them tended to their jobs, their families, and their public duties much as Americans had always done. Nevertheless, the mood that has been described did pervade the land. The rejection of Europe, the erection of tariff barriers, the persecution of minorities, the corrupt management of public affairs, the Prohibition interlude — these events are segments of the historic record which must be placed in calculation if we wish to understand the nature and meaning of American society after the war.

Inflation and Depression

The Emergence of Illusory Affluence: America

In the two decades after World War I, economic conditions were alternately marked by inflation and depression. To one degree or another the whole world was affected. We shall give particular attention to their course and consequences in the United States and Germany where their manifestations and significance are most clearly seen.

At war's end all of the major nations of Europe were burdened with huge debts. Great Britain's public debt, for example, was ten times greater in 1919 than it had been four years earlier. France was even worse off. In addition to her bonded debt, she suffered from the effects of the war's destruction of many of her factories and farms. Moreover, her prewar loans to Russia had been completely repudiated by the new Bolshevik regime. Germany's internal public debt was higher than that of any of the Allied countries. During the war Germany had preferred to finance military operations almost exclusively by loans rather than by taxes. Presumably, this decision was based on the intention to force the Allies to make good the redemption of her bonds after her victory; when Allied victory put the shoe on the other foot, Germany was of course seriously pinched. Among other penalties suffered were the loss of many of her world markets and patent rights. Italy, a perennial pauper among the Great Powers, came out of the war

somewhat richer in territorial possessions, but with an economy that was teetering on the brink of bankruptcy.

Even the United States, the world's newest and greatest industrial giant, experienced a sharp, if passing, depression in the early postwar period (1921–1922). Nearly seven thousand businesses and banks failed in 1921. Unemployment increased by about 30 per cent. Farm prices fell sharply; corn, for example, which had sold in December 1919 for $1.35 a bushel, dropped within twelve months to 68 cents. In certain key industries such as railroads, textiles, coal, and steel, rates and prices remained high while wages were kept disproportionately low. The Federal Government abruptly curtailed its military spending which naturally affected the overall economy. Foreign markets, of course, dwindled as economic conditions in Europe worsened.

But, paradoxically, economic conditions in America did not become really bad until the nation recovered from its brief depression. The fateful "seven fat years" which followed this recovery — the period of the famous boom — masked basic flaws in the economy which were to bring on the severest depression in modern history. But at the time these years seemed to promise the dawn of an endless age of plenty both in their productivity and in the amazing rapidity with which the nation effected its economic about-face.

No consensus has yet been reached to explain America's rapid emergence from "hard times," although certain elements are obvious. One is the country's transformation during the war years from a debtor to a creditor nation; it became, indeed, the world's leading lender. Another element is the telescoping of technological progress effected by the war itself. It is true that many advances in technology were initiated by Europeans (for example, German chemical engineers and English makers of precision machine tools). But, as one writer has put it:

Big Technology is an integral part of the daily living of Americans. . . . [It] has been for Americans what the Cross was for the Emperor Constantine: *In hoc signo vincas.* . . . The American has been a machine-intoxicated man. The love affair (it has been nothing less) between the Americans and their Big Technology has been fateful, for it has joined the impersonal power of the machine to the dynamism of the American character.[2]

Once out of the slump, American economy went on to set production records never surpassed or even closely approximated. Several relatively new enterprises gave substantial impetus to the boom. One was the automobile industry. By the early 1920s the Ford Motor Company and General Motors, together with a number of smaller corporations, were turning out low-cost cars at such a rate that by 1928 about 25,000,000 automobiles were clogging America's streets and highways.* The automobile's consumption of oil, gasoline, and rubber naturally stimulated these industries.

Another mushrooming business was that of motion pictures. "By 1926 there were over 20,000 movie theaters in the United States, with an average attendance of 100,000,000 persons a week, a figure only slightly smaller than the total population." By this time, too, the radio had become sufficiently perfected to create a demand that industry energetically set about to meet. Electrical appliances and machines of all kinds poured in a flood upon the market. Also, the war had stimulated the construction and proved the practicability of heavier-than-air craft, and the aviation

industry was born. Buildings of all kinds—homes, factories, stadia, business houses—were put up with such speed and in such numbers that in the seven years of 1922 to 1929 America underwent a kind of national face-lifting.

The tempo and scope of this economic bustle imparted to many Americans a feeling that material utopia was at hand. In a special sense of the word, inflation overspread the land—a heady confidence that the realization of stimulated desires and newly felt needs was not only possible but imminent. But inflation in its ordinary sense also marked these times. Price levels stayed fairly high. Real estate values were given dollar values that did not correspond with reality. Stocks of almost all the large corporations were sold—increasingly "on margin"—at figures that only a kind of self-induced delusion prevented the buying public from recognizing as fantastic. In short, a jerry-built economy precariously undergirded America's Jazz Age.

German Catastrophe: Inflation

European economies also suffered spiraling inflation. Particularly significant was the German experience. Stripped of a good deal of her working industrial wealth (most of the rolling stock of her railways, for example, was handed over to France and Belgium), burdened by impossible reparations, and inwardly determined to prove the economic provisions of the Versailles Treaty unsound, Germany turned to the printing press for relief. This cure of her economic ills, of course, was worse than the disease itself. A few statistics tell the story. Before the war, 4.2 German marks equaled one American dollar in international exchange; in 1919 the ratio was 8.9 to 1; by late 1921 it took nearly 250 marks to equal the buying power of one dollar. As the Allies prodded Germany into maintaining her reparations payments, her economy began to show signs of collapse. The French government insisted, as we have

2. Max Lerner, *America as a Civilization,* Simon and Schuster, New York, 1957, p. 227.

* Again, it must be emphasized that in an introductory study of civilization it is impossible to present a bill of particulars and implications for many generalizations. In the instance just cited, for example, it must be obvious that these millions of cars would have been quite useless had not counties, cities, and states constructed thousands of miles of hard surface roads.

seen (*supra*, p. 748), that the Germans were deliberately sabotaging arrangements provided for in the treaty settlement and demanded direct Allied intervention. When Great Britain questioned the soundness of this move, French forces occupied the Ruhr.

The occupation at once set off bitter and indignant German reactions. Some Germans, such as the young agitator Adolf Hitler, urged the meeting of violence with violence. Some vented their passions in hysterical denunciations. Most supported the German government's decision to oppose the move by passive resistance. Miners refused to go into the pits; factory workers made only a pretense of tending their machines; railroads deliberately maintained hit-and-miss schedules. As unemployment increased, the German government felt obliged to grant aid to the displaced workers. This aid generally took the form of newly printed money.

Naturally, this flood of unsecured currency gave impetus to the already strong inflationary trend. In July 1923, one dollar was worth 200,000 marks; by September it was worth 100,000,000 marks; by November over four trillion marks. Merchants tried to peg prices to the changing value of the mark, but it was difficult for anyone to know at any given time just what that elusive unit was worth. For buyers, the situation became even more fantastic. A German housewife might leave her home with 400,000,000 marks to purchase a loaf of bread only to discover before she had reached the bakery that the price had jumped to 600,000,000 marks. Sometimes housewives borrowed wheelbarrows or carts, not to bring home groceries but to transport bundles of currency. Great quantities of paper money were doled out to employed and unemployed workers, but never in proportion to the soaring prices. Worst hit of all was the large middle class whose fixed income and investment returns made its ruin inevitable. Suppose, for example,

that Hermann Schmidt, a civil service employee, had purchased a 15,000-mark annuity policy in 1903 which was to run for twenty years. Throughout these years he had cut expenses to pay his premium against the day when his policy would mature and he would begin to receive benefits which would enable him to purchase some of the comforts that he and his family had denied themselves so long. In 1923 his policy matures and he receives a bundle of paper that does not, literally, buy a postage stamp.

When the harassed German government abandoned passive resistance, the nation's leading financial expert, Hjalmar Schacht, was directed to reform the currency system. He created a new monetary unit, the *Rentenmark,* which "redeemed" the old mark at the ratio of about one trillion to one. Although ostensibly backed by the real estate and industrial establishment of the entire country, the stability of the Rentenmark actually rested on the confidence of the German people. At the same time, and as part of the rejuvenation program, Germany negotiated a series of loans from abroad (mostly from the United States). By mid-1924, the runaway inflation was brought under control, and German industry began a rapid recovery. But psychic scars had been cut deeply into the German body politic. In Kafka's words, the ghosts had been dispersed; "only as the night advances do they return, in the morning they have all assembled again, even if one cannot recognize them." Before a decade had passed, Germany's ghosts had assembled in their legions, bedecked with brown uniforms and swastikas. For the present, however, things seemed to be going well. The hum of the factories was heard throughout the land. Science combined with technology to produce a dazzling display of entrepreneurial pyrotechnics. To the hopeful it seemed that the age of peace and plenty had dawned.

The Mirage of the "Four Good Years"

From 1925 to 1929 business conditions in a large part of the Western World made such marked gains that many economists began to talk of a permanent plateau of prosperity. In 1928 a well-known Harvard economist declared: "There is absolutely no reason why the widely diffused prosperity which we are now witnessing should not permanently increase." One of his German counterparts proposed the rather remarkable thesis that capitalism was unconsciously changing into socialism, which almost automatically would ensure the abundant life:

We are in the period of capitalism, which in the main has overcome the era of free competition and the sway of blind laws of the market, and we are coming to a capitalist organization of economy [which] in reality signifies the supersession, in principle, of the capitalist principle of free competition by the Socialist principle of planned production.[3]

Actually, neither enduring prosperity nor socialism matured by capitalism was rooted in the real conditions of the times. Nevertheless, for a while a kind of economic well-being did flourish. Because of American loans, Germany paid its pared-down reparations installments on time and in full. More loans enabled German industry to rebuild itself, this time in the image of its American assembly-line model. France and England revitalized their own industries, partly out of reparations payments. Soon trade and production, in Europe as well as in America, exceeded their prewar levels.

Currency stabilization and industrial recovery allayed tensions and encouraged humane ventures. During this period, for example, turbulence in German political affairs abated. Nazis and Communists still made much noise, to be sure, but their influence was on the wane. Although the German Republic had not yet grown up to its democratic constitution, the auspices seemed good. Franco-German relations improved. In 1925, as we have seen (*supra*, p. 760), the two former enemies, together with England, Italy, and a number of other states, joined in a large-scale effort to deal with some of the unsettling attitudes and conditions caused by the war and by the treaties that had ended it. Altogether the complex of agreements went a long way — although certainly not the whole way — toward alleviating French fears of future German aggression. For Germany the agreements symbolized her readmittance into the European family. The next year the symbol was made substance by Germany's admission into the League of Nations. Buoyed up by a general feeling of optimism and good will, most states ratified the Pact of Paris (1928; commonly called the Kellogg-Briand Pact) which outlawed aggressive war as an instrument of national policy. In 1929 the Young Plan further scaled down German reparations payments.

One must be either an intellectual smart aleck or an ignoramus to hold that all the hopes and achievements of these "good years" were vaporous products of naïve idealism and shallow Babbittry. Many of the industrial and technological developments were real, lasting, and good. Most of the peacemakers, such as the French Premier Briand and the English Prime Minister MacDonald, were social statesmen of stature, vision, and courage.* Nonetheless, the underpinnings of the prosperous Golden Twenties were shaky. In Chapter 32 we shall survey the spiritual wasteland of those years. The fundamental forces and features of the economic system, more jungle than wasteland, were employed in ways which not only invited

---

3. R. Palmer Dutt, *World Politics, 1918–1936,* London, Victor Gallancz, Ltd., 1936, pp. 65–66.

* This assessment does not apply to the later years of MacDonald's tenure as Prime Minister, which witnessed such an appalling deterioration of the statesman's competence and ideals that they tend to overshadow completely his earlier strengths and achievements.

catastrophe but made it inevitable. Together with the United States, the leading industrial powers of Europe of that time—England, France, and Germany—share responsibility for the coming of this catastrophe; but our purpose is best served by concentrating on the developments in America and their European repercussions.

Untouched by invasion and bombings, American farms and factories during the war produced prodigious supplies of goods and foodstuffs, which the Allies bought with cash or with credit of one kind or another. By war's end, Europe owed American investors over ten billion dollars. As the chief debtors, France and England hoped to use reparations funds to meet their own obligations. When these funds failed or were scaled down, both countries asked the United States for commensurate debt adjustments. The United States, however, held that there was no connection between debts and reparations and insisted on complete fulfillment of contractual commitments (as Coolidge phrased it, "They hired the money, didn't they?").

Conceivably, the debtor states could have met their obligations even without the suggested scaling down if the United States had been willing to buy European products freely. Actually, it made a point of buying less. The Fordney-McCumber tariff raised duties to a higher level than ever before in American history. Denied both debt adjustment and ready access to American markets, the debtors faced a serious dilemma. With their own economies in the doldrums, they could scarcely raise the money by increasing domestic taxes; thus only default or repudiation remained. But either of these avenues of escape would seriously impair their credit and financial stability at a time when these could not stand further shock.

For a time the debtors were saved by the Dawes and Young plans. But obviously such loans and payments on other debts paid out of them did not make the best of sense, because mere circularity of exchange creates little new wealth. And, of course,

the whole complicated process would collapse at any time that America decided to discontinue loans to Germany.

The Great Depression

Presumably, such loans could go on forever, provided that the United States' economy remained strong. As we have seen, surface signs did suggest that the United States had made a miraculous breakthrough into permanent prosperity. But the signs were wrong. In 1929, the Great Boom came to an abrupt end, and the long lean years of depression completely dried up the dollar flood to Germany. Deprived of this support, the German economy collapsed. Because Germany was a good customer of England, British economic conditions, which were already suffering recession, seriously worsened. By 1930 and 1931, almost all of Europe was affected by the cataclysmic downturn.

Causes of the Depression

It is natural—and easy—to ask what caused the Depression, which in this country and in much of Europe lasted in one degree or another for a full decade. It is not easy to provide answers that stand the test of serious and informed analysis. The judgments of professional economists, although numerous and elaborate, tend to originate in certain general economic theories. When the theories differ, as they often do, the judgments contradict one another or at least fail to merge into a consensus. Among lay writers, analysis is almost invariably made to fit the political philosophy held by the particular analyst. The analysis here is summary in nature and subject to the same criticism.

If the Golden Twenties had really been golden, there would have existed, among other conditions, a sound economy that served the needs of all citizens equitably. Actually, the economy was anything but sound and basically served the greed of its managers. Throughout the twenties, the national income amounted to approximately

700 billion dollars. Of this about $170 billion, or 25 per cent, went to 5 or 6 per cent of the population. Obviously, levels of profits on the one hand and wages and salaries on the other were out of balance. This disproportion was maintained throughout most of the decade. "Output per worker in manufacturing industries," for example, "increased by about 43 per cent," while wages and salaries increased only 7 or 8 per cent.

Another criterion of a sound economy is a responsible and prudent design and management of the corporate structure. It is true that President Hoover's Conference on Unemployment reported (1929) that our economy was marked by "prudence on the part of management; . . . skill on the part of bankers . . . and [an] organic balance of economic forces." But the structure and activities of holding companies and investment trusts, which by that time dominated our national economy, could better be described as a jungle of exploitative forces. One authority expressed it as follows:

. . . the fact is that American enterprise in the twenties had opened its hospitable arms to an exceptional number of promoters, grafters, swindlers, imposters, and frauds. This, in the long history of such activities, was a kind of flood tide of corporate larceny.[4]

Moreover, at no time throughout this decade had the farmer enjoyed even a modest prosperity; for him the depression had set in as early as 1920. This was due in part to the high tariffs on manufactured goods, which forced the farmer to buy in a dear market while selling in a cheap (world) market. Although the rural population constituted but a minority of the whole, it was a substantial minority whose restricted buying power seriously affected overall economic conditions.

Much of the national "spending" went

4. John K. Galbraith, *The Great Crash,* Houghton Mifflin Co., Boston, 1955, p. 183. For both data and interpretive comment dealing with the causes of the depression, we are particularly indebted to this work. *Cf.,* especially, pp. 173–193.

into capital investment, the profits of which were channeled into further capital investment. In short, the profits of the rich were used in ways which made the wealthy even more wealthy. Obviously, this could not go on forever unless the masses could be counted on to remain satisfied with bare-subsistence living. But, the industrial revolution, and more recently the war, had long since given the masses tastes and expectations hardly calculated to guarantee their easy acceptance of subsistence living conditions.

In 1929 one third of the nation's income was siphoned off by 5 per cent of the population. With its disproportionately small share of the total income, the general public could not buy the flood of goods which steadily poured from the factories. For a while the illusion of a purchasing power commensurate with productive power was maintained by the popular practice of installment buying. But this kind of debt, when long continued, is necessarily self-defeating.

Moreover, the hectic ventures of investment capital during the middle and late twenties encouraged speculation. In the beginning, Wall Street's professional plungers led the way. As the market continued to rise, more conservative men of wealth began to buy and sell. Gradually the good news spread until eager citizens from almost every income level found their way into the market.

In 1927 the increase began in earnest. Day after day and month after month the price of stocks went up. . . . On May 20, when Lindbergh took off from Roosevelt Field and headed for Paris, a fair number of persons were unaware of the event. The market . . . had by then acquired a faithful band of devotees who spared no attention for any celestial matters. . . . Early in 1928, the nature of the boom changed. The mass escape into make-believe, so much a part of the speculative orgy, started in earnest. . . . On March 24 . . . General Motors gained nearly 5 points and the Monday following it went to 199. . . . [John J. Raskob, William Durant, the

Fischer brothers, William A. Cutte, and many other veteran operators] were assumed to have put their strength behind the market that spring. . . . Observing the group as a whole Professor [Charles Amos] Dice [of the Ohio State University] was especially struck by this "vision of the future and boundless hope and optimism. . . ." In noting their effect upon the market Professor Dice obviously found the English language verging on inadequacy. "Led by the mighty knights of the automobile industry, the steel industry, the radio industry . . . and finally joined in despair by many [bearish?] professional traders who, after much sackcloth and ashes, had caught the vision of progress, the Coolidge market had gone forward like the phalanxes of Cyrus, parasang upon parasang and again parasang upon parasang. . . ." [5]

In the last week of October 1929, the market, unable after all to sustain the pace of the fabled phalanxes, collapsed. The Golden Twenties were over.

The Mark of the Depression

The depression which followed the crash (not, it should be noted, essentially *caused* by it) is difficult to describe. Statistics are plentiful enough. Industrial production dropped from a high of 110 in 1929 to 58 in 1932.* The Dow-Jones averages of sixty-five strong, selected stocks plunged from $125.43 to $26.82. Exports declined from over $5 billion to about $1.5 billion. Building construction dropped in the same period from $30 billion to $5 billion. In 1929 approximately 3 per cent of the civilan labor force was unemployed; four years later the unemployed made up about 25 per cent of this force.

But statistics do not really tell the story. One may read that more than 40,000 persons are killed annually by automobiles and yet quite fail to sense the ineffable grief of one father whose child is mangled in a

wreck. On the other hand, some feeling for the depression is required if its nature and significance are to be even dimly understood. The following paragraph evokes some feeling for the disjointing of life which the depression had effected by 1933, some sense of the darkness that enveloped the country.

The fog of despair hung over the land. One out of four American workers lacked a job. Factories that had once darkened the skies with smoke stood ghostly and silent, like extinct volcanoes. Families slept in tarpaper shacks and tin-lined caves and scavenged like dogs for food in the city dump. In October the New York City Health Department had reported that over one-fifth of the pupils in public schools were suffering from malnutrition. Thousands of vagabond children were roaming the land, wild boys of the road. Hunger marchers, pinched and bitter, were parading cold streets in New York and Chicago. On the country-side unrest had already flared into violence. Farmers stopped milk trucks along Iowa roads and poured the milk into the ditch. Mobs halted mortgage sales, ran the men from the banks and insurance companies out of town, intimidated courts and judges, demanded a moratorium on debts. When a sales company in Nebraska invaded a farm and seized two trucks, the farmers in the Newman Grove district organized a posse, called it the "Red Army," and took the two trucks back. In West Virginia, mining families, turned out of their homes, lived in tents along the road on pinto beans and black coffee.[6]

The United States, of course, was not alone in the deepening misery and despair; much of Europe was mired in it too. The capitalist system had experienced contractions and depressions before. In fact, depression had for centuries been one of its fixed features, a kind of seed-rotting on which the system's subsequent grand flowerings depended. This depression was different. The intolerable material and spiritual sickness of the great decline caused millions in Europe and America to question seriously whether such a system

---

5. Galbraith, *op. cit.,* pp. 13–17 *passim.*

* Index numbers 1935–1939 = 100. The statistics cited in this paragraph are from Broadus Mitchell, *Depression Decade,* Rinehart and Co. Inc., New York, 1947, pp. 438–455 *passim.*

6. Arthur M. Schlesinger, Jr., *The Crisis of the Old Order,* Houghton Mifflin Co., Boston, 1957, p. 3.

had not served its day. Indeed, it had already been replaced in Russia where, for all the world to see, economic conditions were anything but depressed.

Out of such questionings came the growing belief that national economies should be made subject to public planning and

A breadline in New York City during the Depression.

management. Nurtured by concerned intellectuals, the collectivist impulse assumed varied forms. In Western Europe (including England) socialist parties grew in strength and respectability. Communism attracted many. In the United States, after the "money changers had fled from their high seats in the temple of our civilization," the people were less sure of what kind and what degree of planning were desirable. But no one could doubt that the majority was ready for almost any innovation and experimentation that could promise food, jobs, and security. Throughout the world it was felt that somewhere there must be a way out of the wilderness, somewhere there must be men who could lead stricken peoples to find that way. And there were. In the United States, Franklin D. Roosevelt improvised a New Deal. In Germany, Adolf Hitler drummed in National Socialism. In France (if only briefly) the Socialist Léon Blum led a "popular front" in instituting a program of mild social reform. For a while the Labour party in England, under Ramsay MacDonald's timid leadership, gave that country its first faint taste of socialism. In the Scandinavian countries (most notably in Sweden) mixed economies developed, which were in part capitalism and in part socialism.

The creation of one or another kind of

Shacks of unemployed along Seattle's waterfront, 1933. Such villages were called "Hoovervilles."

Two of New York City's many unemployed who tried to earn their daily bread by selling apples on the streets of the city.

managed economies, whether spurred by the depression or generated by the revolutionary ferment stirred by World War I, naturally involved wide-ranging political and social changes. In later chapters we shall consider the overall transformations that occurred in Russia, Italy, Germany, and the United States.

SELECTED READINGS

Albrecht-Carrie, René, *France, Europe and the Two World Wars,* Harper & Brothers, New York, 1961.

A very readable account of the main events of Europe's political life, 1914–1939. An epilogue of some 25 pages surveys the "consequences of France's abdication" (in the 1930s) and the impact and consequences of World War II. Particularly worthwhile are the sections on the "false peace"—from Versailles to Locarno—and on the declining power of France after the coming to power of Adolph Hitler in Germany

Brogan, D. W., *France Under the Republic,* Harper & Brothers, New York, 1940.

One of the best general histories of the political life of France between the fall of Napoleon III and the outbreak of World War II.

Carr, E. H., *International Relations Since the Peace Treaties,* Macmillan & Co., London, 1937.

A brief description of international events for the twenty years following the Versailles Treaty. The organization emphasizes the "period of enforcement," 1920–1924, the "period of pacification," 1924–1930, the "return of power politics," 1930–1933, and the "end of the treaties" with the reemergence of Germany.

*Chambers, Clarke A., ed., *The New Deal at Home and Abroad, 1929–1945,* The Free Press, New York, 1965.

A very interesting collection of excerpts from the writings of a number of influential personages of the period—F. Scott Fitzgerald on the Jazz Age; Franklin D. Roose-

velt on the New Deal; Grace L. Coyle on "Rebuilding the American Dream"; Reinhold Niebuhr on the state of religion; Gunnar Myrdal on America's black/white problem; and others.

*Galbraith, John Kenneth, *The Great Crash, 1929,* Houghton Mifflin Co., Boston, 1961.

An informative account of the months that preceded the Wall Street debacle and the weeks that followed it. The reader learns more than who did what with the market; he learns something of the outlook of a people at a moment in history. Written in a very graceful and witty style.

*Havighurst, Alfred F., *Twentieth Century Britain,* Harper & Row, New York, 1966 (2nd ed.).

A detailed examination of British political events.

Jackson, Gabriel, *The Spanish Republic and the Civil War, 1931–1939,* Princeton University Press, Princeton, 1965.

Although his sympathies lie with the Loyalists, the author's careful research and judicious evaluation of issues and events assure the interested reader a more nearly full and well-balanced understanding of the rise and fall of the Spanish Republic than he is likely to obtain from any other single source.

Mitchell, Broadus, *Depression Decade,* Rinehart & Co., New York, 1947.

One of the best attempts to describe in graphic form the events of America's Depression and New Deal years. Its chief fault, from the standpoint of the present-day college student, is that it was written before a generation of research and publication had passed. In other words, sections of it are outdated.

*Rollins, Alfred B., Jr., ed., *Depression, Recovery, and War, 1929–1945,* McGraw-Hill Book Co., New York, 1966.

Although most of the articles of this symposium fall into what many would call the "snippet" category, they are so varied and so well chosen that they can profitably be used by readers who already have a reasonably sound understanding of the broad movements of these times and want or need such source capsules as this collection offers.

Asterisk (*) denotes paperback.

*Shannon, David A., *Between the Wars: America, 1919–1941,* Houghton Mifflin Co., Boston, 1965.

A highly readable, interpretative narration of America's domestic and foreign affairs in the interwar period. Introducing each chapter is a section devoted to what the author believes are misconceptions of the events narrated in that chapter and the author's "corrective" comments. One does not always need to agree with these "corrections" to find them highly stimulating.

Slosson, Preston, *The Great Crusade and After, 1914–1928,* The Macmillan Co., New York, 1930.

Concerned with the impact of the violence of war on the fabric of American society in the years after the war—"the blunted conscience, the overwrought nerves, the growth of intolerance . . . ," and the development of an interest in the materialistic ways of life that were stimulated by a galloping "prosperity."

The Recovery Problem in the United States, The Brookings Institution, Washington, D.C., 1936.

A collection of articles that attempt to point out what obstacles to the return to prosperity lay ahead of the United States in 1936, and what kind of a program should be mapped to overcome them. The first three chapters deal with the background, course, and world impact of the Great Depression.

Toynbee, Arnold J., *The World After the Peace Conference,* Oxford University Press, London, 1925.

An assessment of the general forces at work in the years 1914–1923, forces that brought on the war, and that seemed to prevent its permanent settlement.

Wecter, Dixon, *The Age of the Great Depression, 1929–1941,* The Macmillan Co., New York, 1948.

A volume on the *History of American Life* series. Very readable account of the impact of the Depression on the whole of American culture. Well illustrated.

Werth, Alexander, *The Twilight of France, 1933–1940,* ed. by D. W. Brogan, Harper & Brothers, New York, 1942.

This abridgement of three books includes Rightist groups, Laval, Blum, and interesting accounts of the Popular Front, its response to the Spanish Civil War, the strikes of 1936, France's dilemma *vis à vis* Munich crisis, and an evaluation of the Vichy regime.

28

The Collectivist Trend between the Wars: Russia; Italy

COMMUNIST RUSSIA

Background of the Russian Revolution

The ending of World War I closed one "season of dismay" and inaugurated another, aptly designated by the novelist Arthur Koestler as the "Age of Longing." By then, many traditional attitudes and modes of behavior seemed outworn and unserviceable. Faith in the old frames of reference gradually gave way to a congeries of doubts and discontents. Out of this creeping confusion came an almost universal yearning for new outlooks, new political and social systems, and new manners. The most radical resolution of these longings occurred in Russia when, in 1917, a splinter political party captured power and created a new society.

It surprised no one that the Tsarist regime should one day fall. That it should ultimately fall to a handful of Bolshevik visionaries surprised almost everyone, including many of the Bolsheviks themselves. From the perspective of the present, however, the radical resolution does not appear so remarkable. Because the industrial revolution had come to Russia so late, no sizable middle class existed. Without such a class, a middle course had little chance to emerge. When change came, it was almost certain to be marked by extremism of one kind or another.[1]

1. For a more detailed exposition of this point and those immediately following, see John L. Stipp, *Soviet Russia Today: Patterns and Prospects,* Harper and Brothers, New York, 1956, Chapter 1. A fuller and richer treatment can be found in John Maynard, *Russia in Flux,* The Macmillan Company, New York, 1948, pp. 22–38, from which much of the material in the cited chapter is taken.

The Misery of the Masses: The Peasants

Certain long-standing characteristics of Russian society clearly pointed to a climactic time of troubles. For example, Russia, alone among the great powers, had missed the Renaissance. She did not, therefore, participate in the general reexamination of the meaning and worth of individualism and the escape from medieval inertia that profoundly affected the subsequent development of Western peoples. Russia also missed the Protesant Revolt and the Catholic Reformation that had brought, in the Protesant Revolt, some curb to the repressive force of ecclesiastical power over the peasant and, in the Catholic Reformation, a reinvigoration of the mind and spirit of the clergy.

Cut off from these progressive influences, Russia easily (perhaps inevitably) succumbed to absolutist rule. For nearly 500 years the masses of Russia lived in circumstances that approached the unbelievable. Serfdom, although officially abolished in 1861, still held the impoverished peasant in its grip until the Bolshevik Revolution. The masses were so lacking the refinement of human qualities that they were often referred to in nineteenth-century Russian literature as "dead souls." When, goaded beyond endurance, some rose against their masters, punishment was swift and unmerciful. Peasant families normally lived in squalor inconceivable by their counterparts on American farms. They were always hungry and ill-clad. Their huts, until the twentieth century, commonly consisted of one room. The preponderant masses, both peasant and worker, were illiterate.

The Misery of the Masses: The Workers

As late as 1914, Russia's industrial workers made up less than fifteen per cent of the population. Most of them were transplanted peasants who were hardly a generation removed from the soil. They worked from twelve to sixteen hours a day; in 1914 their average pay was only about $150 a year. Although few in number, Russian factories tended to be much larger than industrial plants in Western Europe or America. Often the worker and his family were quartered on the factory grounds. As Russia stepped up its military preparedness, the state increasingly became the largest single entrepreneur. Under these conditions Russia's industrial proletariat both worked and lived in a military atmosphere.

Unions were forbidden by law until the opening years of the twentieth century. Even then, the unions that were allowed—under the fantastic system called "police socialism"—were designed to thwart rather than advance worker solidarity. They were, in fact, government-supervised company unions. To counter these unions, certain labor leaders created a new organization modeled after the ancient *Mir*. Ostensibly this new instrument—called the soviet—dealt only with such matters as workers' complaints about the malfunctioning of established rules and practices. Actually the soviets held secret meetings to discuss revolutionary ideas and mull over schemes for a general day of reckoning. Since their worker-members were peasants under the skin, and since the soviets came to play a significant part in the revolution to come, the new organization may be regarded as one important element in the (at least partial) successes later achieved by the Bolshevik regime in welding together the interests of worker and peasant.

The Coming of Communism

The March Revolution

We have already considered the infiltration of radical and reformist thought into late nineteenth and early twentieth century Russia (*supra*, p. 669). We have noted, too, the flareup and failure of the Revolution of 1905. But although it failed, the Revolution left memories and sharpened appetites. Another crisis would find the revolutionaries more determined, and the masses more wary of grand, royal promises. This was the case in 1917. By then, Russian armies had been hopelessly smashed by the Kaiser's efficient war machine. Mass desertions were common. Internally, transportation facilities, none too good to begin with, were in a chaotic condition; starvation stalked the cities. Things had become so bad in the House of the Autocrat that even the nobles and gentry were moved to murmured protests.

In February a general strike was called in Petrograd (present-day Leningrad). Within a week it had spread and merged with uprisings throughout the country. The Tsar ordered the dissolution of the Duma. The deputies accepted the order but remained in the capital awaiting developments. Thousands of workers—yesterday's peasants—demonstrated in the streets. On February 27 a significant scene dramatized the rebellious mood of the people. Ordered to disperse the demonstrators, the Tsar's capital guards (numbering about 150,000) not only refused to fire upon the insurrectionists but finally joined them.

By March the Tsar's authority had simply melted away. The strangest thing about the March Revolution was its unrevolutionary character. There were no long drawn out bloody riots; there was little pillaging, little noise and bombast. Soldiers quit fighting; trains stopped running; policemen vanished—in short, the state quietly collapsed. On March 2, 1917, the Tsar of all the Russias signed a simple statement saying ". . . we have recognized that it is for the good of the country that we should abdicate the Crown of the Russian State. . . ." The autocracy, established in the fifteenth century, thus surrendered to the "dark people," and a provisional government took its place. The new government, however, turned out to be composed mostly of bourgeois moderates rather than toilers.

For a short time the new government seemed to enjoy the confidence of the majority of the people. Even the socialist St. Petersburg Soviet supported it. The hated Autocracy had been humbled and harassed from power. A constitutional convention was promised—to be elected by the general adult, male populace. At this point, American, British, and French observers expected, as the next logical step, the setting up of a model of their own bourgeois democracy. Landed aristocrats had stepped out of power; middle-class "democrats" would fill the void, as they had in England in the late seventeenth century and in France in the late eighteenth century.

The provisional government tried to play the role seemingly assigned to it by history. But for middle-class democracy to succeed there must first be a sizable middle class. There also must be available leaders within its ranks who possess political experience and a workable program. In tumultuous times an added ingredient is needed—an iron will. In 1917 Russia, none of these ingredients existed except the iron will. And that, as it turned out, was found only in the leader of the Bolshevik party.

Moreover, it soon became evident that the new regime was more interested in winning a war (which most Russians believed lost) than in reforming the political and social institutions of the land. The St. Petersburg Soviet became increasingly critical. Workers, peasants, soldiers, and sailors— all impatiently demanded an end to their suffering. In July 1917, Prince Lvov, the liberal royalist who had accepted the premiership when the Tsarist regime collapsed, resigned in favor of the much more radical Alexander Kerensky. But the new leader, although eager for socialist reform, felt (no less than his predecessor) the need to honor his country's obligations to her allies. Workers in the cities demanded bread; village peasants demanded land and a fair price for their produce. About all Kerensky and his quarreling colleagues could do was make promises. Thus desertion continued at the front, and chaos spread at home.

The Bolshevik Revolution

Meanwhile, other figures were cueing themselves into the drama. The provisional government promised peace, but only after victory. It promised land and factory reform, but only after a Constituent Assembly could meet and draw up a constitution. The date for the meeting had already been postponed several times. The provisional government neither supported the soviets nor crushed them. On the other hand, Lenin and his Bolshevik comrades were sharp, sure, and simple in their basic strategy and propaganda — almost the only leaders in all Russia who were. Their slogans said what the people wanted to hear: "Peace," now; "Bread," for the cities; "Land," to be taken from the gentry and given to the peasant; and "All the power to the soviets," as the vehicle to effect these aims.

From March to October of 1917, conditions drifted ever closer to pure anarchy. In September, Kerensky launched the last great offensive that, after a faint flicker of success, faded and failed. The Bolshevik coup followed. It was brief, virtually bloodless and, as it turned out, had significant consequence. Lenin and his colleagues already were in controlling positions within the soviets. In October * the Petrograd Soviet, the largest and most powerful in the country, called a Congress of Soviets into session. On the night of the 27th it passed a resolution that declared that all land belonged to the peasants, and all power belonged to the soviets. Back of the Congress stood the peasant-worker army. The provisional government offered only feeble resistance (although in Moscow, Kiev, and several other large cities some sanguinary fighting took place). Within the week, Lenin and the Bolsheviks were in power. Communism had come to Russia.

---

* In 1917 the Russian calendar was thirteen days behind the calendar used in other parts of Europe and in America. Thus, what is "Octobrist" to a Communist is "Novembrist" to a non-Russian. On February 14, 1918, the old Russian calendar was brought into harmony with the one used in the West.

The Ideological Content of Communism

The Basic Concepts

No matter how far-fetched or difficult Marxism-Leninism may strike us, we must give attention to its fundamental ideas, since the greater part of Soviet ideology and practice derives from them.

One basic tenet of Marxism-Leninism is the belief that matter shapes mind; that is, that thought arises from material conditions. Among the material conditions that influence human behavior, economic forces are paramount. These forces are the creators of all societies. They, and they alone, provide satisfactions for the wants that they have created. Mismanaged, they fail and frustrate these wants.

Another tenet holds that the forces of life are fluid, forever flowing. Change is eternal. At any given moment that which is, is becoming that which it was not. But change is not effected by chance (except incidentally). There is a pattern of development that man can discern and develop, even though he cannot alter it. Its features are simple. Every life force meets opposition in its development. Out of this encounter comes that which is neither the original nor the countering element, but an amalgam. In its turn this new element meets its opposing force that merges with it, and creates a new amalgam — and so on.

Class Struggle

Together these two fundamental ideas form the key, in Marxist thought,† that unlocks the mysteries of human existence — past, present, and (up until the establishment of the classless society, at least) future. Proper use of the key produces understandings which, in turn, provide bases for prediction. One understanding is (as the

---

† There are several varieties of Marxists. Here, we refer to the Marxist who claims Lenin and his disciples as the true interpreters of original "scientific socialism."

Communist Manifesto has it) that "the history of all hitherto existing society is the history of class struggles." From earliest times to the present, human beings have been divided into two groups — the exploited and the exploiters. In ancient Rome, plebeians struggled against patricians. In medieval times the serf sought escape from the dominant rule of the landed lord. In modern society the worker is closing ranks against the bourgeois capitalist.

In the past, dominant minorities have ruled every society. This has been true even when, on the surface, the opposite has appeared to be the case. In "democratic," bourgeois republics, for example, the ruling clique is made up of industrial magnates. The people (that is, the masses) may exercise the franchise and believe they are deciding who shall represent them. In reality they elect candidates who, except for occasional mavericks (or popular leaders that arise during a passing time of troubles), know where the real power lies.

In Marxist analysis the elite members of the dominant bourgeois minority dig their own graves. They need immense aggregations of workers to labor in the factories that grow ever larger and more numerous. To garner large profits they keep wages depressed and working conditions unsafe and unhealthy. Working in juxtaposition with one another, the workers exchange grievances, form unions, and test their "bargaining" strength. They lose, try again, and lose again, since the bourgeoisie elite control not only industry but also public office and public opinion. But the economic facts of life are not changed by these capitalist victories. For no national economy can ever achieve permanent prosperity or even solvency as long as buying power lags behind productive power. And under capitalism the economy of scarcity is a prerequisite.

Emergence of Classless Society

Eventually (according to Lenin) nations turn to imperialist adventures. They seek to carve out new markets in undeveloped

Karl Marx, founder of "scientific socialism."

regions. Inevitably this kind of adventure leads to international conflict. The losing powers suffer not only military defeat, but the workers, oppressed beyond endurance, rise against their weakened governments. Radical regimes are established (as, briefly, in France in 1871), or revolutions are staged to bring these regimes into being (as in Russia in 1905). Bourgeois power again asserts itself, but the day of reckoning is only postponed. Experience is gained; memories are cherished. In the end the proletariat, led by strong-willed professional revolutionaries, wrest control from the exploiters, and overthrow the dictatorship of the bourgeoisie. In its place they set up the dictatorship of the proletariat.

According to Marxist thought, the class struggle between the proletariat and the bourgeoisie will be the last of the long series, for the coming victory will represent the overpowering majority of the people. Hitherto, victories were won by small minorities: patricians over plebeians; lords over serfs; bourgeoisie over proletariat. When the workers set up their dictatorship, it will function vigorously but relatively briefly, for when the exploiting minority is tamed or "liquidated," the masses will have no enemy to contend with.

The final stage is reached when the state, having no coercive functions in a gradually perfected, classless society, simply withers away.

Such are the concepts that make up the basic framework of Marxist ideology. However, some of these basic concepts were modified (as we shall see) after the Russian Revolution had ended, when the Bolsheviks turned to the business of managing the political affairs of the nation. But in the main, orthodox Marxist ideology supplied the guidelines for the new rulers.

The Critical Period— 1917 to 1920

"War Communism"

In Lenin's view, World War I was but the prelude to world revolution. Under the leadership of Communist elites, the toiling masses—battered by mounting violence and prodded by a growing understanding of the devouring selfishness of rampant capitalism—would rise up against their bourgeois masters and turn the international imperialist war into a universal class war. Uneven as the pace of proletarian victories might be, the day of the "Big Change" had come. The capitalist *nay* was emerging into the socialist *yea*. Russian Communists might lead the way, but anything short of permanent—that is, global—revolution would miss the goal. And for global revolution, the signs were auspicious. Already in Hungary, Germany, and Austria, Communist leaders were preparing for the takeover. As the revolution gained momentum, national governments (even the bourgeois democracies of the West) would be swept away. Lenin and his colleagues also believed

that they immediately could introduce the full Communist program in Russia.* All land and all industry could (and should) be nationalized at once. True, administrative bottlenecks, even serious and prolonged blundering, would undoubtedly mark the opening phases of the task. But these were details. Once the expropriators were expropriated, the new society could absorb the jolts and jars that inevitably follow when the turning of a grand pivot of history swings one civilization into oblivion and another into being.

Confident that they were reading the curve of history correctly, Lenin and his colleagues set to work. Numerous contacts were established with Communist leaders in other parts of Europe—Bela Kun in Hungary and Rosa Luxemburg and Karl Liebknecht in Germany were outstanding examples. War weariness, linked with postwar social restiveness, seemed to give promise that workers and peasants were ready for radical ventures. A short-lived Soviet Republic was established in Bavaria; Bela Kun, supported by Russian advisers, took over the government of Hungary (March–August, 1918); a Socialist became the first chancellor of the Austrian Republic; in 1919 and 1920, worker unrest in England erupted in a series of large-scale strikes; German Communists ("Spartacists") staged uprisings in Berlin (January–February, 1919). Throughout Europe, classical radical rhetoric took on the flesh and blood of political reality. The Third International (the Comintern), founded in Moscow, served as the organizational center for universal revolutionary activity.

In Russia the new government, calling itself the Council of Peoples' Commis-

---

* Note *introduce,* not put into full scale operation. Historians are in dispute over the basic motivation for "War Communism," some holding it would not have been attempted if the regime had not been threatened by the White armies. For a detailed account written from this viewpoint, see Edward H. Carr, *A History of Soviet Russia,* Macmillan Company, New York, 1952, Vol. II, pp. 147–269.

sars, nationalized banks, land, and factories. A secret police section (the Cheka) was established to deal with reactionary opposition. When the Constituent Assembly, Russia's first and only freely elected national legislative body, convened with a majority of non-Bolsheviks in control, Red guards dispersed the Assembly's members after only a single day's session. The national debt, including of course all foreign loans, was abolished. In March 1918, Trotsky, acting under urgent orders from Lenin, met with German commissioners and signed the Treaty of Brest-Litovsk that took Russia out of the war. History appeared to the coterie of Communist leaders, who held the reins of power, to be running on schedule. Workers of the world were rising under the leadership of men whose mastery of dialectical materialism allowed them perspective and understandings that were denied to others. The words of the famous workers' song, *The International,* seemed quick with life: "Arise ye slaves; no more in thrall! The earth shall rise on new foundations. We have been naught, we shall be all."

Counterrevolution

But the Communists misread both the spirit and conditions of the times. Except for isolated cells in various countries, the workers of the world were not only unready for world revolution but were profoundly unsympathetic toward it. The pull of nationalism was strong. In Germany, it was not an international workers' song but "Deutschland, Deutschland über Alles" that still stirred masses and classes alike. French spines tingled to the "Marseillaise." British proletarians proudly stood at attention to the strains of "God Save the King." The average worker, wherever he lived, wanted more to reform the prevailing economic system than to abolish it. Higher wages, fewer working hours, a chance to move up the social ladder (the Horatio Alger dream in America)—these appealed far more than the vision of pro-

Lenin and Stalin in the early 1920s.

letarian dictatorship in a superstate. In light of these conditions, the "permanent revolution" was doomed from the start.

Meanwhile, the Communist rulers of Russia faced such grave domestic difficulties that the prospect of their survival seemed anything but bright. The war had disrupted the Russian transport system which even in peacetime had never been noted for its efficiency. Confiscation of industrial plants had substituted loyal but untrained Communist managers for experienced bourgeois leadership. On the "nationalized" land, peasants worked fields for their own needs and profit. The combined effects of a seriously disrupted transport system, an amateur, improvised industrial management, and a peasant-centered agricultural economy were almost more than the new regime could cope with.

To these staggering problems two others were added. The Allied powers encouraged the creation of a number of buffer states along Russia's western borders to counter the advantages gained by Germany in the

Treaty of Brest-Litovsk.* Within two months after the November revolution, the Allies recognized the independence of four states that had been formerly a part of Russia—Finland, Estonia, Latvia, and Lithuania. Furthermore, to help local anti-Communist groups to oust their new Red rulers, the Allied governments sent troops to invade or to infiltrate certain regions of Russia.

At the same time, a half dozen "White" armies, led by die-hard Tsarist officers, converged on Trotsky's hastily formed Red defenders. For three years (1917–1920) the masses fed on blood and murder. The advantages of numerical strength, financial resources, and experienced leadership lay with the Whites and their foreign allies. But they were not enough to win the day. The weight of centuries of oppression now made itself felt. With the overthrow of autocracy, Russia's "Dead Souls" experienced a feeling of release that made any attempt to restore the old regime foolish and futile. Many Russians, probably most, opposed Red rule and wished to be rid of it, but not at the price that the Whites demanded, which, by their own admission, was the full restoration of the old regime. Moreover, the general war weariness of the allies was so great that when quick victory seemed impossible, as indeed it was, they one by one withdrew. By late 1920, the counter-revolution had failed.†

The New Economic Policy

The Retreat from "War Communism"

New troubles replaced old ones for the triumphant vanguard of the proletariat.

Military victory had not educated Red factory managers in economic know-how. At the end of the war, all the joints of the economy were unhinged. Peasants refused to plant more crops than for their own needs. If surpluses developed, they were either hid from government agents or were destroyed. In 1920 drought spread famine across the land. By 1921 economic paralysis was almost complete.

Lenin had hoped, and apparently believed, that uprisings in other nations, particularly in industrialized nations, would open the way to proletarian control of the entire Western economy including, of course, international exchange. With the failure of socialist revolutions to materialize or, as in Bavaria and Hungary, to win to victory, Russia stood alone. For the present, at least, whatever way out there was for the stricken country would have to be found by its revolutionary leaders—if found at all.

Late in 1920, rioting occurred among factory workers in Petrograd. It was an ominous sign. Peasant uprisings could be expected. Few farmers dream socialist dreams; even fewer feel enthusiasm for governments eager to confiscate farm produce. But if the *workers* (the proletarians in whose name the dictatorship was established) were to fall away, all would be lost. In February and March of 1921, Red sailors mutinied at Kronstadt where, but four years before, they had sparked the Revolution. Now the government took drastic action. Up until this point Lenin had somehow hoped to force the peasantry to fall into (socialist) step with the city proletariat. But when the city proletariat turned recalcitrant, Lenin laid aside the Marxist book of rules. Why were the workers wavering? They lacked food. How could they be assured of prompt and sufficient supplies? By pacification of the peasants. How could the peasants be mollified without violating the dictates of socialist policy? They could not. For the present, then, policy must yield.

---

* And, almost certainly, to help rid Europe of a socialist state that might serve as an example and rallying point for other peoples who were disillusioned with capitalist ways.

† In 1920, Poland entered the war on the side of the Whites, hoping to slice off a portion of the Ukraine. After a kind of stalemate, the two powers reached a boundary settlement in the Treaty of Riga (March 18, 1921).

The instrument designed to effect agreement with the peasants was called the New Economic Policy (NEP). It essentially was the substitution of a limited grain tax (or tax in kind) for confiscation of surpluses, and the right to trade surpluses for money or goods in the open market. Some limited private production was also permitted. Because of a second and even more severe season of drought, the new policy brought little immediate improvement. Peasants planted beyond their own family needs, and sold the surplus for all that the market would bear. With a fairly steady supply of food, factory workers gradually lost their restiveness. Supplied with funds from a banking system now at least partially capitalistic, small producers and merchants set themselves up in business, and made a profit. Collection of taxes increased. The budget was brought into balance. The value of the ruble was stabilized (although at a rather fantastic figure). War Communism was dead.

The Rise of the Nepmen

For the next five or six years the New Economic Policy performed double service for both Lenin and the Party workers. It lulled to a murmur the haunting question of how socialism could develop in a country as backward as Russia. At the same time, it paradoxically provided the means for transforming the country's economic backwardness into at least a measure of economic strength. Critics of the regime could argue (and did) that NEP proved the impracticability of socialism. But while they argued, Russia grew stronger—under Communist rulers, if not by Communist rule. Lenin made it plain that NEP was a stopgap and that the day would come when two steps forward toward socialism would be possible, because one step backward had been ventured.

In 1921, industrial and agricultural prices had been so far apart that economic collapse had seemed certain. Three years later the two were roughly in the same balance that had existed before the war.[2] In fact, the "step backward" was so successful that new embarrassments developed. The "strong and sober" peasants, once courted by Stolypin, managed their farms so efficiently that they soon outstripped the plodding masses. Month after month the disparity between the rich peasant—the *kulak*—and the poor and middling peasant grew greater. By crafty calculation and manipulation of market opportunities, *kulak* surpluses were transmuted into more acres and still more surpluses. By 1926 the *kulak* class possessed almost a monopoly of Russian draught animals and farm machinery. Those of the middling class who could afford to rent horses and implements from the *kulaks* did so in the hope of making enough profits in a few years to join the owning class. In this way the ranks of the *kulaks* increased. But many middling peasants failed to clear such profits, or even to make their payment on rented animals and equipment. When this happened, they ran the risk of sinking permanently into the lowest stratum, the "poor peasant" class. To the extent that these developments occurred—and they occurred on an increasing scale—Lenin's NEP countenanced, even aggravated, the class struggle of Tsarist times. Certainly, the poor peasant found little substance in the grand promises of the Revolution.

The End of NEP (1928)

If the new policy sharpened conflict among peasant classes, it also divided Red leadership. After Lenin's death in 1924, two of his co-workers, Stalin and Trotsky, began a struggle for power that lasted for nearly three years. NEP was only one of a number of issues over which they quarreled. Trotsky and his followers believed that the purposes of NEP had been achieved. They argued that it was time to begin large-scale efforts to industrialize the country. They

2. Carr, *op. cit.,* p. 191. For a detailed account of the ups and downs of NEP's course, see *ibid.,* Chapter 5.

also insisted upon the necessity for "permanent revolution." Good Marxists, they held, could not give up hope for proletarian victories abroad. Stalin, on the contrary, stoutly argued that the time had not yet come for a new venture in socialist agriculture.

It is difficult to determine how sincere Stalin was in defending this position. Throughout most of the twenties the new policy was unquestionably necessary if the regime was to survive. But unless the transition to socialism was begun soon, the *kulaks* would pass beyond control; the revolution would then surely yield to the long expected Thermidorean reaction. Stalin understood this danger clearly enough. But he also understood that if NEP were abandoned while Trotsky was leading the fight for its abandonment, more than transition to socialism would result—the emergence of Trotsky as supreme leader would be assured.

As General Secretary of the Communist Party, Stalin was in a position to put his men into key party offices. He did this with such thoroughness that, by the mid-1920s, his views had become the Party's views. Therefore, when Trotsky demanded the end of NEP without further delay, Stalin called for a vote by the Party Congress. The decision to continue NEP clearly demonstrated Stalin's supremacy. With power

These wives of field workers are operating a separator on a huge collective farm in the Caucasus region.

now his, Stalin first sent Trotsky to Siberia (in 1927) and then (in 1929) expelled him from the country.

This settled the question of Lenin's successor. But the economic dilemma posed by the Nepmen remained. Stalin met it by adopting Trotsky's program. NEP had allowed the Party to weather the post-revolutionary storm. Now (in 1928) socialist planning could be applied to agriculture and industry. If the Nepmen objected, as they surely would, so much the worse for them.

Socialist Planning

Goals and Methods

The essence of socialism is public ownership and control of all *productive* forms of wealth for purposes of use instead of profit. From 1929 on, this principle was applied to virtually all industrial and agricultural activities. Individual farms were merged into either of two kinds of collectivized farms: the *kolkhoze* and the *sovkhoze*. *Kolkhozes* were based on the cooperative principle—farm lands were cleared by communities and worked by their members. In size, they varied from collectives of seventy-five or eighty "households" to a few of nearly one thousand households. Grains, livestock, and other produce were distributed (in amounts determined by the state), to the *kolkhoze*, to the households, and to the state itself. Each family was given a small individual holding for its own cultivation, in addition to the produce allotted to it from the *kolkhoze*. The *sovkhoze* was given over entirely to state management. Workers lived on these units (usually much larger than their collective counterparts) as day laborers. Of the total land brought under cultivation after 1928, about 95 per cent was made up of *kolkhozes*.

All industry was likewise socialized (except, again, inconsequential fragments). A central planning board was created to fix the kinds, purposes, and amounts of capital investment. It also determined the hours and wages of laborers, prices, and priority of goods to be produced—indeed, all conditions of economic activity of both the individual and the nation. Because Russia lacked power facilities and the machines that produce machines, emphasis was naturally placed on heavy industry. This meant, of course, that consumer goods would be sacrificed for a long time to come. Necessarily, power plants would take precedence over shoe factories, the tool and dye industry over house building, locomotives over automobiles, and so on.

The goals, and the methods to achieve them, were set forth in a series of plans, each originally running for five years (later changed to seven years). The task of drawing up the master blueprint for each period was assigned to the State Planning Commission (Gosplan). The plan for each period stipulated what amount of the nation's total economic energy was to be devoted to agriculture, and what amount was to be devoted to industry. It also provided for the estimated consumer needs of the citizenry, the modes and methods of distribution, the construction needs of heavy and light industry, and the goals and operational procedures of all *kolkhozes* and *sovkhozes*.

Such an undertaking, as unprecedented as it was bewilderingly complex and comprehensive, originally seemed to many beyond what human skill and ingenuity could achieve. How could meeting the needs of tens of millions of persons be planned? More basically, who could determine, or even define, the needs of a nation's population? What criteria of priority should be used? How could gross miscalculations be prevented or remedied? What practicable sanctions could be devised to enforce unpopular decisions? What incentives, consistent with socialist doctrines, would keep the nation at work?

From the days of the first Plan (1928–1935) to the present, Soviet leaders have grappled with these and related questions. It is natural to ask: with what success? Those who believe in the capitalist way of life deny that any people's needs can be planned by a central body, no matter how brilliant and dedicated its leaders may be. Communists point to the historic record. For nearly a half century they have managed an economy that *is* planned; and, of course, it is growing more, not less socialistic. Still, the problems persist.

Party and Government Agencies

A vast complex of Party and government agencies has grown to meet the needs of life in a planned society. Although *Gosplan* drew up the master plan, the Party decided what the basic elements of the Plan were to be. For example, Lenin and his colleagues in the Politbureau early laid down the dictum that Russia's first need was electrification and industrialization. No official in *Gosplan,* no matter how exalted his position, could have altered this decision. On the other hand, once plans had been approved and put into execution by *Gosplan* and its agencies, no local Party official could hope to exempt his community from the plans. Yet, on the local level, considerable discretion was allowed in other ways. For example, local soviets often decided what kind and what amount of recreational equipment and facilities were to be supplied to their communities.

To prevent or to remedy bureaucratic miscalculations, an elaborate system of "self-criticism" was devised. Citizens from whatever part of Russia, or in whatever kind of work, were urged to register complaints about "socialist services" (but not, of course, about policies decided by the Party). Soviet newspapers and magazines regularly published such complaints. In addition to this popular "control," Party inspectors were sent throughout the land to gather information about what seemed to be going either right or wrong. Perhaps the best barometers of public opinion and reaction were the elected officials of the tens of thousands of local soviets (somewhat comparable to our New England town selectmen, or our city councilmen). From their complaints, information and evaluations found their way through the maze of Party and government organizations into the counsels of the Party leadership. Acting on data gathered from all of these sources, the Party leadership decided where pressures were too great to be maintained, how much slack should be loosened in the endless chain of economic activity, and when and where to push forward again.

Behind these agencies and processes loomed the large and dread state organs of sanction—particularly the secret police, Party-packed courts, and concentration camps. In the period of the first Five Year Plan, many *kulaks* refused to cooperate with the government in its drive to collectivize agriculture. Repeating their tactics of a decade earlier, they ignored crop-planting directives, hoarded or destroyed produce claimed by the state, harassed Party officials, and generally sought to wreck the new program. This time the government used the full force of its coercive power. Many thousands of the protesting "rich peasants" were sent to Siberia, where they labored in "work camps" under conditions so mercilessly severe that most of them died before their sentences were completed. Other thousands, both *kulaks* and middling peasants who sympathized with them, were expelled from collective farms and left to starve. Throughout the period the secret police were busy. Thus, arrests, deportations, deliberate starving, and massacres marked the bloody transition from capitalist ways to socialist planning. For many, this was Russia's "long day's journey into night."

Evaluation of Socialist Planning

The general effect of the sweeping collectivist program is hard to assess. Most *kolkhozniks*, as we have seen, resented the socialist form and the nature of collectiviza-

tion. If they could have had their way, they would have become the owners of individual plots, to be worked as they desired. Failing this, they would have preferred a cooperative arrangement, similar to the old *Mir* type. They did not like to labor under terms laid down by the state where goals were fixed, and fixed, moreover, in such a way that the preponderant bulk of the produce of the *kolkhoze* went to the state. For this meant, in effect, that the fruits of their labor were drained off to provide state capital for the industrialization of the country. They resented the constant prodding of Party overseers who held them to a fatiguing tempo of labor. Almost always, the small strips assigned to individual families for their own use yielded too little to satisfy the normal demands of hunger. The portion allotted to them from the collective was also invariably meager. They knew that they were being forced at a fearful price to buy a Communist tomorrow out of their own today's sweat and suffering. The fact that Russia was rapidly becoming a strong industrial nation (as it was) might constitute a hinge of history that later generations could marvel over, but their own days and hours still remained onerous, often miserable. As a result, many peasants took little interest in their work, and devised countless tricks and subterfuges to circumvent the steady pressures of Party planners.

On the other hand, incentives of various kinds were devised to entice both the peasants and the workers to speed up production. On the *kolkhozes,* work was rated according to the skill and effort involved in particular jobs. *Kolkhozniks* were also credited with "labor days" that, at the end of the year, were used as units of exchange to determine how much of the *kolkhoze's* produce was to be allotted to the individual farmer. In the factories, piecework and bonuses encouraged workers to keep at the job. Other incentives were adjustment of prices, issuance of priority ration cards, and the awarding of honor badges and ribbons to workers who produced beyond their quota.

Gains and Costs

The aims of the first Five Year Plan,* as reported by the government, were achieved in four years. A second Plan, also giving emphasis to heavy industry, was set up for the years 1932 to 1937. However, Hitler's schemes of aggression caused it to be modified, sometime after 1935, in favor of military preparedness. But in spite of this economic detour, the second Plan was carried off as successfully as the first (the third Plan, 1938 to 1943, was even more seriously disrupted by the war; even so, its achievements were also substantial).

There can be no doubt that, from the mid-1930s, the standard of living for both farmers and workers rose markedly above that which had so long prevailed in Tsarist times. It is true that food, clothing, and housing remained in short supply, but not nearly as short as before the Revolution. Moreover, a new spirit infused the masses. For the first time in their history they felt as "live souls"; they experienced what one authority has called a release of energy. The regime under which they lived was dictatorial, more absolute than Tsarist autocracy. But it was created and managed for them, not for landed or bourgeois aristocrats. The dread secret police were ubiquitous, but they rarely sought out the peasant farmer or the factory worker. In short, things were looking up. If today was hard, it was only in preparation for a tomorrow that was bright, almost beyond imagining.

On the other hand, the costs of fulfilling the Plans were inhumanely high. Thousands of *kulak* families were deliberately forced into starvation, or into the hell of concentration camps.[3] Many thousands more were subjected to forced labor at gov-

---

* After 1958, Seven Year Plans were substituted.

3. For a realistic view of life in a Soviet concentration camp, see Alexander Solzhenitsyn, *One Day in the Life of Ivan Denisovich,* E. B. Dutton, New York, 1963.

An aluminum plant in the U.S.S.R.

ernment terms (especially during the period 1929 to 1934). Those in supervisory or managerial positions were forever in danger not of mere demotion but of imprisonment and even death if production in their factories or farms consistently fell behind the quotas set for them. For years, *kolkhozniks* were overworked and underfed so that their leaders might buy machinery and hire technicians from abroad. No matter how bright the Soviet tomorrow should turn out to be, millions would be harried to their death before it dawned.

The Purges

Peasant resistance to the strictures of the first Five Year Plan had been so profound and so stubborn that many Soviet leaders demanded a return to NEP, or to some modification of it. But Stalin would not compromise. He was convinced that the forward step had to be taken then, or else all hope given up that it could ever be taken. Perhaps experience would prove the *mouzhik* (the "subsistence" farmer) unteachable. If so, the regime and the Revo-

Premier Josef Stalin.

lution were lost, no matter what was done. But more likely, stern socialist leadership could force the peasant first to tolerate, and then finally to cooperate with that leadership. In any case, all would be lost if the effort was not made soon.

But for a time it appeared that Stalin, after all, would have to yield to the peasants. By 1932, *kulak* destruction of cattle had reached such proportions that the entire agrarian economy was threatened. Moreover, the middling peasant, upon whom the Soviet regime had to depend (or else lose the masses who looked to the middling peasant for leadership and example), showed strong signs of siding with the *kulak*. Stalwart old Bolsheviks such as Bukarin, Kamenev, Rykov, and Zinoviev strongly counseled retreat before it was too late.

But in spite of these pressures, Stalin held his ground—for seven years, during NEP, the *kulak* had been pampered; his strength had come to rival that of the government. What socialist good could come from further pampering? If the old Bolsheviks could not understand a situation as simple as this, their advice was not worth listening to. But it was hard to believe that they had actually misread the signs. More probably, Stalin came to believe, they were conspiring among themselves to rid the regime of his leadership. He remembered Trotsky, of course, and the left "deviationists" of the late 1920s. Then Trotsky's exile and the imprisonment and execution of many of his followers had brought Stalin to power. Now, it seemed, "right deviationists" were plotting his destruction. And if they were, could another purge be avoided?

Since little documentary evidence on the purges is available, conjecture must serve. It seems likely that many of the old Bolsheviks were weary of Stalin's leadership. Lenin, before his death, had cautioned against giving too much power to Stalin. Lenin believed that Stalin was too crude, too rude, and too stubborn. Presumably, most of the "old ones" were of this mind in the early 1930s. It is doubtful, however, whether a real conspiracy to oust Stalin had taken shape. By this time a younger generation of Communists was emerging; many of them had been appointed to high Party and governmental office by Stalin. Indeed, by 1934 both the Central Committee and the Politbureau were dominated by Stalin's followers. Thus, there was not much base left upon which to mount an offensive against the leader. Moreover, the secret police were forever checking against precisely such possibilities. Also, it is hard to understand and to calculate the influence of Stalin's suspicious nature. Presumably a number of Stalin's colleagues wished for a milder program, without at all intending to offer more than verbal opposition to the program proposed by Stalin. But to the edgy Party boss, any opposition increasingly came to be looked upon as treason to the Revolution; he tended, in short, to equate his leadership with the only possible successful completion of the Revolution. And yet, as one authority has pointed out:

it was not ambition alone which had led Stalin in the 20's to amass his great power over the party. The survival in power of the party was at stake during those years, and few communists ever doubted that, for the party to retain its monopoly of power was the first and foremost aim of all policy. But this survival required centralized discipline inside the party, and Stalin was probably the only man who could ensure it . . . since [the] revolution meant an all out war by the communist party against the majority of the population, the peasants, it was unavoidable that Stalin's personal power over party should have increased in the process. . . . Stalin's revolution in agriculture and industry and his assault on the party which consummated this revolution must be seen as integrated parts of one and the same process.[4]

In any case, in the years 1936 to 1938, Stalin purged the Party so mercilessly and so thoroughly that his will emerged as the one voice and guide of the Soviet Union. In this period the "old Bolsheviks" were done away with, almost to the man. In public trials, some of the accused "confessed" heinous crimes against the state. A number of generals, including the commander-in-chief, were condemned to death in secret sessions. In none of these cases can the interested inquirer learn the true facts. Some of the "evidence" has been proved false; as for the rest, we can only surmise that most of the charges were without foundation. However, we cannot be sure. What is certain is that for several years the flaming torch of terror seared the land. When it flickered out in 1939, Russia stood out starkly as a monolithic party-state, still energetic, but purged of all dissent.

From German Marxism to Russian Communism

Twenty years after their overthrow of the provisional government, the Communist revolutionaries had good reason to believe that they were here to stay. The House of the Autocrat was utterly destroyed. Most of the landed gentry and their military colleagues, the White Generals, had been killed or exiled. More recently the whole of the *kulak* class had been wiped out. Although the peasants still had to be convinced of the worthwhileness of collectivization, they were no longer sabotaging the experiment. As for the city workers, they had never given the government real cause for concern. In short, Communism was making its way.

But it had somewhat changed over the years. For example (a rather remarkable example) it had come to power in the absence of either a bourgeois or a proletarian revolution.[5] What Bolsheviks liked to call the proletarian revolution was actually a revolution planned and executed by the "Vanguard," an elite group of professional revolutionaries. Furthermore, Communism, in its original form, maintained that the society that emerged from the revolution would be completely democratic. Russian Communism, on the other hand, had never tried to function under democratic processes, although it always insisted that pure democracy would characterize the ultimate, stateless society. Another modification of German Marxism was Stalin's decision to develop "socialism in one country." Marx and Engels envisioned the proletarian revolution sweeping over all of Europe. Any less effort, they believed, signified both proletarian unreadiness, and the certain collapse of the revolution wherever, in isolation, it might occur. By 1937, Stalin's reading of the curve of history appeared sounder than that of his masters. Clearly, Russia's Communism, although rooted in Marxist theory, was a product of history, mostly Russia's own. The new way of life did not too clearly promise during its first decades that it could transcend the bleak, degrading in-

4. Leonard Shapiro, *The Communist Party of the Soviet Union*, Random House, New York, 1959, pp. 429–430.

5. Cf. John Plamenatz, *German Marxism and Russian Communism*, Longmans, Green & Co., New York, 1954, p. 312, and pp. 306–329.

humanity of that history. But neither did it seem to presage another time of trou- bles. The hopes of both rulers and ruled looked to tomorrow.

FASCIST ITALY

The Spirit and Conditions of Postwar Italy

Disillusionment and Delusion

The aftermath of World War I worked unexpected changes in Italy. After bar- gaining with both sides, she had joined forces in 1915 with the *Entente,* which had promised her substantial territorial gains at the expense of the Austrian and Ottoman Empires (see *supra,* p. 727). As one of the victorious powers she could hope to secure indemnities, much needed for her chronically anemic exchequer. In addition, as a victorious power, her height- ened prestige would lend luster to a politi- cal establishment that had been singularly lacking in grandeur since the days of the Caesars.

In varying degrees, all of these hopes were frustrated within a few years. Al- though territorial gains had been made in the north and north-east, they fell short of what had been promised. Particularly irritating was the creation of the "interna- tional" city of Fiume. Indemnities from both Austria and Germany amounted to virtually nothing. As for glory and prestige, the defeat at Caporetto had dashed, in- deed crushed, Italian spirits so thoroughly that a sense of national shame pervaded the land.

Moreover, war costs had brought the economy close to bankruptcy. Returning veterans could not find jobs. The *lira* stead- ily dropped in value. Much of the land was owned by proprietors who lived in the cities, and left the management of their estates to overseers who paid hired laborers the barest subsistence wage. Millions of share- croppers fared no better. In order to build up her industrial machine so that it might compete with those of her neighbors, Italy needed to import great quantities of coal and iron, of which her Apennine Moun- tains were strangely barren. She also lacked oil, cotton, and wool. But in the gen- eral conditions of financial stringency that prevailed in most of Europe after the war, Italy found little opportunity to borrow the capital required for such expenditures.

Psychic ills were added to depression and disillusionment. The war had warped the value fabric of men who had lived long with violence and death. In a strange, unreasonable way it had sickened many soldiers of the ways of peace.

[They] had grown accustomed to the war with its excitements and rewards, its exalta- tion of the personal feat, its freedom from daily cares and uncertainties. When peace "broke out," as suddenly and unexpectedly as the war it- self, these men experienced a letdown. They un- consciously looked for ways to continue the war- time existence which had lasted so long that it seemed there had been no previous life. [A man might find] in the war self-glorification, fulfillment of his dreams as superman, and an escape from creditors and financial harassment. To him peacetime [meant] a return to debts and old mistresses, and the sad admission that he was getting on in years. To be free from worries and stay young he had to remain a warrior. . . .[6]

Actually, many did remain soldiers. In the new Baltic states, for example, some

6. Laura Fermi, *Mussolini,* The University of Chicago Press, Chicago, 1961, p. 172. The quo- tation specifically refers to D'Annunzio, referred to *infra,* but the observation is applicable generally.

German soldiers continued a kind of guerrilla struggle against the authorities — almost any authorities. In Germany a number of bored officers founded the "Free Corps" with which to harass the new republican regime and keep alive the heroic image of the uniformed man. In Italy the most notorious "permanent soldier" was the romantic poet-politician, Gabriele D'Annunzio, who (in 1920) declared war against his own country and lived to write boastful poems about it.

Lack of Liberal Tradition

Certain conditions rooted in Italy's past compounded her postwar problems. One condition was a citizenry untrained in democratic behavior. The liberal impulse, it is true, had contributed much to Italian unification. But more than impulse is needed to sustain and develop representative government. Particularly important is an alert, educated citizenry; Italy simply lacked this. In fact, as late as 1911, the census returns showed that 40 per cent of Italy's adult population were illiterate. The historic record also showed growing corruption in almost all government agencies and activities. Thus, the machinery of the state was ineffectually run by politicians most of whom felt little responsibility toward the millions that they ruled. It is no wonder that serious socioeconomic problems multiplied as the nation undertook the complicated task of converting the weapons and ways of war into the tools and the modes of peace. The postwar years, then, were a compound of unemployment and sluggish industrial activity, of cynicism, disillusionment, and frustration. In the late months of 1920, workers in the industrial cities of the north "occupied" some factories; here and there, peasants, made desperate by unrelieved hunger and privation, took over land from absentee owners. The national government eventually negotiated settlements that, however, satisfied neither workers nor owners.

Throughout the country there seemed little faith, little hope, much restlessness, and a growing tendency to favor direct — and often violent — action to resolve mounting differences. Landed aristocrats and the bourgeoisie watched the Red tide rolling over Russia. They feared that it could happen to Italy. City and farm workers, on the other hand, wondered when the property-owning classes would learn that exploitation was not the way to the good life, and whether they would learn the lesson before catastrophe overtook them all.

Emergence of Mussolini

The "Cult of Force and Daring"

This was the spirit and the general conditions of the times that prevailed in postwar Italy. Clearly, they pointed to some kind of sociopolitical climax. But this could hardly occur until a forceful and determined leader appeared to work his will upon the roiling furies that stirred the land. For a time it seemed that the Byronic D'Annunzio was the man. He had stormed and taken Fiume, a city supposedly held by a contingent of international troops. He had ruled it for a year by an awesome combination of violent force, poetical pronunciamentos, and thespian talents. But he had departed after one broadside from an attacking naval force, and had retired from politics. His disciple, Benito Mussolini, had many of his hero's strengths and a surer sense of political possibilities. And he was to last longer.

Before the war Mussolini had been a Socialist. He was dropped by the party when he openly espoused Italian intervention. Using financial resources difficult for the historian to trace, he founded a newspaper, *Il Popolo d'Italia,* in which he trumpeted the call to arms. During the war he served as a noncommissioned officer. He returned to his paper before the Armistice. For a brief time he continued to sup-

Benito Mussolini, dictator of Italy (1922–1943), in full Fascist dress, including dagger.

port worker causes, though no longer as a Socialist. In 1919 he founded the *Fasci di combattimento.** The new organization was at first more a movement than a party, and served as an outlet for multiple discontents. Unemployed veterans, passionate nationalists, exploited peasants, former army officers weary of peace, and underpaid workers—all came to see compelling attractions in the Fascists, the self-proclaimed redeemers of Italy's harassed body and soul.

Mussolini's behavior, which normally bordered on the peripatetic, was rooted in a variegated psyche, stirred by longings for power and action. As a young man he had read and responded to the coldly passionate strophes of Machiavelli. The German philosopher Nietzsche made an impression no less profound. Mussolini

* Loosely translated, "groups of fighters." The Italian word *fascio* means "bundle." Its real significance is historic. In Roman days political authority was symbolized by a bundle of rods grouped around an axe. It connoted then—as later—disciplined unity and authoritarian power.

professed to believe that by force of will and high disdain for conventional morality man could become superman. About the time he founded the *Fasci di combattimento* he made this Zarathustrian (the reference is to Nietzsche's, not history's, Zoroaster) declaration: "We who detest from the depth of our soul all Christianity, from Jesus' to Marx's, look with extraordinary sympathy upon this 'resurgence' of modern life in the pagan cult of force and daring." [7]

The Road to Power

The rough treatment that Mussolini's *fasci* gave to demonstrating Socialists caught the eye and interest of industrial and business elements. Throughout 1920 and 1921, street fighting between Red agitators and Mussolini's Blackshirts became distressingly frequent. Army and police units surreptitiously aided the fascist gangs. By 1922, general disorder had become so widespread that the public began to insist on the formation of a government strong enough to keep the peace. Mussolini enthusiastically proclaimed himself in complete agreement with this demand. Communist bands, he said, were trying to disorganize the life of the nation. When Red-inspired anarchy became general, Moscow's minions would take control. He felt that when that happened, the Italian people were finished. Thereafter they would serve as slaves of a vanguard of Marxist racketeers. He believed that only a strong, alert government could forestall this. Liberal parliamentarianism had petered out in futile rhetoric and shameful corruption. The only force standing between the buffeted Italian people and the Red menace was, according to the Fascist *Duce* (leader), himself and his loyal followers.

Actually, there was no serious Communist strength anywhere in Italy. Most Italian Socialists opposed Leninism when they

7. Fermi, *op. cit.*, p. 170.

were not fighting among themselves, which was a common occurrence. More often than not, the street fights were started by the Fascists. If Mussolini had been serious in his repeated demands for domestic order, his first constructive move would have been to disband his *squadristi* (bully-boy street fighters). He was serious about nothing except gaining and keeping power. By 1922, conditions were ripe for his bid for power. Cabinet crises were frequent and pointless. Many local politicians had become fascists; orders from the central government to disarm the Blackshirts received little or no attention. Fascist propaganda stepped up its campaign against the "Red menace." At the same time, Mussolini made it clear that the Royal House had nothing to fear from him. A gauge of the caliber of that institution was its ready acceptance of this supercilious judgment by an upstart agitator.

On October 28, 1922, Mussolini ordered his followers to march on Rome to "restore legality to the representative institutions of Italy." The Prime Minister, Signor Facta, decided to meet force with force, and declared a state of siege. But the king, fearful of civil war (and reassured of Mussolini's good intentions), refused to countersign the declaration. Instead, he invited the Duce to form a new government. In his first interview with the king, Mussolini wore a black shirt, black trousers, and white ankle gaiters. Unconsciously, he had attired himself as the perfect symbol of fascist ruler—political thug and respectable "gent." Thus, fascism came to Italy not in revolutionary storm but in bourgeois spats.

Fascism in Power

The Fascist Credo

In the beginning, Italian fascism had no ideological content. In 1919 Mussolini had declared, "Fascism is a movement of reality, life, adhering to life. It is pragmatist. It has no *a priori* isms. No remote ends. It does not promise the usual heavens of idealism. It does not presume to live for-

Mussolini after the "march" on Rome, 1922.

ever or for long." [8] In a very real sense its prime moving power was the same as that of latter-day beatnik cyclists—"you don't go someplace, man, you just go!" In his famous 1932 essay on fascist doctrines, Mussolini declared: "The Fascist disdains the comfortable life."

By then, fascist "wild ones" had been given a creed. In essence it elevated the state over the individual citizen, exalted the life of action and violence—"the dangerous life"—lauded rule by the elite, and glorified war as the great catalyst of life. Some explication of this creed is given in the following excerpts from Mussolini's *La Dottrina del Fascismo*.

Against individualism, the Fascist conception is for the State; and it is for the individual in so far as he coincides with the state, which is the conscience and universal will of man in his historical existence. . . . Fascism reaffirms the State as the true reality of the individual. . . . Therefore for the Fascist, everything is in the State, and nothing human or spiritual exists . . . outside the State. . . . The State . . . is the creator of right . . . [It] is an absolute before which individuals and groups are relative.

8. Fermi, *op. cit.*, p. 185. Later the Duce changed his mind about fascism's tenure.

Fascism desires an active man, one engaged in activity with all his energies. . . . It conceives of life as a struggle. . . . It does not consider that "happiness" is possible upon earth . . . and hence it rejects all theological theories according to which mankind would reach a definite stabilized condition at a certain point in history. . . . The proud motto of the *Squadrista*, "Me ne frego" ["I don't give a damn"], written on the bandages of a wound is an act of philosophy . . . it is education for combat, the acceptance of the risks which it brings. . . .

. . . . Fascism is opposed to Democracy, which equates the nation to the majority, lowering it to the level of that majority . . . if the nation is conceived, as it should be, qualitatively and not quantitatively [then it may be understood as] the most powerful idea . . . which acts within the nation as the conscience and the will of the few, even of One. . . . [Fascism] affirms the irremediable, fruitful and beneficent inequality of man. . . . If it is admitted that the nineteenth century has been the century of Socialism, Liberalism, and Democracy, it does not follow that the twentieth century must also be [so]. Political doctrines pass; peoples remain. It is expected that this century may be that of authority, a century of the "Right," a Fascist century.

Above all, Fascism . . . believes neither in the possibility nor the utility of perpetual peace. It thus repudiates the doctrine of Pacifism. . . . War alone brings up to their highest tension all human energies and puts the stamp of nobility upon the people who have the courage to meet it.[9]

Consolidation of the Fascist Dictatorship

For several years after taking power, Mussolini respected, at least nominally, the constitutional forms of government. He recognized the right of nonfascist parties to exist and to dispute fascist proposals (provided that they did it reasonably, that is, mildly). He went through the forms of honoring the king. He also refrained from efforts to denigrate the Church. In short, he sang softly while he consolidated his power.

But he did consolidate his power. He quietly purged the bureaucracy and the police. By a decree, his "street squads" were transformed into legal militia units. And in late 1923, he forced through a new election law that provided that any party receiving at least 25 per cent of the popular vote was entitled to two thirds of the seats in the Chamber of Deputies. In the election that followed the next year the Fascists, for the first time, constituted a majority of the Deputies.

In 1924 an event occurred that threatened his regime and then, paradoxically, secured it. The event was the publication by Giacomo Matteotti, a Socialist deputy, of a detailed exposé of fascist corruption and violence. Mussolini was furious. The revelations frightened him, while Matteotti's audacity insulted his image of himself as the new Caesar. To certain confidants he hinted that, for Italy's good, Matteotti ought to be taught a lesson. A few days later the deputy was snatched from the street, bundled into a car and murdered. A wave of indignation surged over Italy. Italians, of course, knew that fascist bully-boys had often brutally broken up meetings, and had often given the castor oil treatment to their opponents. If the average citizen did not give full approval to such tactics, he might have at least believed that they had be-

9. Michael Oakeshott, *The Social and Political Doctrines of Contemporary Europe,* Cambridge University Press, Cambridge, 1939, pp. 164–177, *passim.* It is interesting to compare this 1932 definition of the essence of fascism, as Mussolini then thought of it, with his views after his overthrow in 1943. A few months before his death he made this frank statement to a fascist leader: "Let us not delude ourselves; as a doctrine Fascism contains nothing new, it is a product of the modern crisis, the crisis of man, who can no longer remain within the normal bounds of life with its conventionalism, within the bounds of the existing human laws. I would call it irrationalism. There is such a thing as morality, but we're tired of it; and I'd go further and say that it makes no impression on us. That can be changed by going against the stream. We are tormented people; everyone of us would like to be in the sun, the pole of life for himself and for others. There you have the evil at the heart of the modern man: call it irrationalism, Bolshevism, Fascism." Quoted in Herman Finer, *Mussolini's Italy,* Archon Books, Meriden, Conn., 1964 (this excerpt is taken from the unpaged section following the preface in the new edition).

come necessary. But government-sponsored murder was something else.

For a while, popular support of the regime wavered. Mussolini felt obliged to denounce the crime and to call for apprehension of the guilty ones. For their part, Socialist deputies walked out of the Chamber and vowed that they would not return until the political sins of fascism had been admitted and expiated. But popular indignation faded with the passing of time, and Mussolini, sensing it, regained his courage. Strict press censorship kept the opposition and the public literally out of touch with those who might have led the nation in an assault on the regime. The seats of the "Aventine dissidents" * were declared vacant; many political opponents were rounded up and sent into exile. Local elections were suspended. Mussolini had given himself the power to rule by decree, if and whenever he thought circumstances called for it. Two years after Matteotti's murder the fascist dictatorship was, in all essentials, complete.

It is hard to pass judgment on the average citizen's attitude toward the regime. After 1926 there were no public signs of serious discontent with it but, by that time, coercive instruments of control were in common use. In 1945 Italian mobs mutilated the bodies of the deposed Duce and his mistress; but by then Italy had not only lost the war but had been occupied, first by the Nazis and then by the Allies. After the war Italy repudiated not only fascism but monarchial government as well. Yet as late as the 1960s a widely circulated Italian history textbook blamed the Versailles Treaty almost entirely for Europe's postwar troubles:

. . . the discontent caused by the treaty is described [in the text] as having so disoriented Italian soldiers returning from the war that, "instigated by parties of the Left with a criminal propaganda of hatred against the ruling classes,

they abandoned themselves to public demonstrations, and even fell so low as to occupy factories"; and it was in this political debilitation, against which the "healthy part of the nation reacted," that Mussolini took over the task of rescuing the country from "the bolshevism spreading over the Peninsula." According to [this text's author] Mussolini was a man of "extraordinary dynamism . . . [and] an admirer of the history and grandeur of Rome . . . who let himself be seduced by the idea, noble in itself, of conferring similar fortunes on the New Italy.[10]

Certainly, Italian industrialists and capitalists generally supported Mussolini, as did the army and the Church.† As for the worker and peasant masses, perhaps they welcomed the order and the resurgence of national "glory" that Mussolini so dramatically brought them. Or perhaps they did not like current conditions under the regime, but believed that it was their best promise for a better tomorrow. Or they may genuinely have been attracted to the dynamic Duce whose tones, gestures, and words were always calculated to bring the masses under his spell.

The Paper Corporate State

Beginning in 1926, Mussolini set about the creation of what he called the "corporate state." As it finally (and rather futilely) developed, its basic economic aspects took on these features. At the local level, employees and employers each formed their own organizations. Their activities were supervised by a National Council of Corporations. Strikes and lockouts were declared illegal; differences between labor "syndicates" and employer corporations were submitted to arbitration. In 1934 an elaborate modification of the system was

10. Roland Steel, *Italy,* The H. W. Wilson Co., New York, 1963, pp. 54–55.

---

* The reference is to the withdrawal by the plebeians of ancient Rome to Mount Aventine, where they set up an extralegal government in opposition to patrician rule.

† In 1929 Mussolini, with considerable fanfare, signed a concordat with the Roman Catholic Church that restored normal relations between state and Church. For nearly sixty years the Pope had considered himself a "prisoner" in the Vatican. But in recent years, state-Church relations had improved a great deal. The concordat thus officially recognized a situation that had developed before Mussolini came to power.

effected. All economic activity was divided into twenty-two corporations. These corporations were divided into three groups: one group of eight corporations was concerned with agriculture and non-mineral materials; another group, also of eight corporations, busied itself with mining, construction, and manufacturing; and the third group, of six corporations, administered transportation, finance, and the service industries. Each of the twenty-two corporations was organized as a trade association at the national level. There were also regional associations to mediate conflicts between local and national bodies. In the government the Ministry of Corporations exercised jurisdiction over all local, provincial, and national units.

For the most part, however, the corporate system was a party device used to impose fascism's political as well as economic policies on industrial institutions, particularly as they were concerned with preparations for war, and attempts to achieve autarchy.[11] But, even as such, the system did not constitute a provocation in the eyes of Italian businessmen. Indeed they supported it, as they generally supported the regime. For, in spite of Mussolini's protestation that "Italy is not a capitalist country," it was, as Italian businessmen very well knew. Moreover, in Italy the entrepreneur had economic advantages not found in most industrial states. For example, employers were given the right, by fascist law, "to fine, suspend, or dismiss workers who proved difficult to discipline or who performed acts disturbing to the normal functioning of a concern." Statistics show that even in Europe's boom period of production, Italian workers suffered a reduction in real wages. Actually, Italy experienced the depression well ahead of the rest of the world. "The acceptance of repeated reductions in wages by the workers

was praised by Fascist leaders as patriotic sacrifice and as 'a preparation for tomorrow by the renunciations of today.' And yet in 1934 [Mussolini] asserted: 'We are probably moving toward a period of humanity resting on a lower standard of living. Humanity is capable of asceticism such as perhaps we have no conception of.' "[12]

The Cult of Force in Action

In Africa

These prognostications could hardly have caused jubilation among Italy's masses. Their standard of living was already one of the lowest in Europe. It is reasonable to ask whether the timing of Mussolini's decision to carve out a new African empire was related to domestic miseries.* It is hard to believe that even Mussolini's magic could mesmerize an entire nation into accepting the prospect of permanent poverty. In any case, in 1935 the Duce led Italy down what he thought of as the "glory road" to war. Until the spring of 1936, the nation's attention and energies were absorbed in the conflict with Ethiopia, an underdeveloped, weak country that Mussolini, with a straight face, charged had attacked Italian interests in Africa.

The conquest of this backward state gave the Duce and his people a surge of confidence. Further contributing to Italy's feeling of power was Europe's meek capitulation to overt aggression. Ethiopia had appealed to the League of Nations, whose two chief supporters were England and France. When Mussolini successfully pushed his war in the face of League disapproval, he concluded that he had underestimated fascism's strength and undercalculated democracy's weaknesses. What adventures were not possible if the will was strong and the spirit tough?

---

11. See Witt Bowden, Michael Karpovich, Abbott Usher, *An Economic History of Europe Since 1750*, New York, 1936, pp. 792 ff.

12. *Ibid.*, p. 797.

* The conquest of Ethiopia was decided on in late 1933, at the nadir of the great world depression.

In Spain

Hardly had the African conquest been concluded when, with the outbreak of war in Spain, Italy became involved in new fighting. Reactionary forces under General Francisco Franco attempted a coup against the liberal republican regime in July 1936, which soon turned into a full-scale civil war. Italian troops and material were sent to Spain to help Franco establish his fascist Falangist state. But the new venture led to consequences with which Mussolini had not reckoned. In October of that same year, Italy and Germany signed an agreement which the Duce, with characteristic bombast, labeled the Axis Pact. During the Ethiopian war, Nazi Germany had been the only major power to support Italy's claims. Naturally, Mussolini felt a kind of affinity with his northern neighbor after this experience. Since Hitler was as eager as the Duce to see liberal government liquidated in Europe, he also sent supplies and troops to Franco. It was quite natural that these friends of a friend should themselves become friends.

To dramatize the significance of the new brotherhood, Mussolini paid an official visit to Germany in 1937. What he saw amazed him. Within four years Germany had become one of the strongest military states in Europe. Even more important to the Duce was the clear evidence that Hitler had made only a beginning. Clearly the Prussian power state had been reborn. In contrast, England and France seemed decadent, timid, beguiled by appeasement delusions. In these circumstances, Mussolini modified his general view of things to come. Up to this point he had seen himself as the world's emerging Caesar. Now the ominous stamp of the goose step was again heard in Germany. Another superman had appeared.

The Deflation of Fascism

Soon, other events made even clearer to Mussolini the power dimensions of the new Germany and its leader. Nazi planes, artil-

THE AWFUL WARNING.

FRANCE AND ENGLAND *(together ?).* "WE DON'T WANT YOU TO FIGHT, BUT, BY JINGO, IF YOU DO, WE SHALL PROBABLY ISSUE A JOINT MEMORANDUM SUGGESTING A MILD DISAPPROVAL OF YOU."

Neither England nor France was eager to cross the Duce in his Ethiopian adventure, as this Punch *cartoon makes clear.*

Mussolini and Hitler in 1936.

lery, and infantrymen in Spain performed with merciless efficiency. The Italian effort probably was superior quantitatively, but even a casual comparative study revealed a Nazi striking power and an offensive spirit that Italy could not match. Moreover, in 1938 Germany incorporated Austria into the Reich. This time Mussolini made no protest. The "Greater Germany" towered still higher over its continental neighbors, including Italy. In short, events of the mid-1930s reversed the positions of the fascist leaders and their peoples. For fifteen years the German superman had looked to Rome for inspiration and clues to set up the totalitarian state. But by 1938 the pupil had become the master; hereafter, each passing year was to see the diminution of fascist Italy and the aggrandizement of Nazi Germany. In the end, as we shall see, Mussolini became Hitler's puppet, deprived even of opportunity to hide his sorry state from full view of the world. Ten years after the Italian conquest of Ethiopia, Italy herself was conquered. Fascism longed for action, violence, and war. It got them all. Its leaders had boasted *"me ne frego."* With whatever sincerity, the masses of Italy said, in 1945, "but we do." The adventure of the 1920s had faded out in fury and futility.

SELECTED READINGS

Beloff, Max, *The Foreign Policy of Soviet Russia, 1929–1941,* Oxford University Press, London, 1947 to 1949, 2 vols.

> Probably the best study of this subject up to the time of its publication and still of high worth. The author is not unsympathetic to the problems and position of the Soviet Union.

Carr, E. H., *The Bolshevik Revolution, 1917–1923,* Macmillan & Co., London, 1950–1958, 3 vols., variously numbered according to edition.

> Although sympathetic to the aims of the Russian revolutionists, Carr exercises his ample scholarly talents in a much too disciplined manner to allow his own leanings to seriously affect his work. These volumes offer the best account of the great revolution available to date.

Deakin, F. W., *The Brutal Friendship,* Harper & Row, New York, 1962.

> A long, carefully researched study of the tandem efforts of Mussolini and Hitler to construct a new order in Europe. Mussolini's character and talents appear in a somewhat (but not substantially) different light from that given them by the focus of Kirkpatrick, cited below.

*Deutscher, Isaac, *Stalin, A Political Biography,* Vintage Books, New York, *c.* 1960.

> One of the best studies of Stalin. The author's mild pro-Soviet sympathies are clearly discernible.

Deutscher, Isaac, *The Prophet Armed — Trotsky, 1879–1921,* Oxford University Press, London, 1954.

———, *The Prophet Unarmed — Trotsky 1921–1929* (1959).

———, *The Prophet Outcast — Trotsky 1929–1940* (1963).

> A carefully researched, highly informative trilogy by one who, in his own words, considers Trotsky "one of the most outstanding revolutionary leaders of all times, outstanding as fighter, thinker, martyr."

Finer, Herman, *Mussolini's Italy,* Grosset & Dunlap, New York, 1965.

> Except for a ten-page insert, "From Mussolini's Italy to Italy's Italy," this is the same work that was first published in 1935. Part V, "The Manufacture of Obedience," is especially recommended.

Kennan, George F., *Russia and the West under Lenin and Stalin,* Little, Brown & Co., Boston, 1961.

> In the author's words, this is a "series of discussions of individual episodes or problems," instead of "a chronological account of the happenings of this phase of diplomatic history." Kennan's scholarship, personal experience, and intellectual integrity combine to make each "episode or problem"

Asterisk (*) denotes paperback.

—Brest-Litovsk, the Allies in Siberia, Rappallo, The Soviet-Nazi Pact of 1939, and about 20 others—meaningful beyond any "chronological account" that deals with this material, except perhaps that of Max Beloff's, cited above.

Kirkpatrick, Ivone, *Mussolini, A Study in Power,* Hawthorne Books, New York, 1964.
>The best biography of Mussolini yet published. It is well organized and well documented. The author is not inclined to sympathize with the Duce's dictatorial ways, but his feelings for the dynamic power of the Italian leader show through his fundamentally objective account. This book is particularly worthwhile when read in conjunction with Deakin's work, cited above.

Matthews, Herbert L., *The Fruits of Fascism,* Harcourt, Brace & Co., New York, 1943.
>The author, a journalist, spent many years living in and (for a time) admiring Fascist Italy. The Spanish Civil War gave him, according to his own account, a new and (as he believed) a truer view of the fascist ways of life. This book is a polemic against the evil, inhumane conditions that he believed fascism fastened upon all men who submitted to its authority. It is important for the many illustrative episodes and anecdotes that are not found in the accounts of professional historians.

Maynard, John, *Russia in Flux,* The Macmillan Co., New York, 1948.
>This abridged edition of Maynard's *Russia in Flux* and *The Russian Peasant and Other Studies* is perhaps the best single source for the American reader to use. It stresses the life and outlook of the pre-Revolution peasant—an understanding of which is a prerequisite of any attempt to probe the meaning of the first two decades of Soviet Russian history. Unfortunately, it understresses the inhumanity of early Bolshevik rule.

Moore, Barrington, Jr., *Terror and Progress USSR,* Harvard University Press, Cambridge, 1954.
>The author's main purpose here is to "weigh, with an eye to the future, the sources of stability and the potentialities for change in the Bolshevik regime." He does somewhat more than this as he examines the role of the peasant in a workers' state, Soviet concepts of science and art, and the "function of terror."

Stipp, John L., ed., *Soviet Russia Today,* Harper & Brothers, New York, 1956–1957.
>Selected extracts from various authorities on the theory and practice of Marxism in Russia.

Trotsky, Leon, *The History of the Russian Revolution,* translator, Max Eastman, Simon and Schuster, New York, 1932, 3 vols.
>Both because Trotsky was one of the "three who made the revolution," and because he writes—and is translated—so well, this history of the Russian Revolution invites serious study. If Lincoln had lived to write a history of the Civil War, it would undoubtedly have been denounced by Southern Confederates and Northern Copperheads as a biased, unreliable tract. And probably they would have been partly right. But the work would have been well worth the effort and the reading. This is also true with respect to this 1400 page history of Russia's "civil war."

*Wolfe, Bertram D., *Three Who Made a Revolution,* The Dial Press, New York, 1948.
>The three men are Lenin, Trotsky, and Stalin. They come to life in these pages.

29

The Collectivist Trend between the Wars: Germany; the United States

NAZI GERMANY

Interlude of the Weimar Republic

The defeat of the German armies by the Allies inflicted traumatic suffering upon the whole nation. Right up to the signing of the armistice most Germans expected Allied, not German, surrender. The legend of Prusso-German military invincibility had long been a fundamental part of the psychic fabric that distinguished the Germans as a people. Nothing that the general public was allowed to learn during even the grim later phases of the war had given indication of anything but eventual victory. The sudden capitulation in the fall of 1918 stunned the nation. For many Germans, life would never have worthwhile meaning until German arms had cauterized the wound and made the nation whole again. And, of course, the Versailles Treaty compounded German humiliation and hurt, providing as it did for unilateral disarmament, territorial dismemberment, punitive reparations, and degradation of Germany to the status of a second class power.*

By refusing to deal with the Kaiser and the military, the Allies also encouraged German liberals to set up a German republic to replace Bismarck's "Second Reich." The government of the new state, commonly called the Weimar Republic after the city in which its constitution was written, functioned under severe handicaps. For one thing, its representatives had signed the hated treaty, and thus incurred an odium which persisted, however irrationally, throughout its brief life. For another, its democratic apparatus proved puzzling

---

* For a review of the terms of settlement, see *supra,* p. 737.

to a people long accustomed to authoritarian rule.

For a few years in the mid-1920s the Weimar Republic showed some promise of gaining stability. But at no time did it enjoy the broad public support and imaginative leadership an enduring regime requires. Its troubles were many and began early. In 1919 a Communist uprising (the Spartacist revolt) occurred in Berlin and its environs. Hundreds were killed in the bloody assault and its repulse, including Rosa Luxemburg and Karl Liebknecht, internationally known leaders of the German Marxist Party. The next year monarchist rebels attacked the government. Led by unemployed militarists, the initial thrusts of the insurrection (often referred to as the Kapp Putsch) proved so threatening that the government temporarily abandoned Berlin. In 1923 Adolf Hitler and his Nazi contingents staged what came to be known as the Munich Beer Hall Putsch. All of these attempts proved abortive; but they demonstrated how shaky were the underpinnings of the Republic. Contributing to the general confusion were the restiveness and recalcitrance of the German General Staff. Left untouched by the Versailles Treaty,* the Staff worked secretly and ceaselessly against the day when Junker militarism should regain control of a reborn Reich. Also left virtually untouched were the old imperial civil service and the judicial systems.

Experience has shown that republican regimes are most stable and function most efficiently under the two party system. In the Weimar Republic there were always about a half dozen "major" parties jostling for position and power. On the left were the Communists and Social Democrats. Throughout most of the life of the Republic, the Social Democrats held more seats in the Reichstag (the main governing body) than any other party, but they were never able to command a majority. Until dissolved when the Nazis took over, the Communist party steadily grew in numbers and influence, although at no time did it represent more than about 15 per cent of the total electorate. The Catholic Center party tended to advertise itself as a middle-of-the-road party, but few liberals agreed that the labeling was accurate. The more genuinely middle-of-the-road party was the Democratic party, almost alone in sincerely working to establish a capitalistic republic. It often received less support than either the Communist or Center parties. On the right were the Peoples' party, the Nationalists, and the Nazis. The Peoples' party balanced off the Democrats, the Nationalists balanced off the Centrists; until the last three years of the Republic, Nazi representation in the Reichstag was negligible. In every election a number of splinter parties further complicated the attempt to find a consensus. Despite these troubles, the Republic might have made its way if the army had been kept in its place. But from the beginning, it was not. Friedrich Ebert, soon to be chosen Germany's first president, reviewed returning troops in Berlin and publicly acclaimed them as "unvanquished [on] the field of battle." The General Staff could hardly have asked for a more welcome sign from the leader of the political party that was to play a major role in the new Republic's government.

The Weimar Constitution (adopted in July 1919) seemed to guarantee democratic development. Free speech, press, assembly, as well as freedom of religion were all underwritten by the new basic law. Representative legislative bodies and an elected president were provided. The Reichsrat, roughly corresponding to the American Senate, participated in making laws, but could be overruled by the more popularly elected lower house, the Reichstag. Nevertheless, the new constitution's democratic surface glossed over several potentially autocratic features. For ex-

---

* Technically, the General Staff was abolished by the treaty. In actual practice it reformed under another name.

ample, Article 48 gave the president arbitrary power to issue decrees and laws if he believed public order and safety were threatened. During the fifteen years of the Republic's life, several hundred such decrees and ordinances were enacted.* Indeed, in the two-year period before the advent of Hitler, Germany was governed almost exclusively by decree.

In 1925 President Ebert died. Although hardly an aggressive Socialist he at least was completely devoted to maintaining the republican system. His successor, Field Marshal von Hindenburg, was at best a lukewarm supporter of that regime. Fortunately, a year before, Gustav Stresemann, Germany's one great statesman in the Weimar years, had become the real working head of the government (first as Chancellor, then as Minister for Foreign Affairs). During the war Stresemann had been a strident nationalist. By 1923, he seemingly had come to see the need for genuine rapprochement between his country and France, and for acceptance of the Versailles settlement, at least in its broad outlines. Under his leadership, Germany signed the Locarno Treaties (see p. 760), joined the League of Nations, and accepted the Pact of Paris (the so-called Briand-Kellogg Pact, 1928) that outlawed war as an instrument of national policy. His death in 1929 was a blow that had repercussions reaching far beyond Germany's borders.

The advent of the Great Depression compounded Germany's troubles almost beyond bearing. As unemployment spread, millions of Germans tightened their belts, queued up for public relief, and cursed the Weimar system. Increasingly, they came to hold the government responsible for all the ills that had beset them since that fateful day in November 1918. Their reasoning was simple: never before had Germans suffered so cruelly; never before had Germans allowed themselves to experiment with democratic government. To an extent not amenable to reasonable as-

Dr. Gustav Stresemann, Germany's strongest leader in the new Weimar Republic.

sessment, the doubts and confusions of their present were fused with memories of the past to point to a coming day of rule by "leaders."

Rise of Hitler and the Nazi Party

Cutting through their misery and the general atmosphere of haunting fears, the confident, raucous voice of a rising politician, Adolf Hitler, trumpeted the coming of a new day. Germany, he insisted, had only to awaken, shake off its numbness, and form ranks behind him. There was in National Socialism and its leaders certain salvation for the Fatherland; indeed, more than salvation—a thousand years of power and glory. Scarcely a decade earlier, neither the Nazi party nor its leaders were known by more than a handful of Germans. Formed in 1920, the party mem-

* Technically the Reichstag could rescind such decrees. The party system, however, made this provision difficult to implement.

bership consisted of a strangely assorted company of economic radicals, restless, unemployed junior military officers, and embittered nationalists. Two years earlier a Bavarian locksmith, Anton Drexler, had gotten together a Committee of Independent Workmen. His aim was to create a mass movement designed to set up a sociopolitical system favorable to the little man, and to regain the lost glory of the old German Reich. In the same year a similar movement was organized in Austria under the title National Socialist German Workers Party. In 1919 the limping Committee of Independent Workmen merged with several related splinter groups to form the German Workers Party. It was this party that Hitler joined in September 1919. The next year it took over the name of its Austrian counterpart as well as some of that party's followers. Other recruits were some Free Corps officers, including Captain Ernst Röhm, who yearned for the creation of a German state revitalized by an armed citizenry and a quasi-socialist economy.

The Emergence of Hitler

At no time during this period did any of these parties attract even a moderately large following, until Hitler edged his way into leadership of the National Socialist German Workers Party. By 1923, as we have noted, Hitler considered "his" movement strong enough to attempt an insurrection. But until then, the name Adolf Hitler meant nothing to the German masses. Even for some years after the putsch, the future führer was regarded by most Germans as a rather comical figure destined soon to return to the oblivion from which he had so recently and so unaccountably emerged. Certainly nothing in his record made such a prognosis unreasonable. Born of poor parents in Braunau, a village near Linz, Austria, he had dropped out of school at an early age. As a young man he tried his hand at painting but received no encouragement from professional artists.

Hitler swearing in new members of the Nazi party about 10 years after its founding. Josef Göbbels appears in the background.

After the death of his parents he drifted around Vienna and Munich doing odd jobs. For several years he was so destitute that he was forced to live in flophouses and public charitable institutions. The coming of the Great War gave his life, by his own account, a sense of purpose and direction. He joined a Bavarian regiment and served throughout the war with sufficient distinction to earn the Iron Cross. After the war he worked for the army as a kind of spier-out of subversive activities among dissident civilian groups. In this capacity he attended a meeting of the German Workers party. He so much liked what he heard that within a few months he became a member. Shortly afterwards he resigned his army job and devoted all of his energies to the task of making the organization the nucleus of a movement to "awaken" Germany, break the shackles of Versailles, and create a master Reich.

German Fears of Jews and Communists

The general conditions described above and the new leader's persuasive oratory combined to bring a measure of life to the struggling party. Two other forces also worked to swell Nazi * ranks. When men suffer long and deeply they tend to seek a scapegoat upon whom to load their psychic woes. Hitler well understood this. In his writings and speeches he tirelessly argued that the ubiquitous Jew was fundamentally responsible for most of Germany's troubles. The Jew was represented as an evil genius eternally bent on exploiting the economic resources and systems of all people everywhere. To millions of Germans this was heady talk, especially as many of them, long before Hitler, had nurtured strong anti-Semitic feelings. They looked around and saw affluent Jews untouched by hard times. The Nazi invitation to smash the Jews thus had a double appeal. It offered a way to express pent-up feelings of desperation at the same time that it promised an end of economic conditions which produced such feelings.

Another bogey persistently paraded by the Nazis was the "Communist threat." According to Hitler and his colleagues international communism was actively planning a universal take-over. The precipitating agent, of course, was Red Russia. Unless a mighty force was erected against Russian encroachments, the bolshevization of Germany and the rest of Europe was imminent. National Socialism alone was that force. Actually, at the time the Nazis came to power, Russian Communists were busy following the Stalinist line of "Communism in one country." Moreover, the Communist party in Germany, although stronger than it had ever been, constituted but a small minority of the electorate. Nonetheless, Nazi propaganda made headway among the rank and file members of the bourgeois parties, and especially among the industrial magnates who controlled the economy.

But in spite of powerful forces at work for the new party, most Germans withheld

support from it. Nazi violence and extremism probably frightened away sober elements of the population. To many, National Socialism either suggested rule by rowdyism, or seemed a ridiculous essay in political amateurism, or both. Still, as the Depression deepened, Nazi victories at the polls became increasingly impressive. In 1928, for example, the party had but 12 representatives in the Reichstag; two years later the number increased to 107. By 1933 it was the largest party in the country.

Textbook accounts rarely extend to detailed examination of the doctrinal origins of political parties. The searing—and lingering—impact of the Nazi state was too strong not to require such inquiry in this case.

Nazi Ideology

Darwinism

In general, Nazi ideology was rooted in romantic irrationalism. Instinctive urges, mystical inner feeling were honored above pure intellect. In Freudian terms, the id dominated the ego. Hitler and other shapers of Nazi policy never tired of denouncing reliance upon logic—which they looked upon as a kind of child's game—and respect for conscience, which they thought of as a ghost conjured out of foolish guilt feelings. In place of reason and conscience they stressed intuition and iron will. The real leader, as Nazi ideology pictured him, moved toward his goal with the mystic, unerring certainty of a sleepwalker.

Nazi ideological content was shaped by the thought of a number of scientists and philosophers of the nineteenth century. Particularly prominent was Darwin's theory of the survival of the fittest. To the Nazis, "fittest" meant not only raw, amoral power; it implied a conscious, planned destruction of the nonfit. Quite literally, for them, life was a ceaseless struggle for existence and commanding strength, a struggle which in itself made up the meaning and glory of life. Going beyond Darwin, they argued further

---

* The term comes from *Nationalsozialistische*; the full name of the party was *Nationalsozialistische Deutsche Arbeiter Partei* (National Socialist German Workers Party).

that since power was the goal of life, any scrupulous discrimination between means and ends was ridiculous. Instead, means and ends were interchangeable, like duplicated parts of mass produced machines. Those who could not or would not accept this fact of life were destined to become the manipulated dupes of those who did. Moreover, the amount of power achievable by man was, like physical living space, limited. To achieve power for oneself automatically meant wresting it from another. At any moment of existence the augmentation of an individual or group A necessarily meant the diminution of B.

Philosophic Supports: Elitism, Racism

The philosophy of Friedrich Nietzsche attracted many of the Nazi elite. Actually, Nietzsche was neither a nationalist nor a socialist, but Hitler and his colleagues shopped around in philosophy as one might shop in a supermarket. They were especially attracted by the Nietzschean dictum that the aim of life was to live in an "ectasy of power." They also were interested in Nietzsche's doctrine of the transvaluation of values — the transmutation of values into supervalues. As they saw it, the society of their day exalted the weak and the expedient — that is, evil — and scorned the real good — that is, the frank acceptance of the way of pure power. For example, they believed the whole Versailles world was compounded of hypocrisy and pointless bourgeois strife; its complete and ruthless destruction was an urgently needed good. Unfortunately, most Westerners, including millions of deluded Germans, accepted the Wilsonian principles which undergirded the Versailles system in the foolish belief that these principles, however much violated in practice, derived from eternal Judeo-Christian virtues. For most Nazis, the Christian ethos, characterized by devotion to meekness, gentleness, the turning of the other cheek, was itself a perversion

of the truly good. It was, in short, an abiding madness that led to certain destruction. When the time came, a new race of men — the heroic users of raw power — would know how to deal with this complex of follies and its protagonists.

Another influence bearing upon the Nazi *Weltanschauung* was the pessimistic philosophy of Arthur Schopenhauer (1788–1860), one of the most germinal thinkers of the nineteenth century. According to Schopenhauer, the best that man could hope for was a *realization* of the unachievability of meaning and purpose in life. All thought and will were therefore self-defeating; in the end there is only death. Nazi ingestion of Schopenhauer's pessimistic revelation of the "No Will" led to differing and occasionally self-contradictory beliefs. Hitler professed to have carried certain of the philosopher's works around in his knapsack throughout the whole of World War I. It is difficult to assess the precise nature of Schopenhauer's influence upon the Führer-to-be. Perhaps the philosopher's sweeping rejection of meaning in life was interpreted by Hitler to apply to life as it was then institutionalized. Perhaps the opening sentence in one of Schopenhauer's major works — "The world is my idea" — misled Hitler into believing not in the overriding "No Will" but rather in the power of a hero's will to create whatever world he desired. In any case, and no matter how strangely, the Nazi leader seemed to gain from Schopenhauer confirmation of his own conviction that he could remake the world according to long nurtured and deeply felt desires.

A third force that shaped the Nazi mind and inflated the Nazi spirit was the music and rhetoric of Richard Wagner. For Hitler, Göbbels, Rosenberg,* and other Nazi leaders, the roll of Wagnerian thunder shook loose an earth-bound Germany whose head had been bowed by defeat and whose

---

* Josef Göbbels was minister of propaganda in the Nazi state. Arthur Rosenberg liked to think of himself as the official philosopher of National Socialism.

strength had been shackled by Versailles and by the machinations of the ubiquitous Jew. It can scarcely be denied that Hitler consciously thought of himself as the new Siegfried destined to slay the bourgeois Jewish dragon-world. Until the cares of the war made it impossible, Hitler regularly attended performances of Wagnerian operas. In the panorama of Wagnerian magic, both scored and verbalized, were found all the ingredients of the Nazi creed—reliance upon the mystic dynamism of the *Volk*,* anti-intellectualism, anti-Semitism, and the principle of rule by the elite.

Friedrich Ludwig Jahn, early nineteenth-century nationalist, held a high place in Nazi hagiology. From this superpatriot and his writings, National Socialism fed on a heady antiforeignism. Jahn's fervent nationalism was inspired by visions of a strong, united Germany. In his day there were dozens of quarreling German states, more interested, as Jahn saw it, in defending their petty particularism than in nurturing the *patrie* which their ethnic kinship made inevitable. He spent most of his life preaching the doctrine of "Germany over all." To him, German greatness lay not in the development of Austrian or even Prussian leadership, but in the creation of a holy *Deutschland*. Woven into his fierce plea for *Volkstum* ("folkdom") was Jahn's insistence that physical fitness was a prerequisite for national greatness. In our own century the Jahn heritage helped shape the spirit and formation of Storm Troop battalions.

No little of National Socialism's anti-Semitism was grounded in and strenghened

by the writings of Houston Stewart Chamberlain. Chamberlain, an English-born, naturalized German, elaborated the myth of racism in his *Foundations of the Nineteenth Century*, first published in 1899. Highly praised by Hitler, this work belabored a simple thesis: that blood was the bearer of virtue; that the purest, most virtuous blood was Aryan; that the Germans were Aryan elite; that the worst corruptors of virtuous blood were the Jews. The implication was obvious: as the bearers of the highest culture, Germans were under solemn obligation to harry all Jews out of the coming Aryan dominated world.

The works of Oswald Spengler, German philosopher-historian, were also used by Nazis to buttress their soaring *Weltanschauung*. That Spengler himself rejected Nazism (and finally fled from Germany) merely added a paradox to the Nazi mystique—the belief that the non-Nazi mind often failed to understand its own workings. National Socialists regarded Western society as a cultural cadaver, fit only to be buried. In his *Decline of the West*, Spengler argued that civilization was the sorry mark of the degradation of the human spirit. A vigorous people lives by *élan*, not by effete convention. When it wearies of the call of the spirit it becomes encrusted with complicated status fabrications and falls prey to the scourging power of a new "barbarian" folk. To the Nazi mind the message was clear: the West was a dead waste that needed to be swept away by any means the new elite saw fit to use.

Three Nazi Biases

Anti-Christianity

The above influences helped to shape three great negations which characterized National Socialism, often eloquently declaimed in private, all eloquently denied in public. One negation was the corrupting force of the Christian religion. Publicly, the Nazi regime gave conventional support

* To non-Germans this can be a puzzling word. Literally, it means folk or people. But, in German thought, it was often associated with a union of "blood and soil." Or, as one scholar has put it, "the nature of the Volk is determined by the native landscape." Hence, the Germans, "living in the dark, mist-shrouded forests, are deep, mysterious, profound." See George L. Mosse, *The Crisis of German Ideology*, Grosset and Dunlap, New York, 1964, pp. 4–5.

to Christian institutions. In 1933 Hitler's government recognized, in a concordat with the Vatican, the right of Roman Catholics not only to participate in formal religious services but also to conduct schools and to organize societies (so long as such religious activities were kept free of political involvement). Protestant churches and organizations were given similar formal sanction. But these and other overt practices belied the philosophy and long-term aims of the regime. In private conversation Hitler spoke plainly: "We are not out against the one hundred and one different kinds of Christianity, but against Christianity itself." Writing in 1942, a Nazi soldier expressed the same spirit: "The German God is an omnipotent power, a vision without form, whose presence one can anticipate and sense—but not see. . . . We Germans have by fate been chosen to be the first to break with Christianity."

Fantastic as it must seem to the non-Nazi mind, hate was conceived as one of man's truly "good" basic drives. The heroic, violent deed was the *raison d'être* of life. Without hate, the motivation for the violent deed was lacking. Scraps of Hitler's private "table talk" made this clear beyond misunderstanding: ". . . through work and industry a people has never grown free, only through hatred"; and, "Germany will not be saved by men who fall victim to universal world love but to those who turn universal world hatred against themselves."

But if the Nazi hierarchy rejected a theistic God, many of its members professed faith in a vague, inchoate Providence, or Fate. They believed that when called upon by men of superwill and supersensitivity, this power would respond. But, inconsistently, many at the same time saw blind chance as the determinant force in human life. If a particular effort failed, Providence had willed it for a later good. If the effort was successful, iron will and the caprices of chance were responsible. In a public address in 1935 Chancellor Hitler spoke plainly of his own belief in Providence.

"Fate has meant well for us. It did not let the [1923 putsch] succeed which, had it succeeded, must finally have foundered because of the inner immaturity of the movement and its faulty organizational and spiritual foundations. We know this today. Then, we acted with courage and manhood. Providence, however, acted with wisdom."

Antisociety; Antihumanity

A second fundamental negation in the Nazi creed was directed against the whole corpus of Western institutions, as well as the heritage that had molded it. Except for the instrument of sweeping revolution, nothing was really worth saving. General Werner Blomberg, one-time model of the Nazi military mind, declared:

The existing order is in process of collapse. Apart from that, we are masters of a technique with which we can break all resistance. That is their [the radical Nazis'] contention, and logic is on their side, for progressive radicalization is the law of all revolutionists. . . . Our patterns today are the young generals of the French Revolution. Our model is Napoleon with his pace and his complete change of tactics. It is logical that one should seek in our armies the revolutionary fanaticism of the sans-culottes. And no more of the *bourgeois* patriotism of 1914.[1]

Erich Koch, the notorious *Gauleiter* of East Prussia (later governor of occupied Ukraine), put it in even plainer terms:

There is no longer . . . in Europe anything left in which to believe. Not even "prosperity." Do you suppose [Americans] still believe in their political ideals? Perhaps the political-minded and the literary people do. But there is no longer any life in the old ideals. They are just empty phrases, useful for muddling peoples' heads in peacetime. Let any great upheaval come in that continent, and we shall see that they are no better off than we are here. I tell you, I see such explosions coming as have never before been known in the world.[2]

1. Quoted in Hermann Rauschning, *Men of Chaos*, G. P. Putnam's Sons, New York, 1942, pp. 319–320.
2. *Ibid.*, pp. 81–82.

Special contempt was felt for the midling classes, the bourgeois community that from the beginning had managed the Industrial Revolution and had shaped the substance and style of the "new West." But this did not mean that Nazi leaders felt sympathy for either the old aristocracy or the new proletariat. They hated all classes impartially. Publicly they fulminated against the privileges of the old aristocracy; privately they despised the masses even more than their onetime masters. And at all times they denounced material Thingism and Babbitry. For propaganda purposes they favored a classless society. Actually, Nazi plans for the coming New Order called for the division of human beings into two classes: the elite and the nonelite. Providence had touched some men. For them, schools should be built (and some actually were), so that from early youth the principles of leadership could be nurtured in gifted future führers. The rest were cattle to be herded at the pleasure of their masters. The leaders should not be squeamish about the herding process; otherwise they invited occasional, senseless stampedes. One Nazi leader phrased the idea simply: "Who cares," he said, "about life, fate or interests of the millions, if only the representatives of the racial soul prosper!"

The third bias hardly needs belaboring. In the Nazi outlook, humanity was meaningless as a concept and unspeakably wretched as a phenomenal condition. Pidder Lung, a pedagogue who tried his hand at organizing Nazi philosophy, once said, "Humanity is an abstraction which cannot be translated into practical life." In actual life, inherent human dignity was an illusion. By nature most men were swine. Women were even more inferior than men; essentially they existed as breeding animals, producers of the warrior class. As for children, they were regarded as malleable organisms to be molded as the elite saw fit.

No matter how bizarre these views may seem, they subsumed a terrible program that was soon to be translated into history.

The Nazi State

Alliance with Big Business and the Army

From his first venture in politics, in 1920, Hitler remained confident of ultimate victory, providing only that he could bring into full play his propaganda magic. These things would guarantee revolution: massive rallies throughout the Reich, subsidized Storm Troop units controlling the streets, and sustained newspaper support. But how were they to be paid for? Nazi funds had increased with growing membership lists, but dues would not keep such a program going for even a month. The sums needed could come only from the very rich —from such industrial magnates as Fritz Thyssen (steel) and Gustav Krupp von Bohlen (armaments). But until 1931 the great industrialists had not felt inclined to give much support to Nazi agitation. Partly this was because they took seriously the "socialist" element in the Nazi program; and partly because they distrusted what they thought of as the wild men of the movement. The coming of the Depression changed both their attitude and their behavior. The economic crisis caused many Germans to turn to the left. Worsening conditions could lead to revolution. If they did, only a strong Rightist government backed by the industrialists could save the capitalist system. At this juncture, Hitler's advisers counseled consultation with business leaders. Without their support the Party could not hope to stage the campaigns needed to gain power. With it, victory was certain; and, after victory, the Führer could put whatever construction he pleased on the terms of the bargain. Consequently, each side, compelled by what it considered necessitous conditions, moved closer to the other side.

Besides big business, Hitler needed the army. He doubted (correctly as it turned out) that he could command a parliamentary majority during his earlier days in power. This would necessitate reliance upon power to govern by decree. Under the terms of the Weimar Constitution, only the president could sanction such rule. As president, Field Marshal von Hindenburg assuredly would grant this power only to one who had the confidence of the military. Thus, in 1931 to 1932, Hitler took care to declare publicly that he considered the army the rock upon which any regime must rest, and he assured highly placed military officers of this in many private conversations. Actually, this was in no sense a mere political trick. His grandiose plans of conquest were empty dreams without an efficient military establishment. His courting of the military served a double purpose.

Hitler Appointed Chancellor

A series of cabinet crises brought Hitler to power in January 1933. During the years 1923 to 1929 Germany had made substantial gains both at home and abroad. Most of her recovery resulted from the patient labors of Gustav Stresemann. Stresemann's death in 1929 left the nation leaderless at a time when talents such as his were most needed. Chancellor Heinrich Brüning (Catholic Center party leader) tried to meet the problems created by the Depression. But they proved more than he could handle. Growing national restiveness and lack of a workable parliamentary majority led him to rule by decree. This was of little help, however, for his program for economic recovery was anything but bold and imaginative. As a consequence, parties of both the Left and the Right gained extraordinary support, particularly the Communist and the National Socialist parties. Squeezed into this political vise and harassed by the sharp deterioration of economic conditions, Brüning resigned (1932). He was succeeded by a Junker career diplomat, Franz von Papen, who had neither a program nor the wits to devise one. Seven troubled months later he was replaced by Kurt von Schleicher, a political general

whose behind-the-scenes wirepulling had been responsible for both the rise and fall of his two predecessors. He lasted barely a month.* Confused by the enveloping political chaos and badly advised by his Junker comrades (particularly by von Papen who —typically—believed that he could tame the Nazi Führer), Hindenburg reluctantly gave Hitler his long awaited chance. For Germany, and indeed for much of the world, the hour of the rough beast had come round at last.

Consolidation of Nazi Power

The new leader clearly understood the difficulties that he faced. Most of the members of his cabinet were not Nazis. The Nazi Party lacked a majority in the Reichstag. Big business and the army had accepted him strictly on the basis of temporary sufferance. Intraparty problems were numerous; some were serious (for example, the insistence by some upon genuine socialization of heavy industry; by others, the transformation of Storm Troop brigades into regular army units).

Hitler's first major decision was to call for new elections. In the words of Göbbels the outcome was assured: "The struggle is a light one, since we are able to employ all the means of the State, Radio and Press are at our disposal. We shall achieve a masterpiece of propaganda. Even money is not lacking this time."[3] The results, however, were disappointing. Most Germans voted against Hitler and his regime. True, 288 Nazi delegates were elected to the Chamber, a gain of 92 seats. But opposition parties won 373 seats. Only an agreement between Nazi leaders and leaders of the

---

* The story of political intrigue and conspiracy that attended these events is too detailed and complicated for treatment in a general study. The bibliography at the end of this chapter includes works that relate this story for those who are interested.

---

3. Quoted in Alan Bullock, *Hitler, A Study in Tyranny*, Harper and Brothers, New York, 1952, p. 234.

Nationalist party (with 52 Reichstag members) gave the National Socialist government a shaky majority.

His next move paved the way for outright dictatorship. A bill was presented to the Chamber empowering the government to decree laws when the interest of the state should require it. In order to obtain the necessary two-thirds majority for passage, Hitler outlawed the Communist party—ostensibly because of the burning of the Reichstag building—and denied its representatives their seats in the Chamber. Mixing flat public promises that the "emergency" powers would be used discreetly with private injunctions to the Storm Troopers to soften up the opposition, the new Chancellor got his Enabling Act, as it was called, by the handsome vote of 441 to 84 (all votes against the measure being cast by the Social Democrats). Thereafter, Germany was ruled by the fiat of one will.

Ignoring his promise to use the powers of the Enabling Act sparingly, Hitler proceeded at once to bring the nation's political, economic, and cultural institutions into harmony with the "principle of leadership." Within several months all political parties except the National Socialists were disbanded either by voluntary action of their leaders or by government decree. One of the country's oldest and largest parties, the Social Democratic party, was dissolved on the simple grounds that its philosophy and practice were subversive of the nation's well-being. All of Germany's sixteen states —Prussia, Bavaria, Saxony, and others— were stripped of autonomous powers and came under the rule of governors appointed by the Nazi hierarchy. A new judicial system, capped by a complex of Peoples' Courts, was superimposed upon the old. The chief function of the Courts, put in simplest terms, was to protect and promote National Socialist principles and practices. Thoroughgoing changes were made at all levels of civil service personnel by the Civil Service Law of April 1933. Jews, socialists,

"The Old Consul (to Hitler); 'This is a heaven-sent opportunity, my lad. If you can't be a dictator now, you never will be.'" This Punch *cartoon shows Hindenburg urging Hitler to use alleged Communist violence to build himself into a dictator. Actually, Hindenburg disliked the upstart "little corporal."*

and all other possible opponents of the new Reich were dismissed, and faithful party members were put in their places.

Hitler knew that these revolutionary changes could endure only if the German masses approved them, or could be brought around at least to tolerate them. To this end he took care to establish close control over all media of mass communication. In March 1933, he appointed an Old Guard Nazi, Dr. Josef Göbbels, to head the newly formed Ministry of Propaganda and Enlightenment. Göbbels was not only a brilliant word artist but also an extremely able administrator. He quickly and effectively established control over the nation's newspapers and periodicals, radio, the cinema and theater, literature, art, and music organizations and activities. Thereafter, the German people read or listened to Nazi news, attended Nazi approved plays, read Nazi

Nazi bully boys staged this now-famous book-burning (1933) to keep their compatriots from becoming infected with "radical" ideas.

literature, listened to music calculated to inspire Nazi feelings and emotions. In short, a cultural curtain enshrouded the nation. After a while, many seemed to feel naked without it.

Instruments of Terror

Coercive agencies were also used to fashion consent. One was the *Sturm Abteilung* (Storm Section) or SA. Originally (in the early 1920s) its marching columns were employed to display Nazi strength and solidarity, to whip up public enthusiasm, and to "dominate the streets" during election campaigns. Its rank and file came mostly from the middle and lower middle classes, its officers from the old Free Corps. It appealed to the typical German's love for uniforms and marching; it doled out pittances welcomed by the unemployed; it provided some relief from gnawing feelings of frustration. During the hectic latter years of the Nazi climb to power it broke up Communist and Socialist political meetings, smashed Jewish shops, bullied provincial authorities into giving it special favors, and served generally as the spearhead of the Nazi Revolution (see illustration). When Hitler became Chancellor the brown-shirted Storm Troopers let themselves go in a series of frenzied pogroms directed against Jews, socialists, landlords, aristocrats, and often personal

enemies who could safely be "given theirs" in the general turbulence that prevailed. For a while, Hitler tolerated (even approved) the Brown Terror as a natural expression of exuberant spirits tasting the first fruits of victory. Later he administered a bloody disciplining to some SA leaders who made demands on the army, and had dared to talk about socializing industry. (See section below on the "Second Revolution.")

Another instrument of terror was the SS (*Schutz Staffel*—"protective squads"). Originally it served as Hitler's bodyguard. When the SA swelled to proportions difficult to handle (and increasingly came to include apostates from socialist and radical organizations—to say nothing of a hoodlum assortment of pimps and homosexuals), Hitler made the SS a special cadre of Nazi elite. In 1929 he entrusted its training and program to Heinrich Himmler, one of the most brutal, vicious men of modern times. Under Himmler's direction the SS became a kind of secret state within a state. Above the law and the courts, even Nazi law and Nazi courts, the SS worked to create a "purified" racial body, a nation of Aryan fanatics ruled by a corps of supermen accountable only to the Führer's master will.

Before the SS achieved its dread distinction, the most feared agency in Germany was the Gestapo (*Geheime Staats Polizei*). Created in 1933 by Hermann Göring (Hitler's No. 2 man), it served as the secret investigative agency of opposition to, or disaffection with, the Nazi Reich. The Gestapo, like the later SS with which it was soon affiliated, could (and often did) perform outside the law. If, for example, the unlikely occurred and a political prisoner was found not guilty by a state court, the acquitted might be picked up by the Gestapo as he left the court room and hauled off to a camp for detention or execution.

A number of detention camps, or concentration camps, were set up all over Germany (and just before and during the war, in annexed and occupied territories). Chief among these camps were Dachau, near Munich; Buchenwald, outside of Weimar; Sachsenhausen, close to Berlin; Mauthausen, near Linz (Austria); and Auschwitz, in occupied Poland. Often the main gate to these camps was overarched by the slogen *Arbeit Macht Frei* — "Work Makes Free." But the SS commanders of concentration camps were interested in neither work nor freedom. Their job was to so terrorize the inmates that the very idea of opposition to the regime would die out. In the main they were successful. Many never returned from the camps; their absence was a perpetual reminder to their families and friends of the folly of defiance, or even criticism. Those who did return were often living warnings of what happened to citizens who turned "subversive."

But it is unlikely that Nazi propaganda and Nazi terror, powerful as they were, could have sustained the new regime apart from economic recovery and a growing feeling that Germany was regaining her place among the powers of the world. Within a year unemployment had dropped from around seven million to less than one million. Public works and ambitious rearmament projects mainly accounted for economic rehabilitation. Bold defiance of both world opinion and the remaining restrictions of the Versailles Treaty provided stimuli to create anew the comforting image of national greatness. By mid-1934 the hum of factories was heard throughout the land; by then, too, the world had learned to sit up and listen when the Führer spoke. Germany was becoming herself again.

The Crushing of the "Second Revolution"

Still, all was not well in the Reich. For millions of the SA the taste of recovery was good, but they had not, they insisted, staged a revolution just to get the wheels of industry turning again. They aimed at nothing less than the capture and control of the nation's economy, to be run by them and for them. Also they wanted wholesale absorption of SA military units into the regular army. Hitler had no intention of allowing either. He knew that he needed the support of big business, at least for several years; otherwise, the economic revival, upon which all of his power plans depended, would die aborning. He likewise needed the professional army, for he realized clearly that any day (until, that is, the regime had become firmly rooted) the army wanted to rout the SA rabble and unseat the government it could do it. When, therefore, certain SA leaders increased their agitation for "completion" of the revolution, Hitler publicly warned them against persisting in what he thought of as treasonous behavior. But for large masses in the SA battalions (many of whom had been disappointed at the meager economic and prestige advantages doled out to them in return for their arduous efforts to overturn the "System") the talk about "safe channels of evolution" itself seemed treasonous. Ernst Röhm, leader of the SA, publicly answered his Führer in blunt terms. "Anyone who thinks that the tasks of the SA have been accomplished," he warned, "will have to get used to the idea that we are here and intend to stay here, come what may."[4]

But the combination of Hitler, big business, and the army was more than the little men in brown shirts could handle. In June 1934, Hitler loosed his fury against the dissidents. Within 48 hours all the chief leaders of the "second revolution" were murdered, including Röhm. Many lesser *leiter* were thrown into concentration camps. While they were at it the new rulers settled a number of other accounts. Former Chancellor Kurt von Schleicher was shot down in his home. Several Bavarian politicians who had played a part in crushing the 1923 Beer Hall Putsch were murdered. Vice Chancellor von Papen's chief aide was killed. No accurate count has ever been

---

4. Bullock, *op. cit.*, p. 257.

made of the slain and maimed of that bloody night. But such macabre arithmetic is quite irrelevant. Whatever the number, the nation had learned a lesson in followership not soon to be forgotten.

The next month a venture in foreign affairs came off less happily for the Führer. Long an advocate of the Greater Reich, Hitler judged the time ripe for the annexation of Austria. To this end a coup was staged July 25, 1934. Austrian Nazis raided the Austrian Chancellory, assassinated Chancellor Dollfuss, and took over the national radio station in Vienna. They were thwarted by the prompt action of the Austrian authorities, supported by Mussolini who had sent Italian troops to the Brenner Pass with instructions to move in if the Austrian government showed signs of yielding. Realizing he was not yet ready for this kind of a showdown, Hitler disavowed the putsch and patched up difficulties with Kurt von Schuschnigg, Dollfuss' successor. But Austria's reprieve was short-lived.*

In August, President von Hindenburg died. The old Field Marshal had been the only man in the government with sufficient power and prestige to stand against the upstart Chancellor (and in his latter months, growing senility had made of even this revered soldier-hero just another Hitler puppet). Using a decree long prepared for the occasion, Hitler virtually absolished the office of president by combining its powers with those of the chancellor. Moreover, all members of the armed forces, from field marshals to privates, were required to swear an oath of allegiance not to the state but personally to Hitler. Now, indeed, *der Führer* stood alone in power.

Triumph of the Nazi Way

Across the next several years Hitler sprang surprise after surprise upon fellow Germans and foreign peoples alike. In March 1935, he unilaterally denounced that

section of the Versailles Treaty which limited German armed forces to 100,000 men. Thereafter, a formidable conscript army was raised, trained, and equipped. A year later he ripped another page from the Treaty when he ordered German troops to march into the Rhineland. For the first time since the Armistice, French soldiers now looked across their frontier into the muzzles of German guns. Within a remarkably short time (about two years or less) a vast military establishment bristled in the area once designated a perpetually demilitarized zone. Foreign powers, especially France and England, protested these violations of the Treaty, but their protests were muted. Germans, of course, hailed the creation of a new army and the remilitarization of the Rhineland as the kind of miracles they were coming to expect of their dazzling Siegfried.

By this time the Nazi hierarchy felt strong enough to begin to establish control over their business and military collaborators. The appointment in 1936 of Hermann Göring as economic dictator under a Nazi-devised Four Year Plan officially marked the end of Nazi tutelage under the leaders of German industry. In early 1938 the army received similar treatment. Hitler simply dispensed with the Ministry of War and made himself supreme commander of the *Wehrmacht*. Both business and the military now mulled over possibilities of checking the Nazi tide. But they were late in sensing what had happened. By then, all instruments of government and news were in Nazi hands. The Blood Purge of 1934, the omnipresent Gestapo, the disciplined SS, the concentration camps—all reminded Germans who might want to dispute the Nazi way of the price involved. With few exceptions, the industrial magnates and generals adjusted themselves to the new situation.

Besides, it is doubtful whether many Germans wanted to dispute the Nazi way. Everybody was employed. The Reich was again a power in the world. The Versailles

---

* The union of Austria and Germany—*Anschluss*—is taken up in a later chapter.

Treaty was but an unpleasant memory. There were no unsettling elections, no swift and senseless changes of governments, and no street battles between partisan factions. Some bitter democrats and socialists, it was true, had gone underground, but their grumbling was rarely heard. Foreign newspapers sometimes criticized the regime, but foreigners could hardly be expected to understand the New Order, or approve of the spectacular rise to greatness of the new Germany. Citizens could not, of course, criticize the govern-

ment, even mildly. This was occasionally irritating, as were the haunting stories of Gestapo midnight visitations, and the hard life in the "camps." But prosperity and order demanded some sacrifices, some inconveniences. In the long run it was better, it seemed, to look the other way when now and then a disturbance occurred. Until later when its soldiers floundered in the snows of Russia and its cities rocked under a hail of bombs, the Third Reich's Nazi ways seemed to speak to the longings and to still the fears of most German citizens.

NEW DEAL AMERICA

Thus far, we have considered the collectivist trend as it developed in nondemocratic societies. In the United States the movement was hardly less strong. Between 1929 and 1939 it created a Big Government that made the Hamiltonian dream seem pale and paltry. During the same period, Big Labor grew to proportions no realistic A.F.L. leader would have dared predict a few short years before. Accompanying these changes and making them possible was a new climate of public opinion. Its vital center was the growing conviction that no individual was rugged enough to make his way alone in a complex industrial world. Business, though still big and soon to grow bigger, had failed the test of the Depression. Only the general government, speaking in the name of the people and responsive to their needs, could be trusted to manage the national economy.*

It should not be understood that the new attitude toward the nation's business in general and the business of making a living in particular was adopted by all, nor by many, to the same degree. From about 1934, an increasing number of critics of the New

Deal pointed to this changed attitude as a kind of sickness that must be cured, unless American civilization was to collapse. Much of the criticism came from professional politicians who, as "outs," naturally wanted to get back in. But much of it came from those whom we think of as typical Americans. A sociological study of an Indiana community, published in 1937, reported the following as a kind of consensus of the town's business leaders:

All these big plans they're making in Washington look well, read well—but they just won't work. They're Utopian, and we don't live and try to do business in a Utopia! By what God-given right do those fellows in Washington think they can do so big a job? . . . You can't make the world all planned and soft. The strongest and best survive—that's the law of nature after all—always has been and always will be.[5]

Nor should it be thought that New Deal collectivism was based on a detailed, carefully thought out planned economy that blanketed the nation's business affairs. At no time did Roosevelt and his top advisers suggest such a program; at no time did they

---

* "Manage" is here used in the sense of general supervision, not in the sense of direct, day-to-day control.

5. Quoted in Willard Thorp et al., eds., *American Issues, The Social Record,* J. B. Lippincott Company, Philadelphia, 1955, Vol. I, p. 1012.

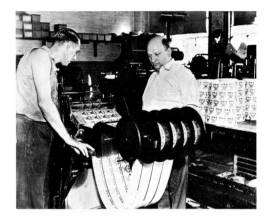

Millions of N.R.A. labels were distributed throughout the country as the new administration sought to rally the country behind its New Deal program.

Civilian Conservation Corps enrollees working on a reforestation project.

give evidence that they had the slightest sympathy for such planning. From first to last, the New Deal was a work of improvisation, always seeking, sometimes desperately, to locate the weaknesses of the established system and to apply effective remedies. And when, in 1939, it faded into national efforts that were more concerned with foreign than domestic affairs, it left no blueprint for a centrally managed economy.*

* Some of Roosevelt's early advisers, such as Rexford Tugwell, did favor large-scale central planning. But this should not be confused with total planning such as Mussolini attempted in the Corporate State or as Stalin inaugurated in Russia in 1929.

Nevertheless, control of the nation's business and the people's outlook regarding that control, despite these qualifications, were fundamentally changed in the years 1933 to 1939. The lure of the American Dream had faded. The glory road from "rags to riches" was relegated to myth. Unrestricted *laissez-faire* was no longer considered tenable as a philosophy of political economy. In 1964 the Republican Party, under the leadership of Senator Goldwater, tested the reality of the "Big Change." No responsible party or statesman is likely soon to repeat the test. For all its improvising on an old theme, or perhaps because of it, the New Deal had made a very real new America.

The First New Deal

Relief Legislation and the N.R.A.

Franklin Roosevelt took up the duties of the presidency in one of the bleakest periods of American history. By March 1933, almost forty million of the country's population were living a hand-to-mouth existence, without a steady income or, in many cases, without any income at all. The index of industrial production had fallen to an all-time low. The nation's banks were in such perilous condition that those that had not already closed their doors to prevent runs were shut down by the President two days after he took office. Near-hysteria gripped the country as day-to-day business and, as it seemed to some, the business of living from day to day itself appeared to be grinding to a stop. In these circumstances, no grand plans to overhaul the economy were worth immediate attention, even if any had been at hand. In his inaugural address the President spoke plainly of what had to come first:

Our greatest primary task is to put people to work. This is no unsolvable problem if we face it wisely and courageously. It can be accomplished in part by direct recruiting by the government itself, treating the task as we would treat the emergency of war. . . .

Lenin Steel Works, *Nowa Huta, Poland. After World War II, Europe sought to revive its shattered economy by means of heavy industrialization. Huge plants such as this steel works, built in 1949, provided employment for large numbers of people. The cabbage patch in the foreground with the modern plant behind it exemplifies the blend of old and new which still characterizes much of the Continent. (Elliott Erwitt, Magnum)*

Wheat Harvesting, *Andalusia, Spain. One of the least industrialized European countries, Spain still depends primarily on agriculture. Andalusia in the southernmost part of the country is a principal area for wheat growing and for horse and cattle raising. There the harvesting of wheat proceeds much as it has for centuries, virtually unaided by modern farming techniques and machinery. Oxen pull primitive threshers, and peasant women separate the chaff from the grain by hand. (Inge Morath, Magnum)*

Tailors on Savile Row, *London. In the present era of ready-to-wear clothing, made from mass-produced textiles and sewn by powerful machinery, the craft of the tailor is fast disappearing. But there are still a few establishments where the well-to-do can have garments made specially to fit their measurements and their tastes. One of the best-known tailoring centers is the Savile Row in London. Lately, however, office buildings have begun to replace many of the old shops. (Burt Glinn, Magnum)*

Enka Factory, *North Carolina. By pioneering in the development of synthetic fibers, the United States made a significant contribution to the standard of living throughout the world. The modern assembly-line worker shown in this photograph is a far cry from the English tailor who painstakingly creates a garment from start to finish, for the factory worker participates in only a single aspect of production and has no control over the quality of the ultimate product. (Bruce Roberts, Rapho Guillumette)*

Cowes Regatta, *England. With the end of World War II, a shorter work day and work week began to be instituted throughout the world. Today people of all classes have more leisure time in which to indulge their interests. Sailing, a sport once restricted to the upper classes, now attracts people from all walks of life, as spectators or participants. The Cowes Regatta is a popular annual event. (Gerry Cranham, Rapho Guillumette)*

Concert Hall, *Prague, Czechoslovakia. Sports, the great class leveller, attracts more people than the arts do, but today more people than ever before have the time either to pursue the arts or to enjoy them as spectators. The number of Sunday painters, amateur musicians, and art collectors has greatly increased in the past few decades. Prague, for centuries one of the foremost cultural centers of Europe, abounds in museums, theatres, concert halls, libraries, and institutions of higher learning. (Elliott Erwitt, Magnum)*

U.N.E.F. Demonstration, *June 1, 1968, Gare Montparnasse, Paris. The strike was first used by trade unions in the 1880's to force individual employers to pay heed to the complaints of their workers. Today, in highly centralized countries such as France, the general strike is used to wrest concessions from the government by paralyzing the whole economy. The 1968 general strike in France was launched by the National Students Union and soon involved workers throughout the nation. However, results were inconclusive. (J. L. Nou, Rapho Guillumette)*

The three months of the special session of Congress that Roosevelt had called were spent first in providing that work, and then in setting up a program designed to promote industrial recovery. Under emergency legislation the nation's banks were opened under strict federal supervision. The same month a Civilian Conservation Corps was established providing jobs for about 250,000 male youths working on a variety of projects—reforestation, flood control, road construction, and prevention of soil erosion. The Federal Emergency Relief Act of May 1933 appropriated millions of dollars for direct relief. Under it, sums were granted outright to states and local communities to finance whatever job programs they could devise. Out of that Act, two other agencies later evolved (1934–1935)—the Civil Works Administration and the Works Progress Administration. Both were concerned with direct supervision by the Federal Government of an extensive program of public works. Farmers were not forgotten. With passage of the Farm Credit Act in June 1933, they became eligible for loans at low interest rates, with which they could refinance their mortgages. Similarly, home owners were granted loans to meet pressing mortgage obligations and delinquent tax bills.

The N.R.A.

More ambitious projects, aimed at getting and keeping the wheels of industry turning, were provided by legislation in this same period. The National Industrial Recovery Act (soon shortened to N.R.A.) was the most important. The Act was designed to effect economic recovery by the creation of a set of codes for each industry in the country. Each code, as it was finally developed, spelled out in detail principles and practices which purported to deal fairly with producers, consumers, and laborers. Representatives from each industry were selected to draw up a general plan under which that industry would conduct its business. To permit this "benign collusion," the N.R.A.

suspended operation of the antitrust laws. By the fall of 1933 almost all businesses in America were operating under such codes. For the most part, industrialists supported the new effort because it allowed them to work together to eliminate the waste and the expensive duplication that are an inevitable part of cut-throat competition. Laborers favored it, both because it promised to provide jobs as industry revived and, particularly, because one section of the new law specifically guaranteed labor's right to organize and bargain collectively. The general public also gave it enthusiastic support since each code, before it became operative, had to be approved by the President who, they believed, genuinely had their interests at heart.

For about a year the N.R.A. seemed to be on the way to meeting many of the stricken country's needs. As unemployment decreased and money began to circulate more freely, the sense of panic subsided. Hopes for a brighter tomorrow sustained millions who still remained unemployed, particularly since the Federal Government, under Section II of the N.R.A., laid extensive plans for the construction of many public buildings and roads. Laborers turned to unionization and the prospects of higher wages through collective bargaining.

A.A.A.; T.V.A.; and S.E.A.

To guarantee American farmers their fair share of the coming planned prosperity, the government set up an Agricultural Adjustment Administration. Its primary task was to promote the restoration of the buying power of farmers. To accomplish this, the new agency arranged for the elimination of surplus crops through agreements with farmers to reduce plantings, and for a bigger "farmer's dollar" through the determining and underwriting of parity prices for certain basic products such as corn, cotton, wheat, and hogs.

Other important New Deal legislation dealt with such diverse problems as rural electrification and regulation of the stock market. Since 1917 the United States government had owned a huge hydroelectric power plant at Muscle Shoals, Alabama. For years Senator George Norris of Nebraska had urged the Federal Government to use the resources of Muscle Shoals and the power of the Tennessee River to upgrade socioeconomic conditions throughout the whole Tennessee watershed region. Republican presidents had vetoed such schemes on the grounds that government must not compete with business. But in the new atmosphere of the "Roosevelt Revolution," things were seen differently. In May 1933, a Tennessee Valley Authority was established, which went far beyond Norris' dreams. During the next decade the T.V.A. constructed power plants that generated and sold electricity directly and cheaply to many farmers in Tennessee, Alabama, North Carolina, Kentucky, Virginia, and Mississippi. It manufactured and sold fertilizers, planned and executed flood control projects, arrested soil erosion, and encouraged the efficient use of the region's water resources. Naturally, private power companies and industries associated with them protested this "socialist innovation," as they thought of it. But for most inhabitants of the vast watershed region (and for many outside it who hoped for like benefits in their own areas), the upgrading of living standards and the hum of renewed industrial activity generated by the T.V.A. dulled the edge of such ideological dialectics.

To prevent the recurrence of stock exchange malpractices that preceded and partly caused the crash of 1929, Congress passed (in 1934) a Securities Exchange Act. Through a commission established by the Act, the Federal Government undertook to weed out unfair practices in securities markets. Promoters of new stocks were required to give solid evidence that their issuance was based upon real capital resources. Price manipulation, of new stocks

and old, was prohibited with severe penalties for infraction of the rules of trading. Buying stocks "on margin," a practice that inflated the exchange boom of the late twenties, was discouraged by restrictive regulations. In short, "it was the New Deal answer to the social control of finance." [6]

The New Deal Moves Left

These and other measures of the first New Deal were based upon curiously conflicting beliefs. From the founding of the Republic until the Roosevelt Administration, presidents and people alike had either never seriously entertained or had consciously rejected the notion that the Federal Government possessed the power or right to directly administer relief to economically distressed citizens. Such an idea constituted, indeed, a kind of affront to the American Dream and to the doctrine of rugged individualism. Three years of the Great Depression had changed much of the popular and political mind about both dream and doctrine. When Roosevelt urged passage of the first federal relief act and the Congress pushed it through almost without debate, both were mirroring the new mood of America.

At the same time, however, both the President and the people seemed to believe that the clearly necessary overhauling of the capitalist system should be entrusted basically to the trained talents of the captains of that system. By 1933, it is true, those captains were no longer regarded with the almost religious awe accorded them in the Golden Twenties. Too many tycoons had publicly stumbled in the wasteland of tickertape for that. Nevertheless, the intricacies of business called for business talents. Moreover, it was reasonable to suppose that the stumbling itself had taught a lesson. Finally, the Federal Government was prepared to act as a surro-

6. Ralph F. De Bedts, *The New Deal's SEC.* . . . Columbia University Press, New York, 1964, p. 205.

gate for the people; its laws would serve as guidelines for the reconstruction of the national economy; its leaders would supervise the activities of the reconstructionists. At any rate, it was to business leaders that the New Deal turned in its first efforts to set the United States on its feet.

As it turned out, the codes approved by the President had little enduring effect on general conditions beyond stimulating a small upturn in business, which gave industrialists disproportionate profits and renewed confidence in "the old way." Labor leaders soon began to refer to the N.R.A. as the "National Run Around." Low wages and long hours were common in spite of certain provisions of the Act designed to give labor a fairer share of economic returns. Some companies kept two sets of books, one for themselves, and one for N.R.A. inspectors. In fact, many of the codes, even if they had been fairly practiced, were loaded in favor of business, in spite of the President's examination and approval of them. A number of them were verbatim copies of plans drawn up for different purposes when Hoover was president. A year and a half after the N.R.A. had gone into operation, the United States (although slowly climbing up from the Depression's depths, and although buoyed and more hopeful of tomorrow) was ready for a cleaner break with the old system. So were the President and most of his advisers. For some time, various radical dissidents had shown signs of capturing substantial followings. In the southwest, Huey Long, demagogue supreme, preached political homilies on sharing the wealth that set that section ablaze and gave him rising hopes of establishing dictatorial control over the whole country. In the midwest, Father Coughlin, a quasi-fascist Catholic priest, blasted the New Deal as communistic and promised national salvation through his own program of social justice. His weekly radio broadcasts reached millions and influenced many who were beginning to

Huey Long in a typical haranguing posture.

The Reverend Gerald L. K. Smith, Father Coughlin, and Dr. Francis Townsend are shown here whipping up interest in "social justice" at an anti-New Deal meeting in 1936.

doubt the efficacy of the New Deal. On the West Coast, Dr. Francis Townsend beguiled many senior citizens with his demand for a government grant of $200 a month for every person over 65.

In 1935 a conservative Supreme Court declared the N.R.A. unconstitutional. Roosevelt was troubled by the decision, but he had already given clear indication (in his annual message to Congress) of a new attack upon the country's economic ills. Hereafter, the Federal Government would point more directly toward a managed economy, with the masses of workers and farmers as the prime objects of its concern.

The Second New Deal

Social Security; Growth of Unions

A sweeping series of reform measures was passed in the period 1935 to 1938. In April 1935, the Government ended its direct relief program and established the Works Progress Administration (W.P.A.). Under the energetic prodding of its director, Harry Hopkins, this agency began a building program that eventually employed more than eight million workers. Before its termination (after the beginning of World War II), it had spent about $11 billion on tens of thousands of projects, ranging from huge public buildings to programs of adult education. Most of the money went directly into wages and salaries, with a consequent jump in mass buying power.

Several months later a comprehensive Social Security Act was passed and put into operation. Among other social services, it provided for unemployment relief, and monthly benefits for those over 65. Under terms of the Act, each state was invited to set up an unemployment insurance plan in cooperation with the Federal Government. Administrative expenses were paid almost completely by the Federal Government, but funds for unemployment benefits came from taxes levied against employer payrolls. Not all workers were covered by the Act—agricultural laborers and domestic workers, for example. But a substantial portion of the American labor force was covered, thus relieving many workers (at least for a period extending to 36 weeks) of the haunting fear of payless Saturdays. Old-age benefits, ranging from $10 to $85 a month, were supplied out of funds provided by taxes paid jointly by employer and em-

ployee. Other provisions of the Act set up funds to be spent on relief of homeless, crippled, and delinquent children, for vocational rehabilitation projects, and for maternity and child care.

One of the most important "second New Deal" laws, although not originally sponsored by Roosevelt, was the National Labor Relations Act, commonly called the Wagner Act. Already before its passage, American labor unions had a century-old history behind them. But they had never enjoyed governmental protection; indeed, quite the opposite was true. Since the Civil War, corporate industry had grown to gigantic proportions; individual laborers could not hope to stand up to its multiplying monopolies and trusts. Now with the United States government guaranteeing their right to organize and collectively bargain, workers were given a truly "new deal." They made the most of it. Within five years the majority of the nation's great corporations had recognized bargaining agents of the workers' own choosing. True, for a while the new unions were put to a severe test. The new law guaranteed the right to organize and bargain; it did not, of course, guarantee that companies would sign contracts. Throughout 1936 and 1937 big unions were formed; both the Wagner Act and the advent of industrial unions, such as the Committee of Industrial Organizations (C.I.O.), assured this. But most big industries, such as United States Steel and General Motors, were determined to draw the line at bargaining; that is, *talk*. To force employers to carry through to contracts, many workers struck and threw close-packed picket lines around company plants. Normally, at this point, industrialists and political leaders joined efforts, almost always successfully, to break both picket lines and union strength. This time the Federal Government and most state governments were controlled by political leaders who either sympathized with the workers or were afraid to oppose them. Consequently the country's business enterprises, large and small, became progressively unionized. For labor the year of decision was 1937. When, in that year, steel companies and the automobile and rubber industries refused union demands for contracts, the workers staged sit-in strikes. Company efforts to dislodge them resulted in bloody fights and considerable property damage. When state and federal government officials showed no signs of coming to their aid, most corporations renewed bargaining negotiations and eventually signed contracts satisfactory to the workers. Big Labor had come to stay.

Other important New Deal legislation was passed in 1935: the Motor Carrier Act, which gave the Federal Government control over conditions of labor, passenger and freight rates, and financial regulations of the country's interstate bus and trucking concerns; the Revenue Act, which sharply increased income, estate, and gift taxes; and the Public Utility Holding Company Act, which forced public utility holding companies to break up their empires of affiliates, empires which had given inordinate financial (and hence political) power to gas and electric monopolies.

In 1938, in what may properly be considered the last year of the New deal, three other significant bills were enacted into law. The Bituminous Coal Act put most of the soft coal industry under federal regulation. A new Agricultural Adjustment Act replaced the earlier one which had been declared unconstitutional (1935) by the Supreme Court. The new "Triple A" gave the Federal Government the power to establish marketing quotas when farm prices slumped; the right to restrict plantings (contingent upon approval of the farmers involved in producing the enumerated crops); and authority to buy and store surplus produce to keep farm prices at a parity with such levels as the Government should decide were just. The Fair Labor Standards Act put a floor under wages and a ceiling over hours of work for about a million wage earners (subsequently, many more) engaged in work that affected interstate commerce.

Significance of the New Deal

Many claims and counterclaims have been made regarding the meaning and worth of the New Deal. Some are too extreme for serious attention as, for example, that the "Roosevelt Revolution" ushered in an age of socialism that would inevitably lead to totalitarian communism; or, on the other hand, that the New Deal brought to as much perfection as human talents allow, the Jacksonian vision of an egalitarian America, secure in both political and economic democracy.

Other claims, more limited but still untenable, are that the New Deal not only did not effect economic recovery but actually retarded it. Or, the other side of the coin, that the New Deal brought America out of the Depression. Statistics prove both of these claims wrong. It cannot be argued soundly that the Roosevelt program retarded economic recovery in the face of these demonstrable facts: from 1933 to 1939 national income increased over 65 per cent; in the same period, unemployment decreased nearly 60 per cent. But, on the other hand, nearly seven million workers were still unemployed in 1938 to 1939, and the income level of the average employed worker was still under what such a conservative body as the Brookings Institute described as the minimum for health and decency. In other words, the New Deal substantially ameliorated the hard times of the 1930s, but it did not "cure" the Depression.

Although still unreconcilable, more reasonable views of the worth and meaning of the New Deal were expressed by the chief protagonists of the old and new views. In his *Challenge to Liberty* (one of our century's most closely and cogently reasoned arguments for the private enterprise way of life), Herbert Hoover made the following charge:

> We cannot extend the mastery of government over the daily life of a people without somewhere making it master of people's souls and thoughts. That is going on today [1934]. It is part of all regimentation. Even if the government conduct of business could give us the maximum of efficiency instead of least efficiency, it would be purchased at the cost of freedom. It would . . . stifle initiative and invention, undermine the development of leadership, cripple the mental and spiritual energies of our people, extinguish equality of opportunity, and dry up the spirit of liberty and the forces which make progress. It is a false Liberalism that interprets itself into government dictation, or operation of commerce, industry and agriculture. Every move in that direction poisons the very springs of true Liberalism. . . . The nation seeks for solution of its many problems. . . . They cannot be achieved by the destructive forces of Regimentation. . . . the restoration of confidence in the rights of men, the release of the dynamic forces of initiative and enterprise are above all the methods by which these solutions can be found and the purpose of American life assured.[7]

In his second inaugural address, President Roosevelt spoke of the nature of the New Deal in these terms:

> When four years ago we met to inaugurate a President, the Republic, single-minded in anxiety, stood in spirit here. We dedicated ourselves to the fulfillment of a vision—to speed the time when there would be for all the people that security and peace essential to the pursuit of happiness. We . . . pledged ourselves to drive from the temple of our ancient faith those who had profaned it. . . .
>
> Our covenant with ourselves did not end there. Instinctively we realized a deeper need— the need to find through government the instrument of our united purpose to solve for the individual the ever-rising problems of a complex civilization. Repeated attempts at their solution

without the aid of government had left us baffled and bewildered. . . . In these last four years, we have made the exercise of power more democratic; for we have begun to bring private autocratic powers into their proper subordination to the public's government. The legend that they were invincible—above and beyond the processes of a democracy—has been shattered. They have been challenged and beaten.

A summary assessment of the New Deal in our own day may stress these developments:

It brought much needed relief to millions of citizens.

It stimulated economic recovery, mainly through governmental spending.

It converted most Americans to a belief in the propriety of governmental regulation of industry and agriculture.

It renovated and strengthened the capitalist system.

The collectivist stamp that the New Deal put upon American life was far stronger than its limited, indeed very brief tenure might suggest. The strengths or weaknesses that it might have developed after 1939 and the new marks that it might have made upon the course of American history cannot be conjectured. For in that year, World War II flamed across Europe, and soon around the world. In the crucible of this new scourge all systems of society were changed, and some were destroyed. But even global war could not erase the collectivist patterns which had emerged out of the first conflict—indeed, it brought them into sharper focus.

SELECTED READINGS

*Buchheim, Hans, *The Third Reich*, translated by Allan and Lieselotte Yahraes, Kosel-Verlag, Munich, 1961.

> There is nothing new in this ninety-page survey of the origin, development, and end of Hitler's Germany. What is interesting

---

7. Herbert Hoover, *The Challenge of Liberty*, Charles Scribner's & Sons, New York, 1934, p. 203.

Asterisk (*) denotes paperback.

about it is its origin and use. It was written as a handbook of the Western German Federal Defense Ministry for "education in history and current affairs."

Bullock, Alan, *Hitler, A Study in Tyranny,* Harper & Brothers, New York, 1952.
As the author makes clear, this is neither a history of Nazi Germany nor of the Hitler dictatorship. It is a biography of Hitler the man, although naturally the main events of German and European history of the period are intimately involved. The book is soundly researched and interestingly written.

De Bedts, Ralph F., *The New Deal's SEC . . . .* Columbia University Press, New York, 1964.
An exciting account of the formative years of one of the basic reform agencies created by the New Dealers.

Freidel, Frank, *Franklin D. Roosevelt,* Little, Brown & Co., Boston, 1952.
A multivolumed work that deals with almost every question likely to be asked about Roosevelt and his place and behavior in the tumultuous times in which he lived.

Harris, Whitney, *Tyranny on Trial,* Southern Methodist University Press, Dallas, 1954.
The first half is devoted to a study of the coercive processes and practices of Hitler's Nazi state; it includes most of the pertinent —and revolting—material on the Gestapo, SS, concentration camps, and crematoria that one needs in order to understand how inhumane modern man can be. The second half details Hitler's plans for war, 1937 to 1940.

Heiden, Konrad, *Der Fuehrer,* translated by Ralph Manheim, Houghton Mifflin Co., Boston, 1944.
This is by far the best account of Hitler's rise to power. It is also the most enlightening study in English of the Führer's family life, boyhood and schooldays, his early encounter with the party that he would soon make his own, and the Beer Hall Putsch.

————, *The History of National Socialism,* Knopf, New York, 1935.
A detailed study of the origins, nature, and activities (up to the early 1930s) of the Nazi party by one of the earliest fighters against the Hitler movement.

Hitler, Adolf, *Mein Kampf,* Reynal & Hitchcock, New York, 1939.
Hitler's own rambling, revealing story of his "struggle." The book is hard to read, since Hitler had no more sense of organization for written work that he had for speechmaking. This is the edition that should be used.

Kubizek, August, *The Young Hitler I Knew,* Houghton Mifflin Co., Boston, 1955.
Three years of the life of Hitler, dispassionately told by the man who shared them with him in Vienna in the early 1900s. An extraordinarily worthwhile study for those in earnest about learning what were the forces that moved this evil genius.

*Mosse, George L., *The Crisis of German Ideology,* The Universal Library, Grosset & Dunlap, New York, 1964.
An important investigation of the intellectual origin of the Third Reich. The attention given to the Volkish slant of nineteenth-century German youth and their teachers is especially worthwhile because this viewpoint is often neglected.

Neumann, Franz, *Behemoth, the Structure and Practice of National Socialism,* Oxford University Press, London, 1942.
Many other works, some of them cited elsewhere in these Selected Readings, tell the story of the rise and rule of the Nazi state at least as well as this one. But none to date has so thoroughly examined in such short compass the economic workings of the Third Reich (Part Two, about 150 pages).

Pinson, Koppel S., *Modern Germany,* The Macmillan Co., New York, 1954.
A solid, scholarly work that, besides these qualities, contains insights and judgments that make it much more than a fact-on-fact recital of German history.

Schlesinger, Arthur M., *The Crisis of the Old Order* (1957); *The Coming of the New Deal* (1959); *The Politics of Upheaval* (1960); Houghton Mifflin Co., Boston.
An exhaustive and sometimes almost exhausting examination of the causes, nature, and course of the New Deal, 1933 to 1936.

Seligman, Lester G., and Elmer E. Carnwell, Jr., eds., *New Deal Mosaic . . .* University of Oregon Press, Eugene, Oregon, 1965.

The contents of this volume are made up of minutes of the meetings of the National Emergency Council created in 1933. The Council held thirty-one recorded meetings from December 1933 to April 1936. These verbatim minutes probably give a better understanding of the New Deal than any other single volume of the many hundreds published thus far. As Professor Frank Freidel has said, "It is the confidential nature of the Proceedings that gives them their value, since the President could speak so much more freely at the Council meetings than in his press conferences." They also give a close up view of leading New Dealers, from President Roosevelt on down through the higher echelons of the Administration. It is so valuable, indeed, that it may be singled out as the one "New Deal" book to read if students somehow find their time too restricted to read more.

*Shirer, William L., *The Rise and Fall of the Third Reich,* Simon & Schuster, New York, 1960.

Despite a good deal of scholarly scolding over this book it is, in general, well researched and well written. The first four chapters, dealing with pre-Nazi history, fall outside of this evaluation; there are many other works that better portray this part of German history, especially Koppel S. Pinson's volume, cited above. But in the remainder of the book, the account is detailed, enlightening, and absorbingly interesting. Unlike a number of other Americans who have written on the subject, Shirer lived in the Third Reich for a number of years, knew all of the highly placed Nazis, and had access to information that gave him a broad knowledge and keen understanding of the spirit of that ill-fated state.

The Third Reich, published by Frederick A. Praeger, New York, under the auspices of UNESCO, 1955.

A collection of 28 essays on various facets of Nazi Germany. Particularly worthwhile are the first and fourth essays on the historical development of German nationalist ideology, the ninth essay on the rise of National Socialism, and the twenty-fourth and twenty-fifth essays on the Catholic and Protestant Churches in Nazi Germany.

*Trevor-Roper, H. R., *The Last Days of Hitler,* Collier Books, New York, 1962 (3rd ed., with a new preface).

This edition should be used in order to profit from the author's updating of events, which are included in the long introduction rather than in the body of the text. The organization is faulty—strict chronology is not an adequate framework for this study. But this is almost the only deficiency of the book. The last three chapters—"The Siege of the Bunker," "Et Tu Brute," and "The Death of Hitler"—are well documented, or they would be quite unbelievable.

*Viereck, Peter, *Metapolitics, The Roots of the Nazi Mind,* Capricorn Books, New York, 1961.

A close—and controversial—examination of historical forces that gave birth to the Nazi "Theology of Terror." This book is especially important when read with Mosse's volume, cited above.

Wheeler-Bennett, John, *The Nemesis of Power,* Macmillan & Co., London, 1953.

The author believes that the outlook and posture of any nation can be gauged by an understanding of the place and power of its armed forces. This book is really an extended warning of what to expect from the new Germanies. It begins with the Kaiser's abdication and ends with the July 20th plot against Hitler. Throughout, the pivotal position and power of the army is emphasized.

30

The World at War Again, 1939 to 1945

The Road to War

The "Have-Not" Powers

By the 1930s, Japan's plight was real, serious, and not altogether of her own making. Her people lived on mountaintops that projected from the sea. The total area was small; tillable soil was severely limited. By the third decade of this century many more people lived on the land than it could decently support. A flourishing industrial economy can overcome most living-space problems; England is an obvious example. But such an economy presupposes access to and control of adequate raw resources as well as highly developed technical know-how. By a kind of miracle Japan, within a generation or two, had mastered the necessary technical skills, but she lacked ready access to both supplies of raw materials and markets for finished products.

A warrior mentality that made violence and aggression a prized way of life was more of Japan's own making. Prodded by promptings of the *samurai* spirit,* the Japanese often formulated both municipal and international policies in terms of raw force. Her attitude toward and resentment of China were an example. China was rich in raw resources of many kinds; she constituted a potential market of almost unlimited demands; she was politically backward and militarily weak. Japan's needs and aggressive spirit naturally tempted her to treat China as an object of exploitation. Inevitably this led to large-scale violence and international turmoil.

Italy, under the leadership of Mussolini, also maintained a posture of belligerence. But Italy was not likely to initiate a general conflict, no matter how pressing her real and imaginary needs were. In spite of his balcony performances and Caesaresque behavior, the Duce well understood where to draw the line in his often dramatic brushes with the other Great Powers.

---

* The strong, warrior mentality of the Japanese gentry and lower nobility.

Weimar Germany, as we have seen, was wracked by political instability, economic adversities, and the psychic strictures of the Versailles Treaty. The "four good years" suggest that the new republic, in spite of all harassments, might have grown in democratic stature and economic health. Enlightened justice from her one-time conquerors conceivably could have cleared the way for genuine democratic development. But it is futile to speculate whether the vision of such enlightened justice might ultimately have been discerned and implemented by peoples and leaders of the time, since the Great Depression (the true "hinge of fate" of these years) turned all nations into desperate seekers after their own salvation.

The Steps to War: Manchuria and Ethiopia

The linking episodes that led to war were many and complicated. Not all can be attributed to Hitler's evil planning. Indeed, the first event occurred in Asia when the German Führer was still struggling to gain power. The Japanese called this event the "Manchurian Incident." For some years Japan had sought to carve out an empire in China. Particularly enticing was the expansive, fertile Manchurian "province," loosely controlled by Peiping, actually governed by local war lords.

In 1931 a portion of track of the Japanese-controlled Chinese Eastern Railroad was blown up. Japan blamed Chinese saboteurs and at once moved large bodies of troops into the area. China appealed to the League of Nations. No one believed the sabotage charge. All informed observers knew the island empire was ready to test its strength in a large-scale imperial adventure.

Legally and morally Japan stood without defense. If unprovoked aggression were to be combated in the name of world order and world peace, it seemed that this was the time and Manchuria was the place to take a stand. But the challenge was allowed to pass. The major nations—preoccupied with domestic difficulties, fearful of the costs of a showdown, and seemingly unconvinced of the practicability of world peace under law—in effect looked the other way while Japan overran the whole of Manchuria.

Thereafter few took the League of Nations seriously, least of all the autocratic rulers of Italy and Germany. In 1933, one year after the new Manchuria was set up (renamed Manchukuo by the Japanese), Mussolini planned the conquest of Ethiopia. The timing obviously suggests the influence of successful Japanese aggression. Undoubtedly, worsening economic conditions at home also moved the Duce to cast about for some diversionary activity. Historic memory probably served as an added stimulus. In 1896 Italian forces had suffered a humiliating defeat when they had tried to overrun and occupy Ethiopia; vindication of Italian honor had thus been a long time waiting. Finally, the Fascist yen for action and dangerous excitement made occasional military activity a normal part of the national experience.

In 1935 Mussolini sent his troops marching on the flimsy pretext that Ethiopian soldiers had violated a frontier zone of Italian Somaliland. Within a year Ethiopia's harassed defenders, matching rifles and spears against airplanes and poison gas, surrendered; later the whole country was annexed by Italy.

Events in Germany

In the meantime Hitler was mulling over plans of his own. As long as Germany remained bound by the Versailles Treaty's provision prohibiting land forces to exceed 100,000 men, the Führer's power dreams must necessarily remain dreams only. Taking advantage of the general confusion caused by Mussolini's preparations to invade Ethiopia, Hitler suddenly announced, in March 1935, the reintroduction of universal conscription. Both France and Great Britain presented the Führer with written protests. But by then a dictator would have to have been a most untypical one to be troubled by such scraps of paper. Throughout the next months and years, Germans heard again the familiar sound of goose-stepping regiments. By 1939 the *Wehrmacht* constituted a formidable fighting machine.

But Hitler knew that even a rearmed Germany must continue to speak softly so long as its western frontier remained open to easy French invasion. According to the terms of both the Versailles Treaty and the Locarno Pacts, fifty kilometers of German territory on both sides of the Rhine were to remain demilitarized in perpetuity. Plans for aggression were idle games unless the front facing France was fortified. Hitler again chose the ides of March—almost a year to the day after his denunciation of the Versailles rearmament restrictions—to announce Germany's intention to remilitarize the Rhineland. Three years later the whole frontier bristled with cannon, tank traps, and antiaircraft installations, manned by tough Nazi battalions.

The Spanish Civil War

The construction of the West Wall in Germany coincided with the destruction of democracy in Spain. Since 1931 various liberal governments in this new republic had tried to redistribute the country's wealth more equitably, to educate the masses to become self-governing, to curtail the power of the Church, to establish a popular educational system, and generally to develop the democratic way of life. The task was formidable. For centuries the monarchy, the Church, and the army had exercised almost total autocratic rule. The common people were uneducated, many were illiterate; wealth was concentrated in the hands of the power elite; provincial separatism was strong; industrial progress slow. By 1936 the forces of reaction felt strong enough to attempt a countercoup which turned into a bloody, three-year civil war. Arrayed against the new regime

These two cartoons reflect general American opinion regarding Japan's naked aggression in Manchuria in 1931.

were the old landlord class, bourgeois wealth, the Church hierarchy and, of course, most of the general officers of the army—one of whom, Francisco Franco, led the revolt.

Since the conflict so closely partook of the ideological struggle that was rending much of the Western world, it soon took on the character of a miniature world war.

Many intellectuals and workers in the free nations sympathized with the Loyalists, as the Spanish republicans came to be called. The Soviet government, always eager to fish in such troubled waters, naturally supported the Loyalists. Fearful that a democratic success might set a bad example for their own peoples, and anxious, anyway, to expand the totalitarian frontier wherever possible, both Mussolini and Hitler sent help to Franco. The attitude of the British government was ambivalent. It continued to give official recognition to the Loyalist regime while withholding tangible aid. France wanted to open her frontier to pass supplies to the Loyalists but was dissuaded by pressure from Britain. But at no time did foreign aid for the republicans equal the German and Italian support finally given quite openly to Franco. In the spring of 1939 the rebels routed the dwindling, starved, and ill-equipped Loyalist forces and soon took over complete control of the country. Among thinking people of the free world there was no need to ask, as the novelist Ernest Hemingway had made clear, for whom this bell tolled.

Renewed Japanese Aggression in China

In 1937, Japan, encouraged by her easy success in Manchuria, began the conquest of the whole of China. Within two years she had captured Peiping, Shanghai, Nanking, Canton, and other areas along the eastern coast. Again the League of Nations and the United States protested. But Japan's warlords now publicly demanded that Britain and the other powers recognize that Japan's "New Order" in the East was beneficent and inevitable. They insisted they were not waging war against China; rather they were laboring to create an expanded, unified "co-prosperity sphere" in which all East Asian peoples could find happiness and fulfillment. No one believed this nonsense, of course; but

no one seemed to know what to do about it. Nagged by internal concerns, conscious of their ambiguous position *vis-à-vis* their own colonial possessions, and without working faith in the international organizations they themselves controlled, the Western powers fretfully watched world affairs drift into hopeless anarchy.

Hitler Plans for War

These conditions, and the bemused spirit that enveloped them, well suited Adolf Hitler's Nietzschean promptings. The League of Nations was dead. Serious domestic troubles beset all of the great powers. Italy and Japan had committed outright and large-scale aggression for which they had been mildly slapped on the wrist. In Germany, masses, business, and army were now firmly under Nazi control (in the case of the masses, "spell" is the more accurate word). New military techniques and units had been tested effectively in Spain. Except for Stalin, the leaders of all European states, Hitler believed, were weak and manageable; and Stalin was too preoccupied with his seemingly endless purges to be feared. These and other favorable developments could not be expected to last forever. Germany's great chance had come.

Impelled by such prognostications and seemingly goaded by restless inner urges, Hitler called his chief advisers into conference in November 1937. His purpose was not to seek counsel on the plans he was to lay before them. Instead, it was to acquaint his subordinates with the shape destiny was taking and to prepare them for their part in the great events to come.

The detailed minutes of this momentous meeting (taken by Colonel Hossbach, Hitler's adjutant at the time) constitute one of the most significant historical documents of modern times. The minutes baldly set forth calculated plans for military conquest, for large-scale aggression that would by necessity involve some if not all of the great European powers.* Hitler made it plain that Germany's basic need was greater living space, realizable only through military conquest (in *Mein Kampf* and his later work, *Hitler's Secret Book,* he specifically referred to Russia's great breadbasket, the Ukraine). Before successful conquest could be assured, however, several immediately pressing problems demanded attention. One problem was the incorporation—"return" in Hitler's unhistorical view—of Austria into the Reich. Another was domination of Czechoslovakia. Other related problems were the unwanted but probably inevitable conflict with France, and the winning of English support if possible or, if not, her conquest. The Polish problem, of course, had also to be solved. The deadline for this grand program was 1943 to 1945.

Anschluss

By 1938 the twenty-years' truce had about run its course. Thereafter, European affairs took their shape and significance from Hitler's grand design for death. In March of that year Austria was absorbed into the Greater German Reich. Nazi plans for the merger dated (as we have seen) from the abortive coup of 1934. In 1936 an Austro-German pact was signed which nominally brought the two states into friendly relations. But neither side seriously honored its terms.

Early in 1938 Hitler arranged a meeting with the Austrian Chancellor, von Schuschnigg, at the Führer's Berchtesgaden retreat. For over two hours he berated his

visitor for going back on his promises, for failing to bring a single Nazi into the cabinet, and for generally pursuing policies which dishonored their common German heritage. Unprepared for such a violent assault, von Schuschnigg bowed to the storm and promised better behavior. Once back home, however, he tried to outmaneuver the outraged Führer by arranging for a (somewhat rigged) plebiscite which would give Austrians the opportunity to approve or disapprove of their Chancellor's policies. This was more than Hitler could bear. Immediately, Austrian Nazis were ordered into action to demonstrate in the streets, to rough up the opposition, and to get von Schuschnigg out of office by whatever means were needed. Unwilling to sanction civil war, von Schuschnigg stepped aside and the Nazi tide rolled in.

Apart from whatever may have been the wishes of the Germans and Austrians, the union itself was of little consequence. But for the broader world, the spirit and tactics displayed in the coup were significant. By both sides, but particularly by Germany, democratic processes were treated with contempt. Beyond this were the cynical chicanery and naked violence of the German manner. Clearly the Nazis' will to power and their reckless use of violence were passing bounds that the Western powers, for all their internal problems and preoccupations, could tolerate.

Conquest of Czechoslovakia

But if Hitler sensed this danger he paid little attention to it. Within six months after tucking Austria into the Reich, he demanded a substantial slice of Czechoslovakia. About three million Germans lived in the part of the Bohemian frontier that flanked Germany, called the Sudetenland after the "southern" mountains which dominated the region. The inhabitants of this area had never been a part of Germany. Moreover, their status as a minority

---

* Some so-called revisionist historians, notably A. J. P. Taylor, dispute the reliability of the Hossbach notes. This is not the place for extended forensics among members of the history fraternity. Let the interested reader go to A. J. P. Taylor, *The Origins of the Second World War*, Atheneum, New York, 1962, and then to a study of the pertinent documents found in the multivolume *Nazi Conspiracy and Aggression* published by the United States Government in 1946 and 1947. A condensed version of these documents is found in John L. Stipp, *Devil's Diary*, Antioch Press, 1955.

group in Czechoslovakia had long been the envy of other ethnic minorities spread across Europe. But the Great Depression had created tensions there as elsewhere. Nazi agitators who were sent into the area played upon these discontents and pointed to the glories of the Greater German Reich. Soon a Sudetenland branch of the Party, headed by Konrad Henlein, was holding stormy meetings demanding autonomy and, implicitly, a "return" to the Reich. The Czech government, one of the most enlightened in Europe (and the lone democracy east of the Rhine), made genuine efforts to satisfy the Sudetenlanders. They were promised more jobs in the Czech civil service and finally, when the agitation had reached hysterical proportions, a substantial degree of home rule. Each concession sent the Führer into new spasms of indignation. In the late summer of 1938 he made it clear that only complete "self-determination" would satisfy the Sudetenlanders, with himself as their protector.

In 1925, France and Czechoslovakia had signed a treaty of mutual assistance as a guarantee against possible German aggression. Ten years later Russia and Czechoslovakia agreed to a similar pact. The same year, France and Russia concluded an alliance which provided that both, if each acted in concert with the other, would go to Czechoslovakia's defense if she were attacked by Germany.

On paper, then, Czechoslovakia seemed reasonably secure despite Hitler's aggressive posture. But by 1938 France was unwilling to stand against Germany under any conditions unless England stood with her. And England—or at least the Chamberlain government then in power—showed no signs of wanting to risk serious trouble with Germany. Nazi brutalities and gaucheries were, of course, deplored. Hitler's tendency to take unilateral action was condemned. But the evidence—in part to be cited presently—suggests that Chamberlain and some of his conservative colleagues con-

sidered the Nazi regime Europe's strongest bulwark against Communism. Without it no part of the Continent, they seemed to believe, would be safe from Soviet imperialism.

As early as 1937 Chamberlain had clearly indicated his intention to appease Hitler. In November of that year he sent Lord Halifax to Berchtesgaden to work out a mutual understanding. No formal agreement was reached, but Halifax returned home with words of praise for the Führer. Nine months later, with the Sudeten issue reaching a crisis, Chamberlain dispatched another appeasement-minded statesman, Lord Runciman, to Czechoslovakia to consult with both Czech officials and Henleinists.

In the meantime, Henlein and Czech officials carried on a series of conversations that produced little change in the situation. The resulting breakdown in negotiations was followed by what can only be called planned disorder. Noisy demonstrations and street fighting occurred throughout the whole region. Against this backdrop of violence, Hitler addressed a Nazi rally at Nuremberg on September 12, 1938. He declared that he could no longer stand by while fellow Germans were being subjected to brutal mistreatment. As at a signal, violence in the Sudetenland increased to almost anarchical proportions. The Czech government declared martial law and indicated that it was prepared, with the help of its allies, to meet German force with force.

The Munich "Settlement"

At this juncture Prime Minister Chamberlain opened a series of conversations with the war-ranting Führer. In all, three meetings were held. In the first two, at Berchtesgaden and Godesburg, prospects for peace appeared alternately bright and gloomy. At Berchtesgaden Chamberlain agreed to the cession of the Sudetenland to Germany. But at Godesburg, where the final arrangements were to be made, Hitler upped his demands beyond even Chamberlain's sense of what was reasonable. For a time war appeared imminent.

The dilemma was resolved by what seemed to be a concession offered by Hitler. Under pressure from various sources — among them his partner, Mussolini, President Roosevelt, and the highest ranking general officers of his own armed forces — Hitler invited Chamberlain, the French premier Daladier, and Mussolini to a conference in Munich (September 29, 1938). A strange scene was enacted there. Hitler offered a program that was in every essential respect the same as the one Chamberlain had earlier refused. Mussolini at once agreed to it (he was the secret author of minor face-saving changes). Chamberlain and Daladier also agreed, satisfied that the principle of multilateral consultation had been honored. Under terms of the agreement (reached, it should not be overlooked, without the consent of or even consultation with Czechoslovakia and Russia), the whole Sudetenland was transferred to German jurisdiction. Occupation by German troops was to begin within forty-eight hours. Certain areas with mixed populations were to vote for or against annexation by Germany. A separate agreement, signed by Hitler and Chamberlain, stipulated that any differences between their two countries in the future would be resolved by negotiation. This so-called settlement, hailed by Chamberlain as the guarantee of "peace in our time," actually brought the world to the threshold of war, over which Hitler would step within the next twelve months.

Occupation of Bohemia and Moravia

Less than a month after signing the Munich Pact, Hitler secretly gave orders to ready Germany's armed forces for the liquidation of the rest of Czecho-Slovakia.* Publicly he had repeatedly asserted that Germany wanted no Czechs in the Reich.

Chamberlain and Hitler at Berchtesgaden as they opened talks on Hitler's Sudetenland demands.

Both before and at Munich he had assured Chamberlain that once the Sudeten question was settled he had no further territorial ambitions. It can be argued that his easy victory at Munich created an appetite for fresh adventures. The loss of the heavily fortified Sudetenland left Czecho-Slovakia defenseless. The recent annexation of Austria had made the new Germany a great pincers lying athwart a helpless state. The Little Entente (see *supra,* p. 747) was a Munich casualty. Finally, Russia, snubbed by the Western powers and conscious of Czecho-Slovakia's easy vulnerability, could scarcely be counted on to repeat her pre-Munich promises of help.

But the "new appetite" argument is specious. Long before Hitler came to power, he had not only formed but published his program of expansion in the East. He spelled it out clearly in *Mein Kampf.* It was reaffirmed in the early 1930s in conversations with Hermann Rauschning, then Hitler's colleague, and published in a widely read book. As chancellor, Hitler's constant public harangues against "Jewish

---

* After the Munich "settlement" the name of the country was given this hyphenated form to emphasize the autonomy newly granted to Slovakia.

EXPANSION OF HITLER'S REICH 1938-1939

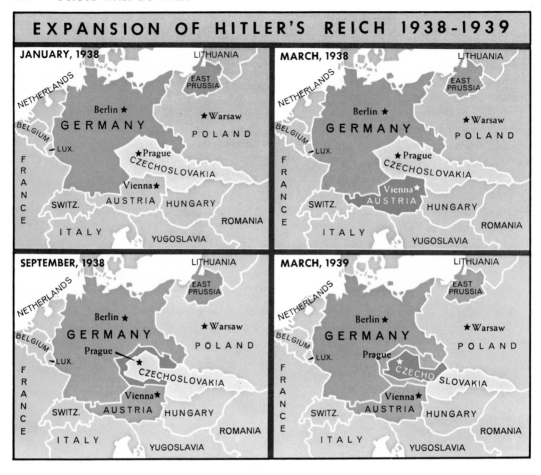

Bolshevism," as well as at least one public reference to what Germany could do with the Ukraine, could leave no doubt about his intentions.

By mid-March, 1939, after covertly stirring up internal strife in the hyphenated Republic, Hitler summoned its president — a political nonentity selected for Benes' place after the Munich settlement — and made a startling announcement. Germany could not, he said, tolerate endless discord in Central Europe. In fact, he said German troops were at that moment on the march (as they were). He "requested" the President to telegraph at once to Prague to offer no resistance. Before the conference was over the President, surrounded by Nazi generals, not only sent such an order, but

signed a statement committing his countrymen to the care of Hitler. Within the week, German troops had occupied all of Bohemia and Moravia. Hungary was allowed to take Ruthenia; Slovakia was recognized as an "independent state."

The Road from Munich

Now, at last, Chamberlain saw Hitler as many others had long seen him. To stop the Nazi tide, he arranged pacts of mutual assistance with Poland, Rumania, Greece, and Turkey. France joined England in these belated gestures of solidarity against rampant German aggression (March–April 1939). Both nations also stepped up military preparations, already accelerated after the Munich crisis. Both served notice that a

German attack upon any of the nations with whom they had signed pacts of defense would be considered an attack upon themselves.

German documents captured by the Allies during and after the war reveal Hitler's decision to push east regardless of pacts and promises. Two months after the occupation of Bohemia and Moravia, Hitler gave secret orders for the attack on Poland to take place "at any time from 1 September 1939 onwards." Hitler never doubted that German forces could easily overrun Poland. What gave him considerable pause was the Russian problem. To deal with it, Hitler prepared for a *detente* with the Soviet colossus. Britain and France had already made a similar decision, but their half-hearted negotiations had merely made Russia suspicious of another Munich "sellout." After a slow start in July 1939, Russian-German discussions moved rapidly from free trade relations, to political accommodations, to the need for a formal alliance. By August 20 the diplomatic revolution had been accomplished. Three days later some of the terms of the agreement were published: neither nation would commit aggression against the other; neither would align itself with a third party or any "grouping of Powers whatsoever which is aimed directly or indirectly at the other Party." A secret protocol provided for a division between them of certain territories in Poland should that state become involved in a war with Germany; it also established spheres of influence in Baltic and Balkan regions.

On August 25, Britain announced its determination to give full support to Poland if Poland were attacked by Germany. Six days later, German troops poured into Poland from three directions. On September 3, Britain and France honored their guarantees to Poland and declared war on Germany. World War II had begun.

THE WAR

Axis Victories: 1939 and 1940

The Polish Campaign and the "Winter War"

The attack launched by the Germans was so overwhelming that the Poles never had a chance to organize their armies for defensive holding, let alone effectively deploy them for subsequent counterattacks. Presently, Russian troops advancing from the east made the struggle altogether hopeless. On September 28, German and Russian diplomats met to settle the final line of demarcation between their spheres of the newly conquered land and to issue a call for a general peace between Germany and her opponents in the West.

Apparently, Hitler believed France and England would seriously consider peace talks. They had given their guarantees to Poland; they had honored them. Now Poland was defeated and occupied. What was there left to fight about? From the first day of the invasion Hitler had ordered his troops on the Western Front neither to attack nor provoke Allied attack. On October 6, Hitler addressed the Reichstag on behalf of peace. He offered to guarantee the British Empire and French possessions in perpetuity in exchange for cessation of hostilities and for Allied recognition of Germany's new position in Europe. When no word came from London or Paris, he professed first puzzlement and then righteous indignation. Clearly, since both countries were in the grip of warmongers, Germany had no choice but to meet force with force.

No doubt Hitler was sincere in wanting to bring the war to an end. His strategy had always been one conquest at a time. He needed to consolidate his Polish gains and make preparations for the next round. Sooner or later, he believed, he would be under the necessity of fighting France, since he was convinced that France would never acquiesce in the creation of a German-dominated continent. But England was another matter. These tired, conservative people could, he believed, be brought to an understanding. With their empire guaranteed, they could come to view German order not as a menace to Europe but as the bulwark against Bolshevism. With England and Germany in agreement, France would be easy to handle when the time came for that showdown.

In the meantime another war broke out not only unplanned by Hitler but much against his wishes. According to the terms of the Nazi-Soviet accord of August 23, as modified by the September 28 decisions, Soviet Russia was given a somewhat free hand in dealing with certain of the small states of Eastern Europe. The quick German victory hustled the Russians into rather precipitate demands on Estonia, Latvia, Lithuania, and Finland. Russia's aim was to gain bases and influence in these countries for the double purpose of preparing against the day of a German attack, and eventually to convert them into Communist satellites. Estonia, Latvia, and Lithuania protested but succumbed to Soviet pressure. Finland simply refused Russian demands for certain bases and territorial cessions.

Confident that it could quickly bring Finland to submission the Soviet government, on trumped-up charges, declared war against her November 30, 1939. But Finnish resistance proved stubborn beyond anything the Soviets had expected. For a month or two it even appeared that Finland, however incredible it all seemed, might force the Russians to sue for peace. England, France, the United States, and many other nations enthusiastically gave the Finnish people moral or financial support. England and France also made plans to send troops and military supplies across Norway and Sweden, if those nations would give their consent. Evidence indicates that such an arrangement was in its final planning stage when, unable after all to stand against vastly superior forces, Finland capitulated in March 1940. She was forced to cede certain strategic areas to the Soviet Union (the Karelian Isthmus, for example). But she successfully resisted pressures to turn herself into a Soviet puppet state (an achievement, it may be added, that still stands).

Nazi Occupation of Norway and Denmark

The ending of the "Winter War" proved particularly embarrassing for the British. They had been planning, as we have noted, to send military support to the Finns. But by March 1940, they had completed other plans only incidentally connected with the fighting in Finland. Much of Germany's wartime iron needs were met by extensive importations from Sweden via Narvik, Norway. If these supplies were shut off, the German war effort would seriously suffer. Moreover, Allied occupation of points along Norway's coasts would simultaneously deprive the Germans of their use and give British and French airmen bases from which to bomb Germany and to break up German naval action in the North Sea. In short, the Allies, in the spring of 1940, planned to occupy a number of strategic areas in Norway. It was hoped that the Norwegian government would approve of the action; but evidence indicates that the project might have been carried out without or possibly even against Norwegian approval.

As it turned out, Hitler relieved the British of the necessity to appear as an aggressor by sending his own forces into Norway just ahead of the Allies (April 9, 1940). Originally he had not thought of this action as either needed or desirable. Certain circumstances combined to bring him around to enthusiastic approval. One was Admiral Raeder's insistence that the war against Britain really required German control of Norwegian ports. Another was Raeder's and Rosenberg's request that the Führer have a talk with Vidkun Quisling, a rabid Norwegian Nazi. Quisling told Hitler that the Norwegian government had agreed not to oppose a British invasion of Norway, thus confirming the Führer's fears. But it was the "Winter War" and England's obvious maneuvering in Scandinavia that convinced Hitler that the project required immediate and serious attention. Plans were well along when the Finnish War ended. Its ending destroyed the political basis for the action; but by that time the idea had become so fascinating to Hitler that he decided to go ahead with it anyway, particularly as he had been kept informed of parallel British planning.

Thus on April 9, 1940, air, naval, and army units struck at Denmark (a purely personal decision of the Führer) and Norway. Denmark was occupied in one day. Fighting in Norway went on for about nine weeks. Norwegian troops fought stubbornly and effectively, in the expectation of substantial help from Britain and France. Allied troops were landed in several coastal areas, and made some headway against Nazi land troops. But the German Luftwaffe smashed communication lines, destroyed much of the attacking and supporting strength of British naval units, and heavily bombed Allied strategic centers. Even so, the Germans might eventually have been driven from Norway if Hitler had not launched an invasion of the Lowlands and France on May 10. This gigantic offensive made it impossible for the Allies to supply or even sustain their forces in Norway. By the beginning of June, Allied evacuation was practically complete. Norway and Denmark remained under German domination for the rest of the war.

Conquest of the Lowlands and France

Originally, Nazi plans to conquer France were fundamentally based on the Schlieffen Plan used in 1914. Attacking troops were to drive through central Belgium, outflank the Maginot Line defenses, turn southward in wide sweeping movements, and encircle and destroy the trapped Allied armies. This time, however, the Netherlands was not to escape involvement. Hitler believed his forces had to use Dutch and Belgian airfields to strengthen his blitz drive against Anglo-French armies and areas, as well as to prevent Dutch ports and airstrips from falling under enemy control. But during the winter months of 1939 and 1940, von Manstein — one of Hitler's most talented generals — persuaded him to order a significant operational change. The new plan called for the major attack to take place north of Liège and drive through to the Channel ports (for these and later references to places in the war zones, see map, p. 838). If successful, Allied forces would not only be cut in two but would be deprived of the use of Channel ports. Without these, the combined and cooperative functioning of French and British forces was impossible. Simultaneously, a group of armies under Colonel-General (later Field Marshal) von Rundstedt was directed to launch a strong attack south of Liège aimed at both preventing French units from giving support to those under attack in the north, and completing the destruction of Allied means of serious resistance.

Before dawn on May 10, German parachutists were dropped near Rotterdam and The Hague. They had been thoroughly coached for the tasks they performed. For example, they knew exactly which parts of strategic bridges contained demolition charges; they knew where the troops were which guarded each bridge; and they knew the strength of the troops at each bridge. Equipped with this information and carefully drilled for these chores, they wrested several strategic areas from the Dutch defenders within hours after dropping from the sky. Meanwhile, armored forces rolled across the Dutch frontier and raced to establish contact with the paratroop units. The blows were so well planned, so powerful, and so swiftly executed that the Netherlands government asked for an armistice within five days. The same tactics employed against the Belgians gained a complete Nazi victory over them in eighteen days. Even Hitler felt some surprise.

The strike against the Lowlands brought the downfall of the tottering Chamberlain government. The glamour of Munich had long since vanished. The conquest of Poland, although hardly chargeable to Chamberlain, had not added to his popularity. The bungling—as many British considered it—in Norway was beyond bearing. When the Lowlands were overrun, Chamberlain did not wait for his parliamentary opponents to rally; he quietly resigned in favor of Winston Churchill, then First Lord of the Admiralty.

With Dutch and Belgian troops knocked out, the German juggernaut pushed relentlessly to the Channel ports. Although French and British forces outnumbered German forces about two to one, neither their troops nor their high commands were prepared for such blitz tactics. By May 20 the German drive had reached the Channel, cutting the defending armies in two. Several attempts were made by both British and French armies to break through the bristling Nazi line; all attempts failed completely. For the British there was nothing to do but try to make it back to their home base. By marshaling a miscellaneous armada of ships ranging from destroyers to fishing smacks (nearly 900 in all), they were able to withdraw from their Dunkerque pocket (May 27–June 4). Over 140,000 French and Belgian troops were evacuated along with about 200,000 British troops. The "miracle of Dunkerque" was rightly made the subject of stirring Churchillian rhetoric; but the fact

remained that, except for some forces south of the Somme, the British had been driven off the Continent in less than three weeks of fighting. And their fighting equipment, perforce, had been left behind.

On June 10 Mussolini, eager to get in on the kill, joined the war and sent his Fascist forces into southern France. They made little headway, but the end for France was near, since now the full force of German might, converging from both north and south, smashed against crumbling French defenses. Although the Maginot Line was never reduced, this mattered little; with German forces of all kinds flanking it, its massed and massive guns now futilely pointed in the wrong direction. By mid-June most of its defenders surrendered. On June 16, Marshal Henri Pétain, famed for the French stand at Verdun in World War I, took over the premiership from Paul Reynaud (Daladier's recent successor) and the next day asked the Germans for an armistice, which was granted on June 22. Under its terms German troops occupied all of France except the inland southern half. A French totalitarian government, under Pétain and Pierre Laval, established itself at Vichy. It set to work at once to mesh its policies and administrative directives with those of Nazi Germany. For Hitler the war seemed over; France had fallen, Britain was isolated, Russia was his ally. West of Warsaw he dominated most of the Continent. Soon the British would get a taste of the Luftwaffe's power. After that he could expect another request for peace parleys. The New Order seemed about to shape a new epoch.

The Failure of "Sea Lion"

Because the fall of France had occurred so quickly, Hitler found himself without a detailed plan for the "battle of Britain." Probably he had not anticipated the need for one; his aim had been to destroy the British and French armed forces on French soil. That done, the war would be over, and peace treaties would be made. But thanks to the evacuation at Dunkerque, Britain—although badly battered—was still unbeaten. Or rather, as Hitler insisted, Britain was beaten but did not seem to know it. To bring home realization of this fact, he ordered an all-out air attack against what he thought of as his stupidly stubborn foe.

In early July the Luftwaffe bombed many English coastal shipping points. Simultaneously, German service troops prepared airstrips and landing fields in various points of northern France and in the Lowlands for the greater assault to follow. It was hoped that, meanwhile, British fighter planes would offer themselves for battle. Experience suggested that they would soon be eliminated as an organized fighting force. Then fleets of German bombers would move inland for the big blow—if that was still needed.

Two weeks of air battle proved somewhat disconcerting for the Führer. British fighter planes were not being knocked out of the sky with the dispatch he had grown accustomed to. Actually, the Luftwaffe itself was taking something of a beating. And, of course, no sounds of surrender were coming from Churchill; quite, indeed, the contrary.

In these circumstances Hitler decided to draw up invasion plans. The code name of the invasion, appropriately enough, was "Sea Lion." In a directive dated July 16, 1940, Hitler laid out the following conditions:

Since England, despite her militarily hopeless situation, still shows no sign of willingness to come to terms, I have decided to prepare a landing operation against England, and, if necessary, to carry it out.

The aim of this operation is to eliminate the English homeland as a basis for carrying on the war against Germany, and if it should become necessary, to occupy it completely.

To this end I order the following:

The *Landing* must be carried out in the form of a surprise crossing on a broad front from Ramsgate to the area west of the Isle of Wight. . . . The preparations for the entire operation must be completed by mid-August.

Before many weeks, however, it became unmistakably clear that British fighter planes excelled their Luftwaffe counterparts in both armament and maneuverability. Newly devised radar equipment proved highly effective. The morale of British pilots, moreover, was savagely high. In short, air superiority was gained by the British, not the Nazis. This meant that the elaborate plans of Sea Lion had to be postponed or (as it turned out) abandoned. For without air cover, invasion was impossible. By mid-September the Germans were so far from establishing that cover that they had practically given up daytime raids in favor of night bombing of inland cities. These raids were numerous and costly; over 20,000 civilians were killed in London alone; a few cities, such as Coventry, were almost demolished. For a year after the fall of France, Britain stood alone before the Nazi fury. Bombings continued, and British ships fell prey to German submarines in fearful and increasing numbers. For a time it seemed that—invasion or not—England could not hold out. How could a small island stand against a continent?

U.S. Aid to Britain

Perhaps England would not have held out if the United States had not furnished massive aid of many kinds. In the mid-1930s, America had sought to isolate itself from Europe by the passage of a series of neutrality acts. By the terms of these acts, the United States was prohibited from shipping arms to any belligerent (either attacker or attacked); United States citizens might travel in belligerent vessels, but only at their own risk; and loans or credits to warring nations were forbidden. As Nazi aggression grew, a number of citizens, led by President Roosevelt, tried to free the country from its isolationist moorings. Before 1939 they made little headway. After the outbreak of war, Congress modified neutrality legislation to permit the "cash and carry" supply of arms to belligerent nations, but isolationist sentiment remained strong. The attack on France led President Roosevelt to ask for vastly increased national defense spending, particularly for aircraft and warships. At his direction the War Department released to Britain millions of dollars' worth of military supplies. In 1940 Congress authorized compulsory military service. The next year, under the "Lend-Lease" Act, seven billion dollars were allocated for the supply of arms and munitions to any country whose defense, in the opinion of the President, seemed vital to the security of the United States. Under the terms of this act, Britain received from the United States vast quantities of goods of almost every kind to meet both civilian and military needs. Anomalously, most United States citizens remained isolationist in sentiment at the time that this country became "the great arsenal for democracy." Beleaguered Britain would have preferred America to become her full-time war ally; lacking this, it gratefully accepted aid that very possibly kept it from defeat.

The Widening of the War, 1940 to 1942

"Case Barbarossa"

In the late fall of 1940 Hitler asked the Spanish government to join him in a move to capture Gibraltar and seal off the British from the Western Mediterranean. The Spanish dictator was willing enough to join a *victorious* Hitler in such a venture. But by then he had begun to have some doubt about Nazi invincibility. England had come off the victor in the air war, and talk of invasion had died down. Hitler might, of course, improvise another victory; but until signs of it were a little clearer, Franco preferred to take no chances. Consequently this scheme came to nothing.

Meanwhile, under the code name "Barbarossa," plans for the conquest of Russia were made ready. Historians have long debated Hitler's motives in taking on Russia

before Britain was conquered. An opinion commonly held is that the Führer was forced into opening a new front by Russia's aggressive moves in the Balkans. There is no question that Russia was very active there. In June 1940, for example, Stalin forced Rumania to cede Bessarabia and Northern Bukovina, largely inhabited by Russians, to the Soviet Union. Soviet diplomatic relations were resumed with Yugoslavia, clearly indicating a resurgence of traditional Russian interest in Balkan affairs. Naturally, these moves disturbed Hitler who had no intention either of yielding control of vital oil resources in this area or of allowing Russia to create a power block that would render more difficult his ultimate aim of carving out *Lebensraum* in the east. Nevertheless, available and ample evidence proves the unsoundness of this view. Instead it makes clear that he was moved by these considerations: sheer inability to mark time militarily; confidence that an attack on Russia would not create a two-front war—France was beaten and England immobilized; the conquest of Russia would force the capitulation of Britain; and, finally, this conquest would bring to realization the ultimate goal of German foreign policy—living space in the east.

Captured German documents also reveal Hitler's original intention to invade Russia in the early fall of 1940. He was talked out of it by Keitel, one of his chief military advisers, who outlined the impossibly difficult military considerations such an attack would involve—rapid transportation of troops from west to east, lack of "necessary physical preparations for the deployment of the masses of troops once they reached their destination," and the few remaining weeks of operational weather. Thus Hitler ordered full-scale planning for an attack that would open in the spring of 1941. In his directive of December 1940, Hitler led off by insisting that Russia was to be crushed "in a quick campaign before the end of the war against England." Repeatedly he stated to his advisers that the whole action should be completed within five or six weeks. Under "General Purpose," the directive declared: "The mass of the Russian *Army* in Western Russia is to be destroyed in daring operations by driving forward deep wedges with tanks and the retreat of intact battle-ready troops into the wide spaces of Russia is to be prevented."

Deflection of the War to the South

D-Day was originally scheduled for early or mid-May 1941; by the end of June or early July, Russia would probably be knocked out, and the surrender of England could be expected soon after. Unfortunately for Hitler's planning, one major and one minor hitch unexpectedly developed that threw off his timing. For one thing Mussolini, envious of his colleague's smashing successes, and resentful of the Führer's sometimes peremptory dealings with his now junior partner, decided on an adventure of his own—the conquest of Greece. This was undertaken by a surprise attack in October 1940. Hitler glossed over his irritation and publicly commended the action. He feared, however, that the move might interfere with his own plans. He was right, since the Greek response was nothing like the Duce expected. Indeed, it soon became apparent that the Italians were in serious trouble. By December their situation was so threatening that the commanding general was relieved, and feverish preparations were made to stave off impending defeat. Hitler realized he would probably have to divert some of his "Barbarossa" troops to rescue his Axis partner.

Three months later the regent of Yugoslavia, a Nazi sympathizer, was ousted and young King Peter II assumed the throne (March 27, 1941). This coup, combined with Italian reverses, caused Hitler to postpone "Barbarossa" in order to put his Balkan house in order. Otherwise, he might expect large British landings along Europe's "soft underbelly" which could wreck his projected one-front war in the east, as well as put in serious danger his oil resources in Rumania. A large contingent of planes, tanks, and infantry troops was therefore detached from the massed forces ready to strike at Russia. In ten days Yugoslavia was overrun and a Nazi government was installed. German troops were then sent against Greek forces and their British allies. By the end of April they had again pushed the British off the Continent and had brought the Greeks to complete surrender. Mussolini, rescued but red-faced, sent occupation troops into Greece. The Allies had suffered another costly and humiliating defeat.

The Invasion of Russia

Hitler now returned to "Barbarossa." His lightning victories in Poland, Denmark and Norway, the Lowlands and France, and now in the Balkans gave him full confidence that his drive against the Soviet Union would shatter, quickly and decisively, the last great continental state and bring with it, too, the capitulation of beleaguered Britain. On June 22, 1941, he sent three large army groups across Russia's western frontier.[*] One group headed for Leningrad, another for Moscow, the third for Kiev and, if necessary, points south and east. The main objective was not territory; it was Russian manpower. Otherwise, the Napoleonic debacle might be repeated.

Hitler's expectations of a quick victory were not altogether unreasonable. The "Winter War" had revealed serious weaknesses in the structure and functioning of the Soviet military machine. In part because of the recent purges, members of the Russian high command were seriously deficient in imaginative planning and ability

---

[*] Partly from pressure by Germany and partly from desire to regain territory lost in the "Winter War," Finland joined in the attack.

WORLD WAR II

GERMAN DOMINATED EUROPE, 1942

Axis Powers

Joined Axis in 1941

Vichy France

Limit of Axis
occupation, 1942

UNITED KINGDOM

IRELAND

*Atlantic
Ocean*

North Sea

THE
NETHERLANDS
1940

BELGIUM
1940

FRANCE
1940

LUX.

SWITZ.

Vichy

PORTUGAL
(Neutral)

SPAIN
(Neutral)

CORSICA

SARDINIA

Mediterranean

SICILY

MOROCCO

ALGERIA

TUNISIA

Sea

NORWAY
1940

SWEDEN
(Neutral)

DENMARK
1940

Baltic Sea

GERMANY

ITALY

FINLAND

ESTONIA

LATVIA

LITHUANIA

1941-42

1941-42

POLAND
1939

1941-42

1942

HUNGARY

RUMANIA

YUGOSLAVIA
1941

BULGARIA

ALBANIA

GREECE
1941

U. S. S. R.

Leningrad

★ Moscow

Stalingrad

Black Sea

TURKEY
(Neutral)

CYPRUS
(Br.)

SYRIA

Map by J. Donovan

to improvise. Officers of the middle class, from colonels to captains, too often were incompetent. Among the troops, individual initiative was conspicuously lacking— a deficiency mitigated (but not wholly compensated for) by a stubborn determination and stolid endurance of conditions that many soldiers would not have found tolerable. Many Russian planes had been destroyed on the ground in the early days of the war; many others were obsolete. The Russians were superior in artillery

and tanks or soon became so; again, however, the tactical use of them (until 1943) was anything but efficient. On the other hand, Russian manpower was vastly superior to that of the Germans. Also, and most important, Soviet propaganda played down the Communist system and emphasized the stark dangers threatening the very life of Mother Russia. Moreover, it soon became apparent that Stalin's "scorched-earth" policy would deny the Germans and their allies the grain, gasoline, and industrial establishments they were so eager to get their hands on.

By mid-August all three German army groups were deep inside Russia. Army Group North was close to Leningrad; Army Group Center was approaching Moscow; Army Group South had penetrated 350 miles into southern Russia, approaching the Dnieper River. Already the Army Chief of Staff had come to believe that the bulk of the Soviet army west of the Dnieper had been destroyed, giving Hitler the feeling that once again an enemy had been conquered, save for the final *coup de grace*. To accomplish this, he ordered renewed attacks by Group North and Group South. Moscow, he insisted, was only "a geographical expression"; for the time being Army Group Center could send part of its forces to support the drive to the south.

Substantial gains were made in the new offensives. In early November it appeared that Leningrad, now almost completely encircled, must fall. In the south, Rostov was taken. Army Group Center, ordered again into action, came to within 25 miles of Moscow. By late November vast Russian spaces were under Nazi control; hundreds of thousands of Russian soldiers had been captured; and Russian casualties were staggeringly high. The end, it seemed, was at hand.

But despite their seizure of vast territories and the inflicting of almost uncountable casualties among Russian troops, the Germans were still not quite victors. They had underestimated the Soviet Union's vast human resources, the stubborn courage of the Russian soldier, and the ability of Russian commanders to learn not only from their own mistakes but also from their enemy's successes. And since Hitler had planned on a scant six weeks' war, German troops were not equipped for winter fighting.

In early December Russian counteroffensives along the whole line combined with the coming of early subzero weather to halt the Nazi sweep. By mid-December

This photograph, showing Nazi troops in Stalingrad, appeared in a Vienna illustrated weekly on September 30, 1941. Part of the caption pointed out that "Each house and factory was converted into a fortress or defended position."

German commanders were calling for the Führer's permission to retreat. Hitler refused to sanction any significant withdrawals. For him, retreat was a kind of non-Aryan concept; victors did not retreat. He also believed that a full-scale withdrawal under existing circumstances would most likely turn into an uncontrollable rout. As a result, all units were ordered to stand where they were and, if necessary, to die there.

By the end of December, Russian thrusts in both the north and the south gave signs of aiming at the encirclement of Army Group Center. Finally sensing the catastrophe that threatened, Hitler ordered a limited withdrawal in mid-January 1942. It did not nearly satisfy the demands of his generals, but it was of sufficient depth to straighten the German line and allow troops that otherwise might have become isolated to guard against strong flanking attacks. Hitler's appeal to the home front for winter clothing for the troops brought enough to give the soldiers some protection against the freezing blasts. Reserve units were also moved up into the line. By early March the Russian offensives had begun to peter out, due as much perhaps to lack of Russian military expertise as to German countermeasures. Soon spring rains bogged down the whole front in mud, so that operations on both sides came to a virtual standstill.

The effects of the winter fighting were of tremendous significance. Hitler's prestige among the troops was raised even higher. Surprised by an early and indescribably severe winter, and bewildered by the seemingly endless raising of fresh armies by the Russians, the German High Command had clamored for a full-scale retreat. Later the generals themselves admitted that it would have been but the prelude to a disastrous rout. Hitler's iron will had infected the frontline soldiers with a spirit that they came to sense only after the ordeal was over. To symbolize the way of the Nazi will—as well as to rid himself of a "mere professional"—Hitler had practically forced the resignation of the army's Commander in Chief (December 1941) and had taken over the position himself. He had seemingly demonstrated that what Napoleon could not master, he could. On the other hand, the Russian people felt a pride in their leadership that many had not felt before. Since 1939 Hitler had romped from victory to victory. Against the Soviet Union he had stumbled and had been brought to a halt, at least for the time being. Russian morale was raised, even among many behind the German lines who had earlier hoped for a German victory.

In the spring of 1942 Hitler planned a new offensive. Although operative along the entire front, it was to concentrate on the Caucasus oilfields. Hitler believed that Russia could not continue to spend blood as it had done in the first campaign. The "Bolshevik beasts," deprived of their chief oil resources and decimated by even more murderous assaults, would finally have no alternative but complete capitulation.

Before the new campaign opened, the Russians launched an offensive of their own, aimed at driving the Germans out of Kharkov, recapturing the great power plant at Dnepropetrovsk, and generally inflicting whatever damage they could on the enemy. Within five days both of the pincers were savagely broken off by newly built-up German units, and the offensive collapsed. The Russians would probably have suffered even greater losses if Hitler's plans for his own offensive had been nearer to completion.

In late June 1942, the Nazi drive opened with gains all along the front but particularly impressive advances in the south. For two months the offensive ground on without, however, either gaining complete control of the oilfields or routing, let alone decimating, Russian ranks which seemed able always to reform after even the most vicious mauling. In mid-October Hitler decided to break off the offensive when his intelligence services informed him that Soviet losses had not been proportionate to their losses in the previous campaign, and that he should anticipate another Russian winter offensive. By this time the new Napoleon doubtless began to understand the magnitude of some of the frustrating problems experienced by the first great conqueror's encounter with the Russians.

The War in Africa, 1940 to 1942

For a year after the fall of France in June 1940, land fighting between the belligerents was confined to North and East Africa.* From Libya the Italians sent exploring columns into western Egypt during August and September. The columns reached a point about 60 miles within the border before being stopped by weak British forces. During the next two months each side worked to build up strength for a vigorous offensive. Early in December the British opened a drive that developed unexpected momentum. In January 1941, Bardia fell—a defeat that cost the Italians 25,000 prisoners and a great deal of war

---

* For places and areas mentioned in the following paragraphs, see map.

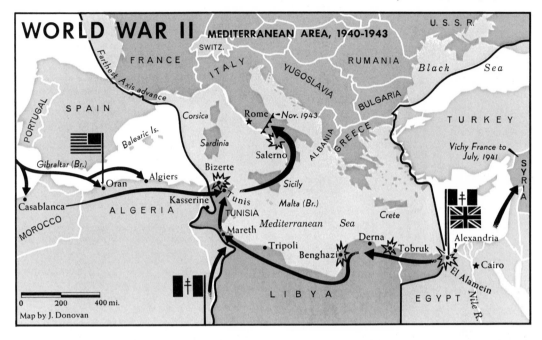

WORLD WAR II   MEDITERRANEAN AREA, 1940-1943

material. Several weeks later, Tobruk (an important fortress-port nearly 100 miles inside the Libyan frontier) surrendered, quickly followed by Derna and Benghazi. By the end of the first week of February the British had captured over 120,000 prisoners, hundreds of artillery pieces, and many tanks. Their own losses in men and equipment were very light. The whole operation had been so surprisingly successful that General O'Connor, the British commanding officer, advised renewing the offensive — which then had pushed 500 miles into Libya — with the aim of expelling the Italians from North Africa.

At this point, however, events in Europe intervened. It will be recalled that Mussolini had staged an invasion of Greece the preceding December and by early 1941 had suffered reverses so severe that Hitler had been forced to effect rescuing operations. In the meantime British forces had joined the Greeks; so that now the question was whether the African offensive should continue, or whether troops and equipment from there should be diverted to save Greece. The Churchill government finally decided to defend Greece, with the dis-

astrous results (April–May 1941) that we have already noted. Somewhat earlier, German troops, under General (later Field Marshal) Erwin Rommel, were sent to Africa to bolster the faltering Italians.*

These developments drastically changed the North African situation. Rommel had under him not only a number of Italian divisions but also his own *Afrika Korps* that was soon to become famous. His daring, drive, and specially trained units combined to push the British out of their advanced positions and back again to the Egyptian border (mid-April 1941). A hastily contrived British counteroffensive failed to regain any of their lost positions but it deterred Rommel from further action until he had built up his forces. The British used the next several months for the same purpose and, under a new commander, launched a smashing attack against Rommel in December 1941. Hitler's drive into Russia caused him to drain off some of Rommel's forces precisely at this time, so that the British

* Other operations subsequently were carried out in Iraq, Syria, and Ethiopia which cannot, in a general study such as ours, be considered. By late 1941 all of these countries were either occupied or dominated by the Allies.

were again able to capture Benghazi, and station outposts at El Agheila. But their stay was brief, for soon Rommel was once again on the offensive. (These somewhat dizzying comings and goings along the rim of North Africa are basically explained by geographic conditions. The coastlines of Egypt and Libya stretch almost 1000 miles. Much of the hinterland is sandy wastes; quite literally, towns are few and far between. A mobile army, if it makes progress at all, can go very far in a relatively short time. However, it also runs into extremely difficult logistical problems, particularly the basic one of water supply. Consequently, unless an army can supply itself on the run *and* keep going until the opposing forces are captured, destroyed, or chased off the continent, the chances are strong that the chaser will soon become the chased. This was the pattern of warfare in North Africa throughout the whole period of 1940 to 1943.)

In late May 1942, Rommel struck again at British and Free French forces, who were themselves preparing for another push. For a while Allied troops held their ground, although at a high price. Soon, however, German-Italian units beat down the defenders and went on to recapture Tobruk and Bardia. They then crossed into Egypt where, at El Alamein, they were stopped — a bare 70 miles from Alexandria. Thereafter, both Allied counterthrusts and Axis attempts to break through British defenses failed; both sides were near exhaustion.

The situation was so serious for the British that Prime Minister Churchill visited Cairo in August to discuss with political and military leaders what was to be done. Out of these meetings came another shake-up in the High Command and a directive by Churchill that the next offensive must be aimed not at gaining ground, but at total destruction of the Axis armies. For the next several months neither side ventured any large-scale action.

The War in the Pacific, 1941 to 1942

In 1941 Japanese leaders, or at least the military people who increasingly had come to dominate the government and to make Japanese policy, schemed to conquer and rule an empire that would stretch from the mid-Pacific to the western limits of China. It would include the Dutch East Indies, the Philippines, Malaya, Indochina, Burma, and Thailand — in short, areas that contained about one half of the world's population.*

Even before the European war (as we have seen), Japan had begun nibbling away at China. With the coming of the war, the most promising possibilities for the consummation of her plans seemed to offer themselves. France was defeated and unable to defend her possessions in Asia; Britain had her hands full staving off her own defeat; the Dutch could hardly offer serious opposition. The most serious obstacle seemed to be the United States, long a champion of the open door in China, and now an unofficial ally of Britain. But America was 6000 miles away. Logistical problems alone would make her striking power weak and uncertain. Moreover, the surprise destruction of her Pacific fleet, stationed in Hawaii, would prevent her from interfering with the construction and consolidation of a sweeping, fortified perimeter that would effectively and permanently shield the new empire from later attacks.

The United States was well aware of Japan's ambitions. Since 1940 she had embargoed iron, steel, oil, and other military or potentially military supplies that would have further strengthened the Japanese war machine. However, her position was complicated and somewhat ambiguous. President Roosevelt believed that involvement in the war, whether in Europe, in Asia, or

---

* For details of this planning see Samuel E. Morison, *The Two Ocean War,* Little, Brown & Company, Boston, 1963, Ch. II, especially pp. 38–45.

on both continents, was inevitable. Millions of Americans did not share this belief. Moreover, among those who did share it there were differences over where the main effort should be applied, if a two-ocean war were to develop. Some favored concentrating on Japan; others argued that if Hitler completely dominated Europe and the British Isles, nothing that we could do in the East would have much meaning.

Although jingo militarists occupied most governmental ministries in Japan, not all Japanese were eager for war. The Prime Minister, Prince Konoye (1941), was not eager, nor was Emperor Hirohito.* In August 1941, Konoye proposed a conference between himself and President Roosevelt to see if a compromise of some sort could be worked out. From the evidence we now have, it does not appear that such a meeting could have done more than postpone hostilities, if it could have done that. In any case the President, acting upon Secretary of State Hull's advice, rejected the offer. (Hull's reasoning was that Konoye could not be trusted and, even if he could, our demands would not be acceptable to the dominant Japanese militarist clique.) Konoye then resigned and was succeeded by General Tojo, who busied himself with perfecting the details of the general plan noted earlier. Mostly as a cover for this planning, Tojo resumed negotiations with the United States which continued until late November 1941. By then Japan felt herself ready to strike.

Because American cypher experts, sometime before, had cracked the Japanese diplomatic code, President Roosevelt and his advisers were fully aware that Japan was about to begin offensive operations. They did not, however, know exactly when or where. Admiral Kimmel, in

This is the group of Japanese statesmen who decided upon the Pearl Harbor attack. Premier Tojo is in the front row, third from the left.

charge of the Pacific fleet stationed in Pearl Harbor, received a warning from Washington, November 27, that "hostile action is possible at any moment." The chief officer of Naval Intelligence requested that another warning be sent December 4, for by that time even more ominous Japanese diplomatic dispatches had been decoded. But the Navy High Command decided to wait for still more specific information. That information came in about five hours before the attack at Pearl Harbor. General George Marshall ordered an alert to be sent at once to the commanding officers at Pearl Harbor. But there "was a foul-up that morning in Army radio, and the officer in charge entrusted the message to commercial channels [Western Union]. A boy on a bicycle delivered it to General Short [in Hawaii] some hours after the attack was over."[1]

The attack on Pearl Harbor on Sunday, December 7, 1941, destroyed half of its large complement of planes, sank or substantially damaged seven battleships, and completely demolished three destroyers. Nearly 2500 lives were lost; hundreds of soldiers, sailors, and civilians were

---

* But it is important to note that Konoye's reluctance to allow Japan to drift into war with the United States did not at all extend to a lessening of Japanese military ventures in China; here he was a thoroughgoing imperialist.

1. Morison, *op. cit.,* p. 53. For details of the "Pearl Harbor Question" see Roberta Wohlstetter, *Pearl Harbor: Warning and Decision,* Stanford University Press, Stanford, 1962.

This scene from a captured Japanese film shows Japanese airmen heading for their planes aboard a carrier to start the raid on Pearl Harbor.

wounded. The nation, though instantly united for war by the savage and unprovoked attacks, suffered a psychic shock. And, as the Japanese had planned, American naval action against Japanese aggression in other parts of the Pacific and in Southeast Asia was seriously hampered for nearly a year. By then most of what the Japanese had blueprinted for their empire—except certain areas of China—was under their control.

On December 13 Guam was surrendered to the Japanese, as was Wake Island on December 20. The same month Thailand agreed to Japanese overlordship, British forces surrendered at Hong Kong, and the Philippines were invaded. Early the next month Manila and Cavite were taken by the Japanese, as the Islands' troops, under General Douglas MacArthur, began a slow retreat first to Bataan Peninsula and finally (a remnant under General Jonathan Wainwright) to the island of Corregidor where the final surrender came May 6. In the same period Japanese forces occupied the Netherlands East Indies, Malaya and Singapore, Burma, portions of New Guinea, and all of New Britain. By late spring of 1942 they

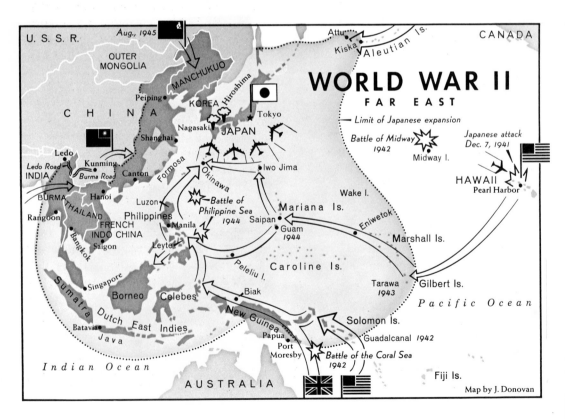

WORLD WAR II
FAR EAST

— Limit of Japanese expansion

Map by J. Donovan

had made what one writer has called "the most rapid, stupendous conquest in modern times." (For the places and names involved in this conquest, see map.)

Allowing itself to become infected by what a Japanese admiral later called "Victory Disease," the Imperial General Headquarters decided on action designed to wipe out the United States Pacific fleet and at the same time to extend its "ribbon defense" to include the Western Aleutians and Midway Island. With these objectives gained, the war (it was believed) would be over and Japan would rule most of Asia, as her Axis partners would soon dominate Europe. Even though the designed action against the United States fleet near Midway was bold, its outcome (for the Japanese) was nearly catastrophic. Although outnumbering United States warships nearly three to one, the Japanese striking force, under Admiral Yamamoto, suffered a defeat so severe in the battle of Midway (June 3–4, 1942) that one American naval historian has said it "thrust the war lords back on their heels, caused their ambitious plans for the conquest of Port Moresby, Fiji, New Caledonia, and Samoa to be cancelled, and forced on them an unexpected and unwelcome defensive role." [2]

But, of course, "the most stupendous conquest in modern times" was not undone at once by the battle of Midway, no matter how decisive that battle ultimately turned out to be. For that, three years and much suffering, death, and destruction were to be the price.

The Year of Decision: 1943

Stalingrad

From September 1939 to late 1942 the Allies had suffered an almost unbroken series of devastating defeats. As we have seen, by the autumn of 1942 German troops had advanced to the Volga; German and Italian forces were within 70 or so miles

of Alexandria; the Japanese had conquered and entrenched themselves in most of the Pacific islands west of Hawaii, in the East Indies, Indochina, Burma, and large parts of eastern China. To the cynic it might have seemed that if the Axis powers now went on the defensive it was because they had no place else to go.[*]

But the situation was not quite so hopeless for the Allies as appearances suggested. For one thing, new Russian armies were being raised, trained, and equipped by Russian officers who were by then much more imaginative and resourceful than they or their predecessors had been a short year before. For another, Axis forces were occupying so many parts of the globe that they were necessarily spread thin. Also, the vast resources and technological skills of the United States were now beginning to be poured into the fearful struggle. Finally, the German submarine, which had played such dread havoc in the "battle of the Atlantic" (1940–1942) that it alone seemed for a while to assure Axis victory, lost its fatal sting when the British perfected "microwave radar and operational research on antisubmarine-warfare methods."

Part of Hitler's directive for the 1942 offense had ordered Army Group B "to develop the Don defences and, by a thrust forward to Stalingrad, to smash the enemy forces concentrated there, to occupy the town, and to block the land communications between the Don and the Volga. . . ." [3] In an earlier section we noted that by mid-October 1942, Hitler had halted the new drive after impressive gains, in order to prepare for the expected Russian winter offensive. The aim of the directive just noted, however, was to be carried out that

---

[*] Since Italian efforts were not of a decisive nature, they are not included in this summary statement. But, as we shall see, Italy remained an Axis partner until September 1943.

2. Morison, op. cit., p. 162.

3. H. R. Trevor-Roper, ed., Hitler's War Directives, 1939–1945, Sidgwick and Jackson, London, 1964, p. 130.

fall. Consequently, the attack in the Stalingrad area continued.

For a while it seemed that the relentless, vicious thrust of German armies would prove too strong for the Russians to withstand. The Sixth Army, under General von Paulus, had penetrated the suburbs of Stalingrad by mid-September. In both armor and aircraft the Germans were, for the time being, superior. The Russian defense, however, was dogged beyond description. When the streets of Stalingrad became the "front" in October and November, Russian soldiers seemed to occupy every house, every factory, every building of every kind.

On November 19 the Russians staged a counteroffensive for which they had been long preparing. Within three days the entire German Sixth Army and part of the Fourth Panzer Army were ringed by rampaging Russian forces. Von Paulus requested permission to withdraw; Hitler curtly refused, and ordered every man to stand or die. Throughout the next two months the terrible encounter went on. On February 2 von Paulus, unable to carry on the struggle and forbidden to retire (indeed, unable at that point to break out of the Russian encirclement), surrendered what was left of his battered army. The great German drive to occupy the "town" and smash the forces concentrated there had ended in disaster. Never again was the dread Wehrmacht to threaten the Volga; indeed, from this time on, its course was, except for one passing moment, backward to Berlin.

El Alamein and "Torch"

Meanwhile, in North Africa, a decisive battle was taking place. We have seen that in the spring of 1942 Axis forces under Rommel had pushed to within 70 to 80 miles of Alexandria. Churchill, gravely disturbed by this threat to the Suez Canal and British control of much of the Near East, ordered General Montgomery (newly assigned to Africa) to make whatever

preparations were necessary to destroy the *Afrika Korps*. To this end Montgomery reorganized the Eighth Army, instituted an elaborate program of tactical training for desert warfare, and built up equipment for the coming task.

Before Montgomery was ready for a new offensive, Rommel again attacked (August 31–September 7, 1942). This time the British lines held. Rommel, unable to break through, and fearing his short fuel supply might leave him stranded in an indefensible position, ordered a general retreat. At this point Churchill urged Montgomery to mount his own attack. But Montgomery insisted that he was not yet ready. He promised that when he did move, in late October, he would not fail. On October 22 and 23 he laid down an artillery barrage designed to destroy Rommel's works on Miteiriya Ridge and then sent his columns forward. For several days each side inflicted terrible punishment upon the other. Finally on November 5 Rommel began to give way. British and New Zealand troops, encouraged by their initial success, increased the fury of their attack until Rommel was in full retreat. Within three weeks Tobruk and Benghazi were again occupied. In January Tripoli and Mareth fell. In less than three months Allied forces, besides routing the famed *Afrika Korps,* had driven forward over 1000 miles and were within striking distance of Tunis, the gateway to Italy and Europe's "soft underbelly."

By this time a new phase of the North African war had developed. In July 1942, Roosevelt had agreed to Churchill's insistent request for an Anglo-American landing in North Africa. The complicated plans for this operation, whose code name was "Torch" and whose overall commander was General Dwight Eisenhower, were worked out by late October. The first landing occurred November 8, at almost exactly the same time as the beginning of Rommel's 1000 mile retreat. Much of the success of "Torch" hinged upon the responses of the French in Morocco and Algeria, technically under the control of the home government at Vichy. As it turned out, French forces, though ordered by Vichy to resist the landings, offered little opposition; within three days all French territories in North Africa were ordered by Admiral Darlan, who had defected from his German-dominated homeland, to co-operate with the Allies. To counter this set-back, Hitler at once decreed the occupation of all of France and readied plans to dis-patch new forces to Tunisia.

The Allies had hoped by their pincer movement — Montgomery from the east, Eisenhower from the west — to close in on Tunis before German reinforcements could be concentrated there. Their hopes ran es-pecially high because of the serious trouble the Germans were experiencing at Stalin-grad which, it was believed, would prevent Hitler from feeling easy about diverting forces to Africa which he would need in the east. Despite his setback in the east, how-ever, Hitler did send substantial reinforce-ments to Africa. During January and Feb-ruary of 1943, powerful attacks were launched against American forces along the Algeria-Tunisia border; for a time it seemed that the Americans might suffer serious de-feat. But by early March they had checked the assault and, concerting now with British troops in the south, began a hard, sustained drive that ended in mid-May with the sur-render of all Axis forces in Africa. The war was far from over; but Churchill's phrase, applied by him to an earlier development, may be used — for the Allies, it was "the end of the beginning."

The Invasion of Italy

In early July 1943, British and American troops made landings along the coasts of southern and southeastern Sicily. For over a month they pushed the defending Axis forces, mostly Italians, to the north and east. By this time the Italians were clearly tired of the war. Although some of their troops fought bravely against the invaders, more seemed indifferent or even inclined to court quick defeat. By the end of July most of the island was conquered. No secret was made of what the next move would be. Soon and certainly the peninsula would be under direct attack. In these cir-cumstances grumblings were raised against the Fascist regime. For three years Italy had suffered humiliating defeats — in Greece, in North Africa, in East Africa, and in Sicily. There was no assurance that Mussolini's warriors — what was left of them, for besides tens of thousands killed, hundreds of thousands had been captured — would be able to stop the Allies once they had gained bridgeheads on the peninsula; indeed, quite the contrary.

Faced with this prospect, the Fascist Grand Council called a meeting in Rome on July 25. Although presided over by the Duce, the Council demanded that King Vic-tor Immanuel III form a new government. Mussolini was arrested, and the King ap-pointed Marshal Pietro Badoglio as the new prime minister. To forestall an immediate German take-over of his country, Badoglio assured the Germans that Italy intended to remain in the war as their ally. Actually, secret negotiations were almost immedi-ately opened with the Allies.

Meanwhile the conquest of Sicily was completed (August 17, 1943). Almost at once plans were begun for the invasion of Italy. Lieutenant General Mark Clark was ordered to lead an amphibious attack on Salerno, just north of Naples, a few days after General Montgomery had crossed the Straits of Messina to advance up the toe of the Italian boot. These operations were car-ried out between September 3 and 9. On September 8 the Italian government an-nounced its withdrawal from the war (in ac-cord with a secret agreement drawn up with the Allies five days before). The "Axis," Mussolini's much-heralded "Pact of Steel," had bent and broken. *Festung Europa* was now under direct attack.

U.S. Marines start ashore from their landing craft on the Guadalcanal beach, August 4, 1942.

Battle of Guadalcanal

Simultaneously with the opening of a new front in southern Europe, American (and later Australian) forces began an offensive in the Pacific. The place chosen was Guadalcanal, one of the southernmost islands of the Solomons (see map, p. 849). Earlier the Japanese had established a formidable base at Rabaul on the island of New Britain.

From Rabaul Japanese air and naval forces were sent out to defend the southern stretches of the "defensive ribbon." If Rabaul could be eliminated, Allied forces would be in a good position to mount an attack on the Philippines and, ultimately, against the main islands of Japan. A second reason for choosing Guadalcanal was its proximity to the Australian base at Port Moresby, New Guinea, then threatened by the Japanese.

In August 1942, about 17,000 Marines landed on Guadalcanal and set about consolidating their position. The Japanese countered with strong air and naval attacks in an attempt to destroy the landing contingent, or at least to cut off its supply line. The first objective was not achieved, the second only partially. They therefore turned to reinforcing their own garrison. By mid-September the Japanese felt strong enough to launch their first offensive which, however, had to be broken off after only two days of fighting.

For the next four months both sides alternated offensive and defensive actions. Although the island was only about 90 miles long and 20 to 25 miles across, the rugged terrain made advances by either side always hazardous and usually costly.

By early February 1943, the Japanese were forced to withdraw from Guadalcanal.

U.S. Marines move through a tropical jungle of Guadalcanal to attack Japanese forces entrenched along a river a short distance ahead.

Japanese prisoners on Guadalcanal. Not many prisoners were taken in the whole operation.

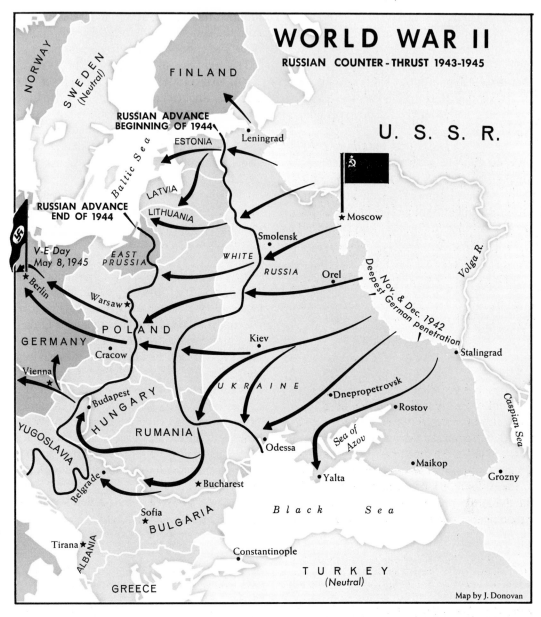

It was the first land battle in which they had been defeated. No more than the German withdrawal from Africa did it signify the imminent end of the war. But, like that defeat, it did mean that a great aggressor nation had had its seemingly invincible war machine brought to at least a temporary halt. For the Allies it meant new hope and greater confidence in plans they were working out for future offensives.

The Road Back, 1943 to 1945

Russian Offensives, 1943 to 1944

The Russian offensive that had begun November 19, 1942 did not stop with the surrender of the German Sixth Army and the reoccupation of Stalingrad. The push continued for three months, sending the

Germans back to Kharkov and, in the south, to Dnepropetrovsk. In an effort to regain the initiative, Hitler ordered a counteroffensive to begin February 18, 1943. A month's heavy fighting brought the reconquest of Kharkov and Belgorod. Then the Russians stiffened, and the German drive bogged down in March mud.

The fact that Hitler mounted no new offensive in the spring of 1943 was a plain indication that the tide of war had turned. Now he had a number of new and ominous developments to contend with. Axis defeat in Africa clearly heralded an Allied invasion of Italy. By 1943, too, Russian partisans behind the German line were proving a serious embarrassment. By this time also, American aid was pouring into Russia on a colossal scale. It is true that for a week in early July a Nazi rally was attempted, but its slow progress, combined with the Allied invasion of Sicily, caused Hitler to call it off and go on the defensive.

The next month the Russians opened a new drive that sent the once-vaunted Wehrmacht reeling backward. The two-year siege of Leningrad was finally lifted; Smolensk, Kiev, and Odessa were retaken. By June 1944, Soviet troops had not only cleared large portions of their homeland of the Nazi invader but were themselves standing on foreign soil (portions of Rumania).

The Invasion of France

Meanwhile the long-awaited second front, carpingly demanded by Stalin, had opened on the Normandy beaches of France. As early as 1942 it had been broached and debated. But Britain had been too weak and America too far from massive mobilization for D-Day to be scheduled that early. By 1943 the changed circumstances we have noted in the preceding sections made realistic planning for that day feasible. In November Roosevelt, Churchill, and Stalin had met at Tehran to work out its broad features and general timing. For

months thereafter about a half thousand American and British personnel pooled their plans, hopes and, often, doubts.

D-Day was originally set for June 5, 1944. All branches and sections of the British, American, Canadian, and Free French forces cooperated fully in an effort to make the landing successful. For several months Allied planes had systematically bombed terminals and transport facilities so that German troops and supplies could not be moved up to the attack area. They also concentrated on further clipping the wings of the once-powerful Luftwaffe. They were more than moderately successful in both efforts. In addition, everything was done to convince the Germans (what they already were quite sure of) that landings would be made in the Calais area, close to England's Dover Beach. Actually, the chosen site was a 60-mile stretch of beach along the eastern shores of the Normandy Peninsula, some five times farther from England than the Calais area.

For their part the Germans had made a large section of the coast facing England a vast and vicious obstacle course: underwater mines and stakes, mined obstacles on the beaches, and a wall of artillery pieces behind which were planted fields of land mines. Strong detachments of German troops were in the area, but the bulk of Hitler's defense forces remained stationed near Calais.

Because of bad weather General Eisenhower, supreme commander of "Overlord," as the whole operation was called, postponed the invasion one day. Then, on June 6, 1944, the giant armada moved against the European fortress. The events of the landings, to be described meaningfully, would take far more space than a general account such as ours allows. Here it can only be emphasized that the operation was far more costly and near to failure than most Americans still realize. Will, courage, indescribable suffering, and some strange

Supply ships unloading along the Normandy coast. Barrage balloons were sent up to protect the operation from attacking Nazi planes.

twists of chance combined to place and maintain parts of seven divisions of Allied troops along that strip of hell. A month later more than a million soldiers had been channeled through the break and had fanned out in three directions.* In mid-August another Allied force invaded southern France. For the next four months the two contending forces mauled each other in a complicated and often confused series of bloody battles.

British troops establishing a beachhead in Normandy, D-Day, June 6, 1944.

---

* It was at this point that the famous "Generals' Plot" to depose Hitler was carried out. On July 20, 1944, a bomb was planted in Hitler's conference room by Colonel Stauffenburg, one of the leading figures in the German resistance movement. The room was wrecked, and two persons were killed, but Hitler escaped with only minor injuries.

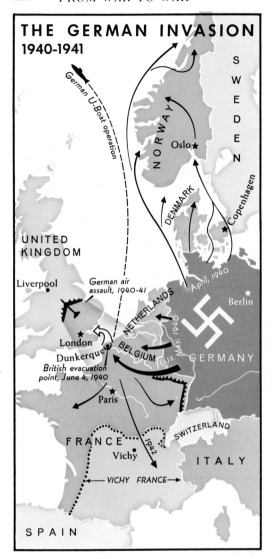

THE GERMAN INVASION
1940-1941

The Collapse of Germany

In the meantime the Russians had launched a new drive (July 1944) that was to evolve, over the next ten months, into a kind of rippling, accordion offensive. At no time were German troops given rest for very long. For a while the Northern Front would explode into action; as it subsided the southern flank would take fire; then the center, then the Northern or Southern Front again until by January 1945 Soviet troops were poised for the breakthrough into Germany. A month before,

Hitler had attempted (in what has come to be called the Battle of the Bulge) to drive the Anglo-American armies back to the coast, establish a new defense line, and turn again to deal with his eastern foes. But by this time he lacked the strength to gain new victories anywhere. German cities and factories were bombed around the clock. Allied forces in Italy had reached the Po Valley. Strong armies were beating in on him from the east and from the west. For nearly six years German armed might had made a terrible and deep mark upon vast stretches of Europe. Now it was opposed by three great industrial powers whose combined populations, armies, navies, air forces, industrial plants, and technological skills were beyond coping with by any single nation.* During the winter and spring of 1945 German armies steadily retreated on all fronts. On April 30, Hitler, who had entombed himself in an underground compound in Berlin, despaired of effecting a breakthrough and committed suicide. In his last will and testament he set up a new government, headed

* By this time the Germans stood practically alone; Italy, Rumania, Bulgaria, and Finland had already succumbed to the same driving power that was now crushing Germany.

THE ALLIED VICTORY
D-DAY JUNE 6, 1944 — V-E DAY MAY 8, 1945

SWEDEN

UNITED KINGDOM

DENMARK

★ Copenhagen

Baltic Sea

North Sea

Feb.-May, 1945

★ Berlin

Russian forces

NETHERLANDS

Oder R.

ALLIED AIR ASSAULT

★ The Hague

March-May, 1945

V-E DAY

★ London

D DAY   Calais •   ★ Brussels

Rhine R.

GERMANY

U.S., United Kingdom and Canadian forces

Sept., 1944   BELGIUM   Battle of the Bulge

• Prague

• LUX.

March-May, 1945

Paris ★

Danube R.

Vienna •

FRANCE

SWITZERLAND

Vichy •

Trieste •

—— VICHY FRANCE —— →

Milan •   April, 1945

ITALY

Free French and U.S. Aug., 1944

Genoa •   • Bologna

Marseilles •

SPAIN

0   100   200 mi.

Map by J. Donovan

by Grand Admiral Karl Doenitz, to carry on the war. But within the week the new government had agreed to unconditional surrender to the Allies. The 1000 Year Reich had lasted barely twelve years.

The End of the War in the Pacific

As we have seen, in the late fall of 1942 American amphibious forces had landed on Guadalcanal and, after six months of severe fighting, had forced the Japanese to withdraw. But only a toehold had been gained. All of the great island cluster groups in the Pacific west of Hawaii still remained under Japanese control; all were heavily fortified. The rim of eastern Asia, from Manchuria to Malaya, likewise constituted a formidable redoubt. Japanese land, sea, and air units were at full strength, and were fired with a savage spirit hard for Westerners to understand. If the Allies were to take as long to conquer all the other islands as was taken to capture Guadalcanal, a half-century would be required.

As finally worked out, Allied strategy called for the conquest of two key areas—

the Philippines and Burma. If the Philippines could be retaken and held, offensive operations by sea and air could be launched, via Formosa and Okinawa, against Japan itself. Reconquest of Burma would open the way into China and territories to the south. To achieve the conquest of the Philippines, MacArthur decided upon what came to be called the leapfrog approach. Many Japanese bases were stationed along the New Guinea coast. To invest and capture all of them would have taken far more time—and cost far more casualties—than the Americans could afford. So the practice was adopted of attacking certain strategic points, securing them, and then bypassing other Japanese-held bases to attack still others farther on. In this way the bypassed stations were sealed off and allowed to "wither on the vine." The second objective was to be achieved by amphibious landings among the Solomon Islands until the whole group was under Allied control. Thereafter each giant pincer would close down on the Philippines. (See map, page 844.)

American and Australian troops under MacArthur spent most of 1943 and 1944 inching along the New Guinea coast. All the way the Japanese offered resistance that again must be labeled indescribable and incomprehensible except to the men who encountered it. One example is offered to indicate the impossible proportions of both description and understanding. Off the northeastern coast of New Guinea lies the island of Biak. It is a very small thrust of coral reef jutting out of the sea, some 50 miles long and 25 miles wide. United States forces were landed there May 27, 1944 with orders to take and secure the airfield, and to clear the Japanese from the island. One participant has estimated that walking distance from where the troops landed to the airdrome was hardly a half hour. It took four weeks of heavy fighting for the troops (finally using tanks and flamethrowers) to secure that airstrip "one half hour away."

Two years of this kind of fighting were required to move Americans and Australians along both areas of the pincers. In October 1944 the United States Sixth Army invaded Leyte in the Philippines. By January 1945 its defenders had been cleared out, and American troops occupied the island. For the next eight months the Japanese, under General Tomoyaki Yamashita, fought to keep their hold on Luzon, the largest of the islands. Meanwhile, other Allied forces attacked and occupied Iwo Jima and Okinawa (February to June 1945) in preparation for the grand assault against the home islands of Japan. (See map, page 844.)

On the mainland of Asia the Allies launched a series of offensives (1944 to 1945) to regain Burma and reopen the road to China. By January 1945, the Ledo Road had been cleared and the way opened to join forces with Generalissimo Chiang Kai-shek's long-isolated armies. This was accomplished in the early spring, breaking Japan's hold on China. By June and July, Chiang's troops controlled nearly 300 miles of the coast north of Hong Kong.

By this time it was clear that Japan's fighting days were numbered. Cut off from the resources of Indonesia by the Philippine-China offensives, open to attack from both the south and the east, her industrial cities under steady bombardment, her carrier force all but annihilated, and her air power seriously crippled, she was unable to mount counteroffensives or even hope to hold on to her severely restricted positions. And, of course, the collapse of Germany in May 1945 meant that even stronger Allied pressures would soon be applied.

On July 16, 1945, the United States completed successful tests of its newly devised nuclear bomb. On August 6 it was dropped on Hiroshima, demolishing almost half of the city and killing some 90,000 persons. Another atomic bomb was dropped on Nagasaki three days later. Simultaneously Russia declared war on Japan and invaded Manchuria. Although

the *samurai* spirit of many of Japan's warriors led them to demand a fight to the finish, the Emperor and his advisors opened negotiations with the Allies. On August 14 Japan's virtually unconditional surrender was accepted, bringing to an end nearly six years of global carnage.

Effects of the War

Before considering the peace settlements and the events of the postwar years, let us make a summary assessment, leaving the details for later discussion. What had World War II accomplished, and at what price? What changes had it worked in the world? What prefigurations had it effected for the future? What had it done to the spirit of man?

The war had, of course, blocked the expansionist schemes of Germany, Japan, and Italy; it had, indeed, caused the prewar areas under their control to be substantially reduced. It had prevented the establishment of Hitler's New Order in Europe, and the creation of a Japanese "Co-prosperity Sphere" in eastern and southeastern Asia. It had discredited the openly avowed Fascist and Nazi ideologies. It had, at least nominally, given a setback to the notion of "heroic" violence as a way of life. These accomplishments, so easily stated, saved contemporary man from degradations and miseries which, in the turmoil of recent years, he may be

tempted to slight. If so, a serious study of the concentration camp culture of Nazi Germany and the savage regimen once imposed over large parts of Asia and the Pacific by the Japanese military—to say nothing of the regimented life concocted by Italy's balcony Caesar—is in order. On the other hand, attention will presently be called to the paradoxical assumption by postwar man, particularly Americans, of some of the totalitarian spirit and habits destroyed at such cost in the years of World War II; neither truth should be allowed to cancel out the other.

The cost in human life and suffering and in material goods is beyond any reasonable calculation. Even if such calculation were possible, the statistical statements would be quite meaningless; the human mind simply cannot personalize abstract figures dealing with such phenomena. Particular statistics may afford a vague hint, hardly more. In Soviet Russia alone military and civilian casualties directly or in-

The battleship Missouri *was the setting for the end of the Pacific War. In the right foreground, General Douglas MacArthur is being saluted by British General A. E. Percival and American Lieutenant-General Jonathan Wainwright. The Japanese delegation, facing the camera, somberly awaits the signing ceremonies.*

directly resulting from the war have been estimated at twenty million; Chinese battle *deaths* (not casualties, which included the wounded) numbered over two million; probably as many civilians were killed. In Germany, *air raid casualties alone,* military and civilian, approximated one million; over three million German soldiers were killed in battle.

Nor can an accurate, or even very meaningful, assessment be made of the shattering impact upon the overall "human condition"—self-respect, the right of a man to decide for himself what he should or should not do, faith in elemental human dignity and worth—effected by massive dislocations of many nationals during and after the war. Large segments of the populations of Poland, Belgium, the Netherlands, Italy and (to a lesser extent) France were taken into Germany during the war as slave laborers. All were mercilessly overworked, underfed, underclothed, and poorly housed. Tens of thousands died from such treatment; many suffered permanent disablement; all were marked by the psychic shock of forced reversion, in the important dimension of decision making, to the dependent status of children. Moreover, millions of Europeans were uprooted from their homelands as a result of the postwar takeover of large areas by Russia and Poland. Naturally, disruption of the normal patterns of living was suffered also by local populations that were forced to make room for and accommodate themselves to the incoming groups.

Out of the war, and partly (although only partly) because of it, emerged two great world powers—the United States and the U.S.S.R. Both had been strong states before the war; in the years that immediately followed it they became, for better or worse, the arbiters of international events. Later—by the mid-1960s—China developed power and influence of such dimensions that it should probably now (despite persisting intra-Party struggles) be counted as the world's third great power.

The war also prefigured certain phases of the developing struggle between capitalism and socialism. Before the twentieth century there was no socialist society (as an organized, sovereign state) anywhere in the world. Between the wars Russia became and remained the sole socialist society.* In the 1960s there were about a dozen socialist states, with combined populations accounting for over one third of the world's total. In a very real sense the contest has taken on aspects closely paralleling the conflict waged in the sixteenth and seventeenth centuries between Protestant and Catholic protagonists. Then, many rulers and peoples alike believed that their opponents were devils, certain to bring destruction to mankind if allowed to preach and practice their doctrines. Then, as now, many on both sides were sincerely convinced that (what today we call) peaceful coexistence was impossible; the only alternatives were conversion or destruction.

This polarization of politico-economic systems naturally led to significant new political alignments. During the war, Britain, France, Russia, China, and the United States were allied against Germany, Italy, and Japan. Spain, under Franco, although not a belligerent, was correctly considered by the Allies as an Axis fellow traveler. Not long after the war an almost complete reversal of commitments developed. As the leader of the so-called free world, the United States came to lean heavily upon the support of West Germany, Japan, Italy and, to a lesser extent, Spain. Conversely, Russia, mainland China, and their allies have become our opponents.

In Africa and Asia, the slogans and energies of the war—as well as the opportunities that were offered at its conclusion—stimulated many of their so-called underdeveloped peoples to shake off colonial

---

* Several nations, such as Britain and Sweden, have either had socialist governments for a period, or have developed a mixed economy. Here the referent is nationwide nationalization of industry and agriculture under seemingly permanent socialist governments.

bonds. In the next chapter we will consider some of the details of this portentous revolution.

Finally, and no less significantly, the war fastened upon the victors, especially the United States, some of the most reprehensible features of the totalitarian way of life that they had risked so much to destroy. Since the war, and in no small part because of it and the events that flowed out of it, the United States itself has taken on some of the features of a militaristic state. No matter how "normal" peacetime conscription may seem to persons under thirty, it is a drastic postwar innovation that runs counter to a humane tradition dating from Jeffersonian times. The United States military budget annually runs to about sixty billion dollars. The country's industrial complex and its military establishments have become so intimately connected that President Eisenhower, a professional soldier, warned against its ominous implications in his farewell message of 1960. As a further example, our federal secret agencies in recent years have become so numerous and so powerful that neither Congress nor the Chief Executive has always been able to control them, or even, on occasion, to know what they were planning. However anomalously, one of the fateful consequences of World War II was that the victors took on some of the features of the violent Sir Society they had vanquished.

THE ROAD TO "PEACE"

Making Peace

New Conditions of Peacemaking

The normal protocol of peacemaking was only partly followed after World War II. In 1919 representatives of the Allied governments met in Paris, debated, decided what was to be done, composed an elaborate document, and presented it to the German delegates for their signature. With less fanfare and ceremony the same general procedure was followed in dealing with the lesser losing powers. Proceedings after World War II were quite different. It is true that treaties with Bulgaria, Rumania, Italy, Finland, Hungary, Austria, and Japan were written and duly ratified. But, for one thing, the time lapse between the ending of hostilities and the ratification of treaties was much greater—ten years, in the case of Austria. For another, not all of the victorious powers signed all of the treaties that were presented to the vanquished. Russia, for example, refused to ratify the Japanese treaty. Furthermore, many provisions were relatively meaningless because of their *ex post facto* nature. In some treaties the amount of reparations was kept low or even passed over, on the surface a generous gesture. Actually much wealth of various kinds had been taken from the defeated countries (Austria, for example) by the occupying power before the treaties were formulated. Finally, the Allies were unable to agree on a solution to the German problem, leaving that nation divided into Eastern and Western states.

Most of these unsatisfactory and confusing developments grew out of two related circumstances. One was the imposition on the defeated powers of unconditional surrender terms; the second followed naturally — the complete occupation and governance of the defeated nations by the victors or their puppets. At Versailles in 1919 a sovereign German state was, as it were, party of the second part. In 1945 there were no sovereign defeated states.* Their official governments were made up of foreign conquerors who ruled without restrictions, for varying periods of time. Under these conditions formal peace treaties were almost superfluous. The victors arranged what they wanted as completely as the possibilities permitted, including the eventual setting up of local governments preconditioned to accept whatever treaty terms the victors should decide upon. A rough analogue is found in our Reconstruction history; then, the North occupied the South, for a while governed it absolutely, and dictated the new state constitutions.

The Peace Treaties

In light of these general circumstances let us briefly note the peace arrangements that followed the ending of hostilities. In the early years of the war, Finland, together with Bulgaria, Rumania, and Hungary (three Nazi puppets), entered the conflict on the side of Germany, as did Austria, then a German "province." Believing that a general settlement with these nations and with their Axis mentors should not be rushed through as had the Versailles settlement of 1919, Russia, Britain, and the United States decided upon a series of preliminary meetings. At these meetings the foreign ministers of Russia, Britain, the United States, France, and China were to explore the victors' legitimate demands and their relationship to the capacities and reasonable needs of the vanquished. It was hoped that a general blueprint would develop that could be submitted to a plenary conference of Allied representatives.

The scheme did not work out quite as planned. Meetings held during the next nine months in London, Moscow, and Paris revealed serious differences between the Western powers and China on the one hand, and Russia on the other. Reparations, boundary adjustments, and the disposition of Italy's African colonies were major objects of disagreement. Beyond these, and more significant, was the rapidly disintegrating rapport between Russia and the other Allies which the war had created and sustained. Nevertheless, agreements for treaties with Italy, Bulgaria, Rumania, Hungary, and Finland were finally reached at a fourth meeting of the representatives (June to July 1946). All of the treaties required the defeated nations to foreswear enactment of legislation that would discriminate against any of their nationals; all required establishment of democratic procedures; all required the relinquishing of some territories; and most provided for moderate reparations.

Continued efforts were directed toward concluding arrangements with Germany, Austria, and Japan. But by this time (1947) friction between Communist Russia and its wartime allies had increased to alarming proportions; further negotiations seemed only to aggravate it. In brief, a "cold war" was in the making, the features and incidents of which we shall consider later. In these circumstances the United States decided to take the initiative for a settlement with Japan, on the grounds that its occupation was no longer necessary and was also prohibitively expensive. Probably both contentions were true; but America's need to mend its foreign fences against a possible encounter with Russia was undoubtedly another, perhaps stronger, consideration. In 1950 a presidential mission sounded out other nations and recommended a general conference to decide upon acceptable terms. More than fifty nations, including the Soviet Union, met the next year for this purpose. The resulting treaty was ultimately ratified (1952) by most of the states. Russia was conspicuous among the non-

---

* With the exception of Finland. It should be understood that the Communist Balkan governments — such as Yugoslavia's — were under the control of directives from Moscow. Technically these countries were not subject to unconditional surrender terms and official occupation; actually Russia or its puppets dominated all of them.

signers.* On the whole the treaty's terms were lenient. No formal reparations were required; the war guilt question was left unmentioned; Japan was invited to join the United Nations; although all of her former colonies and mandated territories were taken from her, her home islands were left intact. Unfortunately for the United States, similar initiative could not be taken to effect a settlement with Germany and Austria, since Russian forces occupied portions of both. Some years later (1955), when relations between Russia and the United States had improved, an Austrian treaty was negotiated not much different from those concluded with the five states mentioned earlier. But the German problem remained unsolved.

Emergent One-Worldism

The Pattern of Conferences

Even before the war's end, plans were made for the creation of a world organization that would prevent the coming of another great conflict. The basic motivation, of course, derived from man's growing realization that civilization and modern war are incompatible. Tactically the planning for a new world organization was made considerably easier by the habit formed during the war by the Big Three's leaders of holding face-to-face meetings to discuss mutual concerns. From 1943 to 1945 no less than five of these conferences brought the Allied heads of state together. Because the meetings dramatized the emergence of an incipient one-worldism (as well as produced decisions we need to note), we may give brief notice to them.

The first conference was set up by Roosevelt and Churchill at Casablanca (1943) to decide upon general matters of strategy and policy. Out of it came the decision to land troops in Africa (Operation Torch, see

supra, p. 844) in preparation for the invasion of Europe, and the policy of unconditional surrender eventually applied to Italy, Germany, and Japan. Later that year Roosevelt, Churchill, and Chiang Kai-shek conferred in Cairo, and Roosevelt and Churchill moved on to Tehran in Persia. This afforded Roosevelt his first opportunity to meet Stalin who, understandably, urged the immediate opening of a Second Front; he also demanded the ultimate breaking up of Germany into a number of small states. In February 1945, as the ring was closing around Germany, the three leaders met again, this time in the Crimea at Yalta. In this meeting certain major decisions were reached: a defeated Germany was to be disarmed, demilitarized, and dismembered, as the Allies "might deem requisite for future peace and security"; Russia promised to declare war against Japan soon after Germany's defeat; certain territories in Asia were to be given to Russia; a new world organization would take the place of the discredited League of Nations. Following Germany's surrender in May 1945, Allied leaders—this time Attlee, who replaced Churchill after a Labour electoral victory, Truman, who became President in April 1945 upon the death of Roosevelt, and Stalin—met at Potsdam, a suburb of Berlin. To the three d's of the German policy outlined at Yalta, two others were added: denazification and democratization; and dismemberment was toned down to decentralization. It was also decided to divide Germany into four occupation zones until a general peace conference could meet and draw up a definite settlement. Berlin, deep in the Russian area, was also divided into four spheres of occupation, one for each of the Big Three, and one for France.

Creation of the United Nations Organization

Plans for peace as well as war brought representatives of the great powers to the conference table from time to time during

---

* In 1956 Russia issued a declaration proclaiming that a state of war with Japan no longer existed.

The Dumbarton Oaks Conference, 1944, was held to lay the groundwork for an organization to take the place of the League of Nations. Key figures, shown above, beginning second from left, are Lord Halifax, British ambassador to the United States, Cordell Hull, U.S. Secretary of State, Andrei Gromyko, Russian ambassador to the United States, and Edward R. Stettinius, U.S. Undersecretary of State.

the war period. In 1941 Roosevelt and Churchill met in Canada to formulate a statement of war aims. To a later generation harassed by seemingly endless crises, the Atlantic Charter, as it came to be called, may seem highly idealistic. Both America and Britain foreswore any intention to annex foreign territories, promised to honor the wishes of the people concerned in whatever territorial changes were to be effected, unequivocally supported the principle of self-determination for every people, and declared their faith in the possibility of creating a world free from fear and want. In January 1943, representatives of twenty-six countries signed a pact embodying these principles. Later in the year the United Nations Relief and Rehabilitation Administration (U.N.R.R.A.) was created to provide food, clothing, and medical supplies to nations ravaged by the war.

When it became apparent in late 1944 that the war was drawing to an end, representatives of Britain, Russia, China, and the United States held a series of meetings in Dumbarton Oaks (in Washington, D.C.)

to lay the groundwork for the creation of the new international organization. Early the next year (April to June 1945) representatives from fifty nations met in San Francisco to draw up a constitution for the new organization, to be called the United Nations. To carry out its purposes—to maintain world peace, to "develop friendly relations among nations," and to "encourage respect for human rights" and freedoms —three main bodies were created. One, the General Assembly, was commissioned to consider world problems of almost any kind and to make recommendations about what should be done. Every member was given one vote; all resolutions required a majority vote for passage. The size of the second body, the Security Council, was limited to eleven members (now fifteen), including five permanent members: the United States, Britain, France, the Soviet Union, and "Nationalist" China. Both the United States and the U.S.S.R. insisted upon the right of each Council member to exercise an absolute veto whenever its national interests indicated the need for it. Thus, although the Council was given the right to sanction the use of military force to oppose aggression, the negative vote of any one of the Council's members could stop U.N. action. None of the great states would have agreed to become working members of the organization if this provision had not been included. Otherwise, they stood the chance of being outvoted on a sanctions measure by small states that could not assume the power responsibility for making the decision effective. The third branch, the General Secretariat, was set up to exercise executive functions much in the manner of the American presidency. Finally, like the old League, the U.N. also was given the authority to set up a number of auxiliary organizations dealing, for example, with labor and health conditions, the world's food supply, and the problem of coordinating international civil aviation activities. It should be emphasized that despite the panoply of powers given to the new world body it was intended to be, and remains, a loose confederation of sovereign states.

At war's end most of the peoples of the world seemed genuinely to want an international body strong enough to prevent a recurrence of war. Naturally the construction and use of the A-bomb played a part in shaping this seemingly strong desire. But the six years of violence even without that bomb undoubtedly played a larger part. Many living then had known the horrors of World War I. For them it was not easy to imagine meaningful existence if man were doomed to look forward to World War III, or World War VIII, or World War XXVIII. On the other hand, no people or its leaders stood then—or now—for the abolition of national sovereignty, without which no world organization could substitute its constabulary for national armies. It is beyond the competence of the historian—as historian—to judge the rightness or wrongness of this position; the fact of the position and the implications rising from it, however, cannot be ignored.

In any case, within ten years after the outbreak of World War II, a new world organization, dedicated to peace and human progress, was operating within and occasionally significantly upon the web of world affairs. But in the succeeding decades of mounting crises and tensions its overall influence, hardly surprisingly, rarely prevailed when opposed by the forces of traditional power politics.

SELECTED READINGS

Bailey, Thomas A., *The Diplomatic History of the American People,* Appleton-Century-Crofts, New York, 1958 (6th ed.).

> The appropriate chapters of this readable text should be consulted, especially for an understanding of how American public opinion helped to shape the diplomatic decisions of this period.

Churchill, Winston S., *The Second World War,* Houghton Mifflin, Boston, 1948–1953 (6 vols.).

Pioneer

A 1945 United States cartoon, expressing the feeling that probably most Americans then held toward the new world peace organization.

> The set, as would be expected, contains very much and very valuable material not found in any other account. But it is not, of course, an unbiased history; and the reader should keep in mind Churchill's admission, made in private conversation before the work was written, that no statesman in writing his memoirs should be so lacking in good sense as to include material which unfavorably reflects upon his own doings and decisions.

*Divine, Robert A., *The Reluctant Belligerent: American Entry into World War II,* John Wiley & Sons, New York, 1965.

> A brief account of, as the author sees it, America's steady bungling in international affairs from the early 1930s to the Japanese attack at Pearl Harbor.

Hall, Walter Phelps, *Iron Out of Calvary,* Appleton-Century Company, New York, 1946.

> An interpretive account of World War II. Where Liddell Hart concentrates on battle plans and actions, Hall tends to subordinate these to narration of why battles turned out as they did, and their political implications.

Asterisk (*) denotes paperback.

*Hersey, John, *Hiroshima,* Bantam Books, New York, 1946.

There are other, fuller, and more up-to-date books on the bombing of Hiroshima. Probably none can match this first one for total emotional impact.

Langer, William L., and S. Everett Gleason, *The Challenge of Isolation, 1937–1940,* Harper & Brothers, New York, 1952.

Detailed examination of America's response to aggression in Europe and Asia.

Langer, William L., and S. Everett Gleason, *The Undeclared War, 1940–1941,* Harper & Brothers, New York, 1953.

A nearly 1000-page examination of the aggressive ventures of Germany and Japan (1940–1941) and their impact on the policies and practices of Britain and the United States. Other nations — Russia (especially), France, China, Greece, Turkey, and Mexico, for example — are brought into the overall picture of the encounter between Axis powers and "Allied" powers. The authors support, in the main, the view that the United States government genuinely tried to keep out of a shooting war.

*Liddell Hart, Basil H., *The German Generals Talk,* Berkeley Publishing Corporation, New York, 1948.

The author held long interviews with many of the leading lights of the *Wehrmacht* and gives here a close, often verbatim account of their views of what went right and wrong with the war.

Morison, S. E., *The Two-Ocean War . . . ,* Little, Brown & Company, Boston, 1963.

An abridged edition of the author's multi-volume history of the global operations of the United States Navy. Despite the salty tang and occasional derring-do rhetoric, this work is a rewarding study of some of the great sea battles of World War II.

*Neumann, Robert, with Helga Koppel, *The Pictorial History of the Third Reich,* Bantam Books, New York, 1962.

By strict category this book belongs on the reading list for the chapter on Nazi Germany.

But it so much depicts the essence of the war spirit that it can, perhaps, most profitably be read with these books specifically dealing with World War II.

Sherwood, Robert E., *Roosevelt and Hopkins,* Harper & Brothers, New York, 1948.

A sympathetic duo-biography of the two men who administered America's foreign policy from 1941 to 1945.

Stipp, John L., ed., *Devil's Diary,* Antioch Press, Yellow Springs, Ohio, 1955.

A condensation of the more important documents relating to Nazi conspiracy and aggression which were collected by the United States government and published in ten volumes.

Von Wegerer, Alfred, *The Origins of World War II,* Richard R. Smith, New York, 1941.

A brief exposition (125 pages) of the events that led to the outbreak of World War II from the standpoint of a well-known German scholar. Written when the Nazi war machine was running wild in Europe, the book is an interesting study of how documents should not be used.

Wheeler-Bennett, John W., *Munich,* Duell, Sloan & Pearce, New York, 1962.

The best account of this very controversial event. The documentation is full, the interpretation is balanced with and based on the facts. The one area insufficiently covered is the British government's knowledge of and reaction to the plot to overthrow Hitler (an area to which, it should be added, no work has yet done justice).

Wohlstetter, Roberta, *Pearl Harbor, Warning and Decision,* Stanford University Press, Stanford, 1922.

A detailed analysis of the operations of U.S. intelligence agencies as they dealt with Japanese "signals" before the attack on Pearl Harbor. In the author's judgment there were no real villains or even very low level incompetents responsible for the general state of U.S. unreadiness at Pearl Harbor on December 8, 1941. Readers may reach a different conclusion after going through the source material provided.

THE WORLD IN FLUX

31

The World in Flux, 1940s to 1960s

DOMESTIC AFFAIRS

To bring the complexity and the pace of national and global events that have crowded the postwar years into a manageable unit of study four categories of developments will be considered: major trends within selected nations; the "decolonization" of Asia and Africa; the revival of Europe; and the more outstanding features of the cold war-coexistence syndrome.

Britain

The New and the Old

An assessment of the meaning of basic developments in Britain since the war is made difficult by our habit of associating, even equating, significant experience with political and economic power. Judged by these two criteria alone, Britain no longer exercises a dominant, at times not even a substantial, influence in affairs that concern the world at large. In a later section we shall see her war against Egypt abruptly called off by the fiat of other powers, particularly the United States and the U.S.S.R. A generation earlier such an event would have been almost unthinkable. Britain no longer rules the seas. Her once great empire has been transformed into a loose, voluntary association of sovereign states. Where once she was somewhat condescending toward Europe, she was now eager to win the approval of continental nations and to associate with them in common economic and political activity. Her economic stature, like her political position, has changed drastically. At the turn of this century, British merchants controlled about 35 per cent of the world's trade; sixty years later this percentage had been cut in half. Since the end of World War II Britain's standard of living, although higher than any in her history, has failed to keep pace with

An American view of what kept Britain poor. As a Socialist, Prime Minister Clement Attlee was expected to recommend a broad program designed to redistribute the wealth and put the economy on an enduringly sound basis.

the rate of rise developed by many other European states. Nevertheless, Britain remains one of the most mature societies, possibly the most mature, of the contemporary world.

Construction of the Welfare State

Probably the dominant theme of British life in the years after the war was the political and economic enlargement of the life of the common man. In feudal and early modern times, as we have seen in earlier chapters of this book, the landed noble— from knight to king—ruled the country. Later, throughout the eighteenth and nineteenth centuries, first the commercial and then the industrial elite gained dominant political power. In the early years of the twentieth century, particularly after 1910, the "little man," under the aegis of the rising socialist Labour Party, jostled with the privileged middle class for a greater share of both economic affluence and political influence. Although the early Labour govern-

ments were short-lived and seemingly ineffectual, they set the national stage for and conditioned the public mind to the program of nationalization that was inaugurated in 1945.

In the general elections of that year the Conservative party, under the leadership of Winston Churchill, suffered a decisive, and rather surprising, defeat. Labour candidates received an absolute majority of the popular vote, and 61 per cent of the seats in the House of Commons. Although Churchill tended to think of the results of the election as a repudiation of his leadership, they were primarily brought about by other considerations. Britons remembered the doldrums that plagued their economic life after World War I when, for most of the period, the Conservatives, either openly or under the cover of the label "coalition," dominated the nation's political life. More important, World War II had worked massive hardships on the home front. The working man was without adequate housing facilities, without prospects of full employment, without reasonable assurance that his subsistence needs would be met, and without a guarantee that his physical and mental health could be ministered to within the limits of his restricted income. On all these counts the Labour party spoke out firmly and in specific detail. The Conservative party, on the other hand, concentrated its efforts on a denunciation of creeping socialism and an acclamation of the merits of free enterprise.

Once in power the new socialist government lost no time in converting its campaign promises into national legislation. By 1947 it had enacted a comprehensive social welfare program that substantially changed the social fabric of the nation. First on its bill of particulars was the national banking system, which was nationalized in March 1946.

In July 1946, Parliament passed the Coal Industry Nationalization Act. This law transferred the entire industry from private to public ownership, with compensation given to the private owners. Civil Aviation and cable and wireless corporations were made public institutions during 1946 to 1947. Control of private investment was effected by passage of the Borrowing Act of 1946. The next year the Town and Country Planning Act empowered local authorities to direct the planning of property development. Also in 1947, wartime legislation dealing with the prices and marketing of farm products was extended. In the same year the Inland Transport Act brought railroads and trucking and bus concerns under government ownership and operations. In late 1946 one of the most controversial of all the socialist proposals was made into law—The National Health Service Act. The medical profession fiercely attacked the measure as it was originally drawn up. In the end, the legislators contrived a measure that went about as far as any legislation could in providing a national health service in which the patient's needs were met within a framework of a patient-physician relationship that was basically similar to that of private practice. Legislation was also passed to provide for housing and educational needs.

In short, under five years of Labour government, Britain was transformed into what is now commonly called the welfare state. Although most industry remained in private hands, government control was close and alertly watchful. In the main the changes were accepted by most classes in the country. Conservative leaders continued to criticize the workings of much of the Labour legislation, but they were careful neither to call for its repeal nor, when they returned to power, to try to turn back the clock.

Economic Problems

Because Britain's economy, more than those of most other powers, fundamentally rests on a favorable balance of trade—selling more than buying from abroad—the short-term value of the many changes that were made depended on a tolerable pros-

perity that unfortunately did not develop. To redress the trade balance Clement Attlee, the Labour Prime Minister, and his colleagues devised an austerity program that discomfited large segments of the population. Labor grumbled at the "Control of Engagements Order" which, although rarely enforced, was designed to direct labor into jobs deemed most important by the government. Meat and gasoline rationing were reintroduced. Temporary monetary laws were passed which precluded the importation of goods from dollar areas. These and other restrictions produced a voter reaction which in the next general election, held in 1950, cut into Labour's Parliamentary majority. In an effort to regain a workable majority, the Prime Minister dissolved Parliament the next year (1951) and directed an "educative" campaign which backfired, resulting in a Conservative victory. For the next fifteen years the Conservative party cautiously combined the more obviously popular achievements of the Attlee government with such dynamics as remained in the free-enterprise system. Although the Conservatives won the elections of 1955 and 1959, the loyalty of Britain's masses to the general Labour outlook and program was not substantially weakened; of the seven general elections held between 1945 and 1966, five produced a popular majority for the Labour party. It came as no great surprise, therefore, when Labour returned to power in 1964 with promises of "more of the same." Two years later, in another general election, its Parliamentary majority was substantially increased. But economic problems, under whatever kind of government, continued to harass the nation throughout most of the postwar years.

France and Italy

France

Even the briefest survey of the history of France since World War II presents unusual difficulties. Encyclopedic details, of course, could be cited at great length — the rise and fall of governments, greater and lesser crises marking intra- and interparty strife, ephemeral "solutions" to colonial problems, the emergence and disappearance of leading political figures, and the many heated disputes over how France might find herself again. Not all of these events, of course, turned out — or seem to be turning out — to be mere details. But even the strategic events are difficult to treat in a general way, because it is hard to delineate the overall profile of France. Granted that in a world in flux the profile of no one collective society is as clear as the student of history would like, the image of France is nevertheless particularly elusive. The very titles of books dealing with France since the 1930s often reflected this blurred view, such as *The Twilight of France,* and *France Against Herself.*

Economic Recovery; Rise in Birthrate

One development that seems to withstand focal distortion is the country's economic recovery after 1947 to 1948. Whether caused fundamentally by the nationalization of certain industries such as banking, coal, gas and electricity, and the major insurance companies, or by a remarkable venture in economic planning (the Monnet Plan, 1947–1951), the French standard of living in the 1950s and 1960s achieved an unprecedentedly high level. France became, for example, the only agriculturally self-sufficient country in Europe; at the same time the income of her industrial workers allowed mass consumption of such items as automobiles, television sets, and sports and vacation equipment.

Concurrently with the rise in living standards, and undoubtedly partly caused by it, there occurred a substantial increase in the population. Since the Napoleonic Wars, France (alone among the large nations of Europe) had suffered a relative decline in population. The unexpected reversal of

ONE CRISIS AFTER ANOTHER

Despite an efficient civil service system, Frenchmen found their everchanging governments a constant source of apprehension and insecurity.

this melancholy tradition had dramatic overtones. In many countries, including the United States, the current population explosion took on a menacing cast. In France, however, the phenomenon was looked upon not only as the actual substance of her new life, but also as a promising symbol of future greatness.

From the Fourth to the Fifth Republic

Probably the most significant postwar event was the establishment of the Fifth Republic in 1958. Earlier we noted the brief, wartime tenure of the Vichy regime. After the war a new constitution set up France's Fourth Republic (1946–1958). Many Frenchmen hoped that under its provisions a way would be found out of the morass of cabinet making-breaking that had marked the tortuous course of the Third Republic (1871–1940). They were disappointed. Premiers rose and fell with the same regularity as before (the average government lasted less than six months). About a half dozen parties sliced up the voting populace so finely and in such a bewildering fashion that no party, with the exception of the highly disciplined Communist party, could ever be sure of its weight from one day to another in the constantly shifting blocs and coalitions. Consequently, consistent policy, for all the vaunted competence of the permanent staff of civil servants, proved teasingly elusive.

Coupled with this embarrassingly carnival aspect of their political life was the tendency of Frenchmen to be plagued by the feeling that their nation had slipped out of the charmed "world-power" circle. Twice within the century they had been rescued from German victory and domination by the intervention of outside powers. If, to many of that time, Europe seemed a diminishing force in world affairs, to sensitive Frenchmen their own country in that shrunken area appeared to count for even less.

De Gaulle's return to politics in 1958 changed this. Sensing the weary despair of his countrymen, he accepted appointment as premier with the express understanding that he would propose drastic constitutional changes making for strong executive leadership. Although some Frenchmen, and all French Communists, saw this as the first move in the creation of a fascist regime, the majority nevertheless seemed to welcome it as the "sole remaining rampart between the Republic and Fascism." De Gaulle's constitution (he personally supervised the construction of every section of it) was submitted to the electorate in the fall of 1958 and received overwhelming approval. Its terms clearly marked the end of the old ways of the Third and Fourth Republics. The president, elected for seven years and eligible for reelection, was given the power to appoint both the prime minister and members of the cabinet. This

meant that the Assembly could no longer overturn ministries at will because the government was not responsible to it. In addition, the Executive exercised the power of suggesting legislation to the Assembly which could approve or disapprove it, as well as initiate legislation itself. Significantly — particularly in view of the current crisis attending the Algerian revolt — the president was also granted the right to issue emergency decrees on his own authority, as well as the power to dissolve the Assembly and call for new elections.

Under the new Republic, France experienced a long period of political stability. Throughout de Gaulle's first seven-year term, only one government exercised power — the longest tenure of any government in the history of republican France. Reelected in 1966 for another seven years, the President gave all signs of maintaining this most un-Gallic record. Although welcoming the end of the old "who's in now?" game, opponents of the regime, especially those of the Left, continued to dispute its — as they saw it — essentially undemocratic character. Particularly objectionable to them was the constitutional clause giving the president the right to rule with full powers in a national emergency. In liberals of almost every hue, this clause stirred further fears by giving to the president, and to him alone, the power to decide what conditions constituted an emergency, and what should be done to meet it.

De Gaulle's France

To the dismay of many Rightists, and particularly the recalcitrant colonialists, de Gaulle insisted on the granting of full independence to Algeria (1962). The next year he caused consternation among the Western European powers making up "The Six" (see *infra*, p. 897) by vetoing Britain's application to join the Common Market. Whatever his official reasons for this action, his real objection lay in his belief that Britain was too closely tied to the United

States for Europe's good, especially as he envisioned Europe's good. In his view a most dangerous situation had arisen with the emergence of the United States and the U.S.S.R. as superpowers. Between them they tended to establish a monopoly on the arbitration of world affairs. For de Gaulle, this was a wholly unacceptable development, which relegated not only France but the whole of Europe to a passive role. Throughout his first term as president, he worked hard to reinstate self-confidence among all European peoples. But his program did not find easy acceptance anywhere. His associates in "The Six" favored the admission of Britain. They and the representatives of other states believed also that, superpower or not, the United States was an indispensable ally whose leadership — and financial aid — should not be underestimated as basic props of the democratic world. They objected, too, to the grand de Gaulle "style," which reminded many of the first Bonaparte.

Nevertheless, by the late 1960s, France under de Gaulle seemed to have achieved a condition at home and a position abroad beyond what the most enthusiastic Francophile could have seriously hoped for a decade earlier. At de Gaulle's insistence, France developed a nuclear power that was sufficiently advanced to give her a place in the atom-bomb club. Also at his insistence, France asserted national independence vis-à-vis the strategic demands of the North Atlantic Treaty Organization,* and went so far as to order (1965) the removal of the United States-dominated NATO bases from French soil. Her new posture regarding the claims of her onetime colonies definitely enhanced her international reputa-

*In a summary history of the contemporary world it it impossible to sharply separate domestic affairs from international affairs. Rather than tediously repeat such directives as "see below" or "discussed in a later section," our account hereafter makes references to related circumstances of this nature on the assumption that the reader will turn to the appropriate parts on his own initiative.

tion. Furthermore, a substantial measure of economic well-being continued to be enjoyed under Gaullist leadership.

Italy

In 1943, as we have seen, Italy disposed of Mussolini and switched from being an Axis partner to a "cobelligerent" of the Allies. But her position was ambiguous. For over twenty years the Fascist way of life had penetrated the interstices of Italy's political and social life. The peremptory dismissal of the Duce, although of course requisite for new policies and a new outlook, could not automatically bring them about. As both an Axis aggressor and an Axis defector, Italy presented, by war's end, a double image that puzzled both herself and the victorious Allies. In the peace treaty of 1947 she was forced to pay an indemnity of $360 million and to agree to a future review of her colonial claims. Eventually she was required to relinquish all foreign possessions.

In 1946 the monarchy was voted out of existence and a parliamentary republic was set up. The first national elections held under it (1948) gave the Christian Socialist party — much more a Catholic center party than Socialist — an absolute majority. Under its able leader, Alcide de Gasperi, the government vigorously attacked the perennial problems of poverty and illiteracy. In 1950 an elaborate ten-year economic program was announced and, primed by Marshall Plan aid, successfully carried out. The living standard rose to a higher level than Italy had ever enjoyed. But the peasant masses still remained underfed, underhoused, and ill-clothed, especially in the regions south of Rome. Relatively generous sums were allocated for educational projects to create a more than barely literate population; here, too, real advances were made, although compared to other Western nations both the quality and the scope of the educational program left much to be desired.

Because of Italy's economic and social deficiencies, the appeal of Communism proved strong. She has the largest and most disciplined Communist party in Western Europe, as well as a large congeries of Socialist parties. Generous United States loans and grants were credited with preventing one or the other of these parties, or a coalition of them, from coming to power. The Church also gave strong support to the Christian Socialist regime. The question of whether that regime will not eventually give way to the radical Left remains another one of Italy's uncertainties.

Because of membership in the Common Market and in the North Atlantic Treaty Organization, Italy's general economic and political situation seems for the present to be reasonably secure. But until the yawning gaps between rich and poor, industrial North and agricultural South, and aristocratic elite and uneducated masses can be narrowed, Italy's future, for all her recent socioeconomic gains, remains none too promising.

The Germanies

Germany in Defeat

The surrender of Germany in May of 1945 was unconditional. This meant that the victorious powers not only occupied all of Germany but exercised complete political control over it. Until a formal overall Allied administration could be set up to govern the conquered land, the occupying powers divided Germany into four zones. Russia was assigned the northeastern provinces lying between the Elbe and Oder-Neisse rivers, Britain occupied a sector in the northwest, and the United States took over the administration of the south German states, from which two Rhineland areas were reassigned to France.

Even if communist-capitalist stresses had not developed among the occupying powers, the job of managing the country would have remained indescribably difficult. The German population, then as in 1918, was stunned by defeat. The problem was confounded by the unprecedented movement and relocation of millions of people who, during the war years, either had been exploited as foreign laborers in Germany or had lived outside the Reich's borders. Among the foreign laborers were hundreds of thousands of Poles, Russians, Italians, Frenchmen, and Balkan peoples. Masses of refugees poured in from areas overrun by Russian troops. In addition, some fifteen million occupying troops and their families moved in, taking over the best living quarters and in general assuming the traditional prerogatives of conquering powers. To impress on the Germans the inhumanity of the Hitler years, the new rulers distributed films, posters, and books that portrayed concentration-camp life and described other acts of Nazi criminality. Thus, guilt feelings merged with resentment and despair to produce inner harassments almost beyond bearing.

Besides multilateral occupation, Germany was forced to accept a sharp reduction in territory. In 1939, Russia took over substantial portions of eastern Poland. After the war Poland was compensated by being given certain eastern areas of the old Germany, including half of East Prussia (the other half going to the U.S.S.R.). Germany was also compelled to accept the dismantling of many of her eastern industrial establishments, which were then shipped to Russia as partial compensation for the massive destruction by German armies of Russian industry in the Ukraine and in other parts of the Soviet Union.

Deemphasis of the "De's"

The original Allied aims of deindustrialization, demilitarization, and denazification were only imperfectly carried out. It soon became apparent, at least to Britain and to the United States, that the revival of European economy depended on the revival of German industry, which automati-

Split Personality

In 1947 Britain and America made one economic unit of their two zones in occupied Germany. Two years later France joined them in drawing up an occupation statute that virtually merged the three zones into one. Meanwhile, Russia had consolidated its control of Eastern Germany. These two cartoons show something of the German predicament that resulted.

ONE VOLK
TWO REICHS
NO FÜHRER

cally meant abandonment of any attempt to "pastoralize" Germany. Decentralization plans eventually yielded to the exigencies of the cold war. Total disarmament was quickly achieved; even many Germans—at the time—supported both the policy and its immediate execution. Denazification was a

more difficult matter. According to the rules of judgment outlined in the Potsdam and Yalta declarations, not hundreds or thousands of Germans were marked by the swastika brand, but millions. To try them under fair court procedures would take years. Compounding the difficulty was the absence of reasonable criteria that could be used to separate active, convinced Nazis from any who had joined the Party or had supported the Hitler regime out of fear of what would happen to them if they did not. In late 1945, twenty-one Nazi leaders were brought to trial at Nuremberg for crimes against the peace, war crimes, and crimes against humanity. All but three were given either sentences of death or terms of imprisonment. Even if we grant the propriety of such trials—which many both in Germany and in the Allied countries did not— the conviction of eighteen leaders hardly denazified Germany. Many trials of lesser Nazi officials were held by Allied and, later, German courts, and a number of those indicted were convicted. Still the basic problem remained—how to root out an ideology that had gripped a large part of the entire nation without immobilizing the economic, political, and social forces that any community requires for even the most elemental kind of organized existence. In the end, the elaborate program of "purification" was allowed to peter out amid the developing agitations of the cold war.*

Capitalist and Communist Germanies

Rising tensions between the Western Allies and Soviet Russia wrecked the original plan to govern Germany as a "unit." In late 1946 Britain and the United States agreed to an economic fusion of their zones and, the next year, set up a German Economic Council to direct a reconstruction

---

* In late 1966, a former Nazi had become Chancellor of West Germany, and the Neo-Nazi National Democratic Party had made substantial election gains.

program. Russia soon countered by creating a German Economic Commission in the Soviet sector. Thereafter, both power blocs moved steadily toward the creation of "new Germanies" in their own image. In the spring of 1949 the three Western powers drew up an Occupation Statute which virtually merged their sectors into one, with substantial political control vested in German officials. This was soon followed by the establishment of the Federal Republic of Germany, with Bonn as its capital. Under the leadership of Konrad Adenauer, its first Chancellor and one of Europe's most gifted statesmen, the new Republic quickly gave signs of spiritual, economic, and political rehabilitation. In reply, the Russians sponsored the creation, in their zone, of the German Democratic Republic. An able statesman, Otto Grotewohl, was named as its Minister President, although real power lay with his Soviet advisers.

Under these circumstances, Western leaders drastically revised the basic provisions of the Potsdam Declaration. They had envisioned the emergence of a new Germany that would be united but weak, sovereign but pliant. Now they worked to make West Germany industrially strong through Marshall Plan aid. Thus stimulated, West Germany's economy soon surpassed prewar levels of production. Indeed, so rapid and so widespread was its recovery that the phrase "economic miracle" came to be used commonly to describe it. Before long, and particularly as the Korean War dramatized the ominous potential of the communist-capitalist conflict, the United States and Britain felt impelled to permit Germany to rearm, with the proviso that the new army would be a part of NATO defense forces rather than an independent organization.

With these developments, little hope remained that a general peace conference would ever be assembled. By 1957, West Germany had become thoroughly aligned with the United States, Britain, and France, just as East Germany had become aligned with the Soviet Union. Constant and serious friction marked their relations with one another. Periodically, West German leaders demanded reunion and restoration of the old pre-Hitler frontiers. East German leaders favored reunion — on their own terms — but remained understandably reticent about boundary changes that both Poland and Russia opposed. Divided Berlin remained a continually festering sore. To the West it was a symbol of the containment of Communism. To the East it was a source of unending irritations. As the recipient of Marshall Plan aid money, West Berlin soon became prosperous almost to the point of ostentatious affluence. Its citizens also enjoyed democratic blessings that were denied to their brothers on the other side of the "curtain." Consequently, many East Berliners moved over into the Western sector until the East German government forbade further migration. When, despite this injunction, many smuggled themselves across the line, the Communist government ordered the erection of a wall along the boundary (1961), which was heavily guarded day and night. Tempers were sharpened on both sides, possible avenues of *rapprochement* were shut off, and the cold war took on new and more menacing aspects.

In short, the makeshift settlements that followed the defeat of the Nazi state aggravated rather than solved the long troublesome "German problem." Nothing in the whole sweep of German history suggests the acceptance by Germans of a permanently divided country. On the contrary, everything in that history, certainly over the past century and a half, points to an eventual resurgence of the unity movement. By itself, this movement would inevitably create international tensions and would in many ways affect general European conditions. The use of each "Germany" as a pawn in the cold war immeasurably complicates the problem. Even if Germans were amenable to treatment as pawns — which they are not — the human chess game being played by the United States and the

U.S.S.R. in the center of Europe cannot, if it is continued, lead to anything but a disastrous "end game." To the world at large this is a deepening cause of concern. To the Germans, it is a prospect too frightening to allow them, however economically affluent they may become, to have the faith and hope that every people must have to construct a humane and stable society.

Russia

Economic Losses and Gains

Though mauled by the ravages of the war more than any other nation, Russia emerged from it strong and confident. To Stalin this was clear proof of the superiority of the Soviet way of life. Not yet half a century old, Communist Russia had faced the greatest fighting force in modern times, had absorbed its most vicious thrusts, and had then gone on to overrun and finally destroy its once seemingly invincible legions. As Stalin saw it, the Red Army had won because it was socialist; but behind that army and sustaining it were a socialist economy and a socialist body politic. One does not have to accept Stalin's analysis of victory to acknowledge the stupendous efforts and achievements of the Russian people in that great struggle. Nor is it possible to deny the almost miraculous economic recovery affected after the war. For some three years the Ukraine and parts of other regions of Russia had been laid waste by the violence of war. Over twenty millions of its people had been killed. Great factories and power plants had been destroyed, and much of its agricultural productivity impaired. Losses in livestock, for example, were so great that, in this sector of the economy, Russia was set back a generation. Soviet officials have estimated that during the war some 70,000 villages, 98,000 collective farms, 40,000 miles of railroad track, 32,000 factories, and nearly 3,000 tractor stations were destroyed.

By 1948, under the fourth Five Year Plan, recovery was well under way. By then the 1940 level of industrial output had already been exceeded by 14 per cent. By 1953 the production of electrical power had increased by 200 per cent, oil by 70 per cent, and iron, steel, and coal by nearly 100 per cent. New virgin lands in Siberia were brought under cultivation, and many new power and industrial plants were constructed in areas east of the Ural mountains. In the 1960s especial attention was paid to the development of the chemical industry which, in Khrushchev's words, "was a mint from which gold flows." At the Twenty-Second Party Congress (1961), Khrushchev called for more than a 500 per cent increase in industrial production by 1980. It is, of course, easy to call for progress; it is also true that in many instances Soviet goals, announced with much gusto, have subsequently been quietly abandoned or put aside. Nevertheless, the economic achievements of the Soviet Union in the postwar years have been, measured by any reasonable criteria, very real and truly remarkable.

The Plight of Agriculture— and of Soviet Man

It would be a mistake, however, to conclude that the Soviets had created overnight a material heaven. For one thing, agriculture, which has always been the weakest sector of the Soviet economy, presented serious problems. During the war many farmers had taken over land and equipment for their private use. Party officials were hard put after the war to regain control over the peasants and redirect their efforts along lines required by the fourth Five Year Plan. Even after this had been achieved—at the cost, not surprisingly, of individual productivity—things did not go well. As always, the greater part of the State budget was allocated to the industrial sector, which meant that equipment needs of the *kolkhozes,* such as tractors and plows, were neglected. Six years after the war, officials publicly admitted that agricultural production did not meet "the demands of the toilers," an admission that can only be characterized as a gross understatement. Nor did the record much improve over the next ten years. In 1961 the government admitted that grain production had missed the planned output by twenty million tons, that the country was suffering from serious shortages of meat and milk, that, indeed, the agricultural situation in general was in an unhealthy condition.

Moreover, many of the gains were made at the expense of elemental human dignity and freedom. To populate the new farms in the east, for example, the State relied heavily on the Political Police.

The labor involved [in one large project] was convict labor, rounded up by the Political Police and transported by them across the tundra. Technically these prisoners were serving sentences of two to seven years under Article 58 of the criminal code, but if they survived and were given their discharge, they were apt to be retained compulsively as "free civilian settlers." How many convict laborers have died in [the] Varkurta [project] there is no means of knowing with any accuracy. A Polish engineer . . . who escaped in 1947, estimated that a million had died there by the end of 1946.[1]

Although much of Russia's economic recovery and progress after the war had no such stigma attached to it, much of it did and, as part of the historic record, should be noted.

Conquest of Space

Even more spectacular than the upgrading of her industrial production were Russia's achievements in science and technology, particularly in the exploration of space. Hard as it may be for Americans — long accustomed to thinking of themselves as the world's most advanced technicians —

1. J. Hampden Jackson, *The World in the Postwar Decade,* Houghton Mifflin Company, Boston, 1956, pp. 208–209.

to accept with any degree of grace, it is nevertheless true that the Soviet Union inaugurated the cosmic age. In 1957 an artificial satellite was successfully put in orbit around the earth; the same year another satellite was sent up, this time carrying a dog. In 1959 a space rocket was fired at the moon and made a direct hit; another rocket, equipped with photographic devices, circled the moon and took pictures of the side that is turned away from the earth. In 1960 a heavy spaceship carrying two dogs was launched and successfully recovered. The next year a 13,000-pound spaceship carried aloft an interplanetary station and discharged it in the direction of Venus. In April of 1961, Yuri Gagarin became the first man to orbit the earth; the same year another manned ship orbited the earth seventeen times. In 1962 and 1963, two "companion ships" were sent up — on one occasion with two men, on the other with a man and a woman. In 1964 the three-man *Voskhod* made sixteen trips around the earth. During this period the Russians also launched a number of satellites to gather various kinds of scientific data and to test the possibility of placing "stations" at various levels in preparation for the grand expedition — the landing of a man on the moon. They were also successful in constructing long-range missiles capable of carrying nuclear warheads.

Expansion in Europe

Not all of Russia's postwar energies were spent in developing her economy and exploring outer space. Equally significant was the extension of Communist control in Eastern Europe. Already before the collapse of the Nazi regime, Russian troops either had occupied or had placed troops and political advisers in Eastern Germany, the Baltic States, Poland, and much of the Balkans. Originally the Soviet Union agreed — on paper — to work with the Western powers toward early free and open elections in the liberated countries. Actually, Stalin and his colleagues did all they could do to prevent them; and by 1950 had largely succeeded. Throughout the 1950s and 1960s, efforts were made to give a semblance of validity to the Russian claim that the governments of the new "Peoples' Democracies" were operating on a mandate from their own citizens—Russian troops were removed and Russian political advisers were sent home. But no one was fooled. Whoever came and went in the presidencies and premierships of the satellite states, each one of them responded quickly and loyally when the Big Slav Brother in Moscow spoke.

There was one exception. For about a year and a half after the war, Yugoslavia under the exceedingly able leadership of Marshal Tito (whose real name was Josip Broz) maintained close ties with the Soviet Union. Tito also concluded a number of economic and political agreements with Poland, Czechoslovakia, Albania, Hungary, and Bulgaria. As one of the founding members of the Cominform, Yugoslavia could reasonably be expected to follow the Moscow line. It did not. By late 1947, Tito had given unmistakable signs of managing the country as he thought its best interests demanded. By 1950 the break was complete and for several years thereafter Yugoslavia and the U.S.S.R. went their separate Communist ways. The subsequent "de-Stalinization" of Russia gave the Kremlin's new rulers an opportunity to restudy the situation. Under Khrushchev, cordial relations were reestablished. Yugoslavia rejoined the Cominform, exchanged diplomatic representatives with Russia and her satellites, and, more often than not, stood with them in the recurring confrontations between the East and the West. Still, she did not give up her right to formulate policy independently and according to her own interpretation of Marxist doctrines, even when this implied and sometimes involved a degree of collaboration with the West. In short, after 1947 the Communist world became two worlds (and after China's break with Russia in the early 1960s, three worlds).

The expansion of Soviet control into almost all of Eastern Europe naturally brought heavy criticism from capitalist governments and peoples. What Communists had called imperialist exploitation when capitalist countries overran African and Asian societies, now seemed to Communists a very proper form of good-neighbor relations, an almost sacrificial effort to effect their "liberation." In capitalist eyes this was sheer hypocrisy which, unless stopped, would lead to the brutal Sovietization of much of the world. There is clearly substantial truth in this charge. Nevertheless, it is not the whole truth. After World War I the Western powers, as we have seen, exerted strong, although short-lived, efforts to overthrow the new regime in Russia. When these failed, the Allies contrived to construct a "cordon sanitaire" around Russia, to isolate it from the community of nations and to weaken its internal position in whatever way they could. Soviet rulers did not forget those years. They were determined that this time the Baltic and Balkan states would not again be used as staging grounds for an eventual assault against their socialist island. Moreover, it should be remembered that some of the Eastern European leaders and regimes, strongly supported by Britain and the United States in the early years after World War II, were reactionary remnants of a past era, which were by no means welcomed by their own people. Our assessment of the nature and meaning of the extension of Russian control in Eastern Europe, therefore, should bring into focus both Western and Soviet images of what Eastern Europe's history was and what its future should be.

"De-Stalinization"

The fourth outstanding event in the life of postwar Russia was its "de-Stalinization." The term can easily be misunderstood. It can be, and unfortunately occasionally has been, construed to mean a consequential deviation from the Marxist-Leninist complex of doctrines that had been administered and developed by Stalin for over a quarter of a century. This is almost completely untrue. Certainly, there has been substitution of one path for another in the post-Stalin era. Soviet leaders have also candidly admitted that the road to socialism may not always be the same for different states. However, the first modification is nothing new in Soviet history. Lenin himself publicly confessed that Bolshevik leaders would have to test out this path and that from time to time to see if it was leading in the direction in which they wanted to go, and this has repeatedly been done. The second "new admission" is truly new, but it is not important from the standpoint of basic Communist goals and basic Communist attitudes. Whether Russian, Yugoslavian, or Chinese, whether dated 1917 or 1967, these goals remain unchanged: the overthrow of capitalist rule; the nationalization of land and industry; the dictatorship of the proletariat (under a "temporary" authoritarian vanguard); the creation of classless society; the final withering away of the state.

More accurately, de-Stalinization signified the following: the replacement of one-man rule with a more truly collective leadership; deemphasis of the power of the police; some relaxation of governmental controls in the creative arts; more reasonable accommodation of the demands of non-Russian Communist regimes; and reforms in education, jurisprudence, and the sciences.

Procedural changes began almost immediately after the death of Stalin in 1953. For about two years Soviet affairs were administered by three men — Malenkov (Stalin's young protégé); Molotov, an "Old Bolshevik" and an expert in foreign affairs; and Khrushchev, newly made head of the Party Secretariat. One of the first signs of the new approach was the arrest and execution of L. Beria, Minister of Internal Affairs. Whether or not he was, as charged, engaged in a plot to gain control of the government and the Party, his execution marked a turning point in the power of the secret police and of the many agencies of the security apparatus. Such democratic safeguards as those of the American Bill of Rights certainly were not brought into use, but terror as an instrument of government was curtailed.

Another sign of the new times was the nonviolent removal of Malenkov as premier in 1955. It is not possible to accept Malenkov's own publicly announced reasons for his resignation — "nonexperience in Ministerial affairs," his "guilt and responsibility for the unsatisfactory state of affairs which has arisen in agriculture," and his admission that his emphasis on the production of consumer goods had been wrong. The important point is that he was dropped from power but not executed or even arrested; as a matter of fact, he retained high posts for several years, and remains today an unmolested citizen not without some influence.

The most dramatic wrench with the past was Khrushchev's "secret" blast against Stalin at the Twentieth Party Congress in February of 1956. In a detailed indictment that stunned his listeners, Khrushchev charged Stalin with a series of crimes ranging from fostering the "cult of personality" to the murder of hundreds of Bolshevik stalwarts. His leadership during the war was denounced as having been marked by hysteria, incompetence, and, in the early stages, defeatism. "After the first severe disaster and defeats at the front, Stalin thought that this was the end. In one of his speeches in those days he said: 'All that which Lenin created we have lost forever.'" Throughout the speech, Khrushchev took care to underscore Stalin's positive contributions to the building of a socialist state, especially during the trying times of the NEP and the first Five Year Plan. These contributions,

Alexei Kosygin and Leonid Brezhnev, who took over the positions vacated by Nikita Khrushchev, clasp hands during an appearance at Moscow's Sports Palace. This picture was taken about four years before they assumed office, Kosygin as Premier, Brezhnev as Secretary-General of the Communist party (1964).

he insisted, should never be forgotten. Nor did he bring into question Stalin's complete devotion to the basic aims of the Party. But, the charge ran, sometime after 1934 the temptations of pure power and self-aggrandizement increasingly affected his behavior until, by the time of his death, he had become a demented tyrant. News of this long polemic and some of its more macabre details were allowed to leak out to prepare the people, as Khrushchev thought of it, for Russia's return to true Marxism-Leninism. The term "collective leadership" was made a shibboleth. Censorship, even though by no means abandoned, was sufficiently toned down to permit writers and composers a measure of freedom not enjoyed since Lenin's time (although even then, it should be noted, truly free expression was not permitted).

The "Thaw"

In short, a politico-cultural "thaw" set in, both making and marking a new style of Soviet life. Many Western critics have made light of the "new departure." They rightly point out that the creative artist is still more a servant of the state than of the muses that move him. When Boris Pasternak was awarded the Nobel Prize in literature, for example, the Party refused to allow him to accept it, arguing that his work, especially his novel *Doctor Zhivago,* was unfairly critical of Soviet life. Uprisings in East Berlin and other East German cities in 1953 were savagely suppressed. Hungarian revolutionists who tried in 1956 to set up a government free from Soviet interference were mercilessly slaughtered. Before Khrushchev had been in power more than a year or two, highly laudatory articles in the press and other periodicals began to appear, reminiscent of the Byzantine-like worship of Stalin. Nevertheless, the "thaw" was real. Poems and novels limn facets of Russian life that are probingly critical despite their subtle phrasing. Most of the satellite states, particularly Poland, have political and cultural elbowroom that they did not have while Stalin lived. Although it often works in collaboration with the Soviet Union, Yugoslavia remains a sovereign power. And, as we have noted earlier, political opponents, although they are still often dealt with harshly, may leave office without necessarily leaving life. Indeed, Khrushchev himself suffered both expulsion from power and rather severe denunciation in 1964 when the Party apparatus installed a new premier, Alexi Kosygin, and a new Party head, Leonid Brezhnev. It is significant that he continued to live in peace and with his family, the same as the leaders whom he himself had from time to time peremptorily dismissed and publicly castigated. It is impossible, of course, to predict what new forms and features Soviet life will assume in the future. Especially is this important to note in view of the return to Stalinist terrorism and naked aggression in the Soviet occupation of Czechoslovakia in the late summer of 1968. Even so, the "thaw" trends seem hardly reversible.

The United States

The main events of American life after the war were industrial expansion accompanied by a general raising of the standard of living, continuing and contentious concern over civil rights, and the emergence of the nation as a consequential arbiter of world affairs.

Economic Affluence

Elaborate reconversion plans, carefully worked out before the end of the war, saved the country from the economic irregularities that followed World War I. As controls were removed, both wages and prices rose substantially, especially prices. However, the inflationary trend was not so marked as had been feared, except in a few areas of the economy such as rentals and meat produce. Nor did another Great Depression prostrate the country, as it had in the 1930s. Returning veterans found jobs, or opportunities to continue their education. In the first five years after the war national production, national income, and consumer income increased by 35 per cent, 30 per cent, and nearly 40 per cent, respectively. After 1950 the indices of all these categories rose even more spectacularly. By the 1960s the trend had continued so markedly that it was commonplace to think of American society as the most affluent of any that the world had ever known.

On the other hand, it should be noted that some critics found both the overall situation and its impact on the national character anything but reassuring. From the end of the Korean War in 1953 to the beginning of large-scale American intervention in Vietnam in 1961 and 1962, the country had suffered three recessions serious enough to give concern to both the government and the general public. Even apart from these periods, the *rate* of America's economic growth did not keep up with, let alone surpass, that of many European and Asian countries. In addition, about 4 or 5 per cent of the population persistently remained unemployed, and nothing that either the government or private industry could do seemed effective. Also, some thought that they saw in the national character a highly developed tendency to measure all meaning of life in materialistic terms. Admittedly man has always craved material comforts and material power. These critics argued, however, that the periods of true human "ascent" have been those when man, however lamentable his failure to put them into practice, held faith in spiritual postulates that subsumed his other activities. They saw contemporary American society headed, therefore, toward the kind of inner crackup which, as they read history, had ultimately destroyed all the great civilizations of the past.

Others pointed to disconcerting conditions beneath the admittedly glittering surface. Most of America's Negroes—over 10 per cent of the country's total population—lived in rural or urban slums. Other segments of the population, such as the white residents of "Appalachia" and of expansive areas in the rural South, lived from birth to death without adequate food, houses, and clothes, to say nothing of educational opportunities. Even many of the so-called white-collar class, wherever they lived, maintained a seemingly comfortable existence only by the grace of the nation's system of installment buying, supplemented by easy access to the funds of numerous loan companies—in short, by living in continuous, virtually unredeemable debt. Finally, some believed that the economic system itself was living on borrowed time. They pointed out that more than one half of the national budget (well over fifty billion dollars) was devoted to war expenditures of one kind or another. If such expenditures were withdrawn—that is, if the country really lived in the peace that it said it believed in and was working for—the economy would collapse overnight. Whether these judgments of the state of

McCARTHY'S RULES OF ORDER

A St. Louis Post Dispatch *cartoon shows McCarthy running the whole show at the hearings which, before they were over, spelled the end of the Senator's career as America's great Communist witch-hunter.*

postwar American economic conditions are wholly or partly valid, the historian, of course, cannot say. However, the serious student of history can hardly be excused from including them in his calculations as he assesses the nature of contemporary American society.

Ordeals Domestic and Foreign: McCarthyism

Another significant development in America's postwar years was the fierce contest between forces that sought to restrict civil rights and the forces that would enlarge them. As used here, the term "civil rights" implies the option of the individual to participate in the general affairs and experiences of the society of which he is a citizen without hindrance, except for the limitations imposed by due process of constitutional law, and without restrictive discrimination because of racial or religious conditions or affinities. American society, as every other society, has never been entirely free from attacks on and infringements of such rights. Some periods of its history have been more marked by them than others; the years following World War II was such a period.

One example of the struggle for dignified "humanhood" was the complex of events that made up the so-called McCarthy era (c. 1950–1955). The outbreak of the Korean War in 1950 stimulated patriotic suspicions, already sensitized by earlier cold war events. The resulting tensions allowed ambitious and unscrupulous persons, both in and out of the government, to play on American fears and confusions in such a way that for a time a condition not far from true hysteria gripped the country. Republican Senator Joseph R. McCarthy, of Wisconsin, became almost overnight the anti-Communist voice of America. Before he died seven years later, he had cowed many of the leaders of his own party, captured the rapt attention of millions of Americans, branded certain national leaders (such as Secretary of State George Marshall) as Communist dupes, attacked prominent figures in the Department of the Army, and caused the nation to fret with festering fears and hatreds that were the stronger because they were beyond reasonable analysis. In this atmosphere of hate and suspicion, legislative measures were enacted at both national and state levels which, in effect, made portions of the Bills of Rights of both federal and state constitutions empty phrases, devoid of positive legal life. Many government officials were dismissed from their posts on the strength of hearsay evidence or because of "guilt by association." Others in private business and in the professions were demoted, dismissed, or viciously harassed. In 1954, McCarthy scathingly denounced an army general for alleged "softness on Communism." The aftermath was a direct confrontation between McCarthy and his aids and the Secretary of the Army and his colleagues. For over a month the televised hearings kept Americans close to their sets. In the end the fantastic and brutal tactics of McCarthy alienated most of the nation and caused the Senate officially to condemn him. Thereafter the country took a more humane, sophisticated attitude toward those accused of subversion by self-serving demagogues, and a more critical attitude toward the accusers. But the price of this "second-look wisdom" had come high.

The Black-White Problem

No less agonizing was another ordeal whose roots lie deep in American history and whose ramifications still blight the life of almost every section of the country. Its essence is the struggle of American Negroes to break the bonds of cultural servitude and degradation fastened on them by the white majority of this country after the Civil War. World War I and its aftermath brought a variety of economic opportunities to the colored population. The war, fought in the name of democracy, also stimulated Negro aspirations for political equality and at the same time weakened ideological defenses against it constructed by the white managers of American society. The revival of Klan activities after the war for a time muted the Negro cry for freedom. So did the cultivated inertia of many white Americans who, although not willing to parade in white sheets and to burn crosses, preferred to look the other way while others did. Nevertheless, white complacency toward and Negro resignation to the Jim Crow way of life were substantially weakened.

The successful revolt of colonial peoples in Asia and in Africa after World War II also spurred Negroes in America to stake out bolder claims. When a black man from a country born only yesterday could stand in the highest council of the nations and command the respectful attention of his white colleagues, American Negroes, who had had cultural advantages for centuries before the advent of the new African states, could not fail to be impressed and to be stimulated to improve their own lot.*

Another landmark in the struggle was the Supreme Court's decision of 1954, which held that the country's public educational facilities must serve colored and white alike. This reversal of an earlier opinion that had supported the "separate but equal" doctrine, enraged the South and opened an era of increasingly violent racial strife. Various artifices were used by Southern lawmakers to circumvent the ruling, such as the nominal transformation of public schools into private schools. In practice almost all Southern schools in one way or another continued to discriminate between the races and to maintain the *status quo.* In one effort to enforce the decision, President Eisenhower sent troops to Little Rock, Arkansas, to protect the handful of colored children who had enrolled in one of the city's "white" schools. Under these circumstances, the colored students were allowed to attend classes, but the tension and harassments to which they were subjected naturally precluded meaningful learning.

In the early 1960s several civil rights organizations, such as the Student Nonviolent Coordinating Committee (S.N.C.C.) and the Congress of Racial Equality (CORE), "invaded" the South in a valiant attempt to break the racial barrier and open the way to integration and the building of a more humane social structure. Before these efforts Southern Negroes themselves had already initiated action designed to give them their rightful place in "the land of the free." This action mostly took the form of boycotting enterprises such as city bus lines which drew the color line, and staging "sit-ins" in all-white restaurants. The sustained efforts of both native

* However, local developments probably counted for more in the developing civil rights struggles than African events.

WHERE THE GRAPES OF WRATH ARE STORED

This cartoon appeared at the time that a new and vigorous race stuggle took shape in the early 1960s.

Negroes and "foreign" whites had the same kind of impact on the social, more general, level as the decision of the Supreme Court had had on education. In 1964 Congress passed a civil rights act which made discrimination by reason of race illegal in all public institutions, such as restaurants, hotels, motels, and theaters. Although sustained by the Supreme Court in a test case and made at least superficially effective in a number of Southern cities, the act did not achieve its main objectives. The same was true of a second civil rights law passed in 1965, which empowered federal officials to supervise the registration of voters in counties where the majority of eligible voters were not registered. It is true that Negro registration picked up noticeably and that more Negroes exercised their franchise. However, pressures of many kinds were used by the whites to keep down both Negro registration and voting. These were so effective that even after 1965 Negroes still did not influence election results to a degree proportionate to their numbers. Because "white promises" and "white laws" seemed, at least to many reform-minded citizens, to fade out in practice, a new mood took over in some of the foremost civil rights organizations. S.N.C.C., for example, in 1965 repudiated its original nonviolent approach and, together with some leaders of CORE, began to speak of "Black Power" as the only path that could lead to the realization of a meaningful life for the Negro. Admittedly an ambiguous term, it nevertheless suggested a turn toward violence in keeping with the views of such very radical Negro organizations as the Black Muslims, which frankly worked for the time when the Negroes could make "Whitey taste a little of his own hell," as one of their leaders put it.

Despite disappointments, setbacks, and sporadic violence, however, the movement for equality between the races is likely to grow in scope and effectiveness. Three hundred years of white domination have

When integrationists tried to use this segregated beach (1964), they were attacked by white youths.

ingrained attitudes and practices that cannot be changed in a generation. But a turning point in race relations was reached in the postwar years, which promises a more humane way of life for both Black and White America.

Great-Power Problems

Besides wrestling with the task of reconciling its split economic and racial selves, the United States endeavored to identify and cope with the responsibilities and prerogatives that devolved upon it as an emergent Great Power. Because it was the possessor of such vast economic and military strength, the United States was naturally regarded as the main support of the Western states, great and small, as they set about the onerous task of rebuilding their war-ravaged lives. It soon became apparent that without massive aid they would certainly founder, bringing ruin not only to the peoples of Europe but eventually also to the American econ-

More than a year after passage of what seemed to be an effective Civil Rights law (1965), Negroes were still living much the same kind of restricted lives they were before the bill was made law. This picture shows a CORE leader addressing a group of demonstrators who are picketing the main post office in Philadelphia against what they called its discriminatory hiring practices and working conditions.

omy whose well-being ultimately depended on a reasonably healthy world market. Moreover, languishing economies meant unemployed and restive populations, amenable to the allurements of Communist propaganda.

In these circumstances the United States embarked upon a colossal rescue mission. Billions of dollars, through loans and grants, were poured into those European countries which most needed help. As outlined by Secretary of State George Marshall, such aid was to be used not only to prime Europe's industrial pump, but to create "political and social conditions in which free institutions can exist." Russia and her satellites refused all assistance on the grounds that the Plan was an elaborate device designed to bring Europe under American domination. Whether intended or not, the Plan, and later assistance that was offered after the Plan was terminated in 1950, did give the United States a substantial, often decisive, influence in determining both the policies and practices of most West European governments.*

Meanwhile the stockpiling of atomic bombs and the construction of the far more potent hydrogen bomb, together with the lavish production of long- and medium-range ballistic missiles, made the United States a military power surpassed by none and rivaled only by the Soviet Union. Increasingly the country came to base its faith in its own security and that of the Western World on this power, thus initiating a trend away from the nation's long-hallowed Jeffersonian tradition of the complete subservience of military to civilian authority.

By the mid-1960s, America seemed to be less the reluctant world leader that it had appeared to be in the 1940s and more the world's self-appointed policeman. Accompanying this seeming change was a reluc-

tance to accept the goals of disarmament and peace by world law as items of practical and negotiable policy. Leaders in all sectors of society continued, of course, to proclaim the worthwhileness and desirability of such goals. But the heady wine of newly sensed power and the growing feeling that economic prosperity depended on flourishing war industries made it difficult to translate these idealistically desirable goals into acceptable reality.

On the other hand, there were signs in the 1960s that America was troubled by its military might and the international reputation that it was acquiring. Peace organizations multiplied, although none developed a broadly popular base. Growing numbers of United States senators and representatives went on public record against the power and practices of such governmental agencies as the C.I.A. and the House Un-American Activities Committee. Public opinion polls showed a marked decrease in popular support for the long-term projects of the "Hawks," as the proponents of the "get tougher with Russia" policy were called. It is impossible to predict what the future character of the American mind and spirit will be, or to foretell what use the nation will make of its ample resources and its growing power. But it is hard to believe that the country's long democratic tradition, its established sense of fair play, and its often tested devotion to the imperatives of the good society (whether Great or not) will vanish amid the perplexities and confusions of a world in flux.

Latin America

Postwar conditions in the twenty-one Latin American nations were characterized by contradictions, ambiguities, and uncertainties. In most of these states the standard of living rose over that of the prewar years, particularly in Argentina, Chile, Brazil, and Uruguay. But nowhere was the increase shared equitably. New industries and increased trade brought spectacular affluence

---

* Although the Truman Doctrine was the natural forerunner of the Marshall Plan, it has been thought best to deal with it in a later section.

to the business elite while heightening the contrast between how they and the illiterate working masses lived. Although most Latin American governments had declared war against the fascist powers, all but a few, such as Chile, Colombia, and Uruguay, were themselves fascist in practice, whatever their democratic professions.

Not surprisingly, the exigencies of the cold war aggravated these conditions. In 1948 all of the American nations joined together in the Organization of the American States (O.A.S.). Although concerned basically with the settlement of inter-American quarrels and problems, the organization lent itself, by reason of the weight of the United States in it, to the checking of Communist moves in world affairs. To effect this, the United States government often favored conservative regimes even when they were corrupt, undemocratic, or both, which more often than not they were. This steadily alienated the Latin American masses from their big "neighbor" to the north and at the same time fomented revolutionary discontent at home. An example of how these forces interacted with one another is the Guatemala crisis of 1954.

In that year the Inter-American Conference of the Organization of the American States met to discuss common problems. The United States was much disturbed by the reform program of the Communist-infiltrated government of Guatemala which had shortly before expropriated lands owned by the American United Fruit Company. To the peasants of Guatemala, and for that matter to the masses in other Latin American countries, this move had been most welcome, signaling the eagerly awaited redistribution of land. To Washington it meant the creation in Latin America of a "beachhead of international Communism." To wipe out this "beachhead," the United States delegation pressured the O.A.S. to approve a resolution holding that "domination or control of the political institutions of any American State by the international Communist movement would constitute a threat to the sovereignty and political independence of the American States, endangering the peace of America." Shortly thereafter an American-financed and trained band of insurrectionists overthrew the Guatemalan government and returned the country to the conditions that had existed before the liberal government had come to power. In the early 1960s a similar coup was executed in Brazil, with strong United States approval, if not direct support. Naturally, such actions by the United States increased the already strong anti-American feelings throughout Latin America and made Communist propaganda even more attractive.

In the 1960s no substantial progress had been made in dealing with any of Latin America's persistent and pressing problems. Landlords and the merchant elite continued to manipulate economic controls almost exclusively to their own advantage. Little progress had been made in reducing mass poverty and illiteracy. Most of the governments were dominated by militarists, often supported directly or indirectly by the Church. Neither the United States nor the Soviet Union showed any tendency to alter their practice of using these nations as pawns in the cold war.

THE DECOLONIZATION OF ASIA AND AFRICA

Asia

The Revolt Against the West

In an earlier chapter we traced the outlines of imperialist ventures in Asia and Africa. By the early 1900s it must have seemed to the empire builders that they were riding the crest of an irreversible tide of world dominion. Scarcely half a century later the white man, perhaps not quite understanding how it had happened, found himself relieved of his burden as colonial peoples everywhere had either reversed or were in the process of reversing the flow of the once strong imperialist tide.

Japan's quick and humiliating defeat of Allied forces in the early years of World War II spurred the revolt. For almost three hundred years the power of the white man over his colored brothers had been successfully, often arrogantly, exploited. Here and there in local actions, as in the Russo-Japanese war of 1904 to 1905, Western states had suffered setbacks, but they were on a small scale. The events at Pearl Harbor and Singapore and the vast Japanese conquest in Southeast Asia completely destroyed the image of white invincibility. Thereafter the colored peoples of the world nursed long-deferred hopes—the dissolution of the sahib-servant syndrome and the setting up of independent communities. The achievement of these aims was expedited by the shaken economies and the disturbed social patterns (and in the British experience at least, guilty consciences) produced by six years of world war and long-sustained exploitation. Another dissolving force was a stratagem practiced by the Japanese when their own defeat appeared imminent. To consolidate their early conquests they had used local leaders as nominal heads of state wherever possible.

The device was transparent and, of course, fooled no one. However, the substitution of eastern masters for western ones, although leaving the ruled far from satisfied, produced a kind of racial psychic gain. More important, as the Japanese pulled back before the advancing American and British forces, they gave full independence to the peoples which they could no longer dominate. Thus, when "liberators" arrived, they were more often than not confronted by nationalist governments savoring the turbulent delights of newly gained independence.*

Indonesia

This was the situation that faced Allied forces entering Indonesia in late 1945. At first the British, who acted as caretakers until Dutch officials could be sent in, gave *de facto* recognition to Sukarno's nationalist republican regime. Their hope was that Dutch and Indonesian leaders could work out a compromise acceptable to both peoples. It was a vain hope. The Dutch failed to understand the new forces at work, and attempted to substitute endless debate for a decisive confrontation of the problem. The Indonesians, supported by world opinion, insisted on self-determination. Lacking the resources to prevent it, the Dutch finally agreed (December 1949) to the establishment of a completely independent Indonesian Republic. For many years thereafter the new nation and its government suffered the buffeting of political strife as militarists fought Communists and both, occasionally (and overtly), fought Sukarno and his bureaucratic apparatus.† Neither economic

---

* For this and the following references to emergent Asian states, see the map on the facing page.
† In 1967 Sukarno was ousted by local anti-Communist forces.

well-being nor political democracy developed to the degree or at the pace idealistic reformers had hoped for. But the white master was gone; whatever harassments came from their many fumblings, the Indonesians at long last enjoyed at least the satisfaction of making their own mistakes.

ASIA, 1967

Countries which gained independence after WW II

Map by J. Donovan

Mahatma Gandhi salutes an audience after an address in which he called for Indian independence and unity. This photograph was taken about a year before India gained her independence and about two years before the Mahatma was assassinated by a Hindu fanatic.

India

Earlier we noted the formation in India of the Congress party. Long before World War II, it had come to demand dominion status for India. When Britain asked for Indian cooperation in the war and promised home rule after the end of the war, Indian leaders proved stubborn. They pointed out that Britain had made a similar promise during World War I. They argued that they should not be asked to fight for a freedom that they themselves did not enjoy. Gandhi, Nehru, and other leaders were finally jailed. But when the war ended, their pronouncements bespoke the attitude of the Indian masses so clearly and faithfully that Britain could not ignore them unless she was prepared to keep an endless armed watch over all the peoples of the subcontinent. This was out of the question, because Britain needed all of

her talents and wealth to restore her own house to some kind of order and comfort. So she began the process of "decolonization."

It was not easy. For years she had used many local princes as willing puppets; they did not welcome the creation of a new state in which they would enjoy neither power nor special privileges. In addition to the problem of the pampered rajahs, there was also the religious rivalry of Hindus and Moslems. Gandhi and most of the leaders of the Congress party wanted a united land with guarantees of religious toleration. Most Moslem leaders insisted on a country of their own. British statesmen lamented these difficulties and divisions but, by 1948, were determined to leave their solution to the Indians themselves. The independence act of that year recognized a free Hindu India and a free Moslem Pakistan. From then on only the bonds of Commonwealth membership bound the three states together, and these of course were voluntary.

Burma and the Malay States

In 1943 the Japanese had given paper-independence to Burma. When the Japanese withdrew two years later, the returning British found a strongly established Burmese government in operation. The British decision to liquidate its imperial position in India made it easy to open negotiations with Aung San, the determined young leader of Burma's national front party. In late 1947 a popularly elected constituent assembly proclaimed Burma an independent republic; in January of 1948 all British controls were removed. Another new Asian nation was born.

Liquidation of British control in the Malay states did not proceed so smoothly. For one thing, Britain wanted to keep Singapore as a naval and trading base. For another, the peoples of this region were of three distinctly different ethnic strains—Chinese, Indians, and Polynesians. Moreover, Communist guerrillas kept up a steady assault against both foreign and local ruling groups. In 1957 Britain ended her protectorate of Malaysia in return for the right to negotiate a separate agreement with the island colony of Singapore (which was concluded the following year). The struggle against the Communists gave the conglomerate peoples of the Malay states a common purpose, thus serving as a kind of substitute for cultural unity.

Indochina, the Philippines, and China

In the following section we shall note the withdrawal of French forces from Vietnam in 1954. The year before, Cambodia and Laos had achieved full independence. France's ultimate withdrawal from Vietnam thus marked both the end of French imperialism in Asia and the heightened development of the struggle of the peoples of Southeast Asia for political, social, and spiritual independence.

Of all the imperialist powers, the United States acted the most promptly in recognizing the new era in Asia. Her dominance of the Philippines, dating from the turn of the century, had never won the whole-hearted, enthusiastic support of her people. The new trend, therefore, presented no such problems for them as it had for the French. With obvious reference to its historic significance, Congress chose July 4, 1946 as the day on which to give assent to legislation granting full independence to its former colony. In return, the new Philippine government consented to the establishment of several United States bases in the islands. Intermittent Communist guerrilla attacks gave clear indication that not all Filipinoes were satisfied with the new government, but in the main the transition from colony to independent nation was effected with much less turmoil than that which plagued so many Asian peoples.

Developments in China, more than in any other Asian country, most clearly epitomized the interrelatedness of the forces opposing Western colonialism and the capitalist system which undergirt it.

By the early 1940s Japan had occupied substantial portions of northern and eastern China. With the collapse of Japan the foreign war turned into a civil war as Communist forces, under Mao Tse-tung, fought with Nationalist troops under Chiang Kai-shek for control of the country. For a while (1945–1947) it seemed that the Nationalists would emerge as the victors. They could field more divisions, they received generous United States support, and they controlled most of the great urban centers. But Chiang's government was both unpopular with the masses and indescribably corrupt. From 1947 on, the stubborn assaults of Mao's highly disciplined troops, combined with Communist promises of a new day for China's exploited millions, wore down Nationalist strength. In 1949 Chiang took what troops he could to Formosa (renamed Taiwan) to wait for the Communist experiment to fail and then, with American support, to return to the mainland.

A 1957 photograph of Chinese Communist leader Mao Tse-tung.

Throughout the civil war, Mao had received help from the Soviet Union. After his victory he asked for continued assistance, especially for strategic supplies and trained technicians. For about ten years Chinese agriculture and industry underwent revolutionary development under Russian tutelage, accompanied by astonishing changes in social conditions and general outlook. Warlords became a thing of the past. Except for the Soviet Union, whose help had been requested, no foreign power had a voice in policy making. Dictatorial as Mao's regime was, it afforded more democracy to the awakening masses than they had ever enjoyed. However it appeared to hostile Western eyes, the new regime seemed to the majority of the Chinese people an instrument with which the doors of a more meaningful and abundant life had been opened. In the early 1960s, ideological and political differences dissolved the Chinese-Soviet entente; but by that time the new China was strong enough to stand alone. Its problems were many and serious: periodically food supplies fell below a level to satisfy even minimum requirements; after the break with Russia, capital and technical assistance were hard to come by; "free nations" repeatedly rejected its bid to join the United Nations; prodded by the United States, many nations not only refused to grant recognition to the new regime but insisted on regarding Chiang's Formosa as the "real China." Nevertheless, by the late 1960s the new nation had established itself as the world's third Great Power, and the old days of kowtowing to the West seemed gone forever.

The Near East

The nationalist surge was no less strong in the Near East. Here the revolutionary forces of the war transformed the whole area from a checkerboard on which imperial powers moved pieces almost at will to a mosaic of independent states, which were often fierce rivals of one another but were also fiercely alert against renascent colonialism in any of its forms.

Syria, Lebanon, and Jordan

With the collapse of Germany, France attempted to regain control over Syria and Lebanon. British and French troops had occupied both countries after the surrender of France in 1940 in order to prevent the penetration of the Axis powers. After the war Britain promptly removed her forces. France, however, pointing to the threat of Communist infiltration, argued that her pre-World War II mandate over both countries gave her a legal right to administer their affairs, and claimed that the Catholic population of the region (mostly concentrated in Lebanon) required her protection. Nevertheless, when Syrian and Lebanese nationalists, with the tacit support of Britain and America, staged violent demonstrations, the French government finally withdrew its troops and recognized the independence of both states.

In 1946 Britain proclaimed the independence of Transjordan (which soon renamed itself the Kingdom of Jordan). But there, as in Iraq, British loans, technical assistance, and military aid made practical independence somewhat unreal. In the next two decades, however, the sustained thrust of Jordanese nationalist agitation made the British game there not quite worth the cost; by the 1960s Jordan was substantially free of all external control. In Iraq, Britain attempted to use a sympathetic royal ruling house as the instrument of its control. But, in keeping with the established pattern, patriotic agitators won a sufficiently strong following to overthrow the Western-tainted dynasty and establish (1958) a truly independent state.

The New Israel and the New Egypt

During and after the war, hundreds of thousands of Jews migrated to Palestine where they and their native coreligionists demanded the immediate creation of the long-promised independent Jewish state. Prompted by the same forces that caused her to withdraw from Greece, Britain announced in May of 1948 that she was taking her troops and administrators out of Palestine. What happened thereafter would be the responsibility of the Jews and Arabs themselves. The Jews immediately proclaimed the State of Israel under the presidency of Chaim Weizmann. Almost its first act was to call up troops to defend itself against Arab attacks. For over a year bitter fighting, broken by temporary truces, bathed the Holy Land in blood. By the summer of 1949, the superior equipment and resources of the Jews, together with crippling dissension among the Arab states, brought an uneasy peace to the region.

Seven years later this peace was broken by a new Israeli-Arab war which, at the prodding of the United States and Russia, the U.N. quickly halted. Again, in 1967, still another war erupted, from which the Israelis emerged completely victorious. Few observers believed that the new "peace" would be much more durable than the old, however.

Although Egypt had been granted official recognition as a sovereign nation in 1922, British controls remained strong. As in Iraq, Britain had kept control with the help of a compliant — and fantastically corrupt — royal house. In 1952 the nationalist surge swept the royal debauchee off the throne, and set up a republican government. Three years later Gamal Abdel Nasser, a powerful leader dedicated not only to Egyptian nationalism but to Arab unity, gave the British the choice of withdrawing the last of their troops from Egypt or fighting to keep them there. The British withdrew. The next year, in a bold action that would have been an exercise in fantasy a score of years before, Nasser took over complete control of the Suez Canal. Britain, joined by France and Israel, made the event a cause for war which was, as just noted above, quickly aborted by the United Nations.

Egypt's victory naturally stimulated Pan-Arabism. In 1958 a new United Arab Republic, made up of Egypt, Syria, and (for a while) Yemen, was created. A revolution in Iraq brought to the fore anti-Western leaders who associated themselves with the new republic, as did the successors of Ibn Saud, Saudia Arabia's founding father. When Jordan and Lebanon seemed, under Egyptian pressure, to be moving in the same direction, Britain and the United States landed troops in Lebanon and announced that they would support any Near Eastern nation threatened by "Communist aggression." This rather ambiguous pronouncement and the action which implemented it were not particularly welcomed either by the peoples of the region or by most of the Western nations. Russia, of course, at once charged both Britain and the United States with imperialist aggression.* Amid recriminations between the capitalist and communist blocs and a rising chorus of disapproval from citizens of the occupying powers, British and American troops were withdrawn. The fiasco might have led to greater cohesion among the Arab states and a widening of the East-West split, had the nationalist force within the Arab states not proved to be so strong. In the four years following the creation of the United Arab Republic, Syria came increasingly to criticize its domination by Nasser. Yemen's local interests steadily separated that little state from loyalty to the U.A.R. Jordan turned toward Saudi Arabia and away from Egypt. Even so, Pan-Arabism remained a strong force in the Near East. Its official instrument, the Pan-Arab League (founded in 1945), served as both a forum of protest

* The American action was planned by the C.I.A., apparently with the interests of American oil companies in mind. If this is true, Soviet Foreign Minister Andrei Gromyko did not altogether miss the mark when he publicly charged that America's greed for oil was the basic force in this operation of the so-called "Eisenhower Doctrine." But the U.S. State Department's fears of Nasser and its desire for military bases were also compelling reasons for the action.

and a rallying center for nearly 300 million Moslems. Whatever differences retarded united action—and they were many and significant—the Arab peoples of the world had made it abundantly clear that Western imperialism was no longer to be borne.

Africa

Libya, Algeria, and Tanzania

The postwar surge of nationalism in the Far and Near East soon spread to Africa. The pace and scope of its development there have produced results so complex, so novel, and so bewilderingly ramifying as to require study quite beyond the aims of this book. Here we can only sketch its main outlines and, in order to give some body to our understanding, sample a few specific developments.

At the end of World War II there were only four independent nations in Africa: South Africa, Ethiopia, Liberia, and Egypt. Within the short span of twenty years, over thirty other independent states emerged (see map opposite). Many specialists in African affairs predict that the few remaining colonies, such as Angola, Mozambique, and South West Africa, will achieve independence within another score of years or less.

The rapid process of decolonization in Africa was carried out in various ways. For example, Libya, which became an independent state in 1951, had its freedom practically thrust upon it. Before the war, as we have already seen, it was an Italian colony. After the war the new Italian Republic showed signs of wanting to regain complete control. Because Italy had been an Axis belligerent, this claim was given little sympathetic attention. More as a move in the cold war, which by then had assumed serious proportions, than as an act of humane justice, the country was made an independent monarchy, with air bases and other accommodations granted to the Western powers, particularly the United States.

Quite different was the course of Algerian independence. For almost a century Algeria had been a French dependency. From time to time small-scale demonstrations and riots, generated by the eloquent pleading and daring of liberation-minded leaders, bespoke nationalistic potentials that lay under the surface of regimented French rule. The collapse of France in World War II gave stimulus to these potentials. By the early 1950s many Frenchmen, including influential members of the government, were ready for negotiations that would ease rising tensions. By this time Algerian leaders, and a majority of their countrymen as well, were insisting on complete independence. Even this might have been considered by the French Cabinet had it felt reasonable assurance that their compatriots in the colony would have accepted such a decision. Tentative proposals made it plain that the settlers would not only refuse the granting of independence but also would not accept any substantial change in the *status quo*. At this point large-scale rebellion broke out. Under the vigorous leadership of the National Liberation Front, Algerians fought with all the resources at their command for the creation of a free, independent Algerian nation. For seven years (1955–1962) terror roamed the land; each side perpetrated atrocities that both would like to forget today. With de Gaulle's return to power in 1958, new efforts were made by the French government to persuade French colonists to either return home or accept Algerian rule. For a time it appeared that civil war would rend France itself. Only when de Gaulle made ready to use the armed forces on a massive scale against the settlers, did they grudgingly yield.

Still another road to independence was taken by Tanzania (formerly called Tanganyika). Long a ward of first the League of Nations and then the United Nations, Tanzania achieved full freedom as an independent state in 1962. Orderly negotiations, rea-

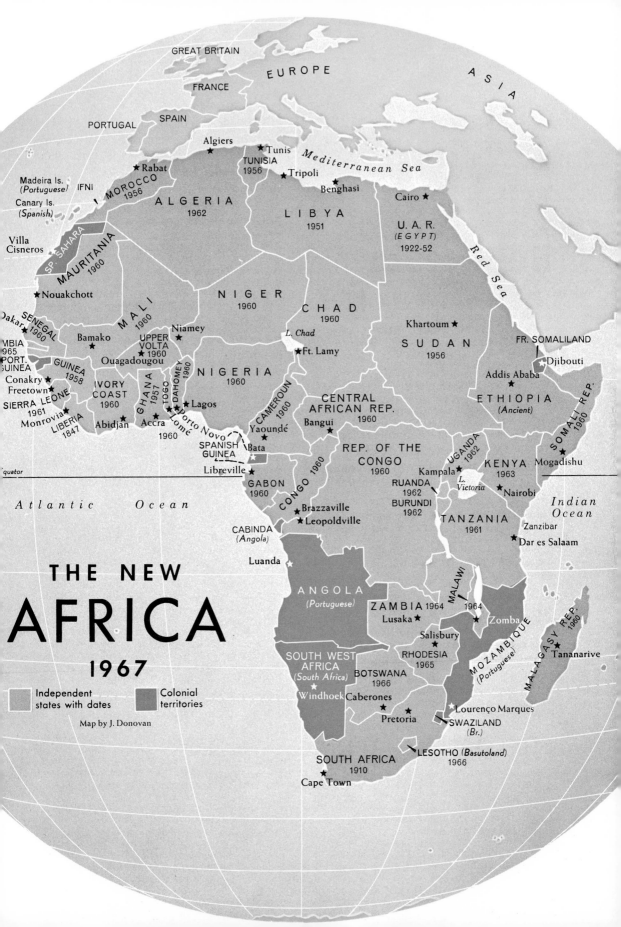

In 1964 a Tanzanian army mutiny led to rioting and looting. President Julius Nyerere, left, speaks at a press conference in his residence at Dar-Es-Salaam. The President, although lamenting the strife, felt that the soldiers had real grievances.

sonable demands, and a mutual recognition of political realities marked the change from colony to nation. Much of the credit for this sophisticated approach to decolonization must go to Julius Nyerere, leader of Tanzania's nationalist party and head of the government. Unlike some African leaders, Nyerere refused to allow excited emotions to affect his judgment of what could be done as against what a long-repressed people would like to see done. For example, he retained large numbers of British civil servants despite the agitation of many of his countrymen to send the white man packing. Without them, he well understood, administrative chaos would follow, intensifying the

growing pains that every new nation must suffer. He even went so far as to severely punish Tanzanian soldiers who mutinied in January 1964, in protest against the retention of British officers in the small Tanzanian army. In return, Britain took care not to allow its citizens who remained in the former colony to subvert the plans and processes of the new government.

The Failure of Nationalism in South Africa

In these three instances of surgent African nationalism, full freedom and independence were achieved. In South Africa, on the contrary, native Africans suffered humiliating defeat. More than two thirds of the population of the Republic of South Africa are Negroes. But all instruments of authority and control are held or dominated by whites. Negroes are denied the right to vote. Their major political parties, such as the African National Congress and the Pan-Africanish Congress, were banned and many of their leaders imprisoned. A detailed and severely enforced program of *apartheid*—segregation—operates at every level of society.

Repeatedly the United Nations has tried, always unsuccessfully, to persuade the Nationalist government to grant basic freedoms to the majority black population. Thus, while in almost all other parts of Africa the native peoples have freed themselves from the yoke of colonialism, in South Africa the nationalist surge has been blunted and almost broken.

THE METAMORPHOSIS OF EUROPE

Regional Groupings

In the early postwar years, Western Europe's influence in world affairs declined as the potentials of leadership passed to

the United States and, to a lesser degree, to Russia. By 1947 Great Britain had come to acknowledge openly that she could no longer support Greece in its fight against Soviet aggression, an acknowledgment that heralded the end of Britain's preeminence as aribter of world affairs. France was nearly prostrate from four years of Nazi occupation and internal dissension. Germany was sundered into two parts. Italy was all but bankrupt both economically and politically. In contrast, the Soviet regime was not only master of its own house but also of most of Eastern Europe. The United States, its homeland unravaged by war, had amassed wealth and power of quite immeasurable dimensions. Europe had not only ceased to "expand" but had shrunk to almost its pre-Columbian condition.

Nevertheless, the early prophets of Europe's doom were more wrong than right. Within twenty years after World War II, Western Europe was again enjoying economic prosperity and, in the main, political stability. Most important, it had taken giant steps towards regional integration; in the years following Germany's surrender, a half dozen or so comprehensive supranational institutions were created.*

The Council of Europe and the European Coal and Steel Community

The first such venture was modest enough. In 1948 Belgium, the Netherlands, and Luxembourg agreed to abolish all tariffs against incoming goods originating within the borders of any of them, and to charge common rates on incoming foreign goods. The resulting enlargement of their free-trade areas stimulated economic activity while it lessened political tensions among them. In 1949 Belgium, Denmark, France, Britain, Ireland, Italy, Luxembourg, the Netherlands, Norway, and Sweden formed a loose political association called the Council of Europe, which came to serve as an important clearing house of debate.

---

* The emphasis here is upon "comprehensive." In all, large and small, these organizations ran into many dozens.

In 1951 the six nations constituting "Little Europe"—France, Italy, Belgium, the Netherlands, Luxembourg, and West Germany—set up the European Coal and Steel Community. In essence this organization, which developed out of what is popularly called the Schuman Plan after its founder Robert Schuman, then French Minister of Foreign Affairs, allowed the member states to pool their basic industrial resources under complicated arrangements designed to do away with restrictive competition and encourage mutually profitable trade. Together with the Marshall Plan it brought Western Europe out of its postwar economic doldrums in a remarkably short time.

The outbreak of the Korean War in 1950 prompted the United States to urge the rearmament of West Germany against the possibility of renewed Communist expansion in Europe. Fearful of resurgent German militarism, the Schuman Plan countries debated a French suggestion for the

This Chicago Sun-Times *cartoon shows Europe's "First Family" happily—and surprisingly—united six years after the holocaust of World War II.*

EUROPE, 1967

NORTH AMERICA
Arctic Ocean
Ural Mts.
ASIA
Atlantic Ocean
Caspian Sea
AFRICA
Indian Ocean

Barents Sea

Atlantic

Ocean

FINLAND
Helsinki ★
• Leningrad

NORWAY
★ Oslo
SWEDEN
★ Stockholm

Baltic Sea

★ Moscow

UNION OF SOVIET
SOCIALIST REPUBLICS

North Sea

Dublin ★
UNITED KINGDOM
IRELAND

DENMARK
★ Copenhagen

West Berlin ★ East Berlin
EAST GERMANY
Warsaw ★
POLAND

• Kiev

The Hague ★
London ★
NETHERLANDS
Brussels ★
BELGIUM
Bonn ★
WEST GERMANY
★ Prague
CZECHOSLOVAKIA

English Channel

LUXEMBOURG
Paris ★
FRANCE

LIECHTENSTEIN
Vienna ★
AUSTRIA
HUNGARY
★ Budapest
ROMANIA

Bay of Biscay

Bern ★
SWITZERLAND

Bucharest ★

Black Sea

Belgrade ★
YUGOSLAVIA

Sofia ★
BULGARIA

ITALY

SAN MARINO

Adriatic Sea

ALBANIA
Tirana ★

Istanbul •
Ankara ★
TURKEY

Lisbon ★
PORTUGAL

ANDORRA

MONACO

Corsica (France)

Rome ★

Sardinia (Italy)

GREECE

Aegean Sea

★ Madrid
SPAIN

Balearic Is. (Spain)

Athens ★

• Gibraltar (Br.)

Mediterranean

Sicily

Crete

Malta (Br.)

Sea

Communist countries

"THE SIX"

"THE SEVEN"

0   200   400 mi.

Map by J. Donovan

formation of a Western European army—
the European Defence Community
(E.D.C.). Ironically, the idea caught on
with all members of the Plan except France
itself. After two years of fretful debate the
French Chamber of Deputies, with visions
of goose-stepping conquerors still fresh,
voted against it. Thus Europe's first serious
move to create a truly international army
came to nothing. But its approval by the
other five nations showed how far along the
road to integration many Europeans had
traveled.

"The Six" and Other Regional Groupings

One of the most momentous steps toward
integration was taken in 1958 when the
busy "Six"—Belgium, the Netherlands,
Luxembourg, France, Italy, and West Germany—formed the European Economic
Community (E.E.C.), popularly called the
Common Market or "The Six." Fundamentally an extension of the Coal and Steel
Community, the new organization set up a
program to eliminate import and export
duties among themselves, to establish a
common tariff policy for trade with the rest
of the world, and to develop common agricultural and transport policies. Like the
Coal and Steel Community, the Common
Market played a tremendous role in re-
vitalizing the economic life of Western
Europe. For a while Britain, originally invited to join the enterprise, felt that her
Commonwealth commitments and advan-

tages overbalanced the attractions of the
new organization. To strengthen her position, she invited Norway, Sweden, Denmark, Switzerland, Austria, and Portugal
to join with her in a similar enterprise which
would still permit her to keep her preferen-
tial tariff arrangements with the Commonwealth states. When trade gains of "The
Seven," as they came to be called, did not
keep pace with those of "The Six," she
reversed her position and applied for admission (1961). But President Charles de
Gaulle of France, fearing that Britain had
become too dependent on America for
Europe's good, refused to give his consent.
Nevertheless, Britain continued her efforts to merge "The Six" and "The Seven."

Meanwhile, other constellations in other
parts of Europe and the world were formed,
such as the Council for Mutual Economic
Aid (1949) made up of the U.S.S.R. and
six satellite Communist countries, the Central American Common Market (1960), and
the Organization of American States
(O.A.S.) which included all nations of the
Western hemisphere. In short, although national sovereignty was not surrendered or
even seriously discussed, in the score of
years following World War II regional communities were established and developed
strength and by that fact diminished traditional national prejudices. If Europe, the
world's onetime master, loosed its grip on
peoples and places, it also created the model
of the "cluster community" that gave promise of an eventual Global Society.

THE CAPITALIST-COMMUNIST CONFLICT

The Cold War

Causes

Parallel with this promise, an ominous
peril appeared—the growing conflict between the capitalist and communist worlds.

Were he alive, Hitler could point with some
gloating to a statement that he made just
before his suicide in 1945: "With the defeat
of the Reich . . . there will remain in the
world only two powers capable of confronting each other—the United states and

Soviet Russia. The laws of both history and geography will compel these two Powers to a trial of strength. . . ."[2] Although we may seek comfort from the fact that one of the age's greatest liars spoke these lines, we cannot deny that the first of the two theses proved itself, at least until the advent of Communist China partially invalidated the Führer's arithmetic.

After the war collaboration between the capitalist and communist worlds came to an abrupt end. It is idle to deny, although some have attempted to, that ideology was a basic cause of the cold war. In 1848 the bourgeois world was horrified at the pronouncements of the Communist Manifesto. A hundred years later it had much more reason to be apprehensive. Even though, as we have seen, Soviet Russia had lost over twenty million of its people in the war and had suffered a scarring of its earth beyond the comprehension of any who did not live there, it emerged from the long "Years of the Gun" with a greater strength than this ancient land had ever known. Its leaders believed that its Marxist way of life had saved it from destruction. Available evidence plainly indicates that its masses, although weary of Stalin, were not of a mind to turn the clock back to pre-Soviet capitalism.[3] For millions in Russia and in other lands, Communism had come to stay. But Communists believed that staying meant encountering, battling, and eventually overcoming the non-Communist world. For their part, many among the capitalist ruling elites believed that the world would never know either peace or prosperity so long as the "Communist menace" existed.

But more than ideology was involved in the renewed struggle. Soviet leaders remembered that after World War I the Western powers had ringed Russia with a tight "cordon sanitaire." This time they were determined to forestall a repetition of this by doing some ringing of their own. Before the war had ended they had annexed Estonia, Latvia, Lithuania, and a portion of Poland. By 1948 they had set up Communist regimes in Czechoslovakia, Albania, Bulgaria, Rumania, and Hungary. The eastern provinces of Germany, occupied by Russian troops since early 1945, were also consolidated into the German Democratic Republic (1949), under Russian domination. Thus the Russian push westward was motivated by a mixture of ideological concerns, determination to revenge the sealing-off strategy of the Western powers after World War I, and plain, old-fashioned imperial aggrandizement.

Crises: Greece and the Marshall Plan

The first serious crisis in the renewed capitalist-communist struggle occurred in the Balkans in early 1947. For several years Communist insurrectionists had tried to overthrow the reactionary monarchial regime in Greece, but had been thwarted by military and economic aid supplied by Britain. In 1947 the British Labour government, as we have seen, frankly admitted that Britain's own pressing needs necessitated the abandonment of this policy. To prevent an otherwise certain Communist take-over, President Truman ordered American intervention. Thereafter American money, arms, and military advisers were sent to Greece in an ever-increasing volume. With this aid the Greek government was finally able to put down the insurrection and consolidate its position (1949). Because Soviet Russia had put similar pressure on Turkey, aid under the "Truman Doctrine" was extended to that nation.

Simultaneously, United States Secretary of State George Marshall urged Con-

2. François Genoud, ed., *The Testament of Adolf Hitler,* translated by R. H. Stevens, Cassell, London, 1961, p. 107.

3. See George Fischer, *Soviet Opposition to Stalin,* Harvard University Press, Cambridge, 1952.

gress to legislate a gigantic economic-recovery program for Europe. Originally the program was designed to stimulate the economic recovery of all of Europe by extending unusually generous loans to countries applying for them. However, between Marshall's formulation of the plan in 1947 and Congressional enactment of it into law in 1948 the occurrence of two events substantially changed its original purpose. One was the American intervention just noted; the other was Soviet Russia's adamant stand against any Communist country accepting American aid. Both events gave the President and his advisers the opportunity they wanted to use the Marshall Plan to forestall the advance of Communism in Western Europe. In short, it became a weapon in the cold war.

Soviet Response: The Cominform and New Conflicts

To counteract Western pressures the Soviet Union, in late 1947, revived the Third International (see *supra,* p. 778) under a new name—Cominform. Ostensibly an agency to facilitate the exchange of information among Communist states, it actually functioned as a political propaganda instrument supporting anticapitalist solidarity around the world. Its influence was soon felt in important developments in France, Czechoslovakia, Italy, and Germany. In November of 1947, French Communist leaders called for a general strike. Because both economic and political conditions in the Fourth Republic were in anything but a healthy condition, the call posed a real threat to the government. For several weeks it appeared that spreading violence and sabotage might actually destroy the democratic system. Strong government action gradually wore down the insurrectionists, however, so that by mid-December the strike was given up. In February of 1948, events took a different turn in Czechoslovakia. For several years democratic leaders there had been able to keep Soviet influence

within moderate bounds. Now Moscow gave the signal for a showdown with which the little country, surrounded by Communist satellite states, was unable to cope. Thereafter it followed a strict Stalinist line. The Communist take-over deeply shocked the Western world and, of course, intensified the cold war.

Soon Italian Communists began a gigantic rally to win mass support for their candidates in the general elections of 1948. Because a majority of Italy's Socialists, under Pietro Nenni, joined with the Communists in what was called the People's Bloc, and because Italy's politico-economic situation was even more unstable than France's, it appeared possible, even likely, that another capitalist regime would fall. But the recent example of Czechoslovakia, combined with American pressure and the Pope's strong support of anti-Bloc efforts, gave the Christian Democrats and their allies a substantial victory.

Much more threatening to the precarious peace of the world was the Berlin crisis of June 1948 to May 1949. To deter the Western powers from creating a West German state, Russia cut off land access to their sectors of divided Berlin, deep within the Soviet zone. Because the city had become a symbol of Western power vis-à-vis Soviet designs in Europe, Western statesmen felt that their sectors of the city had to be supplied at all costs. They therefore organized a gigantic airlift to bring in food, fuel, and other necessities. For a while during the winter months of 1948 and 1949, the city's demands for coal alone almost caused the project to collapse. Somehow enough planes and skilled airmen to fly them were found to carry it off, and in May the Russians admitted defeat by lifting the blockade.

The Creation of NATO

One rather logical result of this crisis was the creation of the North Atlantic Treaty Organization (1949). It was essentially a military alliance, and its basic purpose was to secure the non-Communist states of Europe against Soviet aggression. Although made up of some fifteen states, the United States, Britain, and France in practice bore the chief responsibility for making the organization strong enough to discharge its principal obligations. Eventually, Russia and the Communist states of Eastern Europe formed a similar organization under the terms of the Warsaw Pact (1954). Thus, within ten years after the destruction of Nazi Germany, the major powers, and many of the minor ones, were grouped into two opposing camps, each armed and bitter in its denunciations of the machinations of the other.

The Korean War and Its Aftermath

In 1950 the capitalist-communist conflict developed into a shooting war in Korea. After the surrender of Germany but before the defeat of Japan the United States and Russia agreed, with Britain concurring, to work for an independent Korea to be set up after the war. As a temporary measure the country was to be divided at the 38th parallel, with the United States occupying the southern half and Russia the northern half. Quite naturally, this eventually resulted in the establishment of a communist regime in the Russian sector and a capitalist regime in the American sector. In 1948 and 1949 both Russia and the United States withdrew their troops from Korea. Shortly thereafter a North Korean army crossed over the dividing line in an attempt to unite the country under Communist rule. President Truman at once ordered United States forces to join those of South Korea in repelling the attack, and called on the United Nations to declare North Korea guilty of flagrant aggression. Owing to the temporary absence of Russia from the United Nations Council, the Council unanimously agreed and directed all members of the United Nations to supply military and other aid. Token forces from some United Nations

member states were sent, but the main force opposing North Korean troops was made up of American and South Korean units. General Douglas MacArthur was appointed supreme commander of all forces.

Throughout the period of 1950 to 1952, the war followed a seesaw course. At one point the North Koreans came very close to driving MacArthur's troops into the sea. Not long afterward, a United Nations offensive pushed the North Koreans back to the 38th parallel. MacArthur insisted on continuing the advance until the whole of North Korea was conquered. Sustained by President Truman, MacArthur pushed his forces almost to the Chinese border. At this point Communist China sent massive support to the North Koreans, and the war thereafter settled into a deadlock. To break it, MacArthur insisted on bombing mainland Chinese bases. Because this would have probably moved Russia to intervene and thus might have led to the total war that President Truman was determined to avoid, the President removed MacArthur from command. Under his successor, General Matthew Ridgeway, United Nations troops, although unable to move much beyond the 38th parallel, stubbornly withstood further North Korean and Chinese offensives. After many months of tedious negotiations a truce was signed, which left the general situation much as it was before the invasion began. Even though repeated attempts to frame a definitive peace settlement failed, a general war was avoided.

The ominous strength displayed by Communist China in the Korean War was the partial cause of the creation of still another regional grouping—the South-East Asia Treaty Organization (SEATO), which was made up of Australia, France, New Zealand, Pakistan, the Philippines, Thailand, Britain, and the United States (1954). Thus in Asia, as in Europe, the capitalist-communist conflict spawned rival alliance systems.

As long as the United States could claim

exclusive possession of nuclear weapons, the Communist world naturally operated in world affairs under a severe handicap. From 1950 on, this situation underwent rapid change. From the successful detonation of an atomic bomb the Russians went on to build up a massive arsenal of medium- and long-range missiles. Moreover, in 1957 it announced the successful orbiting of an object in space (the first Sputnik), an event that ushered in the still bewilderingly strange space age. The next year the United States launched its Explorer I, and the cold war took on some of the aspects of fantasy in a kind of Edgar Allan Poe progression — which "side" had the more expert mathematicians and astrophysicists? Which could first send up a man to walk in space? Which would first hit the moon? By the mid-1960s the cold-war equations became even more complicated as China and France joined the lethal "Atomic Club" with political propensities that leaned clearly neither toward the Soviet Union nor the United States.

Coexistence and the "Thaw"

In spite, or more probably because, of the rapidly mounting and increasingly fearful developments in destructive power, the tensions of the capitalist-communist conflict showed intermittent easement after 1954. With the emergence of Khrushchev as Russia's chief policy maker in 1956, a new Soviet note was struck — a note that is perhaps best described as cautious leniency at home and measured tolerance abroad.[4] We have already noted the nature and significance of the de-Stalinization of Party and State. Its influence was also felt in varying degrees in international affairs. In April of 1956, for example, the dissolution of the Cominform was announced. Also, the new Soviet leader made a special point of laboring the thesis that socialism was a

many-mansioned system, and that the roads leading to it were not limited to the one traveled by Russia. The *détente* with Yugoslavia was further cultivated. Under a native Communist leader, Wladislaw Gomulka, Poland undertook the execution of certain nationalist policies — for example, the restoration of limited liberty to the Catholic Church — without retributive action from Moscow. In 1955, President Eisenhower and the foreign ministers of Britain and France met with Khrushchev in Geneva. No specific program for more peaceful East-West relations came from this "summit" conference, but the cordial atmosphere of the informal discussions suggested a welcome lessening of world tensions. Even new Russian threats — such as Khrushchev's "We will bury you" — took on new tone and meaning. Now the emphasis was on *outproducing* rather than outshooting the capitalist world, on winning the so-called backward nations to communism by example rather than by Russian-initiated revolution. The "thaw" was far from complete; as we shall soon note, it was not even reasonably progressive. But it was real and marked a possible turning away from "bomb diplomacy" to grudgingly tolerant exploration and adjustment of world problems.

A recurrence in 1961 of the Berlin crisis emphasized the ambiguity of East-West interchanges. By then migrations from East Berlin to West Berlin, for reasons beyond our detailing here, had reached proportions both embarrassing to and economically crippling for the life and leadership of East Berlin. As its mentor, Khrushchev demanded an end of Western occupation. His blunt words and threatening gestures seemed to make an all-out violent showdown inescapable. A meeting between him and President Kennedy in Vienna (June 1961) did not resolve the issue. Indeed, one of the results of the meeting was the construction by the East German government of a great wall erected to seal off migrations from East to West Germany.

4. See H. Stuart Hughes, *Contemporary Europe; A History,* Prentice-Hall, Inc., Englewood Cliffs, N.J., 1961, pp. 488–489.

Nevertheless, the Vienna exchange probably helped to forestall the violent showdown which haunted both West and East.

The "Refreeze"

The Cuban Crises

Nevertheless, the "thaw" periodically yielded to distressing periods of "refreeze." After Fidel Castro's establishment of a Communist regime in Cuba, many anti-Communist refugees fled to Florida and other areas not too far from their homeland to prepare for the day of their return. Officials of the United States government, particularly those holding important positions in the Central Intelligence Agency (C.I.A.), actively collaborated with a refugee junta to plan the overthrow of the Castro government. The attempt was made in April of 1961—the "Bay of Pigs" invasion. It was promptly and completely repelled when, to the surprise of many Americans, the Cuban masses not only refused to join the invasion forces but supported the government in dispersing them.

A popular American conception of the Cuban crisis of 1962. Khrushchev is the happy "Cuba Meddler."

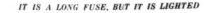

IT IS A LONG FUSE, BUT IT IS LIGHTED

A year and a half later another Cuban crisis occurred when Soviet military technicians began to install and equip missile-launching sites on the island. President Kennedy demanded their immediate removal under threat of military sanctions. This time it was Khrushchev who heeded the voice of caution. The sites were dismantled and their materiel and Soviet personnel were returned to Russia. The resolution of this crisis was of extraordinary significance. Put negatively, it precluded complicating developments that might— some would say almost certainly would— have plunged the nations into nuclear war. Put positively, it resulted in a *détente* which made it possible for the United States and the U.S.S.R. to collaborate in arranging multilateral talks that resulted in a partial nuclear test-ban treaty. It also led to more East-West contacts, although at the cost of heightening Chinese recalcitrance.

The War in Vietnam

In 1965 and 1966, another serious East-West confrontation developed, the background of which must be examined in some detail. For many years (since about 1875) the people of Annam, Tonkin, and Cochin China had been ruled by the French. After an interlude of Japanese overlordship (during World War II), some of them won a kind of independence from the restored French rule in 1946. These included most of the people of Annam, but none of Tonkin to the north or Cochin China to the south. Negotiations between leaders of newly established Vietnam ("southern country") and the French soon ran into difficulties. The Vietnamese insisted on both complete independence and unity, by which they meant unity with their ethnic kin in Tonkin and Cochin China. France refused to grant either and, in December of 1946, the leaders resorted to guerrilla war to gain their ends. The fighting went on for eight years, with France (generously supported by United States dollars and other aid) winning many battles but steadily alienat-

This Associated Press photograph shows a United States soldier waiting for Vietcong guerrillas to emerge from a hideout into which a smoke bomb had been thrown (1966).

Ho-Chi-Minh, the North Vietnam leader, is shown chatting with a group of young people after viewing with them an exhibition in Hanoi that featured examples of Chinese support of the North Vietnamese stuggle against the United States.

ing the peasant population. After the Communist victory in China in 1949, Vietnam was supplied by them with arms and aid of many kinds. By 1954 the Communist-dominated Vietminh ("independence party") ruled most of the countryside, with fairly strong peasant support. In that year the French forces suffered a complete defeat at Dien Bien Phu, and France was forced to negotiate a settlement. Although North Vietnam gained its complete independence, France, aided by Western powers at Geneva where the meetings were held, was able to insist on a temporary continuation of the division of the whole land—at the 17th parallel—until general elections could be held in 1956. The anti-Communist government in South Vietnam, however, refused to honor the elections agreement. Its strong man, Ngo Dihn Diem, whose armies were now organized and trained by agents of the United States government, consolidated his power in a dictatorship as tight as North Vietnam's, without the latter's social program. Indeed, Diem's regime became so corrupt and autocratic that, in spite of increased assignment of United States advisers and aid, it was overthrown in 1963 and Diem was executed. His successors, however—all militarists and by 1966 all except one former officers in the French army who had fought from 1946 to 1954 against their own people—were as little inclined toward reform as he.

When the Geneva agreement was abrogated by the Diem government, the North Vietnamese, under Ho Chi Min (a veteran Communist leader who, because of France's long struggle to keep her Asian colonies,

was able to blend Communism with nationalism), again agitated for unity. Soon Ho sent Vietminh fighters south of the dividing line to rally the countryside against Diem. In 1964 the United States government, fearful that Ho would succeed in establishing Communist rule throughout the whole land, increased its support of the southern regime.* Within three years it had sent well over 500,000 soldiers to South Vietman and had bombed various sections of North Vietnam. Thus in Southeast Asia the cold war had turned into a shooting war, which threatened, despite "peace" talks begun in Paris in the summer of 1968, to develop into a conflict the dimensions and end of which were difficult to foresee.

SUMMARY OF THE FLUX AND FLOW OF CONTEMPORARY EVENTS

The New Europe

The events that we have considered in this chapter clearly indicate the development of far-reaching changes in the terms and conditions of human existence. During the eighteenth and nineteenth centuries, Europe made itself the world's mentor and, often, master. Since 1914 it has been contracting. But, as we have seen, the historic record plainly gives the lie to the pessimistic claims of those who argued that Europe was finished. Developments of the last ten years, indeed, point rather to its revitalization as a "high culture-carrier." Moreover, the emergent peoples of Africa and Asia have been so deeply marked by Europe's brand of civilization that, whatever their political status and their "awareness of a cultural heritage which did not derive from the west and which it was important to retain and integrate into modern life," [5] they are and

will long remain cultural cousins of their ousted masters. Nevertheless, the "Atlantic Community" is now but one of a cluster of communities, part of a global constellation which is both sign and substance of a new age in human history.

The New Masses

Another aspect of the new age is the changed conditions, place, and power of the masses. At no time in the 5000-year record of civilization had mass man counted so much either in his own notion of his worth or in that of the elites who ruled over him. Even in Periclean Athens, we will re-

---

* It should be noted, however, that this was the officially stated aim. Many knowledgeable persons believed that the real purpose of the United States government was consolidation of a base in Asia which could be used in a future struggle against China.

5. Barraclough, *op. cit.,* p. 192.

call, the free citizens of the city constituted a dominant minority. At the other chronological extreme of "democratic life" — nineteenth-century America — the situation was not very different. Except for most Negroes and Indians, adult males possessed the franchise and often used it with telling effect. Still, the American mass man was rarely the chief architect of the conditions of his own life, nor is he yet. However, over most of the world today the "little man" is on the move — either under his own power, as in the American labor movement; or under the "vanguard of the proletariat," as in communist countries; or working through socialist parties, as in Britain and Scandinavia; or, anomalously, under autocratic "chiefs," such as Jomo Kenyata in Kenya. Everywhere in the world the gap between commoner and "gentleman" is still wide. But mass society is in the making, and the trend hardly seems reversible.

Beginnings of the "Breakthrough to Peace"

Paradoxically, this century of violence has been marked by a peace move surging far beyond anything of its kind in all human history. It is true that the doctrine of state sovereignty is still strong, thus weakening the will and ability of peoples to use an international constabulary in place of national armies. It is also true that the might of those armies is stronger than ever. Even so, signs of a revolutionary "breakthrough to peace" are clear. "Peace marches" and "peace sit-ins," for example, indicate a kind of grass-roots drive to abolish war as an instrument of national policy. Many academic communities have seen the creation of permanent "peace-research" groups, which seek to educate both themselves and a wider public. Some large foundation grants subsidize this and other kinds of peace activity. An unprecedented number of young men in the United States, at least, are registering as conscientious objectors to war. And, the

destructive power of the nuclear bomb has caused even the man in the street to pause and ponder the destruction of civilization, unless large-scale wars are somehow relegated to the limbo of outworn human habits. This is not, of course, meant to suggest that contemporary civilization is on the verge of universal disarmament and the creation of a world state under a common law. It is meant rather — and only — to emphasize an unprecedented turn toward peace.

A New Age

Also undergoing fundamental change is the complex value system of the long-dominant ruling class. In the 1960s, the bearded dissenters from conventional society's "rut and rule of living" were striking symbols of this change. Almost every convention and almost every concept with roots has invited challenge, from the propriety of neckties to the existence of God. We shall consider some of the more significant of these challenges and changes in the concluding chapter.

In short, the overall cumulative force of the often bewildering developments of the postwar years constitutes a huge pivot in human history, swinging one age, which we have long since labeled "modern," to the periphery of our life, while swinging another age, not yet named, into its vital center.

SELECTED READINGS

Beloff, Max, *Soviet Policy in the Far East, 1944–1951,* Oxford University Press, London, 1953.

Particularly useful as background for understanding present-day Soviet-Chinese encounters.

*Gatzke, H. W., *The Present in Perspective: A Look at the World Since 1945,* Rand McNally & Co., Chicago, 1965 (3rd ed.).

A brief (200 pages) factual account of the

Asterisk (*) denotes paperback.

cold war, the "restoration" of Western Europe, the major trends of events in the United States, Stalin and Stalin's Russia, the rise of new states in Asia and Africa, and "competitive coexistence."

Jackson, J. Hampden, *The World in the Post-war Decade, 1945–1955,* Houghton Mifflin Co., Boston, 1956.

The events of this decade are grouped under three themes—the power conflict between Russia and the United States; the emergence of nationalism in Latin America, Africa, and Asia; and the more important "home" developments in Russia, the United Kingdom, and the United States.

Kitchen, Helen, ed., *A Handbook of African Affairs,* Praeger, New York, 1964.

Good brief accounts of developments in the struggle that the peoples of Africa are waging to achieve independence and a measure of the dignity that their membership in the human race affords them.

Luthuli, John Albert, *Africa's Freedom,* George Allen & Unwin Ltd., London, 1964.

A collection of source materials that gives the Western student a closer understanding of the aspirations—and agonies—of the emerging peoples of Africa.

*May, Ernest R., ed., *Anxiety and Affluence, 1945–1965,* McGraw-Hill Book Co., New York, 1966.

America's promises and perils, at home and abroad, as shown in "source" excerpts. Examples are the Taft-Hartley Act, Kennedy's "New Frontier" address, the Marshall Plan, a State Department report on the "fate of China," Truman's "Point Four," Kennedy on the Cuban missile crisis, McCarthy on Communists in the State Department, the problem of automation, and the Civil Rights Act of 1965.

Pikles, Dorothy, *The Fifth French Republic,* Frederick A. Praeger, New York, 1960.

A perceptive study of the meaning and methods of de Gaulle's France.

*Robertson, Charles L., *International Politics since World War II,* John Wiley & Sons, New York, 1966.

A summary review of the more significant events and policy decisions of the twenty-year period since the war. The author tries to explain these happenings as they developed out of varying assumptions—not necessarily truths, as he points out—of the policy makers, and the changes worked on the old balance-of-power system by mass ideology, technology, and mass communications.

Saunders, John J., *The Age of Revolution,* Roy Publishers, A.N., New York, 1949.

A pessimistic survey of liberal romanticism and nationalist democracy, which ends with the suggestion that Western civilization may be heading for a new Middle Ages.

Toynbee, Arnold, and Veronica M. Toynbee, eds., *Hitler's Europe,* Oxford University Press, London, 1954.

A volume in the *Survey of International Affairs* series. It covers the years 1939 to 1946. The articles by various authors do not deal with battles or strategy, but with the political and economic structures of Germany, Italy from 1940 to 1943, Vichy France and the Free French Movement, the occupied countries of Western and Eastern Europe, and the satellite states. An excellent reference work.

Ward, Barbara, *Five Ideas that Change the World,* W. W. Norton & Co., New York, 1959.

The ideas are nationalism, industrialism, colonialism, communism, and internationalism. Miss Ward treats them with a strong bias for freedom and human dignity as against the approach of those who pin their hope on cold logic and political expediency as the proper criteria for national behavior in the modern world.

*Wright, Gordon, and Arthur Mejia, Jr., *An Age of Controversy,* Dodd, Mead & Co., New York, 1963.

These "Discussion Problems in Twentieth Century Europe" are concerned with the subjects that you would expect to find in a work with this title—the origins of World War I, the rise and decline of colonialism, Russian totalitarianism, the Depression, etc. Particularly recommended are the sections entitled "Transition to the Twentieth Century," "The Impact of Freudian Thought."

Zagoria, Donald S., *The Sino-Soviet Conflict, 1956–1961*, Princeton University Press, 1962.

A detailed study of the origin and course of the parting of the ways of these two communist giants. The author does not think the conflict, of itself, is necessarily beneficial to the noncommunist world, which, he believes, should not relax in developing its military strength and its ability to respond firmly and rapidly to political challenges. Particularly useful when read with Beloff, cited above.

32

The Travail of Contemporary Man

Not surprisingly, the discontinuities of a world in flux which we considered in the preceding chapter gave contemporary man a sense of insecurity and apprehension. Further disturbing aspects of our unsettled condition were certain changes that took place within the corpus of our institutional life and the frames of reference which encompassed them; and, equally disturbing, at least to the masses of society, the "revolt of the intellectuals" which accompanied and, though not always intentionally, accelerated these changes. The purpose of this brief, concluding chapter is to sketch these two developments. It should be understood that the examples cited, though meant to be typical, can do little more than illustrate them.

THE DISINTEGRATION OF TRADITIONAL INSTITUTIONS AND BELIEFS

The Heritage of Hope

It is a truism that life is a continuum. No age or epoch of human existence is completely divorced from the experiences that precede and follow it. Indeed, in many aspects the desires and dreams, the fears and foibles of twentieth-century man are basically the same as those of the citizens of ancient Babylon. But though the threads of human existence eternally bind the past with the present and bind both with the future, attitudes and patterns of behavior shift and change. Periclean Athens, for example, subscribed to an overall attitude toward life which shaped and gave substance to distinctive institutions and modes of behavior. A hundred years later Athenian life, though organically descended from its Periclean past, was characterized by quite another temper and a very different societal structure. Another random example of evolutionary change is the contrast between the America of Cotton Mather and that of Andrew Jackson.

A similar contrast also characterized the society of the West before the Great War and the society that emerged and developed from it. The war itself both contributed to and dramatized this change. Many came to believe that the established order and the system of values which sustained it were, if not wholly illusory, shockingly flimsy, fancy façades hiding a dangerous and perhaps fatal complacency that was itself at least partly responsible for the outbreak of the war.

> What was the value of the long looked
>   forward to,
> Long hoped for calm, the autumnal serenity
> And the wisdom of age? Had they deceived
>   us
> Or deceived themselves, the quiet-voiced
>   elders,
> Bequeathing us merely a receipt for deceit? [1]

Before this transvaluation of values, most men and women of Western society believed in and labored for the realization of a world for which they thought they had a reasonably clearly drawn blueprint. It was often assumed that in this imagined future the individual would be free from arbitrary control by others whether they were princes, plutocrats, or priests—an ideal partly fostered by the egalitarian sentiments of the American and French revolutions. These and related impulses substantially motivated the revolutionaries of 1848 and 1849, the creators of the French Third Republic, English commoners, Russian revolutionists

and, to a lesser extent, Jacksonian Democrats and, later, Progressives in the United States. In this imagined world, too, man would live a life of moderate affluence based on the machine. Men hoped that technology would one day free humanity from menial drudgery, and the prison house of ignorance and dulled sensibilities which that drudgery had so cruelly built. Conditions and developments of the nineteenth century also led some seers to perceive, however dimly, the lineaments of a world ordered by law. The phrase "peaceful coexistence" had not yet been coined; but the idea it connotes was taking shape in the minds of many, if lesser, latterday Kants.

Subsuming these projected enlargements of life, and sustaining their proponents with hope and strength, was a complex of institutions and beliefs inherited from the past. Among them was a social structure built around the family. In this microcosm of the larger community, children learned the elements of both self-fulfillment and communal behavior—from the techniques of language to group patterns of morals and manners. In it, too, were found psychic resources which nurtured a sense of security and, at least potentially, encouraged each member to "find himself" as a distinct and worthy individual.

Another basic resource was the inherited concept of man as a creature of reason, purpose, and dignity, flawed by the prostitution of his own powers, but still only a "little lower than the angels." Encompassing these and all of the other common postulates and practices of the Western way of life was the Judeo-Christian ethos. This religious matrix, rent though it was by skeptics, hypocrites, ignorant zealots, and sometimes intelligent atheists, nevertheless bound the Western world in a developing humane and purposeful fellowship. Assuredly the golden age of peace and plenty, of learning and law and love, had not yet flowered; nor would it soon flower. But men believed they had at least a taste of it, and would settle for nothing less.

---

1. From T. S. Eliot's *Four Quartets*.

The Impact of Science and Industry

All of these assumptions and ideas, although not completely destroyed in the postwar world, underwent changes so profound that much of their original nature and significance vanished or became suspect. The assault on tradition came from many directions, from the Great War itself, as well as from science, technology, and industry. To gain some sense of the magnitude of the changes that produced the present "time of troubles" we need to sketch the basic outlines of prewar traditionalism, and note to what extent technology, with science as its basis and industry as its beneficiary, repudiated the past and shaped the present.

On Religious Institutions and Beliefs

The Judeo-Christian faith which cradled Western life was formed about 2000 years ago. Its main postulates are these: that "in the beginning God created the heavens and the earth"; that God is good, compassionate, and caring; that He is personal—that is, to His creature, Man, He bears the relationship of father to son and, like an earthly father, when appealed to properly, will provide the help man needs to achieve the good life; that all creation is purposed by Him and ordered in ways that develop that purpose—the ultimate experiencing of pure love; and that He and His way are not limited in time or space, but are "from everlasting to everlasting." Formed out of the still older faith of the Hebrews, it naturally took over many of that religion's beliefs and practices, such as the primacy of revelation as the way to truth, the anthropomorphic nature of God, the concept of the Savior, and the Ten Commandments as the moral requisites of the life of God's chosen. Naturally, too, it accepted the understandings of that time regarding the physical universe:

Famed defense lawyer Clarence Darrow, right, is pictured here in a store in Dayton, Tennessee during the Scopes evolution trial.

the central and stationary position of the earth; the daily revolution of the sun around the earth; and the stars as heavenly "extras" studding the skies for man's delight.

With the advent of science in the sixteenth century the cosmological underpinnings of the Christian faith were severely shaken. Although inspired scripture depicts Joshua commanding the sun to stand still, the findings of Copernicus and Galileo clearly demonstrated that, in relation to the earth, the sun was always "standing still." Even more disturbing to orthodox Christians were the principles set forth by Isaac Newton about 150 years later. By them, Newton explained a complex body of natural laws that set aside the Judeo-Christian concept of direct and interruptive divine intervention in terrestrial affairs, such as the parting of the Red Sea to provide for the exodus of the Jews from Egypt. In the nineteenth century, faith was even more profoundly shaken by Darwin's discovery of the origin of species which brought the sons of God into direct biological relationship to the lower animal kingdom and, at least implicitly, invalidated the accepted Christian concept of immortality.

Moreover, all phenomena took on new aspects and meaning from the hypotheses advanced by Albert Einstein in the early years of our own century. According to

Albert Einstein in 1931. Flanking him are his wife and the then governor of California.

these theories, all phenomenal "objects" take on particular dimensions, characteristics, and "meaning" strictly in relation to the particular motion and position of their observer, with the exception of the speed of light which is constant. This dissolution of the traditional notion of absolutes applied even to mass and energy which, in Einstein's famous equation ($E = mc^2$, energy equals mass multiplied by the square of the velocity of light), were capable of transformation from one to the other. Time, as a coordinate of the dimensions of length, width, and breadth, took on a dimension of its own which was also subject, like space, to its relatedness, from the standpoint of the particular observer, to all other phenomena.

Probings into the nature of matter by other physicists revealed further intricacies and complications so removed from the workaday world of sense impressions

as to rival the mysteries of the religious faith they were discrediting. Only the barest reference to these revolutionary concepts can be made. Around 1900, Max Planck (1858–1947), the German physicist, presented theoretical evidence controverting the hitherto accepted notion that a continuous "flow" marked the emission and absorption of energy by atomic and subatomic particles. Planck held that rather than transmission through waves, energy was transferred in discrete packets, which he called quanta. A few years later Niels Bohr (1885–1962) developed the principle which successfully resolved a number of problems that physicists had long found baffling. But the quantum theory ran into difficulty when its more thorough application posed serious inconsistencies. In the 1920s, through the work of Louis de Broglie (1892–   ), Erwin Schrödinger (1887–1961), and Werner Heisenberg (1901–   )—among others—these inconsistencies were, for the most part, eliminated by a hypothesis which asserted the *wave* character of particles. Thus the "flow" and "packet" explanations of the nature and movement of energy were merged into complementary hypotheses. In addition, Heisenberg advanced the thesis that since the position and speed of an electron can never be simultaneously fixed, scientists must give up all hope of ever determining absolute causality in nature. The dual character of the mode of the transmission of energy, as well as the Heisenberg "principle of uncertainty," continued to be held by most physicists into the second half of this century.

In the life sciences, particularly biology, revolutionary discoveries have been made in recent years. Whereas, for example, geneticists once labored long (and profitably) on the mechanics of heredity alone, their attention now centers on the nature and functioning of gene action. Their application of biochemistry and biophysics to this phenomenon have led them to believe that the "primary carrier of genetic information" is a nucleic acid (deoxyribonucleic acid—DNA). From this they conclude that study of the basis of that acid's strand may lead to a complete understanding of the processes that determine the transmission of characteristics, and thus may bring man close to mastery of the production of those forms of living things that he decides are "good."

These complicated findings of science revealed a new and fascinating world to modern man. But they also made it increasingly difficult for educated persons to hold both to these findings and to the orthodox doctrines of the Christian faith. Although churches continued to be built and their services attended—in increasing numbers, as a matter of fact—the certainties and sanctions of the faith weakened. In short, the 2000-year-old God frame of reference, once sharp and compelling, increasingly tended to take on a disconcerting vagueness that left many Christians groping and confused.

On the Man Frame of Reference

Another troubled frame of reference was man's long-held image of himself. If he had difficulty "picturing" God, he perforce found it unrealistic to view himself as God's son, or as a creature with godly attributes or potentialities. Nor could he rely, as many men of the Enlightenment had assumed he could, upon innate powers of reason and discernment. For here too the impact of science was strong and, to many, disturbing. One such study, of particular significance, was developed by Sigmund Freud, a Viennese psychologist (1856–1939). Fundamental to Freudianism was the hypothesis that men are basically irrational. What man commonly believed to be purposive cognition Freud insisted was a basic response to the sexual frustrations and inhibitions formed in early childhood. By the early decades of the twentieth century this view of man's motives and behavior became quite widely accepted. Its popularization gave many a sense of release from binding and, as they saw them, hypocritical Puritan restrictions and views of the nature and destiny of man. But it also gave to many a growing feeling of alienation from a world which had traditionally been considered to have meaning and humane purpose.

Another twentieth-century view of man was proposed by John B. Watson (1878–1958) and later, in a variant form, by Charles L. Skinner. Watson argued that man had to rid himself of the notion of "mind" if he was ever to understand and control his behavior. All activity is, in this view, grounded in response to stimuli. Like other animals, man has certain needs to meet—such as hunger, sex, and affection. How he responds to these needs ultimately forms his "character." Since responses to stimuli may be conditioned and reconditioned * this character becomes so highly complicated and intricate that it is easy for man to forget—or refuse to believe—that his total personality really rests upon an originally very simple and wholly physical "stimulus-response arc." But, the behaviorists insisted, temptations to accept religious or other nonbehavioristic explanations of man's actions must be resisted, if scientific truth was to be a guide to action.

The double thrust of Freudianism and Behaviorism went far to dim and, for many, to destroy the traditional Man frame of reference. The various images of the "new man," constructed by psychologists and others in the behavioral sciences, like the new universe of the physical scientists, gave to a growing number of men a sense of openness and adventurous growth; most people, however, were left puzzled and bewildered.

* Terms first used, in this context, by the Russian psychologist, Ivan Pavlov (1849–1936). In his famous experiment, Pavlov offered meat to a hungry dog, to cause it to salivate. Later a bell was rung as the meat was offered. Subsequently, merely ringing the bell produced salivation—a "conditioned" response.

Sigmund Freud (1936) whose views of the motivations and workings of the human mind revolutionized, for many, the meaning of human existence.

On Social Institutions

Industrial and technological developments of the late nineteenth and twentieth centuries significantly altered the old framework of Western man's communal life. The introduction of the dynamo vastly accelerated the industrialization and urbanization of society. Powered by electricity now, as well as by steam, giant machines and machines to make machines helped to provide a material abundance that man had never before experienced, and at the same time the machines spawned sprawling megalopolises. Food, clothing, shelter, gadgets, games, places to go and rapid means of going there—all increased in supply, variety, and novelty. But the distribution of the new abundance was uneven, resulting in social tensions and spreading slums. As it put man on wheels, the mechanized life also frayed his nerves and dulled his sense of the worth of the nonmarketable goods of life. And with the

advent, around midcentury, of automation and huge computers, it became increasingly possible to view life as a "program," coldly directed by mysterious engineering elites more interested in models and "games" than in understanding the needs and, as they were once thought of, noble capabilities of human beings.

Corporate Man

Even apart from the "program" aspects of modern industrial society, its corporate structure had become such as to cause, rightly or wrongly, many of its members to feel they had been "depersonalized." The telescoping of new and intricate communication devices had, for example, grafted onto the typical large corporation a giant, composite ear and a giant, composite mouth. Little opportunity was left for the individual to reflect on the processes that engaged him or even the meaning of his individual contribution. Nor was this true of only the lower-echelon workers. Although there were still individual "stars" in industry, the day of the tycoon seemed past. Policy making was usually the function of a team, its end product the result of group discussions which often involved a complicated hierarchy of committees and subcommittees. Moreover, the ramifications of the trend toward mergers, and the ever accelerating growth of the "business mind" were no longer separable from society at large, especially in the United States. Also, although government "interference" in business had steadily increased in the postwar years, industry nevertheless probably had more to say about what the individual—at every social level—thought, said, wore, and valued than any other institution in society, including government. For most workers "the code of practice of the firm—[a kind of] body of common law—seems to them to condition their lives and functions more urgently than the ordinances of the city or the laws of the state or nation."[2] Or again, suppose the executives of a supergiant industry decided to lay out several hundred million dollars for plant expansion. This decision,

may well determine the quality of life for a substantial segment of society. Men and materials will move across continents; old communities will decay and new ones will prosper; tastes and habits will alter; new skills will be demanded, and the education of a nation will adjust itself accordingly; even government will fall into line, providing public services that corporate developments make necessary.[3]

Whether "depersonalized," anonymous, or conformist, many men and women of modern industrial society live their lives on the basis of the frame of reference of the corporation, not that of God or man.

Family

The combination of industrialization and the exigencies of World Wars I and II helped to produce a "new woman" by providing a new place for her in society. As late as the beginning of the twentieth century, the interests of most women centered in home and children. By the second half of the century woman's range of activities and her degree of mobility had increased astonishingly. Almost every occupation, business and profession was opened to her or, more accurately, by her. Besides psychic rewards, she achieved a measure of financial independence which, among other things, changed the nature of marital relationships and responsibilities; more specifically, it made divorce of incompatible partners more practicable and eventually more respectable. With more time, money, and freedom of action at her command, the new woman naturally felt greater concern for her formal education. The effects of these changes meant new family relationships — less time spent with children and husband, and more sexual

freedom, as examples — greater activity in political affairs, more direct influence in the economy, all resulting in greater responsibility for the general ordering of society. Concurrently, the wide acceptance of the idea that children as well as adults had inalienable rights of expression and creativity gave children, too, a new freedom and mobility. These developments, coupled with industry's growing propensity to move men from place to place as its expanding needs and facilities might indicate, created a new rhythm of life, sometimes exhilarating, sometimes bewildering. In short, the old home, unit of the old society, as well as the hierarchy of relationships within society, underwent changes which increased the scope of human movement and endeavor as it decreased man's sense of community, security, and rootedness.

The "Ethical Revolution"

The impact of universal war, science, and technology caused Western man to question the old norms of accepted behavior. After the war, much of what had long been considered the "good life" seemed at best to be irrelevant convention, at worst, unbearable hypocrisy. It was an age of retreating answers and probing questions. Had not the face of Western civilization been revealed as a mask? Was its life a husk which hid or distorted dynamic internal forces? If so, how could Western man trust the traditional value system? For if it had not induced, certainly it had not prevented the catastrophic dimension of his experience. On the other hand, if traditional values were illusory, what values were more sound? Was it realistic to believe in any general code of ethics? Was not, perhaps, each individual answerable to whatever powers might lie within himself, and to these powers alone?

These questions were initially — and insistently — pressed by many of the spokesmen of the famous "Lost Generation." *

2. Frederick Lewis Allen, *The Big Change,* Harper and Row, New York, 1952, p. 253.
3. Quoted in John Brooks, *The Great Leap . . . ,* Harper and Row, New York, 1966.

* Who became most active and vocal in the 1920s.

Their answers, often confused and contradictory, were rooted in rebellion against what they regarded as a phony world and its managers. The new spirit of the times both reflected and shaped the whole range of this generation's thought and behavior. Its chief (and mutually contradictory) characteristics were emphasis upon pure subjectivism, hedonistic abandon, and frank acknowledgment of life's anarchic, often cruel, purposelessness. Although the following example of the new subjectivism deals with art, it is typical of the subjectivist approach to all human experience:

It is true that human imagination can give to the most ordinary object an unexpected distinction; but the magic power of the imagination is put to very feeble use if it serves merely to preserve or reinforce that which already exists. That is an inexcusable abdication. It is impossible in the present state of modern thought, when the exterior world appears more and more suspect, to agree any longer to such a sacrifice. The work of art, if it is to assist in that absolute revision of values upon which we all agree, must base itself upon a purely subjective inspiration or it will cease to exist.[4]

An "ethical revolution" — based in part on the new emphasis on the private, personal, and subjective — led many youths (and no few of their elders) into experiments in hedonism. Possessed of (as well as by) a restless energy created in part by the agitations of the Great War and intolerably dammed up by the frustrations of the aborted peace, these youths sought release in a new warfare against inhibitions. One meaning of the notorious Jazz Age was privatization as exemplified in an endless round of parties, sexual adventuring, shocking stunts, as well as the partly impulsive, partly calculated defiance of convention on any level of life they might happen to find themselves.

The New Nihilism

Mingled with this desperate search for private experience in the external world was a perhaps numbing recognition of life's basic purposelessness. This nihilism affirmed neither existentialist nor hedonistic fulfillment. Instead, its practitioners perceived life as an ongoing, incomprehensible, often hideous nightmare that the individual had somehow to endure, as in E. E. Cummings' *The Enormous Room*. Sensations were felt, events occurred, ideas were conceived; but all were unpurposed, unplanned, unreal, but nonetheless genuinely threatening to both authenticity and even survival. At best, man's elaborate social structures, complex legal systems, and conventional behavior were alluring chimera; at worst, they could destroy first manhood and, eventually, mankind. A clear (and chilling) expression of this view of life is found in Franz Kafka's *The Trial*. Its hero, fittingly nameless, was an assistant bank director who was arrested by authorities of the state Apparatus on an unnamed charge. The case dragged on for months with no intimation to the victim of the nature of his crime. His guilt was assumed; periodically he was interrogated in a vague, ghostly manner. At no time did he face his official accusers; nor was he ever brought to trial. In the end two "warders" led him out to a stone quarry at the edge of town, courteously disrobed him (taking care to fold his clothes neatly), and ran a butcher knife through his heart. Two of many of such entries in Kafka's diaries reflect the hopeless torment that plagued him throughout his brief life:

There are conflicting thoughts always in my head, something like this: My situation in this world would seem to be a dreadful one . . . on a forsaken road . . . where one keeps slipping in the snow in the dark, a sunless road . . . without an earthly goal . . . incapable of striking up a friendship with anyone, incapable of tolerating a friendship. . . . A man is purer [at night] than in the morning; the period before falling asleep is really the time when no ghosts haunt one; they

---

4. Andre Breton, quoted in Quincy Howe, *The World Between the Wars*, Simon and Schuster, 1953, p. 300.

are all dispersed; only as the night advances do they return, in the morning they have all assembled again, even if one cannot recognize them.[5]

In general, these were the attitudes of the postwar generation. With the past discredited and the future frameless, the condition of modern man, on the one hand, paralleled "the position of those few illuminati who, when initiated into the seventh circle of Syria's medieval Order of Assassins, were told the Order's secret of secrets: 'There is no truth; everything is permitted.' Or, to cite an unconscious Broadway jazz echo of the Assassins, 'Anything goes.'"[6] On the other hand, the condition for many of a later period was so characterized by fretful futility that, if they had invented a slogan to describe their condition (which they seemed to beat to bother about), it might have been "nothing counts."

The characteristic anguish of the 1920s was interrupted by the crises of depression and war. But, beginning in the late 1950s, both hedonistic abandon and nightmarish nothingness tended to yield to an almost frantic concern for "identity" as not only the supreme value but almost the only value. Some individuals, such as Salinger's symptomatic Holden Caulfield, probed their inner self for feelings, insights, and powers which, once encountered and recognized, would give some measure of meaning, perhaps even satisfaction, to existence. This effort was doubly paradoxical: it came to affirm the unique properties of the self at the same time it insisted that the lone individual was brother to all men, also lone individuals, and that all were comrades in a corporate existence that one could not pretend to ignore with impunity. It also simultaneously attacked bourgeois materialism while urging the need for contemporary man to face realistically the fact that the new world was an industrial world that simply refused to be buried under an avalanche of protest literature.

Thus by the middle of the twentieth century almost the whole fabric of Western man's culture had undergone or was undergoing cataclysmic change, with little indication that the pace would slacken.

THE REVOLT OF THE INTELLECTUALS

Concomitant with these changes, and in part causing them, was the complex of cries of defiance or despair, protest movements, and startling innovations that characterized the revolt of the intellectuals. As in all ages, these probing venturers constituted a very small portion of the population. But their influence can hardly be measured by their numbers. Long before the average person

5. Max Brod, ed., *The Diaries of Franz Kafka, 1914–1923,* Schocken Books, Inc., New York, 1949, pp. 214, 217.
6. Peter Viereck, "The Revolution in Values: Roots of the European Catastrophe, 1870–1952," *The Political Science Quarterly,* Vol. LXVII, No. 3, September 1952, p. 349.

sensed the superannuation of tradition, the "illuminati" had come to see the need for change even if that change meant sheer destruction, as it did for some. Although initially their work was known only to a few, eventually it filtered down, in part, and in one form or another, into the consciousness, outlook, and behavior of the many. We need, therefore, to note the efforts of at least a few of the intellectual innovators, some of whom were rebels while others acquiesced, who manifested this travail and attempted to sketch the outlines of a new way of life. The examples of revolt that we shall note are representative of the cen-

Woman Combing Her Hair, *a bronze statue by Alexander Archipenko (1915).*

tury's *Zeitgeist,* although a different cast would yield somewhat different results.

Art and Music

In art the revolt against the old ranged from expressionism, "metaphysical art," dadaism, surrealism, cubism, and abstrac-

tionism, to the styles called "pop" and "op." It is enough to illustrate only some of the motivating forces at work.

Metaphysical painting flourished in the first two decades of this century. Its founder, Giorgio de Chirico, sought to "transcend human limitations" by creating on canvas poetic fantasies that bore no resemblance to the experiences of this world. His work was permeated by a nightmare mood that transformed objects, which seemed at first examination to resemble (though distortedly) normal features of life, into desolate other-worldly—or nonworldly—apparitions. Dadaism grew out of revolution against the senseless horrors of World War I. "A whole generation had come to the conclusion that nothing was of any importance. . . . [Dadaism's] aim was to make a clean sweep; its methods were confusion and destruction. It proclaimed that everything, especially art, was nonsense."[7]

Both its chaotic daubings and its strangely disciplined nihilism—the latter strikingly seen in the works of Max Ernst—therefore were not meant to be made sense of. It was a culturally significant and symptomatic temper tantrum. Cubism, on the other hand, although rejecting the traditional concepts of representational art, sought to put mind and order back into art by emphasizing geometric form, and to put the emotions in their place by deemphasizing vivid colors. Some of the early works of Pablo Picasso (who did not long remain in any particular school) effectively portray this approach to reality. The Cubists, however, in their effort to reduce their work to visual symbolic representations of parts, often made the object that embraced these parts so unrecognizable as to destroy it. Contrarily, abstract art had this as one of its primary aims. It tried to break through the "superficial" world of sensory impression to reach the essence of harmony and order. In all of modern art, however—whether coldly ra-

7. Emile Langui, ed., *Fifty Years of Modern Art,* Frederick A. Praeger, New York, 1959, p. 41.

Le Grand Déjeuner, *an oil painting by Fernand Léger (1921).*

Picasso's Seated Woman *(1927).*

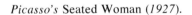

An oil painting by Miro – Dutch Interior *(1928).*

tional, deliberately "insane," or resting somewhere in between—there was clearly discernible the artist's deep concern for coming to terms with a world whose landscape of reality, whatever it might be, was certainly not the one that was once thought to have been so clearly brought into focus.

The same tendency to break from tradition is found in the works of many (though by no means all) modern composers. Charles Ives, for example, created rhythms and harmonies that any music lover a century ago would have found unrecognizable as music and, perhaps, unbearable as naked sound. Ives also felt that the format of traditional composition and performance was often stuffy and cramping. To free composer, performer, and listener alike from "thralldom" to form, Ives wrote some long works without time signature, and in various other ways allowed the performer to establish whatever rhythm patterns appealed to him. He "was a poetic realist in his music. . . . If, for example, he heard several brass bands on the 4th of July marching through the center of his small town of Danbury, Connecticut, he attempted in his music to create what might be called the poetic confusion of these sounds from different points of the compass meeting simultaneously." [8]

Even when the genius of the artist sought to reduce all feeling and thought to cold logical order, the result often was something quite different from the disciplined harmonies and tonal effects of the great masters of the eighteenth and nineteenth centuries. The works of Igor Stravinsky (1882–   ) are perhaps the best examples of this "backing into the future." For Stravinsky, who denied both "inspiration" as a motivating force in the writing of music, and "expression" as an inherent property of it, every valid work was characterized by objectivity and structural order—"Apollonian" (in contrast to the

romantic "Dionysian" style). Yet some of his compositions were frankly based on the works of Tchaikovsky and other romanticists. And his repeated use of irregular rhythms, strong dissonances, and the twelve-tone scale led many to think of him as the "leader of the futurist group in music." In short, although Stravinsky praised constraint and order and in his own way practiced both, that way was itself of the times—bohemian in its protest against bohemianism.

Literature and Philosophy

Much of the serious literature of the twentieth century may be considered as one great polemic against the emptiness and futility of the times. Almost nothing, from general outlook or "spirit" to the most humbly workaday institutions, is spared castigation. In Theodore Dreiser's *An American Tragedy,* for example, man's life is portrayed as a pointless journey through a labyrinth of experiences conditioned by chance beyond man's meaningful control of them. The sociological novels of Sinclair Lewis strip away the conventional masks of "main street" America to reveal it as small and mean in spirit and childishly simple of mind (which Lewis, despite himself, continued to admire). European society is portrayed as equally distraught, as in Arthur Koestler's *Age of Longing.* Examples could be multiplied almost without end. In this summary survey, we are perhaps best served by T. S. Eliot's *The Waste Land* and *Four Quartets.*

In several ways Eliot was not typical of the literary rebels of the twentieth century. In poetics and religion he was conservative; in contrast to many of his colleagues he revered tradition, and sought to preserve, not destroy, form and order. But he was like them in holding up the profound emptiness of modern life.

In *The Waste Land,* which has been called "in many ways the pivotal poem of

8. Peter Garvie, ed., *Music and Western Man,* Dent, London, 1958, p. 285.

the twentieth century," [9] man is portrayed as bereft of faith, wandering through a maze of disconnected experiences without zest or meaningful awareness. In one section a woman sits in her richly appointed bedroom, bored with herself, her surroundings, and the expected visit of her lover who, when he comes, is also bored with what he sees, what he does, and what he is.

> Footsteps shuffled on the stair.
> Under the firelight, under the brush, her hair
> Spread out in fiery points
> Glowed into words, then would be savagely still.
>
> "My nerves are bad tonight, Yes, bad. Stay with me.
> Speak to me. Why do you never speak. Speak.
> What are you thinking of? What thinking? What?
> I never know what you are thinking. Think."
> I think we are in a rats' alley
> Where the dead men lost their bones.
>
> . . . .
>
> "What shall I do now? What shall I do?"
> "I shall rush out as I am, and walk the street
> With my hair down, so. What shall we do tomorrow?
> What shall we ever do?"
>   The hot water at ten.
> And if it rains, a closed car at four.
> And we shall play a game of chess,
> Pressing lidless eyes and waiting for a knock upon the door. [10]
>
> . . . .

In another poem, "East Coker," from *The Four Quartets,* Eliot weighs the burden of modernity:

> The whole earth is our hospital
> Endowed by the ruined millionaire,
> Wherein, if we do well, we shall
> Die of the absolute paternal care
> That will not leave us, but prevents everywhere

And the seeming (but not, probably, in Eliot's own view) finale of man:

> O dark dark dark. They all go into the dark,
> The vacant interstellar spaces, the vacant into the vacant,
> The captains, merchant bankers, eminent men of letters,
> The generous patrons of art, the statesmen and the rulers,
> Distinguished civil servants, chairmen of many committees,
> Industrial lords and petty contractors, all go into the dark. . . .
> And we all go with them, into the silent funeral,
> Nobody's funeral, for there is none to bury. [11]

Philosophy

No more than in any other century did philosophy have but one voice in the twentieth century. For example, in the thought of Henri Bergson (1858–1941), for a time France's foremost philosopher, human existence is powered by a vital force beyond (although not excluding) reason which creatively shapes meaningful existence. On the other hand, logical positivists such as Bertrand Russell (1872–   ) devote almost the whole of their professional study to the determination, by logical analysis, of meaning. And in between these "heart" and "head" schools are a variety of other schools principally concerned with reconciling the new findings of science with a social behavior that does not too radically depart from that which is part of the Western tradition.

Here, however, it will suffice to indicate

---

9. By Wright Thomas and Stuart Brown in *Reading Poetry,* Oxford University Press, New York, 1941, p. 716.

10. T. S. Eliot, *The Waste Land,* Boni and Liveright, New York, 1922, pp.19–22, *passim.*

11. David Cecil and Allen Tate, eds., *Modern Verse in English, 1900–1950,* Macmillan Co., New York, N.Y., 1958, p. 337.

the main lines of only one philosophy, existentialism; or rather the existentialism of Jean-Paul Sartre (1905–   ). Although Sartre's arguments and outlook are not widely—that is, popularly—known, and even less understood, they may be noted here because they appeal to many intellectuals, and because they are so consonant with the modern temper.

The essence of this philosophy is the denial of absolute essence. Things, including man, exist. But "behind" existing things there is no meaning, no pattern, no order—there is, instead, complete *nothingness*. Man is not a creature of goodness, for there is no being or essence of goodness; and if there were he could not know of it. Man is forever confronted with the present and the passing—and meaningless —things of the present. True, he is free; but he is free in a world where all is uncertain, indefinite, and equivocal. His sole satisfaction comes from his ability to exercise choice in ways to engage his freedom, though whatever actions he decides upon are and must always remain wholly unconditioned. Man is therefore radically free to choose; every act is a result of free choice; and every choice carries personal responsibility for consequences. Viewed from any traditional perspective existentialism may afford only small satisfaction. This philosophy denies all historical moral codes, all religious or philosophical purpose, or even—apart from the choosing to act—meaning itself. The best understanding of the everyday meaning of this deeply pessimistic and monstrously demanding philosophy can be obtained from the following excerpt from one of Sartre's dramas (*The Condemned of Altona*, 1956). In it the "hero," Franz, appeals to History, out of his sense of guilt:

Centuries of the future, here is my century, solitary and deformed—the accused. . . . The century might have been a good one had not man been watched from time immemorial by the cruel enemy who had sworn to destroy him, that hairless, evil, flesh-eating beast— man himself. . . . Where does it come from, this rancid, insipid taste in my mouth? From man? From the beast? From myself? It is the taste of the century. [It] knows it is naked. Beautiful children, you who are born of us, our pain has brought you forth. This century is a woman in labor.

To a substantial degree, then, the life of twentieth-century man has been marked by the dissolution of old certitudes and the search for new meaning. Is there God, or No God? Is there purpose in life, and if there is, what is it? Is man a rational creature or a bundle of conditioned reflexes? Where can we hide from purposeless violence, and the shadow of the Great Mushroom? Where can we flee to escape unbearable reality? Mass man did not, of course, fill his days chanting these litanies of despair. He did not voice his uncertainties in the poignant strophes of the poet:

> . . . Alas, who is there
> we can make use of? Not angels, not men:
> and already the knowing brutes are aware
> that we don't feel very securely at home
> within our interpreted world. . . .[12]

The evidence of everyday observation, however, makes clear that mass man's life was marked by abiding tensions and insecurity.

Still, it would be wrong to conclude, however distraught the temper of the times, that man is drifting to inevitable doom. The reflective student of history knows that the 5000-year record of Western civilization is darkened by recurring "seasons of dismay": the two centuries of confusion that followed the collapse of Egypt's Middle Kingdom; the melancholy straying from the golden mean of Periclean Athens; the long night of the dark ages that blacked out the grandeur that was Rome—the list is long. It is not likely that contemporary man, amid

12. The theme of Rainer Maria Rilke's first *Duine Elegy,* quoted in Erich Heller, *The Disinherited Mind,* Farrar, Straus, and Cudahy, New York, 1957, p. 277.

his vanishing frames of reference, will turn away from the genius that has served him so long. Rather, all of history points in the other direction—to his ability to confront the future with that genius, to make new worlds out of old.

SELECTED READINGS

Barraclough, Geoffrey, *An Introduction to Contemporary History*, Basic Books, New York, 1964.

In this provocative work the author holds that the new age—in transition from about 1890 to the late 1950s—is as different from the "modern" age as the Renaissance is from medieval times. Its chief characteristics, he believes, are global life, mass man, and technological society.

Berger, Peter L., ed., *The Human Shape of Work*, The Macmillan Co., New York, 1964.

A study in the sociology of occupations, from the menial tasks of janitoring to the power positions of business executives. It sharply outlines the values system of modern American society as that system and the role of economic man in our times interact upon each other.

Boulding, Kenneth, *The Meaning of the Twentieth Century*, Harper Colophon Books, New York, 1965.

A large-minded, humane economist goes beyond the bounds of his professional discipline to probe, in a very provocative way, such questions as: are we living in an age which is so "new" that it can be compared only to the cultural shift that occurred when man passed from precivilization to civilization; what are the signs that may indicate the need for the creative reforming of the prime categories of human living—family, political organization, religion, for example; what are the responses needed to actually formulate these new attitudes and patterns of life?

Clark, Kenneth B., *Dark Ghetto*, Harper & Row, New York, 1965.

A Negro social-psychologist reveals the facts, fantasies, and frustrations of the Harlem "ghetto," and relates them to the white man's posture of mixed pride and fear. Almost every aspect of the Black-White problem in America is dealt with in one or another way in this frank, preceptive study of the American dilemma.

*Contemporary Civilization, Scott, Foresman & Company, 1959–1964, 3 vols.

Various scholars summarize the more significant happenings of contemporary civilization, relate them to their historic roots, and attempt projection into the future. Sample articles in Volume I are on the crisis in the Communist world, science and technology, the beat generation, and the overall patterns of life today. Volumes II and III update the examination of these and related subjects.

Frankel, Charles, *The Case For Modern Man*, Harper & Brothers, New York, 1956.

The main thesis of this book is a reaffirmation of the liberal interpretation of history and of the potentialities for good in modern man. The author's main method is to detail the arguments of some who oppose that view, such as Jacques Maritain, Reinhold Niehuhr, and Arnold Toynbee, to show how these arguments are invalid.

Goodman, Paul, *Growing Up Absurd*, Random House, New York, 1960.

A strong, sustained attack upon modern society's hypocrisies and futile posturings. He believes the "Organized System," as the author calls the complex of adult social behavior, poses for youth the alternatives of adjusting to a phony way of life and thus growing up absurd, or rebelling against it which, when adults grow wiser and more honest, will seem to these adults the epitomy of absurdity.

**Heilbroner, Robert L., *The Great Ascent*, Harper Torchbooks, Harper & Row, New York, 1963.

In the brief span of 160 pages the author effectively poses the new problem of "development" in the emerging nations of Asia and Africa. He concludes that more, not less, turmoil will mark this development in the years ahead, that the major Western powers should accept this as part of the

Asterisk (*) denotes paperback.

growing pains of a new age, that Western democracy must not be made a condition for aid, and that how far and how steadily the new nations develop will depend upon "reforms at home" among the older, if not always wiser, societies.

Regler, Gustav, translated by Norman Denny, *The Owl of Minerva,* Farrar, Straus & Cudahy, New York, 1959.

An autobiographical account of the life of a German who fought in World War I, fled the Nazis, fought in Spain with the Loyalists, joined and finally left the Communist party, and eventually found himself homeless, disillusioned but still hopeful that new understandings will come out of his harassed grappling with half truths and untruths. This sensitively written work gives the reader a close and poignant feeling for the glory and shame of modern man's confrontations of, and usually retreat from or distortion of, the new world's new issues.

Seldes, Gilbert, *The Great Audience,* The Viking Press, New York, 1950.

An examination of the impact on America's general outlook on life, its morals, manners, and intellectual formulations made by the mass media of communication and entertainment, particularly movies, radio, and television. The author concludes that present use of the popular arts is undermining the forces that make for free men, and for the enlarging development of a free society.

*Sinnott, Edmund, *The Biology of the Spirit,* Compass Books, The Viking Press, New York, 1957.

The author, a world-renowned geneticist, presents the thesis that matter and spirit are one, with protoplasm the fundamental stuff of all life. He suggests that life is teleological and God-designed, though his concept of God is certainly not that included in any orthodox religion.

Smith, Lillian, *Killers of the Dream,* W. W. Norton & Co., New York, 1961 (rev. ed.).

The author, who lived all of her life in the South, tries to probe the mysteries of racial prejudice out of the context of her own experiences and reflections. There is no other work on the White-Black problem like it. The book should be read as a whole; but to whet his appetite, the reader might first turn to a section in Part Two entitled, "The Women."

Illustration Credits

Page
5   Mas-Art Reference Bureau.
8   The University Museum, University of Pennsylvania.
10   Marburg—Art Reference Bureau (Egyptian Museum, Cairo).
12   Art Reference Bureau (British Museum).
21   Art Reference Bureau (Egyptian Museum, Cairo).
32   The University Museum, University of Pennsylvania.
33   Art Reference Bureau (British Museum).
36   Cliché des Musées Nationaux, Louvre.
39   Marburg—Art Reference Bureau (Candia Museum).
41   Art Reference Bureau (Candia Museum).
50   Alinari-Art Reference Bureau (Louvre).
73   Courtesy Museum of Fine Arts, Boston, Pierce Fund.
79   Courtesy Wadsworth Atheneum, Hartford.
86   Copyright Department of Antiquities, Ashmolean Museum.
94   Alinari—Art Reference Bureau (Galleria Spada, Rome).
98   *Upper left,* Alison Frantz, Athens—Art Reference Bureau (Delphi Museum); *lower right,* Alinari—Art Reference Bureau (Delphi Museum).
99   *Lower left,* Alinari—Art Reference Bureau (Musio Nazionale delle Terme, Rome); *upper right,* Alinari—Art Reference Bureau (Olympie Museum).
100   *Upper,* Marburg—Art Reference Bureau (Acropolis Museum); *lower,* Art Reference Bureau.
111   *Upper right,* Art Reference Bureau (Autnahme des Deutsche Archaeologische Institut); *lower left,* The Metropolitan Museum of Art, Rogers Fund, 1909; *lower right,* Alinari—Art Reference Bureau (Museo Nazionale, Naples).
112   Alinari—Art Reference Bureau (Museo della Villa Borghese, Rome).
124   Alinari—Art Reference Bureau.
132   Alinari—Art Reference Bureau (Gliptoteca, Munich).
133   Alinari—Art Reference Bureau (Gliptoteca, Copenhagen).
153   The Metropolitan Museum of Art.
161   *Upper,* Alinari—Art Reference Bureau; *lower,* Alinari—Art Reference Bureau.
186   Alinari—Art Reference Bureau.
195   Art Reference Bureau.
196   Alinari—Art Reference Bureau.
197   *Upper,* Alinari—Art Reference Bureau; *lower,* Alinari—Art Reference Bureau.
198   Alinari—Art Reference Bureau.
199   Alinari—Art Reference Bureau.
206   Copyright British Museum.
216   Anderson—Art Reference Bureau.
221   *Lower left,* The Pierpont Morgan Library; *lower right,* The Pierpont Morgan Library.
227   Art Reference Bureau (Library of the Abbey of St. Gall).
229   Marburg—Art Reference Bureau.
246   Historical Pictures Service—Chicago (French National Archives).
259   Paul Lacroix, *Science and Literature in the Middle Ages and the Renaissance,* 1878.
267   *Upper right,* Alinari—Art Reference Bureau; *lower left,* Alinari—Art Reference Bureau.
285   Alinari—Art Reference Bureau.
296   Historical Pictures Service—Chicago.
308   Historical Pictures Service—Chicago.
318   Courtesy of the Walters Art Gallery, Baltimore.
338   Historical Pictures Service—Chicago.
340   National Library, Paris, in Paul La-

Page

croix, *Science and Literature in the Middle Ages and Renaissance*, 1878.

343   *Upper right,* Alinari—Art Reference Bureau; *lower right,* Alinari—Art Reference Bureau.

345   *Upper left,* Marburg—Art Reference Bureau; *lower left,* Alinari—Art Reference Bureau; *upper right,* Marburg—Art Reference Bureau.

347   Imperial Library, Paris, in Paul Lacroix, *The Arts in the Middle Ages and at the Period of the Renaissance*, 1870.

353   Ms. Ashmole from the Bodleian Library, Oxford.

355   *Upper right,* Campana Museum, in Paul Lacroix, *Science and Literature in the Middle Ages and the Renaissance*, 1878; *lower left,* Genevieve Library, in Paul Lacroix, *Science and Literature in the Middle Ages and the Renaissance*, 1878.

361   Alinari—Art Reference Bureau (S. Caterina, Pisa).

374   The Metropolitan Museum of Art, Dick Fund, 1925.

376   The Pierpont Morgan Library.

378   Historical Pictures Service—Chicago.

379   The Metropolitan Museum of Art, Fletcher Fund, 1933.

380   Alinari—Art Reference Bureau.

381   Alinari—Art Reference Bureau (National Museum, Florence).

382   Cliché des Musées Nationaux, Louvre.

383   *Upper,* Alinari—Art Reference Bureau (Uffizi Gallery, Florence); *lower,* Taurgo Slides (Dresden Museum).

384   Alinari—Art Reference Bureau (Galleria dell' Accademia, Florence).

391   Historical Pictures Service—Chicago.

393   Historical Pictures Service—Chicago.

400   Museo del Prado, Madrid.

402   Vatican Museum.

406   Joseph Gruenpeck, *Ein Spiegel der naturlichen himlichen und prophetischen sehungen aller trubsalen. . . .*, 1508, Bayerische Staatsbibliothek, Munich.

408   Pamphilius Gengenbach, *Der Bundtschu*, 1513, Staatsbibliothek der Stiftung Preubischer Kulturbesitz Marburg.

415   *Upper right,* Historical Pictures Service—Chicago (British Museum); *lower right,* Museo del Prado, Madrid.

417   Bibliothèque publique et universitaire, Geneva (Jean Arlaud, Photographer).

419   Sebastian Munster, *Cosmographie*, 1550, Bibliothèque publique et universitaire, Geneva (Jean Arlaud, Photographer).

Page

422   *Upper left,* Historical Pictures Service—Chicago; *lower left,* The Bettmann Archive.

424   Museo del Prado, Madrid.

425   Museo del Prado, Madrid.

427   Historical Pictures Service—Chicago.

432   *Upper,* Historical Pictures Service—Chicago; *lower,* Courtesy of the American Museum of Natural History.

437   *Upper left,* The National Library of Wales; *upper right,* The Huntington Library, San Marino, California.

439   The Metropolitan Museum of Art, Bequest of Annie C. Kane, 1926.

440   Historical Pictures Service—Chicago.

441   Kunsthistorisches Museum, Vienna.

443   Historical Pictures Service—Chicago.

446   Propriété du Musée cantonal des beaux-arts à Lausanne.

447   Courtesy Museum of Fine Arts, Boston (gift of Gordon Abbott and George P. Gardner).

451   British National Gallery.

455   Essex Institute Collection (Baldwin Coolidge, Photographer).

456   *Upper left,* New York Public Library; *lower left,* Alinari—Art Reference Bureau (Church of S. Maria della Vittoria).

457   Alinari—Art Reference Bureau.

458   The Metropolitan Museum of Art, Bequest of Mrs. H. O. Havemeyer, 1929, The H. O. Havemeyer Collection.

467   Historical Pictures Service—Chicago.

468   *Upper left,* The Bettmann Archive; *middle left,* The Bettmann Archive (from the Bagford Collection, The British Museum); *lower left,* Historical Pictures Service—Chicago (engraved after a painting by Jan Steen in the Braunschweig Gallery).

469   Historical Pictures Service—Chicago.

471   Historical Pictures Service—Chicago (painting by C. Lefevre in the Versailles Museum).

472   Historical Pictures Service—Chicago.

479   Historical Pictures Service—Chicago.

481   The Bettmann Archive (painting by Jean Marc Nattier).

483   The Bettmann Archive.

484   Historical Pictures Service—Chicago.

487   Historical Pictures Service—Chicago.

488   The Bettmann Archive.

492   Courtesy of The American Museum of Natural History.

493   Courtesy of The American Museum of Natural History.

496   Historical Pictures Service—Chicago.

497   Historical Pictures Service—Chicago.

499   *Upper right,* Historical Pictures Serv-

Page

ice—Chicago; *lower left*, Historical Pictures Service—Chicago.

501   Historical Pictures Service—Chicago.

503   The Bettmann Archive.

509   Historical Pictures Service—Chicago (courtesy of Lloyd's).

511   Historical Pictures Service—Chicago.

512   *Upper left*, The Bettmann Archive (Essex Institute, Salem); *lower left*, The Bettmann Archive.

517   The Bettmann Archive (painting by Rigaud in the Wallace Collection, London).

518   Historical Pictures Service—Chicago.

520   *Upper left*, The Bettmann Archive (The British Museum); *lower right*, Historical Pictures Service—Chicago.

522   Historical Pictures Service—Chicago.

523   Historical Pictures Service—Chicago.

526   Historical Pictures Service—Chicago.

528   *Upper left*, Historical Pictures Service—Chicago; *lower left*, Historical Pictures Service—Chicago.

529   Historical Pictures Service—Chicago.

530   Historical Pictures Service—Chicago.

532   Historical Pictures Service—Chicago.

533   The Bettmann Archive.

534   Historical Pictures Service—Chicago.

544   The Bettmann Archive (Versailles Museum).

546   The Bettmann Archive.

549   The Bettmann Archive.

552   The Bettmann Archive.

553   Historical Pictures Service—Chicago.

554   Bulloz—Art Reference Bureau (Carnavalet Museum).

557   Historical Pictures Service—Chicago (Louvre).

559   Courtesy of the Prado Museum.

563   The Bettmann Archive.

569   The Metropolitan Museum of Art, Wolfe Fund, 1931.

570   Copyright, The Frick Collection, New York.

571   The Bettmann Archive.

572   The Bettmann Archive.

573   The Bettmann Archive (painting by Sir Thomas Lawrence).

578   Historical Pictures Service—Chicago.

582   Cliché des Musées Nationaux, Louvre.

583   Historical Pictures Service—Chicago.

584   Historical Pictures Service—Chicago.

586   Marburg—Art Reference Bureau.

588   The Bettmann Archive.

590   Historical Pictures Service—Chicago.

595   Historical Pictures Service—Chicago.

596   Bibliothèque Nationale, Paris, Cabinet des Estampes.

597   Historical Pictures Service—Chicago.

Page

599   *Upper right*, The Bettmann Archive; *lower right*, The Bettmann Archive.

600   *Upper left*, Historical Pictures Service—Chicago; *lower left*, Historical Pictures Service—Chicago.

601   The Bettmann Archive.

603   Historical Pictures Service—Chicago.

605   Historical Pictures Service—Chicago (from the Report of the Royal Commission, 1842).

607   *Upper right*, Historical Pictures Service—Chicago; *lower right*, Historical Pictures Service—Chicago.

608   *Upper left*, The Bettmann Archive; *lower left*, The Bettmann Archive.

609   Historical Pictures Service—Chicago.

613   Courtesy of the Swedish Information Service.

615   Wide World Photos.

621   The Bettmann Archive.

622   Historical Pictures Service—Chicago.

626   Historical Pictures Service—Chicago.

628   Historical Pictures Service—Chicago.

632   The Bettmann Archive.

634   *Upper*, Historical Pictures Service—Chicago; *lower*, Courtesy of the Museum of Fine Arts, Boston, Tompkins Collection.

635   Kunsthistorische Museum, Vienna.

645   Historical Pictures Service—Chicago.

646   Historical Pictures Service—Chicago.

647   Historical Pictures Service—Chicago.

648   Historical Pictures Service—Chicago.

651   Historical Pictures Service—Chicago.

655   The Bettmann Archive (photo by Alexander Gardner).

657   Historical Pictures Service—Chicago.

662   Photo courtesy of W. W. Binns, Portsmouth, Ohio.

666   The Bettmann Archive.

669   Historical Pictures Service—Chicago.

676   Historical Pictures Service—Chicago (from *Harper's Weekly*).

683   *Upper right*, The Bettmann Archive; *lower left*, The Bettmann Archive; *lower right*, The Bettmann Archive.

685   Historical Pictures Service—Chicago.

687   Historical Pictures Service—Chicago.

691   Historical Pictures Service—Chicago.

693   Historical Pictures Service—Chicago.

694   *Upper*, The Bettmann Archive; *lower*, The Bettmann Archive.

700   Historical Pictures Service—Chicago.

705   *Upper*, Historical Pictures Service—Chicago; *lower*, The Bettmann Archive.

707   Historical Pictures Service—Chicago.

715   Historical Pictures Service—Chicago.

729   Wide World Photos.

730   Wide World Photos.

Page

731   The Bettmann Archive.
733   Wide World Photos.
736   Historical Pictures Service—Chicago.
749   Wide World Photos.
751   Historical Pictures Service—Chicago.
756   Wide World Photos.
762   *Upper,* Wide World Photos; *lower,* The Bettmann Archive.
770   *Upper left,* Wide World Photos; *lower left,* Wide World Photos; *lower right,* Wide World Photos.
777   Wide World Photos.
779   Wide World Photos.
782   Wide World Photos.
785   Wide World Photos.
786   Wide World Photos.
790   Historical Pictures Service—Chicago.
791   Historical Pictures Service—Chicago.
795   *Upper,* Wide World Photos; *lower,* Historical Pictures Service—Chicago.
801   Wide World Photos.
802   Historical Pictures Service—Chicago.
809   Historical Pictures Service—Chicago.
810   Historical Pictures Service—Chicago.
814   *Upper,* Wide World Photos; *lower,* Wide World Photos.
817   *Upper,* Wide World Photos; *lower,* Wide World Photos.
825   *Upper,* Historical Pictures Service—Chicago (Talburt in the Washington *Daily News,* 1932); *lower,* Historical Pictures Service—Chicago (Darling in the New York *Tribune,* 1931).
843   Wide World Photos.
848   *Lower left,* Wide World Photos; *lower right,* Wide World Photos.
851   *Top,* Wide World Photos; *bottom right,* Wide World Photos.
852   Wide World Photos (New York *Times*).
855   *Upper left,* Wide World Photos (New York *Times*); *lower right,* Wide World Photos.
860   Wide World Photos.
861   Historical Pictures Service—Chicago.
866   Historical Pictures Service—Chicago (Burck in the Chicago *Sun-Times,* July

29, 1945; reprinted from The Chicago *Sun-Times*).
868   Historical Pictures Service—Chicago (Fitzpatrick in the St. Louis *Post-Dispatch,* October 6, 1955; reprinted by permission of the St. Louis *Post-Dispatch*).
872   *Upper left,* Historical Pictures Service—Chicago (Burck in the Chicago *Sun-Times,* February 23, 1949; reprinted from The Chicago *Sun-Times*); *lower left,* Historical Pictures Service—Chicago (Vicky in the London *Daily News Chronicle,* 1948).
878   Wide World Photos.
880   Historical Pictures Service—Chicago (Fitzpatrick in the St. Louis *Post-Dispatch,* March 23, 1954; reprinted by permission of the St. Louis *Post-Dispatch*).
883   Wide World Photos.
888   Wide World Photos.
889   Wide World Photos.
894   Wide World Photos.
895   Historical Pictures Service—Chicago (Burck in the Chicago *Sun-Times,* August 13, 1952; reprinted from the Chicago *Sun-Times*).
902   Historical Pictures Service—Chicago (Orr in the Chicago *Tribune,* 1962; copyright by the Chicago *Tribune*).
903   Wide World Photos.
912   Wide World Photos.
914   Wide World Photos.
918   Collection, The Museum of Modern Art, New York, acquired through the Lillie P. Bliss Bequest.
919   *Top,* Collection, The Museum of Modern Art, New York, Mrs. Simon Guggenheim Fund; *lower left,* Collection, The Museum of Modern Art, New York, gift of James Thrall Soby (permission by courtesy of James Thrall Soby); *lower right,* Collection, The Museum of Modern Art, New York, Mrs. Simon Guggenheim Fund.

Index

Aachen, 229, 239
Abbasids, 214–215, 268
Abelard, Peter, 279, 352, 356–357
Abraham, as first patriarchal leader of the Hebrews, 55; formulation of first covenant by, 56
Absenteeism, 399
Absolutism, theory of royal, 466
Académie des Sciences, 495
Academy, Platonic, 374
Accademia del Cimento, 495
Accademia del Lincei, 495
The Acharnians, 97
Acre, 271, 273
Acropolis, 101
Actium, battle of, 136
Act of Supremacy (1534), 414
Act of Uniformity (1549), 415
Adages (Erasmus), 377
Adams, John, 516
Adenauer, Konrad, 873
Aduwa, battle of (1896), 658, 686
Aediles, 120
Aehrenthal, Count von, participation of, in "Buchlau Bargain," 713
Aeneas, 148
Aeneid, 148
Aequi, 119
Aeschylus, 96; theme of tragedy, 73
Africa, imperialist thrust into, after 1870, 684; nationalist movements in, 892
Afrika Korps, 841, 846
Agamemnon, 96
Agincourt, battle of (1415), 391
Agricultural Adjustment Administration (AAA), 815; second "AAA," 819
Agricultural revolution, 594–596; origin and nature of, 6
Agriculture, technology in Carolingian Europe, 220–222; Middle Ages and, 250–253, 258, 261–262; open field system, 251; commercialization, 594–596; scientific and mechanized, 609
Ahura-Mazda, 54
Aix-la-Chapelle, Peace of, 521
Akhenaton, reign and religious innovations of, 20; influence of, on Egyptian art, 20
Akkad, 29; *see also* Mesopotamia
Alamein, El, battle of, 842
Alaric, 165
Albania, 742
Alberti, Leon Battista (1404–72), 382
Albigensians (Cathari), 272, 281–282, 285, 300; crusade against (1208), 281–282; Innocent III and, 302–303
Alcabala, 440
Alcuin, 209, 231–232, 234

Aleander, Hieronymus (Italian cardinal) (1480–1542), 409
d'Alembert, Jean le Rond (1717–1783), 508
Alexander I (Tsar of Russia), 558, 560, 574
Alexander II (Russia), 666
Alexander III (Russia), 667
Alexander III (Pope), 301–302, 317
Alexander VI (Pope) (1492–1503), 402
Alexander the Great, military activities of, 103; efforts of, to merge West and East, 104; division of empire of, 104
Alexandria, 110
Alexius I (Byzantine Emperor), 268–269
Alfred the Great (King of England), 239, 241–243
Algeciras, Conference of, 712
Algeria, independence gained by, 869, 892
Allia, battle of, 118
Alliances, as motivated by balance of power forces, 679; system of, re-created at Congress of Berlin, 701; between Germany, Russia, and Austria collapsed (1877), 703; between France and Russia (1894–1914), 705; between England and Japan (1902), 709; between England and France, 709; military talks between France and England (1912–), 710; overpowering force of, by 1914, 710–711; assessment of effect of, 716
Alphabet, Arameans, spreading of, by, 47
Alva, Duke of, 441
American Federation of Labor, 655
American Revolution, 532–534
Amiens, Peace of (1802), 557
Amorites, 46; conquest of Sumer-Akkad by, 30, 31
Anabaptism, 412
Anabaptists, 412
Anachronism as historical idea in Renaissance, 373
Anagni, 309
Anarchism, 626–627
Anarchists, 568
Anarcho-Syndicalism, 626–627
Anatolia, invaded by Greek forces, 741
Anatomy Act (1834), 645
Anaximander, 85
Anaximenes, 85
Angevin Empire, 314, 318–319
Anglo-Saxon England, 310–311; Alfred and, 241–242; end of, 310; institutions of, 310–311
Anschluss, 827
Anthropology, 636–637
Antigonus, 104
Antioch, 110
Anti-Semitism, 631–632
Anti-Trinitarianism, 425
Antoninus Pius, 155–156
Antony, Mark, 133, 135, 136, 137
Antwerp, 239

Apartheid, in South Africa, 894
Apella, as Spartan Assembly, 79
Apostles, twelve chosen by Jesus, 169; work of, in spreading Christianity, 169
Appeasement, British policy of, 828
Appian Way, 124
Aquinas, St. Thomas, 353, 359, 360–364
Arabs, in Palestine, 891
Aragon, 263
Arameans, 45; as chief inland traders of Middle East, 47; widespread use of language of, 48
Arch, 345
Archimedes, 109
Architecture, Gothic, 342–346; medieval, 342–346; Romanesque, 342–345
Areopagus, Council of Elders, 75; powers of, diminished, 76
Argentina, 884
Arianism, 185, 189, 192; medieval thought and, 354–366; Aquinas and, 362; Grosseteste and, 364–365
Aristarchus, 108
Aristides, 160
Aristocratic Recovery in the Renaissance, 397–398
Aristophanes, 96, 97
Aristotelianism, 500
Aristotle, 94
Arius, 178
Arkwright, Richard, 598
Arminians, 486
Armistice, ending of World War I, 736
Army, Byzantine, 194; Charlemagne and, 227; feudalism and, 244–245; fyrd in England, 311
Arnold of Brescia, 300
Arnold, Matthew, 633
Arras, League of, 441
Art, in ancient world: preliterate, 4, 5; Egypt, 13, 16, 20; Mesopotamia, 33; Crete, 40; Persia, 53; Greece, 69, 98, 101, 110, 111; Rome, 160–163; Byzantine, 195; Roman, 195; in Sicily (twelfth century), 266–268; Gothic, 277; Renaissance, 379–380; contemporary, and music, 918–920
Arthur, King, 340
Articles of Confederation, 533, 534
Artois, Count d', 561
Asia, conquest of large areas of, by Japan, 886; effect of Japanese conquests upon growing nationalism in, 886
Asiento, 476
Asquith, Herbert, 649
Assideans (Hassidim), 168
Assignats, 547, 551
Assize of Clarendon, 316
Association Movement, 531
Assyria, cultural borrowings of, 49; early migration into Mesopotamia by, 49; as creators of first true empire, 51; rule by terror of, 50
Athanasius, 178
Athelney, 241
Athens, demography of, 74; class struggles in, 74; political structure of, 74; Draconian constitution of, 75; Solonian reforms of constitution of, 75; role of *Thetes* in, 75; celebration of Festival of Dionysos in, 76; role of Council of Five Hundred in political life of, 76; function of *Strategoi* in political life of, 76; measure of political democracy in, 78; dominance in the Delian League, 101
Atlantic, "Battle of the," 845
Atlantic Charter, 860
Atom Bomb, 854, 861
Attila, 165
Attlee, Clement, British prime minister, 867
Aucassin and Nicolette, 341
Augsburg, Diet of (1530), 413

Augsburg, Peace of (1555), 423, 448
Augustus, Caesar, 133, 136, 144–145
Ausgleich (compromise of 1867), 664
Austerlitz, battle of (1805), 558
Australia, 646
Austrasia, 222, 229
Austria, joined in alliance with Germany (1879), 702; ultimatum of, to Serbia in 1914, 727; surrender of (1918), 736; forced to accept Treaty of St. Germain (1919), 740; annexed by Germany, 827
Austria-Hungary, Turkish wars of, 474; absolutism in, 476; lack of middle class in, 477; commercial interests of, 516; War of Austrian Succession (1740–1748), 520; in Seven Years' War, 521; diplomatic alliance with France (1756), 522; and partitions of Poland, 525; Maria Theresa and Joseph II, enlightened monarchs in, 524–526; in coalitions against revolutionary France, 549, 555, 558, 560; at Congress of Vienna, 562; ascendancy in Central Europe after 1815, 572; in revolt (1848–9), 587; revolutionary aims of rebels (1848), 587; counterrevolution in (1848–1849), 588; Federalism versus Centralization, 664; Compromise of 1867 (*Ausgleich*), 664; social and nationality problems after the Compromise, 664–665; basic aims of, preceding World War I, 681; occupied Bosnia-Herzegovina (1878), 701
Automation, 608
Avars, 228
Averröes, 353–354
Avignon, papacy at, 330
Axis Pact, signing and significance of, 795

Babeuf, Francois (1760–1797), 554
Babylonia, founding of, by Amorites, 36
"Babylonian Captivity," 398, 400; *see also* Hebrews
Babylonian captivity of Hebrews, 59
Bach, Alexander, 664
Bacon, Francis (1561–1626), 500, 501, 594
Bacon, Roger, 287, 365
Bacon's "idols," 502
Badoglio, Pietro, Marshal, 847
Baghdad, in Middle Ages, 214–215, 219; Swedish Vikings and, 240
Baillis, French official, 328, 329
Bakewell, Robert, 595
Baldwin IX, 271, 272
Baldwin, Stanley, as Conservative leader in England after World War I, 752; became prime minister after split in Labour Party, 754
Balfour, Arthur, 648
Balfour Declaration, 757
Balkan peoples, basic aims of, after 1870, 682
Balkan states, consequences of World War I for, 736, 737; dominated by Soviet Russia, 876
Balkans, aims of peoples of, 699; force of nationalism in, 699; formation of the Balkan League, 714; the Bosnian crisis of 1908–1909, 713; wars among the states of the, 1912–1913, 714
Balkan wars, aftermath of, 715
Baltic states, dominated by Soviet Russia, 876
Banking, in High Middle Ages, 261
Bank of England, 489, 518
"Barbarossa," code name of German plans to invade Russia, 836
Barnabites, 422
Barnard, Claude, 630
Baroque, Art, 456
Basel, Council of, 303
Bastille, fall of, 545
Battle of the Bulge, 852
"Battle of Nations" (1813), 561
Bavaria, 228, 248

Bayle, Pierre (1647–1706), 504
"Bay of Pigs" invasion of, 902
Beccaria, Marchese Caesare de (1735–1798), 528
"Beer Hall Putsch" (1923), 800
Beethoven, Ludwig, 569
Behaviorism, 913
Bela Kun, 778
Belgium, 895; France in, 554, 555; French lose (1814), 561; rebellion against Dutch and independence of, 583; industry in, 610; conquered by Germany, 834
Belinsky, Vissarion G. (1811–1848), 665
Benedict of Aniane, 232
Benedict IX (Pope), 292–293
Benedictine Rule, 232
Bentham, Jeremy (1748–1832), 508, 577, 622
Bergson, Henri, 634
Beria, L., 877
Berlin, treaty of, 701; division of, into capitalist and communist sectors, 873; Cold War crisis in (1948–1949), 899
Berlin Conference, 1885, imperialist implications of, 683
Berlin-to-Bagdad railroad, 707, 724
Berlin Wall, 901
Bernini, Giovanni (1598–1680), 456
Bernstein, Eduard, 625
Bessarabia, ceded to Rumania after World War I, 742
Bessemer, Henry, 608
Beza, Theodore (1519–1605), 419, 420
Bible, Polyglot, 375
Bill of Rights in 1689, 488
Biology, 498–499, 627–629, 912
Bishop John Fisher (1469–1535), 414
Bismarck, Otto von, "blood and iron," 590; social insurance system, 612; attacks Social Democrats, 625; and expulsion of Austria from Germany, 659–660; Ems dispatch, 660; and Franco-Prussian War, 660–661; and the German Empire, 661–663; dismissed by Emperor William II, 663; attitude toward Balkans after 1871, 681; attitude toward England after 1871, 681; attitude toward France after 1871, 681; peace as aim of, 1871–1890, 681; work of, at Congress of Berlin, 701; formed Dual Alliance with Austria (1879), 702; instigated Mediterranean Pacts (1887), 703; joined Germany in pact with Russia (Reinsurance Treaty, 1887), 703; weaknesses of diplomacy of, 704
Black, Joseph (1728–1799), 498, 601
Black Death, 396, 400
"Black Hundreds" (Russia, 1905), 670
"Black Power" movement, rise of, in United States, 882
Black-White Problem in United States, as affected by 1954 Supreme Court Decision, 881; sit-ins as involved in, 881
Blanche of Castile, 329
Blenheim, Battle of (1704), 475
"Bloody Sunday" (Russia, 1905), 670
Blum, Leon, 759
Boccaccio, Giovanni (1313–1375), 371
Bodin, Jean (c. 1530–96), 466
Boer War, 684, 685
Boethius, 193
Bohr, Niels, 912
Bolivar, Simon, 579
Bologna, center of Roman legal scholarship, 348–349
Bolshevik Revolution, *see* Communism
Bolsheviks (Russian Social Democratic party), 669, 670; *see also* Communism
Bonaparte III, 586, 587
Bonaparte, Jerome, 561
Bonapartists, 574, 579

Boniface VIII (Pope), 308–310, 330, 398
Book of Common Prayer (1549), 415
Borgia, Cesare (1476–1507), 402
Borromeo, Charles (1538–1584), 424
Borromini, Francesco (1599–1667), 456
Bosnia-Herzegovina, 713; Serbian attitude toward, 682; revolt of, against Turkey, 700; occupied by Austria, 701
Bossuet, Jacques Bénigne, Bishop (1627–1704), 466, 472
Botticelli, Sandro (1444–1510), 382
Boulton, Matthew, 601
Bourbon dynasty, 445, 470, 562, 574, 579
Bourbon monarchists (France), 650, 651
Bouvines, battle of (1214), 304, 319, 327
Bow and arrow, development of, 5
Boxer Rebellion, 693
Boyars, 480, 481
Boyle, Robert (1627–1691), 498
Braganza, regent of Portugal, 579
Brahe, Tycho (1546–1601), 494
Bramante, Donato (1444–1514), 383, 402
Brandenburg, 449, 452
Brandenburg-Prussia, rise of, 478; in War of Austrian Succession, 520; in Seven Years' War, 521; and partitions of Poland, 523, 551; and Enlightened Despotism, 526–527; in wars against revolutionary France, 549, 550, 559, 561
Brazil, 884; American support of conservative regime in, 885
Brest-Litovsk, 779, 780; effects of Treaty of, 735
Brethren of the Common Life, 375, 376, 401
Briand, Aristide, 760
Brissot, Jacques, 549
Britain, *see* England
British North American Act (1867), 646
Brunelleschi, Filippo (1377–1446), 380
Bruni, Leonardo (1370–1444), 373
Brüning, Heinrich, 808
Bucer, Martin (1491–1551), 410, 417
Bucharest, Treaty of, 735
"Buchlau Bargain," as precipitant of Bosnian Crisis of 1908–1909, 712–713
Budé, Guillaume (1467–1540), 375
Bulgaria, surrender of (1918), 736; forced to accept Treaty of Neuilly (1919), 741
Bülow, German Chancellor von, 711
Bundesrat, 662
Bundschuh, revolts, 408
Burckhardt, Jacob, 369
Bureaucracy, in Byzantium, 194; Charlemagne and, 234–235; papal, 276; Norman England and, 312–314; under Henry II, 314; under Edward I, 323–325; baillis in France under Capetians, 325–330
Burghley, Lord (1520–1598), 439
Burgoyne, General (1723–1792), 523
Burgundy, 222, 393
Burke, Edmund (1729–1797), 531, 532, 548, 568
Burma, nationalist agitation in, 888
Burschenschaften, 573
Byzantine Empire, government in, 193–194; heresy in, 194–195; culture in, 195–196; reign of Justinian, 198–200; Swedish invasion of, 238; Seljuk Turks and, 268; Crusades and, 268, 272

Cadets (Russian Constitutional Democrats), 670
Caesar, Julius, 132, 134–135, 137, 151
Caesaropapism, 185, 194; and Justinian, 198; and the Western Church, 209
Cahiers (notebooks of grievances), 543
Cairo, meeting of Roosevelt, Churchill, and Chiang Kai-shek at, 859
Calendar, "Julian" revision of, 135
Caligula, 152

Calonne, Charles Alexander de (1734–1802), 535, 542

Calvin, John (1509–64), 375; life and doctrines, 416–418; views on interest, 428

Calvinism, 416, 418; spread of, 418; and capitalism, 428

Cambyses, 52

Campbell-Bannerman, Sir Henry, 649

Campo Formio, Treaty of (1797), 555

Canaan, peoples of, and conquest of, by Hebrews, 58

Canada, 646

Canning, George, 581, 584

Canon law, 301, 349–350

Canossa, 297, 299, 309

Canterbury Tales (Chaucer), 371

Canute, King of England, 243

Capetian Dynasty, 271, 325–332; rise of, 244

Capitalism, inhibited in Spain, 390; depression of, in Renaissance, 397; and Protestantism, 428; commercial capitalism in nineteenth century, 594; financial capitalism, 609–610; in the United States, 612; *laissez faire* capitalism, 621; Marxism and capitalism, 624; revolt of Anarchism against, 626

Capitularies, 230

Capuchins, 422

Caracalla, 162, 164

Caraffa, Carlo (Cardinal), 425

Caraffa, Giovanni Pietro (Pope Paul IV) (1517–61), 421

Carbonari, 579, 583

Carloman, 222, 223

Carlsbad Decrees (1819), 573

Carlyle, Thomas, 577, 633

Carolingian Empire, 219; rise of, 222; Charles Martel in, 222

Carolingian miniscule, 232

"Carolingian Renaissance," 231–233

Cartels, 610

Cartesianism, 501

Cartesian Revolution, 500

Carthusians, 278, 292

Casablanca, meeting of Roosevelt and Churchill at, 859

Cassiodorus, 193

Castiglione, Baldassare, Count (1478–1529), 374–375

Castile, 264

Castlereagh, Lord, 563

Castro, Fidel, established Communist regime in Cuba, 902

Cateau-Cambrésis, treaty of (1559), 421

Cathedral, 342–346; schools, 346–348, 362; *see also* Architecture

Catherine de Medici (1519–89), 445

Catherine II (the Great) of Russia (1729–1796), 522, 528–529, 549

Catiline, Sergius, 133

Cattulus, 136, 151

Cavaignac, General, 586

"Cavaliers," 454

Cavendish, Henry (1731–1810), 498

Cavour, Count, 656

Censors, 120

Censuses, 597

Center party (Germany), 662

Central American Common Market, 897

Central Intelligence Agency (C.I.A.), 884

Cervantes, Saavedra (1547–1616), 450, 459

Cézanne, Paul, 635

Chaeronea, battle of, 103

Chaldea, origin and expansion of, 51

Chamberlain, Joseph, 649

Chamberlain, Neville, 829, 830; desire of, to appease Hitler, 828

Chambers of Reunion, 473–474, 475

Chambord, Duke of (France), 651

Chansons de geste, 338–339, 343

Charlemagne, 209, 219–220, 226–233, 557; coronation of (800), 229; army of, 244–245

Charles I (King of England) (1625–1649), 452, 454, 455

Charles II (King of England) (1630–1685), 455, 475, 487, 488, 495

Charles III (of Spain) (1716–1788), 529

Charles VI (Emperor), 477

Charles VII (King of France) (1403–1461), 391

Charles I, 394; *see also* Charles V, Holy Roman Emperor

Charles V (Holy Roman Emperor), Charles I (King of Spain, 1500–1558), 394, 409, 412, 414, 439, 499

Charles X (France), 574, 581

Charles XII of Sweden, 481, 482

Charles Albert (Piedmont-Sardinia), 588

Charles of Anjou, 307

Charles the Bald, 233, 236

Charles Martel, 214, 222, 223, 224, 263

Charles the Rash (Duke of Burgundy, 1467–1477), 394

Chartism, 644

Chartists, 632

Chartres Cathedral, 358

Chemistry, birth of modern, 498; in nineteenth century, 627

Chernyshevsky, Nikolai, 667

Chiang Kai-shek, 889; as Dr. Sun's successor, 694

"Children's Crusade" (1212), 272

Chile, 885

China, "Free," *see* Formosa

China, European imperialist thrusts into, 689; European concessionary rights in, 689; internal turmoil invited European intervention, 690; war with Japan, 1894–1895, 691; efforts of, to stand against the West, 692; Boxer Rebellion, 693; revolution of 1911–1912, 693; internal difficulties of, 694; casualties of, in World War II, 856; emergence of, as a world power, 856; refused admittance into the United Nations, 890; nationalist developments in, 889; spread of Communism in, 889; development of conflict with Russia, 890; as third world power, 890; supported North Korea, 900

Chirico, Giorgio de, 918

Choephori, 96

Chopin, Frederic, 569

Christian IV (King of Denmark, 1577–1648), 448

"Christian magistracy," 412

Christianity, origins of, 167; Jewish reactions to, 169; collapse and revival of, after crucifixion of Jesus, 171; spread of, in Roman Empire, 172; turning point of, in conversion of Paul, 173; development and difficulties of "world" evangelism, 173; martyrdom among early leaders of, 173; formation of doctrines of, 174; persecution of members of, 175; prominent martyrs of, 176; "apologies" for, 176; early organizations of, 177; rise of monasticism in, 177; dangers to development of, 178; final triumph of, in Roman Empire, 179; Constantine's conversion to, 184; fourth century conversions to, 185; Roman Empire and, 184–186; Clovis and, 193; Russia and, 201; Benedictines and, 207; Anglo-Saxon England and, 208; Normandy and, 239; Scandinavia accepts, 241; Iberian peninsula and, 264; Poland converted to, 273; heresy in High Middle Ages and, 280–282

Church at beginning of Middle Ages, 205; Charlemagne and, 219; in Carolingian times, 224–225; under Otto I, 249–250; in the eleventh century,

254–255; and lay lords (mid-eleventh century), 254; Albigensians and, 281–282; St. Francis and, 285–286
Church Councils, 303
Churchill, Winston, 866; helped break General Strike of 1926, 753; met with Allied leaders in Cairo, 1942, 842; met with Roosevelt and Stalin at Tehran, 850
Cicero, M. Tullius, 133, 137, 151, 372
C.I.O., *see* Committee of Industrial Organizations
Cistercians, 278–280, 282, 287
City of God, 166, 188
Civate, Battle of (1035), 265
Civil Code of 1804 (France), 556, 559, 561, 563; burning of, in Germany, 573
Civil Constitution of the Clergy, 548
Civil Rights Acts of 1964 and 1965 (United States), 882
Civil Wars in England, 453
Civil Works Administration (CWA), 815
Clarendon Code, 487
Claudius, 152
Cleisthenes, 76
Clemenceau, Georges, 652, 732
Clement V (Pope), 309, 330
Clement VII (Pope) (1523–1534), 414
Cleopatra, 134, 136
Clergy, as social and legal group, 467
Clive, Robert (1725–1774), 522
Clovis (Merovingian king), 193, 204, 222
Cluny, 254, 277–278
Coal in industrialization, 600
Colbert, Jean Baptiste (1619–1683), 470, 471, 510, 556
"Colbertism," 470, 471
Cold War, 858; "Thaw" in the, 878; causes of the, 897–898; crises in the, 898–899; space-race aspects of, 901; "Refreeze" phase of, 902; United States-Russian confrontation in the, 902
Coleridge, Samuel Taylor, 569
Colet, John (c. 1467–1519), 376
Coligny, Gaspard de (Admiral of France), 445
Colloquies (Erasmus), 377
Colloquy of Regensburg (1541), 421
Colonnade of St. Peters (Bernini), 456
Columbus, Christopher, 390, 433
Cominform, 899
Comintern, 778
Comitatus, 190–191, 222
Comitia Curiata, 119, 120
Commerce, Eastern Empire and, 193; Mecca and, 210–211; Bagdad and, 214; under Charlemagne, 235; Vikings and, 241
Commercial Capitalism in the nineteenth century, 594
Commercial crises, 604
Commercial and economic trends in High Middle Ages, 260
Committee of General Security, 552
Committee of Industrial Organizations (C.I.O.), 818
Committee of Public Safety, 551, 552, 553
Commodus, 157
Common Market, 870, 897
Communications, significance of the Crusades on, 273; development of, in nineteenth century, 601
Communism, ideological content of, 776; place of class struggle in, 776; concept of state "withering away" in, 777; concept of classless society in, 777; attempts to establish, in Europe after World War I, 778; critical period of, in Russia, 778; goals and methods of (after 1929), 782; function of Party leadership in Russian, 784; incentives in Russian, 784; gains and costs of Russian, 785; changes in, in Russia, 787; ideology of, held by

rival states, 876; spread of, after World War II, 875; expansion of Soviet, 876; spread of, in China, 889; advances of, in Italy (1948), 899
Communist Manifesto, 623, 624
Communist Party, in Weimar Republic, 800
Communist Revolution, background of, 774; preceded by brief bourgeois revolution, 774–775; in Russia, 776
Competitive State System (1720–1740), 515
Comte, August, 629
Concentration camps, in Germany, 810
"Concert of Europe," 563, 572, 576, 581
Conciliarism, 399
Concordat of Bologna, 472
Concordat of 1801, 557
Concordat of Worms (1122), 298, 304, 313
Condillac, Etienne de, 505
Condorcet, Marquis de (1743–1794), 505, 506
Confederation of the Rhine, 558
Confessions (Rousseau), 509
Congo, conquest of, by Belgium, 683
Congress of Berlin, 723; rewrote Treaty of San Stefano, 701; aftermath of, 701
Congress of Racial Equality (CORE), 881
Congress of Vienna, 561, 656
Congress System (after 1815), 562
Conquistadores, 264, 433
Conrad III (Emperor), 270
Conservation of energy (Physics), 627
Conservatives (England), 644, 645, 647, 648, 752, 753
Conservatives (Germany), 662, 663
Consolations of Philosophy, 193
Constance, Council of (1414–1417), 399
Constant, Benjamin, 577
Constantine, 164, 165, 178, 184
Constantinople, Sancta Sophia in, 199; Moslems attack, 201; in Charlemagne's time, 219; Swedish Vikings and, 240; Venice and, 259
Constitution of 1793 (France), 552
Constitution (United States), 534
Constitutions of Clarendon, 317
Contarini, Gasparo (Cardinal) (1483–1542), 421, 422
Contemporary society, the "new masses" in, 904; "breakthrough to peace" in, beginnings of, 905; summary statement regarding, 909; the disintegration of traditional institutions and beliefs in, 909–910; impact of industry and science on, 911; views in, re religious beliefs and institutions, 911–913; views in, re nature of man, 913; changes in social institutions of, 914; "Corporate Man" in, 914; "new woman" and "new family" in, 915; "ethical revolution" in, 915; the new nihilism in, 916; art and music of, 918–920; search for "identity" in, 917–923; literature and philosophy in, 920–921
Continental Congress, 523
Continental System, 558–560
Cooper, James Fenimore, 569
Copernicus, Nicholas (1473–1543), his challenge to Ptolemaic astronomy, 493
Cordon Sanitaire, 743
Cordova, 216, 263
Corporations, limited liability, 609; coordination of, 610
Corpus Juris Civilis, 200, 349–350
Cort, Henry, 600
Cortés, Hernando (1485–1547), 389
Cosmos, in Greek religious beliefs, 73
Coughlin, Father, 817
Council of Europe, 895
Council for Mutual Economic Aid, 897
Council of Trent (1545–1563), 424, 427
Councils and the papacy, 303, 306
Coup d'etat of Napoleon (1799), 555

Court of High Commission, 453, 488
Court of Star Chamber, 453
Courtier, the (Castiglione), 375
Courtrai, battle of, 330
Cranmer, Thomas, Archbishop of Canterbury (1489–1556), 414
Crassus, Marcus, 132
Crécy, battle of (1346), 391
Crete, early settlements in, 37; cultural developments in, 37; commercial dominance of, 38; political patterns and practices of, 38; economic and religious life of, 39; art forms in, 40; humane character of society of, 40; language and literature of, 41
Crime and Punishment (Dostoevsky), 633
Crimean War (1854–1856), 656, 663
Crispi, F. (Italy), 658
Cro-Magnon man, 2
Crompton, Samuel, 598
Cromwell, Oliver (1599–1658), 455
Cromwell, Thomas (1485–1540), 414
Crusader States, 177, 270
Crusades, background and First Crusade (1095–1098), 268; Pope Urban II and First Crusade, 268–270; capture of Jerusalem, 269; Second Crusade (1147–1148), 270; Third Crusade (1189–1192), 270–271; Fourth Crusade (1201–1204), 271–272; later Crusades, 272; significance of, 273
Cuba, became quasi-proctectorate of the United States, 696; Communist regime established in, 902; "Bay of Pigs" invasion of, 902
Cubism, 918
"Cult of stability," 516, 520
Cultural stages of humankind, 2
Culture, German tribes and, 189–190; Byzantine, 195–196; in Carolingian Renaissance, 231; Norse and European, 241; in Anglo-Saxon England, 242; Ottonian Renaissance and, 250; significance of the Crusades and, 273; Louis IX and, 329–330; high medieval and Greek compared, 335–336
Cummings, E. E., 916
Curia Regis, 321
Custom, 467–469
Czech Brethren, 425
Czechoslovakia, created at end of World War I, 740; harassed by Sudetan problems, 827, 828; dismemberment of, by Hitler, 829; Russian takeover in (1948), 899
Cyclades, as settled by Ionians, 71
Cynics, 107
Cyrus, as creator of extensive empire, 52

Dadaism, 634
Daimler, Gottlieb, 607
Dalton, John, 627
Damascus, 212, 213
Damietta, 272
"Danegeld," 243, 311
"Danelaw," 243
Danilevsky, N. Y., 667
Dante, 342, 371, 493, 583
Danton, Georges (1759–1794), 553
Darius, 88
Darlan, Admiral, 847
Darwin, Charles, 621, 628–629
Darwinism, Social, 619, 629, 630, 631
Das Kapital (Marx), 624, 669
David (Donatello), 380, 389
David, extension of Hebrew kingdom by, 59
David, Jacques Louis (1774–1825), 544, 552
"Dawes Plan" (1924), 749, 767
Dead Sea Scrolls, 168

Decameron (Boccaccio), 371
Decembrist Revolt in Russia (1825), 575
Declaration of Independence, 533
Declaration of Pillnitz, 548
Declaration of the Rights of Man and the Citizen, 546
"Defenestration of Prague," 448
Defoe, Daniel (1660–1731), 518
De Gaulle, General, 892, 897; re-elected president of France (1966), 869; return of, to politics, 869; vetoed England's entrance into Common Market, 870
Deism, 505
Deists, 568
Delacroix, Eugene, 569
Deladier, French premier, 829
Delcassé, French Foreign Minister, involved in first Moroccan crisis (1905), 711
Delphi, religious festivals at, 74
Democracy, theory of rise of, 191; medieval towns and, 259; Parliament and, 321
Democritus, 91, 108
Demos, 75
Demosthenes, 103
Denmark, 241–243, 895
Depression, during Renaissance, 397
The Depression, in Germany (1930s), 801
Der Führer, see Hitler
Descartes, René (1596–1650), 496, 500
De Valera, Eammon, Irish leader, 754
Deventer, 401
De Witt, Jan, 486
D-Day, invasion of Normandy by Allied forces, 850
Dialogue on the Two Principal Systems of the Universe (Galileo), 495
Diaz, Bartolomew (c. 1450–1500), 432
Diaz, Porfirio, Mexican dictator amenable to activities of imperialist powers, 697
Dickens, Charles, 632
Diderot, Denis (1713–1784), 505, 508
Diderot and the Encylopedists, 508
Dien Bien Phu, battle of, 903
Dilthey, Wilhelm, 635
Diocletian, 164, 184, 194
Diplomatic revolution (1756), 522
Directory (France), 554–555
Disarmament, failure of Allied powers to effect, 743; commission created to deliberate on, 749
Disraeli, Benjamin, 632, 645, 647
Dissenters (British), 645, 647
Divine Comedy, 342, 371
Divine right of kings, 385, 389, 427, 460, 466
DNA, significance of, in genetics research, 913
Doctor Zhivago, 878
Doenitz, Karl, Admiral, as Hitler's successor surrendered to Allies, 853
Domesday Book, 312
"Domestic system," 437
Dominican Order, 283–284
Donatello (c. 1386–1466), 380
"Donation of Constantine," Valla and, 230, 373
"Donation of Pepin," 225
Don Quixote (Cervantes), 450, 459
Dorians, 68; invaded Peloponnese, 70
Dostoevsky, Fedor, 633, 667
Draco, 75
Drake, Francis (c. 1540–1596), 443
Dreiser, Theodore, 920
Dreyfus, Alfred, 653
Dreyfus Case, 653
Duce, see Mussolini
Duke of Monmouth, 488
Duke of Somerset (1506–1552), 415
Duma (Russia), 670, 671
Dumbarton Oaks, conferences at, 860

Dunkerque (Dunkirk), evacuation of Allied troops from, 835
Duns Scotus, 363–364
Dürer, Albrecht (1471–1528), 385
Durham, Lord, 646
Dutch, Empire Building, 433; United Provinces, 441, 449; Republic, 465, 467, 473, 486, 489, 491, 503, 518, 594; in French revolution, 555, 557; separated from Belgium, 583
Dutch East India Company, 433, 436, 688

Earth, age of, 1
Eastern Europe, crisis in, 451–452
Eastern Orthodox Church, 373, 425
Eastern Roman Empire, 396
East India Company, 510, 517, 686
East March, 228
Ebert, Friedrich, as first president of the Weimar Republic, 800, 801
Ecclesia, general assembly of Athens, 75, 76
Eck, John (1486–1543), 409
Economic thought, of the Enlightenment, 510; liberal, 620–622
Economy, sixth and seventh centuries, 204; under Charlemagne's influence, 235; village economy in Early Middle Ages, 252–253; in High Middle Ages, 257–262; in twelfth century England, 314–316
Ecstasy of St. Theresa, 457
Edict of Worms, 409, 410, 412
Edington, battle of (878), 241
Education, impact of the Benedictines on, 207; in Charlemagne's time, 231, 233–234; Benedictine power and, 278; St. Dominic and, 283–284; St. Francis and, 287–288; Louis IX and, 330; cathedral schools and, 346–347; universities in eleventh and twelfth centuries, 346–347; *stadium generale*, 347
Edward I (King of England), 323–324, 330
Edward the Confessor (King of England), 243, 250, 254, 311
Edward VI (King of England) (1547–1553), 415, 419, 444
Egypt, 206, 215; early settlements in, 6; chronological chart of political and cultural revolution in, 9; development of writing in, 8; as "land of two lands," 8; government and economic life in Old Kingdom of, 10; founding of first dynasty of, 8; position of women in, 11; medical practices in, 12; creation of calendar in, 11; creation of written language in, 12; religious beliefs and practices in, 13; early architecture and sculpture in, 13; chief gods in religion of, 14; decline of Old Kingdom in, 15; founding of Middle Kingdom in, 15; decline of Middle Kingdom in, 16; beginning of Bronze Age in, 16; religious concepts in, 16; conquest of, by Hyksos, 17; empire period of, 18; imperial conquests of, 18; religious innovations by Akhenaton in, 20; cultural changes of, during Empire period, 19; Aton worship in, 21; decline of Atonism in, 21; spread of Empire in New Kingdom, 22; decline of New Kingdom in, 22; center of Moslem power during Crusades, 272; occupied by England (1882), 684; attempts to achieve independence after World War I, 755; admitted into League of Nations, 755; abandoned monarchy, 891; gained independence, 891
Einhard, 226, 229, 231, 232
Einstein, Albert, 627, 911
Eisenhower, Dwight D., commander of Allied invasion forces in Normandy, 850; as president, sent troops to Little Rock, Arkansas, 881
Electors of the Holy Roman Empire, 394
Electra, 96

Eleusinian cult, 84
Eliot, George, 632
Eliot, T. S., 920
Elizabeth, Empress of Russia (1740–1762), 522
Elizabeth, Queen of England (1558–1603), 416, 442, 444, 452
Elizabethan England, 443–444
Elizabethan Religious Settlement, 444
Emigrés (French Rev.), 548, 549
Empiricists: Bacon and Locke, 501–502
Enclosure of land in England, 595
Encyclopédie, 508, 512
Energy conversion, 607–608
"Energy Revolution," 598–603
Engels, Friedrich, 623, 624, 663
Enghien, Duc d', 557
Engineering, 601
England, Germanic tribes in, 192, 204; Benedictine monks and, 207–209; Viking invasions in, 238, 241; under Alfred the Great, 241–242; medieval agrarian system in, 253; Henry IV and Gregory VII and, 296–298; at end of Anglo-Saxon period, 310; feudalism in, 312; investiture Controversy in, 313; beginnings and evolution of Parliament, 321–325; conquest of Wales by, 325; John of Salisbury and, 358; in Renaissance, 376; Erasmus in, 377; in the Hundred Years' War, 390–393; Wars of the Roses, 393, 397; and heretical movements (Lollards), 400; Henry VIII and succession crisis, 414; in Reformation, 414–416; Catholic restoration under Mary Tudor and Philip II, 416; students from, in Geneva, 418; imperial trade, 436; economic growth in sixteenth century, 437; mercantilism in, 438; Philip II attacks England, 443; Elizabethan religious settlement in, 444; politics under Elizabeth, 444; civil war under the Stuart Kings, 452–455; under Cromwell's Protectorate, 455; control of by King and Parliament, 466; commercial middle classes in, 467; in War of Spanish Succession, 475; and Peace of Utrecht, 475–476; Peter the Great visits, 480–481; and the Restoration of the Stuarts (1660), 487–488; the "Glorious Revolution" in, 488; Revolutionary Settlement and after, 488–489; Whig and Tory factions appear, 489; retains established church, 491; and the Royal Society of London, 495–496; development of chemistry in, 498; public health in, 499–500; empirical tradition in, 501–502; political philosophy of Hobbes and Locke in, 502–504; Methodism in, 511; and the competitive state system (1720–1740), 515; commercial progress in eighteenth century, 518–520; and War of Jenkins' Ear, 520; in War of Austrian Succession, 520; in Seven Years' War and Anglo-French War, 521–523; failure of democratization in eighteenth century, 530–532; the case of John Wilkes, 531; and the American Revolution, 532–534; at war with revolutionary France, 551; in Second Coalition, 555; at war with Napoleonic France, 558–562; and the Continental System, 558–559; represented at Congress of Vienna, 562; conservatism in, 575; aids Greek revolutionaries, 579; aids San Martin, 579; withdraws from Quintuple Alliance, 581; Constitutional changes of 1832, 583–584; Reform Bill of 1832, 583–584, 644; possesses requirements for industrialization, 593; "workshop of the world," 594; mistress of the seas, 594; commercial capitalism, 594; commercialization of agriculture in, 594–595; population growth and industrialization in, 596; urbanization and public health, 597; technological developments in, 598; spread of factory system in, 598–599; coal, iron, and steam

in industrialization, 600–601; development of transportation in, 601–603; and communication, 601–603; organization of industrial society, 603–604; Labour unions in, 604–605; and problems of city life, 605–606; and integration of industrial society, 606; pioneer of "open-ended revolution," 606–607; gains control of Suez Canal, 611; and industrialized warfare, 614–615; liberal economics in, 620–622; Utopianism in, 623; Christian Socialism in, 625; democratization of (1832–1914), 644–650; Victorian Compromise, 644–645; Liberal Nationalism under Palmerston, 645–646; under Disraeli and Gladstone, 646–647; Corn Laws, 645, 648; and the Irish Question, 648, 649; Social Liberalism and the Labour Party in, 648–649; "People's Budget" (1909), 649; Parliament Reform Bill of 1911, 649; suffragettes in, 649; in Crimean War, 656; weakened influence on international crises before WWI, 671; as political arbiter of Europe after 1815, 679; political aims of, preceding World War I, 681; imperialist thrust of, in Africa (1882–1902), 684; conquest of Boer Republics, 684; occupation of Sudan by (1898), 684; imperial interests of, in Asia, 686; crushing of Sepoy rebellion by, 687; imperial conquests of, in India, 688; and "splendid isolation," 702; joined with Austria and Italy in Mediterranean Pacts (1887), 703; reassessed policy of "Splendid Isolation," 707; joined in accord with Russia (1907), 709; joined in alliance with Japan (1902), 707, 708; formed *Entente Cordiale* with France, 709; in the first Moroccan crisis, 712; economic rivalry of, with Germany as a cause of World War I, 724; losses suffered by, from German U-boat activity in World War I, 731; offensive against Turkey in World War I, 730; consequences of World War I for, 736–737; economic difficulties of, after World War I, 751–752; decline of Liberal Party in, 752; political and economic difficulties of, after World War I, 752–754; General Strike in (1926), 753; coalition government in, 753; troubles of, in Ireland, 754; post-war troubles of, in Egypt, 755; troubles of, in Palestine after World War I, 757–758; joined in pacts with Poland, Rumania, Greece, Turkey to stop Nazi aggression, 830; planned occupation of areas of Norway, 832; airforce of, defeated *Luftwaffe*, 835; subjected to all-out bombing by Germany, 835; troops of, fight Nazi and Fascist armies in Africa, 84; construction of welfare state in, 866; general conditions in, after World War II, 865; specific welfare legislation passed in, after World War II, 866; Conservative Party of, formed governments after 1955, 867; economic problems in, after World War II, 867; abortive war against Egypt, 891; landed troops in Lebanon, 891

English Church (Anglicans), 414, 418

English Common Law, development under Henry II, 316; under Edward I, 323–325

English East India Company, 436, 510, 517

Enlightened despotism, 524–530

Enlightenment, 505–510; problem of knowledge, 507–508; economic thought of, 510

Entente Cordiale, 709

Entrepreneurs in nineteenth century industrialization, 604

Ephors, 80

Epic of Gilgamesh, Babylonian reworking of Sumerian saga, 36

Epicurus, 108, 112

Equites, 127, 130, 133, 145, 147

Erasmians, 386, 408, 411, 419, 420

Erasmus, Desiderius (1466–1536), 375, 376–378, 385, 401, 402, 416, 425; "philosophy of Christ," 377; break with Luther, 419

Eratosthenes, 109

An Essay Concerning Human Understanding (Locke), 502

Essenes, 170

Estates-General, origins of, 331

Esterhazy, Major, 653

Estonia, 780, 832

Ethiopia, defeated imperialist thrust by Italy (1896), 686; conquest of, by Italy (1935), 824

Etymologies, 408

Eumenides, 96

Euripides, 95, 96; and theme of tragedy, 73

Europe, in 600 A.D., 204–205; in the eleventh century, 254; in High Middle Ages, 257; at end of High Middle Ages, 288; culture in High Middle Ages, 335–336; territorial expansion of, 431–432; regional groupings in, after World War II, 894–897; the "new," after World War II, 895

European Coal and Steel Community, 895

European Defence Community, failure of Europe to form, 897

European Economic Community ("The Six"), 897

European Revolts of 1820 and 1821, 578–581

Evolution and religion, 629

Evolutionary stages of man, 2

Exodus, of Hebrews out of Egypt, 57

Eyck, Jan, van (c. 1389–1441), 379

Ezekiel, as exilic prophet, 61

Fabian Society, 625

Factory Act (1833), 605

Factory system, 598–599

Fall, Albert, involved in the Teapot Dome scandal, 762

Faraday, Michael, 603

Farel, William (1489–1565), 417

Farnese, Alessandro (Pope Paul III) (1468–1549), 421

Fascist Party (Italian), birth of, 790; road to power of the, 790–791; credo of, 391

Fashoda, encounter between British and French forces at (1898), 684

Fatima, 213

Federal Republic of Germany, 873

Fenian Society, 648

Ferdinand I, Holy Roman Emperor (1503–1564), 414

Ferdinand II (Holy Roman Emperor) (1578–1637), 448

Ferdinand V (King of Spain) (1452–1516), 389, 394

Ferdinand VII (Spain), 574, 578

Ferdinand I (King of the Two Sicilies), 574

Ferry, Jules, 652

Festival of Reason (French Rev.), 553

Feudal law, 315, 316

Feudalism, benefice in, 244–245; vassalage in, 244–245; homage and fealty in, 245; fief in, 245–247; definition of, 245; height of, in France, 247; decline of, 261; Magna Carta and, 320–321; Ficino, Marsilio (1433–1499), 374; establishment of, in England, 312

Finland, 780; "Winter War" of, with Russia, 832

First Coalition, against France, 551, 554

Five Year Plans, 783, 784, 785, 877

Flanders, 259, 393, 397, 428, 456

Fleury, Cardinal (1653–1743), 517, 534

Florence, in eleventh century, 259; Boccaccio in, 371; civic humanism in, 372, 374; Platonic Academy in, 374; expansion of, 388; banking in, 397

Flying buttress, 346

Foch, Ferdinand, Marshal, as supreme Allied military commander in World War I, 735
Fontenelle, Bernard de (1657–1757), 506
Fordney-McCumber Tariff Act (1922), 761
Formosa (Taiwan), 889
Forster Education Act (1870), 647
Fourteen Points, Woodrow Wilson's, 735
Fourteenth Amendment, 654
Fourth Lateran Council (1215), 303
France, genesis of Catholic church in, 193; birth of feudalism in, 244; John I invades (1214), 304; under the Capetians, 325–332; cathedrals in, 342–346; vernacular literature in, 371; humanism in, 375; Hundred Years' War, 390, 397; covets Flanders, 393; invades Italy (1494), 402; Calvin as reformer of, 416; attempts to crush Calvinism in, 418; allied with Ottoman Turks, 425; massacre of St. Bartholomew's Eve, 445; religious and civil wars of the sixteenth century, 445–447; Huguenots in, 445–447, 473; *politiques,* 446, 450, 460; Richelieu brings France into Thirty Years' War, 448; Peace of Westphalia, 449; and Peace of the Pyrenees, 450, 451; under Richelieu and Mazarin, 450–451; and the Fronde, 451; theory of royal absolutism in, 466; famines in era of Louis XIV, 469; under Louis XIV, 469–476; and "Colbertism," 470–471; arts in, 471–472; Gallican Church, 472; religious settlements of Louis XIV, 471–473; wars of Louis XIV, 473–476; losses in Peace of Utrecht, 475, 476; the Enlightenment in, 505–513; Diderot's *Encyclopédie,* 508; Rousseau in, 509; Physiocrats, 510; alliance with England, 516; cult of stability after Louis XIV, 516; effects of "Mississippi Bubble," 516; Jansenists versus Jesuits, 517; productiveness of West Indies, 517; imperial antagonisms with England, 521; Anglo-French conflict in Seven Years' War, 521; and American Revolution, 523; failure of absolutism in, 534; Estates General (1789), 542, 543; Revolution in (1789–1799), 541–555; notebooks of grievances (cahiers), 543; storming of the Bastille, 545; the Great Fear, 1789, 545; Declaration of the Rights of Man and Citizen, 546; Political clubs (Feuillants, Cordeliers, Jacobin Club), 546–547; Chapelier Law (1791), 547; National Assembly, 544, 545, 546, 547; Third Estate, 543, 545, 546, 547; Constitution of 1791, 549; Counterrevolution, 1791, 548; Legislative Assembly, 549, 550; September massacres, 550; Terror and Republic of Virtue, 552–553; Revolution Revolutionized, 550; Republic of the Convention, 550–554; Republic of the Directory, 554–555; Constitution of 1795, 554, 563; "Grande Nation," 555; Concordat of 1801, 557, 653; Expansion, 558–560; The Grande Empire (1804–1815), 558–562; Grand Army, 560; Collapse of Napoleonic Europe, 560–562; Restoration of monarchy after 1815, 574; Ultras, 574; July Ordinances (1830), 582; Revolution of 1830, 581; Revolution and Counterrevolution (1848), 584–587; Industry in, 610–611; from Empire to Republic (1852–1905), 650–654; Liberal Empire and its Fall, 650–651; Napoleon III and the Authoritarian Empire, 650; Commune of 1871, 651; Boulanger Affair, 652; Dreyfus case, 653–654; Third Republic, 650, 651–653; Third Republic and its foes on the Right, 652–653; separation of Church and State (1905), 653; in Crimean War, 656; in Franco-Prussian War, 660–661; basic aims of, after 1871, 681; possessions of, in Africa before 1875, 682; imperial activity of, in Mexico, 695; imperial acquisitions by, of African territories, 1870–1914, 686; imperial conflicts of, in Asia, 686; acquisition by, of Indo-China, 691; at Congress of Berlin, 701; concluded alliance with Russia (1894), 705; formed *Entente Cordiale* with England, 709; and the first Moroccan crisis, 712; and the second Moroccan crisis (1911), 714; 1913 Army Bill of, 716; supported Russia in Balkan crisis (1914), 727; consequences of World War I for, 736; used League of Nations to perpetuate post-war conditions, 747; occupied Ruhr, 748; internal troubles of, after World War I, 758; class struggle in, after World War I, 758; fear of Germany in, after World War I, 759–760; conquered by Germany, 834; divided into occupied and unoccupied zones by Hitler, 834; complete occupation of, by Germans after 1942, 847; rise of birth rate in, after World War II, 868; economic recovery in, after World War II, 868; general situation of, after World War II, 867; independence granted to Algeria by, 869; Fifth Republic of, 869; Fourth Republic of, 868; development of nuclear power in, 870; abortive war against Egypt, 891; withdraws from Vietnam, 903
Franche-Comté (Free County of Burgundy), 439, 473
Francis I of Austria, 573
Francis I (King of France) (1494–1547), 417, 418, 426, 445
Francis II (Austrian Emperor), 558
Francis Ferdinand (Austrian Emperor), 665
Francis Joseph (Austrian Emperor), 588, 651, 664, 665
Franciscan movement, 258, 284–288, 302, 364–365
Franco, Francisco, led rebellion against Spanish Republic, 825
Franconia, 248
Franco-Prussian War, 658, 660–661
Frankfurt Assembly (1848–1849), 589–590
Franz Joseph, visit of, to Bosnia-Herzegovina as a precipitant of World War I, 726
Frederick I, surnamed Barbarossa (German Emperor), 299–300, 301, 306
Frederick II (Hohenstaufen Emperor), 272, 303–306, 387
Frederick the Wise (Elector of Saxony) (1463–1525), 408, 409
Frederick V (King of Bohemia) (1596–1632), 448
Frederick II, "the Great" of Prussia (1712–1786), 480, 507, 520, 522, 523, 526–527
Frederick-William, "the Great Elector" (1620–1688), 452, 478
Frederick William I (King of Prussia) (1688–1740), 465, 479
Frederick William II (Prussia) (1744–1797), 527, 558
Frederick William IV (Prussia), 589, 590
"Free China," 889, 890; *see also* Formosa
French Academy, 635
French Revolution, consequences of, 563–564
Freud, Sigmund, 633, 637, 913
"Friends of God," 401
Fronde, 451

Gabelle (salt tax), 471
Galen, 160, 216, 499, 501
Galileo, Galilei (1546–1642), scientific contributions, 494–496
Gallican Church, 472
Gallipoli, battle of (1915), 730
Gama, Vasco da (c. 1469–1525), 432
Gandhi, Mohandas K. (Mahatma), 888; as leader of Indian Congress Party, 755–757; led "march to the sea" (1931), 756
Gargantua and Pantagruel (Rabelais), 375

Garibaldi, Giuseppi, 657
Gaskell, Elizabeth, 632
Gasperi, Alcide de, 870
Gaul, Frankish kingdom of, 192–193; under Merovingians, 204; defeat of Moslems under Charles Martel, 222; attacked by Vikings, 239–241
Geneva, 417, 418, 420, 509
Geneva Protocol, 749
Geologic ages of earth life, 2
George II, of England (1683–1737), 522
George III of England (1738–1820), 533, 595
George V (England), 649
George, David Lloyd, 648, 649; warned Germany against belligerent action in the second Moroccan crisis (1911), 714; replaced as prime minister, 752
Gerbert of Aurillac, 250
Germania, 189
Germanic Law, 190, 349
German Tribes, 189–193
Germany, Hungarian invasions and, 247; Otto I and, 248–250; medieval expansion of, 274; Henry IV and Investiture Controversy, 295–297, 298; feudalism and, 299–300; Interregnum and, 306–307; humanism in, 375; relationship between Holy Roman Emperor and princes in, 394, 409; decline of cities in, 397; Waldensian heresy in, 400; resentment of the Catholic Church in, 406; economic hardships around 1500, 406; Bundschuh revolts in, 408; "Great Peasants' War," 410; Reformation in, 406–410, 412; wars with Emperor Charles V, 412; Hanseatic League displaced, 433; in Thirty Years' War, 447–450; recognition of three religions in (1648), 449; depopulation in, during Thirty Years' War, 449; baroque art in, 456; rise of Brandenburg-Prussia in, 478–480; in Seven Years' War, 522; enlightened despotism in, 526–527, 530; Napoleon's reorganization of German territory, 558; Confederation of the Rhine, 558; and Kingdom of Westphalia, 559; awakening of nationalism in, 561, 563; German Confederation, 562, 573, 660; romantic literature in, 569; philosophy of romanticism in, 570; pietism and nationalism, 572; unrest in Post-Napoleonic era, 573; German Confederation, Diet of, 589, 659, 660; Liberal-nationalists attempt to unify Germany during 1848 revolution, 589–590; Frankfurt Assembly, 589–590; kleindeutsch (Smaller German), 590; grossdeutsch (Greater German), 590; Industrial preeminence in Europe, 611–612; triumphal march of Germans through Paris (1871), 651; consolidation under Bismarck, 656; Austria's expulsion from, 659–660; Seven Weeks' War, 660; Franco-Prussian War, 660–661; German Empire formed (1871), 661; Falk Laws, 662; Kulturkampf, 662; National Liberals, 662; Failure of democratization under William II, 663; impact of industrial revolution upon, as affecting balance of power in Europe, 680; defeat of France by, as affecting European balance of power, 680; disturbed by British occupation of Egypt (1882), 684; effect of Boer War upon, 685; imperial interests of, in China, 691; joined in alliance with Austria (1879), 702; "New Course" of, under William II, 704; milestones of Kaiser's "New Course" in, 706; fundamental aims of "New Course" of, 707; plans of, for Berlin to Bagdad railroad, 706; new policy of, re Ottoman Empire, 706; in the first Moroccan crisis, 711; in the second Moroccan crisis (1911), 714; economic rivalry of, with Britain as cause of World War I, 724; supported Austria against Serbia in 1914, 726, 727; failure of, to achieve quick victory in World War I, 729;
submarine activity of, in World War I, 731; decision of, to resume unrestricted U-boat activity (1917), 733; defeated Russia in 1917, 734; collapse of military efforts of, in 1918, 735; losses suffered by, under terms of 1914 peace settlement, 738; inflation in, after World War I, 748, 764; abortive attempt to establish Communism in (1919), 778; Catholic Center Party in, during 1920s, 800; Social Democrats in, during 1920s, 800; multiparty system in, during Weimar regime, 800; army in, under Weimar regime, 800; instability of the Weimar Republic of, 799; constitution of, under Weimar Regime, 800; drift of, away from democratic processes, 801; under Nazism, 801–813; Concentration camps in, 810; disciplining of SA in, by Hitler (1934), 810; crushing of the "Second Revolution" in Nazi, 811; attempted to annex Austria (1934), 812; triumph of the Nazi way in, 812; unstable conditions in, as contributing to coming of World War II, 824; annexed Austria, 827; attacked Poland, 831; occupied Norway and Denmark, 832; conquered Lowlands and France, 833; plans of, to invade Russia, 836; invaded Yugoslavia, 1941, 837; invaded Russia, 1941, 837; failure of Nazi troops of, to force quick surrender of Russia, 837; military collapse of (1945), 852; effects of World War II on, 855; failure of Allies to agree on peace treaty with, 858; occupation of, by Britain, France, Russia, and the United States, 858, 859; Nazi trials held in, 872; modifications of original Allied terms regarding, 871; general conditions in, after World War II, 871; relations of the divided parts of, to United States and Russia, 873; divided into capitalist and communist sections, 873; creation of Federal Republic of, 873; creation of Democratic Republic of, 873
Gestapo, power of, 810
Ghibellines, 388
Giolitti, Giovanni, 658–659
Girondins, 549, 550; leaders executed, 552
Glacial record, 2
Gladstone, William E., 645, 646, 648
"Glorious Revolution," James II and, 488
Glossa Ordinaria, 349
Gnosticism, 174
Göbbels, Joseph, 809; as head of Ministry of Propaganda and Enlightenment, 809
Gobineau, Comte de, 631
Godwin, William, 623
Gogol, Nikolai (1809–1853), 633
Golden Bull (1356), 394
Gordon Riots, 532
Gothic realism, 379–380
Göring, Hermann, as No. 2 Nazi and head of Gestapo, 810
Gosplan, 783
Gothic architecture, 342–346
Gothic art, 277, 345
Gothic Wars, 200
Government, in Byzantium, 195; under Charlemagne, 234–235; under Otto I, 248–250; political authority of lords in Early Middle Ages, 253; in medieval towns, 260; in twelfth-century Sicily, 265; in England in 1066, 310; representative governments in England and France, 331; German barbarians and, 406
Goya, Francisco Jose de, 559, 569
Gracchus, Gaius, 130
Gracchus, Tiberius, reforms of, 129–130
Grand Assize, 316
"Grand Embassy," 481
Gratian, 350, 357
Great Depression (1929–1939), 767, 768, 769, 770

"Great Peasants' War" of 1525, 410, 412
Great Schism, 399, 402
Grebel, Conrad, 411
Greece, 898; revolts in (1822–1825), 579; attacked by Italy (1940), 837
Greek civilization, place of, in historical perspective, 67; birth of, 71; early development of, 71; adaptation of Phoenician alphabet in, 71; early political organization and religion in, 72; religious concepts in, 72; relation of man to God in religion in, 73; concept of tragedy in, 73; pantheon of gods in, 73; absence of dogma in religion of, 74; political particularism of, 74; attitudes in, toward other peoples, 74; role of tyrant in, 75; colonial outposts of, 82; class structure in, 81; commercial class in, 83; diminishing role of aristocrats in, 83; religion and philosophy in, 84; everyday life in, 86; early art in, 86; early literature in, 85; stress of athletics in, 87; as influenced by Persian Wars, 87; place of Fate in religious beliefs in, 73; pre-Socratic philosophy in, 91; sophist philosophy in, 92; Socratic philosophy in, 92; Platonic philosophy in, 93; Aristotelian philosophy in, 94; literature of tragedy in, 95–96; literature of comedy in, 96; sculpture and architecture in, 98
"Greek Fire," 213
Gregory VII (Pope), 294–299, 300, 313
Gregory IX (Pope), 287, 307
Gregory of Tours, 203
Gregory the Great (Pope Gregory I), 203, 207–209
Grew, Nehemiah, 499
Grey, Lord, 584
Grey, Sir Edward, 727; actions of, in first Moroccan crisis, 712
Grimaldi man, 2
Groote, Gerard (1340–1384), 401
Grosseteste, Robert, 364–365
Grotewald, Otto, 873
Grotius, Hugo (1583–1645), 460, 503, 504
Guadalcanal, battle of, 848
Guam, occupied by Japanese, 844
Guatemala, American covert intervention in, 885
Guelfs, 388
Guilds, craft, in medieval towns, 260–261, 346
Guiscard, Robert, 265–266, 293, 297
Guise, Henry, Duke of (1550–1588), 446
Guise, House of, 445
Guizot, François, 577, 582, 585
Gustavus Adolphus (King of Sweden) (1594–1632), 448
Gutenberg, Johannes (1397–1468), 378, 630

Habsburg, 421; Rudolph of, 306; Spanish Habsburgs control Italy, 389; superintend Catholic Reformation, 402; Charles V gives eastern lands to Ferdinand, 412; Habsburg Bohemia, 425; Habsburg Hungary, 425, 433; dominance of Spanish Habsburgs, 439–440; dynastic interests in Thirty Years' War, 447–448; revolt of Hungarian leaders against, 474; Austrian Habsburgs gain from Peace of Utrecht, 475; absolutism and particularism in Habsburg lands, 476; title of Emperor becomes empty, 476; decline of Spanish Habsburg Empire, 485; plan to partition Habsburg empire, 520; in same diplomatic camp with Bourbons, 522; fears of Russian power, 524; dynasty and empire in eighteenth century, 524; as enlightened despots, 524–526; Napoleon humiliates, 557; gains territory from, 558; Empire of, as pivot of Continental diplomacy after 1815, 572; paralysis of, in 1848, 587; Prince Schwarzenberg gained control of government of, 588; basis of restored Empire, 588; expulsion of, necessary for unification of Italy and Germany, 590; self-

determination, meaning of, in Empire, 588; hostility of, towards Russia and Crimean War, 656; Empire of (1850–1914), 663–665
Hadrian, 155
Hadrian IV, 300–301
Hammurabi, code of, 36
Hannibal, 126
Hanseatic League, 433
Hardenburg, Baron von, 561
Harding, President, calls for nation to "return to normalcy," 760
Hardy, Thomas, 633
Hargreave, James, 598
Harrington, James (1611–1677), 503
Harun-al-Rashid, 214
Harvey, William (1578–1657), 499
Hastings, battle of (1066), 310
Hatshepsut, national reconstruction of Egypt under, 18
Hatti, *see* Hittites
Hauteville Dynasty, 265–266
Health and Morals of Apprentices Act (1802), 605
Hébert, Jacques (1757–1794), 552, 553
Hebrews, entrance of, into Palestine, 55; origin and settlements of, 55; Exodus of, 56; accompanied Hyksos into Egypt, 56; monolatry of, 56; chief settlements in Palestine of, 57; as ruled by "judges," 57; new covenant of, under Moses, 58; conquest of Canaan by, 58; religious developments of, 60; conquered by Assyrians, 59; conquered by Chaldeans, 59; effect of material success on religious life of, 60; reassessment by, of their status as a "chosen people," 61; concept of salvation of, 61; *see also* Job; religion of, as influenced by Zoroastrianism, 62
Hegel, Wilhelm Friedrich, 571, 623
Hegira, 211
Heidelberg man, 2
Heisenberg, Werner, 912
Heliaea, 102; as popular courts of Athens, 75
Hellas, 67
Hellenes, *see* Greek civilization
Hellenistic society, development of cosmopolitanism in, 105; social conditions in, 105; economic conditions, 106; philosophy in, 106–107; science in, 108–109; literature in, 110; writing of history in, 110; plastic arts in, 110; religions of, 112
Helmholtz, Ludwig von, 627
Heloise, 357
Helots, 79, 80
Helvétius, Claude (1715–1771), 508
Henlein, Konrad, 828
Henry I (England), 312–314
Henry II (England), 298, 317, 318
Henry II (France), 445
Henry III (England), 321, 329
Henry III (France), 446
Henry III (German Emperor), 250; and reform of papacy, 293, 294
Henry IV (France), 446, 447
Henry IV (German Emperor), 294, 295; disposition of, 296, 297
Henry V (England), 391
Henry V (German Emperor), 298, 299
Henry VI (German Emperor), 271, 302
Henry VII (England), 393
Henry VIII (England), 414, 416, 440
Henry the Lion, 300, 302
Henry of Navarre, *see* Henry IV, France
Heraclitus, 85
Herbert, Edward of Cherbury (1583–1648), 504
Herder, Johann Gottfried, 570
Heresies, 400
Heresy, 300; in fourth century, 185; in Byzantium,

194; rise of, 280; Dominic and, 283; Louis IX and, 329

Herodotus, 97

Herzen, Alexander, 665

Hesiod, 81

Hidalgos, 389, 438

High tariffs in United States (1920s), 761

Himmler, Heinrich, as leader of SS, 810

Hindenburg, Paul von, 808; chief German field commander in World War I, 729; as second president of the Weimar Republic, 801; death of, 812

Hipparchus, 109

Hippocrates, 109

Hitler, Adolf, visit of, with Mussolini (1937), 795; and the "Beer Hall Putsch," 800; rise of, 801; early years of, 802; appointment of, as Chancellor of Germany, 808; need of, of army's support, 807; insisted upon Enabling Act, 809; put into practice the "principle of leadership," 809; combined offices of President and Chancellor, 812; introduced military conscription into Germany, 824; fortified Rhineland, 825; war plans of, 826; planned annexation of Sudetenland, 827; ordered occupation of Bohemia and Moravia, 829; *lebensraum* goals of, 829; offered "peace" terms after conquest of Poland, 831; drew up plans to invade England, 835; plans of, to invade Russia, 836; appealed for winter clothing for German troops in Russia (1941), 839; suicide of, 852

Hittites, "federalist" character of empire of, 46; Old Empire of, 46; New Empire period of, 46; religious borrowings by, 46; humane legal codes of, 47

Hiroshima, bombing of, 854

Hobbes, Thomas (1588–1679), 466, 502

Hobson, John A., as socialist critic of imperialism, 677

Ho Chi Min, 904

Hohenstaufen Dynasty, 279, 299–307

Hohenzollerns, 476; scattered lands, 478; join Brandenburg and Prussia, 478; grant Junkers control over rural and urban affairs, 479; tried to stop Louis XIV, 479; rivals of Habsburgs, 524; Frederick the Great, leading Hohenzollern, 526–527; Heavy taxes in Seven Years' War, 527; Leopold of, selected for Spanish Monarch, 660; Prussian Hohenzollern King becomes German Emperor (1871), 661

Holbach, Baron d' (1723–1789), 508

Holbein, Hans (1497–1543), 385

Holstein, Baron von, 711

Holy Roman Empire, 394, 406; origin of, 249; Investiture Controversy and, 295–299; Rudolph of Habsburg and, 306–307; break-up begun at Peace of Westphalia, 449, 476; end of, under Napoleon, 558

Homer, as author of the *Iliad*, 72

Homo habilis, as an omnivore, 2

Homo sapiens, emergence of, 2; special advanced features of, 4

Hong Kong, acquired by England, 689; occupied by Japanese, 844

Hoover, Herbert C., President, 817, 820

Horace, 147, 149–150

Horatian Laws, 121

Horseshoe, development of, 221

Horus, as the living pharaoh, 14

Hospitallers, 273, 280

"Hossbach Notes," 826

House of Orange, 486

House Un-American Activities Committee (HUAC), 884

Hubris, 73

Hugh of St. Victor, 357

Hugo, Victor, 632

Huguenots, 445; rebellion of (1627–1628), 451, 473

Humanism, in Byzantium, 201; Italian, 372–375; civic, 372, 374; Spanish, 375; Northern, in England, France, Germany, 375

Humanists, 370, 372, 373, 374, 375; Erasmian, 385, 408, 411, 419, 420; expulsion from Catholic Reform, 420

Hume, David (1711–1776), 508

Hundred Days of Napoleon, 563

Hundred Years' War, 372, 390, 393, 397, 400

Hungary, 255, 263, 394, 419; settlement of, 238; Calvinism, Lutheranism, and Antitrinitarianism in, 425; movement for autonomy in, 425; revolt against Habsburgs, 474; revolutionary laws of (1848), 587; solution to nationalities problem, 587–588; Hungarian Republic immediately crushed, 588; fear of losing control to Slavs, 664; demands for autonomy ends in *Ausgleich* (compromise) of 1867, 664; policy of Magyarization, 665; forced to accept Treaty of Trianon (1920), 740; made a sovereign nation, 742; abortive attempt in, to establish Communism in (1918), 778

Hus, John (1369–1415), 399, 401

Hussites, 401, 425, 448

Hyksos, conquest of Egypt by, 17; as "ethnic cousins" of the Hebrews, 56

Ibsen, Henrik, 633

Iceland, 241

Iconoclasm, 224; iconoclastic controversy, 225

Iliad, 72

Imperialism, "new," 675; summary definition and account of kinds of, 675; as the "white man's burden," 676; as religiously motivated, 676; as caused by Social Darwinism, 676; as motivated by desire for "color on the map," 677; as an escape from thralldom of the machine, 677; as judged by socialist criteria, 677; as viewed from capitalist outlook, 678; as provoked by desire to hold strategic areas and sea lanes, 679; as an economic liability to colonizing countries, 678; summary account of causes of, 679; thrust of, into Africa and Asia after 1870, 682; as force partitioning Africa, 682; as manifested by Belgian interest in Congo, 683; British development of, in Africa after 1882, 684; as reflected by actions of Powers at Berlin Conference of 1885, 683; as manifested by British conquest of Nigeria, 686; European thrust of, in Asia, 686; thrust of, in the Americas, 694; summation of nature of, 697

Imperial Reichstag (Parliament), 394

Imperial University (France), 558

Impressionism, 634

Incunabula, 378

Independents, 454

Index of Prohibited Books, 425, 571, 629

India, Sepoy rebellion in, 686; conflict in, between Moslems and Hindus, 687; post-war efforts of, to achieve independence, 755–758; friction in, between Hindus and Moslems, 756, 888; development of nationalism in, 888

Indian National Congress, formed in 1885, 687

Indonesia, imperial conquest of, by Dutch, 689; gained independence (1949), 886–888; *see also* Vietnam

Indulgences, 409

Industrial social organization in nineteenth century, 603–606

Industrialization, an open-ended revolution, 606–615; and welfare, 614; responses to, 620–627

Industry and international rivalry, 614–615

Inflation, in United States after World War I, 763; in United States in 1920s, 763; in Germany, 1920–1923, 764; in Italy after World War I, 788

Innocent III (Pope), 302–305, 416; instigates Fourth Crusade, 271–272; the Albigensians and, 281; St. Dominic and, 283; St. Francis and, 285; quarrel with King John of England, 319–321

Innocent IV (Pope), 306

Inquisition, 282, 375, 425, 440, 571, 574, 578

The Institutes of the Christian Religion (Calvin), 417, 418

Institution of a Christian Prince (Erasmus), 385

Instruction of Catherine the Great for a convention, 528

Instrument of Government of England under Cromwell (1653), 455

Integration of industrial society, 606

Intendants, 447, 451, 470, 471, 478

Invasions, 258; after Charlemagne's death, 235–241; renewal of, in tenth-century England, 243

Investiture Controversy, 295–299, 313; canon law and, 349

"Invincible Armada," 443

Ionia, 91; Renaissance of, following Mycenaean settlements in islands and Asia Minor, 70

Ireland, in the early Middle Ages, 205; Norse invasions, 240; starvation in, 648; Land League, 648; in British politics, 648; Home Rule Bill debated, 648, 649; movement to achieve independence after World War I, 754–755

Irish Nationalists, 648, 649

Irish Reform Act (1868), 648

Iron in industrialization, 600

"Ironsides" (Cromwell's army), 454

Isabella (Queen of Spain) (1451–1504), 389, 394

Isaiah, exhortation of, 60

Isidore of Seville, 203

Isis, 113; cult of the goddess, 184

Islam, 211, 255; background and origins of, 210–211; conquests of, 212–214; spread of, 212–216; Tours (battle of) and, 214; culture of, 216; Spain and, 263; Seljuk Turks and, 268

Israel, creation of ancient, 59; cathedrals in, 343–346; gained independence, 890–892; war with Arab states, 891; abortive war against Egypt, 891

Italy, Ostrogoths in, 192; under Theodoric, 192; collapse of Ostrogothic Kingdom in, 204; Charlemagne and, 228; Saracen and Magyar invasions of, 238; invaded by Otto I, 249–250; Normans in southern Italy and, 264–265; consequences of the Investiture Controversy in, 298; Frederick II and, 306; Dante and Tuscan dialect in, 371; humanism in, 372–375; scientific naturalism in art of, 379–382; High Renaissance in, 382; conquered by Emperor (1530), 384; city-states of, 385, 388; heresy in, 400; invaded by France and Spain (1494), 402; papacy in, 401; new religious orders in, 421; Inquisition in, 425; capitalism in, 428; baroque art and architecture in, 456; seventeenth-century depression in, 485; "grand tour" in, 485; Galileo and science in, 494–496; Vesalius and medicine in, 499; French invasion (1795), 554; Napoleon in northern Italy (1797), 555; sister republics in, 555; French lose Italy (1814), 561; Austrian influence and repression in, after 1815, 574; revolts of 1821 in, 579; local revolts (1831) challenge Austria in, 583; *Carbonari* crushed, 583; rebellion in (1848), against Austrian rule, 587–588; consolidation of, 656–658; Kingdom of, formed, 656–658; Cavour, Mazzini, and Garibaldi important in formation of United Kingdom, 657; politics (1871–1914), 658–659; Law of Papal Guarantees (1871), 658; progress in Giollitian era, 659; Catholic Action

groups founded (1905), 659; basic aims of, after 1870, 681; at Congress of Berlin, 701; entered into alliance with Germany and Austria (1882), 702; joined *Entente* powers in World War I, 727; refused to support her alliance partners in 1914, 727; consequences of World War I for, 736; dissatisfaction of, with settlements of World War I, 743; disillusionment in, after World War I, 788; undemocratic characteristics of, 789; post-World War I economic ills of, 789; coming of Fascism to, 790–791; consolidation of Fascist dictatorship in, 792; support of Mussolini by industry, army, and church in, 793; creation of the Fascist "Corporate State" in, 793; Fascist imperialism of, in Africa, 794; Fascist aid given by, to Franco, 795; conquest of Ethiopia by, 824; posture of belligerence in, 823; joined World War II against France, 834; attacked Greece (1940), 837; activities of, in Africa in World War II, 840; invaded by Allied forces (1943), 847; effects of World War II on, 855; Communist Party in, 871; abolished monarchy, 870; position of and conditions in, after World War II, 870

Ivan III, "the Great" of Russia (1440–1505), 395

Ivan IV (The Terrible) of Russia (1530–1584), 480

Ives, Charles, 920–921

Izvolsky, Russian Foreign Minister, involved in the "Buchlau Bargain," 713

J'accuse (Zola), 653

Jacobin Club and Jacobins, 547, 551, 555, 556, 564

James I (King of England), 452

James II of England (Duke of York), 488, 503

Jansenists, 505, 517

Japan, 433, 481, 556; industrialization in, 614; war with China (1894–1895), 691; war with Russia (1904–1905), 692; weaknesses of, in early and mid 1900s, 692; westernization of, 692, Meiji restoration in, 692; joined in alliance with England (1902), 707; as a "have not" power, 823; economic development of, 823; *samuri* spirit in, 823; imperialist designs in China of, 823; conquest of Manchuria by, 824; imperialist aggression of, in China, 826; occupation of much of Asia by (1941–1942), 842; surrender of (1945), 855; effects of World War II on, 855; conquest of much of Asia by, 886

Jaurès, Jean, 625, 653

Java man, 2

Jefferson, Thomas (1743–1826), 533

Jeremiah, warnings of, to his people, 60

Jericho, conquest of, by Hebrews, 57

Jerusalem, capture of (1187), 269–270; Crusader State, 269–273

Jesuits (Society of Jesus), 401, 423, 427, 505, 517, 525, 571, 574, 662

Jesus Christ, life and teachings of, 168

Jews, Islam and, 211; Sicily and, 265; *see also* Hebrews; St. Bernard and, 279; Louis IX and, 329

Joan of Arc (c. 1412–1431), 391

Job, as developer of Hebrew doctrine of sin and salvation, 61–62

John (King of England), 303, 304, 319–321, 327

John the Baptist, 168

John of Jaudun, 354

John of Salisburg, 358

John of Saxony (Elector), 412

John VI (Portugal), 579

Joint-Stock Company, 436

Jordan, 890, 891

Joseph, as Egyptian official, 56

Joseph I (Emperor of Austria), 477

Joseph II (Emperor of Austria) (1741–1790), 524, 525, 527, 559, 573

Josephine Bonaparte, 558
Judah, creation of, 59
Julius II (Pope) (1503–1513), 382, 384, 386, 402
Junkers, 479, 659, 662, 663
Justices of the Peace, 391, 444, 605, 606
Justin Martyr, 176
Justinian (Byzantine Emperor), 198–202, 349
Jutland, naval battle of, 731
Juvenal, 159

Kafka, Franz, 916
Kapp Putsch, 800
Kassites, conquest of Babylonia by, 37
Kaunitz, Count of Austria (1711–1794), 522
Kay, John, 598
Kemal, Mustapha, creator of Turkish Republic (1920), 741
Kennedy, John, President, 901, 902
Kenya, object of British imperialism (1887), 684
Kenyatta, Jomo, 905
Kepler, Johannes (1571–1630), 494, 497; his laws of planetary motion, 494, 497
Kerensky, Alexander, attempt of, to stabilize moderate revolution in Russia (1917), 775
Kett, Robert, 415
"Kett's Rebellion" (1549), 415–416
Keynes, John Maynard, 611
Khayyam, Omar, 216
Khrushchev, 874, 876, 877, 901, 902
Kimmel, Admiral, 843
Kingsley, Charles, 625, 632
Kitchener, General, encounter of, with French troops in Sudan (1898), 684
Knight, 245–247
Knossos, 38
Knox, John (c. 1513–1572), 419
Koch, Robert, 628
Koestler, Arthur, 920
Kolkhoze, 782
Königgratz (Sadowa), battle of (1866), 660
Koran, 211–212, 217
Korea, as scene of conflict between China and Japan, 691
Korean War, 879, 880, 895, 900
Kossuth, Louis, 588
Kronstadt mutiny (1921), 780
Kropotkin, Prince, 635
Ku Klux Klan, revival of, in United States in 1920s, 761, 881
Kulaks, developed during NEP period in Russia, 781, 784, 785, 787

Labour Party (England), 648; first government headed by, 752; became "loyal opposition" after World War I, 752; split in (1931), 754; formed government after World War II, 866
Labor unions, 603–605
Labor unrest, as contributing force leading to World War I, 724
Labrousse, Ernest, 542
Lafayette, Marquis de (1757–1834), 542, 545, 546
laissez faire, 510, 606, 621, 646, 648
Landwehr (Prussian), 561
Lanfranc, 313
Language, in Byzantium, 196, 201; Alfred (England) and, 241–243; Latin and vernacular literature in High Middle Ages, 336–343; translations in High Middle Ages, 358
Laocoon, 112
Latifundia, growth of, in Rome, 129
Latin America, revolts in (1815–1824), 579; as object of imperialist thrusts, 695; extension of United States influence in, 695; general conditions in, after World War II, 884–885; United States

used states of, as pawns in the Cold War, 885; economic and political backwardness of, 885
Latium, plains of, 116
Latvia, 780, 832
Laud, Archbishop (1573–1645), 453
Lausanne, Treaty of (1923), 741, 748
Laval, Pierre, leader of Vichy France, 834
Lavoisier, Antoine Laurent (1743–1794), 498
Law of Papal Guarantees (1871), 658
Law, John (1671–1729), 516
Lawyers, in Louis IX's time, 330
League of Armed Neutrality, 523
League of Augsburg, War of, 475
League of Nations, established at end of World War I, 738; nature and functions of, 738; structure and functions of, 741; settlement of disputes by, 749; inability of, to halt Japanese aggression in Manchuria, 824, 826
Leakey, L. S. B., *hominid* findings of, 2
Lebanon, 890, 891
Lebrun, Charles (1619–1690), 471
Lechfield, battle of (955), 238, 248
Leeuwenhoek, Anton van, 499
Lefébvre d'Etaples (1450–1537), 375
Lefebvre, Georges, 342
Legion of Honor, 556
Legnano, battle of (1176), 301
Leibniz, Wilhelm von (1646–1716), 496
Lenin (Vladimir Ilyich Ulianov, 1870–1925), 542, 669, 776, 778, 779, 780, 877
Leningrad, siege of, by Nazi forces, 839; Nazi lifted siege of (1944), 850
Leo I (Pope), 165, 208, 292
Leo III (Pope), 229
Leo IX (Pope), 293–294
Leo X (Pope) (1513–1521), 409
Leo XIII (Pope), 625
Leonardo da Vinci (1425–1519), 381, 382, 402
Leopold I (Emperor), 465, 475, 476
Leopold II, Austrian Emperor (1747–1792), 526
Leopold II, Belgian King, interest of, in Congo, 683
Leopold of Hohenzollern, 660
Letter of Grace (Catherine the Great), 529
Letters of Obscure Men and Reuchlin case, 376
Levellers, 455
Leviathan (Hobbes), 455
Lewes, battle of, 322
Liberalism, after the Napoleonic Wars, 576; bourgeois and democratic forms, 577, 621; premises of, 577; concept of self-determination of nations, 590; social (England), 648–649
Liberals (England), 646, 648, 649
Liberum veto (Poland), 486
Libya, 892
Liebknecht, Karl, 778, 800
Lister, Joseph, 628
Lithuania, 780, 832
Little Entente, 747, 829
Little Rock, Arkansas, Federal troops sent to, 881
"Little Wars," after World War I, 747–748
Littré, Emile, 630
Livingstone, David, quickened European interest in Africa, 682
Livy, 150
Locarno Pacts (1925), 749, 760, 825
Locke, John (1632–1704), 501, 502, 503, 507
Lodge, Henry Cabot, 740
"Lollards," 393, 400
Lombard, Peter, 357
Lombard League, 300–301, 306
Lombards, 201, 204, 208, 224, 228, 299–302
London, Jack, 633
"Long Parliament," 453
Lorenzo de Medici, 374, 402

Lorraine, 248
The "Lost Generation," 915
Lothar, 236
Louis VI (King of France), 326
Louis VII (King of France), 270, 326–327
Louis VIII (King of France), 327
Louis IX (King of France), 273, 327
Louis XI (King of France) (1423–1483), 391
Louis XIII (King of France) (1601–1643), 451
Louis XIV (King of France) (1638–1715), 515, 516, 556
Louis XIV, Wars of, 473
Louis XV (1710–1774), 517, 534
Louis XVI (1754–1793), 535, 542, 545, 548, 550, 551
Louis XVIII (France), 561, 574, 581
Louis the German, 236
Louis Napoleon Bonaparte, 586; *see also* Bonaparte III
Louis Philippe, 582, 585
Louis the Pious, 232, 235–236
de Louvois, Marquis, 473
Low Countries (The Netherlands), 386, 421, 433, 437, 440, 441, 448, 449, 459, 481, 554, 595
Loyola, Ignatius de (1491–1556), 401, 422
Lucretius, 136, 151
Ludendorff, Erich, 729, 732
Luneville, Peace of (1801), 557
Lusitania, sinking of, 731
Lützen, battle of (1632), 448
Luther, Martin (1483?–1546), 375, 378, 408–411, 412, 416, 417, 422; Ninety-Five Theses of, 409; doctrine of "faith alone," 408, 423; break with Erasmus, 419
Lutheranism, 414, 425, 449
Lutherans, 412, 413, 415, 418, 662
Luxemburg, Rosa, 778, 800
Lvov, Prince, first premier of revolutionary Russia, 775
Lycées (France), 556
Lycurgus, 79
Lydia, as buffer between East and West, 71
Lydians, 45; as inventors of minted money, 48; settlements of, in Asia Minor, 48
Lyell, Charles, 628
Lysistrata, 97

MacArthur, Douglas, General, 854, 900; assumed command of United States forces in the Pacific (1941), 844; dismissed from Korean command, 900
MacDonald, Ramsay, as head of first Labour government (England), 752; as prime minister of coalition government, 754
MacMahon, Marshal (France), 651
"McCarthyism," 880
McCarthy, Joseph, Senator, 880
Maccabean revolt, 168
Machiavelli, Niccolo (1469–1527), 385, 386, 387, 528, 583; his realism, 385, 386–387
Machine tools, 601
Magellan, Ferdinand (c. 1480–1521), 433
Maginot Line, 760
Magna Carta, 320–321
Magyarization, 665
Magyars, 238
Maintenon, Madame de, 473
Malay States, nationalist agitation in, 888
Malenkov, became premier of Russia, 877; dismissed as premier of Russia, 877
Malpighi, Marcello (1628–1694), 499
Malthus, Thomas, 620, 628
Manchuria, conquest of, by Japan, 824
Manfred (King of Sicily), 307
Manichaeism, 179

Manzikert, battle of (1071), 268
Mao, Tse-tung, 889
Marathon, battle of, 87
"March on Rome" (1922), 791
Marconi, Guglielmo, 608–609
Marcus Aurelius, 156
Margaret of Parma, 440, 441
Margaret of Valois (1553–1615), 445
Maria Theresa of Austria, 520, 524, 525
Marian exiles, 444
Marie Antoinette, 552
Marie Louise, wife of Napoleon, 558
Marius, Gaius, 131, 132
Marlborough, Duke of, 475
Marne, battle of (1914), 729
Marshall, George, Secretary of State, 880, 884, 898
Marshall Plan, 873, 884, 898
Martial, 137, 159
Martin-Siemens open-hearth method, 608
Marx, Karl, 619, 622, 623–625, 636, 669; and labor theory of value, 624
Marxism-Leninism, 776; *see also* Communism
Mary Tudor (Mary I) (1516–1558), 416
The *Mathematical Principles of Natural Philosophy* (Newton), 497
Mathematics and the Completion of the Copernican Revolution in Astronomy, 496–498
Matteotti, Giacomo, martyred by Fascists, 792
Maudsley, Henry, 601
Maximilian II (Holy Roman Emperor) (1564–1576), 425
Mazarin, Cardinal, 451, 470, 473
Mazzini, Giuseppi, 578, 588, 657
Mecca, a commercial center, 210; birthplace of Mohammed, 210
Medes, 52
Medina, 211
Mediterranean Pacts (1887), 703
Melanchthon, Philip (1497–1560), 408, 421
Mendel, Gregor, 628
Mendelssohn, Felix, 569
Mennonites, 412
Menno Simons, 412
Mensheviks, 669
Mercantilists, 438, 510
Merovingian dynasty, 204, 222, 224
Mesopotamia, earliest settlements in, 29; establishment of city states in, 30; chronological periods of, 30; development of language and literature in, 32; religious concepts and gods of, 31; architecture and sculpture in, 33; scientific developments in, 33; birth of astrology in, 34; economic conditions in, 35
Messiah, concept of, developed by Hebrews, 62
Mesta, 390
Methodism, 511
Methodology of Science, 500
Metternich, Prince, 561, 573, 583, 587
Mexico, French imperialism in, 695
Michelangelo, Buonarotti (1475–1564), 383, 384, 402, 456
Middle classes, lacking in Russia, 395; in Renaissance, 397, 398, 467; as social group, 467; domains, 477; prestige in 1815, 564; lacking in Habsburg, 567; as basis of Liberalism, 577, 584; and Marx, 623
Midway, battle of, 845
Milan, 388
Militarism, rampant features of 1870–1914, 680; as a cause of World War I, 725
Mill, John Stuart, 622
Millerand, Alexander, 653
Milvian Bridge, battle of (312 B.C.), 184
Milyukov, Pavel, 669

Minnesingers, 341
Minos, creation of Cretan dynasty by, 38
Mir, 666
Missi dominici, 234
Mississippi Bubble, 516
Mississippi Company (French), 516
Mithraism, 139, 178, 184
Mohammed, 210–212, 425
Moira, 73
Molotov, 877
Moltke, General, 659, 660
Monarchy, limited, 191, 200; English birth of, 243; in tenth-century Germany, 249; Investiture Controversy and, 295–299; Church of England and, 317–318; Magna Carta and, 320–321; weakness of (under Capetians), 325; Louis VII and, 326
Monarchy in Theory and Practice, 466
Monasticism, in Ireland, 205; in Early Middle Ages, 205–209; St. Anthony and, 206; St. Benedict and, 206–208; St. Boniface and, 223; Benedict of Aniane and, 232; under Charlemagne, 232; Benedictinism and, 277–278; Cluny, 254, 277–278
Mongol Empire, 397
Mongols, 395
Monk, George (General) (1608–1670), 455
Monnet Plan, 868
Monolatry, birth of ethical, 58
Monophysitism, 195, 199–200
Monroe Doctrine, 581
Monte Cassino, 206
Montesquieu, Baron de (1689–1755), 505, 507, 508, 510, 528, 534, 547; and Historical Empiricism, 506
Montgomery, General, 846
Moors, 263, 303, 389, 390
More, Sir Thomas (1478–1535), 376, 385, 414
Morocco, as scene of power crisis (1905–1906), 711; struggle between France and Germany over (1911), 714
Moscow, 395, 480, 575, 670, 839
Moses, 57; led Hebrews out of Egypt, 57–58
Moses (Michelangelo), 384
Moslems, conquest of Byzantine North Africa by, 201; attacked Constantinople, 201; in Spain, 204; conquest of Persia, 212; spread of, 212–214; defeated by Charles Martel, 222; Frederick II and, 305
"Mountain" in French National Convention, 551
Mozart, Wolfgang, 630
Muentzer, Thomas (c. 1489–1525), 410, 411
Mun, Thomas (1571–1641), 438
Munich "settlement" of Sudeten question, 828
Muscovy, 394, 425
Muslim, League, 687
Mussolini, Benito, 636, 793, 794, 823, 829; ordered occupation of Corfu, 748; emergence of, 789; consolidates power of Fascist regime, 792; effected dictatorial rule in Italy after 1925, 793; growing understanding of, of Nazi power, 796; planned invasion of Ethiopia, 824; ordered attack against Greece (1940), 837; ordered invasion of Greece (1941), 841; deposed (1943), 847
Mycenaeans, conquest of Crete by, 38; as influenced by Cretans, 68; origins and early settlements of, 68; as early Greeks, 67–68; chief cultural characteristics of, 69; development of writing by, 69; conquest of Knossos by, 69; decline of culture of, 70; settlement of colonies by, 69; migration of, to islands and Asia Minor coast after collapse of their civilization, 70
Myron, 98

Nagasaki, bombing of, 854
Nantes, Edict of (1598), 446; revocation of Edict of (1685), 473, 504

Naples, 373, 387, 388, 555, 658; revolts in (1821), 579
Napoleon Bonaparte, Emperor (1769–1821), 555, 558–564; as First Consul, 556
Napoleon III, 626, 650, 651, 657, 660, 695
Napoleonic Government, 556
Narodniki (Populists), 667, 669
Narva, Battle of, 481
Naseby, Battle of (1645), 454
Nasser, Gamel Abdel, 891
National Industrial Recovery Act (NRA), 815
National Labor Relations Act (United States), 818
Nationalism, 276, 563, 577, 643; Magna Carta and, 320–321; linked with Liberalism, 576; and total war, 615; Darwinism and, 630; liberal, 645–646; force of, in the Balkans, 699; as a cause of World War I, 725–726; development of, in Indonesia, 886; large scale development of, in Asia after World War II, 886; development of, in India, 888; movement of, in Burma, 888; movement of, in Malay States, 889; movement of, in China, 889; movements of, in Africa, 892; failure of, in South Africa, 894
Naturalism, literary, 633
Navigation Act of 1651, 439
Navigation Acts (1849, 1859), 646
Nazism, rise of, 801; anti-Semitic appeal of, 803; as a bulwark against Communism, 803; little appeal of (1924–1928), 803; ideology of, 803–805; as anti-Christian, 805–806; as anti-society and humanity, 806–807; alliance of, with big business and the army, 807; consolidation of power of, 808; anti-Semitic laws of, 809; censorship laws of, 809; use of SA troops as instrument of terror, 810; use of the SS guard as an instrument of terror, 810; use of Gestapo to reduce opposition to, 810; effect of, in creating "prosperous" economic conditions, 811; consolidated power of (by 1935), 812
Neanderthal man, 2
Near East, post-World War II developments in, 890–891
Nebuchadnezzar, as conqueror of Jews, 51
Necker, Jacques (1732–1804), 535, 545
Negro, 881–883; *see also* Black-White Problem in United States
Nehru, Jawaharlal, 888; worked for Indian independence after World War I, 756
Nelson, Admiral, 555, 558
Nemesis, 73
NEP (New Economic Policy), 780, 781–782, 786, 877
Neoclassicism, 460
Neoplatonism, 184
Nero, 152, 176
Netherlands, imperial conquests of, in India, 688; conquered by Germany, 833
Neiully, Treaty of (1919), 741
Neustria, 222
Newcastle, Duke of (1720–1764), 530
"New Deal," 813–820; moved left after 1935, 816–818; significance of, 819; summary assessment of, 820
New Logic (Bacon), 502
The "new masses" in contemporary society, 904
"New Model" army, 454
Newcomer, Thomas, 600
Newton, Isaac (1642–1727), 494, 497, 500, 505, 507, 630
New Zealand, 646
Ngo Dihn Diem, 903
Nicea, Council of (325), 178, 185
Nicholas I (Tsar) (Russia), 583, 665
Nicholas II (Russia), 667, 670, 671
Nietzsche, Friedrich, 633

Nigeria, conquest of, by England, 686
Nihilists, 667
Nimwegen, Treaty of, 473
Ninety-Five Theses (Luther), 409
Nineveh, destruction of, 50
Nobility, 467
Nogaret, William, 398
Nominalism, 356
Norman Conquest of England, 311
Normandy, 239, 243, 255, 311–312; Allied landings in (1944), 850
Normans, in Kingdom of Sicily, 265; conquest of England, 311
Norris, George, Senator, urged federal use of power of Tennessee River, 566
North Africa, 204; vandal kingdom of, 192, 200; conquered by Justinian, 200; falls to Moslems, 201
North Atlantic Treaty Organization (NATO), 871, 899
North Korea, supported by China, 900; invasion of South Korea by, 900
Northumbria, 208, 209, 241; St. Bede in, 209; sends monks to Frankland, 223; invaded by Vikings, 239
Norway, 240; conquered by Canute, 243; conquest of, by Germany, 832
Notables, Assembly of (1787), 542
Notre Dame of Paris, 335, 343
Nuremberg Trials, 872
Nyerer, Julius, 894
Nystad, Treaty of (1721), 483

Octavian, 133; *see also* Augustus
Octobrists (Russia, 1905), 670
Odyssey, 72
Oedipus Rex, 96
"Old Believers" (Russian), 668
Old Regime (ancien régime), 515, 527, 577, 606, 622
Oliva, Treaty of (1660), 452
Olivares, Count de, "Castilianization" of, 485
Olympic games, 87; instituted, 74
Omayyad Dynasty, 212–214
"One Worldism," emergence of, 859
On the Fabric of the Human Body (Vesalius), 499
On the Law of War and Peace (Grotius), 503
On the Nature of Things (Lucretius), 136
Opium War (1839–1842), 689
Optimates, aristocratic "party" in Roman Republic, 134
Optimism in enlightenment, 512
The Oratories of Divine Love, 422
"Ordeal," 190
Orders in Council, British, 559
Oresteia, 96
Organization of the American States (O.A.S.), 885
Origen of Alexandria, 186
Origin of Species (Darwin), 628–629
Orleanist monarchists (France), 650, 651
Orphic cult, 84
Ostend Company, 516
Ostrakismos, 76
Ostrogothic Italy, 192
Ottoman Empire, 396, 398, 609
Ottoman Turks, 425, 440
Ottonian kingship, 250
Ottonian Renaissance, 250
Otto of Brunswick, 303
Otto the Great, 248–250
Ovid, 150
Oxford, University of, 364

Pact of Paris or Kellogg-Briand Pact (1928), 766, 801
Padua, 381, 499
Paine, Thomas (1737–1809), 533, 548, 550, 623

Painting, Baroque, 459
Pakistan, independence achieved by, 888
Palacky, Francis, 588
Palatine Elector, 448
Palestine, conquest of, by Hebrews, 59; specific Jewish complaints in, 757; specific Arab complaints in, 757; unrest in, after World War I, 757–758
Palladio, Andrea (1518–1580), 458
Palmerston, Lord, 645
Palmieri, Matteo (1406–1475), 369
Panama, independence of, encouraged by United States, 696
Panama Canal, 696
Pan-Arabism, 891
Pan-Arab League, 891
Pan-Germanism, effect of, on European events, 724
Pankhurst, Emmeline, 649
Pan-Slav Congress (1848), 588
Pan-Slavic Movement, 588, 590, 667
Pan-Slavism, as a force in power politics, 700; effect of, on European events, 724
Pantheon, 162
Papacy, Gregory VII and, 208; support of Benedictines by, 207; iconoclastic controversy and, 224; Pepin the Short and, 225–226; Charlemagne and, 230; in tenth- and eleventh-century Germany, 250; Norman Sicily and, 266–268; Crusades and, 269–273; reform in High Middle Ages, 292–294; Investiture Controversy and, 295–299; Frederick Barbarossa and, 299; Innocent III and, 302–305; in twelfth century, 302; papal decline, 304, 307, 309; in thirteenth century, 307–309
Papal Diplomacy, 402
Papal Election Decree (1059), 294–295
Papal states, 302, 307, 402, 583, 658
Papen, Franz von, as German Chancellor, 808
Pareto, Vilfredo, 636
Paris, 378, 416, 422; "worth a mass," 445, 446, 451; in French Revolution, 545–546, 548–550; massacres in (1792), 550, 551; in the Terror, 553, 561; nonindustrialized city, 584; "gaslit," 650; Commune (1871), 651
Paris, Peace of (1763), 522
Paris, Treaty of (1814), and second (1815), 561, 562
Paris, University of, 330, 360
Parlement of Paris, 451, 516
Parlements, 470, 517, 542, 543, 547
Parliament, 414, 416, 444, 451–455; beginnings of, 321–323; under Edward I, 323–325; compared with Estates-General, 331; and the Glorious Revolution, 487–489, 519, 531, 533; reform (1832), 575, 583–584, 644; Chartists advocate reforms, 644–645; "Victorian Compromise" and, 644–647; laboring men in, 649; Reform Bill of 1911, 649
Parmenides, 85
Parnell, Charles Stewart, 648
Particularism, 299; feudal (in France), 244–247; Henry VI (Germany) and, 302
Partitions of Poland, 523, 551
Pasternak, Boris, 878
Pasteur, Louis, 628
Patarenes, 295
Paul (Saul of Tarsus), 172
Paul II (Pope), 384
Paul III (Pope) (1468–1549), 421
Paul the Deacon, 231, 232
Paulus, General von, Nazi commander at Stalingrad, 846
Pavlov, Ivan, 913
"Pax Babylonica," 35
Peace of Augsburg (1555), 413
Pearl Harbor, attack on, 843
Pearson, Karl, 630

Peasants, 469; in Charlemagne's time, 220; under feudalism, 247, 251–253, 261–262

"Peasants' Rebellion" (1381), 401

Peasants' Revolt (1525), 412

Peel, Sir Robert, 584, 645

"Peelites," 645

Pelagius (c. 360–c. 420), 420

Pepin of Heristal, 222

Peking man, 2

Peloponnesian War, background of, 101; nature and significance of, 102–103

Pepin the Short, 222–226; coronation of, 225, 229

Pericles, 76

Pershing, John J., General, United States military commander in World War I, 733

Persia, origins and early settlements of, 52; development of a cosmopolitan culture by, 53; formulates science of astronomy, 54; collapse of empire of, 55

The *Persian Letters* (Montesquieu) (1721), 506

Persian Wars, 87

Petain, Henri, Marshal, arranged French surrender to Germany, 834

Peter I (the Great) (Emperor of Russia) (1672–1725), 465, 469, 480, 484

Peter's Foreign Policy, 481

Peter III, Tsar of Russia (1728–1762), 522, 528

"Peterloo, battle of" (England), 575

Petition of Right, 452

Petrarch, Francesco (1304–1374), 371, 372

Pharisees, 169–170

Phidias, 99

Philip I (King of France), 326

Philip II (King of France), 327

Philip II (King of Spain), 439, 440; government of, 440; and Tudor England, 443

Philip III (King of France), 330

Philip IV, "the Fair" (King of France), 308, 330–331, 398

Philip IV (King of Spain), 459, 485

Philip V (King of Spain), 485

Philip Augustus (King of France), 271, 303, 319

Philip of Hesse, 411, 412

Philip of Swabia, 303

Philippi, battle of, 136

Philippines, recognition of independence of, by United States after World War II, 889

Philistines, 59

Philosophes, 505–510, 512, 513, 517, 524, 528, 543, 569, 574

Philosophy, medieval, 350–366

Phoenicians, 45; as chief maritime traders of Near East, 47; alphabet of, 47

Physics in the nineteenth century, 627

Physiocrats, 510

Picasso, Pablo, 918

Pico della Mirandola (1463–1494), 374

Picquart, Georges, 653

Piedmont, revolts in (1821), 579

Piedmont and formation of Kingdom of Italy, 656

Piedmont Constitution, 588

Pietism, in eighteenth century, 511

Pietism, German, 460, 572

Pindar, 97

Pisistratus, 76; Greek tyrant, 75–76

Pitt, William (the Elder, Earl of Chatham), 522, 530

Pius II (Pope) (1405–1464), 399

Pius IV (Pope) (1499–1565), 412

Pius VI, Pope, 548

Pius VII (Pope), 557

Pius IX (Pope), 625

Planck, Max, 912

Plantagenets, 314

Plataea, battle of, 88, 101

Plato, 93–94, 351; admired Spartan constitution, 81; in medieval thought, 350–352

Pliny the Younger, 158

Plotinus, 184

Pluralism, 399

Plutarch, 110, 160

Pobiedonostsev, Constantine, 667, 668, 670

Poincaré, Raymond, leader of National Union ministry in France (1926), 758

Poitiers, battle of (1356), 391

Poland, 419, 423, 425, 452; converted to Christianity, 273; baroque art in, 456; and aristocratic decentralization, 485; partitioning of, 520, 524; nobility hails revolution in France, 548; "Congress Poland," 562, 583; response to revolutionary influences from France (1830–1831), 583; reborn after World War I, 742; creation of "new," divided Germany geographically, 742; conquered by Germany, 831; as object of Nazi aggression, 831; territorial acquisitions of, after World War II, 871

Poland-Lithuania, 394, 425

Policraticus, 358

polis, gods of, 74

Polish Corridor, 742

Political theory, 636–637; caesaropapism, 185–186; Henry II (England) and, 316; Magna Carta and, 320–321; representative government and, 321–330; Edward I and, 324, 325; Philip IV and, 330; in medieval England and France, 331–332; Dante and, 342; Roman law and, 348–349; Aquinas and, 360–363

Politics of Reason, 502–504

Politiques, 446, 460

Poltava, battle of (1709), 482

Polybius, 110

Polyclitus, 99

Pompadour, Marquise de (1721–1764), 534

Pompey the Great, 132, 133, 134

Poniatowski, Stanislas (1732–1798), 523

Pontifex Maximus, 120, 123

Pontius Pilate, 171

Poor Clares, 287

Poor Law (1601), 439; administered by Justices of the Peace, 444; centralized (1834), 644

Populares (of Roman Republic), 131

Popular Front, in France (1936), 759

Population, in eleventh-century Europe, 258; Vikings and, 239; growth related to industrialization, 596–598

Portugal, 396; commercial empire of, 432; baroque art in, 456; in Napoleonic wars, 559; revolts in (1820), 579

Positivism, 629–630

Post-Napoleonic Politics, 572–575

Post-World War I Europe and America, seeming affluence of, 766

Potsdam, 526; meeting of Allied Powers at, 859

Power politics, nature of, 680; as shaped by dominant personalities, 680; as framed by aims of the states, 681; effects of English conquests in Africa on, 684; forces of, at work at Congress of Berlin, 701; division of Europe into two armed camps as manifestation of, 711; workings of, in first Moroccan crisis, 711; as manifested in the Balkan crisis of 1908–1909, 714; increased complications of, after 1913, 716; play of Alliance System in, 723

Power transmission, 607

Praetors, 120

Pragmatic Sanction, of Charles VI (1713), 477, 524

Prague, 401, 448

Prague, Jerome of, 399

Prairial law (1794), 553

Praise of Folly (Erasmus), 377

Predestination, Calvinist doctrine of, 417
Preliterate culture, food-collecting as a characteristic of, 4; art forms and practices of, 5; burial rites of, 5; food-producing stage of, 5, 6; domestication of animals as a feature of, 5; savagery as a stage of, 6; development of cities in, 6; barbarism as a stage of, 6
Pressburg, Peace of (1805), 558
Price, Richard (1723–1791), 531
Price Revolution, 438
"Priesthood of all believers" (Luther's doctrine), 409
Priestley, Joseph (1733–1804), 498, 531, 532
The *Prince* (Machiavelli), 386, 387
Prince Henry "the Navigator" (1394–1460), 432
Printing, invention and impact of, 378
Privy Council, 519
Production, organization of in sixteenth century, 436, 437
"Progressivism" (United States), 655–656
Proletariat (Marx's view of), 623–624
Protagoras, 91
Protocols of the Elders of Zion, 632
Proudhon, Joseph, 626
Provisions of Oxford, 322–323
Prussia, 412, 520, 522, 526, 527; attacks France (1792), 549, 554; against Napoleon, 561; at Congress of Vienna, 562, 564, 571, 574, 581; in 1848 revolution, 589–590, 611; and unification of Germany, 659, 660, 662, 664
Psychology in nineteenth century, 637–638
Ptah, as the creator of life in Egyptian religion, 14
Ptolemy, 105; Egyptian ruler, 134
Ptolemy (Alexandrian scholar), 160, 216, 492
Pugachev Rebellion (1773–1775), 529
Punic Wars, 129; significance of first of the, 125; decisive nature of the second of the, 126
Purges, in Russian Communist Party (1935–1938), 785, 786
Puritan religious and social ideals, 280, 453
Pyramids, 343
Pyrenees, Peace of (1659), 450, 451
Pythagoras, 85

Quadruple Alliance, 563, 572
Quakers (Society of Friends), 460, 500, 506, 511
Queen Anne (1702–1714), 488
Queen Anne's War, 475
Quesnay, Francois (1694–1774), 510
Quintuple Alliance, 572; collapse of, 581
Quisling, Vidkun, 833

Rabelais, François (1494?–1553), 371, 375
Racial differentiation, lack of cultural relationships to, 5
Radetzky, General, 588
Raeder, Admiral, 833
Railways, 603
Ramillies, Battle of (1706), 475
Raphael (1483–1520), 383, 402
Rational Religion, 504–505
Realists, romantic, 632
Reason of state (*raison d'etat*), 386, 523, 524
Red China, 889; *see also* China
Red Scare, in post-World War I United States, 761
Reflections on the Revolution in France (Burke), 548
Reform Bill (England) (1832), 583–584; (1867), 647; (1885), 647; (1911), 649
Reformation, German, 406–410; secular background, 406–407; settlement under Henry VIII and Edward VI, 415; Catholic, 421–425; and Eastern Europe, 425–426; and the Modern World, 426–428; and Individualism, 426; and toleration, 426–427; political ramifications of, 427; social and economic repercussions, 427–428

Regensburg (Ratisbon), Diet of, and Colloquy of (1541), 421
Reichstag, 662
Reinsurance Treaty (1887), provisions of, 703; lapse of, 705
Relativism, 629–635
Religion of Humanity, 630
Religious revival and the Restoration after Napoleon, 571
Rembrandt van Rijn (1606–1669), 459
Renaissance, 257; definition, 369; learning during, 370–378; Italian, 369–375; vernacular literature in, 370; Northern, 374–378; classical education, 374; fine arts, 379–388; High, 382–385; Papacy of the, 401–402; Renaissance Popes, 401–402
Renan, Ernest, 630
Rentes, 471
Reparations, 742; payments of, rescheduled under Dawes Plan (1924), 749; difficulty of collecting, 748
Republicans, Florentine, 374; France (1848), 586; (Third Republic), 650–652
Republic of Venice, end of, 555
Republic of Virtue, 552–553
Requesens, 441
Rerum Novarum (Pope Leo XIII), 625
Restoration, Stuart, 487–488
Restoration Settlement, 487
Reuchlin, Johann (1455–1522), 376, 408
Revisionism (Marxist), 625
Revolt of the Low Countries, 440–443
Revolution, as a phase of war, 743–744; Communist, U.S.S.R., 773
Revolution of 1905 (Russia), 668, 669–670
Revolutionary Settlement, 488–489
Rhodes, J. Cecil, as imperialist force in Africa, 684–685
Richard I, the Lion-Hearted (King of England), 271, 318, 327
Richelieu, Cardinal (1585–1642), 448, 449, 450
Ridgeway, Matthew, General, 900
Robespierre, Maximilien (1758–1794), 547, 550, 551, 552, 553, 554
Rocroi, French victory at (1643), 449
Roebuck, John, 601
Roger the Great (Sicily), 266–268
Röhm, Ernst, 802
Roland, Madame, 549, 552
Rollo, 239
Roman Catholic Church, 396, 398, 421, 423, 472, 557; revived after 1815, 571; in France under Napoleon III, 650; in Third Republic, 653; in Italian Republic, 659; in German Empire, 662; in Austrian Empire, 664
Roman Empire, new "Golden Age" of, 144, 146; establishment of Principate in, 143; peace and prosperity of, 145; as autocracy behind republican facade, 145; literature and culture of, 147; paternalistic nature of, 147; literary decline in, 150; literary Silver Age of, 151; period of the Julio-Claudian line in, 151; period of violence in, after death of Tiberius, 152; the "Year of the Four Emperors" in, 152; development of order and advanced culture in Europe by virtue of, 152; period of the "Five Good Emperors" in, 154; rulers of (table), 154; peak of, under Antoninus, 155; end of *Pax Romana* of, 156; beginning of decline in, 157; culture of the Silver Age of, 158; development of medicine and astronomy in, 160; development of architecture and sculpture in, 160; economic conditions in, 163; developing disintegration of, 163; role of army in, 163; endemic warfare in, 164; temporary recovery of, under Diocletian and Constantine, 164;

division of, into two "empires," 164; invasion of, by Teutonic tribes, 165; Christianity made sole religion of, 165; "fall of," 166; legacy of, 166; Christianity and, 184–186

Roman Inquisition, 425

Roman Law, 155, 190, 200, 375, 385, 387, 389, 466, 486; Justinian and, 200; Byzantium and, 201; Inquisition and, 282; medieval Europe and, 349; as base for Napoleonic codes, 556; not found in Russia, 666

Roman Republic, early settlements of, 115; culture in earliest stage of, 116; settlement of Greeks and Etruscans in, 116; Etruscan influence on life in, 117; emergence of Latin tribes in, 116; Greek influence on life in, 117; establishment of, 117; "Revolution of 509" in, 117; territorial expansion of, 118; invasions by Gauls, of, 118; relation of Latin League to, 119; hegemony of, in Italy, 119; political institutions of, 119; early dominance of patricians in, 119; Senate as dominant political institution in, 119; chief political offices in, 120; provision for temporary dictator in, 120; class struggle in, between patricians and plebians, 120; Tribal Assembly in, 121; function of *Comitia Tributa* in, 121; power of *Tribunes* in, 121; creation of Law of Twelve Tables in, 121; *plebiscita* as plebian innovation in, 121; rise of *novi homines* in, 121; early religious life in, 123; Hortensian Law as highwater "democratic" mark in, 123; function of *paterfamilias* in, 123; economic conditions of early, 124; development of practical arts in, 124; impact of first Punic War on, 125; nature and influence of second Punic War on, 126; political and economic changes marking decline of, 127; development of *latifundia* in, 127; rise of *Equites* in, 127; emergence of middle class in, 127; militarization of life of, 127; conquest of East by, 128; century of severe class struggle in, 129; decline of "democracy" in, 129; Gracchan revolution in, 129, 130; major unsolved problems of, 131; wars of, in Africa, 131; "social war" in, 132; First Triumvirate of, 132, 134; political intrigues in, 133; civil war in, 134; culture in the "century of struggle" (c. 150–50 B.C.) in, 136; philosophy and religion in latter years of, 138; economic conditions of, in latter years, 139

Romance, medieval, 339–342

Romance of Renard, 341

Romanesque architecture, 343–345

Romanov dynasty, 484

Romanov, Michael, 480

Romantic Art and Music, 568–569

Romanticism, 568–571

Romantic literature, 569–570

Romantic philosophy, 570–571

Romantic Politics, 570–571

Rome, 380, 382, 384, 395, 402, 410, 414, 422, 459, 555, 658; Visigothic sack of (410), 188, 200

Rommel, Erwin, Field Marshal, in Africa, 841, 842, 846

Roon, General von, 659, 660

Roosevelt, Franklin D., became president, 814, 820, 829; first "Hundred Days" of, 815; led country in effort to supply arms to Britain, 836; met with Churchill and Stalin at Tehran, 850

Roosevelt, Theodore, 655; expansionist plans of, 696

"Roundheads," 454

Rousseau, Jean Jacques (1712–1778), 508, 509, 542, 552, 570

Royal Society of London, 495, 496, 502

Ruhr, occupation of, by French (1923), 748

Rule of St. Benedict, 206–208

Russell, Lord John, 645

Russia, invaded by Swedes, 238, 240; attempts by Teutonic Knights to invade, 273–274; Kievan,

394; emergence of, under Peter the Great, 480–484, 522, 523; administrative absolutism in, 483–484; under Catherine the Great, 528–529; Pugachev Rebellion, 529; Napoleon invades, 560; at Congress of Vienna, 581; after Napoleonic Wars, 374–375; image of, as suppressor of liberties, 583; armies crush Hungarian Republic (1849), 588; industrialization in, 613, 663; Alexander II and emancipation of the serfs (1861), 666–667; Autocracy on Trial, 665–671; Reactionary and Revolutionary Polarization (1863–1881), 667; Reaction after 1881, 667–668; *Zemstvos*, 667, 669; trans-Siberian railroad, 668; formation of revolutionary parties after 1880, 669; war and revolution in (1904–1905), 669–670; Witte's October Manifesto, 670; "Golden Age" (1906–1914), 670–671; basic aims of, after 1870, 681; disturbed by British occupation of Egypt (1882), 684; imperial interests of, in China, 691; war of, with Japan (1904–1905), 692; brought into alliance with Austria and Germany by Bismarck, 702; joined Germany in Reinsurance Treaty (1887), 703; put Balkans "on ice" (1890s), 707; imperialist interest of, in North China, 707; joined in accord with England (1907), 709; yielded to Austria in the Bosnian crisis of 1908–1909, 713; dependence of, upon France (1914) in supporting Serbia, 727; defeated by Germany in 1917, 734; withdrawal of, from World War I, 734; disturbed by creation of *Cordon Sanitaire*, 743; Communist Revolution in, 773; March (1917) Revolution of, 774; collapse of Tsarist regime, 775; brief tenure of moderate revolutionists (1917) in, 775; Communist revolution in, 776; failure of Constituent Assembly in, 779; "White" counter-revolution in, 779; early difficulties of Communism in, 779–780; civil war in, after World War I, 780; introduction of NEP in, 780; rise of *Nepmen* in (1921–1928), 781; Communist goals and methods in, 782–783; place of economic planning in Communist, 783; Party and government agencies in Communist, 783; place of "self-criticism" in Communist, 783; effect of collectivist economy on peasants and workers in Communist, 784; purges in Communist Party in, 785; snubbed at Munich Conference, 829; signed non-aggression pact with Germany, 831; "Winter War" of, with Finland, 832; acquisition of Balkan territory (1940–1941) by, 836; invaded by Nazi Germany (1941), 837; leaders of, emphasized saving of "Mother Russia" (1940–1945), 838; staged counter-offensive at Stalingrad (1942), 846; casualties of World War II in, 855; emergence of, as one of two great powers, 856; development of "Cold War" between United States and, 858; economic conditions in, after World War II, 874–875; explorations of, in Outer Space, 875; "de-Stalinization" of, 876; leaders of, admit roads to socialism may vary, 877; significance of "de-Stalinization" in, 877; dramatic exposé of Stalin by Khrushchev in, 877; return of, to "collective leadership," 878; development of conflict between, and China, 890; reestablished Comintern as Cominform, 899; takeover of Czechoslovakia (1948) by, 899

Russian Orthodox Church, 395, 425, 480, 484, 668

Russification, 668

Russo-Japanese War (1905), 614, 669

Russo-Turkish War (1877–1878), 700

Ryswick, Treaty of (1697), 475

SA (Sturm Abteilung), restiveness among members of, 811

Sabines, 118

Sacraments, 276

Sadducees, 170
Sadler, Michael, 605
St. Albert Magnus, 283–284, 360
St. Ambrose, 186, 295
St. Anselm, 313, 317, 353, 356
St. Anthony, 206
St. Augustine of Hippo, 166, 187–189, 234, 351, 353, 354–356, 372, 420
St. Bede the Venerable, 209
St. Benedict of Nursia, 177, 206, 277–278
St. Bernard of Clairvaux, 270, 279–280
St. Bonaventure, 287–288
St. Boniface, 209, 223–225
St. Dominic, 283–284
St. Francis of Assissi, 284–288, 293
St. Jerome, 186–187
St. Peter, 292
St. Peter Damiani, 295, 352–354
St. Simeon Stylites, 206
St. Thomas Aquinas, *see* Aquinas, St. Thomas
St. Thomas Becket, 316–318
St. Germain, Treaty of, 740
Saint-Just, Louis (1767–1794), 552, 553
Saint-Simon, Henri de, 622
Saladin, 271
Salamis, battle between Greeks and Persians in Bay of, 88
Salerno, University of, 348
Salian dynasty, 250
Salisbury, Lord, 648
Sallust, 137, 151
Salutati, Coluccio (1331–1406), 373
Samnites, 119
Sancta Sophia, 196, 199
Sand, George, 630
Sanhedrin, 169, 170
San Martin, José, 579
Sans-culottes, 549, 550, 551, 554
San Stefano, Treaty of, 700
Sappho, 86
Saracens, 237–238
Sargon the Great, 30
Sargon II, conquest of Israel by, 50
Sartre, Jean-Paul, 922
Satyagraha, "love-force" employed by Gandhi, 756
Saud, Ibn, 891
Saul, as first king of the Hebrews, 59
Savonarola, Girolamo (1452–1498), 374
Saxony, 228, 238, 248, 299
Schacht, Hjalmar, put German mark on firm basis (1924), 765
Schleicher, Kurt von, 811; as German Chancellor, 808
Schleiermacher, Friedrich, 572
Schlieffer Plan, as basis of German military action (1914), 728
Schmalkaldic League (1531), 413
Scholasticism, 351
Schopenhauer, Arthur, 633
Schubert, Franz, 569
Schuman, Robert, 895
Schumann, Robert, 569
Schumpeter, Joseph, as capitalist critic of imperialism, 678
Schuschnigg, Kurt von, 827; as Chancellor of Austria, 812
Schwarzenberg, Prince, 588
Science, Albertus Magnus and, 360; medicine in high medieval Europe, 348; Salerno, medical studies at, 348; ancient Greek science, translations of, 358; Roger Bacon and, 365; impact of, on contemporary civilization, 911–913
Scientific instruments, 496
Scientific philosophy and the new humanism, 500–505
"Scientific Revolution," 491–500

Scientific Societies, 495
Scipio Africanus, 126, 127
Scotland, 419; Irish monks in, 238
Scott, Sir Walter, 569
Scotus, John, 233–234
Scribes, 170
Scripturalism, 417
Scutage, 261
"Sea Lion," code name for German plans to invade England, 835
Second Coalition against France, 555
Second Continental Congress, 533
Second International Workingman's Association, 625
Secret diplomacy, as instrument used to maintain balance of power, 680; main subjects of, in "Bismarckian Era," 703; effect of, upon world events, 724; play of, in bringing on World War I, 726
Secret Treaties, provisions of, published after World War I, 742
Securities Exchange Commission (SEC), 816
Seleucus, 104, 106
senatus consultum ultimum ("the last decree"), 130, 134
Seneca, 158
Senhacharib, conquest of Babylon by, 50
Sepoy rebellion, 646, 686
Septimius Severus, 157
Serbia, incorporation of Bosnia-Herzegovina sought by, 713; and the Bosnian crisis of 1908–1909, 713; increased its pressures on Austria after 1913, 715; reply of, to Austrian ultimatum in 1914, 727
Serfdom, 252–253, 262, 410; abolished in France (1789), 546; abolished in Russia (1861), 666–667
Servetus, Michael, 418
"The Seven" (European economic community), 897
Seven Weeks' War (1866), 660, 663
Seven Years' War, 521–523, 530, 533
Sèvres, Treaty of (1920), 741
Shaftesbury, Earl of, 502
Shakespeare, William (1564–1616), 460
Shaw, George Bernard, 625, 633
Shires, 310; courts in, 311
Sh'ism, 213
Sic et non, 357
Sicilian Vespers, 307
Sicily, conquest by Normans, 266–268; Henry VI, 302–303; Innocent III and, 303; Frederick II, 306; War of Sicilian Vespers in, 307; conquest of, by Allied forces (1943), 847
Siéyes, Abbe, 555, 556
Siger of Brdbrant, 354, 360
Sigismund (Holy Roman Emperor) (1368–1437), 399
Silesia, 520; invaded by Prussia (1740), 526, 527
Simon de Montfort, 322
Simony, 292, 295
Sino-Japanese War, 691
Sistine Chapel, 384
Sistine Madonna (Raphael), 383
"The Six" (European economic community), 869, 897
Six Articles of Faith, in England (1539), 415
Skeptics, 107
Skinner, Charles L., 913
Slavery, in eleventh century, 262
Slavophiles, 666
Sluter, Claus (c. 1350–1405/6), 379
Smith, Adam (1723–1790), 510, 556, 614, 620
Smoot-Hawley Tariff Act (1930), 761
Social Contract (Rousseau), 509
Social Democrats, 625, 662, 663; party of, dissolved in Germany (1933), 809
Socialism, Christian, 625; Fabian, 625; Marxian, 623; Utopian, 622–623
Social revolutionaries (Russia), 669
Social "Scientism," 629–635
Social Thought, late nineteenth century, 635–637

Society, in mid-eleventh century, 292
Society of Jesus, *see* Jesuits
Sociology, 636–637
Socrates, 92
Solomon, splendor of Israel under, 59
Solon, reformed Athenian constitution, 75
Song of Roland, 337
Sophocles, 95, 96; and theme of tragedy, 73
Sorel, Georges, 626, 636
Soul's Secret (Petrarch), 372
South Africa, 646; *Apartheid* in, 894; failure of nationalism in, 894
South East Asia Treaty Organization (SEATO), 900
South Korea, invasion of, by North Korea, 900
South Sea Bubble, 519
South Sea Company, 476, 518
Sovereign state system, definitions and implications of, 679
Soviet Russia, *see* Russia
Soviets, 670, 776
Space explorations, 875
Space-race, as aspect of Cold War, 901
Spain, 388, 390; in Middle Ages, 263; reconquest from Moors, 263; humanism in, 374; printing in, 378, 384; invades Italy, 402; commercial expansion of, in sixteenth century, 433; bid for colonial wealth, 433; dominance of Spain in sixteenth century, 439; government of Philip II, 439; Inquisition in, 440; revolt of the Low Countries against Spain, 440–442; and attack on Tudor England with the Armada, 443; helps Guise faction in France, 445; peace with France, England, and the Dutch, 447; enters Thirty Years' War, 448; Peace of the Pyrenees with France, 450, 485; and baroque art, 456; and baroque literature, 459; and War of Spanish Succession, 475–476; as aristocratic monarchy, 485; joins France against Britain, 523; enlightened despotism in, 529–530; withdraws from First Coalition against France (1795), 554; resistance to Napoleon—"The Spanish ulcer," 559; in Napoleonic Wars, 559; reaction against revolutionary era in Bourbon Spain, 574; Bourbons restored after 1815, 574; revolts in (1820), 578; revolts of 1820s crushed, 578, 579; liberal revolutionaries seek a new monarch in 1868, and start Franco-Prussian War, 660; war with the United States (1898), 696; Civil War in, 825; overthrow of Republic in, 826
Spanish America, 579
Spanish-American War, 696
Spanish Fury, 441
Spanish Habsburg Empire, 485
Spanish Inquisition, 375, 390, 440, 441
Spanish March, 228, 263
Spanish Netherlands, first inherited by Spanish King, Charles I, 394; part of inheritance of Philip II, 439–440; religious wars in, 440; today's Belgium after 1579, 441; sought by Louis XIV, 473, 475; transferred to Austrian Habsburgs, 476, 485
Sparta, monarchy retained, 72; government of, 79; effect upon, of subjugation of Messenians, 78; origin and demography of, 78; large serf population of, 79; function of secret police (*Crypteia*) in life of, 79; place of *Apella* in political life of, 79; place of Council of Elders in political life of, 79; as dominant in Peloponnesian League, 80–81; dominated "people round about" (Perioikoi), 80; raising of male children in, 80
"Spartacists," 778
Spencer, Herbert, 621–622
Speyer, Diet of (1529), 412
The Spirit of the Laws (Montesquieu) (1748), 506
Spiritual Franciscans, 399
Sputnik, 901

Stalin, 781, 874; power struggle of, with Trotsky, 781; exiled Trotsky, 781; "purged" opponents, 786; purposes of, in "purges," 787; met with Churchill and Roosevelt at Tehran, 850; dramatic exposé of, by Khrushchev, 877
Stalingrad, battle of, 845
Stamp Act Congress, 533
Stanhope, Lord, 516, 519
Stanley, Henry, imperialist implications of search by, for Livingstone, 682
Star Chamber, Court of, 393
State Economic Policies, 438
Statute of Laborers, 393
Stavisky, Affair (France) (1933–1934), 759
Steamboat, 603
Steam power, 600
Stein, Baron von, 561
Stephenson, George, 603
Stoicism, 375
Stoics, 107
Stolypin, Peter, 670
Strafford, Thomas W. (1593–1641), 453
Stravinsky, Igor, 920
Streltsy, 481
Stresemann, Gustav, 748, 760, 808; work of, in Weimar Republic, 801
Stuart England, Civil War in, 452
Stuart Restoration, 487–488
Student Nonviolent Coordinating Committee (S.N.C.C.), 881
Studium generale, 347
Subjectivism in philosophy, 633–635
Sudan, occupied by British (1898), 684
Sudetenland, 590, attached to Czechoslovakia, 742; agitation in, for annexation to Germany, 827
Suetonius, 159
Suez Canal, 611; controlled by England after 1876, 684; rights of England reserved in, 755; seized by Egyptians (1956), 891
Suger, Abbot, 326, 345
Sukarno, 886–887
Suleiman the Magnificent (1520–1566), 440
Sulla, as dictator of Rome, 132
Sully, Duke of (1560–1641), 447
Sultan, 396
Sumer, *see* Mesopotamia
Sun, Yat-sen, Dr., led reform movement in China, 693
"Survival of the fittest," 621
Swabia, 248; Hohenstaufens of, 299
Swanscombe man, 2
Sweden, 412, 447, 448, 449, 451, 476, 481, 483, 597; industrialization in, 613; high standard of living, 613
Switzerland, 555, 557; high standard of living, 613
Syllabus of Errors (1864), 625
Synod of Whitby (664), 208
Syria, 890

Taborites, 401
Tacitus, 159, 189
Taff Vale case (1901), 649
Taille, 471
Taiwan, *see* Formosa
Talleyrand, Prince, 555, 561
Tanzania, gained independence, 892
Tarquins, 117
Taxes, papal, 308; John I (England) and, 319–320; consent to (in England), 321; Philip IV and, 331
Technology, 598–603
Tehran, conference of Roosevelt, Churchill, and Stalin at, 850
The *Tempest* (Shakespeare), 460
Templars, 273, 280, 330–331

Ten Commandments, as substance of new Hebrew covenant with God, 58
Tennessee Valley Authority (TVA), 816
Tennyson, Alfred Lord, 629
Terramaricoli, 115
Tertullian, 352
Test Act of 1673, 487
Teutonic Knights, 274, 280
Thales of Miletus, 85
Theatines, 422
Themistocles, 78, 88
Theocracy, 230
Theodoric the Great, 192, 199
Theodosius, 165, 178, 185
Thermidorean Reaction, 553
Thermopylae, battle of, 88
Thespis, 86
Thetes, lowest class of Greek citizens, 75
Thiers, Adolphe, 651
Third International, 778; revival of, as Cominform, 899
Third Republic (France), 651–654
Thirty Years' War, 431, 447, 450, 452, 460, 473, 479
Thomas-Gilchrist process, 608
Thucydides, 97
Tiberius, 151, 152
Tilly, Count of (1559–1632), 448
Tilsit, Treaty of (1807), 558, 560
"Time of Troubles" (Russia), 480
Tirpitz, Admiral von, planned Germany's "risk" navy, 685; pushed naval race with England, 706
Tito, Marshall (Josip Broz), as leader of Yugoslavia after World War II, 876
Tojo, General, planned Japanese attack on United States, 843
Tolstoi, Count Leo, 633
"Torch," code name of plans for Allied invasion of Africa, 846
Tories, 475, 487, 532, 575, 584, 605, 644, 645
Torricelli, Evangelista (1608–47), 496
Tory Democracy, 622, 646
Tours, battle of (733), 215
Towns, at end of Roman Empire, 202; growth of (in Middle Ages), 258–260; craft guilds in, 260; government of, 260; heresies in, 280; Lombard towns and Frederick Barbarossa, 300; vernacular literature, 341; and architecture, 343
Townsend, Francis, Dr., 817
Townshend, Lord, 595
Trade Unions (England), 649
Trafalgar, Battle of (1805), 558
Trajan, 154
Trappists, 280
Treaty of Dover (1670), 487
Treitschke, Heinrich von, 630
Trent, Council of, 303
Trianon, Treaty of (1920), 740
Triennial Act, 453
Triple Alliance formed (1882), 702
Triple *Entente,* formation of, 709–710
Tristand and Iseult, medieval romance, 340
Troppau Protocol (1820), 581
Trotsky, Leon, 779, 780, 782, 786
Troubadours, 338–339
Troy, captured by Mycenaean Greeks, 70
"Truman Doctrine," 884, 898
Truman, President, dismissed General MacArthur from Korean command, 900
Tull, Jethro, 595
Tunisia, occupied by France (1880), 702
Turenne, Marshall, 473
Turgenev, Ivan, 633
Turgot, Baron de, 508, 510, 535
Turkey, 656; Balkan troubles of, 700; wooed by Germany after 1900, 706; defeated by Balkan League states (1913), 715; defeat of English forces at Gallipoli in (1915), 730; consequences of World War I for, 736; forced to accept Treaty of Sèvres (1920), 741
Turks, 396, 409, 474, 482, 485, 558
Tutankhamon, rein of, 21
The Twelve Articles of the German Peasantry (1525), 410
Tylor, Edward, 636
Tyndale, William (d. 1536), 415
Tyrannicide, 358
Tyrant, function of, in Greek political life, 84
Tyrol, ceded to Italy after World War I, 742

Uganda, object of British imperialism (1887), 684
Unam Sanctam, 309
Unionists (England), 648, 649
Union of Soviet Socialist Republics (USSR), *see* Russia
United Arab Republic (UAR), 891
United Nations, organization of, 859–860; office of Relief and Rehabilitation Administration (U.N.R.R.A.) in, 860; limited effectiveness of, 861; support of South Korea by, 900
United States, rise to world industrial preeminence, 612–613; emergence of, in nineteenth century to world power, 654–656; business dominance after the Civil War, 654; the Civil War, 654; the Progressive Era, 655–656; imperialist activities in Latin America, 695; war with Spain (1898), 696; expansionist activities of, in Latin America, 696; effect of sinking of Lusitania on policy of, 731; involvement of, in World War I, 732; consequences of World War I for, 736–737; rejected Versailles Treaty, 739; embraced isolationism after World War I, 747; post-World War I conditions in, 760; restricted immigration after 1924, 761; political corruption in, after World War I, 762; prohibition and "speakeasies" in, 762; summation of post-war mood and issues in, 762, 763; brief depression in, after World War I, 763; inflation in, in 1920s, 763; new industries in, in 1920s, 764; "Golden Twenties" in, 766; causes and nature of the Great Depression in, 767; coming of the New Deal in, 813; nature and achievements of "First New Deal" in, 814; the "Second New Deal" in, 818; New Deal Social Security legislation in, 818; growth of labor unions under New Deal in, 818; furnished extensive aid to Britain, 835; repealed or modified neutrality acts of 1935–1937, 836; emergence of, as one of two great powers, 856; rise of militarism in, after World War II, 857, 884; emergence of secret government agencies in, after World War II, 857; development of "Cold War" with Russia, 858; main events in, in post-World War II era, 879; economic affluence in, after World War II, 879–884; unfavorable conditions in, after 1945, 879; plight of Negroes in, 879; poverty in Appalachian regions of, 879; economy of, dependent upon war preparations and activities, 879; "McCarthy era" in, 880; Army-McCarthy hearings in, 881; Black-White problems in, 881–883; Supreme Court's 1954 decision re segregation in, 881; responsibilities of, as a great power, 883; rise of "Black Power" movement in, 882; passed Civil Rights Acts of 1964 and 1965, 882; as "world policeman," 884; growing agitation for peace in, 884; supported conservative regimes in Latin America, 885; granted independence to Philippines (1946), 889; landed troops in Lebanon, 891; support of South Korea by, 900; extensive involvement of, in Vietnam, 904

Universals, conflict over, in medieval thought, 354–356
Universities, medieval, 346–348
Urban II, 268, 298
"Urban revolution" as prelude to civilization, 6
Urban sanitation, 597
Urbanization, 605
Ursulines, 422
Uruguay, 885
Utopia (More), 376
Utraquists, 425
Utrecht, Peace of, 475, 476, 504, 515
Utrecht, Union of, 441

Valla, Lorenzo (1405–1457), 373, 376
Valmy, battle of (1792), 550
Valois, 389, 421, 445
Vasari, Giorgio (1511–1574), 379
Vasili III, Grand Prince of Moscow (1505–1533), 395
Vassalage, 244–247
Vauban, Marshal de, 473
Vault, 345
Veii, 118
Vendée, revolts in (France), 551
Venice, 259, 378, 384, 388, 422, 459, 465; to Austria (1797), 555, 563
Ventris, Michael, deciphered Mycenaean script, 69
Verdun, Treaty of (843), 236, 248
Verocchio, 381
Versailles, 470, 471, 473; Estates-General at (1789), 543; King taken from, 546, 661
Versailles Treaty, 738, 739, 799, 811, 825
Vesalius, Andreas (1514–1564), 499
Vespasian, 153–154
Vichy, capital of unoccupied France, 834
Victor Emmanuel, King of Italy, 658, 847
Victorian Compromise, 584, 644, 645, 646
Vienna, 477, 481, 525; Congress of, 561; Treaty of, 562, 572; rioting in (1848), 587, 589
Vietnam, large scale intervention in, by United States, 879, 903; war in, 902–904; division of, into North-South Zones, 903
Vikings, 237, 238–241
Villanovans, 115
Villon, Francois (1431–?), 372
Vincent of Beauvais, 359
Virgil, 148–149
Visconti, Bernabó, of Milan (ruled 1378–1385), 388
Visigoths, 188; Justinian and, 200; conquer Byzantine southern Spain, 201
Vives, Juan Luis (1492–1540), 375
Volksgeist, 571
Volsci, 118
Voltaire, François (1694–1778), 505, 506, 507, 516, 527, 542
Voltaire and Humanitarian rage, 507

Wagner, Richard, 634
Wagner Labor Act, 818; *see also* National Labor Relations Act
Waldensianism, 281–282, 300, 400, 409
Waldo, Peter, 281
Wales, conquest of, by Edward I, 325
Wallenstein, Albert of (1583–1634), 448
Walpole, Robert (1676–1745), 518
"War Communism," 778, 780
War and Peace (Tolstoi), 633
War of the Austrian Succession, 520
War of Jenkins' Ear, 520
War of the League of Augsburg, 475
War of Spanish Succession, 475, 517
Wars of the Roses, 393, 453
Warsaw, Grand Duchy of (1805–1815), 558, 560

Warsaw Pact, 900
Warwick, Earl of (1428–1471), 415
The Waste Land (T. S. Eliot), 920
Waterloo, battle of, 561
Watson, John B., 913
Watt, James, 600–601
Wealth of Nations (Smith), 510
Webb, Sydney and Beatrice, 625
Weber, Max (1864–1920), 427, 637
Weimar Republic (*see* Germany)
Weizmann, Chaim, 891
Welfs, 279, 299, 303–304
Wellington, Duke of, 559, 561
Wells, H. G., 625
Wergeld, 190
Wesley, John (1703–1791), 511
Wesleyans, English, 572
Wessex, 241–242, 311
West Germany, *see* Federal Republic of Germany
West Indies, 517, 522
Westphalia, Peace of, 473, 476
Westphalia, Treaty of (1648), 449
Whigs, 487, 519, 531, 584, 644, 645
White Mountain, battle of (1620), 448
Whitefield, George (1714–1770), 511
Whitney, Eli, 598
Wilkes, John (1727–1797), 531
Wilkinson, James, 601
William I of Prussia, 660, 663
William II, 663; constructs "New Course," 704
William III (of Orange), 441, 473, 475, 486, 488
William the Conqueror, 243, 310–314, 316
William of Lorris, 341
William of Ockham, 364
William IX of Aquitaine, 339
Willibrord, 223, 231
Wilson, Woodrow, President, efforts of, to mediate end of World War I, 732; Fourteen Points of, 735; program of, at Peace Conference (1919), 737; attitude of, concerning work of the Peace Conference, 738; role of, in determining fate of Versailles Treaty in United States Senate, 739; "went to the people" to gain United States acceptance of Versailles Treaty, 740
Windischgrätz, Prince, 588
Windmill, development of, 221
Witchcraft, 512
Witte, Count, 668, 670
Wittenberg, 408, 420
Works Progress Administration (WPA), 815
"World Machine," 497
World War I, 670–671; background causes of, 723–724; immediate cause of, 726; immediate events leading to, 727; stalemate in the West (1914–1918), 727; action on the Eastern Front, 729; Germany stopped in, in battle of the Marne, 729; costly offensives of, 730; English action in Turkey in, 730; sea action in, 730; German submarine activity in, 731; development of war-weariness during, 732; Allied resurgence in (1917), 733; final campaigns of, 735; consequences of, 736; peace conference following, 737; minor peace treaties of, 740; peace treaties of, consequences of the settlements of, 741
World War II, the road to, 823; Axis victories in (1939–1940), 831; German invasion of Russia in, 837; failure of Nazis to defeat Russia in winter of 1941 in, 839; in Africa (1940–1942), 840; spread of, in the Pacific (1941–1942), 842; the widening of (1940–1942), 836–845; 1943 as "Year of Decision" of, 845; Allied invasion of Italy in, 847; Russian offensives of (1943–1944), 849; Allied invasion of Nazi occupied France during (1944), 850; Normandy invasion in, 850; col-

lapse of German might in, 852; end of, in Pacific, 853; reconquest of the Philippines and Burma in, 854; general effects of, 855; effects of, in Africa and Asia, 856; "peace" settlements of, 857; peace treaties of, 858
Worms, Concordat of (1122), 298, 304
Worms, Diet of (1521), 409, 410
Worms, Edict of (1521), 409, 410, 412
Wren, Christopher (1632–1723), 471
Wycliffe, John (c. 1320–1384), 399, 400

Xavier, Francis (1506–1552), 423
Xerxes, 88
Ximenes, Cardinal, 375, 390

Yahweh, as tribal god of Hebrews, 58; new concept of, by Hebrews, 61
Yalta, meeting of Allied powers at, 859

Yamashita, Tomoyaki, 854
Yemen, 891
Young, Arthur, 595
Young, Owen D., "Young Plan" (1929), 750, 766, 767
Yugoslavia, creation of, 740, 742; asserted independence from Russia, 876

Zama, battle of, in second Punic War, 127, 128
Zemski, sobor, 480
Zeno, 107, 112
Zinjanthropus boisie, age of, 2
Zionist movement, 632
Zola, Émile, 633, 653
Zollverein, 574, 611
Zoroastrianism, nature and significance of, 53–54; parts of, incorporated into Hebrew religion, 62
Zwingli, Ulrich, 408, 410, 411